Fri
July 18
9:00

Adult
Development
and Aging

FIFTH EDITION

Adult Development and Aging

FIFTH EDITION

William J. Hoyer

Syracuse University

Paul A. Roodin

SUNY College at Oswego

Boston   Burr Ridge, IL   Dubuque, IA   Madison, WI   New York   San Francisco   St. Louis
Bangkok   Bogotá   Caracas   Kuala Lumpur   Lisbon   London   Madrid   Mexico City
Milan   Montreal   New Delhi   Santiago   Seoul   Singapore   Sydney   Taipei   Toronto

McGraw-Hill Higher Education

A Division of The **McGraw-Hill** *Companies*

ADULT DEVELOPMENT AND AGING, FIFTH EDITION

Published by McGraw-Hill, a business unit of The McGraw-Hill Companies, Inc., 1221 Avenue of the Americas, New York, NY 10020. Copyright @ 2003, 1999, 1995, 1991, 1985 by The McGraw-Hill Companies, Inc. All rights reserved. No part of this publication may be reproduced or distributed in any form or by any means, or stored in a database or retrieval system, without the prior written consent of The McGraw-Hill Companies, Inc., including, but not limited to, in any network or other electronic storage or transmission, or broadcast for distance learning.

Some ancillaries, including electronic and print components, may not be available to customers outside the United States.

This book is printed on acid-free paper.

3 4 5 6 7 8 9 0 DOC/DOC 0 9 8 7 6 5 4

ISBN 0-697-36202-7

Vice president and editor-in-chief: *Thalia Dorwick*
Publisher: *Stephen D. Rutter*
Senior sponsoring editor: *Rebecca H. Hope*
Editorial coordinator: *Mary Kate Hanley*
Senior marketing manager: *Chris Hall*
Project manager: *Richard H. Hecker*
Production supervisor: *Enboge Chong*
Media technology producer: *Ginger Warner*
Coordinator of freelance design: *David W. Hash*
Cover designer: *Rokusek Design*
Cover image: @ *Corbis Stock Market*
Senior photo research coordinator: *John C. Leland*
Photo research: *Chris Hammond/PhotoFind LLC*
Senior supplement producer: *David A. Welsh*
Compositor: *Carlisle Communications, Ltd.*
Typeface: *10.5/12.5 Times*
Printer: *R. R. Donnelley/Crawfordsville, IN*

The credits section for this book begins on page C-2 and is considered an extension of the copyright page.

Library of Congress Cataloging-in-Publication Data

Hoyer, William J.
   Adult development and aging / William J. Hoyer, Paul A. Roodin.— 5th ed.
     p. cm.
   Includes bibliographical references (p.) and indexes.
   ISBN 0-697-36202-7 (alk. paper)
   1. Adulthood—Psychological aspects. 2. Aging—Psychological aspects. 3. Life cycle,
   Human. I. Roodin, Paul. II. Title.
BF724.5 .R9 2003
155.6—dc21

                                         2002022715

www.mhhe.com

DEDICATION
WE REMEMBER JOHN M. RYBASH, SCHOLAR, TEACHER, AND FRIEND.
WE DEDICATE THIS BOOK TO JOHN, AND TO JOAN HOYER,
MARLENE ROODIN, AND VINNIE RYBASH, WITH LOVE.

BRIEF CONTENTS

EXPANDED CONTENTS

PHYSIOLOGICAL AND SENSORY PROCESSES 50

COPING AND ADAPTATION 98

MENTAL HEALTH INTERVENTIONS 146

PHYSICAL HEALTH 204

MEMORY, ATTENTION, AND LEARNING 273

8

INTELLIGENCE AND CREATIVITY 310

9

COGNITION, WISDOM, AND EXPERTISE 343

10

PERSONALITY 377

PREFACE

To the Student

Most of the time, when we think about development, we think of childhood or adolescence. However, the first 20 years usually comprise 20-25 percent of the human life span. The next five, six, or seven decades are just as significant as the first two decades of life.

The study of adult development and aging is new. The field is exciting for those who teach and work in it because our knowledge is growing and improving. Our aim in writing this text is to communicate the latest, most accurate information in a way that makes it applicable and relevant to students. Therefore, you will want to keep two perspectives in mind as you go through this text. One perspective is personal; that is, the material is relevant to understanding your own development, as well as the changes your peers, friends, family members, and others have experienced or will experience. Another perspective is professional or practical. You may be interested in the topic of this text because you are preparing for a career in this field as a clinician or researcher. Much of our knowledge about this field derives from the desire to help older adults and their families, and to promote health and effective functioning throughout the adult years.

Because people undergo gains as well as losses during the adult years, we emphasize what individuals can do to promote optimal outcomes in response to everyday challenges as well as to the diseases, declines, and losses that can occur during the adult years.

As you read this book, think about your own development. What will you be like as you grow older? We try to paint an accurate picture of the awesome, complex unfolding of development during the adult years. Not only will you learn important facts about the nature of adult development, you will learn how to apply these facts to your own life as you grow older. What you learn can be a guide to your future development and make you aware of the opportunities and challenges that typically characterize development during the adult years.

To The Instructor

Our aim in writing this text was to organize and present the most up-to-date and important research and theory on adult development and aging in a balanced way, making this information interesting and useful to a wide range of undergraduates. We have tried to engage and motivate students by offering a clear, comprehensive, and current account of the salient issues in the field. After reading this text, your students will have a keen understanding of where the field of adult development and aging has been in the past, where it stands right now, and where it will head in the future.

We have tried to present a balanced treatment of critical issues and of the gains and losses that characterize psychological development through the adult years. We have also given special attention to how different aspects of psychological development may be optimized throughout adulthood.

A number of pedagogical aids have been incorporated into this fifth edition to make the material interesting as well as accessible. Each chapter opens with a chapter outline, and each includes a number of boxed Research Focus inserts containing high-interest, discussion-provoking material. All key terms are highlighted, defined, and thoroughly explained the first time they appear in the text.

Audience

This text is appropriate for all students taking a course in adult development and aging. Such courses are usually titled Adult Development, Adult Development and Aging (or the Psychology of Adult Development and Aging), and Adult Psychology. The writing is geared toward a sophomore, junior, or senior undergraduate who has completed a general introductory-level psychology course. However, the text assumes no prerequisite knowledge of psychology.

Adult Development and Aging would also be useful to instructors who teach a course in life-span development and want to use two books—one on child and adolescent development and another on adult development and aging. The text is equally appropriate for students at two-year and four-year colleges and universities.

Content and Organization

Adult Development and Aging presents current knowledge derived from research findings plus new theories and ideas that view adulthood and aging from an interdisciplinary, process-oriented perspective. The material is organized in terms of the biological, social, and cultural contexts in which change occurs during the adult years. The text consists of 13 chapters, each focused on a major theme or aspect of adult development and aging. The appendix covers research methods used to investigate age-related changes.

Learning Aids

We have written this text with the student in mind, incorporating detailed chapter outlines, Research

Focus boxes, and a comprehensive glossary. All of the terms in the glossary are printed in boldface type when they first appear to alert students to the precise meanings of key terms. Graphs, tables, and figures clearly and concisely illustrate important research findings or summarize facts and theories. Photographs and line drawings give visual emphasis to key concepts and events, as well as to those people, present and past, who have advanced our knowledge of adult development and aging. Finally, a detailed summary and a list of review questions appear at the end of each chapter. Separate indexes for authors and subjects are included at the end of the book.

Instructor's Manual and Test Bank

An *Instructor's Manual and Test Bank* is available to all adopters. The *Instructor's Manual* includes chapter outlines, learning objectives, classroom suggestions, and essay questions. The *Test Bank* includes an expanded selection of objective test items marked as factual, conceptual, or applied to assist you in selecting a variety of test items. Page numbers referencing the text are also provided. These test items are also available on a dual platform computerized test bank CD for both Macintosh and Windows users.

Custom Website

This extensive website, designed specifically to accompany Hoyer and Roodin's *Adult Development and Aging,* offers an array of resources for both the student and the instructor. The password protected instructor side of the site contains the Instructor's Manual, PowerPoint Presentations, web links, and other teaching resources; the student side includes practice quizzes, interactive web links, and other study tools. Visit the website at: www.mhhe.com/hoyer5

PowerWeb

The perfect research-driven resource to complement a research-driven textbook, PowerWeb is a unique online tool that provides students with current articles, curriculum-based materials, weekly updates with assessment, informative and timely world news, referenced web links, research tools, student study tools, and interactive exercises. A PowerWeb access card is packaged for FREE with each new copy of the text. www.dushkin.com/powserweb

Acknowledgments

Special thanks to our Senior Sponsoring Editor Rebecca Hope, Project Manager Rick Hecker, Photo Researcher John Leland, and Developmental Editor Mary Kate Hanley. The fifth edition of this text benefited greatly from colleagues who provided user reviews of the previous edition. For their many good ideas and helpful suggestions, we thank: Paul C. Amrhein, University of New Mexico; Laura Hess Brown, SUNY College at Oswego; David N. Carpenter, Southwest Texas State University; Stephanie Dollinger, Southern Illinois University; Michelle Martin, Vanguard University of California; Daniel L. Segal, University of Colorado; Dorothy Shedlock, SUNY College at Oswego.

Finally, we would like to thank our colleagues and students at Syracuse University and SUNY College at Oswego for their constructive comments and feedback during the preparation of this fifth edition.

1

ADULT DEVELOPMENT AND AGING
An Introduction

> *At first we want life to be romantic; later to be bearable; finally to be understandable.*
> —Louise Bogan

> *Life is what happens when you're busy making other plans.*
> —John Lennon

INTRODUCTION

This chapter lays a foundation for the study of adulthood and aging. You will learn about the different ways developmental scientists describe and explain the adult part of the human life span. In addition, you will learn about some of the controversies that are currently shaping the study of adult development and aging.

Why Study Adult Development and Aging?

People study adult development and aging for many reasons. Some want to understand the processes of development, while others desire to improve the quality of life for themselves or others. Interest in the study of adult development and aging can stem from (1) scientific or factual, (2) personal, or (3) altruistic motives. In fact, the philosopher Habermas (1971) suggested that all human action is largely motivated by precisely these kinds of concerns. First, some of us have a *factual interest* in aging; we want to gain an objective understanding of what happens to people as they grow older. We pursue factual knowledge because we are curious about how and why people change. How does personality or intelligence change with aging? Why is it that some people experience declines in cognitive function, or major changes in their personalities, while others do not? Can we reverse or modify some of the negative changes associated with aging? Do some positive aspects of psychological functioning (e.g., wisdom) emerge only during the later years of life? Questions such as these arise from a factual interest in the aging process.

Second, some of us have a *personal interest* in studying adult development and aging because we want to prepare for the changes, challenges, risks, and opportunities we will face as we grow older. What can this field tell you about your future development and aging? Can you control how you age? How can you become your best self? One can apply one's knowledge of adult development and aging to one's own development. This is especially important when we consider that significant developmental change occurs throughout the entire adult life span—from the twenties onward.

A third reason for wanting to study adult development and aging is *altruistic:* We want to know how to help others. Knowledge within this domain allows us to help others live better lives. We can assist our spouses, friends, confidants, adult children, grandparents, parents, or clients by helping them to negotiate the tasks and challenges of adulthood. For example, we may face the challenge of helping a friend adjust to a new job. Or we may have to learn how to be an effective caregiver for a parent or grandparent with dementia. We may even want to pursue a career in psychology, medicine, or social work that involves direct service to older individuals. Changes in the health care system, combined with the rising numbers of older adults, have created needs within families and opened many employment opportunities in the health and human service professions. In addition, accurate knowledge about the myths and realities of adult development and aging can help dispel oppressive and negative stereotypes about old age and the elderly.

What Is Developmental Psychology?

Developmental psychology has two aims. First, developmental psychologists seek to understand the origins and development of behavior within the individual; this focus concerns the study of **ontogeny,** or **intraindividual change.** Although the intensive study of individual development is a primary goal of developmental psychology, relatively few studies of individual development exist; most of the research in developmental psychology compares groups of individuals of different ages. Studies describing the differences between different age groups have implications for "average" individual development.

Second, developmental psychologists study age-related **interindividual differences,** examining how different individuals develop and change as well as the factors that account for individual differences in development. Thus, the aims of developmental psychology are to study how individuals develop and change as they grow older, and how different people show different patterns of development and change.

With these aims in mind, we can define **developmental psychology** as the study of age-related interindividual differences and age-related intraindividual change. The main goals of developmental psychology are to describe, explain, predict, and improve or optimize age-related behavior change. We use the term *age-related* because age (or time) does not in itself give us a satisfactory explanation for development. The specific events or processes that occur during an interval of time, whether measured in hours, days, years, or decades, are the real determinants of development and aging; time or age itself does not directly cause change. We should also mention that *nonevents,* or events that we do not personally or directly experience, can affect the path of development. That is, we might have developed entirely differently if we had grown up in a different neighborhood or country, not fallen in love, not learned to play a musical instrument, or met different friends or teachers. Someone we know might have developed differently if she had not learned how to read or had not been physically injured in a car accident. We are changed by what we experience, and we develop in ways that are different from others in part because of the consequences of the events we experience or not.

In developmental psychology, *behavior* is the focus of study, because psychology is the study of behavior. Psychologists conceptualize behavior to include just about everything that people do. For example, social interactions, thoughts, memories, emotions, attitudes, and physical activities are all topics of study within the psychology of adult development and aging. We may select particular kinds of behavior for study because they are important in their own right, or because a behavior may provide a reliable measure for an important concept or process that we cannot measure directly.

The term **development** applies to changes in behavior that vary in a predictable and orderly way with increasing age. Developmental change must be relatively durable and distinct from temporary fluctuations in behavior caused by mood, short-term learning, or other factors. We would not identify an infant's one-time utterance of someone's name as evidence of language development. Nor would we identify a one-time failure to recall someone's name as evidence of age-related memory deficit. Development is reversible, and may include increases as well as decreases in behavior, but the changes must be relatively durable to be considered developmental change.

Theoretical Issues in the Study of Adult Development and Aging

Table 1.1 summarizes the major theoretical issues in the study of adult development and aging. As the table shows, those who study adult development and aging generally take the view that development takes place throughout the entire adult life span. In general usage, the term *development* refers to growth, including physical maturation during the early years of childhood and adolescence; developmental psychologists who study the adult years recognize that development or change occurs throughout the human life span.

Development as Gains and Losses

Although the types of changes that occur between birth and 20 years of age differ from those that occur after one's 20th birthday, *gains* and *losses* occur throughout life. Those who study adult development and aging take the view that no age period is any more important than any other period of development. Thus, changes that occur during the adult years are just as significant as those that occur during childhood or adolescence. For example, most people undergo great changes in social maturity during the college years. One's choice of vocation has a strong impact on social and intellectual development, and on health and happiness, during the adult years. Whether someone marries or becomes a parent has a substantial effect on many aspects of development. Perhaps you have noticed changes in the attitudes, motivations, and capabilities of your parents or grandparents as they have grown older. Profound changes continue to occur throughout the life span.

Qualitative versus Quantitative Change

As table 1.1 indicates, developmental changes may be either **qualitative,** abrupt, and stagelike or **quantitative,** gradual, and continuous. Qualitative changes are differences in kinds of behavior, while quantitative changes are differences in amount or degree. For example, developmental change is considered qualitative when an individual dramatically changes in his thinking about interpersonal relationships. Change is quantitative when a person's information retrieval from memory gradually slows.

TABLE 1.1

A Summary of Theoretical Issues in the Study of Adult Development and Aging

Development is a lifelong process.

No age or period of development is any more important than any other age or period of development.

Development includes both increases and decreases, or gains and losses, in behavior.

Development is modifiable or reversible; the individual is active in determining the course of development, and there is plasticity in how an individual develops and changes throughout the life span.

Development can take many different paths, as age-related interindividual differences show.

Development is multidirectional: different rates and directions of change occur for different characteristics within the individual and across individuals.

Developmental change can be quantitative, gradual, and continuous or qualitative, relatively abrupt, and stagelike.

Developmental changes are relatively durable, distinguishing them from temporary fluctuations in behavior.

Development can vary substantially depending on historical and sociocultural conditions.

Development is determined by the interactive effects of nature and nurture; the contributions of environmental and biological influences vary for different aspects of development and for different points in the life span.

The study of development is multidisciplinary; it combines the perspectives of anthropology, biology, psychology, sociology, and other disciplines.

Whether adult development is essentially qualitative or quantitative is both an empirical and a theoretical issue. Most likely, developmental change is *both* qualitative and quantitative (Lerner, 2001).

Stagelike versus Continuous Change

Some researchers and theorists point to identifiable stages of adult development and aging. Others maintain that no universal markers distinguish one stage of development from any other. The notion of stages of development is controversial; researchers disagree about whether distinct stages of development occur during the adult years and about the criteria that might indicate the presence of stages.

A **stage theory** is a description of a sequence of qualitative changes. According to such a theory, Stage 1 must always precede Stage 2. In addition, (1) each successive stage consists of the integration and extension of a previous stage, (2) the transition from one stage to another is abrupt, and (3) each stage represents an organized whole characterized by several particular behaviors or competencies. Thus, if entire sets of behaviors appeared rather suddenly in the development of most individuals at a particular time in life, and if each new set of behaviors incorporated and extended the competencies of the previous stage, then we would have clear evidence for a developmental stage. Evidence for stages of development is rare, however, leading some investigators to doubt the stage concept (Flavell, 1985). Others want to relax the criteria for defining stagelike development (Fischer, 1980; Wohlwill, 1973).

Stage theories imply an abruptness, or developmental **discontinuity,** between stages and **continuity** within stages. Nonstage theories posit that development is *always* continuous. According to social learning theory, for example, the same principles and processes control behavior throughout the life span; imitation, reward, and punishment continually shape an individual's behavior. These mechanisms cause an increase, a decrease, or stability in a behavior over the life span. For example, because of changes in reinforcement contingencies, we can expect that some adults will experience increasing feelings of depression and helplessness as they age.

Researchers who study adult development and aging are concerned with understanding stability as well as gains and losses during the life span. Although adulthood is traditionally characterized as a period of relative continuity (e.g., Shanan, 1991), studies have revealed substantial diversity among adults (interindividual differences), as well as substantial variability within the same person across time (intraindividual change) and across tasks or situations (intraindividual differences). Despite the appearance of stability and continuity, a considerable amount of change appears to occur in various underlying mechanisms (e.g., at the neurophysiological level).

Plasticity versus Nonplasticity of Change

Another issue in the study of adult development and aging is the extent to which behavior exhibits **plasticity** (Baltes, 1997; Hoyer, 2001). Baltes and his colleagues, in particular, have been active proponents of the notion of developmental **reserve capacity,** or the idea that individuals have a finite amount of resources to respond to stresses and challenges, and that this amount may decrease with age. Baltes and his coworkers have thoughtfully discussed the relevance of the concepts of both plasticity and reserve capacity in regard to adult development (e.g., Baltes, Staudinger, & Lindenberger, 1999). Evidence suggests that many kinds of age-related deficits can be remediated through appropriate intervention and health care (e.g., Fries, 1997).

Although the reversibility of some aspects of adult development is an exciting possibility to explore, research indicates that reserve capacity diminishes in later life. That is, older adults are less able to benefit from training designed to optimize performance on cognitive tasks (e.g., Baltes & Kliegl, 1992). The notions of plasticity and reserve have significant implications for the mechanisms that underlie competence and performance. Just as cardiovascular function, muscular efficiency, and other biological systems decrease with age, behavioral efficiency may decrease when stresses or other factors challenge the systems that maintain behavioral or cognitive performance (Kiecolt-Glaser & Glaser, 2001). Reserve capacity decreases with age across many biological systems. The concept of reserve is useful for describing the potential as well as limits of behavioral functioning.

Developmental psychologists must also confront the fact that the same individual performs differently at different times. Theories of adult development and aging must consider this variability, emphasizing what the individual can do under some conditions, some of the time.

Multidirectional versus Unidirectional Change

Another theoretical issue in the study of adult development and aging concerns the directionality of development. **Multidirectionality** refers to the observation that intraindividual differences occur in the patterns of aging. In other words, individuals show stability for some types of behavior, declines in others, and improvements in still others. The developing individual might show an increase in creativity or wisdom and a decrement in some memory functions with advancing age.

In contrast to research and theory in adult development and aging, child-focused views of development, such as those of Piaget and Freud, generally assume a **unidirectional** view of development. These theories argue that all abilities show the same forward trend or direction with maturation.

Determinants of Adult Developmental Change

Why do individuals change and develop as they do? Some determinants or causes of development are universal; they are the same for everyone. Other determinants of development are culture-specific, cohort-specific, or specific to a segment of historical time. Some developmental causes are gender-specific, and some are entirely unique to individuals because of their particular experiences. In this section, we will discuss these three general categories of determinants of developmental change: (1) **normative age-graded factors,** (2) **normative history-graded factors,** and (3) **nonnormative** or **idiosyncratic life events.** These factors interact to determine adult development. Usually it is an error to attribute developmental change to only one of them.

Normative Age-Graded Factors

Some aspects of development appear *normative,* or similar across individuals and even cultures, and development throughout life appears to be subject to a variety of normative age-graded factors. For example, the maturation and deterioration of the brain and nervous system occur at roughly the same ages in all individuals. Reliable age-graded changes also appear in the speed of information processing and in vision and hearing acuity.

Normative History-Graded Factors

Some developmental influences are closely related to specific historical eras or events rather than to age. These events, called normative history-graded factors, produce dramatic effects on the individuals who experience them—effects that may persist for a lifetime (Elder, 1998). Normative history-graded factors include the pervasive and enduring effects of societal events such as wars and economic depressions on individual lives. Think of the personality differences that exist between adults of different ages. Why do many people in their thirties and forties have different attitudes and personalities than individuals in their seventies and eighties? Is it simply because of the different ages of these two groups of adults? Or is it because each age group grew up in different circumstances? In today's world, for example, the consequences of a particular event, the terrorist attacks on the

Many people now choose to marry or begin parenting at a later age. Medical advances and improved family planning allow for a wider range of individual choices in this area of development, and career and financial considerations influence decision making.

Pentagon and World Trade Centers in 2001, or a particular context, the political and economic condition of a nation, may have different effects on different-aged individuals.

We can observe normative history-graded influences by comparing different cohorts of individuals, or groups of individuals born at a particular time. For example, figure 1.1 shows changes in attitude among students of different eras. These data come from annual surveys of over 200,000 first-year college students (Dey, Astin, & Korn, 1991; Sax, et al., 1998). The percentage of entering college students who agree that "It is very important or essential to be very well off financially," gradually increased from about 40 percent in the mid-1960s to about 75 percent in the 1980s and 1990s. And the percentage of college students saying, "It is very important or essential to develop a meaningful philosophy of life," declined from about 80 percent in the mid-1960s to about 40 percent in the 1980s and 1990s.

History-graded or cohort factors have also been shown to affect the level of intellectual abilities in different-aged individuals. Consider the results of the Seattle Longitudinal Study, which began as a doctoral dissertation by K. Warner Schaie in 1956. Careful planning and design allowed Schaie and his colleagues to distinguish the influences of age-related and history-graded changes over six waves of testing (1956, 1963, 1970, 1977, 1984, and 1996). For each wave of data collection, the researchers tested individuals ranging in age from 22 to 70 years and older on measures of verbal meaning, spatial orientation, inductive reasoning, number, and word fluency from the Primary Mental Abilities (PMA) test (Schaie, 1993, 1994, 1996; Schaie & Willis, 1993). As expected, age-related declines occurred for most of the measures of intellectual performance. Considering these cross-sectional data by themselves, it appears that cognitive ability declines with age. However, when the results are examined across the six measurement intervals from 1956 to 1996, the results demonstrate substantial history-graded differences in intellectual performance. These results suggest that both age-related and history-graded factors are responsible for differences in intellectual ability. In Schaie's study, for example, individuals born in 1910 performed worse on all measures of mental ability than individuals

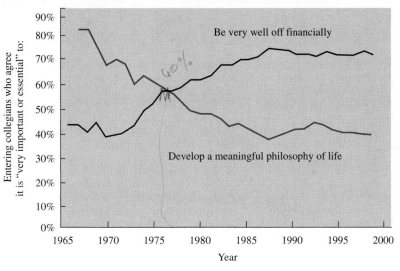

Figure 1.1
Changes in materialism occurred among students first entering college from 1965 through the late 1990s.

Note: From annual surveys of more than 200,000 U.S. students entering college (total sample approximately 6.5 million students). Data from Dey, Astin, and Korn, 1991, and subsequent annual reports, including Sax, et al., 1998.

born in 1917 and later. Generally, subsequent cohorts of individuals experienced better schooling with less discrimination on the basis of race, ethnicity, and gender, better health care and nutrition, and more stimulating intellectual environments. History-graded factors influence many other aspects of psychological functioning, and we cannot overemphasize the importance of distinguishing age effects and history-graded or cohort effects in developmental researches (see Hofer & Slowinski, 2001). Appendix A describes in detail research designs for disentangling age and cohort effects.

Nonnormative or Idiosyncratic Life Events

One of the most important characteristics of adult development is that some changes are unique to the individual. This kind of developmental change is nonnormative, or **idiosyncratic.** Idiosyncratic change is attributed to variations in experiences across a wide range of environmental or societal opportunities and constraints (e.g., Baltes, 1997; Riley, 1985; Riley & Riley, 1994). Age-ordered normative change is much less evident during adulthood than during the childhood and adolescent years. Many of the individual changes and interindividual differences in adult development can be attributed to idiosyncratic influences rather than to universal patterns of developmental change (see Research Focus 1.1). A high degree of interindividual variability is generally evident among adults. Thus, during adulthood, age-ordered, biological, or maturational processes are only one source of interindividual and intraindividual variability, leaving room for a wide range of individual influences.

Many influences on adult development are unique to the individuals who experience them. Some nonnormative life events are common to a small proportion of same-age

Personal Control and Successful Aging

Until recently, most of the studies about successful aging focused on 50- to 60-year-olds, following them into their later years (e.g., see Elder, 1998; Lachman, 2001; Rowe & Kahn, 1997). Recently, Vaillant and Mukamal (2001) made a unique contribution to the understanding of successful aging by following two cohorts of adolescent males for 60 years, or until death. The two groups consisted of 237 college students and 332 core-city youth. Researchers collected complete physical exams on the subjects every five years and psychosocial measures every two years. These measures included "uncontrollable factors" such as parental social class, family cohesion, major depression, longevity of family members, childhood temperament, and physical health at age 50 years, and "controllable measures" such as alcohol abuse, smoking, marital stability, exercise, body mass index, coping mechanisms, and education. The measures selected to assess successful aging at ages 70 to 80 included physical health, death or disability before age 80, social supports, and mental health, as well as two self-rated variables (instrumental activities of daily living, and life enjoyment).

Vaillant and Mukamal found that successful and unsuccessful aging could be predicted by all the variables assessed before age 50 and by the controllable variables assessed after age 50. When an individual controlled the "controllable" variables, successful aging was evident; depression was the only uncontrollable variable that negatively affected the quality of aging. Thus, the results suggest that it is seldom or never too late to begin aging successfully. Older individuals (as well as adolescents and young adults) have much greater personal control over their aging than anyone previously recognized.

From Vaillant, G. E., & Mukamal, K. (2001). Successful aging. *American Journal of Psychiatry, 158*, 839–847.

individuals; others affect only a single individual. Furthermore, nonnormative life events do not happen at any predictable time in a person's life. For example, winning first prize in a multimillion-dollar lottery might profoundly influence a person's behavior. However, it is only likely to happen to a small number of individuals and cannot be predicted to occur at any particular point in a person's life. Nonnormative life events, then, are usually chance occurrences.

Other examples of nonnormative events include accidents, illnesses, business failures, or the death of a young adult. Nonnormative life events also include unintended or chance encounters with new people which may become critically important determinants of many aspects of our lives, including career choice and marriage (Bandura, 1982). How many college students settle on an academic major because of an enthusiastic and inspiring professor they encounter by chance in an elective course? How many young men and women begin their career paths by chance? These important and interesting research questions are open for exploration. The goal is not to count the frequency of occurrence of chance encounters, but to examine how much choice and control we have—or do not have—over the events that affect our future development.

As figure 1.2 shows, the relative importance of normative age-graded factors, normative history-graded factors, and nonnormative life events varies across the life span. Normative age-graded factors, for example, are most likely to influence development at the beginning and end of the life span (figure 1.2). Most of the behavioral hallmarks of infancy (e.g., crawling, walking, and talking) and very old age (e.g., decrements in vision and speed of information processing) are probably due, to a great extent, to age-related biomaturational changes. Normative history-graded factors are

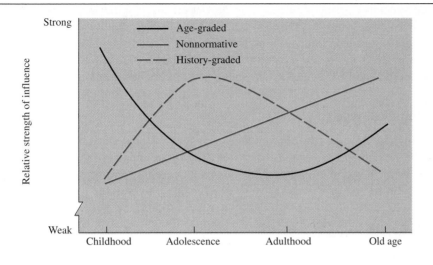

Figure 1.2 The relative influence of normative age-graded factors, normative history-graded factors, and nonnormative life-event factors in promoting developmental change at different times across the human life span.

most likely to produce developmental change during adolescence and young adulthood. These are times when an individual first constructs an understanding of society and his or her relationship to it. It seems obvious, for example, that living through the Vietnam War era and the civil rights movement in the United States had the least effect on extremely young and old individuals and the greatest effect on young adults entering the mainstream of societal life at that time. Finally, nonnormative life events may take on a gradually more powerful role in promoting developmental changes as an individual ages. This may account for the observation that individual differences become progressively more identifiable with increasing age. For example, there is generally more interindividual variability in a group of 60-year-olds than a group of 40-year-olds. As we grow older, the continued emergence and accumulation of unique nonnormative life events helps to shape our personal lives, making individual differences more and more apparent.

Thus, we can distinguish three types of influences on adult development: the normative age-graded factors that most developmental research has emphasized; the nonnormative influences (such as winning a lottery); and the history-graded factors (such as the rise and fall of employment opportunities in e-commerce or health care).

The Concept of Age

The concept of age is *multidimensional.* Time since birth (or chronological age) is not always a good measure of developmental function. Some researchers have thus attempted to develop **functional age** measures as replacements for chronological age. For example, an individual needs a number of skills and abilities (both psychological and physical) to function effectively as the sole occupant of an apartment—the individual has to be mobile and independent to be able to shop, clean, cook, and wash as well as to efficiently plan and remember pertinent information. Not surprisingly, some 75-year-olds are more self-sufficient than some 25-year-olds. Given the fact that chronological age is not always a good predictor of functional age, psychologists find it increasingly important to develop valid and reliable measures of a person's functional abilities. In the following paragraphs, we will describe some of the other dimensions and meanings of age and aging.

Chronological Age

Chronological age refers to the number of years that have elapsed since a person's birth. Chronological age per se is often *not* an accurate index of psychological development; a person's age in and of itself does not cause development. Age is merely a rough marker for the processes that influence behavior over time.

Biological Age

Biological age has been defined as an estimate of the individual's position with respect to his or her potential life span (Birren & Schroots, 2001). This concept of age involves measuring the capacities of an individual's vital organ system. From this perspective, age is an index of biological health. An individual's biological capacities may differ from those of other persons of the same chronological age.

Psychological Age

Psychological age refers to an individual's adaptive capacities—that is, his or her ability to adapt to changing environmental demands. Individuals adapt to their environments by drawing on various psychological characteristics: learning, memory, intelligence, emotional control, motivational strengths, coping styles, and so on. Therefore, adults who possess such psychological characteristics to a greater degree than their chronological agemates are considered "psychologically young"; those who possess such traits to a lesser degree are "psychologically old."

Social Age

Social age refers to the social roles and expectations people hold for themselves as well as those others impose on them. Consider the role of "mother" and the behaviors that accompany that role. It is probably more useful in predicting these behaviors to know that a woman is the mother of a 3-year-old child than to know whether she was born 20 or 30 years ago. Furthermore, individuals are often aware of being on- or off-time with regard to social age. Some older adults, for example, act like perpetual teenagers because they consider themselves "young."

Age Profiles

Given the different dimensions of age, we can develop a comprehensive age profile for any individual. For example, a 70-year-old man (chronological age) might be in very good physical health (biological age), yet be experiencing a number of problems re-

Both women in these photos are 80 years old. Biological and psychological aging occur at different rates for different individuals.

membering and focusing attention (psychological age). The same man might consider himself more an avid golfer than a "grandfather" (social age).

The Concept of Successful Aging

As Lerner (2001) has pointed out, the need has never been greater to increase or improve opportunities for optimal development across the life span. Measures of biological age, psychological age, and social age are relevant to healthy development or **successful aging.** Successful aging refers to a combination of three components: (1) the avoidance of disease and disability; (2) the maintenance of high physical and cognitive capacity in the later years, and (3) continued active engagement with life (Rowe & Kahn, 1997). In many countries, aging is associated with disability, cognitive deficits, and loneliness. But substantial and growing evidence indicates that the risk factors for some diseases, such as cardiovascular disease, can be modified (Vaillant & Mukamal, 2001). Research also shows that cognitive deficits and social disengagement are not inevitable consequences of growing older (e.g., Freund & Baltes, 2002; Simonton, 1997; Willis, 2001).

Conceptual Paradigms for the Study of Adult Development

Paradigms, also called models or worldviews, enable researchers to construct meaningful patterns from otherwise unrelated observations. Paradigms guide scientific activity by

Social age refers to the age-graded prescriptions people hold for themselves and others. Although definitions of social age are becoming more flexible in American culture, we still take notice of individuals who are atypical for traditional age prescriptions— for example, performer Mick Jagger, at age 55-plus.

determining what is important to study, how we should study it, and what kinds of theoretical ideas we can advance on the basis of such study (Kuhn, 1962).

Paradigms are not directly testable; they are too abstract to be objectively verified or falsified. Thus, paradigms are *not* the same as theories. However, paradigms serve to stimulate ideas, issues, and questions that we *can* test. They provide a framework for generating theories, and theories generate research. Paradigms are useful if they serve this purpose, and not in terms of being right or wrong. Historically, psychologists have used mechanistic, organismic, and contextual paradigms to understand human development.

The Mechanistic Paradigm

According to the **mechanistic paradigm,** an individual's development is the product of environmental forces. The mechanistic model assumes that human behavior is machinelike. Machines are passive or not self-evolving; similarly, some or much of behavioral development is reactive to environmental stimuli or life events.

The Organismic Paradigm

According to the **organismic paradigm,** development is qualitative. From this view, the developing individual emerges according to a wired-in blueprint, as a cell or embryo develops. The organismic paradigm shifted the emphasis from the study of simple stimulus-response relationships and quantitative change to the study of internal processes and qualitative change. According to this view, individual development unfolds in a universal, orderly sequence of stages.

The Contextual Paradigm

In recent years, the **contextual paradigm** has become predominant. This paradigm, based on the metaphor of an historical event, suggests that adults, like historical events, are ongoing, dynamic, and not directed toward a particular goal or end-state. Furthermore, the interpretation of historical events may change, depending on the *context* or perspective from which we view such events. A war may be viewed as "moral" from one historical context and "immoral" from another. Similarly, an individual's development may seem either passive or active, depending on the context. The basic concept of this model is that an adult both influences and is influenced by the different contexts of life.

Context is an open-ended term that may apply at different levels. For example, the environmental context pertains to one's physical environment. The social, historical, or cultural context pertains to influences such as societal norms and the expectations of friends and relatives. Further, the biological context pertains to an individual's health and physical skills. In all of these examples, not only do the contexts have an effect upon the individual, but the individual has an effect upon the context. To take a simple example, one's family might make unreasonable demands. When the individual begins to refuse these demands more often, it may alter the family's subsequent demands, which in turn alters the individual's responsiveness to further demands.

The contextual model underlies a broad range of theories that address various aspects of adult development. For example, an adult's ability to remember an event depends on (1) the psychological, social, and physical contexts in which the person initially experienced the event, (2) the unique skills, abilities, knowledge, and motivation that the individual brings to the context in which he must remember, and (3) the special characteristics of this context. As the individual changes, and as the contexts in which he is asked to remember change, we would expect the person's memory to change as well. Thus, we could say that memory is a dynamic process involving the continual *reconstruction* of past events and experiences. Adults seem to serve as their own "historians," constantly revising their pasts from the perspective of the present.

One version of the contextual paradigm is the **dialectical view.** Riegel (1976) argued that individuals and the contexts of their lives are always in a state of flux; that is, adults are constantly changing organisms in a constantly changing world. From Riegel's view, the individual and society are never at rest. Riegel also believed that contradiction and conflict are an inherent part of development and that no single goal or end point is ever reached. The dialectical perspective stresses the inherent multidirectionality of developmental change and the wide-reaching interindividual variability observed with increasing chronological age.

Two current versions of contextualism, perhaps contenders to replace or revise the contextual paradigm, are **action theory** and **goal pursuit theory.** Action theory and goal pursuit theory state that individuals are self-motivated to initiate goal-directed pursuits. Research shows that behavior is optimal when individuals formulate intentions and translate their intentions into action (e.g., Brandstaetter, Lengfelder, & Gollwitzer, 2001; Gollwitzer & Bargh, 1996). Today, most research on social and personality development emphasizes that the individual initiates and implements personal goals (e.g., see Antonucci, 2001; Blanchard-Fields & Abeles, 1996; Carstensen, Isaacowitz, & Charles, 1999; Freund & Baltes, 2002; Mischel, Cantor, & Feldman, 1996). Certainly the idea that development involves selection, optimization, and compensation is based on an integration of some of the principles of action theory and goal pursuit theory with concepts of successful aging (e.g., Carstensen, Pasupathi, & Mayr, 2000; Freund & Baltes, 2002).

New ways of thinking about adult development and aging have emerged in recent years, and these views are largely contextual (e.g., Baltes, Staudinger, & Lindenberger, 1999; Lerner, 2001). These views have emerged from researchers' dissatisfaction with the mechanistic and organismic stress on the negative aspects of aging. Some psychologists also object to an overemphasis on chronological age as the measure of development, and to the lack of emphasis on resiliency, vitality, and adaptation in adult development and aging.

New contextual approaches to development try to take into account individual differences, gains and losses in function during the adult years, and the role of social interaction and conflict in adult development. Another characteristic of the new work in adult development and aging is its greater emphasis on practical aspects of development. Many everyday activities in adulthood and old age are contextually based. Thinking, reasoning, emotions, and other aspects of everyday function in adulthood are constrained not so much by biological aging as by the contexts in which these activities take place.

Paradigms and Issues in Adult Development

Let's compare the mechanistic, organismic, and contextual paradigms with respect to the issues considered earlier in this chapter. As tables 1.2 and 1.3 show, the organismic model places an emphasis on qualitative change, distinct stages of development, and continuity of change. It also is unique in emphasizing the importance of age-graded influences on development. One of the main differences between the mechanistic and contextual models is that the contextual model places greater emphasis on the multidirectional nature of developmental change and on history-graded influences. The mechanistic model emphasizes nonnormative life events at the expense of all other aspects of development. The contextual model also emphasizes nonnormative influences, but not exclusively; it considers history-graded influences as well as individual differences. Indeed, as table 1.3 indicates, the contextual model stresses all aspects of development. From this perspective, development is multifaceted and multidetermined. The contextual model, more than the others, recognizes that individuals help determine their own development.

TABLE 1.2

Overview of the Three Life-Span Models of Adult Development

Questions for Distinguishing among Developmental Models	Models		
	Mechanistic	Organismic	Contextual
What is the underlying metaphor?	machine	cell, embryo	historical event
What is the relationship between the person and the environment?	dynamic environment; reactive person	passive environment; self-evolving person	dynamic environment; dynamic person
What is the focus of developmental psychology?	quantitative changes in behavior	qualitative changes in internal structures	changes in person/ environment transactions

TABLE 1.3

Models and Characteristics of Adult Development

Degree of Emphasis on Different Characteristics of Human Development	Models		
	Mechanistic	Organismic	Contextual
Qualitative change	Low	High	Medium
Stages of change	Low	High	Medium
Continuity of change	Low	High	Medium
Multidirectionality of change	Medium	Low	High
Reversibility of change	Medium	Low	Medium
Multiple determinants of change			
Normative age-graded factors	Low	High	Medium
Normative history-graded factors	Low	Low	High
Nonnormative life-event factors	High	Low	High
Chronological age as a useful variable	Low	High	Medium

Overview of the Text

One of the challenges for those who study adult development and aging is to construct a useful and accurate framework for describing and explaining adult development. Some researchers focus on the factors that *constrain* development at different ages. For example, some social and cultural influences, such as restrictive sex roles, ageism, and racism, limit opportunities for growth during the adult years and constrain individual development. Of course, some biological and health influences also constrain the range or nature of development during the adult years. In this text, we emphasize not only the constraining factors, but also the factors that may *optimize* adult development. Furthermore, we stress the ideas that this development represents a complex interplay of gains *and* losses, and that aging is characterized by a great deal of intraindividual change and interindividual variability. Throughout the text, we illustrate how cultural, biological, and experiential factors influence functioning in different domains of development.

Domains of Development

Adult development occurs in a number of areas or domains. The *biological and physical domain* comprises changes that range from simple alterations in size, weight, and other anatomical features to the genetic blueprint that places constraints on our development from conception to death. The genes we were born with influence our adult development. Scientists are looking closely at the role genetics plays in such adult disorders as schizophrenia, dementia, alcoholism, and depression. Hormones are another aspect of biological makeup that play an important part in adult development; for example, significant hormonal changes accompany the onset of menopause in women. In this text, we will pay close attention to age-related changes in the brain and nervous system. And we will describe how such changes in the aging brain influence psychological functioning.

The *cognitive domain* includes the age-related series of changes that occur in mental activity—thought, memory, perception, and attention. As part of our study of cognitive development, we will explore how adults process information; how intelligence and creativity change over time; and how qualitatively new styles of thinking emerge during adulthood. We will look carefully at declines in memory during adulthood, paying special attention to the issue of how "normal" and "pathological" memory deficits may be distinguished in older adults.

The *personality domain* in adult development usually refers to the properties distinguishing one individual from another. But as we will see, some experts believe that commonalities also characterize individuals at particular points in adult development. Sex-role orientation, perception of self, moral values, and sociability are some of the aspects of personality we will discuss. You will find it is difficult to meaningfully discuss adult personality development without looking at the individual's interactions with and thoughts about the social world.

The *social domain* involves an individual's interactions with other individuals in the environment. Two elderly people consoling each other, a son helping his father, two friends arguing, and a grandmother hugging her grandchild are all examples of interaction in the social world. Social development focuses on how these behaviors unfold as an individual grows older. We shall also study the contexts of social development. As we have seen in this chapter, the contexts in which adult development occurs are important in determining behavior. Some of the most important social contexts of adult development are families, other relationships, and work.

Although it is helpful to study adult development within different domains—to take it apart and examine each aspect—keep in mind the importance of integrating the various dimensions of human development. Biological, physical, cognitive, social, and personality development are inextricably linked. For example, in many chapters, you will read about how social experiences shape cognitive development, how cognitive development restricts or promotes social development, and how cognitive development relates to physical development.

SUMMARY

Developmental psychology is the study of age-related interindividual differences and age-related intraindividual change. The main goals of developmental psychology are to describe, explain, predict, and improve or optimize age-related behavior changes. Some of the guiding principles of developmental psychology are:

1. Development is a lifelong process.
2. No age or period of development is any more important than any other age or period of development.
3. Development includes both increases and decreases, or gains and losses, in behavior.
4. Development is modifiable or reversible; the individual is active in determining the course of development, and there is plasticity in how an individual develops and changes throughout the life span.
5. Development can take many different paths, as age-related interindividual differences show.
6. Development is multidirectional; different rates and directions of change occur for different characteristics within the individual and across individuals.
7. Developmental change can be quantitative, gradual, and continuous, or qualitative, relatively abrupt, and stagelike.
8. Developmental changes are relatively durable, distinguishing them from temporary fluctuations in behavior.
9. Development can vary substantially depending on historical and cultural conditions.
10. Development is determined by the interactive effects of nature and nurture; the contributions of environmental and biological influences vary for different aspects of development and for different points in the life span.
11. The study of development is multidisciplinary; it combines the perspectives of anthropology, biology, psychology, sociology, and other disciplines.

It is important to study development during the adult life span for many reasons. These reasons can be categorized as scientific or factual, personal, or altruistic.

Multiple determinants influence development during the adult years. In addition to the normative age-graded influences traditional developmental theory emphasizes, nonnormative life events (e.g., accidents and chance encounters) and normative history-graded influences (e.g., wars, social and economic conditions) also affect the course of human development.

Although chronological age does not "explain" development or change, age is an important descriptive variable in developmental research. One can construct a useful age profile based not only on chronological age, but also on biological, psychological, functional, and social age.

Paradigms are useful for generating ideas, issues, and questions for research. They also suggest appropriate methodological approaches for exploring these areas of research. In contrast to the mechanistic and organismic models, the contextual model is unique in its broad attention to all types and all determinants of change. Indeed, the contextual model actually seems to encompass the other two.

Development takes place within different domains. Thus, to develop an integrative view of adult development, we must understand how the biological/ physical, cognitive, personality, and social dimensions of individuals change (or remain stable) over time.

REVIEW QUESTIONS

1. Give some examples of scientific, personal, and altruistic reasons for studying adult development and aging.
2. What are the primary goals of developmental psychology?
3. Give examples of intraindividual change and interindividual variability.
4. Define the term *development.* Is development characterized by gains or losses? Is development reversible? What is meant by the *optimization* of development?
5. Contrast the life-span perspective with a child-focused perspective.
6. Give examples of nonnormative factors, normative history-graded factors, and normative age-graded factors in adult development.
7. Explain the difference between the concepts of chronological, biological, psychological, functional, and social age. Why is it useful to make distinctions among them?
8. Develop an age profile for yourself and for someone older (e.g., a parent or grandparent). Compare the profiles.
9. What are the purposes and functions of a paradigm? What is the difference between a paradigm and a theory?
10. Describe the mechanistic, organismic, and contextual paradigms. Which paradigm is currently generating the most impact on research into adult development and aging?
11. Give examples of the different domains in which adult development and aging takes place.

ON THE WEB   www.mhhe.com/hoyer5

For a listing of educational resources and links to new topics in the psychology of adult development and aging, see:

From the home page for Division 20 of the American Psychological Association, you can access resources for educators (for example, syllabi and videotape listings), information about graduate study in the psychology of adult development and aging, publications summarizing new research findings, and conference information.

The Administration on Aging page lists many links to Internet websites on a large variety of topics in aging, as well as a wealth of information about aging and the elderly.

The home page for the American Psychological Society (APS) is a portal for access to APS journals and other resources in psychology.

The Gerontological Society of America (GSA) is a professional organization devoted to advancing research, education, and practice in gerontology.

CULTURAL AND ETHNIC DIVERSITY

*W*e breathe the air of our times.
—Anonymous

*E*verything is perfect in being what it is,
Each person is perfect in being,
Having nothing to do with good or bad,
acceptance or rejection.
You might as well burst out laughing.
—Longchenpa

INTRODUCTION

This chapter describes the wide range of diversity that is evident in adult populations. We examine the influences of social and cultural factors—or norms and expectations—on individual development and individual differences during the adult years. We begin with descriptions of U.S. demographic characteristics and of the projected changes in the numbers of older adults and their proportion of the population. The experience of adult development and aging varies in different communities and countries, for different cohorts, for different racial and ethnic groups, and for men and women. Age roles often serve as prescriptions for social behavior and other aspects of development during the adult years.

Characteristics of the Adult Population in the United States

People change and cultures change—each influences the other continuously. Substantial changes have occurred in the composition of the American population in recent years, most strikingly in regard to age groups and the ethnic composition of the population. The number and percentage of middle-aged and older adults in the United States is growing at an unprecedented rate; the number of adults over age 65 is expected to double in the next 40 years. There is also greater diversity of race and ethnicity in the United States than ever before. For example, more foreign-born residents than nonimmigrants live in Miami and Miami Beach, Florida; in Huntington Park, Santa Ana, and Monterey Park, California; and in Union City, New Jersey. In 2000, the American population was 84 percent non-Hispanic white, 8 percent non-Hispanic Black, 6 percent Hispanic, 2 percent non-Hispanic Asian and Pacific Islander, and less than 1 percent non-Hispanic American Indian and native Alaskan. By 2050, these proportions will be substantially different: 64 percent non-Hispanic white, 16 percent Hispanic, 12 percent non-Hispanic Black, 7 percent non-Hispanic Asian and Pacific Islander, and less than 1 percent non-Hispanic American Indian and native Alaskan. In the sections that follow, we will examine the "graying of America" and the "diversification of America." Then we will consider how demographic trends affect both individual development and social institutions such as the family, the workplace, health care, and the educational system.

The Graying of America

The phrase "graying of America" aptly describes increasing numbers and percentages of older adults in the U.S. population. As shown in figure 2.1, about 3.1 million Americans were aged 65 and over in 1900. In the year 2000, there were more than 10 times as many older adults—34.9 million.

Older adults also represent a much greater proportion of the U.S. population than they did 100 years ago. Since 1900, the percentage of Americans aged 65 and over has tripled. In 2000, about 13 percent of the population was age 65 and over, compared with about 4 percent in 1900. As figure 2.2 shows, by 2030, over 20 percent of the population will likely be aged 65 or older (U.S. Bureau of Census, 2001).

The median age (meaning half are older and half are younger) of the U.S. population in 2000 was 35.3 years, the highest ever. The increase in the median age reflects the aging of the baby boomers (born from 1946 to 1964). In the 2000 Census, the population of 45-to-54-year-olds jumped 49 percent, to 37.7 million. At the same time, the number of 18-to-34-year-olds declined 4 percent. The 65-and-over population actually increased at a slower rate than the overall population for the first time in the history of the census. The slower growth of this older population reflects the relatively lower number of births in the late 1920s and early 1930s.

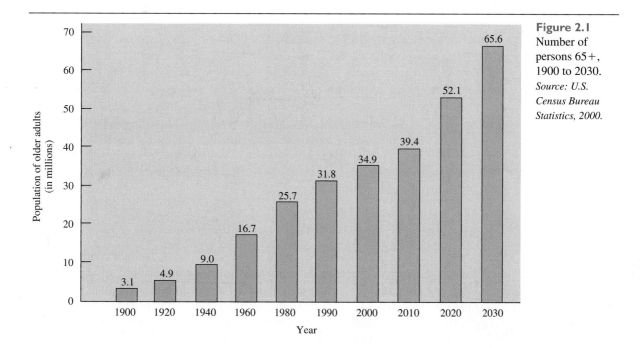

Figure 2.1
Number of persons 65+, 1900 to 2030.
Source: U.S. Census Bureau Statistics, 2000.

Figure 2.2
Percentage of persons 65 or older in the United States, 1900 to 2030. The percentage of individuals 65 or older is expected to nearly double in the next 30 years. *Source: U.S. Census Bureau Statistics, 2001.*

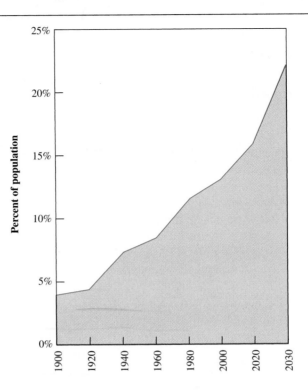

It is projected that the 55+ population will keep growing at a faster rate than other age groups as the baby boomers age. By 2030, 66 million older adults will live in the United States, nearly twice the present number.

Also, the older population is getting older. One of the swiftest-growing segments of the American population is the *old-old,* defined as those aged 85 years and older. The old-old constitute nearly 10 percent of the population over age 65. By 2050, the old-old will represent 25 percent of the population (U.S. Bureau of the Census, 2001). As shown in figure 2.3, between 1980 and 2000, the population of the United States aged 85 and over increased by 90 percent (U.S. Bureau of the Census, 2001).

Finally, the number of *centenarians,* individuals who reach their 100th birthday, increased substantially over the last century, and is expected to continue to grow. In 2000, there were 56,000 centenarians (U.S. Bureau of the Census, 2001). By the year 2050, there may be about 1 million.

Age Structure

One way to show that the United States population is aging is to examine changes in **age structure.** Age structure refers to the percentages of men and women of various ages grouped by age intervals. The top panel in figure 2.4 shows the age structure of the United States in 2000. The second panel shows the projected age structure of the United States for the year 2025. The shapes are quite different; the first graph resembles a pyramid, while the second looks more rectangular. This means that, comparing the age structures

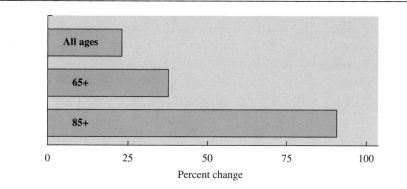

Figure 2.3
Relative change in size of U.S. population 1980–2000. *Source: U.S. Census Bureau.*

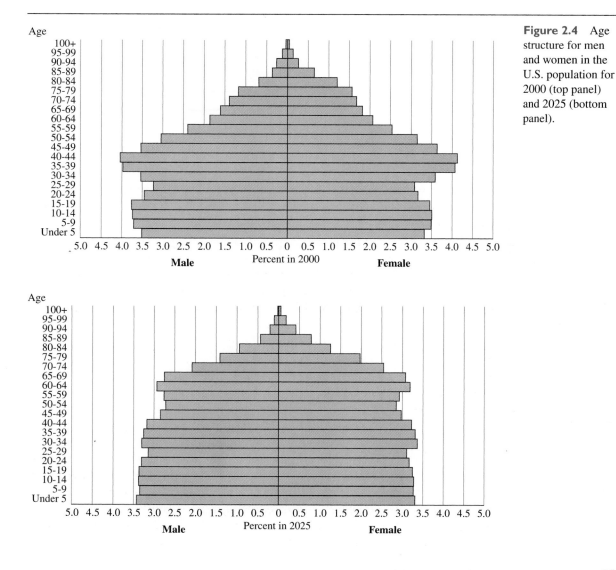

Figure 2.4 Age structure for men and women in the U.S. population for 2000 (top panel) and 2025 (bottom panel).

in 2000 and 2025, we see a trend toward equalization of the percentages of Americans within various age intervals. By the year 2025, the percentages of individuals in each period of life—except for the oldest age groups—will be approximately equal.

The same trend in the shapes of the age structures can be seen for the world population, as shown in Figure 2.5. The age structure for developing countries in Africa,

Figure 2.5 Age structures for men and women in developing countries and developed countries for 1950, 1990, and 2030.

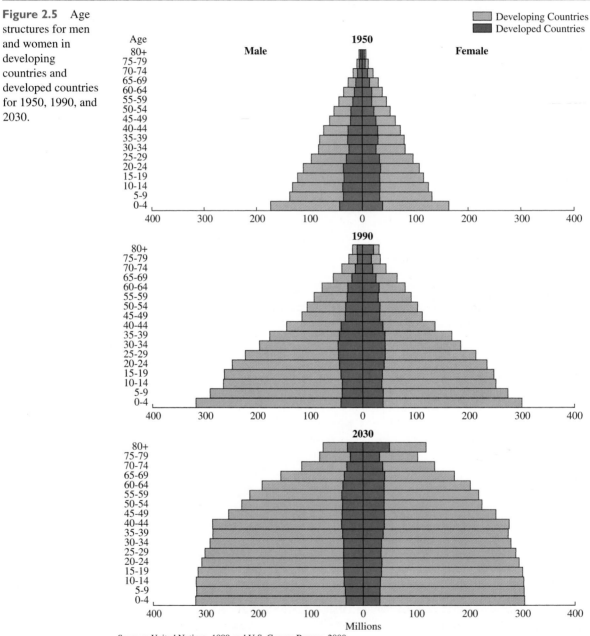

Sources: United Nations, 1999 and U.S. Census Bureau, 2000.

Chapter Two

Asia, Latin America, and the Caribbean will be less triangular in 2030 than it was in 1990 or 2000. The age structure for developed countries in Europe, North America, and Oceania are presented in this figure for comparison. However, the age structures by regions give an incomplete picture for two reasons. First, regional averages hide great diversity among countries. For example, Bangladesh and Singapore are grouped together because they are close geographically, but these countries have substantially different age structures. Second, percentages between age groups hide percentages of growth within age groups. For example, the change in the percentage of elderly adults relative to other age groups in Sub-Saharan Africa is expected to change very little, but the elderly population in Sub-Saharan Africa is expected to jump by 50 percent, from 19.3 million in 2000 to 29 million in 2015 (US Census Bureau statistics, 2001).

Life Expectancy

Life expectancy refers to the predicted length of one's life. Table 2.1 and figure 2.6 show the increase in life expectancy in the United States during the twentieth century. A person born in 1900 had an average life expectancy of about 47 years, whereas a person born in 2000 has an average life expectancy of more than 77 years. This 30-year increase in average life expectancy is greater than the rate of increase through all previous human history. Life expectancy will not continue to increase at this rate (see Research Focus 2.1). Most of the change in life expectancy that occurred during the past century came from improved health care in infancy and early childhood. Life expectancy for those who reached 50 years of age, in contrast, remained unchanged.

Changes in average life expectancy are not uniform across race. The National Center for Health Statistics reported that whites generally live nearly six years longer than blacks, with both groups increasing in life expectancy at roughly the same rate (one year added every two and a half years since the turn of the century). One reason for the differential life expectancy for black men and women is that blacks are dying far earlier in young and middle adulthood. Black children and adults are too often victims of violence in the streets, or of drug abuse; and blacks are more likely than whites to face limited access to medical care, poor nutrition, and substandard housing.

Changes in life expectancy differ for people who live in different countries. Figure 2.7 shows life expectancies for different countries and figure 2.8 shows the overall trend of an increasingly aged population worldwide. During the year 2000, the number of people aged 65 and over in the world increased by more than 800,000 each month (US Census Bureau, 2001). Life expectancy projections must be interpreted cautiously because future changes in infant mortality, in the ability of individuals to resist infectious diseases, in migration, in the quality of medical care, and in social-environmental conditions will influence the health and life expectancy of tomorrow's older adults.

Sex Differences in Life Expectancy

In the United States, data from the 2000 census show that females begin to outnumber males at age 25. This gender gap widens with increasing age. The number of men aged 65 and older (138.1 million) edged closer to the number of females aged 65 and older

TABLE 2.1

Average Life Expectancy in the United States, 1900–2000

Year of Birth	Men	Women
1900	45.2	49.1
1940	60.8	65.2
1950	65.6	71.1
1960	66.6	73.3
1970	67.1	74.7
1980	70.0	77.4
1990	71.8	78.8
2000	74.0	79.6

Source: United States Department of Health and Human Services, 2001.

Figure 2.6 The increased life expectancy of Americans. Both life expectancy at birth and at age 65 have increased over the past century. Eighty percent of Americans now live to age 65. On average, they can expect to live another 18 years after reaching age 65. *Source: U.S. Census Bureau Statistics.*

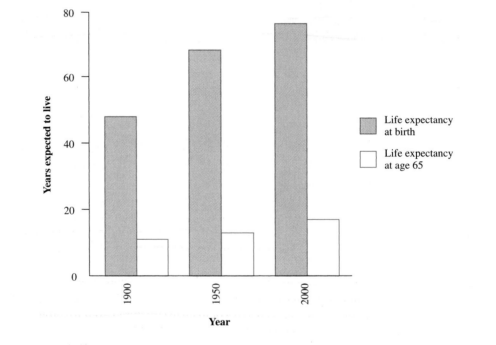

(143.4 million) in 2000; the sex ratio (males per 100 females) increased from 95.1 in 1990 to 96.3 in 2000. By age 75, about 61 percent is female. By age 85 and over, 70 percent is female.

Sex differences in longevity are due to a combination of social, biological, and genetic factors. Social factors include health behaviors and attitudes, habits, lifestyles, and occupational styles. For example, the major causes of death in the United States, including heart disease, lung cancer, motor vehicle accidents, suicide, cirrhosis of the

Sex differences in longevity account for the increasingly higher percentage of females in the older population.

liver, and emphysema are more likely to affect men than women. Such causes of death are associated with habits and lifestyles. For example, lung cancer and heart disease are more likely to kill men because men have historically been heavier smokers than women. Men also have fewer physician checkups than women, which reduces their opportunity for early medical treatment.

If stress at work has a strong influence on life expectancy, we might expect sex differences in longevity to begin narrowing because so many more women have entered the work force in the last 50 years. Actually, it seems that different factors are associated with longevity and physical functioning for older men and women. Income level, educational level, and marital status are strongly associated with changes in physical functioning for men. For women, control over health seems to correlate strongly with changes in physical functioning (Strawbridge, Camacho, Cohen, & Kaplan, 1993). This study suggested that older men stay healthier if encouraged to participate in structured exercise programs, while older women do better by keeping active and doing the things they enjoy.

Biological factors also influence sex differences in longevity (DeLuca et al, 2001). In practically all animal species, females have longer life spans than males (Franceschi & Fabris, 1993). (See Research Focus 2.2 for a discussion of recent research on women's longevity.) Women have more resistance to infectious and degenerative diseases. For instance, estrogen production helps to reduce the risk of atherosclerosis (hardening of the arteries). Further, the two X chromosomes women carry may be linked with the production of more disease-fighting antibodies (Franceschi & Fabris, 1993).

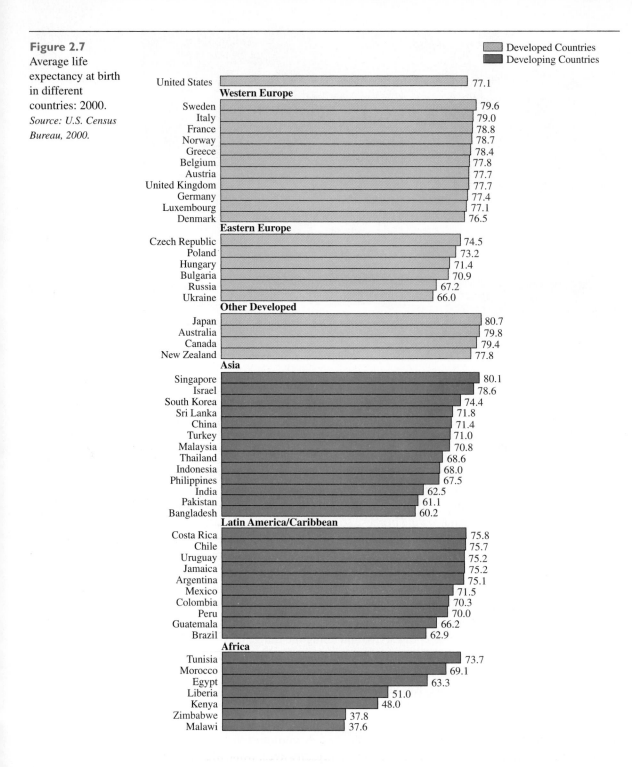

Figure 2.7
Average life expectancy at birth in different countries: 2000.
Source: U.S. Census Bureau, 2000.

Developed Countries
Developing Countries

United States	77.1

Western Europe

Sweden	79.6
Italy	79.0
France	78.8
Norway	78.7
Greece	78.4
Belgium	77.8
Austria	77.7
United Kingdom	77.7
Germany	77.4
Luxembourg	77.1
Denmark	76.5

Eastern Europe

Czech Republic	74.5
Poland	73.2
Hungary	71.4
Bulgaria	70.9
Russia	67.2
Ukraine	66.0

Other Developed

Japan	80.7
Australia	79.8
Canada	79.4
New Zealand	77.8

Asia

Singapore	80.1
Israel	78.6
South Korea	74.4
Sri Lanka	71.8
China	71.4
Turkey	71.0
Malaysia	70.8
Thailand	68.6
Indonesia	68.0
Philippines	67.5
India	62.5
Pakistan	61.1
Bangladesh	60.2

Latin America/Caribbean

Costa Rica	75.8
Chile	75.7
Uruguay	75.2
Jamaica	75.2
Argentina	75.1
Mexico	71.5
Colombia	70.3
Peru	70.0
Guatemala	66.2
Brazil	62.9

Africa

Tunisia	73.7
Morocco	69.1
Egypt	63.3
Liberia	51.0
Kenya	48.0
Zimbabwe	37.8
Malawi	37.6

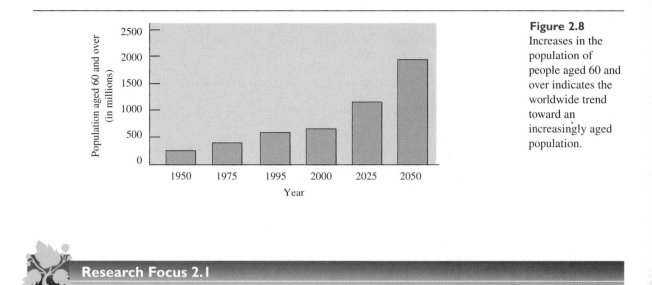

Figure 2.8
Increases in the population of people aged 60 and over indicates the worldwide trend toward an increasingly aged population.

Research Focus 2.1

Long Life Expectancies Are 500 Years Away

Americans can now expect to live 76.9 years on average. Women can expect to live for nearly 80 years, and men can expect to live for nearly 74. However, the increase in life expectancy that accrued over the twentieth century—from about 47 years in 1900 to nearly 77 years in 2000—will *not* continue in the future.

Olshansky, Carnes, and Desesquelles (2001) predicted that more than five centuries would be required for average life expectancy to reach 100 years. This prediction certainly contradicts the optimistic predictions that life expectancy will increase dramatically during the twenty-first century. Olshansky, Carnes, and Desesquelles pointed out that earlier gains in life expectancy were largely attributable to reductions in infant mortality and in deaths from infectious childhood diseases. These investigators noted that if nobody died before age 51, average life expectancy would increase by only 3.5 years. Because death rates are lower in France and Japan than in the United States, it is possible that average life expectancy could reach 100 years in these countries in just two centuries.

The most common causes of death have changed and continue to change. It seems that when one cause of death is eliminated or reduced, another takes its place. For example, in the 1880s in the United States, cancer and heart disease ranked relatively low on the list of killers, while tuberculosis and other infectious diseases ranked high.

Recent research with fruit flies has suggested that a mutation in one gene could almost double the insect's life, from 37 days to about 70. However, it would be a mistake to infer that gene therapy will be equally successful in humans. Aging in humans depends much more on the interaction of many genes, making it difficult or impossible to manipulate only the right ones.

Olshansky, Carnes, & Butler (2001) noted that humans would need to be built differently to live longer. A human optimally designed for long life might have stronger hip and knee joints and thicker vertebrae in the spine to reduce injuries, more hair cells in the ears to preserve hearing, and more valves in the leg veins to improve circulation.

Olshansky, S. J., Carnes, B. A., & Butler, R. N. (2001). If humans were built to last. *Scientific American, 284,* 50–55.

Olshansky, S. J., Carnes, B. A., & Desesquelles, A. (2001). Demography: Prospects for human longevity. *Science, 291,* 1491–1492.

Longevity and Life Expectancy

How long will you live? Some websites will calculate an individual's life expectancy from information about lifestyle, health habits, family, and environment. The term **longevity** refers to the number of years an individual actually lives, while life expectancy refers to demographic projections regarding the average length of life. Although life

Longevity after Menopause

From an evolutionary perspective, it is puzzling that women live as long as 40 years after menopause. Evolutionary theory argues that natural selection favors traits that enhance reproduction. Because postreproductive traits in both women and men are not selected, there is no accepted explanation for why people live for a long time after their reproductive years. Humans are the only primates to enjoy an extended life span after their ability to produce progeny has ended.

Recently, Kristen Hawkes and her colleagues at the University of Utah proposed that women live past the reproductive years because grandmothers provide food crucial to the survival of grandchildren. By providing for grandchildren, grandmothers enhance their daughters' availability for fertility and thereby increase the chances that their genes will be passed. Daughters can breast-feed for shorter periods if grandmothers assist with feeding. Hawkes suggested that women who have help from their mothers can bear more babies during their fertile years than women without helpers. She and her colleagues based their theories on observations of 300 Hadza hunter-gatherers in Tanzania. In the

Hadza culture, women collect berries or dig tubers, and men hunt. The Hadza survive entirely on gathered or hunted food. The anthropologists found that children's weight gains depended on how much time their mothers had for gathering food. When mothers had less time to forage because of the demands of caring for a new baby, the fit and hard-working grandmothers, frequently in their sixties, spent more time foraging. The weight gain of children then depended on the grandmother's foraging success. Researchers have paid relatively little attention to the functions of grandmothers in various cultures. Confidence in the grandmother theory will depend on observations of similar patterns in other cultures.

Source: Hawkes, K., O'Connell, J. F., & Blurton Jones, N. B. (1998). Hazda women's time allocation, offspring provisioning, and the evolution of long post-menopausal life spans. *Current Anthropology, 38,* 551–557; Hawkes, K., O'Connell, J. F., Blurton Jones, N. G., Alvarez, H., & Charnov, E. L. (1998). *Proceedings of the National Academy of Sciences, 95,* 1336–1339.

Physical activity throughout the adult years is one of the predictors of longevity.

expectancy increased dramatically during the twentieth century, the actual upper limit of the human life span has not changed much since the beginning of recorded history.

The upper limit, or the **potential life span,** refers to the maximum age an individual could reach if he or she could avoid all illnesses and accidents. The average maximum potential human life span is estimated to be approximately 95 years of age (Olshansky, Carnes, and Butler, 2001). This means there is a biological limit to how much improved medical care, nutrition, and public health can help to increase longevity.

Improved health care, coupled with a fixed upper limit on the potential human life span, has produced changes in the survivorship curve, as shown in figure 2.9. From ancient times to the present, the curve has become increasingly more rectangular as more people reached the fullest extent of their potential life span. It is generally expected that the survivorship curve will become even more rectangular in the future with continued advances in public health, nutrition, and medicine.

In light of some new and largely unanticipated concerns, some researchers, however, are beginning to question whether the increasing rectangularization of the life curve will ever be realized (Olshansky, Carnes, and Desesquelles, 2001). When medical researchers and demographers proposed the notion of an increasingly rectangular life curve, they were optimistic that medical science would eventually succeed in conquering diseases that shorten the length of the human life span. Remarkable medical achievements, such as the creation of vaccines that eradicated smallpox, polio, and other childhood diseases, boosted optimism. Further, the potential for producing universally available effective

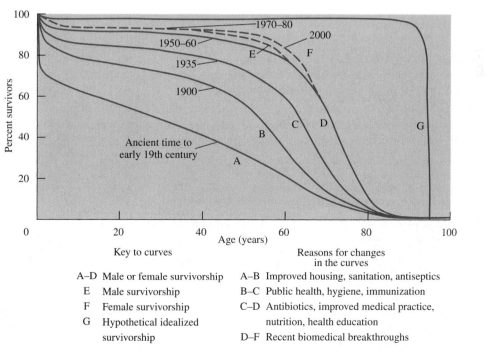

Figure 2.9 The rectangularization of the human life span. This graph shows human survivorship trends from ancient times to the present, illustrating a rapid shift toward a rectangular curve over the past 100 years.

Key to curves

A–D Male or female survivorship
E Male survivorship
F Female survivorship
G Hypothetical idealized survivorship

Reasons for changes in the curves

A–B Improved housing, sanitation, antiseptics
B–C Public health, hygiene, immunization
C–D Antibiotics, improved medical practice, nutrition, health education
D–F Recent biomedical breakthroughs

antibiotics, combined with national trends toward healthier lifestyles, supported the view that people would soon be able to live to the fullest extent of their life spans.

Demographers use the term, **mortality,** refering to either the percentage or incidence of deaths in a population. The term, **morbidity,** refers to the prevalence or incidence of disease in a population. Control of infectious diseases during the past century added about 25 years to the average length of life in the United States. However, infections such as AIDS, cholera, malaria, hepatitis, dysentery, and tuberculosis, as well as nutritional problems and toxic exposure, continue to suppress life expectancy in many regions of the world (see figure 2.7).

Even with the medical and nutritional advances of the past century, life expectancy is still about 15 years short of the potential life span even in many developed countries. One major reason is cardiovascular disease; its complete elimination would add about 10 years to average life expectancy. Reduction or cessation of tobacco use would help eliminate premature deaths from emphysema, lung cancer, and some other forms of cancer, as well as reducing the incidence of cardiovascular and circulatory diseases. Eradication of cancer, the second leading cause of death in many countries, would add about three more years to average life expectancy, and reduction in alcohol dependence would also increase the potential life span (e.g., see Neumark, Van Etten, Anthony, 2000).

Further, as chapter 3 discusses, a good amount of scientific evidence now suggests that moderately reduced caloric intake throughout the life span could increase the average life expectancy of humans by as much as 15 years (e.g., Lee et al., 2001, Roberts et al., 2001). Researchers have also pointed out the role antioxidant-rich fruits and vegetables, antioxidant vitamins such as Vitamin E, and other dietary supplements may play in extending the potential life span and improving health (e.g., Grundman, 2000).

But new diseases are emerging, and "old" diseases are reemerging (see Research Focus 2.1). Human immunodeficiency virus (HIV) infection, pneumonia, and influenza are now ranked among the 10 leading causes of death in the United States. Diseases such as tuberculosis and measles, which not long ago were considered to have been practically eradicated, have reappeared as major diseases in the United States. New strains of tuberculosis and other infectious diseases have developed, and there are no effective treatments for them. Infectious diseases are the leading cause of death worldwide and are the leading cause of serious illness in the United States (Berkelman & Hughes, 1993).

Social and Economic Impact of an Aging Population

The age structure of a society determines, in part, the allocation of its resources. Over the next several decades, larger sums will be needed to meet the needs of a progressively more aged population. One way to quantify how the working members of a society support those who are not working is to calculate the **dependency ratio,** or the ratio of workers to those dependent on them. In the United States, the dependency ratio is expected to drop from 4.5 in 2000 to 2.5 in 2040. This is one of the reasons that the Congress of the United States increased the age for receiving Social Security benefits to 67 years in 2000. Further adjustments to the Social Security system can be expected.

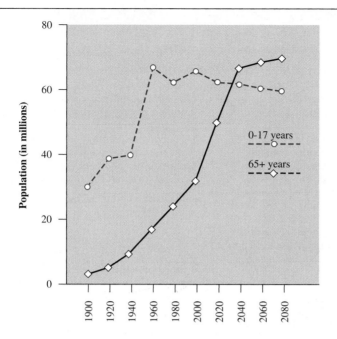

Figure 2.10 The number of persons 65 or older and children under 18 in the United States. By 2040, older adults will outnumber children by 5 million.
Source: U.S. Census Bureau, 2001.

The data in figure 2.10 are particularly striking. The figure indicates that there will be more older adults (over 65 years) than children (under 18 years) in the United States by 2040.

It is difficult in any society to decide how to optmally distribute the economic resources needed to support the young and old. Changing demographic trends as well as increasingly higher health care costs pose sticky challenges for policy makers in the new millennium.

Social Class, Poverty, and Housing

In the United States, the experience of growing older differs for individuals from different social classes, races, and economic levels. If people can't afford to pay for routine dental checkups, eye exams, or physical exams, for example, it is less likely that they will detect and treat a health problem at an early stage. Also, economic and educational factors affect attitudes about health and exposure to health information. In this section, we examine how the effects of social class, race and ethnicity, and economic level impact individual development and individual differences. (See Research Focus 2.3 for a discussion of how African-American women perceive menopause and hormone therapy.)

Social Class

Every culture is stratified by social class, but cultures differ in the strictness or specificity of the prescriptions as well as the nature of social roles. In every culture, occupations vary in pay structure, prestige, and power to influence others. Thus, individuals possess different

African-American Women's Perceptions of Menopause and Hormone Replacement Therapy

Menopause is a life change related to biology, culture, and health. Women from different cultural backgrounds and ethnicities hold different views about menopause. In a recent study, a research team at Michigan State University investigated African-American women's perceptions of menopause and hormone replacement therapy (HRT). The research participants consisted of 55 African-American women who were living in a low-income housing development or who belonged to a women's group at a large urban church. The women were in average or good health and ranged from 46 to 56 years of age. Women discussed their thoughts and feelings about menopause in semistructured group interviews (or focus groups). The main findings were as follows:

1. The women considered menopause a natural transition to late adulthood or old age.

2. Menopause produced physical symptoms of bad cramps, bleeding, and hot flashes.
3. Menopause produced psychological symptoms of mood swings and negative feelings.
4. Women responded differently to the symptoms.
5. Other women and books were good sources of information about menopause.

Some women viewed HRT negatively because of cancer risk, and others viewed it positively because of symptom relief.

Source: Padonu, G., Holmes-Rovner, M., Rothert, M., Schmitt, N., Kroll, J., Ransom, S., and Gladnery, E. (1996). African-American women's perceptions of menopause. American Journal of Health Behavior, 20, 242–251.

economic resources and have different educational and occupational opportunities. Cultural differences in the way the rewards of society are distributed often produce inequities for people of different ethnicities (racism), for men and women (sexism), or for different-aged individuals (ageism). **Ageism** refers to unequal opportunities for older individuals.

Poverty

In 1997, nearly 3.8 million, or 10.5 percent, of the elderly were classified as poor (U.S. Census Bureau 2000). Another 6.5 percent of elders have incomes just above the poverty line. The official poverty rate for 1997, the latest year available at the time of this writing, is $8,183 for a person living alone and $10,473 for a family of two adults. A large percentage of Americans will experience poverty for at least a short period of time during their adult years. Rank and Hirschl (1999) reported that nearly one-half of all Americans aged 60 to 90 experienced at least one year of living near or below the poverty line. The percentage increased sharply for individuals who were black, who were not married, or who had less than 12 years of education. By age 85, about 65 percent of blacks, 38 percent of females, 51 percent of those not married, and 48 percent of those with less than 12 years of education had spent one year at or below the poverty line. By comparison, just under 40 percent of whites, 31 percent of males, 25 percent of married couples, and 20 percent of those with greater than 12 years of education experienced a year in poverty. These figures are based on an income analysis of thousands of Americans for a 25-year period ending in 1992. During this time, the official poverty rates for the elderly fluctuated between 11 and 15 percent.

The percentage of elderly poor would probably be much greater if the statistics included the **near poor** and the **hidden poor.** The *near poor* are individuals

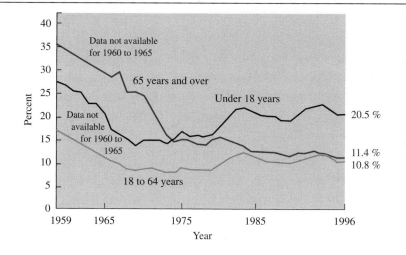

Figure 2.11
Poverty rates by age, from 1959 to 1996. Poverty rates appear to have improved in recent years. However, these statistics are underestimates of the numbers of older adults living in poverty in the United States.
Source: U.S. Census Bureau Population Survey.

with incomes between the poverty level and 125 percent of this level. In total, 20 percent of the older population was poor or near poor in 2000. The *hidden poor* are individuals who could be classified as poor on the basis of their own incomes but who are supported by relatives who are not poor. Estimates place the number of hidden poor at nearly double the rate determined by official census statistics (figure 2.11). The hidden poor live in the homes of family members or friends and are listed in census data as part of that household. About 92 percent of the hidden poor aged 85 years of age and older are women who live in such arrangements and are not classified as poor.

Many elders are unprepared for the reduced income associated with retirement from paid work. Many expect their Social Security benefits to provide the support necessary to live comfortably in retirement, but Social Security is seldom sufficient. Yet in 2000, the major source of income for those 65 years of age and older was Social Security. Social Security accounted for 36 percent of the income of older Americans, with 24 percent coming from assets, 18 percent from pensions, and 18 percent from earnings (U.S. Department of Health and Human Services, 2000). For those who are poor and living alone, Social Security represents a far more sizable percentage of income than it does for those with moderate or high incomes.

In addition, very few older adults are prepared to handle the financial impact of long-term health care. Among those 75 years of age and older and living alone, 46 percent reach poverty levels within 13 weeks of institutionalization in a skilled nursing facility. Twenty-five percent of married couples reach poverty level in 13 weeks and 47 percent reach poverty level in one year. Elderly couples, compared with younger couples, have more out-of-pocket health expenditures.

Race is a significant predictor of poverty among the elderly. In 2000, blacks comprised 34 percent of the elderly living at or below poverty levels, and Hispanics 21 percent, while whites represented just 11 percent (U.S. Census Bureau, 2000). The best predictors of poverty in old age continue to be race (black), education (no high school degree), gender (female), marital status (divorced or widowed), and city living environment.

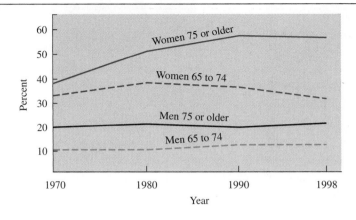

Figure 2.12 The annual percentages from 1970 to 1998 of men and women aged (1) 65 to 74 and (2) 75 and older who lived alone. *Source: U.S. Census Bureau. 1994, 1998. Marital status and living arrangements.* Current Population Survey Reports, *March 1994, p. 20–484; and March 1998, p. 20–514.*

Housing

Although the bulk of research on the living environments of the elderly has focused on special situations such as nursing homes, public housing, mobile home parks, welfare hotels, or retirement communities, the proportion of older Americans in these living conditions is actually small. In 2000, approximately 22.1 million older adults lived in family homes, 10.4 million of them alone (U.S. Census Bureau, 2001, see figures 2.12 and 2.13). Home ownership represents a sign of achievement among all adults, particularly the elderly (National Center for Health Statistics, 1987a). However, the data concerned with housing quality are less positive. The U.S. Senate Special Committee on Aging estimated that 30 percent of the elderly occupy housing that is deteriorating or substandard in 2000.

Suitable living environments directly influence the morale, adjustment, sociability, and intellectual abilities of the elderly. The immediate impact of substandard housing is far greater for the elderly because their lifestyles center so much more on activities in the home. The elderly overwhelmingly prefer to maintain ownership of their own homes, assuming they are physically, mentally, and economically able to do so. For elderly persons who are unable to live independently, those with higher incomes have many more housing options. For example, some elderly can afford to insure themselves against long-term costs and escalating inflation, taxes, and home maintenance by enrolling in *continuity of care retirement communities*. Such individuals pay a substantial initiation or entrance fee as well as a monthly fee. The costs remain constant regardless of the medical and nursing care a resident may require in the future. Unfortunately, only a small percentage of the population can afford to consider such options.

Nursing homes may be the only alternative for older adults with serious, chronic health problems. About 5 percent over 65 were residents of nursing homes in 2000. The percentage increases dramatically as age increases. For example, about 1 percent of those between the ages of 65 and 74 live in nursing homes, whereas 25 percent of those age 85 and over reside in nursing homes.

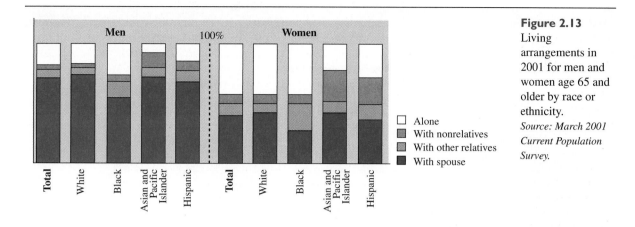

Figure 2.13
Living arrangements in 2001 for men and women age 65 and older by race or ethnicity.
Source: March 2001 Current Population Survey.

Ageism

Stereotypes about the elderly are inaccurate. Ageism, like sexism and racism, is the prejudiced behavior of a society against older adults or negative stereotyping of the elderly (Palmore, 1990). Many older adults in the United States face painful discrimination. For example, they may not be hired for new jobs or be eased out of old ones because older adults are perceived as incapable. Elders are sometimes presumed to be verbose or boring. Infirm elders may be treated without sensitivity, and without regard for who they are and who they once were. Sometimes adult children even push the elderly out of their families because they see them as a burden rather than as positive contributors to the family.

One of the most serious problems facing the elderly in the United States is stereotyping. Misperceptions of aging and the elderly may be either positive (idealizing old age) or negative (viewing the elderly as useless and inadequate). Table 2.2 lists some of the stereotypes.

Some have suggested that even the research that focuses on age, gender, or race differences can be stereotypical and inherently discriminatory (Cole & Stewart, 2001). Researchers need to insure that their studies do not support an ideology in which members of different groups are viewed as fundamentally different and alien.

Aging and Culture

The cultural milieu—that is, the physical and social setting in which adults develop—varies tremendously from culture to culture in regard to aging. The term *culture* refers to the behaviors, attitudes, values, and products of a particular group of people. For example, the culture of the United States, China, and the Caribbean represent different belief systems, languages and dialects, and rituals of daily life. Always, within each culture, there are many subcultures, each with its own distinct set of behaviors and values.

TABLE 2.2

Common Misperceptions About the Elderly That Are Based on Stereotypes

Examples of Misperceptions Based on Negative Stereotypes

1. Most older persons are poor.
2. Most older persons are unable to keep up with inflation.
3. Most older people are ill-housed.
4. Most older people are frail and in poor health.
5. The aged are impotent as a political force and require advocacy.
6. Most older people are inadequate employees; they are less productive, efficient, motivated, innovative, and creative than younger workers. Most older workers are accident-prone.
7. Older people are mentally slower and more forgetful; they are less able to learn new things.
8. Older persons tend to be intellectually rigid and dogmatic. Most old people are set in their ways and unable to change.
9. A majority of older people are socially isolated and lonely. Most are disengaging or disengaged from society.
10. Most older persons are confined to long-term care institutions.

Examples of Misperceptions Based on Positive Stereotypes

1. The aged are relatively well off; they are not poor, but in good economic shape. Their benefits are generously provided by working members of society.
2. The aged are a potential political force that votes and participates in unity and in great numbers.
3. Older people make friends very easily. They are kind and smiling.
4. Most older persons are mature, experienced, wise, and interesting.
5. Most older persons are very good listeners and are especially patient with children.
6. A majority of older persons are very kind and generous to their children and grandchildren.

Source: From S. Lubomudrov, S. (1987). Congressional perceptions of the elderly: The use of stereotypes in the legislative process. The Gerontologist, 27: 77–81. Copyright © The Gerontological Society of America.

A child learns the values of a particular community or culture. A child may have learned that some values were relatively constant among individuals and families, while others varied; or that his/her family seemed the same as some other families, all other families, or no other families. In the United States, considerable variation exists in how families view parents, grandparents, and other older relatives, in part because of ethnic diversity (Bastida, 1987).

In China and Japan, older persons are venerated and encouraged to be active in the family and in other social roles (Kinoshita & Kiefer, 1993). Intergenerational relations are reciprocal rather than linear. **Filial piety** runs high in China; respect and homage to family and community elders is a way of life. For example, one custom is for parents to send weekly or monthly stipends to a married child. This money is not to be spent, even though it is a gift. Rather, the younger generation is expected to safely invest the funds so they can be returned to the parents when the parents reach old age. In Japan, the elderly are more integrated into their families than the elderly in most industrialized countries. More than 75 percent live with their children, and very few older adults live alone. Respect for the elderly in Japan is evident in a variety of everyday encounters: The best seats on public transportation are usually reserved for the elderly, cooks cater to their tastes, and people bow respectfully to them. However, such respect appears to be more prevalent among rural than urban Japanese and among middle-aged than young adult Japanese (Palmore & Maeda, 1985).

It is clear that, with modernization, the status and integration of elders in Japan has declined (Hashimoto, 1996; Kumagai, 1996). Tobin (1987) suggested that Western observers have idealized Japan's approach to old age. Tobin noted that our idealized view of Japanese old age is exaggerated and overlooks the negative aspects. The observance of Respect for Elders Day and the designation of subway seats as "silver seats" for the elderly and handicapped may mean that such policies are *needed* to ensure respect for the elderly. Similarly, although it appears that in Japan more older people live with their children than in the United States, the elderly may yet experience loneliness and emotional distance. Living together does not ensure reverence, respect, and belonging. Finally, Tobin found that the overall percentage of parents living with children in Japan has declined steadily as changes in modernization, housing space, and population have occurred. Japan actually lags far behind the United States in providing housing options for elders (Kinoshita & Kiefer, 1993).

The language used to refer to Japanese old age has also evolved dramatically. Current usage gives a negative connotation to the traditional term *rojin,* or *ecstasy years.* The more preferable *jitsunen,* translated as the *age of harvest* or *the age of fruition* has replaced the older term (Loveridge-Sanonmatsu, 1994).

In earlier times, when fewer individuals reached old age, the elders were granted high status in many cultures. Members of some cultures believed that elders were imbued with special powers and wisdom. Jay Sokolovsky (1986), drawing on the work of Cowgill and Holmes (1972), identified the following seven values that seem universally associated with high status for the elderly:

1. Older people possess valuable knowledge.
2. Older persons control key family and community resources.
3. Older persons are allowed to perform useful and valued functions as long as possible.
4. Fewer role shifts and a greater sense of role continuity take place throughout the life span.
5. Age-related role changes involve gains in responsibility, authority, or advisory capacity.
6. The extended family is an important residential and/or economic unit, and the elderly are integrated into it.
7. Less emphasis is placed on individual ego development.

In some cultures, elders remain in their homes with friends and family regardless of health. Placing an elder in a hospital or nursing home would be unacceptable. In Hindu tradition, for example, there are four life stages (ashrams). Each stage, though distinct, produces a balance and harmony between person, nature, life forces, and one's duty (dharma), and the stages apply to all males except those in the menial caste. The first stage consists of the *celibate student* in adolescence and early adulthood. This is a time when a teacher provides both a home and a mentor relationship in transmitting religious knowledge. The second stage of life consists of marriage and the special obligations of a *householder,* which include bringing children into the world and participating in family life. In traditional Hindu marriages, sons bring their wives into the paternal home, creating an extended family that preserves religious and cultural practices by direct transmission to the next generation.

After the stage of householder and the establishment of family, a man is to voluntarily begin to remove himself from his family. The third life stage is that of a *hermit in the forest.* This is a time for meditating, studying, and totally absorbing Hindu religious thought and ideas. It involves living a life devoted to asceticism, self-control, and the acquisition of inner spiritual power. A man is ready for this stage when he sees "his skin wrinkled, his hair white, and the son of his sons." The final stage is *complete separation from all worldly concerns;* the elderly man abandons all ties to family, possessions, and home. He wanders unencumbered, free to seek harmony between himself and the universe, free to find the common cord between his existence and the existence of others, both animate and inanimate. The goal of the fourth stage is to eliminate the need for spirituality, sensuality, psychological bonds, or social dimensions. The individual has no selfish needs, no real-world concerns; he waits to die. Death is blissful liberation, the deserved attainment of one who has led a perfect life by committing time to religious study, marrying and producing children, and having offered support and help to those in need. Given these accomplishments, the man's life should be in total harmony.

In India, even among the highest caste (Brahmins), few people practice or attain the goals of each of the four stages. Yet these stages provide a culturally prescribed path for successful aging. They provide a direction to life, a target for maturity. Other cultures prescribe different paths. Modern technological societies, for example, emphasize productive personal achievements in the workplace (Valliant, 1977).

Age-Related Changes in Sex Roles

The term **sex role** refers to the characteristics individuals display because of their gender. Sex roles prescribe the behaviors *expected* of males and females. An important aspect of being male or female is gender identity, or the extent to which an individual actually adopts the behaviors and attitudes associated with either the male or female role. Embracing sex-appropriate sex roles results in "masculine" males and "feminine" females. Although in past years researchers assessed masculinity and femininity as distinct categories, current researchers usually take a more continuous view based on the concept of androgyny.

Androgyny

In the mid-1970s, work by Sandra Bem (e.g., Bem, 1974) and others revealed the fallacy of considering masculinity and femininity as polar opposites on a scale. Bem (1974) reported that 30 to 40 percent of men and women have an **androgynous** sex-role identity. That is, when given a list of masculine and feminine attributes (see table 2.3) and asked to indicate how well each trait describes themselves, androgynous individuals score high on both sets. Bem's research suggested that masculinity and femininity involve separate attributes, and that people with androgynous identities have advantages in psychological adjustment. The androgynous person endorses both male traits (e.g., being self-reliant) and female traits (e.g., warmth). Having a broad range of personal attributes enables individuals to adapt competently to a wide variety of situations.

The notion of androgyny has some limitations as it applies to the understanding of sex-role identity throughout the adult life span. Gender roles and gender identity

Socio-Cultural and Cohort Differences in Anxiety

During the past few decades, people in the United States seem to worry more and have more things to worry about than ever before. Are we living in an "age of anxiety"? Levels of anxiety have increased in recent years, and the most likely cause is change in the amount of social connectedness in the larger socio-cultural environment. Many statistics point to a weakening of social connections in America in recent years. Specifically, divorce rates have increased, birth rates have decreased, people choose to marry later in life, and many more people now live alone than ever before (United States Census Bureau, 2000). It has also been reported that people are less likely to join community organizations and visit friends than ever before (Putnam, 2000).

In two recent analyses of the research literature, Jean Twenge (2000) showed that levels of anxiety in children and adults have increased by a full standard deviation between 1952 and 1993. Comparatively, the average individual in the 1980s reported more anxiety than psychiatric patients did in the 1950s! Correlations with divorce rates and crime rates suggest that the rise in anxiety is related to decreases in social connectedness. This interpretation follows from research showing that anxiety is associated with being disconnected from social groups or relationships. Cohort factors, the distinctive socio-cultural characteristics associated with a particular span of time, clearly exert strong influences on personality and adult development.

Source: Putnam (2000). Bowling alone: The collapse and revival of American community. New York: Simon & Schuster.

Source: Twenge, J. M. (2000). The age of anxiety? Birth cohort change in anxiety and neuroticism, 1952–1993. Journal of Personality and Social Psychology, 79, 1007–1021.

TABLE 2.3	
Examples of Masculine and Feminine Items from Bem's Sex-Role Inventory	
Masculine Items	Feminine Items
Acts as a leader	Affectionate
Analytical	Compassionate
Competitive	Feminine
Forceful	Gullible
Individualistic	Sensitive to the needs of others
Self-reliant	Sympathetic
Willing to take a stand	Warm

Reproduced by permission of the publisher, Consulting Psychologists Press, Inc., from the Bem Sex Role Inventory *by Sandra Bem, Ph.D., copyright 1978.*

continue to develop during the adult years. There are several ways to interpret *how* and *why* gender roles change as individuals age (Huyck, 1990, 1999).

Several researchers have studied longitudinal changes in personality and sex-role (e.g., Lowenthal, Thurnher, & Chiriboga, 1975; Neugarten, 1973). In the Kansas City Longitudinal Study, Neugarten (1973) reported that older men were more receptive to their own affiliative and nurturant behavior than younger men, whereas older women were more receptive than younger women to their own aggressive and egocentric behavior. Coming to terms with the emerging dimensions of one's personality (e.g., nurturance or aggressiveness) may be one of the challenges of midlife development. With the acceptance and integration of masculine and feminine dimensions of personality, individuals may become more adaptable in facing the challenges of growing older (Huyck, 1990).

Recent research shows that gender differences in middle-aged and older adults may actually be much less significant than previously realized (Costa, Terracciano, & McCrae, 2001). Observations of gender differences in behavior and personality may really have more to do with factors, such as stress, that are associated with particular family roles (e.g., Almeida & Kessler, 1998; Kiecolt-Glaser & Glaser, 2001). Costa, Terracciano, and McCrae (2001) examined personality inventory data for 23,031 individuals across 26 cultures and found that gender differences are actually very small.

David Gutmann's View of Sex-Role Changes during Adulthood

Gutmann (1977, 1987, 1992) suggested that a critical difference in men's and women's **ego mastery styles** is dominant in the early adult years, but that this difference shifts as adults reach middle age. *Ego mastery* refers to the style one adopts in coping with self and others. It encompasses more than just how we respond or behave; ego mastery style is the underlying organization of values and beliefs that govern external behavior. Two ego mastery styles have been associated with age-related personality changes: active mastery and passive accommodative mastery. **Active mastery** typifies individuals who strive for autonomy, control, and personal competence: One shapes the external environment to fulfill one's own needs and desires. Individuals with active styles may employ strategies centered on achievement. **Passive accommodative mastery,** in contrast, is typical of individuals who gain control over their environments by accommodating others perceived to be in power. By accommodating the needs and desires of others, the individual gains a sense of ego mastery and control.

Each of these styles occurs in both men and women, varying in strength over particular periods in life. According to Gutmann, active mastery generally overshadows passive accommodative mastery in younger men. By middle age, however, the two styles have shifted; passive accommodative mastery predominates. Interestingly, Gutmann suggests that this is frequently reversed for women. The passive accommodative mastery style generally predominates among women in young adulthood, whereas active mastery predominates by middle age. Gutmann's conclusions are based on observations of adults in a variety of cultures (Mayan Indian, Navajo Indian, and Middle-Eastern Druze).

Gutmann offers a socioevolutionary model for age changes in mastery style; he emphasizes the concept of the **parental imperative.** To ensure the survival of our species, parents must develop effective divisions of labor to manage the demands and responsibilities of childrearing. One division of labor, which has evolved over thousands of years, has given rise to the two ego mastery styles. A passive accommodative style is uniquely suited to the nurturing responsibilities of parenting, while the active mastery style is suited to providing the economic and material support needed for family survival. After parenting is over, middle-aged adults begin a process of role reversal. The shift or transition Gutmann identified is gradual, not abrupt. Individuals slowly recognize dimensions of "self" that have previously gone unfulfilled and unrecognized. By middle age, men frequently become more aware of their inner selves, their social connectedness, and their nurturant dispositions. Corresponding changes in women are also evident by middle age.

Gutmann has suggested that men and women change the ways they express mastery after their parenting years. New research suggests that individuals seek to master new "possible selves" throughout their lives.

Critics of Gutmann's theory have questioned whether the observed changes in ego mastery style in middle age actually reflect role reversal or are a description of cohort effects and sociocultural influences. Other theorists propose different reasons for age-related changes in sex roles.

Carl Jung's View of Sex-Role Development in Adult Life

Carl Jung (1933) broke with traditional Freudian psychoanalytic theory to create a theory of personality development that focused on adulthood. In Jung's view, a healthy adult personality establishes an equilibrium among various components, including masculinity and femininity. Early adulthood is marked by a decided imbalance between the two, so that one component dominates to the exclusion of the other. In Jung's view, masculinity or femininity predominates at this time because of society's coercive sex-role stereotyping or modeling. Usually, the dominant orientation to masculinity or femininity matches one's biological sex. By middle age, however, masculinity and femininity balance more as males express more of their feminine characteristics (e.g., nurturance), and females express more of their masculine attributes (e.g., aggression). By old age, Jung suggested, a healthy equilibrium often exists between these personality components. Older males and females see this balance in themselves and recognize that they have *both* masculine and feminine traits.

Conclusions about Sex-Role Changes in Later Life

Some data suggest that by middle age, males and females become increasingly aware of new or underdeveloped aspects of their personalities. Neugarten (1977), for example, described this kind of personality change as the incorporation of opposite sex-role characteristics. Bengtson, Reedy, and Gordon (1985), Gutmann (1987, 1992), and others found a greater expression and acceptance of nurturance in both older men and women. It seems that, as they grow older, both men and women become more aware of personality components they have not previously recognized, fostered, or expressed.

Social Dimensions of Aging

Riley (1997) suggested that the social dimensions of aging are best understood using a conceptual framework that emphasizes *age integration* and the interplay between the developing individual and changing social structures. The meaning of aging is changing in all societies; age integration means that societies are breaking down barriers and bringing people of different ages together. The process of age integration has consequences for a number of social structures, including the family, the community, educational institutions, and the workplace. Riley gives an example of this interplay as follows:

> There [have] been and will continue to be unprecedented increases in longevity. This increased longevity produces changes in the structure of family networks (e.g., there are more middle-aged adults with surviving elderly parents). The caregiving pressures on individuals lead to structural changes in society (e.g., changes in community organizations, federal regulations).

Because of the tremendous variation in cultural and ethnic backgrounds among the aged in the United States, social development must be considered within the con-

Many older adults continue to enjoy and benefit from exercise, especially if they were physically active earlier in life. Dr. Patricia Peterson, shown here, holds a number of world running records in her age group.

text of different and continuously changing cultural systems (Riley, 1997; Riley & Riley, 1994). One lifestyle and set of activities may suit people from one ethnic background better than another. For example, social interaction with family members tends to be more frequent and important for older people of French-American or Hispanic background than for others. Many elderly have adapted to an individualized lifestyle and seek social integration by selectively participating in community organizations.

There are many ways for adults to experience well-being and life satisfaction, and many pathways to successful aging in American society. Some individuals age successfully by staying active, and some by striking a unique balance among a variety of roles and responsibilities. However, social constraints (ageism, job discrimination) may have negative consequences for older adults.

Laura Carstensen's (1999) selectivity theory provides a useful framework for understanding social relationships across adult life. According to Carstensen, social interaction has three functions: (1) it is an information source, (2) it helps people develop and maintain a sense of self, and (3) it is a source of pleasure or emotional well-being. The informational and identity functions of social interactions wane during the later adult years, and the emotional support function gains in significance (see also Carstensen, Pasupathi, Mayr, & Nesselroade, 2000).

SUMMARY

America is "graying." In 1900, about 3.1 million Americans were aged 65 and over. By 2000, the number had risen to 34.9 million, and by 2030, there will be 66 million older adults in the United States. Middle-aged and old-old adults represent the fastest-growing segments of the population.

Although life expectancy has increased substantially in recent years, the average potential human life span has remained stable, with an upper limit of approximately 95 years. Until recently, the increase in life expectancy was mostly due to a reduction in deaths during infancy and early childhood. Improved nutrition and health care could help increase the chances that older adults will live longer. In the future, older adults are expected to have healthier, and more productive lives. Women continue to live longer than men. And differences in life expectancy are associated with culture, race, and ethnicity.

Increases in the numbers of older adults and their proportion of the population in the United States have profound economic and social ramifications. As the population ages and the ratio of workers to dependents diminishes, new policies for the equitable distribution of economic resources will emerge.

Aging takes place within a cultural context, and one important aspect of a culture is social class. One of the major concerns of individuals in late adulthood is the decrease in income they are likely to experience. The poverty rate is higher for the elderly than for any other age group.

Aging in America carries a number of negative stereotypes. Ageist stereotypes are evident in the view that the elderly are inactive, lonely, and bored. China and Japan appear to hold relatively positive attitudes toward the elderly. However, recent social, economic, and demographic changes in these cultures have led to a decline in respect toward the elderly. An examination of various cultural definitions of aging and cultural differences in the treatment of the elderly provides a more accurate view of cultural differences in intergenerational relations.

Aging in America, as in most cultures, differs for men and women. The nature of sex roles and how they change over the life span is highly complex. The concept of androgyny stresses the idea that each individual's personality has both masculine and feminine dimensions. The degree to which an adult with a masculine, feminine, or androgynous sex-role orientation shows effective adjustment depends on the cultural context. Gutmann's work indicates an increase in sex-typed feminine traits in the personality profiles of older men and a corresponding tendency toward masculine traits in older women. Riley's (1997) age integration theory provides a broad framework for understanding the complex social dimensions of aging.

REVIEW QUESTIONS

1. What are the differences between life expectancy, potential life span, and longevity?
2. Who are the old-old?
3. Describe the changing age structure of the U.S. population. What effects will the changing old-age and young-age dependency ratios have on society?
4. What factors seem to contribute most to longevity?
5. Discuss how sex, race, ethnicity, and social class affect life expectancy. What factors account for these differences?
6. Describe the economic hardships that many of today's elderly endure.
7. What is ageism? Trace the historical background of ageist attitudes toward the elderly in the United States.
8. How do attitudes toward the aged in countries like China, Japan, and India compare to the attitudes Americans hold?
9. How do sex roles change during the adult years? What is androgyny?
10. Explain the meaning of the following terms: active mastery, passive accommodative mastery, and the parental imperative.
11. Describe Carstensen's selectivity theory.
12. Is there an optimal way to age? What evidence supports your position?

 ON THE WEB   www.mhhe.com/hoyer5

For a listing of links to the latest information about cultural and ethnic diversity in the United States and to other topics related to this chapter, see:

The main page for the United States Census Bureau provides access to news releases and overviews describing various characteristics of the population of the United States.

The National Institute on Aging site is a component of the National Institutes of Health web page devoted to improving the health of older adults. This site contains new research findings and consumer-oriented information on a wide range of topics of interest to older persons.

The Centers for Disease Control page summarizes trends in health and aging and provides links to information relevant to the study of these topics.

The home page for the American Association of Retired Persons, an organization devoted to advocacy for individuals over age 55, offers a variety of resources, information sources, and services to visitors.

PHYSIOLOGICAL AND SENSORY PROCESSES

I think the brain is the most wonderful organ in the body. But look what is telling me that.
—Emo Phillips

The unpredictable and predetermined unfold together to make everything the way it is. It's how nature creates itself, on every scale— the snowflake and the snowstorm.
—Tom Stoppard

[handwritten annotation: → Longevity = How long a person lives
Life Span = How long a person is expected 2 live]

INTRODUCTION

In this chapter, you will learn about the biological aspects of aging. It is important to distinguish the normal aging processes from the consequences of particular diseases. Although the likelihood of poor health increases in later life, poor health is not the same as aging. Normal aging, or **senescence,** refers to a gradual, time-related biological process that takes place as degenerative processes overtake regenerative or growth processes. All individuals, if they live long enough, will experience senescence. In contrast, diseases associated with later life, such as Alzheimer's disease, arthritis, or cardiovascular disease, affect some individuals and not others. The biological declines associated with normal aging are relatively mild and gradual compared with the severity and swiftness of the impairments associated with disease.

Keep in mind that some individuals are healthy and vital in late life. Researchers distinguish between *normal* aging and *successful* aging. One of the goals of the field of health psychology is to help individuals optimize health and psychological functioning. To accomplish this, we must recognize both the gains and the losses associated with aging and help individuals build on their strengths to help compensate for losses.

Caution is in order when interpreting the research on biological aspects of aging. Most of the available research on this topic focuses on cross-sectional comparisons between young adults and elderly adults. This makes it impossible to distinguish between the effects of age and the effects of a wide range of cohort factors that affect health and vitality across the adult years.

Why Do We Age?

We begin this chapter by asking two fundamental and interrelated questions: "What is aging?" and "Why do we age?" The former may be answered in a rather straightforward manner. *Aging* refers to the orderly changes that occur in both physiological and behavioral function across the adult years. A conceptual distinction is made between the concepts of primary aging and secondary aging. *Primary aging,* which is the same as senescence, refers to changes that are gradual, inevitable, universal, and insidious. These changes occur in representative individuals living under representative conditions; changes associated with primary aging are not a consequence of disease. *Secondary aging* refers to the processes that affect the rate at which primary aging occurs. Intense work-related stress, prolonged exposure to environmental toxins, and the consequences of disease are examples of secondary factors that accelerate the rate of primary aging processes.

The latter question, "Why do we age?", is much more complex and difficult to answer. One early view, called the **wear-and-tear theory,** stated that the human body ages because it "wears out" over time in response to the stresses of life. However, some kinds of exertion or activity, such as challenging work and vigorous exercise, promote vitality and are essential to long life, whereas other kinds of stressful activities are detrimental to longevity (Kiecolt-Glaser & Glaser, 2001). Other theorists proposed that breakdowns or wear-and-tear within a particular organ system—for example, in the immune system, endocrine system, or nervous system—are responsible for aging. One major problem associated with wear-and-tear theories is that it is impossible to determine whether changes in a specific body system *cause* aging or are the *outcome* of a basic genetic, cellular, or molecular process.

Wear-and-tear theories do not explain why we age before we die and why there is an upper limit to the life span. Biologists make a distinction between theories that explain the maximum length of the human life span and theories that explain how and why individuals experience a deterioration in particular biological and psychological functions as they approach the upper boundary of human life.

Recently, Leonard Hayflick (1996) suggested that instead of asking the question "Why do we age?" we should ask: "Why did aging evolve?" or "What is the adaptive significance of aging?" Hayflick (1996) pointed out that the key to understanding the increases in the longevity of the human species is the realization that evolution selects primarily for reproductive success of the species. Species in which individuals attain reproductive age and bear and rear children will flourish; other species will not. One of the best ways to ensure reproductive success is to select for organisms that have very robust systems that allow them to survive environmental variations, disease, and predation. In essence, evolution would select for "overengineered" individuals with a great deal of physiological (and adaptive) reserve capacity and resilience (Olshansky, Carnes, & Butler, 2001).

A species would increase its chance of survival by investing its resources in reproductive success rather than postreproductive longevity. Thus, Hayflick (1996) argues that evolutionary mechanisms select for humans who reach maximum physiological vigor at sexual maturity, and that evolutionary/genetic factors indirectly select for the upper limit of the human life span by directly selecting for reproductive success. In other words, humans (like other animals) live beyond sexual maturity because of physiological reserve capacity that is a by-product of reproductive success. During the postreproductive years, humans age and ultimately die because of breakdowns or glitches in their physiological systems that eventually cannot be compensated for or repaired. The term, *pleiotropy,* refers to the fact that characteristics that evolve to enhance reproductive success may have either positive or negative influences on longevity and health later in life. For example, long life is an outcome of positive pleiotropy, and cancer risk in the ovaries, prostate, and female breast is an outcome of negative pleiotropy.

One way to understand Hayflick's ideas is to think about the design of a space vehicle that will take photographs of a particular planet, say Saturn, and send the photos back to Earth. The engineers of this spacecraft would design a vehicle with at least enough capacity to reach Saturn. After its goal was accomplished, after passing by Saturn, the space vehicle might continue to move through space because of the inherent reserve capacity in its design. However, as time went on, the systems that make up the space vehicle deteriorate. Sooner or later a fatal malfunction would occur.

What particular breakdowns or glitches lead to human aging? Some glitches have a genetic basis. For example, the **genetic mutation theory** suggests that aging is caused by changes, or mutations, in the DNA of the cells in vital organs of the body. Eventually, the number of mutated cells increases to the point that biological functioning becomes significantly impaired. Possible sources for these mutations may be intrinsic factors, such as chance errors in DNA replication or in genes that specifically cause mutations in other genes. Other potential triggers of mutations are extrinsic factors, such as toxins in the air, in water, and in food.

The **genetic switching theory** suggests that certain genes cease to operate, or switch off, causing aging. Information needed to produce DNA is no longer available, so the cells atrophy (Selkoe, 1992). Eventually, genetic switching leads to cell death and the loss of organ functioning. According to this theory, a kind of genetic blueprint in each of the body's cells controls the "off switch."

According to the **error catastrophe theory,** aging is caused by damage to RNA, enzymes, and certain other proteins rather than by errors in DNA. For example, if an error occurs in the RNA responsible for producing an enzyme essential to cell metabolism, the result will be a marked reduction in cell functioning and possibly cell death. The escalating impact of the original RNA error is the "error catastrophe."

One of the most promising lines of new research is motivated by the **free radical theory.** This theory hinges on the fact that certain molecules within a cell display a violent reaction when they encounter oxygen. Specifically, these molecules break away from the cell and form highly reactive molecular fragments called free radicals. These free radicals, which are highly unstable, readily bind with other molecular structures within a cell, and this binding process can damage DNA. These cellular calamities ultimately manifest themselves as the signs of aging (Selkoe, 1992).

Antiaging Interventions

Throughout the centuries, humans have tried to slow down or stop the aging process. Early cultures used metaphors from nature to help them search for the secrets of immortality. For example, snakes are capable of rejuvenating themselves by shedding their skins. Thus, people sought ways of ridding themselves of the confines of their aging body. In fact, the Greek word for old age, *geron* (from which the term *gerontology* is derived), refers to the process by which an animal sheds its skin.

Today, scientists are experimenting with a number of promising techniques to prolong life. The emerging field of regenerative medicine is concerned with interventions for developing new tissues and organs as the old ones wear out, and with ways of rebuilding the body using embryonic stem cells or adult stem cells. Before we discuss some of these techniques, we must distinguish between the influence a particular antiaging intervention might have on *life expectancy* versus the *aging process.* For example, researchers have estimated that the elimination of cardiovascular disease and cancer would increase life expectancy by 13.9 and 3.1 years, respectively. However, we could not say with any certainty that the elimination of these diseases would slow the aging process unless we observed a significant increase in the upper limit of the life span. Increasing life expectancy is not the same as halting the aging process (see Research Focus 3.1).

Caloric Restriction

In the 1930s, researchers discovered that moderate caloric restriction initiated after weaning and continued throughout the rest of life drastically increased the life expectancy of laboratory rats (McCay & Crowell, 1934). This finding has been replicated many times. Research has shown that caloric restriction, even begun in middle adulthood, can extend the longevity of nonhuman primates (Masoro, 1984; Roberts et al.,

Research Focus 3.1

Good Health Predicts Delayed Onset of Cognitive Impairments

McNeal et al. (2001) recently studied whether superior health in old age protects against cognitive impairment and Alzheimer's disease. About 100 optimally healthy individuals who were at least 85 years old were studied for six years. The results of the study showed that superior physical health does *not* prevent or protect against cognitive decline, but does delay the onset of cognitive impairments! That is, the onset ages were much later for optimally healthy individuals than for the general population. For healthy individuals, the median onset age for cognitive impairment was 97 years, and the median onset age for Alzheimer's disease was 100 years. This suggests that finding the factors that postpone the onset of cognitive deficits will help us improve cognitive health in later life. Consistent with previous findings, cognitive impairment began later for individuals who did *not* have the APOE allele and for men rather than women. The results of studies of the effects of estrogen levels on curtailing cognitive decline are mixed. In the McNeal et al. study, estrogen levels had no detectable benefit on cognition.

Research findings on the effectiveness of cognitive interventions are summarized in a recent report prepared by the Institute for the Study of Aging (*Achieving and Maintaining Cognitive Vitality,* 2001). The methods for postponing cognitive decline are as follows:

Exercise. A regular schedule of physical activity reduces the risk of cognitive decline by improving the blood supply to the brain.

Cognitive and social activities. Intellectual and social stimulation promotes brain growth in animals and protects against cognitive decline in humans. Continuing to perform meaningful work or leisure activities and remaining socially active reduce the risk of cognitive decline.

Stress reduction. Because prolonged stress is known to reduce the efficiency of the immune system and the ability to maintain normal physiologic function, stress reduction reduces the risk of cognitive decline.

Sleep. Lack of sleep can negatively affect cognitive function at any age.

Nutrition. Maintaining a healthy diet, and maintaining body weight at the low end of the normal range, could delay cognitive decline.

Achieving and Maintaining Cognitive Vitality with Aging. (2001). Report prepared by the Institute for the Study of Aging. International Longevity Center. McNeal, M. G., Zareparsi, S., Camicioli, R., Dame, A., Howieson, D., Quinn, J., Ball, M., Kaye, J., & Payami, H. (2001). Predictors of healthy brain aging. *Journal of Gerontology: Biological Sciences and Medical Sciences, 56,* B294–B301.

2001). In these studies, *restriction* is typically defined as reducing caloric intake by 25 to 40 percent from free feeding levels while providing an adequate intake of essential nutrients and vitamins. It is important to note that the animals are not malnourished.

One explanation for the beneficial effects of caloric restriction on longevity is that it delays (or even prevents) age-related pathologies in the cardiovascular, renal, and central nervous systems (Lee et al., 2000). Recently, caloric restriction has been shown to have a range of beneficial effects in nonhuman primates studied under laboratory conditions, and the same markers for these benefits appear to occur in humans (Hadley et al., 2001). New research is needed that examines the effects of caloric restriction on human longevity and aging (Roberts et al., 2001).

Antioxidants

Recall that one of the most promising theories of aging focuses on the deleterious effects of free radicals on cell function. Free radicals form when the components of a cell react with oxygen. The major culprit, then, is oxygen: Oxidative stress is a major cause of neural deterioration (Cotman, 2001). The administration of antioxidant drugs might prolong life and delay the aging process.

Some antioxidants, like vitamins E and C, occur in foods. The body manufactures other antioxidants. One such substance is **melatonin,** a hormone produced by the pineal gland within the brain. Melatonin binds, like all antioxidants, with free radicals before they have a chance to harm body cells. Several researchers (e.g., Pierpaoli & Regelson, 1995) have touted a whole range of beneficial effects associated with melatonin; their data suggest that melatonin cures insomnia, lowers cholesterol, increases resistance to cancer, prolongs sexual vitality, and may slow the aging process. This last claim is based on the finding that administering melatonin increases the life expectancy of laboratory mice and rats. However, as with other antioxidants, it is unclear how melatonin achieves its success. Hayflick (1996) cautions, for example, that the taste of melatonin may have inhibited the food intake of lab animals. Thus, the effects of melatonin might actually be attributable to caloric restriction.

Hormonal and Drug Supplements

For women, age-related changes in estrogen levels are an important factor in both normal cognitive aging and in neurodegenerative disease (Finch & Sapolsky, 1999). Alzheimer's disease is more common in women than in men, and researchers have found a relationship between estrogen deficiency and the progression of the disease. Further, some studies have found that estrogen replacement therapy has beneficial effects on memory performance in postmenopausal women (Steffens et al., 1999). However, not all studies find evidence for these effects, and some risks may be associated with using estrogen replacement medications.

Estrogen can work in several ways. First, it seems that estrogen can protect neurons against amyloid-induced toxicity and other toxic effects. Second, estrogen increases the concentration of an enzyme needed to synthesize acetylcholine, a brain chemical critical to memory. Third, estrogen enhances communication between neurons in the prefrontal cortex and hippocampus, areas of the brain that are fundamentally

Health in later life depends on the choices we make in young adulthood. Healthy eating habits are associated with increased longevity and reduced risk of heart disease.

important for learning and memory (Keenan, Ezzat, Ginsburg, & Moore, 2001). The links among N-methyl-D-aspartate (NMDA) receptors, estrogen levels, hippocampal circuitry, and memory function are significant subjects for future research.

Dehydroeplandrosterone (DHEA), a natural precursor of estrogen and testosterone, may play a role in postponing the negative effects of aging. Although DHEA levels decline with age, research does not support using DHEA as a drug supplement (Wolf et al., 1998).

Lifestyle

Many scientific studies seem to confirm the obvious: If we adopt a healthy lifestyle—if we avoid smoking, keep alcohol consumption moderate, reduce our intake of high-cholesterol foods, exercise regularly, eliminate environmental stressors, and so on—we will live longer. However, these interventions affect life expectancy because they reduce disease, not because they have a fundamental impact on the aging process. (See Research Focus 3.1.)

Biological Aging

In a general way, we know what it means to age in a biological or a physical sense. We constantly observe the effects of aging in ourselves and in the people around us. Scientists, however, are interested in identifying the "exact" and "specific" changes that

Physical appearance continues to change as we grow older, and some changes bring on other changes.

accompany the aging process. In this section, we describe the research on age-related changes in physical appearance, and we discuss some of the changes that take place in the functional integrity of some of our most important organ systems during adulthood.

Changes in Physical Appearance with Age

One of the physical manifestations of aging involves the appearance of the skin. Facial wrinkles and age spots become more apparent as we age. Age-related changes in the skin are largely cosmetic; the primary functions of the skin, protecting the internal organs and regulating body temperature, are relatively unaffected by aging. Facial structure also changes with age. The cartilage in the nose and ears continues to grow, although the bones of the face do not enlarge after young adulthood. Scalp hair grays and thins. Some men experience a genetic form of hair loss called *male pattern baldness;* this hair loss begins at the temples, proceeds to the top of the head, and continues until the entire top of the head is bare (the "monk's spot").

For men, height decreases by about a half inch between ages 30 and 50 and by another one inch between ages 50 and 70. The height loss for women may be as much as two inches between ages 25 and 75. These changes in height are associated with postural changes, compression of the cartilage in the spine, and loss of bone density with age.

Loss of bone density occurs at a faster rate for women after menopause (Siris et al., 2001). **Osteoporosis** is a disease that involves significant losses in bone calcium and increased bone brittleness. Individuals with this disease are at higher risk for breaking bones if they fall.

A recently published longitudinal study of more than 200,160 generally healthy post-menopausal women found that an unexpectedly large number of the women had osteoporosis that was not previously diagnosed. Further, the study showed that an unexpected large number of the women had mild losses in bone density, referred to as **osteopenia** (Siris et al, 2001). Seven percent of the women tested had bone density levels indicating osteoporosis, and 40 percent had bone density levels indicating

Figure 3.1   Osteoporosis: reducing the risk. After age 30, and especially after menopause in women, bone loss begins. Osteoporosis is an extreme form of the bone loss and mineralization that ordinarily occur with age. As bones become more brittle, fractures in the wrist, spine, and hip are more likely. Back pain, a bent spine, and loss of height also occur.

A decrease of more than one inch from baseline height at age 20 is a sign that significant bone loss is taking place. Individuals can reduce the risk of osteoporosis by maintaining a good calcium intake, engaging in weight-bearing exercise, and getting a moderate amount of sun (in order to manufacture vitamin D) during young adulthood. Restricting alcohol intake and not smoking also reduce the risk. Women past menopause should consult a doctor about estrogen replacement therapy and calcium supplements.

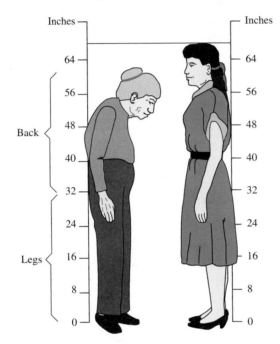

osteopenia. One year after bone-density testing, the participants in the study completed questionnaires assessing risk factors and incidence of skeletal fractures. Compared to women with normal bone density levels, the women with osteoporosis were 4 times more likely to have experienced a bone fracture. The women with osteopenia were 1.7 times more likely to have experienced a bone fracture. The study confirmed that estrogen replacement, maintaining a balanced diet including daily requirements for calcium, and engaging in physical exercise on a regular basis are associated with a decreased likelihood of osteoporosis. Age is associated with an increased likelihood of osteoporosis. As shown in Figure 3.1, a height loss of more than one inch from baseline height at age 20 is indicative of osteoporosis.

It is likely that improved nutrition has had a major effect on height changes in different cohort groups. Young adults today are generally taller than young adults of just a decade ago, and part of this cohort difference is probably due to improved nutrition. Figure 3.2 shows the effects nutrition may have on height for middle-aged and older adults. This figure shows the estimated mean height for groups of middle-aged and

Figure 3.2 This figure shows the estimated mean height for groups of middle-aged and older adults measured in 2000. The solid line indicates *age differences* in height. The dashed line indicates *age changes* for this cohort. These data illustrate two important points. First, some part of the differences we observe between age groups for any measure is due to cohort factors rather than age. Improved nutrition has had a major effect on height and other physical characteristics. Second, some physical dimensions are remarkably stable as individuals age. Do you think the mean height of the middle-aged group tested in 2000 will decline or stay the same?

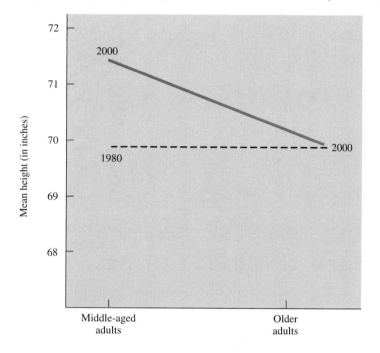

older adults measured in 2000. The solid line indicates age differences in height; the dashed line indicates an age change for this cohort. Although these data are estimations of actual heights for these groups, they illustrate that some part of the difference we observe between age groups for any physical measure is due to cohort factors. Appendix A describes in detail methods for disentangling age and cohort influences.

Studies of age differences and age changes also suggest that muscle tissue gradually declines in strength, size, firmness or tone, and flexibility. Age-related changes in strength and muscle tone can be attributed to tissue changes, but the decline in strength depends largely on one's level of activity.

Changes in Circulation and Respiration

As figure 3.3 illustrates, the major biological systems of the body all begin to decline during one's twenties and thirties. One of the most noteworthy declines occurs in the circulatory (cardiovascular) system. The cells in the human body, in order to survive and function, must receive oxygen and nutrients and must have a way to dispose of waste products. The circulatory system provides for these needs. Figure 3.4 shows the

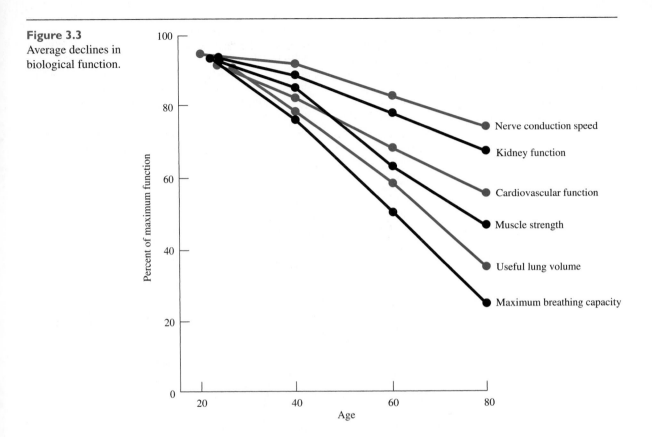

Figure 3.3
Average declines in biological function.

four chambers of the heart and the pattern of circulation. Although the heart muscles become less efficient, and the arteries narrow and become less flexible, normal aging of the circulatory system does not pose a problem for most older adults. However, diseases of the circulatory system, such as heart disease, hypertension, and atherosclerosis, are serious problems for a large number of middle-aged and older adults (Elias, Elias, & Elias, 1990). Although the incidence of heart disease is decreasing, it is still the leading cause of death in the United States. Changes in health behaviors as well as medical advances have helped to reduce the consequences of heart disease.

The circulatory system interacts with the respiratory system. Oxygen, delivered to the body cells via the blood, enters the bloodstream in the lungs. Starting about age 30, maximum oxygen capacity in the lungs decreases by about 5 to 10 percent per decade. Furthermore, collagen fibers begin to build up in the lungs, causing the lung tissue to lose its elasticity. This means that, with advancing age, individuals experience more and more problems when performing anaerobic activities that last for more than a few seconds. For example, it is more common to see a 40-year-old Olympic weight lifter than a sprinter.

Changes in Hormone Regulation and Reproduction

Age-related changes in hormonal regulation occur due to changes in secretion patterns and their effects on target tissues. One system that undergoes hormonal change with ag-

Figure 3.4   Circulation in the heart. The heart is a four-chambered muscle, about the size of a fist. Each side of the heart contains two separate spaces separated by a valve. The thin-walled upper chamber is called the atrium, and the thick-walled lower chamber is called the ventricle.

Used blood returns to the heart via the vena cava, the body's largest vein, and enters the right atrium. It then flows down through the valve into the right ventricle. The ventricle contracts, forcing the blood through the pulmonary artery into the lungs, where carbon dioxide is removed and oxygen is added. The clean, oxygenated blood returns to the heart via the pulmonary veins and enters the left atrium, then flows down through the valve into the left ventricle. The powerful muscular wall of the left ventricle forces the blood up through the aorta, the body's largest artery, and into the systemic circulation. The familiar "lub-dub" sound of the heartbeat comes from the alternating contraction (systole) and relaxation (diastole) of the chambers of the heart.

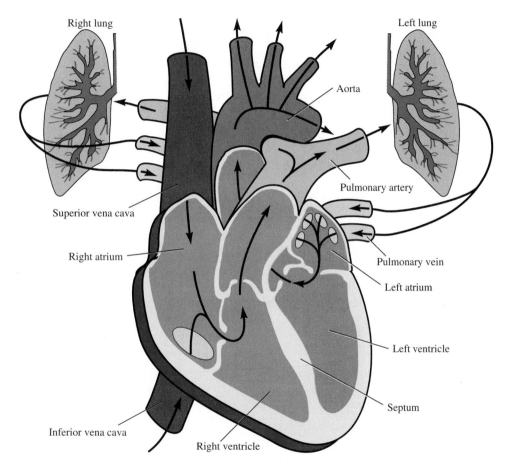

ing is the female reproductive system. The transition from the comparative regularity of the menstrual cycle during young adulthood to increased variation in the menstrual interval in middle age is due to changes in the lengths of the follicular and luteal phases of the cycle. Changes in ovary function determine the timing of the events leading to irregular cycles (Wise, 2001). Changes in anterior pituitary function are also likely to occur with aging. Age-related changes in follicle stimulating hormone (FSH) levels are one of the earliest hallmarks of reproductive aging in women. In regularly cycling women over age 45, FSH concentrations are elevated during the early follicular phase, then fall to normal during the late follicular phase. The mean number of follicles in the ovaries of women who are still menstruating is tenfold higher than in postmenopausal women of the same age. Over the life span, there is a continuous, exponential reduction in ovarian oocytes and follicles. By the time of menopause, less than 1 percent of the original reserve of oocytes and primordial follicles remain.

Men do not generally experience abrupt changes in fertility or other sexual functions. However, during the later adult years, reproductive impairments become more common. The incidence of impotence increases, testosterone concentrations decrease, and the diurnal rhythm in testosterone levels disappears.

Aging and Sensory Processes

We make contact with the world around us through our five primary senses—vision, hearing, touch, taste, and smell. **Sensation** refers to the reception of information by the ears, skin, tongue, nostrils, eyes, and other specialized sense organs. When we hear, for example, the outer ear senses waves of pulsating air; the waves are transmitted through the bones of the middle ear to the cochlear nerve and then sent to the brain. When we see, waves of light enter the eyes, focus on the retina, and travel along the optic nerve to the brain. We now consider the effects of aging on vision, hearing, and other sensory processes.

Vision

Figure 3.5 shows a diagram of the human eye. Although visual function changes relatively little during the early adult years, it changes noticeably during the middle and later years. In the middle adult years, most or all individuals will experience **presbyopia,** or difficulties in near vision tasks such as reading. This is caused, in part, by a substantial decline in the process of **accommodation,** which is defined as the ability of

Figure 3.5
Major structures of the eye.

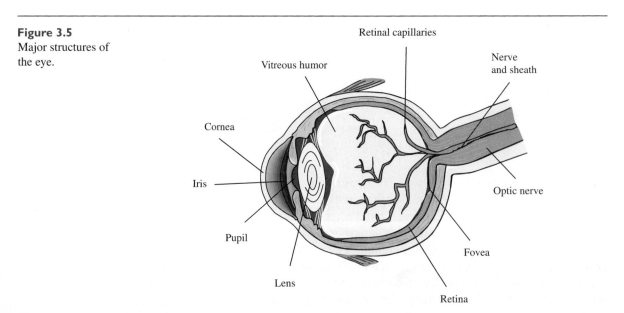

TABLE 3.1

The Percentage of Elderly Adults Who Are Visually Impaired, Grouped by Age, Sex, and Race (1995)

	Men			Women	
Age	70-74	12%	Age	70-74	15%
	75-79	17%		75-79	18%
	80-84	25%		80-84	23%
	85+	26%		85+	34%

	Black			White	
Age	70-74	18%	Age	70-74	13%
	75-79	19%		75-79	18%
	80-84	26%		80-84	24%
	85+	28%		85+	32%

Source: Desai, M., Pratt, L. A., Lentzner, H., & Robinson, K. N. (2001). Trends in vision and hearing among older Americans. Aging Trends: Hyattsville, MD: National Center for Health Statistics.

the lens to focus on near or far objects and maintain a clear image on the retina (Fozard & Gordon-Salant, 2001). The percentages of adults aged 70 and over who are visually impaired appear in table 3.1. Although visual acuity is the most common measure of accommodation, measures of **contrast sensitivity** may provide a more accurate assessment of age-related changes in visual function (see Research Focus 3.2).

Another visual problem associated with the middle-aged years is an increased sensitivity to **glare.** This change is usually noticed after age 45. Age-related changes in glare sensitivity are largely due to changes in the lens; and indeed, the lens becomes progressively thicker, less flexible, and more opaque with age. All of these changes in the lens mean that less light reaches the retina. Also, the number of cones (color receptors) on the fovea (the center of the retina) markedly decreases between 40 and 60 years of age. Such a change has a negative influence on visual acuity (Weale, 1986).

Another visual change relates to our ability to adjust to the dark. As we grow older, the processes involved in adjusting to changes in illumination take longer (Weale, 1986). The term *dark adaptation* refers to the adjustment involved in going from a brightly lit to a dimly lit environment.

The area of the effective visual field also becomes smaller with advancing age. This means that either the size or the intensity of stimuli in the peripheral area of the visual field must be increased to be seen. Thus, events occurring away from the center of the visual field are more difficult to detect (Pringle et al., 2001; Sekuler, Bennett, & Mamelak, 2000). Changes in the size of the visual field are due in part to an age-related reduction in the amount of blood reaching the eye. Researchers have determined that the retina of a 60-year-old receives approximately one-third of the light the retina of a 20-year-old receives (Weale, 1986). Kosnik et al. (1988) surveyed a large number of adults ranging from 18 to 100 years of age about their ability to perform everyday visual tasks. The participants reported that dynamic vision (reading the moving credits at the end of a movie), and visual search (locating a particular type of cereal at the

Age Changes in Contrast Sensitivity

Contrast sensitivity refers to an individual's ability to perceive visual stimuli that differ in both contrast and spatial frequency. *Contrast* is the difference in brightness between adjacent areas of a visual stimulus. A black line on a white piece of paper possesses a great deal of contrast; a light grey line on a white piece of paper possesses a smaller amount of contrast. *Spatial frequency* refers to the number of cycles of bars of light (one cycle consisting of both a light bar and a dark bar of the same width) imaged within a specific area on the retina—very wide bars of light have low spatial frequencies, whereas very narrow bars of light have high spatial frequencies. Psychologists have constructed simple visual stimuli, called *gratings,* that differ in spatial frequency. (See figure 3.A for an example of two simple gratings.) If held at arm's length, grating A has a spatial frequency of 1 (each cycle of one light bar and one dark bar takes up one degree of visual angle on the retina); grating B has a spatial frequency of 3 (three cycles of light and dark bars take up one degree of visual angle). In other words, there are three times as many bars of light in grating B as in grating A.

Think of an experiment in which we present adults of varying ages with a number of gratings that differ in both contrast and spatial frequency. The goal is to determine the *contrast threshold* for different-aged adults, or the minimal amount of contrast needed to perceive gratings that differ in spatial frequency. By doing such an experiment, Owsley, Sekuler, and Siemsen (1983) demonstrated that the contrast threshold changes in a predictable manner from 20 to 80 years of age.

With increases in age, adults (1) need more and more contrast to see gratings with high spatial frequencies, (2) be-

come progressively blind to higher spatial frequencies regardless of the amount of contrast in a grating, and (3) display no alteration in their ability to see low spatial frequencies.

Why do you think scientists are so concerned with the concept of contrast sensitivity and with age-related changes in the contrast threshold in particular? To answer this question, we need to consider the concept of visual acuity. When an adult goes to an optometrist for a routine eye exam, she is typically given a test of visual acuity, or the ability to perceive objects under maximum amounts of contrast. When you take your eye exam, you are placed in a dark room, and the optometrist projects an eye chart consisting of black letters against a white background. Alternatively, contrast sensitivity is a measurement of the minimum amount of contrast necessary to see an object. The standard test of visual acuity provides an incomplete evaluation of visual function. For example, suppose that several older adults complain of poor vision. But when they take the standard test of visual acuity, no deficits are detected. This does not mean that these people are imagining their problem or complaining about nothing. Instead, it means that under conditions of reduced contrast (e.g., driving at dusk or reading in a dimly lit room), older adults may experience a pronounced difficulty in seeing. But when high levels of contrast are available, as in a test of visual acuity, they experience less difficulty.

Contrast sensitivity is a more sensitive and more meaningful measure of a person's visual ability than is visual acuity. For this reason, a person's contrast sensitivity is a better predictor than visual acuity of one's ability to drive a car under conditions of reduced visibility.

---

supermarket) declined very gradually with age, whereas visual processing speed (the time necessary to read a passage or recognize an object), near vision (ability to read small print), and light sensitivity (seeing at dusk or sorting dark colors) declined rapidly with age.

Two of the most common pathologies of the aging eye are **cataracts** and **glaucoma** (Fozard & Gordon-Salant, 2000). A person with a cataract has a lens that is completely opaque—light cannot travel through the lens to project onto the retina. Cataracts can be surgically treated by removing the lens and inserting an artificial one. Glaucoma results from increasing pressure inside the eye, which eventually causes irreparable damage to the retina and the optic nerve. Glaucoma, which affects 2 percent of individuals over the age of 40 and becomes more prevalent with age, can be effectively treated with eye drops. If glaucoma goes unchecked, blindness can result.

Hearing

Hearing remains fairly constant during much of early adulthood and starts to decline during middle adulthood. By age 40, a specific decline in hearing is sometimes evident. By

TABLE 3.2

The Percentage of Elderly Adults Who Are Hearing Impaired, Grouped by Age, Sex, and Race (1995)

	Men			Women	
Age	70-74	35%	Age 70-74	22%
	75-79	41%	75-79	27%
	80-84	47%	80-84	36%
	85+	58%	85+	49%

	Black			White	
Age	70-74	14%	Age 70-74	29%
	75-79	19%	75-79	34%
	80-84	26%	80-84	41%
	85+	32%	85+	53%

Source: Desai, M., Pratt, L.A., Lentzner, H., & Robinson, K. N. (2001). Trends in vision and hearing among older Americans. Aging Trends: Hyattsville, MD: National Center for Health Statistics.

age 50, we are likely to have problems hearing high-pitched sounds (Kline & Scialfa, 1996). Table 3.2 shows the percentages of adults over 70 who report hearing problems. The reduction in the ability to hear high-pitched sounds seems to be caused by a breakdown of cells in the **organ of corti,** the organ in the inner ear that transforms the vibrations that the outer ear picks up into nerve impulses. Sensitivity to low-pitched sounds, on the other hand, does not decline much in middle adulthood. The need to increase the treble on stereo equipment is a subtle sign of this age-related change in hearing high pitches.

Hearing impairment becomes more serious in the later years. About 20 percent of individuals between 45 and 54 years of age experience some hearing difficulty; for those between 75 and 79, this rises to 30 percent (Desai et al., 2001). Hearing loss is usually due to degeneration of the **cochlea,** the primary neural receptor for hearing. **Presbycusis,** the decline in the ability to hear high-pitched sounds, is the most common age-related problem in hearing. Another specific hearing disorder in later life is **tinnitus.** This is a high-pitched "ringing" or "whistling" sound in the ears that is present for nearly 11 percent of those between 65 and 74 years of age (Desai et al., 2001). Though not unknown among middle-aged adults (9 percent) or younger adults (3 percent), tinnitus is a problem the elderly find most difficult to accept. It is constant, distracting, and nearly impossible to "tune out."

With increasing age, it is more and more difficult to hear speech sounds. This becomes especially noticeable when an individual tries to process speech sounds under noisy conditions. Degeneration of certain areas within the brain, as well as age-related changes in the structures and functions of the ear, may be responsible for this phenomenon. Whatever the cause, this deficit has a negative effect on the older adult's ability to communicate with others (Souza & Hoyer, 1996).

Many older adults use hearing aids. Recent technological improvements have made them more comfortable and effective, especially if a professional properly fits them. Some older adults must wear two hearing aids to correct for different degrees of

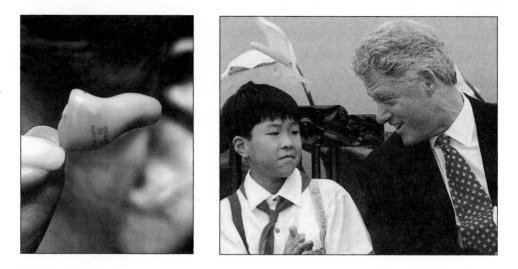

This is the type of hearing aid that former President Bill Clinton began wearing in October of 1997 at age 51 . Note that it is virtually impossible to detect the hearing aid (right).

hearing loss in each ear. If the aids are not properly balanced, or if the individual uses only one, he loses the subtle differences in phase and intensity at each ear that enable him to localize and identify sounds. Localization of sounds helps us to attend to one conversation while ignoring another. When we can't do this well, both wanted and unwanted sounds combine and produce confusion.

Deficits in hearing, like those associated with sight, may have a profound impact on an individual's sense of well-being as well as her ability to meet the demands of everyday life. Recently, Marsiske, Klumb, and Baltes (1997) examined the relationship between visual and auditory acuity and everyday functioning in a sample of 516 people between 70 and 103 years of age. The researchers measured two different facets of everyday functioning: basic living activities (e.g., eating, dressing, shopping) and discretionary social activities (e.g., socializing with friends, playing cards). They hypothesized that sensory acuity would predict an individual's ability to perform basic living activities, but that intellectual and personality variables would predict the types and amounts of a person's discretionary social activities. Surprisingly, Marsiske et al. (1997) discovered that sensory acuity explained most of the age-related variance in both aspects of everyday functioning. This underscores the notion that sensory factors, more than intellectual and personality variables, are powerful determinants of a person's everyday functioning.

Taste, Smell, and Touch

Age-related declines also occur in taste, smell, and tactile sensitivity (Engen, 1977; Schiffman, 1999), although declines in these senses are not as dramatic or noticeable as those that affect vision and hearing. Declines in the sense of taste and smell affect one's enjoyment and intake of food and thus also affect one's choice of diet. For example, some older adults suffer from nutritional deficiencies because they crave highly seasoned but nonnutritious "junk food."

The human tongue contains specialized receptors that detect four different tastes: sweet, salty, bitter, and sour. Bartoshuk, Rifkin, Marks, and Bars (1986) found that

Age-related changes in sensitivity to taste and smell affect dietary preference and may affect how much "hot sauce" we use.

older adults were less sensitive than younger adults to all four basic tastes. Many researchers have suggested that sensitivity to all tastes remains stable until the late fifties, when the ability to detect all tastes steeply declines. However, changes in taste sensitivity do not cause all changes in eating behavior during older adulthood (de Jong et al., 1999). Older adults may eat less because they don't want to bother to cook, shop, and clean up, or for other reasons such as loneliness.

Age-related changes in smell have been very difficult to reliably document (Engen, 1977). This is because smell is one of the last senses to decline with age, and because a number of age-related variables (e.g., health) may affect this sense. Deficits in smell may have disastrous effects. For example, Chalke, Dewhurst, and Ward (1958) reported that as many as 30 percent of adults over age 65 were not sensitive to the smell of lower concentrations of gas.

Age-related changes in touch have also been reported. For example, Gescheider and colleagues (Gescheider, 1997; Gescheider et al., 1994) examined vibrotactile sensitivity (the ability to detect vibrations on the surface of the skin) in individuals between 8 and 87 years of age. They found substantial age-related declines in the detection of high-frequency stimulation, but just moderate declines in the detection of low-frequency stimulation. This suggests that the aging process affects certain types of sensory receptors, such as Pacinian corpuscles, more than others. Corso (1977) has observed that the touch sensitivity of the lower extremities (ankles, knees, etc.) declines more with aging than that of the upper extremities (wrists, shoulders, etc.). Loss of tactile sensitivity in itself is not much of a problem for the typical older adult. It does become problematic, however, when other severe sensory disorders combine with it.

Temperature, Pain, and Kinesthetic Senses

Older adults are less sensitive to temperature changes than young adults (Schieber, 1992). Because older adults may be less able to detect changes in temperature, they are more susceptible to hypothermia, heatstroke, and frostbite. One of the age-related losses in sensory sensitivity, the sensitivity to pain, may have an advantage: Older people are

Falling: The Leading Cause of Accidental Injury Among the Elderly

Among those over age 65, falling is the leading cause of accidental injury. For example, of the 200,000 hip fractures each year in the United States, more than 170,000 occur to this age group. The rate of mortality from falling increases directly with increased age and represents the seventh-leading cause of death in those over 75, surpassing even automobile accidents. About 25 percent of older people require intensive medical intervention and hospitalization from falls. Severe falls are associated with broken bones (fractures of the hip, wrist, and vertebrae), head injury, and multiple facial, skin, and hand lacerations.

Most falls occur in the homes of older people, especially in the living room or bedroom during the regular daytime routine, or while going downstairs. The institutionalized elderly are also at high risk due to the many predisposing medical conditions that require institutional placement. Institutional falls are more common at night, perhaps as older people become disoriented and confused in unfamiliar surroundings. Newly admitted patients in institutions are particularly vulnerable. The causes of falling among the elderly represent a burgeoning area of research. Many studies suggest that the elderly who are most likely to experience severe injury or death from a fall

are those just beginning to undergo physical and psychological decline who have not yet recognized their limitations. On the other hand, those elderly who are frequent fallers and have identified their problem are less likely to be seriously injured in a fall.

The risk of falling is related to poor illumination, dark staircases, and loose rugs. Some of the physical conditions that contribute to falling are arthritis, loss of balance and equilibrium (presbystasis), weakness in the muscles that control coordination of the knees and ankles, impaired vision, impaired hearing (hearing provides critical feedback for walking), and diabetes (leading to reduced sensation in the legs). Several medications can even increase the risk of falling.

Why do falls lead to such severe injury in the elderly? First, because of the generalized age-related slowing of behavior, older people may not be as able as younger people to prepare themselves to break a fall. Second, the age-related phenomenon of osteoporosis, or thinning and weakening of the bones, may cause the spontaneous shattering of brittle, thinning bones (especially in the pelvis) in older people. This sudden breakage can actually cause a fall. Thus, falls can cause broken bones, and brittle or broken bones can cause falls.

---

less sensitive to pain than younger adults (Kenshalo, 1977). Although decreased sensitivity to pain may help the elderly cope with disease and injury, it can be harmful if it masks injuries and illnesses that need treatment. A vast array of important personality and cultural factors influence the reporting and experience of pain.

Simoneau and Liebowitz (1996) reviewed evidence that the elderly are likely to experience impaired kinesthesis. **Kinesthesis** is a person's ability to know where his or her body parts are as he or she moves through space; for example, being able to touch your nose when your eyes are closed. A reduced kinesthetic sense makes elderly adults more susceptible to falls (see Research Focus 3.3).

Aging and Physical Ability

The physical skills of an individual usually peak between his or her early twenties and midthirties. One of the major reasons for a decrease in physical performance during adulthood is a reduction in muscle strength. Muscular strength and the ability to maintain maximum muscular effort both decline steadily during middle adulthood. At age 30, about 70 of a man's 175 pounds are muscle. Over the next 40 years, he loses 10 pounds of that muscle as cells stop dividing and die. By age 50, the strength of a man's back muscles declines to approximately 96 percent of its maximum value. Most men in their late fifties can only do physical work at about 60 percent of the rate that men who are 40 can achieve. Much of this decline appears to be linked to physiological changes such as the thickening of the air sac walls in the lungs, which hinders breathing, and the hardening of connective sheaths that surround muscles, which decreases both oxygen and blood supply. All these age-related changes, identified for the most part by cross-sectional research, are confounded with a variety of other potent variables, such as lifestyle changes and cohort differences in exercise habits. With exercise and training, individuals can reduce the rate of decline in various psychomotor and physical functions (see Research Focus 3.4).

Simple actions that entail little or no effort are just as likely to slow down with aging as are complex behaviors that demand strength, endurance, and skill. For example, finger tapping and handwriting slow dramatically with age (Dixon, Kurzman, & Friesen, 1993). Salthouse (1985) noted that **psychomotor slowing** is probably the most reliable finding in the study of human aging. Older adults, because their motor performance slows, may be less able to adapt to the demands of a changing world. According to Salthouse (1985):

> If the external environment is rapidly changing, the conditions that lead to the initiation of a particular behavior may no longer be appropriate by the time the behavior is actually executed by older adults. This could lead to severe problems in operating vehicles, controlling equipment, or monitoring displays. Despite some claims to the contrary . . . it appears that the speed of decision and response can be quite important in our modern automated society, and, consequently, the slowness of older adults may place them at a great disadvantage relative to the younger members of the population. (p. 401)

Although it is reasonable for individuals to expect age-related changes in health and physical functioning, individual differences are the rule. To a significant extent, we control our own health and quality of life as we grow older. For example, regular exercise has many beneficial effects for the aging individual (King, 2001).

Brain Aging

Age-related changes in the nervous system may have dramatic effects on the behavioral, cognitive, and personality functioning of the aging individual. Thus, we turn our attention to age changes in the human brain.

Major Components of the Brain

The major structures of the human brain, along with some comments about the effects of aging on these structures, appear in figure 3.6. In an evolutionary sense, the **brain stem** is the oldest part of the brain. It controls basic biological functions such as breathing and heart rate. The **ascending reticular activation system (ARAS),** a structure that originates within the brain stem and extends to the other portions of the brain, regulates an individual's state of consciousness and level of arousal. Attached to the brain stem is the **cerebellum.** This structure helps maintain balance and posture and coordinate

Aging and Peak Athletic Performance

Although peak levels of athletic performance are usually attained in young adulthood, age-related changes in athletic performance are smaller than most individuals imagine. Furthermore, older athletes who continue to train display high levels of athletic competence (Schulz, Musa, Staszewski, & Siegler, 1994).

Ericsson and Crutcher (1990) reviewed the research regarding age changes in swimming and running performance. They chose these sports for analysis because (1) the distances of specific races within these sports have been fixed for approximately the last century, and (2) performance is measured objectively by specific units of time (minutes, seconds, etc.)—there is no subjective element in measuring performance in these sports, as in boxing or gymnastics. These attributes allowed researchers to make valid comparisons of changes in swimming and running performance from one era (the 1920s) to another (the 1980s).

Examination of the world records and Olympic gold medal performances in these sports from 1896 (the year of the first modern-day Olympic games) to 2000 reveal four major findings. First, gold medalists and world record holders have generally achieved their peaks during young adulthood, usually when they are between 20 and 30 years of age. Second, world record and gold medal times have steadily and significantly decreased. Third, the shorter the distance of the race, the younger the age of the medalists and/or record holders. Fourth, winners of shorter swimming events are becoming younger (in their early twenties), while the winners of longer running events such as the marathon are becoming older (in their late twenties to mid-thirties).

Box figures 3.A and 3.B show the best times as well as the average times achieved by swimmers between 25 and 75 years of age. Both of these figures show a decline in performance with age. Age-related declines were most evident in the average performance of swimmers over 60 years of age.

Box Figure 3.A Changes in the *best* race times for expert competitive swimmers 25 to 70 years of age.

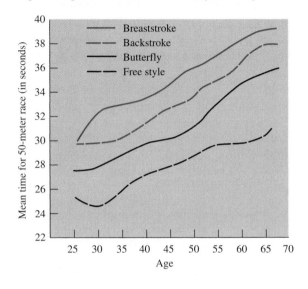

Box Figure 3.B Changes in the *average* race times for expert competitive swimmers 25 to 70 years of age.

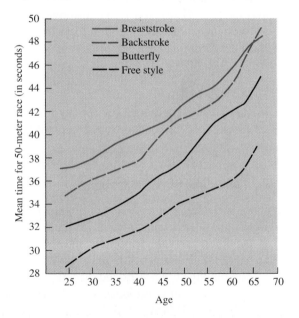

Aging and Peak Athletic Performance

Athletes can maintain (and sometimes improve) their performance through middle and late adulthood. This occurs only if adults maintain or increase their levels of practice and training. Continued exercise is an important factor in minimizing the losses in aerobic power usually observed during adulthood. Aerobic power, which refers to the body's maximal ability to take in oxygen, is arguably the best predictor of performance in endurance events (e.g., long-distance running).

Data reported by Howard Grubb (2001), an applied statistician at the University of Reading, indicate that the effect of age on running speed and swimming speed is about the same regardless of the distance of the event (see http://www.rdg.ac.uk/~snsgrubb/athletics/). The effect of aging on performance was a constant, regardless of the distance of the event, for both men and women athletes. These data are shown in box figures 3.C (running) and 3.D (swimming).

Box Figure 3.C Running speed as a function of age for men and women. Age group performance is shown as a percentage of the overall world record. Each line represents a different running event.

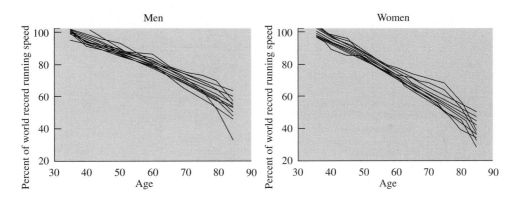

Box Figure 3.D Swimming speed as a function of age for men and women. Age group performance is shown as a percentage of the overall world record. Each line represents a different swimming event.

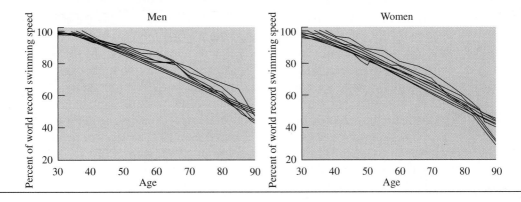

Figure 3.6 Age-related changes in brain structures.

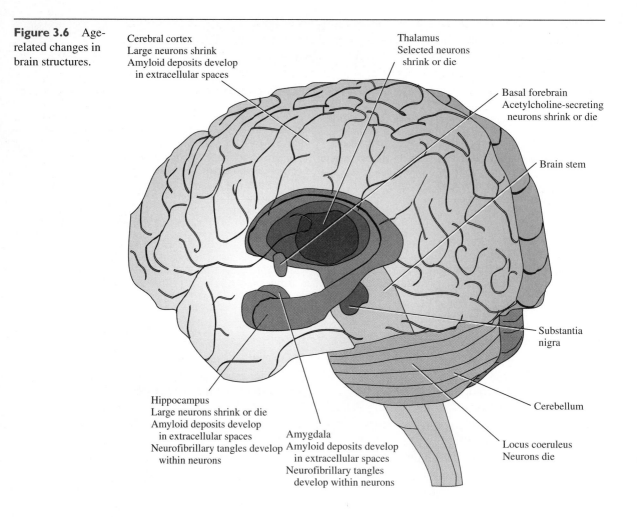

Cerebral cortex
Large neurons shrink
Amyloid deposits develop
in extracellular spaces

Thalamus
Selected neurons
shrink or die

Basal forebrain
Acetylcholine-secreting
neurons shrink or die

Brain stem

Substantia
nigra

Cerebellum

Locus coeruleus
Neurons die

Hippocampus
Large neurons shrink or die
Amyloid deposits develop
in extracellular spaces
Neurofibrillary tangles develop
within neurons

Amygdala
Amyloid deposits develop
in extracellular spaces
Neurofibrillary tangles
develop within neurons

body movements. Also, memories for simple learned responses seem to be stored here (Woodruff-Pak, 1997).

The **limbic system** is a border area between the older parts of the brain (the brain stem and cerebellum) and the newer part of the brain (the **cerebral cortex**). One part of the limbic system, called the *hypothalamus,* controls eating, drinking, body temperature, and sexual activity. Another component of the limbic system is the **hippocampus.** A great deal of evidence suggests that the hippocampus plays a major role in memory (Schacter, 2000). Patients who suffer from amnesia and other disorders characterized by memory failure, display significant damage to the hippocampus (Raz, 2000). Furthermore, biological changes in the hippocampus that accompany normal aging may be responsible, in part, for decline in memory abilities with advancing age (Moscovitch & Winocur, 1992; Raz, 2000).

The cerebrum is the largest, and evolutionarily the most recent, part of the brain. It totally covers the limbic system as well as significant portions of the brain stem and cerebellum. The cerebrum has several important features. First, it is divided down the middle into two halves or **hemispheres**—the right and the left. Second, a tract of nerve fibers called the **corpus callosum** connects the hemispheres. Third, the top covering of the cerebrum is called the **cerebral cortex.** The cortex, from the viewpoint of a psychologist, may be the most important part of the brain. In fact, it is the cortex which makes us "human"; it serves as the source of personality, cognition, perception, communication, and creativity.

The cortex may be divided into four different regions called **lobes,** where various psychological functions are housed. The **frontal lobe** is responsible for basic aspects of personality and social behaviors, planning and execution of complex behavioral sequences, and control of motor movements. In the **temporal lobe** we find structures involved in the consolidation of long-term memories, in the assigning of emotional properties to incoming experiences, and in simple auditory sensation. The **parietal lobe** influences the construction of a spatial representation of one's body. Finally, the **occipital lobe** controls basic visual processing. Despite its importance in human psychological functioning, the cortex is amazingly delicate, fragile, and thin. In fact, the cortex is just a one-eighth-inch-thick sheath covering the cerebrum.

As individuals age, they become more likely to suffer from damage or injury to the cortex. Also with aging, the brain becomes less plastic. This means that uninjured parts of the cortex are less likely to take over the functions of injured cortical areas. Damage to the elderly brain usually results from a stroke or a brain tumor. Strokes occur when brain tissue is deprived of oxygen, often when a blood vessel in the brain becomes clogged, plugged, or broken. In general, damage to the left hemisphere results in **aphasia,** a breakdown or loss of an individual's language abilities. Damage to the right hemisphere typically results in visual-spatial disorders; for example, **agnosia,** a failure to recognize familiar objects or faces. People with right hemisphere damage may become lost in familiar environments (even their own homes or neighborhoods) and may not be able to form a visual representation of all the objects (including their own bodies) in the left half of their visual field.

Neuronal Aging

The brain consists of a diverse array of neurons, glial cells, and blood vessels. A **neuron,** or nerve cell, is the basic unit of the brain and nervous system. Communication between neurons makes behavioral and psychological functions possible. Glial cells and blood vessels support, nourish, and help repair neurons. Every neuron has three major components: **soma, axon,** and **dendrites.** The axon is an elongated structure that relays signals to other neurons that are often a good distance away. The dendrites, typified by branching, receive signals from other neurons. The soma, or cell body, helps coordinate all the processes that take place within the neuron. Figure 3.7 shows a sketch of a typical neuron.

Overall brain weights, as well as the number of neurons in the brain, decrease with age (see figure 3.8). Postmortem or autopsy studies have confirmed reports of age-related neuronal death (Kemper, 1994). At the cortical level, these studies showed that neuronal loss is least likely to occur in sensorimotor areas such as the occipital and parietal lobes

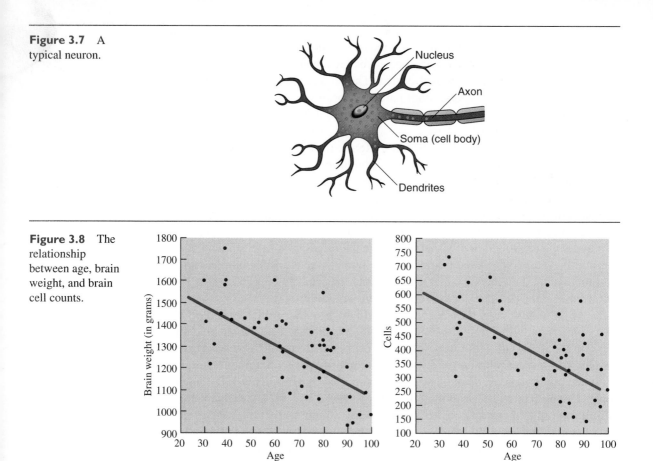

Figure 3.7   A typical neuron.

Nucleus

Axon

Soma (cell body)

Dendrites

Figure 3.8   The relationship between age, brain weight, and brain cell counts.

and is most likely to occur in the areas that control intelligence, memory, and abstract thinking, such as the frontal and temporal lobes. These studies also revealed a substantial amount of cell loss in subcortical areas, particularly in certain parts of the limbic system that are central to memory, especially the hippocampus. (See figure 3.9 for drawings of the dendrites of neurons in the hippocampus for different-aged individuals.) The conclusions derived from postmortem studies must be viewed with a great deal of caution. This is because most postmortem studies were conducted decades ago, when researchers underestimated the prevalence of Alzheimer's disease among older adults. Thus, these studies may have inadvertently included many diseased brains in their "normal" sample.

More recently, however, a number of researchers have pointed out that the consequences of age-related neuronal death may be very much overblown. For example, Albert (1993) was one of the first to show that large numbers of neurons may shrink or atrophy, but not die, with increasing age. In fact, a great deal of recent evidence points to the conclusion that there may be little, if any, cortical neuronal loss associated with normal aging (Wilkelgren, 1996).

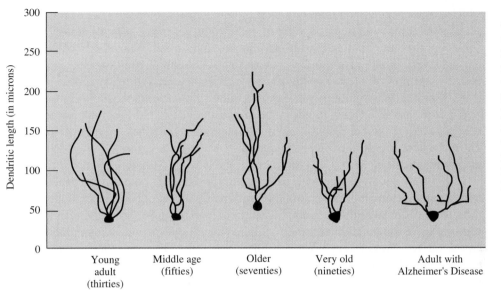

Figure 3.9 Age differences in dendritic branching for healthy adults from middle age to very old age, and for an Alzheimer's patient. The illustrations are drawn from photographs of neurons from the hippocampus.

The term, **apoptosis,** is used to refer to programmed neuron death and the loss of neurons. Although a 25–50 percent loss of neurons occurs in the neocortex and in some areas of the hippocampus with aging, **neuronal viability,** in addition to apoptosis, is a key factor in normal and abnormal brain aging (e.g., Cotman, 2001; Morrison & Hof, 1997; Raz, 2000). Neuronal viability refers to the efficiency of neural functioning. Decline in neuronal viability can result from the generation of free radicals (oxidative stress), acute or chronic inflammation of neural tissue, shrinkage of dendritic branching, change in hormonal processes, and genetic factors.

Genetic risk factors for developing Alzheimer's disease, such as the presence of the apolipoprotein E epsilon 4 allele (APOE), probably reduce neuronal health by affecting the accumulation of amyloid and by triggering the spread of neural inflammation (Cotman, 2001). APOE is a plasma protein involved in cholesterol transportation. In a recent study of 5,888 older adults (65+ years), the presence of apolipoprotein E epsilon 4 allele (APOE) predicted cognitive decline over a seven-year period (Haan, et al., 1999). Many new studies show that the presence of APOE accelerates the onset of Alzheimer's disease (e.g., Miech et al., 2002).

Neurons undergo changes in their internal architecture with aging. For example, the cytoplasm of particular cells of the hippocampus can begin to fill with tangled bundles of protein filaments known as **neurofibrillary tangles.** The development of tangles seems to indicate that certain proteins, particularly those of the cytoskeleton, or internal walls of the cell, have been chemically modified in ways that impair the neuron's signaling efficiency (Selkoe, 1992). Also, Albert (1993) has reported a large age-related decline in the amount of **white matter** (i.e., the fatty myelin sheath that surrounds and insulates long axons). Many scientists claim that losses in white matter, especially in the frontal cortex, account for many of the cognitive declines older adults display (Wilkelgren, 1996).

The discovery that significant numbers of cortical neurons do not die with advancing age opens up a number of exciting possibilities. For example, different types of drug therapies might be developed to prevent neuronal atrophy along with the shrinkage of white matter. This might allow a larger number of adults to display enhanced levels of cognitive function into old age. As figure 3.10 illustrates, a massively complex network of interconnections exists among neurons, with large open spaces between them. With normal aging, the extracellular spaces within the hippocampus, cerebral cortex, and other brain regions gradually accumulate spherical deposits called **senile plaques** (Scheibel, 1996). These plaques are aggregates of a small molecule known as **beta-amyloid protein.** Plaques also accumulate in blood vessels in these regions of the brain.

Neurons communicate with each other by secreting chemical substances called **neurotransmitters.** Normal brain function depends on having normal amounts of neurotransmitters present in the brain. Too little (or too much) of a neurotransmitter may result in brain dysfunction and aberrant behavior. Scientists who study aging have focused on two important neurotransmitters: acetylcholine and dopamine. **Acetylcholine,** manufactured in the basal nucleus, travels along a cholinergic pathway to help neurons in the temporal lobe and hippocampus communicate with each other. Some researchers believe that a small reduction in acetylcholine may cause the memory lapses associated with normal aging, whereas a massive reduction in acetylcholine is responsible for the severe memory loss associated with Alzheimer's disease. **Dopamine** is manufactured in the cells of the substantia nigra and travels along a dopaminergic pathway to neurons in the frontal cortex. Normal age-related reductions in dopamine may account for the fact that older adults cannot plan and execute motor activities (even very simple ones, such as finger tapping) as quickly as younger adults. Age-related diseases typified by the loss of motor control, such as Parkinson's disease, are associated with a massive reduction in the manufacture of dopamine.

Figure 3.10 A 3-D photomicrograph of the interneuronal structure.

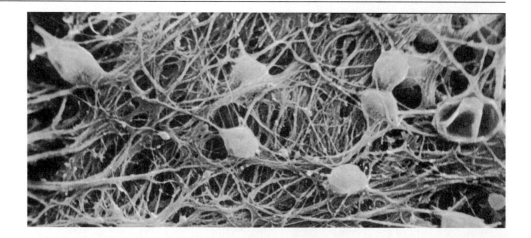

Chapter Three

Measuring the Aging Brain

Recent advances in brain imaging allow noninvasive examination of the status of brain structures of the ways in which changes in neural systems and structures affect behavior (Cubeza, 2000; Langley & Madden, 2000). Prior to the development of brain imaging techniques, the study of normal and neuropathological brain aging was based on autopsy examinations. The emergence of several brain imaging methods and psychophysiological techniques has significantly advanced current understanding of brain aging and brain-behavior relationships (Albert & Killiany, 2001; Madden, 2001). One of the imaging techniques is **structural magnetic resonance imaging** (MRI). Stimulated brain tissue emits signals that a computer transforms into an image. The MRI technique is so powerful that it can identify structures as small as 1 millimeter. Cognitive neuroscientists have used MRI as a tool for identifying regions of the brain that are most sensitive to age-related deterioration.

Another imaging technique is **functional magnetic resonance imaging** (fMRI), which uses the magnetic qualities of water molecules to evaluate the changing distribution of oxygenated to deoxygenated blood, an indirect measure of neuronal activity.

In **positron-emission tomography** (PET) scanning, brain metabolic activity is assessed by measuring changes in the amount of regional cerebral blood flow (rCBF). In PET scanning a radioactive isotope is either injected or inhaled. The pattern of radioactive emissions describes rCBF to different parts of the brain. The idea is that the most metabolically active parts of the brain will emit the highest levels of radioactivity. In one study using PET, Waldemar (1995) showed that age-related declines in blood flow are much more pronounced in the frontal cortex than in the areas involved in basic sensory function, such as the occipital lobe. Grady and colleagues (1995) compared regional blood flow in younger and older adults while subjects tried to learn and remember a series of human faces. Results showed that impaired recognition in the older group was attributable to reduced flow to the frontal cortex during the encoding and retrieval phases of the experiment. Several other PET studies have documented age differences in rCBF when younger and older adults performed a variety of memory tasks. For example, Bennett (2001) examined cortical reorganization during normal aging using PET measures of the brain activity associated with short-term memory for simple visual attributes. Results showed that younger and older adults performed equally well, but that the neural systems correlated with good performance differed for the two age groups. Thus, this PET study showed that the functional networks that underlie visual memory undergo reorganization during aging.

Age-related cognitive declines have been linked to a number of brain aging phenomena such as changes in neurotransmitter substances at the synapse, neural demyelination, disruptions in neural circuitry related to vascular lesions, and increases in the amount of recruitment and activation of brain volume. The results of fMRI studies suggest that older adults require more cognitive resources than younger adults to carry out cognitive tasks (e.g., see Raz, 2000, for a review). In these studies, younger persons showed a relatively well-defined pattern of activation involving the inferior prefrontal-orbitofrontal cortex during the encoding of episodic information and involving the right prefrontal cortex during the retrieval of episodic information. In contrast, older adults showed more widespread activation patterns for encoding and retrieval. Although fMRI studies indicate increased activation in the prefrontal areas for older adults, MRI and PET studies indicate shrinkage of the prefrontal cortex with aging (Madden, 2001). These findings suggest that older adults use more cognitive resources to carry out demanding cognitive tasks.

The most consistent finding from studies using PET and fMRI is that brain activity is less lateralized and less localized in older adults than in younger adults (Cabeza, 2001, Langley & Madden, 2000; Prull, Gabrieli, & Bunge, 2000; Raz, 2000). Figure 3.11 shows brain activity in young and older adults while performing a simple word judgment task (whether words represent concrete or abstract objects) as measured by fMRI. The line through the illustration at the top of the figure indicates the location of the functional "slices" shown in lower illustrations. It can be seen that the pattern of activation is less localized for older adults. This finding suggests that there is an age-related decline in the efficiency of the brain to recruit specialized neural mechanisms.

Figure 3.11 This figure shows averaged fMRI scans for 15 young and 15 older adults as they performed a simple word judgment task. The task required the participants to indicate whether words represented concrete or abstract objects. The line through the illustration at the top indicates the approximate location of the section displayed in the lower illustrations. It can be seen that the pattern of activation is less localized for older adults. This figure is based on data presented at the meetings of the Cognitive Neuroscience Society by Carillo et al. (1998). Reprinted from Prull, M. W., Gabrieli, J. D. E., & Bunge, S. A. (2000). Age-related changes in memory: A cognitive-neuroscience perspective. In F. I. M. Craik & T. A. Salthouse (Eds.), *The handbook of aging and cognition* pp. 91–154). Mahwah, NJ: Erlbaum.

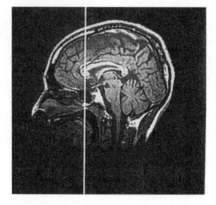

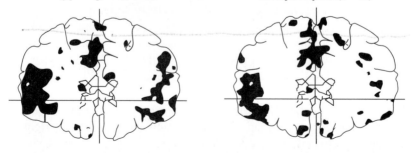

Young participants (n = 15)   Older participants (n = 15)

Cabeza suggested that reduced specialization and bi-hemispheric involvement might actually serve to compensate for structural losses in the aging brain.

It is also possible to measure the general electrical activity of the brain by means of an **electroencephalogram (EEG).** EEG research has yielded a number of important findings. For example, several different patterns of rhythmical electrical activity (i.e., brain waves) have been detected in the brain. Each of these waves is related to a particular state of consciousness. The **alpha rhythm,** the dominant rhythm the brain displays, is linked with alert wakefulness. In contrast, the faster **beta rhythm** characterizes periods of focused thinking and problem solving. The **delta rhythm** is the slowest of all brain waves. It appears when individuals enter the deepest, most restful component of the sleep cycle.

Bashore (1993) examined age-related changes in a particular brain rhythm called the **P300 brain wave.** The P300 is an event-related response (ERP) that occurs somewhere between 300 to 500 milliseconds after a stimulus is presented to an individual. The onset of the P300 seems to signify that a person has recognized or identified a stimulus. Bashore (1993) and others have shown that older and younger groups of adults differ much more on measures of physical reaction time to a stimulus (e.g., pressing a button when a particular stimulus appears on a computer screen) than to the timing of the P300 brain wave. This means that reaction-time tasks may lead researchers to overestimate the extent to which changes in central processes cause behavioral slowing in late adulthood.

Another new and potentially informative tool for the non-invasive assessment of brain function uses **event-related optical signals** (EROS). This method is based on measures of change in the optical properties of active brain tissue. EROS yields images of cortical activity and the processing time of cortical activity (Gratton & Fabiani, 2001).

A point to consider in measuring brain function is that it, like any other organ in the body, may be "over-engineered"; it possesses a significant reserve capacity (just as the heart, lungs, kidneys, etc., possess a reserve capacity that the individual draws upon as he or she ages). See Research Focus 3.5 for more information about this intriguing idea.

Alzheimer's Disease

Perhaps the most devastating age-related brain disorder is **Alzheimer's disease (AD).** The symptoms of AD were first described by a German physician, Alois Alzheimer, in 1907. Alzheimer's disease is a form of **dementia** whose primary symptom is the abnormal deterioration of mental functioning. This type of mental disorder is not part of the primary aging process.

Unsurprisingly, qualitative as well as quantitative differences distinguish the effects of normal aging and dementing illness. The hippocampus seems to be only mildly affected by normal aging, yet substantial atrophy of hippocampal structures appears in individuals in the early stages of Alzheimer's disease. Although degenerative changes usually occur gradually, cognitive deficits are noticeable only after a large amount of structural deterioration has occurred. The **threshold model** observes that a significant amount of damage or deterioration occurs before behavioral consequences are noticed (Cottman, 2000).

Brain Reserve Capacity and Aging

Considering the inevitability of brain aging and the increased prevalence of dementing diseases in later life, how is it possible to maintain effective behavioral and cognitive function? The term *brain reserve capacity* (BRC) refers to an individual's potential for maintenance or restoration of function in response to loss or disease. Recent conceptions of BRC are based on research that shows that some aspects of neural circuitry and synaptic connectivity are capable of growth and repair throughout life. Brain reserve capacity and effective cognitive function may be interdependent; continued active involvement in cognitive activities might serve to facilitate brain plasticity, or at least lead to alternative strategies for effective cognitive and behavioral functioning. The amount of BRC is probably a function of deliberate efforts to restore, protect, or promote plasticity rather than a natural resource.

Links exist between the amount of brain reserve and one's vulnerability to cognitive/functional impairment due to strokes and neurodegenerative diseases such as Alzheimer's disease (Bartzokis, 2001; Satz, 1993). Hoyer (2001) suggested that the amount of BRC could determine the threshold levels at which particular neurological diseases produce observable symptoms. New research is focusing on devising measures that index protection from the deleterious effects of normal brain aging and neurological disorders such as Alzheimer's disease. For example, the neural correlates of processing speed, working memory, learning rates, and sensory function are likely to be reliable measures of BRC. BRC may be called upon when an individual faces high levels of cognitive demand, stress, or the challenge of recovering from a stroke or other kind of neurological insults (Albert & Killiany, 2001).

Albert, M. S., & Killiany, R. J. (2001). Age-related cognitive changes and brain-behavior relationships. In J. E. Birren & K. W. Schaie (Eds.), *Handbook of the psychology of aging* (5th ed.). San Diego: Academic Press.

Bartzokis, G. (2001). Brain still developing in middle age. *Archives of General Psychiatry, 58,* 461–465.

Hoyer, W. J. (2001). Normal brain aging: Behavioral, cognitive, and personality consequences. In N. J. Smelser & P. B. Baltes (Eds.), *International encyclopedia of the social and behavioral sciences.* Oxford: Elsevier.

Description of Alzheimer's Disease

Your mother frequently misplaces her keys. But last Tuesday, she couldn't remember what they were for.

Your grandfather likes to take daily strolls around the neighborhood. But four times in the past month he couldn't find his way home without help from a neighbor.

Your favorite uncle can't remember your name or the names of any family members.

The memory loss, confusing, and disorientation described in these examples are symtoms of Alzheimer's Disease.

AD is a degenerative brain disease that is the most common cause of cognitive failure in older adulthood. The elderly person with AD loses the ability to remember, recognize, and reason. In the final stages of the disease, the afflicted person develops profound physical as well as mental disabilities and typically needs institutional care. AD is the fourth leading cause of death for adults in the United States. Approximately 4 million people were diagnosed as having AD in the United States in 1999 (Corder & Manton, 2001). However, evidence from a series of National Long Term Care Surveys indicates that there has been an unexpected and large decline in the prevalence of severe dementia in the United States for individuals over 65. There has been a decrease from 1.4 million cases of severe dementia (4.7 percent) in 1982 to 0.9 million cases (2.5 percent) in 1999 (Corder & Manton, 2001). Further, there have been unexpected declines in chronic disability in the population of the United States over the same period (e.g.,

Manton & Gu, 2001). The explanation for these positive changes is multi-factorial. One factor is improved medical care, including the development and use of effective medications and technological improvements that serve to reduce the negative consequences of disability. Another factor reflects changes in behavior across cohorts, such as improved diets, healthier lifestyles, and a one-third decline in cigarette smoking from 1960 to 2000. Despite these improvements, however, the prevalence of mild cognitive impairments has not decreased (Unverzagt, Gao, Baiyewu, et al., 2001).

In the past, researchers and clinicians thought that AD was a neurological disease that afflicted an exceptionally small number of middle-aged adults. Consequently, they categorized it as a type of "presenile dementia," believing that dementia in older adults was caused by vascular disorders such as cerebral arteriosclerosis (i.e., a hardening of the arteries that feed the brain). In the 1970s, however, researchers discovered that the symptoms and causes of dementia were identical in both middle-aged and elderly adults (Wurtman, 1985); dementia in both age groups was accompanied by the same neurological abnormalities. This finding revolutionized ideas about the prevalence and causes of AD. Scientists began to realize that AD in old age had been misdiagnosed and misunderstood. Table 3.3 lists facts about AD as well as its warning signs.

Some of the most important findings about AD concern the types of neuronal changes that appear in patients with this disorder. Specifically, AD patients have an excessive number of senile plaques and neurofibrillary tangles. Remember that the presence of plaques and tangles represent two of the prominent features of normal aging (i.e., senescence). This suggests that a quantitative, rather than a qualitative, difference exists between the brains of the healthy elderly and those with AD—the brains of AD patients have more plaques and tangles than those contained in normal aged brains. These plaques and tangles are spread throughout the brain, but they are most concentrated in the hippocampus and in the frontal and temporal areas (Scheibel, 1996).

Stages of Alzheimer's Disease

AD is characterized by a predictable, progressive decline in specific areas of psychological, physiological, and social functioning. Reisberg and his colleagues (Reisberg & Bornstein, 1986; Reisberg, Ferris, & Franssen, 1985) developed the **Functional Assessment Staging System (FAST)** and the **Global Deterioration Scale** to categorize these losses. The advantage of such an approach is that it provides clinicians and family members with the information necessary to provide appropriate intervention and to identify the projected course of the disease. Table 3.4 contains a description of FAST, along with the major clinical manifestations of AD. Note that the early stages (1, 2, and 3) are not specifically descriptive of AD. Stages 1 and 2 are included to inform professionals about the typical patterns of normal aging. Stage 3 describes an early confused state that may be symptomatic of a number of possible disorders.

Causes of Alzheimer's Disease

At present, no one knows the actual cause of AD. Nevertheless, scientists have advanced a number of different theories to account for the development of this disease. One of the most influential theories is the *cholinergic hypothesis,* which states that AD is caused by

TABLE 3.3

Alzheimer's Disease: Stats and Facts

A Look at the Numbers

Alzheimer's disease is a progressive, degenerative disease of the brain, and the most common form of dementia.

- Approximately 4 million Americans have AD. Nineteen million Americans say they have a family member with AD, and 37 million know someone with AD.
- Alzheimer's disease is the fourth-leading cause of death among adults.
- The incidence of *severe* dementia for individuals aged 65 and over in the United States has decreased from 1.4 million (4.7 percent) in 1982 to 0.9 million (2.5 percent) in 1999.
- A person with AD can live from 3 to 20 years or more from the onset of symptoms.
- AD costs society approximately $100 billion a year. Neither Medicare nor private health insurance covers the long-term care most patients need.
- Home care costs an estimated $47,000 annually; typically, insurers pay for $12,000 of that cost. The remainder is the responsibility of families and other informal caregivers.
- Half of all nursing home patients suffer from AD or a related disorder. The average cost for a patient's care in a nursing home is $36,000 per year, but it can exceed $70,000 per year.
- The federal government spent approximately $311 million for Alzheimer's research in 1995. The federal investment in heart disease, cancer, and AIDs is four to seven times higher.
- More than seven of ten people with Alzheimer's disease live at home and are cared for by family and friends.

For more statistical information, visit the web site of the Alzheimer's Association at *www.alz.org*.

Ten Warning Signs

1. **Memory Loss that Affects Job Skills**
   It is normal to occasionally forget assignments, colleagues' names, or a business associate's telephone number and then remember them later. Those with a dementia, such as Alzheimer's disease, may forget things more often, and not remember them later.

2. **Difficulty Performing Familiar Tasks**
   Busy people can be so distracted from time to time that they may leave the carrots on the stove and only remember to serve them at the end of the meal. People with Alzheimer's disease could prepare a meal and forget to serve it.

3. **Problems with Language**
   Everyone has trouble finding the right word sometimes, but a person with Alzheimer's disease may forget simple words or substitute inappropriate words, making sentences incomprehensible.

4. **Disorientation of Time and Place**
   It's normal to forget the day of the week when you are away from your daily routine, or to occasionally drive past your destination. People with Alzheimer's disease can become lost on their own street, not knowing where they are, how they got there, or how to get back home.

5. **Poor or Decreased Judgment**
   People can become so immersed in an activity that they temporarily forget the child they're watching. People with Alzheimer's disease could entirely forget the child under their care. They may also dress inappropriately, wearing several shirts or blouses.

6. **Problems with Abstract Thinking**
   Balancing a checkbook may be disconcerting when the task is more complicated than usual. Someone with Alzheimer's disease could completely forget what the numbers are and what needs to be done with them.

7. **Misplacing Things**
   Anyone can temporarily misplace a wallet or keys. A person with Alzheimer's disease may put things in inappropriate places: an iron in the refrigerator, or a wristwatch in the sugar bowl.

8. **Changes in Mood or Behavior**
   Someone with Alzheimer's disease is likely to exhibit rapid mood swings—from calm to tears to anger—for no apparent reason.

9. **Changes in Personality**
   The personality of a person with Alzheimer's disease can change drastically; they may become extremely confused, suspicious, or fearful.

10. **Loss of Initiative**
    It's normal to tire of housework, business activities, or social obligations, but most people regain their initiative. The person with Alzheimer's disease may become very passive and require prompting to become involved in any activity.

decrements in the neurotransmitter acetylcholine. This theory stems from the research finding that the neurons in the hippocampus and temporal lobe are among the most negatively affected parts of the brain in AD patients, and that these brain structures employ acetylcholine as their primary neurotransmitter. The number of neurons in the basal forebrain that manufacture acetylcholine is substantially reduced in patients with AD, and the brains of AD patients contain significantly less acetylcholine than those of normal individuals (Bartus, 2000). The cholinergic hypothesis has generated a great deal of important research. The major drawback of this theory, however, is that it is difficult to tell whether a reduction in acetylcholine is a cause or an outcome of AD.

Other researchers have put forth a *genetic hypothesis* based on the discovery that early-onset familial AD (usually referred to as FAD) runs in families. In an important study, St. George-Hyslop et al. (1987) discovered that FAD is associated with a defective gene located on chromosome 21. Furthermore, Tanzi et al. (1987) found that the gene responsible for the production of amyloid (the core material of senile plaques) is also located on chromosome 21. This is interesting, since it is well documented that nearly every individual with Down's syndrome (which is most frequently related to extra chromosomal material on the 21st pair) begins to develop the symptoms of AD by about age 40 (Kosik, 1992; Raskind & Peskind, 1992). Thus, the excessive amyloid deposits in the brain and the accumulation of senile plaques in both AD and Down's syndrome patients may have a common origin—chromosome 21. Researchers also know that a mutation in a gene on chromosome 21 is responsible for encoding an **amyloid precursor protein (APP).** APP is the chemical substance that underlies the manufacture of amyloid, the core material of senile plaques. However, as Jarvik (1987) has noted, the genes responsible for the production of APP and Down's syndrome are positioned in very different locations on chromosome 21. Thus, the relationship between AD, amyloid production, and Down's syndrome remains a mystery.

Mutations in the gene on chromosome 21 that manufacture APP underlie a relatively small number of cases of FAD (Selkoe, 1995). In the vast majority of instances, FAD is related to the presenilin-1 and presenilin-2 genes, which are located on chromosomes 1 and 14, respectively (Rogaev et al., 1995; Sherrington et al., 1995). The more common, or late-occurring, form of AD seems to be related to the function of APOE on chromosome 19 (Miech et al., 2002). Thus, several genetic routes may lead to the symptoms of AD. And, as Dewji & Singer (1996) have noted, it remains to be determined how mutations in any of the aforementioned genes can accelerate the production and formation of senile plaques that are the hallmark of AD.

Results of the Nun Study provide important information about behavioral predictors and the neurological correlates of AD. Research Focus 3.6 discusses this research project and one of its exemplary participants, Sister Mary.

Treatment of Alzheimer's Disease

Because we don't know the specific cause of AD, it has been difficult to develop a single effective treatment that cures, delays, or prevents its onset. However, delaying the onset of the disease by five years could reduce the number of afflicted individuals by 50 percent (Marx, 1996)! Thus, scientists are extremely interested in developing drug

TABLE 3.4

Global Deterioration Scale for Age-Associated Cognitive Decline and Alzheimer's Disease

GDS Stage	Clinical Phase	Clinical Characteristics	Diagnosis
1. No cognitive decline	Normal	No subjective complaints of memory deficit; no memory deficit evidence on clinical interview.	Normal
2. Very mild cognitive decline	Forgetfulness	Subjective complaints of memory deficit, most frequently in the following areas: (a) forgetting where one has placed familiar objects; (b) forgetting names one formerly knew well. No objective evidence of memory deficit on clinical interview; no evidence of deficits in work performance or social situations.	Normal for age
3. Mild cognitive decline	Early confusional phase	Earliest clear-cut deficits, manifesting themselves in more than one of the following areas: (a) patient gets lost traveling to an unfamiliar location; (b) coworkers have become aware of patient's relatively poor performance; (c) word- and name-finding deficits have become evident to intimates; (d) patient may read a passage or a book and retain relatively little material; (e) patient may demonstrate decreased facility in remembering names when introduced to new people; (f) patient may have lost or misplaced an object of value; (g) concentration deficit may be evident on clinical testing. Objective evidence of a memory deficit is obtained only when an intensive interview is conducted by a trained diagnostician; when performance decreases in demanding employment and social settings; when denial begins to become manifest in patient; when mild to moderate anxiety accompanies symptoms.	Compatible with possible incipient Alzheimer's disease in a minority of cases
4. Moderate cognitive decline	Late confusional phase	Clear-cut deficit on careful clinical interview, manifest in the following areas: (a) decreased knowledge of current and recent events; (b) some deficit in memory of personal history; (c) concentration deficit on serial subtractions; (d) decreased ability to travel, handle finances, and so on. Frequently no deficit is evident in the following areas: (a) orientation to time and person; (b) recognition of familiar persons and faces; (c) ability to travel to familiar locations. Inability to perform complex tasks; denial is dominant defense mechanism; flattening of affect and withdrawal from challenging situations.	Mild Alzheimer's disease

5. Moderately severe cognitive decline	Early dementia	Patients can no longer survive without some assistance; patients are unable during interview to recall a major relevant aspect of their current lives—for example, their address or telephone number of many years, or the names of close members of their family (such as grandchildren). Frequently some disorientation to time (date, day of week, season) or to place; an educated person may have difficulty counting backward from forty by fours or from twenty by twos. Persons at this stage retain knowledge of many major facts regarding themselves and others; they invariably know their own name and generally know their spouse's and children's names; they require no assistance with toileting or eating, but may have some difficulty choosing appropriate clothing.	Moderate Alzheimer's disease
6. Severe cognitive decline	Middle dementia	May occasionally forget the name of the spouse upon whom they are entirely dependent for survival; are largely unaware of all recent events and experiences in their lives; retain some knowledge of their past lives, but this is very sketchy. Generally unaware of their surroundings, the year, the season, and so on; may have difficulty counting from ten backward and, sometimes, forward; require some assistance with activities of daily living, for example, may become incontinent, require travel assistance, but occasionally display ability to travel to familiar locations; diurnal rhythm frequently disturbed; almost always recall their own name; frequently continue to be able to distinguish familiar from unfamiliar persons in their environment. Personality and emotional changes occur, including (a) delusional behavior (for example, patients may accuse their spouse of being an impostor, may talk to imaginary figures, or to their own reflections in the mirror); (b) obsessive symptoms (for example, persons may continually repeat simple cleaning activities); (c) anxiety symptoms, agitation, and even previously nonexistent violent behavior may occur; (d) cognitive abulia (that is, loss of willpower because individual cannot carry a thought long enough to determine a purposeful course of action).	Moderately severe Alzheimer's disease
7. Very severe cognitive decline	Late dementia	All verbal abilities are lost; frequently no speech at all—only grunting; incontinent of urine; requires assistance toileting and feeding; loses basic psychomotor skills (for example, ability to walk); it appears the brain no longer is able to control the body.	Severe Alzheimer's disease

From Reisberg, B., Ferris, S. H., de Leon, M. J., and Crook, T., (1982). The global deterioration scale for assessment of primary degenerative dementia. American Journal of Psychiatry, 139: 1136–1139. Adapted with permission.

The Nun Study and Sister Mary

In the early 1990s, David Snowdon and other scientists at the University of Kentucky's Sanders-Brown Center on Aging began an ambitious longitudinal study of 678 nuns who belonged to the School Sisters of Notre Dame. The nuns who participated in this study lived in various parts of the United States and averaged 85 years of age (age range: 72 to 102) when the research began. All the participants are evaluated regularly on various tasks of cognitive ability, and, upon death, each participant has agreed to donate her brain for an in-depth neuropathological examination. Thus, the overarching goal of the Nun Study is to examine the relationship between cognitive ability and neuropathological evidence of AD (Danner, Snowdon, & Friesen, 2001).

One way to gain new information in a research project such as this is to analyze data from the entire sample of participants. Another strategy, however, is to intensely examine the data obtained from a single participant. Snowdon (1997) presented some provocative findings obtained from one of the most exceptional individuals in the Nun Study—Sister Mary. Sister Mary was born in 1892 in Philadelphia to working-class parents. After graduating from the eighth grade, she entered the School Sisters of Notre Dame convent in Baltimore and took her religious vows five years later. With her eighth grade education, Sister Mary began teaching the seventh and eighth grades in various schools throughout the eastern United States at age 19. After taking summer courses over a 22-year time span, she received her high school diploma in 1931, when she was 41 years old. (She maintained an A average throughout her studies, with her highest grade, 100, in algebra!) Sister Mary retired from teaching at age 84 but continued to be active in the religious community and was very much concerned about world affairs. She once remarked that: "I only 'retire' at night." In 1990, at the age of 98, she decided to join the Nun Study and donate her body to science. Sister Mary described that day as "one of the happiest days of my life."

Sister Mary was 101.1 years of age when her cognitive abilities were last assessed, and she died eight months later at the age of 101.7 years. Thus she became one of the 118 sisters whose brain tissue has been analyzed by researchers at the Sanders-Brown Center on Aging.

To grasp Sister Mary's intellectual function at 101 years of age, look at box figure 3.E and box table 3.A. As you can see, Sister Mary scored just as well or better than the other sisters (who were much younger and more highly educated) on all cognitive measures. Most interesting was her score of 27 on the Mini-Mental Status Exam. This is a remarkable score, given that she was 101 years of age at the time of assessment, had less for-

mal education than 85 percent of the other sisters in the Nun Study, and was examined less than a year before her death. (The Mini-Mental Status Exam is a brief test used to help make a diagnosis of AD. The average score for functioning, nondemented older adults is between 24 and 30.) If we consider Sister Mary's age and years of formal education compared to that of the other sisters, we would predict that all her cognitive scores would be much lower than the norm. For example, box table 3.A shows that we would predict that Sister Mary's Mini-Mental Status Exam score should be 4!

In contrast to her excellent level of cognitive function, neuropathological examination revealed that Sister Mary's brain contained an astonishing number of the classic neuropathological lesions associated with AD: neurofibrillary tangles and senile plaques (for details, see box table 3.B). In fact, Snowdon (1997) has commented: "Although Sister Mary was not the first to live to a very old age with intact cognitive function, she may have been the first to do so in the presence of such abundant Alzheimer's disease lesions" (p. 155). Sister Mary's low brain weight (870 grams) suggests that she did not avoid the symptoms of AD because of a large surplus of brain reserve capacity, as we discussed in Research Focus 3.5. Instead, the type and location of the tangles and plaques in her brain suggest that she may have had a relatively benign form of AD. This claim is consistent with one of the major findings of the Nun Study: The best predictor of demented cognitive function is the presence of neurofibrillary tangles in the neocortex (which were almost absent in Sister Mary's brain); and the worst predictors of demented cognitive function are the presence of diffuse plaques in the neocortex and hippocampus (which were extremely abundant in Sister Mary's brain). This leads to the more general conclusion that the most severe form of AD manifests itself in individuals with numerous neocortical tangles who possess low reserve capacity (i.e., low brain weight).

To be sure, we will learn much more about the relationship between cognitive function and neuropathological lesions as the Nun Study progresses and more data are collected and analyzed. In order to gain more knowledge about AD, "we need more people like Sister Mary who are willing to make sacrifices. Sister Mary did not benefit directly from participating in the Nun Study, but her friends and family knew that she felt better for doing it. She was willing to lay out her life, her cognitive function, and her brain in all their details. Her only request was that we call her Sister Mary. She did not want to become a celebrity. She did not want accolades. She only wanted to help younger people who would one day reach old age. Surely there are many others who are willing to leave such a legacy." (Snowdon, 1997, p. 156)

The Nun Study and Sister Mary

Box Figure 3.E Age and Mini-Mental Status Exam score and best fit regression line for 678 participants in the Nun Study.
From: Snowdon, D. A. (1997). Aging and Alzheimer's disease: Lessons from the Nun Study. The Gerontologist, 37, 152.

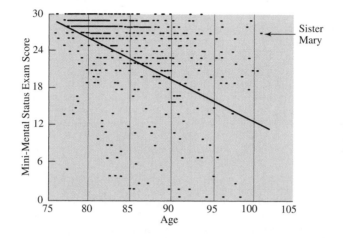

BOX TABLE 3.A

Cognitive Function Test Scores for Sister Mary and Other Sisters Who Died While in the Nun Study

	Cognitive Test							
	Mini-Mental State Exam	Boston Naming	Object Naming	Verbal Fluency	Word List Memory	Delayed Word Recall	Word Recognition	Constructional Praxis
Sister Mary's actual score	27	9	8	8	10	5	8	9
Unadjusted mean in other sisters	17	7	7	8	10	3	5	6
Sister Mary's predicted score based on the other sisters	4	2	2	1	0	0	1	2
P-value for difference between actual and predicted score	0.01	0.05	0.05	0.09	0.09	0.03	0.02	0.02

Note: Predicted scores were adjusted for days between the exam and death, age at time of the exam, and attained education. P-value was based on the Student test, and was a test of the hypothesis that Sister Mary's scores were higher than those predicted based on the scores of the 117 other sisters who died.

Source: Snowdon, D. A. (1997). Aging and Alzheimer's disease: Lessons from the Nun Study. The Gerontologist, 37, 152.

The Nun Study and Sister Mary

TABLE 3.B

Alzheimer's Disease Lesion Counts and Brain Weight in Sister Mary and Other Sisters Who Died While in the Nun Study

	Cognitive Test						
	Neurofibrillary Tangles in Neocortex	Neurofibrillary Tangles in Hippocampus	Neuritic Plaques in Neocortex	Neuritic Plaques in Hippocampus	Diffuse Plaques in Neocortex	Diffuse Plaques in Hippocampus	Brain Weight in Grams
Sister Mary's actual value	1	57	3	6	179	32	870
Unadjusted mean in other sisters	11	20	15	3	92	7	1120
Sister Mary's predicted value based on the other sisters	14	22	10	1	55	4	1007
P-value for difference between actual and predicted values	0.59	0.14	0.60	0.42	0.02	0.001	0.24

Note: Predicted values were adjusted for age at death and attained education. P-values were based on t-tests to test the hypothesis that Sister Mary's values were different from those predicted based on the values of the other sisters who died. Means were based on 110 to 116 sisters (since lesion counts were not possible in some sisters because a brain infarction had obliterated a specific brain region, and brain weight was unavailable for one sister).

Source: Snowdon, D.A. (1997). Aging and Alzheimer's disease: Lessons from the Nun Study. The Gerontologist, 37, 153.

treatment alternatives. One approach to treat some of the cognitive symptoms of AD (memory loss, confusion, and so on) makes use of the neurotransmitter acetylcholine. Initially, there were two variations to this approach. The first was based on the idea that the symptoms of AD should lessen if patients could produce more acetylcholine. This led physicians to advise patients to eat foods rich in choline because choline is a food substance that the brain transforms into acetylcholine. Unfortunately, this approach did not produce any significant changes in functioning among AD patients. More recently, the National Institutes of Health and the National Institutes of Aging have funded large-scale studies examining the effects of estrogen, the female sex hormone, on AD. For example, the Women's Health Initiative Study will ultimately include 165,000 women between the ages of 50 and 79 to try to determine whether estrogen replacement therapy initiated at menopause can prevent (or delay) the onset of AD. A much smaller five-year longitudinal study already conducted by Tang and colleagues (1995) showed that 2.7 percent of older women who took estrogen developed AD, compared with 8.4 percent who did not take estrogen. It seems that estrogen facilitates the production of acetylcholine and also helps to build strong connections between neurons.

The second variation of the acetylcholine approach was based on the theory that patients' AD symptoms should dissipate if they were given a drug that inhibits the activity of acetylcholinesterase. **Acetylcholinesterase** is the enzyme responsible for the synaptic absorption and deactivation of acetylcholine. The inhibition of acetylcholinesterase should allow small amounts of acetylcholine to gradually accumulate on the receptor sites of neurons. (These small amounts of acetylcholine would be quickly deactivated if acetylcholinesterase production resumed its normal level.) Once acetylcholine levels reach a critical threshold, the receptor cell fires—and the person remembers, thinks, and reasons. William Summers and his colleagues (Summers et al., 1986) have gathered impressive results using this strategy, with the degree of success directly related to the patient's stage of AD. Summers and associates administered THA (tetrahydroaminoacridine), a drug usually called tacrine or cognex, to inhibit acetylcholinesterase in a group of AD patients. These patients showed significant improvement on a number of cognitive measures. However, tacrine, like other **palliative treatments,** only treats the symptoms, not the causes, of AD (Bartus, 2000) .

Some other possible drug treatments for AD are listed in table 3.5.

TABLE 3.5

Possible Drugs for Preventing or Treating Alzheimer's Disease

Drug	Activity	Proposed Mechanism of Action
Cognex, Aricept	Inhibit acetylcholinesterase	Compensate for loss of cholinergic neurons
Ampakines	Enhance activity of AMPA receptor	Improve memory by enhancing long-term potentiation
Prednisone, ibuprofen, other NSAIDS	Anti-inflammatory	Prevent inflammatory damage to neurons
Vitamin E	Antioxidant	Protects against free-radical damage
Premarin	Female hormone	Promotes neuronal survival
Nerve growth factor	Maintains cholinergic neurons in brain	Promotes neuronal survival
Calcium channel blockers	Inhibit calcium ion entry into neurons	Reduce calcium toxicity
Cholesterol-lowering drugs	Lower APOE4 concentrations	Prevent APPE4 toxicity to neurons
Protease inhibitors	Block β-amyloid production	Prevent neuronal loss to β-amyloid toxicity

Source: Marx, J. (1996). Searching for drugs that combat Alzheimer's disease. Science, 273, 51.

The picture is somewhat brighter when one considers the noncognitive symptoms associated with AD, such as paranoia, depression, wandering, and so on. These symptoms may be treated with various drugs that have proven effective in psychiatric settings.

Other Dementias

AD is just one of many different types of dementia. Next we briefly describe some of these other dementing conditions.

Multi-Infarct Dementia

Multi-infarct dementia has been estimated to account for 20 to 25 percent of cases of dementia. This disease arises from a series of ministrokes in the cerebral arteries. The condition is more common among men with a history of hypertension (high blood pressure) and arises when the arteries to the brain are blocked (e.g., by small pieces of atherosclerotic plaque that dislodge from the artery walls in other parts of the body and travel to the brain). The clinical picture for multi-infarct dementia differs from that for Alzheimer's disease, since the individual typically shows clear and predictable recovery from the former but gradual deterioration in the latter. Symptoms may include bouts of confusion, slurring of speech, difficulty in writing, or weakness on the left or right side of the body, hand, or leg. However, after each occurrence, rapid and steady improvement usually occurs. Each succeeding occasion leaves a bit more of a residual problem, making recovery from each new episode increasingly difficult. A relatively minor stroke or infarct is usually termed a **transient ischemic attack (TIA).** See figure 3.12 for more information about this disorder.

Mixed Dementia

In some cases, two forms of dementia coexist. For example, Alzheimer's disease and multi-infarct dementia have been estimated to co-occur in approximately 18 percent of cases of diagnosed dementia (Raskind & Peskind, 1992); it is impossible to determine with accuracy the cause of the observed symptoms, although an autopsy may help to determine the cause. Obviously, treatment and intervention for a person with mixed dementia presents an especially difficult challenge.

Creutzfeldt-Jakob Disease

This disorder is a rare form of dementia caused by a slow-acting virus. Under certain uncommon circumstances it can be infectious (Raskind & Peskind, 1992). In experimental studies, an analogous virus has been transmitted from lower animals to other primates. The analog virus in sheep produces a disease called scrapie, whose symptoms and brain tissue destruction are similar to the symptoms of Creutzfeldt-Jakob disease. Scrapie can be transmitted directly to chimpanzees and monkeys in laboratory investigations (Cohen, 1988). Another rare neurologic brain disorder, kuru, can also be virally

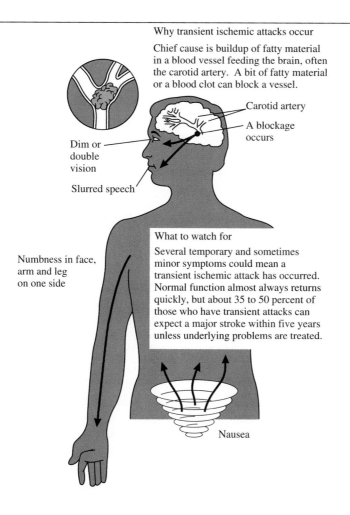

Why transient ischemic attacks occur

Chief cause is buildup of fatty material in a blood vessel feeding the brain, often the carotid artery. A bit of fatty material or a blood clot can block a vessel.

Carotid artery

A blockage occurs

Dim or double vision

Slurred speech

What to watch for

Several temporary and sometimes minor symptoms could mean a transient ischemic attack has occurred. Normal function almost always returns quickly, but about 35 to 50 percent of those who have transient attacks can expect a major stroke within five years unless underlying problems are treated.

Numbness in face, arm and leg on one side

Nausea

Figure 3.12
Recognizing the symptoms of ministrokes or transient ischemic attacks.

transmitted from primate to human (Zarit & Zarit, 1983). This raises the question of whether the more common dementias, such as Alzheimer's, may also be the products of a virus, transmitted either from animal to human or from human to human. Some evidence of direct human-to-human transmission of Creutzfeldt-Jakob disease has been reported (Gorman, Benson, Vogel, & Vinters, 1992). The pattern of symptoms is highly variable, although central nervous system deterioration is commonly present. The rate of decline is rapid, and death ensues within two years (Raskind & Peskind, 1992). The emergence of specific symptoms and the rate of deterioration in cognitive functioning, judgment, memory, and personal and social competence depends on the overall rate and extent of neuron loss, the initial level of intellectual ability, and the availability of a socially supportive and simplified living environment.

AIDS Dementia Complex

This neurological disorder is characterized by progressive cognitive, motor, and behavioral loss. It arises as a predictable part of **acquired immunodeficiency syndrome (AIDS)** (Price, Sidtis, & Rosenblum, 1988; Raskind & Peskind, 1992). **AIDS dementia complex (ADC)** is the result of direct brain infection by the human immunodeficiency virus (HIV). An HIV by-product, a protein called gp 120, is responsible for the death of neuron cells, which ultimately produces dementia. Early symptoms include inability to concentrate, difficulty performing complex sequential mental tasks, and memory loss in tasks requiring concentrated attention (reading, meeting the demands of independent living and working). Motor symptoms include clumsiness and weakness in the limbs; and behavioral changes include apathy, loss of spontaneity, depression, social withdrawal, and personality alterations. As ADC progresses, both mental performance and motor behaviors become noticeably impaired. Fine motor responses weaken, walking without assistance becomes difficult, and bowel and bladder control are lost. The terminal phase is marked by confinement to bed, vacant staring, and minimal social and cognitive interaction (Price et al., 1988). Raskind and Peskind (1992) estimate that approximately 10,000 adults over 60 were diagnosed with ADC in the United States in 1992, with transmission attributable to unprotected sex or infection via contaminated blood.

Focal Brain Damage

The sudden emergence of selective (rather than global) impairment of specific cognitive abilities is typical of focal brain damage. This damage is not considered a dementia and is not marked by progressive deterioration. Localized brain damage due to head trauma, stroke, or tumor is a common diagnosis among young adult patients but is frequently overlooked among the elderly. The defining characteristic of focal brain damage is the rapid and sudden onset of limited, specific cognitive impairments. Once the damage is identified, further losses in intellectual function can be prevented with timely and appropriate intervention.

Parkinson's Disease

Tremors of the voluntary small muscle groups are the most noticeable symptoms of Parkinson's disease, a motor disorder triggered by degeneration of dopamine-producing neurons in the brain (Morgan, 1992). Other classic symptoms of Parkinson's disease include unnatural immobility of the facial muscles, staring eyes, and the inability to initiate simple motor behaviors. This neurological disorder not only produces disturbances in psychomotor functioning but also is associated with depression in about 45 percent of cases, and is associated with dementia in 15 to 40 percent of cases (Raskind & Peskind, 1992). The standard treatment for Parkinson's disease is the administration of a drug called L-dopa, which the brain converts into dopamine. It is sometimes difficult to determine the correct dosage of L-dopa. If Parkinson's patients take too much, they may display schizophrenic symptoms. Conversely, if young schizophrenic patients are given too much of a drug that blocks the effects of dopamine, they may develop what appear to be the symptoms of Parkinson's disease. Another treatment for Parkinson's disease involves transplanting dopamine-producing neurons into the substantia nigra.

Pseudodementia

The clinical picture of depression in the elderly often mimics dementia; some clinicians have even labeled depression as **depressive pseudodementia.** Table 3.6 presents the difference in symptoms between true dementia and depressive pseudodementia. At least 30 percent of the elderly diagnosed with dementia in fact have treatable depressive pseudodementia (LaRue et al., 1985). Symptoms such as apathy, psychomotor retardation, impaired concentration, delusions, and confusion in a depressed elderly person may easily be mistaken for dementia, particularly when they are accompanied by complaints of memory loss. Interestingly, clinicians observe that persons with depressive pseudodementia may complain far more about memory loss than those with true dementia. Although some studies suggest differential brain wave activity during sleep, at present, the only way of definitively distinguishing between depressive pseudodementia and true dementia is by retrospective means (Hoch, Buysse, Monk, & Reynolds, 1992). Thus, if any treatment for depression produces dramatic improvements in a person's cognitive deficits and

TABLE 3.6

Depressive Pseudodementia versus True Dementia: Differential Symptoms

	Depression	Dementia
Onset	Rapid; an exact date of onset can often be identified	Insidious and ill-defined
Behavior	Stable; depression, apathy, and withdrawal common	Labile; fluctuates between normal and withdrawn and apathetic
Mental competence	Usually unaffected; however, may appear demented at times; complains of memory problems	Consistently impaired, takes effort to hide cognitive impairment
Somatic signs	Anxiety, insomnia, eating disturbances	Occasional sleep disturbances
Self-image	Poor	Normal
Prognosis	Reversible with therapy	Chronic; slow, progressive decline

other symptoms, then the correct diagnosis must be depressive pseudodementia (LaRue et al., 1985). Clinicians are thus advised to first treat such symptoms not as dementia, but as depressive pseudodementia.

Given the difficulty of diagnosing either problem prior to treatment, some have questioned the scientific utility of the concept of depressive pseudodementia. Caine and Grossman (1992) suggest that those with depressive pseudodementia may sometimes be "coaxed" into more positive cognitive functioning and improved task performance through techniques such as cued recall; elderly people with true dementia are unable to benefit from these interventions.

Drugs, toxins, and physical illness may also cause reversible dementias. The sedative effects of some drugs (including alcohol) and drug-drug interactions may contribute to memory impairment, delirium, or acute brain syndrome/reversible dementia in older persons (Cohen, 1988; Schuckit, Morrissey, & O'Leary, 1979; Zarit & Zarit, 1983). Disorders of thyroid metabolism (such as hyperthyroidism) may impair cognitive ability and represent still another reversible cause of dementia. And almost any intracranial lesion or tumor may produce memory loss or dementia (Gambert, 1987; Zarit, Eiler, & Hassinger, 1985). Seeking the particular cause of dementia is important because treatment can be somewhat successful in at least 10 to 30 percent of cases (LaRue et al., 1985).

SUMMARY

Researchers have proposed several biological theories of aging because there is considerable controversy about the biological causes of aging. Any such theory must address the relationship between primary and secondary aging. Current hypotheses suggest that evolutionary mechanisms indirectly resulted in the aging process. Interventions such as dietary restriction, antioxidant drugs, and lifestyle changes may increase life expectancy. It is unclear, however, whether these interventions actually slow down the aging process.

The term *sensorimotor development* refers to the changes in the sensory systems that gather information from the environment and in the motor systems that enable us to perform physical actions. Vision and hearing are the two most important sensory systems in adulthood. Visual decline is characteristic of most individuals in late adulthood and can be traced to physiological changes in the eyes, including changes that limit the quality and intensity of light reaching the retina. It is important to distinguish between visual acuity and contrast sensitivity. With increasing age, important changes take place in both.

Hearing usually reaches its peak in adolescence and remains reasonably stable during early adulthood, but may start to decline in middle adulthood. Less than 20 percent of individuals between 45 and 54 years of age have a hearing problem, but for those between 75 and 79, the figure rises to 75 percent. We also become less sensitive to taste, smell, and pain as we grow older.

Motor skills usually peak during young adulthood. One of the most common measures of motor performance is reaction time. Many studies have shown that reaction time gradually slows as we approach older adulthood. Decrements in reaction time may have potentially significant effects on the ability of older adults to function effectively in our complex, modern society. Experts disagree over the extent to which age-related psychomotor slowing is caused by the deterioration of central rather than peripheral processes. With practice and exercise, physical abilities—even demanding physical sports—may be maintained throughout adulthood.

The human brain has three major components: the brain stem (including the cerebellum), the limbic system, and the cerebrum. The hippocampus, a structure within the limbic system, seems to be involved in remembering and storing information. The cortex, the top covering of the cerebrum, is responsible for all higher-order psychological functioning. The cortex may undergo widespread or localized damage in aged individuals.

The brain is composed of specialized cells called neurons, and these neurons communicate by releasing special chemical substances called neurotransmitters. It is generally agreed that we lose a large number of neurons as we grow old, but researchers have drawn few precise conclusions about the psychological effects of neuronal loss. With increasing age comes an increase in the amount of lipofuscin, the number of granular particles, and the number of neurofibrillary tangles inside the neurons. Senile plaques also increase in the synaptic areas between neurons.

It is possible to observe the brain in a noninvasive manner by using PET scan, or fMRI. The electroencephalogram (EEG) is used to measure the electrical output of the brain in general, and the cortex in particular. The alpha rhythm, as measured by the EEG, begins to slow in late older adulthood. Some psychologists have linked the slowing of alpha brain activity to the generalized pattern of psychomotor slowing. The delta rhythm also changes with age. Alterations in delta activity have been linked to changes in sleep patterns and sleep satisfaction among the elderly. Age-related changes in evoked brain potentials are also of interest to gerontologists. Of particular importance is the latency of the P300 brain wave.

Dementia and *senescence* are not interchangeable terms. The former refers to an abnormal condition of aging, the latter to universal processes. Alzheimer's disease is a common cause of dementia among older adults; much research has focused on its causes. Providing care for patients with Alzheimer's and other cognitive dementias remains a challenge for families, service agencies, and our society. There are other dementing brain illnesses besides Alzheimer's disease. Unlike Alzheimer's disease, some respond well to treatment.

REVIEW QUESTIONS

1. What does biological aging have to do with senescence?
2. Explain the differences between the following pairs of terms: *normal aging* and *successful aging; primary aging* and *secondary aging.*
3. Explain how evolutionary mechanisms may have indirectly been selected for the aging process.
4. Discuss the effectiveness of antiaging interventions such as dietary restrictions and antioxidant drugs.
5. Describe some of the changes in physical appearance that accompany the aging process.
6. Discuss the changes in sensory systems that occur during the adult years, focusing especially on vision and hearing.
7. Explain the difference between visual acuity and contrast sensitivity.
8. Describe the changes that take place in motor performance during adulthood.
9. Compare the "peak athletic performances" of younger, middle-aged, and older adults.
10. What are the major changes that take place at the *cortical* and *neuronal* levels as we age?
11. Discuss the advantages of using MRI, fMRI, and PET scans to measure the aging of the human brain.
12. Distinguish between *senescence* and *Alzheimer's disease (AD).*
13. Discuss the pros and cons of the *cholinergic* and *genetic* approaches to understanding the cause of AD.
14. At present, what types of treatments are available for individuals with AD?
15. Compare and contrast AD with other dementing conditions.

ON THE WEB   www.mhhe.com/hoyer5

For a list of links to the latest information about the effects of aging on physiological and sensory processes, as well as to other topics related to the material in this chapter, see:

The Alzheimer's Disease site provides a gateway to a wealth of information about Alzheimer's disease.

The Living to 100 website presents a calculator for estimating longevity potential. The calculation of estimated life expectancy is based on the relationships between longevity and life style and health factors. The average person is born with a set of genes that allows a life span of about 85 years of age. Using average life expectancy as the starting point, people can add or subtract as many as 10 years, depending on individual health factors.

The Howard Hughes Medical Institute site provides information about vision and hearing.

4

COPING AND ADAPTATION

> *Old Age . . . a glorious thing when one has not unlearned what it means to begin.*
> ——Martin Buber
>
> *Life consists not in holding good cards but in playing those you do hold well.*
> ——Josh Billings

INTRODUCTION

In this chapter, you will learn about coping and adaptation in adulthood. We will discuss theories that explain stress management and consider how those who provide care to elders with Alzheimer's disease cope with their responsibilities. We will examine factors that enhance one's ability to cope with stress, including cognitive, emotional, social, and spiritual resources, and we will review the positive and negative outcomes of adapting to stress. Finally, we will discuss individual differences, ethnicity, race, and gender as mediating influences on effective coping and adaptation.

Stress, Coping, and Adaptation

The ability to manage stress effectively is a key factor in promoting health in adult life. Most older adults are in good mental health and are capable of managing the stresses they experience (Gatz, Kasl-Godfrey, & Karel, 1996). As people age, they become better at managing stress; even major mental health problems such as depression are less common among older adults (Joiner, 2000). However, some highly stressful events, such as the death of a spouse, ordinarily occur later in life and tax the survivor's coping resources.

Psychodynamic View of Stress and Coping

Traditionally, clinical psychologists have been interested in knowing why some people do not cope well and are emotionally overwhelmed by stress. Psychotherapists, beginning with Freud, have encouraged clients to improve their basic emotional responses to stress. They work to modify a client's basic personality and character traits through therapy to help the client adapt more effectively to stress.

People who do not cope well with stress can find help. In theory, clinicians can teach clients how to develop more successful coping behaviors and more mature defenses using adults who effectively adapt to stress as models. The coping mechanisms these adults use are often helpful to people who have difficulty managing emotions, dealing with anxiety, and finding support.

People who handle stress effectively and poorly can be distinguished by their defense mechanisms (Cramer, 2000). Defense mechanisms distort reality and help us cope with emotional threats and ego challenges; however, some defenses are more effective than others. George Valliant (1977) conducted a longitudinal study of personality and coping. Adults who effectively coped with stress used more mature defense mechanisms, including altruism, humor (a method of expressing emotions that is free of consequences); suppression (being optimistic in the face of problems, waiting for a desired outcome, or looking for a silver lining); anticipation (planning and preparing for a realistic outcome such as the death of a family member who is gravely ill); and sublimation (channeling unacceptable impulses and emotions into socially valued and personally rewarding activities). Defenses that were less effective included denial, distortion of reality, acting out, passive aggression, and withdrawal. These immature defenses were typical of adults who had difficulty adapting to stress.

In contrast to Valliant's view that denial and distortion of reality are immature, ineffective coping mechanisms, some investigators consider denial to be a healthy mode of adjustment in response to specific types of stress (Aldwin, 1995: Johnson & Barer, 1993; Taylor et al., 1992). In general, adults facing extremely stressful life events are more likely to engage in repression and denial, while the oldest-old who face serious health problems are more likely to cope through denial and distancing. Denial, if used temporarily, can actually give these individuals time to prepare themselves to face a harsh reality and to identify resources to help them cope. For example, adults injured in serious accidents may sustain spinal cord injuries that leave them permanently paralyzed. The sudden event leaves them no time to prepare for a life of disability. However, if they at first deny the seriousness of the injury and are optimistic that full recovery is possible, they may adapt better over the long run. In time, they begin to accept the reality of their situation and abandon their denial and distorted optimism, defenses that have given them a chance to adapt. Unrealistic optimism thus can allow people a sense of control that enhances self-esteem.

Consider a group of HIV-positive men who continued to participate in a variety of health-enhancing activities, including safe sex, to "defend" themselves against AIDS (Taylor et al., 1992). Once the virus has been contracted, health-enhancing behaviors cannot protect against AIDS, although the progression of the disease may be slowed. Some denial and distortion, then, can be helpful in coping, depending on the nature of the stressful event and the length of time for which these defenses are maintained.

The Life-Events Model of Coping and Adaptation

Stress is a physiological response to threatening or frustrating events in the environment. It is well known that stress and physical illness are related. Since the pioneering work of Hans Selye (1956, 1980), many researchers have examined the health risks associated with stressful events and ineffective coping. Threats and challenging events can be external (e.g., an oncoming car) or internal (e.g., thoughts about the behavior of a friend), and the physiological system responds by preparing the body for "fight" or "flight." Stressful events heighten hormonal and neurochemical reactions that trigger disease and illness (Cohen & Herbert, 1996).

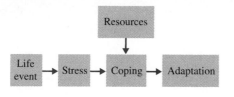

Figure 4.1 The life-events model for coping and adaptation.

Some psychologists have developed scales to represent stressful events and to measure how people manage life experiences. People are asked to rate a variety of stressful life events from high to low, with researchers assuming that the higher-rated events have a higher probability of causing stress-related illness or adjustment problems. By examining natural life stresses, researchers can learn about the thoughts and actions that determine "the quality of an individual's adaptation to adversity" (Coyne & Racioppo, 2000). If most adults use similar strategies to cope successfully with similar life events, these strategies could serve as models for those who struggle to cope. Unfortunately, life-events analyses have not been helpful for clinicians who wish to develop specific intervention strategies for individual clients. Key life events that require individuals to change their basic coping styles are rare; it is difficult to teach clients new ways to handle stress. Figure 4.1 presents a sketch of the life-events model.

Measuring Stress through Life Events

Identifying the events that cause significant stress can help us predict when people are at higher risk for physical and mental health problems. Holmes and Rahe's Social Readjustment Rating Scale (1967) is one index of the amount of stress associated with specific life events (see table 4.1). An anchor point was determined, for example, "getting married," and assigned a value of 50. Adults were then asked how much readjustment would be required if each of the events listed in the table occurred in their lives. For example, would being fired at work require more or less readjustment than marriage? Would the death of a close friend demand more or less readjustment than marriage? While some studies show modest relationships between degree of stress and physical illness, individual differences make predictions difficult. Prolonged periods of stress do appear to wear down the immune system. In one study, caregivers of Alzheimer's disease patients showed reduced immune system function that persisted for more than two years after the death of the person they were caring for (Esterling, Kiecolt-Glaser, Bodnar, & Glaser, 1994).

Since not all persons react the same way to the same stressors, the life-events approach has not been very useful. Individual differences mean that some people handle stress better than others facing the same difficult situation. Yet some patterns do transcend individual difference. Research suggests the oldest-old (85 years and older) use denial and distancing strategies to cope with health problems more than those who are younger (Aldwin, 1995). Still, several unanswered questions persist. Do adults experience more or fewer stressors as they age? Are similar stressors experienced differently

TABLE 4.1

The Social Readjustment Rating Scale

Rank	Life Event	Mean Value	Rank	Life Event	Mean Value
1	Death of spouse	100	23	Son or daughter leaving home	29
2	Divorce	73	24	Trouble with in-laws	29
3	Marital separation	65	25	Outstanding personal achievement	28
4	Jail term	63	26	Wife begins or stops work	26
5	Death of close family member	63	27	Begin or end school	26
6	Personal injury or illness	53	28	Change in living condition	25
7	Marriage	50	29	Revision of personal habits	24
8	Fired at work	47	30	Trouble with boss	23
9	Marital reconciliation	45	31	Change in work hours or conditions	20
10	Retirement	45	32	Change in residence	20
11	Change in health of family member	44	33	Change in schools	20
12	Pregnancy	40	34	Change in recreation	19
13	Sex difficulties	39	35	Change in church activities	19
14	Gain of new family member	39	36	Change in social activities	18
15	Business readjustment	39	37	Mortgage or loan less than $10,000	17
16	Change in financial state	38	38	Change in sleeping habits	16
17	Death of a close friend	37	39	Change in number of family get-togethers	15
18	Change to different line of work	36			
19	Change in number of arguments with spouse	35	40	Change in eating habits	15
			41	Vacation	13
20	Mortgage over $10,000	31	42	Christmas	12
21	Foreclosure of mortgage or loan	30	43	Minor violations of the law	11
22	Change in responsibilities at work	29			

Source: Holmes, T. H., & Rahe, R. H. (1967). The social readjustment rating scale. Journal of Psychosomatic Research, II, 213–218. Oxford, England: Pergamon. Reprinted with permission.

as adults grow older? Do older people become more effective in managing stress, or are they more easily overwhelmed?

The Life-Events Model: A Critique

The life-events model predicts that the greater the severity and number of key events, the greater the stress. Some psychologists believe that the Social Readjustment Scale places too much emphasis on selected events; they challenge the assumption that change itself is stressful. They question whether older adults encounter more stressful life events than younger persons, are unable to manage stress as well, and face an increased risk for stress-related health problems.

As we will see, some people facing stress perceive a challenge or an opportunity, not a threat. Those who have coped successfully with a particularly difficult life event may view the experience as beneficial. With the passage of time, some people reinterpret stressful events as factors that made a significant contribution to their personal development by increasing their sense of mastery, improving their coping skills, enhancing their self-knowledge, creating new values, or building a wider social network (Aldwin, 1995). Thus, the life-events perspective ignores the personal significance (or subjective interpretation), the situational context, and the cognitive-emotional impact of the specific stressor. Consider the following example. The death of a parent may be felt and understood very differently by a 16-year-old adolescent and a 45-year-old adult, depending on the age and health of the parent. The same traumatic event holds very different meanings for each "child" and causes different levels and types of stress.

Finally, experts note that when people in comparable situations face similar events, they choose different coping strategies. Most people select the coping responses they feel will best fit the experience, depending on the strategies they have used in the past (Pushkar et al., 1997).

Life Events: The Importance of Timing

Another perspective on life events suggests that adaptation depends not on the severity of a stressful event, but on the timing of the event. Neugarten and Neugarten (1987) believe that stressful events are handled better when they occur at predictable or expected times in the life course. Those that occur "off-time" are far more difficult to manage. Neugarten suggested that adults construct a kind of **social clock** to compare against their own developmental progress. Each cohort identifies the "right" age for marriage, for having children, and for retirement. Similarly, adults expect to move a parent to assisted living or experience the death of a parent at predictable points in their lives (usually when the adult children are in their forties or fifties). Events that go according to schedule are considered less stressful than those that are off-time. Pregnancy can be a wonderful and fulfilling event for a 30-year-old married woman, yet bring immense distress to an unmarried adolescent girl still in high school. And changing jobs can be a very different experience for a 25-year-old and a 45-year-old.

We can also view life-threatening illness within Neugarten's framework. Older adults generally confront cancer with less anger than younger adults do; the disease is not an off-time event. Similarly, while older gay men with AIDS have decades to bring themselves and others to accept their lifestyles, identities, and relationships, making it easier to focus on coping with their illness, younger gay men with AIDS try to accomplish all this in a highly compressed time frame (Ascher, 1993). Often feeling isolated and estranged from family, many with AIDS attempt the Herculean task of resolving family relationships in the brief amount of time they have left, given the progress of their illness. The off-time character of this task makes coping with a life-threatening illness even more stressful.

The Cognitive Model of Coping and Adaptation

The **cognitive model of coping** and adaptation to stress emphasizes the importance of a person's subjective perceptions of potentially stressful life events (see figure 4.2). It can account for individual differences in how people experience identical life experiences by focusing on individual reactions. The process of determining whether an event is stressful is called **primary appraisal.** The subjective determination of an event as

Figure 4.2
Lazarus's cognitive
model of coping
and adaptation.

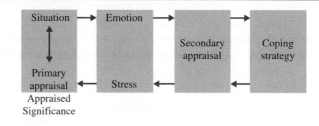

stressful produces emotional reactions of tension, anxiety, and dread, while events considered nonstressful provide challenge and growth, typically stirring the emotions of hope, excitement, and joy (Lazarus & Folkman, 1984). Once a person has made a primary appraisal, he or she can decide how to adapt by choosing resources within themselves (emotion-focused) or within the environment (problem-focused). Then the individual can estimate the costs of using such resources—a process called **secondary appraisal.**

In research on stress in the adult years, Richard Lazarus and his colleagues (DeLongis et al., 1982; Lazarus & Folkman, 1984) found an inverse relationship between stressful life events and age for people aged 45 to 64. Does this mean that people experience fewer stressful life events as they age? Probably not. Most elderly identify fewer stressors in their lives than younger persons do, but it appears that the life-events inventories simply list stressors that we more commonly encounter at earlier points in the life span (Aldwin, 1995). Also, we cannot conclude that because the *frequency* of stressful life events decreases with age, older people experience *less* stress (Kahana, 1992); we must also consider the subjective interpretation of stress (primary appraisal). A simple frequency analysis of the number of stressful life events ignores the different coping demands placed on younger and older people. Older individuals, for example, may find that a single minimally stressful life event, such as leaving home for a vacation, may overwhelm them if they also have to deal with a chronic infirmity such as arthritis and nonsupportive relatives who question the wisdom of their decision to travel. In general, however, the evidence indicates that older people continue to maintain the coping abilities they developed at earlier points in the life span (Folkman and Moskowitz, 2000). Older adults identify themselves as effective at coping; they are not more vulnerable to stress (Aldwin, 1995). An important difference exists, then, between objective and subjective definitions of stressful experiences.

Aging and Cognitive Variables

According to Willis (1996), an important set of cognitive variables determines how adults of different ages deal with stressful life events. Older adults may have an advantage in resolving stressful life situations; they generally have more efficient and effective cognitive problem-solving strategies. For example, in a well-controlled study, older adults were directed to imagine they had contracted an illness and asked how they would resolve it. From a description of symptoms, older persons recognized the severity of the hypothetical illness far earlier than middle-aged adults (Leventhal, Leventhal,

Schaefer, & Easterling; 1993). And when the illness was determined to be "serious," they sought medical attention far earlier than middle-aged adults. Middle-aged adults delayed seeking treatment, despite descriptions that highlighted growing pain. Both age groups had equal access to medical care and equivalent knowledge regarding the severity of the medical condition (Willis, 1996). In another study, older women presented with a hypothetical medical crisis were able to arrive at a treatment decision more quickly than either young or middle-aged women.

Cognitive appraisal is also helpful in managing the stress of the caregiving role. Seltzer, Greenberg, and Krauss (1995) noted that problem-focused strategies appear to be more "proactive" in helping to control stress. Cognitive appraisal leads caregivers to take direct action and is related to positive affect and positive outcomes, particularly for male caregivers attempting to manage disruptive behaviors in care recipients. Some cognitive strategies, such as wishfulness and stoicism, are related to depression and negative affect in caregivers (Schulz & Williamson, 1994; Yee & Schulz, 2000). And emotion-focused coping tends to be predictive of negative mental health outcomes, such as higher levels of anxiety and depression (Kramer, 1997b). Depression is also related to the repetitive use of simple strategies to control disruptive behaviors such as memory deficits, wandering, and repetitive actions. Repeated reliance on strategies such as physical intervention or shouting leads to exhaustion and a sense of failure among caregivers. Moreover, these strategies ultimately prove fruitless in reducing the unwanted behaviors (Kramer, 1997b; Williamson & Schulz, 1993).

Daily Hassles: The Broken Shoelace Syndrome

Daily hassles are the little, irritating annoyances that punctuate our day-to-day existence (Lazarus & Folkman, 1984). Some are relatively infrequent and random, whereas others are everyday occurrences; for example, driving in traffic or feeling annoyed with one's roommates might be frequent hassles for some individuals. Lazarus and his colleagues developed a hassles scale to evaluate the frequency and intensity of everyday stresses such as misplacing one's belongings, not having enough time for family, filling out forms, or breaking a shoelace. They found no differences in the types and frequency of hassles men and women encounter. Interestingly, the measurement of daily hassles is a strong predictor of a person's overall adaptation. The individual's ability to cope with hassles, in fact, is a far better predictor of morale, life satisfaction, psychological symptoms, and somatic illness than the number of major life stresses the person has endured. Why might this be so? Daily hassles seem to have a stronger link to health outcomes because they evaluate proximal aspects of stress, whereas life-event rankings measure distal aspects. *Proximal aspects* are related to adults' immediate perceptions of the environment, while *distal aspects* are more removed perceptions that may not hold common meanings for all people.

Comparing the daily hassles that college students, young adults, and middle-aged adults endure, Lazarus and his colleagues found some age differences. Older people report fewer hassles than young adults, perhaps because of the loss of potentially stressful roles, for example, worker or parental caregiver (Aldwin, 1995). Younger adults report more hassles than older adults in two areas: finances and work (although personal-social concerns were also problematic). Younger college students cope with academic and social problems—wasting time, meeting high standards, being lonely. Older adults, on the other hand, experience hassles in the areas of environmental and social problems, home upkeep, and health. Lazarus's sample was essentially white, healthy, middle-class, and well educated. The daily hassles of adults from other backgrounds would probably vary from this pattern.

Daily Uplifts: Positive Affect in Coping

Counterbalancing daily hassles are **uplifts,** or the positive experiences that we encounter each day. Uplifts co-occur regularly with hassles and stress, providing a respite, or psychological time-out, from stressful events and the demand to cope. They serve as a reminder that there are other dimensions to life besides stress. According to Fredrickson (1998), uplifts provide a positive affect that reduces the physiological and neurochemical phenomena associated with stress; they can even serve as a buffer against depression for those coping with chronic stress. For example, caring for a partner with AIDS was associated with clinical depression among men with high levels of negative affect, while those with more positive emotions did not tend to become depressed (Moskowitz, Acree, & Folkman, 1998).

Folkman and Moskowitz (2000) have identified three processes that seem to enhance positive affect among those who successfully cope with stress. First are *routine events that people infuse with positive meaning.* For instance, in one study of 1,794 people providing care for someone with AIDS, nearly 100 percent identified a positive event each day or "something that [they] did, or something that happened that made [them] feel good and that was meaningful to [them] and helped [them] get through the day" (Folkman, 1997). Most people identified events in everyday life: a magnificent sunset, a beautiful flower, a visit from a friend or neighbor. In other words, embedded in the everyday stresses, people find joy in uplifts, the routine activities and events that others take for granted. Perhaps successful caregivers emphasize ordinary events to reduce the impact of chronic stress and stressors that might otherwise overwhelm them (Hobfall, 1998). A second process that enhances positive affect is *positive reappraisal,* or the application of cognitive strategies to reframe situations in a more positive way. Positive reappraisal gives adults a way to manage difficult situations, seeing some positives in even the most stressful events. Caregivers of older parents, for instance, often reflect positively on the value of the role, their happiness in being able to give back to those who cared for them, and their sense of fulfillment and mastery. Folkman and Moskowitz (2000) suggest that perhaps positive reappraisal of the caregiving role is what sustains caregivers to maintain their commitment to a loved one. Finally, *problem-focused coping* is linked to positive affect. This coping style prods individuals to relieve their distress by resolving the problem, in contrast to emotion-focused coping, which directs attention to the management of the emotions the stress invokes. If people are unable to control a stressful situation, the reasoning goes, they can at least try to control the way they feel about it. Actually, it appears that problem-focused coping and emotion-focused coping often co-occur. But problem-focused coping, even if only marginally effective, helps people regain a sense of mastery, personal efficacy, and control. It directs attention to some of the more manageable dimensions of stress (Scheier and Carver, 2001; Folkman and Moskowitz, 2000; Klinger, 1998). These three processes—infusing everyday happenings with positive meanings, engaging in positive reappraisal, and employing problem-focused coping—help individuals to reinterpret stressful situations and manage the environment successfully and effectively.

The Search for Meaning: Cognitive Distortion, Social Comparison, and Life Management

Adults rarely respond passively to stress. Instead, they attempt to change the circumstances when possible (problem-focused coping) or invoke other strategies to alter the meaning of the situations that they face (emotion-focused coping). Creating meaning from challenging and stressful situations is a hallmark of effective adaptation and an important part of the process of cognitive appraisal (Lazarus, 1999; Folkman & Moskowitz, 2000). Adults who face difficult caregiving situations for lengthy periods of time search for meaning in what they are doing (Farran, 1997). They find a sense of purpose and commitment to older family members. They value their own contributions, develop a sense of mastery, and usually find a social support network to help sustain them. Most caregivers thus identify positive values in the caregiving role, despite its demands. This search for meaning is part of the human condition and is central to existential philosophy and humanistic psychology. It has been popularized in books such as Harold Kushner's *When Bad Things Happen to Good People.* Coping is enhanced when people can find meaning in their roles. And meaning arises within the person from prior history, experiences, and values (Farran, 1997).

The process of creating meaning influences one's cognitive appraisal of stressful events and the choice of coping strategies; it is part of the individual's continuous search for understanding and mastery of difficult situations (Skaff, Pearlin, & Mullan, 1996; Willis, 1996). Taylor and her colleagues explored this in a series of studies of women facing life-threatening breast cancer (Taylor, 1983; Wood, Taylor and Lichtman, 1985). Women responded to the diagnosis by creating a set of active distortions of reality to help them manage their stress (emotional-focused coping). Of 78 women interviewed, 95 percent reported searching for personal meaning through their illness. Many reported discovering new dimensions of their identities (e.g., "I was very happy to find out that I am a very strong person."). A second theme was the attempt to gain "magical mastery" or control; many women believed that meaningful lifestyle changes, dietary changes, or maintaining a positive attitude would help them win their battle over the disease. The search for meaning led them to discover dimensions of their lives that could be improved. A third theme was the attempt to regain feelings of self-esteem. The women found a reference group to compare themselves against that gave them a more favorable view of themselves and their disease (*downward social comparisons*). For example, older women felt better off than younger women, married women felt sorry for unmarried women, and those with a poor prognosis consoled themselves that at least they were still alive. Those who coped most successfully with the diagnosis of breast cancer created personal meaning to help them manage their stress. They showed active attempts to master their illness through active distortion, unrealistic optimism, and taking charge of their lives, despite the reality of the threat they faced. Suzanne Somers, a popular television celebrity, recently disclosed that she had breast cancer. She recognized her choice: "Am I going to be a victim and feel sorry for myself, or can I learn from this and grow?" Many women feel similarly and recognize that severe illness gives new meaning and perspective to life.

Heidrich and Ryff (1993) have found that older adults use downward social comparisons to maintain a stable and positive view of themselves in the face of age-related change. Women in poor health frequently engaged in social comparisons to evaluate their status and condition. They used downward comparisons in three areas: physical health, coping with aging, and level of activity. Surprisingly, the more frequent the comparisons, the more positive their mental health and adaptation; downward social comparisons with women who were in even poorer health bolstered their self-esteem and mental health. The women reported *upward social comparison* in only two areas: physical appearance and friendships. Elderly women were motivated towards continued self-improvement in these domains and looked to specific role models or friends for inspiration.

Adapting to stress has implications for health, well-being, psychological functioning, work productivity, and interpersonal relationships (Taylor et al., 1997). Recently, psychologists studying older people have wondered how they maintain positive self-esteem, feelings of control, and a sense of mastery in the face of an increasing number of changes and losses (Brandstadter, Wentura, and Greve, 1993). Studies show that older adults continue to maintain a strong belief in their ability to control the external environment. This belief is positively related to psychological functioning, physical health, and cognitive-intellectual achievements (Lachman & Burak, 1993; Rodin, 1990). Older adults make choices regarding the areas of life they can still manage and relinquish areas over which they no longer have much control. This, of course, contrasts with younger adults, who have minimal control over life tasks such as schooling, work, or residential location (Brim, 1992; Lachman & Burak, 1993). In this sense, older adults adjust aspirations, relinquish goals, lower expectations, and readjust priorities as developmental changes occur. In the face of age-related developmental change, they maintain a positive view of themselves and their sense of control.

In one account (Brandtstadter et al., 1993), the success of adults in adjusting to and coping with cumulative losses in old age and corresponding threats to self-esteem lies in their ability to use accommodative and assimilative processes. **Accommodative processes** allow older adults to disengage and lower their aspirations from goals they cannot attain. Accommodative processes become more important with advancing age. **Assimilative processes** direct older adults' behavior, actively engage them, and encourage them to strive to achieve attainable goals. Assimilative processes imply directed, intentional activity that prevents or reduces the developmental losses that can damage the older person's self-esteem and personal identity.

The interplay of these two processes allows older adults to maintain both a sense of control and a positive view of self. Figure 4.3 shows how the interplay between assimilative and accommodative processes contributes to the maintenance of self-esteem across the life span. Based on cross-sectional comparisons of 1,256 participants, the figure shows little age-related difference in the gap between perceived self

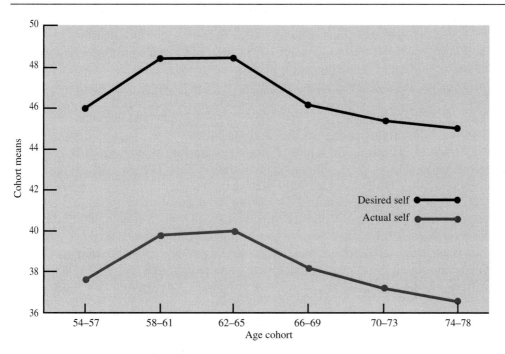

Figure 4.3 Age differences in ratings of desired self and actual self (sum scores). By accommodating normative self-conceptions, older adults can stabilize self-esteem despite perceived developmental losses.

and desired self. Thus, although older adults recognize losses in different domains, they are able to adjust their desires to promote a positive view of self. Self-evaluations in the later years remain virtually unaffected by actual or perceived age-related developmental losses. The data in figure 4.3 show that self-evaluations for each age cohort, measured by the difference between actual and desired self, remain about the same. That is, among successive age cohorts, perceived self-deficits do not increase with age, regardless of real or perceived declines in function (Brandtstadter et al., 1993; Ryff, 1991).

The complementary processes of assimilation and accommodation combine to comprise **life management,** or the process by which individuals protect their view of the aging self. Older persons are able to manage stress and preserve a positive view of themselves based on subjective interpretations of developmental gains and losses. The process of life management offers one explanation for effective coping (e.g., positive self-evaluation and enhanced well-being) despite the adverse effects of developmental changes as people age. Life management is not, however, a process of active denial and repression; older persons are well aware of the changes and losses they face. Rather, positive self-evaluations come through active assimilative and accommodative modes of coping, relinquishing some goals and renewing the commitment to others. Brandtstadter and colleagues (1993) have also begun to apply this model to help us understand how older people preserve a sense of control. These researchers suggest that personal control may be maintained simply by lowering aspirations or devaluing goals that are difficult to attain. This process leads to stability, or even enhancement, of the older person's sense of personal control.

Coping and Adaptation: Assessment and Measurement

As we have shown, stress causes both positive and negative affect. It affords an opportunity for growth, as well as a chance to question one's goals, priorities, and values. Those who adapt well may enhance their current coping strategies and develop new ones. Successful problem-focused or emotion-focused coping can build self-esteem and contribute to a sense of mastery, and successful adaptation makes it more likely that the individual will manage future stresses well (Aldwin, 1995). How can psychologists best assess the success of one's coping and adaptation?

Measuring coping skills and studying adaptation are at the heart of considerable recent debate (Coyne and Racioppo, 2000; Lazarus, 2000, Tennen, Affleck, Armeli, & Carney, 2000). Checklists of stressful life events and simplistic inventories of coping styles are not particularly helpful. First, the questions asked are far too broad ("How do you cope with the death of a parent?"). Second, the results offer little help or direction for those facing similar life events; in fact, personality, situational, and other mediating factors (such as social support) make it difficult to generalize results to any specific individual or group. Third, single measurements of coping may not predict how adults will react to stress across time and in various situations. As Coyne and Racioppo (2000, p. 657) note, "When coping is reduced to a summary score, the likelihood is that crucial aspects of timing, sequencing, and appropriateness will be lost." A fourth reason simple checklists and inventories are not enlightening is that they merely describe the end results of stressful encounters (rating one's own coping success), not the process (Lazarus, 1998). Most studies have relied on group comparisons (**nomothetic comparisons**) at one or two different test sessions but have not examined the process of coping and adapting longitudinally. To study the *process* of stress and coping, it is best to obtain repeated measurements of the same persons (**idiographic comparisons**) over an extended period of time. For example, the same individuals may be asked on a regular, repeated basis to identify their current coping behaviors, list and rate their immediate sources of stress, and rate their emotional states. Idiographic assessments can describe the course of coping as it unfolds naturally over many days or months in the same sample of individuals; these assessments employ a within subjects design. Fifth, by obtaining assessments of coping as stressors are experienced, rather than after the fact, researchers reduce the chances of errors in recall, distortion, and bias in memory (Tennen et al., 2000). Finally, qualitative studies of coping are vital to balance the use of summary assessments and nomothetic comparisons. They capture important insights, convey the richness and complexity of coping, and improve the validity of research conclusions (Lazarus, 2000). Research Focus 4.1 discusses a recent study of coping strategies among people with Parkinson's disease.

Coping and Family Caregiving

An increasingly common role for families is to provide care for an older relative, often a parent. As people live longer, family caregiving for frail elders and those with dementia is becoming more common. Family support helps elders live independently in the community, rather than in costly nursing homes or other supervised settings. Fam-

Coping with Parkinson's Disease: Chronic Health Problems and Stress

People with chronic health problems face many challenges and stressors. Studies of chronic disease have assessed its impact on a range of quality-of-life issues, including limitations in everyday functioning, levels of pain, energy, social function, and psychological well-being. Parkinson's Disease (PD) has a unique constellation of symptoms, including deteriorating motor function with visible tremors, rigidity, and slowness in initiating motor responses. People with PD have difficulty with balance and walking; they have impaired memory, judgment, and confusion (Hobson & Meara, 1999). PD patients have an uneven response to treatment with drugs such as L-dopa, which acts on the brain's center for motor control. Family caregivers recognize the often devastating emotional impact PD has on the person it affects; and research shows that this disease hits 1 percent of people over age 55 (Cummings, 1999). Finding a way to manage the disease, as well as to preserve quality of life and psychological well-being, is difficult.

Frazier (2000) recruited a population of 145 people with PD to examine coping. On average, respondents had been diagnosed and in treatment for about eight years, and most reported that the disease caused mild to moderate symptoms; 60 percent stated that the symptoms responded effectively to medications. The impact of PD on three types of stressors was studied: physical, cognitive, and psychosocial. It was hypothesized that older adults with PD would adopt different coping strategies (problem-focused coping, emotional regulation, and emotional distancing) to fit each of the three different types of stressors. The most stressful physical symptoms for older adults with PD were tremors and rigidity; lack of mental energy was the most troublesome cognitive stressor; while dependency, fear of being a burden, depression, and loss of control caused the most psychosocial distress.

Results showed, contrary to predictions, that participants most often used a single coping strategy, emotional regulation, to cope with stressful symptoms, regardless of whether the stressors were physical, cognitive, or psychosocial. The strategy they were least likely to use was emotional distance. However, respondents with more severe PD and in poorer physical mental health most often used emotional distance as a coping strategy. Many studies report that problem-focused coping reduces stress; however, for adults with PD, problem-focused coping did not. There is little reason to initiate active coping when many of the more troublesome symptoms are beyond one's control (e.g., 40 percent of the sample reported that symptoms irregularly responded to medication). The impact and stress of PD was pervasive and affected all measures of quality of life that the study examined. Those with chronic diseases such as PD develop unique patterns of coping and adaptation.

---

ily caregiving is a responsibility added to the already complicated lives of many adults; yet most feel a strong social or moral obligation to provide for a parent's financial, emotional, and physical needs. Most wish they could provide more help than they do. Some families provide daily visits to elderly parents to help with Activities of Daily Living (ADLs) such as preparing meals and assisting with housecleaning, bathing, and dressing. If an elderly parent moves into the home of an adult child, it is usually because of illness, frailty, or diminished finances. Elderly parents try to give something back to the extended household when this occurs. Studies show many do more than 75 percent of the housework, while others contribute financially to household expenses (Speare & Avery, 1993; Ward, Logan, & Spitze, 1992).

The care of a parent with dementia is particularly stressful for families. When a spouse is not available, this responsibility often falls on middle-aged adults. According to the **gender consistency model,** adult children are most likely to care for a parent of the same gender (Lee, Dwyer, & Coward, 1993). Since the majority of older-adult parents are mothers, the role of caregiver most often falls to daughters who look after their widowed mothers. Daughters express concern about the time constraints of providing care and show considerable anxiety about the complexity and uncertainty of the situation. Elderly mothers receiving care feel angry and helpless about their condition; they feel guilty about the burden they have placed on their families (Walker, Martin, & Jones, 1992).

Caregiving in the home influences everyone in the family to some degree. The resulting stress extends to the entire family system. The greater the health problems and overall frailty of the older person, the more likely that primary caregivers will feel hostility, resentment, and guilt (Light, Niederehe, & Lebowitz, 1994). Studies have shown a significant relationship between the severity of chronic health problems the care recipient is experiencing, and the stress the primary caregiver perceives. However, this relationship also holds true for other family members, including spouses, adult children, and spouses of adult children. The entire family system experiences the "cascading effect" of chronic illness and caregiving.

Women who serve as primary caregivers often must give up their careers, at least temporarily. They drop out of the workforce or significantly reduce their work hours to care for aged relatives. A caregiving role can last for many years and reduce family income as well as the caregiver's contributions to Social Security. In one study, Social Security contributions for women responsible for caring for an older relative cost them $127 in lost benefits per month at retirement (Kingson & O'Grady-LeShane, 1993).

Providing care often pits women's strong feelings of parental obligation and loyalty with resentment over lost time with spouses, children, and personal interests. It is no wonder that caregivers feel guilt, anxiety, and anger. Franks and Stephens (1992) tried to study the role conflicts women experience by examining the meaning attached to each specific role (e.g., caregiver, mother, spouse). They found that adult daughters experience stress and role conflict as they struggle to balance the value of each role to their subjective well-being. For some adult caregivers, role conflicts did not cause much stress, if a particular role contributed only marginally to their sense of well-being. Thus, these caregivers could temporarily abandon a role in order to adopt another role that contributed more to their sense of well-being. Another investigation revealed the negative effects of trying to balance the two primary roles of caregiver and employed worker (Stephens, Franks, & Atienza, 1997). The multiple demands of the two roles produced negative spillover effects on both. Although some research (e.g., Hong & Seltzer, 1995) suggests that multiple role responsibilities may be beneficial to the caregiving role, there were no reported enhancements in balancing employment and caregiving roles. Women experienced role stress and more symptoms of depression trying to do both. Longitudinal studies also show that as caregiving continues, depressive symptoms become more severe among daughters caring for their mothers. Problem-focused coping, more characteristic of caregivers with higher mastery, was related to fewer depressive symptoms over the 18 months of the study. Emotion-focused coping, on the other hand, was more often characteristic of caregivers with lower mastery and was associated with a greater number of depressive symptoms (Li, Seltzer, & Greenberg; 1999). The effects of problem-focused versus emotion-focused coping have been confirmed in many other cross-sectional studies.

The term *sandwich generation* has been used to refer to adults who are caregivers both to elderly relatives and to children. Surprisingly, however, two studies of middle-aged women found few to be "sandwiched" between these roles. In a large cross-national

Canadian study, the majority of middle-aged adult children were not responsible for providing direct care to their parents (Rosenthal, Martin-Matthews, & Matthews, 1996). Most often, daughters in their later fifties, who no longer had childrearing responsibilities at this point in their lives, took on the role of caregiver to aging parents. Soldo (1996) also confirmed that most adult children begin to care for parents at a time when their own children are in or entering adulthood (e.g., entering college, starting a career, or having children). Role conflicts for most middle-aged adults are few; when they do arise, it is at a point later in life.

Social support from friends and family is important to sustain caregivers; yet, most married daughters face interpersonal conflicts with their own siblings that add to the stress they encounter in caring for an elderly parent. Regardless of who actually provides direct care, brothers and sisters hold egocentric perceptions of their own and other siblings' contributions and concern for the parent. They believe that other siblings are less involved, derive less personal satisfaction from their contributions, contribute less time and money, and have more freedom than they do. They believe that if they shared these egocentric perceptions, other siblings would agree with them (Lerner et al., 1991; Suitor and Pillemer, 1993). As we already mentioned, caregivers with higher mastery scores have fewer depressive symptoms than those with lower mastery, and mastery is enhanced when the caregiving role is shared with a sibling. Lower mastery scores are found among caregivers with multiple primary role responsibilities and among those providing care to an elderly person with serious behavior problems (Wailing et al., 1999; Seltzer and Wailing, 2000).

Coping with Alzheimer's Disease: Caregiver Burden

The physical, emotional, social, and financial costs associated with caring for a family member with Alzheimer's disease are profound. Experts have labeled the overall negative impact of providing such care the **caregiver burden,** differentiating between objective and subjective aspects of this burden. The **objective caregiver burden** refers to the disruption in expected routine or lifestyle; it is reflected by changes in finances, family activities, friendships, marital relationships, entertainment, vacations, and travel. The **subjective caregiver burden** centers on emotional reactions to caretaking such as guilt, embarrassment, shame, resentment, anger, and exclusion. Caregivers are not prepared for the progressive decline in function and increase in care that an elderly parent requires. Moreover, the additional care and intervention they provide often threatens the personal autonomy, dignity, and individual rights of the parent. Studies show that those who experience the greatest caregiver burden and role overload provide care to elders with greater memory impairments and more disruptive emotional and behavioral symptoms (e.g., nighttime wandering, hallucinations). Caregivers who perceive a greater burden and more stress are more likely to institutionalize an older relative or parent in a supervised health facility or nursing home (Gaugler, Davey, Pearlin, and Zarit, 2000; Light et al., 1994; Seltzer, Vasterling, Yoder, & Thompson, 1997).

Few caregivers anticipate the extent of the burden or the diminished time for friends, work, and leisure activities (George, 1992; 1990b). Family members have been identified as the "hidden victims" of AD, and their struggles were documented in Mace and Rabins' *The 36 Hour Day* (Gatz et al., 1996; Pearlin, Mullan, Semple, and Skaff,

1990; Zarit, Orr, and Zarit, 1985). Experts encourage all family members to participate in community support groups with other caregivers. They also should prepare themselves for the course of the disease and understand its symptoms. Baum, Edwards, and Morrow-Howell (1993) propose a measurement-based approach to help caregivers manage those with AD. They emphasize the functional strengths that remain as the disease progresses, rather than focus on the losses that many other stage approaches to AD highlight. Using the Functional Behavior Profile (see table 4.2), caregivers can identify the remaining strengths in each stage and work with them. The goals are to reduce the rate at which the person loses behaviors and to preserve the adaptive behaviors still present so that those with AD can function as independently as possible. Many studies of caregivers have recognized the interaction between the home environment, the char-

TABLE 4.2

Functional Behavior Profile Showing Significant Decline Between Stages of Alzheimer's Disease

Item*	Stages					
	0.5–1	0.5–2	1–2	0.5–3	1–3	2–3
Follows three-step command		*	*	*	*	
Learns complex tasks without difficulty	*	*	*	*	*	
Follows two-step command		*	*	*	*	*
Knows the day of the week and/or date	*	*	*	*	*	
Makes complex decisions independently	*	*	*	*	*	
Problem solves without assistance	*	*	*	*	*	
Problem solves with repeated assistance	*	*	*	*	*	
Takes responsibility		*	*	*	*	*
Finishes a task		*	*	*	*	*
Performs neat work		*	*	*	*	*
Concentrates on a task for a time		*	*	*	*	*
Handles tools or instruments		*	*	*	*	*
Performs fine detail				*	*	*
Performs work within a reasonable time		*		*	*	
Engages in activities appropriate to time of day		*	*	*	*	*
Makes simple decisions		*	*	*	*	*
Follows one-step command		*	*	*	*	*
Shows enjoyment in activity				*	*	
Socializes when others initiate				*	*	*
Participates in activities			*	*	*	
Initiates conversation with family				*	*	*
Identifies familiar people				*	*	*
Expresses self appropriately				*	*	*
Performs activity without frustration				*	*	
Makes decisions when given choices		*	*	*	*	*
Continues activities when frustrated		*	*	*	*	
Learns simple tasks without difficulty		*	*	*	*	*

Stage Numbers refer to Alzheimer's Disease: 0.5—Questionable Diagnosis; 1—Mild AD; 2 —Moderate AD; 3—Severe AD.

Source: Baum, C., Edwards, D. F., and Morrow-Howell, N. Identification and measures of productive behaviors in senile dementia of the Alzheimer's type. The Gerontologist, 33, 403–408. Copyright (©) 1993. The Gerontological Society of America.

acteristics of the caregiver, and the functional status of the elder care recipient. These factors help determine the specific types of intervention that may help reduce stress and enhance caregiving (Seltzer et al., 1997). Initially, investigators found that caregivers adopted one of three emotional styles in coping with a parent with AD: confrontational (characterized by emotionality—anger, guilt, and sadness), denial (repression of negative emotions), and avoidant (suppression of negative feelings). Avoidance strategies were associated with a higher incidence of depression among caregivers. Some studies show that these three coping styles may characterize different phases of coping. Avoidance strategies can help older spouses and family members to deal with the immediate impact of stress, such as when a relative is recently released from a rehabilitation hospital and needs home care for a few months. However, if caregivers responsible for elderly persons with chronic problems used avoidance for six months or more, they generally fell prey to depression and other negative outcomes (Light, Niederehe, & Lebowitz, 1994). A 12-month longitudinal study of family AD caregivers found two predictors for depressive symptoms: Caregivers who cared for relatives with serious behavior problems (higher objective primary stress) and caregivers who felt overwhelmed or trapped by the caregiving role (higher subjective primary stress) were at greatest risk of developing depression (Alspaugh et al., 1999).

After reviewing a large number of research studies, Gwyther (1992) reported that (1) initially, families are the primary caregivers for relatives with dementia; (2) caregiving can have both negative and positive outcomes; (3) most studies have examined only the negative consequences; (4) research has taken a simplistic view of the role of caregiver and care recipient; and (5) intervention is helpful to caregivers, but does little to alleviate the stress they experience in managing their multiple roles and responsibilities. Research also suggests that caregivers are at higher risk for mental health disorders such as depression than they are for physical health problems. It appears that the subjective caregiver burden is the better predictor of mental health problems than the objective caregiver burden is (Yates, Tennstedt, and Chang, 1999).

The subjective burden is high among those caring for a relative with AD, and these caregivers are most often women. Most studies find that the caregiver burden among women is associated with a higher incidence of psychiatric symptoms, including depression, than it is among caregiving men (Yee & Schulz, 2000). Wives are more likely to experience depressive symptoms in caregiving for a spouse with AD than are husbands. One explanation for this phenomenon is the *loss of reciprocity* (shared meaning, common activities) in the marital relationship due to cognitive impairment. Reciprocity may be a more important dimension for caregiving wives than for caregiving husbands. One study recently compared men and women caring for spouses with cognitive impairments or with frailty and limitations in Activities of Daily Living (ADL). Husbands caring for a spouse reported fewer stressors and fewer depressive symptoms than wives. Yet the actual caregiving demands, behavior problems, and level of help was the same for men and women caregivers, as was the objective impact of caregiving (e.g., activity restriction, quality of the relationship). Men tend to be more stoic in accepting the responsibilities of caregiving to a spouse. Their perceptions of the caregiving role were different from those of women (Bookwala & Schulz, 2000). A recent study evaluated these relationships by comparing husbands and wives caring for a spouse with Alzheimer's disease or Parkinson's disease (Hooker et al., 2000). Results showed that women caring for a spouse with AD had significantly higher levels of perceived stress, anxiety, and depression than did caregiving husbands. However, there were no gender differences among caregivers of a spouse with Parkinson's disease. Reciprocity losses due to Parkinson's disease are relatively few in comparison to the cognitive impairments associated with AD.

Generally, most adults are resilient and manage the stress of providing care to a family member with AD. The role of caregiver is complex, emotionally demanding, and time-consuming; yet, most people handle their responsibilities effectively. They often manage the burden and accompanying stress for many years, successfully coping with their feelings and making use of community resources. Farran (1997) notes the "majestic serenity, calmness, and sense of 'being at peace' with what they are doing and experiencing" (p. 250). Caregiving may have been portrayed in an overly negative way. Other models represent the more positive dimensions of caregiving. Researchers are examining new models to understand the essential resources needed for success in the caregiving role. Learning about the mediators of successful outcomes can be instructive for those about to face the challenges of becoming a caregiver.

Alzheimer's Disease: Caregiving Decisions

Families make the decision to institutionalize relatives with Alzheimer's disease in different ways and at different points, but the decision is always a difficult one to make. Often the decision comes after a number of years of struggling to manage the increasing physical and emotional demands of caregiving. Caregivers are motivated by altruistic reasons (e.g., feelings of empathy and attachment), social norms (e.g., feelings of generational reciprocity and responsibility), and personal motives (including avoidance of guilt, fear of public censure, or a sense of indebtedness) (Gatz, Bengtson, & Blum, 1990; Biegel, Bass, Schulz, & Morycz, 1993). Yet the consequences of accepting the responsibility to care for an impaired relative are rarely understood until caregiving is well under way.

Following the decision to institutionalize a close relative or parent, caregivers are less burdened in terms of both physical demands (feeding, bathing, dressing) and emotional demands. Older spouses, understandably, make the decision to institutionalize a disabled husband or wife more quickly than middle-aged children decide to institutionalize a parent or relative, presumably because middle-aged children are physically stronger and more able to deal with the physical and emotional demands of caregiving. The immediate impact of institutionalization on caregivers, freed from the day-to-day responsibilities of providing assistance to an impaired elder, is a gain of 1 hour and 47 minutes per day (Moss, Lawton, Kleban, & Duhamel, 1993). Caregivers use this gain in free time for family interaction and activities outside the home. Institutional placement brings relief from the physical demands of caregiving, but it can make family members angry and remorseful. Still, the decision is eventually viewed as a wise choice.

The concerns associated with a move to a nursing home include: (1) orientation and adjustment to the new facility, (2) family and dependency concerns, (3) concerns about the quality and availability of medical care, (4) the provision of tender loving care, and (5) availability of sufficient space (Stein, Linn, & Stein, 1985). Initially, the move to an institution may produce confusion, disorientation, and withdrawal that lasts for about two months (Borup, 1983). Individuals who are effective at expressing their needs and preferences usually make a better adjustment than docile individuals (Simms, Jones, & Yoder, 1982; Tobin & Lieberman, 1976). The nursing home programs that receive high marks from new residents are the ones that provide more "tender loving care" than residents expected (Stein et al., 1986).

Alzheimer's Disease: Personal Perspectives

What is it like to experience the losses associated with AD? Do people realize what is happening to them? What are their fears and feelings? In a book-length narrative, *Living in the Labyrinth,* Diana Friel McGowin (1993) provides some insights into the feelings and experiences of those coping with the disease. McGowin was in her late forties when she was diagnosed with AD. In her diary, written on a computer, she described two of the earliest signs of her problems as (1) memory loss and (2) difficulty in recognizing and negotiating her regular environment. For example, McGowin became lost while driving her car close to home. In the following passage, she describes getting directions from a security guard at a local park.

> "I appear to be lost," I began, making a great effort to keep my voice level, despite my emotional state. "Where do you need to go?" the guard asked politely. A cold chill enveloped me as I realized I could not remember the name of my street. Tears began to flow down my cheeks. I did not know where I wanted to go. He prompted me, his voice soft as he noticed my tears. "Are you heading to Orland, or Windermere?" "Orland!" I sighed gratefully. That was right. I live in Orland, I was certain of it. But where? . . . I felt panic wash over me anew as I searched my memory and found it blank. Suddenly, I remembered bringing my grandchildren to this park. That must mean I lived relatively nearby, surely. "What is the closest subdivision?" I quavered. The guard scratched his head thoughtfully. "The closest Orland subdivision would be Pine Hills, maybe," he ventured. "That's right!" I exclaimed gratefully. The name of my subdivision had rung a bell. . . . Once home, a wave of relief brought more tears (McGowin, 1993, pp. 6–9).

Other feelings persons with AD experience in the early stages include: (1) Lost (1) stigma, originating from the shame one feels in having a particular illness and the fear of having to confront rejection or discrimination because of the illness, and (2) disruption of self-image, occurring as a result of restricted lifestyle, fewer social contacts, and increased reliance on others (Conrad, 1990; Cotrell & Schulz, 1993; Gerhardt, 1990). McGowin wrote about the pain and fear of disclosing the diagnosis of AD to her family:

> . . . I could not bring myself to confide in my children. I could not even accept it myself. Intellectually, I knew my condition was not cause for shame, yet emotionally, I felt ashamed. I was losing my intelligence, losing my memory, and my directional system was really shot to Hades. Embarrassment kept me from confiding in my family and friends. I had no idea of how they would respond. If they were too condescending and made me feel worthless, I would chafe; on the other hand, if they displayed a "so what" attitude, I would be devastated. It would break my heart. I wished I could unload this burden, reveal my

thoughts to someone, state my innermost fears and anxieties, and receive kind support and understanding. . . . What I wanted, no, needed, was someone to assure me that no matter what my future held, they would stand beside me, fight my battles with me, or if need be, for me. I wanted assurance from someone that I would not be abandoned to shrivel away. They would give me encouragement, love, moral support, and if necessary, take care of me (McGowin, 1993, pp. 53–54).

Those with chronic disorders also experience fears of desertion, feelings of social isolation (from relatives and friends), and fears about the future course of the disease (Cohen & Eisdorfer, 1986). These fears, too, were evident in McGowin's writings. And in the early stages of coping with the disease, she tried to cover up many of her problems coping. For example, she describes her continuing attempts to compensate for her difficulties on the job:

I attempted to bluff my way through small talk with the young stranger. As we walked along together, (he said) he was there to interview for a job as a messenger or courier. Could I help him? I threw in the towel and smiled resignedly at him. "Please forgive me. I know that I know you, but it is just one of those days! I simply can't bring your name to mind. I will be happy to put in a word for you, if you could write down your name and other relevant details." "I don't get it," he muttered. "Your name?" I did not waver. "Diana, I'm your cousin, Rich," he said slowly. Tears began to surface in my eyes, and I embraced my cousin, whispering, "I was just trying to keep anyone from overhearing that one of my relatives is applying. Of course I'll put in a good recommendation with the personnel department. Absolutely!" It struck me that while I may forget relatives, coworkers, or the way to the restroom, I certainly could think fast enough when cornered, and come forth with a believable bluff. (McGowin, 1993, pp. 19–20)

Personal accounts such as those of Diana McGowin help to improve the management and treatment of AD. Thus far, psychological studies and treatment approaches for AD have emphasized the assessment and management of functional impairments and disruptive behaviors. Personal accounts suggest that we should pay more attention to helping people cope with adjusting to the disease. Some programs try to build on the positive skills and abilities that remain (Sheridan, 1993). Research Focus 4.2 discusses whether and how to tell a person that he or she has AD.

Mediators of Caregiver Burden

Although many people face similar situations in providing care to a relative with AD, not all people cope similarly. Research has shown that a number of variables can mediate the stress of caregiving, particularly for a relative with AD. Mediators of stress include social support for caregivers, personality variables, financial resources, and the utilization of formal support services (Yates, Tennstedt, & Chang, 1999). Other research suggests that race and ethnicity, emotional support, the quality of the current relationship, and the past relationship serve as mediators of caregiver burden.

Consider the model developed in figure 4.4. Yates and colleagues (1999) described the impact of certain mediators on caregiver burden within a unique conceptualization of cognitive appraisal and stress. They used an index of depression to measure caregivers' psychological well-being. Primary stressors included the care recipient's level and type of

Whether to Tell People They Have Alzheimer's Disease

In recent years, the doctor-patient relationship has been characterized by increasing openness and directness. Physicians and patients speak with each other about cancer or AIDS, yet Altman (1992) suggests that the diagnosis of AD may be medicine's "last taboo." Telling patients that they have a terminal disease is one of the most difficult tasks physicians face; of all fatal diseases, the diagnosis of AD is perhaps one of the most devastating. Because of the special nature of the progressive losses patients with Alzheimer's experience, physicians realize all too well that the disease ultimately "robs people of one of the most fundamental things that makes them human—memory, personality and the ability to think" (Altman, 1992, p. C3). What do you think . . . should physicians tell patients that they are in the early stages of the disease?

Many people believe it is a physician's responsibility and a patient's right to know of a suspected diagnosis. However, sometimes having such information does more harm than good. In deciding what to communicate to the patient and the family, physicians must employ exceptional humanity, sensitivity, and judgment; this is the "art" of medicine. Physicians appear to judge the strength of the personalities involved, the strength of the family unit, and the stage to which the disease has progressed. Also of importance is the source of the referral (patient or family) and when an initial diagnosis is sought. Physicians realize that what is best to share with a person with AD may not be in the best interest of the family. And, conversely, what family members may wish for may be at odds with a physician's appraisal of what the affected patient can handle. For example, patients may have developed strategies to hide their difficulties from family, friends, and coworkers; concerned relatives may have coerced them into an initial visit. At other times, patients themselves recognize that they are having problems and visit a physician. They then may refuse to share the diagnosis with children or a spouse.

Recall that a diagnosis of AD is difficult to confirm and that physicians may be reluctant to apply a label with so much emotional baggage. Often they use general descrip-

tions such as "senile memory problem" or "neurological deterioration" without employing definitive terms. Under such conditions, physicians may rightly be hedging their bets. By the time a clear picture emerges and a more definite diagnosis is possible, the person with AD may not fully comprehend the diagnosis and, thus, may have been spared much emotional anguish. Most patients who can comprehend the diagnosis appear to fear the Alzheimer's disease label and the social stigma attached to it. Perhaps on such grounds, it is argued, it is best to wait for the sake of the patient. Why rush people into confronting such a diagnosis and into depressed moods; what is the benefit?

Telling those in early-stage AD of the suspected diagnosis, on the other hand, has the advantage of allowing all concerned to make sound, responsible decisions. Early in the disease, before they become debilitated, patients can make decisions affecting their finances, their wills, and their health care options. Patients with early Alzheimer's can still exercise good judgment in these matters and may want to play a central role in deciding what they want for themselves. With the opportunity to understand their situation, they might choose to volunteer for experimental treatment programs or to visit special friends. Also, families can begin to prepare for the changes needed to provide continuous care and begin to think ahead about how to intervene as behavioral and functional losses emerge. Sometimes, just being able to prepare for the changes that will ensue is sufficient to help families cope.

However, not all patients with AD want their families to know about their situation. Some may refuse to share information and insist on their physician's strict confidentiality as a means of keeping some control over their lives. Thus, families and physicians may have to confront difficult ethical issues to obtain information related to diagnosis and treatment when the patient wishes to maintain confidentiality. There is little normative statistical data to provide physicians, families, and patients with Alzheimer's with clues as to what is best.

---

disability; unlike other studies, this one considered caregiving assistance to be part of primary appraisal. Primary appraisal of the elder's need for care reflected the caregiver's subjective understanding of the disability and the situation. Each family caregiver appraised the needs of care recipients differently, despite comparable disabilities (the sample consisted of disabled elders over 85 years of age and their informal caregivers). Subjective burden or overload was conceptualized as a process of secondary appraisal. How do caregivers assess their feelings about their energy levels, satisfaction with the level of care they

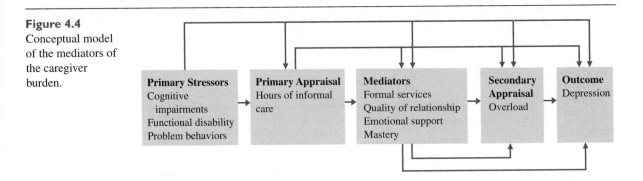

Figure 4.4
Conceptual model of the mediators of the caregiver burden.

Primary Stressors	Primary Appraisal	Mediators	Secondary Appraisal	Outcome
Cognitive impairments	Hours of informal care	Formal services	Overload	Depression
Functional disability		Quality of relationship		
Problem behaviors		Emotional support		
		Mastery		

provide, and available time for themselves? Psychological well-being (level of depression) was a function of the hours of informal care provided (primary appraisal) that led to caregiver burden. In other words, caregiver burden (overload) was directly related to the hours of care provided (primary appraisal) and indirectly related to primary stressors (e.g., caregivers understanding of the elder's level of disability and needs). With greater disability, caregivers were more likely to assess the need for greater care and thus experience greater overload. The relationship between primary stressors, emotional overload, and depression was mediated by the quality of the relationship between caregiver and care recipient. As in other research on mediational factors, a sense of mastery and the presence of social-emotional support reduced the incidence of depression among caregivers.

The Value of Social Support

Some research on informal caregivers of the elderly (e.g., relatives) has confirmed the value of social support. Debate continues regarding the importance of the number of people who provide support versus the type of social support they provide (Lawton et al., 1991; Vitaliano et al., 1991). It has been suggested that social support for informal family caregivers serves as a buffer, protecting them against some of the more difficult stresses of coping with a hard-to-manage chronic illness. Families appear to be able to maintain their caretaking of a frail or ill older parent in the home primarily through social support (Gwyther, 1992; Thompson et al., 1993).

One study compared different types of social support to determine those most effective in reducing the burden of caretaking on family members (Thompson et al., 1993). Engaging in social interaction for simple fun and recreation was measurably superior to other forms of social support in helping family members manage the stress of caring for an older relative. Other types of social support, such as direct aid, physical assistance, emotional support, and validation of self-esteem, were ineffectual in reducing the stress associated with chronic caregiving to an elderly relative in the home. The data suggest that caregivers should engage in regular, pleasant activities with friends and other relatives to best manage the chronic stress associated with their complex and demanding roles (Thompson et al., 1993).

Natural disasters tax the coping skills of individuals throughout the life span in dramatically different ways.

However, the value of the social environment in promoting effective coping can be overstated (Taylor, Repetti, & Seeman, 1997). When the assistance provided by others robs the caregiver or the care recipient of the opportunity for independence, mastery, and self-sufficiency, the risk of dependency, depression, and helplessness can increase. In such situations, the health status of the care recipient can be compromised, and declines occur (Taylor et al., 1997). Unfortunately, the presence and availability of a close and supportive social network does not consistently lead to lower levels of stress among caregivers, nor to greater likelihood of recovery among those facing chronic illness (Bolger, Foster, Vinokur, & Ng, 1997; Coyne & Fiske, 1992).

Caring for a relative with AD is different from other types of family caregiving. AD requires more hours of direct care each week than caring for ill relatives without dementia requires. AD is also associated with more strain on caregivers, a greater burden, and more negative consequences at work for those still employed. Those who provide care for a family member with AD are more likely to experience mental and physical health problems. Caregivers also have less time for other family members and less time for leisure activities (Ory et al., 1999).

Community Programs and Respite Care

The burden of providing care 24 hours a day to those with AD takes a toll on care providers. Depression, a marker of compromised psychological well-being, has been reported in more than 50 percent of family caregivers (Hirsch, Davies, Boatwright, & Ochango, 1993). Among health care professionals whose job is caring for those with AD, the rate of burnout and job-related anxiety is also high. In one study, nursing assistants in a long-term care facility for the elderly reported burnout, perceived job pressure, and burden. When they were given specific training to help them manage elderly residents with cognitive impairments, the nursing assistants felt significantly less job-related stress (Chappell & Novak, 1992).

Family members providing care at home for a relative with AD are encouraged to participate in community-based support groups to help reduce stress. Community programs include various support groups for those providing care; they meet regularly to share their burden, exchange stories, and air their feelings. One of the functions of support groups is to help people see they are not alone and that others face similar challenges. Another function is to provide education about AD and teach families strategies for effective behavioral management. Such programs have been shown to help family members by decreasing their perceptions of the frequency and severity of problems and helping them to react to problem behaviors more appropriately. Psychoeducational intervention also decreases caregiver burden (Ostwald et al., 1999).

Other types of community programs offer caregivers **respite care.** Respite care is any type of service that allows time away from caregiving responsibilities, providing temporary relief so caregivers can take a break. For instance, community members may come to caregivers' homes for a few hours so that the caregiver can go to a movie or have a meal at a restaurant. Some community organizations offer supervision for those with AD in structured groups in a specialized day care or evening care program. Still other community programs offer people with AD a brief stay in an institution so that caregivers can travel or meet other obligations. Community programs also include Meals on Wheels, which delivers prepared meals to homes. This frees caregivers from some of the demands of supermarket shopping and meal preparation.

Many spousal caregivers are themselves old and frail, and they may be unable to provide home-based care without such community support services. Ideally, respite care and other support services should fit the needs of the caregiver and care recipient. Services should also consider how the person with AD functions and be tailored to the background and needs of the caregiver and the family. Cairl and Kosberg (1993) find such targeted intervention based on need to be more effective than generic community programs (i.e., "one size fits all").

Not all community members are receptive to respite programs and other organized interventions. Studies have found racial and ethnic differences in the use of respite care services and caregiver support groups. In one study, investigators compared black and white caregivers who were responsible for a relative with dementia (Hinrichsen & Ramirez, 1992). Caregivers of both races were equally willing to accept the responsibilities and demands of the role. However, black caregivers were less willing to consider institutionalization for their relatives and were more willing to accept the personal distress and burden of the caregiving role than were whites. When asked to identify services that would be helpful, black caregivers listed training in nursing and physical therapy rather than respite programs or participation in AD support groups. Simply making caregivers from ethnically diverse backgrounds aware of the availability of AD support groups may not be an effective way to get them to join these groups. In order to encourage participation in AD support groups, the groups must be created and organized to match the values of the community itself. Look at the basic principles listed in table 4.3. The principles were developed as part of a program to involve both black and Hispanic caregivers who are providing care for a relative with AD in their own home.

Source: Henderson, J. N., Gutierrez-Mayka, M., Garcia, J., and Boyd, S. (1993). A mode for Alzheimer's disease support group development in African-American and Hispanic populations. The Gerontologist, 33, 409–414. Copyright 1993 © The Gerontological Society of America.

Caregivers' Appraisals of Efficacy

Gignac and Gottlieb (1996) studied a group of 87 family caregivers of older adults with AD. Using the cognitive model of coping that Lazarus and colleagues developed, Gignac and Gottlieb identified cognitive appraisals caregivers use to assess their personal efficacy in coping with a family member with AD, assessed the stability of such appraisals, and measured the overall frequency of such appraisals. They identified 12 basic efficacy appraisals that family caregivers employed in managing people with AD; these appraisals ranged across five separate domains: problem-solving, regulating emotional distress, protecting self-esteem, managing social interactions, and self-development. Table 4.4 lists the 12 types of cognitive appraisals of coping efficacy. These data revealed that five of the 12 basic efficacy appraisals were associated directly with either caregiver distress or well-being: nonefficacious coping outcomes, no coping options, no control, improved ability to cope, and means/ends insights. Interestingly, the caregivers varied in their assessments of their individual efficacy in coping with a relative with AD. Stability in their self-assessments of efficacy depended on how successful the interactions with their older relatives were at the time of the evaluation.

The research by Gignac and Gottlieb (1996) suggested that caregivers focus on very broad goals in determining how best to cope with a relative with AD. Coping efficacy was directly related to an individual's subjective appraisal of success or failure. In managing the most upsetting problems, caregivers tended to use "making meaning" and humor as tactics for managing their own emotions. They recognized that their emotional management of distress and the caregiving burden were a key to their efficacy in previous interventions. When disruptive actions associated with AD occurred (e.g., noxious habits, confusion, aggression, and nighttime disruption), caregivers needed to be educated to attribute these problems to the disease, not to the volition of the patient.

TABLE 4.4

Types of Appraisals of Coping Efficacy

Type	Illustrative Quotations
Efficacious coping outcomes: appraisals of efficacious coping outcomes.	"I've tried everything, but that seems to work." "And that makes it a little better." "This has really helped my situation."
Nonefficacious coping outcomes: appraisals in inefficacious coping outcomes.	"But with not much result." "It doesn't do any good." "But it just doesn't register."
No coping options: appraisals that nothing further can be done to manage stressor demands.	"I don't know what to do." "There's nothing I can do." "I'm just helpless."
Control appraisals: appraisals of the control the respondent can exercise over the stressor or over his or her emotions.	"I'm more able to control things now." "I'm fortunate enough to be able to control any upset feelings."
No-control appraisals: appraisals that the respondent is not able to control the stressor or his or her emotions.	"I guess it's a situation that I can't control."
Less stressor reactivity: appraisals that the respondent is able to tolerate the stressor.	"But I'm getting used to that now." "It doesn't upset me like it used to."
More stressor reactivity: appraisals that the respondent is unable to tolerate the stressor.	"I never get used to it." "I just can't get used to the idea of my mother sitting there."
Depletion of energy: appraisals of diminished energy.	"Trying to cope with it all, it's tiring me out." "As much as I love them, it is wearing." "You get to the point where you don't even try."
Improved ability to cope: appraisals of improvements in coping.	"I'm more reasonable than I used to be." "I've learned to cope with it." "The more you know about the disease, the more [you are able] to understand him."
Coping self-criticism: appraisals of shortcomings in coping.	"I should know better." "I realize I should have done something or said something different." "I haven't been able to handle it too well, I guess."
Means/ends insights: appraisals of the relationship between coping efforts and their outcomes.	"Because she gets really upset if I yell at her." [Changes subject] "So she can start thinking about something else." [Hold onto hands] "So he doesn't pull the waitress's arm."
Strategic planning: appraisals of the costs entailed in different coping efforts.	"I wouldn't say anything to hurt her feelings." "You don't want her to feel guilty, you know." "Otherwise, you're going to have a frustrating time your whole life here."

Source: Gignac, M., & Gottlieb, B. (1996). Caregivers' appraisals of efficacy in coping with dementia. Psychology and Aging, 11(2), 214–225.

Using longitudinal data collected from 456 respondents, Skaff, Pearlin, and Mullan (1996) observed that differences in sense of mastery related to changes in the caregiving role. A sense of mastery emerged as the direct result of a lengthy career of caregiving. Most caregivers did not consider mastery a stable personality trait. Skaff and colleagues (1996) also found three distinct patterns related to mastery among the caretakers. For those relatives who continued to care consistently for a family member with AD, the sense of mastery declined steadily; for those who decided that they could not provide adequate care and placed their relative in a full-time institutionalized care facility, the sense of mastery remained unchanged (e.g., it stayed at the level it was just prior to placement). The only group for whom the sense of mastery increased was the group who had experienced the death of their relative and thus ended their caretaking careers (Skaff et al., 1996). Transitions thus occur among caregivers who derive a sense of mastery and efficacy in response to the changing nature of their experience with a family member with AD. The career of care provider is dynamic, with multiple trajectories throughout an extended period of time. In some cases, this time period may encompass a decade or more, and caregivers themselves show increased difficulties in meeting the needs of the older person as they grow older and the physical demands for care increase.

Positive Outcomes of Caregiving

The benefits of caregiving include gains in personal efficacy and mastery as well as enhancement of well-being and self-worth (Kramer, 1997a). Caregivers express positive feelings about their ability to assist a relative, their selflessness in choosing to do so, and their willingness to forgo other interests. Caregiving also may increase feelings of pride and personal achievement, enhance meaning, and heighten the sense of closeness and warmth between caregiver and care recipient (Farran, 1997; Kramer, 1997a). Studies of the impact of caregiving on the larger family also show some positive outcomes. Beach (1997) documented specific benefits among a sample of older adolescents who were living at home with an older relative with AD who was receiving care in the immediate family. Adolescents developed increased empathy for older adults, felt closer to their mothers who were providing care, shared more with siblings through activities, and showed enhanced communication with peers. They were also more selective in their choice of peers, choosing those who understood and were empathic to the family's commitment to provide home care.

It is only through the use of multiple outcome measures that positive benefits have been identified (Kramer, 1997a; Miller & Lawton, 1997). Perhaps most intriguing is the possibility that there may be differential predictors for caregiver burden and caregiver benefits. The literature Kramer (1997a) reviewed suggests that motivational differences in assuming the role of caregiver, attitude, and ethnicity are all predictive of benefits. For instance, both white and black caregivers show satisfaction in being able to assume the role of provider and a positive affect in doing so (e.g., indicators of mental health and well-being are enhanced) (Lawton, Rajagopal, Brody, & Kleban, 1992). White caregivers derived benefits when their motivation for assuming the role of caregiver included maintaining family traditions, showing mutual aid, concern, and reciprocity; however, benefits for black caregivers were not predicted by these motivations (Kramer, 1997a). In a number of studies, satisfaction with the caregiving role was related to the care recipient's level of day-to-day independent functioning, assessed through inventories such as **activities of daily living (ADL)** (Kramer, 1993a, 1997a). Burden and depression were predictable from caregivers' difficulties in managing the care recipient's behavioral symptoms, the length of time engaged in the caregiving role, prior history of the relationship between caregiver and care recipient, and the level of stress created by the care recipient's limitations in day-to-day independent functioning (Kramer, 1993a, 1993b).

Figure 4.5 shows Kramer's conceptual model of some of the predictors of caregiver burden and caregiver gains. The model takes into account background and context variables including (1) care recipient characteristics: the severity of the illness, capacity for self-care, cognitive abilities, disruptive actions, and awareness of memory impairment; (2) caregiver demands; and (3) caregiver attitudes: motivation for helping, value in helping, and goals for helping. The intervening processes in the model include resources external to the caregiver, chiefly social support and organized community services, including adult day care and respite care (in-home and out-of-home). Intervening processes also include resources within the individual, such as coping style and adaptiveness, personal control, appraisal of efficacy, health status, knowledge, and resiliency. Kramer's model accounts for the relationship between strong social support and caregiver gains, and for the relationship between reduced support and perceptions of increased caregiver burden. The model also accounts for poor or declining health among caregivers, leading to negative outcomes, increased strain, and a higher incidence of depression (Kramer, 1997a).

In reviewing 29 studies of the positive aspects of caregiving, Kramer carefully noted some of the methodological weaknesses in this type of research. These include

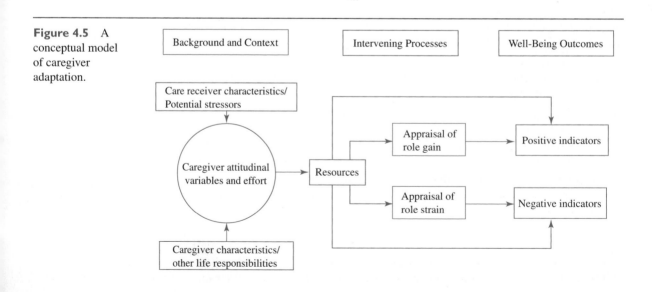

Figure 4.5 A conceptual model of caregiver adaptation.

Husbands as Caregivers for Wives with Dementia

The majority of studies of caregiving have focused on those who most often provide direct intervention and services: women. This is certainly the case for spousal care among the frail elderly. Studies may have oversampled women and may not generalize to today's cohort of older men engaged in caregiving for their wives (Harris, 1995; Kramer, 1997b). Only relatively recently has gender been a focus in studies of caregivers (Harris, 1995). The role of spousal caregiver may be differently experienced emotionally, cognitively, and socially by husbands. It is not clear whether women experience or express greater feelings of burden from caretaking than men; however, males have been found to experience depression in caring for their wives with Alzheimer's disease. Moreover, males who are caregivers to a spouse with Alzheimer's are in poorer overall health than men who are not caregivers (Fuller-Jonap & Haley, 1995). When compared with women, older males appear to have different needs for and different responses to available services both in the community and from friends and relatives.

Based on interviews with husbands, Harris (1995) identified four types of caregiving roles assumed by spouses whose wives suffered from AD: Worker, Labor of Love, Sense of Duty, and At the Crossroads. The Workers modeled their spousal caregiving after their work role. They established small offices in their homes to manage the HMO, Medicare, and Blue Cross paperwork as well as keeping careful track of bills, payments made, and scheduled medical visits. The Labor of Love role described husbands who cared for their wives out of love and devotion, not duty. These husbands continually talked about the love they felt in providing care for their wives. The Sense of Duty role was characterized by husbands who felt highly responsible, conscientious, and committed to the caretaking role; they would never abandon their spouses. Finally, the group of husbands "At the Crossroads" were in the initial period of coping with their wives' disease and were in crisis. They were exploring options for their wives' care as well as beginning to develop a routine system for managing regular caretaking needs associated with AD.

Kramer (1997b) examined the various predictors of positive gain and negative burden experienced by 74 husbands engaged in the role of caregiver for their wives with dementia. Qualitative studies in the past have suggested that most husbands are reluctant to share their inner feelings with others and try to bear up as long as possible with the burden of caretaking. While stoic and reserved, husbands have identified their own feelings of "pride, gratification, satisfaction" in managing the caretaking role. Kramer's cross-sectional study revealed specific stressors, background characteristics of the husbands, and availability of resources that

Box Figure 4.A The buffering effect of (1) duration of illness and (2) satisfaction with social participation on strain in husbands caring for wives with dementia.

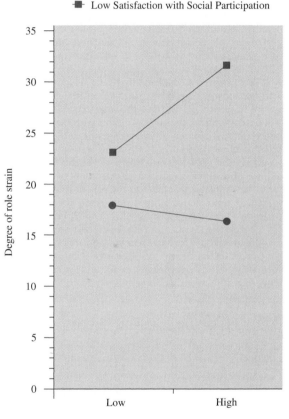

- High Satisfaction with Social Participation
- Low Satisfaction with Social Participation

Degree of role strain

Duration of caregiving

were predictive of husbands' perceptions of gains and losses in providing care to their wives. As in other research, the length of time spent in the caretaking role and the degree of memory difficulties and problem behaviors for the care recipient were predictive of negative burden or role strain. Husbands who experienced higher levels of strain were in poorer health, less satisfied with their level of social interaction, and relied more on emotion-focused coping strategies. Box figure 4.A shows one of the most important results of the regression analysis: The longer husbands spent in the caretaking role and the more satisfied they were with their level of social participation with family and friends, the less role strain or burden they experienced. And husbands also showed positive gains predicted from their satisfaction with social participation, higher levels of health, and greater use of problem-focused coping strategies.

Interestingly, the only personal or background characteristic predictive of caregiver burden for husbands was the health status of the caregiver. When predictors of positive gain in the role of caregiver were examined, a different picture emerged. Husbands' level of education was inversely related to positive outcomes of the caretaking role. Those with lower levels of education derived the highest benefits. The relationship suggesting that lower education is predictive of husbands' perceptions that they have derived positive outcomes from the caretaking role with their wives has been confirmed in two other studies, one with white adult children as caregivers and one with African-American caregivers' (Miller, 1989; Picot, 1995). However, Kramer (1993b) did not obtain this result in an earlier study of caregivers', wives. It is arguable that perhaps the role of caregiver is devalued by more educated husbands when compared with their own previous type of employment (Kramer, 1997b). Or, alternatively, husbands with less education may have lower expectations for their success than wives in the caregiving role. Males appear to place significant value in the caretaking role as a purposeful, direct, and instrumental activity (e.g., it provides a concrete direction for action).

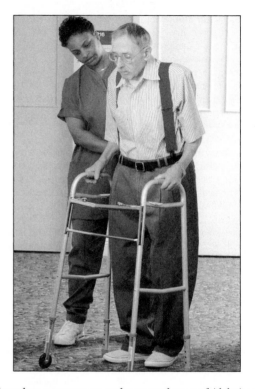

When the management and personal care of Alzheimer's patients becomes too complex and burdensome, nursing home care is sought by most families.

the use of heterogeneous samples that lump together different groups of caregivers (e.g., spouses, adult children, relatives, and friends); the paucity of studies examining gender effects and specifying the type of relationship (e.g., husband versus wife caregiving, adult male child versus adult female child caregiving); the failure to recognize that caregivers are at different points in their caregiving careers; and an overreliance on cross-sectional and quantitative data (see Research Focus 4.3 for a perspective on husbands acting as caregivers to their spouses). It has also been difficult to develop clear and unambiguous definitions of both independent and dependent measures in this research, which makes it difficult to compare studies. Finally, the richness and meaning of the caregiving role is often missing in simple quantitative indicators of caregiver gain or loss. Qualitative research studies highlight the positive value of caretaking. The positive benefits that caregivers identify include: (1) past memories of meaningful relationships with the recipient, (2) feelings of appreciation from the recipient, (3) efficacy and satisfaction with the quality of care they provide, (4) positive relationships within the larger social system, and (5) enhanced feelings of self-worth, mastery, and individual growth as a person. Clearly the gains derived from the role of caregiving include both knowledge and skills as well as emotional enhancements (e.g., growth in self-knowledge, self-awareness, and well-being).

Race and Ethnicity

Folkman and Moskowitz (2000) have noted the importance of a caregiver's social resources and appraisal of the stressful situation in coping research. Both factors mediate successful adaptation, and both have been studied in relation to race and ethnicity. When depressive symptoms among white and black caregivers are compared, black caregivers generally report fewer symptoms. Black caregivers find the responsibility results in fewer intrusions into their lives, causes less of a subjective burden, and produces fewer role conflicts than white caregivers report (Aranda & Knight, 1997; White, Townsend, & Stephens, 2000). In similar fashion, black caregivers report less stress overall in the role, experience less subjective burden, and derive greater personal rewards from parent care (Hughes et al., 1999).

A recent investigation studied the impact of multiple roles on depressive symptoms in black and white women. The women were between 55 and 64 years of age and had cared for a child at home or for an elderly parent or in-law during the past year. Reflecting contemporary black families' experiences, the roles included marriage, employment, care provider, grandmother, and volunteer. Depressive symptoms overall were higher among black women, contrary to other research (Connel & Gibson, 1997). These women were more likely to fill the roles of both caregiver and grandmother than white women. Both groups of women had fewer depressive symptoms if they had marriage and employment roles; however, compared to white women, black women were less likely to occupy these two roles, which were also associated with greater psychological and economic benefits. Employment was most effective in reducing the number of depressive symptoms for black women (Cochran, Brown, & McGregor, 1999).

The strong relationship between caregivers' sense of mastery and psychological well-being has been studied almost exclusively with whites. Caregivers with higher mastery derive greater feelings of psychological well-being. In two studies comparing black caregivers with whites, race was not related to mastery and psychological well-being (Miller et al., 1995; White et al., 2000). Other research examining the prior and current relationship between caregiving daughters and their mothers has found racial differences. Mui (1992) found that the quality of the relationship with the parent predicted more role conflict for white caregivers, but had no effect on role conflict for black caregivers.

Explanations for these results center on fundamental differences in values and principles within cultures. White et al. (2000) has summarized these values and principles and their influence in blacks' attitudes towards aging, their role expectations for caregivers, and their religious beliefs. Black families hold more positive attitudes towards the elderly and treat the aged with dignity and respect. They have a cultural expectation to provide care for older relatives and to fulfill this responsibility despite role conflict (Haley et al., 1996). The sense of obligation to care for others arises from religion and faith, central to the lives of many of these families. This may elevate the role of care provider to a "higher calling" and give the caregiver more inner strength and emotional resources to better manage the stresses associated with caregiving than are found in many white families.

In Korean culture, adult sons and their families are expected to provide for their aging parents. Daughters-in-law are expected to care for their in-laws with AD and handle the majority of the day-to-day responsibilities. Unlike caregivers in black families, Korean family caregivers carry out the duties of caregiving as obligations. Comparisons of traditional families living in Korea, Korean families living in the United States, and white American families who cared for a parent showed that **familism** (e.g., shared family goals, mutual support, unity, in-group emotional identification) was highest among traditional Koreans and lowest among whites in the United States, with immigrant families in between (Youn, Knight, Jeong, & Benton, 1999). Traditional Korean caregivers received little emotional support or help with the physical demands of caregiving from other family members. Similar to other studies of Korean caregivers (e.g., Choi, 1993), this study found that the lack of emotional support and help led caregivers in traditional Korean families to feel trapped and abandoned, rather than valued and appreciated. Familism in this culture contributed to higher levels of caregiver burden and anxiety. In the United States, studies of the caretaking role of daughters and daughters-in-law have been conducted to compare caring for a parent or an in-law. Regardless of the relationship, caregiving produced highly similar patterns and subjective perceptions of stress (primary and secondary appraisal) as well as a general caregiver burden (Peters-Davis, Moss & Pruchno, 1999).

It is more common for elderly Hispanic individuals to move in with their adult children than for other ethnic elderly. This culture has established an expectation to provide care and support in the homes of adult children, rather than turning to impersonal professionals in institutions or community organizations. This cultural support can reduce the level of stress the extended family encounters when an older parent moves in with an adult child initially, but it can also lead to problems as caregiving demands escalate (Speare & Avery, 1993).

Coping Effectively with Stress: Personality, Social Interaction, and Well-Being

In a classic longitudinal study, Marjorie Fiske (1980) assessed the balance between inner resources and deficits among men and women at different stages of life, the relationship between those resources and deficits, and the individual's sense of well-being. Looked at separately, inner resources and deficits are related to life satisfaction in an entirely rational fashion. People with the most resources (such as the capacity for mutuality, growth, competence, hope, and insight) tend to be satisfied with themselves and their lives; those with deficits (psychological symptoms, including anxiety, hostility, and self-hatred) are the least satisfied. But these expected results were found among fewer than one-third of the people studied. Among the other two-thirds, a combination of many positive and negative attributes seemed to increase the individual's sense of well-being. Coping is also influenced by personality dispositions including optimism, neuroticism, and extraversion (Folkman & Moskowitz, 2000).

Well-being and physical health among the elderly have been reported to be related (Angel & Angel, 1995). Well-being includes physical and mental health, financial resources, and social involvement. It is one quantifiable way to represent *caregiver burden,* a term that can be too general for research studies.

Depression leads to reduced involvement with the social environment. It is a common outcome coexisting with a variety of physical illnesses: arthritis, cancer, chronic lung disease, neurological diseases, and heart conditions (Angel & Angel, 1995; Katon & Sullivan, 1990). Well-being is enhanced with higher levels of social interaction and is reduced among adults who have no close confidants and no regular companions (Kramer, 1997b). The elderly with better health are able to initiate and sustain more contacts with their families than those in poorer health (Field, Minkler, Falk, & Leino, 1993). Emotional closeness between the healthier elderly and their families is possible through the mechanism of reciprocity (i.e., mutual giving and receiving of social, tangible, and emotional support). Reciprocity is less likely among family members and the elderly who are in poorer health (Field et al., 1993). This was confirmed as well in a cross-cultural investigation among the rural elderly in China (Shi, 1993). Elderly Chinese with greater resources (such as health, income, and education) were more likely to provide rather than receive assistance in their family social support networks; exchanges were most often in the form of emotional support and/or behavioral assistance (Shi, 1993).

Friendships established earlier in life are frequently maintained through the later years. The degree of contact older persons have with friends and family is nearly comparable to the levels of earlier ages (Rook, 2000). Age by itself is not a good predictor of the type and frequency of social interaction when compared with more powerful variables such as gender, ethnicity, and social class (Antonnuci & Akiyama, 1991a). However, social networks contract around age 70 and then increase dramatically as family members begin to help with daily activities, most typically a necessity near age 85.

Social networks generally become smaller as people age, although many maintain close friendships in the later years. Social activity or frequency of interaction also declines as people age. Since social support is essential to well-being, investigators have studied these age-related changes. Carstensen and her associates have theorized that reductions in social contact are related to changes in the underlying motivation for social interaction (Carstensen, 1998; Rook, 2000). Social interaction stems from three primary psychological motives: (1) acquisition of information, (2) support of self-concept, and (3) regulation of emotion. The first two motives are largely characteristic of younger people, while the elderly are motivated largely by regulating their emotions. Thus, the elderly are more selective in their social interactions and engage in fewer social exchanges. Carstensen's **socioemotional selectivity theory** reflects elderly adults' choices—to engage in fewer social exchanges, selecting people whose companionship they enjoy and who contribute positively to their emotional life. Older adults do not bother with social interactions that are not emotionally rewarding. They find older, closer friendships emotionally gratifying and are likely to preserve them, while treating superficial social exchanges as less emotionally rewarding and therefore expendable. Older adults seem to feel they have limited time for social exchange, and they allocate this time to only those social networks that bring them emotional satisfaction (Rook, 2000).

Many challenges to coping emerge at the same time that the social network changes. Retirement and relocation to retirement communities are two examples. Older adults can compensate for the loss of neighbors and coworkers by finding substitutes for missing network ties, redefining their social needs, or developing nonsocial activities such as hobbies or solitary leisure pursuits (Rook, 2000). Some people are able to replace key members of their social network with other people, either from among former friends or by creating new friendships. Widows sometimes redefine their social needs by broadening their definitions of friendships to include casual social contacts; this allows them to compensate for their limited opportunities to socialize (Johnson & Troll, 1994; Rook, 2000).

Ryff and Keyes (1995) identified six unique dimensions of well-being: (1) positive relations with others, (2) self-acceptance, (3) a purposeful life or sense of meaning, (4) autonomy, (5) environmental mastery, and (6) continued personal growth. Distinctive age trajectories correlate with each of these six dimensions. Figure 4.6 shows that two components of well-being, environmental mastery and positive relations with others, increase with age, whereas two others, personal growth and purpose in life, show significant declines as individuals age. Ryff (1995) also reports gender differences on two components of well-being. Women of all ages reported higher levels of positive relations with others and higher levels of personal growth than men. This may, in part, explain why social support is one of the more critical dimensions contributing to well-being and reducing stress among elderly women. As Kramer (1997a) notes, well-being is no longer considered a single unitary construct, but a multidimensional entity. Examine Research Focus 4.4 for additional insights into the construct of psychological well-being.

Autonomy and Control

Mental health experts recognize the importance of providing the elderly with a sense of control and autonomy. Older persons need to do all they can to remain in charge of their lives. Preservation of mental and physical function, positive affect, and decreases in dependency are the direct results of supportive but not overly intrusive assistance (Seeman, Bruce, & McAvay, 1996). Older people encounter many circumstances that limit their sense of autonomy and control. These include physical impairments, reduced economic resources, and changes in residence (Seeman et al., 1996).

In some studies, researchers have observed that genuine concern may lead a caregiver or human service professional to do too much for an older person. Spouses, relatives, and friends may assume too much responsibility for those faced with disability, illness, and even dementia. Too much helping may unintentionally produce decreased physical function, anxiety, lowered motivation, depression, greater dependency, a loss of sense of control and autonomy, reduced feelings of well-being and life satisfaction, and deficits in cognitive and motor performance among the elderly (Taylor et al., 1997). In a study of elderly over the age of 85, Johnson and Barer (1993) found that coping and a sense of control were associated with a high degree of well-being. Most of the el-

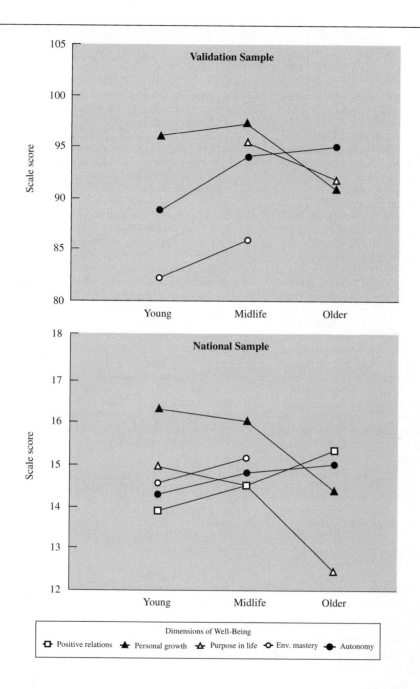

Figure 4.6 Self-ratings on the six dimensions of well-being for young, middle-aged, and older adults. The top graph shows scores from the original sample. Scores on a 20-item scale range from 20 to 120. The bottom graph shows scores from a national sample. Scores on a 3-item scale range from 3 to 18. Only results showing significant age differences are graphed. *Source: Ryff, C. (1995). Psychological well-being in adult life.* Current Directions in Psychological Science, 4(4), 99–104.

derly's coping strategies were directed at specific problems, and they identified these problems by narrowing the social and physical boundaries of their environments. The elderly in this study appear to have redefined themselves (e.g., their long-term survivorship, health status, physical functioning) and moved from a future-oriented to a present-oriented time frame to produce a greater sense of control.

Well-Being and Happiness

The search for factors that promote well-being and happiness comes from outside the traditional theories of psychology. Most psychological theories have focused on the origins of mental disorders, psychological problems, anxieties, and adjustment difficulties. They assumed that the absence of such issues led to well-being, positive outcomes, and overall happiness. The absence of pathology, however, does not guarantee well-being and a positive emotional state.

David G. Myers (1993), in his book *The Pursuit of Happiness: Discovering the Pathway to Fulfillment, Well-Being, and Enduring Joy,* has approached this idea from a totally different perspective. His understanding of contemporary research suggests that well-being and happiness are highly related to four positive traits: (1) high self-esteem, (2) optimism, (3) outgoing personality, and (4) strong belief in the ability to control and master the environment. Well-being is also related to exercise and a positive physical self-image, to the presence of a warm supportive social network of friends, a nurturing marriage, religious commitment and spiritual faith, and the ability to establish realistic expectations and attainable personal goals. To this list, Myers adds the importance of deriving meaning and personal satisfaction from one's work, friendships, and family relationships. It is critical to be well-matched in these areas to derive a sense of well-being and happiness.

The sense of well-being does not show much change across the life span. Well-being and happiness are relatively impermeable to the culturally sanctioned methods that are supposed to enhance them. For example, studies do not find that financial success leads to greater happiness.

The sense of well-being and happiness does appear to be modifiable, according to Myers. His findings suggest the following principles to increase well-being and happiness.

1. When adults are encouraged to behave and speak as if they were happy, optimistic, positive, and in control, they begin to change their basic attitudes and enhance their sense of well-being and personal happiness. Act happy, and you will become happier.
2. Live in the present and savor every moment, regardless of whatever else might be occurring in other spheres of life or what may be in store for the future.
3. Enjoy what you do, especially your work. Become totally invested in work or hobbies that match your personal skills, talents, and unique interests.
4. Develop a sense of mastery by establishing a timetable for accomplishing small goals that ultimately lead to the very important larger goals of life. Feedback and success are important to help maintain direction and enthusiasm.
5. Begin or continue to be involved in regular exercise to maintain physical health.
6. Engage in the process of downward comparison, which allows people to appreciate what they have and what they have accomplished. Comparing yourself with those in worse situations helps you focus on the positive features of your life.
7. Emphasize and make time for close personal relationships, both family and friends.
8. Rekindle your spirituality and practice your religious faith.

Source: Myers, D. G. (1993). The pursuit of happiness: Discovering the pathway to fulfillment, well-being, and enduring personal joy. New York: Avon Books.

When residents of nursing homes and other institutions feel they have control and autonomy, beneficial outcomes result. Interventions include providing choice over the timing of a change in living arrangements; providing options for residents to select in their nursing home environment; giving residents control over the length and timing of student volunteer visits; and having residents care for pets and plants (Langer & Rodin, 1976; Rodin, 1986). These interventions have been reported to improve health, emotions, subjective well-being and satisfaction, activity levels, eating, and sleeping. Encouraging control and autonomy also means discouraging well-intentioned caregivers from **infantilizing** the elderly—treating them as cute children rather than dignified adults. Overprotecting and infantilizing robs the elderly of their dignity, self-worth, mastery, and sense of achievement.

Coping with Loss: Aging and Driving

One of the most important signs of autonomy and control is the freedom afforded adults who can drive a car (Campbell, Bush, & Hale, 1993). For individuals in our society, driving provides the ability to maintain an independent lifestyle, whether residing in a rural environment or in an urban center (Burns, 1999). Among the cohort of older people today, men, in particular, associate driving with independence and are most reluctant to forgo their driving privileges. Persson (1993) revealed the value older adults place on driving in this interview: "Driving is a way of holding on to your life. I was 94 years old, and it was like losing my hand to give up driving." When they were asked to identify what they missed about being able to drive, the subjects in this study responded most often with the following three words: *independence, convenience,* and *mobility* (Persson, 1993). Only a few decades ago, most elderly drivers were males; women who held driving licenses were small in number, often learning to drive later in life. Driving a car is the most frequently used method of travel for older people in the United States, Canada, and England (Burns, 1999). Yet, in one study in the early 1990s, nearly 40 percent of adults over 65 had never driven a car themselves (Marottoli et al., 1993). By the year 2050, drivers 55 years of age and older will comprise 39 percent of all drivers (Persson, 1993).

Society is concerned about the safety of older drivers because of the increased likelihood of impairments in physical, visual, and cognitive capacities (Campbell et al., 1993). There is no unified approach to assessing the driving skills of older individuals, nor is there agreement on using the vision screening tests currently required by all states for an older person's license renewal (Persson, 1993). Investigators have found that the physical skills necessary for safe driving decline dramatically by age 75. However, there is evidence that driving can be problematic even in late middle age. The National Research Council reported that for adults 65 to 74, vehicular crashes are the leading cause of accidental death; for adults 75 and older, they are the second leading cause (next to falls) (Persson, 1993). Studies have shown that as they age, older drivers have difficulty reading signs, particularly at night. In recognition of this, the Canadian government has recommended a ratio of letter size to distance be established for road signs and has also recommended the creation of minimum levels of illumination for signs at night (Charness & Bosman, 1990). When visual images or pictorial signs are used instead of lettered signs, no age differences are reported among younger, middle-aged, and older drivers. As people age, they report increased difficulty driving at night (poor night vision) and overall difficulties navigating.

Burns (1999) defines navigational difficulties as those involving *route planning,* or the preparations people make before driving on unfamiliar roads; and those involving *wayfinding,* or the decisions needed to follow a route and reach an intended destination. Older people appear to have more difficulty with spatial relations and finding their way by reading a map. They take longer to extract information from a route map and may miss key landmarks and information posted on road signs. One way of coping with these navigational problems is to reduce the amount of driving they do. Older drivers drive more than 50 percent fewer miles than younger drivers. They drive fewer miles each week, take fewer trips each week, and generally drive less frequently. Most experts believe that improving road signs would be of great help to older drivers. Newer in-car global positioning navigational systems will also help (Burns, 1999).

Visual acuity and peripheral vision show loss beginning in the fifties, and it becomes more difficult to engage in **dual-processing tasks.** Driving demands this type of physical and visual-cognitive processing of complex and dynamic information; for example, yielding the right of way at an intersection requires complex dual task performance (Kline et al., 1992; Persson, 1993). In one investigation, drivers from 22 to 92 years old were surveyed to evaluate any visual difficulties they encountered in routine driving tasks. The study found that older drivers experienced more problems with routine tasks: unexpected vehicles, vehicle speed, dim displays, windshield problems, and sign reading. These data, plotted as a function of age, appear in figure 4.7. They suggest that the declines in visual functioning reported in other studies are related to the perceived experiences of older drivers. Kline and colleagues (1992) also found the data in figure 4.7 were related to the types of automobile accidents most frequently occurring among older drivers.

The decision to stop driving completely is a difficult one for older persons to make. Campbell and colleagues (1993) found that nearly 50 percent of older drivers who had ceased driving completely, despite the vast majority maintaining a valid license, identified medical reasons for their decision. Specific factors in their decision to stop driving included visual impairments (macular degeneration, retinal hemorrhage), deficits in functional ability (e.g., the ability to physically carry through other daily living tasks), Parkinson's disease, stroke and stroke-related residual paralysis or weak-

Figure 4.7 Mean reported difficulty on visual driving tasks as a function of age.

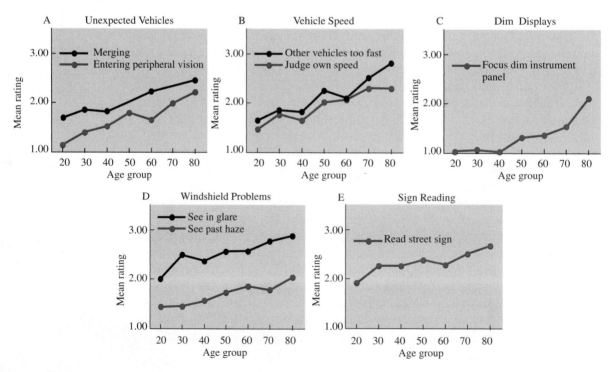

ness, episodes of losing consciousness, and Alzheimer's disease (Campbell et al., 1993; Gilley et al., 1991; Kline et al., 1992; McLay, 1989).

There are people diagnosed with AD who continue to drive for many years. They usually drive slowly, avoid heavy traffic, and easily get lost. Persuading people with AD who wish to drive that they must stop is often difficult; families are likely to enlist the support of doctors, lawyers, insurance agents, or close friends. At times, families have taken away the keys to the car, hidden the keys, disabled the vehicle by disconnecting the battery or starter, or requested that the police or motor vehicle agency suspend the person's license. Now, many states are requiring doctors to report suspected diagnoses of AD to the motor vehicle agency responsible for issuing driving licenses. The rate of traffic accidents is high for older drivers with Alzheimer's disease, reportedly 20 times the average number of accidents per mile as compared to adults of similar ages who do not have AD (*Harvard Mental Health Letter,* 1995a, 1995b).

Some older adults decide to stop driving based on their own assessment of their abilities, their age, the presence of neurologic disease, cataracts, and other limiting disabilities. However, social and economic factors also play a role (Campbell et al., 1993). Among a group of older drivers (Marottoli et al., 1993), 40 percent had stopped driving within the past six years due to physical or visual impairment, increased physical disability, or social factors (economics and retirement). Though all of these factors combined to predict the total cessation of driving, the single best predictor of driving cessation was a social factor, "no longer working." In another investigation, Persson (1993) asked elderly adults to identify why they had stopped driving. The reasons included advice from a physician, increased anxiety while driving, trouble seeing pedestrians and other cars, medical conditions, and advice from family and friends.

Persson (1993) reports that among older adults still driving, 42 percent drive more than 5,000 miles per year. Those who drive more than 5,000 miles have higher incomes, are still employed, are most often male, and are relatively younger and less disabled than those who drive fewer miles or do not drive at all. Other studies suggest that older drivers voluntarily adjust their driving habits in terms of frequency, length of trips, speed, time of day (e.g., daylight hours rather than evening), miles driven, and avoid peak traffic or superhighways (Burns, 1999). Although older individuals can and do make the decision to stop or reduce their driving themselves, little research has examined how the elderly perceive their own driving skills. Some studies report that older drivers individually believe they are both safer and more skilled than other drivers of a similar age (Persson, 1993). It is interesting that older individuals apparently ignore some factors related to safety, such as hearing loss or cognitive difficulties, in making assessments of their own driving skills and abilities. One of the respondents in Persson's investigation jokingly remarked, "I can barely hear, barely see, and barely walk. Things could be worse, though. At least I can still drive." Perhaps this reflects a bias in the sample of respondents typically surveyed—that is, community-residing and ambulatory older adults (Campbell et al., 1993). The point in much of the research is that while most older adults voluntarily decide to stop driving, many elderly individuals with identical problems and circumstances believe they can continue to drive and indeed do so, often in the face of physical problems. For example, consider the presence of medical conditions such as **syncope** (pronounced sin-co-pee; losing consciousness). Florida, along with 13 other states, requires patients with this condition to undergo a

12-month driving suspension. Yet, a recent analysis revealed that 65 percent of older people with syncope continued to drive (Campbell et al., 1993).

It remains difficult to limit the independence and autonomy of older drivers even when conditions appear to warrant revocation of driving privileges. Yet it should be clear from the national statistics on automobile accidents that older persons are increasingly at risk, with a higher rate of accidents than any other age group except teenagers (Insurance Institute for Highway Safety, 1992). Persson (1993) found that physicians have the most authoritative voices when it comes to convincing older adults to stop driving. Adults must realize that with increased age, there truly are declines in some of the basic skills needed to successfully perform the complex task of driving a car.

Religion, Spirituality, and Coping

Until recently, many gerontologists overlooked the importance of religion in the lives of older persons. In a Gallup poll of persons 65 years of age and older, 76 percent identified religion as a very important part of their lives, while an additional 16 percent indicated it was fairly important. More than 52 percent of older adults report attending religious services weekly, 27 percent read the Bible two or more times a week, and nearly 25 percent pray at least three times each day. Adults with the least education have the highest degree of religious participation. Older adults with the lowest levels of self-worth had the least religious commitment (Kraus, 1995a). Ethnically identified and minority elderly have high levels of religious attendance and deep religious faith. Professionals are increasingly recognizing the spiritual needs of older people as part of their mental and physical health.

Spirituality and Religion

There is considerable variability in how investigators have defined and measured spirituality and religion. McFadden (1996) differentiates between functional and substantive definitions of religion. The former highlights the role of religion in giving meaning to life and in providing direction for behaviors leading to social control or psychological support. Substantive definitions of religion focus on the link between a higher power and human existence. Spirituality is also difficult to define conceptually. Some experts consider **spirituality** to be the motivational and emotional cause of the human **search for meaning.** Spirituality usually refers to an individually experienced connection to a higher being. There is an emotional dimension to spirituality, a "felt" experience that provides a sense of connectedness and transcendence.

Obviously, religion and spirituality represent two separate, multidimensional concepts for which a variety of measures can be derived. Most studies employ cross-sectional designs and offer little insight into the patterns of religious belief, commitment, spirituality, and practices of individuals over time. Religion appears easier to measure quantitatively through church or synagogue attendance or degree of religious belief when compared with the complex components involved in assessments of spirituality. Traditional research methods may not be sensitive to all dimensions of spirituality; some of these dimensions may require in-depth individual interviews to assess the meaning individuals derive from their religious faith and commitment (Thomas & Eisenhandler, 1994).

Spirituality, Health, and Coping

Spiritual feelings and beliefs appear to be related to health. Adults report spirituality contributes to enhanced feelings of well-being, inner emotional peace, and satisfaction with life (Marcoen, 1994). Spirituality and participation in formal religious services are regularly identified elements in the lives of many centenarians. Older adults who attend religious services regularly and participate in the formal structures of an organized religion show improved health status, reduced incidence of chronic disease, and more effective coping with stress (Hoeger & Hoeger, 1995). According to some religions, illness can be a "test of faith" or a punishment for sins, and spiritual reasons to avoid illness may even underlie the health-promoting behaviors of the elderly (McFadden, 1996). The importance of social support, as well as the opportunity to give to others in times of need, have been identified as part of the reason that spirituality and religious participation have a positive influence on health.

For the elderly, spirituality is one mode of connecting themselves to God (McFadden, 1996). Spirituality has been linked to hopefulness among nursing home residents (Gubrium, 1993) and underlies the use of prayer in coping with illness and terminal disease. Spirituality is the most frequently addressed topic of home hospice visits with the terminally ill, with death anxiety a distant second (Reese & Brown, 1997). Hospice programs need to consider this important dimension in their service delivery and intervention programs. In another study of how hospice patients cope with terminal illness, those with greater spiritual strength and ego strength were best able to buffer their response to upcoming death. Spiritual and ego strength helped hospice patients overcome their fears of death, view themselves as "whole," and affirm death as a new, challenging, and transformational experience (Kazanjian, 1997).

Religion, Health, and Coping

Among adult populations, religion serves an organizing function. It helps individuals to derive meaning, a sense of purpose, and a coherent framework for their lives (Pargament, 1997). There is mounting evidence that religion and psychological well-being are represented by a U-shaped model. That is, psychological well-being is highest among those who either have a high degree of religious belief or no religious commitment at all; adults with a moderate commitment to their religious beliefs and those with doubts showed the greatest psychological distress and a reduced sense of well-being (Krause, 1995a; Krause, Ingersoll-Dayton, Ellison, and Wulff, 1999). Religion has been linked consistently to longevity, improved health status (e.g., reduced risk of cardiovascular disease and less hypertension), higher self-esteem, and improved psychological well-being (Simons-Morton, Greene, & Gottlieb, 1995; McFadden, 1996). Private prayer has been considered a form of spiritual coping. It is common among those who have had open-heart surgery and is related to better psychological recovery. Private prayer was found to reduce depression and general stress even a year after surgery (Ai, Dunkle, Peterson, and Bolling, 1998).

Competing views attempt to explain the beneficial effects of religious involvement on well-being and subjective health status. Religion serves older persons as an anchor, providing not only continuity to earlier periods in their lives but also stability as "individuals begin to disengage from other roles and formal institutional involvements due to retirement, declining health, or other reasons" (Levin, Markides, & Ray, 1996, p. 461). Older people also report that religion serves as the strategy they most frequently choose to help them cope. Prayer and exercising faith are the most frequent and most effective strategies adopted (McFadden, 1996).

There are different views as to why religious belief leads to effective coping. First, religion provides spiritual support: it provides a belief in a compassionate higher spiritual being who cares for all people, an opportunity to gain pastoral care, and the chance to participate in a variety of religious activities. A church, mosque, or synagogue also provides the elderly with access to regular social support from congregants. Many older adults participate in social programs and volunteer for community service to benefit others. Families may not be the only or the most important source of social support for older adults (Grams and Albee, 1995). Ramsey and Blieszner (1999) found that belonging to a Christian religious community helped women cope with individual loss and the emotional stress of aging. Their faith community helped sustain these women through difficult times and helped them become more resilient. Religion also offers people a way to bring control and self-worth to their lives in times of stress. It offers a framework for deriving deeply personal and emotionally satisfying benefits: hopefulness, preservation of self, forgiveness, and reconciliation with God. Religion has special significance in helping people find meaning in their lives, especially when dealing with serious loss (Krause, 1998; Pargament, 1997). In a national study of more than 800 older retirees, religion was found to buffer the stresses associated with highly valued roles under certain conditions. Respondents with the least education, who relied on their religion to cope with losses in roles most central to their identities, lived longer. Religion contributed to their sense of meaning and gave them strength. However, religion had no impact on coping when stressors occurred in less salient roles (Krause, 1998). As older husbands transition into the role of caregiver for their wives with health problems (not dementia), they report an increase in their participation in religious activities. Caregiving husbands seem to seek religious activities as a substitute for a decline in emotional support. The religious organization provides social continuity and an accepting safe haven for husbands and their wives with health threats. Caregiving husbands were able to spend the same amount of time in social and recreational activities as those whose wives did not require caregiving (Kramer & Lambert, 1999).

Religion and Diversity

Religious participation serves the diverse populations of ethnic older persons especially well. Investigators have repeatedly noted the special significance that religion and religious attendance have on the well-being and life satisfaction of older persons from ethnically diverse backgrounds (Levin et al., 1996). Religion serves to connect such older persons to the cultural traditions and values of their parents, grandparents, and other relatives; it is an especially valued resource as older adults disengage from other roles, retire, and suffer health losses (Post, 1992). While religion offers continuity and hope to most practicing older adults, it particularly helps those from diverse backgrounds to gain a sense of control over their lives (Levin et al., 1996; Koenig, 1995). In Mexican-American as well as black older populations, religious participation plays a major role in well-being. Among a sample of older Mexican Americans and among black Americans, overall subjective health, well-being, and life satisfaction were directly related to religious attendance. For older Mexican Americans, regular religious attendance provided connectedness to both family and cultural traditions. The church, its membership, and its ministers provide social support in times of joy as well as during times associated with loss and conflict (Levin, Chatters, & Taylor, 1995; Levin et al., 1996).

Religion, according to some experts, plays a major role in meeting the physical and mental health needs of many ethnically and religiously diverse populations. For example, for Hispanics, the community (the family, the church, neighbors, and friends) offers social supports to meet the needs of older adults. The value of such primary group support may explain Hispanics' underutilization of programs such as public health clinics, a hypothesis formalized as **alternative resource theory.** Hispanics turn to their families or to the church to help solve their problems before they turn to secondary support groups, community services, or institutional programs provided by local, state, or federal governments (Rogler, Malgady, & Rodriguez, 1989). The inability of family or religious institutions to help them cope is a cultural stigma. Certainly with these central values, Hispanic elderly coping with health and mental health problems will exhaust their family and religious social support systems before they seek out professional care institutions and community agencies. In a recent study, foreign-born older Mexican Americans were more likely to reside in the homes of their adult children when compared with their counterparts born in the United States. Factors related to the decision to reside with an adult child were mutual help, economic needs, and declining health (Angel, Angel, McClellan, & Markides, 1996).

Religion and Aging

There is little consistent support for the view that religious commitment and religious practice change with increasing age (McFadden, 1996). Some studies report an increase in religious faith and practice, whereas others report stability from early adulthood to older age. Certainly, to investigate the meaning of one's religious faith across time, researchers must adopt a longitudinal strategy rather than the more common cross-sectional approaches employed to date. Most older persons appear to be content with their level of spirituality, faith, and time commitment to their religion, although a surprising 35 percent would like to be able to spend more time in religious pursuit (DeGenova, 1992). Some investigators have suggested a relationship between the documented changes in mature thinking (e.g., postformal thought, wisdom, awareness of multiple perspectives, integration of cognitive and emotional realities) and various developmental views of spirituality (the growth of faith, resolution of religious dilemmas and value conflicts, and spiritual questioning) (Fowler, 1981; Oser, 1991). Sinnott (1994) finds that spirituality is understood best from a cognitive developmental perspective. She suggests that the ability to recognize that one coexists at both a physical and spiritual level requires **postformal operational thought.** Thus, not all older individuals who seek spirituality will necessarily realize their goal, since postformal thought is not a universal style of thinking for all adults.

SUMMARY

The ability to cope and adapt to life is an essential dimension of adult life. Three views of coping have been suggested: the psychodynamic, the life-events, and the cognitive models. Historically, clinicians adopted the *psychodynamic view,* which emphasizes the role of defense mechanisms in coping with stress. In this view, coping defenses are associated with specific personality traits indicative of maturity. The *life-events view* emphasizes rankings of key experiences. The greater the stress associated with key life events, the more demands and resources an individual needs to be able to cope. This view neglects to consider subjective interpretations of events and the positive challenge of mastering change. Neugarten emphasized coping with life events that occur on-time versus off-time; this makes the social clock and predictable events in development more important than any specific life event. Lazarus's *cognitive model* of adaptation and coping has been adopted in many research studies. Individuals determine whether an event is stressful in a process called primary appraisal. Secondary appraisal is the process of choosing the resources that can best help the person cope with a stressful event. Resources may be environmental (problem-focused) or within the person (emotion-focused).

The relationship between aging and cognitive resources suggests that older adults cope effectively, tend to use well-practiced strategies, and are generally adaptive over time. Handling the daily hassles of life is a strong predictor of overall coping, morale, life satisfaction, and health. Uplifts counterbalance daily hassles and provide positive affect that helps people handle long-term stressors. They include routine events that people infuse with positive meaning, positive reappraisal of a situation, and problem-focused coping. Uplifts also serve as a buffer against depression for those providing care to chronically ill people.

Making sense of very stressful life events, such as death or a life-threatening illness, plays a central role in effective coping. This search for meaning gives adults a way to manage highly stressful situations. Downward social comparison promotes a positive view of self; upward social comparison provides models for self-improvement. In parallel fashion, adults adjust to age-related losses through the dual processes of accommodation (adjusting expectations) and assimilation (working to achieve attainable goals). Taken together as life management, these processes help aging adults maintain a positive view of self and a sense of control. Assessments of coping skills have relied primarily on between-group (nomothetic) comparisons of successful and less successful adaptation. To best understand the process of adaptation, more longitudinal studies are needed to obtain repeated measures of the same persons as they cope over time.

The demands of caregiving affect the entire family. According to the concept of gender consistency, daughters are most likely to care for their elderly mothers. The objective caregiver burden is identified as the multiple stresses the family experiences from competing demands (role conflict) for caregivers serving as spouses, parents, and members of the workforce. The subjective caregiver burden refers to the emotional impact of providing care. Caregivers experiencing the greatest demands are responsible for elders with severe memory impairments and disruptive behaviors.

Providing care to someone with AD is stressful and demanding; depressive symptoms are common among caregivers. Wives experience more depression than husbands in providing care for a spouse with AD; they are more sensitive to the loss of reciprocity in the marital relationship. Men experience comparable demands in providing care to a spouse with AD, but they perceive the burden as less stressful. The subjective burden is increased when caregivers feel trapped by their role. In the early stages, people with AD may be quite aware of their confusion and memory difficulties. They feel stigmatized by their disease and frightened about their futures.

Mediators of caregiver burden include a sense of mastery or efficacy, positive affect, social support, personality, financial resources, formal services, race, ethnicity, and the quality of the current and past relationship with the care recipient. Greater caregiver burden occurs as providers recognize the need to give more hours of care. Community programs and respite care may reduce caregiver burden; fitting programs to the values of certain ethnic communities will increase their participation. Respite programs temporarily free caregivers from their responsibilities.

Mastery, meaning, and personal efficacy can emerge from the role of caregiver. Other positive outcomes include personal achievement, pride, sense of closeness, empathy, and enhanced communication. Based on different motivational patterns and cultural expectations, black and Hispanic caregivers appear to experience less stress and burden than whites in the role of caregiver. However, when role strain is examined across a variety of different roles, whites are less likely to show depressive symptoms than blacks in the caregiving role. The obligatory care daughters-in-law in traditional Korean families must offer leads to high levels of caregiver burden and depression. Other family members offer little physical or emotional support.

Generally, well-being and physical health are related to personal resources, social interaction, and life-satisfaction. Friendships are important mediators of stress throughout development. The social network begins to contract at about 70 years of age; the number of social contacts increases by age 85 as the elderly need more help with activities of daily living. Older people maintain a social network with the friends who bring positive emotional value to their lives (socioemotional selectivity theory). Replacing members and redefining the social network are two strategies older adults employ.

Researchers have studied well-being extensively. Well-being consists of positive relations with others, self-acceptance, a purposeful or meaningful life, autonomy, environmental mastery, and continued personal growth. A sense of control enhances well-being; providing autonomy and choice to the elderly in nursing homes has beneficial outcomes for health, level of activity, eating, and sleeping. However, the loss of autonomy through infantilizing is a constant risk in institutional environments. Driving is a marker of adult autonomy. Elderly people have difficulty giving up this activity despite visual and cognitive changes that make driving more risky. Older drivers do make adjustments in driving frequency, mileage, time of day they drive, speed, and destinations. Many have navigational difficulties.

There is growing interest in the roles that religion and spirituality play in helping older people cope. Deep spirituality and private prayer give hope and strength to people facing serious health problems, but moderate religious beliefs actually reduce well-being. Religion is reported to be the most frequently used coping strategy of the elderly, especially among ethnically diverse populations. It is an alternate resource in the community, almost as strong a support as the family. Religion offers social support, pastoral care, and a faith (meaning and inner strength) to turn to in difficult times.

REVIEW QUESTIONS

1. Compare the life-events view of coping with the psychodynamic view. What are the basic objections to life-events research?
2. Prepare an outline of the basic features of Lazarus's cognitive model of adaptation and coping. Identify at least three criticisms of research that uses this model.
3. What is the significance of the Neugarten's social clock? Describe both an on-time and an off-time event and explain how each influences stress.
4. What are the three ways that women cope with breast cancer, according to Taylor's research? How does active distortion influence adaptation in this research, compared to its use as a defense mechanism?
5. What role do social comparison processes play in helping people cope with age-related losses?
6. Why do black caregivers show fewer depressive symptoms in caring for relatives with AD than white caregivers? Identify the methodological issues that might account for this pattern and help us understand it.
7. What are the factors that contribute to subjective burden? How do these factors differentially affect men and women?
8. What are the benefits that arise for those who provide care to a relative with AD?
9. Describe the importance of social and emotional support for caregivers of a relative with AD. How does the social support network for older adults differ from that for younger adults?
10. How do mastery, autonomy, and personal efficacy influence caregiver burden and caregivers' coping strategies?
11. Name four challenges that older drivers must face. How do they cope with each of them? Why is driving so important for older people?
12. What is the difference between *religion* and *spirituality?* How does each contribute to an older adult's ability to cope with stressful situations?
13. Describe the basic understanding people in the early stages of AD have as they cope with their disease. What are their short- and long-term concerns?

ON THE WEB   www.mhhe.com/hoyer5

Visit the text website to find links to the following web pages.

Administration on Aging: ElderPage for Older Persons and Their Families

A major government-sponsored site with dozens of web pages that provide caregivers with all types of resources and information. Includes a guide for caregivers, a locator to help caregivers identify local resources for special services, and links to key government agencies.

American Association for Retired Persons

This site has an excellent web page article on Caregiving: Driving and Transportation Concerns. The six pages detail excellent suggestions for older drivers and for those who provide care for the elderly. Tips on how to sensitively approach the topic of continued driving are helpful. Suggestions for alternative community services to transport older adults are also included as well as links to driving safety for elders and a link on independent living.

Caregiver Zone

A site with a complete range of resources, tips, and helpful links to other services. Every major topic related to caregiving is presented. Especially helpful is a section on preventing burnout and recognizing the signs of overload and burden.

CareThere.com

This site contains current information for caregivers seeking to locate local assistance for relatives who live far away. It has been designated a Kiplinger top website for caregivers.

Empowering Caregivers

A site developed by professionals in the caregiving field. In addition to extensive pages of information and guidelines for making residential choices, this site discusses healing music and alternative therapies for care recipients, plus provides inspirational messages for care providers, including prayer and emotional comfort.

Family Caregiving Alliance

A site with targeted information for relatives providing in-home care. It includes an online caregiver support network for caregivers to share their experiences with others in similar positions.

National Aging Information Center

Consult this government site for caregiver information and a listing of top not-for-profit websites as well as commercial sites marketing specialized services and products. The list of caregiver websites has been carefully reviewed and includes a resource directory site. There are also web pages specifically devoted to caregiver issues, care/case management, and Alzheimer's disease.

National Alliance for Caregiving

A site designed for the 22 million or more adults currently providing care to older adults so that they can remain independent in their homes and communities for as long as possible. There are specific pages for developing grassroots community programs, an excellent list of "Tips for Caregivers," and suggestions for preventing burnout.

Well Spouse Foundation

A site providing support for spousal caregivers. This association has a mentoring program, publications, an active regional program of sponsored events, and a virtual community/bulletin board for spousal caregivers to share their experiences and challenges with others.

5

MENTAL
HEALTH
INTERVENTIONS

> *Life is a matter about which we are lost if we reason either too much or too little.*
> —Samuel Butler II
>
> *To know how to grow old is the master work of wisdom, and one of the most difficult chapters in the great art of living.*
> —Amiel

INTRODUCTION

In this chapter, you will learn about methods that optimize and promote effective psychological functioning in older people. Prevention of mental health problems remains one of the keys to success. There are fewer professionals and programs than could ever meet the needs of the older population (Konnert, Gatz, & Hertzsprung, 1999). Implementing preventive programs requires an awareness of the diversity of older adults and sensitivity to their unique cultural, ethnic, and racial backgrounds. Prevention also implies knowledge of the communities in which people live so that professionals and families can help the elderly choose appropriate programs with documented success. Ideally, prevention implies a life-span approach in developing appropriate interventions.

Elderly people who experience difficulty coping and adapting turn to social support networks first, and much later to mental health professionals. Many of today's older adults are reluctant to seek professional help; others do not have ready access to services, and still others do not have the resources needed to use them. Cost, availability, accessibility, and breadth of services are all important considerations in meeting the mental health needs of older people. Common disorders include depression, anxiety, alcoholism, and adjustment to loss or functional disability. Therapeutic interventions include social support from the family, staff, and volunteers in the community as well as through community mental health programs. Older adults who have seriously impaired judgment may require legal protection from inappropriate, risky decisions.

Mental Health and Aging

Healthy People 2010 lists improving the nation's mental health as one of the specific public health goals of the U.S. Surgeon General (U.S. Department of Health and Human Services, 2000). The federal government has defined **mental health** in the same publication as

> a state of successful mental functioning resulting in productive activities, fulfilling relationships, and the ability to adapt to change and cope with adversity. It is indispensable to personal well-being, family, and interpersonal relationships and one's contribution to society.

This definition of mental health implies the absence of psychological disorders and stresses the positive outcomes of coping and adaptation. To effectively manage a wide range of life events, people must possess an accurate perception of reality; a sense of personal mastery; the capacity for independent, autonomous behavior; and positive self-esteem. Successful social relationships, a productive orientation to work and life, and self-actualization also enhance mental health. Since older adults are more likely than younger adults to have some type of physical illness, physical and mental health are more intensely interwoven in later adulthood than in younger adulthood (Deeg, Kardaun, & Fozard, 1996).

Despite the importance of meeting the mental health needs of older adults, many people with significant problems do not receive help. Currently, less than 3 percent of Medicare funding is used to support mental health in the United States. Estimates suggest that 66 to 90 percent of all nursing home residents have diagnosed mental disorders including dementia, yet only a tiny fraction receive treatment (Agronin, 1998; Smyer and Wilson, 1999). And a parallel shortage of outpatient services exists for community-residing adults over 65 years of age. Although older adults may consult their family physicians, these doctors are usually not trained to diagnose and recommend appropriate mental health treatment (Gatz, 2000a).

Aging itself has not been found to be related to an increase in mental health disorders. Gatz and colleagues (1996) estimated that about 22 percent of older adults (65 and over) may be classified as having a mental disorder as defined by the *Diagnostic and Statistical Manual of Mental Disorders of the American Psychiatric Association (DSM-IV)* (American Psychiatric Association, 1994). This percentage includes both cognitive impairments such as dementia as well as emotional disorders such as depression. Depression and other mood disorders are less prevalent in older adults (see figure 5.1).

Growing older does not necessarily increase the risk of mental health problems, but the numbers of older adults are increasing in most countries, and the wide variety of life circumstances older adults face creates a great deal of variability in mental health. For example, for some individuals, mental distress may increase with age as friends and loved ones die or chronic illness sets in; other older adults may show improvements in mental health as they retire from stressful jobs or finish caring for ill parents.

The **diathesis-stress model** describes the relationship between challenging life events (stress) and the individual's degree of frailty or vulnerability (diathesis). Figure 5.2 shows the model and highlights the relationships between life-event stressors and individual vulnerabilities. The threshold point is reached when stresses exceed the individual's capacity to handle them.

[Older adults with mental health problems are often individuals who may have had (a) the same disorder at one or more earlier points in development, (b) a problem in earlier development that blossoms into a more serious mental disorder as the individual ages, or (c) no evidence of any mental health problem earlier in development but one that appears in late life. Some authors suggest that older adults may be less vulnerable than younger adults. For example, some research suggests that older adults coping with physical illness show less anger, fear, or shame than younger persons. Older persons may have developed more successful strategies to cope with illness over their lives or may have adjusted their expectations to accept such problems (Deeg et al., 1996). Other investigators suggest that the severity of certain stressors, such as the loss of spouse, retirement, or relocation may be much harder on older persons than on younger persons. However, other research suggests that younger adults experience a greater num-

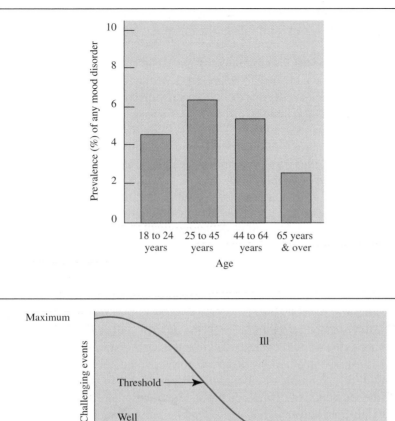

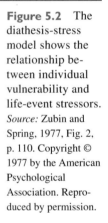

Figure 5.1 One-month prevalence rates of any mood disorder, including major depression, dysthymia, and bipolar disorder, drawn from Regier et al.'s (1988) results.

Figure 5.2 The diathesis-stress model shows the relationship between individual vulnerability and life-event stressors. *Source:* Zubin and Spring, 1977, Fig. 2, p. 110. Copyright © 1977 by the American Psychological Association. Reproduced by permission.

ber of negative events than the elderly. Chronic stress leading to mental disorders such as depression is far more characteristic of younger adults than of the elderly (Gatz, 2000). The risk of depression does not increase with advancing age unless special physical or medical problems occur or unless analyses are restricted to those over 90 years of age (Gatz et al., 1996). Even the patterns of depressive symptoms seen in the elderly are somewhat unique when compared with those of younger adults. Perhaps biological diathesis increases with advancing age.

Prevention and Mental Health

Preventing emotional problems remains one of the keys to success in the field of mental health and aging, given the shortage of trained professionals to work with the elderly (Konnert, Gatz, & Hertzsprung, 1999). As we previously mentioned, creating preventive programs requires an awareness of diversity among older adults and familiarity with high-quality programs in the communities in which older people live. Ideally, effective prevention programs would begin many years before mental health problems emerge (Smyer, 1995).

Preventive mental health programs for older adults can have different goals, including (1) to reduce the incidence of a disorder; (2) to reduce the severity or impact of a disorder; and (3) to eliminate the risk that the specific disorder will appear. Conceptually, prevention can thus occur at three levels. *Universal prevention* targets all individuals in a specific population, regardless of the risk of the disorder for any subgroup or individual; *selective prevention* is designed for those who are at risk for a disorder, but who have no current symptoms; and *indicated prevention* is designed for those who are at high risk of a disorder and are already showing some symptoms (Munoz, Mrazek, & Haggerty, 1996). Older adults are not at greater risk of developing mental health disorders than adults in other age groups. But mental health disorders such as depression are increasingly more likely as health problems and loss of functionality increase (Konnert et al., 1999).

Preventive services can directly target the elderly to reduce the risk of certain disorders. Alternatively, prevention may be indirect and benefit the elderly by targeting those who provide support to them. Indirect prevention, for example, might consist of regular support group meetings for family members providing care to a relative with Alzheimer's disease. Providing social support for caregivers will reduce the risk of depression in caregivers, enhance the care of the elderly, and reduce the risk that those with Alzheimer's disease will contract additional mental disorders. Indirect prevention might also consist of implementing programs for young adults to reduce the likelihood that they will develop chronic disease and health problems in old age. Ultimately, this will reduce the incidence of depression caused by functional disability.

We can illustrate *universal preventive interventions* through volunteer activities for older adults. Elderly volunteers may assist with organized activities in nursing homes, provide career advice to younger workers, provide business assistance to new owners, assist adolescents as surrogate parents, or interact with young children in latchkey programs or other intergenerational programs such as day care. Being needed and valued are essential ingredients that help volunteers maintain positive mental health. In some programs, benefits are greater for volunteers than for the people they assist (Konnert et al., 1999). Other examples of activities that serve as preventive programs include community education programs for older people and political advocacy groups such as the American Association of Retired Persons (AARP) or the Older Women's League (OWL). Community programs that promote universal prevention empower the elderly through action.

Selective preventive interventions target groups of elderly with common issues such as the loss of a spouse or social isolation. Selective interventions are designed to bolster older adults' psychological resources and coping abilities and strengthen their social support networks (Konnert et al., 1999). For example, some community programs enrich the lives of older adults who are socially isolated at home through friendly visits or daily phone calls. Other targeted programs link widows in social support groups.

Indicated preventive interventions include programs that maintain older people's independence and prevent institutionalization in a long-term care facility (Konnert et al., 1999). Visiting nurse programs, in-home health care services, or even Meals on Wheels fit this model of prevention. Having personal "emergency buttons" installed in the residences of frail elderly people or providing emergency call devices for those at high risk of falling to wear around their necks are other examples of indicated preventive interventions.

Utilization of Mental Health Services

Compared with younger adults, fewer older adults use mental health services. It has been suggested that older people hold many stereotypical views and inaccurate beliefs about mental health treatment and diagnoses (Harel & Biegel, 1995).

For example, elderly people may associate treatment with institutionalization in a hospital or psychiatric center or with outmoded labels like "nervous breakdown." They often assume that treatments for mental disorders such as depression are not generally successful. They may be embarrassed by mental health problems, believing that such disorders should be hidden from family and friends or that the person with a disorder should be isolated from the community. Some fear that such disorders will leave a stigma on other family members or may consider mental health problems a sign of genetic weakness. Older persons have not been socialized to self-disclose or discuss personal adjustment issues openly; they frequently believe their problems are not serious enough to warrant attention. They may assume that all therapeutic intervention is based on intensive, expensive, and long-term individual clinical therapy. They may assume that mental health centers and mental health professionals are only for the highly disturbed, for example, those who are "ready for the loony bin" or "crazy" (Dick & Gallagher-Thompson, 1996).

With such a stereotyped understanding of mental health, older persons expect little success from mental health treatment and may be unaware of new and effective clinical advances or innovative services. Many older adults have difficulty recognizing symptoms of mental health problems in others and in themselves (Davies et al., 1994). Although fear of self-disclosure may be responsible, in part, for older adults' under-recognition and underutilization of mental health services, other possibilities remain. Padgett, Patrick, Burns, and Schlesinger (1995) note that older persons may have poor memories for such incidents and a lower level of acceptance of the diagnostic labels indicative of mental disorders. There are higher mortality rates for those with serious and untreated mental health disorders (Joiner, 2000).

Harel and Biegel (1995) note that attitudes toward mental health services vary greatly depending on the ethnic community, gender, and age cohort to which an individual belongs. **Ethnic elderly** populations historically have been at lower socioeconomic levels, in poorer health, underemployed or nonemployed for significant periods in adult life, and recipients of fewer benefits in retirement. These demographic factors are associated with increased mental health needs. These older adults do not readily use the available intervention services government provides. Many are first-generation immigrants, and others have remained isolated but comfortable in their ethnic communities where their extended families meet their basic needs and supply their social support (Morales, 1999). They rarely travel into the larger culture for goods and services; many continue to rely on their own language and are uncomfortable with English. It is difficult for them to value mental health services offered in the larger, dominant culture and difficult to move beyond their comfort zone for supportive programs and intervention. Women from such backgrounds more often access mental health services compared to men (Rivers, 1995).

Some investigators have suggested that being both old and a member of an ethnic subculture results in extra vulnerability to physical and mental health problems; however, others have questioned whether such "double jeopardy" applies to all ethnic elderly (Padgett, 1995). Considerable effort needs to go into removing the barriers that inhibit older people from various ethnic populations from utilizing mental health services. Mental health disorders have quite different defining behavioral symptoms and are treated differently within each ethnic subculture. Psychologists need to be sensitive to the operational definitions of mental health problems in different subcultures to understand the significance of unique presenting complaints and symptoms. This understanding is crucial to the development of culturally appropriate treatment plans and successful functioning within ethnic communities (Dinges & Cherry, 1995; Morales, 1999).

Diversity and Mental Health

The need to understand the relationship between psychological disorders and ethnic aging is being addressed, in part, by educating mental health professionals about the values, beliefs, and cultural assumptions of specific aging ethnic populations. There is an emphasis on improving sensitivity to ethnic groups both in graduate education and among practicing mental health professionals involved in program design and service delivery. By 2030 nearly 25 percent of adults over 65 will be non-white in the U.S. The success of any clinical treatment depends on each therapist's ability to establish trust, build relationships, develop empathy, and listen sensitively to clients as individuals, free from personal prejudice and bias. Successful intervention requires mental health professionals to be caring, compassionate, and curious; who seek to discover the unique individuality of every client. Sensitivity embraces a willingness to understand the culture, values, and background of the client seeking treatment (Wohl, 1995).

Ethnic group membership implies identification with and participation in the unique attributes of that subculture, its heritage, and its values. Yet, there are wide individual differences in the centrality of **ethnic identity** across subcultures, and correspondingly sharp differences within each subculture in acculturation and assimilation to the majority society. Various indexes are used to mark acculturation, such as preferred language, number of years in the United States, age at which migration occurred, ethnic self-identification, or degree of contact with members of other ethnic groups (Rodriguez & O'Donnell, 1995). At least for elderly Hispanics, such indexes are significant because those who are most acculturated access mental health services at higher rates than those who are less acculturated (Morales, 1999; Rodriguez & O'Donnell, 1995).

Historically, older adults from ethnic populations have experienced discrimination, prejudice, and racism in our society. They are most comfortable in their own communities, where they feel isolated but protected. Their strength comes from their culture, traditions, and extended families. Many feel strongly that they are the "kin keepers" for the next generation, passing on stories about family, origins, and customs. They are different from younger adults, and they fear that exposure to the majority culture and government will mean facing the bias they experienced in the past (Morales, 1999). Mental health issues serious enough to warrant treatment are found in nearly one of four ethnically and racially diverse adults over the age of 65. However, certain behaviors may fit Western criteria for mental health disorders, but in reality be quite appropriate for specific ethnic and racial cultures. For example, Angel (2000) notes that a Latina daughter may be devoted to her parents and be committed to providing care despite multiple commitments to her husband and children. This is not pathological devotion or excessive dependency, but a reflection of the duties and expectations of daughters to their mothers within Hispanic culture.

Hispanic elders are more likely to experience symptoms of depression, particularly if they are recent immigrants to the United States and newly exposed to a different culture and language. Hispanics are more likely to have health problems, be poor, and be socially isolated, all of which increase the risk of depression (Black, Goodwin, & Markides, 1998). The caregiving burden can be quite high for Hispanic and black grandparents, who often experience role strain in the extended family trying to fill the roles of parent, grandparent, employee, volunteer, spouse, and in many cases, caregiver to kin (White, Townsend, & Stephens, 2000).

Studies have also shown differences in depressive symptoms for other Hispanic cultures. Mexican-American elders have high rates of depressive symptoms compared to other minority elders; the rates are highest among immigrants, the uninsured, and those with physical health problems (Angel, 2000). Puerto Rican and Dominican elders showed more symptoms of depression than non-Hispanic whites living in the same neighborhoods in Massachusetts (Falcon & Tucker, 2000). The higher scores on depression scales for Puerto Rican elderly have been related to a greater number of health problems, living alone, and being female. Cubans have the lowest rates among all Hispanics.

Black, Asian, and Hispanic families serve as the primary support systems for elderly relatives with mental health problems. Family support and the support of the larger social network are essential links to positive mental health for older adults from minority cultures and are also essential for coping with psychological disorders. Hispanics, particularly Mexican Americans, rely on the family to help them cope with difficult life situations. Cultural gerontologists also point to the *compadrazgo* system; this is "a network of ritual kinships whose members have a deep sense of obligation to each other for economic assistance, often serves as an extension of the nuclear family" (Angel, 2000, p. 504). Being part of a couple contributes significantly to overall emotional health, but is particularly salient for new immigrants to this country. Among Cuban elderly, marriage, education, and contact with economically stable kin helped to promote emotional health. Religious affiliation and religious involvement contributed positively to overall emotional health for elders from ethnically and racially diverse cultures; both were especially important for first-generation elderly immigrants new to the United States (Hao & Johnson, 2000). Among oldest-old blacks, an extended, active, and supportive network of kin is essential to well-being. Unlike whites, however, blacks include in the social support network an expanded definition of kin. First, they make distant kin a part of the immediate family and consider them primary relatives, a process known as **upgrading kinship relationships.** Second, they expand the definition of family member to include **fictive kin,** people who are considered family, even though they are not related by blood or marriage (Johnson, 1999). Fictive kin include those who visit the older black person regularly, provide services such as meals, or who develop a close relationship through church, neighborhood contact, or prior history. Blacks refer to fictive kin as: (1) like family; (2) play relatives; (3) adopted daughters or sons; (4) chosen family; (5) church family.

Older adults from ethnically and racially diverse subcultures have one advantage in coping with mental health problems: Compared to whites, they have a wide range of social support available from the family, extended kinship network, church, and larger community. They will access these resources first, before they consult other formal organizations such as community mental health agencies. It is only when culturally approved interventions have failed that older people reluctantly seek professional mental health services.

The low rate at which ethnically diverse older adults use mental health services has been linked by Rogler and colleagues (1989) to two major explanations: alternative resource theory and barrier theory.

Hispanics, for example, turn initially to alternative resources—family, friends, religious leaders, spiritualists, or folk healers—to help solve their psychological problems before they turn to secondary support groups, community services, or institutional programs provided by government (Morales, 1999). Hispanic culture places a high value on the mutual help provided by the nuclear and extended family. **Mutual help,** according to Rogler and colleagues (1989), is an obligatory norm sustained by both guilt and gratitude. One feels guilt if one should fail to help a relative who is in need, while one experiences gratitude when one's relatives help. Hispanic family members bond closely with each other, are loyal, and are strongly committed to **familism.** The immediate and extended family remains the dominant reference group throughout life, offering emotional security and a sense of belonging. The family cares for all its members and gathers in times of crisis. The Catholic Church and its clergy are another key alternative community resource. Elderly first-generation immigrants benefited by being part of a couple (e.g., experienced better emotional health) than did older Hispanics born in the United States (Hao & Johnson, 2000). Today's elderly Hispanics are likely to be living in multigenerational households and to hold traditional views of authority and power based on age and being male. They expect women to follow traditional roles and meet the needs of the family and children to share responsibilities that often include caring for grandparents (Morales, 1999).

Specific Hispanic cultural values that also lead to underutilization of community mental health services include: (1) *confianza,* or trust in a person over trust in an organization; (2) *personalismo,* or the value of the immediate personal relationship with friend/family over relationship with an unknown, impersonal mental health institution; (3) *respeto,* or the value of respect owed to one's elders; (4) *verguenza* and *orgullo,* or the sense of shame and the value of pride; and (5) *machismo,* or pride in manliness and avoidance of admitting personal defects and weaknesses (Rodriguez & O'Donnell, 1995). Professional community mental health services appear to be a last resort, at least among those who are least acculturated. Traditionally, in a Hispanic community, a person with a mental health disorder is stigmatized if he or she cannot be helped informally. Persons needing formal help are viewed as having lost ties to their family and to their Hispanic community; their social value within the community is significantly reduced (Angel & Angel, 1995).

For elderly Puerto Ricans living in New York City, alternative resource theory has been found to underlie the reliance on family social support to lower stress; this reduces the rate at which this population utilizes professional mental health services. Natural community resources such as social support can be helpful; however, they do not necessarily take the place of needed mental health services among older Puerto Ricans. Social support may delay the search for professional intervention services, may not be as effective as professional intervention in treating mental health disorders, and may take a heavy toll on the caregivers who provide support. In one study, the best predictor of those seeking community mental health services among older Puerto Ricans was the ability to subjectively identify a need for professional services (Rodriguez & O'Donnell, 1995).

Another alternative resource that members of Hispanic cultures use is **folk systems** to heal people with mental and physical disorders. Three distinctive Hispanic cultures have been identified within the United States, each with its own unique view of mental and physical illness and appropriate treatment: *espiritismo* in Puerto Rican subculture, *santeria* in Cuban subculture, and *curanderismo* in Mexican-American subculture. In simplistic terms, each of these traditions views physical, mental, emotional, and interpersonal problems as due to forces outside of the person and his or her awareness. To bring relief, the forces that threaten the ideal balance between the person, the environment, and the spirits or cosmos must be brought to resolution. Healing means restoring harmony and equilibrium to the person (Koss-Chioino, 1995). A healer determines what is out of balance with little or no input from the client. As acculturation proceeds, folk healing decreases among each of these three Hispanic groups.

Barrier theory hypothesizes that institutional obstacles within the mental health system cause ethnic populations to underutilize available services. Consider the perceptions of Hispanic elderly seeking mental health treatment; they identify community agencies as impersonal, in conflict with their basic cultural traditions, and discriminatory in discouraging the use of Spanish language. There are also basic values within Hispanic culture which turn persons away from any agency perceived to be part of a distant, large bureaucratic system and not part of the immediate face-to-face social supports of the community (Morales, 1999). Barrier theory does not necessarily conflict with alternative resource theory. Experts believe that current needs for mental health services are high among the ethnic elderly (Angel & Angel, 1995). Culture, class, and language all appear to be barriers to utilization. Barriers also include the following (see Harel & Biegel, 1995; Vasquez & Han, 1995):

1. Overt discrimination and prejudice
2. Lack of bicultural understanding among professionals in mental health centers
3. Professionals who speak only English
4. Socioeconomic differences between therapists and clients
5. Geographic inaccessibility, with mental health services located outside of the ethnic community
6. Lack of transportation to mental health centers
7. Lack of health insurance and/or income to cover the cost of treatment
8. Lack of ethnic minority mental health professionals and role models
9. Physical and social isolation of the ethnic community itself

Other barriers that inhibit members of ethnic groups from fully utilizing mental health interventions include a lack of education and awareness about mental health, mental health services, and the value of counseling in solving problems (Vasquez & Han, 1995). In some subcultures, specific restrictions exist against discussing personal problems with nonfamily members. And some ethnic subcultures have a unique understanding of, language for, definition of, and representation of mental health symptoms.

In earlier studies, ethnically diverse elders were reported to have a higher incidence of mental health disorders than whites. However, this may be attributable, at least in part, to differing cultural definitions and concepts of mental health disorders, language differences, or a reporting bias for mental disorders (Paniagua, 1994). For example, many ethnically diverse elders' language of preference is not English, and counselors may have difficulty understanding the issues they are presenting and may misinterpret the nature of their concerns. Alternatively, as we have just reviewed, many Hispanic elderly have strong cultural beliefs in folk healing and symbolic healing practices. Professionals in mental health, lacking the knowledge that these beliefs are typical of the culture, may erroneously attribute them to a psychological disorder (Morales, 1999).

Elderly Native Americans living on reservations have been able to maintain some cultural continuity with the past. They pass on oral history, traditions, and native languages. All members of the tribe are responsible for each other; individual identity is secondary to tribal identity. They find it difficult to accept or recognize individual accomplishment or failure since all tribal members are equal. Mutual respect is typical of relationships within the tribe and within a strong family unit (husband-wife, parent-child). Elders expect tribal members to share concerns in open discussion and to resolve concerns through collective problem solving (Morales, 1999). Turning to government-sponsored programs, mental health interventions, and paid professionals is difficult for elderly Native Americans.

Explanations for why older black adults underutilize community mental health services have centered on alternative resource theory, limited availability of services, and institutional barriers. In times of need, these elders seek out alternative resources first, including extensive social supports provided by the immediate and extended family network, friends, and by community institutions like church and clergy (Morales, 1999; Padgett et al., 1995). A number of barriers limit older black adults from utilizing mental health services. For example, the small number of professional black role models on staff at community mental health agencies suggests that these agencies are biased, prejudiced, and discriminatory in attitude, treatment, and service delivery. To older black adults, it appears that perhaps the community mental health needs of the community are being ignored. Economic barriers mean that, with less income and insurance coverage for mental health services, many ethnic populations, including black Americans, are less likely to seek and receive professional treatment. However, it may be that the type of mental health services older black adults seek differs from the type sought by older whites. In one investigation, equal access to mental health services was available to black and white federal workers who received identical mental health insurance coverage. Black and white adults over the age of 55 utilized inpatient health and mental health services at equal rates. Yet older blacks were less likely to make use of outpatient mental health services, as measured by number of visits to the agency, than similarly aged whites (Padgett et al., 1995).

Access and Ethnicity

The rate at which older adults from diverse ethnic populations access mental health services appears to mirror the lower overall rate for elderly persons in the United States (Padgett, 1995). Table 5.1 summarizes some of the special concerns of ethnically and racially diverse elderly people. For example, Barney (1995) noted that within a recent six-month period, approximately 7.1 percent of a Native American population of older persons accessed some mental health services, a figure that is nearly identical to that for non-Native American older persons in national surveys. The best predictor of whether older Native Americans living on a reservation would utilize mental health services was their subjective self-assessment of perceived need. However, for those living in urban settings, degree of mental impairment was the best predictor. Reservation-dwelling elderly have a choice between traditional spiritual healing or standard mental health approaches; those residing in urban settings have only the latter. As Barney noted, "traditional healing, as an option, may assist reservation elderly in having more control over their own self-perceived need for 'treatment'; thus explaining why this variable was so strong in predicting mental health service use for reservation elders and so weak in predicting service use for urban elders" (Barney, 1995, p. 210). Older Native Americans on reservations perceive themselves as more isolated, a reality based on the reduced availability of traditional social support and the decline of the extended family network as younger persons move away. Elderly Native Americans living on reservations may thus be more at risk for psychological disorders and may be in greater need of mental health services today than they were in the past. Older Native Americans residing in urban settings may be more knowledgeable about mental health agencies and in closer geographical proximity to such services than those residing on a reservation.

Comparisons of the rate at which older blacks and whites seek mental health services are rare (Padgett et al., 1995). The assumption has been that underutilization of mental health services among older black Americans should mirror that of younger black adults. Black Americans facing mental health problems are underrepresented in both inpatient and outpatient community mental health programs (Padgett et al., 1995).

Considerable research has focused on the type of mental health disorders that cause elderly from different ethnic populations to seek services. Regardless of specific ethnicity, elderly from diverse backgrounds seek help from their families or their immediate social networks first. Social supports are readily available and accessible for older persons with mental health problems within most ethnic subcultures (Aponte & Barnes, 1995). When primary social supports prove inadequate or ineffective in managing the disorder, older persons from ethnically diverse backgrounds reluctantly seek specific mental health treatment. Older persons from diverse backgrounds, however, are not as likely to access outpatient services as inpatient services. Inpatient treatment is usually appropriate for fairly serious mental health disorders. Harada and Kim (1995) found that 89 percent of older Asians and Pacific Islanders utilizing mental health services sought direct inpatient care. The presenting mental health disorders were severe and required constant monitoring; most had waited until a crisis arose. Mental health referrals for Asians and Pacific Islanders were usually made by health care agencies. In contrast, however, older Vietnamese clients were most often referred by family, friends, or social agencies for less severe mental health problems (e.g., adjustment disorders) than other Asians and Pacific Islanders. The older Vietnamese clients also stayed longer in treatment than their Asian and Pacific Islander counterparts (Harada & Kim, 1995). Depression was the most common presenting problem for older Koreans, Chinese, Japanese, and Filipinos seeking treatment from mental health agencies.

TABLE 5.1   Counseling Elderly from Diverse Backgrounds

Morales (1999) has sensitized mental health professionals to the unique challenges of counseling elderly persons who are ethnically and racially diverse. Each subculture carries its own history, values, and understanding of mental health. To be effective, counselors must develop techniques that recognize the concepts, belief systems, values, and histories of older people from *different* cultural traditions. Using a "one size fits all" approach to counseling not only is ineffective, but it also results in alienation and termination of treatment. Read Morales's suggestions in this table to help counselors understand the reluctance of older Hispanic, Native American, Asian, and black adults to access mental health services and counseling.

Alternate Resources for Elderly Hispanics

Nuclear family
Extended family
Catholic church (faith)
Clergy
Family friends
Family confidants (physician)

Nature of Counseling Relationship

Counselors providing mental health services to elderly Hispanics are seen as part of the extended family. Trust is established based on the similarity between client and counselor. The elderly value counselors who are mature, formal, and professional. Elderly Hispanics maintain a fundamental belief in fatalism, believing that a "divine providence governs the world and that the individual cannot control or prevent adversity" (Morales, 1999, p. 146). Culturally, this represents an adaptive response to stress, although to many counselors unfamiliar with Hispanic culture it would appear to be maladaptive and an indicator of depressive mood. Many elderly Hispanics believe that spiritual forces cause mental health problems, with symptoms they lump together and identify as a "nervous disorder." It may be difficult to explain that medications may not help a particular disorder. Showing respect for professionals means that Hispanic elders rarely criticize or correct statements made in therapy. Morales encourages counselors to provide opportunities for the elderly to clarify issues and to restate their concerns so that they do not feel that they are embarrassing or correcting the counselor.

Alternative Resources for Elderly Native Americans

Tribal identity
Tribal council
Traditional healers
Family relationships (mutual respect)

Nature of Counseling Relationship

Elderly Native Americans who live on reservations have distinctive sensitivities based on their specific tribal heritage. Counselors must be supported and accepted by the tribal council. Elders will first seek help from within the tribe before exploring assistance from the larger community. Mental health services and counseling must be open and flexible; older tribal members will not accept rigid, formal settings, and appointment times. Native American elders make a decision with input from all family members and sometimes only after consultation with tribal leaders and council. Traditional healers, tribal leaders, and key family members may attend counseling sessions (unannounced) with the elders. Elders expect counselors to show them the same respect they receive from tribal members, based on their status and leadership. Native American elders are usually excellent listeners and use nonverbal communication extensively. They think carefully before speaking, and their speech is deliberate and focused. Morales (1999) recommends repeated sessions to establish trust before initiating in-depth questions.

Alternative Resources for Elderly Asians

Nuclear family
Asian community
Professionals (physician)

Nature of Counseling Relationship

Asian elderly are used to expressing problems only within their families. They believe strongly in fatalism and accept adverse situations with patience and tolerance, denying the need for individual action. Exposing problems to community mental health experts is a sign that the family has failed and causes considerable embarrassment, guilt, and anxiety. Sharing problems outside of the family is very difficult. Usually, mental health counseling is sought only when problems reach crisis levels and families can no longer cope. Elderly Asians expect counselors to tell them what to do to resolve their problems. They expect immediate results, and in the course of treatment, they need concrete signs of their progress. Many psychological problems of the Asian elderly present as somatic symptoms. In-patient hospitalization for treatment of psychological problems is difficult for all family members, not just the elderly person, to accept (Morales, 1999).

Alternative Resources for Elderly Blacks

Nuclear family
Extensive kin network
Church and clergy
Community leaders

Nature of Counseling Relationship

Elderly black Americans expect to experience prejudice when they participate in government-supported mental health programs in the larger community. They turn initially to their kin and extensive family network for support and guidance, and then to the church and clergy for help. They may consult respected leaders in the black community long before turning to community mental health programs. Elders expect counseling to be brief and to resolve the presenting problem quickly. Morales (1999) notes that feelings of empowerment and counselor acceptance can help build a trusting relationship.

Source: Morales, P. (2000). *The impact of cultural differences in psychotherapy with older clients: Sensitive issues and strategies.* In M. Duffy (Ed.), Handbook of counseling and psychotherapy with older adults (pp. 132–153). New York: John Wiley.

Mental Health and Psychological Disorders

In the past, psychologists have often overlooked mental health issues in the elderly. With growing interest in this segment of society, psychologists have begun to devote special attention to the more common psychological disorders the elderly experience, such as depression, anxiety, and alcoholism.

The Incidence of Clinical Depression

The incidence of depression reported among older adults varies widely since different methodologies, samples, nationalities, and criteria have been employed in various research studies (Gatz, 2000). There is some agreement that about 4 to 7 percent of the elderly experience **clinical depression** serious enough to require intervention (Anthony & Aboraya, 1992). The incidence of clinical depression in community-residing adults over the age of 65 is 1 to 4 percent, which is lower than that for any other age group (Dick & Gallagher-Thompson, 1996; Gatz, 2000). However, specific subgroups of older individuals show much higher rates of clinical depression (e.g., 10 to 15 percent). For example, clinical depression is often a corollary condition among older persons with serious health problems and is thus quite common among the frail elderly (Dick & Gallagher-Thompson, 1996). Futterman, Thompson, Gallagher-Thompson, and Ferris (1995) found the lowest incidence of clinical depression among community-dwelling older residents, followed by older adults with health problems severe enough to warrant outpatient care. Elderly hospitalized for heart disease or hip fracture show a 12 percent incidence of depression, while nursing home residents show the highest rates, estimated at 15 to 25 percent.

Across the life span, clinical depression affects twice as many women as men, but by old age it occurs at equal rates (Joiner, 2000). Women who are poor and on welfare, less educated, and members of ethnic/racial groups are at highest risk. One of the consequences of depression is the inability to carry through roles such as caregiver for a spouse or partner. In some studies of older couples, it appears that depressive behavioral symptoms in one spouse are likely to result in depressive symptoms in the other (Tower & Kasl, 1995). Interestingly, the closer the preexisting emotional relationship between spouses, the greater the similarity in symptoms. The multiple mechanisms underlying these findings may include, but are not limited to, mate selection, emotional contagion, and common environmental influences (Bookwala & Schulz, 1996). Among institutionalized elderly populations, in particular, deteriorating health and associated clinical depression have been found to be predictive of death (Parmelee, Katz, & Lawton, 1992).

Previous studies that related the incidence of clinical depression to age are subject to criticism. Some used a very narrow age range of older persons (e.g., 65 to 75), a small number of older respondents (e.g., 75 or more years of age), or a measure of age that combined all individuals over the age of 65 into a single group for analysis (Kessler, Foster, Webster, & House, 1992). Other investigators have based their conclusions on nonrepresentative samples (e.g., because older research participants exclude themselves from research participation at high rates). Sometimes being affected by the very phenomenon that is under investigation (i.e., clinical depression), may cause older adults to refuse to participate in research. Without representative samples, researchers will consistently underestimate the incidence of clinical depression in the elderly and have greater difficulty finding significant correlates of depression (Thompson, Heller, & Rody, 1994).

It is important to differentiate clinical depression from the self-reported depressive *symptoms* commonly assessed in research studies. Behavioral symptoms may indicate the existence of subclinical depression, a classification called minor depression in the past (Joiner, 2000). Some studies show that symptoms of depression in older adults over a 13-year period are predictive of functional impairment, cognitive loss, and higher mortality (Gallo et al., 1997). The highest rates of depressive symptoms appear among those older than 65; the lowest rates among those in middle adulthood. The pattern of low incidence of clinical depression and an increase in depressive symptoms with advancing age has been supported empirically (Gatz, 2000). The number of older community-residing adults reporting depressive symptoms has been estimated at 15 percent; that for medical outpatients, 20 percent; for hospitalized inpatients, 33 percent; and for nursing home residents 40 percent (Gatz, 2000).

Depressive symptoms are often dismissed as a "normal" part of aging, a natural response to accumulated and intense loss. As a result, depression is often ignored and left untreated. Depression remains the most common mental health diagnosis in old age, with an average duration of approximately eight months (Joiner, 2000). Depression accounts for more days in the hospital than any other condition but heart disease. In-patient hospitalization for depression typically averages about two weeks, at a cost of more than $5500 per week.

Those who experience depression earlier in life are at higher risk of becoming depressed again. Currently adolescents, young adults, and adults in middle adulthood are showing a surprisingly high incidence of depression. As they enter old age, they will be at increased risk of depression. In the next 50 years, some expect to see an epidemic of depression among the elderly (Joiner, 2000).

Diagnosis of Clinical Depression

Table 5.2 presents the clinical diagnostic criteria of depression in the *DSM-IV.* Clinical depression may be more difficult to diagnose in an older person than in younger persons for several reasons. First, it manifests itself somewhat differently in older and younger populations. Clinical depression among the aged is most often marked by "diminished interest in things around them, fatigue, difficulty with waking early in the morning and not being able to get back to sleep, complaints about their memory, thoughts about death, and general hopelessness" (Gatz et al., 1996, p. 368).

A pattern of depressive symptoms called the **depletion syndrome** that has been identified among the elderly is manifestly different from the symptoms younger persons show (Newmann, Engel, & Jensen, 1991). Depletion syndrome is characterized by lack of interest, hopelessness, and feeling that everything is an effort. It is identified diagnostically as a minor depression, but the current *DSM-IV* does not recognize this diagnosis (American Psychiatric Association, 1994). Some experts disagree that depletion syndrome is truly indicative of clinical depression; they note that many adjustments to old age produce disappointments, anxieties, and motivational difficulties that should not be taken as evidence of clinical depression. Still, the depletion syndrome is useful for describing many of the motivational difficulties older adults experience. It

TABLE 5.2

Symptoms of Depression: Diagnostic Criteria for Major Depressive Episodes

A. Major depressive episode: Five (or more) of the following symptoms have been present during the same two-week period and represent a change from previous functioning; at least one of the symptoms is either (1) depressed mood or (2) loss of interest or pleasure. *Note:* Do not include symptoms that are clearly due to a general medical condition or mood-incongruent delusions or hallucinations.

    1. Depressed mood most of the day, nearly every day, as indicated by either subjective report (e.g., feels sad or empty) or observation made by others (e.g., appears tearful). *Note:* In children and adolescents, symptom can be irritable mood.

    2. Markedly diminished interest or pleasure in all, or almost all, activities most of the day, nearly every day (as indicated by either subjective account or observation made by others).

    3. Significant weight loss when not dieting or weight gain (e.g., a change of more than 5 percent of body weight in a month), or decrease or increase in appetite nearly every day. *Note:* In children, consider failure to make expected weight gains.

    4. Insomnia or hypersomnia nearly every day.

    5. Psychomotor agitation or retardation nearly every day (observable by others, not merely subjective feelings of restlessness or being slowed down).

    6. Fatigue or loss of energy nearly every day.

    7. Feelings of worthlessness or excessive or inappropriate guilt (which may be delusional) nearly every day (not merely self-reproach or guilt about being sick).

    8. Diminished ability to think or concentrate, or indecisiveness, nearly every day (either by subjective account or as observed by others).

    9. Recurrent thoughts of death (not just fear of dying), recurrent suicidal ideation without a specific plan, or a suicide attempt or a specific plan for committing suicide.

B. The symptoms cause clinically significant distress or impairment in social, occupational, or other important areas of functioning.

C. The symptoms are not due to the direct physiological effects of a substance (e.g., drug abuse, a medication) or a general medical condition (e.g., hypothyroidism).

D. The symptoms are not accounted for by bereavement; that is, after the loss of a loved one, the symptoms persist for longer than two months or are characterized by marked functional impairment, morbid preoccupation with worthlessness, suicidal ideation, psychotic symptoms, or psychomotor retardation.

Source: American Psychiatric Association. (1994). Diagnostic and statistical manual of mental disorders (4th ed., rev., pp. 161–163). Washington, DC: American Psychiatric Association. Reprinted by permission.

underscores reports by the elderly that routine daily tasks become increasingly exhausting and difficult to complete. And the depletion syndrome also describes the loss of interest and enjoyment in activities that older people formerly found rewarding.

A second factor making it difficult to diagnose clinical depression in the elderly is that both older persons as well as other family members usually disregard depressive symptoms, believing they are normal for anyone who reaches old age (Blazer, 1993; Dick & Gallagher-Thompson, 1996). Many believe that depressive symptoms are a natural consequence of growing older, reflecting the accumulation of many personal losses (spouse, job, friends, family, housing) and the health problems older adults frequently encounter. More than 50 percent of all older persons believe that manifestations of clinical depression are a "normal" part of aging and a natural response to the illnesses and losses associated with growing old (Katz, 1997).

A third factor contributing to the difficulty of diagnosis is that older persons may not have well-developed strategies for self-assessment, and they fail to recognize depression. The elderly are less likely than younger adults to identify themselves as being depressed or feeling "down" (Gallo, Anthony, & Muthen, 1994). Instead, older adults often report negative feelings to other family members and their physicians in metaphorical terms, expressing (1) cognitive complaints such as worthlessness, demoralization, hopelessness, and despair; and (2) somatic complaints such as difficulty sleeping, low energy, weight loss, intestinal disorders, appetite decline, aches and pains, and nervousness (Blazer, 1993; Dick & Gallagher-Thompson, 1996). It may be that there are age-related differences in the nature of depression itself, both in how it is experienced individually and in how it manifests itself (Gatz, 2000).

Fourth, clinicians find it difficult to identify depression in older persons using the criteria in the *DSM-IV* (Blazer, 1994). The inclusion of many items with a strong somatic component is biased against the elderly, who are far more likely to report symptoms in this domain than are younger persons (Gatz, 2000).

Weiner (1992) notes a final difficulty in the diagnosis and treatment of depression in the elderly. Today's cohort of elderly may be embarrassed to seek treatment for depression and reluctant to admit such personal difficulties to others due to shame, guilt, and fear of public knowledge. The elderly today often hold inaccurate beliefs that mental health issues are highly stigmatizing, incurable, and a mark against one's entire family. Unfortunately, untreated depression places the elderly at a significantly higher risk of suicide compared to younger adults (Gatz et al., 1996).

The decision to seek treatment has been conceptualized as a series of steps beginning with an understanding of mental health and the identification of a psychological disorder, followed by direct observation and recognition of specific mental health symptoms, and concluding with a decision on whether to take action (Davies et al., 1994). With treatment, older people find, as do younger persons, that the manifestations of clinical depression (e.g., negative feelings, thoughts, and behaviors) improve or even disappear. Effective treatments for both older and younger adults include intensive, brief therapy; drug treatments; or some combination of the two (Joiner, 2000).

The diagnosis of depression is sometimes difficult to determine, since the criteria listed in table 5.2 are not adjusted for age. It is often quite complicated trying to separate depression from the typical age-related physical changes, illnesses, and symptoms that occur in the elderly. Dick and Gallagher-Thompson (1996) note that many symptoms of depression in the elderly mimic age-related health complaints: difficulty sleeping; poor appetite; cognitive and memory difficulties; coping with loss, bereavement, and grief; and side effects of various medications. Also, recall from chapter 3 that it is hard to separate mild dementia from depression because they share common behavioral patterns— for example, difficulty with memory, attention, and concentration. Generally, dementia is characterized by slow onset and generally deteriorating functioning, whereas depression is more sudden and clearly noticeable to others as a change in personality (Dick & Gallagher-Thompson, 1996).

Stress-Buffering Effects

With advancing age, the risk of depressive symptoms theoretically should increase. Older adults with high levels of anxiety are at higher risk of developing depressive symptoms (Wetherell, Gatz, & Pederson, 2001). Moreover, aging is related to a higher risk of poor health, the deaths of friends and relatives, retirement, and so on. However, despite the increased risk, depressive symptoms do not increase with age in a linear fashion. Tower and Kasl (1995) hypothesized that stress-buffering effects moderate the risk. **Stress-buffering effects** refer to the effects of social support from loved ones in the nuclear and extended family, from close friends, and from people in community organizations. Social support can buffer the impact of risk factors for depressive symptoms and enhance coping with other negative life events. Stress-buffering effects therefore reduce the likelihood that multiple risk factors will invariably lead to an increase in clinical depression or depressive symptoms. Consider, for example, the surprisingly low incidence of depressive symptoms among the oldest-old (85 years of age and over) given the rate of functional disabilities and physical illness in this population (Haynie et al., 2001). Symptoms of depression and measures of well-being were obtained in a group of elderly Swedish twins with an average age of almost 84 years. Elderly who did not complete the four-year study had significantly higher depression scores at the initial testing session and higher mortality. Those who completed the study were physically healthier and had fewer problems such as dementia, depressive symptoms, or impairment in ADLs. These results suggest that the oldest-old are a remarkably resilient group of "hardy survivors" who remain in overall good physical and mental health (Johnson & Barer, 1996).

Depression has been found among older people with impairments severe enough to interfere with routine activities of daily living (ADLs). When these individuals perceived a strong, supportive social network (e.g., emotionally supportive people making frequent visits), the symptoms and severity of their depression were significantly reduced (Oxman & Hull, 2001). Older adults have smaller social support networks than younger adults, and these networks are dominated by kin. People have less face-to-face contact and live further away from their social support networks as they get older. Blacks generally have even smaller social support networks than whites, and their networks are often exclusively comprised of kin and friends who are treated like kin. However, blacks also have more direct contact with their social networks and apparently live in closer proximity to them than white elderly. These racial differences in social networks become less dramatic with increasing age (Ajrouch, Antonucci, & Janevic, 2001).

Stress-buffering effects can also enhance effective coping in older people. Mittleman and colleagues (1995) have shown the benefits of psychosocial support from spousal caregivers and immediate families in reducing depression among Alzheimer's patients. The multifaceted psychosocial intervention included family counseling, ad hoc counseling as needed, and social support through targeted discussions with spouses facing similar problems. Caregivers showed significantly fewer depressive symptoms than control caregivers without such intervention.

Risk Factors for Depression in Old Age

The best predictors of depressive symptoms in late life are poor health, an accumulation of losses, and minimal social support. Specific stressful life events in themselves, such as the death of a spouse, rarely cause depressive symptoms. Risk factors associated with the onset of clinical depression in late life include health problems, chronic disease leading to functional disabilities, and cognitive impairments associated with dementia (Gatz, 2000; Zeiss, Lewinsohn, Rhode, & Seeley, 1996). The relationship between depression and health, however, appears to be bidirectional. Poor health can heighten the risk of depression, just as depression may increase the probability of illness and disease (Gatz, 2000). Researchers recently examined these relationships in a more detailed way.

Illness that caused impairments in ADLs was found to lead to depression in adults over the age of 60. Having a large, emotionally supportive social network that made frequent visits during the illness and afterwards increased older adults' perception of support. Perceived support, in turn, led to decreases in depression (Oxman & Hull, 2001). Other investigators wondered whether depression led to declines in physical health and an increased risk of illness, disability, and mortality. Among older adults, it appears that short-term health events are related to short-term depressive states. However, when depressive symptoms persist for a longer time, they are considered part of an enduring trait, and they result in a range of negative consequences, including lower self-reported health. Meeks, Murrell, and Mehl (2000) conclude that "illness can affect depressive states; depressive traits, but not states, can affect illness" (p. 108).

The possibility that genetic factors, in part, underlie depression was examined in a 10-year longitudinal study (Carmelli et al., 2000). If depressive symptoms reflect genetics and are an inherent part of depressive traits in personality and temperament, then longitudinal studies should show continuity in these symptoms. By studying older male twins, there researchers hoped to compare the relative contributions of environment and genetics on depressive symptoms. The research found remarkable stability in depressive symptoms obtained when the twins were 63 years old and then again 10 years later. The authors concluded that the genetic contribution (or heritability index) underlying stable depressive symptoms with increasing age was 55 percent. Chen et al. (2000) also examined the course of depression longitudinally. They studied young adults with depression, checking again when these participants reached old age. There was a high probability that depression would reappear later in life, although the type of depression and specific symptoms were not necessarily the same as those experienced in early adulthood. The authors concluded that the type of depression was not as important in predicting depression in later life as the severity of symptoms in early adulthood. Gatz (2000) reports that half of older adults admitted to facilities for psychiatric treatment of depression had experienced depression earlier in their lives.

Physical illness is one of the strongest risk factors for depression (Gatz, 2000). Specific diseases by themselves do not appear to predict depression among the elderly (Zeiss et al., 1996). Clinical depression has also been found to be a predictable but not inevitable outcome of chronic disease (Beckman, Kriegsman, Deeg, & Van Tilburg, 1995). Studies have reported that some older persons make a better adjustment to later-onset chronic disease if they have developed coping skills over their lifetime to deal with stressful events. Older persons who expect to have to deal with chronic diseases as a part of their own aging are not as deeply disturbed or clinically depressed by such problems (Deeg et al., 1996). Apparently, the more severe and more life-threatening the chronic disease, the more often clinical depression results. In one investigation, the rate of clinical depression among older adults in medical settings was reported to be 15 percent (Reifler, 1994). The coexistence or **comorbidity** of clinical depression with chronic disease suggests greater functional disabilities and higher rates of mortality than is found among elderly with the chronic disease alone (Sullivan, 1995). Thus, the treatment of clinical depression among older persons with chronic disease may well have positive benefits not only in terms of mental health, but also in terms of maintaining functional abilities (Deeg et al., 1996).

Coping with chronic disease, as we have seen in chapter 4, can also lead to depression among those who provide direct care (increasing caregiver burden and distress) as well as among other family members. In one investigation of caregivers, depressive symptoms were found to continue even after the older care recipient had died. Bodnar and Kiecolt-Glaser (1994) found comparable levels of depressive symptoms among both those currently providing direct care to a relative with dementia and those who had done so but had stopped due to the death of the relative. Both groups showed significantly higher depressive symptoms than controls who were not and had never provided care to a relative with dementia.

Clinical Depression and Alzheimer's Disease

Among the newer challenges that clinicians face today is treating clinical depression in older persons with Alzheimer's disease (AD). The comorbidity of depression and AD is common, and in the early phases of AD, depression may add "excess" disability that affects day-to-day functioning. The symptoms of depression can be difficult to identify in individuals with AD. Recent studies suggest that one manifestation that has been overlooked may be heightened aggressive behavior, including verbal hostility, toward family members and other long-term caregivers (Menon et al., 2001). Depression is also highly likely in older persons diagnosed with other mild levels of cognitive impairment. And depression is increasingly likely among family members who provide direct care and supervision for a relative with AD. Some research shows that depressive symptoms in the care recipient are mirrored in the persons who provide care; the more depression in the care recipient, the more in the caregiver (Teri, 1996). It is not that depression is contagious, but rather that it adds so much to the burden of caregiving, often serving to negate the rewards and recognition caregivers might receive. In one study, caregivers of depressed patients with Alzheimer's experienced greater depression and burden themselves than caregivers who provided care for nondepressed patients with Alzheimer's (Pearson et al., 1993). In another study, spouses caring for a husband or wife with AD showed greater depression when they lacked flexibility in defining their spousal role (Majerovitz, 1995). With effective treatment, the aspects of depression that limit the AD patient's functioning and that increase the caregiving burden can be alleviated.

Depression and Caregiving

Caregivers at greatest risk of depression are those who provide for an aging relative with behavior problems and cognitive impairments, who have significant role conflicts (e.g., employment and family), and who feel captive in the caregiving role (Bookwala & Schulz, 2000; Stephens, Townsend, Martire, & Druley, 2001). Depression and other psychological disorders are more likely to occur among female caregivers, particularly those with low mastery (Yee & Schulz, 2000). A high risk for depression was reported among daughters with low levels of mastery and multiple caregiving responsibilities among their own families. Daughters with higher mastery and those who shared the caregiving role with a sibling had a much lower risk of depression. Longitudinal studies reveal that as new demands for assistance occur in the caregiving career, the risk for depression rises (Given, Given, Stommel, & Azzouz, 1999).

Caregiving for an aging parent with multiple behavior problems or dementia increases the risk of depression (Li, Seltzer, & Greenberg, 1999). Dementia caregivers, for example, spend many more hours in the caregiving role than nondementia caregivers. They provide more assistance with Activities of Daily Living and Independent Activities of Daily Living and experience more mental and physical health problems themselves. Dementia caregivers also experience significantly more role conflict and role strain and have less time to devote to family, leisure, and employment (Ory et al., 1999).

Elderly husbands serving as caregivers to their wives generally report fewer *primary stressors*—providing personal assistance (in eating, toileting, and transporting), doing heavy housework, and managing behavioral problems—than wives who care for their husbands. Yet wives have more depressive symptoms than husbands in the caregiving role (Bookwala, Yee, & Schulz, 2000). Wives experience the caregiving role as more limiting to their personal and social activities than husbands do; these limitations constitute *secondary stressors*. Caregiving wives also report feeling less emotionally close to their spouses (less intimacy, less sharing, less emotion) than caregiving husbands. Gender differences and perceived types of stress underlie the increased risk of depression among spousal caregivers (Bookwala & Schulz, 2000).

The risk for depression among caregivers is greatest among those who feel captive in the role. Feelings of captivity do not dissipate over time, even with targeted intervention. For example, using adult day care reduced symptoms of depression and role overload in caregivers, but had no effect on feelings of role captivity. Only institutionalization of the care recipient reduced the perception of role captivity (Alspaugh et al., 1999).

Treatment of Clinical Depression

Treatment of clinical depression in older adults can be complex, as Research Focus 5.1 shows. As family and friends can verify, depressed people are difficult to be around, unusually dependent, withdrawn, and demanding. Clinically depressed people generally discourage social contact from the very people who can be most supportive. Thus, families and caregivers need assistance, and depressed older adults need interventions that will mobilize their resources while recognizing their concerns.

Brief psychotherapy based on cognitive-behavioral models, drug interventions, and combination forms of treatment has been effective in treating clinical depression in older adults. Drug therapy for the depressed elderly consists of antidepressants. These drugs can not only improve depressive symptoms, they also benefit those with cognitive impairments. However, cognitive abilities such as memory and personal

Creative Achievement, Eminence, and Psychological Disorders

Experts examining psychological adjustment and coping processes have noted that frequently, though not always, those who make unique and outstanding contributions in their fields are burdened with psychological disorders. Some believe that mental turmoil helps to feed the creative process (Ludwig, 1996). For example, it is curious that many of the musical geniuses of the past two centuries suffered from manic-depression, or bipolar affective disorder. DeAngelis (1989) examined the suffering and personal anguish this mood disorder brought to those in the creative arts. Talented composers such as George Frederic Handel, Hugo Wolf, Robert Schumann, Hector Berlioz, and Gustav Mahler experienced the cyclic effects of intense periods of activity or mania, which probably contributed to their immense musical creativity and productivity. Yet their corresponding bouts of debilitating depression, leading at times to suicidal thoughts or behaviors, also affected these composers.

The following diary excerpts and letters reveal how difficult it was for these composers to cope with their manic-depressive episodes. Berlioz, for instance, described his two moods as "the two kinds of spleen; one mocking, active, passionate, malignant; the other morose and wholly passive." Schumann likened his mood swings to two imaginary people, the first "impulsive, widely energetic, impassioned, decisive, masculine, high-spirited, and iconoclastic; the other gentle, melancholic, pious, introspective, and inwardly-gazing." According to musicologist Robert Winter, Gustav Mahler recognized the emergence of the condition as early as age 19, writing, "I have become a different person. I don't know whether this new person is better; he certainly is not happier. The fires of a supreme zest for living and the most gnawing desire for death alternate in my heart, sometimes in the course of a single hour."

Is manic-depression a prerequisite to creative expression in the arts? Are all creative people likely to experience manic-depression? Though many creative people have experienced manic-depression, the percentages rarely exceed 66 percent in any of the samples selected for study. However, even the more modest estimates that 25 to 50 percent of a sample of creative persons experience and/or have been treated for manic-depressive disorders represents a "disproportionate rate of affective illness in the highly creative," according to Kay Jamison of Johns Hopkins University of Medicine. However, not all persons who are creative, talented, or gifted in the arts experience manic-depressive disorders. Nor are all those with manic-depression necessarily creative.

Current research and theory suggests that manic-depression stems from biological factors that are expressed psychologically. The condition is apparently triggered when an environmental stressor "primes the pump," and the affective disorder begins its inevitable progression. The most effective treatments are based on a combination of psychotherapy and lithium, a drug used to level extreme moods. But researchers estimate that fewer than two-thirds of the more than two million adults with manic-depression are diagnosed or treated. Many of these untreated adults are elderly.

Researchers have observed other types of psychological disorders in creative persons of achievement. Ludwig (1995) identified a sample of 1,000 deceased twentieth-century persons who were prominent in their fields. Their eminence was identified from data on reputation, public recognition, breadth of creative achievements, originality, foresight, influence in their fields, and so on. Those in the creative arts were more likely to experience psychological disorders at some time in their lives—more than 72 percent of the creative fell into this category. Those in social, business, and investigation

personal judgment still do not return to normal levels. Some investigators see a relationship between late-onset depression and a risk for developing dementia (Butters et al., 2000). Combined drug and psychotherapy treatments produced the most improvement in older persons treated for clinical depression, while drug treatments alone had the poorest results. Surprisingly, older persons whose clinical depression was treated either with brief (4 months) psychotherapy alone or with combined psychotherapy and drug treatment showed nearly identical, positive results (Dick & Gallagher-Thompson, 1996). Many physicians, concerned about the side effects of drugs, may not prescribe appropriate dosages to adequately alleviate depression in older adults (Joiner, 2000).

Creative Achievement, Eminence, and Psychological Disorders

professions showed disorders an average of 39 to 49 percent of the time. The most common psychological disorders among artists, composers, entertainers, and writers were depression and alcoholism. Actors and those involved in performance had high rates of drug abuse, while poets were more likely to show evidence of manic-depression and psychosis. Suicide attempts were most often reported among actors, fiction writers, poets, and musical entertainers. According to Ludwig (1996), across all fields in the creative arts, achievements that relied on precision, reason, and logic were less likely to be associated with psychological problems than achievements that tapped into emotional expression and subjective experience. For example, poets and fiction writers showed higher rates of adjustment disorders than those who wrote nonfiction.

Eminence in other areas, such as science, academics, or politics, was not associated with higher probabilities of psychological difficulties either in adolescence or adulthood. Ludwig points out that higher rates of psychological disorder among creative artists does not mean that mental turmoil is a necessary precondition for creative achievement. Those in the arts who were psychologically stable and those with disorders showed similar levels of creativity and eminence. Eminent people who experienced emotional difficulties in Ludwig's sample included Virginia Woolf, Ernest Hemingway, Eugene O'Neill, Paul Gauguin, and Robert Lowell. Those free from difficulties included Albert Einstein, Niels Bohr, Camille Pissaro, Margaret Mead, George Gershwin, and Orville Wright.

Although some believe that turmoil can spur creativity and creative expression, others recognize that the mental anguish associated with psychological disorders can limit achievement and productivity. Ludwig did note that psychological disorders can indirectly lead to a state of perpetual

"uneasiness" and tension that is released through creative productivity. Those who are stable emotionally, however, may generate their own uneasiness by identifying problems that require creative solutions. Both sources of creative achievement produce an individual who is highly motivated, focused, and able to concentrate for long, long periods of time on their work. These people have a sense of total commitment to the productive process, an exclusivity to their work, and a timelessness to the enterprise. This process, identified as "flow" by psychologist Mihaly Csikszentmihalyi, described a state in which individuals lose all sense of time as they become fully absorbed in their work. "Flow" is not restricted to adults who suffer from psychological disorders, nor is it unique to certain fields.

Ludwig concludes that those with the highest attainments among people of eminence, whether they experienced psychological disorders or not, did not find contentment and peace of mind; their successes did not satisfy them for very long. Mental disorders in themselves do not necessarily prove helpful or destructive to the process of creative achievement. "Other personal attributes and circumstances determine the capacity to exploit inner tensions in the service of creative achievement" (Ludwig, 1996, p. 6).

Sources: DeAngelis, T. (1989). Mania, depression, and genius: Concert, talks inform public about manic-depressive illness. *APA Monitor, 20* (1): 1, 24. Copyright 1989 by the American Psychological Association. Reprinted by permission.

Ludwig, A. M. (1996). Mental disturbance and creative achievement. *Harvard Mental Health Letter* (March, pp. 4–5). Copyright 1996 by Harvard Mental Health Letter. Reprinted by permission.

Ludwig, A. M. (1995). *Resolving the creativity and madness controversy.* N.Y.: Guilford Press.

Therapy for depression is often based on cognitive-behavioral approaches and brief psychotherapeutic interventions. **Cognitive-behavioral therapy** attempts to change the negative thoughts, beliefs, and attitudes that depressed individuals hold about themselves, their experiences, and their futures. Carrying negative views leads to ". . . certain errors in thinking that occur relatively automatically and that are self-reinforcing unless they are challenged . . ." and replaced with more accurate thoughts or beliefs (Coon, Rider, Gallagher-Thompson, and Thompson, 1999, p. 488). Once they develop more flexible thought patterns, patients experience an improved emotional outlook that can reduce depression and enhance functioning in everyday life. Depression also causes behavioral withdrawal. Doing less and less leads people to feel worse and worse. Cognitive-behavioral therapy tries to break this downward cycle and encourage participation in everyday activities. Engagement in pleasant activities enhances mood and improves feelings, thereby combatting depression. Even elderly with depression related to chronic illness can be taught to recognize dysfunctional thinking and to engage themselves in pleasant activities (Gatz, 2000; Rybarczyk et al., 1992).

Psychoeducational programs that combine group therapy and education also have a place in the treatment of depression among older adults. Psychoeducational programs employ a specific "curriculum," that presents essential information and also gives participants an opportunity to discuss their problems. A clinical leader encourages active, focused discussion in a supportive environment, inviting participants to share their feelings and concerns with each other and the clinical leader. Psychoeducational programs are also helpful for elderly spouses caring for a husband or wife with dementia (Dick & Gallagher-Thompson, 1996). Antidepressants are available to treat depression in the elderly and are generally highly effective, once appropriate dosages and side effects have been dealt with. The more common antidepressants include the older monoamine oxidase inhibitors, tricyclic antidepressants, and the newer selective serotonin reuptake inhibitors such as Prozac. Older persons with depression have responded best to brief psychotherapy and drug therapy in combination.

Suicide

Undiagnosed and untreated depression is a risk factor for suicide for people of all ages. It has been implicated in two-thirds of the more than 32,000 suicides in the United States each year. Suicide is the seventh leading cause of death among U.S. males, regardless of age; it does not rank among the top 10 causes for women. One of every six elderly persons with severe depression commits suicide. With increasing age, the risk of suicide also increases. Older adults commit 17 percent of all suicides, yet comprise less than 13 percent of the population in the United States. The suicide rate for white men over 85 years of age is 65 per 100,000—higher than for any other age group; it is six times the overall national rate. Compare this to the rate of 11.5 per 100,000 for young adults, 14 to 24 years old (Katz, 1997; National Institute of Mental Health, 2001a).

Other risk factors implicated in elderly suicide include (1) gender, (2) living alone, (3) social isolation, (4) the loss of a spouse, and (5) failing health. For men 65 years of age and older, suicide is the third leading cause of death. Men accounted for 83 percent of suicides among those 65 and older (NIMH, 2001a). The largest percentage increase in suicides is for men 80 to 84 years old; they show a 17 percent increase from only five years ago (National Vital Statistics, 1999). Figure 5.3 shows the suicide rate by age, sex, and race. The suicide rate for older white males is nearly seven times that for older white females, although the incidence of clinical depression is more prevalent among females than males.

Ethnicity and Suicide Mental health professionals who focus on aging have examined the relationship of suicide to ethnicity. Suicide is a more probable outcome of untreated depression among older white males, but not among Asians, Hispanics, or blacks (Conwell, 1994; McIntosh, Santos, Hubbard, & Overholser, 1994). Recent surveys show that white males 65 years of age and older have a suicide rate of 37 per 100,000, versus a national rate of 11.3 (McIntosh, 2001). Analysis by race reveals that white males

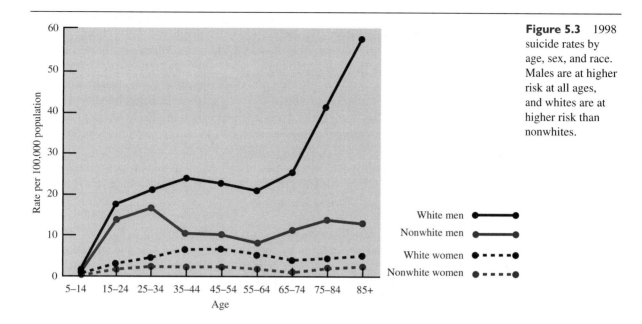

Figure 5.3 1998 suicide rates by age, sex, and race. Males are at higher risk at all ages, and whites are at higher risk than nonwhites.

aged 85 or older have three times the rate of suicide of black males in the same age group. As figure 5.3 suggests, patterns of suicide differ widely among white and black older males, with elderly females showing rather low rates among both races. Whereas older white men show the largest age-related increase in suicide, black American men show two peaks, at about age 20 to 35 and another in later life, beginning at age 80 (Katz, 1997; McIntosh, 2001).

Turnbull and Mui (1995) have suggested that the lower rates of suicide among black men may be due to selective mortality or to better coping skills among this population of hardy "survivors," given the differential life circumstances that separate this cohort of elderly males from their white counterparts. Older black American men, by virtue of their survival, may well represent a group that has succeeded in managing stress and discrimination in their earlier years. Blacks over the age of 75 show a **crossover effect.** Although they are at higher risk for death at earlier ages, those who manage to live into old age represent a select group whose life expectancy is higher than that for people of similar age from other races (Padgett, 1995). Black suicide is highest in urban areas and lowest in the South, where blacks' population density is the highest (Conwell, 1995). Investigators speculate that regional differences may relate to the significant role community institutions play in the South—particularly the black church and the extended family network, which hold older blacks in high esteem.

Native American peoples represent more than 302 separate tribal groups; there-fore, it is difficult to make generalizations about mental health issues such as suicide among this diverse ethnic group. The Navajo of the Southwest, for instance, believe that suicide will lead to bad luck and illness for all family survivors and for any others who were directly associated with the death (Holmes & Holmes, 1995). Perhaps because of this belief, Navajo suicide rates are lowest among Native Americans, with only 12 sui-cides per 100,000 population. Compare this rate to that for the Intermountain Native

American tribes (Blackfoot, Shoshone-Bannock, and Shoshone-Paiute), which is close to 100 per 100,000 population (Group for the Advancement of Psychiatry, 1989). Among the Inuit peoples of Northwest Canada, the Yukon, and Alaska, researchers have documented that high suicide rates among the elderly are the direct result of a cultural acceptance of the practice. When infirmity and disability limit the contributions of the elderly to Inuit society or make the traditional nomadic lifestyle difficult to follow, older persons recognize that they have become a burden and view suicide as an acceptable response. Suicide may also emerge in response to the death of a close relative or loved one. According to Inuit religious belief, through death, especially if it is violent, a person can become reunited with family and loved ones. In general, Native American suicide rates are 1.5 times the national rate, with younger males (15 to 24) accounting for 64 percent of all suicides.

Recognition and Treatment of Suicide Risk   Since many elderly are reluctant to access community-based mental health services, family members, friends, and neighbors play a critical role in recognizing the signs of depression and helping older persons to seek treatment. Many depressive episodes in late life are the direct result of chronic medical problems that lead to functional impairment, and disabilities such as heart problems, lung problems, and other chronic conditions. Unfortunately, more than 50 percent of all older persons believe that depression is a "normal" part of aging and a natural response to the health problems typically associated with growing old (Katz, 1997). They see no reason to seek treatment for what they assume to be inevitable emotional responses.

Reducing the incidence of suicide is one of the mental health goals of the Surgeon General's national health agenda for the next decade, laid out in *Healthy People 2010* (U.S. Department of Health and Human Services, 2000). One strategy for reaching this goal is to educate both families and professionals about the risk factors leading to suicide, particularly in the elderly. **Psychological autopsies** of suicides are *ex post facto* analyses of the psychological state, personality characteristics, and environmental stressors that preceded a suicide. Mental health professionals use the psychological autopsy to discern the warning signs of suicide so that they can provide timely, appropriate interventions and increase public awareness of the risk factors in suicide. Since older persons are usually more likely to be successful in committing suicide than younger people, intervention is directed at preventing the suicide attempt (Katz, 1997; Kennedy, 1996). It is easy to overlook the warning signs of possible suicide in older adults. Many have seen a health care professional within the previous month, usually a primary care physician, to treat the physical symptoms of depression (Kaplan, Adamek, & Calderon, 1999). Signs of potential suicide in the elderly include extreme despair, overwhelming helplessness, and hopelessness about themselves and the future. Most physicians are not trained to recognize the signs of potential suicide in older patients. The general signs of suicide among all at-risk individuals, regardless of age, include:

1. Extreme mood or personality changes (moodiness, withdrawal, hostility)
2. Discussion of suicide or death; verbal threats ("You'd be better off without me.")
3. Preoccupation with the futility of continuing the struggle of daily living and little interest in the future
4. Giving away prized possessions to friends and relatives

5. Disturbances in sleep and eating
6. Severe threat to identity and self-esteem
7. Death of loved ones and/or long-term friends
8. Depression

Elderly adults who have no social support network to monitor depressive and suicidal feelings can move from thought to action. Knowing that an older person has thought about suicide, developed a plan, and has the means to carry it out requires immediate action; the more detailed the plan, the greater the risk. Intervention means telling others about the plan so they can monitor and prevent an older person from carrying it out (Richman, 1999). Other recommendations include (1) talking with the person to show concern and a sincere interest to help, (2) listening closely to the issues, (3) obtaining professional help, even if the person is resistive, (4) not leaving the person alone, (5) not becoming a counselor, (6) not acting shocked, (7) not becoming judgmental (National Mental Health Association, 2001).

Two factors have been identified to explain why suicide attempts among older adults are more likely to be lethal. The most prevalent method of suicide the elderly use is firearms. Nearly 71 percent of all suicides in this population used this method, followed by hanging, poisons, and jumping from heights (McIntosh, 2001). Those choosing firearms were most likely to have less than a high school education, reside in a nonmetropolitan area, and to be married, divorced, or widowed (Kaplan, Adamek, & Geling, 1996). Lethal suicide attempts may also be more common among the elderly because they have more difficulty recovering from their injuries than younger people do. Passive techniques are believed to be underrecognized in the suicide statistics for older adults, particularly among the chronically ill. Passive techniques include starvation, single-car automobile accidents, failing to take medications, overdosing on prescription medications, or mixing medications with other drugs such as alcohol.

Suicide by firearms is the most prevalent active suicide method among older white males (Kaplan et al., 1996). White males over age 85 were more likely to use firearms in a suicide *attempt;* those between ages 65 and 84 were more likely to actually commit suicide using firearms.

Alcoholism

The abuse of alcohol is the most common drug problem, excluding tobacco use, among older adults. The American Medical Association estimates that more than 2.5 to 3 million older persons have alcohol-related disorders, or roughly 5 percent of those 60 years of age and older (Adams & Cox, 1997; Council on Scientific Affairs, 1996). Identifying alcoholism among older adults involves less traditional routes than identifying it among younger adults. Older adults who are problem or heavy drinkers are often first identified at primary care office appointments, on emergency room visits, during hospitalizations, or on admission to long-term care facilities (Dupree & Schonfeld, 1999).

The incidence of alcohol-related problems in the elderly has probably been underestimated. Screening questionnaires may not be appropriate for the elderly, and the consequences of alcohol abuse (depression, inadequate nutrition, congestive heart failure, frequent falls) may be erroneously attributed to medical or other psychological conditions. Nearly 50 percent of nursing home residents have problems related directly to alcohol, while 14 percent of older adults seen for emergency room treatment and 21 percent of those hospitalized for in-patient care show evidence of alcoholism (National Institute of Alcohol Abuse and Alcoholism, 1998; Dupree & Schonfeld, 1999). Careful screening of new hospital patients by staff trained to recognize alcoholism results in even higher percentages. Socioeconomic status plays a significant role in alcohol abuse among the elderly. Those who have had to cope with poverty, unemployment or underemployment, discrimination, and substandard housing throughout their lives are at high risk (Aponte, Rivers, & Wohl, 1995). However, the rate of alcoholism among older white Americans is higher than that among older blacks, Hispanics, and Asians.

Older adults show symptoms of alcoholism that mirror those of younger persons (e.g., amount consumed, alcohol-related social and legal problems, alcohol-related health problems, behavioral signs of drunkenness). Older men are more likely to have problems with alcohol than women. Men over the age of 75 who have lost a spouse have the highest incidence of alcoholism of any group (Glass, Prigerson, Kasl, & Mendes de Leon, 1995). Women turn to alcohol much later in life than men, who seem to continue drinking habits established years earlier. Older women are also at risk for other addictions such as abuse of prescription drugs (NIAA, 1998).

Elderly adults are not likely to receive counseling or seek help for alcoholism. One national survey found less than 4 percent of clients in alcoholism treatment programs were over the age of 55 (Dupree & Schonfeld, 1996). However, like treatment for depression, treatment for alcoholism in older adults is just as effective as it is for younger people. Generally, the shorter the duration of the problem, the better the results. The treatment goals for elderly alcoholics are similar to those for any age group: Stabilize or reduce alcohol consumption, treat coexisting psychological problems, and develop a social support network. Successful treatment programs for older adults with alcoholism share the following features (Schonfeld and Dupree, 1999):

1. Emphasize age-specific group treatment with supportive approaches and minimal confrontation.
2. Focus on negative emotional states (e.g., depression, loneliness, struggling with personal losses such as death of friends and family, poor health, and lowered self-concept).
3. Develop resources to rebuild social support systems.
4. Employ staff with a decided commitment to and extensive experience with the elderly.
5. Develop links with aging and medical services to get appropriate referrals.
6. Create a therapeutic environment with an appropriate pace and content that fits the elderly client.

A three-stage treatment approach represents one model program for older adults (the Gerontology Alcohol Project). Participants are initially screened to identify their drinking behavior patterns. They then learn to recognize the "high-risk" situations that lead them to drink. Finally, they are trained to use self-management and cognitive behavioral skills "to address their personal high-risk situations or antecedents for use, and relapse prevention" (Dupree & Schonfeld, 1999, p. 634). The drinking behavior chain

Figure 5.4 Mrs. S's drinking behavior chain. *Source:* Dupree, L. W., and Schonfeld, L. Management of alcohol abuse in older adults. In M. Duffy (Ed.), *Handbook of counseling and psychotherapy with older adults* (p. 642). New York: John Wiley.

| | | | | | Time → | |
| | | Antecedents | → | Behavior | → | Consequences |
Situations/ Thoughts	Feelings	Cues	Urges	Drink	Immediate or Short-Term	Long-Term
Home, alone watching TV	Depressed about life Bored— nothing to do Restless and tense	Liquor in my cabinet Beer in refrigerator	"This will help me forget." "I'll feel less lonely."	Bourbon or vodka Beer	Less lonely (+) Relaxed (+) Less angry (+) Less depressed (+)	My ulcer will be bothering me (−) I feel guilty over my drinking problems (−) My daughter gets angry if she sees me drinking (−)
At my house, babysitting the grandchildren At my daughter's house babysitting	Angry and pressured about babysitting Angry at babysitting	Phone call from daughter After babysitting grandchildren Supply of liquor at my daughter's house	"I'm angry at her and want to calm down; to relax." "I'd like to take control over my life again. I'm in charge of me."	Bourbon or vodka Bourbon or vodka		

in this treatment model consists of *Antecedents* (situations, feelings, thoughts, cues, urges) that lead to *Behaviors* (drinking) with both short- and long-term *Consequences.* Figure 5.4 illustrates the ABC model for one elderly individual. This treatment approach has been successful, with participants learning to be more sensitive to their emotions (developing self-monitoring skills) and to break the chain linking negative feelings and alcohol. Relapse is common, and usually related to intrapersonal feelings (loneliness, anger, depression, frustration), interpersonal conflict or social pressure (Dupree & Schonfeld, 1999). Once participants identify the feelings that trigger relapse, they can use new cognitive and behavioral skills to prevent relapse or recover from it.

Other successful programs for elderly alcoholics use older peer counselors who have recovered as models and mentors for those facing their addiction. Peer counselors act as "coaches," encouraging alternative coping strategies to deal with the multiple losses of old age. Other interventions include Alcoholics Anonymous or other social support groups, behavior modification, and insight therapy. Some programs train the elderly in "drink refusal," others stress assertiveness, and still others train older people to manage tension and anxiety differently, so that they are not dependent on alcohol for coping. Older adults work at slower pace in any intervention program, but they can become abstinent and successfully self-monitor. If they relapse, they can also learn to recognize when it is time to call others for help (Dupree & Schonfeld, 1996).

With increasing age, the body becomes less able to tolerate the effects of alcohol. As people age, the body experiences a decrease in lean body mass, a lower volume of water, and reduced blood flow. These changes increase sensitivity to alcohol and create higher blood alcohol levels (Dupree & Schonfeld, 1996). Given the increased biological sensitivity of older persons to drugs, intoxication occurs at lower levels of consumption than would be necessary for younger people. Paradoxically, statistics reveal that with increasing age, beginning at age 50, the number of people classified as alcoholics *decreases.* Evidently, those who develop alcoholic behaviors in early adulthood (**early-onset alcoholism**) often do not survive to reach middle or old age, or they develop multiple health problems that force them to abstain. One estimate is that the life span of an alcoholic who starts young is shortened by 10 to 15 years (Institute of Alcohol Studies, 1997). Early-onset alcoholics who reach old age are beset with a variety of physical health problems, including liver damage, high blood pressure, heart disease, and alcohol-based organic brain syndrome. The latter severe condition, called **Korsakoff's syndrome,** is marked by behavioral disorientation, confusion, delusions, and irreversible memory disorder. Patients have an inability to remember new facts and events for more than a few seconds (*anterograde amnesia*) and have difficulties with temporal discrimination, spatial organization, abstraction, and initiative. Alcohol-based organic brain syndrome is related to the destruction of brain cells and reduced metabolism in the frontal cortex and parietal cortex. Malnourishment, vitamin deficiency, and inadequate protein are correlated with the syndrome, as alcoholics typically forgo basic nutritional needs in favor of gratifying their substance dependency (Eberling & Jagust, 1995). Long-term heavy drinking results in increased mortality for both younger and older adults (Gallo, Bradley, Siegel, & Stanislav, 2001).

The existence of **late-onset alcoholism** was disputed for many years, but many studies have now confirmed the phenomenon. It may emerge in one of three forms: (1) as an increase in consumption over earlier periods in development, (2) as a relapse reflective of earlier patterns of overuse, or (3) as a first-time phenomenon. Late-onset alcoholism can often be triggered by situational factors such as failing health, isolation, loneliness, difficulty sleeping, or the death of a spouse. It is usually related to chronic, multiple situational stressors rather than one specific life event and is more common among older women than older men. Late-onset alcoholism is associated with higher socioeconomic status, and is often ignored by family and friends and underdiagnosed by professionals (Dupree & Schonfield, 1999). Late-onset alcoholism accounts for one-third to one-half of all elderly alcoholics (NIA, 2001; Welte & Mirand, 1995). One study investigated the phenomenon of late-onset alcoholism in response to involuntary job loss. Workers who lost their jobs and those who continued their employment were compared on two measures: (1) self-reported daily consumption of alcohol (2) onset of drinking. Using careful analysis of baseline alcohol consumption, and controlling for illness and social class, the results showed that job loss was unrelated to an increase in drinking among drinkers who lost their jobs. However, job loss doubled the likelihood that workers who did not use alcohol to cope would begin drinking (Gallo, Bradly, Siegel, & Kasl, 2001). The choice of dependent variable (increase in drinking or initiating drinking) is an important factor in studying the relationship of late-onset alcoholism to situational stresses.

The **tension-reduction hypothesis** offers one explanation for why problem drinkers turn to alcohol (Glass et al., 1995; Krause, 1995b). Alcohol is a way of managing the tension that negative life events and chronic stress create. Those with limited coping skills and social resource deficits are more likely to use alcohol to manage tension. Support for this hypothesis appears in studies with young adults, but the results are equivocal when older adults are the target subjects. Research Focus 5.2 discusses one study of the tension-reduction hypothesis.

Life Events and Alcohol Use:
The Tension-Reduction Hypothesis

The tension-reduction hypothesis was explored in a three-year longitudinal study with 2,487 community-residing persons 65 years of age and older (Glass et al., 1995). Researchers identified each person's baseline alcohol consumption at the beginning of the study, and then monitored 11 different negative life events common to the experience of older persons over the next 36 months to determine their effect on drinking. Negative life events included the loss of a close friend who moved away from the area, the death of a close relative, having a close relative become sick or injured, being the victim of a crime, hospitalization, or a nursing home stay. The population sample included heavy drinkers, light-moderate drinkers, and nondrinkers.

The major finding of the study was that the initial baseline level of alcohol consumption determined the impact of only certain negative life events on drinking. Most important, not all negative life events had the same effect on alcohol consumption. Interactions appeared between initial levels of alcohol consumption and the type of negative life event. Some negative life events, such as dealing with a sick or injured relative, caused an increase in drinking among those who drank heavily, yet had no effect on light drinkers. Other negative life events, such as being hospitalized or being the victim of a serious crime, were associated with a decrease in drinking, regardless of initial level of alcohol consumption. These results were moderated still further by gender. Taken together, these data offer only moderate support for the tension-reduction hypothesis as an explanation for alcoholism among older persons.

In a related study, Krause (1995) found some support for the tension-reduction hypothesis as a factor in alcohol consumption in the elderly. The salience of the role in which the older person encountered stressors was the major determining factor in increased alcohol consumption. Alcohol did reduce tension or lower stress by helping to buffer the older person from stressors in roles that were not very important to him or her. However, in roles that were highly salient, alcohol was found to increase stress and tension for the elderly (Krause, 1995).

The data showing gender differences are consistent with other studies showing that men and women react differently to negative life events. Women appear to react more strongly to negative life events that affect their social networks, while men react more strongly to negative life events that involve their work or have an impact on their finances (Conger et al., 1993). The data also show that one-third of the men and one-half of the women abstained from drinking completely for at least one year during the study's duration. It was hypothesized that abstinence for a 12-month period was most likely related to medical treatments, medications that could not be taken with alcohol, and illnesses that required hospitalization or extensive nursing home care. Perhaps most interesting, given the current national concern about alcoholism in the elderly, overall alcohol consumption declined from the baseline over the three years of the study, regardless of the initial level of alcohol consumption. Key negative life events, however, were found to delay this general decline in alcohol consumption.

Older alcoholics are more likely to have adopted cognitive and behavioral avoidance responses as a way of managing life stress. Avoidance is linked to a higher incidence of problem drinking, more depression, more physical symptoms, and lowered self-confidence (Dupree & Schonfeld, 1996). Prior problem drinking often reemerges in later life (Dupree & Schonfeld, 1999).

Many health care professionals do not make referrals, even if alcoholism is suspected. They believe identification as an alcoholic is worse for an older person than the occurrence of alcoholism itself. Acceptance of the problem is particularly likely in Hispanic populations, where symptoms of alcoholism such as frailty, depression, senility, or unsteadiness are taken as "normal" aging (Lopez-Bushnell, Tyra, & Futrell, 1992). However, it is important to distinguish between various Hispanic populations and their risk for alcoholism. Cuban-American males, for example, in both middle age and older age tend to have low rates of alcoholism, in contrast to Mexican-American and mainland Puerto-Rican males (Black & Markides, 1994).

Therapeutic Intervention with the Ethnic Elderly

The need to know the backgrounds, values, and assumptions that clients bring to therapeutic treatment becomes clear when we examine the ethnic elderly. Therapists are well advised to understand the cultural backgrounds of older clients from different ethnic traditions before developing intervention strategies and to help with case-management decisions.

Ethnic Sensitivity

Aponte and Barnes (1995) reviewed the importance of intervention strategies that recognize the broad differences between major ethnic groups in the United States. Membership in an ethnic group does not mean that all such individuals share homogeneous characteristics, values, and attitudes. Trimble (1989) originally coined the term **ethnic gloss,** to refer to the tendency to try to make ethnic groups appear more homogeneous than they actually are. Hispanics, for example, may come from Caribbean countries such as Puerto Rico or Cuba; from specific countries of South America; from Central America, including Mexico; or from Spain. Not only do different origins instill different values, they also may reflect different levels of acculturation to Western society. Some families voluntarily choose to become immigrants; others arrive as refugees, migrating involuntarily and experiencing harsh conditions and significant stress; still others have established roots in the United States over many generations; and others may immigrate temporarily (e.g., foreign students or workers from other countries). Despite the appearance of commonality based on ethnicity, each individual is at differential risk for psychological problems (Aponte & Barnes, 1995). The field of psychology has too often ignored individual differences among people with similar ethnic backgrounds. People with different acculturations, different migration histories, and different socialization experiences are not likely to share the same behaviors, regardless of their shared group identity. Thus, it is difficult to develop general mental health recommendations and treatment approaches for older persons from apparently similar ethnic backgrounds.

Case Management

Ethnic elderly clients most often present themselves to health and mental health professionals with diverse symptoms that could stem from any of a number of mental health disorders. Some individuals prefer to share their complaints with physicians, rather than with mental health professionals. This can delay appropriate diagnosis and make treatment challenging and complex.

Historically, mental health professionals have not valued clinical intervention with the elderly, and until recently, few ethnic role models were involved in the delivery of mental health services (Grant, 1995). Ethnic elderly who are particularly likely to need treatment are those who have had adjustment difficulties in the past or whose demographic profiles suggest vulnerability; for example, those subject to financial restrictions, health problems, and lack of health care insurance. Some older persons find it increasingly difficult to manage stress as new coping demands emerge in later life.

Mental health professionals need to pay specific attention to cultural and social environmental factors in understanding the symptoms the ethnic elderly present.

Some ethnic populations do not conceptualize mental health disorders as problems based on "internal psychological" processes. Among some ethnic groups, mental health disorders are expressed primarily through physical complaints (Grant, 1995). Older persons, in particular, may show symptoms that carry special significance for their culture. Psychologists must be aware of the meanings of these symptoms and carefully review how elderly persons from diverse backgrounds adapt and cope in their everyday environments. Functional assessments of physical health, cognition, activities related to independent daily living, and social interactions may be confounded by symptoms of psychological disorders for ethnically diverse elderly. It is important to understand how ethnic differences in expressing symptoms can influence such assessments before drawing any conclusions regarding functional impairment.

Treatment Concerns: Individual Therapy

Professional mental health workers are not all equally effective in working with different ethnicities. Consultation with others who are knowledgeable about a particular ethnic group or culture is one way to build cultural sensitivities. Successful interventions require an appreciation of the multiple factors in the culture, community, and social network that may contribute to a mental health disorder. Therefore, successful intervention with the ethnic elderly often requires professionals from different agencies and disciplines to work together (Markides & Miranda, 1997).

Individual therapy has been successful in helping older people from diverse cultural backgrounds to cope more effectively with adjustment disorders, depression, and anxiety (Grant, 1995). Western models of individual therapy, however, make basic treatment assumptions that may not be adapted to the backgrounds of ethnic minorities. These treatment assumptions include a primary focus on the person; the expectation of open verbal, emotional, and behavioral sharing between client and therapist in an intimate relationship; the adoption of an analytic, linear model of causation in identifying problems and creating solutions; and the tendency to see inner, emotional functioning as separate from physical life (Sue, 1998; Uba, 1994). Traditional therapeutic intervention is also problem-focused, time-limited, and empowering to the client. It is vital for therapists not only to recognize these assumptions, but to clarify them when treating older persons from diverse ethnic backgrounds (Morales, 1999). A therapist may want to consider several questions. For example, what cultural beliefs might the client hold regarding mental illness and its symptoms or behavioral manifestations? What cultural biases might the client have regarding emotional self-expression and gender differences? What beliefs might influence the client's access to mental health services? What expectations govern the amount of time spent in therapy and the treatment outcomes? Asian Americans, for instance, have difficulty placing themselves, their needs, and their individual treatment ahead of family (Morales, 1999). Asian-American therapists were asked to identify the most important cultural values they would like other therapists to know in conducting therapy with Asian-American clients.

Table 5.3 summarizes the results of this survey, placing values in descending order of importance. The therapists were also asked to identify the ethnic-specific problems, values, and concerns that therapists should know in treating Asian-American clients. These data appear in table 5.4.

Culturally aware therapists recognize the discomfort that certain ethnic subgroups will experience in therapy. Some have been reviewed earlier (see table 5.1). Without this awareness, clients may perceive the therapist as lacking in care and concern, empathy, and understanding—factors that can lead to the decision to end treatment long before achieving success (Aponte & Barnes, 1995). Client and therapist may have rather different goals and definitions of success. Thus, therapists must be prepared to be far more active with older ethnic minority clients in order to keep them in treatment for sufficient periods of time. Ethnic elderly may perceive the passive strategies common to most listening therapies as disinterest (Grant, 1995). In addition to indi-

TABLE 5.3
Important Asian-American Cultural Values Therapists Need to Know About
Importance of family   Shame and guilt   Respect for people based on their status and roles   Styles of interpersonal behavior   Stigma associated with mental illness   Restraint of self-expression   Orientation toward group   Achievement   Sense of duty and obligation   Expectations that follow from different roles

Note: Data in table are based on Matsushima and Tashima (1982).

TABLE 5.4
Important Asian-American Ethnic-Specific Problems Therapists Need to Know About
Immigration experiences (presumably including traumas experienced prior to leaving home country)   Cultural conflicts in lifestyle and values   Importance of family issues   Racism   Conceptualizations of mental health and attitudes toward mental health services   Behavioral styles and norms   Language   Ethnic identity   Intergenerational problems

Note: Data in table are based on Matsushima and Tashima (1982).

vidual psychological counseling, therapists may also want to utilize biological, medical, nutritional, and social interventions. This may require them to educate clients about the availability of services and help them to access appropriate resources. Therapists must be prepared to work with the broader social network of the client, including friends and multiple generations in the family, to enlist their support. This can help the therapist to extend the benefits of individual therapy (Grant, 1995).

Treatment Concerns: Group Therapy

Group therapy for older ethnic populations seeking mental health services must be sensitive to clients' specific concerns in seeking treatment. The following guidelines, developed by Vasquez and Han (1995), have been designed to help professionals implement group therapy. These principles are appropriate for any group, including support groups for caregivers overwhelmed by dealing with an older patient with Alzheimer's or for older persons experiencing specific types of adjustment or coping disorders.

1. Focus on each group member's strengths. Ethnically diverse clients may assume more responsibility for creating their problems and solving their difficulties than other clients. Positive evaluation of ethnic minorities' personal strengths will help build self-esteem.
2. Promote the empowerment of group members. Create opportunities for participants to begin to trust their individual emotions and direct observations. Ethnically diverse clients, particularly older women, appear to have had little opportunity to gain validation for their feelings, perceptions, and understandings. Support that helps them express their opinions and exchange their views with others may be beneficial.
3. Promote communication and assertiveness skills. These skills will generalize to other areas and help older persons from ethnically diverse backgrounds to

The challenge of bringing individual or group therapies to the lives of ethnically diverse adults lies in overcoming cultural values that are incompatible with the processes and goals of traditional treatments.

express personal views, indicate personal preferences, and negotiate differences of opinion between close family members.

4. Facilitate the expression of negative feelings. Clients may have difficulty expressing negative emotions (e.g., anger, hostility, disapproval) to others in group settings. The group provides an opportunity to learn how to recognize and express these emotions when they occur in other settings.

5. Promote a focus on the here and now. Help clients face the reality of today and their current emotions. Clients can explore how today's issues relate to their unique past experiences.

6. Focus on sociocultural issues. Help people see how forces outside of themselves have contributed to their development, exploring sociocultural factors, environmental factors, politics, power, and economics.

Treatment Concerns: Language

Language differences for a number of ethnic groups in the United States can have an impact on both the decision to access mental health services and on treatment effectiveness or outcomes. More than 17.5 million U.S. residents over the age of 5 speak Spanish, and another 4.5 million primarily speak a language from Asia or one of the Pacific Islands. One-third of Hispanics over the age of 60 speak English poorly or not at all (Mutchler & Brallier, 1999). Proficiency in English is poorest among recent immigrants to the United States, particularly those with less education and income. Many live in a community with a high concentration of other Hispanics who have weak English-language skills. Dealing with English-only mental health professionals will be very difficult for these individuals. Mental health professionals often show a negative bias regarding those whose primary language is not English. They tend to evaluate such persons as being more disturbed and as having greater pathology and more difficulty expressing affect (Aponte & Barnes, 1995). The decision to leave treatment before attaining a successful outcome can often be traced directly to the perceived effectiveness of both verbal and nonverbal communication between client and professional. Important questions to consider are the following: Are bilingual clients using their preferred language? Does the clinician understand the cultural expressions conveyed by critical words in English? And does symptom expression truly convey the depth of feeling and psychological experience of the client to the clinician (Westermeyer, 1993)? Many older clients belonging to diverse subcultures have identified language differences between themselves and their therapists as one of the primary reasons behind their decision to terminate treatment (Morales, 1999).

Treatment Concerns: Bias and Prejudice

Many obstacles besides language discourage culturally diverse older people from seeking and staying in treatment. Many of these obstacles may stem from an older person's long personal history of discrimination with the majority institutions in our society (Morales, 1999). One oft-mentioned barrier to seeking mental health treatment among older black Americans is healthy **cultural paranoia.** This describes hostility, suspicion, and distrust directed toward mental health programs as well as other community-based services associated with white majority culture. Improving access to mental health services does not automatically lead to better treatment or to the end of prejudice. And, similarly, removing many of the barriers to mental health utilization does not automatically improve outcomes for older persons from ethnically diverse backgrounds. Even **ethnic matching,** which links clients to a professional with similar ethnic characteristics, does not necessarily result in better treatment outcomes (Sue et al., 1992; Sue et al., 1994). Professionals who provide treatment to adults from ethnically diverse cultures must also recognize their clients' strong fear of becoming stigmatized among their communities for seeking mental health services. Ethnicity and race are often predictive of client misdiagnosis, reduced mental health services, inappropriate treatments, and service provided by the least-seasoned among the professional staff (Sue, 1998). Mental health services for ethnically diverse older adults must be available in advance of crises. To make this happen, professionals must develop a delivery system that matches the cultural sensitivities of ethnic and racially diverse elderly and the communities in which they live.

A Developmental Perspective on Intervention

Psychological problems can be related to age if they are brought about by events that are likely to occur at certain points in adult development. As we mentioned in chapter 4, most adults carry an "expected timetable" of normal life events and experience minimal distress when life events occur as anticipated. Much of the information regarding anticipated events is transmitted within the extended family, from the social network of neighbors and friends, and from the mass media. Some may regard this information as a form of "preventive intervention" since it allows adults to prepare for their own futures and plan ahead to avert problems. When events are off-time, occurring earlier or later than anticipated, when the events cause greater-than-expected functional impairments, or when they require coping and adaptation far beyond the ability of the individual to manage, then interventions become necessary. Available resources include both formal and informal social support and one's own inner resources. As we age, our coping resources may change. A woman widowed at 65 may profit from many years of coping with life changes and manage a loss well. She may have developed strengths and skills that were absent when she was 40.

As we have mentioned, older adults in our society, unlike younger persons, seldom define a personal problem in terms of mental health issues. Consequently, they are not as likely to seek mental health services (Padgett, 1995). The way individuals define problems influences the kinds of intervention they seek. The need for mental health services among older adults is likely to increase when today's cohort of young and middle-aged adults reach old age.

Before examining various intervention options, consider the more salient issues in adult development and some of the ways that mental health interventions can be developmentally appropriate.

Intervention in Middle Adulthood

During the transition to middle adulthood, it is common for people to reexamine the choices they made in young adulthood: their goals, vocations, mates, lifestyles, the geographical locations where they live. Levinson (1996) suggested that, early in life, we develop a dream of how life is supposed to be; then, in midlife, we reexamine the dream, either affirming it or rejecting it for another. It appears that we may construct our **life dreams** without much information about what might be required to carry them out. In middle age, many individuals feel a strong need to use their remaining time well, to do the right things, and to make the right decisions while there is time left. Reexamining life dreams is a part of the midlife transition and a time for self study.

Few men and women are able to realize their life dreams and "have it all," attaining the multiple goals of successful or challenging occupation, personal interests, marriage, and children. The cohort of 35- to 45-year-old women in Levinson's study reported, for the most part, that their life dreams were not met. About half of the 45 women in Levinson's intensive study had sought mental health services by the time they reached middle age. They viewed their efforts to combine marriage, motherhood, and full-time career as a partial or massive failure. In other words, they needed to invent a different dream or "new basis for living" from middle age onward.

In time, most adults master the transition of midlife and derive a sense of control over the more important decisions that affect them. They often expand their life goals and priorities, with men seeking more affection and compassion and women more assertiveness and autonomy. Some may revise and redefine marriage relationships, and work may, for some, become a place to mentor others. With middle age also comes the launching of children from the home, plus caring for grandchildren and aging parents. The strains of this developmental period are greatest when the individual feels blocked from making desired changes or is forced to make changes he or she does not endorse. Interventions make it possible for individuals to match their goals and ambitions with opportunities. Obviously people enter midlife with unique developmental histories, which can promote successful transitions or can bring about adjustment problems. Erik Erikson suggests that successful resolution of prior developmental tasks makes it more likely that the midlife transition will be successful, whereas prior problems are predictive of less success within this developmental period.

Intervention in Late Adulthood

Later life is marked by changes, and for some of these changes, interventions are helpful, appropriate, and, in some cases, absolutely necessary. The greatest danger is in providing too much intervention long before it is really called for, thus robbing older individuals of a sense of autonomy and personal control over their lives (Tiffany & Tiffany, 1996). Of course, on the other side of the coin, there are older people who need specific interventions that are not available, not affordable, or not recognized as essential for maintaining their independence. More people now enter their later years in good health than did members of previous cohorts. The elderly are no longer heavily involved in full-time employment, and they are free from concerns about parenting. The "young-old" person wonders how to make the most of this period of life. Generally, older persons who take up activities that are meaningful to them show higher morale and well-being than those who continue their middle-age roles and responsibilities. Options for the young-old include giving more time and energy to volunteer activities, seeking spiritual growth, continuing education, taking up hobbies and recreation, traveling, and taking on part-time employment. Mutchler, Burr, Pienta, and Massagli (1997) have noted that while a single retirement from a career or work role (a so-called crisp exit) is assumed to be normative in society, more than one-half of all older persons experience repeated exits and returns to the labor market (so-called blurred transitions). The most common reason for reentry to the workforce is to sustain or enhance a particular standard of living.

Specialized intervention strategies can enhance physical and mental health at earlier periods of development or reduce the impact of more serious disorders that arise in later life. Such interventions include education, exercise, and nutrition; eliminating behaviors that compromise health; and increasing behaviors that promote mental health, such as early diagnosis and treatment of disorders. By taking a preventive approach to intervention, the quality of life in old age can be enhanced. Of course, therapeutic approaches for older persons can be just as successful as those for younger persons. But, as noted earlier in this chapter, older persons are not as likely to seek or receive treatment for mental health disorders. Older adults are at risk, since they must redefine themselves and their social roles, and adapt to change as spouses, friends, and coworkers die and they themselves face retirement, reductions in income, and threats to health (Pettibone, Van Hasselt, & Hersen, 1996). Depression and adjustment disorders are common mental health concerns of older persons, and effective therapeutic treatments are available for these problems.

Understanding Intervention Options

Intervention can take many forms, but it always begins with a definition of the problem. Many older adults refuse to recognize problems that limit their autonomy or threaten their safety; many adult children are reluctant to face issues that threaten parents' independence—perhaps their inability to live alone or their problems with Activities of Daily Living. The elderly and their children often ignore concerns or try to diminish their seriousness. Professionals advise families not to "ignore the elephant in the living room" when obvious signs of depression or dementia are present or when physical illness compromises autonomy. When families ignore serious problems, they usually lead to greater difficulties and less effective intervention later on.

Once the problem has been defined, it is important to examine presumed causes. This often requires professionals to help with the assessment and diagnosis of the elderly. They can chart the likely progression of the problem, with or without intervention, and they can help to identify a range of intervention options. One of the best ways to determine causation is to examine the outcomes of intervention. A professional may assess **probable causes** for depression in old age by measuring the effectiveness of counseling and drug therapies. If the problem improves as a result of these interventions, then its probable cause has been identified. Table 5.5 summarizes the variety of goals, techniques, settings, and change agents involved in intervention across the life span.

Choosing the optimal intervention requires the mental health worker to evaluate empirical studies of the intervention's previous success. Interventions developed from empirically supported evaluations, or **efficacy research,** work best. This approach however, often systematically excludes specific groups of elders from the research: (1) those

TABLE 5.5

A Framework for Intervention Options

Goals	Settings
Alleviation	Home
Compensation	Work
Enrichment	Institution
Prevention	Community
	Society

Techniques	Change Agents
Clinical intervention/therapy	Self
Education and training	Family members
Psychopharmacology	Friends
Service delivery	Paraprofessionals
Environmental interventions	Professionals
Legislating social and behavioral change	Administrators
	Lawmakers/Governmental leaders

with two or more simultaneous mental health problems, (2) those with mental health issues and chronic disease, and (3) those who are oldest and most frail (Gatz, 2000).

Empirical evaluations of interventions that try to correct psychological disorders are far more common than those that try to enhance mental health function in older people who are free of disorders. Mental health professionals spend little time with non-clinical populations of well elderly, although there are some exceptions. For example, the Berkeley Growth Study studied positive mental health retrospectively in a longitudinal sample. Ratings of psychological health were obtained for each of 236 respondents when they were 14, 18, 30, 50, and 62 years of age. Examples of traits giving high scores on an index of psychological health include: (1) genuinely dependable and responsible; (2) warm and compassionate; (3) productive; and (4) socially perceptive of various social cues. Lower psychological health was marked by: (1) a brittle ego-defense system; (2) feeling cheated and victimized by life; (3) an emotionally bland, flattened affect; and (4) withdrawing when facing adversity or frustration. Adolescent psychological health was stable from 14 to 18 years of age; but not for adults. In adulthood, there were systematic changes in positive mental health associated with advancing age. Adolescents with more positive mental health most rapidly attained the highest levels of positive adult mental health. Adolescents with lower psychological health improved in adulthood, but the gains took longer to achieve. Adolescents also did not attain the same level of adult mental health as those that began adulthood with high positive mental health scores (Jones & Meredith, 2000).

Goals of Intervention

Table 5.5 identifies four general goals of intervention; any particular intervention may entail one or more of these. Goals may be short-term or longer-term; however, interventions with the elderly tend to emphasize short-term goals, since they are often focused on symptom relief and halting or slowing further decline or loss. Resources for intervention are always scarce, limited because of availability and financial cost. Professionals and politicians continue to debate such matters concerning health care access and service.

Alleviation   One goal of intervention is to alleviate or remove an identifiable problem. If an older person is having difficulties with anxiety, for example, a therapist may establish a goal of reducing this feeling in the client. Treatment interventions may involve drugs or individual or group therapy.

Compensation   A second goal may be to compensate for losses contributing to the problem. For example, if a person experienced some brain damage due to a stroke, it might be necessary to create a plan to simplify the individual's living environment in order to permit continued independent functioning.

Enrichment   The goal of this intervention is to raise the level of functioning above normal. Clinical therapy may help clients to enhance their self-acceptance, self-fulfillment, and self-actualization. Some therapists may try to enhance interpersonal flexibility so that an older adult may function more effectively and comfortably in social settings, adjust better to institutional living, and create greater intimacy from interpersonal relationships.

Prevention   Some interventions are designed to prevent problems from occurring or recurring. Prevention programs work best when reasonably good information is available about the factors that place individuals or groups at risk for certain kinds of problems. For example, the risk of developing cancer is heightened among those who smoke, so prevention programs are designed to discourage younger persons from choosing this behavior and to help those who have started smoking to stop. Interventions can also aim to slow down the rate of decline; for example, an improved diet and regular exercise may help those in middle or old age to preserve their physical health. Most psychological problems are not so easily addressed, although health-promoting behaviors seem to fit this model quite well.

Kinds of Functioning

Within any particular area of life, the kind of functioning defined as problematic or pathological may change with age. Older persons often turn to health care professionals, relying on their practical experience and clinical expertise, to help determine whether their level of functioning is typical of other people of the same age or a sign of pathological aging. It is difficult to apply simple rules of thumb (or to assess the degree of interference with everyday functioning) because people at each age express a wide range of acceptable behaviors and abilities. Older persons themselves are quite understanding of such latitude, sometimes tolerating significant pain and discomfort as a "normal" part of aging, while younger people faced with similar problems may seek and obtain intervention.

Symptoms

The symptoms used to identify problems change with age. For example, the symptoms of depression in older persons are somewhat different from those in younger persons. Elderly persons often present a high incidence of somatic complaints that are frequently mistaken for physical illness (a condition called *masked depression*), show psychomotor retardation, have difficulty with memory, and deny their depressed mood. They tend not to report everyday symptoms such as difficulty sleeping, feeling tired, being anxious, feeling down, and having impaired attention, wrongly believing that these are normal consequences of being old (Turnbull & Mui, 1995). Clinicians sensitive to these symptoms in the elderly can openly discuss depression and encourage exploration of treatments. If the symptoms are ignored as "just old age" or treated as illness-related, the individual may experience difficulty.

Techniques of Intervention

A wide range of different interventions are possible. Since professionals tend to develop expertise in only a few specialized techniques, intervention programs can often be enhanced by combining the special perspectives and skills of several intervention specialists.

Psychopharmacology   The **psychopharmacology** technique relies on the use of medications that alter the individual's biological state to attain a desirable mental health goal. This intervention is chosen when the physician suspects that the cause of the problem lies in the biological sphere. These physicians, usually psychiatrists, not only prescribe the drugs, they must monitor their direct and indirect effects. We know that drugs have different effects on people of different ages. As people grow older, physiological changes take place in metabolism and absorption rate as well as decreased drug transport due to reduced arterial flow. Professionals must be wary of the side effects of drugs, the interactive effects different medications may have on each other, the long-term effects of the drugs, and each individual's unique reaction to the same drug and dosage level. Drugs alter the rate and quality of ongoing behavioral processes.

Clinical Therapy   Clinical intervention attempts to restore or enhance functioning by developing the interpersonal relationship between client and professional. As we saw earlier in this chapter, specific Western assumptions prevail regarding clinical therapy, including the need for an intimate, confiding relationship and for both parties to work to help the client change. The length of the relationship, the treatment goals, the content of interaction, and the style of interaction may differ from one type of therapy to another. Outcomes of clinical therapy vary as a function of client characteristics, therapist characteristics, and the setting itself. Therapeutic clinical approaches with the elderly include both individual and group intervention and may be combined with psychopharmacologic treatments.

Education and Training   Another major intervention technique uses education and training to alter or prevent maladaptive behavior. Information about current or future problems is provided, with the expectation that the individual will use the information in beneficial ways. Professionals may teach specific coping skills needed for successful adaptation directly to those participating in psychoeducational programs. Classes and seminars designed to help people prepare for retirement also help the elderly to maintain or enhance mental health. These programs typically provide information about the needs of retirees: health care, money management, social contacts, and marital relationships, to name a few. The goal is to provide some anticipatory planning for the normal stresses associated with changing patterns of work and leisure. Alternatively, programs for individuals with specific health problems help clients learn new methods of salt-free cooking, how to lift heavy objects, or how to lip-read to improve their day-to-day functioning. Adult education experts emphasize discussion and provide each participant an opportunity for personal reflection and group sharing. Most programs are informal, use small lecture-type presentations, permit individuals to proceed at their own pace, have little or no formal evaluation (e.g., tests), meet at neutral places such as local community centers, and use multimedia instructional techniques.

Service Delivery   Services are activities performed by others for individuals who formerly performed these tasks for themselves. Providing needed services is one intervention strategy that can restore overall functioning. For example, when a husband breaks a hip and becomes disabled for a time, his wife with visual problems may be unable to drive, to shop, or to provide for her own needs. This can lead to feelings of abandonment, isolation, and perhaps depression unless the services of a home health aide or a driver are arranged. Relatives, friends, and neighbors often provide such services themselves; community support agencies also do so. Usually, specific services are arranged to restore the individual to normal functioning on a short-term basis until a crisis is over. The goal becomes more complex when disabilities are long-term or permanent. The range of assistance available to permit older persons to remain in their home is impressive: visiting nurses; physical therapists; house cleaners; prepared meals; home health aides who assist with dressing, bathing, or cooking; personal shoppers who search for specific goods; and direct delivery of items purchased over the telephone or Internet. Telephone services call the elderly to check on their well-being, to ensure that they took medications on time, and to remind them of appointments. Services are not always widely available and may be costly. Many people feel ambivalent about the need for services—grateful for their availability, but resentful and depressed about the loss of functioning that makes them essential.

Environmental Interventions   Interventions may involve changes in the larger environment to enhance individual well-being. For example, some individuals or organizations make microenvironmental changes such as making lettering on signs large enough for those with visual impairments to see, or using doorknobs with levers rather than round knobs to help those with arthritis to turn them more easily. Neighborhoods or communities make more expansive changes, offering the resources and services many elderly people need. And at the macroenvironmental level, we can work to expand the availability and affordability of health care, offer older adults security from crime, increase opportunities for employment or encourage respect for all older individuals as part of public policy.

Settings and Agents for Intervention

As outlined in table 5.5, interventions can occur in a variety of settings, including home, work, educational institutions, hospitals, and other health care facilities, specific communities, or the larger society. No one technique is limited to specific settings. A variety of change agents can also be called on to implement intervention. Most problems are the responsibility of the older individual and may involve family or friends. If problems persist, professionals may be consulted. Families will likely become more reliant on professionals' advice in managing problems unique to this segment of the life span. Mental health professionals with specific training in clinical geropsychology, clergy trained to work with the elderly, social workers with expertise in facilitating the welfare of the elderly, and health care professionals who coordinate and/or deliver direct services such as nursing, nutrition, physical therapy, and drug administration are particularly helpful, especially when members of the extended family live many miles away.

Finally, lawmakers and administrators can and do influence interventions through the policies they establish and the practices that ensue. Consider federal programs such as Social Security, Medicare, and Medicaid and the various interventions available to those eligible for support. Think also about the recent interest in insurance for long-term care, especially now that part of the premiums can be deducted from earned income.

Interventions with the Elderly: Illustrations

Intervention with the elderly is designed to preserve and/or enhance independence, self-respect, and autonomous functioning. Well-intentioned intervention may sometimes, however, undermine integrity and create feelings of anger and resentment. Both younger and older adults view unsolicited support and advice as intrusive. They dislike the implication of personal incompetence (Smith & Goodnow, 1999).

Community-Based Intervention: Social Support

One of the most common interventions designed to assist older persons is to provide social support. This support may take the form of actually providing direct assistance to an older relative, friend, or neighbor in times of acute need; having an older parent move into the home of a younger adult child; or offering daily assistance with regular routine activities (e.g., shopping for groceries, driving to a physician's office, cleaning the house, mowing the lawn, or shoveling snow from a walkway). On one level, care recipients appreciate this kind of support. On another level, however, social support may not uniformly result in positive outcomes for the recipient. Older persons can become overly reliant on help from others and may resent the intrusion in their lives and the loss of capacity that necessitates such intervention. Social support, if provided in advance of a real need or if given in situations in which it is unnecessary, can be detrimental to older persons. Krause (1995) identified the long-term risks of providing too much social support. Initially, social support can reduce chronic financial strain and reduce depressive symptoms, but over time, it is associated with increased psychological distress among care recipients. Caregivers may lose their patience or become domineering, abusive, or highly critical as their caregiving careers extend over many months and years. Still, Newsom and Schulz (1996) noted that older persons with limited social supports (e.g., those with fewer contacts with friends, fewer contacts with family, and less objective direct aid) had more impaired functioning than those with more support.

Krause (1995) has suggested, then, that there are limits to the value of social support for the elderly and that any stress-buffering effects are moderated by the care recipient. Ideally, the elderly must determine for themselves the interventions that they need, when they are needed, and who should provide them. Therefore, social support is critical in helping older persons cope well, but the older persons must feel that they are in control. Knowing that others are willing to help, if needed, gives rise to risk taking, personal mastery, and autonomy in the elderly. The subjective perception of support was more predictive of depressive symptoms among older persons than the actual objective measure of support provided. Those who subjectively perceived their support to be low not only had more depressive symptoms, they also had decreased **life satisfaction** (Newsom & Schulz, 1996). Research Focus 5.3 discusses one beneficial form of community-based support.

Institutional Intervention: Reducing Disruptive Behaviors

Older persons living in institutional settings such as health care facilities, assisted living centers, and nursing homes receive many forms of intervention. Some intervention programs aim to increase specific targeted behaviors to foster as much autonomy, awareness, and control as possible; others focus on reducing behaviors that are disruptive or problematic, such as wandering, disruptive vocalization, physical aggression, or unwillingness to walk (Burgio, Cotter, & Stevens, 1996). The Omnibus Budget Reconciliation Act of 1987 prohibited psychoactive drugs from being used alone to control disruptive behaviors in nursing home residents (Burgio et al., 1996). These homes must also make attempts to employ psychosocial and environmental interventions.

One of the oldest environmental interventions is the application of **behavior therapy** to manage disruptive or intrusive responses in the elderly. Behavior therapy uses positive rewards for appropriate behaviors and nonrewards for inappropriate behaviors. The environment is carefully analyzed to see what rewards are reinforcing and maintaining the disruptive behaviors: staff attention, withdrawal from an unwanted activity, or escape from a responsibility are potential rewards (Burgio et al., 1996). Rewards are then applied contingently for appropriate behaviors, particularly for those that are incompatible with the unwanted problem behaviors. This type of intervention requires extensive training of staff and a concerted effort to be consistent in shaping the desired behaviors.

Another common intervention strategy developed to help control older persons' disruptive behaviors in institutional settings is **reality orientation.** In this approach, the elderly are reminded of where they are and the present situation (e.g., day, month, year, residence) through cues in their immediate environment and the direct encouragement and reminders of staff. The goal of such intervention is to help older residents become more aware of their environment and their own place in it. Reality orientation often occurs in group sessions. Analyzing the results from a number of carefully controlled

Building Community Mental Health: Intergenerational Programs

Intergenerational programs link young and old for mutually beneficial exchange. Typically, one age group provides service to another. Older persons serve as teacher aides, foster grandparents, or share a creative skill or hobby; even those with Alzheimer's disease can assist toddlers in day care. Adolescents and young adults help older adults with household tasks, repairs, or to develop biographies; some simply visit with lonely, socially isolated adults living at home or in long-term care facilities. Innovative projects require young and old to work together as partners providing service to their communities. They build playgrounds, beautify neighborhoods, and trace the community's roots in historical projects; intergenerational choirs perform at community events. Intergenerational programs help to reduce age bias and dispel stereotypes while building a sense of community. These programs strengthen the concept of citizenship and the shared responsibility we have for each other's welfare in our democracy.

Young and old can see that age does not limit productivity, leadership, enthusiasm, motivation, or creativity. Sally Newman of the University of Pittsburgh, a pioneer in this emerging field, was one of the first to recognize the interdependency of the generations and their reciprocal needs. "All older adults have needs to nurture, to teach, to have a successful life review, to share cultural understanding, to communicate positive values, and to leave a legacy. And all children have a need to be nurtured, to be taught, to learn from and about the past, to have a cultural identity, to have

a positive role model, and to be connected to preceding generations" (Newman, 2001).

Intergenerational programs recognize that regardless of age or life situation, all individuals need people who care about, value, and respect them. Government can help, but it cannot meet these needs for every citizen; community action and support can reduce the need for government programs. Consider the long-term care needs of a growing population of elderly. Do we want government to build more and larger nursing homes? Who will pay the cost of constructing these "warehouses" and the cost of providing nursing home care? More importantly, is this the best way to meet the needs of older people for long-term care? Could we expand services in the community to keep older people independent and at home for more of their lives? Paul Kerschner, former executive director of the Gerontological Society of America, notes that "too often we devalue our older citizens: we look at them and say, 'Look what they cost us,' rather than 'Look at all they gave and can continue to give....' When all generations can experience each other in positive and supportive ways, society wins in all ways." Intergenerational programs provide one way to enhance the mental health of our communities.

Adapted in part from *Young and Old Serving Together: Meeting Community Needs Through Intergenerational Partnerships.* Washington, DC: Generations United.

---

studies, Spector, Davies, Woods, and Martin (2000) found that group reality orientation with at least 10 participants produced significant improvement in cognitive and behavior measures for those with dementia. Sustaining these benefits seems to require continued program participation.

Reminiscence therapy encourages a sensitivity to the life memories of older persons in institutions. This approach invites older persons to remember their pasts and reflect on their unique experiences; they are encouraged to resolve lifelong conflicts and other **unfinished business.** Reminiscence therapy is often part of the treatment approach taken with patients with Alzheimer's, who are given opportunities and encouragement to reminisce in an organized, focused manner. This intervention reduces agitation, confusion, and wandering by helping institutionalized elderly understand and accept themselves, by providing them freedom to "be" in the institution, and by accepting them and their experiences as they are (Burgio et al., 1996). By giving patients with Alzheimer's permission to live more in the past than the present, reminiscence therapy provides a greater sense of well-being and security. Programs based on reminiscence therapy make use of reminders of the past in the forms of music, posters, furniture, magazines, and appliances.

Milieu therapy is concerned with improving the quality of older persons' interactions with their physical, social, and emotional surroundings. Milieu therapy can also benefit confused or forgetful elderly persons by modifying the living environment of the institution. Rooms are highly individualized, doors to each room may have a distinctive color, and special colored pathways may mark the floors of the hallways to assist residents in getting around and to reduce confusion, wandering, and getting lost (Burgio et al., 1996).

Expressive therapies include art and music therapy. Expressive therapies are designed to help older adults clarify their identities and improve their relationships with others. *Art therapy* improves eye-hand coordination and upper body mobility and provides enrichment and stimulation. It serves as an outlet for emotional expression without risk. Those with Alzheimer's disease participate in decision making and problem solving as they conceptualize and create art (Weiss, 1999). The individual's level of impairment determines the appropriateness of various activities such as simply drawing, illustrating and maintaining a daily journal, or creating symbols from one's life. *Music therapy* provides those with dementia an opportunity to respond to environmental stimulation, particularly to rhythm. Hanser (1999) suggests that people process music at multiple levels: cognitively, emotionally, and physiologically. This means that even when dementia leaves an individual impaired in one processing mode, other channels can remain responsive. Music also evokes strong memories, linking older adults to their childhoods and earlier special life events. Expressive therapies occur in a safe, protected environment with no risk in participation. This intervention usually occurs in groups so that, for those with dementia who are able to take part, participation becomes a way to enhance social interaction.

Therapeutic Benefits of Pets for Institutionalized Elderly

Pet therapy is an intervention that increases an institution-residing older person's sense of autonomy, responsibility, and control. Taking care of a pet increases social participation among institutionalized elderly since it leads to expanded contact with other staff and residents. It also gives residents the opportunity for independent self-expression and creativity, as well as productive participation in a structured activity. Pets are assigned to individual residents during regular days each week through pet visitation programs. Alternatively, pets may be specifically assigned directly to a residential unit and live with the elderly.

The goal of pet therapy programs is to encourage contact between the pet and the elderly, which will generalize the elderly's involvement to the larger social environment (other residents, staff, and family members). Pets offer one solution to dealing with loneliness and improving self-esteem among elderly persons residing in nursing homes (Burgio et al., 1996; National Institutes of Health, 1988). Haughie, Milne, and Elliot (1992) have shown that nursing home residents become more spontaneous, animated, and talkative during the time they care for and visit with a pet. And residents become more aware of their environments as they prepare for the regular visit of the pet and provide routine care for it. For severely depressed residents, pets reduce anxiety, elicit responses (such as care and stroking) when the human environment has been rejected, provide physical reassurance, and help maintain reality, even among those who are terminally ill. Pet visitations two or three times each week help break the cycle of helplessness, hopelessness, dependency, and despair that institutionalization creates. Pets reduce confusion and tension (Crowley-Robinson, Fenwick, & Blackshaw, 1996). Institutionalized older people become less depressed, more communicative, and evidence higher rates of survival than controls who do not participate in such programs (Langer & Rodin, 1976; National Institutes of Health, 1988). Some institutions have maintained cats or dogs for a considerable time for this purpose. Others have developed similar programs using tropical fish, or feeders that attract wild birds. Some concerns arise with pet visits in institutions, including residents' allergies, fear of certain types of animals, injuries due to scratches or bites, and jealousy if a pet has a special affinity for and spends more time with some residents rather than others (Brickel, 1986; Burgio et al., 1996).

Therapeutic Benefits of Pets for Community-Residing Elderly

For the widowed or single individual, pets can play a therapeutic role by allowing pet owners to organize each day. Routine pet care may also help to increase the number of interactions between the pet owner and other people. Miller, Staats, & Partlo (1992) found that among a group of 250 pet owners, 50 to 90 years old, pets provided far more uplifts than hassles; older pet owners were happier, more self-confident, and more responsible than those without pets. Women more than men reported pets to be associated with uplifts, freedom, and positive use of leisure time. Men, on the other hand, associated pets with decreases in social interaction as well as with hassles over time and money.

Pets may help to meet attachment needs and increase the responsiveness of the elderly. They also provide a concrete anchor for those whose lives have undergone major change or loss. Pets may even serve as family substitutes, providing comfort and support

Pet therapy has many benefits for the elderly, including the general enhancement of social responsiveness to other elderly residents and staff.

to those experiencing the negative consequences of aging: death of loved ones, sickness, and feelings of loneliness (Tucker, Friedman, Tsai, & Martin, 1995). Elderly individuals who were most lonely were more strongly attached to their pets (Keil, 1998). Some research suggests that the ability to care humanely for pets gives an older adult meaning, purpose, and a sense of control over his or her environment. And caring for pets provides a sense of independence for elderly adults, allowing them to take care of something rather than be taken care of by others. The older adult's quality of life is enhanced through bonding with a pet. The elderly see pets as allies, supportive in times of loss and stress. They add to the elderly's sense of self-worth and give them nurturance. Pets also give older people a regular daily schedule, a chance to be mobile (e.g., walking the pet, bending or reaching to feed and stroke them), and a way of relaxing (Enders-Slegers, 2000).

However, the long-term benefits of owning pets are not so clear. In one investigation, adults who cared for a pet over a 14-year period were not found to have better health, health-promoting behaviors, perceived health, or lowered mortality risk than those without human-pet interactions (Tucker et al., 1995). Perhaps the positive benefits of pets reported in other studies are restricted to people who have experienced a uniquely stressful event or to special populations such as the institutionalized elderly. In one classic study, owning a pet was the best predictor of survival one year after leaving a coronary care unit in the hospital. Of 53 pet owners, only 6 percent died within one year, whereas of 28 individuals who did not own pets, 28 percent died within the same period. Pets provided a regularity and predictability in routine care that gave a sense of order to these heart attack patients' lives (Friedmann, Katcher, Lynch, & Thomas, 1980). Even having a small aquarium with goldfish or other minimal-care pets helps to reduce the owners' blood pressure and anxiety and to increase leisure satisfaction (Tucker et al., 1995).

Community Intervention: Volunteering

About 70 percent of all adults have engaged in volunteer activities during their lives. Many older volunteers engage in helping roles that benefit others, as volunteering is a vital part of our culture (Van Willigen, 2000). The federal government has recognized the value of volunteer older adults by establishing the National Service Corps (NSC). More than 500,000 older adults donate about 20 hours each per week in one of three volunteer programs; NSC volunteers receive a small stipend. *Foster Grandparents* offer aid and support to children and adolescents who have been abused or neglected, at-risk adolescents, teenage mothers, premature infants, and children with physical disabilities. *Senior Companions* offer assistance and companionship to other elderly people who need some help with Activities of Daily Living to maintain independent living in the community. They help pay bills, shop for groceries, and provide transportation to medical appointments. The Retired Senior Volunteer Program (RSVP) places adults over the age of 55 in local community projects, giving them the opportunity to tutor immigrants in English as a second language, build playgrounds, or help victims of a natural disaster. Volunteers choose from a range of projects, matching their interests and abilities with community needs (Corporation for National and Community Service Corps, 2001). Other Western countries have similar programs to engage the elderly in volunteer service.

Helping others is assumed to affirm self-perception, personal competence, and self-esteem in older adults. The volunteer role contributes to successful aging by providing a productive purpose, direction, and structure to leisure time (Herzog, Franks, Markus, & Holberg, 1998). When adults over 65 volunteer, it enhances their view of self as "agentic" or competent and, to a lesser degree, increases their social connectedness. Over a six-to-seven-year period, older adults from upper socioeconomic classes showed continued enhancement of self-esteem from volunteer activity. Those from lower social classes showed initial benefits on self-esteem, but these dissipated by the end of the study (Krause & Shaw, 2000). Social class thus moderated the long-term impact of volunteering on self-esteem in older adults.

Other studies indicate that older adults experience enhanced well-being from volunteering (Hertzog et al., 1998; Myers, 1999). Well-being has been defined to include life satisfaction, engagement in activities, social support, and access to support networks (Van Willigen, 2000). The greater the number of hours volunteered, the greater the benefits for older adults on most measures of mental health and well-being. Younger adult volunteers, however, showed a negative impact from participating more than 2.7 hours per week. Older adult volunteers (over 60 years of age) report significantly greater life satisfaction and higher scores on measures of perceived health than older people who do not volunteer at all (figure 5.5). For older adults, the volunteer role may serve as a replacement for roles lost through retirement. Alternatively, the meaning and importance of the volunteer role may shift in old age (Van Willigen, 2000). For example, older adults who report intrinsic satisfaction from their volunteer roles also have a higher sense of well-being (Myers, 1999).

Okun, Barr, and Herzog (1998) studied the motivation for volunteering among older people. Older volunteers were strongly influenced by four specific factors: (1) *core values:* the importance of helping others; (2) *understanding and knowledge:* learning about oneself and the world of other; (3) *self-enhancement:* feeling useful and good about oneself; (4) *social interaction.* Younger persons' motivation for volunteering included a dimension of career concern that older adults did not share. In

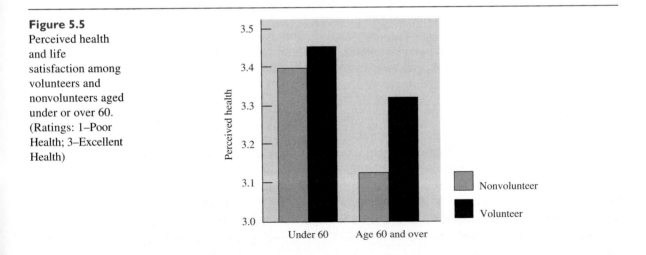

Figure 5.5
Perceived health and life satisfaction among volunteers and nonvolunteers aged under or over 60. (Ratings: 1–Poor Health; 3–Excellent Health)

Australia, the key factors underlying volunteer service among older adults was having available time (in retirement) and committing personal and social resources to the role. It appears that volunteers more often came from higher social classes, were least likely to be self-employed, and most likely to perceive their health status as positive (Warburton, LeBrocque, & Rosenman, 1998). Those who have a history of volunteering and continue to do so as they age generally have higher levels of ego development compared to nonvolunteers or those who become volunteers later in life. Older adults with higher ego development and perceived good health are more likely to be involved in volunteer roles (Morros, Pushkar, & Reis, 1998).

Volunteering to help others has a positive effect on mortality. In a large sample of community-residing elderly, 31 percent reported involvement in volunteer service. Those who volunteered for two or more organizations had a 63 percent lower mortality than those who did not volunteer at all. Volunteers with high religious involvement and perceived strong social support networks had even lower rates of mortality (Oman, Thoresen, & McMahon, 1999). Elderly volunteers involved in only one organization or contributing 40 or fewer hours each year also show somewhat lower rates of mortality. Mortality was enhanced among volunteers who had low levels of informal social interaction. Volunteering may benefit mortality by enhancing an older adult's identity, by reducing role strain, and by adding meaning to life (Musick, Herzog, & House, 1999).

Legal Intervention: Judgments of Competence and Incompetence

In dementia patients, the **competence** to make good decisions is often impaired. When a person's competence to function independently becomes a concern, a formal legal hearing is required; often a psychiatrist or clinical psychologist is asked to evaluate the person and share his or her professional judgments with the court. Competence is always linked to a specific type of task, decision, or judgment; for example, competence to make medical decisions, competence to consent to psychological evaluation, or competence to execute legal matters such as deciding to marry or to complete a will (Pruchno et al., 1995). A legal determination of competence is similarly specific (competent to make health care decisions such as refusing admission to a nursing home, for instance, but incompetent to distribute personal assets through a will). The difficulty for the courts is how to balance individual differences in intellect, ability, and personal values (e.g., what is important, good, or in one's own interest) with a minimal threshold of competence in judgment. There are no absolute, value-free, objective standards for judging competence—each case must be evaluated individually (Haldipur & Ward, 1996).

Competence cannot be called into question every time an older person refuses a medical treatment or makes a decision that family members disagree with. Rather, competence can only be questioned if a judgment appears to be irrational. For instance, the competence of an elderly person to make medical judgments may be questioned when the individual refuses to accept standard treatment for a life-threatening condition if the treatment has minimal side effects, if it is proven effective, and if its refusal will likely lead to irreparable harm or even death (Haldipur & Ward, 1996). Growing concern for the issue of competence can be traced to legislation in the Nursing Home Reform Act and Omnibus Budget Reconciliation Act of 1987, which mandates that nursing home residents participate in decisions about their own care unless they are judged incompetent according to the standards established in the states where they reside.

According to Appelbaum and Grisso (1988), most legal determinations of competency address the following threshold cognitive standards: (1) the ability to communicate a choice, (2) the ability to understand information about a treatment decision, (3) the ability to appreciate the situation and its consequences, and (4) the ability to manipulate the relevant information rationally. Older persons focused only on the here and now, fearing pain in certain treatments, and believing themselves invulnerable (i.e., capable of beating the odds without treatment) may be showing signs of irrationality (Haldipur & Ward, 1996). Depressed persons, for example, may be unable to see the benefits of treatments, may identify only with the risks, and may harbor strong feelings that their own lives are not worth living (Haldipur & Ward, 1996). While older persons may not wish to move to a nursing home, the decision can be rationally framed in terms of the improvements in level of functioning, improvements in level of care, and reduced demands on family caregivers to sustain the older person in present living arrangements (Haldipur & Ward, 1996).

At times, the courts may appoint a **guardian** or conservator, though this is rare and reserved for only the most serious of situations. Guardians are called upon to make substitute decisions for those judged incompetent to make decisions for themselves (Wilber & Reynolds, 1995). Most guardians come from the immediate family and many have served as caregivers. Those who become guardians often experience role strain, burden, personal sacrifice, and overwhelming demands (Wilber, 1997). The courts require documentation of functional deficits in basic mental or physical capacities that make an older person's decisions regarding money management, property, and health care questionable. Some older persons, as a safeguard against the possibility that they may become incompetent and have a court-appointed guardian, choose in advance a specific family member or trusted friend who is given **durable power of attorney.** A person with durable power of attorney can make substituted judgments for an individual if they become incompetent; *durable* simply means that the authority to act on behalf of the older individual continues throughout the time of incompetence and is not revocable without cause. Guardianship remains the intervention of last resort, since all authority for independent decisions is transferred to a surrogate (Wilber, 1997).

A final area of competency of concern to the elderly and their families is that of **testamentary capacity,** or the competence to execute a will. Many individuals postpone making a will until late in life (Haldipur & Ward, 1996). They often need to change the basic document as circumstances change. Changes, called **codicils,** are recorded and legally documented but not always widely shared with other relatives. Only upon the death of the individual do these changes become known, and the codicils then may provoke challenges from dissatisfied family members. These challenges are often based on the mental competence of the older person to have made the changes in a will or on the possibility that the changes were made under some other party's undue influence. Three conditions are used to assess the mental capacity to complete a will: (1) an individual must be able to understand that a will is being created, (2) an individual must know the extent of the property and assets under consideration, and (3) an individual must understand who will benefit from the execution of the will (Haldipur & Ward, 1996). The competence of older persons to make decisions that affect them, their participation in such decisions, and the issue of guardianship will all continue to be important issues in the future.

SUMMARY

Given the predicted growth in the numbers of elderly citizens in our society, preventive mental health programs are acquiring increasing importance. Effective programs consider the racial, ethnic, and cultural uniqueness of the community and its elderly. Three types of prevention include: (1) universal prevention, for all individuals in an age group, regardless of risk; (2) selective prevention, for elderly at some risk for a disorder; (3) indicated prevention, for elderly at high risk for a disorder.

Mental health is defined by productive activities, fulfilling relationships, and flexibility in managing change and diversity. Positive mental health in older adults is often linked to physical health and an absence of chronic illness. The *diathesis-stress model* describes the relationships between vulnerability, challenging life events, and the risk of psychological disorders. Older adults hold many inaccurate, stereotyped views of psychological treatment and hold little hope for its success; they are less likely to utilize mental health services than younger adults. Ethnic and racially diverse older adults are even less likely than whites to seek mental health services. Thus, being older and a member of an ethnic, racially diverse group places individuals in "double jeopardy," at heightened vulnerability for health and mental health problems and with an increased need for services.

Professionals in mental health are becoming more sensitive to the cultural backgrounds of older clients. Elderly from diverse backgrounds, and especially Hispanic and Asian individuals that are less acculturated, usually seek alternate resources (family, friends, religious leaders, or folk healers) in the community to treat mental health concerns before turning to formal programs. Hispanics turn to their families in times of need, with familism defining the bonds of loyalty, commitment, and belonging that sustains the family. Folk systems are also part of Hispanic support systems and offer traditional spirit healing. Among the oldest-old who are black, the definition of immediate family includes supportive distant kin (upgrading kinship relations) and supportive friends or neighbors who function like family (fictive kin). The range of alternative resources is very broad among diverse populations of the elderly; along with family and friends, religious institutions and the clergy play a central role.

Barrier theory identifies institutional obstacles that account for the underutilization of mental health services by ethnic and racially diverse elderly. Culture, class, prejudice, and language are examples of such barriers. Others include lack of professionals from the same culture as the elderly, lack of transportation, and the cost of service. Different cultures conceptualize mental health disorders differently, and some may not value counseling as a way of resolving issues. Native American elderly expect traditional tribal approaches to help resolve mental health problems; tribal councils listen to concerns and participate in collective problem solving. Asian elders have difficulty bringing mental health problems to the attention of professionals. Like Hispanics, they believe that any issue that cannot be resolved within the family is stigmatizing. Asian elders experience shame when they share problems with outsiders or need professional help to resolve their problems. Other than among Vietnamese elderly, formal mental health services are sought only when mental health problems reach a crisis.

Clinical depression is the most common psychological disorder of the elderly, but it occurs at a rate far below that of other age groups. It is associated with cognitive impairment, increases in illness, and chronic health problems that limit function. The comorbidity of depression with chronic disease is associated with higher mortality. Other risk factors include gender, income, education, ethnicity, race, and prior history of the disorder. Some studies suggest a strong genetic component for clinical depression, but not for depressive symptoms. The latter are more common among those over 65 years of age, with the highest rates found among nursing home residents, followed by those in hospitals and medical outpatients, and lowest among the community-residing elderly. Risk factors for depressive symptoms include poor health, experience with loss, and minimal social support. Given the current high rates of depression among adolescents and young adults, there should be a marked increase in the rate of depression as these cohorts advance to old age. Depression in old age is not normal or predictable, and it should be treated aggressively. Depression in the elderly may manifest itself somewhat differently than among younger people; for instance, somatic complaints and metaphorical concerns are more evident. Effective treatment includes brief therapy, drug treatment, or some combination of the two. The stress-buffering effects of social support can moderate many of the risk factors for depression.

The comorbidity of depression and Alzheimer's disease is often reported, and caring for an aging relative with behavior problems or dementia also increases the risk of depression. Caregivers who experience role captivity are at higher risk, as are women who care for a spouse. Depressive symptoms lessen when caregivers have social support, fewer additional role obligations, and higher levels of mastery. Cognitive-behavioral therapy for depression seeks to alter negative thinking about the self, current experience, and the future. Developing logical thought patterns and beliefs improves emotional life. Participation in pleasurable activities also enhances mood, and psychoeducational programs have also been successful in treating depression in the elderly.

The risk for suicide increases with age. Factors related to increased probability of suicide include (1) gender, (2) social isolation, (3) loss of spouse, (4) failing health, (5) untreated depression, and (6) hopelessness about the future. Older white males are at higher risk for suicide than any other racial or age group. Native Americans, depending on tribal identity, have different rates of suicide. Recognizing the signs of suicide in elderly people is essential to reducing the death rate. Psychological autopsies can help identify the predictive factors in suicide by analyzing the psychological state, personality factors, and stressors that contributed to the suicide. Older people are more likely to carry out a plan than younger people, most often using firearms to commit suicide. Passive techniques (starvation, auto accidents, prescription drug errors) may underlie an underreporting of suicides in the elderly.

The incidence of alcohol abuse among the elderly has also been underestimated. At highest risk are those who have dealt with poverty, discrimination, employment issues, and poor housing. Men have a higher incidence than women, particularly if they have lost a spouse and are over the age of 75. One treatment to break the chain of negative emotions and drinking behaviors for older adults is the ABC model (analyzing antecedents, behavior, and consequences). Other programs use abstinent older peer models, social support, insight therapy, and assertiveness training. Early-onset alcoholics have chronic, severe health problems that include organic brain syndrome (Korsakoff's syndrome). Late-onset alcoholism is triggered by situational factors (failing health, loneliness, death of a spouse). Late-onset alcoholism often is underreported by physicians and ignored by friends and family. The *tension-reduction hypothesis* defines drinking as a behavior designed to lessen the emotional pain of negative life events and chronic stress.

Understanding differences in cultures, values, beliefs, languages and the meaning of behavioral symptoms is essential to effective mental health treatment with older adults from diverse backgrounds. It is necessary to overcome older adults' stereotypical perceptions of formal mental health organizations in order to improve the rate of service utilization. Ethnically and racially diverse elderly may misunderstand the values, goals, and methods of Western models of therapy. Strengthening communication, assertiveness, emotional expression, reality orientation, and self-esteem may lead to conflict within their families and communities.

A number of mental health interventions can enhance the lives of older adults. Specialized interventions that preserve physical function and enhance health or mental health are important throughout the life span. Intervention begins with a definition of the problem, identification of its probable causes, and the choice of a strategy using empirical results from efficacy research. Intervention goals include alleviation, compensation, enrichment, and prevention. Intervention options must fit the goals, techniques, settings, and change agents appropriate for each problem.

One type of intervention is social support. Social support for the elderly generally has positive effects on mental health; however, to be most effective, older adults should still feel in control. Intervention strategies to manage disruptive behaviors include behavior therapy, reality orientation, reminiscence, milieu therapy, and expressive therapies (art and music). Pets can also constitute a form of intervention. They improve the psychological status of both community-residing elderly and those in long-term care. Nursing home residents become more animated, less depressed, and less hopeless when they care for pets. Older adults in the community are happier, more confident, and more responsive. Pets serve as family substitutes, provide comfort, and help alleviate loneliness through the close attachment bonds that evolve with their owners. Volunteering is another form of intervention actively encouraged through the National Service Corps. Older adult volunteers remain engaged and productive in later life. Volunteering leads to enhanced self-esteem, well-being, and social connectedness. Helping others even has a positive outcome on mortality. Legal intervention may be needed when an older adult's judgments are called into question. Without a threshold level, it is difficult to establish legal definitions for competence. Differences of opinion among family members are not themselves grounds for legal intervention, but intervention may be needed to prevent a clearly irrational decision that is not based on fact or will cause irreparable harm. In this case, the courts can appoint a guardian to act on behalf of a seriously impaired older adult. Many elderly designate a family member or trusted friend with durable power of attorney to act on their behalf should they become incompetent. Testamentary capacity may become an issue if the elderly person makes changes in his or her will.

REVIEW QUESTIONS

1. Identify two aspects of depression that make it difficult to diagnose and treat in older adults.
2. Explain the relationship between depression and suicide in the elderly. Why are older white males at so much higher risk?
3. List the risk factors for clinical depression and for depressive symptoms.
4. What are the three types of prevention strategies?
5. Explain the differences between early-onset and late-onset alcoholism.
6. List five of the major barriers to effective mental health access and service for ethnic and racially diverse elderly.
7. Identify alternative resources for ethnic and racially diverse elderly with mental health problems. What are the disadvantages in utilizing such resources?
8. What benefits does volunteering offer to older adults?
9. Outline the cultural assumptions, procedures, and values inherent in traditional Western mental health therapy. Illustrate the difficulties that elderly persons from Hispanic, Asian, black, or Native American cultures might experience in traditional therapy.
10. Identify the goals of successful intervention.
11. What are the risk factors for depression among caregivers?
12. Define and provide an illustration of three of the following therapies: cognitive-behavioral, expressive, reality, ABC, milieu, reminiscence, and behavior.

 ## ON THE WEB   www.mhhe.com/hoyer5

The American Association on Suicidology is a nonprofit organization devoted to understanding suicide and reducing its incidence. The website has outstanding links to other relevant sites. Detailed topics include helping family survivors to cope, finding support services, and accessing hotline services for those in immediate danger.

The Corporation for National Service offers special programs for older adults and others interested in providing volunteer service in their own communities. A number of different programs continue to seek volunteers. The website provides direct links to some of the web pages for these programs.

The Department of Health and Human Services has published its national goals for health in the United States for the next decade. This site includes links to other health-related agencies in the federal government.

Depression.com is a well-organized, comprehensive website dealing with a variety of topics. Pages are devoted to living with someone who is depressed, drug therapy treatments, and clinical treatments.

The Institute on Alcohol Studies has an excellent website for those seeking to learn more about alcohol abuse and its relationship to a variety of health concerns and mental health issues.

Mental Help Net contains an immense directory of articles, editorials, and self-help resources. Current research is available on specific psychological disorders as well as organizations interested in those disorders. The site also contains a directory and links to online support and tells how to contact various resources. Major topics such as depression, suicide, and alcohol and drug abuse have links to nationwide agencies, government agency home pages, and current publications.

The National Institute on Aging maintains a web page with extensive coverage of a wide range of issues related to the elderly. Mental health topics include alcohol abuse (see the web page for NIMH), depression, and suicide. This site also discusses health concerns, residential living options, end-of-life issues, and other topics that older adults would find timely and appropriate.

The National Institute of Mental Health's web page contains basic information on a wide variety of mental health issues, psychological disorders, and treatments. These pages deal with suicide, with links to other relevant websites. They also include information on a large range of other mental health concerns.

The National Mental Health Association has a confidential online screening test to assess depression. The website also has reliable and accurate information about depression for families and others simply interested in learning about this important clinical topic. A general fact page with relevant materials on specific psychological disorders and general topics on mental health is also part of this website.

6

PHYSICAL HEALTH AND AGING

Senescence begins
And middle age ends
The day your descendants
Outnumber your friends
—Ogden Nash

Age is not all decay; it is the ripening, the swelling, of the fresh life
within, that withers and bursts the husks.
—George Macdonald

If I'd known I was going to live this long,
I'd have taken better care of myself.
—Jazz pianist Eubie Blake (on his 100th birthday)

INTRODUCTION

In this chapter, you will learn about the effects of aging on physical health. The economics of health care is a growing concern for older adults and for public policy makers in our society. It is essential to plan how we will finance health care in the future and protect public programs such as Medicare and Medicaid. Increasingly, older persons must face difficult health care decisions. When they require services, they question what health care intervention would be best, where it should be received—at home, in the hospital, in an assisted living center, or in a nursing home—who will provide it, and how will it be financed. The cost and availability of nursing home or long-term care is a major issue for older persons. Although some elderly experience impairments in the later years, health care in the United States emphasizes rehabilitation and the preservation of autonomy.

This chapter also explores the importance of a number of health-promoting behaviors, the risks of heart disease and cancer, the relationship of gait to falling, sarcopenia, and muscle loss in the elderly. We highlight the benefits of health-enhancing interventions wherever possible. Finally, this chapter discusses the important roles of exercise and health intervention in helping older persons cope with health-compromising problems.

The Health Status of the Elderly

An analysis of elders over the age of 65 (*Older Americans 2000: Key Indicators of Well-Being*) suggests some startling changes from even a decade earlier (Rosenblatt, 2001). Elders currently enjoy better health than previous cohorts and will likely live longer. Women comprise a larger and larger segment of the elderly population. Women who have just turned 65 can expect to live another 19.2 years, men another 16 years. However, they can also expect to spend an increasingly larger percentage of their yearly income on health care. The longer women live, the greater their odds of being poor. Perhaps this accounts, in part, for their growing dependency on their children and the health care system to meet their medical, social, and physical needs.

The rate of chronic disability is lower for older Americans than ever before. This means that more elderly people are living in the community, with fewer functional impairments or limitations in activities of daily living. While a smaller percentage of elderly will need nursing home care in the future, the growth in sheer numbers needing such care will grow dramatically. Studies suggest that cardiovascular disease, arthritis, and emphysema are declining as new cohorts reach old age; however, asthma, orthopedic limitations, and musculoskeletal problems are increasing (Reynolds, Crimmins, & Saito, 1998).

The hypothesized reasons for improved health include better medical care, new drugs, and advanced medical technology, as well as improved diet, increased exercise, and expanded social networks for older adults. Healthier older people are more likely to be socially active, thus enhancing their health and psychological well-being. Social relationships documented for 70-year-olds over a two-week interval reflected that (1) 92 percent spent time with a family member, (2) 88 percent saw friends or neighbors, and (3) 50 percent participated in group activities such as religious institutions.

The active lifestyle outlined in Rowe and Kahn's model of successful aging was found among 72 percent of the elderly in the study, with only 28 percent reporting a sedentary lifestyle. Most elderly continue to be productive, active, and contributing citizens to society. Recent census data show that more than 4.5 million people over the age of 65 either continue to be employed, work part-time, or are seeking work. More than 80 percent of those over 65 do not want a life of total leisure; they believe their good health and vitality give them an opportunity to continue with the next phase of life, setting new goals and challenges and taking up meaningful pursuits (Freedman, 2000; Rosenblatt, 2001).

Racial Differences in Health

Numerous studies reveal that elderly from ethnically and racially diverse cultures are adversely affected in terms of health and access to health care. Blacks and Hispanics reach retirement and old age in poorer health than other segments of society, and often without health care insurance (Padgett, 1995). The longer they live, the greater the percentage of their income they spend on health care. Ethnic and racially diverse older people suffer the accumulated impact of socioeconomic disadvantage that limits their access to health care. Older black Americans have higher levels of physical and functional impairment than their white counterparts. Black Americans also experience higher rates of mortality, as well as morbidity for a number of diseases including cancer, hypertension, and diabetes. Functional impairments in Activities of Daily Living are also greater among blacks than whites. Self-ratings of health reveal that white older adults consistently feel better about their health than Hispanics or blacks, as figure 6.1 shows. While social class (see figure 6.2) is a factor underlying these differences, it does not explain them entirely (Mui, Choi, & Monk, 1998).

The general health disadvantage of older blacks and other ethnic groups has been linked to a *double-jeopardy hypothesis.* Being old as well as a member of an ethnic minority group creates a double disadvantage. Discrimination and disadvantage have a

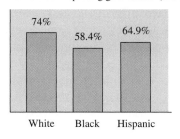

Health

Percent 65+ reporting good health (1996)

74%

58.4%

64.9%

White   Black   Hispanic

Figure 6.1 Self-rated health of white, black, and Hispanic older adults. Whites are most likely to report they are in good health. *Source: Older Americans 2000, Federal Interagency Forum on Aging-Related Statistics.*

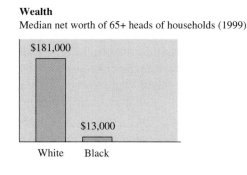

Wealth

Median net worth of 65+ heads of households (1999)

$181,000

$13,000

White   Black

Figure 6.2 Median net worth of black and white older adults. The median net worth for whites is more than 10 times higher than that for blacks. *Source: Older Americans 2000, Federal Interagency Forum on Aging-Related Statistics.*

negative impact on health early in development, and the disadvantages continue to accumulate later in life. Those with less education, reduced income, less access to a regular physician, and a reliance on Medicaid show more rapid declines on many health indicators as they age (Mui, Choi, & Monk, 1998). Similar results are reported for frail elderly black Americans. They have significantly more health problems than their white counterparts, although they may have greater family support to maintain them at home and in the community. At the time of nursing home admission, these differences become evident.

Cuban-American elderly appear to be in better physical health than either Mexican-American or Puerto-Rican elderly. Cuban-American elderly are also less likely to experience impairments in Activities of Daily Living or Independent Activities of Daily Living. Consistent with these data, self-rated health is higher among Cuban Americans that either Mexican-American or Puerto-Rican elderly (Mui, Choi, & Monk, 1998). The reasons for these differences may lie in the differential immigrant experiences of each group. Cubans came to the United States more than 40 years ago and have had more education than other Hispanics. Unlike Mexican Americans and Puerto Ricans, Cuban

Americans have had no opportunity for "return migration" to their country of origin because of political restrictions. Thus, older Cuban Americans tend to participate more in community support networks that preserve their cultural heritage and language.

Native-American elders have difficulty accessing health care and obtaining medical services. One common disease in this population is diabetes. Without regular monitoring and treatment, it can have a devastating impact on those in old age.

Health Care Costs

It is difficult for older persons to meet the increased costs of health care given the typical 30 to 50 percent decline in yearly income following retirement (Gottlieb, 1992). Health care costs are partially covered by Social Security income and Medicare. Some elderly are able to cover the gap in their health care coverage with personal savings; others rely on private insurance coverage (*Medigap policies*). Still other older persons depend on special appropriations through government-sponsored programs for the low-income elderly. The anticipated growth in the *dependency ratio* (a larger number of older adults needing support from a smaller number of workers) may mean shifting some of the costs of health care programs directly back to those who utilize program services, that is, the elderly themselves. Programs that promote health and prevent disease are more effective and less expensive than programs that deliver health care services after illness or disability arise. If aging individuals maintain their health, they have less need for costly interventions; improved psychological, social, and physical functioning; greater life satisfaction; and a higher perceived quality of life.

Health Promotion and Aging

Health promotion within the field of public health is a late twentieth-century phenomenon (Wallace, 2000). In the nineteenth century, scientists discovered that communicable diseases were preventable by reducing the spread of germs. One hundred years ago, pneumonia, tuberculosis, diarrhea, and enteritis were the major diseases causing death; less than half of the population lived past age 65. Public health measures subsequently put into place included instituting proper sanitary procedures such as providing safe water free of bacteria, eliminating rats and mice from human habitation areas, reducing human overcrowding, and inoculating humans to prevent disease.

Today the three major causes of death are coronary heart disease, cancer, and stroke; together, they account for 60 percent of all deaths (National Center for Health Statistics, 2001). These are chronic conditions that arise slowly over many years of an individual's life. They result in progressive, long-term disabilities in old age, diminished quality of life, and, ultimately, death. To help prevent these chronic diseases, public health officials have included health promotion and education as a major part of our national public health agenda.

Health promotion advocates recognize that it is preferable for people to enter their later years in good health than to try to cure them of chronic diseases. "It is no longer enough to reduce death rates—the new goal is to 'add life to years,' not just 'years to life' " (Wallace, 2000, p. 374). Rather than thinking of good health as the absence of disease, today's health educators and health care providers define healthy aging or *successful aging* as including three features: a low probability of suffering from disease or disease-related disabilities; high cognitive and physical functioning; and active engagement with life (Rowe & Kahn, 1999). Today, over 80 percent of our population can expect to live to age 65.

How can people grow old in good health? Good health in old age stems from multiple factors, including genetics. However, some behaviors definitely promote health. First, individuals are encouraged to make lifestyle choices that will lead to successful aging. People have personal control over their diets, smoking, use of alcohol, and exercise, to list some well-recognized controllable variables. Second, we can empower people to determine how they will age by strengthening their belief that they have personal control over health choices (Wallace, 2000). At a more general level, government has focused attention on a third factor: identifying environmental hazards (such as auto accidents and AIDS) that increase the risk of disability in old age or reduce the probability of survival. Seatbelt use, safe sex, and not driving and drinking are encouraged for elders. Finally, social engagement and social networks provide documented benefits; they play a role in promoting good health in later life (by encouraging active engagement with life). Adults who enter old age with a greater number of social relationships and a strong social support network are not only physically healthier than those without such support, they are also psychologically healthier and can expect to live longer. Good health in later adulthood is more common among those who take on meaningful roles by volunteering or pursuing a hobby or a religious affiliation. The elderly who continue active engagement with life report higher energy, less depression, and more life satisfaction. There are many pathways to successful aging, and adults are encouraged to become actively responsible for initiating healthy behaviors (Rowe & Kahn, 1999). It is never too late to make beneficial changes.

Evidence for Rowe and Kahn's model of successful aging was obtained in a sample of 224 older adults (average age of 73) who completed a survey about their activities and social support. Participants who maintained goal-directed and high-demand leisure activities (e.g., swimming, woodworking, walking, or gardening) had higher scores on measures of physical health. Low-demand leisure activities (reading, watching television, or listening to music) were typical of those with lower physical health scores. In this study, however, social support was not related to either physical health or active engagement (Evearard, Lach, Fisher, & Baum, 2000).

Other studies have found a positive relationship between social networks or social support, health indicators, and lower **mortality** rates among older adults. Gump, Polk, Kamarck, and Shiffman (2001), for example, found that measurements of marital partners' blood pressure were significantly lower when they were participating in social interactions with their partners rather than alone or with other adults. Blood pressure has been found to be a valid indicator of cardiovascular health and mortality for adults. Another study assessed social support over nearly a 50-year period. Having fewer living children and belonging to fewer organizations was related to a significantly higher mortality risk for both men and women (Tucker, Schwartz, Clark, & Friedman, 1999). Men who had experienced the dissolution of a marriage, regardless of their present status (divorced, separated, or widowed), were also at higher mortality risk. Remarriage for men over 70 was associated with reduced mortality risk, but for those under 70, it was related to higher mortality. The beneficial effects of remarriage on mortality therefore appear to depend on age, with older men deriving the greatest benefit. Generally, marriage has beneficial effects on health and mortality in older adults. In addition to providing social benefits and emotional support, marriage encourages a healthy and active lifestyle (Schone & Weinick, 1998).

Intervention

The needs of the elderly and provision of intervention services are important dimensions of health and psychological well-being. One goal of intervention programs is **optimization**, that is, to enhance and preserve independent functioning throughout the later years. Programs also rely heavily on the concept of **functional assessment**, that is, determining the basic abilities necessary for adequate functioning in our society. Interventions to preserve independence are possible at different functional levels. Functional abilities deemed important in assessments include physical health, mental health, complex cognitive skills, and social roles. Figure 6.3 shows one hierarchical model of functional abilities.

A number of factors have restricted the application of useful interventions to the older adult population. First, health care workers must be encouraged to work with the elderly and to see that they benefit from various types of therapeutic intervention. Second, health and mental health care must be made both affordable and widely available. Third, the number of health care professionals (e.g., geropsychologists, physicians, nurses, social workers, and physical therapists) who are interested in working with the elderly must increase to improve intervention services and enhance the quality of care for the elderly. Perhaps this goal could be accomplished, in part, by advocating that courses on aging be required for those in fields such as psychology, human services, nursing, the allied health care professions, and sociology. If students find the study of aging and gerontology interesting and challenging, they may commit to a career work-

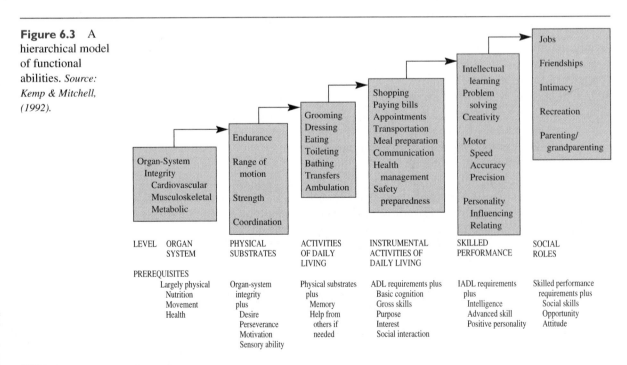

Figure 6.3 A hierarchical model of functional abilities. *Source: Kemp & Mitchell, (1992).*

ing with the elderly. On the McGraw-Hill Developmental Psychology website (www.mhhe.com/developmental) you will find further discussion of careers in applied gerontology.

Functional Assessment of Health

More older adults today are healthier than ever before, although aging is associated with declines in health. Figure 6.4 shows the proportion of healthy and disabled adults projected over the next two decades. Older adults report fewer sick days compared with previous generations, spend fewer weeks in the hospital, and have fewer physical and mental disabilities and limitations. The number of days on which activities are restricted because of illness or injury increases with age, averaging one month per year among those over 65 years of age (Manton, Corder, & Stallard, 1993).

The assessment of health status is an important factor in determining an older person's capacity to live independently and a critical variable in determining the nature and timing of intervention services. Many older individuals live successfully without much intervention or assistance, and others do so despite serious illness and physical restrictions. Psychologists recognize that self-assessments can be biased. Some people err in the direction of enhancing self-function to avoid relocation and maintain their autonomy;

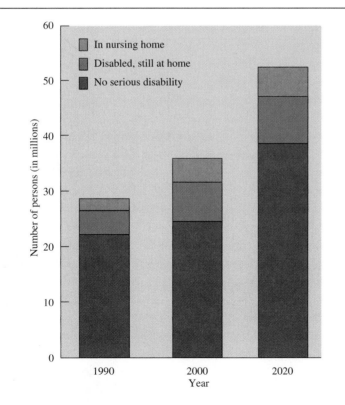

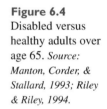

Figure 6.4
Disabled versus healthy adults over age 65. *Source: Manton, Corder, & Stallard, 1993; Riley & Riley, 1994.*

others overemphasize losses and seek assistance far beyond what they really need (Kart, Metress, & Metress, 1992).

To assess the physical skills necessary for self-care and maintenance of functional health, gerontologists developed **activities of daily living (ADL) scales** for older adults. The activities assessed include: bathing, dressing, toileting, getting in or out of a bed or chair, walking, getting outside of the home or apartment, and feeding oneself. The activities just listed are ordered toward increasing dependency; for example, bathing is the most common limitation among older persons, and the inability to feed oneself indicates the most severe restriction in physical functioning. Identification of specific deficits in the elderly creates an opportunity for environmental intervention to optimize independence and physical functioning (see figure 6.5). Most studies show a relationship between health status or physical functioning as assessed by ADL and demographic variables. Those who are oldest, female, live in poverty, are nonwhite, and come from rural regions of our country show the most restrictions in ADL. Nearly 90 percent of adults up to age 64 show no restrictions in ADL, compared with 50 percent of those over the age of 85 (Kart et al., 1992).

Another comprehensive assessment of autonomous functioning has also been developed, the **instrumental activities of daily living scale (IADL).** This assessment evaluates personal self-care as well as more complex dimensions of functioning: preparing meals, going shopping, managing money, using the telephone, doing light and heavy housework. IADL tasks are more complex, multidimensional, and physi-

Figure 6.5 An older person's ability to continue using a bathtub can be enhanced by installing such features as a hand-held shower, grab bars, a bench-type seat, nonskid strips on the bottom of the tub, and lever-type faucet handles.

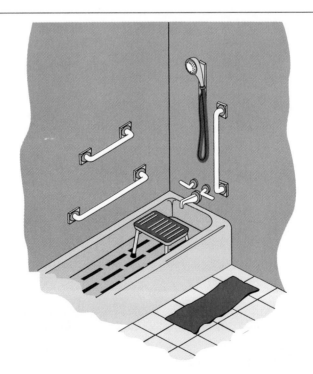

cally demanding than ADL tasks; functional declines are thus more likely to appear in assessments of IADL than ADL. For example, nearly 33 percent of those over the age of 85 reported four or more limitations in IADL tasks. Limitations in multiple IADL tasks predict that the person will be house-bound, will need significant levels of assistance on a regular basis, and will be at high risk for relocation to an institutional living arrangement.

Rudberg, Parzen, Leonard, and Cassel (1996) reviewed a national sample of more than 5,000 community-residing older adults to see whether functional limitations as measured by number of restrictions in ADL were related to or predictive of death. The results indicated that although death was predictable from age alone, it was not predictable from knowing the number of ADL impairments. Even when the number of functional limitations held constant, death was predicted by increasing age. For example, women aged 70 to 79 who had difficulty in three activities of daily living had a 21 percent probability of dying within two years, whereas those aged 90 or older with the same number of functional impairments had a 52 percent probability of dying within two years. Interestingly, gender differences showed up for people with similar numbers of functional restrictions; the risk of dying was greater for men than for women when the two had similar functional impairments. Declines in functional abilities are predictable, however, from data on the age of onset and the typical course of a disease (e.g., heart disease, diabetes).

Although women live longer than men, women are more likely to be in poorer health than men in their later years and more affected by symptoms of their illness. Being unmarried doubled the chances of being severely restricted, whether the subjects were men or women; those who smoked or abused alcohol also exhibited more functional impairments.

One implication of these findings is that health care costs will increase substantially in the future because greater numbers of adults will reach old age and require costly medical services. Of those age 85 and over, 50 percent will be severely restricted in their last year of life. As figure 6.6 shows, disability levels are greater in adults over age 85 because people with heart disease, cancer, and other diseases are living longer than ever before (Olshansky, Carnes, & Cassel, 1993). On the other hand, data suggests that disability rates among the elderly are declining when compared with the growth of this segment of the population (see figure 6.4); (Rosenblatt, 2001).

Frailty

Until recently, health care professionals have widely used the term **frailty** without establishing a common definition. It is important to understand frailty so that it is not mistaken for other reversible medical conditions. Family members, physicians, and the frail elderly themselves can then adjust their expectations and make better treatment decisions (Gillick, 2001). Frailty refers to a wasting of the body and is associated with general muscular weakness and poor nutrition. A recent study highlights the behavioral markers of frailty (Fried et al., 2001). Frailty is marked by at least three of the following: unintentional weight loss (more than 10 pounds in the past year), self-reported exhaustion, weakness (grip strength), slow walking speed, and

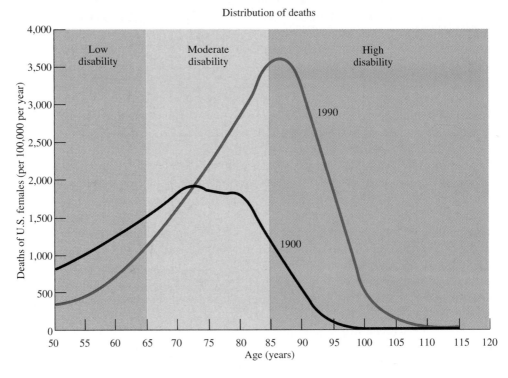

Figure 6.6
Patterns of disability and death are shifting. With healthier lifestyles and improved medical care, people are surviving longer than ever before, even with heart disease, stroke, and cancer. Because of extended survival, those 85 years of age and older may live with a high level of disability.
Source: Olshansky, S. J., Carnes, B. A., & Cassel, C. K. The aging of the human species. Scientific American, 268, 46–52. Copyright © 1993 by Scientific American, Inc. All rights reserved.

low physical activity. Fried et al. (2001) noted the predictive power of this definition among a group of nearly 6,000 adults over the age of 65. Frailty was increasingly common with advancing age and associated with higher rates of mortality, falls, hospitalization, and institutionalization. A cycle of frailty (see figure 6.7) suggests a pattern of declining reserve to "withstand acute illness or emotional upheaval or physical dislocation" (Gillick, 2001, p. M135). One implication of the behavioral markers of frailty is that weakness and declining strength alone cannot be used to define frailty, although they are among the most commonly encountered symptoms. Older adults with any three of the criteria of frailty are considered highly vulnerable and likely to experience steady declines in function.

Self-Assessment of Health

Older adults bring their personal histories and understanding to the assessment of their own health. The same chronic disease may mean very different things to different individuals. Some are able to maintain their integrity, self-worth, and dignity in the face of serious functional losses; others crack and crumble in the face of relatively minor losses. Successful adjustment to old age does not require one to maintain autonomy and a lifestyle exactly as it was in earlier life. Experts have criticized models that equate old

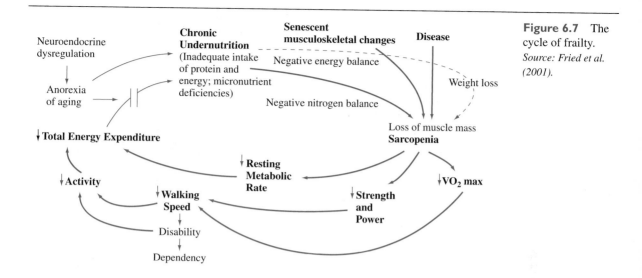

Figure 6.7 The cycle of frailty.
Source: Fried et al. (2001).

with young or that advocate an "ageless self," one that shows no change after middle age. These models overemphasize sameness and label even the slightest deviation in health status as evidence of increased vulnerability and dependence (Smyer, 1995).

Self-assessments of health in the elderly have been reported to correlate strongly with mortality, future health problems, recovery from illness, and overall functional abilities. Recent research has also examined the relationship between self-assessment of health and positive health outcomes, including positive mood or affect and active involvement in life, among elderly residents of a retirement community. These factors were just as predictive of current self-assessments of health as traditional "negative" indicators: negative mood, use of medications, and functional ability (Benyamini, Idler, Leventhal, & Leventhal, 2000). To understand self-rated health in the elderly, we must examine both positive and negative relationships.

Most older adults are in fairly good health and live a lifestyle that in many ways continues the pathways they chose when they were younger. Many live independently in their own homes or apartments and function as part of a community (Smyer, 1995).

Older individuals usually show some increase in health-related problems as they age. Of all the factors that predict how individuals will adjust to aging and that predict their subsequent mortality, health is the most powerful. Among persons 62 years of age and older, perceived health declines with the onset of new illnesses and the associated increase in the number of visits to physicians for care, or with preexisting illnesses that worsen (Rodin & McAvay, 1992). Among older adults, perceived health is also predicted by higher scores on tests used to measure depression and by lower scores on a life satisfaction index.

Studies of the trajectories of chronic disabilities suggest that factors such as poor self-concept, lower self-perceived health status, depressive symptoms, or the presence of multiple chronic diseases accelerates the rate of functional decline. Those with more negative perceptions have increased mortality, independent of the severity of their disease. And, as might be expected, with each new disease or medical emergency, older persons who already have a chronic illness experience greater functional loss than those facing these illnesses initially (Deeg, Kardaun, & Fozard, 1996).

Health can be defined in many ways: by number of illnesses, chronic conditions, disabilities, number of restrictions, limitations, physical pain, emotional status, or cardiovascular capacity, to cite but a few. Increasingly, older Americans are able to take control of their own health status, as Research Focus 6.1 explains.

Economics of Aging and Long-Term Health Care

The "graying of America" has meant that we now find people living 20, 30, and 40 years past retirement. Some senior organizations have been effective in influencing health care policy. Older adults worry about whether they will be able to live independently or whether they will require in-home assistance or have to move to an institution. Many are concerned about the availability of financial resources to meet

Research Focus 6.1

Taking Charge of Health

Americans of all ages are increasingly turning to the medical marketplace to address many of their health concerns. Older adults can purchase a blood pressure or cardiac device to monitor their status at home, or they can visit the local pharmacy and use such equipment for free. Other home use devices are available for diabetics or others who need to check their blood sugar levels or those who wish to check for colorectal cancer. Assessing health status has become a topic of conversation among the elderly. Just as people discuss stock market changes or baseball scores, they ask each other "How's your cholesterol?" The at-home monitoring movement is only about a decade old and shows no signs of tapering off (Rozhon, 2001). There are kits for HIV testing, pregnancy, body fat monitoring, as well as computer chips and miniature cameras that can monitor a stroke patient's rehabilitation and exercise techniques. One university is developing a wearable computer chip that monitors all of the basic physiological functions and triggers an alarm if one becomes problematic.

One negative consequence of self-monitoring and the increased demand for equipment is that physicians may not be seen early in the disease process. Another may be an obsession for self-diagnosis and a tendency towards overassessment. A third possible negative consequence is that consumers may jump to conclusions without consulting a medical expert. Just as medical testing is subject to error, these monitors can be fallible. In fact, most manufacturers are careful to provide information about the limits of the results the devices reveal. Insurers are reluctant to cover the costs of these in-home devices, unless a physician specifically prescribes them. And they may not cut down on costly office visits. Rozhon (2001) has reported just the opposite, that any change in test readings leads users to call or visit the doctor.

There are some very positive outcomes, however. The trend toward home monitoring devices has many benefits for older people. They may better adjust their medications and tailor dosages to changing conditions. They establish a sense of partnership between patient and physician. There is mounting evidence that when physicians actively consult with patients, making them partners in their own health care, better outcomes accrue all around. Patients feel more in control and accept responsibility for their own health, rather than putting themselves in a totally dependent relationship with a medical expert. The trend towards self-monitoring will continue for many years to come as devices become more sophisticated, miniaturized, and easier to use.

their health care needs. Who will pay for the costs of health care? Because of their concerns, many older adults pay attention to the politics of health care cost containment and access (Will benefits be capped for individuals? Will health maintenance organizations limit access to controversial treatments? Will they offer high-cost interventions such as transplants only to those who have the resources to pay for them?).

Social Security and Health Care

Today, Americans are focused on the economic survival of Social Security and its four component trust funds: (1) Old-Age Survivors Insurance, (2) Disability Insurance, (3) Hospital Insurance Trust Fund—Medicare Part A, and (4) Supplementary Medical Insurance—Medicare Part B. Health care experts and politicians question the capacity of the Social Security program to expand to meet the projected growth in numbers of eligible recipients as the baby boomers retire.

Social Security is the federal government's income and insurance program for those who have worked a minimum of 10 years in jobs that earn credit and accumulate benefits. Social Security represents a significant source of income for more than 36 percent of the elderly (National Academy on Aging, 1996). In 2001, 187 million persons were working in jobs covered by Social Security, but not every worker is a part of Social Security (Social Security Administration, 2001). All eligible workers must contribute to Social Security based on a percentage of their earnings. Workers, or survivors if the worker dies, receive benefits upon retirement. Although retirement benefits can be accessed beginning at age 62, they are reduced in proportion to what the person would have received when eligible for full benefits.

In June 2001, 28.8 million retired workers were drawing benefits from the Old Age and Survivors Insurance Trust. The average monthly benefit was $849. Benefits are based on each worker's highest average earnings. Today, eligible workers contribute 5.26 percent of their earnings to the Old Age and Survivors Insurance Trust and 0.94 percent to the Disability Insurance Trust. There is a limit on the maximum contribution a worker must make. The Hospital Insurance Trust Fund (Medicare Part A) has no maximum limit on workers' earnings, which are assessed at 1.45 percent of earnings. Benefits that retirees receive are tax free and employees match these contributions; self-employed adults pay double these rates.

Since health care costs represent an increasing burden to older adults on fixed incomes, it is important to understand how Social Security programs, both income and hospital coverage, help to meet these costs. Older persons in the United States living outside of a nursing home spend about 25 percent of their yearly income on health care (TIAA, 2000). For a significant segment of older Americans, federal programs are the only means to meet the costs of long-term nursing care. By 2030, the number of nursing home residents is predicted to be 3.5 million people, with in-home care offered to nearly 9 million additional elderly. The costs associated with this growth in long-term care are staggering; some predict the figure to top $200 billion by 2030. While there are sufficient numbers of nursing homes and beds available nationwide, community-based adult day care is in short supply. The current need is for 10,000 adult day care centers (Connole, 1999). How will this demand be met, and how will it be financed?

Pensions

Having a yearly pension from an employer, in addition to Social Security benefits, has a significant impact on the financial well-being and health care of an older adult (Burkhauser & Salisbury, 1993; Lillard, Rogowski, & Kington, 1997). In several European countries, such as Sweden, Germany, France, Great Britain, and the Netherlands, as well as in Australia, nearly all older persons receive a substantial pension and subsidized health care at government expense. In the United States, by comparison, pensions provided by private employers are modest and available to only a relatively small group of older adults (Quinn & Smeeding, 1993). Thus, few retirees in the United States receive a comparable level of support to that of retirees in these six other countries. And although Social Security gives older adults a base of financial support from the federal government, it leaves many retired individuals living a meager life if this is all they have to draw upon.

Increasingly, people are beginning to anticipate the need for multiple levels of support to sustain them into old age. Table 6.1 identifies the traditional "passive" economic supports available to older people, including Social Security, pensions, earnings, and assets. There is considerable disparity in such sources of income as a function of marital status, ethnicity, and race. As table 6.1 shows, Social Security is the single most important source of income for retirees. According to Snyder (1993), unmarried older African Americans derived more than 70 percent of their total retirement income from Social Security, Hispanics more than 74 percent, and whites, 54 percent. Many married women, in particular, discover that the death of a spouse may mean the end of supplemental pensions and other types of income supports. Often, pensions and other benefits such as health insurance are available to former employees until they die but do not necessarily transfer to a spouse. Postretirement health insurance is a significant benefit that can increase the value of a pension; this type of deferred compensation is offered by some companies to workers who have remained on the job for many years (Lillard et al., 1997).

Hospital and Home Health Care

When major health problems strike older people, they often require short-term nursing or medical care. Nursing home care and reimbursement guidelines are linked to current health care policies designed to contain hospital and medical costs. National health care policy requires that each patient with a specific medical condition, or within a **diagnostic related group (DRG),** conform to the average cost and length of treatment in a hospital based on other patients with this condition. Hospitals receive federal support for each patient in a specific DRG based on this average. If some patients require longer stays or more complex treatment, the hospital must absorb the differential in cost between the patient care they provide and the amount reimbursed by federal programs such as Medicare.

Treating patients within the norms of the DRGs for comparable conditions is difficult. The hospital and physician must subsidize hospital stays and medical costs above DRG averages; those under the averages qualify for the standard reimbursement. With the rise in the use of DRGs to control hospital reimbursements, interest has risen

TABLE 6.1

Sources of Passive Income for Retirees by Marital Status, Gender, Race, and Hispanic Origin

Income Share and Amount	White	Black	Hispanic
Married Men and Their Wives			
Total number (in thousands)	521.2	40.3	12.5
Median amount	$18,240	$11,980	$12,700
Total income	100.0%	100.0%	100.0%
Social Security	34.5	44.1[a]	42.4[a]
pensions	19.9	23.3	10.4[a,b]
earnings	19.8	25.1[a]	31.0[a]
assets	21.1	3.6[a]	10.0[a]
other	4.7	3.9	6.2
Married Women and Their Husbands			
Total number (in thousands)	335.1	21.8	7.9
Median amount	$17,780	$10,790	$13,040
Total income	100.0%	100.0%	100.0%
Social Security	37.3	48.3[a]	44.9[a]
pensions	16.2	21.7[a]	19.4
earnings	24.5	24.6	25.9
assets	18.0	2.0[a]	8.3[a]
other	4.0	3.4	1.5[a]
Unmarried Men and Women			
Total number (in thousands)	239.0	41.5	11.3
Median amount	$9,940	$5,570	$5,210
Total income	100.0%	100.0%	100.0%
Social Security	40.3	53.8[a]	52.9[a]
pensions	18.8	14.4	12.6[a]
earnings	14.0	21.8[a]	17.9
assets	20.0	3.6[a]	9.1[a]
other	6.9	6.3	8.5

Source: Data from Richard V. Burkhauser and Dallas L. Salisbury (Eds.), Pensions in a Changing Economy, Copyright © National Academy on Aging, Department of Health and Human Services, Washington DC. Data also from new Beneficiary Survey, 1982.
[a]Significantly different from whites at the 0.95 level of confidence.
[b]Significantly different from blacks at the 0.95 level of confidence.

in discharging older persons "quicker and sicker" into home care, nursing homes, and other institutional arrangements. Home health care is an appealing alternative to nursing home or hospital care. Home health agencies include governmental, institution-based, for-profit proprietary, and nonprofit community-based agencies such as visiting nurses. Services covered by Medicare Certified Home Health agencies include skilled nursing, home health aides, physical and occupational therapy, speech pathology, and medical social work services (Ondeck & Gingerich, 1999). Care is provided to individuals in their homes with an emphasis on patient and caregiver education. Today, highly sophisticated interventions such as tube feedings, intravenous chemotherapy and antibiotics, physical therapy, and respiratory therapy can be carried out at home.

The economic incentives for home health care are clear. Whereas hospital charges may total over $2,000 per day, home care with a single daily nursing visit costs about $120 and is usually covered by private insurance or Medicare. Unless an older patient requires extensive intervention throughout the day and evening or has severe Alzheimer's disease, home care is preferable to hospital or nursing home care. There are often so many home health services arranged that a specialized hospital staff member is assigned the role of "discharge planner." These professionals focus on determining the services older adults need and arranging for community resources to meet those needs. Working with multiple agencies, discharge planners coordinate visits and schedule services to coincide with patients' return home.

Many adults still think of nursing homes as the one alternative for intervention services and do not realize the range of choices that exist. With an average cost of $50,000 per year or $4,200 per month, nationwide, nursing homes are expensive (Sabitini, 2001). In some urban areas in the Northeast, nursing homes can cost more than twice this amount. Yet adult children cannot always take time away from work and personal responsibilities to help make arrangements and supervise the care of a parent who requires assistance with day-to-day needs. Many live hundreds or thousands of miles from their aging parents. Professional **geriatric care managers** can develop a plan of intervention services and identify appropriate service agencies in the community for each older client. They assess the medical, social, emotional, nutritional, and physical status of the client as well as the current residence, the client's ability to function independently, functional level, and financial situation. They identify alternative living arrangements, if needed, and appropriate interventions for an older parent within the financial restrictions of the family. Table 6.2 shows a typical Home Environment Assessment used with the elderly (Ondeck & Gingerich, 1999).

Assisted Living

Assisted living describes a philosophy of care, according to the American Association of Retired Persons Policy Institute, that enhances the capabilities of frail elders so they can live as independently as possible in a homelike atmosphere that supports the autonomy and privacy of each resident (Matthews, 1999). Assisted living is a less costly alternative to nursing home care for those having difficulties with routine ADL and IADL skills. Residents live in apartment-type settings or single dormitory rooms and may gather for group activities or meals. Assisted living facilities can help foster successful aging and enhance day-to-day functioning. Residents, despite needing help with ADLs or IADLs, can maintain as much independence as possible in other spheres. Social services and informal social support are also provided, and residents report being happier than those in nursing homes.

Assisted living offers "health and personal care to an increasingly more impaired and disabled senior population in the least-restrictive and most homelike environment possible" (Mitchell & Kemp, 2000, p. P117). Elderly people respond best to assisted living (in a quality of life assessment) when given as much choice and control as possible and when receiving strong social support through facility-sponsored activities and regular visits from friends and family. The residents' perception of quality of life is strongly influenced by the social climate of the facility (in terms of cohesion, conflict, and independ-

TABLE 6.2

Assessment of the Home Environment

The Physical Environment

Are the following present ...
- sturdy hand railings in stairwells?
- wide doorways for ease of access with ambulation aids?
- water temperature below 110°?
- grab bars in the shower and tub area?
- nonskid bathtub surface?
- equipment and supplies for activities of daily living (ADLs) within easy reach?
- side rails on the bed, if applicable?
- food and beverage in appropriate quantity and quality?
- telephone for emergency access?
- lifeline, if indicated?
- running water?
- heating and cooling, as needed?

The Safety Environment

Are the following present ...
- smoke and fire detectors?
- fire extinguishers?
- fire exit plan?
- no frayed electrical cords?
- grounded electric plugs for all medical equipment and appliances?
- good lighting?
- clear pathways and stairwells?
- secured medications and biologicals?

The Cognitive Safety Environment

Are ...
- all pools, spas, and ponds fenced in?
- doors locked securely or camouflaged by draperies?
- gates placed at all stairwell entrances?
- medications stored in a locked enclosure?
- cognitively impaired individuals equipped with an identification card in the event that they wander off?

Source: Pratt, J. R., (Ed.). (1999). Long-term care: Managing across the continuum (p. 209). Gaithersburg, MD: Aspen.

ence); not all facilities are similar on these dimensions. Those residents with higher quality of life maintain a positive view (in a subjective appraisal) of themselves and their environment, have generally positive affect, and show high levels of life satisfaction and well-being. Assisted living is a form of environmental intervention that enhances successful aging; positive outcomes include *biological criteria* (morbidity, health status), *psychological criteria* (mental health status, absence of pathology), and *personal autonomy/control criteria* (cognitive and social efficacy, productivity, and life satisfaction; Smyer, 1995).

The average assisted living costs for rent and basic services in the Northeast is over $3,000 per month, with subsidies sometimes available for the poor. Residents may

Nursing homes vary in the kinds and quality of services they offer.

contract for additional services, such as help with bathing, dressing, or other routine tasks; the typical services that older persons need cost about an additional $1,000 each month (Kindleberger, 1996). Assisted living is obviously not easily within the reach of most older persons (Kindleberger, 1996). Massachusetts, for instance, recently built an assisted living complex with almost half of its 69 apartments set aside for low-income elderly. Low-income residents qualified for up to $1,000 of Medicaid funding to help with their expenses; however, even when linked with Social Security Supplemental Income benefits of $500 to $700 each month, these low-income residents could not afford all the services that might have helped them (Kindleberger, 1996).

Long-Term Care

Long-term care encompasses a wide-range of supportive services and assistance to people who, as the result of chronic illness or frailty, are unable to function independently (Seperson, 2001). Long-term care includes medical intervention, social support services, and personal care assistance to help chronically ill or disabled elderly cope with basic day-to-day activities. In the past, this type of care was referred to as custodial care. The day-to-day care activities older persons may need assistance with include personal care activities such as dressing, bathing, toileting, and walking. Some long-term care is delivered in the home; these services include help with cooking, shopping, or feeding. Other long-term care is provided in specialized centers such as those offering physical rehabilitation, supervised adult day care for a person with Alzheimer's disease, community-based visiting nurse programs, home health aide services, or respite programs for those with Alzheimer's disease and their families. Table 6.3 illustrates the differences between long-term and acute care, using an example of the treatment and delivery of services to an older person who has experienced a stroke. As is true of the treatment for any impairment, the goal of long-term care is to help the older person regain skills and maintain as much independence as possible. Table 6.4 shows that with advancing age among adults over 65, the need for some long-term care services becomes

TABLE 6.3

Types of Care

This chart shows the possible types of care given to someone who has suffered a stroke, illustrating the differences between acute care and long-term care.

	Acute Care	Long-Term Care
Care objectives	Improve patient's ability to function	Maintain patient at current level of function
Where care is received	Hospital and rehabilitation unit	At home
Who provides care	Physicians, nurses, therapists	Family member, home health aide
Type of care	Medication, X rays, IV feedings, physical therapy	Help with bathing and dressing, shopping, and housework
Length of care	4 weeks in hospital and rehabilitation	Ongoing
Who pays for care	Medicare and private supplemental insurance	Patient most likely pays out of pocket

Source: Long-term care—A guide for the educational community. Copyright © 1992 by Teachers Insurance and Annuity Association (TIAA).

TABLE 6.4

Percentage of Persons Over 65 Years of Age Reporting Difficulty with Selected Personal Health Care Activities

Age	Personal Care Activity						
	Bathing	Dressing	Eating	Transferring	Walking	Getting Outside	Using Toilet
65 years and under	9.8	6.2	1.8	8.0	18.7	9.6	4.3
65–74 years	6.4	4.3	1.2	6.1	14.2	5.6	2.6
65–69 years	5.2	3.9	1.2	5.3	12.2	4.9	2.2
70–74 years	7.9	4.8	1.1	7.1	16.6	6.6	3.0
75–84 years	12.3	7.6	2.5	9.2	22.9	12.3	5.4
75–79 years	9.8	6.4	2.1	7.5	19.5	9.9	4.1
80–84 years	16.8	9.7	3.2	12.4	29.0	16.8	7.8
85 years and over	27.9	16.6	4.4	19.3	39.9	31.3	14.1

Source: National Health Interview Survey, National Center for Health Statistics, 1984.

increasingly likely; estimates are that nearly 60 percent of adults will require such services at least once in their lives.

The cost of long-term care for the elderly is substantial, and many people have little knowledge of the economics involved until such services are needed (see figure 6.8).

Long-term care is most frequently delivered in nursing homes. With an expected annual rise in nursing home costs of 5 percent per year due to inflation, an institution charging only $150 a day in 2001 will be charging more than $430 in 20 years. The typical nursing home stay is about 75 days, but long-term care needs may require a six- to seven-year

Figure 6.8 The increasing cost of long-term care. In 1965, the average cost in the United States for one year of nursing home care was $2,900. By 2003, the average cost for one year of nursing home care will be $53,600.

Note: Costs cited from 1965–1984 are based on unpublished data from the *Office of National Health Statistics, Health Care Financing Administration, Office of the Actuary.* Cost cited for 2003 is based on a 5 percent annual increase over the 1997 cost of $40,000 per year. *Source: TIAA, 1997.*

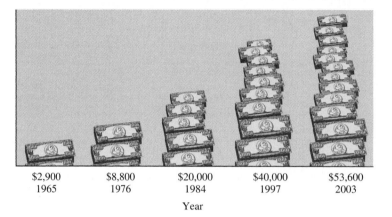

| $2,900 | $8,800 | $20,000 | $40,000 | $53,600 |
| 1965 | 1976 | 1984 | 1997 | 2003 |

Year

Figure 6.9 Who pays for long-term care? Today, a large portion of the costs in the United States are paid out of private, personal resources. *Source: Office of the Assistant Secretary for Planning and Evaluation, DHHS. (1995). Congressional Research Service Issue Brief, March 22.*

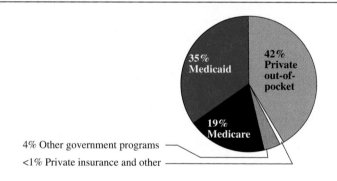

35% Medicaid

42% Private out-of-pocket

19% Medicare

4% Other government programs

<1% Private insurance and other

stay, or even longer. Who pays for these services? Medicare and Medicaid are federally subsidized programs that provide some of the health care coverage older people need. Ordinarily, these programs do not cover the complete cost of long-term care (see figure 6.9).

Medicaid

Medicaid is a federal insurance program that provides matching funds to the states to help pay for the medical care of lower-income elderly. To be eligible for Medicaid, one must be over the age of 65 and at or near the poverty level. Medicaid is provided to states only if the states offer minimum basic benefits, although individual states may establish restrictions on the types of services offered and the level of support they offer to older persons. Medicaid typically covers about two-thirds of the cost of the medical health services the poor elderly require, including some psychiatric services (Liska, Obermaier, Lyons, & Long, 1995).

If older people have significant assets, of course, Medicaid cannot help them with long-term care expenses. However, when such assets are depleted to a minimal level due to long-term care costs in a process called **spending down,** older people can become eligible for Medicaid. In 2001, Medicaid payments were restricted to (1) $645 per month for a community-residing single individual with maximum assets of $3,750; (2) $920 per month for a community-residing couple with maximum assets of $5,400; (3) $2,175 for a husband or wife whose spouse was in a nursing home and who had maximum assets of $87,000, excluding the value of a home. To be eligible for Medicaid in 2001 a community residing single person is allowed to keep $3,750 in assets and earn $625 per month of income. A married couple may keep $5,400 of joint assets and earn $920 per month of combined income. And, a husband or wife whose spouse is in a nursing home may hold $87,000 of combined assets, excluding the value of a home, and keep $2,175 in monthly income. More than a third of Medicaid funds were used to provide long-term care, including community-based services, home health care, nursing, and individual personal care (Burwell, 1996; Weiner, 1996). Elderly adults received more than 60 percent of all Medicaid funds assigned for nursing home care; nearly 70 percent of all nursing home residents were covered either fully or partially from Medicaid funds.

Medicare

Medicare is funded from the Hospital Insurance Trust Fund–Part A of the Social Security system. It provides some support, but not complete coverage, for medical services for any individual over age 65. More than 42 million people were covered by Medicare in 2001, including not only the elderly, but also individuals with end-stage renal disease and disabled younger persons who pay a monthly premium for coverage. Medicare has no fee or premium and covers hospitalization for each illness for up to 150 days, less deductibles, if the older person requires medical treatment. There are no limits to the number of hospital stays it will cover as long as 60 days have elapsed between discharge and readmission. Medicare will also cover nursing home services (a maximum of 100 days) for each medical condition as long as a physician has "prescribed" such services (Health Care Financing Administration, 2001).

Medicare is designed to deal with acute illnesses or accidents, not chronic conditions that require intervention. The only home care Medicare covers is for a condition or need related directly to recovery from an acute illness. A physician must file a written recovery plan for the patient, including needed home health services (Health Care Financing Administration, 2001). The elderly person is assumed to be housebound, under the direct care of a physician who has developed and filed a written plan for intervention and recovery, and to require only intermittent skilled nursing or other therapy (e.g., speech therapy, physical therapy, or occupational therapy). Services must be provided by a certified home care agency.

For an additional monthly premium of $50, extended hospital coverage benefits are available to older persons under a voluntary Supplemental Medical Insurance–Part B program. Basic covered services are reimbursed at 80 percent of allowable charges, less a $100-per-year deductible (Health Care Financing Administration, 2001). Nearly 98 percent of those who are eligible for Hospital Insurance–Part A also elect extended coverage under the Supplemental Medical Insurance–Part B program. The Part B Trust Fund is funded from general revenue from the federal government, monthly premiums, and trust fund interest. Medicare remains the leading insurance provider in the United States, accounting for 28 percent of all hospital payments and 20 percent of all physician payments (National Academy on Aging, 1995). In 2001, there was a deductible for each inpatient hospital stay ($792) and a daily copayment ($198) for hospital stays extending for 61 to 90 days. Coverage for hospitalization beyond three months is limited to 60 additional days in a lifetime (Health Care Financing Administration, 2001).

Physicians receive reimbursement from Medicare based on customary, prevailing, and reasonable rates that the government establishes. Reimbursement rates for physician services reflect the integration of (1) the typical costs for similar services charged by physicians in a community, (2) the lowest cost for specific services, (3) the charge for specific services by other physicians, and (4) a historical review of charges for similar services (Gottlieb, 1992). There are no limits on medical or surgical benefits for Medicare recipients (e.g., lifetime costs, costs per illness, or number of visits for treatment). Inpatient psychiatric coverage is set at a lifetime maximum of 190 days. Currently, clinical social workers and psychologists may receive direct reimbursement as independent providers, although Medicare only covers half of the costs for outpatient mental health. Skilled nursing care directly related to a condition that required hospitalization is covered completely for the first 20 days and for a $99-per-day copayment for the next 80 days. Skilled nursing and intravenous medical care are covered in a home setting only if a physician prescribes them and only if they relate directly to the condition for which hospitalization was required. Nearly all hospice care for the terminally ill is covered for up to 210 days, including home care services, some prescription drugs, and counseling (Health Care Financing Administration, 2001).

Long-Term Health Care Costs

Medicare was never intended to cover all of an older person's long-term health care needs, since it excludes personal home care services as well as nursing care, except under highly restrictive situations (Seperson, 2001). Some states have permitted private insurance companies to fill in the missing coverage with **Medigap policies.** These policies, for an additional fee, provide coverage for home-based personal care and other health expenses not fully covered by Medicare. For example, Medicare does not cover the costs of prescription drugs, routine physicals, hearing aids, eyeglasses, or nonsurgical dental care. Kington, Rogowski, and Lillard (1995) found that 44 percent of the elderly required dental services in one 12-month period, and only 13 percent had dental insurance to meet even part of the costs. Similarly, one of the most underutilized services covered in the Medicare program has been treatment for psychiatric disorders.

By the time adults reach age 65, they have a 40 percent chance of needing some long-term care intervention (Balch, 1997). Private long-term care insurance is available to reduce the direct costs of such services, but the insurance itself is costly. Only 10 to 20 percent of older persons can afford the premiums (Weiner, 1996). Table 6.5 shows comparative costs for one national insurance company. As with most policies, the younger the purchaser is, the lower the cost. A policy is nearly five times more costly for someone 80 years of age to purchase than for a 60-year-old. Insurance policy costs also vary considerably based on coverage, as table 6.5 shows; better policies with higher lifetime benefits cost three times more than basic policies. A standard long-term care policy with a high deductible, no inflation protection, modest $100 per day coverage, and a 90-day waiting period is only half the cost of a premium policy. Compare this coverage with the costs in figure 6.8, which illustrates national costs for nursing home care.

Insurance companies may exclude those most likely to use nursing home services—older people with prior illnesses, prior nursing home utilization, and/or chronic disabilities. Many policies specifically exclude disorders such as Alzheimer's disease or require that nursing care supervision must be continual to protect the person or others (TIAA, 1996). Finally, most policies provide a fixed daily rate of reimbursement

TABLE 6.5

Long-Term Care Insurance Costs

Premiums for each plan are based on the purchaser's age at the time the policy is issued.

	Plan A-96	Plan B-96	Plan C-96
Lifetime Benefit Maximum	$109,500	$182,500	$255,500
Nursing Home Daily Benefit Maximum	$100/day	$100/day	$100/day
Home Health Care/Adult Day Care Daily Benefit Maximum	$50/day	$50/day	$50/day
Waiting Period	90 days	90 days	90 days

Illustration of Long-Term Care Insurance Costs

Age	Plan A-96 Quarterly	Plan B-96 Quarterly	Plan C-96 Quarterly
40	50.52	59.11	62.79
45	64.37	75.41	80.08
50	81.28	95.28	101.12
55	109.05	127.74	135.37
60	152.89	178.85	189.08
65	219.25	256.49	270.59
70	319.61	374.93	395.15
75	485.72	572.97	603.45
80	754.33	898.73	945.68
84	1042.62	1253.85	1316.97

(indemnity) rather than meeting the actual costs of services required. The reimbursement rates in a standard policy ordinarily do not increase year by year to take inflation and the generally escalating costs of nursing home stays into account. When people purchase policies 10 to 15 years in advance, they often discover that their own projections of nursing home costs are far below real charges (Coronel & Fulton, 1995; Weiner, 1996).

In practice, however, only 4 to 5 percent of older people have purchased long-term health care insurance, most often when they are close to retirement (Weiner, 1996). Among retirees, wealth is the best predictor of whether an individual will invest in long-term care insurance protection. Older black Americans, women-headed households, and those with less education tend not to purchase supplemental coverage. Interestingly, health status is not related to the decision to buy private health care insurance (Lillard et al., 1997). Lillard and colleagues (1997) reported that many elderly fortunate enough to have private long-term care insurance received policies from the companies they retired from as a reward for long, continuous employment.

To reduce Medicare expenditures on long-term care, the government has periodically considered a range of incentives to encourage individuals to purchase private long-term care insurance. Incentives under consideration at the time of this writing include tax deductions for the cost of individual policies, allowing elderly who have purchased policies to hold on to more assets, and offering employer-sponsored policies to younger workers (Weiner, 1996). The government has also considered meeting the growing Medicare funding gap through increased payroll taxes, shifting contributions from the other Social Security Trust Funds, increasing premiums, instituting a $5 copayment for services, and contracting with managed care systems and health maintenance organizations for services. Other alternatives are under discussion, including raising the age of eligibility for Medicare from 65 to 67, requiring higher-income retirees to pay higher premiums, reducing reimbursement rates to specialty physicians, freezing hospital reimbursement rates, and permitting older persons special tax-free medical savings accounts to purchase private health care insurance (Gavin, 1997).

Nursing Homes

There are 17,000 certified nursing homes in the United States, with an occupancy rate of 83 percent. Average annual costs were estimated to be $53,000, or about $150 per day, in 2001; costs are expected to increase by 5 percent per year. Without certification, nursing homes cannot receive reimbursement for services from Medicare and Medicaid (AARP, 2001). The government conducts certification reviews of nursing homes and home health care agencies. Nursing home abuses in the past have reinforced the need for vigilance and regular monitoring. Only 15 years ago, more than one-third of skilled nursing homes were seriously deficient in at least one major area and therefore not eligible for reimbursement. Even today, nursing homes may have difficulties with certification if they fail to meet the minimum standards for availability of physicians, pharmacists, and other rehabilitation professionals (e.g., occupational and physical therapists). Certification also ensures compliance with Public

Law 100–203, which protects the patient's rights to privacy, open access to medical information, a lifestyle that fits his or her mental and physical capacities, safety, and personal items.

The National Center for Health Statistics has undertaken a comprehensive analysis of 1,500 nursing homes. From the most recent data available, they have compared changes in residents from 1985 to 1997 (Sahyoun et al., 2001). The number of nursing home residents is predicted to increase to 3 million by 2020, almost double the number of residents in 1997. The past 12 years has seen the nursing home population become somewhat more racially diverse and older, as figure 6.10 illustrates. In 1985, the average age of residents was 81.1, compared to 82.6 in 1997. In 1997, more than half of all nursing home residents were over the age of 85. Women residents continue to outnumber men three to one. Most new nursing home residents are widows.

Table 6.6 shows that the length of nursing home stays has become shorter. This table also shows that in 1997, 30 percent of older persons were being discharged from nursing homes to live in the community, compared to only 18 percent in 1985. Over the 12-year period, the elderly have been discharged more rapidly to the community. Earlier, circulatory diseases (hypertension, stroke) and cognitive/mental disorders were the most common problems. A pattern of cognitive impairment, incontinence, and functional decline, however, most often underlies nursing home admissions today (Tomiak, Berthelot, Guimond, & Mustard, 2000).

Nursing home residents in 1997 were more functionally impaired as measured by the need for assistance on the six basic activities of daily living (ADLs): bathing, dressing, eating, transferring from bed to chair, toileting, and walking. In 1985, nursing home residents needed help with an average of 3.8 ADL tasks; by 1997, the average was 4.4. Nursing home residents were less independent upon admission, perhaps because they received more in-home health care, medical technological assistance, and family assistance in the community. Older persons seem to be living longer in their communities and entering nursing homes sicker and more frail than in the past. Home health care has increased dramatically in the past 12 years, making it possible for the elderly to live longer in their communities (Sahyoun, 2001). Quality of life is higher

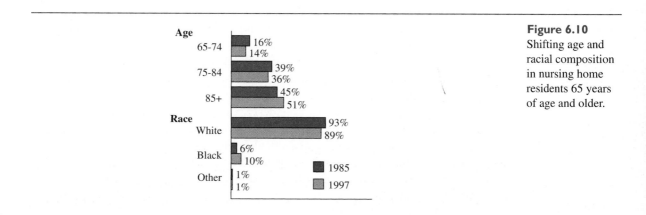

Figure 6.10
Shifting age and racial composition in nursing home residents 65 years of age and older.

TABLE 6.6

Reasons for Nursing Home Discharge, 1985 and 1997

	1985	1997
Recuperated/back to community	18%	30%
Moved to hospital or other nursing home	49	36
Death	31	25
Unknown/other	3	9

Average Number of Days Residents Lived in Nursing Homes, 1985 and 1997

	1985	1997
Current resident:		
from admission to interview	1,026	903
Discharged residents:		
to community/recuperated	89	45
to a hospital/other nursing home	400	284
death	653	562

among elderly living in the community than in nursing homes. The challenge is to find support for older adults to remain in the community. Home health care (physical therapy, visiting nurses, and aides), assisted living, adult rehabilitation, and day care are all part of the solution, as is a work environment that supports family caregivers.

The risk of mortality in nursing homes is highest among recent admissions with dementia. In one investigation, nearly 25 percent did not survive the first six months in care (Aneshensel, Pearlin, Levy-Storms, and Schuler, 2000). Moving from home care to nursing care is associated with a doubling of mortality risk for those with dementia. Certain effects predict nursing home admission for those with dementia: being a white male in poor health and having advanced age are the predictive factors identified in research. Mortality has also been examined in nursing home residents who did not have dementia (O'Connor & Vallerand, 1998). Over a four-year period, mortality was found to be related to the psychological adjustment variables of self-evaluation and life evaluation. Survival (controlling for age, health, and gender) was most strongly related to an individual's self-evaluation of their own self-esteem and depression. Only modest relationships were found for mortality and general evaluations in life satisfaction and meaning in life. Figure 6.11 reveals differential mortality rates for each of three levels of psychological adjustment.

The decision to institutionalize an elderly relative is not easy; most family members do not want to "put away" a person who has loved and cared for them. Often, caregivers persist in the face of increased physical demands as basic ADL skills decline. It appears that certain forms of family assistance reduce the likelihood of institutionalizing a relative with dementia. Those who can provide overnight help to an impaired relative and provide help with routine ADLs are less likely to elect nursing home care

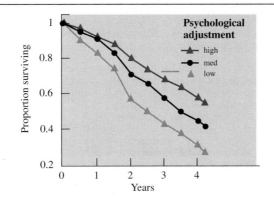

Figure 6.11
Nursing home survivorship curves for three levels of psychological adjustment: the mean ("med"), 1 standard deviation *(SD)* below the mean ("low"), and 1 *SD* above the mean ("high"). *N* = 128.

(Gaugler et al., 2000). However, incontinence may be a task outside the boundaries of routine care for relatives and may trigger the institutionalization of an older adult (Sahyoun et al., 2001). Urinary incontinence is a primary risk factor for skin breakdown and infections, especially among nursing home residents. Nearly one-third of nursing home residents have lost bladder control (Schnelle, McNees, Crooks, & Ouslander, 1995).

Another predictor of nursing home admission is loneliness. Loneliness may simply reflect the inability of caregivers to provide for the needs of the elderly. Without adequate caregiving, older adults are increasingly at risk for nursing home admission (figure 6.12). Those who were most lonely were more highly educated, had more chronic illnesses, reported lower levels of well-being, participated in fewer organizations, and had fewer friends than those who were least lonely (Russell, Cutrona, Wallace, & de la Mora, 1997).

Agitation in residents with dementia can be difficult to manage. Using two broad factors, researchers have reported comparable levels of agitated behavior in both the U.S. and Japan. One factor consists of physically aggressive acts and was seen in 10 to 20 percent of those with dementia; the second factor, verbal agitation, was seen in a smaller percentage. The most frequently observed agitated behaviors were wandering, general restlessness, and verbal acts such as repetitive questioning, cursing, and complaining. In both cultures, these behaviors were most likely to emerge while a staff member was assisting with personal care, especially bathing (Schreiner, Yamamoto, & Shiotani, 2000). Ombudsman programs may be helpful to both staff and residents when problems occur (Research Focus 6.2).

Cognitive Impairment and Environmental Intervention

Physical disabilities and limitations that limit independence in the elderly usually result in predictable types of environmental support and interventions to preserve autonomy. Much less agreement exists regarding treatments and interventions for older adults with cognitive impairments. The goal of intervention for this population is to strengthen independent function, preserve self-worth, and minimize the impact on families.

Figure 6.12 Age and risk of nursing home admission.

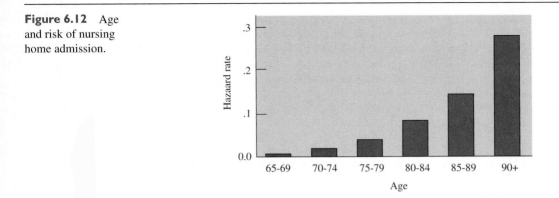

Ombudsman Programs in Long-Term Care

A long-term care ombudsman is concerned for the welfare of elderly who reside in nursing facilities and other supervised group settings. An ombudsman helps protect the health, safety, and individual rights of the institutionalized elderly and monitors quality-of-life and quality-of-care issues. Ombudsman programs began in the 1970s as poor-quality nursing home care and abuse came to light. Each state has established an Office of Long-Term Care Ombudsman; ombudsman programs are part of the requirements for certification and federal reimbursement under Medicare. National standards for ombudsman programs and assessment procedures have been recently suggested (Huber et al., 2001).

Ombudsmen receive training to enhance their skills in listening, observing, facilitating, educating, mediating, problem solving, and advocacy. They provide a link between the institution (staff and administration) and the larger community the residents are a part of. Often, elderly in long-term care are shut away from the mainstream of society; many have no family or friends to represent their interests or needs. Some residents may not fully understand their basic rights and benefits or mistakenly believe that institutional living takes away many personal freedoms. Ombudsmen work with institutional staff to find the best possible solution to care issues. Most long-term care administrators cooperate fully with ombudsmen and help to resolve resident concerns. Residents should not fear retaliation or punishment from institutional staff or administration for reporting their concerns to an ombudsman; residents are not to be abused or belittled by staff nor intimidated by other residents. Ombudsmen are encouraged to approach problems systematically, from a broad perspective, and to help change policies as well as educate staff, families, and residents. As advocates of the elderly in long-term care, ombudsmen encourage community participation as well as active resident councils (regular meetings at which long-term care residents air their concerns, free from staff monitoring (Harris-Wehling, Feasly, & Estes, 1995).

Generally, ombudsmen respond appropriately and quickly to residents' concerns, although ombudsmen in rural areas may make infrequent visits to long-term care facilities because of distance. The use of hotline telephone numbers for residents to report complaints has come under criticism. First, residents may be too cognitively impaired, frail, or fearful to initiate a call to an ombudsman. Second, telephone inquiries may not result in a rapid or detailed investigation. Finally, telephone calls too often result in a follow-up inquiry with the institution's staff or administrators, not the resident. Evaluations reveal that 75 percent of ombudsmen feel that they have been responsive to resident concerns and effective in dealing with these concerns. The definition of the ombudsman role provided in training helps volunteers understand the scope of their responsibilities and increases their feelings of effectiveness (Nelson, 1995). Ombudsmen value initial training and believe it leads to success in the volunteer role. Those who felt most positive about their training were able to approach the role of ombudsman with a greater sense of efficacy and less anxiety (Keith, 2000).

Community and Home Care

Long-term care of the cognitively impaired begins with intervention provided by un-paid family and friends. Those without support networks are at increased risk of being institutionalized (Seperson, 2001). The *substitution hypothesis* explains how formal community services are provided to older adults who are without a network of sup-portive family or friends or who have a network that is unable or unwilling to provide help. The hypothesis is based on the idea that communities can provide replacement services directly to impaired elders. Alternatively, communities may offer respite serv-ices to an older adult's support network so that they can continue their support respon-sibilities. Respite services might include support groups or respite care. Alternatively the *supplementation* or *linking hypothesis* provides a rationale for supplementing the contributions of family and friends to a cognitively impaired elder (George, 1992). Caregivers may link with services that they themselves are not trained or able to pro-vide; task differentiation helps to identify the nature of the services needed and the available resources in the community (for example, meal preparation, bathing, or adult day care). With appropriate support from the community, friends and family can help keep an impaired older adult from becoming institutionalized for quite some time.

Environmental Design for the Cognitively Impaired Elderly

Regnier and Pynoos (1992) developed a set of 12 principles to enhance the institutional settings and home environments of cognitively impaired elderly. These principles can help professionals responsible for the architecture, interior design, and aesthetics of in-stitutions focus on critical environmental dimensions known to influence both the be-havior and quality of life of cognitively impaired older persons. For example, the "L" design or "toe-to-toe" placement of beds shown in figure 6.13 provides more privacy for residents than placing the beds side by side. And when cognitively impaired resi-dents with AD are able to see their bathrooms and toilets from bed, incidents of incon-tinence are significantly reduced (Brink, 1993; Regnier & Pynoos, 1992). Such princi-ples are outlined briefly in table 6.7 (for a more complete account see Regnier & Pynoos, 1992, pp. 763–792). It is hoped that cognitively impaired elderly will continue to experience better, safer, and more secure environments to optimize their capacity for independent living.

Wandering and Cognitive Impairment

Institutional and home care for the cognitively impaired elderly must also address the difficulties and safety concerns associated with wandering. Wandering is a common problem among older persons with dementia and a special burden on those providing home care (Martino-Saltzman, Blasch, Morris, & McNeal, 1992). In the past, care-givers and nursing homes were permitted to use physical restraints and even strong drugs to reduce wandering, but these methods, when used indiscriminately, violate the legal rights of older persons as well as their humanity and dignity (Namazi, 1994). Wandering includes "pacing, trying doorknobs, entering other people's rooms, talking about going 'home,' attempting to leave or leaving an institution against advice, getting

Delivering prepared food (Meals on Wheels) is a service found throughout communities in our society.

Figure 6.13 Two basic room configurations are commonly utilized in skilled nursing facilities today: (a) two-bed room, toe-to-toe, and (b) two-bed room, side-by-side. Configuration (a) provides more privacy.

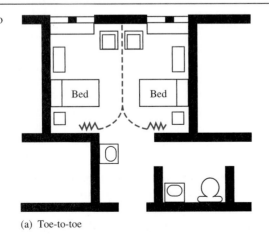

(a) Toe-to-toe

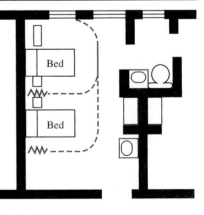

(b) Side-by-side

TABLE 6.7

Twelve Environment-Behavior Principles for Cognitively Impaired Older Persons

Privacy: Provide seclusion from company or observation, where one can be free from unauthorized intrusion. Privacy may mean having one's own room and the time to be away from others, free from unnecessary surveillance.

Social Interaction: Provide opportunities for social exchange and interaction. For cognitively impaired individuals, social interaction can be therapeutic, and even the wide corridors of institutions can become "streets" for seeing others, and for friendly exchange.

Control, Choice, and Autonomy: Promote opportunities for residents to make choices and control events. Older persons need to have some sense of control and mastery over their environments.

Orientation and Way Finding: Foster a sense of orientation within the environment that reduces confusion and facilitates way finding. Provide an environment that is easy for those with cognitive impairments to negotiate and understand.

Safety and Security: Provide an environment that ensures each person will sustain no harm, injury, or undue risk.

Accessibility and Functioning: Consider manipulation and accessibility as the basic requirements for a functional environment. Utilize environmental features that are easy to manipulate (doors, windows) and require simple decisions.

Sensory Aspects: Changes in visual, auditory, and olfactory senses should be accounted for in environments. Meet the needs of older residents to sustain social and physical interaction with their environment; provide sufficient audition and illumination.

Stimulation and Challenge: Provide a stimulating environment that is safe but challenging. Stimulating environments minimize boredom and passivity and challenge the older person to maintain alertness and awareness.

Familiarity: Environments that use historical references can provide a sense of familiarity and continuity. Encourage the use of personal objects, particularly in new settings, to provide the impaired individual a familiar frame of reference and a sense of continuity.

Aesthetics and Appearance: Design environments that appear attractive, proactive, and noninstitutional. Avoid living conditions that depersonalize and stigmatize residents; build residential models that humanize and individualize the living experience.

Personalization: Provide opportunities to make the environment personal and mark it as the property of a single, unique individual. Maintain self-identity by individualizing the space the individual occupies; demonstrate the older person's uniqueness.

Adaptability: An adaptable or flexible environment can change to fit changing personal characteristics. Environments can be adapted to the changes the elderly encounter to permit them to "age in place" rather than to have to move to new settings; this permits redesign within existing structures, for example, to enhance safety. An illustration of such an environment appears in figure 6.13 which displays the relatively simple but essential adaptations necessary to help the cognitively impaired older adult negotiate the risk of bathing.

Source: Regnier, V., & Pynoos, J. (1992). Environmental intervention for cognitively impaired older persons. Handbook of mental health and aging. Orlando, FL: Academic Press, Copyright © 1992.

lost on a walk, or simply behaving in a way that someone considers disoriented." In one investigation, nursing home residents with dementia and identified as wanderers were compared with a group of residents in the same nursing home who were not wanderers. Martino-Saltzman et al. (1992) identified four types of travel patterns, seen in figure 6.14, based on their analysis of more than 10,000 events that were video-recorded in the nursing home over a one-month period, 24 hours each day. Although developed from a small sample of dementia residents, the results summarized in table 6.8 suggest

Figure 6.14

Travel patterns of nursing home residents identified as wanderers and nonwanderers. Lapping was more common among wanderers.

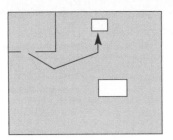

(1) **Direct**

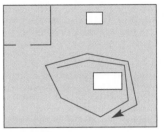

(2) **Random**

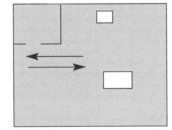

(3) **Pacing**

(4) **Lapping**

TABLE 6.8

Characteristic Wandering Patterns among Nursing Home Residents with Different Levels of Dementia

Pattern of Travel	Mild/No Dementia	Moderate Dementia	Severe Dementia
Direct	94.7%	92.5%	72.0%
Random	0.2	1.0	1.7
Pacing	1.5	0.0	0.03
Lapping	3.6	6.5	26.0

Source: Adapted from Martino-Saltzman, D., Blasch, B. B., Morris, R. D., & McNeal, L. W. (1992). Travel behavior of nursing home residents perceived as wanderers and nonwanderers. The Gerontologist, 31 (5), 666–672.

that with more severe dementia, patterns of travel become more indirect, and lapping is significantly more common.

Others have also studied pacing and its relationship to cognitive impairment in the elderly (Cohen-Mansfield, Werner, Marx, & Freedman, 1991). Pacing, when examined across a 24-hour period of study, was found to increase most dramatically in the evening hours, from 7:00 to 10:00 P.M., consistent with other observations of **sundowning** in dementia patients. The peak for nondirective travel was 7:15 P.M.; table 6.9 shows the distribution of nondirective travel (e.g., random, pacing, and lapping) across the day and evening hours.

These findings suggest that the overall travel of wanderers, particularly those with severe dementia, and the difficulties they present to nursing homes may be overestimated. With the greater likelihood of lapping, many institutions use structured or

TABLE 6.9

Percentage of Nondirective Independent Travel Events at Selective Time Periods for Nursing Home Residents with Various Levels of Dementia

Time Period	Mild/No Dementia (n = 12)	Moderate Dementia (n = 11)	Severe Dementia (n = 9)
10 pm–4 am	4%	1%	31%
4 am–7 am	2	13	26
Breakfast	2	5	19
9 am–12 noon	2	7	31
Lunch	4	5	15
2 pm–5 pm	7	6	32
Dinner	4	8	23
7 pm–10 pm	15	12	31
Total	5	7	28
Total excluding meal times	7	8	31

protected walking environments. Regnier and Pynoos (1992) describe an institution that incorporated AD wandering gardens to provide "restless patients" the chance to walk unencumbered in a safe, controlled area. And other institutions have found effective techniques to permit dementia patients to wander, including disguising emergency exits (e.g., by placing cloth covers matching the color of the walls on tamperproof doorknobs). Restricting visual accessibility helps reduce exiting behaviors. These visual barriers, used singly or in combination, were effective in redirecting wandering in one institution without compromising safety or fire codes (Namazi, 1994).

Restraints

Nursing homes have been mandated to reduce the use of physical restraints, and they are now required to record the use of such restraints as outlined in the Nursing Home Reform Act of 1987. The percentage of nursing home residents who are restrained today is about 20 percent, or 300,000 older people, a figure that represents a 50 percent reduction from 1989. Restraints include vests, mittens, belts, wrist or ankle ties, and *gerichairs,* or chairs with locking trays (Castle, 2000). In the past, residents were tied to beds, chairs, or wheelchairs by lengths of cloth wrapped around their waists, hips, chests, arms, or legs. Some residents were even chemically restrained, or administered antidepressants or other psychoactive and mood-altering drugs. Residents, according to law, have the right to be free from physical restraints. Use of restraints is permitted only under the following conditions: (1) because of a physician's order—restraint is required for medical treatment; (2) with the informed consent of the resident or a designated proxy; (3) as part of a nursing care plan for the resident that ultimately targets the complete elimination of restraints; (4) with documentation that alternatives to restraint were attempted but failed; and (5) with the proviso that residents must function at the highest possible level. Castle (2000) found more than 1 in 9 nursing homes had received formal citations for failure to comply with the requirements of the Nursing Home Reform Act governing restraints. Citations were more likely among larger, for-profit nursing homes affiliated with a hospital and less likely in facilities with higher ratios of staff to residents and training programs for nurse's aides.

Burton et al. (1992) studied the use of restraints among elderly persons admitted with "mental illness" to a nursing home facility. The more severe the cognitive impairment and the more difficulty the person had in managing independent daily living skills, the more likely staff were to employ physical restraints. Clear differences emerged in the use of restraints among the eight nursing homes studied, with high-use institutions tending to restrain persons who needed assistance in walking and low-use homes not engaging in this practice. Burton et al. (1992) suggest that staff attitudes predominately account for differences among high- and low-use nursing homes; in high-use homes, staff try to protect residents from falling and are quick to provide assistance with daily living tasks such as walking and dressing. They report considerable latitude in staff adoption of the use of physical restraint rather than mandated policies within the nursing home.

A number of studies have shown that appropriate education of staff tends to reduce the use of physical restraints. For example, when staff use behavioral prevention strategies, they are more successful in managing aggressive and agitated residents than when they use restraints (Chappell & Reid, 2000). Moreover, there are few negative outcomes when restraints are eliminated. There is no increase in the incidence or in the severity of falls. In fact, the use of restraints has actually been linked to an increase in falling among residents. When freedom of movement is limited, muscle atrophy can occur and lead to an increase in functional decline (Rubenstein, 1997). Understanding the variables that predict the need for restraints in institutional facilities can lead to further reductions in their use. Research focus 6.3 discusses the dangers of using restraints without careful monitoring.

Health and Impairment

The fact that physical functioning and health are at their peak in early adulthood is in some ways a risk. Young adults do not notice any immediate negative consequences of poor diet, alcohol abuse, stress, smoking, and lack of exercise. It is difficult to take better care of one's health when the consequences of one's choices are many decades away. Nine out of 10 people between the ages of 17 and 44 view their own health as good or excellent. Young adults have few chronic health problems.

Verbrugge and Jette (1994) noted that the health care community is particularly interested in eliminating specific risk factors that accelerate the rate of decline in illness or chronic disease and promoting behaviors that can delay, reverse, or even prevent the occurrence of illnesses. Healthy life choices can help people reach old age in the best of physical condition. Aging can be slowed, and the premature death associated with chronic illnesses can be prevented (Deeg et al., 1996). The following sections discuss some of these risk factors and interventions. A national effort is taking place to mobilize people of all ages to become aware of the importance of lifestyle, behavior, and individual choice in promoting good health and longevity.

The Use of Restraints in Nursing Homes

The use of restraints in nursing homes is controversial. It is one of many practices under which nursing home residents receive federal protection under a bill of rights, established in 1987 under the Omnibus Budget Reconciliation Act. Although penalties for nursing homes that fail to comply are still evolving, the bill of rights specifies that residents have the right to a physician, to be informed about treatment, to refuse treatment, to complain without fear of reprisal, and to be free of restraints (Brink, 1993). Investigators (Burton et al., 1992; Miles & Irvine, 1992) suggest that many considerations govern the use of restraints by staff. Schnelle, Simmons, and Ory (1992), for example, reported that staff failed to provide release from physical restraints (wrist, mittens, vest, and gerichairs) among nursing home residents whom they perceived as verbally aggressive, physically aggressive, and generally unpleasant. The continuous use of restraints for any extended period must be carefully monitored. Restrained residents require as much as 15 percent more time from nursing home staff than those who are unrestrained, and restraints over extended periods limit independence such as toileting and may contribute to painful pressure sores (Brink, 1993). Miles and Irvine (1992), using an ex post facto analysis, report that the ultimate risk in using restraints continuously without supervision and without regular monitoring in nursing homes is death. Their analysis revealed that death is most likely to occur to a nursing home resident who is female, about 81 years old, and diagnosed with dementia. Miles and Irvine (1992) estimate that about 1 in 1,000 nursing home deaths could be linked directly to the use of restraints, and they advocate a dramatic reduction in their use; they suggest short-term use of restraints only to ensure medically necessary therapy for acutely ill, delirious older persons. From their analysis of case records, a composite scenario has been developed to illustrate the way in which restraints can accidentally cause death:

A nurse or aide applies a vest or strap restraint. While unobserved for ten minutes to several hours, the patient slides off the bed or chair so that the restraint bears her weight and prevents her from sliding further down to a weight-bearing surface. She is confused and unable to use her arms or legs to return to a safe position in her bed or chair. Her weight, transmitted through the restraint, creates a force about her chest. As she struggles, the restraint gathers, thus concentrating the pressure around her chest. She asphyxiates, usually because she cannot inhale, less often because the restraint slides up and gathers to act as a ligature on her neck. (Miles & Irvine, 1992, p. 765)

An illustration of such a situation is provided below.

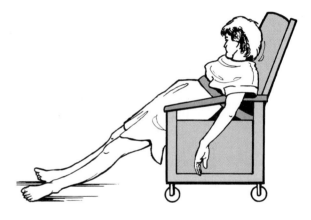

Source: Miles, S. H. & Irvine, P. (1992). Deaths caused by physical restraints. *The Gerontologist, 32* (6), 762–766.

Attitude, Disease, and Psychoneuroimmunology

Medical experts, psychologists, and health care professionals have expressed a consistent interest in the role of attitude in promoting wellness. Cohen and Herbert (1996) reviewed some of this research within the context of a simple model (see figure 6.15). According to the model, a person's psychological state can trigger a set of neurological, hormonal, and behavioral responses that can directly alter the functioning of the immune system. **Psychoneuroimmunology** is the study of those multifaceted changes in the central nervous and immune systems that heighten or lower a person's susceptibility to and recovery from disease. The immune system protects the body from potentially damaging or fatal

Figure 6.15 Psychological factors can influence the onset and progression of an immune system-mediated disease through several pathways. For simplicity, arrows are drawn in only one direction, from psychological characteristics to disease. No lack of alternative paths is implied. *Source:* Cohen, S., & Herbert, T. B. (1996). Health psychology: Psychological factors and physical disease from the perspective of human psychoneuroimmunology. *Annual Review of Psychology, 47,* 113–142.

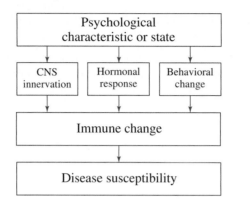

bacteria, viruses, fungi, and parasites. Immune system cells (e.g., white blood cells, antibodies) circulate in the blood to fight these disease-causing organisms.

Psychological stress can reduce the effectiveness of the immune system, as studies on rheumatoid arthritis have shown. **Rheumatoid arthritis** is an autoimmune disease characterized by swelling of the joints and, over time, by degeneration of the cartilage in the affected joints and loss of joint function. Adults coping with stressful life events and without a strong social support network appear to be more susceptible to the onset of this disease and more prone to flare-ups (Cohen & Herbert, 1996).

A great deal of work on psychoneuroimmunology has focused on the possible psychological triggers that might depress immune system function and lead to cancer. By and large the results are not consistent, perhaps in part because the research has failed to recognize (1) that cancer is not a single disease entity and (2) that stress and depression are not stable attributes, but traits that change as the individual ages and as the disease progresses or slows down (Cohen & Herbert, 1996). Two general types of studies have been conducted: (1) predictions of who will develop cancer among a population of older persons free of the disease, and (2) predictions of those who will survive longer following a diagnosis of cancer. Some studies show that cancer patients survive longer if they have positive rather than pessimistic attitudes toward life and their disease. Other studies show the same survival rates when access to social support is readily available. However, the relationship of survival to positive attitude and access to social support appears to hold for younger adult cancer patients, 40 to 59 years of age, but not for older adults with the disease (Schulz et al., 1996).

Cancer

Cancer is not a single disease, but a group of different diseases that share a common feature: rapid and uncontrollable growth of abnormal cells, resulting in a cancerous or malignant tumor. Unless the growth of the malignant tumor is halted through some treatment or combination of treatments, death will occur. Malignant tumors can easily spread or metastasize to other sites and organs because cancerous cells travel throughout the body via the blood and lymph systems. Scientists are focusing on why the normal process of cell division suddenly goes awry and produces cancer cells that multiply uncontrollably. They have found genetic links in certain kinds of cancers, as well as defects in genetic codes—some that cause cell division to speed up, and some that fail to limit it. One mechanism, *angiogenesis,* permits small tumors that have been dormant to grow larger and larger by promoting the growth of the blood vessels, nutrients, and blood supply surrounding the tumor. Researchers do not know what triggers angiogenesis to overcome the other processes that kept the tumor under control. A number of effective cancer treatments use antiangiogenic drugs or angiogenesis inhibitors, which can slow blood vessel growth and thereby eliminate or reduce tumor size. These new treatments include interleukin-12, angiostatin, and alpha-interferon, and they are often part of multiple, combined treatments (*Stopping Cancer in Its Tracks,* 1995).

If a malignancy is detected early, before any cancer cells have had a chance to migrate or metastasize to other body organs, **oncologists** (physicians who specialize in cancer treatment) report that treatment success is quite high. In 2001, for example, nearly 1,268,000 persons were newly diagnosed with cancer; more than half would be cured, and only 43 percent were to die of the disease (Cancer Facts and Figures, 2001). The American Cancer Society estimates that 80 percent of all cancers are diagnosed at age 55 and older. Following heart disease, cancer is the second leading cause of death in the United States. Currently more people die from lung cancer than any other type. More than 10 million new cancer cases have been diagnosed since 1990; current statistics show that one of every four deaths in the United States is from cancer (*Cancer Facts and Figures,* 2001). Figure 6.16 shows the age-adjusted death rates due to different types of cancers for men and women from 1930 to 1997.

There are three major classes of cancerous tumors, identified by the type of cells responsible for their genesis. The most common malignancies are called *carcinomas.* They arise from the epithelial layers, or outside layers of the cells of the body: the skin, the outside layers of glands (e.g., breast, uterus, prostate), the outside layers of the respiratory tract and lungs, the urinary tract, and the gastrointestinal tract (e.g., colon, rectum, stomach, and mouth). *Sarcomas* are malignant tumors that develop from cells of the connective and fibrous tissue of the body (e.g., bone, muscle, and cartilage). *Lymphomas* are cancers that arise in the lymph nodes, or in the infection-fighting system of the body. Leukemia is a cancer that arises in the bone marrow, resulting in the overproduction of mutant white blood cells and the reduction of red blood cells. The abnormal white blood cells cannot effectively protect the individual from infection and disease; the loss of red blood cells produces anemia and fatigue since oxygen transport is compromised (Insel, Roth, Rollins, & Peterson, 1996).

Breast Cancer   The most common cancer among women in the United States is breast cancer. If all women lived to age 85, recent statistics indicate that one in nine could expect to have a diagnosis of breast cancer. Statistics also indicate that 1.6 million women currently have the disease, and that there may be as many as 1 million undiagnosed cases. According to the American Cancer Society, there were more than 192,000 new cases of breast cancer in women in 2001. Nearly 80 percent of women with breast cancer survive

Figure 6.16
Age-adjusted
cancer death rates
in the United States
from 1930–1997
for (a) males and
(b) females.
Source: US Mortality
Public Use Data
Tapes 1960-1997, US
Mortality Volumes
1930-1959, National
Center for Health
Statistics, Centers for
Disease Control and
Prevention, 2000.
America Cancer
Society, Surveillance
Research, 2001.

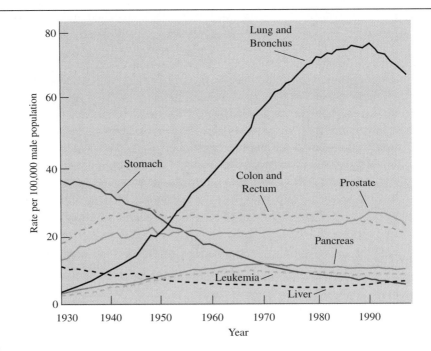

(a)

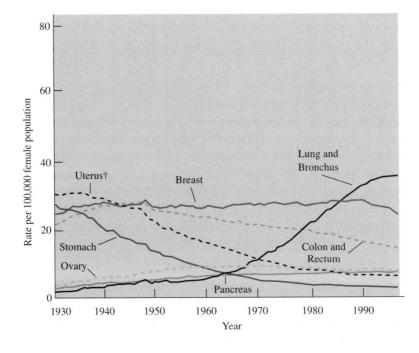

(b)

for at least five years following the initial diagnosis; the 10-year survival rate is 65 percent, and the 15-year survival rate is 56 percent (Frieswick, 1997). The incidence of breast cancer is lower in black women than in white women, yet more black women die of breast cancer. The risk of breast cancer doubles every five years between ages 30 and 45, and the risk increases by 10 to 15 percent for each five-year interval beyond age 45. There is some evidence that younger women who are premenopausal have less favorable survival statistics, given the higher rate of recurrence of the disease (de la Rochefordiere, Asselain, & Campena, 1993).

Risk factors for breast cancer include increased age, genetic history, high-fat and low-fiber diet, sedentary lifestyle, obesity, alcohol consumption, oral contraception, early menstruation, late menopause, extended exposure to postmenopausal estrogens, recent use of oral contraceptives, never having children or having a late-in-life first childbirth (*Cancer Facts and Figures,* 2001). Early detection is a key to successful treatment, although some question the risk of regular exposure to radiation. The routine use of **mammography** (X-ray screening for breast cancer detection) reduces the risk of death by 60 percent, according to recent data from the American Cancer Society (Haney, 2001). Unfortunately, only 50 to 60 percent of women in the United States routinely obtain mammograms, usually only beginning after age 50. In Sweden, for instance, mammography is more common, and 85 percent of women participate in the testing at least every two years after age 40. In addition to mammography, the American Cancer Society urges women to conduct their own self-examination each month; mammography misses some 10 to 15 percent of breast cancers (Breast Imaging, 1995).

Treatment of breast cancer is determined by the specific characteristics of the malignant tumor, whether it has metastasized, patient preferences, and the age and health of the woman. With no metastasis to lymph nodes, breast cancer treatments allow 97 percent of women to survive at least five years (*Cancer Facts and Figures,* 2001). Treatment for breast cancer may involve removal of the tumor and the lymph nodes under the arm (**lumpectomy**), removal of the entire breast and the lymph nodes (**mastectomy**), and/or administration of radiation, chemotherapy, or hormone therapy. Usually, some combination of treatments is in order. Surgeons and oncologists continue to debate when lumpectomy or mastectomy is preferable. Some studies suggest that with small breast tumors, survival rates with lumpectomy followed by radiation treatments are the same as those following mastectomy and radiation (Posner & Wolmark, 1994).

Older and younger women differ in how they process information related to diagnosis and treatment for breast cancer. Older women arrive at treatment decisions more quickly than younger women. Young women tend to focus on detailed information and bottom-up processing; older women tend to approach information with a balanced problem-solving approach, seeking information within the context of their expertise and choice of treatment alternatives (Meyer, Russo, & Talbot, 1995; Sinnott, 1989). Older women (65 to 88 years of age) generally seek less information before making a treatment decision for breast cancer. Interestingly, in these research studies, the actual treatment decisions younger and older women made were virtually identical. Younger women (18 to 39 years of age) just tended to seek more information and more detail before coming to a resolution regarding treatment.

Women face a nexus of psychological reactions to the diagnosis of breast cancer, some lasting for the rest of their lives. The initial diagnosis is met with disbelief, shock, anger, and denial. In time comes acceptance and a desire to conquer the illness. Feeling in control is empowering to women. Developing a "fighting spirit" against the disease, creating a sense of control, hopefulness, and personal responsibility, seems to enhance a woman's chance to beat breast cancer, its treatment, and the quality of life (Cohen & Herbert, 1996). In a longitudinal study, Greer (1991) first showed that women with a "fighting spirit" were more likely to live longer than other breast cancer patients who maintained a "stoic acceptance" or hopeless/helpless attitude regarding the disease and their recovery. In a related study, Phillips, Todd, and Wagner (1993) reported that among Chinese Americans facing breast cancer, those who believed they were "ill-fated" and "gave up" did not live as long as those who believed they could be cured. The conclusions from this research, however, are somewhat complex, since age appears to play a role in the results. It also appears that optimism and pessimism provide differential predictions for treatment outcomes and must be evaluated separately to understand their role in promoting survivorship (Schulz et al., 1996).

Every woman facing breast cancer must cope with some degree of helplessness and anxiety; the disease is proof of one's mortality and vulnerability. There is also a deep sense of loss—the potential loss of one's future, the fear of missing out on the continued growth and development of family members, and the loss of a breast if surgery is required. Mastectomy causes the loss of a critical element of gender identity and can lead to a profound sense of loss of sexuality. Clinical psychologists and psychiatrists help women who feel depressed and unattractive after breast cancer surgery. Some women seek reconstructive breast surgery, although no reconstruction can ever psychologically replace the breast that has been lost (Frieswick, 1997). In some cases, depending on the ensuing treatments and on patient characteristics, certain reconstruction procedures can be performed at the time of mastectomy (*Cancer Facts and Figures, 2001*).

Research suggests that the quality of a woman's primary relationship with a partner or husband can help in coping with the diagnosis and treatment of breast cancer. In some intervention programs, support is given to both the patient and her significant other (Frieswick, 1997). Breast cancer patients are encouraged to share their emotions and not try to protect other loved ones in their families. Patients are helped to express their concerns, deep emotions, and basic fears. One program at Harvard University's Brigham and Women's Hospital offers 10 sessions in a "Partners in Coping" program. It helps couples work on and improve coping strategies, enhancing communication, listening, intimacy, sharing responsibilities, caring for children, and living with breast cancer itself. The disease puts strains on partners and their relationships; poor relationships get worse, and strong relationships are challenged. Couples need to speak openly and honestly about their concerns to help each other adjust. Since strong social support is so important to improving the quality of life for those with cancer, the American Cancer Society offers women with breast cancer an opportunity to talk to a volunteer who has survived the disease in its "Reach to Recovery" program. Often, the physical recovery from mastectomy, radiation, and chemotherapy can proceed far more rapidly than a woman's emotional adjustment (Frieswick, 1997). With every checkup throughout each passing year, it is common for survivors to experience anxiety that their cancer has reappeared.

Prostate Cancer   The most common cancer among men is prostate cancer. This carcinoma affects the prostate gland, which lies at the base of the bladder. In 2001, more than 198,000 new cases were reported in the United States (*Cancer Facts and Figures, 2001*). Cancer of the prostate is increasingly more common as men age; 80 percent of diagnoses are made in those over the age of 65, and African-American men have the highest rate in the world, with a 66 percent higher rate than that for white males. Some experts believe that nearly every male over the age of 80 has the disease, but the rate at which it grows and threatens survival can be quite slow.

As with other cancers, early detection is a key to successful treatment. Many men with prostate cancer have no noticeable symptoms. A yearly physical should include a routine rectal examination to permit a physician to monitor the size of the prostate gland and the presence of smaller tumors on its surface. In some cases, ultrasound tests detect extremely small malignancies in the prostate. A blood test that assesses the level of **prostate-specific antigen (PSA)** can be very helpful in providing an early warning. The American Cancer Society recommends this blood test for all men over age 50 and for those over 40 if they have a family history of prostate cancer or are African American. A single reading is not as helpful diagnostically as a series over a number of years to help determine any problem. PSA testing has improved early detection of prostate cancer by more than 25 percent since 1986 (Ferraro, 2001). Note that a condition unrelated to cancer of the prostate—*benign prostatic hypertrophy (BPH)*, or enlargement of the prostate—naturally occurs with aging. BPH can cause difficulty in urination, interrupted urine flow, frequent urination, reduction in the flow of urine, and difficulty in emptying the bladder fully.

Treatment for prostate cancer is most effective when there has been no metastasis beyond the gland, and current statistics suggest a five-year survival rate of 99 percent under such conditions. Overall, five-year survival rates are about 93 percent; 31,500 men died from prostate cancer in 2001. The mortality rates are twice as high for African-American males (*Cancer Facts and Figures, 2001*). Various treatment options are available, including chemotherapy, implanting radioactive pellets in the gland, laser surgery, destruction of tumors by selective freezing or high heat, hormone therapy, surgery to remove the prostate, or radiation to shrink it. Men are understandably concerned about any treatment for prostate cancer since some of the treatment options are associated with an increased risk of incontinence and sexual impotence. For example a common surgical procedure to remove the prostate, *transuretheral resection (TUR)*, cuts the nerves responsible for establishing an erection in nearly 40 percent of cases. Men in their late seventies and eighties find their physicians advise them to simply live with slow-growing prostate cancers if they are not an imminent threat to survival, rather than be exposed to unnecessary risks from surgery, chemotherapy, or radiation. Physicians find "watchful waiting" appropriate for older men with early-stage tumors (*Cancer Facts and Figures, 2001*; PSA Debate, 1995).

Lung Cancer   In the United States, lung cancer remains the leading cause of death among all forms of cancer. Nearly 157,400 persons died from lung cancer in 2001, and there were 169,500 new diagnoses of lung cancer the same year (*Cancer Facts and Figures, 2001*). The American Cancer Society has identified the single most significant risk factor in this disease: cigarette, cigar, and pipe smoke. Lung cancer has clear early warning signs, including a persistent cough, pain in the lungs or chest area, and frequent bouts of bronchitis. Only 15 percent of lung cancers are detected early, and the five-year survival rate is only 48 percent in such cases. Surgical removal of the carcinoma if it has not metastasized is the most common treatment. Surgery involves removal of one or more of the lobes of the lung (lobectomy) and follow-up treatment with radiation or chemotherapy. Since detection usually occurs very late in the disease, metastasis has commonly occurred, and chemotherapy and radiation are needed in combination with surgery. Statistically, lung cancer survival rates for five years or more for all cases are only about 14 percent (*Cancer Facts and Figures,* 2001).

Human Immunodeficiency Virus and AIDS

Another threat to the health of adults, both young and elderly, is AIDS. Health care professionals are concerned with the growing number of elderly persons (50 years of age and older) who have contracted HIV or AIDS. There is neither a vaccine nor a cure for AIDS. Therefore, preventing the transmission of the virus that causes AIDS, the human immunodeficiency virus (HIV), is the primary goal of public health programs. A second goal is to contain the virus once someone has it. Not every person exposed to the virus develops AIDS.

Older adults may be more likely than younger adults to become HIV-infected and to develop the symptoms of AIDS for three reasons. First, the efficacy of the immune system declines with age. Older adults have a shorter HIV incubation period than younger adults (5.8 years versus 7.3 years, respectively). Second, older adults are more likely to receive blood transfusions, which increases the risk of infection through contaminated blood. Third, postmenopausal women usually experience a thinning of the cells of the vaginal wall. Since AIDS is transmitted by sexual contact, the thinning vaginal walls of the older woman provide more potential sites for HIV infection. Although AIDS is generally thought of as a young adult disease, it is occurring most rapidly among those 50 and older. Older women are advised to be wary of exposure to the virus during unprotected sexual relations with "condo cowboys." Safe sex in this instance is a mandate.

Weight Management, Obesity, and Health

In 2001, 60% of our population was overweight, including obesity, according to the U.S. Surgeon General. Weight is a critical public health issue since being overweight is associated with an increase in chronic disease and mortality. For older people, extra weight limits mobility, function, and independence. It contributes to their need for support services and increases their impairment in activities of daily living.

Weight gain in adulthood is a consequence of the reduced rate of **metabolism** (i.e., the rate at which calories are burned) that comes with advancing age. Most people become more sedentary as they age, but continue to eat as they did when they were younger. To avoid weight gain, adults can eat less or exercise more to burn the calories they consume. Eating the same amount of calories per day without an exercise increase eventually results in accumulated body weight.

As adults age, the total amount of fat they store in their bodies increases; it is typically stored in abdominal tissue. The increase in body fat from early adulthood to age 85 is approximately 18 percent for men and 11 percent for women (Evans, 1995b). Baumgartner, Stauber, McHugh, Koehler, and Garry (1995) validated these data for men over 80, but women over 80 showed a significant decrease in body fat related to reduced calorie intake, perhaps as a result of frailty. In a 28-month study, reducing the quantity of food intake was predictive of mortality among frail elderly women residing in a nursing home. Intervention strategies that focus on food intake, rather than nutritional value per se, may improve health and mortality among frail elderly in nursing homes (Frisoni et al., 1995). Nutritional needs are determined by body size, level of physical activity, and rate of metabolism; however, little is known about age-related changes in these areas (Fahey, Insel, and Roth, 2001).

Our country has a passion for weight control—but data reveal that our attempts are predictably unsuccessful over the long haul. Without a commitment to alter lifestyle and eating choices on a permanent basis, weight losses through dieting are transitory. Statistics show that at any given time, 47 percent of Americans are actively trying to control their weight, including 24 percent who identify themselves as on a diet to lose weight.

Figure 6.17 shows that in 2000, more than 124 million people identified themselves as dieting. Unfortunately, less than 5 percent will be able to sustain their diets and maintain weight loss for more than a year. Figure 6.18 shows some of the reasons why dieting has such predictably poor results. To change eating behaviors, people must make a lifestyle and lifetime commitment; magic cures, two-week diets, and quick weight loss programs are not the answer (Fahey et al., 2001).

Obesity refers to the condition of being far enough over healthy body weight that one's life expectancy is reduced. In the past, obesity was defined as 20 percent above ideal body weight. Today it is based on a formula called the **body mass index (BMI)** that compares height and weight; nationwide, slightly more than 23 percent of the adult population is considered obese (Department of Health and Human Services, 2000). A simple calculation determines the BMI from pounds and inches:

$$BMI = \frac{\text{weight in pounds}/2.20}{(\text{height in inches}/39)^2}$$

Figure 6.19 shows the body mass index for adults and the corresponding values for overweight and obesity. Adults are considered obese if they have a BMI of 30 or above. Obesity is estimated to lead to 300,000 premature deaths each year. It is implicated in an increased risk for heart disease, stroke, diabetes, and some types of cancer: breast cancer among postmenopausal women, plus endometrial, uterine, and ovarian cancer, and colon and prostate cancer among men (*Cancer Facts and Figures,* 2001). It remains the second leading preventable cause of premature death, led only by smoking. The American Heart Association in 1998 identified obesity as a major risk factor in coronary heart disease; prior to this time it was considered to be only a contributing factor. Controlling or eliminating obesity can reduce the incidence of death and disability due to coronary heart disease (American Heart Association, 2000a).

Figure 6.17
Fewer Americans diet as people recognize that traditional dieting (deprivation over the short term) spells failure. Instead, it takes permanent lifestyle changes to take and keep weight off. Only 24 percent of U.S. adults *(51 million people)* are currently dieting.
Source: Calorie Control Council National Consumer Survey, 2000.

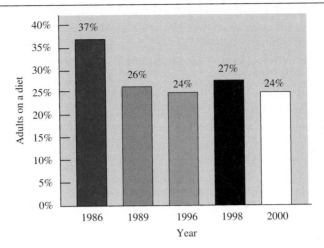

Figure 6.18
Why do we fail? There are several reasons why Americans are not successful at maintaining their desired weight.
Source: Calorie Control Council National Consumer Survey, 2000.

Percentage of adult Americans reporting that they need to lose weight who…

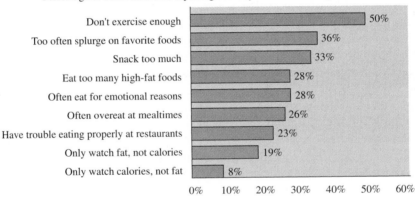

Research has documented the advantages of reduced caloric intake in promoting longevity in animal species (Lee et al., 2001). Reduced calorie diets promote longevity in species such as laboratory rats, spiders, and guppies.

The mechanism most likely at work is at the cellular level, specifically within the **mitochondria,** the "power plants" of cells. In creating energy, mitochondria release **free radicals** (reactive molecules with an unpaired electron); free radicals will rapidly and indiscriminately oxidize or destroy other electrons. Some biological theories of aging hypothesize that the accumulation of free radicals accelerates the aging process. As the cells themselves become less efficient, and as more free radicals are produced, the body's tissues and organs are compromised, deteriorate, and become less able to respond to the demands imposed on them (Weindruch et al., 2001). Research with animals suggests that a restricted calorie diet and the reduced production of free radicals

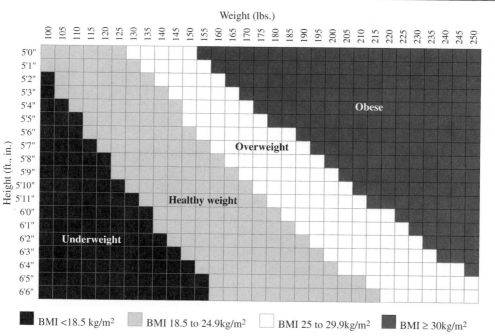

Figure 6.19
Body mass index chart for adults 20 years of age and older.
Source: American Cancer Society, Surveillance Research, 2001.

Weight (lbs.)

Height (ft., in.)

Obese

Overweight

Healthy weight

Underweight

■ BMI <18.5 kg/m²   ▨ BMI 18.5 to 24.9kg/m²   □ BMI 25 to 29.9kg/m²   ■ BMI ≥ 30kg/m²

may slow down the rate of aging. Does a low-calorie diet increase the efficiency of the mitochondria so that fewer free radicals are produced in humans?

Heart Disease and Lifestyle

Coronary heart disease is the leading cause of death for men and women in the United States, and stroke is the third leading cause (Center for Disease Control and Prevention, 2001). Almost 25 percent of those who die from coronary heart disease experience sudden death due to cardiac arrest, most often *ventricular fibrillation,* the rapid, uncontrolled beating of the heart. A heart attack (**myocardial infarction**) is the end result of **atherosclerosis,** the narrowing of the arteries that supply blood to the heart muscle due to a buildup of fatty deposits or plaque (American Heart Association, 2001a).

    Cardiovascular disease (CVD) includes coronary disease, stroke, congestive heart failure, and high blood pressure or **hypertension;** CVD accounts for 1 of every 2.5 deaths, or 41 percent of the total deaths in 2000. More than 60 million people have some type of CVD. Major risk factors that cannot be controlled include family history, aging, being male, and ethnicity. Controllable major risk factors include smoking and exposure to smoke, high blood pressure, high cholesterol, sedentary lifestyle, obesity, nutrition, and diabetes. Secondary factors that are also controllable include psychological and social factors: stress, chronic anger/hostility, suppressing psychological distress and anger, depression, anxiety, and social isolation (Fahey, Insel, & Roth, 2001). Currently, so-called 'statin' drugs are available for those with multiple major risk factors and unacceptable levels of LDL cholesterol. These drugs reduce cholesterol levels substantially. New guidelines define candidates for statin drugs based on a sliding scale of LDL levels and the presence of major risk factors (American Heart Association, 2001b). Eligible adults include those with LDL cholesterol above 190 mg/dl (no disease, fewer than two risk factors); 160 mg/dl (no disease, two or more risk factors), or 130 mg/dl (heart disease present).

As figure 6.20 indicates, age is related to the risk of heart attacks, with a dramatic rise beginning at age 65. A milder increase in heart attacks also occurs among men after age 45 and among women after age 55 (American Heart Association, 2001b). The impact of heart disease differs with age. Women's mortality from the disease continues to rise until age 70, but the rate is constant for men beginning at age 60. Statistics show that men are more likely to experience heart attacks, more likely to have them earlier in life, and more likely to survive them. Women are less likely to survive a heart attack and, if they do, more likely to experience another one. Women are also considered at greater risk for functional impairments associated with heart disease than men are (Clark et al., 2000).

Death rates due to heart disease vary by ethnicity. Black Americans have higher rates of coronary heart disease, stroke, and hypertension than whites. Hispanics and whites have similar rates of hypertension. Asian Americans have historically had significantly lower rates of coronary disease than whites, although this is changing as they adopt the higher-fat diet of Western countries (Fahey, Insel, & Roth, 2001).

The heart and coronary arteries begin to show changes in middle adulthood. Under comparable stress, the heart of a 40-year-old can pump a much smaller number of liters of blood per minute (23) than the heart of a 20-year-old (40). Older persons may experience difficulties with the heart muscle itself as it loses its elasticity and its ability to pump blood throughout the body. When the muscle can no longer easily pump blood, fluids may accumulate in the body tissues and lungs. If this persists, the person may end up with pneumonia and ultimately die. This condition, *congestive heart failure,* is common in older people. They are treated with drugs to increase the strength of the beating heart muscle and diuretics to reduce the amount of fluid in the body (*Harvard Health Letter,* 1995).

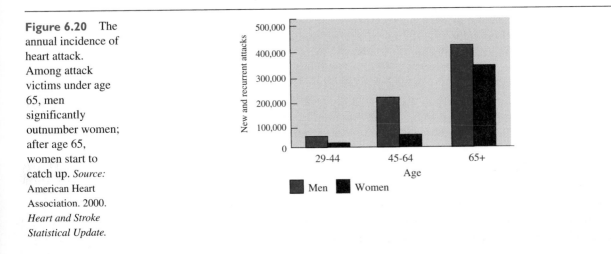

Figure 6.20 The annual incidence of heart attack. Among attack victims under age 65, men significantly outnumber women; after age 65, women start to catch up. *Source: American Heart Association. 2000. Heart and Stroke Statistical Update.*

The **coronary arteries** that supply blood to the heart narrow during middle adulthood, and the level of cholesterol in the blood increases with age (at age 20, the average is 180 mg/dl; age 40, 220 mg/dl; age 60, 230 mg/dl). Cholesterol begins to accumulate on the artery walls, which themselves begin to thicken. Total cholesterol is a risk factor for heart attacks for middle-aged and older adults. However, the presence of good cholesterol (high-density lipoprotein or HDL) reduces the risk of death due to heart disease, just as the presence of bad cholesterol (low-density lipoprotein, or LDL) increases the risk of death due to heart disease. Total cholesterol readings that are high (e.g., above 240 mg/dl) are associated with a high risk of dying from heart disease for middle-aged men and women, but in older populations, these readings are predictive of higher risk only for women. Heart attack risk for adults of all ages is best predicted by the ratio of total cholesterol to HDL cholesterol (e.g., total cholesterol divided by HDL). A ratio of 4.5 or lower is highly desirable (*Harvard Health Letter,* 1995).

With increasing age, the arteries increase the pressure on the arterial walls, which makes the heart work harder to pump blood and makes a stroke or heart attack more likely. High blood pressure can be related to personal stress, obesity, diet, and family history. Without treatment, high blood pressure can cause a break in the artery wall (an aneurysm) and be fatal. If the arteries continue to narrow, a blood clot or small piece of plaque may prevent blood from moving through and reaching vital organs. If the heart is deprived of blood, the result is a heart attack: the neurological equivalent of a heart attack is a **stroke,** characterized by the death of blood-deprived brain cells (*Harvard Health Letter,* 1995). A stroke can occur if a blood vessel supplying the brain itself is blocked; the consequences can be nominal or severe.

Lifestyle, diet, physical condition, stress, and family history are risk factors for heart disease. One intriguing theory relates individual behavior styles to either a high risk (**Type A**) or low risk (**Type B**) of heart disease (Friedman & Rosenman, 1974). A person with a Type A behavior style is excessively competitive, accelerates the pace of ordinary activities, is impatient with the rate at which most events occur, often thinks about doing several things at the same time, shows hostility, and cannot hide the fact that time is a struggle in life. By contrast, a person with a Type B behavior style lacks these behavioral tendencies. About 10 percent of the individuals studied clearly had Type A or Type B styles, although most people were mixtures of the two. High achievement and Type A behavior style seem to be related (Friedman & Rosenman, 1974). An analysis of Type A behavior style, however, shows "the true picture seems to be one of a person with one or more negative emotions: perhaps someone who is depressed, aggressively competitive, easily frustrated, anxious, (or) angry . . ." (Booth-Kewley & Friedman, 1987, p. 358). An "angry" or "hostile" personality was related not only to heart disease but also to general disease.

Health and Coping

The probability of developing disease or chronic illness increases with advancing age. A majority of individuals who reach the age of 80 will likely have some type of health impairment; this is simply part of normal aging. It is very rare to find anyone over the age of 80 or 85 who is completely free from disease or illness.

Heart disease and cancer are the most serious health concerns in late adulthood. Other diseases, such as arthritis, can severely limit physical functioning, mobility, and the quality of life of older adults. Almost two of every five people between the ages of 65 and 75 have some impairment that limits their physical functioning. After age 75, the rate rises to three of every five persons. Some of the most common chronic conditions that compromise the health of the elderly are arthritis (38 percent), hearing impairments (29 percent), vision impairments (20 percent), and heart conditions (20 percent). Studies indicate that elderly women are more likely to have a higher incidence of arthritis, hypertension, and visual problems, but are less likely to have difficulty with hearing than men.

Many elderly awake in the morning feeling tired and report difficulty functioning during the daytime. Older adults spend less time in deep sleep, awaken more frequently at night, and endure longer periods of wakefulness (Riedel & Lichstein, 1998; 2000). These symptoms, typical of *primary insomnia,* define the collective changes in sleep that affect about 25 percent of the elderly. The perception of a good night's sleep is best predicted by the amount of time older adults spend in deep sleep stages versus the time they spend in light sleep, along with the time it takes to fall asleep (reduced sleep latency). *Secondary insomnia* refers to similar sleep patterns that originate from medical conditions, medications, or psychiatric disorders. Secondary insomnia is associated with greater impairments in daytime functioning, affecting mood, memory, and attention more profoundly than primary insomnia does (Lichstein, Durrence, Bayen, & Riedel, 2000).

The best approach for optimizing health throughout the adult years, including coping with disease and chronic illness, is to use optimistic attitudes to manage behavior and emotions effectively (Rodin, 1986). Mental health experts recognize the importance of providing the elderly with a sense of control and autonomy. Without individual control, human beings experience emotional distress, depression, lowered motivation, reduced feelings of well-being and life satisfaction, and deficits in cognitive and motor performance (Tiffany & Tiffany, 1996).

Health Promotion and Wellness

Individuals take responsibility for their own health status through active, direct, and deliberate behavioral practices (Wallace, 2000). Adults can make choices and adopt lifestyles designed to promote effective functioning. The health choices people tend to make are related to income and education (Benson, 1997).

Diet and Nutrition

Proper nutrition combined with caloric restriction produces beneficial effects with regard to life expectancy, biological integrity, and behavioral abilities. A proper diet consists of a low-fat, high-fiber, low-salt, low-sugar, and moderate-calorie regimen. The Food Guide Pyramid (U.S. Department of Agriculture, 1996) provides guidelines for healthy eating. The pyramid suggests a specific number of servings across six different food groups each day to promote health:

1. Bread-cereals-pasta-rice (6–11 servings)
2. Vegetables (3–5 servings)
3. Fruits (2–4 servings)
4. Meat, poultry, fish, beans, eggs, nuts (2–3 servings)
5. Milk, yogurt, and cheese (2–3 servings)
6. Fat, oils, sugars (minimal, no recommended servings)

An adult following this diet and the recommended serving sizes would consume about 1,600 calories per day. Many companies that manufacture and process foods have adopted the food pyramid guidelines to comply with federal laws requiring manufacturers to disclose nutritional content on food labels (i.e., serving sizes and percentage by weight of fat, saturated fat, cholesterol, protein, dietary fiber, and sodium). Adults are not forbidden to eat specific foods. Rather, the guidelines suggest a balance over days, weeks, and months. Adults are encouraged to select a wide variety of different foods from among the pyramid's six groups. They can work toward preserving a reasonably healthy body weight with a diet that limits cholesterol to 300 to 500 milligrams a day, restricts fats to no more than 30 percent of total calories, and keeps both saturated fats and sugars to a maximum of 10 percent of total calories each. The American Heart Association (2001a) is also stringent, recommending that no more than 10 percent of the calories consumed each day come from saturated fat. Hidden fats occur in meats, processed foods, oils, butter, dairy products, and certain vegetarian sources such as seeds, nuts, avocados, and tropical oils (coconut and palm). Americans are reducing their total fat intake in a variety of ways. They substitute leaner choices of meat or fish, steam or broil foods rather than deep fat fry them or cook them with oils or butter, and increase the consumption of fruits, vegetables, legumes, grains, and carbohydrates while reducing their intake of meats, processed foods, and dairy products (Fahey, Insel, and Roth, 2001). A healthy diet includes sufficient vegetables, fruits, and grains to reach the goal of eating 20 to 35 grams of dietary fiber a day for maximum protection against cancer.

Most younger adults are unlikely to believe that good nutrition is essential for their health in later adulthood. Health and diet usually become major concerns in middle adulthood. Middle adulthood is characterized by an increasing awareness of gradual losses in optimal physical functioning and health. The negative results of poor nutrition usually do not show up for many years; there are often no observable difficulties until a major illness strikes. It is only when a disease or other threat to one's health occurs that people show a willingness to change their behaviors.

Exercise

The beneficial effects of regular and consistent aerobic exercise on aging and longevity have been documented for more than four decades. Adults who engage in at least 30 minutes of regular exercise nearly every day are at significantly reduced risk of developing heart disease. The type of exercise is less important than the regularity for a person who has been sedentary (Evans, 1995b). Even routine activities such as housecleaning, mowing the lawn, climbing stairs, or walking can enhance cardiovascular fitness and increase longevity. Moderate exercise sufficient to burn 150 calories per day provides health benefits, and those who are the most fit live the longest (Evans, 1995b). The body is quite responsive in adapting to the demands of exercise. The principle of **progressive overload** describes the process of gradually increasing the amount and intensity of exercise to improve fitness. It is also clear that fitness can be lost as demands on the body are reduced, a principle called **reversibility of fitness** (Fahey et al., 2001).

The positive benefits of regular exercise in promoting longer life are identifiable for adults at virtually any age. The greatest enhancement of life expectancy accrues from regular exercise. Exercise does not have to be continuous or sustained, although this is ideal, but can be intermittently engaged in throughout the day (Evans, 1995b). To improve physical fitness and quality of life significantly, however, the American College of Sports Medicine recommends at least 20 minutes of sustained aerobic exercise (exercise that boosts the heart rate) three to four times each week. Many older adults plan for specific exercise times in their daily routine, perhaps jogging, cycling, or swimming. Exercise has many beneficial effects, including stress reduction, blood pressure reduction, an increase in the "good" type of cholesterol (HDL) levels, and weight control.

Physical exercise has different consequences depending on its intensity. For example, more sustained and vigorous exercise is needed to improve physical fitness and quality of life than to merely improve life expectancy (Evans, 1995b). Moderate-intensity physical activities can fit every individual's lifestyle and preferences. For example, many older adults may choose a brisk walk going two miles in 30 to 40 minutes (Evans, 1995b). Most research suggests that the more exercise, the longer the exercise regimen; and the more intense the workout, the better the overall impact on health. However, some moderate exercise is better than no exercise at all.

Training, exercise, and physical activity consistently slow the declines associated with aging in areas such as strength, grip, and lifting. Exercise can enhance mood and reduce physical limitations in some ADL tasks for even the oldest-old (Brill, 1999; Femia, Zarit, & Johansson, 2001; Tsutsumi, et al., 1998). The leading risk factors in early death include smoking and failure to exercise coupled with poor nutrition. Physical activity is like an insurance policy for older adults; it protects them from many diseases and reduces the risk of enduring disabilities and dependency. There is no age limit on who can benefit from exercise (AARP, 2001). Most experts recommend at least 30 minutes of exercise 5 to 7 days each week, a regimen that

1. Protects against osteoporosis and strengthens bones
2. Enhances immune system functioning by reducing stress
3. Strengthens the heart muscle
4. Reduces blood pressure
5. Lowers cholesterol
6. Strengthens muscles, joints, and tendons associated with mobility, reducing the probability of falling
7. Reduces the joint swelling associated with arthritis

Physical competence is a concept that combines physical fitness and expertise—that is, expertise derived from practice. It is used to assess the impact of physical exercise and training (Stones & Kozma, 1996). It is difficult for scientists to obtain valid measures of physical competence for people of different ages. In the case of the oldest-old, it may be difficult and often very expensive to bring them to an exercise laboratory for precise assessments. There also may be potential safety or health risks concerning the age group under study that may make such measurements inadvisable (Stones & Kozma, 1996). And, of course, some tasks may simply be impossible for certain populations, such as the frail elderly (Stones & Kozma, 1996). When investigators have to change tasks for one age group, it becomes difficult to compare performance; there is no single index of physical competence that they can apply universally to all persons throughout the life span (Stones & Kozma, 1996). Common measures used to assess physical function are an index of independent activities of daily living and simple tests of physical fitness such as grip strength, endurance capacity, or trunk flexibility. Determining a person's *functional age,* or, more precisely, *psychophysical fitness,* requires researchers to make field-based assessments of four variables: flexibility, balance, vital capacity, and digit symbol memory (Stones & Kozma, 1996).

The overall benefits of exercise affect the cardiorespiratory system, strength, and strength endurance (Stratton et al., 1994). Some studies have even found generalized improvements in cognitive/neuropsychological performance with exercise programs lasting only a few weeks or months (Stones & Kozma, 1996). For example, in one study, nursing home residents in their eighties improved their cognitive performance on a semantic memory task by 20 percent over baseline with a simple physical exercise program (Stones & Dawe, 1993; Stones & Kozma, 1996). However, sustained physical exercise, or **chronic exercise,** rarely enhances cognitive performance. Stones and Kozma (1996) speculate that perhaps it is easier to demonstrate the benefits of short-term exercise programs on psychomotor competence and cognition in older adults because the participants are often in poor condition at the outset. In such people, it may be easier to demonstrate the immediate benefits of exercise with a single intervention session or with one lasting only a few days or weeks. Gains in physical health, however, are subject to "a law of diminishing returns, with the extent of gain varying negatively with the baseline level" (Stones & Kozma, p. 349).

Investigators have noted that physical inactivity relates directly to a decrease in aerobic exercise capacity in older men and women (Spina et al., 1996). Reversing the process through aerobic exercise activates different physiological mechanisms in men and women. In men, improvements in cardiac function increased aerobic exercise capacity, primarily through changes in the left ventricle of the heart that lead to stronger blood flow volume at each heartbeat and improved filling of the ventricle itself. For women, improved cardiac function resulted from increased oxygen transport through the arteries and veins (Spina et al., 1996).

No exercise can completely eliminate the normal developmental changes associated with senescence. Rates of senescence have been documented in a national sample of more than 54,000 adults between the ages of 30 and 70 (Sehl & Yates, 2001). Using statistical modeling, the authors estimated the rate of loss for 13 different biological functions and organ systems. The results show that loss rates per year ranged from 0–2 percent; however, endocrine, thermoregulation, and gastrointestinal functions showed somewhat higher losses per year, up to 3 percent. The losses were linear and appeared to be associated with senescence.

Corporations know that a healthier workforce is more productive, less likely to make medical claims, and less often out of work (Peters, 1996). Fewer than 55 percent of companies with 750 workers or more offered corporate fitness programs in 1985; by 1992, more than 83 percent provided this option to their workers (Peters, 1996). Promoting wellness in corporate America makes good financial sense in other ways, as the comparisons between high- and low-risk workers in table 6.10 show. The highest cost differences appear in four categories: (1) drinking alcohol, (2) physical health, (3) life satisfaction, and (4) physical activity. Carrier Corporation has built one of the largest

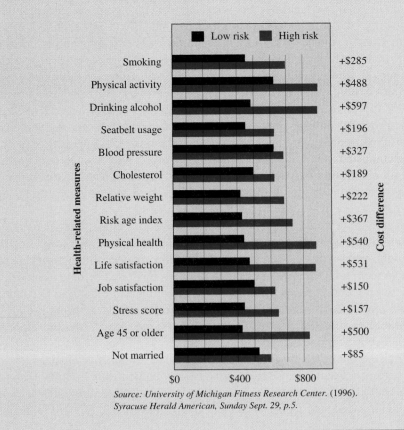

TABLE 6.10

Some Workers Cost More

High-risk employees—those who use tobacco, abuse alcohol, don't exercise, and are at risk because of other factors, such as age—cost companies considerably more in medical claims each year. Here's a comparison of health-claim costs for high and low-risk workers.

Health-related measures	Cost difference
Smoking	+$285
Physical activity	+$488
Drinking alcohol	+$597
Seatbelt usage	+$196
Blood pressure	+$327
Cholesterol	+$189
Relative weight	+$222
Risk age index	+$367
Physical health	+$540
Life satisfaction	+$531
Job satisfaction	+$150
Stress score	+$157
Age 45 or older	+$500
Not married	+$85

Source: University of Michigan Fitness Research Center. (1996). Syracuse Herald American, Sunday Sept. 29, p.5.

business-based wellness centers in the nation. The 40,000-square-foot center has a track for running, jogging, or walking on an upper level, which overlooks a fully equipped, high-technology fitness area, complete with treadmills, weight-lifting machines, and steppers (Peters, 1996). Preventing illness rather than providing costly health care to employees who develop illnesses can improve the bottom line. For example, each heart bypass operation prevented will save $30,000 to $35,000 in medical insurance claims. Clearly, promoting fitness and wellness (i.e., prevention) is more cost-effective than bearing the higher costs of treatment once employees become ill.

Measurement of health and physical function is complex. Many methods are available, depending on the physical system one is interested in assessing. For instance, overall cardiovascular endurance can be determined by assessing one's overall aerobic capacity, or **maximal oxygen uptake (VO$_2$max).** Table 6.11 provides standard values of VO$_2$max levels for adult men and women, as well as a method—running 1.5 miles—for

TABLE 6.11

Cardiorespiratory Fitness Classification

Age (years)	Maximal Oxygen Consumption (ml/kg/min)				
	Very Low	*Low*	*Moderate*	*High*	*Very High*
Women					
Under 29	Below 24	24–30	31–37	38–48	Above 48
30–39	Below 20	20–27	28–33	34–44	Above 44
40–49	Below 17	17–23	24–30	31–41	ABove 41
50–59	Below 15	15–20	21–27	28–37	Above 37
60–69	Below 13	13–17	18–23	24–34	Above 34
Men					
Under 29	Below 25	25–33	34–42	43–52	Above 52
30–39	Below 23	23–30	31–38	39–48	Above 48
40–49	Below 20	20–26	27–35	36–44	Above 44
50–59	Below 18	18–24	24–33	34–42	Above 42
60–69	Below 16	16–22	23–30	31–40	Above 40

Determining Maximal Oxygen Consumption Using the 1.5 Mile Run/Walk Test

1. Convert your running/walking time from minutes and seconds to a decimal figure. For example, a time of 14 minutes and 25 seconds would be 14 + (25/60) or 14.4 minutes.
2. Insert your running time in the equation below, where

T = running time (in minutes)
$VO_{2max} = (483 \div T) + 3.5$

For example, a person who completes 1.5 miles in 14.4 minutes would calculate maximal oxygen consumption as follows:
$VO_{2max} = (483 \div 14.4) + 3.5 = ml/kg/min$

Source: Preventive Medicine Center, Palo Alto, CA, and a survey of published sources. As published in Fahey, Insel, & Roth, 1997.
Source: Brooks, G.A., & Fahey, T.D. (1987). Fundamentals of human performance. New York: MacMillan.

estimating an adult's individual aerobic capacity from performance. The higher the oxygen consumption per minute, the more effective the cardiovascular system and the greater the overall endurance (Hafen & Hoeger, 1994). A standard 1.5-mile test should be conducted *only* under a physician's supervision for men over age 40 and for women over 50, and *only* after adequate aerobic training (e.g., six weeks) prior to taking the test. The test is simple—it consists of an "all-out" 1.5-mile run. From the time the individual takes to complete the run, it is then possible to determine the individual's fitness classification. Acceptable cardiovascular endurance is indicated by scores at the upper end of average, good, and excellent. People who score in the poor, fair, and lower range of average would benefit from training and fitness programs. Recall that some changes with age are not modifiable through exercise. The heart pumps less blood with advancing age, and the maximum heart rate also declines with increased age (Fahey et al., 2001). Research Focus 6.4 features an individual who has continued intense exercise into his eighties.

Research Focus 6.4

The Marathon Man

A group of investigators led by Leslie Katzel at the Baltimore Veterans Administration has been comparing the health and physical abilities of sedentary people and master athletes over the age of 60. One individual participating in these studies is 80-year-old Don McNelly, a true marathon man. Beginning in his late 40s, McNelly transformed his sedentary life and began running marathons; he found he really enjoyed the 26-mile long-distance event. Up until age 70, McNelly ran most marathons in under 4 hours, or under 10 minutes per mile. The marathon continues to be his passion in old age. McNelly has run 568 marathons, and he ran more than half (297) while he was in his seventies. His pace has slowed however; the grueling distance event takes him about 7 hours, or 16 minutes per mile, now that he is 80. His goal is to reach 600 marathons by the end of 2002. McNelly believes his training, lifestyle, and mental toughness have allowed him to realize his goals, making him dramatically different from other 80-year-olds. Indeed, only two other individuals in the United States, regardless of age, have run more marathons than McNelly (*New York Times,* 2000). He is a wonderful example of an individual who has taken charge of his own health and aging through exceptional endurance training.

Other master athletes have similar philosophies and commitments to their own health. These individuals show a wide range of physiological advantages that derive from their exceptional activities. For example, the rate of decline in VO_2 maximum capacity for these athletes is only half the ordinary rate of about 1 percent per year after age 25 (Morley, 2000). Master athletes 50 to 80 years of age not only have greater VO_2 max, they also have a higher ratio of good cholesterol (HDL) to bad (LDL) and better overall blood chemistry and metabolisms predictive of better health and longevity (Goldberg et al., 2000). Some wonder if genetics helps lead master athletes to participate in such demanding physical activities. Others wonder about the limits of the physical demands our bodies can endure in old age. Can McNelly continue to be a marathon runner in his nineties?

Recent studies of nursing home residents show that physical and cognitive dysfunction increases most rapidly among those 95 to 100 years old (Fries et al., 2000). Using a cross-sectional design, researchers evaluated 193,000 nursing home residents over the age of 80 on physical and cognitive measures; 6,500 of the subjects were centenarians. Results showed that the oldest-old had the greatest rates of dysfunction in activities of daily living, cognitive functions, and arthritis, as well as in 18 other measures of everyday functioning such as falls, inactivity, and weight loss. The rate of dysfunction rose dramatically in the oldest group, those 90 years of age and older. Were any of these nursing home residents former master athletes? Following McNelly as he and other master athletes become centenarians will help shed further light on the relationship between physical aging and endurance training.

Age and Fitness: Is It Ever Too Late to Exercise?

The basic variables used to assess an individual's physical fitness include cardiovascular endurance, muscular strength and endurance, muscular flexibility, and body composition (weight and percentage of body fat). Physical exercises and training can enhance fitness at any age, and the benefits include better functional health as well as greater cognitive and emotional well-being. In some studies, sustained exercise was found to trigger the release of important neurotransmitters responsible for boosting alertness, to improve cerebral blood flow, and to improve cognitive performance as measured by reaction time, short-term memory, and nonverbal reasoning skills (Fahey et al., 2001).

Current research suggests that older men and women can improve their cardiovascular endurance, strength, and flexibility as a result of increased physical activity. Hoeger and Hoeger (1995) note that the effectiveness of such interventions with the elderly depends on the initial fitness level and the type of activities chosen for training. Kasch and colleagues (1990) estimated that one-third of the loss in VO_2max from middle age to old age is the direct result of aging itself, while two-thirds comes from physical inactivity and a sedentary lifestyle. Documented improvements in VO_2max occur among older persons who train extensively. And although such gains require a longer time to produce, they are comparable to those seen in younger persons. Research Focus 6.5 presents an analysis of the rate of normal physiological decline as gifted athletes age.

Older persons up to 90 years of age have also been able to improve their strength with regular and sustained training programs. Results of training programs to improve strength often appear in a matter of a few weeks, even among nursing home residents. It is not necessary to undertake intense weight training to achieve beneficial results. Programs that last 10 to 15 minutes and are repeated a few times each week seem sufficient to produce beneficial results. As in all intervention programs for the elderly, care should be directed to choose activities that do not cause a large increase in blood pressure or place an undue strain on the heart (Hoeger & Hoeger, 1995).

Insel and colleagues (1996) summarized some of the benefits of exercise for the elderly (p. 312): (1) increased resiliency and suppleness of arteries; (2) better protection against heart attack, and enhanced probability of surviving a heart attack should one occur; (3) sustained capacity of lungs and respiratory reserves; (4) weight control through reduction of fat tissue; (5) maintenance of physical flexibility, balance, agility, and reaction time; (6) significantly preserved muscle strength; (7) protection from ligament injuries, dislocation, and strains in the knees, spine, and shoulders; (8) protection against osteoporosis; (9) increased effectiveness of the immune system; and (10) maintenance of mental agility and flexibility, response time, memory, and hand-eye coordination.

Strength Training

Evans and other experts suggest that the single most important exercise to actually reverse the process of aging is **strength training** (Evans, 1992; Liebman, 1995). Most healthy adults of any age can enhance their lives through exercise and strength training, reducing the likelihood of injuries and the impact of chronic diseases. Experts have

How Fast Do We Age?
Exercise as an Indicator of Biological Decline

The degree to which declines in physical function reflect true biological aging processes has been debated for many years. Bortz and Bortz (1996) examined this basic question from an unusual perspective. They suggested that many studies which have documented declines in physical capacities (e.g., cardiovascular, respiratory, and kidney problems, sarcopenia, and muscle strength) do not really reflect age or biological factors per se, but are more the result of atrophy due to physical inactivity and a sedentary lifestyle. The majority of the participants in past studies were themselves typical sedentary adults, rarely in top physical shape, and rarely involved in regular exercise.

To assess the effects of biological processes on the rate of decline in physical function in adulthood, the investigators used the national records attained by a special cohort of adult Master athletes 35 years of age and older. These athletes were "free of the artifacts of disease and disuse...." Adult Masters are older athletes who have, by virtue of their accomplishments in sports, maintained their major body systems as well as anyone else of similar age. They are in superb shape, as evidenced by their athletic success. Using the national records established by elite Master athletes from 35 to over 85 years old, the researchers compared three endurance events: the marathon, the 100-meter run, and 2,500-meter individual rowing. Results showed declines with advancing age in Masters record performance—a .5 percent decline per year from age 35 to age 65. After age 65, however, the rate of decline accelerated, perhaps due to more rapid physiological decay or to reduced participation.

Although the analysis of record times from an elite subsample of Master athletes may not represent the population of older adults as a whole, the rate of change was assumed to be identical to that in nonathletes of similar age.

These data were consistent with other cross-sectional studies showing losses of .3 percent per year in timed swimming speed events (Whitten, 1992), equivalent to an 11 percent decline in performance overall from 35 to 65 years of age. Master record holders in field events (e.g., shotput, high jump, javelin throw) showed even faster rates of loss with advancing age than those in running events. The data Bortz and Bortz (1996) reported also closely approximate the estimated biological decline of 0.5 percent in VO_2max that Kasch and colleagues (1990) obtained with athletes 35 to 70 years of age participating in several different events. And the studies also match the reported decline of 0.5 percent per year Schaie (1994) identified for cognitive/intellectual loss across the life span.

Bortz and Bortz (1996) noted that a rate of 2 percent per year loss in physical function has routinely been estimated from previous research with adults who were not highly trained athletes. This figure does not appear to differ greatly from the 0.5 percent found in this investigation with records from highly trained athletes. However, if these rates are compared cumulatively after two or three decades, the differences can be quite striking. Bortz and Bortz have helped clarify the contribution of biological factors in the decline in physical function in adulthood.

---

noted that by increasing muscle strength through regular exercise, even the oldest-old can show benefits. Strength training requires resistance against a mass or load in order to produce muscle contractions, and it is the only way to stop muscle atrophy (Liebman, 1995). Research has confirmed that from the twenties through old age, if you are not building muscle you are losing muscle (Liebman, 1995).

Strength training and physical exercise may reduce the severity of chronic conditions, in some cases entirely eliminating hypertension, obesity, arthritis, and diabetes. Simple strength training coupled with walking can reduce symptoms of chronic conditions, increase mobility, increase range of motion, and assist in weight reduction (Liebman, 1995). Evans (1995b) reported that after only three months of strength training, older adults increased the calories they burned by 15 percent, which led to a loss of body fat.

Among sedentary middle-aged and elderly adults, inactivity produces a "stiffness" in the joints with advancing age. This stiffness may cause poor or unnatural posture, leading to chronic back pain, but regular stretching programs and strength training that expands the range of motion can relieve the pain to some degree (Fahey et al.,

Preparing for a Longer, Healthier Life

Adults can take preventive actions to prepare for their later years and prolong their health, independence, wellness, and sense of well-being. The following 10 *biomarkers* developed by Evans, Rosenberg, and Thompson (1991) help us assess our need to take such actions.

1. *Muscle mass.* The rate at which adults lose muscle mass accelerates after age 45, although muscle mass begins to shrink far earlier. By using the muscles, pushing them to the limits of their capacity, one can increase muscle mass no matter what age one begins. With even a moderate program, older persons can increase muscle mass by 10 percent and show a corresponding 200 percent increase in strength (Evans, 1992). A program of weight lifting to increase muscle mass would provide significant improvements in strength within three to four months.

2. *Strength.* By 30 years of age, or even earlier, most individuals begin to lose muscle cells, and the nerves that provide connections to contract the muscles lose function. To regain strength, one must initiate physical exercise such as weight training.

3. *Basal metabolism rate.* The number of calories burned at rest drops by 100 calories per decade starting at age 20. Older persons need less oxygen to fuel their smaller muscle mass. By building up muscle mass, older persons can increase the number of calories they burn.

4. *Body fat percentage.* It is possible to reduce the amount of body fat each of us carries. It is a fact of American life that we show a steady increase in body fat as we age. Reducing calories can be a significant way to lose fat, but unless adults also exercise, a

reduction in muscle mass will also occur as a consequence of calorie reduction.

5. *Aerobic capacity.* An increase in aerobic capacity is one of the most significant markers of enhanced life expectancy.

6. *Blood-sugar tolerance.* Maintaining high tolerance through exercise and a high-fiber and low-fat diet means less body fat overall and an increase in the muscle response to insulin. With low tolerance comes a higher risk of heart disease and diabetes.

7. *Total cholesterol/HDL ratio.* The lower the ratio of total cholesterol to high-density lipoprotein (HDL), the less risk of heart attack and coronary artery disease. The recommended ratio is 4.5 or lower; overall cholesterol should be lower than 200 mg/dl. Proven techniques that can increase HDL include regular exercise, body fat loss, and cessation of smoking.

8. *Blood pressure.* Some research has shown that regular exercise increases blood volume, which lowers the risk of high blood pressure.

9. *Bone density.* Weight-bearing exercise (e.g., walking, jogging, running, or bicycling) can reduce the rate at which adults lose bone.

10. *Body-temperature regulation.* Older persons show heightened susceptibility to dehydration and injuries caused by heat or cold. Aerobic exercise can improve one of the ways the body regulates temperature—the ability to sweat.

Source: Evans, W., & Rosenberg, I. H., with Thomson, J. (1991). *BioMarkers—The 10 determinants of aging you can control.* New York: Simon & Schuster, by permission.

1997). For older persons, strength-training programs provide increased strength and elasticity of tendons and joints as well as reductions in muscle stiffness (Liebman, 1995). Similarly, stretching programs help older persons recapture some of the body's **flexibility,** defined as the ability to move the joints through their full **range of motion.**

In addition to the documented gains in physical health, exercise also provides benefits in other areas. People engaged in strength training and stretching programs feel better, have better mobility, enjoy increased energy and endurance, and show improvements in their sleep (Cox, 1997). Those who are physically fit report a higher quality of life, experience better overall health, and are able to improve their functional health status. And, of course, with psychological (both cognitive and emotional) and physical gains, the probability of maintaining autonomy and living independently rises (Hoeger & Hoeger, 1995). Examine the suggestions in Research Focus 6.6 to see how adults may better prepare for old age.

Muscle Atrophy: Sarcopenia

One of the most generally recognized and predictable physical consequences of aging is skeletal muscle mass atrophy, or **sarcopenia** (Roubenoff and Hughes, 2000). The term *sarcopenia* is derived from two words: *sarco* or "flesh" and *penia* or "reduction in amount or need" (Evans, 1995a). Health experts have explored the phenomenon of skeletal muscle mass atrophy in old age extensively, because it is one of the chief causes of decreased muscle strength as people grow older. The effects of sarcopenia explain, in part, the reduced mobility, limitations in ADL, and physical disabilities commonly seen in old age. Loss of muscle mass makes even the simplest tasks of daily living—such as climbing a flight of stairs, doing yard work, or getting up from a chair—difficult or impossible. Sarcopenia affects all muscle groups and is implicated in upper body and arm weakness, postural stoop and balance, and increased difficulties in walking and general mobility (Evans, 1995a; Roubenoff and Hughes, 2000). Interventions are particularly important, since studies reveal that strength training can reduce the rate of muscle atrophy, preserve current functioning, or reestablish greater muscle mass. Even among the oldest-old, lost muscle mass and strength can be regained through training. Muscle atrophy can be reversed and muscles retrained in a matter of a few weeks or months through regular exercise programs.

Sarcopenia is often attributed to normal aging, but it appears to be more a function of lifestyle changes as people age and become more sedentary. The data suggest that targeted activities such as exercise and strength training can improve the level of overall functioning in older persons, especially in the frail and in the institutionalized elderly. Sarcopenia may also underlie the decrease in functioning associated with many age-related chronic diseases (Roubenoff and Hughes, 2000). In the sections that follow, we will examine the role of sarcopenia in falls, fractures, walking or gait velocity, and balance.

Muscle Power

The concept of **muscle power** comes from exercise physiology. It refers to the product of the force and the velocity (speed) of muscle contraction; put simply, it is a measure of the ability to generate force quickly, or do work per unit of time, as muscles shorten (Evans, 2000; Foldvari et al., 2000). Studies have found that leg power can be more important than muscle strength (force without speed), endurance, and other such measures in predicting everyday function among the elderly in such activities as climbing stairs, walking, or standing from a seated position (Foldvari et al., 2000). Muscle power is needed to sustain many activities of daily living (ADLs); rapidly generating force is essential for walking (Evans, 2000). Muscle power increases from infancy to young adulthood and then begins to taper off with advancing age. Martin, Farrar, Wagner, and Spirduso (2000) found that muscle power declines at a rate of 7.5% per decade due to reduction in muscle size and muscle fiber type. They reported that muscle volume declined significantly from roughly 8 to 70 years of age, as did the rate of loss of specific muscle fibers associated with efficient power output (type II fibers).

Evidence suggests that incremental resistance exercises can enhance muscle strength and size in older adults; both are critical for day-to-day functioning, mobility, and independence among the elderly. Further research is needed to see if enhancement of muscle power can help sustain independent living or delay dependency, especially for the frail elderly (Foldvari et al., 2000). But muscle power appears to be a better predictor of disability, mobility, and independence than other measures (Evans, 2000).

Balance and Postural Stability

An older adult may fall easily when sensory perceptual systems are impaired, when she plans movements inaccurately, or when she initiates an inappropriate motor response (Simoneau & Leibowitz, 1996). During the aging process, the vestibular organs progressively deteriorate, making it more difficult for older adults to sense head position, body position, and bodily motion in space. It is also more difficult for the elderly to make postural corrections as the vestibular sensory system functions less adequately.

The visual system provides feedback that assists a person in controlling balance and in postural stability. Because the aging visual system transmits less light to the retina and is characterized by reduced visual acuity and slowed responsiveness to changes in illumination, the aging eye also may contribute to postural instability and falling. Reduced sensitivity to the position and movement of the joints as well as reduced muscle strength and muscle mass (sarcopenia) add to an older person's potential for dangerous falls.

Evidence indicates that the elderly find that postural stability demands effort (Rankin, Wollacott, Shumway-Cook, and Brown, 2000). Older persons display more sway or body movement when standing than do younger adults. Some studies have found body sway can predict the risk of falling; however, increases in body sway do not always indicate difficulty with balance and postural stability.

Balance requires lower extremity strength and is affected by sarcopenia (Wolfson, Judge, Whipple, & King, 1995). Balance is also influenced directly by gait speed, and vice versa. Other factors coupled with balance may also play a role in restricting an older person's mobility, independence, and functioning, including fear of falling, pain, joint impairment, visual difficulties, and reduced sensation (Brown, Sinacore, & Host, 1995). The sense of balance is involved in lifting and carrying, and when balance is not steady, an older person's range of movement and functioning is restricted. Figure 6.21 shows the direct consequence of sarcopenia on other muscle groups (e.g., back and thoracic muscles) and how this compromises balance. From this figure, we can see how sarcopenia is related to the sense of balance and the postural adjustments required in bending, moving, and lifting. It is understandable how fear of losing one's balance and falling can become a preoccupation for some elderly.

Falls

In any given year, one of every three people over age 65 falls, and two of every five people over the age of 80 fall (Simoneau & Leibowitz, 1996). The leading cause of death from accidental injury in people over the age of 65 is falling; nearly 10,000 people over the age of 65 died from injuries related to falling in 1998. For older adults, fatal falls

Figure 6.21 Tracings of photographs show that when this woman with scapulo-thoracic muscle weakness brings her arm forward, her thoracic kyphosis increases, and her center of mass moves forward. The shift in center of mass is even more pronounced when she is holding something. Thus, scapulo-thoracic weakness can increase the risk of falling. *Source: Brown, M., Sinacore, D. R., & Host, H. H. (1995). The relationship of strength to function in the older adult. Journals of Gerontology Series A, 50A, (special issue), 55–59. Reprinted by permission.*

occurred most often at home (60 percent), followed by public places (30 percent) and in nursing homes (10 percent). Falling is the most common cause of injury and hospital admission for older adults, and falls cause 87 percent of all fractures in the elderly. The greatest risk of death from a fracture occurs with hip fractures, 80 percent of which occur in women. Almost 340,000 hip fractures occurred among older adults in 1998. By the year 2040, it is predicted that there will be 500,000 hip fractures each year, at a total cost of $240 billion. More than 50 percent of the elderly with a hip fracture are unable to live independently after falling. Hip fracture is more common in Western society than in other parts of the world; countries that have a diet rich in vegetable protein rather than animal protein have a lower incidence of hip fractures (Frassetto, Todd, Morris, & Sebastian, 2000). Vegetable protein supplies sufficient acid intake that, according to the investigators, reduces the risk of hip fracture.

Among older adults living independently, 55 percent were found to be fearful of falling and as a result restricted many activities. Those who were most fearful were women with fewer social contacts and a past history of having fallen (Howland et al.,

1998). Those who restricted their activities did not share their concerns about falling, had less social support, and could identify a person in their immediate environment that had experienced a fall.

Intrinsic risk factors for falling can be the result of either normal aging or disease that leads to cognitive, sensory, neurological, or musculosketel deficits (e.g., those associated with sarcopenia). Individual factors that contribute to falling include problems with gait, balance, medications, dementia, and poor vision. Muscle atrophy with an accompanying decline in strength appears to underlie both gait and balance problems that lead to falling. Falls are more likely when lower muscle strength is weak and mobility is impaired (Wolfson et al., 1995). Other intrinsic risk factors include disability of the knees, legs, ankles, or feet; gait and balance abnormalities; poor vision; and disease. Fear of falling is particularly common among elders who experience dizziness, especially if they also had difficulties with ADLs, symptoms of depression, and difficulty maintaining stability in a standing position (Burker et al., 1995).

Falling in older adults may also be the result of tripping, slipping, or side effects from medications. Extrinsic factors that heighten the risk of falling include medications, alcohol, and environmental hazards such as slippery surfaces, uneven floors, poor illumination, loose rugs, unstable furniture, and objects on floors (National Center for Injury Prevention and Control, 2001a). Older adults are most likely to fall while walking, changing position, or tripping over an obstacle (Draganich, Zacny, Klafta, & Karrison, 2001). It is important to predict which community-residing elderly are at high risk for falling, particularly if they live alone. A risk index comprised of three dimensions helps determine the risk of falling. These dimensions are (1) history of falls in the past 12 months, (2) clinical pattern of dizziness or balance problems, and (3) physical problems affecting mobility. The index showed a range from 10 percent (low risk) to 51 percent (highest risk) for elderly adults with an average age of 81 years (Covinsky et al., 2001). Targeted interventions with at risk elderly have been effective in reducing the risk of falling. Most programs focus on improving balance, upper body strength, and lower leg power and reducing environmental-hazards (Yates & Dunnagan, 2001). Any intervention that reduces or eliminates the probability of falling is important, since risk factors are additive (Simoneau & Leibowitz, 1996).

Wojik and colleagues (1999) have found that older women recovering from a near fall take larger steps to regain their balance than younger adults do. Other studies, however, suggest that older women take multiple shorter, lateral steps to keep from falling (McIlroy & Maki, 1996). In an experimental setting to prevent injury, Hsiao and Robinovitch (2001) studied how community-residing elderly (mean age of 75) regained their balance from a potential fall with instructions to "try to take only one step." Half of the sample was able to recover balance from a backwards fall with only a single step. An additional 27 percent in the study recovered their balance by using two steps. The ability to recover balance from a backwards fall was dependent on the relationship of body lean angle, or tilt, to stepping angle. The greater the trunk deviated from upright/vertical (the greater the postural stoop), the more steps were needed to recover balance. The relation between posture and stepping angle determined whether a single large step or two or more smaller steps was needed to prevent the fall. Other studies show that going up a step can lead to falling, since older adults adopt a strategy that is not as safe as that of young adults (Begg & Sparrow, 2000). Specifically, the elderly leave too great a distance between the leg that is raised and the leg that remains trailing. Younger adults use shorter distances that allow an opportunity to correct a mistake. Older adults cannot easily recover if their initial foot placement goes awry. They should be encouraged to assess the environmental demands carefully before initiating stepping movements.

Falls occur for about half of the more than 1.5 million nursing home residents each year. Residents are more frail than those living in the community and tend to be older, more cognitively impaired, and at greater risk of falling. General weakness and difficulties with gait are the most common causes of falls among nursing home elderly. Other factors include environmental hazards (e.g., wet floors, poor lighting, lack of bed rails, bed height), and medications such as those for depression (Avorn, 1998). The tricyclic antidepressant amitriptyline causes slower walking (gait velocity) and interferes with the movements needed to step easily over an obstacle; the newer antidepressants (e.g., SSRIs, or selective serotonin reuptake inhibitors) do not have comparable effects on psychomotor skills. Depressed elderly taking amytriptyline need to be encouraged to take slower, more deliberate movements to safely navigate the environment (Draganich, Zacny, Klafta, & Karrison, 2001).

Prevention of falls in nursing homes is based on strengthening, conditioning, and rehabilitation exercises to improve gait and endurance. Environmental assists such as lowered bed height, handrails in hallways, and grab bars in key locations are particularly helpful. Early screening for risk factors helps target the interventions needed for specific deficits. The Frailty and Injuries: Cooperative Studies of Intervention Techniques (FICSIT) project is a pioneering attempt at targeted intervention. Elderly at very high risk of falling were given training to improve strength, endurance, balance, and other physical skills; they also improved their nutrition and wore protective hip pads to protect them from falls, and environmental hazards around them were monitored (National Center for Injury Prevention and Control, 2001b). Monitoring involved assessing the lighting, especially in hallways and stairwells; checking for availability of grab bars in bathrooms and railings in hallways and on stairs; checking for appropriate footwear; and removing area rugs. Results are quite promising.

Prevention of Falls and Fractures

Older persons and the frail elderly are likely to experience sarcopenia as they age because of muscle disuse, disease, and an increasingly sedentary lifestyle (Evans, 1995b). Institutionalized and frail elderly are particularly at risk. Atrophy of muscle mass and decreasing muscle strength corresponds to an increased risk of falls and fractures. However, exercise programs targeted to strengthen specific muscle groups related to strength, balance, stability, and endurance can significantly reduce the risk of falling. In an institutionalized population aged 87 to 96 years old, significant improvements in leg strength and quadriceps muscle size were apparent after only an eight-week program of training. The participants also improved their gait speed and functional mobility. Such gains, once established, can be maintained with minimal programming; for example, with strength-training exercises as infrequently as once a week (Evans, 1995b).

Strength training helps stability and balance and can lower the risk of hip fractures due to falling by 30 to 40 percent (Cox, 1997). Various types of strength, resistance, or weight training reduce the risk of fractures in some groups of older persons, such as postmenopausal women who have adopted a sedentary lifestyle (Evans, 1995b). Strength training appears to increase bone density in postmenopausal women as well as to reduce the likelihood of falls and the subsequent risk of bone fractures among those who have osteoporosis. Fractures due to falling are more likely to occur among the elderly who have poor balance, poor gait, and reduced lower-extremity leg strength (Liebman, 1995).

If they are not used, the muscles used to run, climb a flight of stairs, get out of a chair, or even just stand will atrophy. However, it is possible to rebuild important muscle groups and to enhance an older person's independence and sense of control in the process. It is not any easier to get older persons to exercise than it is younger persons. But older adults, both men and women, show gains comparable to those of younger adults when they engage in similar strength training programs (Evans, 1995b). Generally, the greater the intensity of the exercise program, the greater the benefits (Evans, 1995b). And, not surprisingly, benefits will decline and disappear unless some program continuity is maintained.

Gait Velocity

When older persons face threats to their mobility, especially limitations in walking, their autonomy is challenged (Simoneau & Leibowitz, 1996). Some challenges may be alleviated through exercise and strength training, while others are psychological and appear less responsive to exercise. Judge, Davis, and Ounpuu (1996) identified normal aging with a reduction in **gait velocity** (walking speed) for most elderly. Gait velocity reduction is, in part, the result of a shortened step length among the elderly as compared to that of younger adults. There is also a corresponding loss of power from decreased ankle flexion at the "push-off" phase of gait, which is the result of shortening or reduction of the flexion of the ankle itself. This is recognized more simply as flat-footedness in the appearance of the elderly as they walk (Simoneau & Leibowitz, 1996). Reductions in gait velocity are also characterized by an increase in the amount of time both feet are on the ground simultaneously, a decrease in the length of the step taken, and an increase in stride width. Others have found that a loss of strength in the leg muscles (quadriceps and hamstring), coupled with declines of other lower-extremity muscle groups, cause a reduction in gait speed (Brown et al., 1995). This is a particularly common occurrence among older persons with arthritis. The elderly also experience a power loss due to muscle atrophy and reduced ankle flexion, which some counteract with an increase in power from hip flexion. One way to increase gait speed, then, could come from exercises that strengthen ankle flexor muscles and increase leg strength by targeting muscles of the lower extremities in weight training (Judge et al., 1996).

There are many reasons for a reduction in gait velocity beside sarcopenia and reduced ankle flexion. These usually relate to the older individual's stability, postural balance, and concern for personal safety. In one study, less than 1 percent of people aged 72 or older walked at normal speeds (about four feet per second) that would permit them to cross the street at intersections in the time allowed by stoplights (Langlois et al., 1997). A comparison of gait velocity in active versus sedentary older adults revealed that the latter were more cautious and slower in their style of walking. They took shorter steps both while walking and to overcome obstacles (Rosengren, McAuley, & Mihalko, 1998). Gait velocity was predictable from older adults' individual judgments of efficacy; those who moved faster expressed more self-confidence in walking, climbing stairs, stepping over obstacles, and going up and down from a curb. In another investigation of factors associated with reductions in gait speed among the elderly, Buchner and his colleagues (1996) identified a psychological variable—an indicator of depressive symptoms—was related to gait speed. It seems likely that declines in physical health status can have a direct impact on depressive symptoms, and these factors together can contribute to slowness in gait velocity. Slow gait speed is predictive of institutionalization, mortality, and physical functioning in general since it is highly correlated with both strength and aerobic capacity in older adults (Buchner et al., 1996).

SUMMARY

Today's adults are reaching old age in better health and living longer. Successful aging means being able to make productive contributions to society, maintain a social network, continue an autonomous life, and engage in an active lifestyle. The rate of chronic disease is lower than in previous cohorts, and the elderly are increasingly able to maintain an independent lifestyle and avoid nursing home care. Racial differences in health are evident, partly as a result of social class, access to health care, discrimination, and disadvantage accumulated over the life course (certain races face double jeopardy). Women are more likely to be in poorer health than men in old age. Most elderly cope successfully with chronic disease or disability.

Health status has an impact on activities of daily living (bathing, dressing, toileting, getting out of bed or chair, walking, getting outside of the residence, and self-feeding) and instrumental activities of daily living (personal self-care, meal preparation, shopping, money management, telephone use, light and heavy housework). Assessment of these skills is an essential first step in developing interventions to optimize independent functioning in the later years. Frailty is associated with difficulties in ADL and IADL. It is defined as a wasting of the body along with muscular weakness and poor nutrition and is marked by a loss of more than 10 pounds in a 12-month period, self-reported exhaustion, weakness, slow walking speed, and low physical activity. Self-reported health among older adults is a strong predictor of overall mortality and predictive of future health problems, recovery from illness, and functional ability in the elderly. Black and Hispanic elderly have lower self-perceived levels of health than whites. Generally, elderly with symptoms of depression and lower life satisfaction report lower levels of perceived health.

The costs of health care become an increasing burden to older adults on fixed incomes. Social Security is the federal government's income and insurance program for retired workers that qualify. It consists of four trust funds: (1) Old-Age Survivors Insurance, (2) Disability Insurance, (3) Hospital Insurance Trust Fund—Medicare Part A, and (4) Supplementary Medical Insurance—Medicare Part B. Some workers receive retirement pensions in addition to Social Security benefits. Hospitals and physicians attempt to manage the costs of health care by following Diagnostic Related Group standards, which are based on the average cost and length of treatment for patients with similar illnesses. Older people are discharged from hospitals "quicker and sicker" to go to home care and long-term care facilities where the costs of recovery are lower. Discharge planners can help make appropriate referrals to assisted living facilities, nursing homes, or home-based services such as visiting nurses.

Assisted living is care for the frail elderly that enhances their independence, autonomy, and privacy in a homelike atmosphere. Quality of life in assisted living is determined by the social climate of the facility, the freedom to make choices, and regular visitations from friends and family. Long-term care includes medical intervention, social support services, and personal care assistance (in ADLs) for chronically ill, frail, or disabled elderly. The cost of long-term nursing home care is substantial ($150 per day in 2001) and is projected to increase 5 percent per year ($430 per day in 2021). A typical nursing home stay is about 75 days. For adults aged 65 years and older, there is a 40 percent chance that such services will be needed. About 5 percent of older adults have obtained private long-term care insurance to help meet these costs.

Elderly residents of nursing homes are sicker and more frail than in the past; community-based health care has enabled many older people to live longer in their own homes with complex diseases before they need nursing home care. Mortality is high among new admissions to nursing homes, particularly those with dementia, and those who have recently been moved to a new facility. Residents who live longest in nursing homes have higher levels of self-esteem, lower levels of depression, and a positive overall psychological adjustment.

Family members caring for an older relative at home are often not prepared for the demands of the role. The elderly family member's urinary incontinence is often a trigger for the decision to move him or her to a nursing home. Isolation and dementia are also factors that predict a move to a nursing home. An advocate for the welfare of elderly residing in nursing homes is called a long-term-care ombudsman. An ombudsman serves as a mediator between the resident and the policies, staff, and administration of the institution.

Medicaid is a federal insurance program for lower-income elderly; many older adults have to "spend down" or deplete their assets before they can quality for coverage. Medicare is a part of the Social Security system that provides partial medical insurance for persons over the age of 65. It is designed to deal with acute illness, not chronic conditions, although Supplemental Medical Insurance can be purchased from the federal government to help pay additional medical costs. Some states permit private insurance carriers to underwrite Medigap policies for services that government programs do not cover, such as personal home care, prescription drugs, or hearing aids. The financial viability of Medicare is an ongoing concern. Various policy changes have been considered, and the age of eligibility for full Social Security retirement benefits has already been raised to age 66.

Environmental interventions can assist those who have cognitive impairments. Elders who do not have supportive family can access formal services (substitution hypothesis); other community services such as respite provide support for family members who serve as caregivers (supplementation hypothesis). Using restraints to control cognitively impaired nursing home residents is becoming less common as staff are educated about alternative control methods. By law, residents may not be restrained except under very specific conditions; those that are must be monitored regularly. Wandering and pacing are characteristic of those with dementia, especially in early evening (a phenomenon called sundowning).

Health promotion can have beneficial effects for adults and the elderly. Risk factors for the leading causes of death (heart disease, cancer, and stroke) have been identified, as have important preventive choices related to diet and exercise. We examined three types of cancer (breast, prostate, lung) and HIV to understand the importance of early detection, attitude (psychoneuroimmunology), and treatment options. Weight management can be effective in controlling obesity, a major risk factor for both cancer and coronary heart disease. Weight loss programs are rarely effective over the long run, however.

Adults enter old age today stronger, healthier, and with fewer disabilities and chronic diseases than previous cohorts. Both moderate and intense exercise have positive effects throughout the entire adult life span. Through exercise (progressive overload), people improve cardiovascular and respiratory fitness, strength, endurance, and muscle power. Exercise can reduce the rate of decline in many physiological systems; this benefit will be lost as exercise demands are reduced or programs abandoned (fitness is reversible). Exercise can protect against osteoporosis, reduce the risk of falling, strengthen heart muscle, improve mobility, reduce blood pressure, lower cholesterol, and reduce joint swelling from arthritis. It is never too late to begin an exercise program. There are, however, normal developmental changes that exercise cannot prevent; senescence describes biological losses that occur at a rate of about 2 percent per year. For example, age-related changes in maximal oxygen uptake (VO_2 max) may be delayed but not prevented. Sedentary lifestyles lead to atherosclerosis, myocardial infarction, stroke, and congestive heart failure.

Strength training has value in overcoming sarcopenia (muscle atrophy). Strength training can reverse, to some degree, the effects of muscle atrophy at any age. Muscle atrophy and muscle power relate to balance, postural stability, and falling in the elderly. Falling is a common occurrence for the elderly, but the risk can be reduced through intervention on intrinsic and extrinsic factors. Exercises that strengthen the muscles involved in walking enhance the gait and improve endurance, reducing the risk of falling. Similarly, exercise can strengthen the muscle groups associated with balance, stability, and strength.

REVIEW QUESTIONS

1. Discuss the difference between health promotion and disease prevention as these concepts apply to aging.

2. Explain the significance of activities of daily living and instrumental activities of daily living. How are these used in the field of aging?

3. What are the reasons that the health status of black and Hispanic elders is lower than that of white elders?

4. What are the basic components of successful aging?

5. Define the concept of frailty and indicate the behavioral markers used to identify it.

6. How are Medicare and Medicaid different? What is the significance of "spending down" in each of these programs?

7. Identify at least five principles of environmental design to assist the cognitively impaired older adult.

8. Under what conditions are restraints used in nursing homes? What is the role of a long-term care ombudsman in a nursing home?

9. What are the major risk factors for heart disease and cancer?

10. Design a program to offset the impact of sarcopenia and explain each of the dimensions the program will implement.

11. Define the risk factors related to falling in the elderly. How can falling be prevented?

12. Identify at least 10 benefits of regular exercise for the elderly.

ON THE WEB   www.mhhe.com/hoyer5

The Agency for Healthcare Research and Quality publishes on its website a variety of practical guidelines for caring for a wide range of different physical and medical conditions. This is a good site for those seeking information on how to help older adults with disease prevention and wellness.

The American Heart Association website contains current statistics and educational information on medical procedures, including surgeries and drug treatments, for various forms of heart disease. The site has buttons to assess risk for heart attack and to outline healthy diets and exercise programs. A number of excellent links to other health-related sites are included.

The American Heart Association also provides a special site on fitness, exercise, and adopting activities to enhance heart function and reduce the likelihood of coronary artery disease. Lots of events are publicized for those interested in participating in nationally coordinated activities or in regionally sponsored programs.

The Calorie Control Council is an organization sponsored by the food industry—those who manufacture, prepare, and sell low-calorie and reduced-fat food. The site contains useful facts central to the concerns of the nearly one-quarter of Americans who embark on diets each year.

The Family Caregiver Alliance provides services to people seeking care for their family members when they cannot meet their needs at home. The Alliance has a variety of out-of-home options for families, along with helpful definitions and guidelines.

The National Association of Geriatric Care Managers sponsors a website for those seeking an assessment of the support services necessary to sustain an older adult's independent lifestyle. For a fee, a case manager will make recommendations, identify appropriate resources, and even arrange for care. Services are frequently provided for families living far from an older relative.

The geriatric care manager can also review financial, medical, and legal issues and consult with the family.

The National Center for Injury Prevention and Control (a division of the Center for Disease Control) maintains a web page specifically directed at injuries among the elderly. The site has information on the causes of falling and its economic, psychological, and health consequences, including fractures. Other common injuries are also examined on this site, and there are excellent links to other health and aging sites.

The National Heart, Lung, and Blood Institute has a website with useful information on various cardiovascular diseases. The site includes pages to help focus on reducing heart disease risk factors, such as a calculator to determine body mass index and another to calculate ideal weight.

The National Sleep Foundation supports an active website with excellent background on various sleep disorders. There are links to national and international organizations, current studies, and practical guidelines to assist those having sleeping difficulties.

7

MEMORY, ATTENTION, AND LEARNING

> *Memory is sometimes so retentive, so serviceable, so obedient—at others, so bewildered and so weak—and at others again, so tyrannic, so beyond control!*
> —Jane Austin, *Mansfield Park*
>
> *That's what learning is. You suddenly understand something you've understood all your life, but in a new way.*
> —Doris Lessing

INTRODUCTION

Imagine an older man driving to the supermarket to buy some groceries. While driving to the store he asks himself, "I know I have to buy orange juice, dish detergent, and lettuce, but what are the other two items my wife wanted me to buy?" After finding some of the items he was supposed to buy, the man is standing in a checkout line when an elderly woman walks past him. As he sees the woman, he thinks, "I'm certain I met that woman a couple of weeks ago, but I don't really remember where, and I can't remember her name." Upon leaving the supermarket, he roams the parking lot and repeatedly asks himself, "Where did I park my car?" After he locates his car and begins the drive home, he says to himself, "I can't remember things as well as I did when I was younger." He begins to wonder if his memory problems are "normal," or if his forgetfulness signals the onset of dementia.

What are your reactions to the preceding scenario? Do all adults experience these kinds of memory failures? Do older persons invariably experience the deterioration of all or most aspects of memory? Or are only particular kinds of memory losses associated with aging? How does health influence memory? What types of age-related memory loss, if any, are predictive of the onset of dementia? In this chapter we address these questions.

Self-Conceptions of Age-Related Memory Loss

One way to assess the degree to which aging affects memory is to ask individuals to rate the quality of their memories, to estimate the frequency of their memory failures in everyday situations, and to predict how they think they would perform on a memory test. Self-ratings of memory performance are measures of **metamemory** or the self-appraisal or self-monitoring of memory. Studies of metamemory gauge how well each of us understand, the efficacy of our own memory. Some studies have found that older persons' metamemory is mostly accurate, whereas other studies have found that older adults exaggerate their memory failures (Hertzog & Hultsch, 2000). In a recent study by Turvey and colleagues (2000), for example, older people (aged 70 years and over) were asked if they believed their memory was excellent, very good, good, fair, or poor. They then took a cognitive assessment derived from the Mini-Mental Status Exam. In general, people's assessments of their own memory corresponded with their actual performance on memory measures. However, a large number of the research participants inaccurately assessed their memory skills. People who reported depression and impairment on activities of daily living were more likely to report an impaired memory, even though they performed adequately on the memory measures. Hess and Pullen (1996) also pointed out that older adults have a much more negative view of their memory ability than younger adults, report more memory failures in real-life contexts than younger adults, and expect to perform much worse on laboratory tasks of memory compared with younger adults.

Why are there discrepancies between metamemory and actual memory performance? There are at least four reasons. First, it may be the case that people confuse their self-perceptions of everyday memory failures with age-related changes in physical and/or mental health status. A wealth of research reinforces this idea, showing that deficits in vision, hearing, and overall health status, as well as the incidence and severity of depression, are all related to the frequency of self-reported memory complaints among the elderly. Second, older adults (and their relatives and health care providers) tend to overestimate the number of memory difficulties they experience in everyday life. Older adults seem to be more sensitive to their memory failures than younger adults. They are more likely to be concerned about minor forgetfulness in comparison to younger adults and exaggerated concern about memory failure is especially likely to occur in novel or stressful situations. In other words, older adults may hold "ageist" attitudes and stereotypes about themselves that distort their memory assessments. A third reason for the discrepancy between metamemory and memory performance is that self-report measures may, in actuality, assess the complexity of an individual's psychosocial environment rather than his or her memory. Rabbitt and Abson (1990) argued that memory in most adults from their late fifties to early seventies continues

Have you ever had difficulty remembering where you parked your car at the mall? As we get older, we pay more attention to encoding such things as where we park as a way of avoiding memory failures.

to function effectively in demanding environments. These older adults continue to work, manage busy family schedules, and so on. Under such circumstances, individuals might be overly concerned about trying to keep track of many details. Old-old adults (say, in their eighties) may have less complicated lives and notice fewer memory lapses. Thus, memory problems would be underreported in the oldest-old.

A fourth reason why self-reports of memory problems do not predict actual memory performance is that peoples' ideas about the structure, function, and organization of human memory may be inaccurate. People sometimes think of memory as a filing cabinet for storing diverse pieces of information for later retrieval. Remembering is equated with conscious recollection of the distant past. These individuals assume that the major function of memory is to provide a fully detailed and precise reproduction of previous events and experiences.

One way to approach the topic of memory is to take a *multiple memory systems* point of view (Schacter, 2000; Schacter & Tulving, 1994). This chapter is organized from this theoretical perspective. Multiple memory systems theory suggests that the human brain has a number of different memory systems, each of which possesses a different fundamental goal and achieves its goal using different operations and different neural mechanisms. At the most basic level, we can distinguish between **short-term memory** and **long-term memory.**

Short-Term versus Long-Term Memory

More than 100 years ago, the psychologist and philosopher William James (1890) pointed out the distinction between primary memory and secondary memory. James identified *primary memory* with conscious awareness of recently perceived events. He defined *secondary memory* as the retrieval of events that had left consciousness. James's ideas about the differences between primary and secondary memory were derived from introspection, but now this basic distinction is supported by a great deal of evidence.

The model of memory shown in Figure 7.1 includes a system of sensory stores or buffers in addition to short- and long-term stores. Note that figure 7.1 outlines processes that transfer information from one store to another. Transfer from sensory to short-term memory entails attention, whereas transfer from short-term to long-term memory requires rehearsal and elaboration. In this model, three different types of forgetting correspond to the three memory stores. Forgetting from sensory stores is thought to result from simple decay; this information is lost within less than a second. Forgetting from short-term memory results from displacement; new information replaces old information. Forgetting from long-term memory results from interference between the memory

Figure 7.1
Three-stage model of memory.

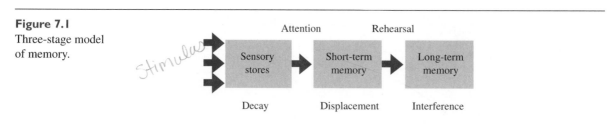

for one piece of information and that for another bit of information learned previously or subsequently. Indeed, some researchers have reported that interference does not destroy information in long-term memory, but simply impairs its retrievability.

Are there age-related differences in the capacity of short-term memory? Younger adults can hold approximately seven pieces of information in short-term memory (Miller, 1956). Do older adults have the same capacity? One way to answer this question is to give younger and older adults a digit- or letter-span task. In forward-span tasks, individuals are asked to repeat a sequence of numbers or letters of the alphabet. The lists vary in length from 1 to say 12 items. In backward-span tasks, the person is asked to recall the items in reverse order. These tests show that memory capacity is hardly, if at all, affected by aging (Gregoire & Van der Linden, 1997). (Consider the findings shown in Figure 7.2.)

Working Memory Relatively substantial age-related declines are found on memory tasks that require juggling a lot of information at once. When an individual is performing tasks that entail the active and simultaneous processing and storing of information, he or she is using **working memory.** One way to understand the concept of working memory is to think of a desktop. During the course of a day, new pieces of information (memos, reports, work requests, and maybe empty pizza boxes) constantly accumulate on an individual's desk. The individual has to determine (1) which information is the most important, (2) which pieces of information require further processing, (3) which processing strategy to use, and (4) which pieces of information are cluttering up the

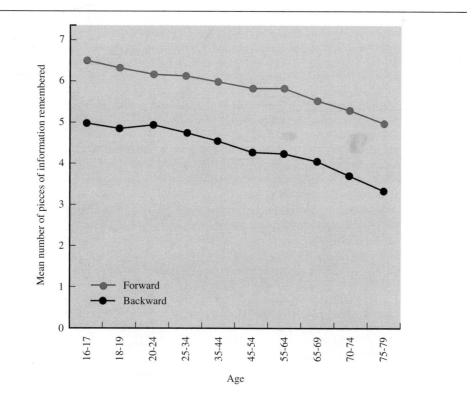

Figure 7.2
Forward and backward digit span scores for 1,000 research participants ranging from 16 to 79 years of age. *Source:* Adapted from Gregoire, J., & Van der Linden, M. (1997). Effect of age on forward and backward digit spans. *Aging, Neuropsychology, and Cognition, 4,* 140–149.

desktop and should either be discarded or stored. Working memory tasks require individuals to simultaneously select, coordinate, and process incoming information.

Baddeley (1994) theorized that working memory consists of three major components: a central executive, an articulatory loop, and a visual scratch pad. The central executive is responsible for making decisions about what information is processed in working memory and how that information is to be processed. For example, the central executive helps you remember what you need to buy at the supermarket. It may accomplish this goal by devising an elaborate encoding procedure that involves the assistance of the other parts of working memory. If, for example, you need to buy strawberries, chicken, milk, and cereal, the central executive may instruct the visual scratch pad to develop a mental image of "a chicken sitting down to a breakfast of strawberries, milk, and cereal." Or it may instruct the articulatory loop to rehearse the sentence "Chickens like milk and strawberries on their cereal" as you drive to the store.

Age-related deficits in working memory may have far-reaching consequences. A breakdown in working memory means that a person cannot keep her mind on a particular task (cannot inhibit intrusive thoughts and distractions) and cannot manipulate the contents of working memory to solve a complex problem. Consider the following working memory task that typically yields a substantial age difference in performance, favoring younger adults: Individuals listen to a tape recording of a list of "things you can drink" (e.g., *coffee, soda, water, milk,* etc.); and, at the same time, see a list of "things you can eat" (e.g., *pizza, spinach, crackers, apple,* etc.) presented one at a time on a computer screen. The participants are told to ignore the auditory words but remember the visual words. Immediately after the presentation, participants must repeat the visual words beginning with the one you would be most likely to eat if you were on a diet (e.g., *apple*) and ending with the word that represents the item you would be least likely to eat if you were on a diet (e.g., *pizza*). Older adults perform poorly on this task compared to younger adults because they must selectively attend to some information (the visual words), ignore other information (the auditory words), and manipulate the visual words held in working memory according to a specific rule (how healthful each food item is).

Everyday tasks often require functional working memory. Age-related declines in complex tasks have been attributed to a number of factors, including limited processing resources and the costs of having to switch attention from one task to another.

In a recent study, Lustig, May, and Hasker (2001) investigated the possibility that *interference* is the source of age-related difficulties in working memory. Younger and older adults were given a working memory span task either in the standard format or in one designed to reduce the impact of interference. Reducing the amount of interference in working memory raised the span scores for both groups. These authors suggest that age differences in working memory capacity may be due to differences in the ability to overcome interference.

Researchers have also suggested that age differences in long-term memory are the result of the central executive's tendency to use ineffective strategies when it encodes (or retrieves) information from long-term memory. For example, instead of using one of the previously mentioned strategies to remember a shopping list of strawberries, chicken, milk, and cereal, an older adult may try to remember a list by simply repeating the words on the list to herself or by forming a mental image of the words on the list.

Memory Search　　Along with being better at manipulating the contents of working memory, younger adults are faster than older adults in searching or scanning the contents of memory (e.g., Fisk & Rogers, 1991). Researchers measure memory search by presenting a person with a set of items (usually digits, such as 6, 3, and 9) to hold in memory. Then another digit (e.g., 9) is presented, and the individual's task is to decide whether the digit matches one of the digits in the memory set. Memory sets of varying lengths are used, and as might be expected, response times increase (answers are given more slowly) as the size of the memory set increases. Figure 7.3 shows the results from one early study (Anders, Fozard, & Lillyquist, 1972) that compared the speed of short-term memory search for individuals in early, middle, and late adulthood. Note that longer memory sets produced longer response times, and that the slope (i.e., the steepness) of the response-time curve is slightly greater

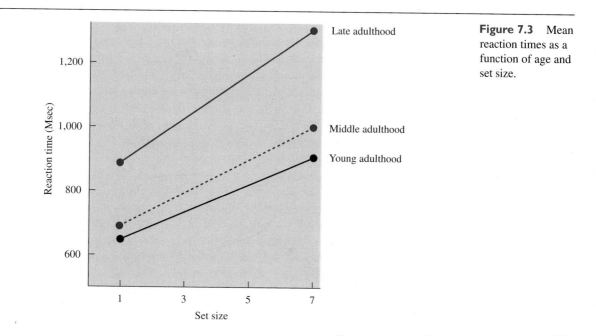

Figure 7.3　Mean reaction times as a function of age and set size.

for individuals in late adulthood than for those in early adulthood. This difference in slope indicates that older adults scan through items in short-term memory at a slower pace than younger adults.

Even though there appear to be interactive effects of age and set size, the most prominent effects associated with aging have to do with a general slowing in the speed of performance. Age-related slowing in information processing speed accounts for a substantial part of the age-related decline in memory across a wide range of tasks (e.g., for comprehensive reviews, see Cerella, 1990; Salthouse, 1996). Older adults perform at a ratio of about 1.4 to 1.7 of the performance of young adults. That is, a typical older person needs 1.4 to 1.7 seconds for every 1.0 seconds a younger person needs to carry out mental processing. Age-related slowing in memory performance may be associated with a number of changes in the brain such as changes in neurotransmitter substances at the synapse, neural demyelination, disruptions in neural circuitry related to vascular lesions, and increases in the extent of recruitment and activation of brain volume (Raz, 2000).

Divisions of Long-Term Memory: Multiple Memory Systems

What about the effects of age on long-term memory? Long-term memory is typically defined as the retrieval of information that was processed more than one minute ago, or the retrieval of information that has left consciousness. For many years, psychologists were certain that long-term memory underwent a significant deterioration in older adults. This "fact," as we have previously noted, is certainly consistent with one of the most common self-perceptions among the elderly: "I can't remember as well as I did when I was young."

Within the past decade, research in cognitive neuroscience has radically changed our understanding of the nature of human memory. Endel Tulving, Daniel Schacter, John Gabrieli, and Larry Squire have contributed to the development of the *multiple memory systems theory* of long-term memory (Prull, Gabrieli, & Bunge, 2000; Schacter, 2000; Schacter & Tulving, 1994; Squire, 1994; Squire & Knowlton, 1995). Long-term memory consists of two major systems that are functionally and neurologically distinct: declarative memory and nondeclarative or

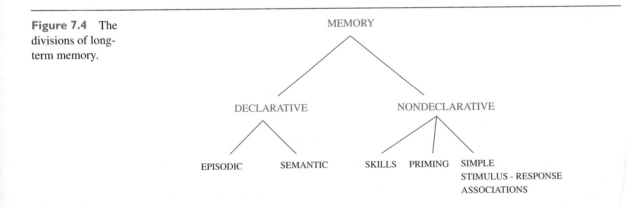

Figure 7.4 The divisions of long-term memory.

procedural memory (see figure 7.4). **Declarative memory** involves the conscious recollection of the past. When people use their declarative memory system, they "remember that" something has happened in the past. In fact, declarative memory is responsible for the remembrance of previous events that can literally "be declared." An example of declarative memory would be "I remember that the first car I ever drove was a _____."

Nondeclarative memory, in contrast, reveals itself by the influence that past events have on a person's current behavior. When people use their nondeclarative memory system, they "remember how" to do something because of past experience. An example of nondeclarative memory would be remembering how to drive a car.

Figure 7.4 shows the major subdivisions of declarative and nondeclarative memory. In the next several sections, we discuss the effects of aging on these different memory systems.

Episodic and Semantic Memory

Episodic memory refers to the conscious recollection of specific details of previous events. Most importantly, episodic memory is accompanied by a sense of remembering, pastness, and autonoetic awareness (Tulving, 1993; Wheeler, Stuss, & Tulving, 1997). *Autonoetic awareness* is the feeling that a remembrance actually happened to us. It is a type of "self-awareness" that indicates we are mentally reexperiencing a specific event from our personal past.

Try to remember the first (or last) time you flew in an airplane. If you can mentally transport yourself back in time and reexperience the way the inside of the plane looked as you moved toward your seat, the mannerisms of the flight attendant and the person who sat next to you on the plane, what you saw and how you felt when you looked out the window, and so on, you are experiencing the output of your episodic memory system.

Semantic memory refers to the remembrance of acquired knowledge about the world. Semantic memories are not accompanied by any of the autonoetic characteristics that mark episodic memories. When we remember something via the semantic memory system, we do not feel as if we are remembering anything from our personal pasts. This is because our semantic memories are accompanied instead by *noetic awareness*—the awareness that we possess certain pieces of information and that this information is objective rather than subjective in nature.

To illustrate the salient features of semantic memory, let's return to our example of trying to remember your first airplane flight. Suppose that the first time you flew you were going to Chicago, and you remember ticketing and security procedures, but you have no personal recollection of actually being on the airplane and cannot remember the personal experiences you had during the flight. You would be experiencing a semantic, but not an episodic, memory.

A great deal of neuropsychological data points to the validity of the distinction between episodic and semantic memory. Tulving, Hayman, and MacDonald (1991) studied a brain-injured patient named K. C. who displayed a severe amnesia for all of the episodic, but not the semantic, memories he had acquired during the course of his life. After his brain injury, K. C., who loved to play chess, could still remember how to play chess, could remember the fact that his father taught him to play chess, and could remember the fact that he had played chess with his father on several occasions. But K. C. could not remember a single instance in which he had actually played a game of chess! When asked "What was the saddest day in your life?," K. C. replied it was the day of his brother's funeral. Yet, despite being able to remember when and where his brother's funeral took place, K. C. could not remember actually being at this sad event.

In other research, Tulving (1989) used positron emission tomography (PET) to distinguish between the episodic and semantic memory systems. These experiments have shown that areas in the frontal cortex become activated when individuals retrieve episodic memories, whereas more posterior brain regions become activated during the recall of semantic memories.

As Research Focus 7.1 describes, cognitive psychologists have devised a sensitive technique for revealing age-related difference in episodic and semantic memory. The findings provide clear evidence that age negatively affects episodic, but not semantic, memory. In the next few sections, we provide other examples of how aging affects these two memory systems.

Recall and Recognition

Episodic memory can be assessed using a variety of measures, including those that measure **recall** and **recognition.** Both of these types of tasks make use of the same study items—say, a list of 20 common words. In a recall task, research participants would be instructed to say or write down as many of the 20 study items as possible without any hints or clues. A recall score is calculated by subtracting the number of intrusion errors (the false recall of words that were not on the list) from the number of items correctly recalled.

In a recognition task, participants would be presented with all of the 20 study items, along with another 20 distractor items that were not on the study list. They would then be asked to indicate which of the 40 words were presented at study. Recognition ability is determined by subtracting the number of "false alarms" (the number of items not on the study list that were mistakenly identified as on the study list) from the number of "hits" (the number of items on the study list that were correctly identified).

Figure 7.5 shows the results of a classic experiment by Schonfield and Robertson (1966) that contrasted the recall and recognition abilities of different-aged adults. The lower line shows an age-related decline for recall. In contrast, the top line indicates that recognition is relatively unimpaired by aging.

Why should aging have a detrimental effect on recall, but not recognition? It could be that recall and recognition tap the efficacy of the episodic and semantic memory systems, respectively. When performing a recall task, most participants try to think back to the study session and "remember" words they actually studied. When performing a recognition test, however, participants may be guided by feelings of familiarity rather than actual recollection. Thus, when given a recognition task, an individual can look at a test item and have the vague feeling that he "knows" the word was on the list, even though he can't actually remember studying it.

Age Differences in Remembering
versus Knowing the Past

Endel Tulving (1993) has proposed that when we experience an episodic memory, we feel as if we *remember* something, while when we experience a semantic memory, we feel as if we *know* something. An interesting paradigm used to understand the differences in remembering versus knowing the past has been developed by Gardiner and colleagues (Gardiner & Java, 1990; Gardiner & Parkin, 1990). In this methodology, each participant is given a study list of common words or faces. Then the participant is given a recognition task in which he is required to classify each of the items he claims to have recognized as an item that he either remembers (**R response**) or knows (**K response**) was on the study list. Interestingly, increasing the length of the study-test interval and making participants divide their attention during study has a detrimental influence on the frequency of R responses, yet no influence on K responses. These data are important because they reinforce the idea that R and K responses reflect the operations of different memory systems.

Parkin and Walter (1992) used this paradigm to examine age differences in the episodic and semantic memories. The results of their research are shown in box figure 7.A, which shows that younger people make more R than K responses, but older individuals make more K than R responses! Furthermore, Parkin and Walter (1992) found that the elderly participants' tendency to display a decrement in R responses was related to poor performance on a neuropsychological test of frontal lobe function.

The data Parkin and Walter reported support the contention that, as a result of frontal lobe dysfunction, older individuals experience a deficit in episodic memory and compensate for it by relying on semantic memory. How could this pattern of impairment and preservation affect the everyday life of the typical older adult? When they encounter events, persons, or things from the recent past, older individuals may experience vague feelings of "familiarity" and "just knowing." In contrast, they may process memories from the distant past (childhood and adolescence) on an episodic basis. Thus the older person might "remember" the past, but just "know about" the present.

Box Figure 7.A Recognition as a function of response type in a group of older subjects and a group of younger subjects matched on overall recognition accuracy. *Source:* Parkin, A. J., & Walter, B. M. (1992). Recollective experience, normal aging, and frontal dysfunction. *Psychology and Aging, 7,* 293.

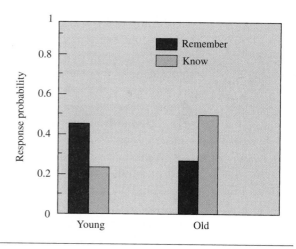

Another reason why recall is harder than recognition is that good recall performance may demand that individuals engage in complex processes when learning (or encoding) the information they must subsequently remember. Three types of encoding processes appear especially important: organization, semantic elaboration, and mental imagery.

Effective **organization** of information means that individuals categorize study items in some conceptual manner. In experiments within this line of research (Backman, Mantyla, & Herlitz, 1990; Hultsch, 1971), some participants receive instructions to sort (or organize) a number of words by category. Other individuals are merely told to remember words. They are not instructed to organize the study items in any particular way. When recall is tested, older adults perform much worse than younger adults

Figure 7.5
Recognition and recall scores as a function of age.

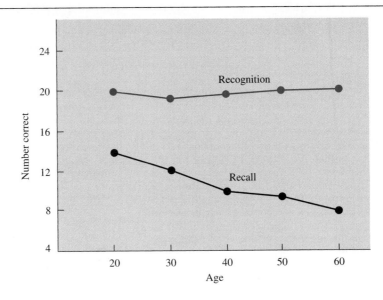

in the no-organization condition, whereas age differences are minimized in the organization condition. Furthermore, younger adults tend to recall just as many items regardless of whether they are told to organize them at study, whereas older adults recalled substantially more items when they were instructed to use an organizational strategy. This suggests that younger, but not older, adults spontaneously use complex organizational strategies when they study material they expect to need to remember.

Semantic elaboration means embellishing a study item by linking it to some piece of conceptually-related information. Smith (1977) required adults to study a list of words under three different conditions. Adults in the no-cue condition were shown a list of words (e.g., *apple, yellow, horse,* etc.) and instructed to learn it. Those in the structural-cue condition saw each word on the list along with its first letter (*apple*—A). Those in the semantic-cue condition saw each word on the list along with a category the word belonged to (*apple*—fruit). Age-related differences in recall appeared in the first two conditions: The young group (aged 20 to 39) had the best recall, the late-adulthood group (aged 60 to 80) had the poorest, and the middle-aged group (aged 40 to 59) was intermediate. However, in the semantic-cue condition, recall was approximately equal in all age groups! These findings suggest that an age-related decline in recall might be eliminated by incorporating semantic elaboration at the time of study.

Another process known to affect long-term memory performance is **mental imagery.** One study (Mason & Smith, 1977) focused on the recall of individuals in early, middle, and late adulthood. Those in the imagery condition were instructed to form mental images for each word on a list, but those in the control condition were given no instructions to aid recall. Imagery instructions did not affect recall in the early- and late-adulthood groups but did improve recall in the middle-adulthood group. Indeed, middle-aged adults in the imagery condition performed as well as young adults, though in the control condition their performance fell below that of young adults. These results indicate that using imagery at encoding serves to eliminate age differences in recall.

However, the imagery encoding procedure effective with middle-aged adults was not effective with elderly adults.

In summary, the research suggests that organization, elaboration, and imagery might be less efficient or less likely to occur in old age, and that with appropriate techniques, older adults can overcome or at least reduce deficits in recall. Most puzzling, of course, is the question of why most older people don't use these strategies naturally to aid memory.

Source Memory

Source memory is the ability to remember the context (i.e., the exact time and/or place) in which a particular piece of information was learned. Remembering that last Saturday evening at 8:00, while you were cooking dinner, your best friend telephoned to say that she is moving to California, is an example of a source memory. In contrast, remembering that your best friend is moving to California but not remembering how and/or when your learned this information is an example of fact memory.

Traditionally, source memory has been measured by presenting subjects with fictitious facts (Tom Hanks's stepfather was a firefighter) or obscure facts (Bingo is the name of the dog on the Cracker Jack box). At a later date, individuals take a recall test (What was the occupation of Tom Hanks's stepfather?) or recognition test (Tom Hanks's stepfather was a: (1) police officer, (2) firefighter, (3) baker, or (4) mechanic). They are also asked to provide information about when and/or where they learned each fact that they correctly recalled or recognized (How did you first learn that Tom Hanks's stepfather was a firefighter? Did you read it in a magazine or hear about it on TV?). Problems with source memory are apparent when individuals can remember facts but are incapable of remembering the exact context within which they first learned a fact.

Using this methodology, researchers (Janowsky et al., 1989) have found that neurological patients with damage to the frontal cortex display pronounced source memory deficits despite the fact that their ability to recall or recognize factual information is as good as that of control subjects. It has also been shown (Craik, Morris, Morris, & Loewen, 1990; McIntyre & Craik, 1987; Schacter, Kasniak, Kihlstrom, & Valdiserri, 1991) that elderly adults are more likely to commit source errors than younger adults—even when younger and older individuals match on the amount of fact memory! Finally, the magnitude of source error rates among the elderly is related to their performance on neuropsychological tests that measure the integrity of the frontal cortex.

Consider the following scenario in order to grasp some of the real-life consequences of a breakdown in source memory. A younger and older adult walk through a supermarket checkout line and notice the following headline on a tabloid newspaper: "Wearing a Copper Bracelet Will Cure Insomnia." A few days later, both of these individuals remember the fact that they recently became aware of the claim that a copper bracelet is a valid treatment for insomnia. Since the younger adult has intact source monitoring skills, he dismisses this claim as nonsense because he remembers that he read about it in an unreliable source. The older adult, because he possesses poor source memory skills, "remembers" that he heard about the advantages of wearing copper bracelets by listening to a world-renowned physician who was interviewed on a credible TV news program. Consequently, the older person begins wearing a copper bracelet.

It is not commonplace to directly ask an individual to recall the source of a particular piece of information. Thus, assessing source memory via the traditional methodology may yield an overly liberal estimate of an individual's ability to monitor sources within real-life contexts. Source monitoring usually takes place implicitly as a component of some ongoing cognitive activity. This indirect and unintentional form of source memory may have the greatest impact on everyday behavior and decision making.

Because traditional tests of source monitoring may not generalize to situations outside the laboratory, Larry Jacoby and his colleagues (Jacoby, Kelley, Brown, & Jasechko, 1989) developed an alternative methodology—the Fame Judgment Task. In this paradigm, research participants read a series of nonfamous names, such as Bruce Hudson. Then they are shown a list of names and are asked to indicate which are famous. Items consist of previously presented nonfamous names (e.g., Bruce Hudson), nonfamous names that the participants were not previously exposed to (e.g., Shawn Johnson), and famous names (e.g., John Milton). Individuals are reminded that all of the names they previously read were nonfamous and that some of these names may appear on the current list. If a person consciously recollects that he or she previously read a name on the list, the participant should judge the name as "nonfamous" without hesitation. Alternatively, if a person fails to remember that a name appeared on the reading task, but is nevertheless familiar with the name due to the prior exposure, the person might mistakenly judge the name as "famous." A misattribution of fame to a previously presented nonfamous name is defined as a source error. Thus, the Fame Judgment Task allows an experimenter to determine if, in the absence of conscious recollection, an individual can monitor the source of the familiarity that surrounds a test item.

Dywan and Jacoby (1990) found that elderly adults are much more likely than younger adults to display source errors on the Fame Judgment Task. In other words, they are much more likely than college students to claim that "Bruce Hudson" is, in fact, a famous person. Thus, older adults are not able to use their conscious recollection of when and/or where they last saw the name "Bruce Hudson" to oppose the effects of familiarity and prevent a source error.

Dywan and Jacoby (1990) offered several examples of how an inability to monitor source on an implicit basis might affect an older adult's ability to function in everyday life. For example, sitting down to play cards with a group of friends may serve as a cue for an older adult to remember a funny story from her distant past. Telling the story the first time at the card table might unconsciously influence her by later making the story pop into her mind during future card games with her friends. If her conscious memory of telling the story does not oppose her unconscious tendency to repeat it, she may retell the story countless times to her card-playing companions.

First Memories and Infantile Amnesia

Until now, we have discussed the results of laboratory studies of age differences in memory. In these experiments, participants are given lists of arbitrary items to learn, and their memories are tested shortly afterward. This research, while important, may not tell us much about how aging affects the everyday or personal aspects of human memory.

When people are asked to remember a real-life experience, they are engaging in an autobiographical memory task. For example, can you remember something that happened at your high school graduation, or the last time you ate a pizza? Autobiographical memory allows each of us to become our own personal historian. We are continually engaged in the process of writing, editing, and updating the stories of our own lives (Nelson, 1993).

An individual's first recallable autobiographical memory usually comes from the middle of the fourth year of life. Psychologists have coined the term **infantile amnesia** to describe the fact that the typical adult cannot remember life experiences from the first three and one-half years of life. Psychoanalysts, such as Sigmund Freud, speculated that infantile amnesia was caused by the repression of traumatic sexual experiences. Later, psychologists and researchers suggested that infantile amnesia was due to the neurological immaturity of the declarative memory system (Moscovitch, 1986). Without an "up-and-running" declarative memory system, there could be no conscious recollection of the past. Several lines of more contemporary research, however, have made it clear that the declarative memory system is operative within the first year of life (McKee & Squire, 1993). Nowadays, theorists believe that the offset of infantile amnesia is linked to the development of a rudimentary sense of self or self-consciousness that emerges during the fourth year of life. It seems we cannot remember events from our early lives until we develop a "self" that is capable of experiencing (and remembering) those events (Howe & Courage, 1993; Nelson, 1993; Usher & Neisser, 1993). This theoretical perspective suggests that cognitive function and personality and social processes are interconnected.

The vast amount of research on infantile amnesia has focused on children. Not much is known about the first memories of elderly persons. Do older adults have earlier- (or later-) occurring first memories in comparison to younger adults? What types of psychological variables predict the age of younger and older adults' first memories? Rybash and Hrubi (1997) conducted two studies that examined the roles that intellectual and psychodynamic factors play in the first memories of younger and older individuals. They found that the relationship between IQ test scores and age of first memories was identical for members of both age groups; younger and older adults who scored above average on various facets of IQ had earlier first memories than individuals who displayed below-par performance. This finding replicated Rabbitt and McInnis's earlier research (1988) that showed that "smarter" older adults tend to have earlier first memories.

Rybash and Hrubi (1997) also found that psychodynamic factors affect younger and older adults' first memories. They reported that the need to reminisce about the past to prepare for death was more typical (as well as more adaptive) for older than for younger adults. Reminiscing as part of death preparation was negatively related to the age of an older adult's first memory, but positively related to the age of a younger adult's first memory. It makes sense that older adults who think about the past to prepare themselves for death would have deeper, richer, and earlier memories of their childhoods than those who do not reminisce for this purpose. These individuals may be facing the final portion of the life span with a sense of ego integrity (Erikson, 1968). Alternatively, it may be that younger individuals who have a developmentally inappropriate way of reminiscing have a difficult time gaining access to their personal pasts.

Another point to consider is that the elderly participants in Rybash and Hrubi's (1997) research reported first memories that occurred later in life (at approximately 4 years of age) than did younger adults (approximately 3.5 years of age). This finding could reflect a genuine age difference in the ability to remember one's personal past, or a conservative bias in older adults' willingness to estimate the age of their earliest memory. Whatever the basis for this age difference, Rybash and Hrubi recorded the narrative rather than the historical truth about the exact age at which participants' first memories occurred (cf. Bruner, 1986). Rybash and Hrubi argued that the retrieval of early memory is a constructive process representing the interaction of diverse systems that operate according to similar (or different) rules across different developmental periods.

Not all remote memories from the distant past are autobiographical. Bahrick, Bahrick, and Wittlinger (1975) investigated memory for high school classmates after a long interval. The research assessed face recognition, name recognition, and name-face matching. It also evaluated free and cued recall of names in response to faces. The participants differed in the number of years that had elapsed since their high school graduation (from 3 months to 47 years since graduation). Figure 7.6 shows that recognition and matching performance were nearly constant (and nearly perfect) up to a retention interval of 34 years. Adults in their midfifties were performing about as well as 18-year-olds. In contrast, the recall measures, particularly free recall, showed clear evidence of an age-related decline that began shortly after graduation. Of special interest is the steady drop in free recall from the 3-year interval (adults about 21 years old) to the 47-year interval (adults about 65 years old). Bahrick and his colleagues found similar results when they measured long-term retention of academic information (e.g., geography and foreign language) learned in high school.

Flashbulb Memories and the Reminiscence Bump

Some events are indelibly printed in memory, such as the events of September 11, 2001. A **flashbulb memory** is an exceptionally vivid, detailed, and long lasting mental image of a personal experienced event. Fitzgerald (1988) asked a group of older adults (approximately 70 years of age) to write a paragraph describing three different **flashbulb memories.** Participants wrote about vivid memories that occurred at any time over the course of their lives. Fitzgerald also asked the research participants to rate each vivid memory on several dimensions. These dimensions included personal importance, national importance, frequency of rehearsal, and intensity of emotional reaction.

Fitzgerald (1988) showed that participants were unlikely to recall vivid memories from middle adulthood or old age. Instead, these older adults were most likely to recall vivid memories from their late adolescence and early adulthood. The tendency for older adults to recall more vivid memories from an early time period has been called the **reminiscence bump** (see figure 7.7). The data for the study were collected shortly after the *Challenger* explosion in the early 1980s, yet, none of the participants included this event in their list of vivid memories. Some of the older adults' vivid memories possessed a

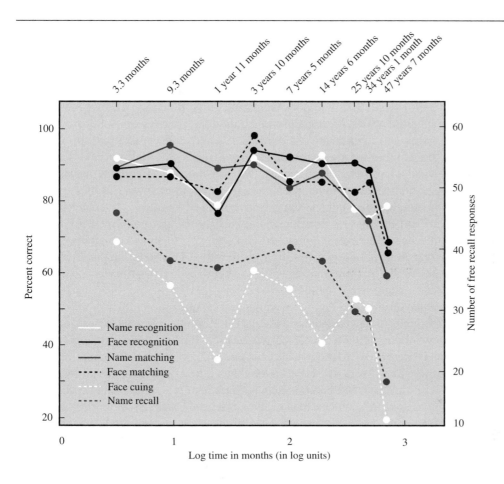

Figure 7.6
Recognition and recall of names and faces of high school colleagues.

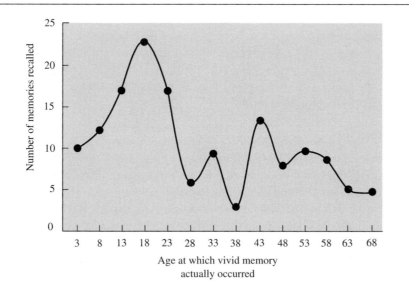

Figure 7.7 Age at which vivid memories occurred for older adults.

great deal of emotional importance (e.g., a soldier remembering his friends dying in combat, and a mother remembering the birth of her daughter). Recently, Finkenauer et al. (1998) showed that emotional processes play a role in memory for salient events.

Why does the age distribution of vivid memories yield a reminiscence bump rather than an orderly pattern of retention? Fitzgerald (1988, 1996) speculated that adolescence and young adulthood may be the period of the life span when we are forming unique personal identities. We may use this period as a marker or anchor from which to begin the story of our adult psychological selves. Thus, because of the special status we attach to this time, we may have distinctive memories from this period. Fitzgerald (1988, 1996) also suggested that because we live in a youth-oriented society, older adults may be motivated to maintain a storehouse of vivid memories from a time when they were young, healthy, and had their lives in front of them.

Jansari and Parkin (1996) offer an explanation of the reminiscence bump that complements the one Fitzgerald proposed. They suggest that we have a bias, in an unconstrained recall task, to report first-time memories ("The first time that X happened to me was when . . ."). There may thus be an abundance of first-time memories from late adolescence and young adulthood.

Others have suggested that older adults have a much more difficult time forming flashbulb memories than younger individuals. For example, Cohen, Conway, and Maylor (1994), who worked with a large sample of individuals from the United Kingdom, showed that 90 percent of younger adults, but only 42 percent of older adults, had flashbulb memories for a distinctive event in the news media—the unexpected resignation of British prime minister Margaret Thatcher. These results are intriguing because in the vast number of instances, older adults who experienced flashbulb memories scored the same as older adults who did not on several encoding and rehearsal variables surrounding the prime minister's resignation (e.g., How much did you think about her resignation?, How surprising was her resignation?, How intense was your reaction to her resignation?, How interested are you in politics?, etc.). In fact, both groups of older adults' scores on these questions were essentially identical to the scores of younger adults who did possess flashbulb memories! The low incidence of vivid memories among the older adults could not have been caused by low levels of rehearsal, interest, or reactivity. Cohen et al. (1994) speculated that the neurological factors that underlie age differences in source memory (i.e., the inability to remember the exact contextual details of a given piece of information) may be responsible for age-related deficits in forming flashbulb memories as well.

False Memories

If older adults are less capable of remembering events that actually occurred, are they also more likely to remember events that never happened to them? Recently, the issue of false memories has become an extremely controversial topic. There have been several cases, chronicled in the media, in which adults have experienced "recovered memories" of traumatic childhood events such as being the victim of sexual abuse or witnessing a murder. On the basis of these recovered memories, a wide range of individuals, including family members, priests, and day-care workers, have been accused (and sometimes convicted) of serious crimes (Loftus & Ketcham, 1994).

Some recovered memories are, in actuality, *false memories* implanted in people's minds by unscrupulous or biased psychotherapists (Loftus & Ketcham, 1994). Consequently, scientists have become very interested in developing methodologies that help crime investigators to distinguish true from false memories, and in determining the extent to which different groups, especially young children and elderly adults, are susceptible to the false memory effect.

One of the best ways to study false memories has been popularized by Roediger and McDermott (1995). If you were a participant in their research, you would be instructed to listen to a list of words such as *nurse, sick, health, hospital, office, cure, operation,* and *medicine.* Then you would be asked to recall as many of the words as possible. (Close your eyes and try to recall the list items as accurately as you can.) Roediger and McDermott selected a false target word that was not presented on the list but was strongly associated with the other list items. For this list, the false target word was *doctor.* Roediger and McDermott (1995), who did their original research with college students, found that a large percentage of the participants confidently claimed that they remembered listening to the false target item on the study list. (Did you recall reading the word *doctor*?) In fact, college students were given 12 word lists to study, and the typical student displayed, on average, false memories for 5 of the 12 lists!

What psychological mechanisms are responsible for this false memory effect? It is possible that hearing a list of words such as *nurse, sick, health, hospital,* and so on evokes semantically related words such as *doctor.* When given a recall task, the individual can remember the word *doctor,* but he cannot remember whether he heard it on the list or just thought about it. If this theory is correct, a person's false memory of having heard the word *doctor* is a source memory error.

If false memories constitute source errors, we would expect that older adults would be more likely than younger adults to display such memory distortions. To test this hypothesis, Rybash and Hrubi (2000) presented college students, elementary school children, and elderly adults with Roediger and McDermott's word lists. Right after some of the lists were presented, participants were asked to "generate" words that were related to the list items but not on the list. The purpose was to prevent false memories by making the person think of the target item (*doctor*) and reinforcing the notion that the target item was not on the study list. Compared with a baseline condition, this generate condition reduced the incidence of memory distortions in young adults, but had no beneficial effects on either the children or the elderly.

These results, along with data from several other studies (see Schacter, 1996), lead to the conclusion that older individuals are more likely than younger individuals to experience memory distortions. However, Karpel, Hoyer, and Toglia (2001) have reported that older adults are *not* disproportionately worse in terms of memory suggestibility. That is, the effects of age on real and suggested memories were of practically the same magnitude.

Nondeclarative Memory

Nondeclarative memory does not involve the conscious recollection of past events or previous knowledge. Instead, it involves being able to do something effectively because of the beneficial effects of past experience. Being able to drive a car is an example of a nondeclarative memory. Your ability to start the engine, use the brake and accelerator pedals, turn the wheel, and so on as you drive to your friend's house depends on your ability to retrieve information from your nondeclarative memory system. Yet, as you drive you don't feel as if you are remembering anything (e.g., your driver's education class), and you don't experience any sense of pastness—you just feel as if you are doing something.

Many everyday activities involve nondeclarative memory, especially perceptual-motor skills. Activities within this category include driving a car, playing golf, playing a musical instrument, using a word processing program, tying your shoelaces, and so on.

One way to better understand the general distinction between declarative and nondeclarative aspects of memory is to consider the distinction between "memory as an object" and "memory as a tool." See Research Focus 7.2 for details.

Memory as an Object versus Memory as a Tool

What is the difference between an object and a tool? This may seem a simple and trivial question. An object is something we can look at, inspect, hold onto, and so on. A tool, in contrast, is something we could use to perform some sort of function or task. This distinction notwithstanding, it is important to realize that a particular item could be both an object and a tool. For example, a hammer is certainly an object. You can hold it in your hand, inspect it, and so forth. At the same time, a hammer is a tool. You can use it to pound a nail. A hammer becomes an "object of inquiry" versus a "tool to be used" because of the circumstances we find ourselves in. When we go to the hardware store with the intention of buying a hammer, the hammer becomes an object. When we repair a roof that has been damaged in a storm, the hammer becomes a tool.

What does the object-tool distinction have to do with memory? Our everyday, intuitive conceptualization of memory is that it is an object. A memory, it would seem, is an experience stored in mind. It is something we may inspect, analyze, and attend to. If you remember what you did last fourth of July, your memory is an object of inquiry within your conscious mind. Beyond any doubt, the object-like aspect of memory diminishes with age. Older adults have greater difficulty than younger individuals in deliberately retrieving and inspecting bits of their past lives.

Darlene Howard (1996) and James Howard suggest that the tool-like properties of memory are much less obvious—but just as important—as its objectlike characteristics. To il-

lustrate this point, Darlene Howard gives an example of showing one of her favorite films, which had a rather fuzzy and garbled soundtrack, to a psychology class. As she watched the film, she had no trouble hearing what the main characters were saying. However, the college students in her class had great difficulty deciphering what they heard. What was responsible for this effect? Was her hearing better than that of her students? Was she sitting closer to the sound system than her students? (The answer to both of the questions is a definite "no.") She suggests instead that since she had seen the film several times before, she was using her memory of the film's soundtrack to help her comprehend what she heard. The students could not do this because they were seeing the film for the first time. Most important, she was using her memory of the film in an unintentional and automatic way. In fact, she was unaware that she was remembering anything at all when she listened to the film; she had the illusion she was "hearing" the sound when she was actually "remembering" it. This shows how memory may be used as a tool for performing some current task that seems totally unrelated to memory. Memory facilitates perception of the present!

Do you think that a song you have heard several times in the past is easier to understand than a song that you're hearing for the first time? Why?

Does the tool-like quality of memory decline with age? See the sections on Priming and Implicit Memory and on Age Differences in Implicit Memory for the answer.

Priming and Implicit Memory

One way to study nondeclarative memory is to assess participants' performance on various types of priming tasks (Schacter & Buckner, 1998). In a **priming task,** individuals are asked to identify or make judgments about stimuli that were (or were not) presented during an earlier phase of an experiment. Priming is demonstrated if exposure to items during a study phase enhances performance (e.g., if there is a reduced latency of response or an increased accuracy of response) during a test phase. Consider the following priming format. Participants study a list of familiar words such as *motel.* Later they are presented with three-letter stems for items on the study list (mot____ for *motel*) and an equal number of word stems for items that did not appear at study (sha____ for *shape*). Participants are instructed to complete as many stems as possible with the first letters that pop into their minds that spell valid words. Priming is demonstrated if more stems are completed correctly for study items than for control items. This task, referred to as *word-stem completion,* provides a measure of **implicit memory** because individuals are not directly asked to complete test items with words from the study list. Their memory for the study items is instead assessed in an indirect manner.

On the other hand, in **explicit memory** tasks, an individual is instructed to deliberately recollect a previous event. Traditional tests used in memory research, such as recognition, recall, and cued-recall tasks, measure explicit memory. In a cued-recall task, for example, participants are shown a series of three-letter stems for items that were presented (mot____) or not presented (sha____) at study. They are then asked to complete as many stems as possible that spell words from the study list and to guess on the stems for which they cannot produce studied words. Explicit memory, which draws on the resources of the declarative memory system, is demonstrated if participants complete more stems for study items than for control items.

Psychologists have become excited about the distinction between explicit and implicit memory for two reasons. First, a wealth of evidence shows that brain damage has dramatically different effects on how well individuals perform implicit versus explicit memory tasks. For example, patients who suffer from amnesia display no memory whatsoever for lists of common words when tested on explicit tasks, yet the same individuals display robust levels of performance when tested on implicit tasks. The finding that amnesics perform exceptionally well on priming tasks, despite the fact that they are unaware they are remembering on an indirect basis, has led some psychologists to categorize implicit memory as memory without awareness. Second, with non-brain-injured individuals, various independent variables have differential effects on implicit versus explicit tasks. For example, consider an experiment in which participants encode common words (e.g., *sharp*) in a shallow ("Is there an e in this word?") or a semantic ("Is this word the opposite of dull?") manner. Research demonstrates that semantic encoding facilitates explicit memory more than shallow encoding. In contrast, these two encoding procedures have the same effect on implicit memory. Furthermore, a long delay in the study-test interval (e.g., one week) significantly reduces individuals' performance on explicit tasks, but has no effect on their performance on various implicit tasks.

This evidence points to the conclusion that implicit and explicit tasks reflect the operation of distinct memory systems that are associated with different brain regions (e.g., Schacter, 2000). Most researchers would agree that performance on explicit tasks is under the control of the declarative memory system, which has its neurological basis in the hippocampus, frontal cortex, and diencephalon. The issue of which brain regions control performance on implicit tasks is a much more complex and controversial issue. Daniel Schacter (Schacter 1994, 1996) has argued that priming is regulated by posterior neural regions that process information about the physical/surface (but not the semantic) features of words and objects. Schacter labeled these brain areas the Perceptual Representation System (PRS).

Age Differences in Implicit Memory

One implication of the growing body of research suggesting that memory systems can be experimentally dissociated in normal and brain-injured populations is that we can more easily compare younger and older adults' performance on implicit and explicit tasks. Obviously, this may help us achieve a better understanding of the stabilities and losses that characterize the aging of human memory. For example, perhaps aging has an influence on memory identical to the one associated with amnesia: A person's ability to perform explicit tasks is impaired, but his or her ability to perform implicit tasks is spared.

Normal aging, Alzheimer's disease, and amnesia do not impair performance on priming tasks that are highly perceptual, that depend solely on posterior brain regions such as the PRS, and that make minimal retrieval demands (Rybash, 1996). An example of such a priming task is called *word naming*. In this task, a person reads words such as *motel* that appear one at a time on a computer screen, and the experimenter measures the exact number of milliseconds it takes to read each item. At another time (e.g., one hour, one day, or one week later), the participant reads another list of words, half of which were read at study (*motel*) and half of which were not (*shape*). Priming is measured by comparing the speed at which the participant reads study versus control words. The fact that aging, AD, and amnesia have no ill effect on some types of priming opens up the possibility that psychologists might develop memory rehabilitation programs based on implicit memory for brain-injured or demented individuals (Camp, Foss, O'Hanlon, & Stevens, 1996).

On the other hand, it seems that aging has a slight, but statistically significant, effect on a person's ability to perform priming tasks such as word-stem completion. These tasks seem to draw on both conceptual as well as perceptual abilities, possess a strong retrieval component, and are controlled by the interaction of anterior and posterior brain centers. It is interesting to note that patients with AD, but not amnesia, perform in a subpar manner on word-stem completion tasks.

Based on the available evidence, Rybash (1996) concluded that the performance of older adults across a wide range of priming tasks is more similar to the performance of patients with AD than to that of individuals with amnesia. This suggests that amnesia does not serve as an adequate model for understanding age-related changes in human memory, while the memory changes associated with AD and normative aging are united by a common thread. However, these conclusions do not necessarily imply that AD represents an acceleration of the normal aging process.

One drawback associated with priming task methodology is that explicit memory may contaminate implicit memory performance, especially in non-brain-damaged individuals. This means that when performing a word-stem completion task, some individuals may deliberately try to remember words from a study list in order to complete word stems, whereas other persons may unintentionally recall study items when they are attempting to complete word stems under implicit instructions. Furthermore, one could argue that the age difference favoring younger adults on priming tasks such as word-stem completion is an artifact of developmental changes in conscious recollection that favor younger adults. Research Focus 7.3 provides information about an ingenious approach for studying "memory without awareness." The approach in the Research Focus article is very different from the priming paradigm.

Conclusions about Aging and Memory

It seems that older adults are at a distinct disadvantage when they perform explicit tasks for recently acquired information that focus on the objectlike properties of memory that the declarative memory system controls. Explicit memory for events from the distant past, however, seems to hold up remarkably well with age. Likewise, older adults perform almost as well as younger individuals when performing implicit tasks that draw upon the tool-like aspects of memory that the nondeclarative memory system controls.

Along with age-related changes in some aspects of memory performance, changes in the subjective dimension of memory also occur. The younger adult's memory of a past experience is accompanied by a sense of remembering, whereas the older person's recollections of the past are marked by feelings of knowing. Another way to think of the relationship between memory and aging is to draw a distinction between memory processing and memory knowledge. As we have seen, aging is associated with a decline in the speed and efficiency of the processes responsible for establishing new memories. This decline, however, does not affect the amount of knowledge already stored within memory, which is still available for many different tasks. Thus, age-related declines may be restricted to tasks in which a person's prior knowledge is not used. Tasks that capitalize on previously learned information may show no age-related declines; indeed, on such tasks, older people may even outperform young adults. The distinction between remembering and knowing is similar to the distinction between fluid and crystallized intelligence (discussed in chapter 8), and to the theory of encapsulation (discussed in chapter 9).

A final point to consider is that individuals possess varying amounts of knowledge in selected domains of work, sports, hobbies, music, and other areas. Access to such knowledge is unaffected by aging. Individuals maintain their ability to use well-learned knowledge, strategies, and skills throughout middle age and into old age (Rybash, Hoyer, & Roodin, 1986). Tests of factual knowledge (e.g., vocabulary or news events) typically show no decline from young adulthood to old age (Hoyer & Touron, 2002).

It may be unnecessary and inaccurate to suggest that there are specific types of memory aging deficits, because most of the age variance in memory performance can be

Process Dissociation Procedure

The priming methodology, even though it has yielded a wealth of important data, possesses a serious drawback. Individuals may, on either a voluntary or involuntary basis, use their explicit recollection of a study list when they are performing a priming task. Thus, their explicit memory may contaminate their implicit memory. At the same time, it is possible that unconscious memory processes may influence a person's behavior on an explicit memory task!

How can we eliminate the unwanted influence of conscious recollection on implicit tasks, and unconscious recollection on explicit tasks? Larry Jacoby (Jacoby, 1991; Jacoby, Yonelinas, & Jennings, 1996) has proposed a novel approach to this problem. He developed a technique called the **Process Dissociation Procedure (PDP)** that estimates the degree to which conscious and unconscious (or automatic) factors independently contribute to performance on memory tests. The key to the PDP is a comparison of individuals' performance on inclusion and exclusion memory tasks. In an inclusion task, conscious and unconscious processes work in concert because participants are asked to respond with items that appeared at study. In an exclusion task, however, conscious and unconscious processes work in opposition because participants are asked to respond with items that did not appear at study. Comparing the degree to which individuals respond with studied items on an inclusion task and on an exclusion task yields separate estimates of conscious and unconscious influences on memory.

For example, say a group of individuals learns a list of common words such as *motel,* and their memory is tested by having them complete word stems such as mot_____ . In the inclusion condition, participants are told to complete the stem with a word they remember from the study list and to just guess if they cannot remember a word from the study list. Given these instructions, pretend a person does what we tell him to do. He completes the stem as *motel.* Why? Jacoby suggests that the response *motel* could have occurred because the person consciously recollected *motel* or because the person unconsciously recollected *motel* but experienced a failure of conscious recollection.

In the exclusion condition, participants would be told to complete the stem with a word that was not on the study list. Given these instructions, say a person does what we tell him not to do. He completes the stem as *motel.* Why? Jacoby argues that the response *motel* could have occurred because the person unconsciously recollected *motel* but experienced a failure of conscious recollection.

Given these assumptions, the strength of conscious recollection is determined by subtracting the probability of producing study items on the inclusion tasks from the probability of producing study items on the exclusion task (Conscious Recollection = Inclusion − Exclusion). An estimate of the strength of unconscious recollection is determined by dividing the probability of producing study items on the exclusion task by the failure of conscious recollection [Unconscious Recollection = Exclusion/(1-Conscious Recollection)].

Research using the PDP has consistently shown that older adults display lower levels of conscious recollection than younger adults (Jennings & Jacoby, 1993, 1997; Rybash & Hoyer, 1996b; Rybash, DeLuca, & Rubenstein, 1997; Rybash, Santoro, & Hoyer, 1998). However, it remains unclear as to whether age differences occur in unconscious contributions to memory.

One of the most exciting aspects of the PDP approach involves detecting age- and disease-related memory deficits (Jacoby, Jennings, & Hay, 1996; Jennings & Jacoby, 1997). For example, telling the same story to a friend on more than

---

attributed to a general aging factor. The evidence suggesting that the effects of aging on memory are about the same regardless of type of memory being measured comes mainly from meta-analytic studies (e.g., La Voie & Light, 1994; Verhaeghen & Marcoen, 1993; Verhaeghen, Marcoen, & Goossens, 1993). In the Verhaeghen, Marcoen, and Goossens (1993) meta-analysis, the average size of the age difference between younger and older adults in recall from episodic memory was about one standard deviation for all studies that used different measures of episodic memory. La Voie and Light (1994) reported the same effect size for episodic recall and a somewhat smaller effect size for episodic recognition. Thus, there really are age-related deficits in memory (Zacks, Hasher, & Li, 2000).

Process Dissociation Procedure

Box Table 7.A

Estimated Strength of Conscious and Unconscious Memory Processes for Repeated Items in the 3 and 12 Lag Conditions

	Conscious Processes		Unconscious Processes	
	Lag 3	Lag 12	Lag 3	Lag 12
Younger Adults	.90	.83	.64	.66
Older Adults	.71	.51	.67	.74

one occasion (i.e., unnecessarily repeating yourself) certainly represents a failure of memory. However, we would be much more concerned about an individual who repeats the same story after five minutes than a person who repeats himself after an interval of five weeks.

How capable are older adults at detecting and avoiding unwanted repetition? What role do conscious and unconscious memory processes have in promoting (or avoiding) repetition? To address these issues, Jennings and Jacoby (1997) conducted an experiment in which younger and older participants studied a list of words. Then the participants were given inclusion and exclusion versions of a recognition task that contained previously studied words as well as control words not on the original study list. Most importantly, some of the control words only appeared once on the memory tasks. In contrast, other control words were repeated after 3 or 12 intervening test items occurred. (These items were said to be in the 3 and 12 lag conditions, respectively.) On the inclusion task, participants were instructed to say yes to study items and repeated control items, and no to brand new control items. On the exclusion task, participants were instructed to say yes to study items and no to both repeated and nonrepeated control

items. This methodology allowed Jennings and Jacoby to compute the estimated strength of conscious and unconscious contributions to memory for repeated control words at each lag condition.

The results of the experiment (as shown in box table 7.A) were clear-cut. Namely, age differences in unconscious processes were not found at either lag interval. However, older adults were much less likely to consciously recollect that a control item was repeated during the test phase of the experiment, even when only three words intervened between the repetitions of a control word. This suggests that older adults repeat themselves because of a failure to consciously use recollection to oppose the unconscious tendency toward repetition—not because unconscious processes, by themselves, are more powerful in the elderly. (Note that Ste.-Marie, Jennings, & Finlayson [1996] found this same pattern of performance in younger brain-injured adults.) A final observation is that older adults exhibited large deficits in conscious recollection compared with younger adults. This suggests that previous reports of spared recognition memory in older individuals was probably due to the contaminating influence of unconscious memory processes on conscious recollection.

Attention

Probably too much emphasis is given to the study of memory, and too little emphasis to the study of attention and learning and how these processes affect the encoding and retrieval of information. The term *attention* refers to the capacity or energy necessary to support information processing (Plude & Hoyer, 1985). The limited attentional capacities of humans become evident when we observe a wide variety of cognitive activities. There are varieties of attention, including alertness, ignoring distractions, selecting relevant from irrelevant information, and handling multiple sources of information simultaneously. The two aspects of attention most affected by aging are selective attention and divided attention (McDowd & Shaw, 2000).

Selective Attention

Selective attention refers to the ability to distinguish relevant from irrelevant information. Selective attention is required when we are trying to concentrate on something we are reading while trying to ignore irrelevant or interfering information such as loud or unpleasant music.

In the laboratory, researchers frequently use *visual search* tasks to study age-related differences in the factors that affect selective attention. In a visual search task, the participant decides if the target item is present in displays containing different numbers of distractor items. Typically, older adults are more affected by the number of distractors than are younger adults. It has been reported that older adults are at a disadvantage when the target can appear anywhere in the display to be searched, and the task is to find or localize the target (Plude & Hoyer, 1986). Age differences are smaller or nonexistent in *filtering tasks;* in these tasks, the target item is always in the same location, and the person's task is to identify the item in the presence or absence of distractor information. It is well established that age-related declines occur in the ability to attend to relevant information while trying to ignore distracting information (McDowd & Shaw, 2000).

Divided Attention

Divided attention deficits are evident when there are problems in distributing attention across multiple sources of information. Doing two tasks at once, or having to pay attention to two things at the same time, would probably be more difficult for older adults than for younger adults. Generally, when we have to do two or more tasks at once, our performance on each of the tasks suffers; for example, we find it difficult to track two conversations at the same time, or to concentrate on what we are reading while also listening to an interesting conversation. Divided attention deficits may be responsible for the difficulties that older drivers experience in some situations. For example, driving a car in heavy traffic in unfamiliar surroundings while looking for a specific road sign is a real-life divided-attention task. Although it is frequently reported that there are age-related deficits in divided attention, older adults do not fare more poorly than younger adults in relatively simple divided-attention situations (McDowd & Birren, 1990) or when initial age differences in nondivided attention are taken into account (Salthouse & Somberg, 1982). It can be concluded that age-related differences in divided attention emerge when performance in complex tasks is assessed, but age-related decrements are negligible when simple and relatively automatic tasks are used. In fact, McDowd and Craik (1988) suggested that overall task complexity, rather than the requirement to divide attention per se, may account for age-related performance decrements on divided-attention tasks. The ability to ignore or inhibit irrelevant information affects our performance in many kinds of tasks. One of the primary hypotheses in cognitive aging is that age decrements in inhibitory processes can account for many aspects of aging and cognitive functioning (e.g., Zacks, Hasher, & Li, 2000).

An important related area of research concerns the effects of aging on **task switching** and **executive control processes.** It has been reported that there are age-related deficits in situations that require switching mental sets or that require the coordination active control of task switching (e.g., Kramer, Hahn, & Gopher, 1999; Mayr, 2001; Verhaeghen, Kliegl, & Mayr, 1997).

Limited Attentional Resources

Age-related differences in attention have been described in terms of limitations in *general-purpose processing resources.* Although several kinds of evidence suggest that age-related limitations exist in processing resources, researchers must avoid circular explanations of aging phenomena. That is, age differences should *not* be attributed to a decline in some resource or capacity that cannot be measured. Again, it is worth noting that there is very little age variance left to be explained after speed of processing is taken into account (Cerella, 1990; Verhaeghen & Salthouse, 1997).

Learning

Pronounced age differences have been reported for many types of learning (e.g., see Hoyer & Touron, 2002; Kausler, 1994). For example, in an early study by Thorndike, Bregman, Tilton, and Woodyard (1928), right-handed young adults between the ages of 20 and 25 years and right-handed older adults between the ages of 35 and 57 years were given 15 hours of practice writing left-handed. Large age differences occurred in the rate at which writing speed improved with practice. Recent studies of the effects of age on technology use have also revealed that acquisition is slower for older adults than for younger adults (e.g., Czaja, 2001; Rogers & Fisk, 2001).

Researchers have reported that there is an age-related deficit in associative learning; that is, older adults require more presentations to learn and remember simple associations (Jenkins & Hoyer, 2000). An age-related deficit in developing cognitive skills has also been reported (e.g., Touron, Hoyer, & Cerella, 2001).

Did I take my pills today? Older adults frequently rely on a mnemonic aid such as a time-coded pill box to keep track of complicated medical regimens.

Explaining the Effects of Aging on Memory, Attention, and Learning

We now turn our attention to three different approaches to the study of age-related memory deficits: with neuroscience, information processing, and contextual. Each of these approaches attempts to understand the aging of memory from a different perspective or level of analysis.

Neuroscience Approach

The **neuroscience approach** maintains that age-related memory deficits may be traced to changes in brain function. As we mentioned in chapter 3, several structural changes occur at the neuronal level as we age, such as the emergence of senile plaques and neurofibrillary tangles. Concentrations of neurotransmitters, including acetylcholine, diminish with age. These changes, along with cell death and atrophy, occur in varying degrees throughout the brain, but are especially prominent within the frontal cortex (Raz, 2000).

There are several ways in which age-related deterioration of the frontal cortex explains the most prominent losses in explicit memory that older adults display. For example, Moscovitch (1994) proposed that the hippocampus and frontal cortex are involved in the automatic retrieval and strategic retrieval of declarative memories, respectively. Automatic retrieval occurs when an individual perceives a specific environmental cue so that a memory spontaneously pops into a person's mind. For example, seeing an ad in the newspaper for an Italian restaurant may automatically trigger your recollection of the last time you and your friends had a pizza together (as well as a salivary response). Strategic retrieval occurs when a person is not provided with external cues to prime memory. In other words, the individual must use an effortful strategy to retrieve a particular memory. For example, you would have to develop a strategy to find the memory that answers the following question, "When was the last time you had pizza?"

Retrieval of a declarative memory requires a conscious, "on-line," deliberate strategy. Generating and using a retrieval strategy sometimes requires working memory. As you would guess, the frontal cortex (not the hippocampus) regulates this aspect of memory (Schacter, 2000; West, 1996).

Recently, Schacter et al. (1996) used the PET methodology to examine some of the claims Moscovitch made. These researchers found that blood flow increased to the frontal lobes when individuals tried to search for a memory (strategic retrieval), whereas blood flow increased to the hippocampus when a memory was actually recollected (associative retrieval). Furthermore, their data showed that older adults showed less activation of the frontal cortex during strategic retrieval than did younger adults. Age differences in blood flow to the hippocampus were minimal. This suggests that age differences in memory crop up when strategic retrieval is called for, and that age declines in the frontal cortex underlie age differences in strategic retrieval (see also Raz, 2000).

New findings show how a particular protein in the brain is responsible for converting short-term memories into long-term memories (Frankland et al., 2001). In a healthy brian, the hippocampus stores information on a temporary basis. When information is converted into long-term memory, the hippocampus interacts with the prefrontal cortex. If problems occur in either the hippocampus or the cortex, memory impairment results. To better understand this interaction, Frankland and his colleague trained mice to accomplish certain tasks. Half the mice were genetically normal, and half had reduced levels of a key protein known as a-CaMKII. The genetically altered mice had normal hippocampal function. Both groups of mice showed an equivalent ability to learn, indicating proper functioning of the hippocampus. When memory testing took place several days later, the normal mice remembered their training. However, the memories of the genetically altered mice were impaired, showing that the protein-deficient cortex did not convert learning into memory.

Information-Processing Approach

The **information-processing approach** emphasizes the kinds of cognitive processes involved in memory. Some researchers have focused on the nature of age differences in the encoding, storage, and retrieval aspects of memory (Zacks, Hasher, & Li, 2000). Encoding refers to the registration or pickup of information. Storage refers to the retention of information in memory and retrieval refers to finding or using information in memory. Interestingly, a large amount of evidence suggests an age-related encoding deficit, and an equally large amount of evidence suggests an age-related retrieval deficit. An **encoding deficit** suggests that elderly persons are less capable of engaging in the organizational, elaborative, and imagery processes that are helpful in memory tasks. A **retrieval deficit** implies that older adults cannot develop the strategies that would help them find stored information.

Current research using the PET and MRI methodology has increased our understanding of the nature of the encoding and retrieval processes. For example, Nyberg, Cabeza, and Tulving (1996) have shown that younger adults display a very specific pattern as blood flow increases in the left frontal cortex during encoding and in the right frontal cortex during retrieval. Interestingly, several researchers (Cabeza, 2001, Cabeza et al., 1997; Grady et al., 1995) have consistently shown that older adults exhibit diffuse and bi-lateral patterns of neural activation during encoding and retrieval. This suggests that aging is associated with *both* encoding and retrieval deficits.

Another line of research within the information-processing perspective is illustrated by the work of Tim Salthouse (2000). Salthouse has examined mediating variables that are correlated with age on memory performance; mediator variables include speed of information processing or working memory, for example. Figure 7.8 illustrates Salthouse's research strategy.

The three circles in figure 7.8 signify age, the mediating variable, and memory performance. Of crucial importance are the two areas of overlap: a and b. Area *a* represents the extent to which age is related to memory performance independent of the mediating variable; area *b* represents the extent to which performance on the mediating variable accounts for age-related differences in memory performance. In other words, this methodology allows us to determine if, after we control for the mediating variable, age still shares a significant relationship with memory.

Figure 7.8 Venn diagram showing the common variance among age, memory, and a mediating construct. The overlap in circles represents shared variance. *Source:* Smith, A. D., & Earles, J. K. J. (1996). Memory changes in normal aging. In F. Blanchard-Fields & T. M. Hess (Eds.), *Perspective on cognitive change in adulthood and aging* (p. 210). New York: McGraw-Hill.

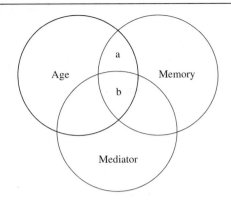

a = Proportion of variance in memory performance associated with age and not with a mediator

b = Proportion of variance in memory performance associated with both age and a mediator

Smith and Earles (1996) reviewed several studies that used this technique to examine the relationship between age and memory performance. They concluded that noncognitive mediators such as years of education and self-reported health status did little to attenuate the relationship between age and memory. However, when cognitive mediators were considered, a very different picture emerged. Smith and Earles (1996) reviewed several studies that showed that processing speed—for example, in performing very simple cognitive operations like matching abstract symbols to different numbers (+ = 3, * = 7, ≈ = 4, etc.)—mediates age differences in both working memory and free recall. And, as you will see in chapter 8, a great deal of the relationship between age and intelligence is mediated by speed of information processing. It seems that performance on measures of processing speed give us clues about the efficiency of the mind and brain.

Contextual Approach

The **contextual approach** suggests that age differences in memory can be explained by understanding the relationship between the characteristics of the memory task and the characteristics of the individual performing the task. Many characteristics of the task and of the person apart from age can determine performance in memory tasks. For example, person characteristics that might affect memory include attitudes, interests, health status, intellectual abilities, and style of learning.

Craik, Byrd, and Swanson (1987) performed an experiment inspired by the contextual approach. They studied memory ability in three groups of elderly people who ranged from 64 to 88 years of age. Group 1 consisted of highly intelligent and relatively affluent individuals. Group 2 was composed of individuals of somewhat lower intelligence and socioeconomic status who were actively involved in the community. Group 3 consisted of individuals of lower intelligence and socioeconomic status who were not involved in community or social affairs. Craik et al. also studied a group of college students matched on verbal intelligence with the first group of elderly participants. All participants received lists of words to remember. The participants differed, however, in the number of cues (the contextual support) they received at encoding and/or retrieval. Some participants were provided cues during the initial presentation of each word on a list (e.g., "a type of bird—*lark*"), but not during recall. Other participants were given this cue during recall, but not during presentation; others were cued during both presentation and recall; and still others were not cued during either presentation or recall. Age-related differences in memory were found to depend on both the amount of support offered in the task and the characteristics of the persons performing the task. Among the participants who received the greatest degree of support (cued presentation and cued recall), all of the elderly groups with the exception of group 3 (low IQ, low socioeconomic class) performed just as well as the college students. Among the participants who received an intermediate amount of support (noncued presentation and cued recall), only the first elderly group performed as well as the college students. When participants were not provided with any support (noncued presentation and noncued recall), the college students performed better than all of the elderly groups. Research Focus 7.4 discusses memory improvement.

Normal versus Pathological Memory Loss

Until now, we have focused mainly on age differences in cognition among healthy adults. Older adults who are in good health and who do not have any debilitating disease usually exhibit only minor declines in their everyday cognitive functions. As individuals age, however, they are more likely to have diseases that produce memory loss and other deficits in cognitive function. For example, AD, which causes progressive and severe memory and attentional losses, is most likely to develop in the seventh or eighth decade.

It is important to differentiate normal memory loss from memory loss due to AD and other kinds of dementia. The nonpathological loss of memory has been labeled as **age-associated memory impairment (AAMI).** This type of memory impairment is benign because it does not interfere with a person's ability to function in everyday life. Some adults notice a decline in memory function in the fifth decade, although it is more common to become aware of memory problems after 60 years of age. In many instances, the elderly become very concerned about their memory. They want to know if their memory function is normal or abnormal for their age. Schacter (1996) has given some general advice about how to distinguish normal from pathological memory loss. He stated that, ". . . the next time you forget where you put your car keys, you need not worry that you are headed for Alzheimer's. Nor do you need to become concerned the next time you fail to come up with the name of a friend that feels like it is on the tip of your tongue. But if you forget that you possess a car or you can't remember your own name, then there is clearly cause for concern" (p. 285).

Can Memory Be Improved?

Research on the effectiveness of memory training in older adults is important for practical and theoretical reasons. Research on this topic is motivated by a desire to improve memory in older adults. Memory training research also has important implications for theories of aging because description of the potentials and limits of memory function bear on questions of cognitive plasticity.

It is a fact that decrements in memory functioning occur with advancing age (see La Voie & Light, 1994). The negative effects of aging on memory depend in large part on age-related declines in the efficiency of brain mechanisms (for a review, see Raz, 2000). However, memory performance depends not only on neurobiological mechanisms, but also on the strategies used for remembering and retrieving information. Training studies demonstrate that some portion of the memory decline in older adults is related to the use of nonoptimal learning and memory strategies, and that older adults can learn to use more effective strategies in order to improve memory.

Programs designed to improve memory in older adults do produce improved memory performance. In a meta-analysis of 32 studies based on data from 1,539 persons, Verhaeghen, Marcoen, and Goossens (1992) reported that memory training boosted performance by 0.73 standard deviations. The effects of training on performance were larger than the effects of just retesting (0.38 standard deviations) or placebo treatments (0.37 standard deviations). The meta-analysis also showed that the effects of memory training appear to be durable, lasting six-months or longer after training. Across studies, the performance gains associated with training were greater when participants were told in advance about the nature of the training.

Memory training programs can produce improvements in the person's subjective evaluations of memory as well as in actual memory performance. Subjective evaluations of memory functioning come from self-report questionnaires. In a meta-analysis of the 25 studies that examined the effects of memory training on subjective measures of performance, Floyd and Scogin (1997) reported that the magnitude of improvement is less on subjective measures than on objective measures. Subjective evaluations of memory performance improved by about 0.2 standard deviations as a result of memory training. Like objective measures, subjective measures were enhanced by including pretraining information about the use of memory skills such as imagery.

According to the Verhaeghen et al. meta-analysis, no one type of training procedure was superior. In a study directly comparing the effectiveness of several types of memory training procedures, Rasmusson, Rebok, Bylsma, and Brandt (1999) also reported that there was no evidence to suggest the superiority of any one type of training. Rasmusson, Rebok, and Bylsma gave residents of a retirement community a microcomputer-based memory training program, a commercially available audiotape memory improvement program, or a group memory course that took place in weekly 90-minute sessions for nine weeks. All three training programs were successful.

The retrieval of information from memory is likely to be better when information is distinctly encoded and systematically organized, stored, or filed. Frequently, the procedures used in memory training studies are variations on a method that teaches individuals to associate to-be-

Cotman (2000) identified a continuum from normal memory aging, or AAMI, to mild cognitive impairment (MCI), to dementia (see figure 7.9). However, keep in mind that only a small percentage of adults will experience severe dementia (Corder & Manton, 2001). Specifically, 2.5 percent of those aged 65 or older were severely demented in 1999. Prevalence of severe dementia for people aged 80 and over was 6.4 percent in 1999 (Corder & Manton, 2001). However, 19.2 percent of those aged 65 or older experience cognitive impairment that is not irreversible dementia (Unverzagt et al, 2001).

A distinction can be made between apparent memory deficits and genuine memory deficits (Grober & Buschke, 1987). **Apparent memory deficits** are memory problems resulting from ineffective encoding and retrieval strategies. Apparent memory deficits can be overcome by inducing individuals to process information

Can Memory Be Improved?

remembered items with a familiar series of locations. In this method, called the method of loci, individuals are taught to remember lists of items by forming visual associations between the nth item in a list and the nth place or locus within a familiar sequence of loci. Retrieval of the items occurs by mentally travelling through the familiar sequence, and retrieving the associated item at each locus. Some writers have noted that ancient Roman orators used this procedure to remember the main points or themes in long speeches. The orators would first memorize a large number of places in a serial order, so that each locus could be clearly visualized. Next, after a speech was prepared, its content was divided into a series of visual images that represented key words or themes in the speech. Each of these images was serially associated with one of the loci. For example, the first theme in the speech would be visually associated with the entrance to a building; the second idea would be associated with the first room in the building, and so on. To recall the main themes of the speech, one simply imagined traveling through each of the places in the building. The orator could mentally "walk through" the series of places in order to remember the main points of any speech.

A similar mnemonic technique is the peg word method. Images of concrete objects rather than locations are used as the "pegs" to attach the images to be remembered. This method requires that the person can readily retrieve both the peg words and their order. In a rhyming peg-word method, for example, each peg word rhymes with the number indicating its position in the list: "One is a bun, two is a shoe, three is a tree," and so on.

It is important to emphasize that improvements associated with memory training are specific to the type of training provided. That is, there is little or no evidence to suggest that general-purpose memory function can be improved by training. In other words, memory training probably does not affect general processing speed or brain plasticity per se, but instead provides beneficial effects by teaching strategies for the effective retrieval of specific kinds of information. There is little if any work on the training of working memory or on the training of speed of processing that seems to underlie most if not all age-related deficits in cognitive performance. Measures of the extent to which training can improve the fundamental processes of memory might provide a description of individual differences in the potentials and limits of cognitive plasticity (e.g., Verhaeghen & Marcoen, 1996).

Rasmusson, D., Rebok, G.W., Bylsma, F.W., & Brandt, J. (1999). Effects of three types of memory training in normal elderly. *Aging, Neuropsychology, and Cognition, 6,* 56–66.

Verhaeghen, P., & Marcoen, A. (1996). On the mechanisms of plasticity in younger and older adults after instruction in the method of loci: Evidence for an amplification model. *Psychology and Aging, 11,* 164–178.

Verhaeghen, P., Marcoen, A., & Goossens, L. (1992). Improving memory performance in the aged through mnemonic training: A meta-analytic study. *Psychology and Aging, 7,* 242–251.

Verhaeghen, P., Marcoen, A., & Goossens, L. (1993). Fact and fiction about memory aging: A quantitative integration of research findings. *Journal of Gerontology: Psychological Sciences, 48,* P157–P171.

more effectively or by providing them with effective retrieval aids. **Genuine memory deficits** are memory problems that persist even after individuals have carried out effective encoding and retrieval activities. In other words, genuine memory deficits are largely irreversible (Grober & Buschke, 1987). Nondemented individuals (both normal elderly and depressives) would be more likely to experience apparent memory deficits than genuine memory deficits. See Research Focus 7.5 for more information about how Grober and Buschke distinguished between apparent versus genuine memory deficits.

Recent work suggests that there is a substantial amount of preclinical dementia in samples of "healthy" community-dwelling older adults (Sliwinski, Lipton, Buschke, & Stewart, 1996; Backman, Small, Wahlin, 2001).

Figure 7.9 Model for phases of brain aging. In this model, memory changes progress through age-associated memory impairment (AAMI) and mild cognitive impairment (MCI) to dementia. At some stage in dementia, irreversible damage occurs. *Source:* Adapted from Cotman, C. W. (2000). Homeostatic processes in brain aging: The role of apoptosis, inflammation, and oxidative stress in regulating healthy neural circuitry in the aging brain. In P. C. Stern & L. L. Carstensen (Eds.), *The aging mind: Opportunities in cognitive research* (pp. 114–143). Washington, DC: National Academy Press.

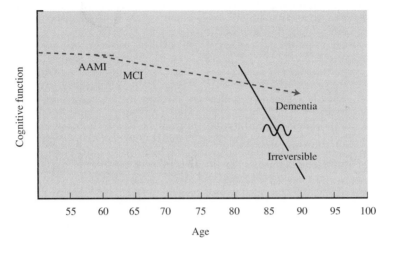

Research Focus 7.5

Memory Abilities in Normal and Demented Elderly

Ellen Grober and Herman Buschke (1987) developed a methodology that distinguishes between genuine memory deficits and apparent memory deficits. In the controlled-learning component of their paradigm, groups of normal and demented elderly were given a list of 16 common items drawn from different conceptual categories. The items were presented four at a time on four different sheets of paper. Each item was presented as a picture (e.g., a bunch of grapes) with the name of the item boldly printed above the picture (GRAPES). The participants were given the name of a conceptual category (in this case, "fruit") and were told to point to and name the picture on the card that corresponded to the category. After identifying all four items on a sheet of paper, the participants were given an immediate recall task in which they had to recollect the names of the four items they had just identified. If a participant could not recall the items, the sheet of paper was re-presented, the identification procedure was repeated, and the participant was given another chance to recall the item. This entire procedure was repeated again if necessary. Then, the remaining 12 items (four items drawn and labeled on three different sheets of paper) were presented, identified, and recalled in the same manner. All of these controlled-learning procedures ensured that the

Box Figure 7.B Free recall (open circles) and total recall (closed circles) for 16 unrelated pictures by elderly adults with and without dementia. Total recall is obtained by adding items remembered from cued recall to the number remembered from free recall. *Source:* Data from Grober, E., & Buschke, H. (1987). Genuine memory deficits in dementia. *Developmental Neuropsychology 3,* 13–36.

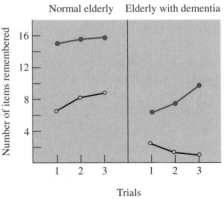

Memory Abilities in Normal
and Demented Elderly

Box Figure 7.C Free recall (open circles) and total recall (closed circles) by (A) a normal 89-year-old man, (B) a normal 87-year-old woman, and (C) an 86-year-old woman with Alzheimer's disease. *Source:* Data from Grober, E., & Buschke, H. (1987). Genuine memory deficits in dementia. *Developmental Neuropsychology 3,* 13–36.

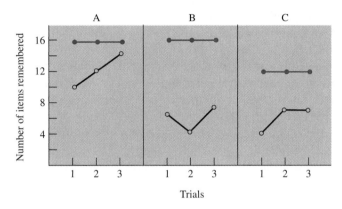

participants attended to all of the items, briefly stored the items, and could immediately recall the items.

Twenty seconds after the controlled-learning phase was over, the participants were given three separate recall trials for the entire 16 items. Each recall trial consisted of two distinct tasks: a free recall task and a cued-recall task. During the free recall task, participants had two minutes to remember as many of the 16 items as possible. In the cued-recall task, participants were provided with conceptual cues for the items they did not remember in the free recall task. (For example, a researcher might ask, "What was the type of fruit pictured on the card?") Two different types of recall scores were obtained for each participant: a free recall score and a total recall score. The free recall score represented the number of items retrieved without cues on each trial. The total recall score consisted of the total number of items recalled on each trial by both free recall and cued-recall methods.

Grober and Buschke (1987) reasoned that the total recall score should provide a valid estimate of the total number of items stored in memory and potentially available for recall. Thus, a participant's total recall score, rather than free recall score, should be a better predictor of whether he or she belonged to the normal or demented group.

The results of the study were straightforward. First, as box figure 7.B shows, free recall dramatically underrepre-

sents the amount of learning and memory that takes place in both the normal and demented groups. Box figure 7.B also shows that the normal group, because they had near-perfect total memory scores, had stored all 16 test items. The demented group, on the other hand, stored only about one-half of the 16 items.

From the evidence illustrated in box figure 7.B, it appears that free or total recall scores should be equally useful in predicting if a person is demented. The data in box figure 7.C, however, indicate this is not the case—total recall is better than free recall at distinguishing normal from demented elderly. Box figure 7.C shows the free and total recall scores of three participants. Graph A represents the scores of an 89-year-old normal participant who had exceptionally good free recall. Graph B represents the scores of an 87-year-old normal participant who had an average range of free recall scores. Graph C represents the scores on an 86-year-old participant with AD whose free recall scores are almost identical to those shown in graph B. But the normal participants (A and B) had perfect total recall scores, while person B and the demented person (C) had identical free recall scores but differed in total recall. In other words, total recall proved to be a better indicator of dementia, because normal elderly, but not demented patients, displayed near-perfect performance on the total recall score regardless of their free recall scores.

SUMMARY

In this chapter, we have described age-related changes in memory. The capacity of short-term memory does not undergo significant change with age. However, age-related deficits in working-memory tasks and in the speed at which an individual searches the contents of short-term memory have been reported. Older adults perform more poorly than young adults on tasks of long-term memory, especially when episodic rather than semantic memory is involved. Memory in the elderly is better when it is measured by implicit rather than explicit memory tasks.

When older adults are instructed in how to use efficient encoding strategies, they show an improvement in their ability to remember. Age-related differences in memory are unlikely to occur when older adults draw upon previous knowledge to help them remember. Researchers try to explain age-related changes in memory using three perspectives. The biological perspective suggests that the age-related deterioration of the brain causes decrements in memory. The information-processing perspective suggests that age-related changes in memory are the result of speed-of-processing or strategy differences for encoding and retrieving information. The contextual perspective stresses the relationship between the task and the person.

There is an age-related decline in the ability to remember episodic information. This type of age-associated memory impairment does not seriously affect an older adult's ability to function in everyday life. Psychologists and cognitive neuroscientists have developed techniques that help distinguish normal from pathological memory loss.

REVIEW QUESTIONS

1. Discuss the accuracy of older adults' self-perceptions of memory.
2. Compare and contrast short-term and working memory. What type of memory is more likely to become impared with aging?
3. In general, what are the assumptions of multiple memory systems theory?
4. Describe the differences between declarative and nondeclarative memory, episodic and semantic memory, and implicit and explicit memory.
5. What types of memory systems and/or memory performances are spared (or impaired) by aging? What factors are responsible for the observed pattern of age-related preservation (or impairment) in memory?
6. Are there differences in the performance of younger versus older adults on priming tasks?
7. Explain the advantages associated with using the Process Dissociation Procedure in the study of memory and aging.
8. Compare and contrast the biological, information-processing, and contextual approaches to the study of age-related memory changes. Is one of these perspectives more useful or valid than the others?
9. What is age-associated memory impairment (AAMI)?
10. Explain the differences between the memory impairments that occur in the normal elderly and those that occur in someone who has a dementia such as AD.

ON THE WEB   www.mhhe.com/hoyer5

For a listing of links to the latest information about normal and neuropathological changes in memory, attention, and learning, and links to new topics related to the material in this chapter, see:

http://www.neuropsychologycentral.com/ This page provides access to sources and links for topics in neuropsychology, including the assessment of dementia.

http://www.cogneurosociety.org/ This is the home page for the Cognitive Neuroscience Society. It provides updated links to graduate and research programs in cognitive neuroscience.

http://www.usewisdom.com/fun/java/reactiontime.html#null/On this page you can measure your own speed of reaction time.

http://www.7minutescreen.com/ This site tells about a screening test for Alzheimer's disease that takes seven minutes to administer. The brief test was developed to identify individuals with Alzheimer's disease, and it is meant to distinguish memory deficits associated with dementia from normal age-related memory deficits.

http://www.serendip.brynmawr.edu/bb/ This site features an interesting variety of exhibits of cognitive phenomena and examples of tasks used in cognitive studies.

8

INTELLIGENCE AND CREATIVITY

In the desert there is no sign that says, Thou shalt not eat stones.
—Sufi Proverb

We work in the dark—we do what we can—we give what we have.
Our doubt is our passion and our passion is our task. The rest is the
madness of art.
—Henry James

INTRODUCTION

This is the second of the three chapters that focus on adult cognitive development. In this chapter, we consider the **psychometric approach,** a measurement-based view that has sparked debate on the definition and assessment of intelligence. How and why does intelligence change during adult years? We summarize the research examining the effects of physical health and the generational (or cohort) influences on adult intelligence. We also discuss the relationship between scores on intelligence tests and performance in everyday situations. Next, we examine the differences between creativity and intelligence and chart the developmental course of creativity over the adult years. Finally, we examine the relationships between aging, intelligence, education, and work. How do age-related changes in intelligence affect occupational productivity during the adult years?

The Nature of Intelligence

Intelligence is a concept that is easy to understand but hard to define. The word *intelligence* is derived from Latin words that mean "to choose between" and "to make wise choices." But how can a researcher objectively measure whether an individual has made a wise choice? Is there a measurable as well as meaningful definition of intelligence?

One of the questions concerning the nature of intelligence is whether it is a single ability or a collection of independent mental abilities. Charles Spearman (1927) argued that intelligence was a single ability that an individual could apply to any task. Spearman called this unitary ability the **g factor**—g for "general capacity." Spearman assumed that because of the g factor, an individual performs at roughly the same level of proficiency regardless of the type of task he or she undertakes. A college student with a high g level would show a high level of understanding in most or all of his or her courses. The notion that intelligence is best conceptualized as a single, general ability was also held by Alfred Binet. Binet was the French psychologist who developed the first intelligence assessment in 1906. Today, Spearman and Binet would be likely to conceptualize intelligence as a computer program that could solve a wide variety of problems. Other psychologists have suggested that intelligence consists of a number of separate, independent mental abilities. Thurstone (1938) originally advocated this position, proposing that there are a small number

TABLE 8.1

The Primary Mental Abilities

Verbal comprehension: The principal factor in such tests as reading comprehension, verbal analogies, disarranged sentences, verbal reasoning, and proverb Interpretation. It is measured by vocabulary tests.

Word fluency: The principal factor in such tests as anagrams, rhyming, or naming words in a given category (e.g., "list as many boys' names as you can", or "list as many words as you can that begin with the letter B."

Spatial reasoning: The principal factor in tests that assess spatial relations and the identification of changes in spatial relations. It is measured by figural relations test.

Associative memory: The principal factor in tests that tap the extent to which one uses associative strategies to remember information. It is measured by tests of memory for paired associates.

Perceptual speed: The factor in tests that assess quick and accurate identification of visual details, and similarities and differences between objects. It is measured by tests of how long it takes individuals to compare the visual features of objects or strings of letters or numbers.

of **primary mental abilities.** Table 8.1 describes them. K. Warner Schaie adapted Thurstone's test for use with older adults; the **Schaie-Thurstone Adult Mental Abilities Test** (Schaie, 1985) has been used in many studies of adult intellectual development. Applying the computer analogy, Schaie would take the view that intelligence consists of a number of separate computer programs, each designed to carry out a particular kind of task.

John Horn (1998; Horn & Noll, 1997) has argued for the existence of two components of intelligence that subsume the various primary mental abilities: crystallized intelligence and fluid intelligence. **Crystallized intelligence** represents the extent to which individuals have incorporated the valued knowledge of their culture. It is measured by a large inventory of behaviors that reflect the breadth of culturally valued knowledge and experience, comprehension of communications, and the development of judgment, understanding, and reasonable thinking in everyday affairs. Some of the primary mental abilities associated with crystallized intelligence are verbal comprehension, concept formation, logical reasoning, and induction. Tests used to measure the crystallized factor include vocabulary, simple analogies, remote associations, and social judgment.

Fluid intelligence represents an individual's "pure" ability to perceive, remember, and think about a wide variety of basic ideas. In other words, fluid intelligence involves mental abilities that are not imparted by one's culture. Abilities included under this heading are seeing relationships among patterns, drawing inferences from relationships, and comprehending implications. Some of the primary mental abilities that best reflect this factor are spatial reasoning and perceptual speed. Tasks measuring fluid intelligence include letter series, matrices, and figure relations. It has been suggested that fluid intelligence represents the integrity of the central nervous system. Figure 8.1 shows examples of tasks that measure fluid and crystalized intelligence.

Figure 8.1
Examples of test items that measure fluid and crystallized intelligence.

Matrices   Indicate the figure that completes the matrix.

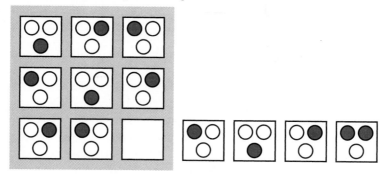

Letter series   Decide which letter comes next in the series.
A   D   G   J   M   P   ?

Figure relations   Decide which shape comes next in the series.

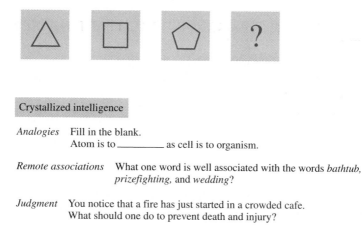

Crystallized intelligence

Analogies   Fill in the blank.
Atom is to _____ as cell is to organism.

Remote associations   What one word is well associated with the words *bathtub, prizefighting,* and *wedding*?

Judgment   You notice that a fire has just started in a crowded cafe. What should one do to prevent death and injury?

The Measurement of Intelligence

It is one thing to develop a theory of intelligence and another thing to develop valid and reliable measures of intelligence. A psychometrician must consider several factors in developing an intelligence test. First, it is important to realize that intelligence does not really exist! Intelligence is a **hypothetical construct** rather than a real entity. It is not possible, for example, to look inside the brain of an individual and see the amount of intelligence she possesses in the same way one can look inside a refrigerator to see the amount of food stored there. This means that psychometric tests must measure intelligence indirectly by examining a person's performance on tasks that depend on the use of intelligence.

A second factor psychometricians must consider, since no psychometric test can directly measure intelligence, is that many factors other than intelligence influence test performance. These factors include personality characteristics, motivation, educational background, anxiety, fatigue, and so on.

A third consideration for psychometricians to remember in developing an intelligence test is that it is necessary to present individuals with a wide variety of tasks to evaluate whether intelligence is a single ability, such as a g factor, or a number of independent abilities. This is why contemporary intelligence tests consist of a number of different scales or subtests. One of the most commonly used tests to measure adult intelligence is the **Wechsler Adult Intelligence Scale (WAIS-R).** This test consists of 11 subtests with six composing a verbal scale. These six subtests include general information, digit span, vocabulary, arithmetic, comprehension, and similarities. The items on this scale tap language and numerical skills. The remaining five subtests make up a performance scale. The subtests on this scale include picture completion, picture arrangement, block design, object assembly, and digit symbol substitution. On this scale, a person is required to make a nonverbal response (e.g., arranging a number of pictures in a logical sequence to tell a story) after a careful appraisal of each problem. Table 8.2 contains a brief description of the subtests the verbal and performance scales of the WAIS-R.

TABLE 8.2

Subtests of the WAIS-R

Verbal Scale

Information: Answer questions about general information. For example, Who is John Glenn? Or, name five classical or modern famous painters and five classical or modern famous musicians or composers.

Comprehension: Answer questions about social circumstances, or explain the meanings of proverbs or quotations. For example, explain why there is a legal drinking age. Explain what it means when people say, "Don't count your chickens before they hatch."

Arithmetic: Solve simple arithmetic word problems. If Paul has $20.00, and he buys two sandwiches that cost $5.97 each, how much change does he receive?

Similarities: Explain how two things or concepts are similar. For example, describe how a pencil and a tree are alike.

Digit span: Listen to a series of numbers, then repeat the numbers in the same order in which they were presented (forward span), and in reverse order (backward span).

Vocabulary: Define the meanings of words. For example, what does *perfidious* mean?

Performance Scale

Digit symbol substitution: Write down symbols that are paired with numbers using a key or code showing the pairings. The person's score is the number of symbol substitutions completed in 90 seconds.

Picture completion: Identify a missing part of a picture.

Block design: Arrange blocks in different patterns of colors to form a design identical to one the examiner presents.

Picture arrangement: Arrange a set of cards in a logical sequence.

Object assembly: Arrange cut up pieces to form a familiar object.

Note: The examples are intended to illustrate the types of questions that appear on the WAIS-R subtests; they are not actual questions from the WAIS-R.

Another thing to consider in developing intelligence tests is that although we can construct subtests, this does not necessarily mean each subtest measures a different aspect of intelligence. Each subtest might measure the same mental ability—the g factor, for example—but in a different way. To determine whether the various subtests of an intelligence test are measuring a single ability or a number of special abilities, researchers developed the factor analysis technique. **Factor analysis** (discussed in appendix A) is a statistical procedure used to determine how scores on a large number of tasks intercorrelate (or fail to intercorrelate) with one another. Using factor analysis, Thurstone discovered the different primary mental abilities. Cattell and Horn also used factor analytic procedures to discern the difference between crystallized and fluid intelligence.

Finally, it is important for psychometricians to understand how a person's IQ score is calculated. The first intelligence tests were constructed solely for children and young adolescents. These tests computed IQ by multiplying the ratio of mental age to chronological age by 100 (IQ = MA/CA $\times$ 100). A child's mental age was measured by the number of items passed on the IQ test. For example, if a child passed all of the items that a typical 6-year-old could pass but could not pass any of the items solved by children 7 years of age and above, a mental age of 6 years was assigned to that child. Then the child's IQ could be computed by determining the ratio between the child's mental age and chronological age and multiplying the answer by 100. For example, if the child with a mental age of 6 is 6 years old chronologically, the child's IQ is 100 (IQ = 6/6 $\times$ 100). Thus, an average IQ, regardless of the age of the person tested, is always 100.

Psychometricians discovered it was very easy to classify the mental ages of children. However, the concept of mental age broke down when applied to adults. It is relatively easy to develop questions that distinguish between children with mental ages of 6 and 7, but it is impossible to develop questions that distinguish between adults with mental ages of 66 and 67. The IQ formula used for children would thus be useless for determining adult intelligence. To resolve this problem, researchers determine an adult's IQ by comparing the number of correct answers a person achieves on the whole test to people of the same chronological age. A score of 100 is arbitrarily assigned to those performing at the average for their age group, while IQs of greater or less than 100 are assigned according to the degree of statistical deviation from this average.

Using this scoring system, it is possible for different-aged adults to perform in an identical manner yet receive radically different IQ scores. To take a simple example, suppose that the average 25-year-old can pass 65 questions on an IQ test, while the average 75-year-old can pass 45 questions on the same test. Thus, a 25-year-old who passed 55 questions would be assessed as having a below-average IQ, while a 75-year-old who passed 55 questions would be assessed as having an above-average IQ. This discovery leads to an interesting question. How should we examine developmental changes in adult intelligence? Should we use the raw scores (the total number of questions correctly answered) obtained by adults of different ages or use the adjusted IQ scores (the comparison of the raw score to the average score for a particular age group) for different-aged adults? It seems that examining raw scores provides more valuable information about developmental changes in test performance than examining the adjusted scores (the IQ scores).

Developmental Changes in Intelligence

There is no doubt that the scores on intelligence tests decline with age. However, the age at which decrements in test performance first begin, as well as the magnitude of the decline, depend on the research design employed to measure developmental change. In this section, we compare various cross-sectional and longitudinal studies of adult intellectual development. Overall, we will see that declines in intelligence (1) occur much later, (2) affect a smaller number of individuals, and (3) affect a smaller number of intellectual abilities than we earlier thought.

Cross-Sectional Studies

Initially, a number of cross-sectional studies (Garret, 1957; Jones & Conrad, 1933; Wechsler, 1939) showed that raw or unadjusted scores on intelligence tests decreased in older age groups. Decrements in test scores began in late adolescence and early adulthood (at about 20 years of age) and steadily continued over the remainder of the life span. These results suggested that intelligence peaked early in life, a conclusion not at all surprising to psychologists of this era. At this point in time, psychologists held a child-focused perspective on developmental change that assumed that adulthood can only be characterized by intellectual decline.

Researchers began to notice that adults displayed a steeper rate of decline on some types of intellectual tasks than on others. With increasing age, the scores on performance subtests of the WAIS declined more rapidly than the scores on the verbal subtests. However, performance subtests are speeded, while verbal subtests are nonspeeded. A speeded subtest is one in which individuals must make their responses as quickly as possible, while in a nonspeeded test, individuals can take their time answering items. These data suggested that speed of response may underlie the poor performance of the elderly on nonverbal tasks. However, many older adults continue to perform poorly on the performance subtests of the WAIS even if given unlimited time to respond (Botwinick, 1977).

A study conducted by Schaie and Willis (1993) illustrated, rather nicely, that various components of intelligence decline at different rates. These researchers administered a battery of tests that measured the primary mental abilities of inductive reasoning, space, number, verbal ability, speed perception, and associative memory to 1,628 community-dwelling adults between 20 and 90 years of age. The results of this study appear in figure 8.2. Three findings are noteworthy. First, age-related decrements occur in all of the primary mental abilities. Second, verbal ability is least affected by age, whereas perceptual speed is most affected. Third, after midlife, performance on the different mental abilities varies more.

Similarly, when one analyzes the developmental changes in crystallized and fluid intelligence in a cross-sectional manner, an interesting pattern emerges. With advancing age, crystallized intelligence shows increases up until the sixth decade of life. On the other hand, fluid intelligence exhibits a steady decline beginning in early adulthood. The net effect is that the increases in crystallized intelligence tend to cancel out the decreases in fluid intelligence. Therefore, if one did not make a distinction between crystallized and fluid abilities, one would conclude that intelligence, as a general ability, remains relatively sta-

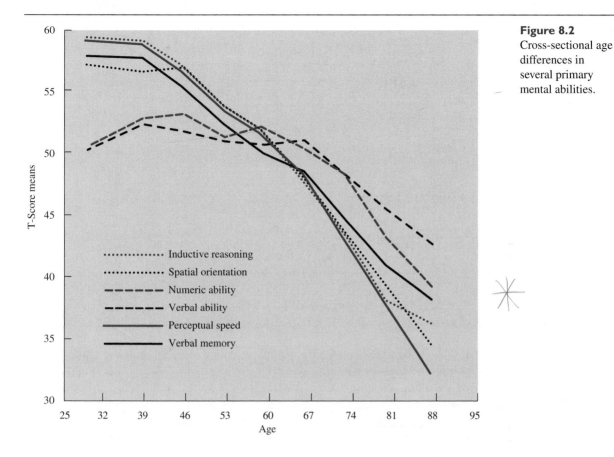

ble until the onset of late adulthood. Figure 8.3 contains a schematic representation of the relationship between crystallized intelligence, fluid intelligence, and general intelligence.

In summary, cross-sectional research seems to indicate that intellectual and physical development follow the same pattern of steady decline—a pattern of irreversible decrement. Furthermore, researchers have consistently shown that scores on nonverbal or fluid abilities display an earlier, steeper decline than scores on verbal or crystallized abilities. The tendency for nonverbal abilities to deteriorate more rapidly has been referred to as the classic aging pattern (Botwinick, 1977). How can we understand this phenomenon? John Horn and colleagues (Horn, 1982; Horn & Donaldson, 1976) have proposed that age spares crystallized intelligence because it reflects the cumulative effects of experience, education, and acculturation, whereas age impairs fluid intelligence because of the gradual deterioration of the physiological and neurological mechanisms necessary for basic intellectual functioning.

Longitudinal Studies

Longitudinal studies offer a very different impression of adult intellectual development than cross-sectional studies. A number of longitudinal studies were initiated during the

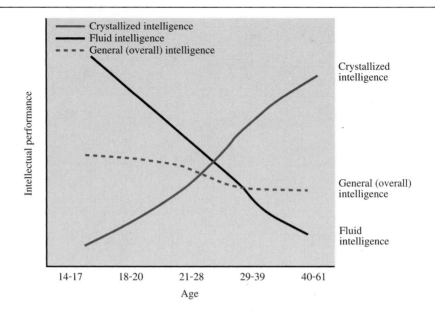

Figure 8.3 Age-related changes in crystallized intelligence, fluid intelligence, and general intelligence from adolescence to older adulthood.

Crystallized intelligence
Fluid intelligence
General (overall) intelligence

Crystallized intelligence

General (overall) intelligence

Fluid intelligence

Intellectual performance

14-17   18-20   21-28   29-39   40-61

Age

early 1920s. At this time, incoming groups of college freshmen in the United States took intelligence tests on a routine basis. Psychologists kept track of these individuals as they grew older, retesting them at different points during adulthood. Surprisingly, the participants in these longitudinal studies showed an increase in test performance up to approximately age 50 (Owens, 1966). After age 50, these gains were usually maintained or sometimes evidenced a small decline (Cunningham & Owens, 1983).

In one longitudinal study, Schwartzman and colleagues (1987) analyzed the intelligence test scores of a group of 260 men. These men were first administered intelligence tests when they were army recruits during World War II. Forty years later, the men were retested when they were approximately 65 years of age. They had completed, on average, nine years of formal education. One of the interesting twists of this study was that at the 40-year retesting, the men took the intelligence test under two different conditions: a normal-time condition in which participants had the standard amount of time to answer the test questions, and a double-time condition in which participants had twice as much time. Overall results showed a slight decline in test scores under the normal-time condition, but a reliable and significant improvement in scores in the double-time condition! Gains were most likely to occur in those portions of the test that measured verbal abilities (e.g., vocabulary), with losses in essentially nonverbal abilities (e.g., spatial problem solving). Three other findings are especially noteworthy. First, individual differences in test scores remained very stable over the 40-year time span. Second, gains were more highly associated with the number of years of formal education the men had attained than with their ages at the retesting. Third, self-reported activity levels and personal lifestyle differences were related to test scores at both times of testing.

One way to compare the results of cross-sectional and longitudinal studies of adult intellectual change is to examine the information in figure 8.4. The cross-sectional data

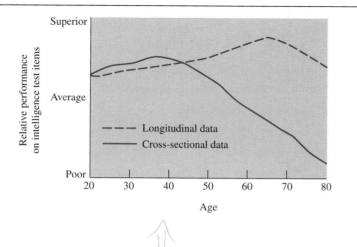

Figure 8.4 A comparison of the results of cross-sectional and longitudinal studies investigating the relationship between age and verbal intelligence. *Source:* Data from Schaie and Willis, 1986.

indicate that adults show a peak in verbal ability at 35 years of age, followed by a significant decline thereafter. The longitudinal data, on the other hand, show that verbal ability peaks at about age 55. In addition, the longitudinal data show only a very small decline up until 70 years of age, while the cross-sectional data show a larger and earlier rate of decline.

One of the most informative investigations of adult intelligence is the Seattle Longitudinal Study (SLS) of K. Warner Schaie and his associates (Schaie & Hofer, 2001). This investigation used a sequential research design (i.e., a combination of both cross-sectional and longitudinal methods of data collection). The study began in 1956 when 500 participants between 22 and 70 years of age were administered the Primary Mental Abilities Test. These individuals, along with new groups of individuals, were retested at seven-year intervals in 1963, 1970, 1977, 1984, 1991, and 1998. Overall, this research project, which consists of six cross-sectional studies and one longitudinal study covering a 35-year period, has tested more than 5,000 individuals. A large number of published reports have summarized the outcomes of the SLS (Schaie, 1996; Schaie, Maitland, Willis, & Intrieri, 1998; Schaie, & Willis, 1996). Generally, the cross-sectional comparison exhibited the typical pattern of decline across all of the different primary mental abilities. The longitudinal findings, however, tell a different story. They indicate that intelligence test scores either increase or remain stable until approximately age 60, when a small decline becomes evident. Figure 8.5 illustrates the results from one of the first reports of this investigation. This figure, based on the findings of Schaie and Labouvie-Vief (1974), compares the cross-sectional data collected in 1963 (black lines) with the cross-sectional data collected in 1970 (colored lines). The longitudinal data is signified by the dashed lines connecting the black and colored lines.

In another report, Schaie (1990) examined the effects of age on the mental abilities of verbal meaning, spatial orientation, inductive reasoning, number, and word fluency. He collected longitudinal data on individuals from ages 53 to 60, 60 to 67, 67 to 74, and 74 to 81. Table 8.3 reveals that, as age increased, participants were more likely to display a decline. However, only about one-third of the participants showed a significant decline on any ability between 74 to 81 years of age. Likewise, table 8.4 shows

Figure 8.5 A comparison of cross-sectional and longitudinal findings concerning the relationship between age and intelligence based on data from Schaie and Labouvie-Vief (1974). *Source:* Schaie, K. W., & Labouvie-Vief, G. (1974). Generational versus ontogenetic components of change in adult cognitive behavior: A fourteen-year cross-sequential study. *Developmental Psychology, 10,* 305–320.

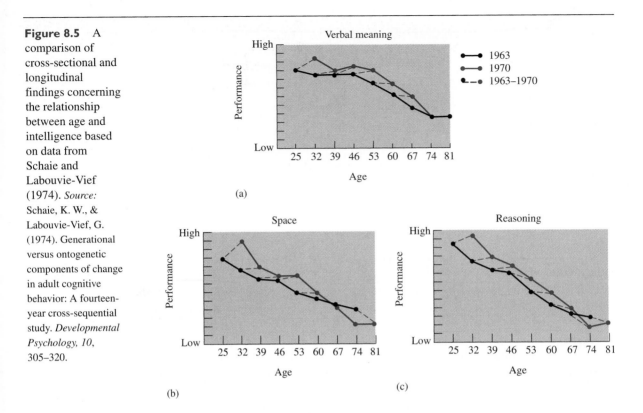

(a)

(b)

(c)

that very few individuals showed global intellectual decline. For example, at age 60, about 75 percent of the participants maintained their performance on at least four out of five primary mental abilities. This maintenance level was also found for slightly more than half of the 81-year-olds in the sample. Only 2 percent of the participants showed a decline on all five abilities between 74 to 81 years of age. Finally, Schaie discovered that no participants displayed constant intellectual decline on all five primary mental abilities over the 28 years of data collection! Overall, these results suggest that constant, linear, and all-pervasive intellectual decline is mythical. More positively stated, these data show that a significant percentage of individuals maintain most of their intellectual abilities well into old age.

All of the research we have reviewed, until now, has focused on the relationship between age and intelligence. A related question, of course, is the relationship between societal changes and intelligence. For example, has the availability of the Internet and other new technologies served to improve adult intellectual functioning? Research Focus 8.1 describes some very interesting data pertaining to this issue.

We also want to know whether and how individuals become more (or less) intelligent as they grow older. The role of heritability on intelligence is substantial, so how can environmental factors have much influence? Dickens and Flynn (2001) discuss the massive gains in IQ during the past several decades (as discussed in Research Focus 8.1). They

TABLE 8.3

Proportion of Individuals Showing a Decline in Specific Intellectual Abilities

Intellectual Ability	Age 53 to Age 60	Age 60 to Age 67	Age 67 to Age 74	Age 74 to Age 81
Verbal meaning	15.2%	24.8%	26.8%	35.7%
Spatial orientation	21.1	27.0	29.6	32.6
Inductive reasoning	14.0	26.5	23.6	27.9
Number	17.2	26.2	26.2	31.8
Word fluency	23.6	28.4	27.5	37.2

Source: Data from Schaie, K.W. (1990). The optimization of cognitive functioning in old age: Prediction based on cohort-sequential and longitudinal data. In P. B. Baltes and M. Baltes (Eds.), Longitudinal research and the study of successful (optimal) aging (pp. 94–117). Cambridge, England: Cambridge University Press.

TABLE 8.4

Proportion of Individuals Showing Decline in Intellectual Abilities

Number of Abilities	Age 53 to Age 60	Age 60 to Age 67	Age 67 to Age 74	Age 74 to Age 81
None	41.3%	26.7%	24.3%	15.5%
One	35.3	35.1	37.7	37.2
Two	17.0	22.0	21.8	24.8
Three	4.8	10.3	11.3	14.0
Four	1.2	5.0	3.9	6.2
All five	0.5	0.8	1.1	2.3

Source: Data from Schaie, K.W. (1990). The optimization of cognitive functioning in old age: Prediction based on cohort-sequential and longitudinal data. In P. B. Baltes and M. Baltes (Eds.), Longitudinal research and the study of successful (optimal) aging (pp. 94–117). Cambridge, England: Cambridge University Press.

use a sports analogy to show how these IQ gains are largely the result of environmental factors. It is quite unlikely that genes for either intelligence or basketball have improved very much in recent years, yet consider how the level of play of college and professional basketball has changed. The huge improvements in shooting percentages, rebounding, and virtually all dimensions of game performance for men and women must be attributed to environmental factors—from more practice and better coaching to starting earlier and attracting more talented players to supportive programs. Even seemingly modest changes, such as providing more television time for high school, college, and professional basketball can trigger a small rise in skills, leading to yet another small rise, and so on. Dickens and Flynn refer to these upward snowball effects as *social multipliers*.

Factors Responsible for Developmental Changes in Intelligence

Several investigators have suggested that the deterioration of the central nervous system causes intellectual decline. Without doubt, age-related changes in the brain have a

Societal Changes in Intelligence

You have probably heard many people lament the idea that the media and popular culture are "dumbing down" society in the United States. In support of this viewpoint it is generally assumed that today's teenagers and children can't read, write, or do math as well as their parents did. The data show the opposite. Average IQ scores have increased dramatically over the course of this century (see box figure 8.A). In fact, the average 20-year-old tested in the 1990s scores about 15 points (or one standard deviation) higher than the typical 20-year-old tested in the 1940s. This startling fact, discovered by James Flynn (1984, 1987, 1996, 1999), has been dubbed the **Flynn Effect.** Flynn's careful analyses of the IQ data from 14 countries revealed that scores have increased by 5–25 points in the past fifty years!

Remember how IQ scores are constructed. Raw scores may vary from age group to age group, but the average scores for individuals within any particular age group are always set at 100 IQ points. The same logic applies to the Flynn Effect. As box figure 8.A shows, the average IQ score over the last 70 years has been a constant 100. However, the raw scores that underlie IQ test performance have risen substantially. It is the increase in raw IQ scores that constitutes the Flynn Effect.

Consider the fact that psychologists make a distinction between IQ test items (or subscales) that measure crystallized versus fluid intelligence. What aspect of intelligence (crystallized or fluid) do you think underlies the Flynn Effect? Most probably, you answered "crystallized," since this dimension of intelligence seems most likely to be affected by schooling and life experience. Surprisingly, generational changes in measures of fluid intelligence are responsible for the Flynn Effect! This aspect of intelligence, which measures abstract reasoning and information processing speed, is much less likely to be affected by schooling than crystallized intelligence. In fact, the IQ gains associated with the Flynn Effect have not generally been accompanied by gains in school achievement.

Ulric Neisser and colleagues (Neisser et al., 1996) considered several possible explanations for the Flynn Effect. First, there are striking differences in the nature of everyday life for successive generations of individuals. Today, practically every aspect of life is much more fast-paced and more dependent on technological devices than it was in the past (Czaja, 2001). Perhaps the increasing demand to keep pace with emerging new technology in practically everything that we do drives gains in IQ. Second, better nutrition and health care may have boosted IQ. Third, changes in IQ may reflect increasingly higher levels of educational attain-

Box Figure 8.A The Flynn Effect. *Source:* Flynn, J. R. (1987). Massive IQ gains in 14 nations: What IQ tests really measure. *Psychological Bulletin, 101,* 171–191.

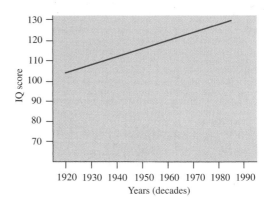

ment among parents. On average, the number of parents attending college increased by 75 percent from 1970 to 2000, whereas the number of minority parents attending college jumped by 350 percent over the same time span. These data are consistent with the finding that the average difference in IQ scores between blacks and whites in the United States has been reduced by half since 1970. Fourth, given the dramatic gains in measures of intelligence over the last several decades, perhaps intelligence isn't a fixed capacity. Maybe it merely represents some sort of abstract problem-solving ability that improves with use. For example, Neisser and colleagues (1996) noted that in 1952 about 0.4 percent of the individuals tested in the Netherlands had IQs indicative of genius (140 or greater), whereas in 1982 approximately 9.1 percent of the Dutch population had IQs in that range when their performance was scored by 1952 norms. If IQ truly reflects intelligence, the Netherlands should be experiencing an unrivaled cultural renaissance.

Most of the research on the Flynn Effect has focused on college-aged individuals. However, it is also quite likely that the intellectual abilities (Dickens & Flynn, 2001) of older adults have also increased during the last 30 years. We touch on this topic at a later point when we discuss the issue of "cohort" (or generational) changes in IQ.

significant impact on adult intellectual functioning. However, these changes alone cannot account for the patterns researchers have found, nor can they adequately explain the individual differences that dispute the claim of universal biologically based loss. In this section, we discuss a variety of factors that have a profound impact on intellectual performance during adulthood.

Cohort Effects

Why do cross-sectional studies paint a more pessimistic picture of adult intellectual change than longitudinal studies do? The answer may be that in cross-sectional studies, age-related differences are confounded with cohort differences. **Cohort** you'll recall, means the generation one is born into, or the year of one's birth.

In a cohort-sequential analysis of the data from the Seattle Longitudinal Study, Schaie (1994, 1996) showed that adults' intellectual performance changed as a function of both age and cohort. Figure 8.6, adapted from Schaie's (1994) data, illustrates the profound influence of cohort effects on five different primary mental abilities. This graph represents the test performances of individuals from 10 successive birth cohorts (1889 to 1952). Notice the multidirectional manner in which the abilities change. The graph shows that inductive reasoning, verbal meaning, and spatial reasoning have increased in a linear manner over time. Number ability seems to have peaked with the 1924 cohort and declined since then. Finally, word fluency declined steadily until the 1938 cohort; since then it has displayed a slight upward movement.

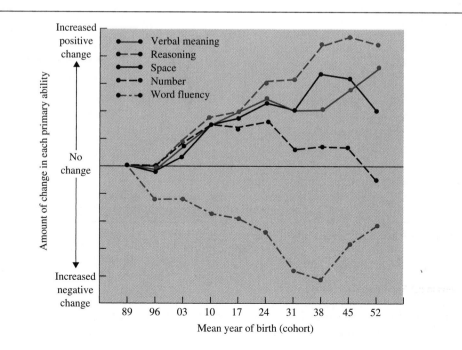

Figure 8.6
Cohort changes in the primary mental abilities.

Cohort effects on intellectual development can be relatively negative or relatively positive. Paul Baltes (1987) described three different ways in which cohort differences can boost intellectual performance: in terms of education, health, and work. First, successive generations have received increasingly more formal education. Educational experience has been positively correlated with IQ scores. Second, each succeeding generation has been treated more effectively for a variety of illnesses (e.g., hypertension) that are known to have a negative impact on intellectual performance. Third, changes in work life among more recent generations have placed a much stronger focus on cognitively oriented labor. Many of our grandfathers or great-grandfathers may have been farmers or manual laborers. Today, we are more likely to find jobs in service fields, working as emergency medical assistants, paralegal aides, or computer operators. This emphasis on occupations demanding cognitive skills most assuredly enhances intellectual abilities.

Selective Dropout

The **selective dropout** of participants may mean that longitudinal studies provide an overly optimistic view of adult intellectual change. The concept of selective dropout is based on the idea that as information is gathered during a longitudinal study, it becomes harder and harder to keep one's original sample intact. Participants who are unhealthy, unmotivated, or who believe they are performing poorly on an intelligence test are not likely to return for repeated testing. As a longitudinal study progresses, a positively biased sample of participants is thus likely to evolve. This biased sample consists of adults who tend to do well on measures of intellectual functioning—that is, those who are highly educated, successful, motivated, and healthy.

Health

It seems obvious that individuals who are in good physical health can think, reason, and remember better than those in poor health. Even 20-year-old college students may find it difficult to concentrate during an exam if they are ill with the flu. The problem for developmental researchers, of course, is that older adults are much more likely to suffer from chronic illness than younger people are. The relatively poor health of the elderly population can bias both cross-sectional and longitudinal studies. The older the population studied, the greater the number of persons with health problems in the research sample.

Developmental psychologists must concern themselves with two interrelated issues. First, they must recognize that health may become much more of a determinant of intellectual functioning as individuals move through the life span. Second, they must try to develop methodologies that separate the effects of aging from the effects of disease.

Research has shown that hypertension (high blood pressure) is related to a decline in intellectual abilities (Elias, Robbins, Ebers, & Streeten, 1998). Schaie (1990) found that hypertension was a better predictor of the intellectual performance of older adults than was a measure of overall health status. Elias, Robbins, Ebers, and Streeten (1998), in a longitudinal study of middle-aged adults, reported that non-hypertensive participants displayed increases in performance on the WAIS, whereas hypertensives showed no significant change.

At a more general level, recent studies have investigated the degree to which a healthy lifestyle influences intellectual abilities. Hultsch, Hammer, and Small (1993) found that, for a sample of adults between 55 and 86 years of age, self-reported health status, alcohol and tobacco use, and level of participation in daily activities predicted performance on a wide range of mental abilities. More specifically, Hultsch et al. (1993) found that these measures were better predictors of fluid rather than crystallized measures of intellectual function, especially for older participants. In a related study, Hill, Storandt, and Malley (1993) charted the effects of a yearlong aerobic exercise program on a group of 87 sedentary older adults. They reported that long-term exercise increased cardiovascular fitness and morale and prevented an age-related decline in verbal memory.

Likewise, Schaie and Willis (1996) reviewed a number of studies that highlighted the complex relationship between IQ and health-related behavior. In general, these studies showed that adults who scored high on various IQ measures were likely to have healthy diets that excluded sodium and fat and to engage in a number of self-initiated health practices, such as exercise, use of seat belts, regular medical checkups, and so on. These relationships held true even when participants' ages and educational achievements were taken into account.

One important aspect of an individual's overall health status is his or her level of sensory function. See Research Focus 8.2 for a discussion of some research that focused on the relationship between adults' ability to see and hear and their IQ scores.

Terminal Drop

Closely associated with selective dropout and health status is the notion of terminal drop. **Terminal drop** refers to the tendency for an individual's psychological and biological abilities to decrease dramatically in the last few years prior to death. Terminal drop occurs when individuals have terminal, chronic illnesses that drain them of their strength, energy, and motivation. Most older people die of chronic diseases rather than accidents or injuries. Chronic diseases reduce older adults' capacities for clear thinking, undivided attention, and mental effort. As a result, their scores on cognitive tasks drop dramatically (Small & Bäckman, 2000). Further, Bosworth and Schaie (1999) reported that the effects of terminal drop are much more prevalent among the old-old (75 or more years) than among the young-old (65 to 74 years). The intelligence test scores of older adults are much more likely to reflect terminal drop and the possibility of early or undiagnosed dementia than the test scores of younger adults.

Processing Speed

As mentioned previously, one of the most ubiquitous findings in developmental psychology is an age-related slowing of behavior and information processing. Because the slowing of cognitive processing is so pervasive, could the decrement in processing speed be the

Sensory Acuity, Intelligence, and Aging

It seems obvious that how well we can see, hear, touch, taste, feel, and smell has no relationship whatsoever to our intellectual prowess. To prove the obvious, a number of researchers have shown that sensory ability is, in fact, independent of cognitive functioning.

Ulman Lindenberger and Paul Baltes (Baltes & Lindenberger, 1997; Lindenberger & Baltes, 1994) noted that previous research on the topic of sensory functioning and intelligence has focused on middle-aged adults. They wondered if sensory functioning and intelligence might be strongly related in very old individuals (those between 70 and 100 years of age). They based their hunch on Baltes's (1987) claim that there may be fundamental discontinuities in the correlates of cognitive functioning at different times during the life span. For example, Lindenberger and Baltes agree that there is nothing to suggest that sensory acuity would be related to intelligence in a group of healthy 20-year-olds. However, they offer two hypotheses on why these variables might share a powerful relationship during advanced old age. The sensory deprivation hypothesis suggests that age-related declines in cognitive functioning reflect the cumulative effects of reduced high-quality sensory stimulation in the oldest-old. It is difficult, if not impossible, for very old individuals to engage in intellectually stimulating activities if they cannot see and hear well. The common cause hypothesis, on the other hand, maintains that deficits in sensation and intelligence in advanced old age are the result of a common factor—the physiological deterioration of the brain (Christensen et al 2001). It is reasonable to assume that negative brain changes lead to impoverished cognitive performance. However, it seems just as intuitive to believe that changes in visual acuity are caused by deleterious changes in the eye. Surprisingly, recent research has shown that a great deal of the age-related deterioration of visual acuity is caused by changes in the brain, not just the eye!

To explore these ideas, Lindenberger and Baltes (1994) tested 156 older adults who were part of the Berlin Aging Study. The average age of the individuals in this research was 85 years, and the age range was 70 to 103 years of age. All participants were given 14 different tasks that measured five basic intellectual functions: speed, reasoning, memory, knowledge, and fluency. They were also administered standard measures of visual acuity (the Snellen reading task) and auditory acuity (an auditory threshold test for pure tones).

The data were analyzed by a complex statistical technique called structural equation modeling. This methodology allows a researcher to construct a graphic representation of the probable causal pathway between a number of variables, all of which may be correlated with each other. As box figure 8.B shows, age was correlated with visual and auditory acuity. More important, visual and auditory acuity were related to intelligence. Thus the pathway between age and intelligence was mediated by sensory acuity. In fact, when taken together, visual and auditory acuity account for 93 percent of the age-related variability in intellectual task performance!

In another study (Baltes & Lindenberger, 1997) involving 680 individuals between 25 and 103 years of age, these researchers showed that the average proportion of individual differences in intellectual functioning related to sensory function increased from 11 percent in adulthood (25–69 years of age) to 31 percent in old age (70–103 years of age). In fact, Baltes and Lindenberger (1997) have shown that sensory function is a better predictor of intellectual ability than sociobiographical variables such as occupational prestige and years of education.

What are the implications of the exceptionally powerful link between sensory and intellectual functioning in very old adults? Baltes and Lindenberger (1997) offer several provocative suggestions about the outcome of their re-

general determinant of intellectual decline in older adulthood? Lindenberger, Mayr, and Kliegl (1993) examined this hypothesis. They administered measures of processing speed (e.g., the digit symbol substitution task) as well as tasks of fluid (reasoning and associative memory) and crystallized (knowledge and verbal fluency) intelligence to 146 individuals between 70 and 103 years of age. Results showed that the negative age differences on all measures of crystallized and fluid intelligence were mediated through age differences in processing speed. In other words, the amount the variability in performance due to speed by itself, and speed in combination with age, was exceptionally high. It is interesting to note that processing speed was highly related to performance on knowledge tasks even though these measures were untimed! Lindenberger et al. (1993) suggested (figure 8.7) that age

Box Figure 8.B Age, IQ, and sensory activity. *Source:* Lindenberger, U., & Baltes, P. B. (1994). Sensory functioning and intelligence in old age: A strong connection. *Psychology and Aging, 9,* 348.

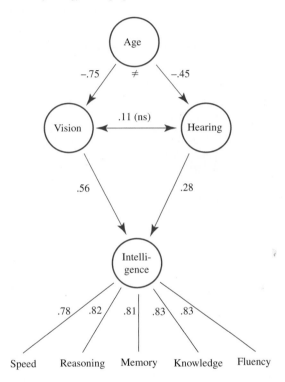

search. Most interestingly, they speculate that ". . . the assessment of visual and auditory acuity is 'transformed' into a task of cognitive functioning with advancing age " (p. 352).

Thus the standard clinical assessment of sensory function may provide a great deal of insight into the operations of the aging mind.

affects speed of processing, which negatively affects general intellectual ability, which, in turn, affects performance on individual tasks. These findings reinforce the claim that any legitimate theory of cognitive aging must address the centrality of age-related changes in the speed of basic processing and how age changes in processing speed affect higher-order cognitive processes.

Mental Exercise and Training

One of the assumptions of the successful aging view is that the brain is like a muscle, and to prevent or postpone the negative effects of aging on cognition, we must "use it or lose it" (Hultsch, Hertzog, Small, & Dixon, 1999).

Health status is a major factor affecting intellectual functioning.

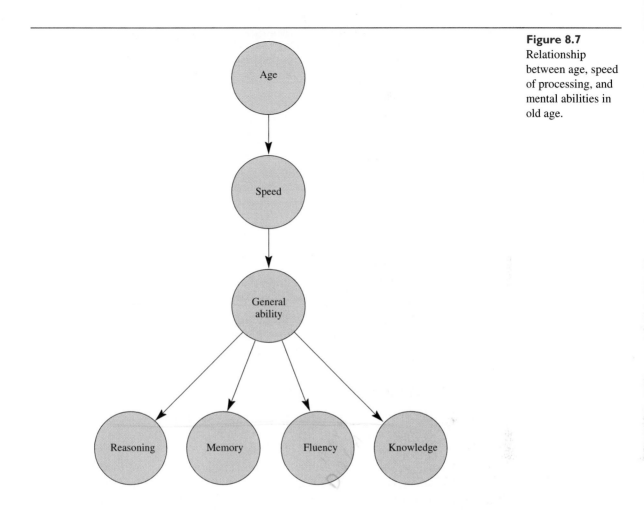

Figure 8.7
Relationship
between age, speed
of processing, and
mental abilities in
old age.

The idea that we can improve mental abilities by training, experience, or exercise has intrigued psychologists for many years; this idea is consistent with notions of cognitive plasticity. The concept of plasticity suggests that older adults have substantial cognitive reserve capacity and that training makes use of untapped reserve. Baltes and Kliegl (1986) hypothesized, for example, that older adults have little everyday experience with test items that measure fluid intelligence. But they also assumed that older adults possess the reserve capacity to raise their levels of performance on fluid-intelligence tasks. These researchers found that adults between 60 and 80 years of age who were exposed to a cognitive training program exhibited performance levels on fluid tasks comparable to the performance levels of a group of untrained younger adults. Baltes et al. (1989) have even shown that older adults can train themselves to become more proficient in fluid-intelligence tasks.

Even though training programs may significantly boost the intellectual abilities of older adults, training seldom transfers to a large range of other measures (Willis, 2001). Further, training has a much more beneficial effect for younger than older adults. It is certainly possible to teach older adults to display better performance on

TABLE 8.5

Factors That Reduce the Risk of Intellectual Decline During Older Adulthood

Absence of cardiovascular and other chronic diseases
Favorable environment mediated by high socioeconomic status
Involvement in complex and intellectually stimulating environment
Flexible personality style at midlife
High cognitive status of spouse
Maintenance of high levels of perceptual processing speed

Source: From Schaie, K.W. (1993). The Seattle longitudinal studies of adult intelligence. Current Directions in Psychological Science, 2, 171–174.

some components of intelligence in comparison to untrained younger adults. But, all things being equal, younger adults show greater gains from training and greater transfer of training than do their older counterparts (Touron, Hoyer & Cerella, Verhaeghen & Kliegl, 2000). See table 8.5 for a general summary of the factors that K. Warner Schaie believes reduce the risk of intellectual decline during later adulthood.

Intelligence and Everyday Problem Solving

As figure 8.8 shows, everyday problem solving may be unaffected by aging. There seems to be a number of reasons why intelligence test scores are poor indicators of an individual's ability to deal with the demands of everyday life. First, the types of items—such as defining unusual words, solving arithmetic problems, arranging pictures in a particular sequence, and so on—seem to have little in common with the problems adults face in real life. Second, many of the tests are speeded. This puts older adults at a disadvantage, because their responses are slower than those of younger adults. Third, older adults are not as accustomed as younger adults to taking tests and as a result may be more anxious or cautious. Fourth, older adults seem to be less motivated than younger adults to perform at optimal levels. Fifth, the original goal of intelligence tests was to predict school success or failure among groups of children and adolescents, and not real-world functioning.

Despite these factors, many psychologists have found that scores on various psychometric intelligence tests are somewhat predictive of real-life problem-solving ability. Allaire and Marsiske (1999) examined the relationship between a battery of everyday cognition measures and traditional psychometric tests. Their data revealed that performance on each of the everyday cognition measures was strongly correlated with the basic cognitive abilities.

One important aspect of everyday functioning that would seem to demand a blend of both analytic and practical intelligence is job performance. Research Focus 8.3 provides some information concerning the speculation that intelligence is related to occupational success.

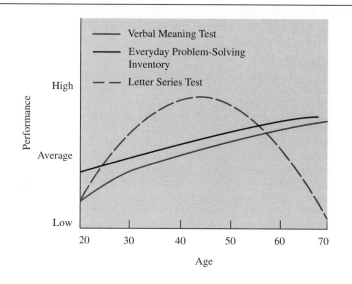

Figure 8.8 An illustration of age-related changes on the Everyday Problem-Solving inventory, the Verbal Meaning Test, and the Letter Series Test. *Source:* Cornelius, S. W., & Capsi, A. (1987). Everyday problem solving in adulthood and old age. *Psychology and Aging. 2;* 144–153. Washington DC: American Psychological Association.

Conclusions about Adult Intellectual Change

One of the major goals of this chapter was to answer what seems a relatively simple question: What happens to intelligence as one ages? As we have seen, however, there is no simple answer to this question. Cross-sectional studies show a more dramatic, steeper rate of intellectual decline than longitudinal studies.

Cross-sectional studies, because they are often contaminated by cohort effects and terminal drop, are likely to paint an overly pessimistic picture of adult intellectual change. Longitudinal and sequential studies indicate that intelligence remains stable (or actually increases) until approximately 60 years of age, after which a slight decline may occur. This conclusion seems most valid, however, for healthy, well-educated adults. Furthermore, selective dropout may contaminate the findings of longitudinal studies.

We have also seen that different types of intelligence show different patterns of change over age. Crystallized and verbal components of intelligence seem to increase with age, while fluid intelligence and measures of performance decline with age. Despite these predictable patterns of age-related change, a great deal of plasticity characterizes adult intelligence. It is possible to train adults to increase their scores on intelligence tests, even on tasks that measure fluid abilities. But training effects are more significant for younger than older adults.

The finding that fluid intelligence can be boosted among older adults is important within the context of Earl Hunt's (1993) remarks about the productivity of older workers. Hunt noted that older people are not adept in performing jobs that require them to make quick decisions, recognize stimuli embedded in a noisy background, and keep track of several pieces of information at once. However, these are the kinds of tasks that computers excel at. Thus, older (as well as younger) workers

Intelligence and Occupational Success

Initially, intelligence tests were designed to predict academic success (or failure) in school-aged individuals. In their extensive review of the psychometric literature, Neisser et al. (1996) concluded that IQ tests have achieved this goal remarkably well. The average correlation between IQ test performance and school grades is +.50. What else should IQ test performance predict? Should IQ relate to the type of job a person takes during adulthood and her success in her occupation? After all, IQ is related to educational success, and we hope that school success predicts occupational success. Again, Neisser et al. (1996) have found that IQ test scores possess a great deal of predictive power along these lines. For example, individuals with blue-collar jobs (e.g., truck drivers) typically have IQs of about 100, whereas white-collar workers (e.g., physicians) have substantially higher IQs, approximately 125. Also, job performance within a variety of occupations, as measured by supervisor ratings, productivity, work quality, and so on, correlates about +.50 with IQ scores. In effect, IQ scores may be the best "single predictor" of job success. However, as Neisser et al. (1996) have cautioned, other characteristics of the individual—

such as motivation, personality, and interpersonal skills—probably play just as important, or perhaps even more important, a role in predicting occupational success.

Psychologists are just beginning to understand the complex relationship between IQ and career success. Cognitive psychologist Earl Hunt (1995) has put forth one of the most interesting perspectives on this relationship. Hunt argues that there is a nonlinear, rather than a linear, relationship between IQ and job performance (see box figure 8.C). As the figure shows, a linear relationship is characterized by a straight line—distance on one axis of the graph is proportional to distance on the other axis of the graph. A nonlinear relationship is characterized by a curved line—distance on one axis of the graph is *not* proportional to distance on the other axis of the graph. This nonlinearity suggests that eventually. It is important to have enough intelligence, but having lots of it does not add that much. Hunt suggests that having a certain level of IQ is important for getting into an occupation. However, once one has mastered the essentials of an occupation, motivational, interpersonal, and experience-based factors—not IQ—drive job performance.

Box Figure 8.C   The nonlinear or "curvilinear" relationship between IQ and job performance. *Source:* Hunt, E. (1995). The role of intelligence in modern society. *American Scientist, 83,* 361.

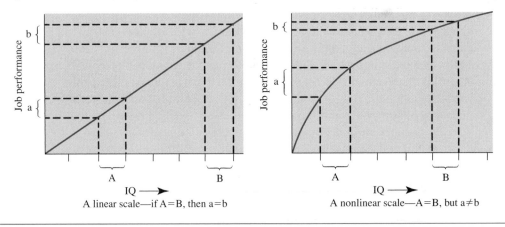

who possess the skills needed to perform highly speeded perceptual-motor tasks run the risk of being replaced by machines. On the other hand, machines are not capable of dealing with the "novel" problems that arise in any industry or occupation. Hunt maintained that fluid intellectual abilities are needed to solve these types of problems. He also suggested that understanding why fluid intelligence declines during middle adulthood and how this might be prevented or ameliorated will be of major economic necessity. Hunt's message to the employers (and employees) of the twenty-first century is straightforward: "The simple fact is that fluid intelligence will be in demand. Crystallized intelligence is only of use in a crystallized society" (Hunt, 1993, p. 597).

Finally, we reported that traditional measures of intelligence are modestly related to measures of practical or social intelligence during adulthood. This finding does not mean that traditional tests are invalid. Rather, it suggests that psychometricians need to develop a more differentiated theory (and tests) of intelligence—a theory that does full justice to the broad array of intellectual abilities adults manifest as they age. Research Focus 8.4 presents the basic ideas that underlie some new theoretical viewpoints about the nature of human intelligence.

Creativity

What is it about someone like Thomas Edison that made him able to create so many inventions? Was he simply more intelligent than most people?

Surprisingly, when Edison was a young boy, one of his teachers told him he was too dumb to learn anything! There are many examples of unnoticed creative genius in early development. Walt Disney was fired from a newspaper job because he did not have any creative ideas. Winston Churchill failed one year of secondary school. Consider the following comments made by John Lennon: "People like me are aware of their so-called genius at ten, eight, nine. . . . I always wondered, 'Why has nobody discovered me?' In school, didn't they see that I'm more clever than anybody in this school? Why didn't they put me in art school? Why didn't they train me? I was different, I was always different. Why didn't anybody notice me?" (quoted in Gardner, 1983, p. 115).

One of the reasons people overlook creative ability is because we have such difficulty in defining and measuring creativity.

Older adults, unlike college students, are often unfamiliar with standardized tests and testing situations.

New Conceptions of Intelligence

Howard Gardner and Robert Sternberg have developed theories that challenge the traditional psychometric views concerning the measurement and meaning of intelligence. In this research focus, we outline the basic tenets of these theories.

In a controversial book entitled *Frames of Mind,* Howard Gardner (1983) proposed a **Theory of Multiple Intelligences.** This theory suggests that different human intelligences are each localized in a different area in the brain. The different intelligences Gardner identified are linguistic, logical-mathematical, spatial, musical, bodily-kinesthetic, and personal intelligence. Each of these intelligences makes use of a different symbol system through which individuals represent or structure experience. For example, we can symbolize experience through words; other symbols include logical-numerical relationships; visual images; tones, pitches, or rhythms; body movements; and so forth. Gardner maintains that traditional IQ tests measure only the first three of the preceding intelligences. Gardner's criteria for identifying specific types of intelligences include the following: (1) Each intelligence can be independently represented in the brain and destroyed by damage or injury to a localized brain site; (2) exceptional individuals, child prodigies, and idiot savants may exhibit extraordinary performance in one form of intelligence, but moderate or poor performance in other forms; (3) each intelligence has a unique developmental history; (4) each intelligence consists of a core set of opera-tions that particular types of experience or information automatically trigger; (5) each intelligence has an evolutionary history; (6) the existence of each intelligence can be demonstrated by laboratory experiments and psychometric research; and (7) each intelligence possesses its own unique symbol system.

The vast majority of the research on Gardner's theory has focused on children, especially within the context of educational policy. Unfortunately, Gardner's theory has not been assessed in adult and/or aged populations. Based on the extant psychometric literature, however, we might expect that logical-mathematical and spatial intelligence would decline with age, whereas linguistic and personal intelligence might remain stable (or perhaps increase) with age.

Similar to Gardner's notion of personal intelligence is Daniel Goleman's (1995) concept of **emotional intelligence.** Emotionally intelligent people are aware of the needs, feelings, and motives that operate in themselves and in others. More important, they can effectively manage their emotional states (and those of others) to achieve a number of desirable goals. Consequently, they may have tremendously successful professional careers despite the fact that they may not possess extremely high IQs or "academic smarts." Researchers need to determine how best to measure emotional intelligence and how emotional intelligence interacts with more traditional notions of intelligence.

Definition and Measurement of Creativity

Creativity refers to the ability to produce novel ideas that are high in quality and task-appropriate (Sternberg, 2001). The prevailing belief of psychologists who study creativity is that intelligence and creativity are not the same. If intelligence and creativity were identical, there would be no reason to make a distinction between them! We could choose one of these terms—intelligence or creativity—to describe the same phenomenon.

Distinguishing between creativity and intelligence is a difficult task. David Ausubel (1968) emphasized that *creativity* is one of the most ambiguous and confusing terms in psychology. He believes the term *creative* should be reserved for people who make unique and original contributions to society. Surely a list of creative individuals, from this point of view, would include Marie Curie, Charles Darwin, Thomas Edison, Georgia O'Keeffe, Pablo Picasso, and William Shakespeare—they possessed creative genius, or **exceptional creativity.** The creative acts of these individuals have shaped and influenced our world. Several other researchers (e.g., Mumford & Gustafson, 1988; Simonton, 1988, 1990, 1997) have also agreed that psychologists should focus their attention on the study of exceptional creativity.

New Conceptions of Intelligence

Robert Sternberg (1999a, 1999b, Sternberg et al., 2001) has put forth a **Triarchic Theory of Intelligence.** This theory suggests that intelligence consists of three independent facets: analytic, creative (or insightful), and practical (or street smarts). The analytic aspect of intelligence refers to an individual's ability to process information and solve problems. This component, according to Sternberg, is very closely related to traditional psychometric conceptualizations of intelligence. Put somewhat differently, Sternberg argues that psychologists have all but ignored the creative and practical aspects of intelligence.

To get a feel for Sternberg's theory, think of the following individuals who are about to enter college. Tom's strength is analytic intelligence. He has extremely high SAT scores and gets very good grades in college, but his professors do not consider him a "great student." George's forte is creative intelligence. His SAT scores and grades are about average, yet he amazes his professors by sudden flashes of insight and brilliance. They wonder why such a gap exists between his grades and the quality of his ideas. Sam possesses a great deal of practical intelligence, which we might think of as common sense, or street smarts. His grades, along with his insight, are average. However, he is very well liked by all of his professors. After graduation, he finds a much better array of job opportunities than either Tom or George.

One of Sternberg's most important goals is to develop adequate measures of creative and practical intelligence.

Note that problems that measure analytic intelligence are clearly defined, have a single correct solution, and are somewhat divorced from everyday experience, whereas tasks that measure creative and practical intelligence possess the opposite characteristics. How could you develop and score measures of creative and practical intelligence?

Sternberg, Wagner, Williams, and Horvath (1995) have adopted the following strategy to assess practical intelligence within the area of business management. They have developed a number of vignettes that describe various problems that arise in real-life business situations, and they ask the participants in their research (actual managers) to rank order a number of possible solutions to each vignette. (Note that the quality of these solutions is determined by the ratings these individuals, who are excellent managers, assign to them.) This research has shown that scores on the questionnaires are relatively independent of performance on traditional IQ tests, yet performance on the questionnaires correlates very highly with measures of actual job performance.

Sternberg's theory is especially important when one considers that practical intelligence may become increasingly important to individuals as they journey through the adult life span. Sternberg's model has been confirmed in three different international samples as well (Sternberg, et al., 2001).

Robert Weisberg (1986) argued that it is also important to understand ordinary creativity. **Ordinary creativity** refers to the creative behavior of "ordinary" adults in "ordinary" real-life situations. People we interact with everyday show their creativity in conversation, in their work, in their dress, or in managing on a small budget.

Divergent thinking, one of the dimensions of intelligence J. P. Guilford (1967) proposed, is a kind of creativity. **Divergent thinking** refers to the ability to produce many different answers to a single question. In contrast, **convergent thinking** is the ability to derive the one correct solution to a problem. For example, there is one correct answer to the question, How many quarters can you trade for 60 dimes? This question calls for convergent thinking. But many possible answers exist to the question, What are some of the possible uses for a coat hanger? This question requires divergent thinking.

Rebok (1987) suggested that the generation of novel ideas (divergent thinking) should be viewed as a necessary but not sufficient condition for creativity. Creativity depends in part on possessing a critical amount of knowledge about a particular domain. For example, it would be impossible to be a creative composer if one did not know anything about musical composition. Researchers interested in creativity should simultaneously assess an individual's thinking style and the degree of knowledge he or she possesses within a particular domain. This suggestion may be especially important for understanding creativity in older adults. As individuals age, they develop a substantial base of knowledge through activities and experience.

Georgia O'Keeffe is someone who maintained artistic creativity in older childhood.

Another concept of creativity is based on Csikszentmihalyi's (1997) ideas about the relationship between discovery (or creativity) and autoetelic activities. *Autoetelic activities* are those we do purely because we enjoy them, not because we have to, and not because of external rewards such as money or prestige. A writer who creates a wonderful poem, a play, or a novel for its own sake, regardless of salary or fame, is working creatively. For example, you might love to write poems, or play tennis, or play music, or swim in the ocean. You are more likely to engage in the creative process when you are doing such an autoetelic activity. For Thomas Edison, for example, discovering the principles and applications of electricity was probably autoetelic.

Developmental Changes in Creativity

Because there are different types of creativity—ordinary and exceptional—this section consists of two parts. First, we discuss age-related trends in exceptional creativity—the creative accomplishments of well-known people in various fields of specialization. Second, we discuss age-related differences in ordinary creativity. Researchers have measured this form of creativity by administering psychometric tests of creativity to individuals who represent the general population.

Exceptional Creativity

Many older adults are exceptionally creative. Some examples appear in table 8.6. Lehman (1953, 1960) and Dennis (1966, 1968) conducted the earliest and most influential research on age-related changes in exceptional creativity in adulthood. Lehman (1953) charted the ages at which adults produced highly creative works that had a significant impact on their fields. As figure 8.9a shows, the quality of productivity was highest when individuals were in their thirties; then it declined. About 80 percent of the most important contributions of creative individuals are completed by age 50. In fact, he concluded that ". . . genius does not function equally throughout the years of

TABLE 8.6

Some Creative Accomplishments of Older Adults

Accomplishment

George Burns received an Academy Award at age 80 and was still acting in his late-90s.
Mahatma Ghandi launched the independence movement in India at age 72.
Nelson Mandela was awarded the Nobel Peace Prize at age 75.
Grandma Moses began to paint in her mid-90s and was still painting at age 100.
Pablo Picasso was still painting at age 92.
Arthur Rubenstein performed at Carnegie Hall at age 89.
Bertrand Russell was active and influential in international peace efforts at age 94.
Albert Schweitzer headed a hospital in Africa at age 89.
George Bernard Shaw wrote his first play at age 48 and was still writing plays at age 93.
Mother Teresa was influential as a missionary in India at age 87.
Frank Lloyd Wright completed the design for the Guggenheim museum at age 91.

adulthood. Superior creativity rises rapidly to a maximum which occurs usually in the thirties and then falls off slowly" (Lehman, 1953, pp. 330–331).

Unlike Lehman (1953), Wayne Dennis (1966) studied the total productivity, not just the superior works, of creative people in the arts, sciences, and humanities who lived long lives. Figure 8.9b shows that the point at which creative production peaked in adult life varied from one discipline to another. For example, in the humanities, people in their seventies appeared equally creative as people in their forties. Artists and scientists, however, began to show a decline in creative productivity in their fifties. In all instances, people were least productive in terms of creativity during their twenties.

Dennis (1968) also examined the creative output of famous scholars, scientists, and artists who lived until at least 80 years of age. Dennis discovered that, on average, these individuals were the most creative during their sixties! Scientists produced 35 percent of their total output after age 60—20 percent while they were in their sixties, and 15 percent while they were in their seventies. Famous inventors produced more than half of their major work after age 60. And artists produced about 20 percent of their total output after age 60. A study of Nobel laureates in science found that the average age at which they published their first major paper was 25. All of the laureates in this study who were past 70, however, continued to publish scholarly papers in scientific journals. Therefore, by relaxing the criteria for defining exceptional creativity (i.e., by examining the total creative output of individuals, not just the best work), we see that creativity may not decline as early as Lehman (1953) suggested. It seems as if individuals who are bright and productive in early and middle adulthood have a good chance of maintaining their creativity in older adulthood. This conclusion is consistent with Simonton's statement that the most creative individuals "tend to start early, end late, and produce at above-average rates" (1988, p. 253).

Over (1989) examined the relationship between age and exceptional creativity by analyzing the percentage of both high- and low-impact articles scientists published at

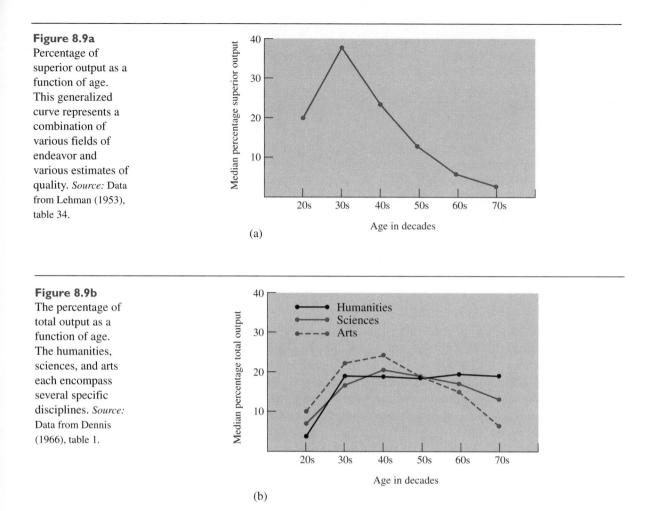

Figure 8.9a
Percentage of superior output as a function of age. This generalized curve represents a combination of various fields of endeavor and various estimates of quality. *Source:* Data from Lehman (1953), table 34.

(a)

Figure 8.9b
The percentage of total output as a function of age. The humanities, sciences, and arts each encompass several specific disciplines. *Source:* Data from Dennis (1966), table 1.

(b)

different ages. He discovered that young scientists published both more high-impact and more low-impact works than older scientists. This finding is consistent with Simonton's (1990) conclusion that the "periods in a creator's life that see the most masterpieces also witness the most easily forgotten productions . . . the 'quality ratio,' or the proportion of major products to total output per age unit, tends to fluctuate randomly over the course of any career. The quality ratio neither increases or decreases with age" (p. 323).

Ordinary Creativity

What happens when we administer psychometric tests of creativity to "typical" as opposed to "exceptional" individuals? Does ordinary creativity show age-related change? Alpaugh and Birren (1977) conducted one of the first studies on this topic. Their cross-sectional sample consisted of 111 teachers between 20 and 84 years of age. These individuals took the WAIS as well as a battery of psychometric tasks that measure creativity. Within this well-educated sample, scores on the WAIS remained stable across adulthood. However, scores on the measures of creativity peaked at 30 and declined thereafter.

In another study, Ruth and Birren (1985) tested 150 persons enrolled in adult education classes in Finland using several psychometric tests of creativity and several measures of crystallized and fluid intelligence. Participants in this study were between 25 and 75 years old. Results indicated that performance on the creativity measures declined with age. The great majority of the decline in creativity occurred between young and middle adulthood.

In one of the most comprehensive studies of aging and creativity, McCrae, Arenberg, and Costa (1987) combined cross-sectional, longitudinal, and cross-sequential methods of data collection. As part of the Baltimore Longitudinal Study of Aging, 825 well-educated men were tested at regular intervals between 1959 and 1972. The men ranged from 17 to 101 years old. All of the participants performed several different divergent-thinking tasks. These tasks involved (1) associational fluency—the ability to provide synonyms for specific words; (2) expressional fluency—the ability to write sentences with words beginning with particular letters; (3) ideational fluency—the ability to name objects in specific classes; (4) word fluency—the ability to write words containing a designated letter; and (5) consequences—the ability to imagine unusual, novel outcomes for particular situations. The participants were also given the vocabulary test from the WAIS.

Results indicated that scores on the measures of creativity and vocabulary were distinct. This is surprising, given the fact that the vocabulary test and all of the measures of creativity were verbal in nature. Furthermore, all the methods of data collection and analysis (cross-sectional, longitudinal, and cross-sequential) revealed that scores on the measures of creativity declined with age. Based on these results, McCrae et al. (1987) concluded that creativity, like fluid intelligence, declines with age. However, the correlations between age and performance on the measures of creativity, although statistically significant, were in the modest range ($-.10$ to $-.30$). Also, McCrae and his colleagues administered the tests of creativity under standardized conditions with strict time limits, a procedure that may be especially disadvantageous to older participants.

Perhaps the complex and somewhat confusing nature of developmental changes in creativity may be best understood by approaching creativity from a contextual perspective. A contextual view suggests that a number of cognitive, neuro-biological, and social changes may influence creativity during adulthood. In a discussion of life-span creativity, Jean and Michael Romaniuk (1981) provide an example of how incentives for productivity may influence an individual's creativity. In the academic world, tenure and the pressure to publish may affect creative accomplishment. Shifts in career interests and activities, such as transferring from research to administrative activity, changing one's career goals or job security, or refining earlier creative accomplishments, may also influence creativity. And the opening of new research fields, along with the saturation of existing fields, may influence creative accomplishments.

At a more general level, it seems that as people age, they may become less interested (due to internal as well as external pressures) in generating new ideas. Alternatively, they may become more interested in reflecting on the meaning of already created knowledge and on using that knowledge to come to grips with the meaning of their own lives and to help their culture evolve in an adaptive manner. Thus, as Simonton (1990) has suggested, the need to be wise may replace the desire to be creative. This viewpoint is consistent with Simonton's (1988) observation that older individuals occupy positions of power and leadership within a number of social, political, and religious institutions, whereas younger adults are more likely to create new institutions and to revolutionize existing ones. For example, a typical pope of the Roman Catholic Church assumes his position at approximately double the age at which Jesus of Nazareth ended his ministry. This seems to support Hall's (1922) position that ". . . men in their prime conceived the great religions, the old made them prevail" (p. 420).

In summary, we have seen that creativity is an elusive concept, difficult to define, measure, and chart. Exceptionally creative individuals may continue to function creatively well into middle and late adulthood; in fact, many creative people do some of their best work late in life. The need to be creative, however, may decline with advancing age for a variety of psychosocial as well as intrapersonal reasons.

Genius

There are many exceptionally creative and highly intelligent adults. However, there seems to be a quality above and beyond creativity and intelligence—genius. What factors are responsible for the development of genius? At what age can genius first be identified? Until what age can it be maintained? At present, many developmental psychologists are attempting to answer questions such as these. In a book entitled *Creating Minds* (1993a), Howard Gardner has analyzed the lives of seven geniuses of the modern era: Einstein, Freud, Picasso, Stravinsky, T. S. Eliot, Mahatma Ghandi, and Martha Graham. What can we learn about genius by studying these individuals?

First, we can recognize that intelligence and creativity are a necessary but not sufficient condition for the development of genius. Second, geniuses are not content with solving problems. They relish the enterprise of **problem finding.** As Begley (1993) observed, Freud's genius was not displayed in his interpretations of dreams; rather, Freud's genius was that he recognized the role dreams can play in revealing human motivation. Third, geniuses seem to approach their work with a sense of childlike enthusiasm and obsessiveness. Geniuses work hard, and they gain their fundamental insights by asking questions that are childlike in nature. For example, Einstein wondered about space and time (things that you may have thought about as a child) from a scientist's point of view. Fourth, geniuses seem to synthesize different modes of thought to produce their work. Composers, for example, often say they can see music, whereas painters often remark that they experience sounds as visual symbols. Fifth, there seems to be a critical amount of knowledge a person must possess about a particular domain to make a genius-like contribution. Too much knowledge or too much time spent thinking about the same problem may be just as antagonistic to genius as too little knowledge or too little thought. This may account for the fact that genius is a phenomenon of middle adulthood. The young adult may be brilliant. The older adult may be wise. But the individual who creates a major revolution in art, science, or literature is likely to be in her thirties.

Although relatively little is known about the developmental trends for geniuses and creative people, we do know that the effects of giftedness in intellectual and academic domains are long-lasting (see Research Focus 8.5).

Where Are They After Twenty Years?

Twenty years after finding that gifted boys were better at math than gifted girls (Benbow & Stanley, 1980), a follow-up study of these same students revealed that early giftedness predicted adult careers and life choices (Benbow, Lubinski, Shea, & Eftekhari-Sanjani, 2000). In the follow-up study, the researchers sent questionnaires to 2,752 men and women who were first tested as 12- to 14-year-olds. Replies came back from 1,975 individuals. Women tended to choose careers in which they could work with people, and men tended to choose careers in the physical sciences or engineering.

Both sets of participants tended to attain high academic achievement, with more than 90 percent earning bachelor's degrees and 25 percent earning doctoral degrees—25 times the national average! The participants reported a relatively high level of happiness and satisfaction with their life choices and careers.

Benbow, senior author on the follow-up study, coauthored the original study when she was a graduate student at Johns Hopkins University. She plans to study where these people are in another twenty years!

Benbow, C. P., Lubinski, D., Shea, D. L., & Eftekhari-Sanjani, H. (2000). Sex differences in mathematical reasoning ability at age 13: Their status 20 years later. *Psychological Science, 2000,* 11, 474–480.

Benbow, C. P., & Stanley, J. C. (1980). Sex differences in mathematical ability: Fact or artifact? *Science, 210,* 1262–1264.

SUMMARY

The psychometric approach emphasizes a measurement-based orientation to the study of adult intellectual change. Psychometricians differ on whether intelligence is a general ability or a constellation of separate abilities. We assess intelligence, from the psychometric perspective, through standardized tests. One of the most widely used tests to assess adult intelligence is the Wechsler Adult Intelligence Scale (WAIS). This test contains both verbal and performance scales.

Different types of developmental studies have reflected differing patterns of age-related changes in intelligence. Cross-sectional studies show that intelligence declines sharply from early adulthood onward. Longitudinal studies, on the other hand, indicate that intelligence remains stable until late adulthood, then may undergo a slight decline. Verbal intelligence is likely to improve with age, while nonverbal or performance components of intelligence are likely to decline with age. Put somewhat differently, crystallized intelligence has been found to increase with age, but fluid intelligence seems to decrease. Several factors appear to contribute to these age-related changes in intelligence, including cohort effects, selective dropout, health status, reduced processing speed, and terminal drop. It has been shown that adults who actively exercise specific mental abilities, or who receive special training in certain abilities, do not display significant age-related decrements in those abilities.

Research on developmental changes in exceptional creativity suggests that in the arts and sciences, creative thought may peak in the forties, whereas in the humanities, creativity continues at a high level well into the early part of late adulthood. Regardless of when creativity reaches its peak, research shows that for the majority of individuals, creative output continues throughout mid-adulthood to later life. Research designed to study everyday creativity in typical individuals has shown a modest, but statistically significant, decline in divergent thinking over the adult life span. However, various methodological problems (including the speeded nature of tests of creativity) reduce confidence in these findings.

REVIEW QUESTIONS

1. What does the term *psychometric* mean?
2. Explain how psychometricians determine intelligence scores for adults of different ages.
3. What does it mean to say that intelligence reflects the operation of a single g factor? Have researchers obtained data supporting the g factor theory?
4. Explain the difference between crystallized and fluid intelligence. How do these forms of intelligence change over time?
5. Explain the different results obtained by cross-sectional versus longitudinal studies of adult intellectual change.
6. Explain how cohort effects, selective dropout, health status, and terminal drop influence IQ test scores.
7. Discuss the concepts of mental exercise, plasticity, and cognitive intervention in late adulthood.
8. Describe two different approaches to the study of creativity and explain what you think is the best way to measure creativity.
9. How do developmental changes in exceptional creativity differ from those in ordinary creativity?
10. Give some examples of the cognitive, cultural, and social factors that might stimulate the development and maintenance of creativity and genius throughout adult life.

ON THE WEB   www.mhhe.com/hoyer5

For a listing of links to new information about intelligence and creativity, and to other topics related to the material in this chapter, see:

The National institute on Aging, a component of the National Institutes of Health, has a website devoted to improving the health of older adults. The Behavior and Social Research program and the Neuroscience and Neuropsychology of Aging Program support research on cognitive aging. Results of new studies are highlighted on these pages.

Secretsofaging.com offers links to information about the aging mind.

9

COGNITION, WISDOM, AND EXPERTISE

> *The questions which belong to different domains of thought, differ very often not only in the kinds of subject matter that they are about, but in the kinds of thinking that they require.*
> —G. Ryle, Dilemmas

> *The fool thinks he is a wise man, the wise man knows he is a fool.*
> —Anonymous

> *Great minds do not think alike.*
> —Anonymous

INTRODUCTION

We have indicated in the preceding chapters that some cognitive decline is an inevitable aspect of aging. There are no measures of intelligence, learning, or memory for which older adults reliably outperform younger adults. Research stemming from the information-processing and psychometric perspectives demonstrates that as you age, you become slower at processing information, and less able to remember.

In some situations, however, some older adults seem to show high levels of cognitive proficiency. Further, some older adults have the extraordinary mental characteristic referred to as wisdom. **Wisdom** is a particular mental quality associated with the cognitive abilities of some aged individuals, but not with younger individuals. Those who possess wisdom combine reflective abilities such as self-analysis and introspection along with affective components such as empathy, gentleness, and peacefulness. Wisdom is characterized by reflection, affect, and knowledge. Psychometric and information-processing theories of cognition have little, if anything, to say about the development of wisdom during older adulthood.

Which is the more valid account of the cognitive abilities of the older adult? Are the elderly forgetful, inattentive, and unintelligent, or wise, knowledgeable, and sage? To help you make a meaningful choice between these two contrasting portrayals, this chapter describes the stage theory approach to the study of adult cognitive development. Stage theories stress the idea that new, more sophisticated ways of thinking emerge during adulthood.

We begin this chapter with a description of Piaget's theory of cognitive development, paying special attention to the concept of formal operations. This stage was originally thought to be the final, most advanced stage of cognitive development. Next, we consider new research that has sought to identify an even more advanced stage of cognitive development. This stage, which only emerges during the adult years, is referred to as postformal operations. We review the basic characteristics of postformal thinking, especially as they apply to social cognition—or how people understand and resolve everyday interpersonal problems.

Next we discuss the encapsulation model of adult cognitive development. This model, developed by John Rybash, William Hoyer, and Paul Roodin, integrates and extends three different theoretical perspectives (the psychometric, information-processing, and developmental stage theories) that bear on the topic of adult cognition. We illustrate the basic tenets of the encapsulation model by describing the research on aging and cognitive expertise and the growth of wisdom during the adult years.

Stage Theories of Adult Cognitive Development

People often say, "He's in a stage," or "She's going through a phase," when describing someone's development. However, it is important to be precise when describing stage-based sequences of development. Developmental psychologists use a set of specific criteria to identify and define the stages of development.

Characteristics of Cognitive Stages

A set of cognitive stages must satisfy five different criteria: invariant movement, qualitative change, hierarchical integration, universal progression, and structured wholeness.

The notion of **invariant movement** suggests that individuals must pass through a single, unchangeable sequence of stages during development. For example, if a stage theorist maintains that cognitive development consists of a four-stage sequence, then individuals must move through the stages in order: stage 1 → stage 2; stage 2 → stage 3; stage 3 → stage 4. It is impossible to skip stages, or to go through the stages in a different order.

The concept of **qualitative change** suggests that at each stage an individual uses a completely different set of rules to represent and understand reality. These thought structures are assumed to differ from one another as much as apples differ from oranges. A stage theorist would describe a person's cognitive functioning in terms of how the individual understands reality, not in terms of the quantity of information the individual possesses.

Hierarchical integration implies that at each stage in a developmental sequence, an individual should have incorporated as well as extended the stage that preceded it. This means, for example, that the thought structures laid down in stage 2 of a cognitive sequence form the basis of stage 3. It also means that stage 3 extends the structures laid down in stage 2.

The idea of **universal progression** suggests that all individuals in all cultures progress through a set of stages in the same invariant sequence. A valid stage theory must apply to all individuals, regardless of social class, race, ethnicity, educational level, or culture.

Structured wholeness, which may be the most stringent of the criteria for a stage theory, implies that individuals can only understand reality one stage at a time. This means, for example, that if an individual is at stage 2 within a particular cognitive sequence, she will think about all or at least most problems from the perspective of that stage. In other words, a person would not be expected to reason about mathematical problems from the perspective of stage 4 and interpersonal problems from the perspective of stage 2; such an inconsistency would violate the concept of structured wholeness.

Piaget's Stage Theory

Beyond any doubt, Jean Piaget (see Piaget, 1970; Piaget & Inhelder, 1969) formulated the most important and far-reaching stage theory of cognitive development. He identified four stages of intellectual development: the sensorimotor stage, the preoperational stage, the concrete-operational stage, and the formal-operational stage. The **sensorimotor stage** lasts from birth to about 2 years of age and is synonymous with the period most people refer to as infancy. Piaget (1954) argued that infants cannot think about the world by using internal mental symbols (such as words, visual images, etc.). Instead, infants experience events in terms of sensory-motoric relationships.

During the **preoperational stage,** which begins at about 2 years of age and lasts until 7 years of age, children can form internal mental symbols. However, preoperational children have a great deal of difficulty in distinguishing between concrete and imaginary events and objects. Preoperational thinkers cannot reverse mental operations—they might, for example, have difficulty grasping the idea that addition is the reverse of subtraction. A preoperational thinker might not understand that the best way to solve the subtraction problem $? - 7 = 1$ is to transform it into the addition problem $7 + 1 = ?$.

In the **concrete-operational stage,** which lasts from approximately 7 to 12 years of age, children can distinguish between mental symbols and real-life events or objects. Also, they begin to think in a reversible manner. Not only can concrete thinkers understand the complementary relationship between addition and subtraction, they can understand a relationship from different or reversible points of view. For example, when shown two pairs of sticks, the concrete thinker can understand that (1) if the red stick is taller than the blue stick (R > B), and (2) the blue stick is taller than the green stick (B > G), then the red stick must be taller than the green stick (R > G). Put another way, the concrete thinker is able to reason that "If the blue stick is shorter than the red stick but taller than the green stick, then the red stick must be taller than the green stick."

Concrete thinking has its limitations. Consider, for example, the following problem: "Three girls are walking down the street. Mary is taller than Jane but shorter than Susan. Who is the tallest of the three?" This problem is very similar to the stick problem, but the stimuli in the former problem were concrete (they could actually be seen and touched), while the stimuli in the latter task were hypothetical (they had to be imagined). Piaget maintained that it is only during the fourth and last stage of cognitive development, the stage he termed **formal operations,** that individuals can reason about hypothetical, abstract relationships.

Formal Operations

The stage of formal operations, which according to Piaget emerges somewhere around early adolescence to midadolescence, has occupied an important place in the study of adult cognition because it represents Piaget's view of mature adult cognition.

Characteristics of Formal Operations

Piaget and his associate Barbel Inhelder (Inhelder & Piaget, 1958; Piaget & Inhelder, 1969) identified three characteristics of formal thinking:

1. An ability to reason about abstract ideas
2. An ability to think in a hypothetical-deductive manner
3. A capacity to think about the nature of thinking

With regard to the first characteristic, Piaget suggested that a concrete thinker's understanding of reality consists of generalizations based on specific, real-life experiences. At the level of concrete operations, therefore, real experiences are more important than possible (or hypothetical or abstract) experiences. Formal thinkers, however, are capable of reversing the relative importance they attach to real versus possible experiences. This allows formal thinkers to think logically about verbal propositions, or pure ideas. The truth value of a verbal proposition depends on its logical relationship to other propositions, not on its relationship to concrete, real-life events. Thus, formal thinkers can reason about contrary-to-fact ideas and experiences. For example, think about the following problem: Would the weather be any different if snow was black, not white? A concrete thinker would probably argue that this is a silly problem, because in real life, snow is never black. Formal thinkers, on the other hand, can rise above the constraints of reality. They understand that even though snow is never black, it is logical to conclude that if it were, the temperature would change (if large portions of the earth's surface were covered by a black substance, the earth would become warmer because the dark surface would absorb heat).

The ability to engage in hypothetical-deductive thinking means that formal thinkers are capable of reasoning like scientists. They can create abstract hypotheses and then test the validity of these hypotheses by observing the results of well-controlled experiments. Thus, scientific thinking is deductive; it proceeds from the general (the abstract hypothesis) to the specific (creating a single experiment designed to test the theory).

The notion of thinking about thinking means that formal thinkers can ponder the meaning and significance of their mental experiences from multiple points of view. For example, an individual at the formal operational stage can think, "I want to be married," and can then generate a number of hypothetical explanations of the meaning and significance of that thought from his point of view as well as from the points of view of others (e.g., his parents). The ability to think about thinking explains why adolescents and adults often become armchair psychologists who find it intriguing to analyze their own mental activity as well as the thoughts and feelings of others.

Measurement of Formal Operations

Inhelder and Piaget (1958) developed several different types of tasks to determine whether an individual has reached the stage of formal operations. In this section, we discuss two of these tasks: the proportional-thinking task and the isolation-of-variables task. A *proportional-thinking task* refers to a type of problem that an individual can solve only by using simple arithmetic (a concrete operational strategy) or algebraic reasoning (a formal operational strategy). For example, consider the following:

> A psychologist takes a cup, dips it into the large bowl filled with beans, and pulls out 80 beans. Next, she takes a felt-tipped pen and places a large X on each of the 80 beans. She puts the marked beans back into the bowl and randomly mixes the beans. Then she dips the cup back into the bowl and extracts another sample. She discovers that there are 75 beans in the cup and that 15 of the 75 beans have an X on them. What would you estimate the total number of beans in the bowl to be?

A concrete thinker, using simple arithmetic, might answer 140 (adding the 60 unmarked beans in the second sample to the 80 marked beans in the first sample). A formal thinker, using algebraic reasoning, might say 400 (if one-fifth of the beans from the second sample were marked, it is logical to assume that one-fifth of the total number of beans were obtained and marked on the first sample. Therefore, if 80 is one-fifth of the total number of beans, there are 400 beans because $5 \times 80 = 400$).

In an *isolation-of-variables problem,* a person must determine which of a large number of variables produces a specific outcome. One of the most widely used problems of this type is the pendulum task, which asks a participant to determine the factors that influence the speed at which a pendulum swings back and forth. These factors include the length of the pendulum string, the weight of the object placed at the end of the string, the height at which the pendulum is released, and the force applied to push the pendulum.

Participants are given a pendulum apparatus that comes with two different strings (long and short) and two objects of different weights that can be placed on the ends of the strings (heavy and light). Given these materials, the participants are told to do as many experiments as they need to solve the problem. This task measures formal operational thinking because it requires participants to behave like scientists. They must develop a theory about what controls the oscillation of the pendulum and then perform the crucial experiments to test the theory. Only at the formal operational stage do individuals approach this problem in a scientific and systematic manner; that is, they evaluate each of the potential factors one at a time (keeping all other factors constant). Using this approach, they discover that the length of the string, not any of the other factors, determines the speed of oscillation.

Research on Formal Operations

Piaget (1972) assumed that individuals begin to develop formal operational thinking skills at about 11 years of age and that they fully complete the transition from concrete to formal operations no later than 15 to 20 years of age. A great deal of research has examined Piaget's assertions about these ages. Surprisingly, researchers have discovered that a significant percentage of young, middle-aged, and older adults do not attain the stage of formal operations. Furthermore, even when one is able to solve one type of formal-thinking task, that does not guarantee that the person will be able to solve another type of formal-thinking problem (Berzonsky, 1978; Brainerd, 1978). For example, adults who are able to solve an isolation-of-variables task are not necessarily capable of solving a proportional-thinking task, and vice versa.

Complex logical problem solving remains a salient feature of adult thinking.

Reconceptualizing Formal Operations

The tasks used for assessing formal thought focus on problems from the fields of mathematics and physics. Without the prerequisite educational and cultural background, many adolescents and adults are at a distinct disadvantage when faced with these tasks.

In an important paper published in 1972, Piaget modified his view on formal operations. Piaget argued that the stage criterion of structured wholeness may not apply to formal operations. Depending on aptitude, educational experience, motivation, professional specialization, and other factors, adults may develop formal thinking in some, but not all, areas. For example, an experienced garage mechanic may use formal reasoning to diagnose (and correct) the problem with a faulty automobile engine, but the same mechanic may have a concrete understanding of a critically ill patient's right to refuse medical treatment. On the other hand, a physician may reason at the formal level when thinking about problems involving medical ethics, but continue to use concrete thinking to figure out why her car keeps stalling.

Michael Berzonsky (1978) proposed that Piaget's theory can be conceptualized as a tree (see figure 9.1). The first three stages of the theory make up the trunk of the tree; the formal operational stage represents the branches. These branches, which are based on Guilford's (1967) ideas about the different dimensions of intelligence, represent the areas within which an adult could develop formal thinking skills. Thus, it would be possible to develop formal reasoning in any of a number of different domains (e.g., interpersonal relations; art, music, and literature; mathematics or physics).

Critique of Formal Operations

Formal operational thinking provides a powerful, but somewhat limited, mode of thought. In this section, we discuss six limitations of formal thinking.

Figure 9.1 An illustration of Berzonsky's branching model of formal operations.

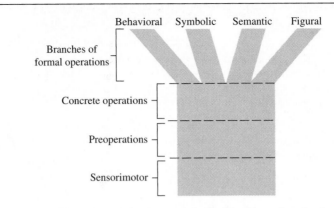

The behavioral branch involves an understanding of interpersonal and intrapersonal psychological processes.

The symbolic branch involves the representation and manipulation of arithematic and algebraic symbols.

The semantic branch involves the representation and manipulation of ideas within a verbal medium.

The figural branch involves the representation and manipulation of ideas and concrete objects within a visual medium.

1. Formal operations overemphasizes the power of pure logic in problem solving. The following passage expresses this limitation:

   Reason reveals relations within any given context. . . . But there is a limit. In the end, reason itself remains reflexively relativistic, a property which turns reason back upon reason's own findings. In even its farthest reaches, then, reason will leave the thinker with several legitimate contexts and no way of choosing among them—no way, at least, that can be justified through reason alone. If he still is to honor reason he must now also transcend it; he must affirm his own position from within himself in full awareness that reason can never completely justify him or assure him. (Perry, 1968, pp. 135–136)

2. Formal operations underemphasizes the pragmatic qualities of real-life cognitive activity. Labouvie-Vief (1984) reinforced this point when she noted that upon entry into adulthood, ". . . there is a concern with the concrete constraints of real life or the refusal to sever cognition from its affective, social, and pragmatic ties" (p. 159).

3. Formal thinking is only suited for problems that call for scientific thinking and logical mathematical analysis. Piaget assumed that the goal of the cognitively mature adult was to reason like a scientist or a mathematician. Consequently, he did not examine how one applies cognition to real-life social or interpersonal problems. In connection with this point, Flavell (1977) maintained, "Real problems with meaningful content are obviously more important in everyday human adaptation (than abstract, wholly logical problems), and it is possible that these are the kinds of problems our cognitive apparatus has evolved to solve" (p. 117).

4. Formal operations is geared for the solution of closed-system, well-defined problems. A closed-system problem is one in which a person determines how a limited number of controllable and specific variables produce a specific and reliable outcome. For example, in the pendulum task, a series of miniexperiments helps to determine how a limited number of controllable and specific variables influence the oscillation of a pendulum. Closed-system problems are also well defined, with a single correct solution (it is the length of the string that controls the oscillation of the pendulum). Real-life problems, in contrast, are open, or characterized by an unlimited number of uncontrollable, fuzzy variables (see Basseches, 1984; Koplowitz, 1984). For example, a woman must consider a large number of constantly changing variables when deciding whether to pursue her business career or take time off when having a child. Furthermore, open-system problems are ill-defined because they emerge from changeable and uncontrollable variables and do not have just one correct solution.

5. Formal operations does not recognize the relative nature of knowledge and the need to adopt multiple frames of reference. Thinking from a relativistic standpoint has been referred to as "intersystemic thinking" by Gisela Labouvie-Vief (1982).

6. Formal thinking places a greater emphasis on problem solving than on problem finding. This means that formal thought is best suited for generating and testing hypotheses that aid in solving closed-system, well-defined problems. Problem finding, in contrast, represents the ability to generate new questions that arise from ill-defined problems. It reflects the ability of adults to ask novel questions about themselves, their work, and the events that surround them. Arlin (1984) observed that Wertheimer (1945) described the essence of problem finding. Wertheimer suggested that "the function of thinking is not just solving an actual problem but discovering, envisaging, and going into deeper questions. Often in great discovery the most important thing is that a certain question is found" (p. 46). Problem finding is observed in particular scientific fields at particular times when faulty assumptions are challenged by new discoveries and questions.

Postformal Cognitive Development

The shortcomings of formal thinking have set the stage for a major conceptual revision of Piagetian theory. It is now assumed that a unique form of thinking, called **postformal operations,** emerges during the adult years.

Characteristics of Postformal Thinking

There are six characteristics of postformal reasoners. First, postformal thinkers possess an understanding of the relative, nonabsolute nature of knowledge. Second, postformal thinkers accept contradiction as an inherent aspect of reality. For example, a physicist might come to understand light as being both waves and particles; or an individual might realize that his feelings about another person are best described by the simultaneous existence of love and hate—apparently conflicting emotions. Third, postformal thinkers are capable of dialectic reasoning. They possess an ability to synthesize contradictory thoughts, emotions, and experiences. Instead of viewing a contradictory situation as a choice between alternatives, the postformal reasoner views it as a call to integrate alternatives.

A fourth characteristic of postformal thinkers is that they tend to use a contextual approach to problem solving. That is, they solve problems by continuously creating new principles based on the changing circumstances of their lives—rather than by applying a set of absolute principles across all contexts and circumstances. This may be especially true when adults reason about the ill-defined problems characteristic of everyday social life. Fifth, postformal thinking seems to be domain-specific in nature. This means that adults develop postformal thinking within some, but not all, areas of knowledge. And sixth, postformal thinking is more directed toward problem finding than problem solving.

Research on Postformal Thinking

William Perry (1968) was one of the first researchers to address the topic of postformal thought. In conducting a longitudinal study in which he questioned university students about their educational and personal experiences, Perry found that first-year students approached various intellectual and ethical problems from a dualistic (formal) perspective. These students assumed that any problem or ethical dilemma could have only one correct answer, and that it was the task of authority figures (in their case, perhaps, professors) to teach them the correct answer. In time, they began to realize the inherent subjectivity of experience. This led the students to conceptualize knowledge and values—even those espoused by authorities—as relative and nonabsolute. At this level, the students felt as if they were adrift in an ocean of uncertainty. They thought that any problem could be approached from a variety of viewpoints, each of which seemed to possess equal merit and validity. Finally, some students reached a developmental level, termed *contextual relativism,* that indicated postformal thinking. They still understood the relativity of knowledge, but they were no longer overwhelmed by it. These students became committed to a self-constructed intellectual and ethical point of view in which they both accepted and transcended relativity. These issues as they apply to college students today are discussed in Research Focus 9.1.

Jan Sinnott (1981, 1989) maintained that relativistic thinking can be applied to several different intellectual domains, but it is easiest to understand the relativistic nature of postformal reasoning within the area of interpersonal reality. Sinnott applied the term *necessary subjectivity* to describe relativistic thinking within interpersonal relations. Necessary subjectivity means that when adults solve interpersonal problems, subjectivity, or mutually contradictory frames of reference, is a basic characteristic of interpersonal reality. This contrasts with the typical view of physical reality, in which subjectivity is considered to be faulty thinking and is eliminated from problem analysis. To examine the relativistic nature of adult cognition, Sinnott (1984) presented a group of adults between 26 and 89 years of age with a variety of problems designed to detect the presence of formal and relativistic thinking. The results showed that older

Postformal Thinking in College Students

In an early study, Perry (1968) examined the forms of intellectual and ethical development that occur during the college years. This provided a foundation for the study of postformal thinking in young adults. Perry described the development of Harvard students during their four years at school in the 1960s. Recently, Richard J. Light, a professor at the Harvard Graduate School of Education, reported on the concerns of today's college students at Harvard. Unlike Perry's study, Light's book is not based on a systematic study of longitudinal change during the college years. However, some postformal themes emerge in Light's suggestions for optimizing the college experience and in the students' comments about approaching the demands of the college years. In contrast to college students in the 1960s and 1970s, today's college students seem to place less of a premium on independence. Over 70 percent of the students interviewed agreed strongly that they needed advice and structure regarding academic as well as nonacademic matters. Light took the opportunity to offer advice to some of his students. In particular, he urged his advisees to get to know at least one professor as a resource each semester.

Second, he urged his advisees to select a mix of required courses and elective courses or small-enrollment seminars each semester, right from the start. The happiest and wisest students in Light's view were those who balanced their own interests with curriculum requirements. Light noted that one of the main differences between students who prospered and students who struggled was time management. Successful students were effective at balancing time for study and time for play, and were careful to schedule and protect their time. One busy student said, "Every day has three parts: Morning, afternoon, and evening. And if I can devote any one of those blocks of time to getting my academic work done, I consider that day a success."

Light's theme was how to make the most of the college experience. Successful development during the college years can be considered an application of postformal thinking in domains such as personal and intellectual growth.

Light, R. J. (2001). *Making the most of college: Students speak their minds.* Cambridge, MA: Harvard University Press.

---

adults were more likely to use relativistic thinking to deal with real-life rather than abstract problems. Younger participants were more likely to solve all types of problems by adopting a nonrelativistic, formal mode of thinking.

Rakfeldt, Rybash, and Roodin (1996) examined the relationship between postformal thinking and the ability to profit from psychotherapy. The participants in this study were adult, first-admission patients in a psychiatric hospital. The researchers discovered that patients who displayed relativistic thinking tended to have a more efficacious understanding of themselves, their disorders, and their relationships with others. These patients also seemed to take a more active role in their healing. In contrast, patients who adopted an absolute (or formal) perspective seemed to make less significant therapeutic gains. Formal thinkers believed it was the duty of authority responsibility of their therapists—to discover the "true" disorder they suffered from, and to treat or fix the problem. Rakfeldt et al. concluded that relativistic thinking allows patients to better understand the complexities of their psychiatric disturbances as well as the options open to them within the therapeutic encounter.

Arlin (1984, 1989) studied postformal thinking in a group of young adult artists, all of whom performed equally well on measures of formal thought. The artists were classified as either formal or postformal in their cognitive orientation depending on their answers to questions such as, "Could any of the elements in your drawing be eliminated or altered without destroying its characteristics?" The formal thinking artists viewed their works as fixed, unalterable, and finished, while the postformal artists viewed their works as changeable and unfinished. Arlin suggested that the more creative artists were postformal thinkers who (1) did not adopt a single, fixed, and absolute view of their work, (2) accepted the idea that their work could evolve and change over time, and (3) actively tried to find new perspectives from which to view their work.

It is important to point out that older adults perform just as well or better than young adults in some kinds of logical decision-making tasks. For example, Tentori, Osherson, Hasher, and May (2001) showed that older adults are more rational than younger adults in several kinds of decision-making tasks. In these tasks, a decision maker was considered "irrational" if she would choose B from a set consisting of A, B, and C, but not choose B from a set consisting of A and B. For example, it would be irrational to prefer vanilla ice cream in a choice between vanilla and chocolate, but choose chocolate in a choice between vanilla, chocolate, and strawberry. College students exhibited more irrational choices than older adults did in a decision-making task using hypothetical discount cards for supermarkets. The results were interpreted in terms of a strategy older adults use to protect themselves from excessive spending.

Conclusions about Postformal Cognitive Development

Clearly, some adults are capable of conceptualizing reality in a postformal manner. The postformal cognitive orientation these adults display is very different from the formal orientation adolescents have. Postformal thinking seems to be a necessity if adults are to truly appreciate the complexities of both physical and social reality. It would be a mistake, however, to believe that all adults display all of the characteristics of postformal development.

Reasoning about social matters clearly occupies a central role in post-Piagetian attempts to identify the levels or stages of postformal cognitive development. Indeed, one characteristic of all of the Piagetian revisionists this chapter describes is their perspective that adult cognition involves the interchange of the individual with his or her social world (Sinnott & Shiffren, 2001). Reasoning about the social and interpersonal world is termed **social cognition.**

Some psychologists believe that postformal thinking reflects a genuine stage of cognitive development Lamberson and Fischer (1988) made a distinction between the optimal and functional levels. The *optimal level* refers to the best or highest level of stagelike performance a person can achieve under ideal conditions. The *functional level* refers to a person's stagelike performance under normal, nonoptimal conditions when the individual has little environmental support. Lamberson and Fischer argued that it is only possible to observe genuine stages of development if we measure an individual's optimal level, not his or her functional level. They also suggest that we focus our attention on an individual's developmental range—the gap between the person's optimal and functional levels. Other psychologists have suggested that developmental changes in thought beyond formal operations, even when measured under optimal conditions, may not meet the criteria that define genuine cognitive stages. Rybash et al. (1986), for example, argued that postformal development is best understood as a set of styles of thinking (absolute, relativistic, or dialectical; see figure 9.2) that emerge during adulthood rather than a stage.

Finally, several developmental psychologists have expressed reservations about the need for the stage concept itself. For example, Brainerd (1978) commented that the cognitive performance of children and adolescents is so inconsistent and variable that it is difficult to embrace the idea of a set of stages that comprise cognitive development. Certainly, adult cognitive performance may reflect even greater individual variability due to the accumulation of different experiences.

Adult Cognition: An Integration

In the last three chapters of this text, we have reviewed the theories that bear on the different approaches to the study of adult cognition: the psychometric approach, the neuroscience approach, the information-processing approach, and the stage approach. Each of these approaches provides valuable information and perspective about adult cognitive development. However, each of these views also focuses on a different aspect of cognition, and each has limitations. In this section, we describe the encapsulation model, a theory that tries to integrate the basic features of several approaches to the study of adult cognition.

The Encapsulation Model

The **encapsulation model** assumes that cognition consists of three interrelated dimensions: processing, knowing, and thinking. *Processing* refers to the way we use our cognitive architecture to process (encode, store, and retrieve) information. *Knowing* refers to the way we use known information to aid information processing and problem solving. *Thinking* refers to our understanding or perspective on the knowledge we have accumulated during development. Usually, psychologists examine these three facets of cognition in relative isolation from one another.

In general, researchers working within the information-processing, neuroscience, and psychometric approaches view adulthood as a period of negative developmental change. They conclude that adults become less adept at general problem solving because they process information in a progressively slower and less efficient manner or because information is lost more quickly.

Knowing is the primary focus of the cognitive-science perspective on cognition. The dominant concern within this tradition has been with the growth and representation of knowledge. Cognitive scientists assume that the source of intelligent problem solving is in the size and reach of the individual's knowledge base rather than in the power of the individual's general mental abilities (fluid intelligence), mental capacities (attention, memory), or thought structures (postformal thinking). Research conducted within the context of this approach is essentially nondevelopmental. Charness (1988) has suggested, however, that research within the cognitive-science tradition has important implications for the study of adult cognitive development. Adulthood is the portion of life during which individuals develop domain-specific cognitive expertise. Thus, older adults are likely to display sophisticated cognitive performance in their areas of specialization because they have developed an expert knowledge base. Read Research Focus 9.2 to gain a better understanding of the cognitive-science approach to the study of cognition.

The Cognitive-Science Approach

Psychologists studying cognitive development during adulthood are faced with an apparent paradox. Research based on the psychometric and information-processing theories indicates a deterioration of generalized cognitive ability with age, while everyday observation of adults within their occupational roles, social interactions, and hobbies indicates that with increasing age comes stability (and sometimes even enhancement) of cognitive performance.

The cognitive-science approach to the study of cognition offers an important line of research that bears on this paradox. This approach suggests that intelligent problem solving lies in the possession and utilization of a great deal of specific knowledge about the world. Waldrop (1984), in tracing the influence of the cognitive-science approach on the study of artificial intelligence (AI), comments: "The essence of intelligence was no longer seen to be reasoning ability alone. More important was having lots of highly specific knowledge about lots of things-a notion inevitably stated as, 'Knowledge is power'" (p. 1280). Thus, in contrast to the earlier approaches (such as the psychometric and information-processing perspectives) that represented human problem solving as a generalized mental process, contemporary cognitive scientists suggest that problem solving in adulthood requires expert knowledge.

Importantly, expert performance has been found to be domain-specific and independent of generalized mental abilities. For example, Chase and Simon (1973) and de Groot (1965) carried out a number of groundbreaking studies on chess experts and novices. These researchers found that chess grand masters could reconstruct the positions of approximately 25 chess pieces arranged in a real game configuration after seeing the display for only five seconds; novice players, on the other hand, could only remember the positions of about six or seven pieces. When the same 25 pieces were arranged in a random configuration on a chessboard, both the experts and the novices remembered the positions of the same number of pieces—approximately seven. Furthermore, experts and novices were not found to differ with regard to generalized measures of memory span and short-term memory. And expert players did not evidence a superiority in general intellectual ability as measured by an IQ test. It seems safe to conclude that chess experts have exceptionally good memories for positions of pieces on a chessboard when the arrangement conforms to a real game because of the vast amount of specific knowledge they possess about chess game configurations. In fact, it has been estimated that chess experts have stored, in long-term memory, approximately 40,000 different game configurations!

Ceci and Liker (1986) investigated the ability of gamblers to handicap horse races. The individuals in the study were avid horse-racing enthusiasts who went to the racetrack nearly every day. Ceci and Liker gave all these participants an early form of a racing sheet. This allowed the gamblers to study the past performances of the horses that would be competing in all 10 races the next day at a real racetrack. The researchers asked the men to pick (1) the favorite in each of the 10 races, and (2) the top three finishers in each of the 10 races in the correct order. Then they compared the men's selections with the post-time odds for the horses in each race as well as with the actual order of finish for each race. Based on their analysis, Ceci and Liker identified 14 "experts" and 16 "nonexperts." The experts selected the horse with the best post-time odds in 9 out of the 10 races and the top three horses in at least one-half of the races: The nonexperts performed much more poorly. The experts used very complex mental models to make their selections, taking seven different variables and their interactions into account: the horse's times during the first and last quarter-miles of a race, the quality of the horses it had competed against in the past, the jockey riding it, and so on. In comparison, the nonexperts used very simplistic models to make their picks.

Most surprisingly, Ceci and Liker found that the experts and nonexperts did not differ on a number of variables that would seem to be good predictors of their handicapping skill. For example, these two groups did not differ in IQ score, years of education, occupational status, or number of years of handicapping experience—both groups had been going to the track for about 16 years! Ceci and Liker concluded that expertise in handicapping is not purely dependent on past experience or general intelligence.

Developmental changes in thinking are the focus of research inspired by Piagetian theory. Neo-Piagetian theorists view adulthood as a period of positive developmental change marked by the transition from formal to postformal styles of thinking. Postformal thinking permits adults to view reality in relativistic and dialectic terms. Such thinking styles provide the necessary basis for solving both well- and ill-defined problems and for discovering new perspectives from which new problems may be identified. The postformal approach certainly has its merits. Postformal theorists, however,

Advanced intellectual skills remain functional in highly specific domains throughout adult life.

appear to paint an overly optimistic picture of aging. They fail to acknowledge the cognitive losses and declines that play a salient role in development during the middle and later years of adulthood.

The encapsulation model suggests that basic mental capacities and fluid mental abilities become increasingly dedicated to and encapsulated within specific domains of knowledge during the course of adult development. As general processes and abilities become encapsulated within domains, knowledge becomes more differentiated, accessible, usable, and "expert" in nature. The encapsulation model also suggests that the acquisition of new knowledge (knowledge unrelated to that already encapsulated in specific domains) becomes increasingly less efficient with age. Mastery of new domains is somewhat uncharacteristic of older adults; they are not ideal "learning machines." Childhood and adolescence are periods of the life span characterized by the acquisition of new knowledge in a variety of ever-expanding domains. Adulthood may be a time during which individuals refine and develop a perspective on their knowledge.

The reduced capacity to acquire new knowledge during adulthood may be offset by the development of expert knowledge within existing domains and by the development of a postformal perspective on that knowledge. Once adults conceptualize their domain-specific knowledge in a relativistic, dialectic, and open-ended manner, they become capable of solving the ill-defined problems of real life, finding new problems and new perspectives from which these problems may be solved and producing creative and sophisticated works within defined areas of expertise.

The encapsulation of thinking and knowing within specific domains seems to represent a necessary and adaptive feature of adult cognitive development. Thus, the

World-renowned British astrophysicist Stephen Hawking, at age 59. Hawking, who authored the book A Brief History of Time, *suffers from a motor neuron disease, cannot walk or talk, and communicates with the help of a voice-equipped computer.*

TABLE 9.1
Basic Assumptions of the Encapsulation Model

1. Any comprehensive theory of adult cognitive development must address the three dimensions of cognition: processing, knowing, and thinking.
2. The processes associated with the acquisition, utilization, and representation of knowledge become encapsulated within particular domains as one grows older.
3. Mental capacities appear to decline with age when they are assessed as general abilities but show minimal age-related decline when they are assessed within encapsulated domains.
4. Adult cognitive development is characterized by the growth of expert knowledge and the emergence of postformal styles of thought. Adult styles of thinking and forms of knowing are the result of encapsulation.

Source: Conclusions from Rybash, J. M., Hoyer, W. J., and Roodin, P. A. (1986). Adult cognition and aging: Developmental changes in processing, knowing, and thinking. Elmsford, NY: Pergamon Press.

age-related loss of general intellectual abilities reported in psychometric and information-processing research may have little functional significance for most adults in most situations. Although age-related declines in mental capacities are indeed documented, these findings seem to result from assessing mental processes apart from their normal contexts. Age-related differences in the component processes of cognition (memory, attention, etc.) cannot be meaningfully assessed apart from the domain in which they are encapsulated. Table 9.1 summarizes the encapsulation model.

We can illustrate the basic claims of the encapsulation model by examining two different lines of research. First, we present the results of several studies that have examined the relationship between aging, information processing, and cognitive expertise. Second, we review studies on the growth of wisdom during adulthood.

Aging, Information Processing, and Cognitive Expertise

The encapsulation model suggests that adults continue to accumulate knowledge that becomes increasingly refined with age and experience. Accumulated domain-specific knowledge can take on a compensatory function for older adults. This means that older adults can continue to function effectively in tasks that allow them to draw on their expert knowledge (e.g. Meinz, 2000; Morrow et. al., 2001). This occurs in spite of the significant reduction in generalized information-processing skills and/or fluid intellectual abilities that accompanies the aging process (Masunaga & Horn, 2001). Evidence for this point of view comes from several sources. Timothy Salthouse (1984, 1990), Neil Charness (1981, 1985, 1988), and Stephanie Clancy-Dollinger and William Hoyer (1994, 1995) have all shown that expert knowledge can compensate for general losses in cognitive functioning in older adults.

Typing

Salthouse (1984) conducted an experiment with typists who differed in age (from 18 to 72 years) and skill level (novices versus experts). As might be expected, Salthouse discovered that the older typists performed more poorly than younger typists on tasks assessing (1) simple reaction time, (2) the fastest speed at which they could tap their fingers, and (3) digit-symbol substitution. The digit-symbol substitution task is a measure of fluid intelligence that requires one to match a series of numbers with a series of abstract geometric patterns as quickly as possible. More important, Salthouse discovered that the participants' typing speed was uncorrelated with age but was significantly related to the participants' skill level: The expert typists (both young and old) were significantly quicker than the novice typists (both young and old). Salthouse was able to determine that older expert typists compensated for age-related declines in speed and reaction time by looking farther ahead at printed text, which gave them more time to plan their next keystroke. Salthouse's findings illustrate the domain-specific nature of older adults' compensatory mechanisms. Older expert typists did not employ the same look-ahead strategy on any of the other tasks Salthouse administered (e.g., digit-symbol substitution), although the implementation of this strategy would have improved their performance.

Using a different approach, Charness, Kelley, Bosman, and Mottram (2001) showed the benefits of experience for older adults when learning a new word processing program. These researchers taught novice and experienced adults representing three age groups (young adults, middle-aged, and older adults) to learn to use a new word-processing program. Age-related differences in learning the new program were largest for the novices. Age differences re-training on the new word processing program were very small for the experienced adults.

Chess

Charness (1981, 1985) reported that older chess experts were found to be as competent as younger experts in choosing the best move from four possible alternatives. More specifically, older experts were found to search just as many moves ahead as younger

Figure 9.2 Age and chess performance. *Source:* Charness, N., & Bosman, E. (1990). Expertise and aging: Life in the lab. In T. H. Hess (Ed.), *Aging and cognition: Knowledge, organization, and utilization* (p. 358). Amsterdam: Elsevier.

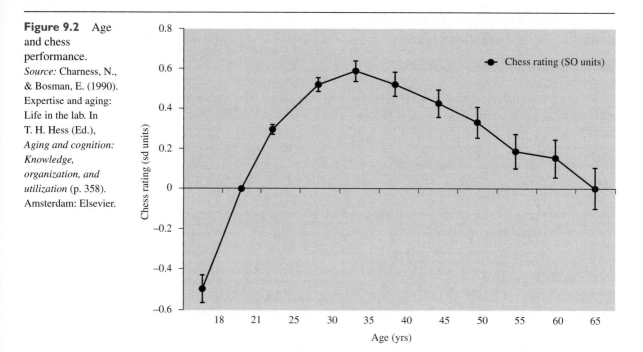

experts. But they were also found to entertain fewer possible moves than their younger counterparts, showing even greater efficiency. Charness concluded that older chess experts compensate for general processing and memory deficits by using an elaborate knowledge base acquired over years of practice. The growth of this vast and highly organized knowledge base allows older experts to search for appropriate moves as quickly as (and perhaps even more efficiently than) younger experts.

However, there is difference between maintaining expertise and maintaining one's best performance. As figure 9.2 shows, the performance of a chess grand master (a very select group indeed) peaks at about age 35. But the typical 65-year-old grand master plays on a par with the average 21-year-old grand master.

Medical Diagnostics

Clancy and Hoyer (1994) conducted an experiment with medical laboratory technologists who differed in both age (younger versus older adults) and skill level (novices versus experts). Keep in mind that a medical laboratory technologist, as an integral part of his or her job, performs a number of complex visual identification tasks such as looking at slides of tissue or blood under a microscope to identify certain diseases. Clancy and Hoyer (1994) examined the effects of age and experience on information processing by administering domain-general and domain-specific visual search tasks to the two age groups of medical laboratory technologists and control subjects. The domain-general task involved finding a letter of the alphabet in a briefly presented visual display. In the skilled task, participants searched a visual display for a specific type of bacteria specimen. Just prior to the presentation of the bacteria samples, participants were shown word cues that were informative, noninformative, or neutral with regard to the target specimen. Results indicated that middle-aged control participants performed more poorly than younger control individuals on both the domain-general and domain-specific tasks. When the data from the experts were analyzed, a different pattern emerged. Middle-aged experts performed worse than younger experts on the domain-general task but not on the domain-specific task. Both expert groups benefited to the same extent when informative cue words were presented prior to the domain-specific search task.

Limits of Expertise

Skill or expertise is not powerful enough to completely compensate for age-related reductions in mental and physical skills (Meinz, 2000; Morrow et al., 2001). For example, performance in such sports as golf, tennis, basketball, and football declines with age, even among individuals who possess a great deal of expertise in these sports. On the other hand, performance within domains that allow more time for planning and reflection, that demand fewer snap decisions and less physical exertion (e.g., musical composition or visual art), may actually improve because of the cumulative effects of age and experience. In connection with this point, Charness (1985) has commented that ". . . when people can draw upon domain-specific knowledge and when they have developed appropriate compensatory mechanisms, they can treat us to a memorable performance, whether on the keyboard of a typewriter, a piano, or on the podium of an orchestral stage. When the task environment does not afford the same predictability or opportunity to plan ahead, however, as is the case in fast-moving sports environments, degradation in hardware cannot be compensated for by more efficient software" (p. 23).

Furthermore, for expertise to aid problem solving, there needs to be an exact match between the older person's knowledge and the task he or she must perform. In other words, expertise does not enhance (or even maintain) the domain-general abilities the expertise seems to be based on. The conclusion is based on the work of Lindenberger, Kliegl, and Baltes (1992) and Salthouse et al. (1990). In these studies, older adult experts in architecture and graphic design—occupations that place a premium on visual cognition—displayed significant declines in domain-general visual thinking and mental imagery.

One of the most perplexing questions surrounding the issue of aging and expertise is: "Why does an individual become an expert in a particular area?" See Research Focus 9.3 for a discussion of some of the most current theories on expertise.

Wisdom

Wisdom is a mental characteristic or ability that has long been associated with aging within both Eastern and Western cultural traditions (Sternberg & Lubart, 2001). Beyond any doubt, the most exciting and provocative work on the topic of wisdom has been conducted by Paul Baltes, Ursula Staudinger, and their colleagues at the Max Planck Institute in Berlin, Germany. Baltes & Staudinger (2000) distinguish between philosophical wisdom and practical wisdom. **Philosophical wisdom** refers to an understanding of the abstract relationship between one's self and the rest of humanity. **Practical wisdom** refers to the ability to display superior judgment with regard to important real-life matters. Baltes and Staudinger (1993)

What Does It Take to Become an Expert?

What accounts for the extraordinary performance of a musician, the outstanding contribution of a scientist or writer, or the unique feats of an athlete? Sir Francis Galton (1869/1979) was one of the first individuals to examine the development of expertise from a scientific perspective. He argued that excellence within a particular field is due to three factors: innate ability (or talent), a burning desire to become the "best," and extensive and laborious practice. Galton assumed that these last two factors (i.e., motivation and practice) were necessary but not sufficient conditions for achieving exceptional performance. In other words, practice is necessary for greatness (even Michael Jordan had to practice), but extensive practice, by itself, will not guarantee success (extensive practice alone will not turn the most dedicated basketball player into another Michael Jordan). This means that individual variability in optimal performance must, in the final analysis, reflect individual differences in innate talent, giftedness, or natural ability—or "unmodifiable genetic good luck."

This view has both intuitive appeal and scientific credibility. One of the leading proponents of the talent-based approach to expertise is Howard Gardner (1983, 1993a, 1993b, 1995). As you may remember from the chapter on intelligence, Gardner put forth the theory of multiple intelligences. Gardner's theory emphasizes (1) the neurological basis of different symbol systems (e.g., linguistic, musical, visual-spatial, bodily-kinesthetic, etc.), which lay the basis for various human intelligences, and (2) the wide-ranging variability that exists both between and within individuals in terms of the inborn strength of these different symbol systems (i.e., the differences between individual brains in terms of how they are "hardwired" via genetic mechanisms to excel at different types of intelligence). The biggest selling point of Gardner's theory is the observation that certain individuals—namely, childhood prodigies and mono savants—display superior performance in a single domain (e.g., music or mathematics) but exhibit average (or below average) performance in all other areas. Most certainly, the psychometric or Piagetian approaches cannot account for this pattern of behavior.

Despite its intuitive appeal, Gardner's talent-based approach is not without its critics. Ericsson and Charness (1994, 1995), for example, do not deny the fact that childhood prodigies and mono savants exist. However, they point out that the vast majority of prodigies develop their skills because of continued practice in combination with constant support from teachers and parents, that hardly any childhood prodigies become exceptional adult performers (e.g., it is extremely rare to see a childhood prodigy like Mozart become a world-renowned musician during adulthood), and that most exceptional adult performers were not identified as childhood prodigies (e.g., based on his performance relative to his agemates in elementary or high school, there was no basis for the prediction that Michael Jordan would become one of the best basketball players ever). Finally, Ericsson and Charness (1994) argue that it is possible to train "normal" individuals to achieve the high levels of performance savants display in areas such as mental arithmetic, calendar calculation, memory span, and so on, and that the special skills

---

defined this latter form of wisdom as ". . . an expert knowledge system in the fundamental pragmatics of life permitting exceptional insight, judgment, and advice involving complex and uncertain matters of the human condition" (p. 76). They suggested that wisdom may be characterized by a set of dimensions that many diverse cultures have identified as important over human history (see figure 9.3). Note that these characteristics reflect the essential features of knowledge encapsulation and postformal thinking.

Fluid Mechanics and Crystallized Pragmatics

Baltes's approach to the study of wisdom is based on the view that the human mind possesses two fundamental dimensions (Baltes, & Staudinger, 2000). First, the **mechanics of mind** involves the raw, basic operations of our human information-processing system. It represents the elementary "mental hardware" such as sensation, perception, and memory. These processes are typically measured by the speed and accuracy with which people can

and abilities prodigies and savants exhibit do not develop all at once, as suggested by popular myths and stereotypes. Their detection may be sudden, but the skill probably took a great amount of deliberate practice to develop and was fostered by supportive conditions.

Ericsson and Charness (1994, 1995) have argued for a practice-based model of exceptional performance. They discount the innate abilities position and suggest that expertise is the end result of many years (and thousands of hours) of deliberate practice and hard work under the watchful eye of a coach or teacher. In fact, evidence from a number of sources suggests that approximately 10 years of intense preparation and practice is necessary to achieve an exceptionally high level of performance across a wide range of domains. This 10-year rule seems to apply to such diverse areas as chess, athletic events, literary achievement, and scientific research. Moreover, the practice that leads to expertise is both deliberate and tedious. It is not necessarily fun and does not lead to immediate personal, social, or monetary rewards. Ericsson, Krampe, and Tesch-Römer (1993) showed that top-level teenage violinists had practiced, on the average, more than 10,000 hours, which was approximately 2,500 hours more than the next most accomplished group, and 5,000 hours more than those who were categorized at the lowest expert level. Interestingly, Ericsson and Charness (1994) suggest that genetic factors might be responsible for expertise, but only indirectly; the genetic mechanisms indirectly affect expertise by directly influencing temperament and motivation. Humans might be more likely to inherit genes for hard work and perseverance than

for musical talent. This is consistent with Charles Darwin's statement that "... men do not differ much in intellect, only in zeal for hard work" (quoted in Galton, 1869/1979, p. 290).

Ericsson and Charness (1994, 1995) raise two other points. Both refute the assumption that exceptional performance rests upon unmodifiable abilities. First, the basic biological, behavioral, and cognitive capacities of experts do not differ from those of nonexperts. For example, elite basketball players and boxers do not have simple reaction times and perceptual abilities that differ from the average individual's; chess grand masters have not been found to have out-of-the-ordinary generic memory skills and visual-spatial abilities. Second, the cultural evolution of expertise occurs at a pace that certainly exceeds any large-scale biogenetic changes in our basic biological structure. For example, today's high school students are capable of grasping mathematical concepts and procedures (e.g., calculus) that two centuries ago were only understood by the world's most advanced mathematicians. Today's typical elite musicians consider several pieces (e.g., Tchaikovsky's violin concerto) to be part of their standard repertoire, whereas performers at the turn of the century considered these selections unplayable. And progress in sporting events has been so fast-paced that the winner of the 1896 Olympic marathon would barely qualify for next year's Boston Marathon.

Given the basic tenets of the talent-based versus practice-based models of exceptional performance, what advice would you give individuals who strive for superior performance? What factors would you look for if you wanted to discover people who would become the "best" at what they do?

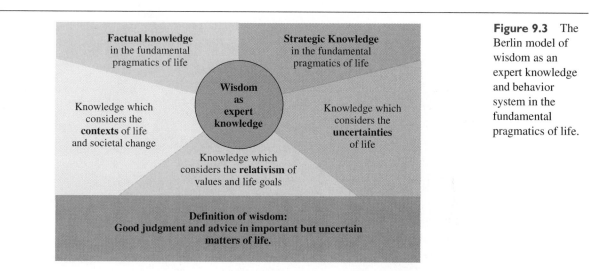

Figure 9.3 The Berlin model of wisdom as an expert knowledge and behavior system in the fundamental pragmatics of life.

perform simple tasks. In general, mental tasks that reflect the basic cognitive-neural mechanisms are referred to as measures of fluid intelligences. A gradual age-related decline in performance takes place on measures of fluid intelligence.

In Baltes's view, the second dimension of the human mind is the **pragmatics of mind,** which refers to the "mental software" that encompasses the general system of factual and strategic knowledge accessible to members of a particular culture, the specialized systems of knowledge available to individuals within particular occupations and avocations, and an understanding of how to effectively activate these types of knowledge within particular contexts to aid problem solving. Most important, the pragmatic quality of mind allows us to develop a strategy—wisdom—for negotiating the major and minor obstacles of everyday life. Furthermore, since cultural (not biological) factors influence mental pragmatics, it may be that aging is accompanied by cognitive growth—a growth in wisdom.

Testing the Limits of Cognitive Reserve

To evaluate his ideas about the mechanics of mind, Baltes and his coworkers have used the technique of **testing the limits** of maximum cognitive reserve. In this methodology, groups of younger and older adults are required to recall a list of 30 familiar nouns (*plane, chair,* etc.) in the order they were presented. Then they learn a mnemonic strategy—the method of loci—to increase their recall. In this memory enhancement procedure, individuals are instructed to create mental images that associating list items with familiar landmarks. For example, a person may think about driving to work in the morning while visualizing list items. One might imagine an airplane at the end of one's driveway, a chair perched on the top of the stop sign at the end of one's street, and so on. When given a memory test, the person re-creates these images one location after another.

Wisdom-related skills and personal intelligence are characteristics related to being an effective leader, therapist counselor, or mentor.

Using this technique, Baltes and Kliegl (1992) gave groups of younger (20-year-old) and older (70-year-old) participants 35 training and testing sessions over a period of one year and four months. Across all sessions, each participant performed 4,380 trials of trying to generate a mental image that linked a familiar location to a list item. Figure 9.4 shows the results of this research.

In the initial testing session, participants remembered about six words, and younger adults performed slightly better than older adults. With extended practice, the memories of both younger and older participants increased in a spectacular fashion. Now a large proportion of the participants could remember between 20 and 30 words in the correct order. However, the training increased (rather than decreased) the difference in memory performance between the two age groups. In fact, the older adults who displayed the best performance at the end of the experiment seemed to be on a par with the younger adults who displayed the worst performance! And, after all of the training sessions, the older adults still did not achieve the performance level that the younger adults exhibited after just a few sessions. Baltes and Kliegl suggested that older adults do not benefit from practice as much as younger adults because of an age-related deterioration in mental reserve capacity that is similar to the loss of reserve capacity in biological domains such as cardiovascular or respiratory potential (see also Vernaeghen & Kliegl, 2000).

In an interesting twist on the preceding research, Margaret Baltes and her associates (Baltes, Kühl, & Sowarka, 1992; Baltes, Kühl, Gutzman, & Sowarka, 1995) used the testing-the-limits methodology as a diagnostic strategy for the early identification of Alzheimer's disease (AD). The major idea behind these experiments is that at-risk elderly should possess less reserve capacity than healthy elderly, and therefore should not profit as much from cognitive training as healthy elderly. In these experiments, therefore, healthy older adults as well as older adults who were at risk for AD were given several training sessions on various measures of fluid intelligence such as figural relations and inductive reasoning. Results shows that the at-risk group of older adults

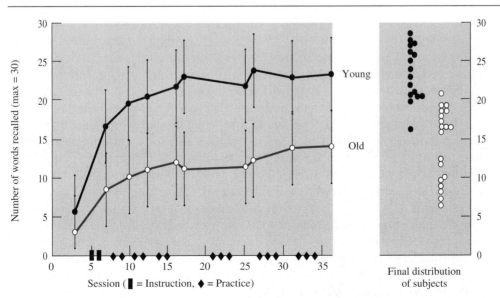

Figure 9.4
Performance by younger and older adults in recalling lists of words in order as a function of training in the method of loci (left panel). (The bars indicate standard deviations. In the right panel, individual scores are given for the last assessment sessions [36/37]. Max = maximum.)

benefited far less from training than their healthy counterparts. Thus, the testing-the-limits strategy may become an important clinical screening tool.

Wisdom and Aging

Are the inevitable declines in the mechanics of mind offset by positive changes in the pragmatics of mind—in wisdom? This is a complex question, because living a long life would seem to be a sufficient condition to produce a decline in basic mental abilities; but, a long life, by itself, does not seem to be a sufficient condition for the growth of wisdom. Consequently, Baltes and his colleagues (Baltes & Staudinger, 2000) hypothesized that wisdom is the end result of a coalition of three factors: (1) advanced chronological age, (2) favorable personality traits such as openness to experience, and (3) specific experiences in matters relating to life planning and the resolution of personal, ethical dilemmas.

Staudinger et al. (1992) investigated the growth of wisdom via the **age-by-experience paradigm.** Specifically, Staudinger et al. (1992) tried to find groups of individuals who differed in age as well as exposure to life experiences that would help develop wisdom. For example, they argued that pursuing certain professions, such as clinical psychology, might provide life experiences more conducive to developing wisdom than the life experiences associated with a career in a nonhuman services field such as accounting. This research strategy enabled Staudinger et al. (1992) to assess the separate, and interactive, effects of age and experience on wisdom.

Staudinger et al. (1992) selected a subject sample that consisted of younger (average age 32 years) and older (average age 71 years) women who were either clinical psychologists or professionals from an area other than psychology (e.g., architects, journalists, and natural scientists). All of the participants, regardless of age and professional specialization, were similar in terms of formal education and socioeconomic status and displayed identical scores on a measure of crystallized intelligence. As would be expected, however, younger adults performed better than older adults on a measure of fluid intelligence.

In the main part of the experiment, Staudinger et al. presented the participants with a "life review problem" in which the main character was either a young or an elderly woman who had to reflect on her decision to have a career rather than a family (see table 9.2 for the actual problems and a list of the standard probe questions). Participants' responses to the life review problems were scored on the five different dimensions of wisdom Baltes and his colleagues identified. Table 9.3 contains examples of wise responses to the life review problems from the perspective of each of these dimensions.

Results of the Staudinger et al. study were straightforward (see figure 9.5). First, younger and older women did not differ in their overall level of performance. Second, clinical psychologists exhibited a greater number of wisdom-based responses than non-clinicians. Third, older adults displayed better performance than younger adults when the life review dilemma involved an elderly woman; but younger and older adults performed identically when the life review problem focused on a young woman. Fourth, when the top 25 percent of the responses to the life review problems were examined, the researchers found that the older clinicians were most likely to generate wise responses. Fifth, participants' performance on standardized measures of fluid and crystallized intelligence accounted for very little of their performance on the life review tasks.

TABLE 9.2

Two Life Review Problems

Young Version

Martha, a young woman, had decided to have a family and not a career. She is married and has children. One day Martha meets a woman friend whom she has not seen for a long time. The friend had decided to have a career and no family. She is about to establish herself in her career.

Old Version

Martha, an elderly woman, had once decided to have a family and not a career. Her children left home some years ago. One day Martha meets a woman friend whom she has not seen for a long time. The friend had decided to have a career and no family. She had retired some years ago.

Standard Probe Questions for Both Versions on the Life Review Problem

This meeting causes Martha to think back over her life.

1. What might her life review look like?
2. Which aspects of her life might she remember?
3. How might she explain her life?
4. How might she evaluate her life retrospectively?

Source: Staudinger, U. M., Smith, J., & Baltes, P. B. (1992). Wisdom-related knowledge in a life review task: Age differences and the role of professional specialization. Psychology and Aging, 7: 271–281. Copyright 1992 by the American Psychological Association. Reprinted by permission.

Overall, these findings are important for several reasons. First, unlike fluid mechanics, wisdom-related tasks eliminate age differences, and older adults seem to display the "best" levels of performance. Second, life experience and professional specialization seem to interact. The highest level of performance was displayed by older adults responding to a dilemma involving an older person. Younger adults, on the other hand, were not capable of using knowledge about their own life stage when responding to the dilemma involving a younger person.

Although certainly thought provoking, the findings Staudinger et al. (1992) reported do not clarify the roles of professional training and life experiences in the development of wisdom. For example, "Would it be possible for older (or younger) adults who were not trained as psychologists to display wisdom?" Clearly, the notion of "wisdom" would lose a great deal of its appeal if it hinged on one's professional training and occupational experiences. See Research Focus 9.4 for more information on this matter.

One final observation is that wisdom is not an isolated object or skill found within an individual. Rather, wisdom typically manifests itself within the context of human social interaction. (For example, when faced with a difficult problem, we typically ask other people for their opinions. We usually don't act on our own hunches.) This insight led Staudinger and Baltes (1997) to conduct an empirical study in which pairs of individuals between 20 and 70 years of age were assigned to different experimental conditions that varied in the participants' degree of interactions with each other as they tried to solve various wisdom-related problems. Results showed that experimental manipulations that increased social interactions had a very beneficial effect on wisdom-based responses. Even more interesting, the older adults benefited much more from this interaction than did the younger adults.

TABLE 9.3

Illustration of the Characteristics of a Wise Response to the Life Review Tasks

Dimension of Wisdom	Characteristics of an Ideal Wise Response
Factual Knowledge	Knowledge about the human condition as it relates to the life review situation (e.g., achievement motivation, emotions, vulnerability, and societal norms). Knowledge about life events relevant to a mother's versus a professional woman's life.
Strategic Knowledge	Cost-benefit analysis: developing various scenarios of life interpretation. Means-goals analysis: what did/does the woman want and how can she/did she try to achieve it?
Contextualism	Discussion of the life review tasks in age-graded (e.g., timing of childrearing and professional training), culturally graded (e.g., change in woman's roles), and idiosyncratic (e.g., no money for education) contexts. The three contexts are discussed across different domains of life (e.g., family, profession, and leisure) and across time (past, present, future). The contexts are not independent; sometimes their combination creates conflict and tension that can be solved.
Relativism	Life goals differ depending on the individual and the culture. The origins of these differences is understood and the differences are respected. No absolute relativism, but a set of "universal" values is acknowledged.
Uncertainty	Plans can be disrupted; decisions have to be taken with uncertainty; the past cannot be perfectly explained nor the future fully predicted (e.g., marriage does not work out, children handicapped, or professional failure). One can work, however, from experience and knowledge-based assumptions and continuously modify them as new information becomes available.

Source: Staudinger, U. M., Smith, J., & Baltes, P. B. (1992). Wisdom-related knowledge in a life review task: Age differences and the role of professional specialization. Psychology and Aging, 7: 271–281. Copyright 1992 by the American Psychological Association. Reprinted by permission.

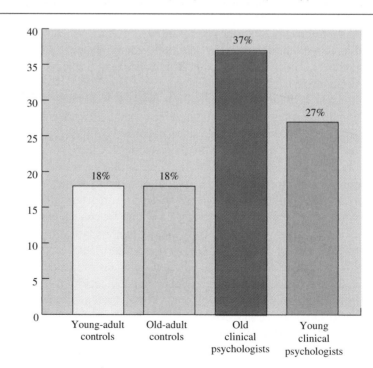

Figure 9.5
Distribution of the top 25 percent of responses in a wisdom-related life review task. Clinical psychologists are professionals with exposure to situations that concern the meaning and conduct of life. Clinical psychologists outperformed matched control subjects. *Source: Data from Baltes and Staudinger, 1993.*

Wisdom and Professional Expertise

The research of Paul Baltes and his associates has contributed to our understanding of wisdom. This team of researchers has shown that wisdom is an attribute that does not exhibit an age-related decline. Using an age-by-experience paradigm, Staudinger et al. (1992) have shown that older clinical psychologists were more likely to generate high-quality, wise responses to a life review problem than were younger clinical psychologists, and that both groups of clinicians performed better than younger and older controls. Despite the intuitive appeal of these findings, the Staudinger et al. (1992) research has two drawbacks. First and foremost, it's unclear if the older clinical psychologists preformed exceptionally well on the wisdom task merely because they were psychologists. Wisdom, in other words, may be a form of expertise tied to the profession of psychology. This would mean that the concept of wisdom Baltes advanced is much too limited in scope. Perhaps Baltes and colleagues, because they are psychologists, unconsciously biased their conception of wisdom to make it consistent with psychological principles. Second, the life review problem used in the Staudinger et al. (1992) study may not have been the best task by which to measure wisdom. Perhaps another type of problem would have placed a greater premium on generating truly wise responses.

Several years ago, Baltes, Staudinger, Maecker, and Smith (1995) conducted a study that addressed both of the preceding shortcomings. In their research, they compared younger and older clinical psychologists (along with age-appropriate control subjects) to a group of older nonpsychologists who were "nominated" to be wise. To select these "wisdom nominees," Baltes et al. contacted 21 top journalists of various political persuasions in Berlin and asked them to identify citizens who were active in public life and could be categorized as wise. This procedure yielded a list of 159 names. Then, the journalists were asked to rate all of these individuals via a seven-point scale on three criteria: life knowledge, wisdom, and personal familiarity. Next Baltes et al. only considered those nominees who were well known to each journalist (i.e., who scored five or higher on personal familiarity) and scored above average on the life knowledge and wisdom dimensions. This winnowing procedure resulted in a list of 22 persons, 14 of them younger than 80 years of age (see box table 9.A for details), who were selected as the primary participants in the research. Baltes et al. characterized this group of individuals as ". . . highly regarded citizens who lived extraordinary lives" (p. 157). About half of these people had published autobiographies, and approximately one-third of them had been involved in the resistance movement against the Nazi

Box Table 9.A

Characteristics of the Research Participants

Groups of Participants	Number per Group	Mean Age (and Range)	Males	Females
Wisdom nominees	14	64 (41-79)	9	5
Academics/science	2			
Cultural life	6			
Media	1			
Political life	2			
Theology	3			
Old clinical psychologists	15	66 (60-76)	7	8
Young non-human-service professionals	20	29 (25-35)	10	10
Old non-human-service professionals	20	68 (60-80)	10	10

Wisdom and Professional Expertise

regime or had emigrated during the Third Reich. Based on one's perspective, these individuals represented the "cream of the crop" or a "very biased subsample" of the older adults in Berlin.

Also, Baltes et al. (1995) used two different tasks to assess wisdom (see box table 9.B). They hypothesized that the highest level of wise responses would be given to the existential life management problem (suicide) rather than the life planning task (business) because issues involving human suffering and death are at the core of the construct of wisdom.

The results of the Baltes et al. research tell a most interesting story. When the overall pattern of results were considered for individuals between 25 and 80 years of age (see box figure 9.A) no age differences were found in wisdom-related performance. However, when the top 20 percent of responses were examined, it was discovered that wisdom nominees and psychologists performed significantly better than controls. This finding reinforces the idea that wisdom in older adults is not the outgrowth of a professional specialization in psychology. It is interesting to note, however, that performance among the nominees falls off between 80 and 90 years of age. This is consistent with Baltes and Graf's (1996) speculation that the ninth decade of life, at least under current cultural conditions, represents a critical threshold point at which gains in the pragmatics of intelligence can-

not offset losses in cognitive mechanics. Thus, there seems to be a point at which very old individuals may no longer be able to compensate for their declining biological and psychological resources.

Another point to consider is illustrated in box figure 9.B. The wisdom nominees (but not the clinical psychologists) produced more wise responses to the existential life management task than the control subjects. However, on the life planning task, the clinicians scored higher than both the nominees and the controls. This is important because the existential (i.e., suicide) task seems to be more central to the concept of wisdom than the life planning problem, and because one might assume that the clinicians would excel on the suicide task due to their professional training. This suggests that wisdom may be a more powerful force than professional training when dealing with the resolution of certain life matters.

In summary, the Baltes et al. (1995) research reinforced the idea that wisdom is not constrained by age, occupation, or professional training. Beyond any doubt, these are encouraging results. They show that individuals from a wide range of domains may achieve wisdom. Do these findings have any bearing on your beliefs about the capability of older individuals to occupy leadership roles in the major political, cultural, and religious institutions of our society?

Box Table 9.B

Wisdom-Related Tasks

Existential Life Management

You get a phone call from a good friend who says that he/she can't go on anymore and that he/she has decided to commit suicide. What should you consider and do?

Life Planning

Joyce, a widow aged 60 years, recently completed a degree in business management and opened her own business. She has been looking forward to this challenge. However, she has just heard that her son has been left with two small children to care for. Joyce is considering the following options: She could plan to give up her business and live with her son, or she could plan to arrange for financial assistance for her son to cover child care costs. Formulate a plan that details what Joyce should consider and do for the next three to five years. What extra pieces of information are needed?

Wisdom and Professional Expertise

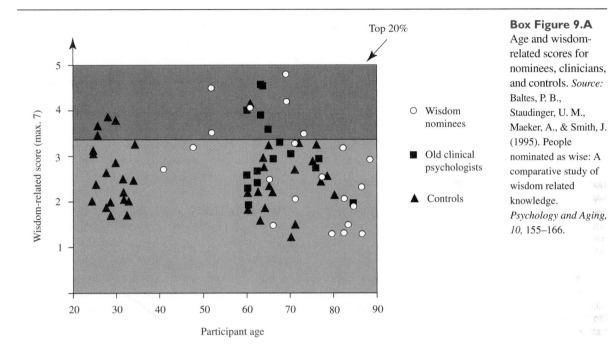

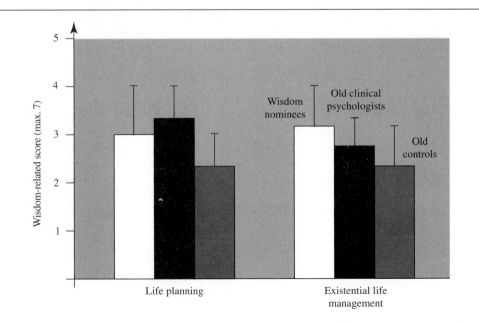

Box Figure 9.A
Age and wisdom-related scores for nominees, clinicians, and controls. *Source:* Baltes, P. B., Staudinger, U. M., Maeker, A., & Smith, J. (1995). People nominated as wise: A comparative study of wisdom related knowledge. *Psychology and Aging, 10,* 155–166.

Box Figure 9.B
Wisdom-related scores for nominees, clinicians, and controls on the life planning and existential life management tasks. *Source:* Baltes, P. B., Staudinger, U. M., Maeker, A., & Smith, J. (1995).

Selective Optimization and Compensation

Given the results of the research studies that have investigated age-related changes in the mechanics and pragmatics of mind, psychologists should realize that cognitive aging is a dynamic process that involves a changing gain or loss ratio in which the accumulation of expertise may offset decrements in reserve capacity. Baltes and Baltes (1990) have developed a strategy for successful aging, termed **selective optimization with compensation,** based on the insights gained from this research. The notion of *selection* means that individuals should restrict their life work to fewer intellectual domains because of an age-related loss in adaptive ability and reserve potential. They should select these domains based on their personal (and societal) importance and relevance. *Optimization* means that adults should engage in activities that maintain their mental reserves and increase their domain-specific knowledge to maximize the satisfaction their chosen life path gives them. The term *compensation* involves the use of a new strategy or technique to adapt to a life task when a long-used psychological (or physical) ability is lost or falls below a critical level. This model, which was originally developed to foster successful "intellectual aging," also offers valuable insight about how to maximize nonintellectual facets of development across the adult years. Table 9.4 provides insights about how nursing home residents, athletes, and musicians might use the principles of selection, optimization, and compensation to maintain (or enhance) their performance upon entry into older adulthood.

Recently, Abraham and Hansson (1995) wanted to determine whether well-educated white-collar working adults between 40 and 69 years of age used, on a natural or sponta-

---

TABLE 9.4

Illustration of the Principles of Selection, Optimization, and Compensation

Type of Individual	Principle
Nursing Home Resident	Selection—become responsible for a few, but important, aspects of daily life (domains) Optimization—get extensive practice in the selected domains Compensation—use technological aids and medical interventions that support functions affected by diminished reserve capacities
Marathon Runner	Selection—give up those activities that take away from running Optimization—increase the quality and quantity of training and develop better dietary habits Compensation—pay close attention to buying proper running shoes and seeking out new techniques for healing injuries
Musician* **(*comments made** **by the pianist** **A. Rubenstein during** **a TV interview)**	Selection—reduce your repertoire, play fewer pieces Optimization—practice more Compensation—slow down playing speed prior to fast movements, thereby producing a contrast that gives the impression of "speed" in the fast movement

Source: Baltes, P. B. & Baltes, M. (1990). Psychological perspectives on successful aging: The model of selective optimization with compensation. In P. B. Baltes and M. Baltes (Eds.), Longitudinal research and the study of successful (optimal) aging (pp. 1–49). Cambridge, England: Cambridge University Press.

neous basis, the principles of "selection," "optimization," and "compensation" (SOC) in their occupational lives. One of the ideas behind this study was that the use of SOC strategies might become more necessary for maintaining high levels of job performance among older adults because older individuals are apt to experience declines in their biological and psychological reserve capacities. The results of this research showed that older adults were just as likely to use SOC strategies as younger individuals; SOC is applicable to, and used by, individuals across the adult life span. More interestingly, however, Abraham and Hansson (1995) reported that the use of SOC strategies was more highly related to job performance and goal attainment among older than younger workers. Thus SOC strategies seem especially useful for older workers.

SOC may apply not only to behaviors that are physical, artistic, intellectual, or occupational in nature, but to many aspects of successful interpersonal and intrapersonal functioning. For example, Baltes and Graf (1996) examined the relationship of age, intelligence, and subjective well-being in a group of individuals between 70 and 105 years of age. The results of this study, which took into account a subgroup of adults suspected of suffering from dementia, appear in figure 9.6. As would be expected, general intelligence declined with age, especially for demented individuals. However, the most interesting aspect of the data was that there was no relationship between age and subjective well-being. What accounts for this highly paradoxical and counterintuitive finding? Why should older adults still experience a strong sense of personal control and

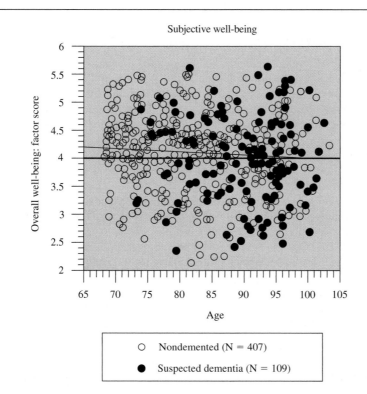

Figure 9.6 Age and subjective well-being. *Source:* Baltes, P. B., & Graf, P. (1996). Psychological aspects of aging: Facts and frontiers. In D. Magnusson et al. (Eds.), *Individual development over the life span: Biological and psychological, perspectives* (pp. 1–34), New York: Cambridge University Press.

self-esteem despite the significant losses they experience in functioning? Perhaps these last two questions should be recast in the following manner: How (and why) have older adults chosen to select and optimize their sense of well-being at the expense of other aspects of their selves? What types of strategies are they using to help them compensate for age-related losses in reserve capacity? Baltes and Graf (1996) suggest that older adults may enhance their sense of subjective well-being in a number of different ways. For example, consider an older individual who has suffered a heart attack and has the intuition that his memory and mental quickness have recently declined. This person may begin to view himself from a new perspective (he may think of himself as a "lover of music" instead of "an executive who is an avid golfer"), change his goals and aspirations (he may adopt the primary goal of helping his grown children achieve their life goals—by giving them financial aid, advice, etc.—rather than seeking new work-related challenges for himself), or change the way he compares himself to others (he may start to compare himself to other retired individuals who have cardiovascular disease rather than to healthy, middle-aged executives).

One of the important aspects of the SOC approach is that individuals of all ages may use the principles of selection, optimization, and compensation in a very positive manner. But during older adulthood, the principles of SOC take on added significance.

Wisdom, Biological Limits, and Society

At its most general level, we may view the work of Baltes and his associates as an attempt to understand the relationship between wisdom, biology, and society. Baltes and Staudinger (1993) made this point in this way:

> . . . because of the enriching and compensatory power of culture and knowledge-based factors, we have come to believe that the potential for future enhancement of the aging mind is considerable despite biological limits. Why? From the point of view of civilization, old age is young; it is only during the last century that many people have reached old age. Therefore, there has not been much of an opportunity for the development and refinement of a culture for and of old age. Culture, however, has the power not only to "activate" whatever biological potential is available, but also, within certain limits, to outwit the constraints (losses) of biology.
>
> Our concluding kernel of truth is this: The complete story of old age cannot be told based on the current reality about old age. . . . What also must be considered are the special strengths of *Homo sapiens:* the unrivaled ability to produce a powerful stream of cultural inheritance and cultural innovation and to compensate for biological vulnerability. Searching for a better culture of old age is not only a challenge for the future. It is the future, because the future is not something people enter, it is something people help create. In this sense, research on wisdom offers a challenge to look beyond. (p. 80)

SUMMARY

The stage approach to the study of adult cognition offers an important alternative to the psychometric and information-processing perspectives. Genuine cognitive stages must meet a strict set of criteria. These criteria include (1) invariant movement, (2) qualitative restructuring, (3) hierarchical integration, (4) universal progression, and (5) structured wholeness. Jean Piaget developed the most significant stage theory of cognitive development. Originally, Piaget argued for the existence of four different cognitive stages. The fourth stage, formal operations, which Piaget thought emerged during adolescence, was considered representative of mature adult cognition. Piaget viewed formal operational thought as a form of scientific thinking, and described it as hypothetico-deductive, logical, and abstract. Formal thought seems best suited for the solution of well-defined, closed-system problems.

In the mid to late 1970s, it became clear that Piaget's stage of formal operations did not capture the essential features of mature adult thought. Thus, psychologists began to search for a fifth, postformal stage of cognitive development. Postformal thought allows adults to solve ill-defined, open-system problems as well as to focus on problem finding, not just problem solving. However, postformal development may be best understood as a number of unique styles of thinking that emerge during adulthood, not as a genuine stage of cognitive development. Postformal accounts of adult cognition place an emphasis on social cognition, or reasoning about the social, interpersonal, and ethical problems characteristic of everyday living.

We briefly described the encapsulation model of adult cognition. This model integrates the psychometric, information-processing, cognitive-science, and cognitive-stage perspectives. It suggests that the salient dimensions of cognition are processing, knowing, and thinking. It also suggests that the most important characteristics of adult cognition (the development of domain-specific expert knowledge and postformal thinking) result from the encapsulation of basic cognitive processes and abilities. We illustrated the encapsulation model through a discussion of the relationships between aging, cognitive expertise, and information processing. In the last sections of this chapter we discuss concepts and measures of wisdom, and the theory of selective optimization with compensation.

REVIEW QUESTIONS

1. Describe each of the criteria that define genuine cognitive stages.
2. Discuss the essential features of formal operations. Describe some of the problems that may be used to test for the presence of formal thinking.
3. Why did psychologists become disenchanted with Piaget's contention that formal operational thinking was the final stage of cognitive development?
4. Describe the essential features of postformal cognitive development. Which aspect of postformal thinking (relativistic thinking, dialectic thinking, or problem finding) do you think has generated the most meaningful and important research? Why?
5. Compare and contrast the psychometric, information-processing, and cognitive-stage approaches to the study of adult cognition. Indicate the focal point as well as the strengths and weaknesses of each approach.
6. Explain the basic tenets of the cognitive-science approach to the study of cognition. What are the research implications of this approach?
7. Explain the basic features of the encapsulation model. Explain the differences between processing, knowing, and thinking.
8. Discuss the research studies that suggest that adults continue to function effectively on tasks in which they have cognitive expertise.

9. Explain how psychologists have attempted to study the concept of wisdom. What insights have they gained about the relationship between the biological and cultural dimensions of aging?
10. Explain how Baltes's distinction between the mechanics and pragmatics of mind relate to the basic features of the encapsulation model.
11. Explain how the concept of *selective optimization with compensation* may be used to help boost the performance of younger and older adults.
12. Explain the significance of research that uses the *age-by-experience paradigm* as well as the technique of *testing the limits* of cognitive reserve.
13. Briefly describe the contrasting approaches to explaining the growth of cognitive expertise.
14. What role, if any, does professional training in psychology play in the development of wisdom?

ON THE WEB   www.mhhe.com/hoyer5

For a listing of links to new information about cognition, expertise, and wisdom, and to related topics, see:

The home page for the John D. and Catherine T. MacArthur Foundation supports the activities of "networks" of scholars and scientists on selected topics, including several relevant to the material in this chapter. This site contains lists of publications and other resources related to the study of midlife development.

The base-berlin.mpg site describes the Berlin Aging Study and lists publications related to a variety of topics in cognition, expertise, and wisdom.

10

PERSONALITY

> *Integrity simply means a willingness not to violate one's identity.*
> —Erich Fromm
>
> *The greatest and most important problems of life are all in a certain sense insoluble . . . They can never be solved but only outgrown.*
> —Carl Jung
>
> *One of the benefits of being 91 years of age, according to Charles Costantino who is still working as a trainer for professional boxers, "There is very little peer pressure."*

INTRODUCTION

In this chapter, we examine the changes as well as the continuities of adult personality. We begin by defining personality, and then we present Erik Erikson's, Jane Loevinger's, and Daniel Levinson's stage theories of adult personality development. Next, we turn to the results of longitudinal studies of personality stability and change. Then, we describe how life events affect adult personality. Finally, we examine the development of morality during the adult years. We devote special attention to the growing interest in positive psychology and personality.

What Is Personality?

Personality refers to a person's distinctive patterns of behavior, thought, and emotion. Sometimes, the term *personality* is used to refer to a person's most unique characteristics. For example, we might notice that someone we know is "shy," while another is an "extrovert." The concept of personality rests on the assumption that individuals have distinctive qualities that are relatively invariant across situations and over time (Mischel & Shoda, 1995).

Researchers and theorists often differ substantially in their views about how personality develops. Sigmund Freud emphasized the importance of unconscious motives outside the adult's awareness as determinants of personality development. B. F. Skinner (1990), in contrast, stressed the importance of learning and reinforced experiences in understanding how personality develops. Skinner suggested that the things a person does—his or her overt behaviors, not unconscious wishes—compose personality.

How do we measure something as complex as an adult's personality? One way is to ask a person about his or her personality; however, people do not always perceive themselves objectively. Another way is to observe personality directly as it functions in everyday life or under particular conditions. Other ways to assess personality involve administering tests, surveys, or questionnaires.

Regardless of the method of measurement, it is necessary to consider the effects of sociohistorical influences when trying to assess age-related changes. The personality characteristics of younger adults today differ from those of older adults today; when younger adults age, they will still be unlike older adults today (e.g., Kogan, 1990).

The Stage Approach to Adult Personality Development

Some theorists have proposed that personality development can be described as a progression of stages. In this section, we describe the stage theories of Erik Erikson, Jane Loevinger, and Daniel Levinson.

Erik Erikson's Eight Stages

One of the earliest and most prominent theories of life-span personality development is Erik Erikson's eight-stage theory of psychosocial development. Freud influenced Erikson, but unlike Freud, Erikson recognized that personality development takes place in the context of a social system.

Erikson's theory (Erikson 1963, 1968, 1982; Erikson, Erikson, & Kivnick, 1986) is particularly important because it was one of the first to cast a life-span frame of reference on development. Erikson accepted the basic outline of Freud's theory that early **psychosexual development,** the ways in which developing individuals deal with pleasurable body sensations, affects and shapes personality development. At the same time, however, Erikson called attention to the individual's **psychosocial development** across the life span. Erikson placed strong emphasis on the lifelong relationship between developing individuals and the social system they are a part of. Erikson envisioned a dialectic relationship between the individual and society: society and individual both change each other and are changed by each other.

According to Erikson, personality changes or develops in a predictable manner. Erikson's theory is based on the premise that development throughout life is influenced by **epigenesis,** or an in-common genetic plan that unfolds with age. However, this genetically programmed unfolding of the personality occurs in a particular social and cultural context, and that context modifies the outcome of the genetic plan. According to Erikson, human cultures guide or facilitate the emergence of epigenetic development. His theory emphasized the interaction between epigenesis (genetics) and culture (environment) in understanding human development. To quote Erikson:

> The human personality develops in stages predetermined in the growing person's readiness to be driven toward, to be aware of, and to interact with a widening social radius; and society, in principle, tends to be constituted so as to meet and invite this succession of potentialities for interaction and attempts to safeguard and encourage the proper rate and the proper sequence of their unfolding. (Erikson, 1963, p. 270)

Each of Erikson's eight stages centers around a distinct emotional concern stemming from epigenetic pressures within the person and sociocultural expectations outside the person. The individual resolves the concerns or conflicts at each stage either in a positive and healthy or in a negative and unhealthy way. Each conflict offers a polarity that predominates all other concerns for a time. The person must resolve earlier stage conflicts satisfactorily for the successful resolution of conflicts at subsequent stages.

Successful resolution of a stage crisis is not necessarily entirely positive. Exposure to a conflict's negative dimensions is often necessary for a healthy solution.

Table 10.1 lists Erikson's stages of psychosocial development. The table indicates (1) the social sphere each conflict occurs in, (2) the self-definition that arises during the course of each conflict, and (3) the virtue (psychological strengths) that may evolve if an individual resolves a conflict in a positive manner.

The first stage, *trust versus mistrust,* corresponds to the oral stage in Freud's theory. An infant depends almost entirely on parents for food and comfort. The caretaker is the primary representative of society to the child. Erikson assumed that the infant is incapable of distinguishing self from caregivers. When responsible caretakers meet the infant's needs with warmth, regularity, and affection, the infant will develop trust toward the world and in self. The infant will have a comfortable feeling that someone will care for his or her needs, even when the caretaker is not always present or available. Alternatively, a sense of mistrust or fearful uncertainty can develop if the caretaker fails to provide for these needs.

Autonomy versus shame and doubt is the second stage in Erikson's theory; it corresponds to the anal stage in Freud's theory. The infant begins to gain control over bowels and bladder. Parents begin to expect the child to conform to socially acceptable methods for eliminating wastes. The child may develop a healthy sense of self-control over his or her actions (not just bowel and bladder), or he or she may develop feelings of shame and doubt because of failure in self-control.

Initiative versus guilt corresponds to the phallic period in Freud's theory. The child is experiencing an Oedipal conflict or an Electra conflict, competing with the same-sex parent for the love of the parent of the opposite sex. The child's exploration and discovery of ways to overcome feelings of powerlessness leads to a self-view of being competent and effective. Alternatively, the child may fail to discover how to overcome feeling powerless, leading to feelings of guilt about being dominated by primitive urges.

Industry versus inferiority corresponds roughly to Freud's period of latency. This stage includes the middle childhood years when the child is involved in learning new cognitive and physical skills. The child is drawn into his or her culture because many of the skills are socially prescribed and occur in interactions with peers or siblings. If children view themselves as basically competent in these activities, feelings of productivity and industry will result. On the other hand, if children view themselves as incompetent, particularly in comparison with peers, they develop feelings of inferiority.

Identity versus identity confusion is roughly associated with Freud's genital stage. The major focus during this stage is the formation of a stable personal identity. For Freud, the important part of identity formation resided in the adolescent's resolution of sexual conflicts; for Erikson, the central ingredient is the establishment of a sense of mutual recognition or appreciation between the adolescent and key persons in his or her social context. The adolescent who successfully completes this stage comes to view society as decent, moral, and just and comes to believe that society values his or her existence. This mutual appreciation leads to feelings of personal identity, confidence, and purposefulness. Without mutual appreciation, the adolescent feels confused and troubled.

Erikson described three stages of adult personality development. These stages, unlike the earlier ones, do not have parallels in Freud's theory. The first of these adult

TABLE 10.1

An Overview of Erikson's Theory of Psychosocial Development

Epoch of the Life Span	Psychosocial Crisis	Sphere of Social Interaction	Self-Definition	Virtue
Early infancy	Trust vs. mistrust	Mother	I am what I am given	Hope—the enduring belief in the attainability of primal wishes in spite of the urges and rages of dependency
Late infancy/ early childhood	Autonomy vs. shame	Parents	I am what I will to be	Will—the unbroken determination to exercise free choice as well as self-restraint in spite of the unavoidable experiences of shame, doubt, and a certain rage over being controlled by others
Early childhood	Initiative vs. guilt	Family	I am what I can imagine	Purpose—the courage to pursue valued goals guided by conscience and not paralyzed by guilt
Middle childhood	Industry vs. inferiority	Community, school	I am what I learn	Competence—the free exercise of dexterity and intelligence in the completion of a serious task
Adolescence	Identity vs. confusion	Nation	I am who I define myself to be	Fidelity—the ability to sustain loyalties freely pledged in spite of the inevitable contradictions of value systems
Early adulthood	Intimacy vs. isolation	Community, nation	We are what we love	Love—the mutuality of devotion greater than the antagonisms inherent in divided function
Middle adulthood	Generativity vs. stagnation	World, nation, community	I am what I create	Care—the broadening concern for what has been generated by love, necessity, or accident
Late adulthood	Integrity vs. despair	Universe, world, nation	I am what survives me	Wisdom—a detached yet active concern for life bounded by death

stages occurs during early adulthood and is termed *intimacy versus isolation.* Young adulthood usually brings opportunities to form a deeply intimate relationship with another person as well as meaningful friendships. A feeling of isolation results if one is not able to form valued friendships and an intimate relationship.

At the same time that young adults are becoming strongly interested in developing close relationships with others, they also experience a strong need for independence and freedom. Development during early adulthood involves a struggle between needs for intimacy and commitment on the one hand and needs for independence and freedom on the other. Although the balance between intimacy and independence is a concern throughout the adults years, Erikson suggested it was a predominant theme in the early adult years.

The chief concern of middle-aged adults is to resolve the conflict of *generativity versus stagnation.* **Generativity** refers to caring about generations—one's own generation as well as future generations. Generativity could be expressed through parenting or helping others' children, or through working as a caring contributor to society. Thus, generative individuals place themselves in roles that involve caring and giving in meaningful ways to those who will outlive them.

It is during this stage that adults may experience a midlife crisis. For example, middle-aged adults may feel a sense of stagnation because they feel their interpersonal relationships and work have no meaning. Occupations such as teacher, minister, nurse, physician, and social worker appear to be generative, but being a builder, artist, entertainer, community volunteer, or any occupation can be generative depending on how one carries it out. The interpretation that each individual gives to his or her actions is the primary determinant of feelings of generativity or stagnation. Consider Erikson's remarks about nongenerativity, as follows:

> The only thing that can save us as a species is seeing how we're not thinking of future generations in the way we live. . . . What's lacking is generativity, a generativity that will promote positive values in the lives of the next generation. Unfortunately, we set the example of greed, wanting a bigger and better everything, with no thought of what will make it a better world for our great-grandchildren. That's why we go on depleting the earth: we're not thinking of the next generations. (quoted in Coleman, 1988)

In one study, McAdams, de St. Aubin, and Logan (1993) examined age differences in generativity among young adults (22 to 27 years), middle-aged adults (37 to 42 years), and older adults (67 to 72 years). McAdams et al. (1993) collected data on four different dimensions of generativity: generative concern—the extent to which an individual feels concerned about the welfare of future generations; generative strivings—the specific things an individual would like to do to help and nurture the next generation; generative action—the specific generative behaviors that one has actually performed; and generative narration—the degree to which salient past memories reflect the basic theme of generativity. Erikson's theory suggests that generativity should peak during middle adulthood and progressively decline throughout old age. Results in the McAdams et al. study partially supported Erikson's position. As expected, younger adults displayed, by far, the lowest levels of generativity. Contrary to expectation, however, the scores of middle-aged adults and older adults did not differ. Thus, it would seem as if the need to be generative guides the daily lives of middle-aged and older adults much more than those of younger adults. This finding is illustrated by the responses to the open-ended question, "I typically try to . . . " (see table 10.2). Finally, McAdams et al. (1993) reported that, within each age group, participants who scored highest on the generativity measures also displayed the greatest amounts of life satisfaction and happiness.

In the later years, adults enter the stage of *ego integrity versus despair.* This is a time when individuals face their own deaths by looking back at what they have done with their lives. Some older persons construct a positive view of their pasts and see their lives as meaningful and satisfying (ego integrity). However, some older persons look back on their lives with resentment, bitterness, or dissatisfaction. Sadly, some older adults feel that they were unable to create the life that they wanted for themselves, or blame others for their disappointment (despair). Erikson's own words best capture his rich thoughts about this crisis:

> A meaningful old age, then . . . serves the need for that integrated heritage which gives indispensable perspective on the life cycle. Strength here takes the form of that detached yet active concern with life bounded with death, which we call wisdom. . . .
>
> To whatever abyss ultimate concerns may lead individual men, man as a psychosocial creature will face, toward the end of his life, a new edition of the identity crisis which we may state in the words, "I am what survives me." (1968, pp. 140–141)

Robert Butler (1963) has given a special name to the older adult's tendency to look back in time and analyze the meaning of his or her life: the **life review.** Others use the term **reminiscence** to capture the process of reflecting on the past.

Erikson arranged the crises of the life span in a linear manner; moving through these stages is a bit like climbing a ladder. The bottom rung is the crisis of trust versus mistrust, and the top rung is ego integrity versus despair. This is not the picture of the

TABLE 10.2

Some of the Strivings Reported by Younger, Midlife, and Older Adults

Age of Participant	Examples of Responses to the Statement "I typically try to . . ."
26-year-old woman	"make my job more interesting" "figure out what I want to do with my life" "be well liked" "make my life more interesting and challenging" "keep up with current events" "make others believe I am completely confident and secure"
40-year-old woman	"be a positive role model for young people" "explain teenage experience to my son and help him work through difficult situations" "provide for my mother to the best of my ability" "be helpful to those who are in need of help"
68-year-old woman	"counsel a daughter who was recently let go from a job due to cutbacks" "help a daughter with her sick child" "help as a volunteer at a nonprofit organization" "offer financial aid to someone, friend or relative, if needed"

Source: McAdams, D. P., de St. Aubin, E., & Logan, R. L. (1993). Generativity among young, midlife, and older adults. Psychology and Aging, 8, 221–230. Copyright 1993 by the American Psychological Association. Reprinted with permission.

life span, however, that Erikson intended. Erikson envisioned the life span as cyclical. He thought the individuals who are just beginning life (infants and very young children) may be profoundly influenced by individuals who are about to leave life behind (the elderly). Erikson stated his thoughts on this matter: "And it seems possible to paraphrase the relation of adult integrity and infantile trust by saying that healthy children will not fear life if their elders have integrity enough not to fear death" (1963, p. 268).

Research Focus 10.1 presents information about the relationship between sex roles and health in adulthood. The research described in this box seems to relate to Erikson' final stage in his model of personality development.

As Erikson himself reached old age, he wondered whether there was a ninth stage of development. But it was difficult to conceptualize a new stage because old age was not yet well represented in society. The oldest-old remained largely apart from the rest of society, overlooked, abandoned, and shut away from regular intergenerational exchange. He commented that "lacking a culturally viable ideal of old age, our civilization does not really harbor a concept of the whole of life" (Erikson, 1997, p. 114). This reinforces the notion that the life cycle can only be understood within its social context. Erikson's wife, Joan, recently tried to outline a ninth stage of development, given changes in society towards the very old. She identified this stage as **gero-transcendence,** a broad perspective on life, universe, and the cosmos (see Research Focus 10.2). Gero-transcendence moves beyond the self, beyond the here and now; it transcends (e.g., rises above) the material, rational world. With ties to spirituality, faith, belief and hope, gero-transcendence may be the last stage of human development, providing inner peace, life satisfaction, spiritual contentment, and the freedom to withdraw from everyday concerns for self and others. Similarly, Riley Kahn and Foner (1994) have identified a structural lag in that our society has not provided roles, structures, or meaning to the added

---

Research Focus 10.1

Sex Differences in Well-Being, Personality, and Health

It is puzzling that the average life expectancy is longer for women than men, but that women have higher rates of illness (or morbidity). In the United States and in a number of other countries, women experience more acute illnesses and stresses than men (as discussed in chapter 6). Helgeson (1994) has suggested that these sex differences in physical well-being are related to sex role differences.

Some of these differences in physical well-being may have to do with sex differences in how men and women are socialized. For example, men have greater mortality from accidents, which may be because of greater risk-taking. Women report more "illness behavior" than men, as measured by a larger number of days of restricted activities, more frequent use of health services, and taking more medications. Helgeson suggests that women may be more responsive to stressors that affect friends and others, and that women may also be generally more affected by stressors

that involve relationships. Evidence for the deleterious effects of having an "other orientation" comes from physiological studies. Women showed greater negative immunological effects than men when discussing marital conflict (Kiecolt-Glaser et al., 1993).

Helgeson examined sex differences in agency and communion. Agency and communion are considered fundamental styles of being. Agency refers to one's existence as an individual, and communion refers to the participation of an individual in relationships, groups, or communities. Helgeson suggested that both agency and communion are required for optimal functioning and well-being. When one exists in the absence of the other, negative health outcomes occur. Possible sex differences in agency and communion may account for sex differences in health and mortality. Sex roles that balance agency and communion may be associated with optimal health and longer life.

Beyond Stages: The Development of Gero-Transcendence

According to stage theory, the hallmark of personality development is the attainment of ego integrity. Ego integrity is achieved as individuals look back and reaffirm their lives in the face of impending death. According to stage theory, ego integrity would not occur unless the person developed a well-differentiated self.

Lars Tornstan (1994) doubts that ego integrity truly describes the personality changes that are characteristic of older adults. Tornstan suggests that the basic distinctions between "self versus other" and "present versus past" reflect an orientation to reality more representative of younger and middle-aged adults. With advanced old age, Tornstan believes that individuals experience a fundamental paradigm shift. They move from a rational, dualistic, and material view of life to one that is more cosmic and transcendent. Tornstan uses the term **gero-transcendence** to refer to this perspective. Some of the most salient features associated with gero-transcendence appear in box table 10.A.

The construct of gero-transcendence, although not explicitly religious in nature, has much in common with the guiding principles of Eastern religions. For example, the overarching goal of the aging Hindu in Indian culture is to become a nonperson, devoid of the need for spirituality, sensuality, psychological bonds, or social dimensions. The individual strives to have no self, no real-world concerns. Death is blissful liberation, the deserved attainment of one who has led a perfect life by having committed time to religious study,

BOX TABLE 10.A

Significant Features of Gero-Transcendence

Decreased concern for one's personal life and an increased emphasis on the flow of life

Decreased emphasis on the distinctions between self-other and past-present-future

Increased time spent in meditation and decreased interest in social interactions and material objects

married and produced children, and offered support and help to those in need. Given these accomplishments, life should be in total harmony. The emphasis on ego integrity, self-awareness, and personal wisdom in American culture contrasts sharply with the values of Eastern religions.

To test his notion of gero-transcendence, Tornstan (1994) administered a series of questionnaires to 912 Danish adults between 74 and 100 years of age. Of primary interest was the percentage of participants who expressed agreement with 10 statements indicative of two aspects of gero-transcendence: cosmic transcendence and ego transcendence. The results, shown in box table 10.B, are consistent with a shift to gero-transcendence with increasing age.

BOX TABLE 10.B

Percentage of Participants Who Agreed with Statements Indicative of Gero-Transcendence

Statements Indicative of Cosmic Transcendence	(% Agree)
Today I feel that the border between life and death is less striking than when I was 50.	60%
Today I feel to a higher degree how unimportant an individual life is, in comparison to the continuation of life.	55%
Today I feel a greater mutual connection to the universe than when I was 50 years of age.	32%
Today I often experience a close presence of persons, even when they are physically elsewhere.	36%
Today I feel that the distance between past and present disappears.	42%
Today I feel a greater state of belongingness with both earlier and coming generations.	49%

Statements Indicative of Ego Transcendence	(% Agree)
Today I take myself less seriously than earlier.	60%
Today material things mean less than when I was 50.	74%
Today I am less concerned with superficial social contacts.	53%
Today I have more delight in my inner world than when I was 50.	57%

continued

Beyond Stages: The Development of Gero-Transcendence

Most interestingly, Tornstan found that endorsing statements indicative of cosmic and ego transcendence was positively correlated with measures of life satisfaction, affirmative coping, and social activity. However, he also discovered that participants who were the most likely to agree with transcendent statements were the least likely to maintain that social interactions were necessary for life satisfaction! Thus, gero-transcendence entails a rather paradoxical relationship between the need to be alone and the need to be with others. This is clear evidence that successful aging does not represent a simple disengagement or withdrawal from society.

In conclusion, it seems that if Tornstan's (1994) ideas about gero-transcendence are correct, we face the interesting possibility that psychologists (typically younger or middle-aged adults) have failed to capture the essence of aging. This is because, by virtue of their age, they have used a worldview to study older adults that is antithetical to the perspective with which older adults live their lives. As members of an aging society, we all face the challenge of constructing social roles for older individuals that are consistent with their transcendent orientation.

---

years of life that adults now enjoy. "Seen in this light lower levels of life purpose and continued growth among the aged may be individual-level manifestations of a society that has yet to address the needs for purposeful engagement and talent utilization among its growing older population (Ryff, Kwan, and Singer, 2001, p. 483)."

Jane Loevinger's Theory of Ego Development

Jane Loevinger's (1976) theory emphasizes that personality development involves an increasingly more differentiated perception of oneself. That is, each person develops a more precise understanding of oneself and one's relationships to others. Table 10.3 summarizes the adult stages of her theory. Several stages preceding the ones listed in the table apply to childhood and adolescent developmental issues. Loevinger states that not everyone will go through all stages. Indeed, attainment of the last two stages is relatively rare. Loevinger also emphasizes that no one stage is any "better" than another, even though individuals may aspire to higher stages.

Loevinger observed that people seldom backslide to ways of thinking associated with an earlier stage. She suggested that backsliding is rare because the stages are in a sense *earned* by the individual through struggling with personal feelings and thoughts. Along these lines, Johnson and Barer (1996) and Troll and Skaff (1997) observed that many older individuals, especially individuals over 85 years of age who had experienced a variety of hardships, radiated an "aura of survivorship" demonstrated by greater tolerance, serenity, and acceptance of what life has to offer.

According to Loevinger, people are continually directing their energies toward becoming or achieving their true selves. One's real self, or *ego,* develops slowly toward the point at which no discrepancy exists between who one really is and how one acts. The ego is the chief organizer of our values, goals, and views of ourselves and others. In Loevinger's theory, the development of the ego comes about because of (1) basic feelings of responsibility or accountability, (2) the capacity for honest self-criticism, (3) the desire to formulate one's own standards and ideals, and (4) nonselfish concern and love for others.

TABLE 10.3

Loevinger's Six Stages of Ego Development During Adulthood

Conformist	Obedience to external social rules. Preoccupied with appearance, belongingness, and superficial matters.
Conscientious-Conformist	Increased awareness of one's own emerging personality. Increased realization of the consequences of one's actions on others.
Conscientious	Intense and complete realization of one's own standards. Self-critical.
Individualistic	Recognition that one's efforts and actions on behalf of others are more important than personal outcomes.
Autonomous	Respect for each person's individuality. Acceptance of ambiguity. Continued coping with inner conflicts contributes to an appreciation the actions and approaches of other individuals.
Integrated	Resolution of inner conflicts. Renunciation of the unattainable for oneself. Cherishing the individuality of others.

Source: Adapted from Loevinger, J. (1976). Ego development. San Francisco: Jossey-Bass.

Daniel Levinson's "The Seasons of Life"

Daniel Levinson's vision of adult development was first set out in his book *Seasons of a Man's Life* (1978). His view grew out of his interviews with middle-aged men who were hourly workers, business executives, academic biologists, and novelists. Though Levinson's major interest was the midlife transition, he described a number of phases, stages, and transitions in the life cycle, as indicated in figure 10.1.

From 1982 to 1992, Daniel Levinson, Judy Levinson, and their colleagues interviewed women regarding adult developmental transitions. They discovered that the framework in figure 10.1 also extends to the development of women during the adult years. An account of their research on women's development during the adult years was published in *Seasons of a Woman's Life,* in 1996.

The most important concept in Levinson's theory is the individual's **life structure.** The term *life structure* refers to the ". . . underlying pattern or design of a person's life at any given time" (Levinson, 1986, p. 41). A person's life structure is revealed by the choices he or she makes and one's relationships with others. For example, one person may choose to devote a significant amount of time and energy to her occupation, forsaking her relationships with spouse, children, and friends. Another individual may choose to use his time and energy to help others acquire new competencies and job skills and to become closer to family members. Levinson reminds us that the choices we make concerning marriage, family, and occupation are the most important facets of our life structure. The relationships we have with others, as well as with our work, ". . . are the stuff our lives are made of. They give shape and substance to the life course. They are the vehicle through which we live out—and bury—various aspects of ourselves and by which we participate, for better or worse, in the world around us" (Levinson, 1986, p. 6). Finally, Levinson argues that the life structure changes and evolves over different periods of the adult life span.

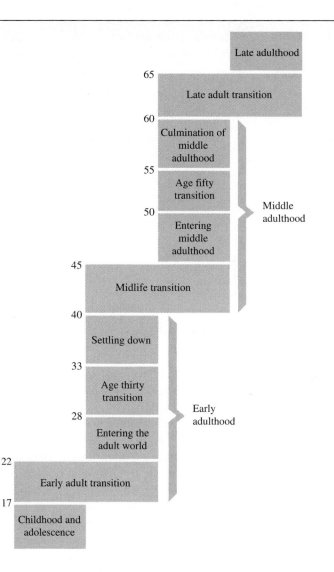

Figure 10.1
Levinson's sequence of eras and transitions for personality development during the adult years.

According to Levinson, the human life cycle consists of four different **eras,** each with a distinctive character. Levinson emphasizes that developmental tasks must be mastered during each of these eras. The eras partially overlap one another; a new era begins as an old one comes to an end. These periods of overlap, or **transitions,** last for approximately five years. As Levinson notes, "The eras and cross-era transitional periods form the macrostructure of the life cycle, providing an underlying order in the flow of all human lives yet permitting exquisite variations in the individual life course" (1986, p. 5).

The first era, preadulthood, lasts from conception to about 17 years of age (see figure 10.1). During this time, the individual grows from being a highly dependent infant to beginning to be an independent, responsible adult. The years from 17 to 22 compose the early adult transition. At this time, the developing person first starts to modify his relationships with family and friends to help build a place in the adult world.

The next era, early adulthood, spans the ages of 22 to 40. This is an era characterized by the greatest energy, contradiction, and stress. The major tasks are forming and pursuing youthful aspirations (fulfilling a dream), raising a family, and establishing a senior position in the adult world. This period can be immensely rewarding in terms of love, occupational advancement, and the realization of one's major life goals. But, due to the demands of parenthood, marriage, and occupation, this era can also be marked by conflict. One's ambitions as well as the demands of family, community, and society can be overwhelming.

The midlife transition lasts from about 40 to 45 years of age. By the time many individuals enter this transitional period, they realize they have not accomplished what they set out to do during early adulthood. This leads to feelings of disappointment and forces the individual to recast earlier life goals. Alternatively, some individuals meet or even exceed their initial dreams. These individuals may soon realize, however, that their outstanding accomplishments did not insulate them from feelings of anxiety and crisis. These negative emotions emerge from several different sources. First, individuals start to experience themselves as older and physically vulnerable. They become aware of their own aging, as well as the aging (and deaths) of their parents. They also begin to view themselves as next in line to die and as the oldest surviving members of their families. Individuals still want to accomplish much, but they feel they have little time left. In essence, these feelings are the characteristics of what others such as Gould (1972, 1980) and Sheehy (1995) refer to as the *midlife crisis*. The successful resolution of the midlife transition leads men and women to refine their goals and prove themselves while separating from their mentors and parents. This process is one of "becoming one's own self."

Levinson suggested that the midlife transition is a time of crisis and soul searching that provides the opportunity to either become more caring, reflective, and loving or more stagnated. The transition's success depends on how we accept and integrate the following polarities of adult existence: (1) being young versus old, (2) being masculine versus feminine, (3) being destructive versus constructive, and (4) being attached versus separated from others.

The third era, middle adulthood, lasts from about 45 to 60 years of age. This is the time period during which most individuals have the potential to have the most profound and positive impact on their families, their professions, and their world. Individuals no longer concern themselves with their own ambitions. They develop new long-range goals that help them to facilitate the growth of others. Adults of this age sometimes become mentors to younger individuals. They take pride in the competence and productivity of younger individuals rather than being threatened by them. Furthermore, as individuals enter middle adulthood, they are more able to reap the benefits of family life. In essence, Levinson's ideas about middle adulthood correspond to Erikson's notion of generativity.

The late adult transition occurs from ages 60 to 65. During this time, older adults experience anxiety because of the physical declines they see in themselves and their age-mates, and because they are now "old" in the eyes of their culture. In the late adulthood era (65 years of age to death), the individual must develop a way of life that allows him or her to accent the realities of the past, present, and future. During this era, the individual must come to grips with a crisis similar to Erikson's idea of ego integrity versus despair.

Levinson (1996) reported that this sequence of eras and transitions holds true for women as well as for men from different cultures, classes, and historical epochs. In a review of four doctoral dissertations, Priscilla Roberts and Peter Newton (1987) found that several aspects of Levinson's model applied to the personality development of young and middle-aged women. This was especially true for Levinson's suggestion that a significant transition occurs at about 30 years of age. There was, however, a major sex difference with regard to the type of dreams that young adults construct. Recall that a "dream," according to Levinson, refers to a set of aspirations that allows an individual to break away from the preadult world and establish an overarching goal for his/her adult life, and that the dreams of young men focus on career-related issues (e.g., rising to a position of responsibility within a law firm). Roberts and Newton (1987) reported that women's dreams were far more complex. In fact, women were likely to experience a split dream, expressing concerns with both interpersonal relationships and with occupational accomplishments. Most important, women with split dreams tended to have unstable lives. These women were likely to experience a sense of dissatisfaction with either their family lives, their husbands, or their careers. They took longer to settle into an occupation, and they established fewer mentor relationships. Further work is needed to determine if these observations are cohort-specific or age-related changes.

Conclusions about Adult Stage Theories

The theories of Erikson, Loevinger, and Levinson describe a similar road map of adult development. Adult development begins with a shift away from identity toward intimacy. Next, it moves away from meaningless activity toward generativity in family and interpersonal matters. Last comes integrity, the result of searching for meaning in life (in the face of death). Although each theorist labels the stages differently and views the processes responsible for developmental change uniquely, the underlying themes of adult development are similar. (See figure 10.2 for a comparison of Levinson's and Erikson's viewpoints.)

Stage theories have intuitive appeal, but they suffer from four major limitations. First, stage theories are extremely difficult to verify through empirical research. How can you determine whether an individual has experienced a particular stage of development? You might follow Erikson's and Levinson's technique of probing the depths of an individual's personality by conducting a series of intensive interviews. You might decide to use Loevinger's Sentence Completion instrument to determine the stage level. Or you might decide to use a questionnaire or survey that asks adults how they feel about themselves. The interview method is extremely costly and time-consuming, and the information collected could end up being from a rather small (and perhaps nonrepresentative) number of participants. The sentence completion method is also costly and time-consuming. The survey method is less expensive and less time-consuming and may be used to test large numbers of participants. But could a researcher really capture

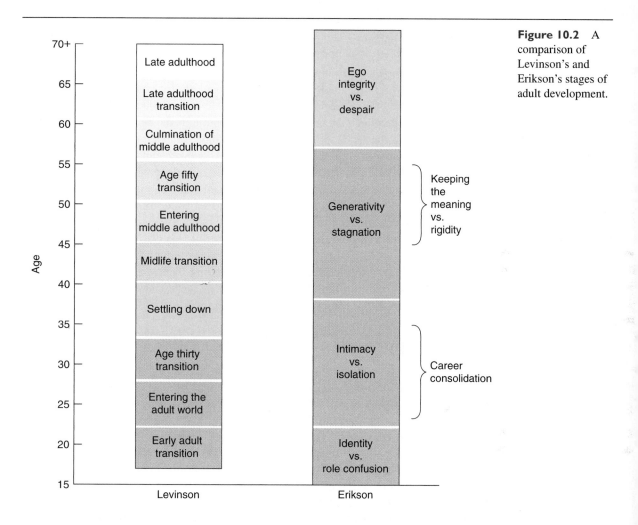

Figure 10.2 A comparison of Levinson's and Erikson's stages of adult development.

the essence of the stages and crises using a paper-and-pencil survey or questionnaire? Given these problems, it should come as no surprise that there is considerable debate about the testability of stage theories (i.e., whether they can be confirmed or rejected).

A second limitation of stage theories is that these theorists have a tendency to focus too extensively on stages as crises in development, particularly in the case of the midlife crisis. Only a small percentage of the adult population actually experiences a midlife crisis, and those who do have typically experienced traumas and psychological upheavals throughout their lives. Middle age can be the "best" time of life. Experts often see middle age as a time free from the stresses of young adulthood (relationships, careers, and finances) and free from the physical declines of old age (Northrup, 2001). It is not about becoming, but about being. Certainly it is a time for shedding illusions and dreams as well as a time for living and enjoying the present.

A third limitation is the increasing tendency for theory and research on adult development to emphasize the importance of personal life events (e.g., a change in occupational or marital status) and major sociocultural factors (e.g., a war or economic depression) rather than using stages or phases to organize development. Most of the individuals Levinson studied were born around the time of the Great Depression. What was true for these individuals when they reached age 40 may not be true for the members of more recent cohorts when they reach 40. Do you think changes in society, particularly for women, will heighten or diminish the tendency for members of future cohorts to experience a crisis at midlife?

Fourth, stage theories may focus too much attention on the development of the individual self as well as the self's ability to review and understand its own existence. For example, the mature individual in our culture is said "to become a unique person," "to know who she is," and "to be able to accept her life." In contrast, the goal of personality development in Eastern societies like India is to lose oneself and one's individual identity. An Indian cultural-religious ideal directs the individual to separate from all worldly concerns to seek harmony with the universe and to understand the common cord connecting one's existence with the existence of others. The developmental goal is to become a nonperson, abandoning ties to family, possessions, and home and to relinquish real-world concerns but embark on an inner quest for peace and understanding. This search for connectedness and wholeness is certainly different from the Western ideas that development leads to greater self-understanding, maturity, and individual growth.

The Trait Approach to Adult Personality

The degree to which personality is stable or changes is a major issue in adult development. To what extent do childhood personality characteristics predict adult personality characteristics? Does a shy child become a shy adult? Will an extroverted 25-year-old still be extroverted at the age of 65?

Instead of looking at the stability of a single personality characteristic across time, researchers are frequently interested in examining the predictability across time of combinations of characteristics present at particular points in the life cycle. They are also interested in how social experiences, family experiences, and work experiences predict personality characteristics later in life.

To the extent that some personality traits exhibit consistency or continuity from one period of time to another, we usually describe personality as being stable. In contrast, to the extent that there is little consistency from one period of time to another, we refer to change or discontinuity in personality.

Personality theorists are often categorized by whether they stress stability or change in personality across time and across situations. Personality theorists called *personologists,* or **trait theorists,** argue for consistency and stability; contextual, life-events, or stage theorists maintain that personality changes over time.

Ryff, Kwan, and Singer (2001) note that

"... personality in adulthood and later adult life is characterized by stability AND change. What is increasingly clear, however, is that there is considerable variation in how much chance (or stability) occurs, and for whom. .... Whether one finds evidence of personality change or stability is driven powerfully by how one conceptualizes personality and how one measures change (p. 480, 481)."

Characteristics of Traits

What is a trait? What are the major assumptions that underlie the trait approach to personality? Traits are conceptualized by some personality theorists as hierarchical. Cardinal traits or factors are few in number (5 to 10) and influence only a limited number of central traits or facets, perhaps a few dozen or so. Central traits or facets, however, can influence hundreds of other surface traits (Hershey & Mowen, 2000). Paul Costa and Robert McCrae (1980), two of the most influential psychologists studying adult personality, have listed a set of principles underlying the trait approach:

1. Traits may be regarded as generalized dispositions to thoughts, feelings, and behaviors that endure over substantial periods of time.

2. Traits have relatively little to do with the determination of single, specific behaviors. Specific behaviors are usually controlled by situational influences. Traits do, however, show an appreciable influence over behaviors that are averaged over long periods of time and over a range of diverse situations.

3. Traits, by their inherent nature, are highly interactive (e.g., trait anxiety is the tendency to experience fear when threatened, sociability involves the tendency to act friendly when in the presence of other people, and so forth). Thus, trait theory recognizes the importance of the Person $\times$ Situation interaction.

4. Traits are not merely reactive. Traits possess dynamic, motivating tendencies that seek out or produce situations which allow for the expression of certain behaviors. For example, a person who is open to experience may react with interest when presented with a new idea and may actively seek out new situations (by attending lectures, reading books, or changing an occupation) that lead to new experiences.

5. The enduring quality of general traits may manifest itself through the emergence of seemingly different types of behaviors that occur at different times in the adult life span. For example, an anxious person may be afraid of rejection in high school, economic recession in adulthood, and illness and death in old age.

6. Traits need not be purely inherited or biologically based. The origin of personality traits can (and should) remain an open question.

7. Traits are most useful in describing and predicting psychologically important global characteristics in individuals. Since traits are sensitive to generalities in behavior, trait theory is especially useful in giving a holistic picture of the person. It is this feature of trait theory that makes it the ideal basis for the study of personality and aging. If one adopted a strict interactionist or contextual model of personality, one would never attempt to address such global matters as how personality changes with age.

8. The aims of trait theory are compatible with the aims of longitudinal and sequential research. If traits are assumed to endure over time, they must be measured over time. And the influence of cohort and time of measurement on trait assessment must be differentiated from the influence of age and true developmental relationships.

Over time, different lifestyles and activity patterns have decidedly different consequences on the aging process.

Now that we have a general understanding of the trait approach, let's look at some of the major studies of personality development that shed light on the stability-versus-change issue as it relates to personality in the adult years.

Baltimore Longitudinal Study of Aging

Much of Costa and McCrae's work demonstrating the consistency of personality traits across the adult life span is based on data from the Baltimore Longitudinal Study of Aging (BLSA). The BLSA is based on a very large sample of relatively well-educated, primarily white, mostly healthy men. Participants ranged in age from 20 to 80 years. Data collection began in the late 1950s to mid-1960s and is ongoing; the way the data were collected allowed for cross-sectional, longitudinal, and sequential analyses. Thus, researchers could determine the effects of age, cohort, and time of measurement. Finally, participants in both of these studies took an extensive battery of standardized psychometric personality tests. These personality tests, called *self-report inventories,* are designed so that a participant must report his or her opinions, feelings, and activities on a wide range of topics.

Costa and McCrae's research (Costa, 1986; Costa & McCrae, 1977, 1978, 1980, 1982, 1985, 1986; McCrae & Costa, 1984, 1987, 1990) has yielded two important findings. First, they discovered that personality can best be conceptualized as consisting of five independent dimensions or factors: neuroticism, extraversion, openness to experience, agreeableness, and conscientiousness. These five dimensions make up what Costa and McCrae call the **five-factor model of personality** (see figure 10.3).

"Adults in later years often choose to spend time reflecting on memories and experiences from the past."

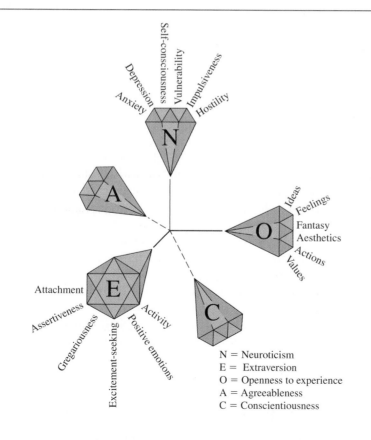

Figure 10.3
Costa and McCrae's five-factor model of personality.

N = Neuroticism
E = Extraversion
O = Openness to experience
A = Agreeableness
C = Conscientiousness

The vast majority of the research on this model involves an analysis of the dimensions of neuroticism, extraversion, and openness to experience. Each of these dimensions of personality contains six different facets. **Neuroticism** encompasses how anxious, hostile, depressed, self-conscious, impulsive, and vulnerable the individual is; **extraversion** measures the individual's attachment, gregariousness, assertiveness, activity, excitement-seeking, and positive emotions; and **openness to experience** pertains to the individual's openness with respect to fantasy, aesthetics, feelings, actions, ideas, and values.

The second major finding of this research is that these three dimensions of personality remain remarkably stable over the adult years. This is especially true when the data from these studies are analyzed in a longitudinal or sequential manner rather than in a cross-sectional manner. This is not to say that the men did not change in a number of ways. In fact, some of the men and their lives changed a great deal. For example, men who were found to be open to experience were likely to change occupations, live eventful lives, and experience good as well as bad in very forceful ways. Individuals who rated high in neuroticism found new things to complain, worry, and become dissatisfied about. What endured over time, of course, were the cardinal traits or factors that the men used to structure their lives.

One potential problem associated with the self-report methodology is that the stability of personality may be a personal illusion. People may construct self-images that suggest the major facets of their personality are stable, when in fact these traits change considerably over time; or they may believe their personalities have changed when they haven't. One investigation compared self-reports of personality change and stability over a 6 to 9 year period among men and women (39 to 45 years of age) participating in the University of North Carolina Alumni Heart Study. The majority of people felt that their personalities had remained the same; only 9 percent reported that they had changed a good deal. Objective measures were better than self-reports in identifying those who changed and those whose personalities remained stable (Herbst et al., 2000). Costa and McCrae (1988) also analyzed self-reports of participants in the BLSA and compared them to wives' ratings of the men's personalities. Results showed that, over time, the wives' ratings of the husbands' personalities remained stable on all of the traits in the five-factor model. Similar high stability has been reported in a recent study of the BLSA with only small declines in neuroticism, extraversion, and openness by midlife. Life events, in general, had little impact on personality factors, although changes in marital status and job did cause some slight shifts (Costa, Herbst, McCrae, & Siegler, 2000). On the other hand, Conley (1985) found that the traits of neuroticism and extraversion remained stable over periods between 20 to 45 years regardless of whether self-reports or spouses' and peers' ratings were analyzed. And remarkably consistent results from cross-cultural studies also show that personality as measured by the five-factor model shows little or no change with advancing age in the Philippines, Germany, Italy, France, Portugal, Croatia, or South Korea (McCrae et al., 1999). The studies identifying age changes in personality are usually cross-sectional and reveal cohort differences.

Perhaps the results of these studies can be best summed up by examining the following excerpt from an interview with Paul Costa:

What changes as you go through life are your roles and the issues that matter most to you. People may think that their personality has changed as they age, but it is their habits that change, their vigor, their health, their responsibilities and circumstances—not their basic personality.

There is no evidence for any universal age-related crises; those people who have a crisis at one point or another in life tend to be those who are more emotional. Such people experience some degree of distress through most of life; only the form of the trouble seems to change. After twenty-five, as William James said, character is set in plaster. (quoted in Goleman, 1987)

The Seattle Longitudinal Study

Schaie's longitudinal study based in Seattle, Washington, has generated several important findings about personality development as well as about intellectual development (as discussed in chapter 8). Schaie and Willis (1991) examined the scores of 3,442 participants on measures of behavioral rigidity, attitudinal flexibility, and social responsibility in 1956, 1963, 1970, 1977, and 1984. The participants ranged from 22 to 84 years of age and were from 10 different birth cohorts from 1896 to 1959. Because of the complex nature of this study, Schaie and Willis were able to examine the separate (and interactive) influences of age and cohort on personality development. As would be expected, cross-sectional analyses showed that individuals became more rigid and inflexible as they aged, whereas the longitudinal data showed that most traits remained stable until the late sixties, and then displayed small negative changes thereafter. Furthermore, more sophisticated sequential methods of data analysis indicated that the age differences the cross-sectional analysis yielded were, in reality, due to cohort or generational influences. This led Schaie and Willis (1991) to conclude that, over the last 70 years, there has been a substantial change toward more open and flexible behaviors, attitudes, and personality styles in successive generations. The continuation of this trend would mean that future generations of individuals will more effectively adapt to rapid social change.

Berkeley Older Generation Study

The Berkeley Older Generation Study is a longitudinal study of approximately 420 men and women who were first interviewed in Berkeley, California, in 1928 and 1929. The participants in the study were tested over a 55-year time span that encompassed their young adulthood, midlife, and older years. Field and Millsap (1991) analyzed the information gathered in 1969 and 1983 from the surviving participants in this study. In 1969, two distinct age groups were interviewed: a group of young-old adults (individuals who averaged 65 years of age), and old-old adults (individuals who averaged 75 years of age). In 1983, a group of 47 old-old adults (average age of 79) and 21 oldest-old (average age of 89) were reexamined. Given this design, Field and Millsap were able to compare personality stability for members of two cohorts across a 14-year time span.

All of the participants were administered a rather intensive open-ended interview that assessed the traits of intellect, extraversion, agreeableness, satisfaction, and being energetic. These traits, except for being energetic (the degree to which a person feels fresh, energetic, restless, etc.) were very similar to the traits of openness to experience, extraversion, agreeableness, and neuroticism that play a dominant role in Costa and McCrae's model of adult personality development.

The results of this study tell an interesting story. When data from all participants were taken as a whole, satisfaction and agreeableness remained stable. In fact, satisfaction was, by far, the most stable trait. With regard to this finding, Field and Millsap (1991) commented that it seems very hard for younger persons to understand the continuing satisfaction that older people derive from life considering the fact that old age is accompanied by significant losses in the interpersonal and physical domains. On the other hand, the researchers noted moderate declines for intellect, being energetic, and extraversion. However, as figure 10.4 illustrates, traits of intellect, agreeableness, and energetic changed in a different manner for individuals who, between 1969 and 1983, made the transition from young-old to old-old, and from old-old to oldest-old. Figures 10.4a and 10.4b show, for example, that scores on the dimensions of intellect and energetic declined over time for the people who became the oldest-old, but not for the old-old. And figure 10.4c shows that individuals who made the transition to the status of old-old increased in agreeableness, while those who became the oldest-old exhibited stability on this trait. In conclusion, Field and Millsap (1991, p. 307) argued that there is a

> normative developmental increase in agreeableness, accompanied by what may be a normative decline in extraversion, as well as relative stability in two other traits, satisfaction and intellect, in advanced old age. These findings help shatter the common stereotype that personality becomes rigid in old age, or that people become more conservative or cranky as they age.

Overall, the data Field and Millsap obtained, as well as the data other personologists mentioned in this section obtained, have shown that adult personality is remarkably stable over the adult years. There may be profound individual differences, how-

Figure 10.4
Personality change over time: Comparing the old-old and the oldest-old.

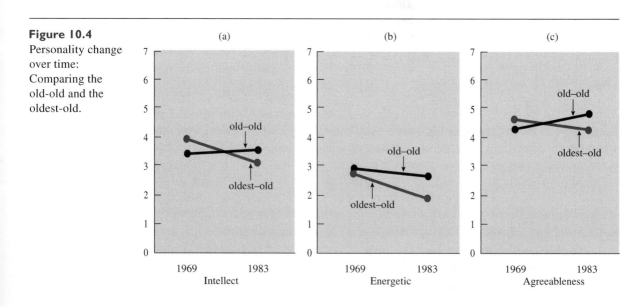

ever, in the stability (or instability) of personality over time. Research Focus 10.3 presents some rather surprising data about the mortality rates of older adults who exhibit stable versus unstable patterns of personality.

The Berlin Aging Study

The Berlin Aging Study provides another important source of information about personality and aging. The Berlin Aging Study examined the effects of aging on personality development, social relationships, and intellectual functioning from a systemic-wholistic view (Baltes, Mayer, Helmchen, & Steinhagen-Thiessen, 1993; Baltes & Smith, 1997).

The data from the Berlin Aging Study is distinct in several ways from the other longitudinal data sets just described. First, very old participants (95–103 years of age) were deliberately included in the study at the outset. In other major studies of aging, such as the Berkeley Older Generation Study and the BLSA, the initial data collections did not include older participants. These studies began as investigations of early development and became longitudinal studies of aging as the participants (and investigators) grew old during the course of the study. In the Berlin Aging Study, very old participants were tested at the beginning of the study.

A second unique feature of the Berlin Aging Study is the emphasis on including equal numbers of men and women within each of the selected age groups (70–74, 75–79, 80–84, 85–89, 90–94, and 95–103 years). In most other studies, the samples usually have different numbers of men and women, and fewer and fewer men at later testing occasions because of differential mortality rates for men and women.

A third feature of the study is the wide range of assessment measures used. Approximately 10,000 individual measures were taken, including objective and subjective measures of physical health and appearance; mental health, personality and well-being; cognitive and sensory functioning; social and family roles; and economics, work history, and residential situation. The Berkeley Older Generation Study, the BLSA, and several other major longitudinal studies also use a range of physical, psychological, and social measures, but not as many as in the Berlin Aging Study.

In a recent report from the Berlin Aging Study, Smith and Baltes (1997) examined personality and self in relation to measures of intellectual and social functioning. The findings of the study revealed that nine distinct subgroups, or *profiles,* of individuals with similar characteristics could be identified. More of the very old participants (85 to 103 years) and more women than men belonged to profiles associated with poor health, less successful functioning in social and family matters, and other less positive characteristics. Preliminary reports from the Berlin Aging Study suggest that the profiles observed at initial testing are relatively stable in old age.

Conclusions about the Stability of Adult Personality

Costa and McCrae observed that adult personality is characterized largely by stability and continuity rather than by extensive change or decline and reorganization. The adult personality seems to be an organized system of traits that resists major alteration. Imagine

Stability of Personality and Survival Rates in Old Age

Some individuals exhibit significant changes in personality during the adult years, whereas others do not. Hagberg, Samuelsson, Lindberg, and Dehlin (1991) wondered if interindividual differences in the stability of personality were related to survival rates during older adulthood. They suggested that a change in personality could be the end product of a fragile individual personality structure coming into contact with a number of harsh psychological and/or biological stressors (e.g., loss of a loved one, or illness). This led them to hypothesize that older adults who displayed stability in personality would live longer than those who exhibited a significant change in their personality.

To test their hypothesis, Hagberg et al. employed a unique measure of personality called the rod-and-frame task (RFT).

In the RFT, a participant is asked to look into a darkened chamber that contains an illuminated square-shaped frame surrounding a straight, illuminated glass rod. The frame is tilted, by the experimenter, 20 degrees to the right or left, and the participant is asked to turn a knob so that the rod rotates to a true vertical position. Two distinct patterns of performance emerge on the RFT. Some individuals (see box figure 10.A) are categorized as *field independent.* They are capable of aligning the rod in a true vertical position without being influenced by the tilted frame. Other people (see box figure 10.B) are labeled as *field dependent.* They align the rod in a vertical position relative to the tilted frame, but they think they are positioning the rod in a truly vertical manner. In other words, the terms *field independent* and *field dependent*

Box Figure 10.A   A field-independent response on the rod-and-frame task.

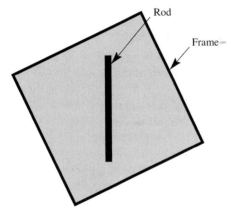

Box Figure 10.B   A field-dependent response on the rod-and-frame task.

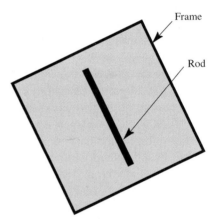

---

how difficult it would be to adapt to the changing demands of our lives if our core personalities underwent frequent change, or if the personalities of our friends and family members did so. Krueger and Heckhausen (1993) have shown that individuals across the adult life span tend to have subjective conceptions about adult personality development that are characterized by the growth and/or stability of personality traits until about 60 years of age, followed by a slight decline thereafter. In fact, Krueger and Heckhausen (1993) found that elderly adults were much more optimistic about late-life personality development than were younger or middle-aged adults.

Ruth and Coleman (1996) pointed out that many of the apparent personality differences between young, middle-aged, and older adults are really caused by generational (cohort) differences rather than by age-related differences. One of the most salient predictors of adult personality is year of birth rather than chronological age. Roberts and Helson (1997) note that an apparent emphasis on individualism from the 1950's to the 1980's in the culture of the United States was reflected in personality. American women

signify the degree to which an individual's perceptual judgments are affected by elements within the visual environment. The perceptual styles of field independence versus field dependence have been found to be related to the personality traits of extraversion, locus of control, and flexibility as well as self-concept and identity status.

Hagberg et al. (1991) conducted a longitudinal design in which they administered the RFT to 113 men and 79 women every second year during a six-year period. Testing began when each participant was 67 years of age. The psychologists calculated the proportion of survivors expected when the participants should have reached 69, 71, 73, 75, 77, 79, 81, and 83 years of age. It was found that about 20 percent of the older adults displayed an unstable pattern of performance on the RFT (i.e., they changed from field independence to field dependence [or vice versa] over the six-year testing period). These "unstable" participants (see box figure 10.C) were less likely to survive than the elderly adults who displayed a consistent pattern of performance. This finding held true for both males and females. Finally, whether participants were classified as field independent or dependent was found to be unrelated to survival rates.

Hagberg et al. concluded that human personality is a tremendously intricate system. In fact, personality is probably so complex that various sorts of perturbations (psychological stress, disease, etc.) that accompany the aging process, as well as aging itself, can have a significant destabilizing effect. This would help explain why personality change is a sensitive predictor of mortality.

Box Figure 10.C   The relationship between stability of performance on the rod-and-frame task and survival rates for older males and females.

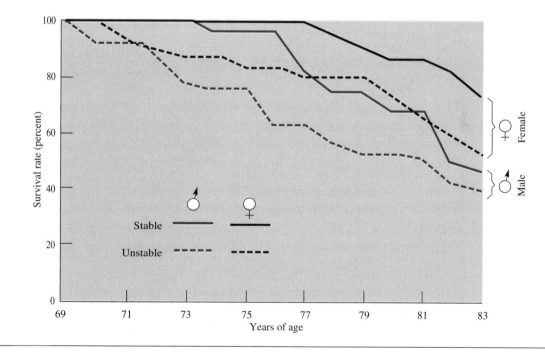

became less bound by normative rules of society and more self-focused and concerned with individuality.

New theories of personality emphasize that despite the apparent stability of adult personality, there is considerable potential for change. Ruth and Coleman (1996) suggest that research on personality and aging is moving away from looking for average personality descriptions at different ages toward the study of individual lives. Research on ego development by Loevinger (1976) and by Labouvie-Vief and her colleagues (1982, 1984, 1985), and on life stories by McAdams (1995) and others, exemplify this new approach.

There is also a trend in the measurement of personality away from the use of questionnaires and tests and toward the use of direct observations and interviews to capture the richness of people's personalities and lives. In new research on personality, there is also an emphasis on trying to understand adaptive competence—that is, whether one is effective in using one's unique resources to change oneself, to re-create situations for optimal development, or to override limitations.

It should be mentioned that the trait approach to adult personality is not totally antagonistic to the stage approaches. For example, it is possible that an individual may go through adulthood with a constellation of stable, enduring personality traits, yet may use these traits to tackle the different tasks and psychosocial crises that writers such as Erikson and Levinson have identified. A person may deal with an identity crisis in adolescence, a midlife crisis at age 40, and a life review at age 75 with the same stable degrees of openness to experience, intraversion-extraversion, and neuroticism. It is reasonable to assume that personality development involves both change and stability.

The Life-Events Approach

An alternative to the stage and trait approaches to adult personality development is the life-events framework or contextual model. Earlier investigators suggested that major life events (e.g., the death of a spouse, divorce) produce taxing circumstances for individuals, forcing them to change their personalities. More sophisticated versions of the life-events framework emphasize the factors that mediate the influence of life events on adult development—physical health, intelligence, personality, family supports, income, and so forth. Some individuals may perceive a life event as highly stressful, whereas others perceive the same event as a challenge.

It is important to consider the sociocultural circumstances that life events occur within. For example, divorce may be more stressful after many years of marriage, when individuals are in their fifties, than when they have only been married a few years and are in their twenties. Also, individuals may be able to cope more effectively with divorce in 2002 than in 1952 because divorce is more common in today's society.

Bernice Neugarten and Nancy Datan (1973) suggested that understanding the nature of adult personality development depends on an analysis of the sociohistorical and personal circumstances that adult life occurs within. They also suggested that chronological age has little, if any, bearing on adult personality. For example, Neugarten (1980a, 1980b, 1989) proposed that the admonition "Act your age" has become progressively less meaningful since the middle part of this century. We are constantly aware of adults who occupy roles that seem out of step with their chronological ages (e.g., the 28-year-old mayor, the 60-year-old father of a preschooler, and the 70-year-old college student).

Neugarten also has deep-seated doubts about an increasing number of popular books that emphasize predictable, age-related life crises. People who read such books worry about their midlife crises, apologize if they don't seem to be coping with them properly, and appear dismayed if they aren't having them. These crisis theories, Neugarten maintains, do not really define the typical pattern of adult development. It may be that adults change far more, and far less predictably, than many oversimplified stage theories or crisis theories suggest. As Neugarten (1980b) has asserted:

> My students and I have studied what happens to people over the life cycle. . . . We have found great trouble clustering people into age brackets that are characterized by particular conflicts; the conflicts won't stay put, and neither will the people. Choices and dilemmas do not sprout forth at ten-year intervals, and decisions are not made and then left behind as if they were merely beads on a chain. (p. 289)

Neugarten (1968) argued that the social environment that the members of a particular generation evolved in can alter their social clock—the timetable according to which individuals are expected to accomplish life's tasks, such as marrying, establishing a career, and even experiencing a monumental crisis at midlife. Social clocks provide guides for our lives. Sociohistorical events and trends unique to specific cohorts "set" the social clock for that cohort.

In earlier periods in our society, it may have been reasonable to describe life as a series set of discrete, predictable stages or crises. More people seemed to experience the same life events at the same ages. People knew the "right age" for marriage, the first child, the last child, career achievement, retirement, and even death. In the last few decades, however, Neugarten (1989) has argued that chronological age is nearly irrelevant as an index of such significant events within adult development.

During the latter part of the twentieth century, our social time clocks changed dramatically. New trends in work, family size, health, and education produced phenomena unprecedented in our history. We see, for example, a significantly longer empty nest period after the children leave home. This may require major readjustments in the parents' relationship. Also, we see an increase in the numbers of great-grandparents as well as those who start new families, new jobs, and new avocations when they are 40, 50, or 60 years old.

Some of the life tasks that used to be associated with a particular age or stage of development seem to recur over the entire course of the adult life span. Neugarten articulated this point:

> Most of the themes of adulthood appear and reappear in new forms over long periods of time. Issues of intimacy and freedom, for example, which are supposed to concern young adults just starting out in marriage and careers, are never settled once and for all. They haunt many couples continuously; compromises are found for a while, then renegotiated. Similarly, feeling the pressure of time, reformulating goals, coming to grips with success (and failure)—these are not the exclusive property of the forty-eight to fifty-two-year-olds, by any means. (Neugarten, 1980a, pp. 289–290)

Applying a Life-Course Perspective to Life Events

It is important to make connections between age or life stage, the probability of certain events taking place, and the power of the event as a stressor. Some events, such as a serious automobile accident, are not necessarily age-linked and have a low probability of occurring. Therefore, we are seldom prepared for such events psychologically. However, other events, such as menopause, retirement, or the death of a parent have stronger ties with age. This allows us to anticipate the events and to develop coping strategies that may help alleviate some of the stress these events engender. Figure 10.5 shows how a life-course perspective might apply to life events (Hultsch & Plemons, 1979). This figure considers variations in the probability of certain events, their timing and sequencing, the motivational factors the events stimulate, the coping resources available for dealing with them, and adaptive outcomes.

The life-events framework in figure 10.5 describes four main components: antecedent life-event stressors, mediating factors, a social/psychological adaptation process, and consequent adaptive or maladaptive outcomes. From this perspective, all life events, regardless of whether they are positive (marriage, being promoted at work) or negative (divorce, the death of a spouse), are viewed as potentially stressful. Factors that may mediate the effects of life events can be categorized as internal (physical health or intelligence) or external (salary, social support network). Social-psychological

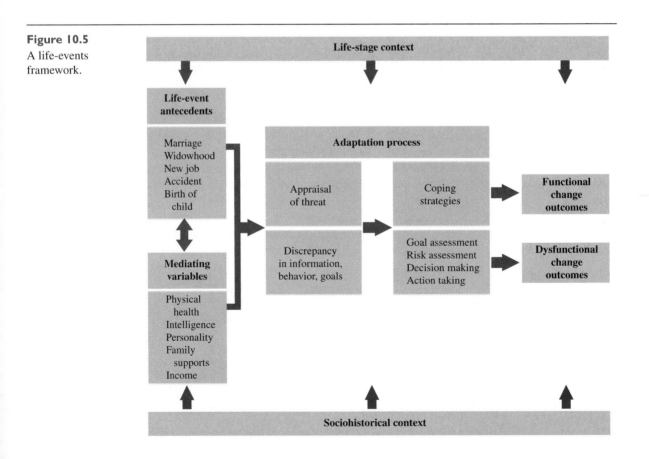

Figure 10.5
A life-events framework.

adaptation encompasses the individual's coping strategies, which may produce either a positive or negative outcome.

As figure 10.5 indicates, it is also important to consider both the life stage and the sociohistorical context in which a life event occurs. Two time lines that are important in our lives are **individual time** and **historical time**. An event (such as the death of a spouse) that occurs at age 30 may have a different impact on the individual than if it occurred at age 73. Similarly, an event (such as early retirement at age 55) would have a different impact if it occurred in 2000 rather than 1960.

The life-events framework provides valuable insights into adult development. Like all the other theories described in this chapter, however, it is not without flaws. One of the most significant drawbacks of the life-events framework is that it may place too much emphasis on change. It does not recognize the stability that characterizes much adult development. Another potential drawback is that this perspective may place too much emphasis on major life events as primary triggers of personality change. Enduring a boring and tense job, a dull marriage, or living in poverty do not qualify as major life events. Yet the everyday pounding we take from these types of conditions can add up to a highly stressful life. Some psychologists (e.g., Lazarus, 2000) believe that we can gain greater insight into life's stresses by focusing on daily hassles and uplifts rather than on catastrophic life stressors.

Recognizing Individual Variation

Broadly speaking, there are two theoretical approaches to the study of personality development—one focuses on similarities, the other on differences. The stage theories of Erikson and Levinson attempt to describe universal forms of intraindividual change that take place during adult development. The life-events framework, as championed by Neugarten, focuses on the interindividual variability characteristic of adult personality change.

In a longitudinal study of women through mid-life, Agronick and Duncan (1998) found wide-ranging support for individual differences in personality development. They examined the interface of social change (e.g., the women's movement) and personality and found that not all women reacted similarly. Women's early adult personality profiles in conjunction with unique adult life experiences such as career trajectories, timing of child-bearing, and commitment to family were predictors of their reaction to the women's movement.

Think about yourself and other people you know. You have certain things in common with others, yet you also differ in many ways. Individual variation must be an important aspect of any viable model of adult development.

Levels of Personality

Theories of personality yield, at the very best, an incomplete description of the individual. Consequently, Dan McAdams (1995) proposed a novel approach that would allow personality theorists to get to know the people they study. The key to McAdams's viewpoint is that a "full description" of an individual entails three different levels of analysis.

Level I is referred to as the *dispositional level.* Here, the individual is described in terms of basic personality traits or dispositions such as extraversion, neuroticism, openness to experience, and so on. For example, say you attend a party and meet a person named George who behaves in a manner that is socially dominant, entertaining, moody, and anxious. It might strike you that your newfound acquaintance scores high on the traits of extraversion and neuroticism. The strength of Level I descriptions is their generality. George, in relationship to other individuals, will typically behave in an extraverted and anxious manner. The greatest strength of Level I is also its greatest weakness—Level I only provides general, decontextualized information about another person. As McAdams points out, "No description of a person is adequate without trait attributions, but trait attributions, by themselves, yield little beyond a 'psychology of the stranger' " (1995, p. 365).

To gain a better understanding of George, you need to know something about the nuances of his personality; these are the focal points of Level II, the *personal concerns level.* At this level, we could come to understand George by measuring his values and coping styles, as well as the defense mechanisms he uses to reduce anxiety. And we could look to stage theories like Erikson's and Levinson's to get an understanding of how all these aspects of George's personality might change across time. For example, the coping styles and defense mechanisms George uses to deal with issues of intimacy in younger adulthood may be different from the ones he uses to establish a sense of generativity during middle age.

The last, and perhaps most important, piece of information we need to gather in order to know George is his answer to the question, "Who am I?" Identity formation is the focal point of Level III—the *life story level.* Within McAdams's model of personality, identity is best conceptualized as an internalized and evolving personal myth or life story. According to McAdams,

> Contemporary adults create identity in their lives to the extent that the self can be told in a coherent narrative that integrates the person into society in a productive and generative way and provides the person with a purposeful self-history that explains how the self of yesterday became the self of today and will become the anticipated self of tomorrow. Level III in personality, therefore, is the level of identity as a life story. Without exploring this third level, the personologist can never understand how and to what extent the person is able to find unity, purpose, and meaning in life. (1995, p. 382)

Level III of personality, unlike the preceding levels, is not revealed by scores on standardized tests. Instead, Level III reveals itself through long-term intensive interactions with others. Thus, individuals who share special intimate relationships with each other, such as friends, lovers, spouses, and siblings, have a good chance of knowing each other at the life story level.

It may prove interesting to speculate about the factors that influence personality at each of the levels McAdams elaborated. For example, it could be argued that, perhaps genetic factors influence personality at the dispositional level. This might account for the remarkable stability of traits over time. At the other end of the spectrum, a myriad of cultural, developmental, and idiosyncratic factors might influence personality at the personal concerns and life story levels. McAdams's (1995) model suggests strong links between personality structure and basic cognitive processing. For example, there seems to be a very strong relationship between the notion of personality as a "life story" and the active, reconstructive nature of human autobiographical memory processes, as mentioned in chapter 7. In one study, adolescents and young adults used uniquely constructed narrative strategies to connect disparate life events into an explanation for their own life transitions. McAdams and Bowman (2001) identified this cognitive element as a key to self-understanding and creating meaning.

Moral Development

Morality is conceptualized in terms of three interrelated aspects. The first component is moral reasoning: How do people think about the rules of ethical conduct? The second issue involves moral behavior: How do people behave in real-life situations where a moral principle is at stake? The third domain is moral emotion: How do individuals feel after making a moral decision and engaging in a behavior that is ethical (or unethical)? Although Kohlberg's theory of moral development focuses primarily on moral reasoning, it has some implications for how adults adjust to emotionally charged life events and how adults behave in moral contexts.

Kohlberg's Theory

Kohlberg (1958, 1987, 1990) argued that moral development involves a gradual stage-like progression in which the individual passes through three different levels of moral thought, with two different stages within each level. Kohlberg maintained that these levels and stages represent an invariant, universal, and qualitatively distinct sequence.

Kohlberg measured moral development by evaluating an individual's response to a number of hypothetical dilemmas. One of his most well-known dilemmas, "Heinz and the Drug," is as follows:

> In Europe a woman was near death from cancer. One drug might save her, a form of radium that a druggist in the same town had recently discovered. The druggist was charging $2,000, ten times what the drug cost him to make. The sick woman's husband, Heinz, went to everyone he knew to borrow the money, but he could only get together about half of what the drug cost. He told the druggist his wife was dying and asked him to sell it cheaper or let him pay later. But the druggist said no. The husband got desperate and broke into the man's store to steal the drug for his wife. Should the husband have done that? Why? (Kohlberg, 1969, p. 379)

A person's stage of moral development is determined by his or her answer to the question "Why?," not by the answer about what Heinz should do. In other words, it is the type of reasoning a person uses to justify his or her judgment that counts; whether the person thinks Heinz should or should not have stolen the drug is unimportant. Put somewhat differently, Kohlberg's theory places primary emphasis on the structure of moral judgment, not its content. The former refers to the underlying rule system that gives rise to a specific moral decision; the latter refers to the decision itself.

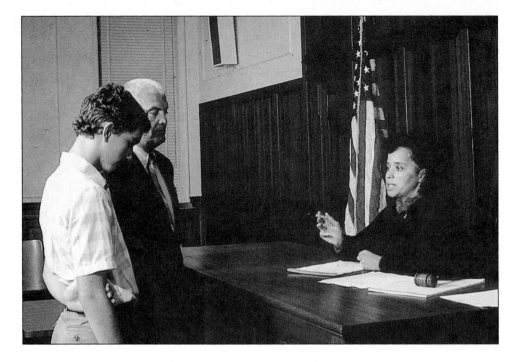

Middle-aged and older adults often have positions with the responsibility of making moral judgments.

The first two stages compose the **preconventional level,** because the individual interprets moral problems from the point of view of physical or material concerns (punishment and reward, the maintenance of power and wealth, etc.) or his own hedonistic wishes. At the preconventional level, then, rules and social expectations are viewed as external to the self.

The third and fourth stages make up the **conventional level.** Here, the individual's understanding of morality depends on her internalization of the expectations other individuals (such as friends, family, or society) have of her. Maintaining these expectations leads to interpersonal trust and loyalty as well as the preservation of the social system. At the conventional level, therefore, the person has internalized the rules and expectations of other individuals or of a more generalized social system.

The **postconventional level** consists of the fifth and sixth stages in Kohlberg's sequence. At this level, the individual becomes capable of distinguishing between basic human rights and obligations, which remain constant over different cultures and historical epochs, versus societal and legal rules, which can change over sociohistorical contexts. In other words, the postconventional reasoner can construct a set of universal moral principles by differentiating his or her moral view from the rules and expectations of others. Table 10.4 provides a more complete description of the different stages and levels that make up Kohlberg's theory. Table 10.5 provides examples of the type of moral reasoning an individual at each of Kohlberg's stages might generate.

TABLE 10.4

An Overview of Kohlberg's Theory of Moral Development

Level and Stage	What Is Right	Reasons for Doing Right	Sociomoral Perspective
Level I— **Preconventional** Stage 1—Heteronomous mortality	To avoid breaking rules backed by punishment, obedience for its own sake, and avoiding physical damage to persons and property.	Avoidance of punishment, and the superior power of authorities.	*Egocentric point of view.* Doesn't consider the interests of others or recognize that they differ from the actor's; doesn't relate two points of view. Actions are considered physically rather than in terms of the psychological interests of others. Confusion of authority's perspective with one's own.
Stage 2—Individualism, instrumental purpose, and exchange	Following rules only when it is to someone's immediate interest; acting to meet one's own interests and needs and letting others do the same. Right is also what's fair, what's an equal exchange, a deal, an agreement.	To serve one's own needs or interests in a world where you have to recognize that other people have interests, too.	*Concrete individualistic perspective.* Aware that everybody has his own interest to pursue and these conflict, so that right is relative (in the concrete individualistic sense).
Level II— **Conventional** Stage 3—Mutual interpersonal expectations, relationships, and interpersonal conformity	Living up to what people close to you expect or what people generally expect of people in your role as son, brother, friend, and so on. "Being good" is important and means having good motives, showing concern about others. It also means keeping mutual relationships, such as trust, loyalty, respect and gratitude.	The need to be a good person in your own eyes and those of others. Your caring for others. Belief in the Golden Rule. Desire to maintain rules and authority which support stereotypical good behavior.	*Perspective of the individual in relationships with other individuals.* Aware of shared feelings, agreements, and expectations which take primacy over individual interests. Relates points of view through the concrete Golden Rule, putting yourself in the other guy's shoes. Does not yet consider generalized system perspective.

continued

TABLE 10.4 *continued*

An Overview of Kohlberg's Theory of Moral Development

Level and Stage	What Is Right	Reasons for Doing Right	Sociomoral Perspective
Stage 4—Social system and conscience	Fulfilling the actual duties to which you have agreed. Laws are to be upheld except in extreme cases where they conflict with other fixed social duties. Right is also contributing to society, the group, or institution.	To keep the institution going as a whole, to avoid the breakdown in the system "if everyone did it," or the imperative of conscience to meet one's defined obligations.	*Differentiates societal point of view from interpersonal agreement or motives.* Takes the point of view of the system that defines roles and rules. Considers individual relations in terms of place in the system.
Level III— Postconventional, or Principled Stage 5—Social contract or utility and individual rights	Being aware that people hold a variety of values and opinions, that most values and rules are relative to your group. These relative rules should usually be upheld, however, in the interest of impartiality and because they are the social contract. Some nonrelative values and rights like *life* and *liberty*, however, must be upheld in any society regardless of majority opinion.	A sense of obligation to law because of one's social contract to make and abide by laws for the welfare of all and for the protection of all people's rights. A feeling of contractual commitment, freely entered upon, to family, friendship, trust, and work obligations. Concerns that laws and duties be based on rational calculation of overall utility, "the greatest good for the greatest number."	*Prior-to-society perspective.* Perspective of a rational individual aware of values and rights prior to social attachments and contracts. Integrates perspectives by formal mechanisms of agreement, contract, objective impartiality, and due process. Considers moral and legal points of view; recognizes that they sometimes conflict and finds it difficult to integrate them.
Stage 6—Universal ethical principles	Following self-chosen ethical principles. Particular laws or social agreements are usually valid because they rest on such principles. When laws violate these principles, one acts in accordance with the principle. Principles are universal principles of justice: the equality of human rights and respect for the dignity of human beings as individual persons.	The belief as a rational person in the validity of universal moral principles, and a sense of personal commitment to them.	*Perspective of a moral point of view from which social arrangements derive.* Perspective is that of any rational individual recognizing the nature of morality or the fact that persons are ends in themselves and must be treated as such.

Source: Kohlberg, L. (1976). "Moral stages and moralization in Thomas Lickona (Ed.), Moral Development and Behavior. Copyright © 1976 by Holt, Rinehart and Winston. Reprinted by permission of Thomas Lickona.

TABLE 10.5

Responses at Each Stage Level to the "Heinz and the Drug" Dilemma

Stage 1

Pro	Con
It's not really bad to steal the drug. It's not like he did not ask to pay for it first. The drug really isn't worth $2,000; at most it costs about $200. Also, letting your wife die would be the same as killing her—and God's commandments say that killing another person is wrong.	Heinz shouldn't steal; he should buy the drug instead. Also, if he steals the drug he'd be committing a big crime and the police would put him in jail for a long time. Finally, God's commandments say that stealing is wrong.

Stage 2

Pro	Con
Heinz should steal the drug because he'd be lonely and sad if his wife dies. He wants her to live more than anything else. Anyway, if he gets sent to jail (that would make him sad), but he'd still have his wife (and that would make him really happy).	Heinz should not steal the drug if he doesn't like his wife a lot. Also, the druggist isn't really a bad person; he just wants to make a profit from all his hard work. That is what you are in business for, to make money.

Stage 3

Pro	Con
If I were Heinz, I'd steal the drug for my wife. Heinz could not be so heartless as to let his wife die. The two partners in a marriage should naturally expect that they will come to each other's aid. Also, you can't put a price on life: and, any decent person should value life above anything else.	Heinz shouldn't steal. If his wife dies, he cannot be blamed. After all, everybody knows that Heinz is not cruel and heartless, he tried to buy the drug legally. The druggist is the selfish one. He deserves to be stolen from.

Stage 4

Pro	Con
When you get married, you take a vow to love and cherish your wife. Marriage is not only love, it's an obligation as well. Marriage is like a legal contract that must be obeyed. Also, by stealing the drug and going to court, Heinz will be able to show the members of his society how dumb the laws about stealing are. This might lead to positive changes in the judicial system.	It's a natural thing for Heinz to want to save his wife, but it is still always wrong to steal. If everybody took the law into their own hands—like Heinz wants to do—his society would be in total chaos. In the long run, nobody in Heinz's society will benefit from this; not even Heinz and his wife!

continued

TABLE 10.5 *continued*

Responses at Each Stage Level to the "Heinz and the Drug" Dilemma

Stage 5

Pro	Con
The law is not set up to deal with the unique circumstances of the Heinz case. Taking the drug in this situation is not correct from a "legal" point of view. But there may be a set of basic human rights (such as the right to life) that must be preserved regardless of what the law may happen to say. The law of the land should protect peoples' basic rights. It certainly isn't in this case. Therefore, Heinz should steal the drug.	You cannot completely blame Heinz for stealing; but extreme circumstances do not really justify violating the law. This is because the law represents a commitment that Heinz and the other members of his society have made to one another.

Stage 6

Pro	Con
Heinz has to act in terms of the principle of preserving and respecting life. It would be both irrational and immoral to preserve the druggist's property right to the drug at the expense of his wife's right to life. After all, people invented the concept of personal property; it is a culturally relative concept. Alternatively, the right of a person to claim their right to life should be absolute.	Heinz is faced with the decision of whether to consider the other people who need the drug just as much as his wife. Heinz ought to act not according to his own feelings toward his wife but on his consideration of all of the lives involved.

Age-Related Changes in Moral Reasoning

Kohlberg's initial research led to the conclusion that individuals completed the moral stage sequence by the end of adolescence. However, longitudinal data collected by Kohlberg and Kramer (1969) showed that the adolescents who had attained postconventional morality during high school regressed to a preconventional level in their college years. Such a clear violation of the stage criterion of invariant progression forced Kohlberg and his associates to make major changes in the theory and measurement of moral development.

Using a revised and more stringent scoring system, Colby, Kohlberg, Gibbs, and Lieberman (1983) reanalyzed Kohlberg and Kramer's longitudinal data and found no evidence of regressive stage movement. Furthermore, Colby et al. (1983) analyzed the data from a 20-year longitudinal study of moral development that began in the late 1950s. The results of this study appear in figure 10.6. As you can see, a clear relationship emerges between age and moral reasoning. Over the 20-year period, reasoning at stages 1 and 2 decreased. Stage 3 peaked in late adolescence or early adulthood and declined thereafter. Reasoning at stage 4 did not appear at all among the 10-year-olds in the study; yet it was reflected in 62 percent of the judgments of the 36-year-olds. Stage 5 moral reasoning did not appear until the age of 20 to 22. Furthermore, it never rose above 10 percent of the total number of the participants' judgments. Armon (1991) obtained similar results.

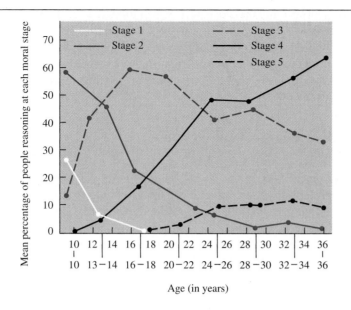

Figure 10.6
Age-related
changes in moral
reasoning.

Based on these results, Kohlberg (1987) suggested that children and young adolescents reason at the preconventional level, most older adolescents and adults reason at the conventional level, and a small percentage of adults (mostly middle-aged and older) reason at the postconventional level. Therefore, it seems as if adulthood (not adolescence, as originally suggested) is marked by the ability to construct a universal set of moral principles. Kohlberg's main discovery was that moral development occurs during all epochs of the life span—childhood, adolescence, and adulthood.

Determinants of Moral Development

What causes a person to move from one moral stage to the next? There is no reason to believe that chronological age, by itself, is a prime determinant of moral change. Some researchers have shown that the attainment of postconventional morality depends on formal operations; however, formal operations, by itself, is not sufficient to automatically produce postconventional morality. Roodin, Rybash, and Hoyer (1984) have suggested that advanced moral reasoning depends on the growth of postformal styles of thinking within the domain of personal knowledge. In fact, it seems that postconventional morality has much in common with Paul Baltes's concept of wisdom discussed in chapter 9.

In addition to logical thinking, psychologists have examined several other factors responsible for transitions in moral development. After all, if moral development is nothing more than logical thinking applied to moral problems, there is no need to have a separate theory of moral development. Theories of cognitive development would explain moral development, too. Kohlberg (1976) suggested that moral development is heavily dependent on the social perspective a person brings to a moral problem (refer to table 10.4). These stages of perspective taking are actively constructed through the reciprocal interactions that take place between an individual and his or her social environment. Moral development should thus be promoted by social environments that (1) give the individual a broad range of role-taking experiences, so that the person becomes aware of the thoughts, feelings, and attitudes of other people and/or adopts the perspectives of various social institutions; and (2) place the individual in real-life positions of moral responsibility.

The Importance of Moral Development

What is the practical significance of being a postconventional rather than a conventional moral reasoner? Should one try to promote moral development in adults, and if so, how? These important questions can be answered in a variety of ways.

First, as individuals progress through the different moral stages, they should be able to make better or more effective decisions about the moral dilemmas that arise in their own lives. This does not mean that advanced (postconventional) moral reasoners are better people than lower-level moral reasoners. It means that postconventional reasoners bring a broader, more all-encompassing, and balanced point of view to a moral problem. A postconventional point of view does not have its primary roots in self-centered interests or social/interpersonal expectations. Thus, it allows individuals to more fully consider the conflicting claims that surround a moral dilemma.

Second, it has been shown that a person's level of moral reasoning is related to a person's moral behavior. Kohlberg and Candee (1984) have shown that as individuals progress through the moral stages, they engage in more consistent moral action: honesty, altruism, and political and civil rights activism. Furthermore, they are less likely to comply with the immoral orders of authority figures.

Third, Kohlberg's theory may provide valuable information about how adults comprehend and cope with real-life moral issues. For example, Rybash and Roodin (1989) have discussed the manner by which different moral orientations influence adults' understanding of the right to self-determination in medical contexts (i.e., the right to accept or reject medical treatment for a life-threatening illness). Research Focus 10.4 contains more detailed information about the relationship between coping and moral reasoning.

Alternatives and Criticisms to Kohlberg's Theory

A number of studies have supported Kohlberg's claims about the invariance and universality of moral stages (see Colby & Kohlberg, 1987; Demetriou, 1990). However, there are some limitations to Kohlberg's theory.

Kohlberg's view is not as applicable to women as it is to men. Carol Gilligan (1982) pointed out that adult males, on average, score higher (stage 4) than adult females (stage 3) on Kohlberg's measure of moral reasoning. This difference does not mean that men are more moral than women. Instead, Gilligan argues, this sex difference in moral reasoning has its basis in the different orientations men and women bring to moral problems. A man's orientation toward morality is based in abstract principles of justice, whereas a woman's orientation toward morality is grounded in her relation-

Moral Reasoning and Coping

Edward Lonky, Cheryl Kaus, and Paul Roodin (1984) examined the relationship between life experiences and adult moral development. Their research had its basis in John Gibbs's reformulation of Kohlberg's theory of moral reasoning.

Gibbs (1977, 1979) proposed two distinct phases of moral development: the standard phase and the existential phase. The **standard phase** consists of the preconventional and conventional levels of Kohlberg's theory. Gibbs used the term *standard* to mean "normal" or "expected." That is, it is the norm for the majority of adults to progress through the first two levels in Kohlberg's theory. These levels, he assumed, are tied to changes in logical thinking and perspective taking that occur in the vast majority of adults. The **existential phase** incorporates the postconventional level. Gibbs argued that the two stages (5 and 6) within this level do not meet the criteria that define true developmental stages. For example, stages 5 and 6 are (1) only displayed in a very small percentage of adults in Western culture and are absent in several non-Western (or traditional) societies and (2) subject to reversals and regressions.

More specifically, Gibbs argued that the existential phase only develops when an adult comes to grips with the core needs that underlie human existence. These core needs, which Erich Fromm (1955) first identified, are relatedness (the need to overcome feelings of aloneness), transcendence (the need to surpass passivity and demonstrate competence), rootedness (the need for warmth, protection, and

security), identity (the need to control one's own destiny and be aware of oneself as a separate entity), and meaning (the need for a guiding set of principles and beliefs).

Gibbs (1979) proposed that these core needs are experienced within the context of salient life events. He also noted that once an individual experiences a need, she seeks a mode of coping with it. Coping may be characterized as either **affirmative coping** (essentially positive) or **abortive coping** (essentially negative and nonproductive). These speculations led Lonky et al. (1984) to wonder whether an abortive coping style would be related to a fixation at the standard phase of moral development, while an affirmative mode of coping would be associated with the existential phase. They studied a group of adult women who had experienced a major loss or separation (the death of a loved one, divorce, and so on) during the past 12 months. These women participated in a semistructured interview that assessed how they coped with their negative life experiences. The researchers also measured the women's level of moral reasoning. Results indicated that women in the standard phase of moral development (conventional reasoners) tended to deal abortively with the needs they experienced within the context of these life events, whereas women in the existential phase (postconventional reasoners) dealt with the same needs in an affirmative manner. Lonky et al. (1984) also showed that affirmative coping was related to the personality trait openness to experience, and to an active coping style called problem-focused coping.

ships with others. These differences have their basis, according to Gilligan (1982), in the socialization of the sexes during childhood. Thus, Gilligan maintains that women score lower on Kohlberg's assessment of moral stage reasoning because Kohlberg's measure is biased in favor of males (i.e., Kohlberg's test measures a person's understanding of abstract principles of justice, rather than the sense of connectedness that binds individuals together). Research inspired by Gilligan's theory (Gilligan & Belenky, 1980; Lyons, 1983) has found that women have a care orientation and make moral judgments by focusing on responsibilities to people: their families, their friends, and themselves. However, some psychologists have not observed the sex differences in moral reasoning that Gilligan reported (Glover, 2001). Therefore, Gilligan's viewpoint has not achieved unequivocal support.

Rybash, Roodin, and Hoyer (1983) have raised another criticism of Kohlberg's theory. They argued that the problems that adults, especially older adults encounter in real life, may have little in common with the hypothetical dilemmas Kohlberg uses to measure moral development. In a 1983 study by Rybash et al., elderly participants described problems relating to family and medical matters, such as whether to give advice to an adult child who is having an affair, give financial support to an adult child who keeps squandering money, move into a nursing home or remain in the home of an adult child, discontinue life support for a terminally ill spouse, and so on. This suggests that older adults may be at a disadvantage using Kohlberg's assessments of moral reasoning. Most interestingly, Rybash et al. found that a significant proportion of the elderly indicated that they were free from personal moral dilemmas. Consider the following response from a 73-year-old man:

> At this point in my life I feel that there are no moral decisions I have to make. I have reached a point in my life where I have peace of mind and am content with my life. I'm in good health and live each day not worrying about having to make moral decisions. There were times when I was younger that I had to make moral decisions, but now all I have to decide about is where I want to go and what I want to do. You come to this point in your life, and I feel everyone about the same age as me feels the same way. (Rybash et al., 1983, p. 257)

How would you categorize this response? Is it representative of gero-transcendence?

Personality and Positive Psychology

Positive Psychology

Positive psychology is the "scientific study of ordinary human strengths and virtues," or the qualities that contribute to effective functioning (Sheldon & King, 2001, p. 216). This field seeks to facilitate optimal functioning and successful adaptation among individuals, communities, and societies (Seligman & Csikszentmihalyi, 2000). Those who study positive psychology examine the values and traits that allow human beings to flourish: hope, love, joy, trust, contentment, interest, pride, life satisfaction, courage, flow, optimism, happiness, and well-being. The study of positive psychology begins to bring balance to decades of research on negative emotions and disorders such as depression, anxiety, and anger. Until recently, positive traits have received little attention. Myers (2000) notes more than 136,000 published studies over the past 115 years on depression, anxiety, and anger, but fewer than 9,500 on topics such as joy, life satisfaction, and happiness. Adult development is as much marked by these positive traits as by negative ones. After all, most people are able to cope, to master their environments and "live lives of dignity and purpose" (Sheldon & King, 2001).

Positive Emotions

"Positive emotions serve as markers of flourishing or optimal well-being" (Fredrickson, 2001, p. 218). The significance of positive emotions has led Fredrickson to develop the **broaden-and-build theory of positive emotions.** Fredrickson's theory links a range of positive emotions such as joy, love, contentment, interest, and pride that broaden the range of adults' thoughts and actions. Experiencing positive emotions opens people up to a wider range of possible actions and thoughts than they would have been able to generate without these feelings. Some believe that positive emotions free people from habitual thoughts and actions; others see positive emotions promoting creative thinking and action. Fredrickson (2001) notes that when people experience joy, they are freer to be creative, to play, and to push the limits in social, intellectual, artistic, and physical endeavors. When people find experiences interesting, it expands their need to explore, to learn new information, and to participate in new experiences. And pride creates the need to share successful accomplishments with others and envision higher future goals.

Broadening an individual's array of thinking and behaviors has long-term benefits. It creates enduring personal resources in the physical, intellectual, social, and psychological domains. Once new ways of thinking or acting have been initiated, they can become habitual and "outlast the transient emotional states that led to their acquisition" (Fredrickson, 2001, p. 220). Newfound personal resources can generalize to different situations, strengthen adaptation and coping, or remain in reserve to be called upon when needed. Individuals are more likely to develop new thoughts and actions when experiencing positive emotion.

The Nun Studies

David Snowdon and his colleagues at the University of Kentucky in 1986 began an extensive longitudinal study of aging, happiness, and dementia with 678 older nuns (Snowdon, 2001). Participants from the School Sisters of Notre Dame agreed to annual physical examinations, blood tests, cognitive assessments, and neuropathology studies from autopsies when they died. Snowdon obtained autobiographies written almost 60 years earlier when the sisters were 18 to 32 years of age for a subsample of 180 of the nuns, now between 75 and 93 years old. Analyses of the written autobiographies examined emotional content, idea (proposition) density, grammatical complexity, and grammatical correctness. Idea density shows "how much information can be packed into a sentence, relative to the number of words. High scores reflect an economy of expression, whereas low scores reflect vague, repetitious, and redundant expression" (Kemper et al., 2001, p. 228).

The differences in the nun's essays in early adulthood corresponded amazingly well to differences in their lives in later adulthood. The nuns who expressed positive emotion in their writing in early adult life lived as much as a decade longer than nuns who expressed fewer positive emotions. The more often the nuns expressed positive emotions in their essays, the longer they lived. Key words expressive of positive emotion in the written autobiographies included *happy, joy, love, content,* and *hopeful.* This suggests that positive emotional states can help prevent serious disease and even prolong life (Danner, Snowdon, & Friesen, 2001). The use of negative emotional words was unrelated to mortality. However, other investigators believe negative emotional states like anger or depression may have a cumulative effect over time and increase the risk of heart disease, stroke, and immune system diseases such as cancer.

Snowdon reported that the essays with less emotional content, low idea density, and low grammatical complexity were predictive not only of earlier death, but of poor cognitive function, dementia, and Alzheimer's disease in later life. Data revealed that even "a one-unit decrease in idea density (one idea expressed per ten words) in a sentence in early adulthood was associated with a 49 percent higher risk of death" by a particular age (Snowdon et al., 1999, p. 103).

The nun studies have provided important insights into the predictive power of emotional expression and language complexity in early adult life as they pertain to mortality and dementia. However, the studies are not without critics. Some argue that differential educational attainment among the nuns or differences in social class and birth cohort might have influenced the results. The autobiographies were not all obtained at a uniform age (the nuns ranged from 18 to 32 years of age), and some studies used slightly different methodologies to predict age of death from earlier predictors. In addition, the studies' choice of a dependent variable raises questions. Does low idea density in a written autobiography validly reflect both lower cognitive ability in early adult life and suboptimal cognitive and neurological development in later adulthood? Might idea density itself be related to other variables that give a different explanation of the correlation between cognitive decline and increased mortality later in life? Finally, Gergan and Gergan (2001) have questioned whether these results generalize to other populations, given the unique lifestyle of the nuns.

Subjective Well-Being: The Study of Happiness and Life Satisfaction

Expressions of happiness and life satisfaction, taken together, are called **subjective well-being.** Psychologists who are interested in identifying the factors that contribute to subjective well-being over the lifespan have focused on the special characteristics of people who report high levels of subjective well-being as well as the unique characteristics, traits, and situations that contribute to their happiness (Myers, 2000). According to Diener (2000), subjective well-being

> refers to people's evaluations of their lives—evaluations that are both affective and cognitive. People experience abundant subjective well-being when they feel many pleasant and few unpleasant emotions, when they are engaged in interesting activities, when they experience many pleasures and few pains, and when they are satisfied with their lives. (Diener, 2000, p. 34)

Subjective well-being is comprised of pleasant and unpleasant affect (that is, mood and emotion), but each makes its own *independent* contribution. In other words, these two variables are not merely two opposite poles of the same dimension, but they actually represent two separate factors. Costa and McCrae's personality dimension of extraversion is most often associated with positive life experiences and is predictive of positive affect and pleasant emotions (Siegler & Brummett, 2000). Negative life experiences, on the other hand, are associated with the personality dimension of neuroticism and lead to negative affect and emotion. Diener (2000) finds support for the notion that positive affect and negative affect have their origins in different biological systems.

The importance of separating measures of positive and negative affect was highlighted in recent studies of health and well-being. Self-rated health is a critical measure that correlates with overall mortality and is predictive of functional ability, morbidity, recovery from illness, and hospitalization. Self-ratings of health were obtained from each of 851 residents in a retirement community. The two strongest predictors of self-ratings of health turned out to be positive affect and level of activity. Other independent predictors of health self-rating scores included negative affect, functional ability, and medication use (Benyamini, Idler, Leventhal, & Leventhal, 2000). In another study, older adults who experienced functional limitations in their everyday lives due to health problems showed significant declines in well-being. Using data from the Berlin Aging Study, another investigation assessed chronological age and functional health as predictors of well-being. Older people with limitations due to health generally showed an absence of positive well-being, rather than the presence of negative well-being. Age itself was not a predictor or cause of decline in well-being, but functional health was (Kunzmann, Little, & Smith, 2000).

Men and women have similar overall levels of subjective well-being unless extenuating circumstances prevail. For instance, spousal caregiving for a husband or wife with Alzheimer's disease reveals gender differences in subjective well-being. Caregiving wives are reported to experience more negative emotions (and more symptoms of depression) than caregiving husbands. However, older husbands and wives have comparable levels of well-being when free of such spousal care responsibilities (Rose-Rego, Strauss, & Smyth, 1998). Investigators speculate that gender differences may occur because women are more sensitive and more aware of negative emotions than men. They also note that female caregivers provide more demanding personal care and household tasks than do men in the spousal caregiving role.

Cross-cultural studies show that subjective well-being among the elderly is as high as that in any other age group (Diener & Suh, 1998; 1999). The regular experience of positive emotions appears to be the key to subjective well-being. The level or intensity of positive emotions is not as important as the frequency with which they are experienced (Diener, 2000). In fact, highly intense positive emotions are not common in adult development. And, when they do occur (perhaps upon receiving a large bonus at work or a job promotion), people adapt quickly so that there is little impact on subjective well-being. It is the repeated experience of moderately pleasant emotions that makes for "happy" people.

Longitudinal studies show people who are happy tend to remain so despite changing life circumstances as they advance in age. Happy people employ cognitive and motivational strategies that ensure long-term happiness; unhappy people rarely use such strategies. For instance, older adults who plan ahead have greater life satisfaction than those who do not (Prenda & Lachman, 2001). Lyubomirsky (2001) reports that happy people perceive, recall, and interpret events in more positive ways than unhappy individuals. Happy individuals tend to recall both positive and negative life events more positively, by using humor or learning lessons from even negative events. Happiness then, is subjective and is constructed cognitively. Long-term stability in happiness is taken as evidence that an underlying genetic component or genetic predisposition, in part, may account for happiness, positive affect, and subjective well-being (Lyubomirsky, 2001). Of course, subjective well-being may be influenced by different factors for older and younger adults. For example, older adults tend to have higher scores on well-being measures when their social relationships are satisfying, their overall health is good, and their religious faith is strong (Myers, 2000).

Social support, friendships, and close relationships are generally characteristic of adults with higher levels of well-being throughout development. Those with less support experience greater illness and increased mortality. Marriage has been consistently linked to greater happiness. Figure 10.7, which summarizes the results of 24 years of

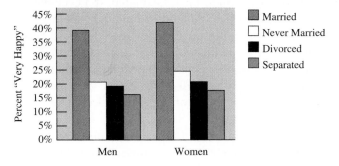

Figure 10.7
Marital status and happiness.

Note: Data from 35,024 participants in the General Social Survey,
National Opinion Research Center, 1972 to 1996.

national surveys, shows that 40 percent of married adults report being very happy to almost twice the number of never married adults (Myers, 2000). Marriage is one antidote to loneliness and isolation for many people.

A recent meta-analysis of nearly 300 studies evaluated a number of socioeconomic factors that related to older adults' perceptions of well-being. The quality of an elder's social network was a strong predictor of well-being, far better than the quantity of social contacts. Older people derived greater well-being from quality contacts and relationships with children than from friends. However, the quantity of social contact with friends enhanced well-being more than the quantity of social contact with family (Pinquart & Sorenson, 2001). A modest correlation also appears between well-being and income. Evidently, a threshold of financial support is needed to provide for essential needs. Once basic financial needs have been satisfied, however, additional wealth does not predict greater happiness (Myers, 2000). In other words, there is a law of diminishing returns for income and well-being; greater and greater income does not result in greater and greater happiness (Seligman & Csikszentmihalyi, 2000). Studies have shown, however, that the absence of trauma or tragedy in life is associated with greater levels of happiness (Lyubomirsky, 2001).

People are more likely to report happiness and well-being when they are fully engaged affectively and cognitively in challenging tasks. Adults actively create their own environments and derive pleasure from selecting tasks and pursuits that are appropriate to their intellectual levels and personal interests. Csikszentmihalyi (1990, 1999) calls the creation of a match between person and environment **flow.** When people engage in flow activities, they enter a "zone" and experience greater happiness and well-being. Flow can occur from any number of self-created, self-selected activities or from certain tasks at work or leisure pursuits. Flow has been described as "unselfconscious self-absorption in mindful challenge" (Myers, 2000, p. 58). Flow occurs when: (1) task demands are neither so unchallenging, boring, or repetitive nor so demanding that they tax a person's patience or abilities; and (2) the nature of the task matches an individual's intrinsic interests. When individuals are engaged completely in tasks that fully challenge them, they lose track of time, place, and context. The type of tasks and activities are secondary to the challenge and the *emotional engagement* they demand. Flow cannot be artificially created by external factors or rewards; for example, few blue or white collar employees identify flow at their workplaces. Executive positions, repetitive jobs, and passive activities such as watching television are not associated with flow or happiness (Massimini & Delle Fave, 2000). Many professionals, artists, teachers, and human service employees, however, do identify their work as a source of flow. Others find flow from activities such as sports, social contact, woodworking, and gardening. Flow demands intense focus, heightened motivation, value attributed to the task, and value in its successful completion. Flow brings gains in well-being and great individual happiness.

Optimism and Hope

Optimism has been related to a variety of positive outcomes, similar to those identified for happiness and subjective well-being. Research studies have found optimism to be highly correlated with health, longer life, achievement, goal-directedness, positive mood, success (occupational, educational, athletic, and political) and, of course, happiness (Peterson, 2000). Demonstrable individual differences exist in optimism as assessed through self-ratings. For example, Scheier and Carver (1992) initially proposed a personality variable, *dispositional optimism,* that guided goal-oriented behaviors. Individual differences in dispositional optimism show that some people expect the future to hold primarily good things and rarely bad; this belief underlies their self-regulation and persistence towards goals. "Dispositional optimism leads to efforts to attain the goal, whereas pessimism leads to giving up" (Peterson, 2000, p. 47). Hope has been conceptualized similarly by Snyder (1994) to involve goal-directedness; however, Snyder has added the concept of pathways. The latter dimension involves the recognition that multiple plans can be created to reach the desired goal.

Peterson (2000) suggests that optimism can operate at a lower level, leading to an expectation for success in a highly specific outcome such as running a 10K race or attending a college reunion. Or, it may lead to generalized expectations that ultimately provide vigor and resilience for adults in many areas of life. It is at this broader level that genetics may play a role. The relationship of optimism to other variables depends on the level at which investigators are working, other individual differences or personality characteristics, the outcome measures selected, and the life-span developmental context (Norem, 2001a).

Pessimism

Pessimism might appear to be the mirror image of optimism, but it is not that simple. Just as negative affect and positive affect are differential, independent predictors of happiness and well-being, so, too, are pessimism and optimism. Pessimism is related to a higher incidence of depression and reduced health status. Encounters with major negative life events such as trauma or heightened stress, however, can lead to significant reductions in optimism and well-being, but not necessarily to heightened pessimism (Peterson, 2000). Experts suggest that pessimism has little value for adults, but this is not altogether true.

Pessimism can play an important role in helping adults cope. Norem (2001b) suggest that some people use *defensive pessimism* as a way of protecting themselves from the possibility of adverse outcomes. Preparing for a public presentation, they might imagine the worst possible scenario. They can then take measures to eliminate the chance of such events actually happening. Mental rehearsal, for defensive pessimists, lowers their stress and helps enhance performance, because they have prepared themselves for every possibility. Establishing a baseline of lower expectations for success, may also help free people to strive for higher success, assuming the lower outcomes are virtually guaranteed.

There is also some value in expressing pessimism and its associated negativity. Pennebaker (1999) identifies the advantages of bringing particularly distressing events out in the open and sharing in the forum that is most comfortable for the individual: dialogue, group discussion, or writing. Disclosure and sharing among those who have experienced psychological trauma reduces stress and is associated with improved health. People who can express negativity and their fears for the future usually feel better after unloading their emotional baggage (Smyth & Pennebaker, 2001). Sharing the burden with other people is also a way of soliciting social support and reassurance. Mild complaints are important for mental health. Complaining helps people discover solutions to problems in living. It can also lead to group problem solving and more effective outcomes than those developed by one person (Held, 2001).

Many people have difficulty sharing personal difficulties and their deepest individual concerns. They believe that they should cover up negative emotions (such as fear and anxiety) and try to act differently from the way they feel. This strategy is not usually beneficial in the long run since it denies the authenticity of their true feelings. Some adults report feeling pressure to be "perpetually" optimistic and upbeat; they feel worse when they cannot meet such unrealistically high expectations themselves (Held, 2001).

Realistic pessimism may be better than unrealistic optimism. Unrealistic optimism can lead to underestimates of risk, for example, of health hazards (Schneider, 2001). People with "optimistic illusions" may assess a lower risk than appropriate for hazards like smoking or using a handheld phone while driving (Schneider, 2001). Denying negative emotions and relying on unrealistic optimism are associated with higher levels of stress and more intense reactions to stressors. Schneider notes that most adults show moderate distortion in maintaining a bias towards unrealistic optimism; this seems to be part of human nature. However, there is a danger of distorting reality so much that unrealistic self-deception is the result (Schneider, 2001).

SUMMARY

Personality refers to a person's most distinctive patterns of behavior, thought, and emotion. Some personality theorists adopt a stage perspective. Freud saw little change in personality from adolescence through the adult years, whereas Erikson stressed personality changes throughout the entire adult life cycle. His theory of ego psychology incorporates social influences and hypothesizes eight stages in development, with four occurring in adulthood: identify versus role confusion, intimacy versus isolation, generativity versus stagnation, and ego integrity versus despair. Resolution at each stage allows an individual to successfully meet the challenge of the next stage. Gero-transcendence is characteristic of those in old age who experience heightened spirituality, faith, inner peace, and universal dimensions of human existence.

Jane Loevinger's theory of ego development emphasizes that development is marked by an increasingly more differentiated perception of the self. Over time, adults develop a more precise understanding of themselves and their relationships to others. The ego helps organize personal dimensions of development: values, goals, self-perception, and self-understanding.

Daniel Levinson developed a stage theory to explain the transitions in adult development, particularly those at midlife. The life structure describes individual choices made throughout development concerning relationships, work, leisure, residence, and the changes that occur in the life structure. Levinson described four distinct eras and overlapping transitions that bridge one era to the next. Midlife transitions require people to come to terms with four conflicts: (1) being young versus old, (2) being masculine versus feminine, (3) being destructive versus constructive, and (4) being attached to others versus separated.

Developmental stage theories share a common view that development is an interweaving of individual self-understanding, personal choice and values, social influences, and individual relationships. While Levinson and Erikson represent these as polarities, they also can be described in terms of the personal growth processes Loevinger outlines. Regardless of the theorist, there are a number of methodological weaknesses in the theories of Erikson, Loevinger, and Levinson.

Traits are enduring characteristics or dispositions that help to organize a person's thoughts, feelings, and behaviors. Some traits are conceptualized as hierarchically organized: Cardinal traits are fewer in number and influence central traits, which in turn influence surface traits. Costa and McCrae adopted this hierarchical view in the Baltimore Longitudinal Study of Aging. They have found five cardinal traits (neuroticism, extraversion, openness to experience, agreeableness, and conscientiousness) that remain remarkably stable throughout the adult years. These results have been confirmed in cross-cultural studies. Self-perception of change in personality is not supported by objective assessments using these five factors. The results of the Seattle Longitudinal Study suggest similar stability in personality from cross-sectional comparisons. However, underlying this stability is the existence of cohort or generational influences. Over more than 70 years, people have become more flexible and open in behavior, attitude, and personality style in each succeeding generation. This was confirmed, in part, by the Berkeley Older Generation Study. From adulthood through old age, the researchers found stability in life satisfaction and agreeableness, but declines for being energetic, for intellect, and for extraversion. Overall, these data suggest a pattern of relative stability, rather than the acquisition of new traits such as stereotypical rigidity, conservativeness, or crankiness. Similar stability in personality using trait patterns or profiles was revealed among both men and women, ranging in age from 70 to 103, in the Berlin Aging Study. Changes in adult personality are usually only documented using subjective reports or cross-sectional methods (e.g., ignoring cohort effects). Current research on personality emphasizes the study of individual lives and the richness of the data obtained from personal reports and structured interviews.

Life-events theorists believe that personality changes in response to unique life events that people experience in adulthood. Neugarten, a pioneer in examining the significance of life events, has emphasized the role of sociohistorical circumstances, or the context in which life events occur. She suggests that the timing of key events (the social clock) is of major importance in understanding the impact of such events. Both sociohistorical circumstances and timing, she suggests, are more significant than chronological age. Life-events theorists believe that too much emphasis has been placed on stages of adult development, universal principles of intraindividual development, and stability. McAdams suggests redirecting attention to the interindividual development of personality by using an approach with three levels: dispositional, personal concerns, and life story.

A person's sense of morality is an important component of his or her personality. Kohlberg reported a series of stages from his analysis of people's reasoning in complex moral dilemmas. He identified three levels of moral thought: preconventional, conventional, and postconventional. Adult moral thought is most often at the conventional level; a small percentage of adults do attain postconventional moral reasoning. Attainment of postconventional moral reasoning requires formal operational thought. This level of moral reasoning leads to more effective coping with negative life events (affirmative coping) than conventional moral reasoning (abortive coping). It also leads more often to moral action than either preconventional or conventional reasoning. Gilligan has suggested a gender bias in Kohlberg's approach to moral thinking. The dilemmas are associated with higher scores for men, who are more likely to commit to abstract principles of justice, while women are more likely to emphasize caring for others and individual connectedness, dimensions that lead to lower scores of moral reasoning in Kohlberg's stage theory. Critics suggest that a wider range of measures should be used to assess moral development. They also suggest using dilemmas that are more typical of those that adults face in their everyday lives.

Positive psychology is the study of ordinary human strengths and personal virtues that lead to effective functioning. Traits that help people flourish in adult life include hope, love, joy, trust, contentment, interest, pride, courage, optimism, flow, and well-being (a combination of life satisfaction and happiness). The benefits of these positive dimensions to adult personality and life have emerged in research studies.

Positive emotions enhance adult well-being. Fredrickson has incorporated positive emotions in the broaden-and-build theory. Positive emotions make people freer to be creative in thought and action; they help build enduring personal resources in the physical, social, intellectual, and psychological domains.

The nun studies highlight the role expressed happiness in early adulthood plays in disease prevention and in prolonging life. Negative emotion carries risks over a longer period of time; it is a separate predictor of cognitive function and longevity. Criticisms of the nun studies include the fact that the researchers ignored the nuns' differential educational attainment, that the autobiographical essays were obtained from a wide age range in early adulthood, that the relationship of dependent measures to other more specific measures varied, and that the results may not generalize to other adults.

Subjective well-being is comprised of happiness and life satisfaction. Research shows that pleasant and unpleasant affect each contribute independently to measures of subjective well-being. Pleasant affect is associated with extraversion and positive life experiences; negative affect is associated with neuroticism and negative life experiences. Self-ratings of health are influenced by positive affect and level of activity. However, independent predictors also include negative affect, functional ability, and medication use. Health limitations lead to an absence of positive well-being, but are not necessarily related to negative well being. Health limitations (functional health) are correlated with a decline in well-being; but age is not correlated by itself. Special stress such as caregiving leads to gender differences in subjective well-being. Women caregivers experience greater loss in subjective well-being than do men, probably because they provide more demanding personal care and do household chores. Cross-cultural studies show that older adults experience as high a level of subjective well-being as those at younger ages. Older adults' subjective well-being is higher when they experience satisfying and meaningful social relationships, social support, good health, and strong religious faith. Different factors emerge among younger adults with high subjective well-being.

The regular experience of positive emotions leads to sustained subjective well-being. The level or intensity of the emotions is not as important as the frequency. Happy people tend to utilize cognitive and motivational strategies that ensure long-term happiness. Their strategies include planning, recall, perception, and the use of humor. Marriage is consistently linked to greater happiness. Some experts believe there is a genetic predisposition to happiness, given its stability. Surprisingly, income shows only a modest relationship with happiness; once a minimum threshold of income has been attained, greater wealth does not necessarily translate into greater happiness. The absence of tragedy or trauma is also associated with higher levels of happiness.

People engaged in tasks that affectively and emotionally challenge them are most likely to report happiness. When the match between person and environmental challenge is ideal, the individual experiences a sense of flow. Flow activities find individuals completely absorbed in the tasks, losing their sense of time, place, and context. These activities produce a state of extreme happiness and intense energy, leading to their successful completion. The challenge, interest, and emotional engagement is primary; the nature of the task is of secondary importance.

People who are realistically optimistic and hopeful have better health, longer life, greater achievement, greater goal-directedness, more positive mood, and more overall success. They are very similar to those who are happy. Individual differences in optimism can be revealed by scales that measure dispositional optimism, or the expectation of what the future will bring. Optimism and hope are related to goal-direction and to one's expectation for success.

Pessimism is related to a higher likelihood of depression and poor health. Defensive pessimism protects individuals from adverse outcomes by preparing them for negative possibilities. Negativity is one technique that elicits social support and reassurance; disclosure of traumatic events is also a beneficial form of sharing. Realistic pessimism may have greater benefits than unrealistic optimism. However, both can distort reality and may lead to an increase in stress.

REVIEW QUESTIONS

1. What are the basic differences among trait, stage, and life-event theorists in conceptualizing personality development? How does each account for change?
2. Identify similarities and differences in the stage theories of Erikson, Loevinger, and Levinson.
3. Define *gero-transcendence*. How does it differ from Erikson's eighth stage of development (ego integrity versus ego despair)?
4. Explain the concept of midlife crisis from two viewpoints: (1) Levinson's (2) Neugarten's. What criticisms have been directed at the notion of midlife crisis?
5. Identify the basic factors of Costa and McCrae's five-factor model of personality. How has the model been used in longitudinal investigations?
6. Describe the relationship of the five factors to central traits or facets in Costa and McCrae's model. Indicate the general results of at least two areas of research using the model.
7. Outline the three basic levels of McAdams's model of personality and indicate how they differ from each other. Why is the third level needed?
8. What are the basic stages and levels in Kohlberg's theory of moral development? Identify an alternative view of adult moral thinking using either Gibbs's reformulation or the work of Carol Gilligan.
9. What is positive psychology? Describe its contribution to adult personality development.
10. Explain the roles of optimism and pessimism in adult personality and coping.
11. How does positive emotion contribute to problem solving and creativity, according to Fredrickson?
12. Define the concept of subjective well-being. What factors enhance subjective well-being for older adults?

 # ON THE WEB   www.mhhe.com/hoyer5

The Positive Aging Newsletter, coedited by Ken and Mary Gergen, is committed to sharing "productive dialogue between research and practice." This newsletter contains brief commentary and summaries of empirical research, articles from the popular press, new books, reader comments, a calendar of events and wonderful NET RESOURCES, all devoted to the theme of positive aging.

The Administration on Aging is a major clearinghouse for information on more than 2,500 government programs available to older adults and those who care for them. A wealth of helpful information and resources are listed on this web site.

The Gerontology Center at Pennsylvania State University has an excellent site with links to a broad range of information on gerontology, aging, and professional health services. Issues related to personality, midlife, and other topics are easy to assess. The major search engines are also online at this site for those needing more research and specific topic information.

Take a quick assessment of your character and temperament on this website that contains two of the most widely used standardized instruments. The Keirsey Inventories provide a quick, general guide to individual strengths and link nicely with career guidelines that fit specific personality profiles.

The Third Age is a general website with relevant information for adults at midlife and beyond. Check out the advice and discussion for older adults interested in breaking new ground. User-friendly articles are plentiful; they focus on dating, remarriage, volunteering, second careers, education, and personality issues, to name a few.

The American Society for Aging is the largest organization for professionals in the field. It has a wonderful key word search that provides up-to-date articles, research publications, and popular press reports on virtually any topic related to aging. Personality issues and related topics are well-covered and thorough.

The American Association of Retired Persons (AARP) conducts its own research and publishes current articles on timely and controversial issues in the field of aging. Their website has a number of excellent articles dealing with contemporary topics in personality and aging for those 50 years of age and older. There are also excellent links to other sites, particularly government-sponsored sites.

RELATIONSHIPS

Seems like by now I'd find a love, a love who'd care, care just for me
Then we'd go runnin' on faith
All of our dreams would come true
And our world would be right
If love comes over me and you
—Eric Clapton

Love is an irresistible desire to be irresistibly desired.
—Robert Frost

The only gift is a portion of thyself.
—Ralph Waldo Emerson

INTRODUCTION

In this chapter we explore the personal relationships and emotions of adults. We examine the core dimensions of adult relationships: love, intimacy, and friendship. We discuss marriage and other forms of close relationship, and examine how these relationships develop and change during the adult years. We discuss sexuality and how sexual relationships change during adulthood. We also examine parenting and grandparenting roles, and the decision to be a nonparent.

Building Relationships: Love, Intimacy, and Friendship

There are mainly two kinds of interpersonal relationships in adulthood—one an emotional, intimate attachment to another person (such as a partner or spouse); the other, close friendships.

Attachment and Love

Though not easily understood or objectively measured, love is a fundamental aspect of adulthood. Adults seem to want to be loved and to love others. Love stories and romantic songs and poems pervade all cultures. Often we are touched by love letters, by stories or movies about love, and by the lyrics of songs about love relationships.

A distinction can be made between liking and loving. *Liking* refers to a broad range of positive feelings toward another person. *Loving,* on the other hand, refers to a deep range of feelings. Love is sometimes or often accompanied by feelings of exclusivity.

Meanings of love seem to have changed over time. Allan Bloom (1993) observed that in earlier times the word *love* was reserved for describing the overwhelming attraction of one individual for another. In modern times, *love* seems to refer to a much more diverse range of ways of relating to another person.

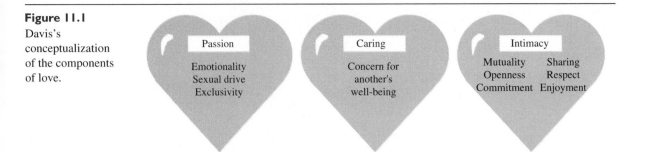

Figure 11.1
Davis's conceptualization of the components of love.

Passion
Emotionality
Sexual drive
Exclusivity

Caring
Concern for another's well-being

Intimacy
Mutuality   Sharing
Openness   Respect
Commitment Enjoyment

Berscheid (1988), Davis (1985), and Sternberg (1986) suggested that love is characterized by three themes: (1) emotionality or passion, (2) a sense of commitment or loyalty, and (3) a degree of sharing, openness, or mutual expression of personal identity. These three themes appear in different proportions in each theory. Davis (1985) views love as composed of intense emotion, a sense of genuine regard and sincere concern for the one who is loved, and also a degree of intimacy unmatched in other relationships (see figure 11.1). Berscheid (1988) suggests that the intensely arousing passions we call "being in love" cannot be sustained. Sternberg (1986), who agrees with Berscheid, describes the passionate phase of relationships as predominant in initiating and establishing a love relationship (see Lemieux & Hale, 2000).

Intimacy

Intimacy becomes an increasingly important factor as love relationships develop and mature. Erik Erikson observed that intimacy is a primary concern in early adulthood. Erikson (1968) suggested that intimacy is only possible after individuals are well on their way toward forming a stable personal identity. Erikson commented:

> As the young individual seeks at least tentative forms of playful intimacy in friendship and competition, in sex play and love, in argument and gossip, he is apt to experience a peculiar strain, as if such tentative engagement might turn into an interpersonal fusion amounting to a loss of identity. . . . Where a youth does not resolve such a commitment, he may isolate himself and enter, at best, only stereotyped and formalized interpersonal relations; or he may, in repeated hectic attempts and dismal failures, seek intimacy with the most improbable of partners. (p. 167)

An inability to develop meaningful relationships may have negative consequences. Lack of intimacy and social engagement has a negative impact on physical health (see Research Focus 11.1).

Friendships

Friendship involves *enjoyment* (enjoying time with friends); *acceptance* (valuing friends as they are without trying to change them); *trust* (believing that friends act on our behalf); *respect* (knowing that friends have the right to make their own judgments); *mutual assistance* (helping and supporting friends and allowing them to do so for us); *confiding* (sharing experiences and confidential matters with friends); *understanding*

Intimacy, Social Engagement, and Health

Having ties to others is universally endorsed as central to cognitive and physical health and optimal living (Ryff & Singer, 2000). Research has shown that shrinkage of a person's social network because of loss of spouse and friends has negative health consequences. Bassuk, Glass, and Berkman (1999) have shown that there is a relationship between social engagement and the prevention of cognitive decline, even after adjusting for poor physical health, activities of daily living, socioeconomic status, sex, and ethnicity. The researchers assessed the relationship between cognitive function and social engagement longitudinally (in 1982, 1985, 1988, and 1994) in 2,812 noninstitutionalized adults aged 65 and older. They measured cognitive function using the Short Portable Mental Status Questionnaire (SPMSQ) and measured social engagement in terms of (1) number of social ties and amount of contact with friends and family and (2) participation in social activities. Haan (1999) pointed out one problem that limits the strength of the conclusions we can draw from this study: The SPMSQ is not a comprehensive measure of cognitive status, and it is not known to be a valid measure of normal cognitive function. This test was constructed for the purposes of assessing mild to moderate levels of dementia. Further work is needed to fully examine age-related changes in the relationship between social en-

gagement and health using more comprehensive measures of cognitive and physical health.

Another way to look at the potentially beneficial effects of social and interpersonal engagement on health is to try and assess the positive aspects of relationships. Instead of focusing on loss and shrinkage of social contacts, Ryff and Singer (2000) suggest that a worthy goal for new research is to examine the relationship between the factors that make interpersonal relationships satisfying and fulfilling and positive health outcomes. The study of the quality of close ties and positive health has only recently gained the attention of researchers.

Finally, one study has shown that even relatively minimal and artificial disengagement can have negative effects on our feelings and mental health. Williams, Cheung, and Cho (2000) studied the effects of being ignored on the Internet. They assessed the performance and feelings of 1,486 participants from 62 countries in an online experiment. The participants played a virtual tossing game with two others (who were actually computer-generated and -controlled). The more participants were ostracized or ignored by other "players," the more they reported feeling bad, losing control, and experiencing feelings of not belonging. Ostracized participants were also more likely to conform on a subsequent task.

(feeling that friends know us well and understand what we are like); and *spontaneity* (doing and saying as we like with friends; Davis, 1985).

Marjorie Lowenthal and her colleagues suggested that the presence of a *confidant*—an extremely close friend—is a critical aspect of psychological adaptation to aging as measured by morale, avoidance of psychosomatic symptoms, and the ability to cope with stress (Lowenthal et al., 1975). The presence of a close confidant or mentor helps adult males in their twenties and early thirties to become successful in their careers (Levinson, 1986). The mentor serves as coach to those beginning their careers, providing a supervised internship as well as support and encouragement. By contrast, extreme social isolation is associated with psychiatric illness, poor achievement, failure to thrive, and limited job success. Indeed, being embedded in a network of close interpersonal ties is related to general life satisfaction and a sense of belonging, competence, and self-worth (Sarason, Sarason, & Pierce, 1989).

Connidis and Davies (1990b) found that adults are likely to reveal confidences to their relatives, but are more likely to seek out spouses and friends as companions. That is, people usually tell their personal secrets and problems (e.g., complain about poor health or finances) to their relatives but do things (e.g., go out to dinner) with their friends. It may come as no surprise, therefore, that Crohan and Antonucci (1989) reported that relationships with friends are more strongly related to psychological well-being than relationships with family.

It has been suggested that female friendships are characterized by more intimacy than male friendships (Antonucci, 1990). Indeed, females are much more likely to disclose themselves to males than vice versa and are much more prone to share their private inner lives than males. Females bring the capacity for intimacy to courtship and then train males to be intimate. The importance of friendship among older women in our society continues to emerge in more recent investigations. In one study, friendships and family supports were equally effective in helping both married and never-married women to negotiate loneliness and isolation (Essex & Nam, 1987).

Friendships are marked by many of the same characteristics as relationships between spouses or lovers (Davis, 1985). Both share the characteristics of acceptance, trust, respect, confiding, understanding, spontaneity, mutual assistance, and happiness. However, relationships with spouses and lovers, unlike friendships, are marked by strong emotion (passionate love) and caring. Sometimes relationships with friends are more stable or reliable than relationships among spouses or lovers (and of course, sometimes not).

Friendships during the Adult Years

Newly married young adults often have more friends than adolescents, middle-aged adults, or the elderly. Young married couples often report that friendships established in their single days are likely to dissipate. Friendships among young married adults are frequently based on a four-person relationship (two couples) rather than on a two-person relationship; the two couples may go out to the movies, have dinner together, and so forth.

By middle adulthood many friends are "old friends." Closeness and convenience seem less salient in establishing friendships during midlife than in early adulthood. In one investigation of 150 middle-aged adults who had moved within the last five years, a majority of the individuals named someone from their former locale as their best friend (Hess, 1971). This indicates that the friendship role does not need to be filled by someone who is physically present. Many people keep closely connected with friends who are physically distant via electronic mail. E-mail contact with friends and family helps to ease the transition of moving away from one's hometown to college or the disruptive relocation of a move. What seems to matter is the perception that "there is someone out there who really cares about me."

Antonucci (2001) used the term **social convoy** to describe the network of close relationships that accompany an individual throughout life. The size of the social convoy—most people have somewhere between two to five close relationships—does not seem to change much during adulthood. Of course, the actual members of the convoy may change because of death, illness, or change of residence. Interestingly, younger and middle-aged adults are more likely than elderly adults to perceive the size and emotional intensity of their convoys as inadequate.

Throughout the adult years, women seem to have larger social convoys than men, and they maintain their friendships longer than men do (Antonucci, 1990). Women in old age expect friendships to be as reciprocal as they were in middle adulthood, even though they expect their children to provide more for them than previously (Ingersoll-

Dayton & Antonucci, 1988; Rook, 1987). O'Connor (1993) has shown that older women tend to have especially meaningful cross-gender friendships with men. These are typically platonic relationships in which men provide a range of domestic services (e.g., grocery shopping and window washing) as well as closeness and support.

Because women have larger social convoys than men, and because women live longer than men in most societies, they usually experience more loss of friendships.

Loneliness

According to Robert Weiss (1973), there are two kinds of loneliness: *emotional isolation,* which results from the loss or absence of an emotional attachment; and *social isolation,* which occurs through the loss or absence of social ties. Either type of loneliness is likely to make an individual feel empty and sad. Weiss suggested that one type of relationship cannot easily substitute for another to diminish the loneliness. Consequently, an adult grieving over the loss of a love relationship is likely to still feel very lonely even in the company of friends.

Similarly, people who have close emotional attachments may still feel a great deal of loneliness if they do not also have friends. Weiss described one woman who had a happy marriage but whose husband had to take a job in another state where they knew no one. In their new location, she listened to her husband describe all the new friends he was developing on his new job while she was home taking care of the kids. She was bored and miserable. Eventually, the family moved to a neighborhood where each was able to develop friendships.

Being alone is different from being lonely. Most of us cherish moments when we can be alone for a while, away from the hectic pace of our lives. Rubin (1979) has commented that for people in high-pressure jobs, aloneness may heal, while loneliness can hurt. In our society we are conditioned to believe that being alone is to be dreaded, so we develop the expectation that solitude may bring sadness. However, research has revealed that people who choose to live alone are no more lonely than people who live with others (Rubenstein & Shaver, 1981).

An older person's health affects the amount of contact he or she has with family and friends and the amount of closeness (or loneliness) he or she experiences. Field and colleagues (1993) reported that elderly adults who were in very good health had *more* contacts with relatives and friends than elderly individuals who were in poor health. Thus the participants who experienced the most loneliness, in reality, should have received the most social support. These results strongly suggest that to maintain closeness with family members and friends, older adults need to possess a certain threshold level of physical vitality. Without health and vitality, it may be difficult, if not impossible, to maintain reciprocal interpersonal relations.

Development of Marital Relationships

For the vast majority of individuals, the most intense and important relationship they enter during adulthood is marriage. From the time two people marry, an average of two years pass before they have their first child. This parental period, if it occurs, represents a major part of adulthood; however, the typical married couple experiences more than one-half of their total years together *after* their last child leaves home. This extended period of shared time is a recent occurrence. Since the turn of the century, due to increased longevity, 10 years has been added to the average length of married life. In the average family of 1900, a couple had less than two years of postparental marriage. Today, both parents are usually alive and healthy when their youngest child becomes independent, and they often live long enough to experience 20 to 30 years of postparental marriage (Trudel, Turgeon, & Piche, 2000). Moreover, the median age of first marriage has steadily increased over the past 30 years, as shown in figure 11.2.

Courtship

How do we choose a spouse or partner? Initially, physical appearance is often an important factor. The choice of a mate often entails a selection process based on mutual interests and sharing similar values. As a rule, opposites do not attract. However, being different from your mate in complementary ways is very important in mate selection. For example, if one person tends to be introverted, a socially outgoing spouse may complement him or her. Not all marital choices, of course, are made on the basis of complementary traits. Most people choose a mate who has some characteristics similar and some that are not (Katz & Beach, 2000).

The Early Years of Marriage

In 2000 in the United States, the median age to marry was 25.1 for women and 26.8 for men (see figure 11.2). Both men and women are frequently dealing with the demands of full-time employment as well as with new personal and interpersonal challenges during the early years of marriage. Life is busy for individuals in their twenties. Typically, the first few years of marriage are filled with exploration and evaluation. Gradually, a couple begins to adjust their expectations and fantasies about marriage to correspond with reality. For couples who have lived together before marriage, many adjustments

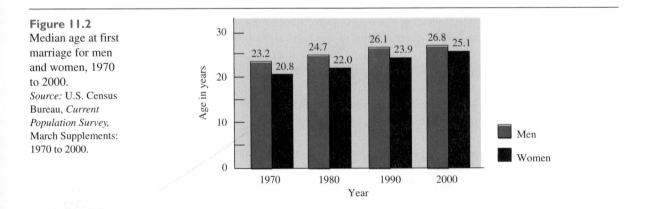

Figure 11.2
Median age at first marriage for men and women, 1970 to 2000.
Source: U.S. Census Bureau, *Current Population Survey,* March Supplements: 1970 to 2000.

need to be made. Couples who live together prior to marriage face exactly the same challenges as other couples in their early years of marriage; in fact, cohabitation and marital satisfaction were reported to be *inversely related* for couples in first-time marriages (Demaris, 1984)! Certainly, every member of a couple has had the experience of realizing that their "perfect" mate has faults, defects, and flaws that they previously overlooked. Cohabitation does not eliminate these early phases of marital adjustment.

Frequently, newly married couples are not only getting to know their marriage roles, but are also becoming established in occupations. In Research Focus 11.2, we describe new research aimed at predicting marital quality and possible divorce.

The Parenting Years

Historically, childbearing and childrearing have been associated with the very beginning of the adult portion of the life span. David Gutmann (1987) described this as a period in which adults respond to a *parental imperative* designed to make maximal use of the division of labor between the sexes and to ensure the continuity of the social community. Recent trends show that many couples are opting to delay parenting until early middle age. Compared with previous decades, couples are more likely to have fewer children or one child (McKibben, 1998). Often, couples opting to remain nonparental are highly educated and career-oriented. Approximately 5 to 10 percent of married couples who choose to be nonparental make the decision in their late thirties or early forties. Other individuals or couples decide not to have children in their teens or twenties. These individuals, called *early articulators,* usually convey their decisions to their

Research Focus 11.2

Predicting Marital Outcomes

It is estimated that between 50 and 67 percent of first marriages end in divorce. For second marriages, the failure rates are even higher. Is it possible to predict which marriages will last and which will end? Research by John Gottman and his colleagues has demonstrated that it is possible to predict which marriages will end in divorce based on observations of how the couples interact. In one study, Gottman and Levenson (1999) showed that it was possible to predict with 93 percent accuracy not only *if* but also *when* a particular couple would divorce over a 14-year period. Seventy-nine couples were studied. The average age of husbands and wives was about 30 years at the beginning of the study. The combination of variables that predicted divorce was marital satisfaction, thoughts of marital dissolution, and direct observations of affective interaction in conversions. The four patterns that are consistently characteristic of ailing marriages were:

1. negative affect
2. withdrawal
3. more negative behavior than positive behavior
4. criticism, contempt, defensiveness, and stonewalling

Interestingly, emotional expression and affective interactions are relatively stable within couples over time (Gottman & Levenson, 1999). How husbands and wives interact with each other is the key factor in marriages (Gottman, 1998). In another study, Carrere and Gottman (1999) showed that it was possible to predict marital outcome over a six-year period using just the first three minutes of a discussion between husbands and wives about a marital conflict. The marital conflict discussions of 124 newlywed couples were coded and analyzed using the Specific Affect Coding System.

prospective spouses before marriage. Other individuals, called *postponers,* delayed the decision to have children until it became obvious that children were not going to be a part of the marriage. These couples seemed to let the decision to remain child-free emerge by placing other priorities (e.g., their relationship, careers, personal freedom, travel) ahead of childbearing. Early articulators have been found to be more expressive of affection toward each other than postponers (Callan, 1987), and early articulators report slightly more satisfaction with their marriages than postponers (Bram, 1987).

Having Children

For the majority of couples who desire children and who are fertile or willing to adopt, parenting brings many stresses as well as immense pleasures. It is during the early years of the child's life that parents report a high degree of dissatisfaction and frustration with marriage (Shapiro, Gottman, & Carrere, 2000). With the birth or adoption of a child, couples no longer have as much time to nourish their own relationship.

In most cultures, the financial responsibilities of parenting are considerable. Couples frequently report that the demands of parenting have profound effects on their lives. For example, being a parent often changes the number and kinds of friendships an adult can have, as well as free-time involvements. Often, both parents must work to meet the costs of raising children, and adults must juggle the demands of work and parenting.

As couples become parents, they experience a decline in marital satisfaction, a decrease in positive interchange, and an increase in conflict. A longitudinal study by Shapiro, Gottman, and Carrere (2000) identified factors in couples' marital interactions

Being parental carries many unanticipated joys and responsibilities.

in the beginning months of marriage that predicted the stability of or a decline in marital satisfaction over the transition to parenthood. Shapiro and her colleagues followed 82 newlywed couples for six years. During the interval of the study 43 couples became parents, and 39 couples remained childless. Couples were interviewed about the values that were important to them in their relationship. The factors that predicted stable or increasing marital satisfaction for mothers were the husband's expressions of fondness toward her, the husband's high level of awareness of her and of their relationship, and her awareness for her husband and their relationship. In contrast, the factors that predicted a decline in marital satisfaction were the husband's negativity toward his wife, the husband's disappointment in the marriage, and the husband or wife describing their lives as chaotic.

Postchildrearing Years: The Empty Nest

Sooner or later, children usually become emotionally and financially independent from their parents. Parents and adult children often develop new bases for their relationship with each other, and at the same time develop new or stronger relationships with others. Parents and offspring gradually begin interacting with each other as one adult to

An "empty nest" may enhance marital satisfaction.

Figure 11.3
The upswing hypothesis: the relationship between marital satisfaction and stage of marriage.

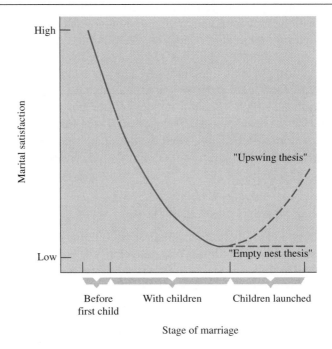

another. The growing realization of adult children that a parent is an adult like themselves, with strengths and weaknesses, is called **filial maturity.**

This period is a time of reorganization, especially for parents. Couples who have learned to relate to each other through their children no longer have their children to buffer their relationship. They must now rely more on their relationship with each other (Rhodes, 1977). It is not surprising to find that this is another point in life when the incidence of divorce rises.

When adolescents or young adult offspring leave home, *some* parents experience a deep sense of loss called the **empty nest syndrome.** Usually, the parents' experience of adult children leaving home carries mixed emotions. Some aspects are quite positive for parent as well as child; the empty nest brings an easing of role conflict and stress (Antonucci, 2001; Stewart & Vandewater, 1999). As evidence that some couples adjust positively to the empty nest, consider the oft-cited data showing marital satisfaction and the **upswing hypothesis** (see figure 11.3). The upswing hypothesis suggests that marital satisfaction is highest before childrearing begins, declines during childrearing, and increases when children have left the nest (Anderson, Russell, & Schumm, 1983). Thus, some couples seem to find renewal in their relationship when the nest is empty. They appreciate the increased free time for individual self-enhancement, plus greater involvement with a spouse, hobbies, and the community. In general, rates of depression are lower for married individuals than for others, as shown in figure 11.4.

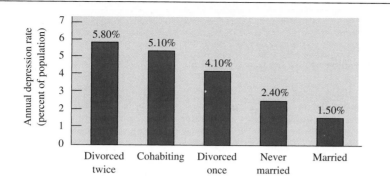

Figure 11.4
Marital status
and depression
rate. *Source:* Data
from Robins and
Regier, 1991, p. 72.

The Aging Couple

The time from retirement until the death of a spouse signals the final stage of the marriage process. Retirement undoubtedly alters a couple's lifestyle and requires some adaptation in their relationship. The greatest changes may occur in families in which the husband works and the wife is a homemaker. The husband may not know what to do with himself, and the wife may feel uneasy having him around the house all the time. In such families, both spouses may need to move toward more expressive roles (Carstensen et al., 1995).

Marriages in which both husband and wife have worked take on a somewhat different pattern of adjustment to retirement, one marked by a simpler transition. In retirement, these couples display more egalitarian and far more cooperative relationships. Among retired working-class couples interviewed in one study, the dual-career couples derived more happiness, satisfaction, and involvement in retirement than single-wage-earner couples (Tryban, 1985).

Married older adults appear to be happier and are less likely to be depressed than those who are single. Such satisfaction seems to be greater for women than for men, possibly because women place more emphasis on attaining satisfaction through marriage than men do. (See Research Focus 11.3 for a discussion of other research on the sources of conflict and pleasure for middle-aged and elderly couples.)

Widowhood

As figure 11.5 shows, a substantial percentage of the older population of the United States is widowed. Not surprisingly, women are much more likely than men to experience the death of a spouse. In fact, widows outnumber widowers nearly six to one (U.S. Bureau of the Census, 2000).

When a spouse dies, the surviving marital partner goes through a period of grieving. The bereavement process in the year or so after a spouse's death is referred to as **grief work.** Women seem to adjust better than men to the death of a spouse, and older

Sources of Conflict and Pleasure in Middle-Aged and Elderly Couples

Levenson, Carstensen, and Gottman (1993) noted an interesting paradox. Marriage has the potential to be the most long-lasting and intimate of all close relationships. But the vast majority of psychological research on the topic of marriage has focused on young and middle-aged couples, especially those whose marriages end in divorce. Why don't psychologists study long-term marriages? Do the members of an older marriage experience greater levels of satisfaction and pleasure than the members of a middle-aged marriage? Or, do older married people feel "stuck" and dissatisfied with each other more than middle-aged married people do?

To examine these issues, Levenson et al. (1993) studied groups of middle-aged and older married couples. The middle-aged and older couples were between 40 and 50 or 60 and 70 years of age and had been married for at least 15 or 35 years, respectively. Overall, couples within these two age groups did not differ in terms of educational background, physical and psychological health status, alcohol consumption, or income. The vast majority had children. And, as would be expected, the children of the older couples (on average, 36 years of age) were older than the children of the middle-aged couples (on average, 17 years of age).

Each spouse within the 156 couples in this study was asked to rate the potential sources of conflict and pleasure he or she perceived in marriage. Participants were presented with 10 potential conflict domains (e.g., money, communication, sex, children, etc.) and 16 potential areas of pleasure (e.g., vacations, children, watching TV, etc.). Participants rated each of these 26 items on a scale of 0 to 100. The higher the rating, the greater the perceived conflict or pleasure.

Table 11.A shows the results. In general, it seems that older marriages enjoy lower levels of conflict and higher levels of pleasure than middle-aged marriages, and that older and middle-aged couples rank-order sources of conflict and pleasure in a similar way. More specifically, older couples attributed less conflict than middle-aged couples to money, religion, recreation, and children; they attributed more pleasure than middle-aged couples to children, things done together, dreams, and vacations. It seems children become a greater source of pleasure and a lesser source of conflict as marriages grow older.

Overall, these results paint an encouraging picture of long-term marital relationships. The positive condition of these marriages could provide a firm foundation for the increased interdependencies that marriage partners experience in their later years. It has also been observed that *responsive listening* is a characteristic of long-married couples (Pasupathi, Carstensen, Levenson, & Gottman, 1999). On another level, the findings Levenson et al. (1993) obtained are consistent with the concept of selective optimization with compensation. As couples age, they may actively seek to maximize the amount of satisfaction they experience with each other (Carstensen, Pasupathi, & Mayr, 2000).

---

people seem to adjust better than younger people. Most widows and widowers, despite having experienced a deep and close relationship with their spouse, adapt effectively to the loss. Many develop new interests, meet new friends and develop meaningful relationships, and learn new skills in response to becoming alone. Thus, the outcome of grief work may be a new and positive identity for the individual.

Parenting and Grandparenting

Before beginning our discussion of parenting and grandparenting, it is important to point out that the composition of households and families and the living arrangements of adults in the United States have changed substantially in recent years (Fields & Casper, 2001). One notable change is that the proportion of households consisting of one person living alone has increased from about 17 percent in 1970 to about 26 percent in 2000, as figure 11.6 indicates.

Sources of Conflict and Pleasure in Middle-Aged and Elderly Couples

TABLE 11.A

Rankings of Sources of Conflict and Pleasure for Middle-Aged and Older Couples

Middle-Aged Couples		Older Couples	
Rank	Topic	Rank	Topic
Sources of Conflict			
1	Children	1	Communication
2	Money	2	Recreation
3	Communication	3	Money
4	Recreation	4	Children
5	Sex	5	Sex
6	In-laws	6	In-laws
7	Friends	7	Friends
8	Religion	8	Religion
9	Alcohol and drugs	9	Jealousy
10	Jealousy	10	Alcohol and drugs
Sources of Pleasure			
1	Good times in the past	1	Children or grandchildren
2	Other people	2	Good times in the past
3	Children or grandchildren	3	Vacations taken
4	Vacations taken	4	Things done together recently
5	Things done together recently	5	Other people
6	Silly and fun things	6	Plans for the future
7	Plans for the future	7	Television, radio, and reading
8	Television, radio, and reading	8	Casual and informal things
9	Casual and informal things	9	Silly and fun things
10	Accomplishments	10	Accomplishments

Source: Levenson, R. W., Carstensen, L. L., & Gottman, J. M. (1993). Long-term marriage: Age, gender and satisfaction. Psychology and Aging, 8; 301–313. Copyright © 1993 by the American Psychological Association. Reprinted by permission.

In 2000, 10 percent of the households in the United States contained five or more persons. This percentage is down from 21 percent in 1970. The percentage of households with one or two persons increased from 46 percent in 1970 to 59 percent in 2000. The average number of people in a family household has declined from 3.14 in 1970 to 2.62 in 2000. The most prevalent kind of family in the United States in 2000 has two working spouses (Perrone & Worthington, 2001).

Over the same period (1970 to 2000), the number of single mothers increased from 3 million to 10 million. The number of single mothers remained constant during

Figure 11.5
Percentages of
men and women
or who never
married, who are
married, widowed,
or divorced by age.
Source: March 2001
Current Population
Survey.

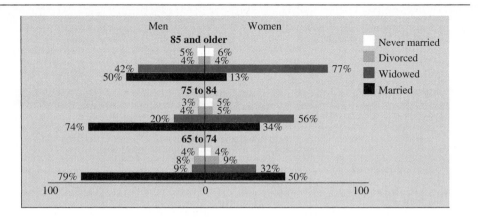

Figure 11.6
Households by
type, 1970–2000
(percent
distribution).
Source: U.S. Census
Bureau, *Current*
Population Survey,
March Supplements:
1970 to 2000.

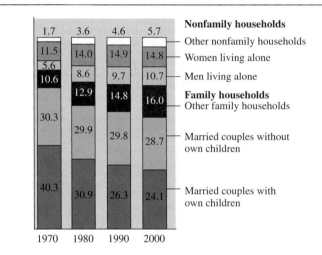

the very end of the twentieth century, but the number of single fathers increased 25 percent from 1.7 million in 1995 to 2.1 million in 2000.

Of the 102 million households in the United States, about 69 percent are *family households.* A family household has at least two people related to each other by blood, marriage, or adoption. The share of family households fell 12 percent between 1970 and 2000. The biggest change has been in the number and percentages of married couples with children, as figure 11.6 shows—from 40 percent in 1970 to 24 percent in 2000.

Sociodemographic variations have changed the nature of parenting and grandparenting. For example, there has been a dramatic increase in the numbers of grandparents who help to raise their grandchildren in recent years (Silverstein & Marenco, 2001; Wallace, 2001). Grandparents pitch in when there are problems of parental drug abuse, teen pregnancy, child abuse or neglect, parent incarceration, and so on (Wallace, 2001). In general, there appears to be a greater need as well as interest for grandparents to interact with their grandchildren now than in the recent past (Silverstein & Marenco, 2001; see Research Focus 11.4).

Why Do People Care about Other Generations?

The term *generativity* refers to caring about the next generation as well as to being productive in meaningful ways. Erik Erikson theorized that both men and women experience a crisis of generativity versus stagnation in midlife. The generative person is motivated to make an important and meaningful contribution to the next generation. And, somehow, the generative person has an increased capacity and commitment to have a meaningful influence on others. Some research has suggested that measures of generativity are higher in middle-age than at other ages (e.g., see McAdams, Hart, & Maruna, 1998). However, other findings suggest no clear pattern of developmental differences in measures of generativity. Stewart and Vandewater (1998) suggested that these conflicting results can be resolved by recognizing that there are different forms of generativity, each with different developmental trajectories. One form, *generative desire,* peaks in early adulthood and declines thereafter. A second form, the *capacity for generativity,* rises and peaks in midlife and then declines. The third form, *gen-*

erative accomplishment, rises slowly during the adult years and peaks in late adulthood.

It has also been reported that differences exist between African Americans and whites in generativity. Hart, McAdams, Hirsch, and Bauer (2001) examined the relation between generativity and social involvement in a sample of 253 community adults between the ages of 34 and 65 years. Approximately half of the participants were African Americans and half were whites. Individual differences in generativity were positively associated with having strong social support from family and friends, involvement in religious activities, and political participation. Parents who were particularly generative emphasized prosocial values, viewing themselves as role models and sources of wisdom for their children. African Americans scored higher on generativity than whites on measures of generative concern and generative acts as well as on indices of social support, religious participation, and parenting as a role model and source of wisdom.

Parenting

In comparison with earlier times, couples today tend to have fewer children and to choose the time for having children. The number of one-child families is increasing. However, even with smaller families, parenting is as much of a time commitment as it has ever been. Frequently, both mothers and fathers are working outside the home. Even with day care services, most parents find that their lives bear little resemblance to their lives before they became parents.

Over the last few decades, three trends in parenting have arisen: (1) women balance the responsibilities of parenthood with work outside the home; (2) men are more invested in parenting; and (3) parental care in the home is supplemented by care outside the home (day care).

The parenting role differs from other roles because it is a life-long commitment. A person can choose to quit one job and take another. A person can choose to divorce or to end a friendship. However, a parent cannot choose to return to being a nonparent. Some adults are relatively prepared for the investments in time, energy, emotion, and money required for parenting, whereas others learn by doing. Table 11.1 summarizes some of the myths about parenting (Okun & Rappaport, 1980).

Grandparenting

Frequently, people who become grandparents say that they did not realize how meaningful the role would be for them. People generally think of grandparents as old, but

TABLE 11.1	
Myths about Parenting	

1. The birth of a child will save a failing marriage.
2. Because the child is a possession or extension of the parents, the child will think, feel, and behave as the parents did in their childhoods.
3. Children will always take care of parents in old age.
4. Parents can expect respect and obedience from their children.
5. Having a child means that the parents will always have someone who loves them and who will be their best friend.
6. Having a child gives the parents a second chance to achieve what they should have achieved.
7. If parents learn the right techniques, they can mold their children to be what they want.
8. It's the parents' fault when children fail.
9. Mothers are naturally better parents than fathers.
10. Parenting is an instinct and requires no training.

there is a wide age range for becoming a grandparent. The average ages for first-time grandmothers and grandfathers are 50 and 52 years old, respectively. According to Hagestad (1985), with increased life expectancy and modifications in fertility patterns, the duration and experience of grandparenting has significantly changed in the following ways:

1. More people become grandparents than ever before.
2. The entry into grandparent status typically occurs at midlife, and many people spend four or more decades as grandparents.
3. Multigenerational families are common, and many grandparents also become great- and even great-great-grandparents.
4. Parenthood and grandparenthood have become distinct from each other, both as life experiences and as two kinds of family status.

It appears that the way in which grandparents and grandchildren interact is partially a function of the age of the grandparents. Younger grandparents are nontraditional in their interactions with their grandchildren. A relatively traditional grandparent role is more likely to be seen among great-grandparents or great-great-grandparents than among grandparents. Younger grandparents are more responsible for their grandchildren in terms of discipline, caretaking, and childrearing advice than older grandparents.

Regardless of age, grandparenting is a role that has few norms in our society. In one early investigation (Neugarten & Weinstein, 1984), 70 pairs of grandparents were interviewed about their relationships with their grandchildren. At least one-third of the grandparents said they had some difficulties with the grandparent role, in terms of thinking of themselves as grandparents, in how they should act as grandparents, and in terms of conflicts with their own children over how to rear the grandchildren.

Kivnick (1983) examined: (1) the meaning of the grandparenting role—*role meaning;* (2) the behavior a grandparent adopts—*role behavior;* and (3) the enjoyment of being a grandparent—*role satisfaction.* For some individuals, the role meaning in being a grandparent was related to feelings of biological renewal (youth) or extensions of the self and family into the future (continuity). For others, being a grandparent meant emotional self-fulfillment, feelings of companionship, and satisfaction from the development of a relationship between adult and grandchild that was often missing in the original parent-child relationship. For still others, the grandparent role was remote; the role had little importance in their lives.

In addition to evaluating the meaning of grandparenting, researchers have assessed the behavioral roles grandparents exhibit in interacting with their grandchildren. In fact, this dimension of grandparent role behavior is the most frequently studied aspect of grandparenting (Silverstein & Marenco, 2001). Three styles of grandparenting have been identified: formal, fun-seeking, and distant-figure. The *formal role* involved performing what was considered a proper and prescribed role. The *fun-seeking role* was typified by informality and playfulness. Grandparents adopting this role viewed their grandchildren as a source of leisure activity and emphasized mutual satisfaction. The *distant-figure role* was characterized by benevolent but infrequent contact between grandparent and grandchild.

Grandparents often play a significant role in the lives of their grandchildren. In one investigation (Robertson, 1976), 92 percent of young-adult grandchildren indicated that they would have missed some important things in life if they had had no grandparents present when they were growing up; 70 percent of teenaged grandchildren reported that they do not see grandparents as boring. The grandparent-grandchild relationship is reciprocal.

Differences exist between the roles of grandmother and grandfather. Grandmothers, for example, tend to outlive grandfathers, thus occupying their role for a longer time and potentially having a different impact on their grandchildren. Grandmothers typically have closer ties to grandchildren of both sexes than grandfathers do (Hagestad, 1985), whereas grandfathers appear to establish closer ties with their grandsons than with their

Grandparents communicate with their grandchildren at many levels, such as directly teaching them skills and cultural traditions.

About three-quarters of adults in the United States become grandparents before the age of 65. Caring for a new generation is a thoroughly enjoyable experience for many adults.

granddaughters (Bengtson, Mangen, & Landry, 1984). Generally, maternal grandparents have more contact with grandchildren than paternal grandparents (Kahana & Kahana, 1970). In times of crisis, the maternal grandparents are more frequently sought for help and more frequently provide assistance (Cherlin & Furstenberg, 1986).

In a recent survey of 40 grandparent-grandchild pairs, Block (2000) compared the perceptions of grandparents and grandchildren in terms of meaning of the grandparenting relationship, the amount of contact, the quality of contact, and the closeness of the relationship. There were no differences between grandmothers and grandfathers, or between granddaughters and grandsons, in the perception of the grandparenting relationship. Grandfathers had significantly more telephone visits and shopping trips with granddaughters than with grandsons. Grandsons participated in more activities with grandfathers than with grandmothers. Grandparents and grandchildren indicated that the amount of contact was less than they would wish. Grandparents and grandchildren reproted a high degree of closeness, and this perception did not differ by gender of grandparent. The finding of no differences between grandfathers and grandmothers in terms of role perception contrasts with the results of an early study by Thomas (1986) that suggested that grandmothers derived greater satisfaction from the grandparent role than grandfathers. There is no doubt that older adults can play a meaningful role in the lives of young children. Grandparents can be deeply affected when the parents of their grandchildren divorce (Hill, 2000; see Research Focus 11.5).

There are cultural and ethnic differences in grandparenting. Black grandmothers, for example, tend to adopt roles that allow them considerable control and authority over

Grandparents' Visitation Rights

During the last 10 to 15 years, most states have passed laws granting grandparents the right to petition a court to legally obtain visitation privileges with their grandchildren. Hill (2000) noted that this is a significant change from traditional laws that gave grandparents visitation rights only if the child's parents consented. Now grandparents may be allowed visitation privileges even if parents object.

What made legislators change their minds about grandparents' visitation rights? One of the most important factors is the emerging political influence of older adults. Also, lawmakers seem to believe that grandparent visitation is a way of preserving intergenerational ties within a family, and that grandparents provide their grandchildren with a powerful source of psychological support.

The benefits that children derive from interacting with their grandparents are directly related to the quality of the relationship between the grandparents and the child's parents. For example, if this relationship is typified by ill will and hostility, little, if any, benefits may be derived from grandparent visitation. In fact, children may even suffer from extended contact with their grandparents if significant intergenerational conflict exists. With regard to this issue, Thompson et al. (1989) commented that:

Grandparents are likely to turn to the courts only if they cannot come to an agreement with the child's parents about visitation with grandchildren. Children are likely to encounter loyalty conflicts during the judicial proceedings, and if a visitation is granted, loyalty conflicts are likely to be maintained as the child remains the focus of intergenerational conflict. Because a child already experiences distress owing to the triggering conditions linked to a visitation petition (for example, parental divorce or death), it is hard to see how further legal conflict between the family members can assist the child in coping. (p. 1220)

By granting visitation privileges to grandparents, the courts have broadened the degree of "extraparental" parenting the child is exposed to. This has eroded the traditional notion that parents have virtual autonomy in childrearing matters. Also, grandparent visitation privileges may inadvertently foster changes in how the family resolves disputes. Bargaining between parents and grandparents over visitation privileges now takes place within legal guidelines (Hill, 2000).

---

their grandchildren. White, Asian, and Hispanic cultures tend to be far more varied in their grandparenting styles (Cherlin & Furstenberg, 1985). In one investigation, Bengtson (1985) reported that Mexican-American grandparenting was marked by many more intergenerational relationships (more children, grandchildren, and great-grandchildren) than black or white families.

The role of *great-grandparent* has emerged with increasing frequency among the elderly. Families composed of four living generations represent a fairly new area for study. There is evidence that younger individuals with living grandparents and great-grandparents maintain very positive attitudes toward the elderly as well as great love and affection for these relatives (Bekker, DeMoyne, & Taylor, 1966; Boyd, 1969). These feelings seem to be reciprocal; in a study of 40 great-grandparents (35 women and 5 men), 93 percent indicated very favorable attitudes toward and emotional significance in their new role (Doka & Mertz, 1988). Most viewed the acquisition of great-grandparenthood as a positive mark of successful aging or longevity.

Abusive Relationships

Parental and spousal abuse have become an increasingly visible part of American life. Some psychologists believe that all forms of family violence are the reflection of a violent society. Because of varying definitions and state reporting standards, the estimate of the incidence of elder abuse in the United States varies from 1 to 10 percent (Wilber & McNeilly, 2001). In a large metropolitan city, a random sampling of incidents of physical violence, verbal aggression, and neglect revealed rates of 32 per 1,000 among older adults (Pillemer & Finkelhor, 1988). Estimates put the national incidence of elder abuse at between 700,000 and 1.1 million cases per year (Pillemer & Finkelhor, 1988). A comprehensive definition of elder abuse includes physical, psychological, and financial dimensions (see table 11.2).

Passive forms of neglect are more prevalent than active forms of physical violence. It is estimated that four of every five cases of elder abuse in the United States go unreported and uninvestigated (Church et al., 1988). Elder abuse is usually a repetitive pattern of behavior, not an isolated or single occurrence.

The elderly are most often abused by their own spouses (Pillemer & Finkelhor, 1988). The rates of abuse are nearly equal for older men and women (Pillemer & Finkelhor, 1988). Other abusers of the elderly are typically relatives acting as caregivers (Pillemer & Wolf, 1986). And it appears that abuse is far more likely among the elderly who live with a spouse, child, or another relative than among the elderly who live alone.

The causes of elder abuse are varied. Investigators have focused their attention on a recurrent stress pattern found among both abused and abuser (Pillemer & Wolf, 1986). The constant responsibility for the care of an older, frail adult often falls on those who neither choose this relationship nor are able to cope with the financial, interpersonal, and time demands placed upon them. Abusers frequently have experienced marital problems, financial hardships, drug abuse, alcoholism, and child abuse (Church et al., 1988). Pillemer (1986) observed that dependency is commonly a factor in the background of the abused elderly. Initially, researchers focused on the abused's dependency on the perpetrator (Quinn & Tomita, 1986). However, other data (Pillemer, 1986) suggest that caretakers who abuse the elderly are often dependent on those whom they abuse. The abuser may be dependent on the elderly victim for housing, for assistance with routine household tasks, or for financial support.

Research also supports the notion that through abuse, the caretaker is able to continue a cycle of abuse that characterized the relationship at earlier periods of development (Steinmetz, 1978, 1981). Resentment over lack of freedom and free time

TABLE 11.2

Forms of Elder Abuse

Physical Abuse: Lack of personal care, lack of supervision, visible bruises and welts, repeated beatings, and lack of food

Psychological Abuse: Verbal assaults, isolation, fear and threats

Financial or Material Abuse: Misuse or theft of money or property

Extremely Unsatisfactory Individual Environment: Dirty home, urine odor in the home, hazardous living environment

Violation of Constitutional Rights: Reduction of personal freedom and autonomy, involuntary commitment, guardianship, protection, psychiatric "incompetence," false imprisonment are also implicated in the development of abusive patterns by those who care for the elderly. The demands of caring for an elderly parent or relative are substantial. The amount of sacrifice required is often not sufficiently recognized or appreciated, which sometimes leads to further cycles of abuse (Myers & Shelton, 1987). In providing care for an elderly parent, for example, adult children in middle or later adulthood have to limit or adjust their work and leisure activities. Finally, elderly victims of neglect are generally old, frail, and mentally and/or physically impaired; they view themselves as helpless and dependent (Myers & Shelton, 1987; Pillemer & Wolf, 1986). See Research Focus 11.6.

Nonmarriage

A large proportion of adults opt to remain single. In 2000, 26.7 million individuals lived alone in the United States, accounting for 26 percent of all households (U.S. Bureau of the Census, 2000). In 1970, by comparison, approximately 17 percent of the women and men in the United States lived alone or with nonrelatives (see figure 11.7 for data on living arrangements in the United States).

Television sitcoms give us a variety of stereotypes about being single. These stereotypes, of course, do not represent real lives. Frequently, single adults' concerns center around issues of career priorities, balance between intimacy and independence, and finding a place in a marriage-oriented society. Singles sometimes feel annoyed at the urgings of their family members and friends to get married. Some individuals see

Research Focus 11.6

Love and Nonmarriage

Individuals change, and relationships change. Edgar Allen Beem, a freelance writer, described one poignant example of the many possible paths that a young adult might take in relationship to another. Beem's story appeared in the December 23, 2001 issue of the *Boston Globe Magazine*. Fern Dorresteyn and Michael Ciborski met in 1988 when they were both 16 years old. The activities, emotions, and experiences of their high school years were not atypical of that age and time. For each, it was *not* love at first sight. Michael was loud, arrogant, and rebellious. Fern was quiet and had a deep reverence for nature. Michael began to change, and they started to do volunteer work together. On one field trip to a nursing home, a young boy happened to watch Michael play the piano while Fern danced for the residents. The young boy later asked Michael, "Are you going to marry Fern?" Fern and Michael then went outside, and talked to each other for a long time in the rain and dark. They began to be with each other often, and after high school graduation in 1990, Fern and Michael attended the same college.

They became engaged to be married in 1991. However, they did not marry, and soon found themselves on separate journeys toward self-understanding, compassion, and mindfulness. As they changed, their love for each other became more spiritual and less physical. Later, as Buddhist monk and nun, each declared vows of celibacy. Now, twelve years later, Michael and Fern feel that their love for each other is just beginning. Fern says that it is quite different to love someone when you still need things from him than to love someone when you do not want anything for yourself. You see the person clearly, you set him free, and you want to help him in ways that you can. Michael adds that lovers tend to need things from each other, such as sexual fulfillment, emotional security, an affirmation of self, a sense of possession. Fern and Michael say with sincerity that they no longer have these needs.

Beem, E. A. (2001). From earthly to spiritual bliss. *Boston Globe Magazine*. December 23, 2001.

Figure 11.7
Note: Ethnic and
gender differences
in living
arrangements in the
United States,
2000. These data
refer to the civilian
noninstitutional
population. *Source:
March Current
Population Survey.*

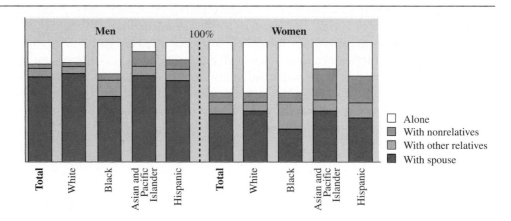

many advantages to remaining single during the early adult years. These include having the time and opportunity to make one's own decisions about the course of life; time to develop the personal and financial resources to meet goals; freedom to make autonomous decisions and pursue one's own schedule and interests; opportunity to explore new places and try out new things; and maintaining privacy.

Choosing a single lifestyle offers flexibility. This freedom partially explains why some adults choose to marry later in life and why the number of single people aged 35 and under is rapidly growing. Another factor in this choice is the attitude change among many women and men toward careers and personal fulfillment. Many choose to develop their careers before assuming marriage responsibilities.

One of the potential drawbacks associated with a single lifestyle is a lost sense of posterity. Rubenstein, Alexander, Goodman, and Luborsky (1991) found that never-married, childless, elderly women developed close, enduring ties with family members and friends during late life and led successful generative lives. Yet many of these women felt that something was missing. They reported that they did not experience the sense of "cultural validation" that is afforded members of society who have children. They saw more than their individual lives ending upon their death. As one of the informants in the Rubenstein et al. study said, "It's hard to think there'll be nothing of you left when you are gone" (1991, p. 276).

Homosexual Relationships

Often the recognition that one is homosexual is initially difficult to accept. In one investigation, homosexual males reported that they continued to question their sexual orientations despite clear evidence that they were homosexual (Remafedi, 1987). Young homosexual adults, concerned about the attitudes or reactions of parents, straight peers, and coworkers, continue to protect themselves from disclosure. Despite legal mandates prohibiting discrimination, homosexuality can bring subtle forms of discrimination in hiring and career advancement.

Close relationships of any sort can bring joys as well as challenges.

Short-term relationships seem to be the norm for young gay adults, particularly for men up to their mid- to late thirties (Kimmel, 1995). Middle-aged and older lesbians and gay men are more likely to develop meaningful long-term relationships (Kimmel & Sang, 1997).

Studies of long-term homosexual relationships suggest that commitment emerges after an extended period of time as single dating partners. The period when gay adults make such commitments is often just prior to middle age (in the mid- to late thirties for males). Homosexual couples committed to each other may elect to maintain closed, monogamous relationships or open, nonmonogamous relationships. Closed relationships have been found to be associated with greater levels of social support, positive attitudes, and lower anxiety levels than open relationships (Kurdek & Schmitt, 1986).

Quam and Whitford (1992) sought to measure how older gay men and lesbian women adapted to the aging process. As table 11.3 reports, the majority of older homosexual adults has positive expectations about aging and displays high levels of life satisfaction. Most of the respondents indicate that being lesbian or gay has helped them adjust to aging. One man comments, "I've been aware of an enhanced psychological and spiritual scope because of the stresses of being in a sexual and a social minority." Similarly, a woman maintained, "My lesbian 'family'—in which I am the oldest—has been a constant source of support. We are learning about aging as a group" (Quam & Whitford, 1992, p. 373). The major areas of concern for aging gay men and lesbian women are the same as those of most heterosexual adults—loneliness, health, and finances.

Divorce

Until recently, divorce was increasing annually by 10 percent, although the rate of increase slowed in the 1990s (Cherlin, 1996). Though divorce rates are high in all so-

TABLE 11.3

Percent of Aging Gays and Lesbians Indicating Different Levels of Life Satisfaction, Loneliness, and Acceptance of Aging

	n = 80 Total	n = 49 <60	n = 31 >60	n = 41 Women	n = 39 Men
Age					
50–59	61.3			74.4	48.8
60+	38.8			25.6	51.2
Gender					
Male		40.8	67.7		
Female		59.2	32.3		
Acceptance of Aging Process					
Very accepting	35.0	27.1	48.4	26.3	43.9
Somewhat accepting	42.5	43.8	41.9	55.3	31.7
Neutral	3.8	6.3	0.0	5.3	2.4
Somewhat unaccepting	16.3	20.8	9.7	10.5	22.0
Very unaccepting	1.3	2.1	0.0	2.6	0.0
Life Satisfaction					
First quartile	6.3	6.7	6.1	5.1	7.5
Second quartile	11.4	6.6	14.3	5.2	17.5
Third quartile	31.6	30.0	32.7	25.7	37.5
Fourth quartile	50.6	56.7	46.9	64.0	37.5
Loneliness a Problem					
Yes	20.0	20.4	19.4	10.3	29.3
Sometimes	47.5	49.0	45.2	56.4	39.0
No	31.3	28.6	35.5	30.3	31.7

Source: Quam, J. K., & Whitford, G. S. (1992). Adaptation and age-related expectations of older gay and lesbian adults. The Gerontologist, 32: 367–374. Copyright © 1992 The Gerontological Society of America.

lower socioeconomic classes, several factors are associated with divorce, including marriage at an early age, low levels of education, and low income (U.S. Bureau of the Census, 2001).

Although divorce rates have declined from 1992 to 2000 by as much as 10 percent, this might not mean that people are now happier in their marriages. Part of the reduced rate may be due to the fact that baby boomers past the "age of divorce" constitute an increasing proportion of the married population. The lower divorce rate might also mean that young adults are evaluating the commitments of a long-term relationship more seriously before marrying. Figure 11.8 shows the percentages of divorced and separated adults by age groups.

Parenting by Divorced Men and Women   During the first year after a divorce, the quality of parenting a child receives is often poor; parents seem to be occupied with their

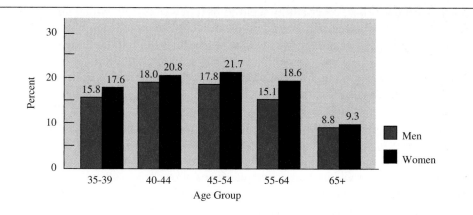

own needs and adjustment. This has a negative impact on the parents' ability to respond sensitively to the child's needs. During this period, parents tend to discipline children inconsistently, are less affectionate, and are somewhat ineffective in controlling children. During the second year after a divorce, parents typically become more effective. The parenting capabilities of the father and mother are central to a child's ability to cope with the stress of divorce.

Support for Divorced Families   Most information about divorced families emphasizes how the loss of one parent in the child's daily life affects the relationship between the custodial parent and the child. Support systems such as the extended family and school- and community-based programs are important for assisting children affected by divorce. Support for single or divorced parents with infant and preschool children can help these persons juggle the demands of work and parenting.

Divorce in Later Life   Although the amount of research on divorce has increased in recent years, psychologists have paid little attention to how this critical life event may influence those with long-term marriages (Chiriboga, 1982a; Kaslow & Schwartz, 1987). One view suggests that since middle-aged adults have more maturity and greater resources, divorce in middle age allows them to simplify life patterns and end an incompatible relationship (Golan, 1986). However, the emotional commitment to a long-term marriage is not easily cast aside. Many middle-aged individuals perceive the divorce as the failure or repudiation of the best years of their lives. The partner initiating the divorce may view it as an escape from an untenable relationship; the divorced partner, however, usually feels betrayal, sadness over the end of a long-standing relationship, and emotional grief over the loss of trust and commitment (Golan, 1986).

David Chiriboga (1982a) evaluated the psychosocial functioning of 310 recently separated men and women ranging in age from 20 to the mid-70s. Included in the analyses were measures of morale, psychiatric symptoms, time perspective, self-reported physical health, social disruption, and divorce-induced upset. Divorce affected people in their fifties the most negatively. With late-age divorce, both men and women feel they lack resources and choices, especially when it comes to dating or in the search for new friends. Thus, older adults seem to have fewer options following divorce. In fact, Uhlenberg, Cooney, and Boyd (1990) found that divorced men over age 50 were unable to anticipate what their lives would be like one year into the future.

Remarriage   In the United States, remarriage has become less prevalent than it was nearly two decades ago (Fields & Casper, 2001). Increased mobility and higher rates of cohabitation may account for these data, but remarriage is still a popular choice among couples who have experienced divorce for the first time. Approximately 80 percent of all divorced people decide to remarry; yet, of these remarriages, 60 percent will end in divorce (versus a 50 percent rate of divorce for first marriages). Wallerstein and Blakeslee (1988) remind us that second marriages often come with excess baggage such as "his and her small children, lowered income, and the ghost of a failed marriage."

The number of remarriages involving children has steadily grown. Remarried families are referred to as stepfamilies, blended families, or reconstituted families. About 10 to 15 percent of all households in the United States are composed of step-families (U.S. Census Bureau, 2001). Projections into the remainder of the first decade of the twenty-first century estimate that approximately 25 to 30 percent of all children in the United States will be part of a stepfamily at some time before their 18th birthday.

Sexuality

One of the most important elements of adult relationships is sexuality. In this section, we discuss several aspects of adult sexuality and focus on age-related changes in sexual functioning.

Sexual Attitudes and Behavior

Although there is usually little biological decline in a man or woman's ability to function sexually in middle adulthood, middle-aged adults usually engage in sexual activity less frequently than they did when they were younger. Career responsibilities, work schedules, and family concerns may contribute to a decline in sexual activity (Trudel, Turgeon, & Piche, 2000). Menopause and age-related declines in hormonal or endocrine function in men and women also play a role.

Menopause

Menopause is defined as the end of menstruation and the cessation of childbearing capacity. The term, **perimenopause**, refers to the 3-5 year period leading to menopause when there is a reduction in the production of estrogen. Menopause is considered to have occurred when 12 consecutive months have passed without a menstrual period.

Women experience a range of reactions during perimenopause (see the web page of the North American Menopause Society: www.menopause.com). In particular, decreasing estrogen levels lead to two physical changes, hot flashes and atrophy of the vagina.

The *hot flash* is a feeling of extreme heat that is usually confined to the upper part of the body and often is accompanied by a drenching sweat. This is the most commonly experienced symptom of perimenopause. Hot flashes gradually diminish in frequency and generally disappear completely within a year or two. *Atrophy of the cells of the vaginal walls* means that the vagina becomes drier, the layer of cell walls thinner, and the amount of lubricants secreted during sexual arousal reduced.

A variety of physical and psychological effects may be directly or indirectly associated with menopause (see table 11.4). As mentioned, hot flashes and atrophy of the vaginal walls are the direct result of decreased estrogen levels. On the other hand, *osteoporosis* (thinning of the bones) is caused by reduced uptake of calcium to strengthen bones; this, in turn, is indirectly caused by a reduction in available estrogen. Osteoporosis is a common cause of the postural stoop in older people and is a contributor to the brittleness of bones. The psychological effects of menopause are not directly related to the physical changes that accompany menopause.

Wilk and Kirk (1995) suggested that menopause is best understood as a developmental process, and not as a medical problem. Wilk and Kirk reported that 70 percent of the women willing to discuss menopause said that menopause means "getting old." About 44 percent of the women in this study reported that menopause means a change in sexuality and in feminine identity.

One of the most controversial aspects of menopause concerns the use of *hormone replacement therapy (HRT)*. HRT involves replacing the estrogen that a woman's body no longer produces; physicians usually prescribe it only in severe cases, using the lowest dosage for the shortest possible period of time. Schmitt and his associates (1991) have noted the many benefits and risks of HRT. On the positive side, HRT may reduce hot flashes, relieve vaginal itching and dryness, and prevent osteoporosis. On the negative side, the chances for endometrial, uterine, and breast cancer increase with HRT. To reduce the cancer risk, estrogen is often administered along with a second hormone called *progestin*. Unfortunately, progestin may cause the reoccurrence of cyclical bleeding. And, at present, the risks associated with long-term progestin treatment are unknown. This is important, because much of the danger associated with HRT occurs when women take the medication for a long period of time.

TABLE 11.4

Effects Associated with Menopause

Physical Effects

1. Blood pressure disturbances and "hot flashes"
2. Osteoporosis (thinning of the bones, calcium absorption deficiency)
3. Atrophy of the vaginal walls, vaginal shortening, and reduced lubricity
4. Increase in incidence of cardiovascular disease

Psychological Effects (Wide Ranging, Great Degree of Interindividual Variability)

5. Insomnia
6. Anxiety
7. Depression

The Male Climacteric

The precise term for the age-related decline in reproductive capacity that occurs for both men and women is the **climacteric**. For men, there is a gradual decrease in the production of *testosterone*, the male sex hormone, after age 40 (Handelsman, 2002; Morales, Heaton, & Carson, 2000; Sternback, 1998). Between the ages of 40 and 70 years, mean testosterone levels decrease by about one percent per year.

There are large individual differences in the extent to which age impacts male sexual health and reproductive capacity. Male fertility persists throughout life but decreases gradually with age usually because of reduced sexual activity and vascular and hemodynamic changes that affect erectile function. The oral drug, *Viagra*, is known to be an effective treatment for erectile dysfunction in older men (Burls, Gold, & Clark, 2001). Health status and the partner's responsiveness are also key factors affecting male sexual functioning (Bortz, Wallace, & Wiley, 1999). There is little evidence to suggest that male fertility declines because of reduced sperm count or function.

Sexuality in Late Adulthood

Aging is associated with a gradual reduction of the sexual response for both men and women (Comfort, 1980; Masters et al., 1991). It takes longer for both men and women to become aroused and to reach climax. Erections are softer and not maintained as long. Climax is less intense, with fewer spasms, and the volume of ejaculation is diminished. For women, estrogen levels decrease, the vaginal walls become thinner and less elastic, and the vagina itself shrinks. However, even when frequency of intercourse is reduced by infirmity, physical health, or hospitalization, the desire for the intimacy associated with sexuality remains strong. Feelings of closeness, physical touching, emotional intimacy, sensuality, and being valued as a man or a woman continue to be important.

Most elderly adults continue to have meaningful sexual relationships. Among people between 60 and 71 years old, almost 50 percent have intercourse on a regular basis. Fifteen percent of those over 78 years old regularly engage in intercourse (Comfort, 1980; Matthias, Lubben, Atchison, & Schweitzer, 1997).

There are no specific or universal limits to sexual activity in later life (e.g., Masters et al., 1991). Adults who have always placed a high priority on their sexual lives approach old age with the same values. Healthy older people who want to have sexual activity are likely to be sexually active in late adulthood (Comfort, 1980). Men and women who are sexually active are more likely to maintain their sexual vigor and interest into their older years.

The results of a 1991 national survey of a large number of married people over 60 years of age provide convincing evidence that older adults maintain their sexual activity (Marsiglio & Donnelly, 1991). As table 11.5 shows, 53 percent of the entire sample and 24 percent of those 76 years old or older had intercourse at least once a month. And most people who are sexually active reported having sex about four times per month. Furthermore, Marsiglio and Donnelly (1991) found that an older person's sense of self-worth and his/her spouse's health status were among the most powerful predictors of sexual activity in their sample.

TABLE 11.5

Descriptive Data on Sexual Frequency Patterns for Married Persons 60 Years of Age and Older

Sociodemographic/Health Variables	Percent Having Sex at Least Once Within the Past Month (N = 807)		Mean Frequency of Sex Among Those Sexually Active Within the Past Month (N = 423)	
	%	N	M	N
Total	53	807	4.26	423
Gender				
Male	54	(427)	4.15	(229)
Female	51	(380)	4.41	(194)
Age				
60–65	65	(340)	4.54	(221)
66–70	55	(206)	4.52	(111)
71–75	45	(140)	3.51	(62)
76 and older	24	(121)	2.75	(29)
Race				
White	53	(711)	4.34	(373)
Black	55	(68)	2.88	(39)
Other	43	(28)	3.54	(11)
Educational Level				
Less than 12 years	46	(288)	4.02	(130)
High school graduate	54	(322)	3.88	(176)
Some college	58	(84)	5.30	(49)
College graduate	62	(113)	4.77	(68)
Personal Health Status				
Excellent/good	58	(524)	4.27	(299)
Fair	45	(222)	4.60	(100)
Poor/very poor	36	(61)	2.97	(24)
Spouse's Health Status				
Excellent/good	58	(524)	4.29	(291)
Fair	46	(234)	4.90	(96)
Poor/very poor	36	(49)	3.48	(36)

Source: Marsiglio, W., & Donnelly, D. (1991). "Sexual relations in later life: A national study of married persons. Journal of Gerontology: Social Sciences, 46: 338–344. Copyright © 1991 The Gerontological Society of America.

The greatest obstacles to continued sexual expression are the lack of an available partner, interfering health problems, and susceptibility to societal attitudes that discourage sexual intimacy in old age. However, societal attitudes are changing, even for elderly living in nursing homes (see Research Focus 11.7).

Sexuality and the Institutionalized Elderly

In most nursing homes and elder care institutions, staff generally ignore the sexual needs of the elderly residents. Nursing homes often have sex-segregated floors or wings, and institutional personnel tend to "discourage" sexual forms of expression. Elderly who express an interest in, genuine caring for, and emotional attachment to each other are often teased and ridiculed. For instance, staff might ask a woman how her "date" behaved at the movie, or they might ask a man to explain his interest in his "girlfriend". Adult men and women should *not* be treated as children or adolescents simply because they reside in an institution. They are entitled to the same privacy and respect that any other responsible adult receives.

Institutionalization of elderly adults does not necessarily mean the demise of sexual interest. Even institutionalized elderly with dementia sometimes maintain the competency and interest to initiate sexual relationships, although well-intentioned staff may thwart such interests (Lichtenberg & Strzepek, 1990). Following is one example of guidelines written to help staff determine the competencies of institutionalized elderly to engage in intimate relationships:

1. Patient's awareness of the relationship
   a. Is the patient aware of who is initiating the sexual contact?
   b. Does the patient believe that the other person is a spouse and thus acquiesce out of a delusional belief, or are they cognizant of the other's identity and intent?
   c. Can the patient state what level of sexual intimacy they would be comfortable with?

2. Patient's ability to avoid exploitation
   a. Is the behavior consistent with formerly held beliefs/values?
   b. Does the patient have the capacity to say no to any uninvited sexual contact?

3. Patient's awareness of potential risks
   a. Does the patient realize that this relationship may be time limited (placement on unit is temporary)?
   b. Can the patient describe how they will react when the relationship ends? (Lichtenberg & Strzepek, 1990, p. 119.)

SUMMARY

Our relationships with others are extraordinarily important to us as adults. Those who do not have emotional attachments or social ties often suffer from loneliness. It is generally important not only to develop an emotional attachment, but also to have a network of social ties to adequately round out one's life as an adult. Emotional attachments give us comfort and security, and social ties provide us with a sense of group identity. In new relationships, physical attraction, the perceived similarity of the loved one, self-disclosure, romance, and passion seem to be important; security, loyalty, and mutual emotional interests are more germane to enduring relationships.

Intimacy is a key ingredient in relationships with a spouse, lover, or close friend. Erik Erikson believed that people develop intimacy after they have developed a stable and successful identity. Intimacy is a part of development in middle and late adulthood as well as in early adulthood. Indeed, building a network of close interpersonal ties appears to be closely linked with life satisfaction throughout adulthood.

One's choice of a spouse or partner may be influenced by personal similarities and complementary needs and interests. Early communication patterns set the tone in a marital relationship. Couples opting to have children face increased responsibilities and demands. One particularly difficult task is to successfully juggle career and parenting responsibilities. Parents often experience mixed emotions when their children leave home, but research suggests that the "empty nest" is associated with increased marital happiness. The time from retirement until the death of a spouse is the final stage of a marriage. Eventually, one spouse dies and the surviving spouse must adjust to being a widow or widower.

Parenting requires interpersonal skills and emotional sensitivity, responsibility, and substantial commitment. Many young adults have idealized views about parenthood. Various meanings have been attributed to grandparenthood. Researchers have identified different interaction styles among grandparents as well as great-grandparents.

The diversity of lifestyles today includes an increase in the number of single adults. Single adults are often concerned with establishing intimate relationships with other adults, confronting loneliness, and finding a place in a marriage-oriented society. Unique issues face homosexual adults, as well as the large number of divorced adults. Divorce is a process that all family members find complex and emotionally charged. The most stressful impact seems to occur during the period just after separation, but over the course of several years, the divorced adult seems to adjust to being single. Divorced mothers may be particularly vulnerable to stress because of increased economic and childrearing responsibilities. A number of factors can mediate the effects of divorce on children, including postdivorce family functioning and the availability of support systems, particularly for women. Marital separation in later life may be more traumatic than in earlier adulthood because of a greater commitment to the marriage, fewer resources, and more uncertainty about the future. The number of stepfamilies is increasing; it is estimated that during the early part of the twenty-first century, one-fourth to one-third of all children under age 18 will have lived in a stepfamily at some point.

Sexuality consists of biological, behavioral, and attitudinal components. Sexual activity is a source of great pleasure among married couples of all ages. Menopause—the end of menstruation—is surrounded by many myths. The majority of women cope with menopause without having to undergo medical intervention, and for some women, menopause can be a positive event. Although males do not experience comparable rapid hormonal changes during middle age, they do seem to undergo a climacteric, involving a gradual decline in sexual interest, potency or fertility, and sexual functioning.

Sexual activity and enjoyment may continue among many individuals in late adulthood. However, many elderly adults who have strong sexual interests do not have the opportunity to fulfill their needs in this important area of life.

REVIEW QUESTIONS

1. Describe Erikson's ideas about intimacy. Discuss why he believed we must go through the intimacy stage in early adulthood.
2. How do close relationships and marriages change over time? What kinds of adjustments must be made over the course of a marriage?
3. What is the empty nest? Describe the upswing hypothesis.
4. Discuss the challenges associated with widowhood.
5. What are the reasons for choosing to marry or not to marry?
6. Discuss the impact of divorce on men, women, and children.
7. How does adjustment differ when separation or divorce occurs in later life?
8. What are the important characteristics of the grandparenting role? Discuss the meaning of grandparenting to both grandparents and grandchildren from intact families as well as from divorced families.

9. Discuss the biological aspects of sexuality in adulthood. Describe menopause and the male climacteric.
10. Describe the behavioral and attitudinal dimensions of sexuality during the adult years.

ON THE WEB   www.mhhe.com/hoyer5

For a listing of links to new information about interpersonal relationships, and to other topics related to the material in this chapter, see:

The refdesk.com site is a virtual encyclopedia of information about interpersonal relationships.

Seniornet provides access to a large variety of links relevant to seniors. It includes discussion groups on topics such as grandparenting, feminism, caring for a disabled adult child, and gay, lesbian, and bisexual seniors. For example, ten searches of Seniornet on different days revealed from 74 to 83 personal entries about the meaning of love.

The site for grandparentsuniversal.com provides links and useful resources about many aspects of grandparenting. You can access informative discussions of the challenges and joys of being a grandparent.

The health4sex.tripod.com site provides links to information about male and female sexual health, including age-related changes in the physiological and psychological aspects of sexuality.

womenatmidlife.com provides resource information about matters of importance to women between the ages of 30 and 60. This page provides links to new research findings on the physiological and psychological dimensions of menopause and perimenopause.

12

WORK, LEISURE, AND RETIREMENT

> *Work*—*what you do so that some time you won't have to do it any more.*
> —Alfred Polgar
>
> *Your work is to discover your work, and with all your heart to give yourself to it.*
> —Buddha

INTRODUCTION

A major part of our waking life is spent working. In most societies, work provides the means for purchasing food, shelter, clothing, and for supporting a family. In addition, work can promote a sense of satisfaction and well-being as adults develop skills, show competence, apply knowledge, and build self-esteem. Sometimes work is interesting and challenging, provides one with a chance to learn or discover new ideas, meets a desire to be useful or to contribute, and provides an opportunity to socialize and develop relationships with people.

In this chapter, we outline the changes that take place in work across the adult years. These changes may involve occupational choice, finding a place in the world of work, adjusting to work, attaining and maintaining occupational satisfaction, and working in late adulthood. We evaluate the varied meanings of work and examine midlife career change, older workers, and the impact of unemployment. Then we examine perhaps the greatest change in the labor force in the last 40 years: the increasing number of working women.

Often, to work effectively, one must balance work with leisure; it's been said, "One can work 10 months in 12 months, but one cannot work 12 months in 12 months." We discuss forms of leisure during adulthood and what it is like to leave one's work or to retire. We describe theories of retirement and factors predictive of successful adjustment to retirement.

The Historical Context of Work

Society in the United States was preindustrial during the nineteenth century. The majority of families farmed land, worked together, and functioned as a unit. Townspeople also worked as family units; a son would apprentice to be a blacksmith or a carpenter, for example. By the end of the nineteenth century, the United States was becoming urbanized and industrialized. By 1910, only one-third of the men were farmers or farm laborers.

The year 1910 is often considered the beginning of the Industrial Revolution in the United States. Factories multiplied, and the labor force changed so dramatically that by 1950 half of all male workers were involved in some form of manufacturing or construction. In an industrial society, machines that operate with mechanical energy substantially increase productivity. Coal, petroleum, and natural gas allowed worker productivity to rise, along with the profits of industrial owners. Since that time, the world of work has undergone yet another revolution.

The World of Work Today

The workplace of the twenty-first century is quite different from that of the Industrial Revolution. Our economy has shifted from manufacturing and producing goods to focusing on service. Employers in the new service economy want highly trained workers who are technologically advanced, who regularly update their work skills, and who are flexible in accepting the challenges of rapidly changing work roles. The greatest asset in any organization is its human resources; good people are hard to attract and hard to keep (Ginzberg, 1995). Today's workers will probably assume three to four different "careers" during their lifetimes. They are prepared for change and realize that career success requires moving from one company to another. Each new position builds on the skills, knowledge, and attitudes they developed from prior jobs. Workers seem to view their career paths as "helicopter landing pads; "they work for a time in one career, only to swoop away and land somewhere else. Compare this to earlier times, when loyal employees joined a company and remained "on the train tracks" until the retirement "station" was reached. Now each job helps strengthen a set of transferable job skills that contribute to employee success regardless of the type of work or the nature of the organization. For example, computer expertise, word processing, and data analysis are all work skills that can transfer from one job setting to another, regardless of the field. Employers value transferable skills that contribute to success and productivity (Carter, Ozee, & Bolinger, 1998). And they know the skills they most want in new hires (see figure 12.1). Employers also value a set of personal qualities in workers, qualities that they believe relate to a variety of performance variables, such as productivity, efficiency, and getting the job done. Look at the list of top ten personal qualities sought in recent job candidates (table 12.1) to see how you compare.

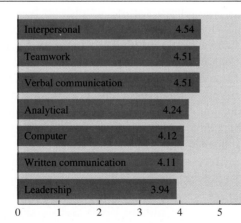

Figure 12.1 The skills employers seek most in new hires.

(Assessed on a 5-point scale where 1 = not important and 5 = very important)
Source: Job Outlook 2000, National Association of Colleges and Employers.

TABLE 12.1

Top Ten Personal Qualities Employers Seek in Job Candidates

1.	Communication skills	6.	Interpersonal skills
2.	Motivation initiative	7.	Technical skills
3.	Teamwork skills	8.	Honesty/integrity
4.	Leadership skills	9.	Work ethic*
5.	Academic achievement (GPA)	10.	Analytical/Problem-solving skills*

*tied ranks
Source: Job Outlook 2000. National Association of Colleges and Employers, p. 20.

Telework: The Future of Work?

Telework or telecommuting is defined as work done at locations distant from the employing organization, performed by mobile employees using computer-based and other high-technology strategies. Telework is one way work has been redefined for the twenty-first century. There are already a growing number of employees choosing to utilize location-independent work sites such as the home or suburban technology-rich community centers (teleservice centers) rather than commute to a job. In 2000, 16.5 million adults over the age of 18 were employed full-time in telework. Given a yearly growth rate of over 20 percent, there will be an estimated 30 million teleworkers by 2004 (Telework America, 2000). Information technology enables employees to work at remote locations, away from a central office, away from supervisors, and away from other employees. Employees do not have to be face-to-face with other workers or supervisors to be productive; nearly one-third of companies in the United States provide workers some telecommuting options. The outmoded concept of a 40-hour work week at ". . . a central location is a vestige of an industrial economy with separate spheres for men and women" (Loscocco, 2000, p. 295).

There are many benefits to telework. First, employees better manage the competing demands of family and work. Teleworkers tend to be older, veteran employees; those working exclusively at home are typically in their early forties. They value their flexibility and increased autonomy in arranging work hours. Second, employees appreciate saving commuting time and travel expenses (Claes, 2000; Nilles, 1998); some studies find traditional workers commute 2 to 3 hours every day in addition to their regular 8 hours on the job. A third benefit affects all of us. The federal government in 1993 established an initiative to support telecommuting through the Environmental Protection Agency and Department of Transportation because telework reduces commuter traffic, conserves energy, and improves air quality. Employers have been pleased with telework arrangements and report reduced staff turnover. Workers have reported higher work satisfaction, productivity, morale, and longer work hours (Hill, Miller, Weiner, & Colihan, 1998). Self-reported increases in productivity averaged about 15 percent for home-based teleworkers and 30 percent for those who utilized a teleservice work center (Telework America, 2000). Employers also do not have to allocate an office to each employee; offices can be shared (a practice called *hoteling*) because of employees' infrequent visits to a central site. Worker stress among those who telecommute seems to center on balancing time between family and job (time management), technical problems at the home-based computer, communication issues with supervisors, coworkers, and clients, and feelings of isolation (Konradt, Schmook, Wilm, & Hertel, 2000; Robertson, 1999; Standen, Daniels, & Lamond, 1999). It will be interesting to see how people resolve these issues as telework becomes even more prevalent.

Work Over the Life Cycle

In this section, we examine career exploration, planning, and decision making. Then we discuss entry into an occupation as individuals attempt to find their places in the world of work. Subsequently, we evaluate the flexibility of careers in middle adulthood, occupational satisfaction, and work in late adulthood.

Occupational Choice

When you think about choosing a career, you may think about a single choice and a commitment to a single career throughout your life. Most employees experience three or four major career changes in their lives, however. Some career changes will challenge and enhance our lives. Others will be forced on us as corporations reduce the size of their workforces or "downsize." Still other career changes will be self-imposed. Some occupations are best suited to a particular age range, and as we change, a particular occupation may no longer be appropriate or possible. For example, in Research Focus 12.1 we discuss professional athletes who "retire" in their late twenties.

Individuals enter occupations, and begin new careers, at different ages. Although career choices are often accidental, unplanned, or uninformed, they are among the most significant decisions of our adult lives. Work decisions have implications for many dimensions of our lives including our sense of identity. Your choice of work says something to others about your abilities, motivation, and personality (e.g., whether you are aggressive, achieving, independent). Further, your choice of work places you in your community and determines your friendships, lifestyle, and leisure opportunities.

It is wise to explore a variety of occupational alternatives before selecting or changing a career. Traditional theories of occupational choice also stress the importance of exploration and knowing oneself. We examine three theories of occupational choice: those Donald Super, Eli Ginzberg, and John Holland proposed.

Super's Theory   Donald Super (1980, 1994) maintained that occupational choices are influenced mostly by self-concept: People select particular careers or vocations that best express their self-concepts. This theory suggests the presence of five stages in vocational development, with each stage reflecting predictable changes in self-concept as one's vocational choice becomes more or less successful. Super suggests that occupational

The Career of the Professional Athlete: Preparation for Retirement?

Few careers are as intense, emotionally involving, and physically demanding as that of the professional athlete. In the early years of childhood and adolescence, outstanding athletes are advantaged in terms of leadership, autonomy, sense of self, and self-esteem; they are admired, sought by peers, the object of media attention, and recruited by colleges and professional teams (Baillie & Danish, 1992). Yet those who are selected and who participate at the professional level often have short-lived athletic careers. Football players in the National Football League average a professional career of 3.2 years. The majority of players end their careers because of injuries, and many experience difficulties in adjusting to retirement and in identifying new career paths (Baillie & Danish, 1992; Webb, Nasco, Riley, and Headrick, 1998). Many also experience financial, interpersonal, and substance abuse problems. The competitive demands and all-consuming nature of a professional sports career, the competition for a place on the team and a contract, as well as physical conditioning and training during the off-season, mean there is little opportunity for players to devote time and energy to other dimensions of personal development and to planning for life after sports. Professional athletes enjoy huge salaries while playing but are often unprepared for the change in lifestyle and loss of earnings when their playing days are over

(Shahnasarian, 1992). Only a handful of professionals in any sport ever realize personal and financial success and a continued career in the same field in upper management or as an announcer, scout, or coach. In the case of professional football players, Shahnasarian noted that "young men—most retiring in their mid-20s—who have committed a lifetime to pursuing a passion and a dream too often one day find that they are ill-prepared to make the career transition from football" (1992, pp. 300–301).

Retirement from a career as a professional athlete in early adulthood is a difficult life transition leading to predictable stresses. Research suggests that a gradual transition is easier to manage than a precipitous transition to retirement (Baillie & Danish, 1992). There is then more time to prepare and develop career plans beyond the individual's limited but powerful identity as a professional athlete. Retirement is hard not only on the athlete, but also on the athlete's family. When retirement is the result of a permanent injury, the stresses are further compounded, and life satisfaction indicators are significantly diminished (Baillie & Danish, 1992; Shahnasarian, 1992). Some teams encourage players to participate in counseling programs designed to help individuals plan for retirement (financially, emotionally, and socially).

---

choice is a continuous developmental process from adolescence to old age, with the person making modifications, reassessments, and redirection throughout the life span as self-concept becomes more distinct.

Super refers to the first stage of career development as *implementation*. At this stage, individuals, usually adolescents, simply try out a number of part- or full-time jobs to explore the world of work. Part of the exploration involves finding the boundaries of acceptable work-role behavior: dress, communication, punctuality, social networks, supervisor expectancies, reward structures, and so forth. In this stage, exploration is healthy and a reflection of adolescent self-concept. Even young adults through the mid-twenties are neither systematic nor intentional in their exploration and decision making about careers.

The second stage, the *establishment* stage, involves the transition to a specific career choice. Again, this stage mirrors a young adult's self-concept. Super predicts considerable stability in vocational choice for those at this stage. There will be little movement away from the specific career they have selected, although some young adults will try to move up the career ladder by changing positions within a company or by moving to a different company. It is usually in midlife that an adult may become serious about a completely new vocation. Such changes occur after an individual takes stock of the opportunities for self-development within his or her initially chosen career.

For the majority of people who stay within the career they chose in young adulthood, the *maintenance* stage describes the period from roughly the midforties to the midfifties. This is a time when most people either achieve the levels of occupational success they hoped to attain or recognize that they will not reach these levels. Super describes this decade of vocational development as early preparation for the disengagement expected with retirement. Individuals remain occupationally involved, committed, and focused, but with reduced intensity on personal achievement and success.

About 10 to 15 years prior to actual retirement, Super believes the individual enters the *declaration* stage. This stage reflects active preparation for retirement as individuals prepare themselves emotionally, financially, and socially. For workers who have made work a central focus in their lives, this stage represents a significant challenge. The last stage in Super's model is *retirement.* The individual physically separates from work and begins to function in life without a career or vocation.

Super's theory has been criticized for its narrow focus on self-concept as the prime factor responsible for occupational choice. He largely ignores the roles of factors such as social class, education, family, and chance. Moreover, his theory implies that most young adults are articulate, mature, and reflective individuals who are able to reason, evaluate, and rationally compare alternative career pathways. Such assumptions have not been fully tested empirically. Another criticism of Super's theory is that it may not account for the career development of women. Additionally, Super's approach implies that career choices are stable and predictive throughout adulthood; however, the stages leave no room for the possibility of career change (forced or voluntary), nor for the many entries and exits into the workforce that are characteristic of women's career pathways (Ornstein & Isabella, 1990).

Super has broadened his theory in response to some of these criticisms by examining the interplay of five major life roles: (1) study or education, (2) work or occupational choice, (3) home and family, (4) community service or citizenship, and (5) leisure. He has adopted a life-span perspective to account for the relative importance of specific life roles at key points in development. Some roles assume ascendancy and must be resolved, while others remain dormant for a time (Kulenovic and Super, 1995).

Ginzberg's Theory   Eli Ginzberg (1971, 1972) has also developed a stage theory of occupational choice. The essential principle underlying his *fantasy, tentative,* and *realistic* stages is the emergence of more and more realistic vocational decisions. The fantasy stage occurs as a child imagines and practices various occupations for a few hours, days, or weeks. The tentative stage begins in early adolescence. Adolescents may closely monitor adults (models) in various careers; they also read about and discuss occupations with family members and friends. The realistic stage begins as the young adult (from high school graduation to the midtwenties) carefully and rationally analyzes career choices. This stage involves a realistic assessment of the necessary education, apprentice period, and personal qualities (values, attitudes, and aptitudes) required to pursue particular careers. The process of realistic assessment begins in young adulthood but continues through the life span. Ginzberg's theory has been criticized for being overly rational in its analysis of occupational choice, with too much emphasis placed on cognitive processes. Also, Ginzberg makes no provision for career change in midlife as a part of his theory.

Holland's Theory Holland's (1996, 1997) RIASEC theory of career choice is quite different from the stage views of Super and Ginzberg. Holland suggests that career selection is based on the best fit between an individual's personality and the demands of the vocation. A good match between an individual's personality and a specific vocation will lead to job satisfaction and stability, whereas a bad match will lead to job dissatisfaction and the search for a different career. In Holland's view, adults seek careers that are most compatible with their personalities. Holland's model is comprised of six basic personality types (RIASEC is the acronym for them) and the corresponding careers that best match each personality type. His typology is used to explain vocational choice, job satisfaction, and career stability or change. Psychological tests have been developed to assess and match personalities with specific careers. Holland's RIASEC model describes the following personality types:

1. The *realistic* personality (concrete, materialistic, mechanical, practical, asocial): This person might be a computer programmer, an engineer, or a mechanic.
2. The *investigative* personality (strong curiosity, intellectual, rational): People of this personality type make good researchers and scientists.
3. The *artistic* personality (creative, emotionally expressive, innovative, original, reflective): This personality might enjoy being an architect or a designer, or working in fashion-related industries.
4. The *social* personality (cooperative, helpful, social orientation, understanding of human relations): People of this type enjoy being counselors, personnel managers, psychologists, teachers, and social workers.

One change in employment patterns among older adults is the increase in part-time work and volunteering.

5. The *enterprising* personality (high energy and motivation, need to be in control, strong, outgoing, and socially gregarious): This personality thrives in business, management, private companies, and sales work.

6. The *conventional* personality (concern for conformity, efficiency, somewhat shy and inhibited): This person might become a bookkeeper, secretary, receptionist, or typist.

Some critics of Holland's approach suggest that few adults have the capacity to see themselves, their personalities, and the demands of specific jobs, as he suggests. Do adults have the ability to deliberately compare potential careers to their own unique personal qualities? Few people are as accurate in their individual self-assessment as Holland suggests. Only recently has Holland recognized that developmental change in self-knowledge in adulthood can be a factor in career change and job satisfaction. Still, Holland's typology is founded more solidly on basic principles of psychological testing and measurement theory than stage theories of careers. His work serves as a starting point for career counselors; most student career centers offer computer-based assessments of personality and career interests that are derived from Holland's theory.

Career Exploration, Planning, and Decision Making

Some individuals prefer to do their own exploration of career options (e.g., by searching the Internet), whereas others seek or receive assistance. Because it is difficult to know what a particular career is really like, it is often useful to have expert guidance and accurate information about career options. College placement centers usually provide assistance with practical matters such as preparing attractive résumés and developing appropriate interview skills.

Career planning is not restricted to any one portion of the adult life span. Discovering and doing one's work is a lifelong developmental process. For some careers, the path or track can be described in four stages: *selection and entry, adjustment, maintenance,* and *retirement* (see figure 12.2). These stages apply to careers that move in an orderly progression. For other careers, the person may be continuously selecting and adjusting, and entering and exiting different work roles.

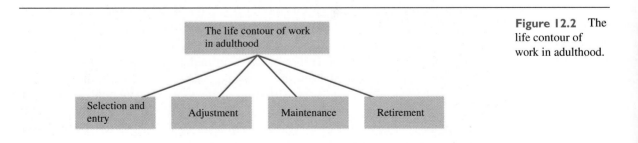

Figure 12.2 The life contour of work in adulthood.

Source: New York Times, April 20, 1997. ©Arlie Russell Hochschild. Reprinted with permission.

Entering an Occupation

At some point during early adulthood, one usually *enters an occupation.* For the first several years, an occupation may take an inordinate amount of a person's time, so that other aspects of life, such as marriage or starting a family, are put on hold. Of course, the demands of getting started in an occupation are different for different career tracks. Most young adults are concerned about their job performance and acceptance by other workers. As workers increase their time and commitments to work, family time becomes compressed and a source of stress—a reminder of the imbalance in their lives (Loscocco, 2000). Hochschild (1997) suggests that men and women increasingly find work rather than family a safe haven. The workplace provides relief from the high demands of family and the hectic pace required to meet the needs of various kin. Sometimes the workplace provides an escape from some of the inequalities of the larger society and the stress of family responsibilities.

Adjustment to the Occupational World

Adjustment is the main concern during the second stage of the occupational cycle (figure 12.1). This is the period that Daniel Levinson (1996) calls the *age-30 transition* in men and women. According to Levinson, once a person has entered an occupation, he or she must develop a distinct identity in the occupational world. Along the way, he or she may fail, drop out, or begin a new career path. The person may stay on a single track or try several directions before settling firmly on one. This adjustment phase lasts several years. Some professional tracks, such as medicine or law, require many years of preparation and apprenticeship, whereas other professional tracks, such as in the business world, require climbing a ladder consisting of a series of lower- or middle-management jobs.

Levinson (1996) reported that women pursuing careers are faced with the same challenges in embarking on a career as men, yet they also give more attention than men do to balancing the competing demands of work and family. A comparative study of 10,339 workers in the United States, Europe, Russia, and Japan identified a set of common occupational concerns: (1) the ability to balance work and personal life; (2) work that is truly enjoyable; (3) security for the future; (4) good pay; and (5) enjoyable coworkers. Russian workers were the only ones who ranked good pay first, just ahead of balancing work and personal life. Workers generally noted a gap between their concerns and the way employers meet those needs. And two of three employees indicated that they would change jobs without question if there were a chance for career advancement, more flexible hours, or a salary increase of at least 10 percent (Yankelovich & Gemini Consulting, 1998). In a study of over 1,000 employed males between ages 20 and 39, having a schedule that gave them time for family responsibilities was rated more important than higher wages or having challenging work (Harris Interactive, 2000). Knowing workforce concerns may help employers manage workers' job satisfaction and productivity as well as facilitate their adjustment to the occupational world.

The Generations at Work

Organizations today are increasingly comprised of workers from different generations. Work teams may include people who are 25, 30, or even 40 years younger or older than teammates. During our working lives, we may report to managers who are 10 to 20 years younger than ourselves or supervise people who are older than our parents. Today's entry-level jobs may be occupied by recent college graduates or by older adults who have just earned a degree and reentered the job market. Supervisors at computer software companies may be in their twenties, and chief executive officers not many years older. Younger workers supervising older workers is a reality in today's workplace. For example, the prohibition against mandatory retirement, other than in a few occupations, means that older employees can continue working into their seventies or eighties.

Zemke (2000) has recognized the challenges managers face when they develop teams of productive workers from employees of different ages. There are few guidelines to govern age relations at work. Each generation brings a different set of expectations, cohort experiences, and perspectives. Veteran older workers (60 and older) are thought to value tradition, expertise, and formality at the workplace. They expect interpersonal, face-to-face communications from supervisors rather than e-mail, as a sign of respect. Baby Boomers (in their forties and fifties) on the other hand, value the close bonds created through teamwork. They are oriented towards service to staff and clients, a factor that drives their work success. They tend to be workaholics, putting in considerable overtime each week, and they appreciate the chance to share their views regularly with other project members. Generation X employees, or X'rs (under 40), seem to value technology and informality at the workplace. For example, they view supervisors as consultants, not managers, dislike formal reporting structures, and value the dress-down business work environment. More than 50 percent of X'rs do not expect to stay with a single job throughout their work career (Families and Work Institute, 1997). And, the Nexters, the new generation of young employees born in the 1980s, will also be unique. Nexters are polite, formal, ready to learn on the job, and extraordinarily computer savvy. They should be good at multitasking, based on the overscheduled lives many led as children and adolescents.

Occupational Satisfaction and Productivity

In middle adulthood, most men and women who have worked full-time reach their highest status and income levels. Employers realize that neither pay nor benefits are as important to working adults in midcareer as the quality of the jobs and the supportiveness of the workplace to help manage the conflicting demands of family and career. The competing demands of family and work peak in midlife and are at the heart of worker conflict and stress (Loscocco, 2000). With challenging jobs and supportive work environments that help employees manage these competing demands, employers promote productivity, job satisfaction, worker loyalty, and retention (Families and Work Institute, 1997; 1998). Workers thrive when assigned high-quality jobs that provide autonomy, an opportunity for learning, meaningful work, a chance for promotion, and greater job security. In a sampling of more than 1,000 profit and not-for-profit businesses and organizations with more than 100 workers each, employees uniformly showed the negative effects of excessive work demands and reduced quality time for self and family. These contributed to burnout, decreased productivity, low morale, and greater absenteeism.

Workplace support can counter some of these negatives. Support comes from supervisors, a positive work culture, caring coworkers, freedom from discrimination, and equal opportunity for advancement. The most important form of support for employees is flexibility in work arrangements so that they can (1) adjust their own hours, such as starting or quitting times; (2) schedule day-to-day flex time to meet the demands of family members as well as themselves; and (3) create telework arrangements, either at home or at a central office away from other employees. Almost 90 percent of workers attributed greater job satisfaction and productivity to these three options, but the ability to schedule day-to-day flex time in response to family needs had the greatest positive impact on workers (Center for Work and Family, 2000). Today, many companies offer workers time off to enroll in college and to meet child-care responsibilities. Many also offer workers the chance to move from full- to part-time employment and back; fewer offered telework arrangements. However, slightly fewer than 50 percent of the companies surveyed perceived that the benefits of providing flexible work arrangements were worth the costs.

Companies supportive of family-oriented policies such as flex time had a larger percentage of women in key executive positions. Linda Hall Whitman, President of Ceridian Performance Partners notes:

> The strong correlation between presence of women and people of color and companies providing more favorable benefits is truly astounding. I wonder which comes first—enlightened companies attracting/promoting women and people of color, and also endorsing work-life assistance for the same reasons, or if it is the women and people of color who advocate once there? (Families and Work, 1998, p. xii)

What leads employees to be satisfied or dissatisfied with their work? The factors that lead to occupational satisfaction are different for younger and older workers (Warr, 1992). Younger workers are concerned about salary, job security, opportunity for advancement, and relationships with both supervisors and coworkers. By midlife, established workers focus on different factors: autonomy on the job, the opportunity for individual challenge and mastery, personal achievement, freedom to be creative, and the need to see one's work as contributing to a larger whole. These factors again emerged in a national study of 3,400 workers asked to identify the *most* important reasons why they selected their current job. Figure 12.3 lists the ratings of importance, which indicate that across small, medium, and large companies, workers value factors other than salary and benefits. Most wish to find a way to balance their lives at home, work, and in the community (Galinsky, 1993). They spend considerable effort to find a balance between work and family responsibilities. We know very little, however, about how younger, middle-aged, and older workers might differ in achieving this balance (Human Capital Initiative, 1993). Informally, we see women moving back and forth from part- to full-time employment, middle-aged workers seeking flexible work arrangements to care for sick children or assist with elder care, an increase in dual-wage-earner families, and men assuming slightly more responsibility for home-based tasks (Families and Work Institute, 1998). Experts have suggested that perhaps age integration would offer another solution to some of these concerns.

Figure 12.3 What workers want: Reasons considered "very important" in deciding to take a job. *Source:* Data from Families and Work Institute.

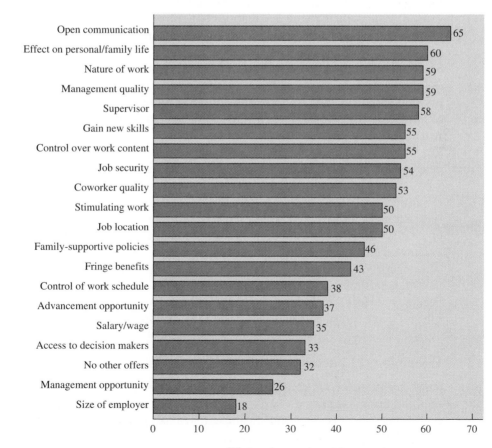

What workers want most, by percentage

Middle-aged workers find job security and the opportunity to rise to a position of influence—external signs that validate their success—very satisfying. Most older workers are satisfied with their work, have derived recognition (and enhanced self-esteem) for their abilities, and will rarely change companies even if offered higher salaries. Middle-aged and older adults are quite reflective and accurate in their assessment of their contributions and the skills necessary for continued occupational success (Fletcher, Hansson, & Bailey, 1992). They also seem to be able to gauge their own work performance accurately, assess their ability to learn new skills for continued occupational success, and apply their knowledge of the organization to serve their needs far better than younger workers. Thus, middle age becomes a kind of "plateau" for many employees. Workers are generally satisfied with their jobs as they move closer to retirement.

Warr (1992) studied this plateau by examining occupational well-being in relation to age. *Occupational well-being* is operationally defined along two broad parameters: (1) job anxiety versus contentment, and (2) job enthusiasm versus depression. Across a wide variety of different kinds of occupations, those who experienced the highest degree of well-being in their jobs were both younger and older workers. Middle-aged workers showed the lowest level of occupational well-being; the data reflected a clear U-shaped curve across the 1,686 people studied. In Warr's sample, new workers found occupations both novel and interesting and experienced a sense of belonging with their coworkers. Investigators have speculated that by middle age, people often experience boredom in their occupations and recognize career limitations as well as the diminished likelihood of advancement, which together promote diminished job satisfaction (Warr, 1992). By later life, among those workers who remain in their occupations, job satisfaction increases as individuals come to terms with their roles in the company, their contributions, and the opportunities work affords them (Warr, 1992).

There are, of course, interesting exceptions to these trends; for instance, some people in middle adulthood start over and select a new career. Many men and women who have had relatively routine jobs deliberately seek work that is more interesting and rewarding. For some, a change is brought about by disappointment in a "dead-end" career; for others, changing jobs represents the need for new challenges; and for still others, it is a response to increased job stress. Perhaps this helps describe the shift traditional women have made from housework to careers. At present, just over 50 percent of women aged 40 to 59 are in the workforce, many of them having obtained jobs as they were raising or immediately after raising a family. And some people change jobs because they feel they are not physically fit for the work required of them (e.g., police officers, professional athletes, and armed forces personnel).

Psychological Factors in Midlife Career Change

What are some of the factors that motivate individuals to change their careers at midlife? Daniel Levinson (1978, 1996) suggested that one important challenge in midlife involves adjusting idealistic hopes to realistic possibilities in light of how much time is left in an occupation. Middle-aged adults often focus on how much time they have left before retirement and the speed at which they are reaching their occupational goals. If individuals believe they are behind schedule, or if they now view their goals as unrealistic, then readjustment is necessary. People in midlife want to be affirmed in the roles they value most. At about age 40, Levinson's sample fixed on some key event in their careers (e.g., a promotion or an award) as carrying the ultimate message of affirmation or devaluation by society.

It is important to consider the deeper meanings of career change during the middle years. Midlife career changes are often linked to changes in attitudes, goals, and values. Though some people hang onto their jobs despite intense dislike for their work, others change careers even when still satisfied with their jobs. The decision to remain with a career is in itself no guarantee that an individual has not revised personal attitudes, goals, and values. Even if nothing in the individual's external life changes, the individual may change. Middle-aged people begin to see themselves, their life situations, and their careers more introspectively, reflectively, and sensitively. Levinson (1996) and Sheehy (1995, 1998) have noted the importance of these internal psychological changes that give different meanings to life, work, and self.

One additional stress on careers in midlife is the existence of fiscal events that influence career decisions. For example, in some families, midlife is a time of financial strain as children enter college. In other families, a reorientation toward the retirement years causes concerns about financial resources. And with the advent of the empty nest, women often embark on new occupations, complete or extend their educations, or resume with greater intensity interrupted or part-time careers (Levinson, 1996).

Work in Late Adulthood

Productivity in old age seems to be the rule rather than the exception: People who have worked hard throughout their lives often continue to do so in old age. Given the changing demographics of the U.S. population, there is a need to invigorate the workforce with older, productive workers. With lower birth rates and fewer younger workers to support retirees, we will need to employ older workers to maintain national productivity. Furthermore, it would be wasteful to have nearly one-third of the adult population out of the workforce (Human Capital Initiative, 1993).

Some older workers keep schedules that would exhaust younger workers, and many continue to be productive and creative, sometimes outperforming their young and middle-aged adult coworkers (see Research Focus 12.2 for a discussion of the effects of overwork on older adults' health). Older workers, despite identifiable declines in cognitive functions outside of their work, seem to develop special strategies to maintain or enhance their performance on the job. In some cases, they compensate for declines in motor performance or speed of processing by applying expertise and acumen developed over many years. Corporations have begun to identify how older workers could function in new roles to improve overall quality and productivity. However, older workers are less likely to be chosen for training programs since employers believe they will get a minimal "return" on investment (Human Capital Initiative, 1993).

In general, a modest but positive relationship exists between age and productivity that favors the older worker. Younger workers have less commitment to their employers

Taking Time Off: Are Vacations Good for Your Health?

One of the benefits extended to workers is the opportunity for time-off. Holidays and vacation days offer employees and their families a chance to rest and relax, free of the daily stress of work. Few investigations have examined the impact of vacations. In one 20-year study of coronary heart disease in women, a relationship was reported between infrequent vacationing and an increased incidence of heart attack or death due to coronary heart disease (Eaker, Pinsky, & Castelli, 1992). Following up on these results, Gump and Matthews (2000) studied more than 12,000 middle-aged men who were at high risk for coronary heart disease. They were initially selected for a nine-year longitudinal project to determine some of the factors that predicted survival or mortality. The men participating in this study agreed to yearly interviews, medical evaluations, and laboratory testing. One of the factors studied was stress. However, rather than utilize standard indexes of stress, the authors chose a simple question. During the first 5 years of the annual visits for medical evaluation they asked each volunteer, "Within the last 12 months, have you taken a vacation?" The authors assumed that workers electing to take an annual vacation had a respite from the job stress and the regular stress of everyday living. They also assumed that regular vacations provided a kind of short-term protective function or inoculation from stress for men. Having a break from stress, they

reasoned, might contribute to longer-term survival, as the earlier study showed for women. Of course, there are many factors other than stress that are related to heart disease and mortality.

Gump and Matthews were particularly careful to control for variables that might lead to spurious results. For example, they noted that those from higher socioeconomic groups might be better able to afford an annual vacation, and those in worse health (perhaps having already experienced a heart attack) might be less inclined or even unable to take an annual vacation. When these factors were controlled statistically and evaluated, a clear set of results emerged. Middle-aged men at high risk of coronary heart disease who took annual vacations substantially reduced their risk of death. Those in the sample who did not regularly take vacations showed an elevated risk of mortality due to heart disease as well as other causes (e.g., cancer). This study supports the idea that stress reduction benefits health. Men on vacation were able to avoid stressors, even for a brief time, as well as to provide themselves a safety net against anticipated stress. Vacations often are a time for enhanced physical activity as well as social contact with friends and family. The authors offer convincing evidence in their carefully controlled analyses and conclude: "Vacationing may be good for your health" (p. 608).

than older workers who have invested decades with a company. Older workers have 20 percent less absenteeism than younger workers. Many older workers are more reliable and derive greater satisfaction from their jobs than do younger workers. Older workers also have fewer disabling injuries and accidents than young adult workers. However, fatal injuries or permanently disabling injuries show a U-shaped function across age (Sterns et al., 1985). In addition, older workers are at increased risk for certain safety problems and injuries. When comparable accidents occur on the job, younger workers have a greater possibility of recovery and a lesser likelihood of permanent disability. The older worker experiencing severe injury may become disabled, preventing further employment, or may even die. Thus, the consequences of accidents and on-the-job injury are far more serious for older than younger workers.

Older workers also experience differential levels of stress when compared with younger workers in certain settings. For example, in one investigation, three age groups of workers (19–28, 30–44, and 53–59 years old) were compared on their adjustment to working a night shift (Harma, Hakola, & Laitinen, 1992). The oldest workers in this sample clearly had the most difficulty in adjusting (particularly when consecutive night shifts were required) and actually decided to retire early as a result (Harma et al., 1992).

Work Performance and Aging

When does age become a factor in work performance? In a variety of work situations, older individuals frequently hold highly responsible positions. For many kinds of real-world job skills, ranging from routine clerical tasks to artistic and scholarly creativity to executive or professional decision making, management, and leadership, performance is largely unaffected by aging throughout the working years (e.g., Salthouse & Maurer, 1996).

Findings from many studies show no relationship between age and the quality or effectiveness of work performance. This finding is accurate in general, averaging across many individuals and different kinds of jobs. For specific kinds of work, a more-detailed pattern emerges. With age, people improve in the skills required for some kinds of work and decline in other kinds of work behavior. Some aspects of work performance, especially speeded performance, show substantial age-related declines (Salthouse, 1996). Compared with younger workers, older adults may experience more difficulty in learning new work tasks such as using new computer systems and in benefiting from training programs (Schooler, Caplan, & Oates, 1997). Age-related declines are also apparent in physically stressful kinds of work, such as building construction, farming or mining, and professional sports.

Other aspects of work performance, especially the performance of familiar non-speeded tasks, appear to be well-maintained across the adult years. Indeed, age-related impairments in work performance are the exception rather than the rule. When the performance of an older worker is impaired, it is probably due to a change in health rather than to normal aging.

The apparent lack of age-associated work impairments is striking, and it contrasts with the findings discussed in chapter 7 that describe age-related declines in basic cognitive and perceptual abilities (see e.g., Schaie, 1996). How do older adults maintain effective functioning in their work, despite laboratory evidence indicative of age-related declines in the basic requisite processes?

One explanation involves the benefit of experience. Although age-related differences do appear in learning new tasks and in using new technologies (e.g., see Hoyer, 1998), the execution of well-practiced skills is generally unaffected by aging (Lincourt et al., 1997; Salthouse & Maurer, 1996). For very demanding kinds of work, effective functioning depends on accumulated knowledge and learned skills. However, age-related declines do affect the speed and efficiency of information processing. Research concerning job performance and aging is difficult to understand without examining the methods used in research studies. Overall, it appears that older workers, despite declining cognitive and sensory processes, are able to maintain high levels of productivity (Human Capital Initiative, 1993). Many studies suggest that older people perform as well as or even better than younger workers (Salthouse & Maurer, 1996).

Decisions about Work

Situational and personal factors influence the amount of energy and effort that individuals give to their work. Job performance and motivation are in part dependent on (1) physiological and cognitive aging, (2) personal and work history factors, and

(3) prevailing conditions in the workplace and society. These factors then affect the choices individuals make about work and jobs.

Job withdrawal refers to resigning, volunteering to be laid off, and retiring. *Work withdrawal* refers to work behaviors such as tardiness, absenteeism, leaving work early, and reduced commitment.

People usually make personal decisions about work thoughtfully, but both objective and subjective factors influence those decisions. Individuals carefully evaluate whether they can afford to retire by determining their retirement income and benefits relative to their anticipated expenses. Family caregiving responsibilities and health factors (e.g., increased difficulty in continuing to work) also come into consideration. However, subjective factors also affect decisions about work. For example, being fed up with the annoyances of work could influence a retirement decision.

In examining the factors that lead individuals to make a decision to leave work, Ekerdt, DeViney, and Kosloski (1996) found that individuals frequently attribute their decisions to objective factors. For example, a response to the question "Why did you retire?" might be, "I reached retirement age," or "They made me an offer that was too good to refuse." However, further interviewing frequently reveals that the decision to retire was influenced by many events in the everyday work environment. For example, conversations with coworkers at lunch about the demanding new boss, about unfair treatment of a coworker, or about increased job requirements might trigger thoughts that it is time to leave the job. An accumulation of minor unpleasant events, such as having to sit through nonproductive meetings, having to complete more new types of paperwork, or hearing age-biased derogatory comments from a coworker could be enough to cause an individual to reevaluate his or her investment in work. So, like many human decisions, decisions about work and retirement depend on "comfort level" as well as on multiple objective factors.

Capable and energetic older workers often meet with subtle suggestions that it is time to consider retiring. Subtle forms of age discrimination are also prevalent in some work environments. Older workers may find it tiresome to adapt to new methods and technologies. Some older workers may find it difficult to continue facing the pressures and rapid pace of work.

Frequently, employers encourage older workers to quit or retire, even when the worker is performing well. Further, little effort is made to adjust the work situation to make it optimal for older workers. For example, an older worker may want to transfer to a different position within the company, the position may be available, and the person may be perfectly suited to the position, but the company hires someone else. Older workers frequently find it hard to change jobs. Even highly skilled and highly motivated individuals in their forties and fifties find it difficult to make any sort of job change or to become reemployed after being out of work. Such factors contribute to older workers' feelings of being unwelcome and undervalued.

Antecedents that lead to job withdrawal and work withdrawal include pay inequity; health factors; dissatisfaction with supervisor, coworkers, or work requirements; and work stress. Factors such as work history, personal values, family situations, coworker pressures, and personal finances also influence work and job withdrawal.

The effects of such factors on work behavior and attitudes are best understood by observing individual differences (Hanisch, 1995). Three individuals, Pat, Kim, and Chris might be equally dissatisfied with their jobs, but each might react by engaging in different behaviors. Pat is unable or unwilling to resign or retire, but is frequently absent and arrives late and leaves early as much as possible. Kim actively pursues plans for an early retirement. Chris chooses to work harder to make positive changes and decrease her dissatisfaction. Researchers need to consider individual differences in reactions to changes in the workplace. As suggested in the research by Ekerdt, DeViney, and Kosloski (1996) and Maurer and Tarulli (1994), self-appraisals of work behavior may take on new significance for older individuals, and these workers might be particularly sensitive to criticism and negative remarks about aging.

Sometimes one's work is who one is. At social occasions, people talk about what they do—their work. Thus, work often defines the person's intelligence, personality, motivation, and so on. Work carries a measure of prestige or status and brings people into social contact. Work may even determine our friends and leisure choices, to some extent. Table 12.2 presents a list of some of the meanings individuals assign to their jobs and links these meanings with more universal functions of work.

Some individuals love their work and refuse to retire. The decision to continue to work is certainly also related to health, finances, and job satisfaction. What is emerging, however, are other models of work among older adults. There has been significant growth in part-time employment among older adults. And many productive older workers trade one job for another, as figure 12.4 indicates.

TABLE 12.2

The Relationship between the Functions and Meanings of Work

Work Function	Work Meanings
Income	Maintaining a minimum sustenance level
	Achieving some higher level or group standard
Expenditure of time and energy	Something to do
	A way of filling the day or passing time
Identification and status	Source of self-respect
	Way of achieving recognition or respect from others
	Definition of role
Association	Friendship relations
	Peer-group relations
	Subordinate-superordinate relations
Source of meaningful life experience	Gives purpose to life
	Creativity, self-expression
	New experience
	Service to others

Source: Friedmann, E., & Havighurst, R. J. (1954). The meaning of work and retirement. Chicago: The University of Chicago Press. Copyright © 1954, The University of Chicago Press, Chicago, IL. Reprinted by permission.

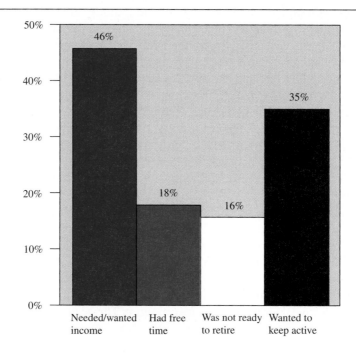

Figure 12.4
Reasons for working following retirement. Many people reenter the workforce after retiring for financial reasons. *Source:* Cornell Retirement and Well-Being Study, Phase 1, 1995.

The Culture of the Work Environment

The meaning of work, and the workplace itself, is undergoing rapid change. Likewise, what we do at work constantly changes. Therefore, quickly adjusting to change, being able to make smooth transitions from one job to another within and across organizations, and being committed to continually upgrade one's skills and learning are essential requirements for today's workers. Corporations may also value a worker's ability to function as a team player in an increasingly diverse workforce (in ethnicity, race, gender, and age).

Many of the changes in corporate attitudes and culture encourage strong motivation, organizational commitment, worker satisfaction, and ultimately, quality and productivity. Considerable emphasis has been placed on management innovations such as team building, quality circles, and Total Quality Management (TQM) approaches.

As the nature of work and the work environment change, the meaning and significance of work also continues to change. Young workers in organizations tend to be concerned with extrinsic factors such as salary, job security, and continuity in their careers, whereas workers with more seniority focus on intrinsic rewards such as independence, quality and meaning of work, and the authority to set goals and achieve them in line with corporate priorities (Galinsky, 1993; Families and Work Institute, 1998). Those workers who welcome change, can manage change, and can initiate and sustain change derive the highest degree of personal success and pleasure from their careers (Belasco, 1991). Evidence is mounting that today's workers are questioning the value of company loyalty and increasingly placing greater value on balancing work and family concerns. The workplace must take into account that nearly 85 percent of all salaried employees live with and care for other family members including children, elderly parents, or spouses with health problems (Families and Work Institute, 1998).

Work and Successful Aging

Models of successful aging describe the positive dimensions of aging and how these dimensions contribute to carrying out work roles. You probably know older individuals who keep up with every workplace innovation or even set the pace in the workplace. Often there is an optimal match between the changing demands of the work context and the particular abilities, skills, and personal characteristics of an individual. Workers of all ages have the potential to make unique and valuable contributions within specific workplace contexts.

Measurement issues must be considered in understanding the apparent discrepancy between real-world job performance and age-related declines in basic cognitive abilities. Only about 4 to 25 percent of the variance in job performance can be accounted for by standardized tests of ability. It is better to assess performance on tasks typical of actual performance on the job for predicting and evaluating job performance.

Introducing new technology in the workplace can help workers to be more productive and enhance work quality by complementing or supporting workers' skills (Hunt, 1993). New technologies can minimize the tedium of repetitive work or allow more time for creativity. Unfortunately, more often than not, new technologies allow a company to displace older workers rather than help workers improve on the job.

Unemployment

Unemployment produces stress regardless of whether the job loss is temporary, cyclical, or permanent. The psychological meaning of job loss depends on a number of factors, including the individual's personality, social status, and resources. For example, a 50-year-old married worker with two adolescent children, a high school education, no transferable job skills, and no pension would not react the same way to the shutdown of an automobile assembly plant as a 21-year-old unmarried man.

Being middle-aged and unemployed today may be as bad, or in some cases even worse, than it was in the Great Depression of the 1930s. The unemployed in the 1930s had a strong feeling that their jobs would reopen. Because many of today's workers have been replaced by technology and drastic corporate downsizing, expectations that jobs will reappear are not very realistic. This suggests that many individuals will experience a number of different jobs during their adult years—not a single occupation, as in the past. Workers who experience job loss must deal with the economic, emotional, and social consequences not only for themselves but also for their families.

As noted earlier, to be successful, workers need to view education as a lifelong process, not something completed during two to four years in young adulthood and marked by the receipt of a degree or the end of a lengthy apprenticeship in the trades. Older, less-educated workers, particularly those with lowest self-esteem, have been reported to have the most difficulty coping with job loss and unemployment (Kinicki, 1989). Job counseling programs and "executives-out-of-work" self-help groups assist those who find the job loss most debilitating. Such interventions take a commonsense approach by offering practical help with résumés and interviewing skills; understanding the resources and skills needed to assist in a job search, such as networking; identifying the skills workers have acquired and can apply to any work setting; and giving emotional support to help individuals begin to reorganize their personal lives. Successful coping with job loss involves being able to distance oneself from the loss, effectively seek or prepare to seek new employment, and balance work issues with other values and activities in life.

Work and Families

In the United States, 85 percent of salaried wage earners live with family members, providing routine care, financial assistance, and other basic support for them (Families and Work Institute, 1997). Among "traditional" families headed by married partners, 78 percent report that both spouses work, which equals the figure for dual wage-earner households where adult partners live together. Recent data show that 13 percent of all full-time employed workers hold a second part-time job for about 13 hours per week. Workers living in families are typically responsible for dependent children under age 18. Single parents also manage family responsibilities and work responsibilities; one study reported that 23 percent of mothers in the workforce were single parents (Galinsky & Bond, 1996). One quarter of all salaried workers provided 11 hours per week to elderly family members within the past 12-month period; one third had to take time away from their jobs to do so (Families and Work Institute, 1997; Loscocco, 2000). And providing care for both a child *and* for an elderly relative during the past 12 months was part of life for 20 percent of workers in this study. Galinsky notes that:

> With today's smaller families, single-parent families, and two-career couples, the pool of able-bodied, nonemployed adults available to provide elder care is shrinking just as demand for care is rising. It is not clear that anyone—employees, employers, community agencies, or government—is prepared for the substantial impact that growing elder care responsibilities will have on the labor force in the coming years. (Families and Work Institute, 1997, p. 15)

The Federal Family and Medical Leave Act passed in 1993 recognizes the multiple responsibilities employees have to work and family. Eligible workers at large organizations can take up to three months of job-protected, unpaid leave to (1) care for a seriously ill child, spouse, or parent; (2) stay at home to care for their newborn, newly adopted, or newly placed child; or (3) take time off when they become seriously ill (Family and Medical Leave Survey, 2000). Since 1993, more than 35 million employees have benefited from the program; employers have not experienced declines in productivity, profits, or growth by being responsive to workers' needs. Most employees increasingly appreciate the leave policy, although more than 50 percent struggle with the lack of income during their time away from work. Some employees cut short their leave because they cannot manage without this income; others come back to work early because they fear losing their job although the Act is meant to prohibit this (Family and Medical Leave Survey, 2000).

Salaried wage earners usually work full-time, spending nearly 44 hours per week on work activities. Women are more likely than men to work part-time. Given the long hours devoted to work, employees have little free time for leisure or personal activities. Life satisfaction ratings are not high, and many workers report declines in well-being, and in their comfort level with family and marriage. In a word, employees are burned out—their jobs are demanding, and family is often forced into second place.

Because balancing these competing demands is difficult, employees appreciate flexible work arrangements, family leave options, and understanding, supportive supervisors and coworkers. Without support, workers become overloaded with family demands and become irritable employees with negative attitudes and lower productivity (Families and Work Institute, 1997).

Gender and Work

The main source of work-family conflict is the erosion of the gender division of labor that was the foundation of the industrial era and the age-segregated life course. With women caring for children and running households, men had been able to focus their energies on work. By 1992, only 18 percent of families followed the traditional model of employed husband and homemaker wife (Reskin & Padavic, 1994). Even mothers of young children, that last bastion of female reserve, have a labor force participation rate of 63 percent, five times higher than it was in 1950 (Cherlin, 1998, as quoted in Loscocco 2000, p. 293).

Although job opportunities for women continue to expand, women still face vexing issues in the work world, led by wage inequity. Federal law established equal pay for equal work in all occupations. Pay differences may only be based on seniority, experience, or documented performance. Yet in the most recent census, women on average are reported to earn 74 cents for every dollar men earn. Minority women experience even greater disparity, with black women earning 65 cents and Hispanic women 57 cents for each dollar earned by men. Such inequities mean the loss of substantial income over a working career; current estimates suggest a loss of more than $500,000 and pensions that are, on the average, less than half the value of men's (Career Women, 1998). Some argue that these differences are the result of women working part-time to help raise a family, of women returning to full-time careers in midlife after stopping to launch a family, or of differential levels of education. These factors, however, cannot account for all wage inequities. Consider the substantial differences for career women: (1) female lawyers' median weekly pay is almost $300 less than male lawyers'; (2) secretaries are paid $100 per week less than male clericals on average; (3) female physicians' median earnings are $500 less each week than male physicians; (4) female professors receive a median paycheck worth $170 less each week than men's; and (5) primary school teachers receive $70 less each week than men (Career Women, 1998).

To compound the problem, women who begin careers in middle age or who choose nontraditional jobs frequently do not have mentors. **Mentors** are experienced, successful employees who help individuals get started in careers by imparting advice, guidance, friendship, and perspective through example. Nontraditional jobs for women are defined as any occupation that employs less than 25 percent women (Department of Labor, Bureau of Women, 2000). Despite growth in equity in hiring, this list includes almost 100 occupations in which women hold only a small percentage of jobs, such as physicians (24.5%), dentists (16.5%), architects (15.7%), clergy (14.2%), law enforcement (14.4%), engineers (10.6%), machinists (5.6%), and aircraft pilots/navigators (3.1%). Though women's participation in some occupations has improved over the last two decades, other fields have not changed much. Figure 12.5 compares the percentage

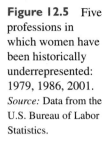

Figure 12.5 Five professions in which women have been historically underrepresented: 1979, 1986, 2001. *Source:* Data from the U.S. Bureau of Labor Statistics.

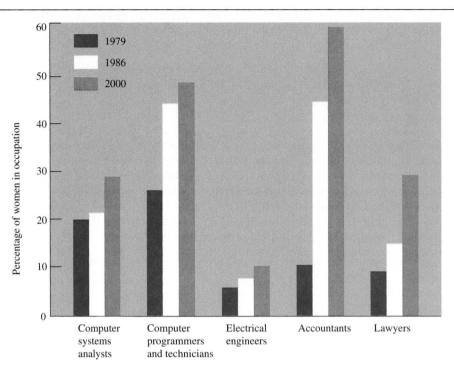

of women in five fields that were historically considered nontraditional careers. Success may be linked to:

Greater equality and access to education and training opportunities

The growth of new occupations requiring special technical skills (e.g., computer technology and computer applications)

Encouragement of companies to comply with affirmative action policies and the imposition of penalties for those that consistently fail to make progress

Development of technologies and work environments that reduce the requirements for physical strength in a particular job

Consider the Department of Labor's recent projections for the 10 fastest-growing occupations from 1998 through 2008 in table 12.3. Interestingly, these are not exclusively "male" or "female" occupations; they are indeed open to all.

There has been some change in household and family responsibilities for husbands and wives with children. In comparison with data from 20 years earlier, fathers are spending about 30 minutes more with their children each day. Fathers on average devote 2.3 hours each day caring for and interacting with their children. Mothers, on the other hand, spend about 3.3 hours each day, about the same amount of time as 20 years earlier. Household tasks are still not shared equally between married spouses, although there is movement towards equity. Compared to two decades earlier, mothers devote 36 fewer minutes each day to household tasks, while men spend 60 more minutes each day. However, figure 12.6 shows, women are more likely to cook, clean, shop,

TABLE 12.3

Predicting the 10 Fastest Growing Occupations, 1998–2008

Occupation	Employment (thousands of jobs)		Percent Growth
	1998	2008	
Computer engineer	299	622	108+
Computer support specialist	429	869	102+
Systems analyst	617	1,194	94
Database administrator	87	155	77
Desktop publisher specialist	26	44	73
Paralegal/legal assistant	136	220	62
Personal care/home health aid	746	1,179	58
Medical assistant	252	398	58
Social/human service assistant	268	410	53
Physician's assistant	66	98	32

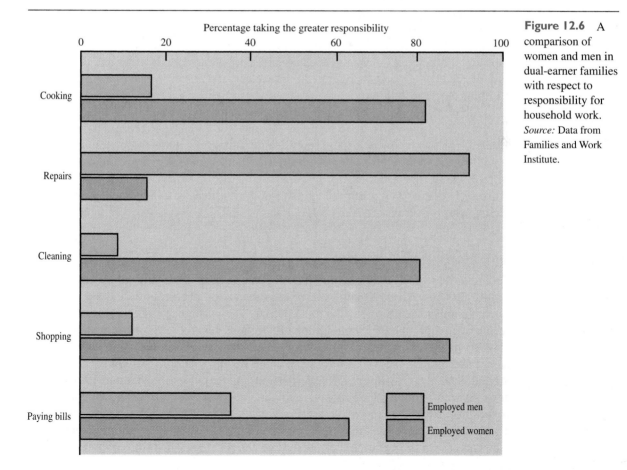

Figure 12.6 A comparison of women and men in dual-earner families with respect to responsibility for household work. *Source:* Data from Families and Work Institute.

and pay the bills. Mothers are also four times more likely than their husbands to take time away from work to care for an ill child (Families and Work Institute, 1997).

Seeking Older Workers

The Baby Boomers are aging; America will have more than 76 million people over the age of 65 by 2011. Some companies recognize the special talent, expertise, and resources of older workers. They retain those over 55 or 60 by creating incentives such as phased retirement, part-time employment, consulting, or contracting for time-limited periods on assigned projects. Some companies call such employees "ambassadors" or "consulting partners" and assign them roles appropriate for senior managers. Other companies use older employees as mentors for younger ones. Mentors serve as job coaches and help direct younger managers moving up the corporate ladder. Older workers may be a resource in easing labor shortages; indeed, they are a growing part of the workforce, as shown in figure 12.7. In 2001, more than 94 percent of workers were employed nationwide, and many job openings went unfilled. Older workers were in great demand for jobs at hourly wages in the service sector, working in fast food, retail sales, or managing inventory for small businesses. When older employees leave their primary careers, some may have to work at least part-time if they haven't saved sufficient funds for a long retirement. Retirees today can expect to live 15 to 25 years or more, yet few expect to outlive their savings—although this does occur. In addition, substantial differences in wealth exist among older white male workers and their black and female counterparts, as figure 12.8 indicates (AARP, 2001; National Academy on an Aging Society, 2000).

Retirement will be defined differently as Baby Boomers reach their sixties and seventies. First, they will be in better health and live longer than retirees a generation earlier. Secondly, many prefer to keep working rather than retire completely. In a 1998 AARP survey, nearly 80 percent of Baby Boomers said they expected to continue to work even after they had officially retired. Work allows this population to maintain a sense of worth as they reach old age and provides them with additional income and feelings of productivity (AARP, 2001).

Career Tracks for Women

Today, most women and men embark on careers upon completing their educations. Employed women have higher levels of life satisfaction, feelings of adequacy, and self-esteem compared to women who do not work. The psychological benefits of employment are greater for educated, middle-class women than for less well-educated, lower-class women (Coleman & Antonucci, 1983). Many women expect to combine both career and family responsibilities and to share the responsibility for household chores with their partner. However, such equity is difficult to achieve (see figure 12.6). Dual-career families with children rely on family members or day care centers for child care, or hire babysitters or live-in nannies. For some couples, the demands are so great that one of the partners, often the woman, moves from full- to part-time employment. Some women cease working completely only to restart a career when the children are older

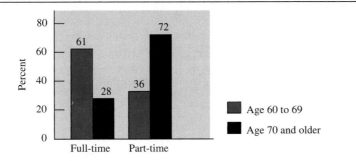

Figure 12.7
Work status of older workers, by age. *Source:* National Academy on an Aging Society analysis of data from the 1993 panel of the *Survey of Income and Program Participation* and the 1993 study of *Assets and Health Dynamics Among the Oldest Old.*

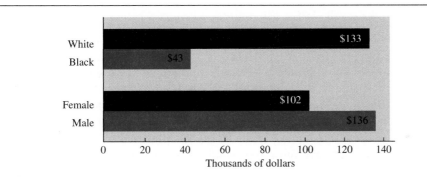

Figure 12.8 Net median household wealth for workers aged 60 and older. *Source:* National Academy on an Aging Society analysis of data from the 1993 panel of the *Survey of Income and Program Participation.*

or when additional income is needed to help with college tuition. Four distinctive career patterns for professional women have emerged (Golan, 1986): (1) the *regular career pattern*—the woman who pursued her professional training immediately after graduation and who continued to work with no or minimal interruption through the years; (2) the *interrupted career pattern*—the woman who began work in the regular pattern but interrupted her career for several years, usually for childrearing, and then went back to work full-time; (3) the *second career pattern*—the woman who started her professional training near or after the time the children left home or after a divorce; and (4) the *modified second career pattern*—the woman who started her professional training while the children were at home but old enough not to need full-time care, then started to work, possibly part-time, until the last child left home, at which time the woman shifted to a full-time career.

Women show a strong commitment to their professional careers regardless of whether they have worked full-time, part-time, or ceased working for a time and then rejoined the work force. While continuously employed professional women may eagerly anticipate retirement, the data suggest that they do not anticipate the stress of losing a significant part of their identity. Those with continuous work histories experience a profound loss of professional identity in retirement. They also lose important social contacts developed at work and miss the challenges their careers provided (Price, 2000). In fact, there are times when individuals might prefer work to being at home. Sometimes the demands of family or home are actually more stressful and chaotic than those of the workplace; or sometimes, home does not seem to offer enough challenge or interaction with other adults.

Thus far, we have discussed a number of aspects of work. Individuals must also relax. Let's now look at the nature of leisure in adulthood.

Leisure

> *I* think that there is far too much work done in the world, that immense harm is caused by the belief that work is virtuous . . .
> —Bertrand Russell (1932), "In praise of idleness"

Aristotle recognized the importance of leisure, stressing that we should not only work well but also use leisure well. In our society, the idea that leisure is the opposite of work is common. Some see leisure as wasted time and thus antithetical to the basic values of our society: work, motivation, and achievement. John Neulinger (1981), a leading investigator of leisure in the United States, poses this dilemma: Is humanity's ultimate goal a life of leisure? Clearly, most of us would disagree that leisure is what motivates us or is the measure of our life's success. Yet the puzzle remains: What is leisure? How important is it in our lives?

The word **leisure** has usually been used in four different contexts. Burrus-Bammel and Bammel (1985) discuss the *classical* view that leisure is a state of mind. Free time alone is neither a necessary nor sufficient condition for leisure; rather, it is how one chooses to define tasks and situations that is the critical variable (Neulinger, 1981). Thus, some persons define their work as leisure, while others define leisure as activities other than work. Generally, the higher one's occupational status and income, the greater the identification with work rather than leisure (Burrus-Bammel & Bammel, 1985; Neulinger, 1981). Viewing work as leisure may also be influenced by the nature of the rewards derived—intrinsic or extrinsic. Intrinsic rewards characterize leisure when the leisure activity itself is rewarding. Leisure may also depend on *social class*. Historically, only the elite were free to choose and pursue self-selected activities, while those from lower social classes were destined to constant work. Leisure may also lead to particular kinds of *activities* apart from work roles, such as recreation, entertainment, education, or relaxation. Finally, leisure may refer to the availability of *free time* (Burrus-Bammel & Bammel, 1985; Kraus, 1978). Our industrial society provides leisure time to retired workers or to employees who choose activities during nonwork hours.

Attitudes toward leisure are becoming more positive in our society (Clebone & Taylor, 1992). Among four generations of women within the same family, attitudes were sampled to investigate patterns and transmission of beliefs in a number of areas, including leisure. Overall, each succeeding generation of women displayed increasingly more positive attitudes to a variety of areas and toward leisure specifically.

The Nature of Leisure Activities

The average work week in 1900 was 71 hours, compared to today's average of 37.5 hours per week. Meeting work responsibilities is easier, too, with flex time options such as working 12-hour shifts over three consecutive days followed by four days off, working at home via computer (telework), completing projects by working weekends, and banking extra work hours to use for free time, vacations, or family priorities. Today's workers exercise considerable autonomy over their work schedules, which seem to offer more free time. However, dual obligations to career and other family members such as a child or older parent leave today's employees with *less* time to pursue personal interests, hobbies, and leisure activities than workers had 20 years ago (Families and Work Institute 1998). Riley and Riley (2000) note the difference between our current **age-differentiated society,** which puts leisure off until retirement, and an ideal age-integrated society, in which leisure, as well as work and education, are pursued regardless of age (see figure 12.9). No matter how much time they spend, people can derive considerable pleasure from both work and leisure, as Research Focus 12.3 describes.

Older adults may spend their time in traditional leisure activities such as watching television, socializing with friends, reading, pursuing hobbies such as music or gardening, playing games, exercising, and caring for others. However, analyses of how older adults spend their leisure time may not reflect how older adults would prefer to spend their time. Watching television takes a significant part of an older adult's day;

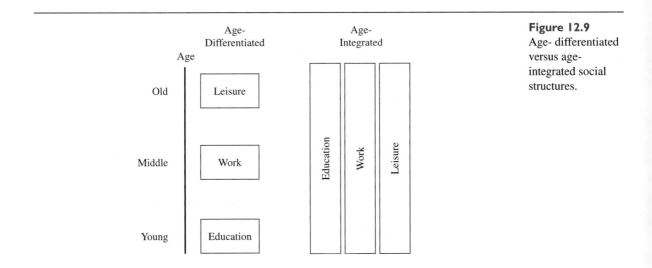

Figure 12.9
Age- differentiated versus age- integrated social structures.

The Experience of Enjoyment or Flow in Work

In *Finding Flow: The Psychology of Engagement with Everyday Life,* Mihaly Csikszentmihalyi (pronounced "CHICK-sent-me-hi-ee") tells about a letter he received from an 83-year-old man. This man enjoyed the challenges of his young adult years, but reported that the next 60 years of his life were uneventful and routine. However, in his eighties, he rediscovered how to experience exhilaration in life. He began to do things he had always wanted to do but never tried. He took up gardening, actively listening to music, and other activities that revived his enjoyment of life. According to Csikszentmihalyi, individuals are in a state of **flow** when they are doing something they really enjoy. Flow can be described as having what we want, how we feel, and what we do all on the same page. Any kind of work or leisure activity, no matter how trivial or how creative and esteemed, can produce the experience of flow. Work is onerous and resented only when it is perceived as *pointless.* Individuals work tirelessly when they really enjoy what they are doing. Working purely for external compensation becomes pointless, unsatisfactory, and eventually impossible to do.

In part, the psychology of flow is about taking steps to enhance the experience of working and leisure by reclaiming ownership of our lives. Absorption and active engagement in what we do are the keys. Csikszentmihalyi's view is based on a substantial amount of research using the Experience Sampling Method (ESM), a behavior sampling tool. Individuals use the ESM to indicate where they are, what they are doing, what they are thinking, and who they are with whenever a signal goes off at random times within two-hour segments during the day. Individuals also indicate how happy they are, how much they are concentrating, how strongly they are motivated, and their self-esteem at the time of the signal.

Research using the ESM has revealed that people are happy when they are fully engaged in what they are doing. Athletes and musicians might describe the experience of full engagement or flow as "being in the zone." Flow is reported when a person is doing his or her favorite activity—bowling, gardening, being creative at work, painting, cooking, driving an automobile, rock climbing, sailing, being with one's partner or friend. Flow is rarely reported in passive leisure activities such as watching television or wasting time. For further information, see the web page http://www.flownetwork.com

---

one study estimated that elders spend more than 40 hours a week on this leisure activity (Bell, 1992). Yet, this may not be what older adults would really prefer to be doing.

There are few realistic portrayals of older adults on television. Television presents a distorted view of aging that Palmore calls **positive ageism,** a classic form of stereotyping. Televised elderly are middle-class, white, free of major health concerns, and able to maintain an active, independent lifestyle. Positive ageism ignores the diversity of ways in which people grow old, evading the special challenges widows, minorities, or the socially isolated face. These elderly may see their own aging as largely negative when they compare their lives to what they see on television.

Americans spend much leisure time pursuing sports, either through direct participation or vicariously by attending sports events, watching televised competitions, discussing sports with friends, listening to sports radio shows, or participating in online chat rooms. Physical declines usually mean that active participation in some sports becomes difficult as adults age, but other sports can be continued for a lifetime such as golf, tennis, or running. As adults grow older, they begin to make adjustments such as reducing the intensity of their participation. For instance, rather than running five miles each day, older adults may reduce the length of their run, the frequency of the run, or build in an extra day off between runs. Research studies suggest that the more physically active people have been in young adulthood and middle age, the more likely they will continue to be involved in physical activities in old age (McAuley, Lox, & Duncan, 1993). This suggests some continuity in leisure activities across the life span.

Regular physical exercise helps maintain health during the adult years. Physical exercise benefits the body as well as the mind; people who exercise show less anxiety and stress and improved morale (Hill et. al, 1993). Exercise is also associated with improved cardiac fitness, endurance, muscle tone, flexibility, strength, cardiac output and respiratory efficiency, and even longevity, no matter at what age we begin (Blumenthal et al., 1991; Hill et al., 1993).

In one study, the ability to initiate and sustain a moderate exercise program over a five-month period was found to enhance feelings of self-efficacy and control. Adults from 45 to 65 years of age enhanced their beliefs about their personal capacity, endurance, and motivation for physical exercise. As in other research, enhanced self-efficacy leads older adults to engage in more health-promoting behaviors and to make additional commitments to exercise. Despite the short-term nature of the intervention, the participants continued to demonstrate enhanced self-efficacy perceptions for nine months following program completion (McAuley et al., 1993). Physical exercise such as walking has also been found to have beneficial effects on the symptoms of depression in older people, particularly somatic symptoms (McNeil, LeBlanc, & Joyner, 1991).

It is difficult for sedentary adults to turn over a new leaf. Most older adults prefer the leisure activities they have pursued for most of their adult lives and rarely turn to new activities. Mishra (1992) has found that men with a high level of life satisfaction are more likely to engage in active leisure pursuits and to seek out friends and join volunteer organizations. Sports activities and group participation allow older adults to escape the rigors and pressures of everyday life, even if only for a few hours per week.

Leisure at Midlife

Middle age is a time for questioning or reassessing priorities. Midlife seems to be a time when adults want more freedom and the opportunity to express their individuality.

Leisure may be a particularly important aspect of middle adulthood because of the many changes we experience at this point in development: physical changes, changes in relationships with spouse and children, changes in self-knowledge, and career changes. With college expenses ended, mortgages paid off, and women embarking on careers, couples find themselves with more spendable income, more free time, and more opportunity for leisure. For many people, midlife is the first time in their adult lives that they have the opportunity to diversify their leisure interests. In midlife, adults may select from a number of intrinsically interesting, exciting, and enjoyable leisure activities. Their participation is largely on their terms, at their pace, and at times they select. Younger adults, by contrast, must often carefully program their leisure activities to match social convention and center them around the "right" people for social and/or career success.

Adults at midlife need to start preparing both financially and psychologically for retirement. Workers by and large have not been very focused on preparing financially for their retirement. Economists find that most employees have insufficient resources to support themselves in retirement. Typically employees wait far too long to begin a retirement savings program; most begin in the mid-forties. Those that do prepare show

(1) greater self-rated financial knowledge; (2) more emotional stability and conscientiousness that leads to; (3) a future time perspective that projects them years beyond their current situation (Hershey and Mowen, 2000).

Many preretirement counseling programs that help workers prepare for retirement include leisure education. Retirees find information on financial management, pursuing hobbies, and maintaining physical health most helpful in preretirement programs (Gee & Baillie, 1999). In our society, with its strong work ethic, people need to be educated about how to use their leisure time and to begin to develop leisure pursuits in middle age. Constructive and fulfilling leisure activities developed in middle adulthood are important to this preparation. Leisure activities that can be continued at some level into retirement may help to ease the transition and role loss.

Leisure Activities in Retirement

What do older people do with their time when they retire? Studies reveal that retirees in their sixties and seventies engage in more activities than they did in their preretired years, probably because work and family responsibilities dominate adult lives. Common leisure activities retirees choose are visiting family and friends, television, reading or writing, arts and crafts, games, walking, physical exercise, gardening, organization and club participation, and travel.

Carpenter, Van Haitsma, Ruckdeschel, and Lawton (2000) asked a sample of adults over the age of 60 to anticipate the kinds of activities and personal lifestyles they would want as they grew older and became more dependent on others. In the domain of leisure activities, the adults ranked their preferences as: (1) getting around town independently; (2) displaying mementos in their residence; (3) going out to eat at restaurants; (4) having free time to relax; (5) doing household chores; (6) watching television; (7) snacking; (8) being able to stay around their own homes; and (9) drinking alcoholic beverages. These preferences reflect an assumption that leisure activities will become more restricted as future retirees become more dependent. These results were partially confirmed in a recent investigation with very old retirees. Horgas, Wilms, and Baltes (1998) studied a longitudinal sample of German elderly with an average age of 85 (from 70 to 102 years old). The authors tracked the retirees' activities and the time spent on each activity by asking for an account of "Yesterday." The elderly described the previous day in terms of mandatory activities (e.g., personal care, IADLs), discretionary activities (e.g., watching TV, reading), and time spent resting. The most common leisure activities these retirees chose in their typical 16-hour day appear in table 12.4.

Retirees spent 5 1/2 hours in obligatory activities such as bathing, dressing, shopping, cooking, and eating. They spent more than 7 hours a day in leisure activities, and rested about 3 hours. Watching television was the most frequent leisure activity (2 3/4 hours per day), with reading (1 1/2 hours per day) and socializing (1 hour per day) also common. Perhaps most surprising was the amount of time the participants spent engaged in active leisure pursuits. Another project reported on the activities of 500 community-residing elderly, 85 years of age or older. More than half of the respondents lived alone. Activities in the previous 30 days showed that one-third helped family, friends, or neighbors by shopping or doing errands;

TABLE 12.4

Description of an Older Retiree's Typical Day: Frequency and Duration of Activities

Activity	Duration	Frequency
	Mean Number of Minutes	**Mean Number of Different Activities**
Obligatory	**337**	**15.6**
Personal	150	7.8
IADL	180	7.6
Discretionary	**439**	**7.2**
Watching TV	163	1.7
Reading	93	1.7
Other leisure	116	2.3
Paid work	7	.7
Socializing	67	1.6
Resting	**177**	**2.7**

Source: Adapted from Horgas, A. L., Wilms, H. U., & Baltes, M. M. (1998). Daily life in very old age: Everyday activities as an expression of successful living. The Gerontologist 38(5), 556–568.

provided child care; helped with household chores; cared for pets; and provided meals for or visited home-bound elderly or those who were ill. Participants were in good health, had no cognitive impairments and were active, engaged, and self-sufficient—43 percent still drove a car (Silverman, 2001).

Guinn (1999) has tried to determine the kind of leisure activities that bring the most satisfaction to retirees. Generally, specific types of activities are less important than older adults' orientation and attitudes. Regardless of the specific leisure pursuit, retirees derive higher life satisfaction if they feel the activity allows them to show competence, express their unique self-determination or choice, and challenge them. Challenge in leisure activities was found by the more than 400 adults in this study to involve (1) the presentation of novel stimuli and new situations and (2) the stretching of their limits, pushing them to new heights. Retirees that experienced such leisure activities had the highest scores for life satisfaction.

Compared with a decade or two ago, older people are choosing leisure activities far more like those of people 20 years younger than themselves. Gender differences have been noted in each new cohort of retirees. Studies in the 1980s found that women tend to engage in home-centered and community-centered activities, whereas men preferred outdoor activities, sports, and travel. Retirees by 2000 reflect the first wave of women committed to balancing full-time employment and family. Career women accepted primary responsibility for the family with little free time for leisure. Retirement gives women a chance to explore personal interests, hobbies, and special interests, now that the children have been launched successfully. Having spent a lifetime balancing work and family, their own personal interests, hobbies, and social lives were put "on the back burner" (Barnett & Rivers, 1996). These women feel comfortable participating in leisure pursuits and their own personal interests. For men, retirement is a time to renew commitments to family (including spouse, children, and grandchildren) that may have suffered in favor of a career; men are less involved in family during their work careers (Szinovacz & Davey, 2001).

When asked to reflect on their lives and consider things they might wish to do differently, most retirees feel they have adequately balanced and prioritized their lives in terms of leisure as well as friendships, family, work, religion, and health. It is only in the area of education and the development of their intellect that retirees feel they would have liked to have devoted more time if they could live their lives over again (DeGenova, 1992).

Between the ages of 60 and 70, many people retire from their occupations. For a person whose job is the central focus of life, retirement can be a difficult and unwelcome experience. For others, retirement is problematic because it is the result of declining health. And still other retirees relish their new freedom and fill their lives with enjoyable leisure activities, volunteerism, and friendships. One goal for our society is to rethink when and why people retire in view of the increasing retiree/worker ratios (Human Capital Initiative, 1993).

Retirement

In the past, employees accepted retirement as an entitlement to be taken as soon as they could afford to exit the labor market. As figure 12.10 shows, labor force participation for men aged 65 and over has declined steadily during the twentieth century.

In 1900, about 60 percent of older men were working, compared to less than 20 percent in 1990. Data from the past 20 years show that the average age of retirement has dropped from 65 to 63. For women aged 65 and over, the work participation rate has consistently remained about 8 to 10 percent. Surprisingly, retirement at

Figure 12.10

Average retirement age of men from 1910 to 1999.

Source: Burtless, G., & Quinn, J.F. (2000). Retirement trends and policies to encourage work among older Americans. *Prepared for the 12th Annual Conference of the National Academy of Social Insurance, January 26–27, Washington, DC.*

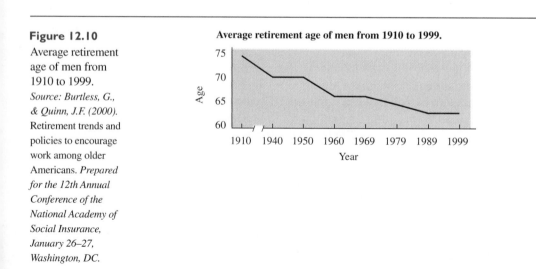

Average retirement age of men from 1910 to 1999.

early ages may not be associated with wealth. Some early retirements are forced due to poor health, accidents, or physical impairments. Averages suggest younger retirees are not as well off financially as those who retire at older ages, but of course some very wealthy young adults retire early. Those elderly who continue to work must be in good health. Both younger and older retirees in good health have high life satisfaction, active community involvement, and optimism (National Academy on Aging Society, 2000).

Experts believe that our view of retirement will change dramatically in the next decade. There are already some signs. Employees have begun to elect to remain working in their sixties and beyond (Quinn, 2000). Examine the data in figures 12.11 and 12.12 to see a surprising reversal of the expected pattern of earlier and earlier retirement. Both men and women aged 60 to 64 years have chosen to remain working in far greater numbers than predicted. There are benefits to such change. Employed older adults help bolster a tight labor pool that has been at nearly full employment. The unemployment rate declined from 10 percent in 1982 to about 5.6 percent in 2002. Second, older workers can help companies be more productive, given their expertise and experience. They can also contribute to reduced labor costs

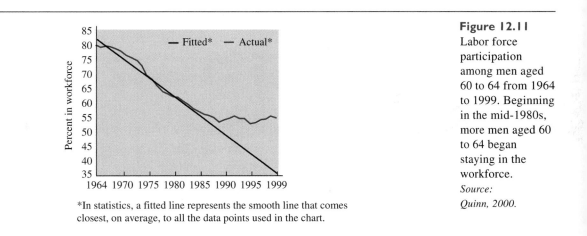

*In statistics, a fitted line represents the smooth line that comes closest, on average, to all the data points used in the chart.

Figure 12.11
Labor force participation among men aged 60 to 64 from 1964 to 1999. Beginning in the mid-1980s, more men aged 60 to 64 began staying in the workforce.
Source: Quinn, 2000.

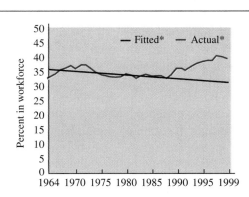

Figure 12.12
Labor force participation among women aged 60 to 64 from 1964 to 1999. Beginning in the mid-1980s, more women aged 60 to 64 began staying in the workforce.

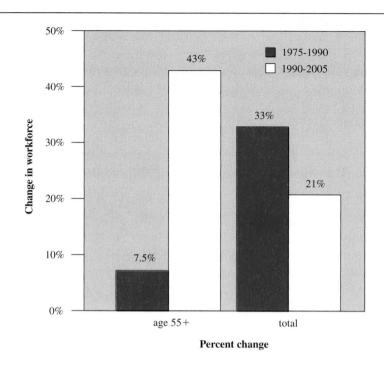

Figure 12.13 In the United States, the number of persons aged 55 or older in the workforce is expected to grow faster than the number of workers in any other age group. *Source: Bronfenbrenner et al., 1996.*

if they work part-time, since they then do not qualify for expensive benefits. Most older adults seeking employment prefer part-time work and flexible work arrangements. The increase in the number of older workers is illustrated in figure 12.13. Older workers are encouraged to remain on the job since there is no longer mandatory retirement, except in a few careers. And since part of the Social Security retirement earnings test has been eliminated, this gives incentives to older adults to pursue employment. Currently, 3 percent of the elderly over age 75 are employed. It appears that those over 70 who are still working tend to be in jobs with minimal physical demands; service, professional, and managerial occupations account for 53 percent of these jobs nationwide. However, there are significant differences by race, as figure 12.14 shows. While 17 percent of white workers over 70 worked in service careers, 59 percent of employed blacks 70 years of age and older were service workers. Service careers provide less pay and benefits than other kinds of work. These racial differences, in part, appear related to education (National Academy on Aging Society, 2000d).

Those that retire often report they were less able to keep pace with the increasing demands of the workplace or experienced subtle pressure to leave. Other retirees believe they have earned the right to relax and want to enjoy their later years while they are still healthy and active. And still others leave their jobs as soon as they can afford to retire or when they are forced out because of illness or job loss. Regardless of the circumstances, the decision is very subjective.

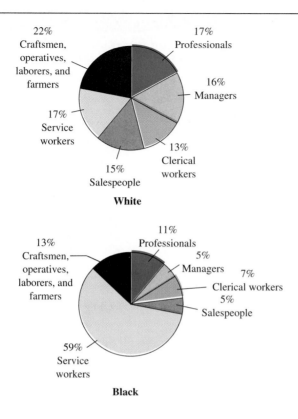

22%
Craftsmen,
operatives,
laborers, and
farmers

17%
Professionals

16%
Managers

17%
Service
workers

13%
Clerical
workers

15%
Salespeople

White

11%
Professionals

13%
Craftsmen,
operatives,
laborers, and
farmers

5%
Managers

7%
Clerical workers

5%
Salespeople

59%
Service
workers

Black

Figure 12.14
Occupational status of workers aged 70 and older, by race.
Source: National Academy on an Aging Society anaylsis of data from the 1993 study of *Assets and Health Dynamics Among the Oldest-Old.*

In the early part of this century, most individuals did not have a choice between work and retirement. The Social Security system in 1935 established benefits to workers who retired at the age of 65; most private pension plans adopted a comparable age. Only recently has the benefit age changed. The change means that each year, new participants become eligible for full support at slightly older ages. So, depending on one's birth year, full benefits may be accessible at age 65, 66, or 67 years of age, reflecting increases in life expectancy (see table 12.5). This will be a further incentive for older adults to continue their employment and one way to preserve the solvency of Social Security. Social Security was originally designed to *supplement* an employee's personal savings for retirement; however, for many retirees, Social Security Income is their only means of support. In 2001, the average benefit for a single individual retiring at age 65 was $845 each month; for couples with only one spouse who has worked, $1,410. Older widows, most of whom did not work during their lives, received $811 per month on average (Social Security Administration, 2001).

The development of a retirement option for older workers is a late-twentieth-century phenomenon. It has emerged for two basic reasons: (1) a strong industrial economy that provides sufficient funds to support the retirement of older workers, and (2) the institutionalization of retirement nationwide through public and private pension systems (Palmore et al., 1985). Today's workers will spend

TABLE 12.5

Social Security Full Retirement Age and Maximum Retirement Benefits

Year of Birth	Full Retirement Age Eligibility
1937	65
1938	65 and 2 months
1939	65 and 4 months
1940	65 and 6 months
1941	65 and 8 months
1942	65 and 10 months
1943–1954	66
1955	66 and 2 months
1956	66 and 4 months
1957	66 and 6 months
1958	66 and 8 months
1959	66 and 10 months
1960	67

Source: Health and Human Services, Social Security Agency. (2001). Think of retiring? Consider your options. Washington, DC: U.S. Government Printing Office.

nearly 10 to 15 percent of their total lives in retirement. In 1967, the Age Discrimination Employment Act (ADEA) made it federal policy to prohibit firing, forcibly retiring, or failing to hire workers strictly on the basis of age. In 1986, legislation banned mandatory retirement in all but a few specific occupations with specific qualifications. These **bona fide occupational qualifications (BFOQ)** permit mandatory retirement only when *all* workers in a specific job classification, because of age, are not able to function safely and efficiently. Such jobs include police officers, firefighters, airline pilots, and foreign service officers (the latter retire at age 60 because of "the rigors of overseas duty"). Employers may not fire older workers who have seniority and higher salaries just to save money. The courts, in vigorously opposing age discrimination in the workplace, have carefully evaluated the justifications employers make when they claim mandatory retirement in BFOQ jobs (see Research Focus 12.4). Some research investigators have questioned whether sufficient data support mandatory retirement at age 60 among airline pilots (Stuck et al., 1992). The authors of the study found no published studies relating declines in cognitive functioning to increases in age among airline pilots. They argued further that there are no validation studies to support a link between tests of cognitive ability and safety performance among experienced airline pilots; that is, there is no evidence that declines on tests of cognitive ability relate in any way to the job performance of older pilots. With mandatory retirement in our country virtually disappearing, and experts continuing to question the remaining BFOQs, older individuals will be confronted with the decision of *when* to retire rather than being forced to retire (Human Capital Initiative, 1993). In the next section, we look at factors related to retirement and the different phases people go through when they retire.

Police Officers and Mandatory Retirement: Application of the Bona Fide Occupational Qualifications

In some jobs, compelling reasons exist for mandatory or forced retirement at specific ages. Such designated jobs are called positions of bona fide occupational qualification (BFOQ). Employers must show, if challenged in court, that a BFOQ job cannot be handled safely and efficiently by older workers. Church et al. (1988) reviewed some of the challenges that have proven successful in demonstrating age discrimination (e.g., when the job was not BFOQ, and employers forced retirement to save the company money). Age discrimination may also be evidenced by selective dismissal of or failure to hire qualified older workers. The work of police officers is particularly enlightening in helping us see what the courts accept as a valid BFOQ occupation.

In one case, *Equal Employment Opportunity Commission v. Missouri State Highway Patrol* (748 F.2d 447 1984), an officer challenged the policy mandating forced retirement at age 60 for all officers. The courts ruled in favor of the highway patrol department policy based on evidence that at age 60, most individuals would not be physically able to keep up with the demanding routine of a police officer. The safety of the public might be jeopardized by continuing to employ police officers over this age. Nearly 90 percent of older police officers, according to experts, would not have the aerobic capacities needed to handle standard emergency situations officers typically encounter on the job. Further, older officers would be at a disadvantage in terms of vision, auditory response, reaction time, physical endurance, and physical strength. And any person over the age of 60 would be at far more risk for heart attack. The importance of individual differences in such global descriptions was noted in the record; that is, some 60-year-olds are physically fit and capable of meeting the demands of the job. However, the court accepted the difficulty faced by the Highway Patrol in

developing, utilizing, and interpreting a battery of tests to measure physical abilities to help them screen which of the 60-year-olds could remain on the job. The policy was justifiable, and the selected age was consistent with expert opinion on the specific behavioral demands and physical requirements for the job of a police officer.

The courts have further supported the right of police departments to maintain mandatory retirement policies at similar or even younger ages. A state police officer challenged the right of the Commonwealth of Massachusetts to force his retirement at age 50 in *Massachusetts Board of Retirement v. Murgia* (427 US 307, 1976). The Supreme Court accepted the retirement policy of Massachusetts as "rationally" based on the performance demands of the job of a police officer, despite the fact that the officer currently was in excellent health, able to handle the requirements of the job on all dimensions, and faced serious psychological and economic hardships due to forced retirement at such a young age. In a similar case, *Equal Employment Opportunity Commission v. Commonwealth of Pennsylvania* (645 F. Supp. 1545, 186), the court accepted that the demanding job of a police officer made mandatory retirement throughout the department appropriate and necessary. All officers had to be prepared to respond to crises, even though such crises materialized infrequently, if at all, for most of the police force. However, the demands that routinely emerged and presented obvious difficulties for older officers included "assisting stranded motorists in snowstorms, pushing disabled vehicles off the roadway, chasing suspects on foot, chasing suspects by vehicle at speeds of seventy to eighty miles per hour, subduing suspects, and removing victims of accidents from wrecked vehicles" (cited in Church et al., 1988, p. 102).

Factors Related to Retirement

As retirement draws near, workers engage in a *preretirement role exit process*. The closer workers are to retirement, the more they discuss it with coworkers and begin to find their jobs increasingly burdensome (Ekerdt, Kosloski, & DeViney, 2000; Ekerdt & DeViney, 1993). Almost every worker engages in some preretirement planning. Among black professionals, those who did the least planning were highly committed to their careers, had fewer financial investments, and relied on work for social interaction (Richardson & Kilty, 1992).

Several factors influence the decision to retire, including finances, health, attitude toward work, job satisfaction, and personal interests (Human Capital Initiative, 1993).

Do older adults possess the physical abilities necessary for some kinds of work?

The factors influencing retirement are unique to each individual and life situation. For many adults, a single factor is weighted more heavily or more importantly, table 12.6 indicates. Over one-half of those responding felt that only a single factor had led to their retirement, and nearly one-quarter cited only two major factors. Most retirees identify Social Security benefits and pensions as one factor in their decision to retire, but rarely are these comparable to factors such as health or the loss of a job (Henretta, Chan, & O'Rand, 1992). Based on the factors in table 12.6, a recent study investigated two types of predictors for retirement decisions: work characteristics (work demands, work environment, etc.) and nonwork characteristics (finances, health, etc.). Among almost 200 workers taking early retirement, the best predictor of employees' retirement age in the work traits category was "being tired of working," while the best predictor for nonwork characteristics was household wealth (Beehr, Glazer, Nielson, & Farmer, 2000). Among dual-wage-earner couples, the one partner's decision to retire early required the full support of the other. In a study of workers aged 55 to 59 in the Netherlands, dual-wage-earner couples revealed the breadth of discussion and involvement in the decision when one of the partners planned early retirement. Rather than being a matter of individual choice, an early retirement decision was considered a household decision with multiple effects on the entire family unit (Henkens, 2000). Early retirement is influenced by subjective appraisals of health, attitude towards work, and wealth (Ekerdt, 1998). Most experts feel that people retire when they are forced to or when they are subjectively ready to and can afford to do so. Elder and Pavalko (1993) studied the retirements of Terman's original population of gifted individuals. Nearly half reduced their work roles gradually, while only 30 percent left the workforce abruptly and completely. Regardless of how they exited their careers, only 16 percent ever worked following retirement.

Remember that some older adults, even though retired, do wish to work, perhaps on a part-time basis, or with the same company but not in the same job. Teltsch (1991) conducted a comprehensive study of workers over 50 years of age employed at three companies: Days Inn of America, Travelers Insurance Corporation, and B + Q (England's

TABLE 12.6

"Most Important" and "Important" Reasons for Retiring

Most Important Reason							Proportion Mentioning Other Reasons				
	N	%	Wanted to Retire	Health	Lost Job	Compulsory	Social Security	Care for Others	Pension	Didn't Like Job	Spouse Retired
Wanted to retire	763	47.4	—	8.0	1.6	6.3	29.5	1.8	34.1	1.7	1.6
Health	401	24.9	25.4	—	2.7	5.5	12.5	4.0	13.2	0.2	0.7
Lost job	160	9.9	9.4	6.9	—	3.1	6.2	0	2.5	0.6	0
Compulsory	139	8.6	21.6	7.9	5.0	—	17.3	3.6	14.4	0	2.7
Social Security	49	3.0	47.0	12.2	2.0	10.2	—	2.0	40.8	0	2.0
Care for others	40	2.5	17.5	5.0	0	0	2.5	—	7.5	0	2.5
Pension	29	1.8	51.7	0	3.4	0	24.1	6.9	—	0	3.4
Didn't like job	24	1.5	54.1	0	4.2	0	8.4	4.2	20.8	—	0
Spouse retired	6	0.4	83.3	0	0	0	33.3	16.6	50.0	—	0
Other	123	7.6	22.0	8.9	4.9	4.1	11.4	2.4	12.2	3.2	0
Percent citing as a reason			56.6	28.5	11.2	12.4	21.8	4.7	23.4	2.5	1.5
Percent most important responses that are *only* response		48.2	59.8	76.2	56.1	30.6	75.0	37.9	37.5	16.7	

Source: From Henretta, J. C., Chan, C. G., & O'Rand, A. M. (1992). "Retirement reason versus retirement process: Examining the reasons for retirement typology." Journal of Gerontology: Social Sciences, 47:1–7. Copyright © 1992, The Gerontological Society of America.

largest do-it-yourself hardware chain). Each company encouraged hiring older workers and shared records to evaluate the success of the hiring policies. Travelers Insurance, for example, actively recruited their own retirees to fill open positions on a short-term or part-time basis; they reported hiring 250 former employees and documented the productivity and overall success of these workers on the job. At Days Inn of America, older workers accepted job responsibilities well and had less absenteeism and lower rates of job turnover than younger employees. Older workers did take longer to learn new procedures and spent longer time on the telephone with customers seeking room reservations than younger workers. However, older workers were more successful in getting customers to commit to a room reservation. At B + Q, older workers were more familiar with home repair and construction problems. They were better able to direct customers to buy products sold at the store that were necessary to complete the project.

Phases of Retirement

Some social scientists believe that many people go through a series of phases before and during retirement. One such perspective has been developed by Robert Atchley (1983).

Atchley reports that people's attitudes toward retirement are generally positive, regardless of sex or age. The only group who seem somewhat less enthusiastic about retirement are those who would like to work but because of other factors (forced retirement, adverse labor market, financial needs, or poor health) cannot maintain their jobs.

Atchley lists seven phases of retirement: remote, near, honeymoon, disenchantment, reorientation, stability, and termination. The sequence of these phases appears in figure 12.15.

Most individuals begin work with the vague belief that they will enjoy the fruits of their labor at some point in the distant future. In this *remote phase* of retirement, most people do virtually nothing to prepare themselves for retirement. As they age toward possible retirement, they often deny that they will eventually quit working.

Only when workers reach the *near phase* do they sometimes participate in preretirement programs. Preretirement planning programs help workers make the transition to retirement and are common in American businesses. Preretirement programs help familiarize workers with the benefits and pensions they can expect to receive as well as discussing more comprehensive issues such as physical and mental health. Retirement preparation programs attract employees with higher retirement incomes; they engage in more activities after retirement and hold fewer stereotyped beliefs about retirement than workers who did not participate in preretirement programs. Of course, not all people go through all of these phases, nor do they necessarily follow them in the order indicated in the figure. How significant each phase is in the retired person's adjustment depends on subjective factors such as psychological preparedness, finances, preretirement expectations, and the ability to make decisions.

It is not unusual for people to initially feel euphoric during the *honeymoon phase* just after retirement. They may be able to do things they never had time for before, and they may derive considerable pleasure from leisure activities. However, people who are forced to retire, or who retire because they are angry about their jobs, are less likely to experience the positive aspects of this phase of retirement. The honeymoon phase eventually gives way to a routine. If the routine is satisfying, adjustment to retirement is usually successful. Those whose lifestyles did not entirely revolve around their jobs before retirement are usually able to make the retirement adjustment and develop a satisfying routine more easily than those who did not develop leisure activities during their working years.

Even individuals who initially experience retirement as a honeymoon usually feel some form of letdown or, in some cases, feelings of depression. Preretirement fantasies about the retirement years may be unrealistic. Atchley calls this the *disenchantment*

Figure 12.15
Seven phases of retirement.

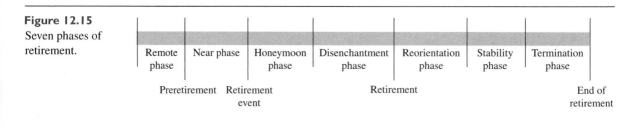

phase. For some, the disenchantment with retirement centers on the experience of loss—loss of power, prestige, status, income, and purpose. Many retired persons also experience the loss of specific work roles (and their own importance) as well as the loss of routine and of work-related friendships (Myers, 1999).

At some point, most individuals who become disenchanted with retirement begin to reason realistically about how to successfully cope with it. The major purpose of this *reorientation phase* is to explore, evaluate, and make some decisions about the type of lifestyle that will likely enhance life satisfaction during retirement. The *stability phase* of retirement is attained when individuals decide on a set of criteria for evaluating choices in retirement and how they will perform once they have made these choices. For some, this phase may occur after the honeymoon phase, whereas for others the transition is slower and more difficult.

According to Atchley, at some point the retirement role loses its significance and relevance in the eyes of the older person. The autonomy and self-sufficiency developed in the stable phase may begin to give way to dependency on others, both physically and economically. This final phase of retirement is called the *termination phase.* Because people retire at different ages and for a variety of reasons, there is no immutable timing or sequencing to the seven phases of the retirement process Atchley describes.

Some experts question the need for a phase approach (Myers, 1999). They see retirement, like other life transitions, as a lengthy process of adjustment. Ekerdt, Bosse, and Levkoff (1985), for example, evaluated the adjustment of 293 men to retirement over a three-year period. Examination of life satisfaction and leisure activities at six-month intervals revealed little support for a phase approach to retirement. The men simply took different amounts of time to examine and make choices about this new era in their lives. These authors suggest that retirement is best conceptualized as an adjustment process.

Retirement Adjustment Styles

Other experts studying retirement consider the importance of factors such as previous lifestyle or the importance of work for the individual. Hornstein and Wapner (1985), for instance, questioned whether all individuals experience retirement in the same fashion that phase theorists such as Atchley suggest. Through in-depth interviews of 24 individuals obtained one month prior to and six to eight months following retirement, Hornstein and Wapner identified four distinctive retirement styles. The first style they called *transition to old age.* Individuals who typified this style felt that retirement was a time to disengage or wind down rather than undertake new activities. One respondent reported it was too late to create new hobbies or interests: "If you've never been a gardener, you're not going to become one now." The adults in this group believed that retirement marked a transition to old age, much as rites of passage mark transitions at other periods of development. For them, retirement meant shedding pressure-filled work roles and the adoption of a restful and enjoyable lifestyle as they moved into old age.

A second style, the *new beginning,* viewed retirement as a welcome opportunity, a chance to live life on one's own terms and to have the freedom to devote time and energy to oneself. For individuals in this group, retirement was marked by feelings of renewal, revitalization, enthusiasm, and increased vigor. These individuals responded to

Retirement for some means a continuation of mentally challenging skills such as the Japanese board game Go and social participation with friends.

retirement enthusiastically: "It's a whole new life. There's so much I want to do that I almost don't know where to start." People with this style view the future positively as a time to gain control over long-overdue goals and pleasures (hobbies, interests, volunteerism, etc.) and to become the person they always wanted to be. Retirement for these individuals is a new beginning and wholly unconnected to becoming old.

A third style was that of *continuation*. For individuals who adopted this style, retirement carried no major personal impact. These adults were able to continue working, despite having retired. They either changed positions, shifted careers, or devoted greater time to a special skill, hobby, or interest. Thus, work remained a central organizer in their life structures because they voluntarily chose to continue. These individuals differentiated preretirement and retirement not by activity, but by the lessened pace and intensity of the work role. Retirement for people with this style was essentially a nonevent that signified neither an end nor a beginning.

The last retirement style, *imposed disruption,* represented a significant role loss. The people with this style saw retirement in largely negative terms (loss of work, the inability to continue achievement). For the individuals representing this style, work was a role in which they had invested significant parts of their self-identity; without work, a crucial part of their identity was terminated. Although in time these retirees develop substitute activities, an underlying sense of frustration and loss persists. Nothing seems to replace work for these individuals, and they never accept retirement well. Table 12.7 summarizes these four unique styles of adapting to retirement. Hornstein and Wapner

TABLE 12.7

Dimensions of the Four Modes of Adaptation to Retirement

Dimension	Group 1—Transition to Old Age	Group 2—New Beginning	Group 3—Continuation	Group 4—Imposed Disruption
Significance or central meaning of retirement	End of working life; time to slow down; beginning of transition to last phase of life (old age)	Beginning of new phase of life; time to live in accordance with *own* needs, not those of others	No major significance except as time to continue preretirement activities in more self-chosen way	Loss of most highly valued activity; period of frustration, lack of focus
Style of making the transition itself	Gradual disengagement from work; transition taken as very meaningful	Rapid disengagement from work; desire to plunge ahead into retirement itself	Minimal sense of transition	Abrupt break with work; "in shock," at a loss for how to proceed
Dominant emotions during the transition period	Reflectiveness; introspection	Excitement; enthusiasm; revitalization; sense of freedom	Quiet satisfaction	Depression; anger; powerlessness
Attitude toward work	Enjoyable but pressured; often frustrating in recent years	In many cases, unsatisfying; in others, satisfying, but pressured and draining	Either highly valued and satisfying or not very meaningful, no real investment	Main source of self-definition and identity; allowed time to actualize valued parts of self
Relation of retirement to sense of self	No change—continuity of self before and after	Retirement allows for birth of new part of self	No change—continuity of self before and after	Retirement represents loss of valued part of self
Orientation toward time	Past is satisfying but over; future is constricted; focus is on present	Relief that past is over; future is expanding, filled with opportunity; focus is on actualization of future in present	Future is expanding, but based on past; focus is on continuing past in present and future	Past is highly valued; future is constricted; present is "a void," focus in on maintaining past in the present

continued

TABLE 12.7 *continued*

Dimensions of the Four Modes of Adaptation to Retirement

Dimension	Group 1—Transition to Old Age	Group 2—New Beginning	Group 3—Continuation	Group 4—Imposed Disruption
Extent of change in overall life focus	Preretirement focus abandoned	Preretirement focus replaced with new focus	Preretirement focus maintained in slightly changed form	Attempt to maintain preretirement focus despite changed circumstances
General level of activity (postretirement)	Tired, less energy than before; generally passive	Highly active, energetic	Moderately active; no real change	Largely immobilized (in a psychological sense); passive, low activity
Nature of retirement goals and activities	No clear sense of direction; too late to start major new projects; mainly continuation of earlier activities and hobbies on diminished level but in satisfying way	Either clearly articulated specific goals for new projects and activities or movement toward articulation of such goals	Clearly articulated goals but no new activities; previously valued activities continue in generally same form	Some goals, but not experienced as satisfying; frustrated attempt to find activities to substitute for work; mainly involved with daily activities, hobbies in nonsatisfying way
Attitude toward old age	Inevitable next stage of life; no choice but to accept it	Denial of connection between retirement and old age; no sense of identification with "old people," "retirees"; feel younger, not older	No particular feelings about it; no clear sense of connection between retirement and old age	Feel as if others see them as old; feel they are not old and should be working; apprehension about idea that retirement is connected to old age

Source: Hornstein, G.A., & Wapner, S. Modes of experiencing and adapting to retirement. International Journal of Aging and Human Development, 21(4):302–303. Copyright © 1985, Baywood Publishing Company. Reprinted by permission.

help us see that the transition to retirement depends on a person's previous orientations to work, to life, and to self. These four styles were also reported among workers 40 years of age who were asked to anticipate their future retirement on an inventory based on Hornstein and Wapner's work. Both men and women expected their retirement to reflect a new beginning, but those who found their work personally involving expected to encounter imposed disruption upon retirement. These predictions were remarkably similar to those for retirees that had found work compelling and who were indeed dissatisfied with their current leisure activities (Gee & Baillie, 1999).

Braithwaite, Gibson, and Bosly-Craft (1986) have also examined the differential styles of adjusting to retirement. Their research focused on the elderly who really never come to terms with their retirement and continue to have problems coping. Those poorly adjusted to retirement generally showed (1) poor health, (2) negative attitudes toward retirement, (3) difficulty making transitions and adjustments throughout the life span, and/or (4) inability to confront job loss. The first two traits predicted retirements characterized by low levels of activity and involvement, physical and mental health problems, insufficient income, and low levels of life satisfaction. The latter two traits were problems for the short term only; these individuals usually made more adaptive responses to retirement over time.

Adjustment to Retirement: Activities, Lifestyles, and Volunteering

There is no evidence that one single lifestyle will bring about a successful adjustment to retirement. However, it is important that retirees feel they have choices and control over how they experience retirement. The fewer choices a person perceives, the greater the dissatisfaction with retirement. If social contacts are sought and maintained, individuals in retirement will be happy. On the other hand, some retirees derive considerable pleasure from having the freedom to spend time alone. Larson, Zuzanek, and Mannel (1985) reported that retired persons spend 50 percent of the waking day alone. Even married couples in retirement spend 40 percent of the waking day in solitude. The investigators hypothesize that the social needs of some older individuals are less intense than those of younger people, since the retirees did not view time spent alone negatively.

In contrast, satisfaction with retirement was directly proportional to the total number of activities in which men and women aged 53 to 88 were involved. Moreover, when retirees perceived such activities to be "useful," their satisfaction in retirement was enhanced. Hooker and Ventis (1984) provide support for the **busy ethic,** a theory of successful retirement Ekerdt (1986) developed. Ekerdt believes that in retirement, individuals must transfer or channel the work ethic into productive, useful activities. By keeping busy, retirees remain productive within the freedom retirement provides. Among the most common activities are community service, skill development and enhancement, profitable hobbies, and education. The retiree retains the feeling of being useful and a contributing part of society. In addition, these activities provide justification for taking time out for oneself (e.g., scheduling vacations between volunteer activities or resting after a morning of running errands for a friend). The busy ethic also provides a way to distance oneself from the effects of aging.

Evidence for the busy ethic comes from older adults committed to volunteerism. One study estimated that half of all adults participate as volunteers, providing $77.2 billion worth of services (Independent Sector, 1998, cited in Hendricks & Cutler, 2001). Some older people view volunteering as a substitute for lost work roles; others find volunteering an opportunity for social exchange. Most appreciate being needed and useful and find that volunteering gives them a way to give back to their communities (Cohen, 2000, Freedman, 2000). Hendricks and Cutler (2001) reported that membership in volunteer associations grows steadily from young adulthood to 59 years of age and then remains stable to age 85. Through memberships in volunteer organizations and other formal institutions such as religious groups, clubs, and professional associations, adults are able to remain active and productive contributors to their communities. Some volunteer efforts are coordinated nationally, such as the Retired Senior Volunteer Program or the program run by the Small Business Association, which recruits professionals with business expertise to serve as free consultants to people starting a business. Older adults through their eighties enjoy continued participation in civic responsibilities and contributing to the common good. Volunteering enhances their feelings of self-worth and competence (Atchley, 1999).

The impact of bridge employment among retirees who choose to engage in work was studied by Mor-Barak, Scharlack, Birba, and Sokolov (1992). Those who used their retirement to engage in other work roles were able to create significantly larger social networks of friends. Van-Tilburg (1992) reported that among recent retirees who did not work, the size of social networks decreased because of the loss of friends from work. However, those friendships that remained, although smaller in number, became more intense and emotionally supportive and were sustained through reciprocity.

The importance of work friends in later life is the focus of research using a *convoy model* of social support (Antonucci & Akiyama, 1991; Bosse et al., 1993; Francis, 1990). The convoy model suggests that older individuals take along with them into aging close friends, family, neighbors, and relatives who define their immediate social support network. Convoys provide one direction for the busy ethic by offering the older person an opportunity to contribute directly to the welfare of others in the social convoy, for example through reciprocity. Morgan, Schuster, and Butler (1991) found that from middle age through age 85, people report giving more instrumental and emotional support than they receive. However, black women were less likely than white women to provide instrumental support to others, but were more likely than white women to receive instrumental support in old age (Silverstein & Waite, 1993). Convoys allow coworkers to maintain their self-esteem, "provide continuity between past and present and forge an integrated continuous sense of self," and help in adapting to discontinuities in later life (Francis, 1990). Retired men appear to experience consistent levels of qualitative support from their most trusted coworkers; yet, the overall number of coworkers with whom retirees maintain contact and exchange support is quantitatively smaller in size (Bosse et al., 1993). The busy ethic provides one way for retirees to be valuable and contributing parts of society. Of course, not all retirees adhere to this ethic (see, e.g., Hornstein & Wapner, 1985), nor should they.

Adjustment to Retirement: Predictive Factors

Who adjusts best to retirement? Overall, older adults who adjust best to retirement are healthy, have adequate incomes, are active, are well educated, have extended social networks including both family and friends, and usually were more satisfied with their lives before they retired (Palmore et al., 1985). Older adults with inadequate incomes, poor health, and other stresses that occur at the same time as retirement, such as the death of a spouse or health concerns, have the most difficult time adjusting to retirement (Stull & Hatch, 1984). Women appear to be more vulnerable than men in making a positive adjustment to retirement given the economic disadvantages they experience throughout their work lives (Perkins, 1992). Increasingly, our society is also encountering women who were previously married but who enter retirement alone, economically disadvantaged, and at greater risk of adjusting poorly to retirement (Hatch, 1992). Women who cope best are those with higher levels of education and better health status (Szinovacz & Washo, 1992).

Overall, about 15 percent of older people have major difficulties adjusting to retirement. The most frequent difficulties in adjustment are found among workers whose health limitations force a retirement decision (Henretta et al., 1992; Ruchlin & Morris, 1992). In recent years, investigators have also focused their interest on retired workers from the business world, retirees who were college professors, and retired professionals who leave their employment voluntarily (Cude & Jablin, 1992; Dorfman, 1992). Among retired professors, their perception of the importance of their own scholarship, academic work, or creative effort was the most consistent predictor of their adjustment to retirement. For workers in business, however, a paradoxical finding emerged. Those workers who were most strongly committed to their work roles and identified with the company had the most difficulty in disengaging from work and accepting retirement. Cude and Jablin (1992) suggest that while organizational commitment leads to productive workers with high morale, acceptance of retirement is more difficult for such workers. These individuals may benefit most from preretirement education and preparation for retirement roles.

Theories of Retirement

We have considered three classes of retirement theories. Stage theorists such as Atchley see a predictable set of adjustments that emerge over a number of years. Other theorists focus on retirement as a negative life transition or crisis. They identify retirement with losses in occupational identity, health, self-worth, social roles, and income. Finally, a third class of theories view retirement from the perspective of continuity or positive adaptation. Retirement may reflect some role losses, but it is largely a time for self-enhancement, self-fulfillment, and leisure pursuits. Old friendships become stronger and new ones are created. Retirees become indulgent and follow personal interests and hobbies that may have been put on the back burner in favor of work and family commitments. And retirement can be a time to open new doors to travel, self-discovery, and service to the larger community. This latter view of retirement assumes retirees are in good health, emotionally stable, and financially secure. Retirement is a challenging opportunity to structure, define, and positively adapt not to a single event, but to a long-term process over the remainder of the life course.

SUMMARY

The nature of work, its role in our culture, and its impact on society have changed substantially over the past century. We are witnessing a shift from a manufacturing to a service economy and a much greater reliance on technology, for example in telecommuting. Choosing an occupation and establishing a career identity are described by Super and Ginzburg as a series of stages; Holland examines the fit between personality and vocational environment. Employers recognize the job skills and personal qualities needed for success in new hires as well as their ability to manage change. Today's workforce is different from that of 20 years ago. The labor market has become ethnically and racially diverse, more gender-balanced, and more age-integrated; this brings special challenges for productivity, supervision, and team building. Younger workers are concerned about their coworkers' performance and acceptance; those in midlife focus more on autonomy, personal challenge, significance or meaning, and flexibility in their jobs. Job satisfaction, retention, and productivity are characteristic of companies that develop policies to help employees balance the competing demands of work and family. Providing flexibility in work arrangements is critical to worker success, satisfaction, and retention. Effectively managing the stress of the dual commitment to family and work is the greatest challenge workers face. The Federal Family and Medical Leave Act recognizes the competing demands in these two spheres. Women and minorities continue to experience the disadvantage of pay inequity, though there have been advances in job opportunities for women. New fields seem particularly welcoming compared to those in which women have been traditionally underrepresented. Women follow different career tracks than men; they may follow an interrupted, second career, or modified tracks. Equity in dual-career households is difficult to achieve, although men have increased their commitment to some household responsibilities. Regardless of gender, the greater the commitment to career, the greater the difficulties in retirement. Unemployment through job loss and downsizing is becoming more common. Some older workers decide not to try and find another job. Both work withdrawal and job withdrawal have predictable antecedents: pay inequity, health concerns, work dissatisfaction, and stress.

Workers need to prepare for employment in different fields, rather than to expect a career with a single organization; some job changes are forced, while others are the result of personal choice, often in midlife. Older workers are able to remain a vital, productive, and contributing force in most work environments. They have fewer disabling injuries and show greater overall productivity than younger workers; age-related impairments in work performance are the exception rather than the rule. With mandatory retirement restricted to only a handful of special careers, and with longer life expectancy, changes in Social Security, and a desire to remain a productive part of the workforce, older men and women are reversing the trend towards earlier and earlier retirement. Organizations are creating opportunities to utilize the special expertise of older workers and recent retirees.

The dual commitments of workers to career and family means little time for leisure activities or to develop leisure interests. The consequences appear in retirement, with many older adults not quite sure of how to spend their time. Retirees enjoy visiting with friends, watching television, and participating in sports, exercise, and volunteering. Television has stereotyped portrayals of older adults (positive ageism). The very old spend time alone, resting about 3 hours per day, and have nearly 7 hours to devote to recreational and leisure interests. Atchley sees the retirement process as a series of phases, while others view it as marked by crisis. An examination of the styles of adjustment that retirees use suggests that it takes a long time to make the transition from work. Forced retirements are more difficult to manage than those that are chosen. Individual differences appear in the centrality of work to one's identity that can influence adjustment to retirement. Older adults participate in a variety of activities consistent with the busy ethic. They volunteer at a very high rate, substituting this role for their former work role. Retirees also take along a social convoy from earlier periods in their life. The social convoy is a part of their immediate social network.

REVIEW QUESTIONS

1. What are the benefits (for both employer and employee) to telecommuting?
2. Describe Super's, Ginzberg's, and Holland's theories of occupational choice.
3. What are the primary job skills and personal qualities that employers seek in new hires?
4. Outline the issues younger workers face in becoming successful in a job. What are the more important concerns in choosing a job?
5. How does age integration affect today's workforce? What are some of the ways in which older workers and retirees contribute to the workforce?
6. Outline the factors that promote and the factors that limit productivity and job satisfaction.
7. What evidence suggests that older workers are productive and successful on the job?
8. What are the antecedents to retirement? What are the psychological meanings that people attach to the experience?
9. What are the special concerns of working women, and how do these concerns influence their career track?
10. Describe the importance of leisure in adult life. What is the relationship between retirement and leisure activities? Outline the differences between leisure at midlife and in retirement.
11. Trace the historical trends in retirement, paying special attention to the role of women in the labor market.
12. List the factors that are most related to the decision to retire. Outline the three views of the retirement process: (a) stage, (b) crisis, and (c) positive adjustment.

ON THE WEB   www.mhhe.com/hoyer5

The International Telecommuting Association and Counsel provides current information on the changing work environment and on the application of telecommuting in a variety of business organizations. The site also includes reports and media releases on telework and analyses of the trend nationwide.

Mother.com has links to a number of work-related sites on issues including gender, family-work issues, state-relevant organizations, and a host of research updates.

The American Society on Aging offers information on work and aging, leisure, and retirement. There is an excellent embedded link to media reports and current research on these topics. This is a comprehensive site for the largest association in the United States for all professionals working with the elderly.

Agingstats.gov is a link to a number of government reports related to aging. It includes current information available on employment, workforce trends, and retirement issues.

The Families and Work website of the Work Life Institute in New York City has all of its current reports available for online viewing. The National Study of the Changing Workforce and the Business Work Life Study are two of particular interest; work-family issues, employee stress, gender issues, and the nature of work are some of the topics covered.

13

APPROACHING DEATH

INTRODUCTION

Montaigne the philosopher suggests that we can deprive death of its fearfulness, strangeness, and power by getting used to it and learning about it. We also deprive death of its power by being ready for it.

Approaching death raises questions about the meaning of life. Whether we turn to religion, look deep within ourselves, or read about the topic, the answers often remain unsatisfactory. Confronting death stimulates personal reflection on the meaning of life. Confronting one's own death means facing with honesty the loss of oneself.

People approaching death may be comforted by a belief that the spirit or soul is immortal. They may believe in spiritual rebirth or in reincarnation (that the spirit or soul is reborn in a different physical form). But death is the end of existence as we know it. Death makes life meaningful. As we move closer to death, we appreciate the preciousness of time and the nature of life (Shneidman, 1992). People can be anxious about death; they want to know how best to face life's final challenge. There are as many ways to approach death as there are ways to live.

In this chapter, we consider how death is defined, the sociohistorical and sociocultural contexts of death, and the issue of euthanasia, as well as the legal, medical, and ethical issues surrounding other end-of-life decisions. We describe attitudes toward death at different points in the life cycle. In our discussion of approaching death, we critically evaluate Elisabeth Kübler-Ross's theory on the stages of dying, and then outline the phases of dying E. Mansell Pattison proposes. Next, we turn to the contexts in which people die—in hospitals, at home, and with the assistance of hospice. We examine grief, including stages of grief, impediments to successful grieving, and widowhood. Finally, we detail various forms of mourning, consider the importance of death education, take a critical look at funeral rituals, and consider deaths that are especially difficult to resolve.

Definitions of Death

With advances in medical technology, the definition of death and the time of death have become increasingly precise. Death is inherently irreversible. But if a patient's life depends on life-support systems, how can we determine exactly when he or she is no longer really living?

Physicians accept brain death indicators as criteria for death. In the United States, laws define **brain death** as equivalent to cardiopulmonary death. Research Focus 13.1

Brain Death Criteria

Following are the guidelines for Brain Death proposed by Medical Consultants on the Diagnosis of Death to the President's Commission for the Study of Ethical Problems in Medicine and Biomedical and Behavioral Research.

Statement: An individual with irreversible cessation of all functions of the entire brain including the brain stem is *dead.* The determination of death must follow accepted medical standards.

1. *Cessation* is determined by evaluation of a *and* b:
   a. *Cerebral functions are absent*—Deep coma with unreceptivity and unresponsivity; confirmation by flat EEG (no electrical activity) or blood flow analysis/angiography showing no circulating blood to brain for at least ten minutes may be done to confirm evaluation.
   b. *Brainstem functions are absent*—No pupillary reflex to bright light in either eye; no extraocular movements (no eye movements when head is turned from side to side or when ear canals are irrigated with ice water); no corneal reflex when the cornea is lightly touched; no gag reflex when a tongue depressor is touched against the back of the pharynx; no cough reflex; no respiratory (apnea) reflexes. Note that some primitive spinal cord reflexes may persist after brain death.

2. *Irreversibility* of death is determined when evaluation discloses a *and* b *and* c:
   a. The cause of coma is determined and is sufficient to account for the loss of brain functions.

b. The possibility of recovery of any brain function is excluded.
   c. The cessation of all brain functions persists during a reasonable period of observation and/or trial of therapy; and confirmation of this clinical judgment, when appropriate, is made with EEG or blood flow data (cessation of blood flow for at least ten minutes).

Conditions Limiting the Reliable Application of the Above-Mentioned Criteria:

a. *Drug and metabolic conditions*—If any sedative is suspected to be present, there must be toxicology screening to identify the drug.
   b. *Hypothermia*—Temperature below 32.2 degrees C/90 degrees F.
   c. *Developmental immaturity*—Infants and young children under the age of five have increased resistance to damage and greater potential for recovery despite showing neurologic unresponsiveness for longer periods of time than adults.
   d. *Shock*—Produces significant reduction in cerebral blood flow.

From the *Journal of the American Medical Association,* November 13, 1981:2184–2186. Copyright 1981, American Medical Association.

---

outlines the criteria for brain death. *Brain death* means that all electrical activity in the brain, as determined by an electroencephalogram (EEG), has ceased for a specified period of time. If an individual's heartbeat has stopped but is restored through cardiopulmonary resuscitation (CPR), then a person who has technically died can be revived. This is because lower brain stem centers (such as the medulla) that monitor heartbeat and respiration may die somewhat later than higher brain centers. However, when the higher brain centers have been deprived of oxygen for more than five or ten minutes, the individual will either never recover mental and motor abilities or will recover them only with severe impairment.

One criticism of the criteria for determining brain death has been that the criteria are difficult to apply in practice. Rarely do patients meet all of the criteria completely. A second criticism is that applying the criteria makes it difficult for medical personnel and families to obtain organs for transplantation. By the time the criteria are met, the organs are often far too damaged for transplantation (Jonsen, 1989). Third, several specific conditions make the application of brain death criteria invalid: drug or metabolic intoxication, hypothermia, developmental immaturity, or shock.

Others have suggested that qualitative criteria should be used for defining death. For example, minimal electrical brain stem activity sufficient to control respiratory reflexes or heartbeat does not assess or describe quality of life. Questions of ethics, medical responsibility, law, and personal values make the issue of defining death of central concern to society. In at least one state, New Jersey, an exception is made for persons whose religious beliefs are in conflict with the application of the criteria for brain death.

Physicians and hospital staff have the authority to "pull the plug" and terminate life-sustaining interventions. But family members rarely discuss in advance to what extent they would like to rely on life support. Ideally, each person should have a chance to communicate with a physician regarding their status, their chances of survival, and the possibility of recovery. Because people generally, perhaps appropriately, avoid the topic, family members must judge how the person would react to the use of life-sustaining interventions. Physicians may hear a family member say, "Mom was always an active person. She would never want to be hooked to a respirator. Please unhook this machine and let her die." Should a physician act in accordance with such statements from the family? What if not all family members agree?

Gaining closure in these debates is difficult. Even when death of the entire brain occurs, there is no assurance that all brain functioning has ceased (Kolata, 1997). Despite meeting the criteria of brain death, in some individuals in rare instances brain activity includes continuation of neurohormonal functioning, cortical functioning consistent with deep coma and indexed by EEG, and brain stem functioning as revealed through evoked potentials. Halevy and Brody (1993) suggest that any further attempt to try to distinguish between life and death based on brain functioning is "biologically artificial." Kolata (1997) has focused on the growing controversy over the "exact moment of death," which more and more assumes importance as it relates to the harvesting and transplantation of organs. Some people believe that the concept of brain death was created mainly to permit the harvesting of donor organs. Brain death is not a fixed, finite event or end point, but is a process that can potentially be delayed or extended through life supports and other medical interventions. It has become as difficult to objectively define the end of life as the beginning of life.

Halevy and Brody (1993) suggest that we need to consider three questions regarding death, and three answers in response: (1) When may organs be harvested?—When current brain death criteria have been satisfied; (2) When can care be unilaterally withheld?—When there is irreversible cessation of conscious functioning; (3) When can funeral directors begin their services?—When there is no evidence of any blood flow (e.g., absence of any blood pressure). This revises the way we conceptualize life and death and avoids the impossible task of creating a single criterion and a single definition that is theoretically satisfying and speaks practically to each of the three important preceding questions. How and when we intervene is determined by the nature of the concerns that we bring to the process of death itself. Definitions of death are matters of "policy choice" or consequences: Can the respirator be disconnected? Can a spouse be permitted to remarry? Regardless of which definitions of death are applied, mistakes will be made. In what direction do we wish to make them—in the direction of protecting the dying individual and family members, or maximizing the availability of organs for the living (Kolata, 1997)?

One of the most troubling of interventions occurs when individuals have incurred severe brain damage and coma but also show signs of a "sleep-wakefulness" cycle without any detectable signs of awareness, a condition called **persistent vegetative state** or **PVS** (Multi-Society Task Force on PVS, 1994a, 1994b). Karen Ann Quinlan experienced this at age 22 when she was brought to a hospital following cardiopulmonary arrest and her breathing was supported by a respirator. She died 10 years later, never having regained consciousness, and became a classic example of the difficulty families have in removing a relative from a respirator. Although her family wished to remove her from the respirator after a number of years, the medical staff responsible for her care refused to disconnect the machine. After much legal battling, the New Jersey Supreme Court ruled that the respirator could be stopped. Similar legal issues have been raised over tube feeding for other PVS patients such as Nancy Cruzan. When her parents asked for the tube feedings to end, the U. S. Supreme Court overruled the state courts, concluding that only patients themselves can choose to withdraw from treatment. In the case of a PVS, a patient must have either written instructions or evidence regarding such interventions as tube feeding or have corroborative testimony from friends, relatives, and others regarding their wishes. It was corroborative testimony subsequent to the Supreme Court ruling that permitted the family to direct physicians to terminate life-sustaining tube feedings for Nancy Cruzan (Insel et al., 1996).

PVS is a temporary or permanent condition characterized by the absence of "any behaviorally detectable expression of self-awareness, specific recognition of external stimuli, or consistent evidence of attention or intention or learned responses" (Multi-Society Task Force on PVS, 1994a, p. 1500). Individuals are unconscious, completely unaware of self and the environment; yet they maintain a sleep-wake cycle and evidence functioning of the autonomic system in the brain stem as well as the hypothalamus. Thus, individuals in PVS show no evidence of sustained, reproducible, purposeful, or voluntary behavioral responses to visual, auditory, tactile, or noxious stimuli; show no evidence of language comprehension or expression; have bowel and bladder incontinence; and have variably preserved cranial nerve and spinal reflexes. PVS is said to be present if such conditions are present one month following acute brain trauma or nontraumatic brain injury or are evident for one month in persons with degenerative or metabolic disorders. Any recovery from a nontraumatic PVS after three months is exceedingly rare; and in cases of trauma, recovery is unlikely after 12 months. Survival for more than 10 years is highly unusual. The cost of care can be extraordinary, with the first three months of care estimated at nearly $150,000, and extended care costs at about $100,000 for each year thereafter.

The distinctions outlined in table 13.1 distinguish PVS from coma and brain death. The decision to withhold or withdraw life support is difficult when the person smiles occasionally, cries, or makes sounds. It appears that PVS diagnosis will aid decision making about when to provide or withhold life support.

TABLE 13.1

Characteristics of the Persistent Vegetative State, Coma, and Brain Death

Condition	Self-Awareness	Sleep-Wake Cycles	Motor Function	Experience of Suffering	Respiratory Function	EEG Activity	Cerebral Metabolism	Prognosis For Neurologic Recovery
Persistent vegetative state	Absent	Intact	No purposeful movement	No	Normal	Polymorphic delta or theta, sometimes slow alpha	Reduced by 50% or more	Depends on cause (acute traumatic or nontraumatic injury, degenerative or metabolic condition, or developmental malformation)
Coma	Absent	Absent	No purposeful movement	No	Depressed, variable	Polymorphic delta or theta	Reduced by 50% or more (depends on cause)	Usually recovery, persistent vegetative state, or death in 2 to 4 weeks
Brain death	Absent	Absent	None, or only reflex spinal movements	No	Absent	Absent	Absent	No recovery

Source: Multi-Society Task Force on Persistent Vegetative Stage. (1994a). Medical aspects of the persistent vegetative state. New England Journal of Medicine, 330(21): 1499–1508.

Decisions Regarding Health Care: Advance Directives

Health care decisions cannot always be made with the full, clear, and unequivocal participation of the dying person. *Advance directives* are legally binding medical treatment decisions in which adults can define which treatment options are acceptable before they are required. Advance directives include living wills, medical directives, and durable powers of attorney for health care. Even when older persons are apparently able to communicate effectively, their choice of medical treatments may be influenced by current conditions or context. Cohen-Mansfield, Droge, and Billig (1992), for example, asked 97 hospitalized elderly patients about their views regarding three different hypothetical treatments that might arise under three different conditions, such as when they were mentally intact, confused, or comatose. Most elderly respondents considered a clear set of personal values, religious beliefs, and prior experiences with the illnesses of others in determining treatment preferences. But for 12 percent of the sample, each hypothetical treatment scenario was considered uniquely; there was no underlying theme to link the responses. The way older persons view themselves and their health care choices is complex, multidimensional, and highly dependent on context.

Living Wills, Medical Directives, and Durable Powers of Attorney for Health Care

The **living will** helps ensure the right of an individual to choose whether heroic measures will be used to sustain his or her life. This document (see figure 13.1) allows an individual to declare his choice of how, when, and under what circumstances life-sustaining treatments should be provided or withheld. It establishes a contract between the person, the medical community, and close relatives. Individuals are advised to use a living will document valid in their state of residence.

A living will, in principle, is intended to make life-sustaining treatment a less complex decision for physicians and family members. In actual practice, many difficulties arise. For example, if one relative objects to the wishes outlined in a living will at the time of a medical crisis, the will may not be enforced (Choice in Dying, 1996). Another possible complication is that physicians, relatives, and the patient may be at odds regarding treatment outcomes. Sometimes the person's wishes and acceptable medical treatment standards may conflict. For instance, a patient may not want to accept tube feeding to sustain life, yet a physician may be unwilling to withhold nutrients and water, knowing the consequences will be death.

The **medical directive** (see figure 13.2) has been proposed to deal with such problems. It anticipates specific conditions not covered in detail in the living will. The medical directive, sometimes called an advance directive, empowers the individual to make decisions regarding treatment before special conditions exist, such as brain injury, stroke, or other extreme conditions, rather than leaving family members or physicians to make such choices. The courts also accept a **durable power of attorney for health care** (see figure 13.2), which specifies a surrogate decision maker (relative, physician, lawyer, or friend) to make health care choices if the individual becomes mentally incapacitated. High (1993) noted that every state has come to accept ". . .

legally binding living wills or powers of attorney for health care decision making in the event of a terminal illness or decisional incapacity necessitating surrogate decision makers" (p. 342). Yet, despite state legislation giving living wills durable powers of attorney for health care, and advance medical directives legal validity, surprisingly few older persons have actually used these options. High's (1993) review of studies showed at most an 18 percent rate among people 60 years of age and older, with usage sometimes as low as 0 to 4 percent. Even with deliberate educational intervention such as free legal assistance and lecture and discussion presentations, elderly individuals were only slightly more willing to complete a living will or advance directive. Among a sample of 293 older people (65 to 93 years old) living independently and participating in an educational intervention explaining advance directives, the overall percentage increase in use among the sample was modest—22 percent to 32 percent. Compare this with the 76 percent of this same sample who had filed a legal will directing disposition of their assets. Table 13.2 lists the reasons people give for failing to authorize an advance directive (a living will or a surrogate appointment/health care proxy) despite having participated in an educational intervention designed to increase use.

The assumption underlying living wills, durable powers of attorney for health care, and medical directives is that individual self-determination is preferable to interdependent decision making among family members. Some believe that family members' judgments are biased in choosing health care options for relatives. They suggest that families will make poor decisions, be influenced by self-interest, or be unwilling to carry out the wishes of loved ones (Zweibel & Cassel, 1989). The illusion is that it is the individual's self-determination at work when a family decision is made. Outside agents are assumed to be capable of making judgments closest to those the individual would have made. Is the converse true, however? Are the elderly less well served when family members participate in health care decision making (High, 1991)?

The benefits of family-shared decision making in advance regarding medical decisions are that the process (1) is empowering to the older person, (2) alleviates emotional

TABLE 13.2

Reasons for Not Executing an Advance Directive

Living Will (n = 151)	n	(%)
Deference to others and putting it off	75	50%
Barriers and difficulties in getting documents executed	30	20
Accept/rely on present arrangements or state of affairs	27	18
Other reasons	19	12

Surrogate Appointment or Health-Care Proxy (n = 63)		
Deference to others and putting it off	31	49
Barriers and difficulties in getting documents executed	7	11
Accept/rely on present arrangements or state of affairs	15	24
Other reasons	10	16

Source: High, D. M. Advance directives and the elderly: A study of intervention strategies to increase use. *The Gerontologist, 33*:342–349. Copyright © 1993, The Gerontological Society of America.

FLORIDA LIVING WILL

Declaration made this _____ day of _____, _____,
(day) *(month)* *(year)*
I, _____, willfully
and voluntarily make known my desire that my dying not be artificially prolonged under the circumstances set forth below, and I do hereby declare that:

If at any time I am incapacitated and

_____ I have a terminal condition, or
_____ I have an end-stage condition, or
_____ I am in a persistent vegetative state

and if my attending or treating physician and another consulting physician have determined that there is no reasonable medical probability of my recovery from such condition, I direct that life-prolonging procedures be withheld or withdrawn when the application of such procedures would serve only to prolong artificially the process of dying, and that I be permitted to die naturally with only the administration of medication or the performance of any medical procedure deemed necessary to provide me with comfort care or to alleviate pain.

It is my intention that this declaration be honored by my family and physician as the final expression of my legal right to refuse medical or surgical treatment and to accept the consequences for such refusal.

In the event that I have been determined to be unable to provide express and informed consent regarding the withholding, withdrawal, or continuation of life-prolonging procedures, I wish to designate, as my surrogate to carry out the provisions of this declaration:

Name: _____
Address: _____
_____ Zip Code: _____
Phone: _____

INSTRUCTIONS

PRINT THE DATE
PRINT YOUR NAME

PLEASE INITIAL EACH THAT APPLIES

PRINT THE NAME, HOME ADDRESS AND TELEPHONE NUMBER OF YOUR SURROGATE

© 2000
PARTNERSHIP FOR CARING, INC.

I wish to designate the following person as my alternate surrogate, to carry out the provisions of this declaration should my surrogate be unwilling or unable to act on my behalf:

Name: _____
Address: _____
_____ Zip Code: _____
Phone: _____

Additional instructions (optional):

I understand the full import of this declaration, and I am emotionally and mentally competent to make this declaration.

Signed: _____

Witness 1:
Signed: _____
Address: _____

Witness 2:
Signed: _____
Address: _____

PRINT NAME, HOME ADDRESS AND TELEPHONE NUMBER OF YOUR ALTERNATE SURROGATE

ADD PERSONAL INSTRUCTIONS (IF ANY)

SIGN THE DOCUMENT

WITNESSING PROCEDURE

TWO WITNESSES MUST SIGN AND PRINT THEIR ADDRESSES

© 2000
PARTNERSHIP FOR CARING, INC.

Courtesy of **Partnership for Caring, Inc.**
1035 30th Street, NW Washington, DC 20007 800-989-9455   6/00

Figure 13.1a Florida living will.

I further affirm that this designation is not being made as a condition of treatment or admission to a health care facility. I will notify and send a copy of this document to the following persons other than my surrogate, so they may know who my surrogate is:

PRINT THE NAMES AND ADDRESSES OF THOSE WHO YOU WANT TO KEEP COPIES OF THIS DOCUMENT

Name: _____

Address: _____

Name: _____

Address: _____

SIGN AND DATE THE DOCUMENT

Signed: _____

Date: _____

WITNESSING PROCEDURE

TWO WITNESSES MUST SIGN AND PRINT THEIR ADDRESSES

Witness 1:

Signed: _____

Address: _____

Witness 2:

Signed: _____

Address: _____

© 2000
PARTNERSHIP FOR CARING, INC.

Courtesy of **Partnership for Caring, Inc.**   10/99
1035 30th Street, NW Washington, DC 20007 800-989-9455

INSTRUCTIONS

FLORIDA DESIGNATION OF HEALTH CARE SURROGATE

PRINT YOUR NAME

Name: _____

(Last)   *(First)*   *(Middle Initial)*

In the event that I have been determined to be incapacitated to provide informed consent for medical treatment and surgical and diagnostic procedures, I wish to designate as my surrogate for health care decisions:

PRINT THE NAME, HOME ADDRESS AND TELEPHONE NUMBER OF YOUR SURROGATE

Name: _____

Address: _____

_____ Zip Code: _____

Phone: _____

If my surrogate is unwilling or unable to perform his or her duties, I wish to designate as my alternate surrogate:

PRINT THE NAME, HOME ADDRESS AND TELEPHONE NUMBER OF YOUR ALTERNATE SURROGATE

Name: _____

Address: _____

_____ Zip Code: _____

Phone: _____

I fully understand that this designation will permit my designee to make health care decisions and to provide, withhold, or withdraw consent on my behalf; to apply for public benefits to defray the cost of health care; and to authorize my admission to or transfer from a health care facility.

ADD PERSONAL INSTRUCTIONS (IF ANY)

Additional instructions (optional): _____

© 2000
PARTNERSHIP FOR CARING, INC.

Figure 13.1b Florida destination of health care surrogate.

MY MEDICAL DIRECTIVE

This Medical Directive shall stand as a guide to my wishes regarding medical treatments in the event that illness should make me unable to communicate them directly. I make this Directive, being 18 years or more of age, of sound mind, and appreciating the consequences of my decisions.

SITUATION A

If I am in a coma or a persistent vegetative state and, in the opinion of my physician and two consultants, have no known hope of regaining awareness and higher mental functions no matter what is done, then my goals and specific wishes — if medically reasonable — for this and any additional illness would be:

- ☐ prolong life; treat everything
- ☐ attempt to cure, but reevaluate often
- ☐ limit to less invasive and less burdensome interventions
- ☐ provide comfort care only
- ☐ other *(please specify)*: _____

Please check appropriate boxes:

	I want	I want treatment tried. If no clear improvement, stop.	I am undecided	I do not want
1. Cardiopulmonary resuscitation (chest compressions, drugs, electric shocks, and artificial breathing aimed at reviving a person who is on the point of dying).		*Not applicable*		
2. Major surgery (for example, removing the gallbladder or part of the colon).		*Not applicable*		
3. Mechanical breathing (respiration by machine, through a tube in the throat).				
4. Dialysis (cleaning the blood by machine or by fluid passed through the belly).				
5. Blood transfusions or blood products.		*Not applicable*		
6. Artificial nutrition and hydration (given through a tube in a vein or in the stomach).		*Not applicable*		
7. Simple diagnostic tests (for example, blood tests or x-rays).		*Not applicable*		
8. Antibiotics (drugs used to fight infection).		*Not applicable*		
9. Pain medications, even if they dull consciousness and indirectly shorten my life.		*Not applicable*		

SITUATION F

If I am in my current state of health (describe briefly): _____

and then have an illness that, in the opinion of my physician and two consultants, is life threatening but reversible, and I am temporarily unable to make decisions, then my goals and specific wishes — if medically reasonable — would be:

- ☐ prolong life; treat everything
- ☐ attempt to cure, but reevaluate often
- ☐ limit to less invasive and less burdensome interventions
- ☐ provide comfort care only
- ☐ other *(please specify)*: _____

Please check appropriate boxes:

	I want	I want treatment tried if no clear improvement, stop.	I am undecided	I do not want
1. Cardiopulmonary resuscitation (chest compressions, drugs, electric shocks, and artificial breathing aimed at reviving a person who is on the point of dying).				
2. Major surgery (for example, removing the gallbladder or part of the colon).		*Not applicable*		
3. Mechanical breathing (respiration by machine, through a tube in the throat).		*Not applicable*		
4. Dialysis (cleaning the blood by machine or by fluid passed through the belly).				
5. Blood transfusions or blood products.				
6. Artificial nutrition and hydration (given through a tube in a vein or in the stomach).		*Not applicable*		
7. Simple diagnostic tests (for example, blood tests or x-rays).		*Not applicable*		
8. Antibiotics (drugs used to fight infection).		*Not applicable*		
9. Pain medications, even if they dull consciousness and indirectly shorten my life.		*Not applicable*		

Figure 13.2 Medical directive (excerpts from the medical brochure).

522

ORGAN DONATION

—I hereby make this anatomical gift, to take effect after my death:

I give
- [ ] my body
- [ ] any needed organs or parts
- [ ] the following parts _____

to
- [ ] the following person or institution _____
- [ ] the physician in attendance at my death
- [ ] the hospital in which I die
- [ ] the following physician, hospital storage bank, or other medical institution: _____

for
- [ ] any purpose authorized by law
- [ ] therapy of another person
- [ ] medical education
- [ ] transplantation
- [ ] research

—I do not wish to make any anatomical gift from my body.

HEALTH CARE PROXY

I appoint as my proxy decision-maker(s):

_____
Name and Address

and *(optional)* _____
Name and Address

I direct my proxy to make health-care decisions based on his/her assessment of my personal wishes. If my personal desires are unknown, my proxy is to make health-care decisions based on his/her best guess as to my wishes. My proxy shall have the authority to make all health-care decisions for me, including decisions about life-sustaining treatment, if I am unable to make them myself. My proxy's authority becomes effective if my attending physician determines in writing that I lack the capacity to make or to communicate health-care decisions. My proxy is then to have the same authority to make health-care decisions as I would if I had the capacity to make them, EXCEPT *(list the limitations, if any, you wish to place on your proxy's authority)*.

I wish my written preference to be applied as exactly as possible / with flexibility according to my proxy's judgment. *(Delete as appropriate)*

Should there be any disagreement between the wishes I have indicated in this document and the decisions favored by my above-named proxy, I wish my proxy to have authority over my written statements / I wish my written statements to bind my proxy. *(Delete as appropriate)*

If I have appointed more than one proxy and there is disagreement between their wishes, _____ shall have final authority.

Signed: _____   _____
      Signature   Printed Name

      _____
      Address   Date

Witness: _____   _____
      Signature   Printed Name

      _____
      Address   Date

Witness: _____   _____
      Signature   Printed Name

      _____
      Address   Date

Physician *(optional)*:

I am _____ 's physician. I have seen this advance care document and have had an opportunity to discuss his/her preferences regarding medical interventions at the end of life. If _____ becomes incompetent, I understand that it is my duty to interpret and implement the preferences contained in this document in order to fulfill his/her wishes.

Signed: _____   _____
      Signature   Printed Name

      _____
      Address   Date

Revised 7/95

Figure 13.2 (continued)

strain on both the older individual and the family members, and (3) is helpful to those having to make substituted judgments about health care choices for the older person. Legal remedies, based on property law, could be helpful in mediating those special instances in which family members disagree about health care decisions, when the possibility of coercion has arisen in making treatment choices, or when a conflict of interest arises. Most family relationships permit intimate moral relationships to flourish, and genuine care and concern are communicated in open dialogue (Kapp, 1991; Lambert, Gibson, & Nathanson, 1990). "The family can be presumed to be the best decision maker, not only regarding knowledge about and concern for the relative but because family members embody the social nexus of values shared by the family unit" (High, 1991, p. 617). It is through such dialogue that society will ensure that older individuals preserve their autonomy in governing their health care choices.

DNR Orders

Do not resuscitate (DNR) orders in the charts of hospitalized patients specifically direct physicians and hospital staff to not initiate resuscitation measures (such as CPR, electric shock, medication injected into the heart, open chest massage, or tracheotomy) when breathing or heartbeat has stopped. Similar DNR orders apply to nursing home residents who will not be transferred to a hospital for these procedures. Hospital and nursing home residents themselves can request and consent to a DNR order prior to or during hospitalization either orally (provided two witnesses are present, one of whom is a physician) or in writing (as long as two adults are present to sign as witnesses). Limits on DNR orders can also be established in advance (e.g., do not resuscitate if a terminal illness or irreversible coma exists). A physician given a DNR order has three choices: (1) enter the order as given in the chart and follow the specifications; (2) transfer a patient requesting DNR orders to another physician; or (3) bring the DNR order to the attention of a mediation panel in the hospital or nursing home (mediation panels cannot overrule a patient's request for a DNR). For patients who are incapacitated or mentally unable to elect a DNR decision, proxy decision makers may be appointed. The proxy decision must represent the patient's own wishes, religious and moral beliefs, or best interests. For those with no one to serve as proxy, a DNR decision may be made if two physicians agree that resuscitation would be medically futile. DNR orders may be changed by informing the relevant health care staff of the changes using appropriate notification procedures (New York State Department of Health, 2001).

Compliance with DNR orders, durable powers of attorney for health care, and advance medical directives is not a simple matter for hospitals, nursing homes, and families. Hansot (1996) has documented the difficulty in transmitting this information from one hospital division to another (e.g., from routine care to intensive care or emergency care). Unless medical personnel are directed otherwise by family, hospital staff, or patients, aggressive actions will be taken to save the life of an individual using heroic measures or artificial means. When DNR orders identifying a patient's right to prevent heroic measures are placed in a hospital computer, this does not ensure that hospital personnel will consult the file in an emergency situation. And a family physician may not be present at the time of hospital admission, particularly during an emergency, to notify medical personnel of a patient's wishes regarding advance directives, especially if a patient enters an unfamiliar hospital.

Most physicians and nurses have not been trained in the clinical aspects of withdrawing life support systems (Brody, Campbell, Faber-Langendoen, & Ogle, 1997; SUPPORT, 1995). When faced with a decision to implement what they know how to do (intensive intervention and life support) or undertake what they have not received training to do (withdrawal of life support), physicians and nurses will choose aggressive treatments designed to prolong life. Few guidelines are available for health care professionals and family members regarding withdrawal of life supports. Brody et al. (1997) have focused attention on compassionate care and the identification of the strategic goals of both the patient and family members. Strategic goals include promoting the comfort of the patient, preserving the patient's ability to communicate, withdrawal of burdensome interventions, and permitting death to occur. The most common treatments that appear to cause patient discomfort when they are withdrawn are mechanical respirators/ventilators, kidney dialysis, artificial nutrition, and hydration. Physicians appear more prone to withdraw costly, scarce, or invasive interventions or ones that lead rapidly to death rather than ones that have been in place for a considerable time or are less costly (Asch & Christakis, 1996; Brody et al., 1997). Not all patients die as soon as mechanical respirators are withdrawn; the process can be quick (in minutes) or quite lengthy (days, months, or years). The strategic goal of patient comfort requires frequent monitoring and the administration of drugs, including morphine and other opiates when needed. Artificial hydration and nutrition intervention have no unique status as life-sustaining treatments since death after withdrawal is usually comfortable. By encouraging training in the methods used to eliminate patient discomfort, health care professionals can become more compassionate and offer more legitimate and palatable choices to the dying patient and the family.

Organ Donation

The struggle that patients, families, and physicians face in deciding when and how death arrives becomes quite clear in the case of organ donation. Nearly 75,000 Americans wait for transplants, and 8 to 10 persons die each day still waiting (see figure 13.3). Those awaiting transplants are placed on a waiting list with priorities established based on specific criteria such as length of time on the list, urgency, and so on. The number of deaths each year that result in transplantable organs reaches only 12,000 to 15,000. Although nearly 70 percent of adults in the United States claim that upon their deaths they would be willing to donate their organs, less than one-third of those eligible to donate organs do so. Usually the failure to make organ donation is the result of family members' lack of awareness of or unwillingness to comply with the wishes of the deceased (Monmaney & MacIver, 1995). Organ transplantation requires the utmost teamwork following the consent decision, and time is critical to maintain the viability of harvested organs. Doctors have only three to five hours to transplant a heart, up to 12 hours to transplant a liver, and 24 to 48 hours for kidney transplantation, which may help explain why the kidney is the most commonly transplanted organ (Monmaney & MacIver, 1995). After national centers across the United States match donor to recipient, harvested hearts and other organs are rushed to waiting recipients by courier.

Figure 13.3 The nation's transplant waiting list has grown much faster than the number of transplants performed. As of April 2001, more than 75,000 patients nationwide are waiting for an organ transplant. *Source:* United Network for Organ Sharing

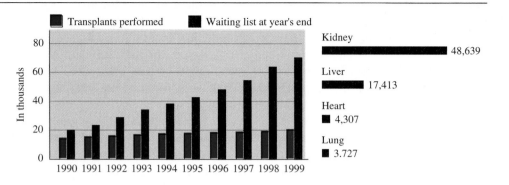

Organ donor cards or signatures permit organ donation under the Anatomical Gift Act. In the event of an automobile accident, driver's licenses in 18 states indicate the license holder's desire to donate organs for transplantation. Organ donor cards allow individuals to identify which specific organs or tissues (heart valves, corneas, kidneys, lungs, liver) may be donated. Cards are available through the United Network for Organ Sharing, a private, nonprofit corporation with a federal government contract to provide a registry of people needing transplants and a national distribution and procurement system. The legal status of donor cards has been questioned, however, and in practice doctors consult with family members about organ donation regardless of signatures on cards and licenses. Families also actively participate in life-support decisions that are designed to give maximum time to medical personnel to best find a match and a recipient for the donor organs and tissues to be harvested.

As long as there has been no element of force in the decision, ethicists support an individual's decision to control the disposition of their organs since it preserves a person's autonomy even after death. Traditional Jewish, Buddhist, and Muslim religious practices prohibit the mutilation, desecration, or dissection of the dead. Recent developments in Jewish law suggest that organ removal expressly for transplantation is permissible when the donated organ will save the life of another. Similarly, Buddhist and Islamic practices permit organ donation if the explicit consent of the donor has been obtained prior to death (Kimura, 1995; Sachedina, 1995). Japanese cultural practices permit transplantation of kidneys and corneas, but rarely of other organs.

Does each person in our society have the right to obtain an organ transplant, and does our society have an obligation to provide this option to all who are in need? On the one hand, it would seem responsible for a society to restrict the number of transplants to efficiently control the health care costs, rationing services and the available organs. On the other hand, it is difficult to determine who should then receive such scarce resources. Should younger candidates have higher priority because of the greater number of productive years they have left to live? Should older persons receive less-than-perfect transplantable organs, while younger persons receive organs without defects or damage? Should those who can afford to pay for some of the cost of the transplant be granted priority over those who cannot?

Euthanasia

Euthanasia, meaning "the good death," is often referred to in the popular press as "mercy killing." **Active euthanasia** refers to deliberate, intentional action such as the injection of a deadly drug or the administration of a drug overdose to hasten the death of an individual with a terminal illness, a massive disability, or an intensely painful disease. **Passive euthanasia** refers to death induced by the failure to act or the withdrawal of a life-sustaining medication or machine. Physicians, in taking the Hippocratic Oath, have vowed to act "to benefit the sick" and to "do no harm," choosing treatments believed "most helpful to patients." Any form of euthanasia is antithetical to these principles, although some ethicists have argued that there is a difference between killing someone (taking deliberate action—an act of commission) and allowing them to die (failing to act—an act of omission). Similarly, it is illegal for laypersons to engage in euthanasia in every country worldwide, although the Netherlands exempts a few specific conditions.

Are there cases in which euthanasia is justified? Could families be spared agonizing decisions, painful memories, guilt, and considerable financial expense if euthanasia were legal? Should hospitals and the health care system use increasingly scarce resources and expensive nursing and medical care for patients with little or no hope of recovery? These decisions are matters of concern for society as a whole, as well as for individual patients, physicians, and family members (see Research Focus 13.2).

Research Focus 13.2

Is There a Duty to Die?

Because of the tremendous advances in medical technology, many people today survive into old age with serious conditions that would have led to their deaths in earlier generations. In hospitals and nursing homes, for example, those with severe dementia survive for years, even when they have virtually no conscious awareness or any serious quality of life. Should society provide essential medical support to prolong life, or do citizens have a duty to die? One group of ethicists argues for the latter, based on two principles: (1) *beneficence:* people have a duty to limit the manner and the degree to which they are a burden to others; and (2) *justice:* one person may not claim an unfair share of scarce, costly health care resources that might be distributed equitably to improve the lives of more people. The basis for making some health care decisions today is thus to minimize burden and to provide a fair allocation of resources. For example, a family member near the end of life may elect a DNR option to protect her loved ones from the financial and emotional pain of an extended life ending. If money is not allocated for personalized special care, it might help other family members to reach important life goals (purchasing a home or attending college or graduate school). Health maintenance organizations (HMOs) decide each year how to allocate benefits to members, given a fixed amount of money available to spend. Providing less costly care for many HMO members may mean not being able to support expensive care for any single member. Society is not yet ready to bring this issue to a vote, and there are strong arguments against the duty to die. First, there are no definitions or guidelines to govern when or how this decision should be made. If you are mentally or physically disabled, or very elderly, should someone else have the right to decide you have a duty to die? Second, there are no methods for enforcing the decision. Third, even when we save resources, there is no guarantee that health care will be improved for more people because we have no method for redistributing the health care savings.

Source: Kissell, J. L. (2000). Grandma, the GNP, and the duty to die. In J. M. Humber & R. F. Almeder (Eds.), *Is there a duty to die? Biomedical Ethics Review,* pp. 191–204. Totowa, NJ: Humana Press.

In complex situations, the physician, the ill person, and family members share moral responsibility for treatment decisions. However, it is important to consider the types of decisions made and the degree of responsibility different individuals accept. For example, when a decision is made to *withdraw* a life-sustaining treatment such as tube feeding, and the outcome will be death, the moral responsibility is typically shared among family members. But when a decision is made to *withhold* treatment that could delay a person's death, such as through DNR orders, the moral responsibility appears to lie with the person him or herself. Slomka (1992) raises the possibility that the assignment of moral responsibility in either withdrawing or withholding treatment is designed to give all participants an illusion of choice; that is, physicians, family members, and older persons near death negotiate a set of meanings about impending death, share moral responsibility differentially for the failure of medicine, and eventually are able to accept the death.

Physician-Assisted Suicide

Physician-assisted suicide is a form of euthanasia in which physicians end the lives of patients who request a lethal injection or medication. If we value cooperative responsibility for patient-physician decisions and the rights of patients to exercise self-determination, then why do so many of us view physician-assisted suicide and voluntary euthanasia as morally troubling? Is the only difference between euthanasia and physician-assisted suicide determined by whether physician or patient actually administers the lethal drug?

In 2001, the Netherlands broadened its already liberal euthanasia law to permit physician-assisted suicide under special guidelines (Deutsch, 2001). There must be an enduring doctor-patient relationship, and patients must be legal residents of the Netherlands. Doctors may assist with patient-requested suicide: (1) when the patient's suffering is deemed "irremediable and unbearable"; (2) when a second physician agrees after completing an independent evaluation; (3) when the patient is aware of all other available options; and (4) when the patient is of sound mind. Such cases presuppose that patients' requests are voluntary, persistent, and without undue influence; in fact, physicians are prohibited from suggesting the suicide option to patients. If these criteria have not been met, a regional review committee can recommend criminal prosecution. Under the new law, doctors could also honor the wishes of those with terminal diseases to end their lives when they reach a specific point, such as an advanced stage of cancer. For children between 12 and 16, parental consent is required under this new law; teens 17 and older can decide for themselves, but they must provide evidence that they have discussed their decision with their parents. The Dutch have been pioneers in the decriminalization of social practices and a model for some in the United States. Oregon, for example, since 1997 has legalized certain types of assisted suicide under the Death with Dignity Act (Richburg, 2000).

Dr. Jack Kevorkian, a Michigan pathologist, has been an advocate of physician-assisted suicide. He created a device to permit patients to administer an intravenous infusion of an anesthetic (thiopental), followed one minute later by a lethal concentration of potassium chloride (salt) that quickly causes a deadly heart rhythm (Basta, 1996). He has assisted people who were facing terminal cancer, amyotrophic lateral sclerosis

(ALS) or Lou Gehrig's disease, multiple sclerosis, Alzheimer's disease, and severe pain to commit suicide (Basta, 1996). Kevorkian believes that helping others commit suicide is warranted in order to meet patients' goals of self-determination and avoidance of future suffering. Despite creating his device so that the patient triggers the sequence of drugs leading to death, Kevorkian was charged with aiding a patient's suicide, had his license to practice medicine revoked, and was imprisoned. Letting a hopelessly ill patient die, he believes, is humane and defensible; however, there is a significant difference between "letting" a patient die and "making" a patient die. In 1997, the United States Supreme Court ruled that states have the right to ban physician-assisted suicide, although they did not establish a federal ban on the practice in all states. In a unanimous opinion, they found no constitutional right to physician-assisted suicide. Each of the nine justices defended the ban differently, leaving room for legal challenges.

Brock (1989) noted that there are few conditions patients face that cause such hardship and pain that suicide becomes the only alternative. Many newer drugs alleviate pain, and innovative treatments can provide relief to patients with chronic conditions such as terminal cancer. Kevorkian has argued that physician-assisted suicide permits a more peaceful, humane, and dignified death. Those opposed to physician-assisted suicide fear the loss of public trust in the medical community's commitment to fight disease and death, as well as possible undue influence from family members or doctors, and the possibility that depressed or pain-ridden patients may seek suicide when they could be successfully treated for depression or chronic pain. For many years, ethicists and physicians have raised the "slippery slope" argument, suggesting that once society endorses even a few cases of physician-assisted suicide, it will become easier and easier to permit other instances that are far removed from the specialized cases the practice was initially permitted to address. The positive and negative consequences of physician-assisted suicide will be debated for some time.

A final issue in the debate over physician-assisted suicide is the role of the physician's intent. Any direct intentional action designed to assist a person to commit suicide is morally unacceptable to many; however, a physician can take actions that indirectly help to hasten death and may be morally justifiable. The best example of this difference is seen in physicians' administration of morphine to patients in the final stages of cancer. The specific levels of morphine must be increased systematically to alleviate severe pain. Physicians recognize that an inherent, but remote, danger in using higher doses of morphine is that the patient's respiration may be seriously depressed (Brody et al., 1997). The very drug administered to alleviate pain may therefore actually accelerate a patient's death by suppressing respiration. A physician can foresee that the patient may experience an earlier death due to respiratory depression, yet still provide convincing evidence that this was not the goal.

Compare the administration of morphine to a terminal cancer patient on the one hand and Kevorkian's assistance in administering potassium chloride on the other hand. Are there differences? Do the physicians in both cases intend to alleviate a patient's suffering? Is there a difference in intent? The answers are not clear or easily reached. Will you be able to choose a painless death at home surrounded by friends and family, or will death come as you lie in a high-tech hospital connected to tubes, pumps, and machines (Basta, 1996)? How much choice should you have over when and how you die?

Sociohistorical and Sociocultural Views of Death

> *I don't want to achieve immortality through my work. I want to achieve it through not dying.*
> —Woody Allen

In earlier times, death occurred with roughly equal probability among young infants, young children, adolescents, young adults, and older individuals. As we have advanced in the treatment of disease and improved the likelihood that infants will reach adulthood and old age, growing old has acquired a parallel meaning: Aging means drawing close to death. Over the years, death has become closely associated with old age, although with the increase in AIDS-related deaths throughout the life span, including infancy and childhood, our society is beginning to recognize that death is not exclusively an old-age phenomenon.

Attitudes toward Death

The ancient Greeks faced death as they faced life—openly and directly. To live a full life and die with glory was the prevailing objective among the Greeks. Currently, our society largely avoids or denies death. Such denial can take many forms:

(1) the tendency of the funeral industry to gloss over death and to fashion lifelike qualities in the physical appearance of the dead; (2) the adoption of euphemistic language for death, such as "passing on," "passing away," and "no longer with us"; (3) the persistent search for the fountain of youth in cosmetics, plastic surgery, vitamins, and exercise; (4) the rejection and isolation of the aged, who remind us of the inevitability of death; (5) the appealing concept of a pleasant and rewarding afterlife, suggesting we are immortal; (6) emphasis by the medical community on prolonging biological life, even among patients whose chances of recovery or quality lifestyle are nil; (7) the failure to discuss emotional reactions to death with our children; and (8) the attempt to cover up emotions at funerals and afterward as mourners adopt a "stiff upper lip" or are encouraged to "get over it quickly and get on with life."

Death is rarely discussed openly in our society and is not part of traditional family life or schooling. Americans are better prepared to operate a VCR than they are prepared for death (Cloud, 2000). Is it any wonder that our society is uncomfortable with death? Grief, the natural human response to loss, is almost considered an illness (Silverman, 2000b). Loss brings about change in our lives and overwhelming emotion. American society attempts to hurry people through death and mourning, providing "support" to help them "get over it" and regain their former roles. We find it uncomfortable to be in the presence of those who grieve; we try to divert them rather than accept their pain and loss. The more quickly an individual overcomes feelings of sadness, isolation, depression, and longing, the healthier the individual's recovery is said to be. But from Silverman's research and that of others, the death of those closest to us is something we never really get over. We revisit the death again and again, approaching it from different perspectives based on our growing maturity and understanding at different points in our lives.

Death and grief are as much a part of the natural life cycle as birth or adolescence. In other cultures and societies, death is simply part of life. Americans may try to believe they are nearly immortal, but people in other cultures are far more realistic.

Death crowds the streets of Calcutta and war-torn nations such as Afghanistan. The presence of dying people in the house, large attendance at funerals, and daily contact with those who are dying help prepare the young for the realities of death.

In one study conducted in the United States, college students were asked to identify their first experience with death. The average age reported was nearly 8 years and centered on the death of a relative for 57 percent of the sample or the death of a pet for 28 percent. Even years later, students recalled their reactions vividly. Most recalled that they cried, and they remembered the reactions and comments of others, as well as very specific details of the funeral (Dickinson, 1992).

Most societies throughout history have had philosophical or religious beliefs about death, and most societies have some form of ritual that surrounds death. For example, in the past, the elderly Eskimo who could no longer contribute to their society might walk off alone, never to be seen again, or they might be given a departure ceremony at which they were honored, then ritually killed. In most societies, death is not viewed as the end of existence; although the body has died, the spirit is believed to live on. This is true as well in most religions. Ardent Irish Catholics celebrate a wake as the arrival of the dead person's soul in God's heavenly home; the Hindu believe in the continuation of the person's life through reincarnation; Hungarian gypsies gather at the bedside of a dying loved one to ensure support and make sure that there is always a window open so that the spirit can leave and find its way to heaven. Perceptions of why people die are many and varied. Death may be punishment for one's sins, an act of atonement, or the action of a higher being or deity. In some societies, long life is the reward for having performed many acts of kindness, whereas in other cultures, longevity is linked to having wisely conserved one's energy and vitality in youth.

A Developmental View of Death

In general, we adopt attitudes toward death consistent with our culture, our family values, and our cognitive and emotional maturity (Doka, 2000). Clearly, attitudes toward death change as we age.

Children 2 or 3 years old are rarely upset by the sight of a dead animal or by hearing that a person has died. Children at this age do not easily comprehend the meaning of death. The egocentrism of children may lead them to blame themselves for the deaths of those closest to them, illogically believing that they caused the death by disobeying the person who died. For young children, death is equated with sleep. They expect that someone who has died will wake up and return to be with them. Five-year-olds, for example, do not believe that death is final and expect those who have died to come back to life (Ward-Wimmer and Napoli, 2000). Although few cross-cultural comparisons have been conducted, given the Piagetian cognitive characteristics of preoperational thinking, children up to 7 or 8 years of age do not appear to understand that death is universal, inevitable, and irrevocable. Most preoperational children (those of preschool age) assume that dead people continue to experience the same life processes as they did when they were alive. The dead simply have "moved away" to live in Heaven, working, eating, bathing, shopping, and playing. Preschoolers believe that those who die continue to have the concrete needs, feelings, and experiences they did when they were alive. Children older than 7 or 8 years of age view death as an event that will occur for some people, but not all. Usually by age 9 or 10, children recognize that they will die and understand the inevitability, finality, and universality of death. Young children become cognizant of death between 5 and 7 years of age (Corr, 2000) although some may have had an experience with death somewhat earlier. Most adults recall their first personal confrontation as the death of a relative (usually a grandparent) or a pet.

The awareness of death increases with age, yet older persons also show a greater acceptance and less fear of death than younger or middle-aged individuals (Woodruff-Pak, 1988). Adolescents and young adults are most fearful of death. Adolescents typically deny death, especially the possibility of their own death. The topic is avoided, kidded about, neutralized, and controlled as adolescents distance themselves from death. Adolescents do, nonetheless, experience a good deal of anxiety about death.

Older people are most concerned about the circumstances surrounding their deaths, especially the context and situation in which they will die (Kastenbaum, 1992). DeVries, Bluck, and Birren (1993) have also reported that, in contrast to younger adults, middle-aged respondents tend to focus more detail and attention on the process of dying than on the event of death. Kalish (1985) first noted that the elderly show (1) greater awareness of the limits of their life and a more realistic assessment of their longevity; (2) an awareness that many significant life roles are no longer available; (3) a sense of achievement in being able to live beyond normal life expectancy, or alternatively, a sense of loss if they are unable to reach an expected age of survival; and (4) a sense of sadness, loss, and emptiness as loved ones and close friends die—but also relief and guilt as they continue to escape death.

Fear of death and death anxiety, however, may not represent a single, unidimensional construct for individuals at any age. Many adults actively deny and avoid the topic of death. Kastenbaum (1985) found that nearly 25 percent of all patients near the end of life deny that they are dying, and Callan (1990) noted a strong belief in invulnerability among gay men with AIDS.

Kastenbaum (1981) first suggested that the elderly may experience **bereavement overload** from the cumulative effects of having to cope with the deaths of friends, neighbors, and relatives in a short time span. The elderly are forced to examine the meanings of life and death much more often than those in middle age or young adulthood. Bereavement overload has also been reported among gay men coping with the cumulative effects of multiple losses of close friends and partners (Neugebauer, Rabkin, & Williams, 1992). The greater the number of losses, the more common and intense the bereavement reactions. There are also, of course, considerable individual differences. Some elderly persons see their lives drawing to a close and accept the ending, whereas others cling passionately to life, savoring each activity, personal relationship, and achievement.

Although it is generally reported that older adults are more accepting of death and dying than younger and middle-aged adults, a person's past experiences and confrontations with death, rather than age, are the better predictors of acceptance of death. Numerous therapeutic death education programs have recognized the need to provide an opportunity for children and adolescents to explore their responses to the deaths of people close to them (Doka, 2000).

Death educators help prepare children, families, and staff for the regular and repeated experience of loss that is a part of life. They help children to learn the language of grief and bereavement and to identify and label their feelings. With enhanced language, they can express their feelings and derive greater support and comfort from friends and family. Adolescents are encouraged to understand that loss is a painful and intense emotion, one that even adults find overwhelming. Death education programs are designed to be preventative, like an inoculation to prevent an illness. They include "a formal curriculum that deals with dying, death, grief, and loss and their impact on the individual and humankind" (Stevenson, 2000, p. 199). Benefits include (1) preparing students for future loss; (2) lessening death-related fear and anxiety; (3) providing greater feelings of personal control; (4) helping students to see that life is precious; and (5) exploring different groups' grief practices to enhance appreciation of cultural diversity (Stevenson, 2000). Some programs chart the typical responses of younger children and adolescents. For example, children grieve intermittently, which family members often find distressing. They alternate periods of happiness, play, and ordinary behavior with periods of crying, sadness, and loneliness. Younger persons have fewer coping strategies to manage the intense pain associated with loss. When negative emotions become too strong, they just turn them off (Ward-Wimmer & Napoli, 2000). Death educators also expose issues that youngsters usually keep to themselves, such as fears for their own safety and security ("Who will care for me if my remaining parent dies? Where will I live? Will I die, too?"). Counselors know young people express loss through behaviors symptomatic of their personal conflict and pain: anger, difficulty concentrating, a drop in grades, fighting with friends, abusing drugs and alcohol, or losing interest in formerly pleasurable pursuits. Often grieving young people are not even aware of their emotions and how they affect their lives (Stevenson, 2000). Research Focus 13.3 illustrates some of the common myths our society holds about the experience of loss for children and adolescents.

Death education programs help prepare individuals for the deaths of loved ones. In these programs, whether for children or adults, counselors emphasize honest and open exchange as the best strategy to help people cope with death. In one investigation of the attitudes of 30,000 young adults, more than 30 percent said they could not recall any discussion of death during their childhoods; an equal number said that although death was discussed, the atmosphere was uncomfortable (Shneidman, 1992). Generally, the more freedom to discuss death, the more mature (emotionally and cognitively) are the attitudes toward death. It seems that even religious orientation plays a role. The data suggest a U-shaped pattern. That is, either strong or weak religious beliefs are associated with less fear of death than are moderate levels (Kalish, 1985).

There are two types of death education programs: instruction-centered (didactic) and person-centered (existential). In the first type, people enroll as they might for a course and study the subject matter of death intellectually. The course features lectures, videos, and trips to hospitals, nursing homes, funerals, cemeteries, and hospices.

Eight Myths: Children, Adolescents, and Loss

1. **Children do not grieve, or they only grieve when they reach a certain age.**
Children grieve at any age. The ways they manifest grief will vary, depending on the child's age, development, and experiences.

2. **The death of a loved one is the only major loss that children and adolescents experience.**
Children and adolescents experience a range of losses. These can include the normal developmental losses incurred when growing older (giving up childhood activities, making school transitions, etc.), losses of pets, losses of dreams, separations caused by divorce or relocations, losses of friends and relationships, losses caused by trauma (such as a loss of safety), as well as losses due to illness or death. All of these losses generate grief.

3. **It is better to shield children from loss, as they are too young to experience tragedy.**
Much as we like to protect children from loss, it is impossible. It is far better to provide children and adolescents with support as they experience inevitable loss. We can teach and model our own ways of adapting to loss if we include rather than exclude children and adolescents. Exclusion only increases fears and breeds feelings of resentment and helplessness.

4. **Children should not go to funerals.**
Children should always attend funerals.
Children and adolescents should have the choice as to how they wish to participate in funeral rituals. For that choice to be a meaningful one, they will need information, options, and support.

5. **Children get over loss quickly.**
No one gets over significant loss. Children, like adults, will learn to live with the loss, revisiting that loss at different points in their development. Even infants will react to a significant loss and, as they get older, may question the events of the loss and experience a sense of grief.

6. **Children are permanently scarred by early, significant loss.**
Most people, including children, are resilient. While early significant losses can affect development, solid support and strong continuity of care can assist children as they deal with loss.

7. **Talking with children and adolescents is the most effective therapeutic approach in dealing with loss.**
There is much value in openly communicating with children and adolescents. But there is also great value in using approaches that allow the child or adolescent other creative means of expression. Play, art, dance, music, activity, and ritual are examples of creative modes of expression that children and adolescents may use to express grief and adapt to loss.

8. **Helping children and adolescents deal with loss is the responsibility of the family.**
Families do have a critical responsibility. But it is a responsibility shared with other individuals and organizations such as hospices, schools, and faith communities, as well as the community at large. In times of significant loss, it is important to remember that the ability of family members to support one another can be limited.

Source: Doka, K. J. (2000). *Living with grief: Children, adolescents, and loss.* Washington, DC: Hospice of America, Bruner Mazel.

Person-centered programs allow participants to share loss experiences, feelings, and existential thoughts. Story telling and reminiscence are used to explore the meanings of life and death (its finite nature, its uncertainty), and counselors work to overcome the tendency to "intellectualize" the death. For death education programs to be effective, they must offer individuals an opportunity to personalize learning (Attig, 1992). Some didactic programs have a reflective component, and these have resulted in lowered scores on a Death Anxiety Scale when compared to person-centered death education programs (Hutchison & Scherman, 1992).

Evaluating outcomes of death education is difficult. First, those who participate represent a sample bias, and control populations are difficult to identify. Second, investigators have relied on single measures of program success, most often using short-term attitudinal change rather than behavioral change. Third, little is known about long-term effects (Durlak & Riesenberg, 1991). For example, do changes in attitudes enhance participants' subsequent interactions with those who are near death? Do those who complete death education approach their wills, advance medical directives, or organ donation differently from those who have not participated?

Facing Death

In his book *The Sane Society,* Erich Fromm (1955) comments, "Man is the only animal that finds his own existence a problem which he has to solve and from which he cannot escape" (p. 24). We know we must die. It is this knowledge that we will someday die that gives meaning to life, causes us to establish priorities, and encourages us to use our time wisely.

Most dying individuals want to make some decisions regarding their death. Some want to complete unfinished business, for example, resolving problems and mending fences in personal relationships. When asked how they would spend their last six months of life, younger adults described activities such as traveling and accomplishing things they previously had not done; older adults, in contrast, described more inner-focused activities such as contemplation and meditation (Kalish & Reynolds, 1981). Research Focus 13.4 describes such a shift in focus among classical musical composers nearing the end of life.

Near-Death Experiences

Moody (1975) initially identified striking similarities among people who had come perilously close to dying. The **near-death experience (NDE)** has been studied using formal interviews, questionnaires, and scales to objectify results (Ring, 1984; Sabom, 1982; Sabom, 1998). An entire journal, *Journal of Near Death Studies,* is devoted to scholarly studies and analyses of this phenomenon. Many people who have had an NDE report similar sequences of phenomena, although not everyone experiences each one: (1) an inexpressible feeling of tranquility, peace, and quiet; (2) constant noise; (3) a perception of entering a dark tunnel or void; (4) a feeling of being outside of one's body—for example, observing doctors working to save them; (5) seeing others who have died; (6) being in the presence of intense white light; (7) reviewing their life; and (8) coming back after reaching a border or dividing line. Sabom "classified these elements into two categories; the first, *autoscopic,* entails visualization of the body or body images, the second, *transcendental,* entails descriptions of objects and events that transcend concrete reality, (Gibbs, 1997, p. 262). Those with NDEs tell of their experience with awe, recognizing the profound impact it has had on them. They fear death less since they have already traveled its path (Ring & Valarino, 1998). Recently, Sabom (1998) conducted interviews with more than 160 people who were unaware of the purpose of his work and who had had NDEs. He found the NDE contributed to a greater sense of faith, belief in God, and heightened religious commitment. There was also a stronger belief in an afterlife and in the existence of a soul, life force, or essence beyond physical death. Other aftereffects included a diminished interest in material gain

Swan Songs: Characteristics of Last Compositions

In an article in the journal *Psychology and Aging,* D. K. Simonton from the University of California at Davis reported the results of his analysis of the final musical works of 172 classical composers. He wondered whether there would be any unique characteristics in the very last musical work or "swan song" of each of these composers.

In a series of complex computer analyses performed on these varied pieces, Simonton surprisingly discovered some commonalities in these final musical compositions. Seven basic variables were used to compare earlier works with the last work of the composer: melodic originality and variation, repertoire popularity, aesthetic significance, listener accessibility, performance duration, and thematic size. Unlike earlier investigators' attempts to examine swan songs, Simonton was able to statistically rule out contaminating factors such as the average age at which the last composition was written and individual differences in terms of fame, reputation, and success. In examining each individual composer's last musical work, or swan song, and comparing it to earlier compositions, Simonton found that the last work was somewhat shorter in length. Swan songs were also typically far more simple in their organization or structure. Also, the swan songs have become some of the most enduring, well-recognized, and cherished pieces in the field of classical music. These musical finales are characterized by a degree of aesthetic significance that earlier works do not have. Examples of legendary swan songs include Mozart's *Requiem,* Tchaikovsky's *Sixth*

Symphony, and Schubert's *Unfinished Symphony.* As composers near the ends of their lives, their musical works seemed to reveal personal contentment, inner harmony, and acceptance rather than depression, sorrow, or tragedy.

The ability of composers to construct such enduring works at the ends of their lives remains puzzling. The swan song structure Simonton found is understated in its aesthetic beauty and simplicity. Yet the simplicity is not that of a country melody or peasant folk tune. What emerges is the elegance of a musical composition that is not too complex, not too simple; music that is "just right." The swan song demonstrates that the composer knew how to produce a work that presented the pure essence of a feeling, mood, or theme in the clearest and most direct fashion. It might be argued that this happened because the composers knew that their lives were nearly over. However, most of the composers did not know they were near death; they did not consciously attempt to produce a final composition. The swan song phenomenon is even more striking when juxtaposed against possible "false alarms"; many of the composers produced musical works against the backdrop of serious disease that brought them to the brink of death. Yet during these near brushes with death, the musical compositions created were similar to those produced at other times throughout their careers. It is only the swan song that contains the unique qualities that separate it from a composer's earlier musical compositions.

---

and an increased interest in prayer and meditation (Gibbs, 1999). Survivors were profoundly moved and reported being forever changed. Other investigators (Siegel, 1980) have been more skeptical, believing that these reported events are largely hallucinations caused by physiological changes in the brain during heightened stress from oxygen deprivation or trauma.

In the next section, we examine the often-cited psychological stages of dying developed by Elisabeth Kübler-Ross, and then we explore the dying phases or trajectories. We also consider the concept of appropriate death, as well as the variety of coping strategies individuals develop to deal with the stress of knowing they are dying.

Kübler-Ross's Theory

The most widely cited view of how people cope with death was developed by Elisabeth Kübler-Ross. This view has been applied to many loss experiences, for example, to loss of a job or loss through miscarriage. The stages, however, have received little direct empirical support and have been the subject of much theoretical criticism (Shneidman,

1992). Kübler-Ross's theory, which suggests the existence of stages in dealing with the dying process, helped focus professional concern on death education and counseling—topics that had been largely ignored. In her psychiatric work with hospitalized patients dying from cancer, Kübler-Ross (1969, 1981) first identified and reported the existence of five stages: denial/isolation, anger, bargaining, depression, and acceptance.

In the first stage, a common initial reaction to terminal illness is **denial/isolation.** The individual denies that death is going to occur, saying, "No, it can't happen to me," "It's not possible," or "There must be a mistake, an error in the laboratory or in the diagnosis." Denial is like shock and is considered a transitory defense. It is eventually replaced with increasing acceptance when the individual confronts matters such as finances, unfinished business, and arrangements for surviving family members.

In the second stage, **anger,** the dying individual recognizes that he or she can no longer maintain denial; anger, resentment, rage, and envy are expressed directly. Now the issue becomes, "Why me?" At this point, the individual becomes increasingly difficult to care for as anger is displaced and projected onto physicians, nurses, hospital staff, family members, and God. The realization of loss is great, and those who symbolize life, energy, and competent functioning are the targets of the dying individual's resentment and jealousy.

In the third stage, **bargaining,** the individual develops hope that death can somehow be postponed or delayed. Some individuals enter into a brief period of bargaining or negotiation—often with God—as they try to delay their deaths. Psychologically, these people are trying to buy a few more weeks, months, or years in exchange for leading a reformed life or for choosing a life dedicated to God or the service of others.

In the fourth stage, **depression,** the dying individual begins to accept the certainty of his or her death; as she or he recognizes the growing severity of specific symptoms, a period of depression or preparatory grief may appear. The dying individual is often silent, refuses visitors, and spends much time crying or grieving. Shneidman (1992) finds individuals at this point mourning their own death, the loss of their special talents and abilities, the loss of their former sense of contentment and well-being, and the loss of their experiences (past, present, and future). Kübler-Ross advises that attempts to cheer up dying individuals at this stage should be avoided because of the dying person's need to contemplate and grieve over his or her impending death.

In the fifth stage, **acceptance,** the individual develops a sense of peace, a unique acceptance of fate, and in many cases, a desire to be left alone. This stage may be devoid of feeling; physical pain and discomfort are often absent. Kübler-Ross describes this stage as the last one before undertaking a long journey and reaching the end of the struggle.

No one has yet been able to provide independent confirmation that people actually go through all five stages in the order Kübler-Ross describes (Kastenbaum, 1981; Shneidman, 1992). Theoretically and empirically, the stages have raised many questions, although Kübler-Ross feels that she has often been misread and misinterpreted. For instance, she maintains that she never intended the stages to represent an invariant sequence of developmental steps toward death, and she has consistently recognized the importance of individual variation in how we face death. Nevertheless, Kübler-Ross still believes that the optimal way to face death lies in the sequence she has proposed. Numerous advocates have seen the stages as prescriptive rather than descriptive and tried to hurry dying patients through the individual stages. But the stages are ultimately only descriptive; they make no claim on how all persons should die.

Other investigators have not found these five stages, and many report that a single stage (e.g., depression or denial) dominates the entire dying experience, while others identify dying patients as being in two or three stages simultaneously (Kalish, 1985; Shneidman, 1992). The fact that Kübler-Ross used primarily interview data from young or middle-aged adults without sophisticated statistical evaluations is yet another criticism of her work. Marsall and Levy (1990) suggest that among her respondents, the experiences of anger, bargaining, and depression are far more likely than among older individuals. Even in Kübler-Ross's earliest work, it is clear that many of the cancer patients she studied remained at one of the first stages (denial or anger) and never passed through all five stages of the sequence. And other studies have found that some patients move backward or regress into stages already completed (Shneidman, 1992). We are left with a provocative and historically important theory of dying, but one that has few developmental or stage properties. In the minds of many critics, the theory, other than serving to stimulate interest and research on the topic of death and dying, has had little utility.

An Appropriate Death

In a certain sense, the ways in which people face death may simply reflect how they face life. The concept of an **appropriate death** suggests that individuals should be granted the freedom to face dying as they choose, a death that fits each person's expectations and style of coping (Weisman, 1972). An appropriate death permits people to die with dignity on their own terms. There is no mandate to move through a set of stages, no requirement to push to acceptance, no social pressure to face death in a prescriptive way. By permitting individuals an appropriate death, we allow them to maintain a sense of hopefulness. Hopefulness refers to the positive anticipation of the future: birthdays, wedding anniversaries, visits from friends or relatives, seeing the new year arrive.

As studies suggest, hopefulness provides one means of control or mastery over terminal illness and allows the coexistance of living and dying (Kalish, 1985; Kastenbaum, 1981). Some dying persons continue to participate in living each day, resisting rather than denying death. Their spirit and hope should not be confused with outright denial; resisting death implies an active decision. With an appropriate death, individuals can maintain their dignity, their self-esteem, their identity, and their individuality. Kalish (1985) identified three factors necessary to permit an appropriate death: (1) warm, intimate personal relationships with family, friends, or health professionals; (2) an open environment in which emotions, information, and the terminal condition can be discussed by all involved; and (3) a sense of meaning derived from this experience, from one's life, or from religion.

Pattison's Living-Dying Interval

E. Mansell Pattison (1977) has defined the **trajectory of life** as our anticipated life spans and the plans we make for the way we will live our lives. When an illness or serious injury causes a revision in our anticipated life span, the life trajectory must also be revised. Pattison calls the time interval between our discovery that we will die sooner than we had thought and the time when we actually die the *living-dying interval.* This interval is characterized by three phases: acute, chronic, and terminal. The goal of those who counsel individuals in the living-dying interval is to assist them in coping with the first or acute phase, to help them to live as reasonably as possible through the second, or chronic phase, and to move them into the third or terminal phase (see figure 13.4). Pattison sees a pattern to the phases. Depending on the nature of the illness, different people may spend vastly different periods of time in each phase. For example, some illnesses allow a pattern of chronic living-dying for only a few weeks; others allow a more protracted period of months or even years, as with a slow, lingering illness or disease or with someone who has a deteriorating condition.

Pattison describes each phase in terms of the individual's reactions and coping needs. In the *acute phase,* individuals face what is probably the most severe crisis in their lives—the realization that they will die sooner than they thought and will not get to accomplish and experience all they had hoped. People in this stage feel immobilized, experience high levels of anxiety, and call into play a number of defense mechanisms to deal with their extreme fear and stress. In this phase, they need a great deal of emotional support from others and need help to deal rationally with the reality of death.

In the *chronic phase,* Pattison believes that individuals begin to directly confront their fear of dying. Fears about loneliness, suffering, separation from loved ones, and the unknown often surface. Health professionals can assist dying people by helping them put their lives into perspective, working through some of their defense mechanisms, and allowing the open discussion of death and basic fears.

In the *terminal phase,* individuals begin to withdraw as their hope of getting better gives way to the realization that they are going to get worse. At the end of this phase, individuals turn inward, distancing themselves from people and everyday experience.

Just as Kübler-Ross's stages are neither fixed nor invariant, Pattison's dying phases do not represent a single trajectory descriptive of every person's death; each person spends different amounts of time in each of the three phases. Some have questioned

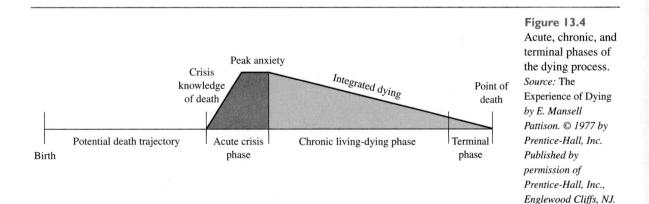

Figure 13.4
Acute, chronic, and terminal phases of the dying process.
Source: The Experience of Dying *by E. Mansell Pattison.* © 1977 by Prentice-Hall, Inc. *Published by permission of Prentice-Hall, Inc., Englewood Cliffs, NJ.*

the need to describe the time spent in each phase of Pattison's dying trajectory, preferring to examine the process of dying; for some people, dying is rapid and sudden, with little time to prepare, while for others the preparation lasts for years.

Marsall and Levy (1990) have considered that a dying person is involved in a dying career, which begins with the realization that one's time left to live is limited and finite. McCain and Gramling (1992) documented the dying careers of 17 people (21 to 71 years old) who were coping with AIDS. The dying career was marked from the initial diagnosis of being HIV positive, through the diagnosis of AIDS, to impending death. McCain and Gramling (1992) identified three processes involved in the dying career: (1) living with dying, (2) fighting the sickness, and (3) getting worn out. Each of us begins his or her dying career from the time that we realize emotionally that we are mortal, like all human beings. As each generation dies before us (great-grandparents, grandparents, and parents), we come to understand that our own time is drawing closer. With the death of parents, we have no one left to stand before us. We understand that our generation's death is next and our dying career is reaching its end.

Communication: Listening to the Dying Person

Often friends and family are unable to listen and communicate with the dying person in an accepting way. This inability to talk honestly isolates the dying person at a time when it would be most helpful to be able to express thoughts and feelings. For Kalish (1985), the advantages of an open-awareness context include (1) closing life in accord with one's own ideas about proper dying; (2) completing plans and projects, making arrangements for survivors, and participating in decisions about a funeral and burial; (3) conversing and reminiscing with others who have been important in one's life; and (4) having a better understanding of what is happening within one's body and the treatments being received. It may be easier to die when people we love can converse freely with us about what is happening, even if it entails considerable sadness. Research Focus 13.5 describes a circumstance in which open communication with a dying person proves beneficial.

For the dying person, external accomplishments and continued achievements become less likely or important. The focus of communication thus needs to be directed more at internal processes, past experiences, endearing memories, and personal successes. A caring relationship is a very important aspect of the dying person's life. But such caring does not have to come from a mental health professional; a concerned nurse, an attentive physician, an interested member of the clergy, a sensitive spouse, or a caring friend may provide important communication resources for the dying person. In such interactions and communications, we want to emphasize the person's strengths and help them prepare for the remainder of life. In one investigation, adult hospital volunteers who were assisting families in coping with impending death and subsequent bereavement were surveyed about the care and management dying persons received. The volunteers felt that the illness and the person's death had been very well managed when appropriate, caring relationships and open communication had been established among family members, health care professionals, and the dying person (Couldrick, 1992).

Open Communication with the Dying Person

My 81-year-old aunt was extremely ill and had been for two years; the indications were that she would probably not live for many more weeks. My home was 800 miles away, but I was able to get to visit her and my uncle for a couple of days. It bothered me to see her hooked into a machine that held her life; the ugly wig she had worn during the past couple of years had been discarded, and there were only a few wisps of hair left, but at least they were hers. Her teeth had been placed in the drawer by her bed since she couldn't take solid food, and at this point she was not concerned about how she looked.

My uncle and I were in her room talking with her as she moved in and out of awareness. He was standing at the foot of the bed and I was sitting next to her, holding her hand. He began to talk to her about coming to visit me as soon as she could get up and around again, probably next summer. I noticed that she tuned his comments out. Then I found a pretext to get him out of the room.

When we were alone, I stood up and kissed her. I'd like to say that it was easy, but it really wasn't. I told her that I loved her, and I realized that I had never said that to her before, hadn't even thought about it, hadn't even consciously thought that I loved her. I just . . . loved her.

Then I said, "Bea, I have to leave now. I may never see you again, and I want you to know how much I love you." Her eyes were closed and she was breathing strangely, but she winced at my words, and I became frightened that I'd said too much, so I hesitated. "Well, I hope that I'll see you again, but I might not." And I left.

She died before I could visit again, and I always wondered whether I should have said what I did, but it seemed important to say it. Even if it pained her to hear me, she knew it was true, and she had not shrunk from painful situations before. It had been easy for me over many years to talk and write about death and dying, but it was very difficult for me to be in the situation where someone I loved was dying. I did what I have told other people to do, and it wasn't at all natural—I had to force myself. But when I heard, three weeks later, that she had died, I considered myself fortunate to have had the chance to be with her before she died and to have been both caring and honest. (p. 172)

Source: Kalish, R. A. (1981). *Death, grief, and caring relationships* (2nd ed.). Pacific Grove, CA: Brooks/Cole. Copyright © 1981 by Wadsworth, Inc.

Likewise, the need for open disclosure of dying is vitally important and has an impact among the institutionalized elderly (Lavigne-Pley & Levesque, 1992). Older individuals who are institutionalized do not want to be kept in the dark regarding the conditions of roommates, acquaintances, or friends who reside with them. Of 25 institutionalized elderly in one exploratory investigation, 21 reported that they wanted to be informed of the impending death of a close peer. When asked if the institutional staff had provided or withheld this information in the past, 20 of the 25 residents reported having an experience in which the staff did not communicate with them that a peer was dying (Lavigne-Pley & Levesque, 1992). One of the consequences of withholding this information was that residents believed that the staff who cared for them were indifferent to the death of an elderly person.

Denial of Death

Not all people close to death can communicate honestly and openly. Denial is characteristic of some people's approach to death. In fact, it is not unusual for some dying individuals to continue to deny death right to the end. Denial serves to protect people from the reality that they will soon die and provides a measure of hopefulness. While some psychologists believe that denying death until the very end may be adaptive, others report a negative relationship between denial and acceptance of death (Shneidman, 1992).

Denial of death takes many forms. Refusing to acknowledge the implications of a disease or a life-threatening situation is one form of denial. For example, a man scheduled for an operation for cancer of the colon may deny the facts and believe that the operation is for benign polyps. Or a person may accept the presence of a severe kidney disease but deny its life-threatening consequences. Some individuals, while accepting the concept of biological death, maintain faith in their spiritual immortality.

Denial can be used adaptively to delay dealing with one's death. But denial can have maladaptive features if it causes one to persistently distort reality. For example, it may keep a person from seeking medical diagnosis and treatment when life-threatening symptoms appear, or it may block communication and other forms of adjustment to dying.

The use of denial must be evaluated in terms of its adaptive qualities for the individual. Taylor and her colleagues (1992) have reported that denial and active distortion were characteristic of a group of gay men who had tested HIV positive. These men believed they would not develop AIDS, despite the evidence that they were carrying the virus. Taylor and her colleagues (1992) suggest that such "unrealistic optimism" helped these men cope with the predictable progression of the disease, and ultimately death. Denial, avoidance, and active distortion are common among people facing the inevitability of death. Such strategies help people cope and actively manage the stress related to imminent death.

Coping well with dying is not necessarily age-related. It appears that the elderly more frequently must face loss, death, and their own mortality. While coping with death often involves some elements of denial, some older persons turn to religious beliefs, prayer, and spiritual faith for help. The homebound elderly are particularly likely to turn to prayer in coping with death, especially when they are uncertain about an afterlife (Fry, 1990). Corr (1992) believes that coping with dying should be approached from a task-based perspective. The coping tasks identified for the dying include coming to terms with four dimensions: the spiritual, the social, the psychological, and the physical. While many find solace, help, and hope through religion and spirituality, others find little comfort in such institutions and beliefs.

Where We Die

The majority of individuals, when asked where they would want to die, indicate a preference to be at home. Of the nearly 2.9 million Americans who died in 2001, however, only 25 percent died in their own homes. More than 49 percent died in a hospital, and 25 percent died in a nursing home. Few young adults asked to imagine their death scene actually visualize themselves dying in a hospital (Kastenbaum & Norman, 1990). Dying at home is most likely among hospice participants; 78 percent died either at home or under hospice care in a nursing home. Despite the media attention devoted to end-of-life issues, 35 percent of Americans have not given any thought to such concerns nor shared their thoughts on the matter with anyone else. Yet a recent survey suggests that 83 percent believe that end-of-life preferences are very important and must be honored by family and doctors (National Hospice and Palliative Care Organization, 2001).

Dying people sometimes feel they may be a burden at home, recognize the problem of limited space, and know they may place undue stress on family members. Hospitals offer professional staff members who are available around the clock and access to advanced medical equipment. Yet a hospital may not be the best location for the dying person to engage in meaningful, intimate relationships or to retain autonomy. Dying at home, often under the watchful eye of a hospice program, is a choice many elderly individuals make, despite their requirements for extensive medical and nursing care and their failing condition (Levine, 1995).

Hospice Programs

The term *hospice* originally referred to a shelter for weary travelers returning from religious pilgrimages. Today, hospice defines a philosophy of care for those who are dying. The care is *palliative,* that is, designed to control pain and physical symptoms; no treatment exists or is offered to cure the terminal illness. The care is designed to humanize the end-of-life experience for the terminally ill and all those who interact with them. The terminally ill receive social support and as much personal control as possible over all decisions. Hospice has helped foster a broad model of care in medicine that permits the terminally ill to die "on their own terms."

The pioneering work in London, England of Cicely Saunders, medical director of St. Christopher's Hospice, established the hospice movement (Saunders, 1977). Hospice programs have three goals: (1) controlling pain for dying individuals; (2) creating an open, intimate, and supportive environment to share the end of life with loved ones and staff; and (3) maintaining the humanity, dignity, independence, and personal identity of each dying individual. Hospice teams include paid professionals (physicians, nurses, mental health experts, clergy) and community volunteers, many of whom have experienced the benefits of hospice in their own families. Team members visit patients in their homes, monitor their status, and provide helpful services such as assisting with personal care, routine household tasks, or simply listening to the terminally ill and their family.

Hospice volunteers and professional staff provide comfort, counseling, and support to family members.

Pain management is under the direction of the terminally ill and medications are self-requested and self-administered to maintain independence and a sense of control. Drugs are used that preserve alertness wherever possible, and pain management is essential. In one study, 3,357 family members, most of whom were not in hospice, reported 40 percent of their terminally ill relatives experienced severe pain; 25 percent reported moderate to great anxiety and depression prior to death (Lynn et al., 1997). The terminally ill remain an integral part of their family throughout hospice care. Family members and the patient participate in death education and counseling and are encouraged to share their feelings over the impending death and the meaning of the loss. Hospice also provides *postvention* bereavement programs for survivors up to a year following the death. Postvention typically includes a memorial service, sharing educational literature, bereavement counseling, and survivor support group meetings (Hospice Net, 2001; Hospice Foundation of America, 2001). Hospice programs also provide counseling and support to staff members. Death takes its toll on all health care workers, and they regularly need a chance to share their feelings (Brody et al., 1997). Most studies suggest that hospice team members become less anxious about death, grow more competent in dealing with death, and better manage death than those without these experiences. Hospice patients show benefits from their participation in many studies, although there are wide-ranging individual differences. Those with greater ego strength and spirituality were best able to cope with their own death. Interestingly, the most frequently addressed topic of home hospice visits was spirituality, with death anxiety the second most common topic of discussion (Kazanjian, 1997; Reese and Brown, 1997).

More than 3,100 hospice programs existed nationwide in 2001, an increase of more than 33 percent from 1990. Hospice offers services to individuals of any age; 700,000 people received hospice care in 1999, or almost 30 percent of all Americans who died that year (National Hospice and Palliative Care, 2001). Most adults over 65 seeking hospice care have a primary diagnosis of cancer (71 percent), with heart disease the second most common diagnosis. Elderly with end-stage dementia are rarely a part of hospice programs; those that are involved usually have dementia that is secondary to a terminal illness (Hanrahan & Luchins, 1995). Currently, 44 states include hospice under Medicare insurance. Eligibility requires (1) written documentation that patients have chosen this care over standard care benefits, (2) certification of a prognosis of death within six months by two physicians, and (3) recertification for patients who survive for more than six months. As table 13.3 shows, hospice care is cost-effective. The total cost of hospice for those receiving Medicare insurance was less than

TABLE 13.3			
Cost Analysis for Hospice, Hospital, and Skilled Nursing Facility in 1998			
	Hospice	Skilled Nursing Facility	Hospital
Daily costs	$113	$482	$2,177

Source: Hospice Foundation of America, 2001.

1 percent of the total Medicare budget. In 1999, 28 percent of all Medicare costs supported care for people in the last year of life; almost 50 percent of these expenditures were expended in the last two months of life. Currently, the average length of hospice stay is only 64 days, with a median length of service of 29 days. Experts note that with longer participation periods (due to earlier enrollment), these cost comparisons may not be quite as impressive (Hospice Foundation of America, 2001; Hospice Net, 2001).

Dying on Our Own Terms

Sensitive, humane, and personal care of the terminally ill has only recently assumed importance in medicine and nursing, probably in part as a response to the growth of hospice programs and in part as a response to the demographic changes in our society. There is even a new certification for physicians from the American Board of Hospice and Palliative Medicine for an "interdisciplinary approach to the study and care of patients with active, progressive far-advanced disease for whom the prognosis is limited and the focus of care is quality of life. It recognizes the multidimensional nature of suffering, responds with care that addresses all of these dimensions, and communicates in a language that conveys respect, mutuality, and interdependence" (ABHP, 2001). What do Americans want in a "good death?" Surveys show that most would like to die at home. But 75% die in medical facilities (Cloud, 2000). The terminally ill are often treated by physicians whom they have never met before, yet most would like to have someone they know caring for them at the end of life. Reform is based on providing options, particularly pain medications that leave patients comfortable but not unconscious. When physicians prescribe such drugs, they may be investigated, or concerns may arise that patients may become addicted—an exceptionally rare event. The simple truth is that physicians have little training and education in managing pain and treating common end-of-life symptoms (Cloud, 2000). And, physicians, nurses, and clergy receive little preparation to help the dying. People facing terminal illness need supportive care providers to help them live well to the end, as comfortably as possible, and in an atmosphere that encourages open dialogue.

Coping with the Death of a Loved One

To everything there is a season, and a time to every purpose under heaven. A time to live and a time to die . . .
—Ecclesiastes

Loss, like love, comes in many forms in our lives. The term **bereaved** describes a person or family who loses a loved one to death. **Grief** is the human reaction to loss—to divorce, death of a pet, loss of a job. No loss is greater than the death of someone we love deeply. In rating life stresses, the death of a spouse is consistently identified as the most stressful. Grief is one of the most powerful of human feelings; it produces intense emotional pain. People who grieve experience deep sorrow, anger, and confusion.

The members of this Tibetan family are conducting a ritualistic ceremony as a memorial on the first anniversary of the death of a loved one.

Doka (1999) notes "grief is a long, uneven process that affects individuals on a variety of levels—physical, emotional, cognitive, spiritual, and behavioral . . . (p. 5). "The process of grieving is essential to recover from the loss of significant people and deep attachments in our lives. **Mourning** is the overt behavioral expression of grief by the bereaved. It follows specific cultural, social, and religious customs, usually in the form of various rituals—burial practices, styles of dress, recitation of prayers, and so forth. Table 13.4 summarizes some of the religious rituals associated with mourning. Reactions to death are influenced by a variety of demographic factors, including age, gender, culture, family background, and social class, as well as dynamic factors including faith and religious commitment, physical and emotional health, support networks, and personal insight on and understanding of grief. Each person grieves in his or her own unique fashion (Doka, 1999). There are, however, some commonalities.

Forms of Mourning and the Funeral

There are many cultural differences in mourning. For example, **sati** is the ancient and infrequently practiced Hindu ritual of burning a dead man's widow alive to increase his family's prestige, enhance the importance of the village, and create an image of the widow as a goddess. Prayers are offered in her memory at the site of the funeral pyre. Other cultures hold a ceremonial meal for the mourners; in still others, mourners wear black armbands for one year following a death. In the United States, the funeral offers a variety of ways to express loss. Table 13.4 describes some of the different religious practices used at funerals.

TABLE 13.4

Funerals of Different Religions: A Summary of Practices and Customs

We all wish to provide comfort and support to friends, coworkers, neighbors, and others in our communities who have experienced a death. However, we are sometimes unfamiliar with the religious practices or customs to be followed at funerals, concerned about behaving inappropriately, and anxious not to feel out of place. Often our concerns keep us away from the funeral or house of mourning when those who are bereaved would most appreciate our presence. Sweet (1994) has provided a succinct summary of some of the traditions that take place in various religions in hopes of breaking down some of the barriers for those who would like to offer support and comfort. Knowing some of these funeral customs may make the expression of support more appropriate and consistent with the customs of the mourners. They will most likely appreciate your respect and understanding of their faith.

Islam

Traditional Muslim custom is to bury the dead as soon as practically possible—ideally, within 24 hours. The brief funeral service occurs in a mosque and is marked by readings from the Quran and ritual chanting by the Imam or religious leader. In the mosque, people remove their shoes and sit on the floor; women are expected to wear loose-fitting clothes as well as a scarf, veil, or head covering, and the sexes will be kept in separate sections. At the conclusion of the service, each person files past the body and pays their last respects. A brief burial service is conducted at the cemetery, and people then return to the mosque for additional prayers and to express condolences to the family. Family members wear black. After burial, at the conclusion of services, a family meal is eaten at the mosque. Sending flowers and sympathy cards is appropriate.

Hindu

Hindu custom is to conduct a funeral service before sundown of the day of death. This service is held at a funeral home and conducted by the firstborn son. At the funeral service, family members wear white out of respect and others in attendance are expected to wear dark clothes (without bright colors). Family members may individually place flowers upon the deceased. All Hindus are cremated, and following the cremation a brief service takes place. Family members enter a period of formal grieving for a least 13 days, depending on their caste. Flowers may be sent to the family.

Christianity

Protestant faiths conduct a service for the deceased at a funeral home or church. The funeral service usually occurs within three days after the death and is conducted by a minister. The family will hold visiting hours at the funeral home the day and/or evening before the day of the funeral service. The corpse is embalmed and the casket open during visiting hours. Family members may wear black or dark clothing, but rarely will cover their heads. There is growing participation from family and friends in the funeral service; those at the service are asked in advance if they wish to participate. Visitors are not obligated to participate, although there may be a time set aside for personal testimonials and vignettes that reflect on the life of the deceased. Sending flowers, cards, and offering gifts to charities in the name of the deceased are all appropriate.

Roman Catholics usually conduct a funeral service in the church, although the body may be viewed first in a funeral home before being transported in a hearse for the church service. At the funeral home, brief prayers lasting about 15 minutes will be offered by a priest. The body is embalmed, and the casket remains open for viewing. Visitors may participate or simply sit quietly until the service is concluded. At the church, mourners and visitors of the Catholic faith will bow at the knee when they enter, a practice that others should not follow. All who are in attendance at the service should stand at appropriate times; kneeling is not obligatory; only those of the Catholic faith will go forward to take communion from the priest. Only family members and

(continued)

TABLE 13.4 *continued*

those who are extremely close to the family will join the family at the cemetery for burial. Sending flowers and cards, and offering gifts to charities in the name of the deceased are all appropriate. Catholics may purchase mass cards, which may be displayed at the funeral home or the home of the family of the deceased.

Buddhism

Buddhist funerals are conducted in a funeral home and only rarely in a temple. The funeral home is arranged with a low table with candles and incense burning until the body is moved to the cemetery for burial. Friends and family participate in viewing the body for one evening only, the night prior to the funeral. The family is seated at the front of the room close by the casket, which is open for viewing. The immediate family wears white to show their grief, and other family members and visitors may wear black to express their respect. After meeting with the immediate family to offer condolences, visitors go directly to the casket and bow before viewing the body. The deceased wears new clothes and shoes (shoes are to be removed only when entering a Buddhist temple). People may stay in the viewing room for a little while, seated or standing, and then quietly depart. The following day a funeral service is conducted by a monk. At the service, men and women may sit together and will hear special prayers and chanting; visitors are not expected to participate in the funeral service. As a group, visitors will participate at the end of the service and congregate in front of the casket and bow together in a final show of respect for the deceased.

Judaism

Jewish funerals are usually conducted as soon as possible following death, often within 24 hours. The family of the deceased recognizes support from the extended family and visitors through their attendance at the funeral service held at either a Jewish temple or funeral home and at a brief service that occurs at the cemetery. Judaism has three distinct branches, each with somewhat different religious practices at the funeral service. Orthodoxy, for example, requires men and women to sit separately and to wear a head covering (a skullcap called a yarmulke or keppah); Conservative practice is to have men and women sit together with only men covering their heads; and Reform practice is to permit both sexes to sit together and people to choose whether or not to cover their heads.

Appropriate head covering is provided at the funeral and cemetery service for all in attendance according to the family's branch of Judaism. Immediate family members will wear a sign of mourning such as a small piece of black fabric that has been cut and attached to a shirt, blouse, or jacket, or they will wear some article of clothing that has been similarly cut, such as a tie or collar. Mourners wear dark clothes, and visitors are expected to do the same. Traditional Jewish practice does not permit an open casket, but this has become more a matter of family choice than a matter of doctrine in recent times. Cremation has traditionally been frowned upon, but it is not prohibited.

At the cemetery, it is customary that family and close relatives shovel some of the earth on the casket so that each mourner has a share in the burial and a private moment marking their separation from the deceased. Mourners may wash their hands after the burial either at the cemetery or before entering the home to mark the end of one phase of life and the beginning of the next (life without the deceased). The burial service is followed by a meal, prepared and served by friends and extended family to the mourners out of respect for their loss, at the home of an immediate family member. The immediate family also receives visitors during a week of shiva which occurs in the home of a surviving spouse or another member of the immediate family. Regular prayers are to be recited daily in the synagogue or temple for many months by close family members. The family's loss is central, and only after burial occurs is it appropriate to visit the family personally or telephone them. It is also not appropriate to send flowers to the family or to the funeral home. To show one's support and respect for the deceased and the family, it is acceptable to make a donation to the family's preferred charity in the name of the deceased.

Source: Sweet, L. (1994). In memoriam: A user's guide on how to behave at funerals of different faiths. Toronto Star, August 27, p. A10.

The funeral industry has been charged with taking advantage of the bereaved at a time when they are most vulnerable. Undertakers have offered expensive but needless rituals, services, and merchandise to those who can ill-afford such luxuries. The Federal Trade Commission (FTC) requires funeral homes to provide written price lists to help consumers identify their options and expenses as part of its 1994 Funeral Rule (see table 13.5). A set of standard definitions for specific funeral practices was also created to help consumers understand the services and merchandise they purchase. A funeral ceremony is a service commemorating the deceased with the body present; a memorial service is a ceremony commemorating the deceased without the body present; and an immediate burial is a disposition of human remains without formal viewing, visitation, or ceremony with the body present, except for a graveside service.

Consumers need not have the most elaborate or most expensive funeral to respect the memory of a relative. A casket is the most expensive product in a traditional funeral, with an average cost of nearly $2,200. Until recently, most caskets were sold to consumers by funeral homes who charged 50 percent or more above their cost. Today caskets

TABLE 13.5

Itemization of Funeral Services and Merchandise (1999)
Average Cost of Services and Merchandise

Most Commonly Selected Services		Average Cost	Range
Professional service charges		$1,182	($963–$1,290)
Embalming		$ 400	($319–$466)
Cosmetic preparations (hair, make-up, etc.)		$ 150	($109–$178)
Visitation/viewing		$ 314	($175–$374)
Memorial service at funeral home		$ 357	($311–$406)
Transfer of body to funeral home		$ 159	($117–$175)
Hearse		$ 179	($135–$196)
Service car or van		$ 87	($ 66–$134)
	Subtotal	$2,828	
Merchandise			
Acknowledgment cards, register book, death notices, and cemetery equipment		$ 169	($ 73–$ 265)
Casket		$2,176	($880–$6,228)
	Subtotal	$2,345	
Cemetary expenses Vault or burial liner		$ 758	
	Total	$6,032	

Source: National Funeral Directors Association (2000).

can be purchased through cemeteries and even directly from manufacturers through the Internet at significant savings, with a 24-hour delivery guarantee. Under the federal Funeral Rule, no extra charge can be levied on consumers who purchase a casket from a source other than the funeral home (AARP, 2001a).

An average funeral costs about $6,000 which includes $4,600 for funeral home use and services as well as an additional $1,000 to cover flowers, limousine service, obituary notices, acknowledgment cards, and vaults (AARP, 2000). Burial in a cemetery adds on average an additional $2,600. For most families, a funeral is one of the most expensive purchases they will make; yet few compare prices or negotiate fees with funeral homes. Choices are largely based on prior experience, location, and reputation (AARP, 2001, NFDA, 2000). Figure 13.5 shows the rising costs for funerals from 1992 to 1999 reflecting nearly an 42% increase in costs over this 7 year period. The funeral industry projects increases in costs of 5 percent per year.

Because it is difficult for the bereaved to make funeral decisions, some elderly individuals are deciding in advance exactly what funeral arrangements they wish to have. Funeral homes have adopted **prior-to-need (or preneed)** funeral plans so that survivors may be spared the difficulty of making decisions and paying for services while they are intensely grieving. Cemeteries also have their own preneed plans to cover burial expenses. More and more people have opted for prior-to-need arrangements. One study found that more than a third of all U.S. funerals in 2000 were the result of preneed planning; this represents nearly 900,000 funerals. Among adults 50 years of age and older, 32 percent, or nearly 21 million, have prepaid some or all of their funeral and/or burial expenses (AARP, 2001b; Funeral Consumers Alliance, 2000). Most bodies in the United States are placed in caskets in the ground or in mausoleums; in-ground burial adds at least $1,000 to $2,000 in cemetery charges in addition to the cost of the funeral and merchandise (NFDA, 2000). America's funeral practices are undergoing significant change, although a viewing of the body still occurs in 84 percent of all funerals and cremations. Many experts suggest that open caskets help survivors face the reality of loss, but the decision is the family's (NFDA, 2001).

Figure 13–5 The average cost of a funeral for an adult rose 42 percent from 1992 to 1999. *Source:* Federated Funeral Directors of America.

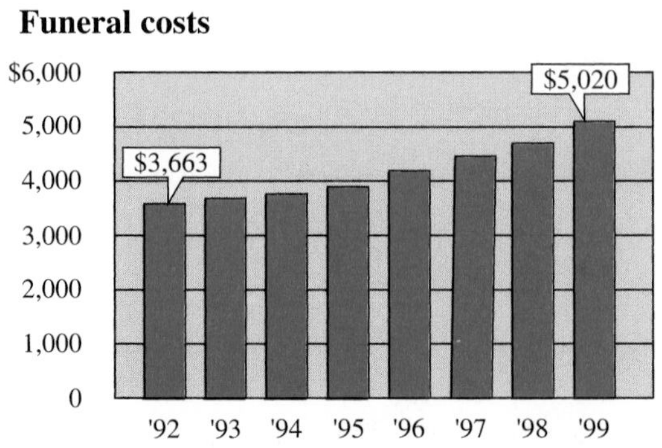

Funeral costs

In 2000, 25 percent of those who died in the United States were cremated. Some states (Alaska, Arizona, Hawaii, Montana, Nevada, New Hampshire, and Florida) report rates of 50 percent or higher. Projections are that by the year 2010, nearly 40 percent of all funerals will involve cremation rather than in-ground burial. This mirrors the results of a national study indicating that 46 percent of Americans intend to be cremated themselves or will choose cremation for a relative (Cremation Association of North America, 2001). The three primary reasons for choosing cremation are: (1) it is less expensive than traditional funerals, (2) it is environmentally preferable and uses less land, (3) it is simpler, involves less emotion, and is more convenient. Cremation requires that the body be enclosed in a casket or strong container that meets standards of respect and dignity. Through heat, the body is reduced to its basic elements or remains. The remains are not ashes, as many suppose, but rather bone fragments. Some families receive a portion of the remains in a sealed urn that may be memorialized. One form of memorial is the **columbarium,** a special building or a wall of a building with single niche spaces for individual family urns. Niches are recessed compartments to hold the urns and have glass fronts or decorative fronts with the name of the deceased and the date engraved on them. Other memorials include an urn garden, a family plot, or a scattering garden. As a matter of safety, certain medical devices, such as pacemakers, must be removed from the body before cremation because they become dangerous under extreme heat. Recently implanted radioactive pellets used to treat prostate cancer can continue to emit radioactivity and so must also be removed. (Cremation Association of North America, 2001).

The Grieving Process

Grief often follows certain phases, although how the phases are expressed or experienced, as well as the duration of the phases, can vary. The phases are associated with emotional, physical, and behavioral reactions. In the initial two or three days, people experience numbness, shock, and disbelief ("this can't be happening"), along with considerable weeping, agitation, and disorientation. Survivors may panic, shriek or moan, and even faint. They may have a heavy feeling in their chests and an emptiness. During the second phase, survivors experience intense longing, with vivid memories and visual images of the deceased often on their minds. People imagine they are still in the presence of the deceased and report seeing, hearing, being held, kissed, touched, and even talking to the one who has died. The desire to recover the dead is very strong, and some survivors even contemplate suicide as a way to reunite with a loved one. Physical symptoms of grief during this phase include insomnia, body pains, listlessness, headaches, fatigue, compulsive pacing or walking, and restlessness. A range of emotional reactions includes survivor guilt, anger, fear, anxiety, intense sadness, irritability, and even relief (AARP, 2001; Doka, 1999). This phase usually peaks about two to four weeks after death and subsides after several months, but it can persist for one or even two years.

The third phase is the realistic appraisal of what the loss means. This phase is characterized by the separation reactions of survivors, which produce disorganization and despair as it becomes clear that the deceased is no longer physically close and will never return. Common responses include heightened anxiety and fear for one's safety.

Survivors may even express anger toward the deceased for leaving them and causing them such sorrow, or may channel their anger (displaced aggression) towards the health professionals who cared for the dead. Survivors may show strong guilt in this phase, regretting things they said or did to the deceased or did not have a chance to say or do. They wonder if they did the right things or somehow helped to hasten the death: Did they call the ambulance soon enough? Could they have recognized the signs of serious illness earlier? Did they use the right doctor or hospital? Doka (1999) notes a spiritual dimension in this phase, as survivors try to make meaning out of their loss. Some become more committed to their faith, others feel alienated and estranged. The experience of grief implies a set of challenges to be faced: (1) accepting the reality of the loss, (2) feeling the depths of pain and sorrow, (3) building a life without the deceased, and (4) balancing and reordering priorities without forgetting the past (AARP, 2001c). This

An AIDs quilt serves as a concrete tie between victims and survivors dealing with the grief and sorrow that accompanies such untimely deaths.

last phase of grief is marked by new interests, looking forward to the future, taking charge of one's life, and accepting personal responsibility for one's self.

Reorganization and recovery usually occur within a year after the death, as survivors resume ordinary activities and social relationships. Many survivors identify with the deceased, adopting his or her personal traits, behaviors, speech, mannerisms, gestures, habits, and concerns (Stephenson, 1985). Through identification, the dead person becomes a part of the mourner, internalized so that the dead person is still a part of the living. At this point, survivors realize they can continue to live without the dead. They recognize the sources of pleasure, love, and support they derive from relatives, friends, and community.

Therapists and counselors recognize the immense energy that must be expended to cope with loss. The term *grief work* aptly describes the intensity and duration of this process. It is difficult, all-consuming, and pervasive work for those who mourn (Davidson and Doka, 1999). Grief work may be arrested and remain incomplete if individuals deny or delay facing their loss and their feelings about it. Experts have found the existence of **delayed grief reaction** among such individuals. Delayed grief, emerging long after the deaths of those we love, appears as an overreaction to the death of a distant relative, a pet, or even a near stranger. **Anticipatory grief** or **anticipatory mourning** is a form of grief that appears before a loved one dies. Family members begin to mourn weeks or even months in advance of the actual death. It does not appear that anticipatory grief makes adaptation to the actual loss easier. Some experts find that dying persons experience grief, too. They grieve for their own loss and show depression, sadness, and isolation in anticipation of their demise (Davies, 2000b).

The Experience of Grief

Grief can be experienced in many ways—as anger, guilt, or idealization. One of the most common is through **grief pangs.** These feelings include somatic distress occurring in waves and lasting 20 minutes to an hour, a tight feeling or knot in the throat, shortness of breath, the need to sigh, an empty feeling in the stomach, and sobbing and crying. Research has shown that intense grief can raise the levels of corticosteroids (hormones) that may, in part, account for the psychological and physical symptoms of grief. Among the recently bereaved, the rate of serious illness and death is higher. At special times survivors are reminded of their loss, and they experience grief as an **anniversary reaction.** It might occur each year on the day of the deceased's birthday or coincide with the day, month, or season of the death. At holidays or family gatherings, some experience this reaction as a deep longing for the lost relationship and feelings of intense loneliness.

Men and women show differences in grief reactions (Lund, 2000). According to Martin and Doka (1999), men are more likely to be *instrumental grievers* who experience their grief intellectually or physically. Some find involvement in physical activities such as hobbies a way to handle their distress. Women are more likely to be *intuitive grievers.* They experience a wide range of different emotions at different times. Women share these emotions with families and friends as they become aware of them. This means they derive more comfort and emotional support than men as they grieve.

Adjustment leads to a renewal of interest in living and in the self. After a year or so, people begin to make major decisions again. They might change the wallpaper or paint a room, buy a new car, rearrange the furniture, or travel. However, the experience of death has an impact for the rest of their lives. They can never return to the life they formerly knew; they are forever transformed. Thus, grief cannot result in complete closure or total resolution.

Making Sense Out of Death

One of the most important aspects of grieving is that it stimulates people to try to make sense of their world and to search for new meanings in life (Lieberman & Peskin, 1992). In a study of recently bereaved spouses, 27 percent reported they had grown from the experience by creating new ways of responding, finding new methods for completing tasks, thinking about themselves differently, and discovering components of their individual identities. Edmonds and Hooker (1992) published an investigation in which 49 college students, all of whom had recently experienced the death of a close family member, were asked to complete measures assessing their distress as well as the significance of the loss in terms of its personal or existential meaning, its religious meaning, and its meaning in terms of life goals. A significant inverse relationship was found between depth of grief and personal or existential meaning. Further, college students indicated a positive change in their life goals as well as a correlated change in the existential meaning of the loss. The deeper the levels of grief they experienced, the more likely students were to refine their religious beliefs. The authors concluded that bereavement can bring about positive changes in one's life, and grief itself may be an impetus for individual growth in the search for the personal or existential meaning of the loss (Edmonds & Hooker, 1992). For one young person's description of the grieving process, see Research Focus 13.6.

Grief is an overwhelming emotion that many younger individuals have little experience with. It is particularly difficult to grieve alone or in secrecy. Yet, in recent years, death due to AIDS has sometimes led to such private grief; survivors may receive little help if they cannot fully share openly with friends or family. Without the opportunity to talk, experience, and fully explore the range of emotions associated with the loss, friends and relatives of those who have died of AIDS remain remorseful over a long period of time. They often ruminate over the years in which they may have distanced the loved one from themselves. As Ascher (1993) notes, grieving for those who die of AIDS means realizing it is too late to ever relive the years of separation and too late to "remedy failed love."

Predictable or expected deaths allow survivors to develop an appropriate personal narrative of the relative's or friend's death. Each person interprets the facts uniquely: whether a different physician would have been better, whether a different treatment would have cured the disease, which relatives showed their concern. From this search through the experience, they build a narrative of the life that has ended and the meaning of the relationship. Survivors struggle to find meaning in death (Why did Uncle Brad have to die? Why does death have to happen at all?).

Loss of a Sibling: It's Impossible to Tell Someone How to Grieve
Maggie Smith

To me, it's impossible to tell someone how to grieve. You can help someone, but never instruct them. I've been to a few grief camps and groups for the loss of my brother Gary and my grandfather Robert. At both, they showed us movies or diagrams about the grieving process. I never really understood them. To me, everyone grieves in a different way, and you shouldn't analyze that, or tell them how it works.

When I lost my brother, it wasn't a shock to me. He had been ill for a long time. There will always be a void in my soul that no one else can ever fill. It was a hole in my entire family, each of us experiencing different pain. To my parents, it was the loss of a son. To me, it was the loss of a brother and a friend. It was an empty room in the house, an empty room in all of our souls.

Of course, there were things that helped, and things that didn't. Without certain people, I never would have gotten through this as I did. One of them was a social worker. She came into our lives after Gary had already lapsed into a coma, so she knew him through me. She was always there to listen when I needed her. She was an escape for me because she was a happy, fun-loving person, but serious when she needed to be.

The constant support and prayers of our local parish and priest were an extreme help to my whole family. Our priest was always there when my mom needed to talk, or when we needed a prayer in a shaky moment, or just for comic relief! How he found the time as the only priest in the parish, I'll never know. I recall one time, my mother was alone at the hospital when my brother was rushed to an emergency CAT scan. As she was walking down the hall, Father Ron appeared around the corner at the exact moment when she needed him the most. She said afterward that he appeared like an angel. And I truly believe he is.

Certain things were not helpful. I'm never sure whether my friends seeming to ignore the fact that my brother had

brain cancer helped or not. We were young then—only ten years old. I think back and say to myself, "What could they have done?" They just let me continue in my own way. I suppose it helped me to maintain a normal life outside the hospital, but I could have talked to them.

Another thing was that people would ask, "How's your brother, Maggie?" But they seemed to forget about me. I was still there! But there were also many people who were concerned about me as well as Gary. People would also say to me, "I know how you feel," or, "I understand." But they didn't! Unless your brother died from brain cancer with you watching in a hospital when you were eleven, you have no clue how I feel. I think people were uncomfortable because they didn't know what to say to a little girl in my place.

Another annoying thing that people did, mainly my friends, was to try to cheer me up when I felt sad, try to make me laugh and forget about it. It was well intentioned, but I wanted to cry. I needed to cry. I couldn't forget. I wanted to talk about it, not to laugh at something.

My advice to anyone talking to a person in mourning is just to be kind, gentle, and a constant support. Offer to talk, but don't pressure them. They will trust you and if they need to talk, they will seek you out. When a brother dies, it's hard to say how it feels. It is a hole in my life, an unfixable void. I miss him a lot, but I must go on with my life. Everyone needs to move on. But whatever you do, you don't have to face it alone.

Note: At the time this was written, Maggie Smith was thirteen years old and in the eighth grade. She enjoyed field hockey, reading, writing, and using America Online.

Source: Doka, K. J. (Ed.). (2000). *Living with grief: Children, adolescents, and loss.* Washington, DC: Hospice of America, Brunner Mazel.

Types of Deaths That Are Difficult to Resolve

Some deaths are more difficult to resolve than others. The most challenging struggles occur when a death is ill-timed (e.g., a newlywed, someone a semester away from graduation) or when the circumstances surrounding the death are troubling (e.g., suicide, homicide, accident, self-neglect, military missing in action with no body recovered). Survivors have great difficulty making meaning of such deaths, which are also highly stressful for professionals—police officers, doctors, or nurses—who must carry the

Work, Grief, and Loss

Employees may grieve the loss of a coworker as deeply as a family member. Coworkers are together every day, sharing their lives for many years. Supervisors are encouraged to recognize grief and its expression at work, accepting the depth and intensity of this reaction. Many coworkers feel guilty over having survived or for not taking action to possibly prevent the loss ("Why didn't I insist that Deborah see a doctor earlier?"). Others become angry with the company for the long hours it expects workers to put in or disillusioned with a Supreme Being who took a friend "too early." Coworkers, reminded of their own mortality, feel vulnerable and wonder how others at work would react should they die.

Supervisor and coworkers need to recognize these various expressions of grief at the workplace. Crying, talking about the loss, sharing feelings, memories, and stories are helpful. Coworkers need encouragement to express these feelings over a period of months, not days. Ideally, a service or some form of remembrance or memorial should take place at work. Some employers help to construct a memorial board of pictures capturing special moments; others arrange a fundraiser for a special cause, prepare a book of coworkers' memories for the family, or arrange a luncheon

for office staff to gather and talk about their unique relationships with the deceased. And all of the personal effects of the deceased should be gathered carefully and returned to the family; coworkers need to see that the company cares about its employees. Most employers grant three days of paid funeral or family leave to the bereaved and may offer only a few hours to coworkers to attend the funeral; neither policy recognizes the reality of the grieving process. Sensitive supervisors might make adjustments in work schedules, lower performance expectations, and seek out employees regularly, listening nonjudgmentally to their expressions of loss. Workers understand through such flexibility and sensitivity that the company cares about them. This means enhanced productivity in the long run.

Source: AARP.org. (2001). *Coping with grief and loss: Grief in the workplace.* @ www.aarp.org

Davidson, J. D., & Doka, K. J. (1999). *Living with grief: At work, at school, at worship.* Washington, DC: Hospice Foundation of America, Brunner Mazel.

National Funeral Directors Association. (2001). *Consumer resources: Caregiving information, coworker death.* @ www.nfda.org

---

news to family members. In one study of 240 professionals providing death notifications, nearly 40 percent had never received classroom or any other training for this phase of their job. Survivor reactions that were most troublesome for professionals included self-harm and harm to others, physical acting out, and overwhelming anxiety. Sources of support for these courageous professionals came from their own families, from open discussions with coworkers, and from time spent alone (Stewart, Harris, & Mercer, 2000). See Research Focus 13.7 for a discussion of how people react when it is a coworker who has died.

Death of a Young Child

The death of a young child produces such intense grief and is such a devastating loss that parents may not ever recover; local support groups for those who have experienced such a loss (parents, siblings, grandparents, friends, and relatives) are particularly helpful. The unexpected death of a child due to accident or the sudden onset of a disease is even more difficult. If the death is due to an accident, parents experience enormous guilt, accepting responsibility far in excess of what is appropriate. When the death is anticipated, parents are encouraged to be honest and open with their child rather than engaging in mutual pretense. Anticipatory mourning or grief is often encouraged as parents and other family members are forced to face the dying process, usually through terminal illness (Davies, 2000b). Parents may alleviate the child's fears of loneliness, separation, and pain rather than trying to help the child to understand the concept of death itself. For most parents, the death of a child produces an existential crisis of meaning or purpose and a search for cognitive mastery. Some parents are able to view the death as ultimately enhancing their lives by helping them to connect to other people in the community, by strengthening their values and beliefs, by preserving the memory and their connections to their child, and by experiencing personal growth in overcoming the trauma of loss. Most parents found meaning in their lives within the first year following the death of their child; yet, they continued their pursuit of meaning as intensely as those who had not yet found meaning (Davis, Wortman, Lehman, & Silver, 2000; Wheeler, 2001).

Death of an Adult Child

The death of an adult child can also be devastating for an elderly parent. It is unexpected for a parent to survive a child, and for some older parents it is the most difficult death to accept—generating fears of isolation, insecurity regarding their own care, as well as intense guilt and anger over the loss of a lifetime identity as parent. The loss of an adult child is at least as intense as that of the loss of a spouse or one's own parent. Some investigators have found that the death of an adult child leads to more intense despair, guilt, anger, anxiety and symptoms of physical illness than the deaths of a spouse or parent. Insurance industry statistics indicate that as many as 25 percent of women over the age of 65 with an adult son will have to cope with the death of their adult child (Moss & Moss, 1995). These parents grieve for the loss of a child and for their grandchildren's loss of a parent (Reed, 2000).

Goodman and colleagues (1991) reported cultural differences in how elderly women (61 to 93 years of age) coped with the death of an adult child. Jewish women in the study appeared to be more grief-stricken and more depressed than non-Jewish women in having lost a fundamental role, focus, and identity in their lives. Among Protestant and Catholic women, the investigators found somewhat more acceptance and an ability to place the death of their adult child into a larger perspective so that they could move beyond the loss and continue with their own lives. Quantitative indicators of well-being, affect, generativity, and personality showed Jewish women to be far more intense in openly expressing the meaning of the death of an adult child and their personal loss than Protestant or Catholic women.

Moss and Moss (1995) have identified six major themes underlying the death of an adult child: (1) the untimeliness of the death and its destruction of the parents' worldview; (2) the loss of the bond established between child and parent and the threat to a major component of parental identity (e.g., the protective parent); (3) intense survivor guilt; (4) disequilibrium and strain in the parents' marital relationship and relationships with other children, as well as the children of the deceased child; (5) loss of social and instrumental support in old age (e.g., someone to share, help, and provide for the parents, especially in times of need) and (6) change in meaning for the future, with generativity needs unfulfilled.

Death of a Sibling

The death of a sibling for young children and adolescents is difficult to resolve (see Research Focus 13.6). Brothers and sisters not only feel the loss deeply, they may cognitively distort the meaning of the loss and accept responsibility for the death. Counselors recognize that children may not have the language to represent their emotions and often work with them through play, art, and music rather than talking. Girls seem to experience the death of a sibling, particularly a sister, more intensely than boys. Boys are more impacted by the death of a parent than a sibling (Worden, Davies, & McCown, 1999). Because parents are intensely grieving, siblings rarely have enough support or recognition of their feelings from family members and may turn to neighbors or friends; bereaved siblings are "the forgotten grievers" (Davies, 2000b). When given a chance to ask doctors questions about a family member's death, children and adolescents most want to understand the cause of death, followed by wanting to know the likely life span for themselves and family survivors (Thompson & Payne, 2000). When children are given appropriate support, information, and an opportunity to share their feelings, their ability to cope with loss is enhanced (Davies, 1999; Melvin & Lukeman, 2000).

The death of an adult sibling is a normative experience for the elderly, so it is curious that this type of loss has received little research attention. Sibling bonds represent the family bond of longest duration (Bedford, 1995). Clinicians, relatives, and friends do not seem to realize the significance of the loss, the intensity of the attachment bond, or the depth of grief among surviving siblings. One study examined the experience of bereavement among three groups of elderly (67 to 85 years old): bereaved siblings, bereaved spouses, and bereaved friends. Bereaved siblings were more impaired functionally and cognitively than bereaved friends and also rated themselves in worse health overall than either bereaved spouses or bereaved friends (Hays, Gold, & Peiper, 1997). Many adults lose siblings earlier in the life cycle due to AIDS-related deaths. Bereaved siblings reminisce, renew their ties, and find comfort and solace in the relationship with surviving siblings. It is as if ties with the deceased sibling are preserved symbolically in the relationship and renewed bonds with surviving brothers and sisters.

In some studies, it appears that ties with the children and spouse of a deceased sibling are also strengthened. In many cases the deceased sibling has served as a role model or standard of comparison, a major contributor to another brother or sister's sense of self; such losses are hard to accept. Moss and Moss (1995) note that whenever a same-aged peer or relative dies, the sense of one's own distance to death is shortened. Siblings may anticipate similar health patterns, similar life endings, and similar life expectancies.

Death of a Parent

The death of a parent shows persistent long-term effects whether it occurs in childhood, adolescence, or adulthood. Children face separation and loss as well as a reduction in the love, affection, and attention they have received. Parental death often means other significant life changes such as moving, a reduction in the standard of living, changes in friends, and stepparenting. Early parental loss can have lifelong effects persisting well into old age. When young children experience the death of a parent, they often have no one to replace the lost parent; in single-parent families, they usually assume adult roles, including work and financial support, far earlier than children from two-parent, intact homes. Children who lose a parent experience financial strain, increased social isolation, and a 20 percent incidence of psychiatric or psychological disorder. Children most often display intense grief, distress, and blunted affect. Boys have a higher rate of difficulty than girls, and boys are less likely to share their feelings, either with the remaining parent or with professional counselors (Dowdney, 2000). It may take many patient interactions, just being with children, before they feel comfortable expressing their feelings or exploring their grief. One of the most helpful questions counselors can ask children is, "Tell me about (the person who died)." From open-ended questions and a genuine personal interest in the child, the meaning and significance of the relationship can be understood and successful intervention initiated (Davies, 2000 a, b).

The death of a parent is a life-cycle transition that is off-time in the lives of young children and adolescents. The surviving parent must adopt some of the responsibilities and roles of the deceased parent; neither mothers nor fathers are prepared for the increased workload. Studies suggest that children cope better with parental death when the remaining parent openly communicates feelings, acknowledges the reality and impact of the loss, and encourages children to share their emotions (Silverman, 2000a, b). It is not the age of the child alone that determines the impact of parental death, but the child's experience with the death itself through family discussions of the loss, the freedom of survivors to share emotions, and the opportunity to continue the relationship symbolically. Grief counselors support a symbolic relationship with the deceased to preserve connections (Silverman, 2000a, b). For example, a counselor might affirm a child's desire to mow the lawn "because I know how angry Dad would be if it didn't look nice." The death of a parent means providing for the needs of surviving children at a time when a spouse is deeply mourning. Sibling conflict may increase (Fuller-Thomson, 1999–2000), perhaps in response to competition for the much-needed support of the surviving parent. It is not helpful to ask children to move on, to keep their emotions to themselves, or to live through memories of the past. Silverman suggests that children need social support, assurances that they remain an integral member of the continuing family unit, and opportunities to link themselves to the deceased parent.

Even for middle-aged or older adults, the death of a parent is an enormous loss. The way in which survivors cope emotionally following the death of any close relative has been studied using depression as the primary outcome variable; but depressive symptoms are not the same as an index of grief (Moss & Moss, 1995). Grief can involve preoccupation with the parent, intense loneliness, and periods of crying without necessarily indicating depression. In one investigation, the relationship between grief expression and social-cultural roles was studied (Klapper, Moss, Moss, & Rubinstein, 1994). A form of **selfish grief** was identified in which daughters were reluctant to display outward, visible signs of emotional expression following the death of their mothers. Rather than expressing their grief, the daughters repressed it, believing that emotional displays such as crying or sobbing would reflect their personal wish to have their mothers still alive with them, ignoring the physical pain and suffering that their mothers experienced at the end of their lives. These daughters experienced this tension between an outward emotional expression of grief and the prolonging of a mothers' pain and suffering as "selfish grief." They resolved it by hiding or controlling the feelings that were a natural part of their loss.

The death of an elderly parent can be somewhat less stressful than the death of a younger parent. There is some evidence that in the former instance, adult children have an opportunity to prepare themselves for the death as they witness their parents becoming older and more frail (Moss & Moss, 1995). Regardless of circumstances, most adult children believe that a parent who has died did not live long enough. The death of a parent also signifies that there is no other older generation standing between the adult child and death.

Death of a Spouse

The death of a spouse is one of the most common relationship losses among the elderly and leads to overwhelming bereavement and personal challenges. Older women are more likely to outlive their husbands since they usually marry men somewhat older than themselves and have a longer life expectancy. As table 13.6 reveals, widows outnumber widowers by almost 4 to 1 from age 65 on. Women who are widowed usually remain unmarried; the older they are, the less likely they will remarry. Being widowed for older men is somewhat more traumatic than for women, although there are no basic differences in the experience of grief (Blieszner & Hatvany, 1996). Older men depend on women for many traditional household responsibilities and as a primary resource for support and friendships. Widowers often feel at a loss in such matters; this may, in part, explain why men are likely to remarry following the loss of a spouse. Nearly 77 percent of men aged 65 or older resided with a spouse, while only 17 percent lived alone (Population 2000).

Experts recognize that reactions to being widowed change over time, and surviving spouses may experience different emotions simultaneously (Blieszner & Hat-

TABLE 13.6				
Marital Status of Men and Women Aged 65 and Over, 1998				
	Men		Women	
	Married	*Widowed*	*Married*	*Widowed*
65–74	79%	9%	55%	32%
75–84	74%	20%	34%	56%
85+	50%	42%	13%	77%

Source: Population 2000. (2000). Older Americans 2000: Key indicators of well-being. www.agingstats.gov/chartbook2000/population.html

vany, 1996; Lund, 2000). Older widows and widowers begin to identify their strengths and vulnerabilities, think about their future without a spouse, and recognize their growing closeness to their own death. Bereavement is not always debilitating, since many survivors find meaning in their loss and recognize the existential growth that occurs. In the early phases of bereavement, younger surviving spouses appear to undergo far more intense grief reactions, whereas older surviving spouses show better early adjustment but more intense feelings of grief months later. Widows, unlike bereaved widowers, do seek social support from other women who have also experienced the loss of a spouse. Yet, compared to older widows, younger widows more often pursue close social supports, derive the support they need from a wider network, and have overall fewer adjustment problems (depression, addictive behaviors, visits to physicians and hospitals, higher mortality; Blieszner & Hatvany, 1996; Parkes, 1993). Living alone is not the same as being lonely or socially isolated. Social support helps to overcome loneliness, but neither replaces the loss of a significant attachment bond nor the loss of security or support—emotional, physical, and financial—that a spouse provides (O'Bryant & Hansson, 1995).

The death of a spouse ends a longstanding attachment bond and has an impact on virtually every area of life. Surviving spouses lose a friend, companion, sexual partner, support, and protector. Recently bereaved women experience unbearable loneliness, particularly at mealtimes. Widows eat less and find meals less pleasurable. On average, they lose 7.6 pounds, but they regain weight as their grief subsides (Rosenbloom & Whittington, 1993). Widows are challenged to pursue new roles, live with a new status, and cope with the loss of a major support system. Most are at increased risk of mortality, have less effective immune systems, and are at increased risk of various psychological and physical disorders. While widows who have cared for a dying spouse are relieved of caregiving obligations and can "reclaim" their lives, they face a host of new responsibilities. Widows must learn to handle finances, insurance, home maintenance, lawn and garden, and upkeep of the family car. Those most independent and in control during marriage have fewer difficulties in widowhood and in managing their grief than those who were highly dependent on their husbands (Blieszner & Hatvany, 1996). In one study, surviving spouses in their sixties were asked to offer commonsense advice to newly bereaved spouses. They suggested staying involved, continuing with one's roles, and maintaining formerly valued and rewarding social relationships as essential to recovery. Younger widows showed better recovery and fewer adjustment difficulties when they preserved a symbolic emotional tie with the deceased spouse and maintained identity continuity through past roles and activities (Bergstrom & Holmes, 2000; Bonanno, Mihalecz, & LeJeune, 1999). Surviving spouses are encouraged to continue to use the name of the deceased in conversations, to express their feelings to others, to turn to others for support, to cherish past memories, and to be patient with themselves as they grieve. Holidays, anniversaries, and birthdays can be particularly difficult, and some try to establish new ways to recognize the day, rather than long for days gone by (AARP, 2001d).

Widowhood may be experienced in many ways (Blieszner & Hatvany, 1996; Lopata, 1987b). Some are unable to reengage in social relations, and may let friendships with other couples wane after the death of a spouse; however, others create new support systems and reimmerse themselves in their families, neighborhoods, communities, occupations, or volunteer organizations. Some widows display long dormant personal abilities, enjoying their newfound talents. Some widows remarry to overcome their loneliness and loss of attachment. Others enjoy their new independence. They have no interest in marriage or in another experience of intense loss or providing care to a seriously ill partner (Blieszner & Hatvany, 1996; Lopata, 1994). Elderly widows are more likely to change their residence when health and functional disability occur since they do not have the additional support from a spouse to manage the routine household tasks and chores of daily living (Bradsher et al., 1992).

Research investigators believe that widows who derive significant social support, develop mastery over the social contexts in which they live, who are positive copers, and who have adjusted to life crises successfully in the past will best manage and recover from the loss of a spouse (Lieberman & Peskin, 1992; Parkes, 1993).

Suicide

The impact of suicide on family survivors is immense, particularly for a spouse. In addition to feeling intense, overwhelming grief, survivors also harbor hostility and feelings of rejection. Family members believe that perhaps they might have been able to somehow prevent the suicide. And rather than reach out for support from neighbors, friends, and clergy, most families become closed to discussion about the death and their own reactions (Bailley, Kral, & Dunham, 1999). Middle-aged and younger spouses show heightened, intense bereavement reactions that include denial, depression, uncontrollable grief, and physical symptoms severe enough to require medical and hospital diagnostic testing. Two-and-one-half-year follow-up studies of surviving spouses 55 years of age and older show those dealing with natural death experience a reduction in grief after six months, while suicide-surviving spouses show strong grief reactions through the first 18 months after the death. Suicide-bereaved spouses rate themselves as having more mental health problems, including depression, distress, and anxiety, than natural death-bereaved spouses. By 30 months after the loss, both groups showed comparable bereavement reactions and feelings of loss, isolation, and sadness. Child survivors of suicide (5 to 14 years of age) tend to internalize their grief, experience depression, and show poor school performance and adjustment difficulties (Farberow, Gallaher-Thompson, Gilewski, & Thompson, 1992). Children also report a high incidence of suicidal thoughts, and experts recommend close monitoring and early intervention if psychiatric disturbances or social maladjustment emerge sometime later (Pfeffer, Martins, Mann, & Sunkenberg, 1997). Bereaved children need (1) information appropriate to their maturity, but not every detail, (2) social support from family and friends; (3) to see family members express their grief openly; (4) an opportunity to grieve openly themselves; and (5) a chance to remember and share the importance of the deceased in their life (Stokes et al., 1999). Most family members feel awkward and stigmatized by their loss and are hesitant to share their emotions with others. All family members need to speak openly about the suicide; trying to protect children by not using the word *suicide* is inappropriate. If their elders try to hide the truth, young children may hear it from others rather than from those they love (NFDA, 2001 a, b).

SUMMARY

Despite the inevitability of death, it remains an uncomfortable topic in our culture. Recent medical advances have made the determination of death complex. For example, brain death can occur even though critical organs such as the heart and lungs continue to function. Today we are faced with ethical questions concerning the practices of euthanasia and physician-assisted suicide, and when we should prolong a person's life. Several states have enacted laws to determine when a dying person may not be resuscitated, to facilitate the use of living wills, and to establish durable powers of attorney, health care proxy, and advance medical directives. Controversy continues over the definition of brain death and its relation to the process of death. Depending on what policy decisions are being made about the process of death, competing definitions may be entirely acceptable.

It is important to consider the sociohistorical and sociocultural contexts of death. There is more avoidance and denial of death in American culture than in many other cultures. Individual experience with death and dying may contribute to cultural differences in attitudes. A growing emphasis is being placed on death education to help those facing death as well as those who have experienced the death of someone close to them. Near-death experiences have been documented and evaluated to identify similarities, and those who have had them seem to be changed in their feelings about life and death.

Elisabeth Kübler-Ross suggested five psychological stages of dying: denial and isolation, anger, bargaining, depression, and acceptance. Researchers have been unable to verify that dying people go through the stages in the prescribed sequence; however, Kübler-Ross has contributed significantly to society's emphasis on humanizing the dying process. E. Mansell Pattison has suggested three phases of what he calls the living-dying interval: acute, chronic, and terminal. The dying process is multifaceted and involves much more than descriptive stages or phases; some have even explored the "dying career." Denial is one aspect of the coping process for the dying person. For many dying people, denial may help them cope. An open system of communication with the dying is an optimal strategy for the dying person, staff, and family members.

The contexts in which people die are also important. Hospitals ensure medical expertise and sophisticated equipment, but more intimacy and autonomy is usually possible at home. Hospice represents a humanizing approach to those facing death. The hospice movement stresses patient control and management of pain as well as a philosophy based on open communication, family involvement, and extensive support services.

The loss of someone with whom we have developed enduring attachment bonds, such as a spouse, is among the most stressful of life events. Coping with the death of a loved one has been described in terms of bereavement, or the state of loss; mourning, the overt, behavioral expression of bereavement; and grief, the most powerful of human emotions. Mourning takes many forms, depending on one's culture, ethnicity, and religious practices. In the United States, the mourning process usually involves a funeral, which is followed by burial or cremation. In recent years, controversy has arisen about the funeral industry, and steps have been taken to improve consumer understanding of its services, charges, and products.

Grief may be seen as a series of phases—shock, despair, and adjustment. However, people do not have to go through each phase to cope adaptively with grief. One of the most common ways of experiencing grief is through grief pangs. Denial is also part of grief, just as it is part of the dying process. One aspect of grief is existential and involves making sense out of the world and trying to solve the puzzle of death. Difficult deaths to resolve include the death of a young child, the death of an adult child, the death of a sibling, and the death of a parent. Suicide has an immense impact on survivors, and bereavement is both more intense and more extended when death is self-inflicted.

REVIEW QUESTIONS

1. How is death defined? Describe two controversies surrounding the definition.
2. Describe the requirements governing euthanasia in the Netherlands.
3. Identify developmental patterns in understanding death in children and adolescence. Explain the corresponding attitudes and beliefs about death.
4. Outline Kübler-Ross's five psychological stages of dying. Describe the concerns of those who have tried to validate her work.
5. What are the distinctions between bereavement, grief, and mourning?
6. List the benefits of death education and explain its role in contemporary society.
7. What is hospice, and what are its goals?
8. What are the eight myths related to loss for children and adolescents?
9. Describe the concept of dying on one's own terms.
10. Indicate some of the basic changes occurring in the funeral industry today.
11. What are the phases involved in the grieving process? How do people grieve?
12. Choose one of the deaths that are difficult to resolve discussed at the end of the chapter and indicate the basic conflicts survivors experience and their characteristic methods of coping.

 ON THE WEB www.mhhe.com/hoyer5

For additional information on topics discussed in chapter 13, check out the following websites.

The National Hospice Foundation site provides current perspectives on the hospice-movement nationwide. It also offers information and booklets explaining end-of-life options for families and advice for encouraging open family discussion.

The National Funeral Directors Association publishes regular statistical reports and updates for consumers. The association provides information, booklets, and resources on its website for families dealing with death.

The Cremation Association of North America identifies funeral homes, cemeteries, and crematoriums that offer services. The association also provides general information for consumers, guidelines for explaining cremation to family members, particularly children, and ways to memorialize a loved one.

The general AARP (American Association of Retired Persons) site offers information on a number of relevant topics, including helping widows and others who are bereaved to get through the holiday season, coping with loss, choosing a health care proxy, and preparing a will, living trust, or medical directive.

DEVELOPMENTAL RESEARCH METHODS

INTRODUCTION

Imagine you are a researcher studying whether creativity declines with age. How should you proceed? You suspect that many opinions about aging and the decline of creativity are rooted in negative prejudices and stereotypes of the aged, or are based on different standards for people of different ages. You are interested in obtaining an accurate description of changes in creativity across the adult life span. How should you proceed?

One approach might be simply to ask people of different ages to rate their creativity (using a seven-point scale, for example). But your goal is to gather objective data on creativity, not subjective impressions. Another approach might be to collect ratings on people's creativity from friends and relatives. This might get around the problem of self-distortion, but the data are still subjective. Moreover, how well can friends and relatives judge a person's creativity? (Do your friends and relatives know exactly how creative *you* are?) Another approach might be to use a questionnaire or structured interview. Rather than simply asking people about their creativity, you might ask them about a variety of items such as lifestyle (Are they unconventional?), work habits (Do they waste many idle hours until spurred by a creative burst?), and motivations (Do they enjoy following orders and being told what to do, or do they prefer to set their own tasks and goals?). Responses could be scored or weighted for creativity, and a total creativity score derived. Unfortunately, participants might guess the purpose of your study and try to produce answers that appear creative.

Perhaps it would be better to test people's ability to find creative solutions to problems rather than to ask them about creativity. You could develop a test or use a test that has already been constructed to measure creative problem solving. This approach seems promising, but you must know the reliability and validity of your test. Does the test give consistent estimates of creativity if the same individual is tested twice or more? This demonstrates *reliability*. Does the test truly measure creativity, or does it measure intelligence, wisdom, or something else? This question involves *validity*.

Even if a test shows high reliability and high validity with young adults, the test might not be as reliable and valid for elderly people. Further, age differences in creative problem solving might not reflect age per se, but, cohort differences in other factors such as educational background or health. Some of these factors could be measured by using a longitudinal design, testing the same individuals every 10 years from ages 20 to 70. But do you have 50 years to complete your study? And how many of the participants you test today will be available 50 years from now?

The problem of extraneous factors and the difficulty of conducting longitudinal designs might lead you to use archival or historical data. For example, you might investigate the typical ages at which people have produced great artistic or scientific achievements. Unfortunately, the evidence archival investigations provide is indirect; many factors in addition to creativity determine at what age someone might produce a great artistic or scientific accomplishment. (Indeed, many social and cultural factor may influence the time course of adult creative achievement.) Further, the accuracy and completeness of archival data are always concerns.

Faced with all of these problems, you might choose to use animals as subjects in your research. With animal subjects, it is possible to control many factors (diet, experiences in infancy, etc.) that cannot be controlled in humans. Also, many animals have relatively brief life spans, making longitudinal research more feasible. But how do you devise a creativity test that animals can complete? And can results obtained with animals be generalized to humans?

How, then, should you investigate aging and creativity? There is no one right answer—only alternative approaches with varying advantages and disadvantages. Furthermore, there is ample room for your own ingenuity in selecting, combining, and even modifying approaches to suit your own research goals. Indeed, the need for innovation in science is part of its challenge and appeal.

The fundamental task of science is measurement. We begin this chapter with a discussion of two basic issues related to measurement: the reliability and the validity of measurements. Then we discuss several techniques used for collecting observations: the structured interview and questionnaire, standardized tests, and behavioral research. Next, we'll consider some of the ways to describe and interpret measurements. Then we'll explore the topic of research design, first considering simple correlational designs and then more powerful experimental designs. We will also discuss quasi-experimental designs. The appendix closes with a section on sampling, a critical problem in all psychological research but particularly important in research on adult development and aging.

Basic Issues of Measurement

Measurement—a major task of science—sounds simple. However, to make accurate and meaningful measurements is far from simple. Let's look at two basic issues we must consider when making scientific measurements.

Reliability of Measures

Suppose you are assisting on a research project focusing on age changes in **reaction time,** the amount of time it takes to respond to a simple stimulus. You are asked to construct a task that will measure the reaction times of all the adults participating in this study. After a great deal of thought, you develop the following reaction-time task. You ask participants to sit individually at tables and place a set of earphones on their heads. Directly in front of each participant on the table is a telegraph key. You tell the participants that every now and then they will hear a beeping sound delivered to both ears via the earphones. You instruct them to press the telegraph key as quickly as possible whenever they hear a beep. Within this context, you define reaction time as the amount of time it takes a participant to press the key after the beep has initially sounded. Furthermore, you decide to measure the participants' reaction times by using a handheld stopwatch that measures time in hundredths of seconds. You plan to start the watch when the participant hears the beep (you will also wear a pair of earphones connected to the same sound source). And you plan to stop the watch when the participant presses the key.

Suppose you tell the principal investigator of the research project about your plan to measure reaction time. You assume she will be very impressed with the task you have developed. However, she seems concerned about the reliability of your measure. What exactly is the principal investigator worried about? How can you reassure her? Essentially, the concept of **reliability** refers to the degree to which measurement is consistent over time. Given your inexperience at measuring reaction time, there are many reasons why the measurements you collect might be inconsistent and unstable. For example, were all of the participants instructed to press the button by using the index finger on their preferred hand? Did some of the participants position their fingers directly on top of the telegraph key before some of the trials but place their fingers on the table before some of the other trials? If the participants positioned their fingers in different locations before each trial, you would collect very unreliable data. (Remember, you want to measure the time it takes to press the key, not the time it takes to move a finger to the key and *then* press the key!) Also, when did you plan to begin measuring the participants' response times—as soon as they begin to perform the reaction-time task, or after several practice trials? Until a participant becomes familiar with the experimental task and apparatus, his or her reaction times could vary considerably from trial to trial. Finally, the principal investigator may wonder how accurately you can measure reaction time by using a handheld stop watch. Is it possible for you to start your watch at the exact split-second the beep sounds and stop the watch at the exact instant the participant depresses the telegraph key? Even if you could accurately measure reaction time at the beginning of the experimental session (which is extremely doubtful), might you become increasingly tired, inattentive as you measured more and more reaction times? As you can see, there is a variety of factors that affect the reliability of even very simple measures of behavior.

Assessing Reliability   How can we assess the reliability of measures? There is a variety of techniques for assessing the consistency of observations.

Test-retest reliability can be assessed by obtaining the same set of measurements on two different occasions. The question is whether measurements (numerical scores of some kind) on occasion 2 are predictable from observations gathered on occasion 1. Thus, after a familiarization period, we could administer 100 reaction-time trials to participants on day 1 and 100 trials on day 2; if the test is reliable, we should obtain predictable measurements of the participants' reaction times. Of course, test-retest reliability is meaningful only when the variable we are measuring is assumed to be stable over time. If a person was in a different mood on Day 1 than on Day 2, or healthy on one day and not the other, or had learned something on Day 1 that influenced performance on Day 2, we would not assess test-retest reliability.

Interrater reliability should be assessed whenever measurements involve a subjective, judgmental component. This is frequently the case in studies that collect observational data. The technique is to assess the degree of agreement among two or more observers. High agreement implies high reliability.

Interitem reliability can be examined whenever measurements entail multiple items. A common procedure for assessing interitem reliability is to divide the items into halves (for instance, the odd-numbered items versus the even-numbered items) and to determine the extent to which measurements (average scores) on one half are predictable from measurements on the other half. High predictability implies high reliability.

Ways of Improving Reliability One method for improving reliability is to refine the procedures and tools we use for measurement. In our example of measuring reaction time, we could improve reliability by using a carefully structured set of procedures (e.g., instructing participants to place the index finger of their preferred hand on the telegraph key). The use of a computer (with an internal clock to record reaction time—in milliseconds—between the onset of the beep and the depression of the key) would improve the reliability and accuracy of measures.

Reliability is a concern in all psychological research. However, reliability problems are particularly bothersome in developmental research, especially when individual differences are at issue. If a group of people is given an IQ test at age 18 and again at age 45, it is probable that some individuals will show gains from the first test to the second, whereas others will show losses. Are there true differences between the gainers and the losers in intelligence, or are we simply seeing the effects of an unreliable measuring instrument? Although statistical methods can be applied to this problem, reliability remains questionable. Furthermore, envision a situation in which every person tested at age 45 scores exactly 10 points higher on the IQ test than they scored at age 18. Since we could exactly predict a person's IQ at age 45 from his or her IQ at age 18, we would conclude that the test used to measure IQ is highly reliable—it possesses a perfect level of test-retest reliability. However, it is obvious that not one of our participants has the same IQ score at both times of testing, making the test's stability questionable. Therefore, since the concept of reliability entails both the predictability and the stability of measurements, separate measures of predictability and stability should be developed and used.

Validity of Measurement

In our example of measuring reaction time, the principal investigator questioned the reliability (essentially, the repeatability) of the measurement. What if she also doubted the **validity** of the measure itself? A measure is valid if it actually measures what it purports to measure. The measure of reaction time, therefore, is valid if it really measures the amount of time it takes adults to make a simple motor response once they hear a sound. The principal investigator might suggest that the task you developed to measure reaction time could actually measure how well participants can hear the beep rather than how fast they react to it. If older adults have trouble hearing, they will have difficulty reacting to the beep. Thus, to make certain that the measure of reaction time is valid, all of the prospective participants in the study will have to be screened for auditory sensitivity.

Although there are many different types of validity, the type we are currently addressing is **construct validity.** Constructs are abstract entities that cannot be directly observed but are presumed to influence observable phenomena. Intelligence is a construct; so are anxiety, creativity, memory, self-esteem, and other aspects of personality and cognition. We often attempt to observe phenomena that we believe might reflect these constructs. The question of whether the observed phenomena actually do reflect the constructs is at the heart of the issue of construct validity.

Even when observations are highly reliable, they do not necessarily have high construct validity. Were we to devise a test of creativity, we might be able to demonstrate high test-retest reliability as well as high interitem reliability. However, the test could still be vulnerable to the charge that it really measures intelligence, not creativity—or to the charge that creativity may not even truly exist.

Students of adult development and aging must consider whether a given test or measurement might have reasonable construct validity for young adults but not for elderly people. For example, a test of long-term memory might be reasonably valid for college students who are accustomed to memory tests. But the same test might be intimidating to elderly people who have not taken a memory test for decades. Hence, the performance of elderly people might reflect anxiety more than memory per se.

Basic Techniques Used for Collecting Measurements

Psychologists collect data in a number of ways to test hypotheses about adult development. In this section, we discuss the salient features of these different techniques.

Interviews and Questionnaires

Many inquiries on adult development use interviews and questionnaires. An **interview** is a set of questions asked face-to-face or interactively. The interview can range from being very structured to very unstructured. For example, a very unstructured interview might include open-ended questions such as, "Tell me about some of the things you do with your friends," or "Tell me about yourself." On the other hand, a very structured interview might question whether the respondent highly approves, moderately approves, moderately disapproves, or highly disapproves of his friends' use of drugs. Responses from highly unstructured interviews can be useful for clinical purposes or for developing more focused measures for future efforts.

Structured interviews conducted by an experienced examiner can produce valuable data. However, structured interviews are not without problems. Perhaps the most critical of these problems involves the response bias of social desirability. In a face-to-face situation where anonymity is impossible, a person's responses may reflect social desirability rather than her actual feelings or actions. In other words, a person may be reluctant to say what she actually thinks on some topics.

A **questionnaire** is similar to a highly structured interview except that adults read the questions and mark their answers on a sheet of paper rather than responding orally to the interviewer. One major advantage of questionnaires is that they can easily be given to a very large number of people. A sample of responses from thousands of people is possible. However, survey items should be concrete, specific, and unambiguous.

Another problem with both interviews and surveys or questionnaires is that some questions may be retrospective in nature; that is, they may require the participant to recall events or feelings from some point in the past. It is not unusual, for example, to interview older adults about experiences they had during adolescence or young adulthood. Retrospective data are prone to memory distortions, but there are ways to increase the reliability and validity of self-report measures (Ericsson & Simon, 1984; Stone, et al., 1999).

Behavioral Research

Regardless of advances in our understanding of verbal reports, they probably will never be adequate, by themselves, as a basis for psychological research. Apart from problems of response set or memory, verbal reports obviously depend on conscious awareness. Yet many aspects of cognition, personality, and social behavior apparently are subconscious. Thus, we must go beyond what people tell us about themselves and examine how they behave.

Behavioral research does not depend on participants' verbal reports regarding the issue under study. For example, a questionnaire might be based on verbal reports of the memory problems the elderly experience. In contrast, a behavioral study of memory might actually assess the accuracy of verbal recall by the elderly. (For instance, the researcher might present a list of words, followed by a test of verbal recall for these words.) Both approaches involve verbalization on the part of participants, but only the questionnaire involves verbalization about memory itself. Interestingly, evidence indicates that reports of memory problems are not strongly associated with true deficits in performance on memory tasks. Marion Perlmutter has collected both questionnaire and performance data on memory in young and older adults. Overall, she found that older adults report more memory problems on a questionnaire and that they also perform more poorly on some (but not all) memory tasks. But reported memory problems have proved to be a poor basis for predicting actual memory performance in this type of research (Perlmutter, 1986). For example, a person reporting many memory problems might actually perform very well on a memory test, and vice versa.

Behavioral Research in Laboratory Versus Field Settings

In behavioral research, it is frequently necessary to control factors that might determine behavior but are not the focus of the inquiry. For example, if we are interested in studying long-term memory in different age groups, we might want to control motivation as well as the conditions of learning (study time, distracting noises, etc.). Even extraneous factors such as temperature and time of day might be important. Laboratories are places that allow considerable control over many extraneous factors. For this reason, behavioral research is frequently conducted in laboratories.

However, conducting laboratory research is costly, and some of these costs are especially high when developmental issues are being addressed. First, it is impossible to conduct research in a laboratory without letting the participants know they are in an experiment. This creates problems with reactivity. **Reactivity** occurs when participants think they should behave in a specific manner because they are in an experimental setting. Second, the laboratory setting is unnatural and might cause the participants to behave unnaturally. This problem can be particularly severe with elderly participants, who may find the laboratory setting even more unnatural than young adults do. Finally, certain phenomena, particularly social phenomena, are difficult if not impossible to produce in the laboratory. The effects of "job-related stress on marital satisfaction," for example, might be difficult (and unethical) to investigate in a laboratory setting.

Because of these problems with laboratory research, many psychologists prefer to do their research in real-world settings. Such settings include job sites, shopping malls, senior citizen centers, nursing homes, or classrooms. The main drawback of field research is limited control over extraneous factors. However, this drawback is frequently outweighed by the benefits of low reactivity, natural contexts, and access to interesting phenomena that are difficult to observe in the laboratory.

Laboratory and field research are two points on a continuum, a continuum that can be labeled *naturalism versus control.* If some laboratory experiments employ conditions or tasks of a decidedly natural character, these experiments belong in the middle area of the continuum. For example, a laboratory study of memory might examine recall of events from one's past. A laboratory study of possible age difference in marriage might bring couples into the lab to measure emotional responses. Researchers find that many benefits of field studies can be enjoyed in the laboratory if the activities of the participants are to some degree natural. This is an important lesson for psychologists interested in adult development and aging. It is frequently necessary to collect data in a laboratory-like context (perhaps a simple room with few distracting stimuli). This does not mean that the tasks participants perform must be unnatural and uninteresting. Such tasks might put elderly people at a disadvantage.

Standardized Tests

Standardized tests attempt to measure an individual's characteristics or abilities as compared with those of a large group of similar individuals. Such tests may take the forms of questionnaires, interviews, or behavioral tests. To maximize reliability, a good test should have a reasonably large number of items and should be given in an objective, standardized manner. The **standardization** of tests actually refers to two different qualities: the establishment of fixed or standard procedures for administration and scoring, and the establishment of norms for age, grade, race, sex, and so on. Norms are patterns or representative values for a group. Hence, the performance of an individual can be assessed relative to that of a comparison group (people of the same age, sex, etc.).

Many standardized tests have good reliability, but their construct validity can be questioned. IQ tests, for example, show impressive reliability, but there is considerable uncertainty about what such tests actually measure. The problem is compounded by the possibility that a single test might measure different things at different ages—for example, an IQ test might measure intellectual ability in young adulthood but anxiety in old age. This possibility is critical in interpreting developmental research that shows that IQ performance can change with age.

There are standardized tests for intellectual functioning, for psychopathology or mental illness, for life satisfaction, creativity, and many other aspects of personality and cognition. Such tests are used for a wide variety of purposes and are invaluable in developmental research. However, when using any test, it is important to consider construct validity. Does the standardized test truly measure the construct in question?

Physiological Research

There is no question that a biological or physiological level of analysis offers a great deal of information about adult development and aging. This is not to say that psychological and sociocultural factors are unimportant; indeed, there is good reason to believe that there are multiple determinants of adult development. Moreover, physiological factors and sociocultural factors interact during the course of adult development.

Basic Strategies for Describing and Interpreting Measurements

In most scientific studies, a vast number of measurements allow researchers to collect considerable amounts of raw data. To understand these data, we must describe and interpret them objectively. In this section, we summarize some of the statistical techniques researchers use to make sense of raw data.

Measures of Central Tendency and Variability

Most people are familiar with the procedure of averaging. Given a set of *n* scores (where *n* refers to the total number of scores in a data set), we add their values and divide by *n*. The result is the **mean,** by far the most common—but not the only—measure of **central tendency.** Another such measure is the **median,** which is a value in the middle of the distribution of scores (so that as many scores fall above the median as below it). The **mode** is the most frequently appearing score in the set.

Measures of central tendency such as the mean provide important but incomplete information. Reporting the mean score is like telling another person that the score of a baseball game is 3–1 but failing to tell which team is ahead and which inning it is. For this reason, we often need information on the variability of scores as well as their mean.

The simplest measure of **variability** is the **range,** which is a comparison between the lowest and highest scores in a data set. A much more meaningful measure of variability is the **standard deviation.** The standard deviation is a mathematical index of the degree to which every score in a distribution of scores differs from the mean. The more the scores in a distribution vary from the mean, the larger the standard deviation. The less the scores in a distribution differ from the mean, the smaller the standard deviation.

Means and standard deviations are reported frequently in research on adult development. There are several reasons for this, but none is more important than the relevance of these measures to individual differences in the course of adult development. For example, it is possible that a group of young adults and a group of older adults would both remember the same mean number of items on a test of memory ability (each group could recognize, on average, 20 words from a list of 35). However, we might discover that the standard deviation for the older group was 7.4, while the standard deviation for the younger group was 3.1. These results would suggest that there is much more variability in the performance of older persons than in that of younger persons. This important point would be obscured if the investigator only reported the mean score.

Correlations between Variables

To understand the concept of correlation, one must first understand the meaning of the term **variable.** A variable is something that can vary—that is, that can take on different levels or values. Age, for example, is a variable because it can take on values between 0 and 100 years or more. Other common variables are IQ, height, weight, and years of education. Some variables can take only two different values (biological sex, e.g., can be only male or female).

A **correlation** is a measure of the relationship or strength of association between two variables. During adulthood, there is usually a correlation between a person's age and the number of grandchildren he or she has—generally, the older the adult, the greater the number of grandchildren.

Correlations can be either positive or negative. A **positive correlation** exists when high values of one variable are associated with high values of the other. During the adult years, the variables of age and onset of chronic illness are positively correlated—the older a person is, the more likely she is to develop a chronic illness such as arthritis. A **negative correlation** exists when high values of one variable are associated with low values of the other. In contemporary American society, a negative correlation exists between age and years of education; young adults in their thirties, on the average, have completed more years of formal education than older adults in their seventies and eighties. This is because of the relative lack of educational opportunity available to many individuals during the early part of the twentieth century. Remember that a positive correlation does not necessarily reflect a "good" finding, nor does a negative correlation automatically reflect a "bad" finding. There is obviously nothing "good" about the finding that as individuals grow older they are more likely to encounter a greater number of health problems.

Whether positive or negative, correlations can vary from weak to strong. A correlation is strong if the values of one variable are very predictable from the values of the other. A perfect correlation exists when the values of one variable are perfectly predictable from the values of the other. The strength of a correlation can be measured quantitatively by computing the **Pearson product moment correlation coefficient,** which is abbreviated as r. A perfect correlation will yield an r of either $+1.0$ or -1.0, depending on whether the association between the variables is positive or negative. As the association becomes weaker, the r score drops in absolute value from 1.0 to .90, .60, .40, and so on, to 0.00. A correlation of 0.0 indicates that there is no relationship between the measures. Perfect correlations (1.0) are seldom obtained, but even moderate correlations (say, those with r values of .30 to .60) can be very meaningful.

Two final points need to be made about correlational analyses. First, measures of correlation, such as Pearson's r, reflect the strength of the **linear** association between variables. This is fine in many cases, but sometimes **curvilinear** associations occur between variables. For example, it is doubtlessly true that most people have little personal income in childhood but that their income increases and then falls again as they grow older. Such a curvilinear association between age and income cannot be measured by Pearson's r. Second, correlational techniques are typically used to measure the relationship between two variables at a time. Thus, we could examine the correlations between

IQ and income, income and years of education, and IQ and years of education. But correlational analyses are not usually used to examine how income and years of education, taken together, predict IQ scores.

Multiple Regression

Multiple regression is a powerful statistical method that allows an investigator to go beyond correlational analyses. Using this technique, a researcher can set up a complex model to determine whether a number of variables, in combination with one another (or independent of one another), predict another variable. For example, a psychologist could determine how age, years of education, social class, gender, and need for achievement predict IQ scores. And the psychologist could also find out whether age predicts IQ independent of years of education, social class, gender, and need for achievement. Finally, multiple regression may be used to measure curvilinear relationships. Thus, a regression model could describe the finding that marital satisfaction progressively declines as children move through adolescence but begins to increase once children leave home and attend college.

Factor Analysis

To understand adult development, it is sometimes necessary to examine many variables and to assess the pattern of correlations between these variables. For example, we might be interested in examining the variable of age with mathematical ability, creativity, health, income, occupational status, and life satisfaction. That would give us seven variables in all, with a myriad of possible correlations. How do we make sense of so many correlations? How do we get a view of the forest, not just the trees?

Factor analysis can be useful for producing a kind of summary of many correlations. The goal is simply to reduce a large number of correlations to a smaller number of independent sets called factors. Put somewhat differently, the purpose of this procedure is to discover what variables are significantly correlated with one another but totally uncorrelated with all the other variables. For example, if health, exercise, life satisfaction, and income all correlated with one another but were mathematically independent of all of the other variables, we might want to say that these variables make up a factor we could label as "general well-being" or "vigor." Through this process, we would replace four original variables with a single derived factor.

A potential problem with factors derived from patterns of correlations is their meaning. Once we identify and label a factor as representing x (well-being or vigor, for example), there is a tendency to believe that x truly exists (that there is, in fact, a separate "trait" of well-being or vigor and that people differ on this trait). In reality, a factor is only a summary of a pattern of correlations. Our label for a factor is just that, a label. It can be wrong or misleading.

Significance Tests

Suppose we conducted a study to determine whether early retirement results in high levels of life satisfaction. We might ask a group of adults who opted for early retirement and a group of their age-mates who are still working to complete a standardized measure of life satisfaction. After collecting the data, we discover that the mean scores for the early retirees versus the workers were 101 and 77, respectively. At this point we might wonder if there is a significant difference between the two groups on the measure of life satisfaction. Or we might wonder if there is a significant relationship between the participants' work status (working versus retired) and their scores on the measure of life satisfaction.

To determine the **statistical significance** of the results of a research study, it is first necessary to determine the probability of obtaining the observed results by pure chance alone. Through any of a number of sophisticated statistical techniques, it is possible to determine mathematically the probability of getting the results we obtained in our study by chance. Although it is not within the scope of this text to show you how to obtain these probability estimates, you should know how these estimates are interpreted. If a researcher determined that the probability of obtaining the observed results by pure chance is 5/100 or less, she would conclude that the two groups in her study reflected differences so great that they are unlikely to have occurred by chance alone. Thus, differences this substantial would be viewed as "significant." Conversely, if the researcher determined that the probability of obtaining the observed results by chance is high (say 80/100 or more), she would conclude that the differences between the groups in her study were "not significant" and that the two groups responded in much the same way. Specifically, psychologists consider probabilities of 5/100 or less as indicative of statistical significance. To return to our original example, if we discovered that the probability of obtaining the observed differences between the workers and early retirees on the life satisfaction measure by pure chance was 5/100 or less, we would conclude that (1) the two groups differ significantly on their responses to the life satisfaction measure, and (2) there is a significant relationship between work status and life satisfaction.

Basic Strategies for Research Design

In preparing to conduct a research project, it is especially important to consider design principles. The research design will determine the relationships assessed and/or the comparisons made. It will also determine how valid our conclusions are. In general, there are two types of research designs: correlational and experimental designs.

Correlational Versus Experimental Strategies

It often is said that the experiment is the principal tool of any research scientist. Yet the vast majority of studies on adult development and aging are not true experiments; rather, they are correlational studies. What is the difference between the two? Why are correlational strategies so often used to study development? Do developmental researchers pay a price for not performing true experiments?

A **correlational study** is one in which associations among variables are merely observed. An **experimental study** also assesses the associations among variables, but makes a distinction between dependent variables, which are measured or observed, and independent variables, which the experimenter manipulates. Thus, the manipulation of independent variables and the observation of dependent variables are critical features of experiments.

A concrete example may help to clarify the differences between correlational and experimental studies. Suppose we develop the hypothesis that living in a dull, nondemanding social environment causes a deterioration in the memories of older adults, whereas living in a stimulating, demanding social environment causes older adults to maintain their memories. We could investigate this hypothesis by conducting a correlational study. This might entail administering a standardized test of memory to two groups of older adults who live in two different types of environments: a nondemanding environment (perhaps a nursing home), and a demanding environment (living independently at home and being actively involved in a senior citizens center, doing volunteer work, etc.). From this study, we might discover that the level of demand or challenge in the social environment is positively correlated with memory performance—that is, as the demands of the environment increase, participants' scores on the memory test increase. Regardless of the strength of this correlation, however, we could not conclude that changes in the environment cause differences in memory. It may be that older people who remember and think well are more likely to choose to live at home, while people who have more difficulty remembering and who are not self-sufficient wind up in nursing homes. Thus, it could be that the ability to remember determines the type of environment in which a person lives, rather than vice versa. The real purpose of a correlational study is to make accurate predictions (not to determine cause-effect relationships). For example, from this study we could predict that people who live in nursing homes often have poor memories, but we would not know why.

To determine cause-and-effect relationships, it is necessary to perform an experimental study that manipulates an **independent variable.** Ellen Langer and her associates (Langer et al., 1979) conducted an experimental study that bears on the hypothesis just described. The investigators randomly divided a sample of the residents of a nursing home into different groups or conditions. In the contingent condition, residents were told that they would be visited several times during the next few weeks and would be asked a number of questions such as, "What did you have for breakfast two days ago?" These residents were given a poker chip for each memory question they answered correctly. The poker chips could be exchanged for gifts at a later date. The participants in the contingent condition thus lived in a demanding social environment. In the noncontingent condition, residents were asked the same memory questions over the same time period. At the end of each questioning session, these residents were given some poker chips as a "memento." (Care was taken to equate the number of chips given to members of the contingent and noncontingent groups.) Residents in the noncontingent group were told that the number of chips they received did not depend on the accuracy of their memory. They were also allowed to exchange their chips for gifts. The participants in the noncontingent condition, therefore, lived in a nondemanding social environment. After three weeks of treatment, all participants were administered a number of memory tests. Results indicated that the residents from the demanding environment (the contingent condition) performed significantly better on the memory tests than those from the nondemanding environment (the noncontingent condition). Thus, the initial hypothesis was confirmed. In this experiment, the manipulated independent variable was whether participants received poker chips under contingent or noncontingent conditions. The observed or measured **dependent variable** was the way the participants scored on the memory tests. But could other factors besides the conditions the participants were assigned to account for the results of this experiment? How do we actually know that it was the independent variable that produced the differences between the participants in the two conditions?

One approach to this problem is to match the two groups on **extraneous variables** that are suspected to be important. For example, we could give IQ tests to all participants, making sure that the groups were matched with respect to IQ. Such matching can be useful; but **random assignment** is a much more powerful technique. In an experiment, individuals are always assigned to a specific group on a random basis. If assignment to groups is random and if the number of participants is reasonably large, we can assume that all extraneous factors will be randomly distributed between the two groups. This includes extraneous factors that we could never have thought of in advance, as well as the more obvious factors that might be handled through matching.

Manipulations between and within Research Participants

Random assignment of participants to different groups is one way to manipulate an independent variable. Such manipulations are **between-subject manipulations.** There are also within-subject manipulations, which involve observing each participant in an experiment under two or more conditions. For example, if we suspect that a certain drug improves memory in patients with Alzheimer's disease, we might measure memory ability in each individual after administration of this drug and after administration of a placebo. Each individual then could be examined under the drug condition and later under the placebo condition to determine the effect of the drug. Counterbalancing would be advisable in such an experiment—we would test one half of the sample first in the drug condition and later in the placebo condition, and we would test the remaining sample first in the placebo condition and later in the drug condition. Counterbalancing controls the effects of the time at which variables are manipulated within subjects.

Quasi-Experimental Strategies in Developmental Research

All "true" experiments involve the manipulation of variables. Unfortunately, some variables are difficult if not impossible to manipulate. Age is one of these variables. Since we cannot manipulate a person's age, we cannot perform true experiments to examine the effects of age on a person's behavior. Despite the fact that most studies involving age are not true experiments, they often resemble true experiments in the ways in which they are designed or analyzed; age is treated as an independent variable even though it is not actually manipulated. Thus, we look for effects of age—actually, effects related to age—on one or more dependent variables. Because they are similar to true experiments, but we cannot manipulate the independent variable—age—such studies are called **quasi-experiments.**

Let's consider what it means to say that a person's age cannot be manipulated. Suppose we are conducting a study on adult development and succeed in finding individuals who are willing to serve as participants. We can observe their behavior under a variety of conditions that are under our control. For example, we might present one of several different types of instruction, or administer several different types of drugs. It is up to us, the experimenters, to decide which conditions or treatments each participant will receive. But we can't decide each participant's age; we cannot alter the number of years each person has lived.

Of course, we can assign any one participant to a group of similarly aged individuals and compare this group to another group of younger or older individuals. We can also plan to test our participants not only today but again several years from now. Using these strategies, we can compare functioning at different ages and gather evidence about effects and phenomena that are related to age. But clearly these strategies do not entail the actual manipulation of age. They simply allow us to take advantage of differences and changes in age that occur independently of our study and that are beyond our control.

The Problem of Internal Validity   Perhaps you feel that the difference between an experiment and a quasi-experiment is rather subtle and has no practical importance. If so, you are right about the subtlety but wrong about the importance.

The concept of **internal validity** concerns the role an independent variable plays in an experiment (or quasi-experiment). An experiment possesses internal validity if the results of the experiment reflect the influence of the independent variable rather than the influence of any extraneous or uncontrolled variables.

Internal validity is a concept developed by Donald Campbell and Julian Stanley in their classic book *Experimental and Quasi-Experimental Designs for Research* (1963). Campbell and Stanley enumerate several threats to internal validity and show that quasi-experimental studies, which include most studies of adult development and aging, are much more vulnerable to these threats than are true experiments.

One of the possible threats to internal validity is **selection.** This threat is especially troublesome when different-aged groups are compared. In such cases, the procedures used to select groups can result in many extraneous differences among these groups, differences that do not pertain to age per se. For example, a young-adult group and an elderly group might differ with respect to years of education, health status, and so on. These differences between the members of the different cohorts may make the results of a research study very difficult to interpret.

A second threat to internal validity is **history.** This is especially serious when we test the same individuals at different ages. The problem is that between one time of testing and another, many events can have a profound effect on the person's behavior; also, of course, the person is growing older between testings. Possible historical effects include attitudinal changes (e.g., social attitudes toward aging), economic events (increases in Social Security), and social changes (the development of new senior citizen's centers), among others. These changes might have a positive effect on an aging population if, as individuals grow older, they (1) are looked on more positively, (2) have more money to spend, and (3) have more opportunities for social and intellectual stimulation. Thus, these individuals are likely to function in a more adaptive psychological manner not because they are getting older, but because of positive sociohistorical changes.

A third threat to internal validity is **re-testing.** Taking a test on one occasion can affect test performance on a subsequent occasion. Obviously, the re-testing threat can accompany the history threat whenever we test the same individuals at different ages. However, the re-testing threat is especially serious when we are measuring some type of behavior that can change as an individual practices. (Many types of intellectual performance can change with practice.)

Suppose that we had a machine that could make someone 20 years old, or even 90 years old, by turning a switch (and that we could bring the person back to his or her original age with no harm done). We could take a sample of individuals and randomly assign half of them to a 20-year-old condition and the other half to a 90-year-old condition, and then compare them on many different dependent measures (e.g., creativity). Random assignment would take care of all extraneous differences between the two age groups (the selection threat). History would not be a factor because we could test all participants on the same day. Further, we would test each person only once, thus avoiding the threat of testing. Under these ideal conditions, we could solve all problems of internal validity. Unfortunately, we have no such ideal situation. In developmental research, we must live with threats to internal validity and compensate for them as best we can.

Next we consider several different types of quasi-experimental design that are used in research on adult development and aging. We will see that different designs compensate for different threats to internal validity. We will also see that the time span of a research design is a critical factor in determining what kinds of threats it can handle.

Quasi-Experimental Designs for the Study of Adult Development and Aging

Discussion of quasi-experimental research designs can be complicated. Let's start with the simplest designs: the cross-sectional and longitudinal designs, which are the basis for all developmental research. Then we'll describe more complex designs called sequential designs, which are actually further elaborations of the basic cross-sectional and longitudinal designs. There are ways in which all of these designs compensate, or fail to compensate, for the various threats to internal validity. Table A.1 provides a summary of each design, its susceptibility to internal validity threats, and other distinguishing features. It may be helpful to consult this table throughout the discussion that follows.

Cross-Sectional and Longitudinal Designs

Consider two different ways in which we might attempt to examine the impact of aging on behavior. First, we might perform a **cross-sectional study,** comparing groups of people in different age ranges. A typical cross-sectional study might include a group of 18- to 20-year-olds and a group of 65- to 70-year-olds. A more comprehensive cross-sectional study might include groups from every decade of life from the twenties through the nineties. The investigators could compare the different groups on a variety of dependent variables, such as IQ performance, memory, and creativity. They could collect data in a very short time; even a large study can be completed within a few

Summary of Quasi-Experimental Designs in Adult Development and Aging

Design	Description	Threats to Internal Validity	Other Properties
Simple cross-sectional	Two or more age groups are compared at one time of testing	Selection, especially cohort effects; differences between groups might reflect differences in time of birth	Easy to conduct; can be useful as a pilot study
Simple longitudinal	A single group of subjects is tested repeatedly at different points in time	Time-of-testing (history) effects: historical changes might produce effects that appear to be age-related changes; repeated testing might influence measures (testing effects)	Those subjects who stay in the study may not be the same as the subjects who drop out prior to completion in what is called selective dropout (this threatens generalizability of findings); allows assessment of individual differences in developmental change
Cohort-sequential	Two or more longitudinal comparisons are made on different cohorts	Time-of-testing and testing effects as for simple longitudinal (can remove testing effects with independent samples)	Requires two time periods to examine change over one time period; allows separate examination of age-related effects and cohort effects
Time-sequential	Two or more cross-sectional comparisons are made at different times of testing	Cohort effects, since every cross-sectional comparison could be influenced by cohort as well as age	Allows separate examination of age effects and time-of-testing (history) effects
Cross-sequential	Two or more cohorts are compared at two or more times of testing	Neither time-of-testing nor cohort effects are independent of age-related changes	Provides no clear information on age-related changes

months. The major purpose of a cross-sectional study is to measure age-related differences. As we shall see, a cross-sectional study allows us to determine whether one age group of individuals differs from other age groups. Cross-sectional studies, however, do not allow us to measure age-related change (i.e., the extent to which age-graded factors, by themselves, cause developmental change).

Another way we might explore the effects of aging on behavior is to perform a **longitudinal study.** In this case, we would take a single group of individuals, all the same age, and test them today and on one or more occasions in the future. For example, we might decide to examine creativity at ages 50, 57, 64, and 71. Longitudinal studies clearly take a long time to complete. Furthermore, the purpose of a longitudinal study is to measure age-related changes, not age-related differences. As we shall see, simple longitudinal studies are not always successful in measuring such changes.

One advantage of cross-sectional designs, then, is time efficiency. Further, cross-sectional designs are virtually free of two important internal validity threats: There is no history threat because all participants are tested at the same time, and there is no testing threat because it is necessary to test each individual only once. For these reasons, cross-sectional designs are enormously popular. However, as mentioned earlier, cross-sectional designs are highly susceptible to the internal validity threat of selection. We often do not know the extent to which the results of a cross-sectional study reflect the effects of age versus the effects of countless extraneous factors.

Many extraneous factors involved in cross-sectional designs pertain to **cohort effects.** Cohort effects are caused by a person's time of birth or generation but not actually by her or his age. For example, cohorts can differ with respect to years of education, childrearing practices, health, and attitudes on topics such as sex and religion. These cohort effects are important because they can powerfully influence the dependent measures in a study concerned with age. Cohort effects can look like age effects, but they are not.

Since cross-sectional designs do not allow random assignment of individuals to age groups, there is no way to control cohort effects or other extraneous variables. Our only approach to controlling these variables is through matching. For example, if our young participants are all college students, we might make sure that all our elderly participants are also college students. Unfortunately, matching for extraneous variables is sometimes impossible. (We may be unable to find an adequate number of elderly college students who are willing to participate in our study.) Further, we can only match for the extraneous variables whose importance we recognize. Finally, matching can have the unwanted side effect of producing unusual or nonrepresentative groups—elderly people in college may differ in many ways from the average person of their age. Selection poses a serious threat to cross-sectional studies, and matching is not truly adequate to remove that threat.

Figure A.1 contains a diagram of a simple cross-sectional study that addresses the issue of whether IQ changes from 50 to 60 to 70 years of age. This study, if it were conducted in the year 2000, would employ participants of different ages (50, 60, and 70) representing different cohorts according to the year in which they were born (1930, 1940, and 1950). Interpreting the data obtained in this study would be impossible because changes in age are confounded (i.e., confused with) changes in cohort. For example, we might find that 70-year-olds have lower IQ scores than 50-year-olds. But we would not know if this is because of the ages of the participants, the amount of education received by individuals born in 1930 versus those born in 1950, or some other extraneous factor.

Although longitudinal studies are time-consuming, they are valuable because they remove the threat of selection, or cohort effects. This is because individuals from a single cohort form the participant pool for a longitudinal study. Further, longitudinal studies have the great advantage of allowing us to track changes that take place within individuals over a long time interval. If one's primary concern is the study of intraindividual change over the course of development, longitudinal designs are indispensable.

Unfortunately, the threats of history, testing, and selective dropout are especially troublesome in longitudinal designs. Selective dropout refers to the possibility that participants who either perform poorly on a particular test, or are unmotivated or ill, will be less likely to undergo repeated testing over the course of a longitudinal study. To illustrate, consider the longitudinal study diagrammed in figure A.2. This study measures IQ changes in individuals from the 1930 birth cohort as they move from 50 to 60 to 70 years of age. The study begins in the year 1980 and concludes in the year 2000. The same participants are retested at 10-year intervals. Interpreting the data ob-

Figure A.1
A cross-sectional design measures age-related differences between different cohorts.

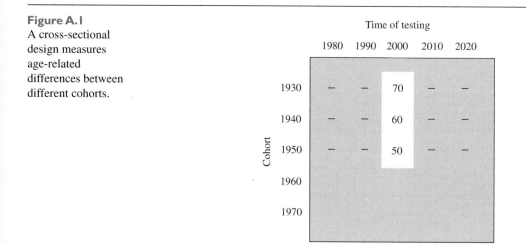

Figure A.2
A longitudinal design measures age-related changes for a selected cohort.

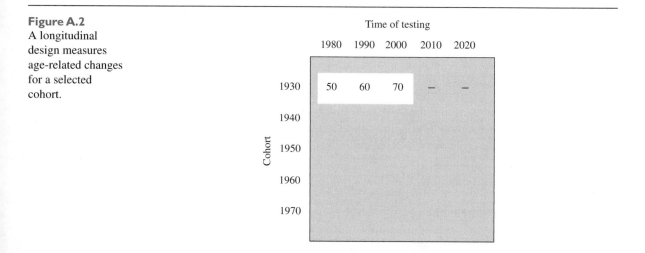

tained in this study would be very difficult. For example, we might find that the participants display higher IQ scores at age 70 than age 50. This finding might be due to any number of facts; for example, it could be true that (1) people actually become more intelligent as they age; (2) between 1980 and 2000, our society changed so that life became more stimulating, enriching, and enjoyable for the typical older person; (3) the participants became more familiar with the IQ test each time they were tested; or (4) at the end of the study in 2000, we were left with a very biased group of participants—those who were exceptionally bright, motivated, healthy, and so on.

It may be possible to remove the threats of testing and selective dropout by adding new or independent samples of participants at each testing. For example, we could collect data on a new group of randomly selected 60-year-olds in 1990 and compare their IQ performance to those participants tested for the second time in 1990. And we could also add another group of randomly selected 70-year-olds in 2000. This procedure, however, would still not remove the history threat.

Cohort-Sequential Designs

Sequential research designs may be used to correct some of the inadequacies of cross-sectional and longitudinal research. A **cohort-sequential design** entails two or more longitudinal studies, each covering the same range of ages, conducted over differing lengths of time. An example of a simple cohort-sequential design appears in figure A.3. Three different cohorts are selected—a cohort born in 1930, a second cohort born in 1940, and a third born in 1950. A sample from each cohort is tested on three different occasions—first when the participants are 50 years old, again when they are 60 years old, and a third time when they are 70 years old. As in the simple longitudinal design, independent samples could also be drawn at the different times of testing to control the threats of testing and selective dropout.

The cohort-sequential design corrects for the major drawback associated with the simple cross-sectional design; that is, it allows us to estimate the relative importance of

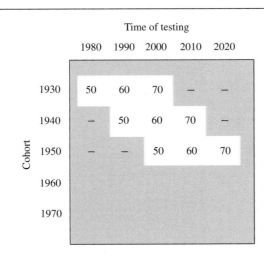

Time of testing

Cohort	1980	1990	2000	2010	2020
1930	50	60	70	—	—
1940	—	50	60	70	—
1950	—	—	50	60	70
1960					
1970					

Figure A.3
A cohort-sequential design involves two or more longitudinal studies covering the same age ranges over different time eras.

age effects in comparison to cohort effects. For example, we can compare performance by the 1930 versus 1940 versus 1950 cohorts by looking across the rows in figure A.3. This tells us something about how cohort-related factors might influence our measure. We can also compare the performance of individuals from each of the three age groups. This is accomplished by looking at the diagonals in figure A.3—we could calculate the average score of all of the 50-year-olds and compare it with the average score for all groups of 60-year-olds, and so on. This tells us how age influences our measure independent of cohort. Further, the design allows us to assess interactions between cohort and age. We can see if the age effect is constant across the two cohorts, or if it varies between cohorts. This can obviously be very important if there are different rates of aging in different cohorts.

The main weakness of cohort-sequential design is that it doesn't compensate for the history threat. We would have no understanding, in other words, of how the historical changes that occurred from 1970 to 2010 affected the behavior of our participants. Another weakness of the design is that it takes a great deal of time to complete. As you can see from figure A.3, to study aging and cohort effects on IQ at 50, 60, and 70 years of age, we need 40 years to collect the data.

Time-Sequential Designs

The **time-sequential design** corrects for the major limitation of the longitudinal design. This design is capable of differentiating age effects from historical changes (or time-of-testing effects). Time-sequential designs involve two or more cross-sectional studies, each covering the same range of ages, conducted at different times. An example appears in figure A.4. According to this figure, in 2000, we examine the performance of three age groups: 50-, 60-, and 70-year-olds. In 2010 and also in 2020, we again examine the performance of individuals at these three age levels (these are, of course, entirely new samples of participants).

The strength of the time-sequential design is that history effects—or time-of-testing effects—can be examined explicitly, in addition to differences related to age. That is,

Figure A.4
A time-sequential design differentiates age effects from historical changes.

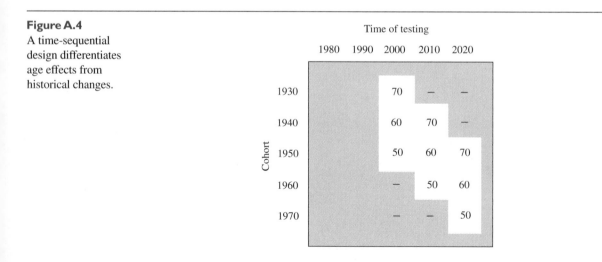

looking at the columns in figure A.4, we can examine differences between performance in 2000, 2010, and 2020; this tells us directly about history effects. Independent of history, we can look at the diagonals to examine differences between the 50-, 60-, and 70-year-olds; this gives us information relevant to aging. Furthermore, we can examine the interactions between age and time of testing. If age-related differences in 2010 are smaller than age-related differences in 2000 and 2020, it might support some interesting conclusions about history-related changes in the course of adult development.

Another advantage of the time-sequential design is that it is more time efficient than the cohort-sequential design. In our example (figure A.4), age and history effects can be studied over a 20-year span (compared with a 40-year span for the cohort-sequential design). Also, note that the time-sequential design (figure A.4) takes the same length of time to conduct as the longitudinal design (figure A.2)!

The disadvantage of the time-sequential design is that it does not consider cohort effects. At each time of measurement, we must be concerned with the possibility that differences between our age groups may, in part, reflect differences in their respective cohorts.

Cross-Sequential Designs

Cross-sequential designs are a kind of hybrid of cross-sectional and longitudinal designs. They are not fundamentally relevant to adult development and aging because they do not separate age effects from either cohort or history effects. Rather, cross-sequential designs separate cohort and history effects from each other.

The technique used in a cross-sequential design, illustrated in figure A.5, is to examine two (or more) cohorts, covering different age ranges, at each of two (or more) times of testing. Differences between cohorts can be examined independently of differences between times of measurement. Unfortunately, neither of these differences can be separated from age. The cohorts differ on an age dimension, and participants must obviously be older at the second testing than the first.

Perhaps this is a good time for you to stop and review the various quasi-experimental designs in adult development and aging. Going over them once or even twice probably

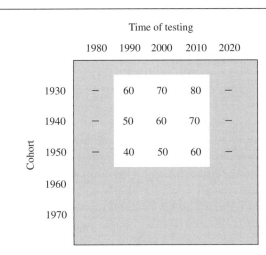

Time of testing

Figure A.5
A cross-sequential design combines the cross-sectional and longitudinal designs.

won't be enough. Take some time to study the material in table A.1, which summarizes the main characteristics of each of these quasi-experimental designs.

Schaie's Most Efficient Design

We can summarize the preceding discussion by saying that the cohort-sequential design is a useful extension of simple longitudinal designs and that the time-sequential design is a useful extension of cross-sectional designs. Furthermore, we could conclude that these sequential designs are far superior to the simple cross-sectional and longitudinal studies they are derived from. However, the various sequential designs are still less than perfect. History or time-of-testing effects threaten the internal validity of cohort-sequential designs. Cohort effects threaten the internal validity of time-sequential designs. So what are we to do to ensure the internal validity of our research?

One answer is to use both the cohort-sequential and time-sequential designs, and then add the cross-sequential design for good measure. Incorporating all of these designs at once is more difficult than performing one of them alone. K. W. Schaie, an authority on sequential designs, has developed the **most efficient design** to combine the best features of the other designs.

The most efficient design is illustrated in figure A.6. Individuals in five different cohorts are studied: 1930, 1940, 1950, 1960, and 1970. Measurements are made at five different times: 1980, 1990, 2000, 2010, and 2020. Finally, it is necessary to collect data from new, independent samples of each cohort at each of the different times of testing (though retesting of the original samples is also recommended). If all this is accomplished, it is possible to perform a cohort-sequential analysis, a time-sequential analysis, and a cross-sequential analysis all at once, as shown in figure A.6.

Such analyses provide a wealth of interesting comparisons. Certain patterns can reveal strong evidence for age-related changes, cohort differences, and history effects. Consider the following possible outcome in a study of creativity: The cohort-sequential analysis may suggest a strong effect of cohort, but only a weak effect of age. The time-sequential analysis supports only weak effects of time of testing and age. Finally, the cross-sequential analysis supports, again, a strong effect of cohort but only a weak effect of time of measurement. In this hypothetical case, we would have clear indications that cohort is an important variable but that age and time of measurement are not.

We must always be mindful of the tremendous difficulty of collecting the data for such complex analyses. Faced with this difficulty, it may frequently be advisable to first conduct simple cross-sectional studies, controlling as much as possible for extraneous, cohort-related variables known to be important. Examining the effects of different treatments in such designs can also help isolate the ways in which younger groups differ from older groups at a particular time in history. Subsequently, once important differences between younger and older groups have been isolated, longitudinal and even sequential strategies can be carried out, allowing a much more complete understanding of the causes of these differences.

Stated somewhat differently, cross-sectional studies seem to be the logical starting point in developmental research. If this type of research establishes reliable age differences in behavior, then other types of designs can be carried out to determine the underlying causes of the apparent age difference.

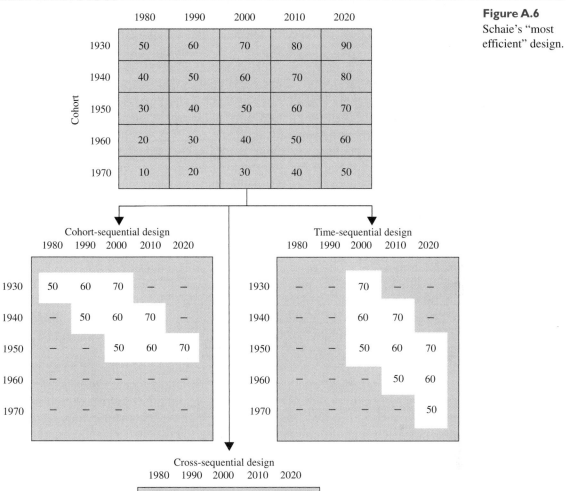

Figure A.6
Schaie's "most efficient" design.

Meta-Analysis

As you have seen from reading this appendix, there are a vast number of ways to engineer a research study. It is possible to use a correlational, experimental, or quasi-experimental research design. One drawback associated with any particular research study, no matter how elegant its design, is the fact that it is a *single* study. As scientists, we want to get the "big picture" on a particular topic. This is accomplished by putting together the results of a number of individual studies.

The problem faced by researchers about *how* they should interpret the results of several different experiments is similar to the one they experience when they interpret a single experiment: Should they come to some personal or *subjective* conclusion about the results of an array of studies? Or should they use some sort of *objective* methodology to reach a conclusion? The technique of **meta-analysis** was developed to provide an objective account of the results of many studies taken together.

When a researcher conducts a meta-analysis, she examines each individual research study to determine the number of individuals within particular groups, group performance means, and group performance standard deviations. These variables are used to estimate the effect size of a certain independent variable on a particular dependent variable. Then, all of the estimates of effect size from the individual studies are grouped together via a mathematical procedure to determine the overall effect size for all of the studies, and to determine whether this overall effect size is statistically significant.

The utility of the meta-analytic technique is illustrated by the following example. Say we want to determine whether a particular training program improves the memory performance of patients with AD. We begin by reading 30 different experiments that have been conducted on this topic. Ten of the studies show that the training program has a statistically significant beneficial effect on the patients' memory. Another 10 of the studies indicate that the training program had a slightly positive impact on the patients' memory, but this beneficial effect just missed attaining statistical significance. And the remaining 10 studies reveal that the program had no beneficial effect on patients' memory whatsoever. If we just "eyeballed" all of these data, we'd most likely become confused and conclude that no firm conclusions may be drawn. A meta-analysis of all of these studies, however, might lead to a definitive conclusion that the training program did (or did not) boost the memory of the AD patients.

Note that a meta-analysis is an extremely handy tool when the individual studies have extremely small sample sizes (as is usually the case in experiments that use groups of demented patients). This is because the smaller the number of individuals within different groups, the larger the mean group difference needs to be in order to achieve statistical significance.

Problems of Sampling in Developmental Research

When we decide to study a certain group of individuals (say, 60-year-olds who have recently retired), we obviously cannot collect measurements on everyone in that group. Rather, we must study a sample of the entire population of individuals. Although we study only a sample, we want to generalize our findings to the rest of the population. Thus, the sampling procedures form a very important aspect of research methodology.

A **representative sample** has the same characteristics as the larger population it comes from. The best way to achieve a representative sample is through the technique of random sampling, a technique in which every member of the population has an equal chance of being in the sample that we study. For example, the ideal way to find a representative sample of recently retired 70-year-olds would be to compile a list of every such individual in the world and then to pick randomly a number of these individuals to be in our study. Obviously, truly random sampling can rarely be employed. Indeed, we often must struggle to find people with certain characteristics who are willing to participate in our studies.

Investigators of adult development seldom can be sure that their samples are representative. This fact produces two consequences, one pertaining primarily to cross-sectional designs and the other primarily to longitudinal designs.

Nonrepresentative Samples in Cross-Sectional Designs

In cross-sectional designs, the problem of nonrepresentative samples adds to problems of internal validity. Specifically, selection threats may be due partially to nonrepresentative sampling. If we find differences between a group of young persons and a group of elderly persons but do not know whether either sample is representative, it is difficult to be sure whether age or cohort is responsible for the differences. Perhaps these differences occurred because we selected a group of young adults with below-average intelligence for individuals of their age and a group of older persons with above-average intelligence for individuals of their age. The solution to this problem is to measure various extraneous variables (e.g., IQ) that are suspected to be important. We must measure the IQs of the two groups and relate them to the norms for their age groups. Though not ideal, this approach is much better than ignoring these issues.

Nonrepresentative Samples in Longitudinal Designs

The problem of sampling in longitudinal studies is not just a hypothetical problem; it has been demonstrated to occur. It frequently takes the form of selective dropout. As we have already mentioned, selective dropout refers to the fact that some participants drop out of a longitudinal study before all of the testings are complete. The problem is that those who drop out of a study are likely to differ significantly from those who continue until the end. Indeed, people who return for testing in a longitudinal study often have greater intellectual abilities than those who do not (Hofer & Sliwinski, 2001; Schaie & Hofer, 2001). Further, longitudinal declines in intellectual ability are more likely to occur among those who drop out of a study after several testings than among those who remain.

At another level, sampling problems can threaten the external validity of longitudinal research. **External validity** refers to the degree to which we may generalize the results of a scientific study. When we use nonrepresentative samples, we often do not know whether age trends observed in one longitudinal study are representative of age trends in the population at large. The external validity of cross-sectional designs, of course, may be threatened for the same reason.

SUMMARY

Two basic problems of measurement are reliability and validity. Although the problem of reliability is serious, effective methods for assessing reliability (e.g., the test-retest method) and for increasing reliability (e.g., collecting data on multiple items) do exist. The problem of validity is more troublesome because many psychological concepts, such as creativity and self-concept, are highly abstract. When we attempt to evaluate such abstract concepts, it is often arguable that we are not truly measuring what we think we are.

Among the basic measures used for collecting observations are the interview and questionnaire, behavioral research, standardized tests, and physiological research. Each has strengths and weaknesses. Interview and questionnaire studies can often be conducted when other sorts of studies are impossible or, at best, impractical. However, these types of studies are especially susceptible to the problem of reactivity, particularly the problem of response bias. Moreover, interviews and questionnaires are highly dependent on the participants' conscious impressions of themselves, and these impressions can be at variance with actual behavior.

Behavioral measures are many and varied and can be collected in laboratory settings or in the field. Behavioral studies in the laboratory allow impressive control over many extraneous variables. However, they often can be artificial, even anxiety-provoking, to individuals. Further, laboratory studies produce problems of reactivity, and they cannot be used to study certain kinds of real-world phenomena. Field studies allow fewer controls, but they can be very naturalistic, can reduce problems of reactivity, and can reveal real-life phenomena that are not reproducible in the laboratory. Standardized tests are useful for comparing a particular sample of individuals to representative samples of individuals tested previously. However, the validity of such tests is often questionable. Further, it is frequently the case that no previously developed test can measure exactly what we want to measure. Physiological measures can be invaluable for an increased understanding of behavioral data, and they can suggest ways to reduce or remove undesirable age-related differences in behavior.

Among the basic strategies for summarizing data are measures of central tendency and variability. Correlations are used to determine the degree to which two variables are related to each other. However, many studies produce so many correlations that interpretation is difficult. In these cases, factor analysis can help reduce many correlations to a smaller number of factors. Significance tests are used to determine whether the results of a study are due to chance.

In terms of research design, correlational studies must be distinguished from true experiments. Experiments involve the manipulation of independent variables and actually provide evidence for cause-effect relationships between independent and dependent variables. Quasi-experiments are similar to true experiments, but quasi-experiments do not involve the actual manipulation of independent variables. Since age cannot be manipulated, studies of this variable are considered to be quasi-experimental. Three threats to internal validity that are problematic in such quasi-experimental studies are selection, history, and testing.

Several types of quasi-experiments are used to study adult development and aging. Simple cross-sectional and longitudinal designs are limited in their usefulness. Cross-sectional designs suffer from cohort effects, whereas longitudinal designs suffer from both testing and history effects. Among the sequential designs, the cohort-sequential design allows independent assessment of age and cohort effects but does not solve the problem of history effects. The time-sequential design allows independent assessment of age and history effects but does not solve the problem of cohort effects. The use of both designs together, along with the cross-sequential design as well, can in principle allow us to distinguish age, cohort, and history effects. A greater investment of time and resources is necessary to use all these designs together, however.

Researchers must frequently sample their participants from different age groups (cohorts), and this sampling can introduce bias; samples may be nonrepresentative. The problem of sampling is unavoidable, but we must keep it in mind when we are interpreting the data in studies of adult development and aging. Particularly vexing is the problem of selective dropout or experimental mortality, which occurs when participants drop out of a longitudinal study. Those who drop out are likely to differ systematically from those who remain. This can threaten the generalizability of longitudinal studies.

REVIEW QUESTIONS

1. How can we assess reliability? How can we improve the methods we use to assess reliability?
2. What are the central issues involved in the validity of measurement?
3. Describe the basic types of measures used for collecting information about adults. Include the advantages and disadvantages of each type.
4. What are the basic strategies for summarizing measurements?
5. Explain the logic behind the technique of factor analysis.
6. Provide an overview of correlational and experimental strategies in research design. Include information about manipulations between and within individuals.
7. Discuss quasi-experimental designs and the problem of internal validity.
8. Compare and contrast the simple quasi-experimental designs (cross-sectional and longitudinal) with the complex quasi-experimental designs (sequential designs) used to study adult development and aging.
9. What are some of the main sampling problems in conducting research with adults?

GLOSSARY

Abortive coping A form of adjustment to life events which is predominantly negative, nonproductive, and limiting to human growth.

Acceptance The fifth and final stage of Kübler-Ross's psychological stages of dying; in this stage, patients end their struggle against death and show acceptance, peacefulness, and solitude.

Accommodation The eye muscle adjustments that allow the eye to have the greatest clarity of image (resolution); the ability to focus and maintain an image on the retina.

Accommodative processes Processes involved in helping older persons adjust to cumulative losses and threats to self-esteem by disengagement and the lowering of aspiration from unattainable goals.

Acetylcholine A neurotransmitter necessary for brain activation, responsiveness, and communication. Composed essentially from choline, it travels from the axon across the synaptic cleft to the dendrites of another cell.

Acetylcholinesterase The substance responsible for the deactivation of acetylcholine; it limits the length of time a neuron is stimulated.

Acquired immunodeficiency syndrome (AIDS) The HIV-caused failure of the body's immune system that leaves afflicted individuals vulnerable to a variety of diseases and ultimately to death.

Action theory A theory that individuals are self-motivated to initiate and pursue personal goals (same as goal pursuit theory).

Active euthanasia Inducing death in an incurably ill person by some direct action, such as injecting a lethal dose of a drug.

Active mastery A style of relating to the environment that changes with age in different ways for men and women. It allows the adult more direct control over the environment.

Activities of daily living (ADLs) The basic functions necessary for individuals to maintain independent living, which include feeding, meal preparation, bathing, dressing, toileting, and general health and hygiene. The long-term needs of the elderly are assessed through these activities, which serve as a guide for appropriate intervention.

Affirmative coping A form of adjustment to life events which is positive, productive, and enhancing to human growth.

Age-associated memory impairment Age-related declines in memory function that are not due to disease or neuropathology.

Age-by-experience paradigm A methodology used to assess the role of age and expertise on some aspect of cognitive ability.

Age-differentiated society A society that assigns separate roles or tasks to its members at specific ages.

Age structure The percentage of males and females within various age intervals in a given society.

Agnosia The inability to visually recognize familiar objects.

AIDS dementia complex (ADC) A set of cognitive dysfunctions associated with brain infection caused by the HIV virus.

Alpha rhythm The dominant brain rhythm, linked with alert wakefulness.

Alternative resource theory The search by ethnic minority families for help first from family and the church rather than from secondary community resources such as government-sponsored programs; helps account for underutilization of services such as community mental health.

Alzheimer's disease (AD) Irreversible dementia characterized by progressive deterioration in memory awareness, and body functions, eventually leading to death.

Amyloid precursor protein (APP) The chemical substance that underlies the manufacture of amyloid, which is the core material of senile plaques.

Androgynous Having both male and female characteristics in one person.

Anger The second of Kübler-Ross's stages of dying; in this stage, persons realize that denial cannot be maintained, causing them to become angry, resentful, and envious.

Anniversary reaction Feelings of loneliness that occur on holidays, birthdays, etc. following the death of a loved one.

Anticipatory grief Feelings of grief, loneliness, and despair that precede the death of a loved one.

Anticipatory mourning

Aphasia A breakdown or loss of an individual's language abilities.

Apparent memory deficits Memory losses that can be attributed to faulty encoding and retrieval processes and that are potentially reversible through intervention or instruction.

Appropriate death A death that fulfills the wishes and ideals of the dying person (e.g., to be given the freedom to die as one has been given the freedom to live).

Ascending reticular activation system (ARAS) A brain system that controls levels of awareness or consciousness.

Assimilative processes Processes that help direct older adults to specific activities and goals that are personally derived and that effectively reduce the cumulative impact of developmental losses to self-esteem and personal identity.

Assisted living Apartment-style residences where elderly receive individual services to maximize their independence such as prepared meals and help with dressing, bathing, or administration of medications.

Atherosclerosis Coronary artery disease caused by the accumulation of fatty deposits (plaque) on the arterial walls of vessels supplying blood to the heart.

Axon The part of the neuron that transmits information.

Bargaining The third of Kübler-Ross's stages of dying; in this stage, patients hope that death can be postponed by negotiating with God.

Barrier theory An explanation for the underutilization by Hispanic, black, and Asian minorities of government health and mental health programs. Minorities see these as large, bureaucratic organizations that are impersonal, inaccessible, and distant, with few professional staff from underrepresented groups.

Behavior therapy The application of positive rewards for appropriate behavior and nonrewards for inappropriate behavior.

Behavioral research Research that relies on the direct observation and recording of behavior, including experimental approaches.

Bereaved The status of a person or family who has survived the death of a loved one.

Bereavement overload The inability to work through the deaths of loved ones that occur close to one another in time.

Beta rhythm A fast brain rhythm that characterizes an attentive, alert state.

Beta-amyloid A protein that makes up senile plaques.

Between-subjects manipulations The random assignment of subjects to groups in an experiment.

Biological age The relative condition of an individual's organ and body system.

Biological approach The idea that age-related memory deficits may be traced to the deterioration of the brain.

Body mass index A mathematical formula that compares height and weight.

Bona fide occupational qualifications (BFOQ) Legislation that mandates that workers in selective jobs (e.g., police or airline traffic controllers) retire at a specific age due to the abilities or traits demanded for successful performance.

Brain death That point at which all electrical activity has ceased in the brain as determined by an EEG.

Brain stem The primitive part of the lower brain that controls the basic biological processes associated with respiration and heartbeat.

Broaden-and build theory Based on the premise that experiencing positive emotions makes it possible for people to consider a wider range of thought, problem-solutions, and actions; positive emotions free people from habitual ways of thinking and behaving.

Busy ethic A theory of successful retirement developed by Ekerdt.

Cancer A group of diseases characterized by rapid, uncontrollable growth of abnormal cells that form a malignant tumor.

Cardiovascular disease The category of disease that includes coronary artery disease, stroke, congestive heart failure, and high blood pressure or hypertension.

Caregiver burden The intense reactions common to adults caring for the emotional, social, intellectual, and physical needs of an elderly relative in their own home.

Cataracts Opacity in the lens of the eye that can cause blindness if not corrected.

Central tendency The manipulation of a given set of scores to determine the mean, median, or mode.

Cerebellum A primitive part of the brain that controls balance, motor programming, and simple conditioning.

Cerebral cortex The outer covering of the cerebrum.

Cerebrum The largest and evolutionarily most recent part of the brain.

Chronological age The number of years since a person's birth.

Climacteric Age-related decline in reproductive capacity for both men and women.

Clinical depression A constellation of behaviors, thoughts, and emotions characterized by intense loneliness and isolation, extreme sadness, crying, feelings of worthlessness, perfectionism, guilt, anxiety, dread, and being unloved.

Cochlea The primary neural receptor for hearing.

Codicils Changes or amendments made to a will that has already been legally filed or recorded.

Cognitive-behavioral theory Treatment designed to change the negative thoughts, beliefs, and attitudes that characterize the thinking of depressed individuals about self, experiences, and the future.

Cognitive model of coping A model of coping and adaptation development by Lazarus that emphasizes the person's subjective perception of potentially stressful life events; cognitive processes underlie subjective perception through primary and secondary appraisal.

Cohort A group of people born in the same time period; the shared or distinctive characteristics of a generation.

Cohort effects Differences in behaviors found among people born at different times in history.

Cohort-sequential design A complex research design that allows a research investigator to distinguish between age effects and cohort effects.

Columbarium A separate building or wall of a building with individual niche spaces to hold the urns containing the remains of loved ones that have been cremated.

Competence A legal term informed by professional input from a psychiatrist or clinical psychologist that describes an older person's capacity to make independent decisions affecting their care, medical treatment, and disposition of assets through a will.

Computerized axial tomography (CT scan) A radiological technique that yields a three-dimensional representation of the structure of the brain.

Concrete-operational stage The third stage of Piaget's theory of mental development that highlights a type of thinking limited to concrete ideas and experiences.

Construct validity The extent to which a psychological test or assessment measures a hypothetical entity, e.g., intelligence.

Contextual approach The viewpoint that the effectiveness of a person's memory depends on the context or setting within which the person is required to learn and remember information.

Contextual paradigm The model that suggests that adults, like historical events, are ongoing, dynamic, and not directed toward an ideal end-state.

Continuity The notion that the same processes control development.

Contrast sensitivity An individual's ability to perceive visual stimuli that differ in terms of both contrast and spatial frequency.

Conventional level The third and fourth stages of Kohlberg's theory of moral development in which moral thought is based on the desire to preserve good interpersonal relations (stage 3) and to comply with formalized rules that exist in society (stage 4).

Convergent thinking A type of thinking designed to arrive at a single correct answer for a problem.

Coronary arteries The vessels that provide blood directly to the heart muscle.

Corpus callosum A band of nerve fibers that connects the brain's two hemispheres.

Correlation A relationship or association between two variables that can be either positive or negative and vary from weak to strong.

Correlational study A type of research in which associations between variables are merely observed.

Crossover effect Black Americans at higher risk for death at earlier ages who reach old age represent a select, hardy group of survivors whose life expectancies are higher (i.e., cross over) relative to those of similar age from other races.

Cross-sectional study A study in which individuals of different ages are observed at different times to obtain information about some variable, usually contaminated by cohort effects.

Cross-sequential designs A complex research design that allows an investigator to distinguish time-of-testing effects from cohort effects.

Crystallized intelligence The type of intelligence that involves skills, abilities, and understanding gained through instruction and observation.

Cultural paranoia The suspicion, hostility, and distrust that African Americans have toward white middle-class community-based programs such as mental health programs; it limits their willingness to seek services when needed.

Curvilinear An association of variables that is represented by a curved line when plotted on a graph.

Declarative memory Conscious recollection of the past.

Dehydroepiandrosterone (DHEA) A hormone produced by the adrenal glands. Age-related decreases in DHEA are related to functional declines in physical and mental health in men and women.

Delayed grief reaction A delayed and heightened reaction to the death of a loved one that is elicited in response to the death of someone to whom the individual is not emotionally attached.

Delta rhythm The brain wave associated with deep sleep.

Dementia An organically based disorder of late adulthood characterized by a deterioration of intelligence and behavior.

Dendrites The component of a neuron that receives information.

Denial/isolation The first of Kübler-Ross's psychological stages of dying; in this stage, persons react to terminal illness with shock, denial, and withdrawal.

Dependency ratio A reflection of the number of workers relative to the number of people deriving support from these workers, most typically children under the age of 15 and elderly persons 65 years of age and older.

Dependent variables The values that are measured as a result of experimental manipulations.

Depletion syndrome A form of minor depression among the elderly characterized by lack of interest and the feeling that everything requires enormous effort, even the simplest of daily tasks.

Depression The fourth of Kübler-Ross's stages of dying; in this stage, persons become silent, spend much time crying, and want to be alone in an effort to disconnect themselves from objects of love.

Depressive pseudodementia Depression that mimics dementia.

Development Refers to a form of change that is organized and adaptive (positive) in nature.

Developmental psychology The study of age-related interindividual differences and age-related intraindividual change.

Diagnostic related group (DRG) National health care definitions of specific medical conditions to permit construction of average costs and lengths of treatment in a hospital for insurance reimbursement purposes.

Dialectical view The view that individuals are constantly changing organisms in a constantly changing world.

Diathesis-stress model Descriptive account of the relationship between a person's current level of vulnerability or frailty (diathesis) and the capacity to manage challenging life events (stressors).

Discontinuity The idea that development is abrupt and controlled by different processes.

Divergent thinking A type of thinking closely related to creativity that produces many different answers to a single question.

Divided attention The ability to simultaneously attend to two different pieces of environmental information.

Do not resuscitate (DNR) Specific orders that physicians are not to initiate heroic measures (e.g., electric shock, drugs to restart a stopped heart) when breathing or heartbeat has stopped.

Dopamine A neurotransmitter implicated in Parkinson's disease and schizophrenia.

Dual-processing (tasks) A person's ability to attend to and perform two tasks at once; this ability declines with advancing age.

Durable power of attorney Legal appointment of a surrogate (relative, friend, physician, lawyer) designated to make health care choices in the event a person becomes decisionally incompetent or incapacitated; the surrogate is legally authorized to accept or refuse any medical interventions the person has not specified in advance.

Early-onset alcoholism The development of alcohol addiction through adolescence to middle age.

Efficacy research The evaluation of prior research outcomes before choosing a clinically effective treatment approach.

Ego mastery styles The style adopted in coping with self and others that reflects the underlying organization of values and beliefs that govern external behavior.

Electroencephalogram (EEG) A machine used to measure the electrical activity of the cortex.

Emotional intelligence The ability to understand the needs, feelings, and motives that operate in one's self and in others.

Empty nest syndrome A group of symptoms, typified by anxiety and depression, thought to be experienced by parents as their children begin leaving home.

Encapsulation model A model of adult cognitive development designed to explain age-related changes in processing, knowing, and thinking.

Encoding deficit A memory failure that may be traced to the inability to acquire to-be-remembered information.

Epigenesis In Erikson's theory, the belief that all growth has an underlying structure that determines the occasions during which specific psychosocial crises may occur.

Episodic memory Memory of the details of personally experienced events, such as the ability to accurately recall details about the source or the context of remembered information.

Eras Major portions of the life span, according to Daniel Levinson.

Error catastrophe theory The theory that errors occur in the RNA responsible for the production of enzymes that are essential to metabolism, resulting in a reduction of cell functioning and possible death.

Estrogen The primary female sex hormone, the depletion of which is associated with menopause.

Ethnic gloss The tendency to make ethnic groups (e.g., Asian, Latino, Blacks) appear more homogeneous than they actually are.

Ethnic identity A person's membership in an ethnic group based on shared customs, heritage, values, history, language, and race.

Ethnic matching Identification of a mental health professional with ethnic characteristics similar to those of a client; facilitates mental health treatment and continuity of treatment.

Euthanasia The act of painlessly putting to death people who are suffering from incurable diseases or severe disability.

Event-related optical signals (EROS) A non-invasive method for assessing brain function by measuring changes in the optical properties of brain tissue.

Exceptional creativity Another term for creative genius.

Existential phase The term Gibbs uses to describe the last two stages in Kohlberg's theory of moral development.

Experimental study A study in which an independent variable is manipulated and a dependent variable is observed.

Explicit memory A task in which a subject is directly instructed to consciously remember a previous event or experience.

Expressive therapies The use of art activities and music activities in helping to express emotions, enhance social relationships, improve eye-hand coordination, mobility, representational skills, and memory in a safe, protected environment.

External validity The extent to which one may generalize the results of an experiment.

Extraneous variables Variables that are not measured nor manipulated but that are suspected to be important.

Extraversion One of the dimensions of Costa and McCrae's five-factor model of personality.

Factor analysis A statistical technique that summarizes many correlations.

Familism A value indicating shared commitment to members of one's immediate family and common among various ethnic groups such as Korean, Hispanic, and Asians; developed and sustained by shared family goals, supportive relationships, and emotional cohesion.

Fictive kin People who are considered family relatives, although they are not related by blood or marriage; usually those who have close physical and emotional contact with an older adult.

Filial maturity The growing ability to view one's parents as separate persons and personalities.

Filial piety The cultural belief in Eastern society that the elderly possess a higher status and deserve more respect than younger people.

Five-factor model of personality Costa and McCrae's theory that adult personality consists of five stable and independent personality traits: neuroticism, extraversion, openness-to-experience, agreeableness, and conscientiousness.

Flashbulb memories Vivid, detailed, and long-lasting mental representations of personally experienced events.

Flexibility The range of motion in a joint or group of joints; directly related to muscle length.

Flow The experience of being fully engaged in an activity.

Fluid intelligence The basic information-processing abilities of the mind independent of life experience and education; measured by relational thinking tasks such as block design and digit-symbol substitution.

Flynn Effect The tendency for IQ scores to increase over time.

Folk systems In Hispanic cultures, the assumption that mental and physical disorders may be resolved by restoring balance between the person, the environment, and the spirits/cosmos (life forces) through informal, community-based healers.

Formal operations The fourth stage in Piaget's theory of intellectual development in which individuals are capable of abstract, hypothetical thinking.

Fraility A wasting of the body and associated general muscular weakness and poor nutrition.

Free radicals By-products of incomplete or inefficient cellular metabolism characterized by a free, unpaired electron.

Frontal lobe A portion of the cortex that controls higher-order executive processes.

Functional assessment The determination of an older person's basic abilities necessary for adequate functioning, including physical dimensions, mental health status, social skills, and intellect; used to determine whether intervention services, if any, are needed.

Functional Assessment Staging System (FAST) Reisberg's conceptualization of the predictable, progressive declines that occur in patients with AD.

Functional magnetic resonance imaging (fMRI) A noninvasive measure of brain activity that uses the magnetic qualities of water molecules to evaluate changes in the distributions of oxygenated and deoxygenated blood.

G factor Spearman's term for general intelligence.

Gait speed/velocity The rate at which a person normally walks; normative changes occur in walking speed with age.

Gender consistency model The assumption of caregiving roles and responsibilities by the child of the same sex as the dependent elderly parent.

Generativity Caring about future generations of people and about contributing to society.

Genetic mutation theory The idea that aging is caused by changes, or mutations, in the DNA of the cells in vital organs of the body. Eventually, the number of mutated cells in a vital organ increases to the point that the efficacy of the cell's functioning is significantly impaired.

Genetic switching theory A theory that attributes biological aging to cessation of operation in selected genes.

Genuine memory deficits Memory impairment due to the brain's inability to store new information.

Geriatric care managers Master's-level professionals, usually social workers, who are hired by families to identify appropriate services, determine level of independence, and identify level of functioning for an older person having medical, social, emotional, nutritional, or physical problems.

Gero-transcendence A view of the world characterized by decreased concern with personal and material interests, and greater concern with the deeper meaning of life.

Glare The reflection of light that has the capacity to limit vision beginning in middle age.

Glaucoma An increase in pressure within the eye that may lead to blindness if left untreated.

Global Deterioration Scale A method used to describe the stages of AD.

Goal pursuit theory A theory that individuals are self-motivated to initiate and pursue personal goals (same as action theory).

Grief The sorrow, anger, guilt, and confusion that usually accompany a significant loss.

Grief pangs The somatic experience of grief, which includes tightness in the throat, nausea, difficulty in breathing, and sobbing.

Guardian A court-appointed designee who makes substituted judgments on behalf of an older adult who is not competent to make certain kinds of decisions for him or herself.

Hemispheres The halves of the cerebrum.

Hemispheric asymmetry reduction hypothesis The hypothesis that there is an age-related decline in the efficiency of the brain to recruit specialized neural mechanisms and that brain function becomes less lateralized with aging.

Hidden poor Those individuals who could be classified as poor on the basis of their own income but who reside with friends or relatives who are not poor.

Hierarchical integration One of the criteria used to identify cognitive stages; current stages incorporate (and extend) the characteristics of preceding stages.

Hippocampus A portion of the limbic system involved with memory processes.

Historical time The sociohistorical context within which a life event occurs.

History A potential threat to the internal validity of a quasi-experiment; it is most likely to occur when the same individuals are tested at different times.

Hypertension High blood pressure, the cause of which is often the narrowing of arterial walls, familial, or unknown (idiopathic).

Idiographic comparisons Repeated measurements of a single person on specific psychological dimensions.

Idiosyncratic change Development unique to an individual.

Implicit memory A memory task that does not require a subject to consciously remember a previous event.

Independent variables The variables that are manipulated within an experimental study.

Individual time The time in an individual's life at which an event occurs.

Infantalizing the elderly Treating older persons as if they were children; seeing them as helpless, dependent, immature, and cute.

Information-processing approach The idea that age-related memory deficits are caused by the inefficient encoding, storage, and retrieval of information.

Instrumental activities of daily living (IADLs) Basic and complex dimensions of daily living: preparation of meals, shopping, money management, telephone use, light housework, and heavy housework; used in assessment of older adults to determine appropriate intervention and services.

Interindividual differences The different patterns of developmental change that may be observed between different adults.

Interitem reliability The extent to which measurements on one-half of the items on a test are predictable from the measurements on the other half.

Internal validity The extent to which an independent variable determines the outcome of an experiment.

Interrater reliability The assessed amount of agreement between two or more observers who make independent observations in behavioral studies.

Interview A method of data collection in which individuals have a verbal conversation with each other.

Intraindividual change Different patterns of developmental change observed within individual adults.

Invariant movement A criteria of developmental stages; suggests that individuals must progress through developmental stages in an unchangeable manner.

Kinesthesis The ability to sense the position of one's body parts in space.

Korsakoff's syndrome A disorder manifested by chronic alcoholics and typified by severe memory loss.

Late-onset alcoholism Alcoholism emerging in middle to late life, usually as a response to multiple stressors such as the loss of loved ones, reaction to retirement, or chronic conditions; currently underdiagnosed.

Life expectancy How long, on the average, one is expected to live.

Life management The integration and application of both assimilative and accommodative processes used to protect the aging self in the face of the cumulative effects of developmental change and to preserve positive self-evaluation and well-being.

Life review A looking-back process, set in motion by nearness to death, that potentially proceeds toward personality reorganization; the attempts to make sense of one's own life and experiences through reflection.

Life structure Levinson's theoretical construct that defines the context in which adult development occurs, including the people, the places, the work, and the situations through which people choose to define themselves.

Life-events model A view that suggests that some life events produce taxing circumstances for individuals, forcing them to change their personalities and value orientations; it is thus also important to consider the sociohistorical circumstances in which those events occur.

Limbic system A part of the brain that controls memory and emotional responsiveness.

Linear A straight-line relationship between two variables.

Lipofuscin A pigment that accumulates in progressive fashion with age in specific organ systems of the body.

Living will A document in which an individual identifies for a physician and/or family members the specific conditions under which life-sustaining measures may be implemented or withdrawn.

Lobes A name used to describe different areas of the cortex of the brain.

Longevity The theoretical upper limit of the life span that is genetically fixed and species-specific.

Longitudinal study A research design in which data are collected from the same group of individuals on multiple occasions.

Long-term care Intervention (medical, social support, personal care, health care, etc.) designed to assist the chronically ill elderly or disabled in meeting their daily needs; may be home-based or delivered in specialized centers offering rehabilitation, respite care, adult day care, or nursing care.

Long-term memory A test of long-term memory in which an individual is asked to recall as many items as possible from a given list.

Lumpectomy Removal of a breast tumor and associated lymph nodes without removal of the entire breast.

Magnetic resonance imaging (MRI) A radiological technique for assessing brain structures.

Male climacteric The decline of sexual potency that usually begins when men are in their sixties and seventies and progresses at a much slower rate than female menopause.

Mammography A procedure used to screen for breast cancer using low-radiation X-ray imaging.

Mastectomy Removal of the breast and associated lymph nodes under the arm.

Maximal oxygen uptake (VO$_2$max) One of the standard methods for establishing a person's overall aerobic capacity; the higher the oxygen consumption per minute per kilogram of body weight, the better one's cardiovascular system and the greater one's overall endurance.

Mean The statistical average for a set of numbers.

Mechanics of mind The basic operations of our human information-processing system. Includes mental hardware such as sensation, perception, and memory.

Mechanistic paradigm The model that suggests that adults are passive machines that merely react to environmental events.

Median The value in the exact middle of a distribution of scores.

Medicaid A federal- and state-supported health care program for low-income persons.

Medical directive An explicit written statement of a person's wish to accept or reject particular forms of medical intervention; it preserves the right of the person to self-determination when he or she becomes incompetent or is unable to make decisions or express wishes.

Medicare Federal health insurance for adults 65 and older and the disabled (regardless of age) that provides short-term in-patient hospital care and limited skilled care at home or in a nursing home.

Medigap policies Health care insurance designed to meet the shortfall between actual medical treatment costs and funds provided by Medicare.

Melatonin A hormone produced by the pineal gland that binds with free radicals.

Menopause The permanent cessation of menstruation and the ability to bear children.

Mental health A state of successful mental functioning resulting in productive activities, fulfilling relationships, and the ability to adapt to change and cope with adversity . . . indispensable to personal well-being, family, and interpersonal relationships and one's contribution to society.

Mental imagery The process of forming mental images as a means of enhancing memory performance.

Mentor An adult who guides or advises another, typically younger, adult about personal, social, or occupational goals.

Meta-analysis An objective account of the results of several studies taken as a whole.

Metabolism A measure of the rate at which an individual burns calories.

Metamemory Knowledge about one's own memory abilities; being able to accurately assess one's memory and to accurately report what one knows.

Milieu therapy Improving the quality of an institutional environment by modifying physical, social, cognitive, and emotional dimensions to maximize the needs of its residents.

Mitochondria Structure of the cell responsible for producing energy through breakdown of nutrients into basic elements.

Mode The most frequently appearing score in a distribution of scores.

Morbidity The prevalence or incidence of disease in a population.

Mortality The frequency or rate of death occurring for a defined population.

Most efficient design The complex design that allows investigators to separate out the specific effects of age, time of testing, and cohort.

Mourning The overt behavioral expression of grief that is heavily influenced by cultural patterns.

Multidirectionality The idea that there are intraindividual differences in the patterns of development and aging.

Multiple regression A statistical method by which a researcher can determine if a number of variables, in combination with each other (or independent of each other), predict another variable.

Muscle power The product of the force and the velocity (speed) of muscle contraction; a measure of the ability to generate work per unit of time.

Mutual help A significant value in Hispanic culture that sustains intergenerational patterns of care through an obligatory norm based on guilt and gratitude.

Myocardial infarction Blockage of one of the coronary arteries sufficient to cause the heart to be deprived of blood and causing irreversible damage to the heart muscle (heart attack).

Near-death experience (NDE) A sequence of subjective phenomena reported by individuals who have come perilously close to dying.

Near poor Those individuals with incomes between the poverty level and 125 percent of this level.

Negative correlation A pattern of association between two variables in which higher scores on one variable are related to lower scores on another.

Neurofibrillary tangles Intertwined fibers that interfere with normal neuronal functioning.

Neuron A nerve cell that is the basic unit of the nervous system.

Neuronal viability Refers to the effciency of neuronal function.

Neuroticism One of the personality traits in Costa and McCrae's Five-Factor Model of adult personality.

Neurotransmitters Chemical substances that carry messages across a synapse.

Nomothetic comparisons Comparisons of groups of individuals to examine differences on any specific psychological measure; comparisons are obtained on a minimum of 2 different testing occasions.

Nondeclarative memory The influence that past events have on a person's current behavior.

Nonnormative life events Influences on development that do not follow a prescribed social or biological order.

Normative age-graded factors Influences on developmental change that are closely related to an individual's chronological age.

Normative history-graded factors Influences on development that are closely related to societal events.

Obesity Having body weight far enough over healthy weight to reduce one's life expectancy.

Objective caregiver burden The measurable disruption of an adult's routine or expected lifestyle (e.g., finances, travel, friendships, family interactions) caused by having to care for an older parent or close relative.

Occipital lobe The portion of the cortex involved in visual perception.

Oncologists Physicians who specialize in the diagnosis and treatment of cancer.

Ontogeny The study of maturation of the individual. The term *ontogeny* can be contrasted with *phylogeny,* which refers to the study of species development.

Openness to experience One of the personality traits that comprises Costa and McCrae's Five-Factor Model of adult personality.

Optimization A goal of the field of gerontology to understand how to best preserve a positive life for all adults (e.g., independence, freedom, personal autonomy, dignity) in keeping with an age-irrelevant view of society.

Ordinary creativity Creativity exhibited by "ordinary adults" in everyday situations.

Organ of Corti The organ in the inner ear that transforms sound vibrations into nerve impulses.

Organismic paradigm The model that views development as genetically programmed and following a set progression of qualitatively discontinuous stages.

Organization A strategy useful in enhancing memory performance.

Osteopenia Mild losses in bone density in women.

Osteoporosis The thinning and weakening of the bones due to calcium deficiency in older people, especially women.

P300 brain wave A unique pattern of brain activity associated with the identification of novel stimuli.

Palliative treatments A treatment that focuses on the symptoms rather than the cause of a disease.

Paradigm A theoretical approach or perspective that helps researchers organize and interpret their observations.

Parental imperative The tendency of the birth of a child to trigger heightened sex-role differentiation between mother and father in order to assist with the division of labor.

Parietal lobe A portion of the cortex involved in short-term memory and the representation of spatial relationships.

Passive accommodative mastery style (passive mastery) A style of coping in which individuals fit themselves to the environment rather than try to change the external environment.

Passive euthanasia Inducing a natural death by withdrawing some life-sustaining therapeutic effort such as turning off a respirator or heart-lung machine.

Pearson product moment correlation coefficient Abbreviated as *r,* this computes the quantitative strength of a correlation on a scale of −1.00 to +1.00.

Perimenopause Refers to the 3–5 year period leading to menopause when there is a reduction in the production of estrogen. Menopause is considered to have occurred when 12 consecutive months have passed without a menstrual period.

Persistent vegetative state A clinical condition of complete unawareness of the self and the environment, accompanied by sleep-wake cycles but no evidence of purposeful or voluntary behavioral responsiveness to environmental stimuli, no language comprehension or expression, and no bowel or bladder control. It lasts for at least one month following an injury or a degenerative or metabolic disorder.

Personality The distinctive patterns of behavior, thought, and emotion that characterize each person's adaptation to the situations of his/her life.

Pet therapy Regular contact with domestic animals that encourages autonomy, responsibility, well-being, control, and improves an older person's general social responsiveness.

Philosophical wisdom Refers to an understanding of the abstract relationship between one's self and the rest of humanity.

Plasticity The range of function that can be observed in individuals; frequently used to refer to the extent to which cognitive or physical performance can be improved by practice or training.

Positive ageism A form of stereotyping that glorifies aging and portrays as models those who are free from the typical problems (chronic health, financial, social) that most older adults encounter.

Positive correlation An association between variables so that high scores on one variable are related to high scores on another variable.

Positive psychology The study of the strengths, virtues, and qualities that contribute to effective functioning in everyday life; traits include joy, love, life satisfaction, happiness, trust, contentment, interest, pride, courage, optimism, well-being, and flow.

Positron-emission tomography (PET scan) A noninvasive method of measuring the metabolic activity of the brain.

Postconventional level The last two stages within Kohlberg's theory of moral development; at this level, individuals are capable of generating moral rules based on universal principles of justice.

Postformal operations The generic term used to describe qualitative changes in thinking beyond Piaget's stage of formal operations, characterized by an acceptance of relativity, dialectic thinking, and problem finding.

Potential life span The maximum age that could be attained if an individual were able to avoid illness and accidents.

Practical wisdom The ability to display superior judgment with regard to important matters of real life.

Pragmatics of mind The mental software that encompasses the general system of factual and strategic knowledge accessible to members of a particular culture, the specialized systems of knowledge available to individuals within particular occupations and avocations, and an understanding of how to activate these different types of knowledge within particular contexts to aid problem solving.

Preconventional level The first two stages in Kohlberg's theory of moral development; characterized by the construction of moral rules based on the fear of punishment and the desire for pleasure.

Preoperational stage The second stage in Piaget's theory of cognitive development; characterized by illogical thinking marked by irreversibility as well as the inability to distinguish fantasy from reality.

Presbycusis The general term used to describe age-related problems in hearing, especially hearing high-pitched sounds.

Presbyopia The reduction in the efficacy of near vision; usually first observed during middle adulthood.

Primary appraisal The process of choosing whether an event is stressful and requires the implementation of coping strategies.

Primary mental abilities Thurstone's belief that intelligence consists of the following mental abilities: verbal comprehension, word fluency, number, space, associative memory, perceptual speed, and induction.

Priming task An implicit memory task in which subjects are asked to identify or make judgments about stimuli that were (or were not) presented during an earlier phase of an experiment.

Prior to need (or preneed) The practice of arranging funeral expenses long before the need arises, when the individual is healthy and well.

Probable causes The use of ex post facto analysis of treatment success to determine the source of a psychological problem such as clinical depression; successful intervention indicates the likely source of the problem.

Problem finding The identification and construction of sophisticated problems to resolve.

Process dissociation procedure (PDP) A method of estimating the degree to which conscious and unconscious (or automatic) factors independently contribute to performance on a memory test.

Progressive overload Training principle that increases stress on the body to cause adaptations that improve fitness; too much stress can cause damage, and too little will be insufficient to enhance fitness.

Prostatic specific antigen (PSA) Blood test used to screen males for prostate cancer.

Psychological age An individual's ability to adapt to changing environmental demands in comparison to the adaptability of other individuals of identical chronological age.

Psychological autopsies The analysis of suicides *ex post facto* to determine individual and interactive predictive factors such as psychological state, personality traits, and specific environmental stressors that are predictive in certain populations.

Psychometric approach An approach to adult intellectual development that involves the administration of standardized adult intelligence tests such as the WAIS and PMA.

Psychomotor slowing The age-related slowing of behavior.

Psychoneuroimmunology The study of multifaceted changes in the central nervous system and immune system in response to life events, stressors, and special challenges that heighten or reduce a person's susceptibility to disease.

Psychopharmacology The administration of prescription drugs to alter a person's biological state in order to attain a desirable goal, e.g., modification of behavioral, affective, or physiological states.

Psychosexual development The study of how individuals of different ages deal with pleasurable body sensations.

Psychosocial development The study of the lifelong relationship between the developing individual and the social system of which she or he is a part.

Qualitative change Abrupt, stagelike differences in kind rather than amount that occur in development.

Quantitative change The differences in amount rather than kind that occur in development.

Quasi-experiments Studies that resemble true experiments in design and analysis but contain an independent variable that cannot be manipulated.

Questionnaire A method of data collection in which an individual responds to a standardized list of questions.

Random assignment The technique of assigning individuals to exposure conditions on a random basis in order to evenly distribute extraneous factors.

Range The simplest measure of variability; revealed by the lowest and highest score in a set.

Range of motion The full motion possible in a joint.

Reaction time Experimental assessments of the time elapsed between the appearance of a signal and a person's responding movement.

Reactivity The way in which an individual reacts to being tested or observed within a psychological study; a threat to the internal validity of an experiment or quasi-experiment.

Reality orientation Providing elderly regular reminders of where they are and of their present situation (e.g., day, date, residence).

Recall A type of memory task in which individuals must remember information without the aid of any external cues or supports.

Recognition A basic strategy for assessing memory ability.

Reliability The consistency of test results for the same person(s) from one time to another.

Reminiscence Memory for biographical events and personal experiences.

Reminiscence bump The tendency for older adults to remember a disproportionately large number of memories from late adolescence and early adulthood.

Reminiscence therapy The encouragement of older persons to recall their pasts, reflect on their memories, and bring closure to personal-family conflicts, e.g., resolve "unfinished business."

Representative sample A sample that has the same characteristics as the entire population.

Reserve capacity The amount of resources available to the individual for responding to physical or psychological challenges. The amount of reserve capacity, or the range of plasticity, of particular physiological systems may be limited with aging.

Respite care Temporary assistance to relieve family members from the physical, emotional, and social demands of caring for an older person at home. Such assistance is often provided by volunteers, friends, relatives, or through community agencies including adult day care programs.

Retrieval deficit Memory impairment due to the inability to successfully access stored information.

Reversibility of fitness The loss of fitness and conditioning that occurs when people curtail their training.

Rheumatoid arthritis An autoimmune disease marked by swelling of the joints and, over time, degeneration of cartilage in affected joints and a resultant loss of joint function.

Sarcopenia Atrophy of skeletal muscle mass; one of the most predictable consequences of aging.

Sati The ancient Hindu practice of burning a dead man's widow to increase his family's prestige and establish her image as a goddess in his memory.

Schaie-Thurstone Adult Mental Abilities Test A standardized test of adult intelligence adapted from Thurstone's Primary Mental Abilities Test.

Search for meaning The existential quest for understanding the human condition and one's purpose in life.

Secondary appraisal When facing a life event determined to be stressful, a person's assessment of the range of available resources and the "cost" of implementing such resources.

Selection A threat to internal validity when the procedures used to select individuals for research result in extraneous or unintended differences in the groups selected for study, e.g., young vs. old subjects may differ not only on education but also in health.

Selective attention A type of attention in which we ignore irrelevant information while focusing on relevant information (e.g., ignoring a television program while listening to a friend).

Selective dropout The tendency for particular individuals to drop out of longitudinal studies (e.g., the infirm, the less able, those who move from the area) and thus skew the results.

Selective optimization

Selective optimization with compensation A technique by which older adults alter their behavior in such a way as to preserve (and perhaps enhance) specific cognitive, behavioral, or physical abilities.

Selfish grief The conflict experienced by daughters who fear that overt expression of grief over the loss of their mothers would mean that they wished to prolong the suffering and pain that their mothers experienced; they suppress their emotional reactions to the loss of their mothers, appearing to readily accept their deaths.

Semantic elaboration A strategy used to enhance memory.

Semantic memory Use of acquired knowledge about the world; thinking about the meanings of words or concepts without reference to when or how we acquired such knowledge.

Senescence All of the changes associated with the normal process of aging.

Senile plaques The accumulation of spherical masses of amyloid surrounded by degenerating axons and dendrites; senile plaques prevent normal communication between neurons.

Senility An outdated term referring to the abnormal deterioration of mental functions in old people.

Sensation The reception of physical stimuli at a sense organ and the translation of this stimulation to the brain.

Sensorimotor stage The first stage in Piaget's theory of cognitive development in which the child discovers the world using the senses and motor activity.

Sex role The behaviors that are expected of individuals because they are either male or female.

Short-term memory Information stored and retained for a brief period, usually less than 60 seconds.

Social age Refers to the social roles and social expectations people have for themselves as well as those imposed by society.

Social clock The internalized sense of timing that tells people whether they are experiencing predictable/normative life events on-time or off-time (e.g., too fast or too slow).

Social cognition Cognitive development focused on the individual's reasoning about social and interpersonal matters.

Social convoy The network of close relationships that accompany an individual throughout life.

Social Security A federal program designed to provide benefits to adults who become disabled or retire. Comprised of four separate trust funds: (1) Old Age Survivors Insurance, (2) Disability Insurance, (3) Hospital Insurance Trust Fund–Medicare part A, (4) Supplementary Medical Insurance–Medicare part B.

Socioemotional selectivity theory The choice of older adults to engage in social exchanges with fewer people e.g., those whose companionship they truly enjoy and who provide positive emotional value.

Soma The cell body of a neuron.

Source memory The ability to remember the context in which a particular piece of information has been learned.

Spirituality The motivational and emotional source of an individual's search for a personally defined relationship with a higher being; leads to enhanced feelings of well-being, inner peace, and life satisfaction.

Stage theory A theory that suggests that development consists of a series of abrupt changes in psychological functions and processes, marked by qualitative change at each stage.

Standard deviation A common measure of variability that reveals the extent to which individual scores deviate from the mean of a distribution.

Standard phase Gibbs's term for the first four stages in Kohlberg's theory of moral development.

Standardization The establishment of fixed procedures for administration, scoring, and norms for age, grade, race, sex and so on.

Statistical significance A mathematical procedure to determine the extent to which differences between groups of data are due to chance factors or the independent variable.

Strength training Directed physical activity requiring resistance against a mass or load to produce muscle contraction.

Stress-buffering effect The reduction in the impact of stressful events due to the moderating influences of social supports (family, peers, neighbors, and community), which lead to decreased likelihood of depression in older adults.

Stroke Blockage of one of the arteries supplying blood to the brain, causing destruction of associated areas, and corresponding loss of function; e.g., loss of language center leads to various speech disorders such as aphasia, loss of certain motor centers leads to paralysis, etc.

Structured wholeness A criterion for determining developmental stages; implies that individuals' cognitions are consistent with their current stage of development.

Subjective caregiver burden The emotional reactions of adults providing care for an older parent or relative that include embarrassment, shame, guilt, resentment, and social exclusion.

Subjective well-being The experience of people who feel positive emotions, engage in interesting activities, feel little pain or negative emotions, and who are generally satisfied with their lives.

Successful aging Avoiding disease and disability, and continued active engagement in life.

Sundowning Heightened incidence of wandering, pacing, and generalized restlessness found among elderly with dementia, which occurs in the early evening (e.g., 7–10 P.M.).

Syncope Temporary loss of consciousness ("blackouts") often due to medical conditions, prescription drugs, or special physical conditions.

Temporal lobe The portion of the cortex involved in audition, language, and long-term memory.

Tension-reduction hypothesis The use of alcohol to manage the tension and anxieties associated with negative life events and chronic stress.

Terminal drop A decline in psychological functioning, revealed in standardized tests, that precedes death by about five years.

Testamentary capacity Having the mental capacity and judgment necessary to create a will directing the disposition of one's assets (real estate, valuables, stocks, bonds, jewelry, clothes, etc.).

Testing A threat to internal validity that is based on the readministration of the same instrument on more than one occasion.

Testing the limits The technique used to measure age differences in maximum cognitive reserve.

Test-retest reliability The degree of predictability that measurements taken on one test on one occasion will be similar to those taken on another occasion.

Theory of Multiple Intelligences The position that there are several neurologically based types of human intelligences.

Threshold model

Time-sequential design A complex research design that allows an investigator to disentangle age effects from time-of-testing effects.

Tinnitus A constant high-pitched or ringing sound in the ears reported in about 10 percent of older adults.

Trait theorists Personality theorists who believe there is some consistency and stability to human personality over time.

Trajectory of life According to Pattison, our anticipated life span and the plan we make for the way in which we will live out our life.

Transient ischemic attack (TIA) A temporary, reversible minor stroke.

Transitions According to Levinson, the periods that overlap one era with another; transitions last for approximately five years.

Triarchic Theory of Intelligence The theory that suggests that intelligence consists of three independent facets: analytic, creative, and practical.

Type A behavior style Behavior reflecting excessive competitiveness, accelerated pace of normal activities, time-urgency, hostility, and aggressiveness.

Type B behavior style Behavior reflective of a relaxed, less hurried, and less preoccupied lifestyle.

Unfinished business Resolution, where possible, of the interpersonal problems created in social relationships; the desire by dying persons to bring closure to the different dimension of their lives.

Universal progression A criteria for the presence of developmental stages; the belief that all individuals in all cultures progress through all stages in the same invariant sequence.

Upgrading kin relationships The process of bringing distant relatives into the immediate family and making them a part of the primary family unit.

Uplifts The small positive experiences we encounter in daily living that counterbalance the hassles that occur in everyday life.

Upswing hypothesis The contention that there is an increase in marital satisfaction when children leave home.

Validity The soundness of measurements in terms of measuring what they are intended to measure.

Variability The statistical description of distribution scores; includes range and standard deviation.

Variable Anything that may change and influence behavior.

Wear-and-tear theory The idea that aging occurs because of physical wear and tear on the body caused by hard work.

Wechsler Adult Intelligence Scale (WAIS) A standard test of adult intelligence that provides both a verbal IQ and performance IQ as well as an overall IQ score.

White matter Another name for the fatty myelin sheath that surrounds and insulates long axons.

Wisdom An expert knowledge system in the fundamental pragmatics of life permitting exceptional insight, judgment, and advice involving complex and uncertain matters of the human condition.

Working memory The active manipulation of information in short-term memory.

REFERENCES

Achieving and Maintaining Cognitive Vitality with Aging (2001). Report prepared by the Institute for the Study of Aging. International Longevity Center.

Adams, W. L., & Cox, N. S. (1997). Epidemiology of problem drinking among elderly people. In A. Gurnack (Ed.), *Older adults misuse of alcohol, medicines, and other drugs* (pp. 1–23). New York: Springer.

Adler, T. (1992, February). For depressed elderly, drugs advised. *American Psychological Association Monitor,* pp. 16–17.

Adrain, M. J. (1981). Flexibility in the aging adult. In E. L. Smith & R. C. Serfass (Eds.), *Exercise and aging: The scientific basis.* Hillsdale, NJ: Enslow.

Agronin, M. E. (1998). The new frontier in geriatric psychiatry: Nursing homes and other long-term care settings. *The Gerontologist, 38,* 338–391.

Ai, A. L., Dunkle, R. E., Peterson, C., & Bolling, S. F. (1998). The role of private prayer in psychological recovery among midlife and aged patients following cardiac surgery. *The Gerontologist, 38* (5), 591–601.

Ajrouch, K. J., Antonucci, T. C., & Janevic, M. R. (2001). Social networks among blacks and whites: The interaction between race and age. *Journal of Gerontology, 56B* (2), S112–S118.

Albert, M. (1993). Neuropsychological and neurophysiological changes in healthy adult humans across the age range. *Neurobiology of Aging, 14,* 623.

Albert, M. S., & Killiany, R. J. (2001). Age-related cognitive changes and brain-behavior relationships. In J. E. Birren & K. W. Schaie (Eds.), *Handbook of the psychology of aging* (5th ed.). San Diego: Academic Press.

Albert, M. S., & Stafford, J. L. (1988). Computed tomography studies. In M. S. Albert & M. B. Moss (Eds.), *Geriatric neuropsychology* (pp. 211–227). New York: Guilford.

Aldwin, C. (1995). The role of stress in aging and adult development. *Adult Development and Aging News, 23,* 3, 7, 16.

Allaire, J. C., & Marsiske, M. (1999). Everyday cognition: Age and intellectual ability correlates. *Psychology and Aging, 14,* 627–644.

Almeida, D. M., & Kessler, R. C. (1998). Everyday stressors and gender differences in daily distress. *Journal of Personality and Social Psychology, 75,* 670–680.

Alpaugh, P., & Birren, J. E. (1977). Variables affecting creative contributions across the life span. *Human Development, 20,* 240–248.

Alspaugh, M. E. L., Stephens, M. A. P., Townsend, A. L., Zarit, S. H., & Greene, R. (1999). Longitudinal patterns of risk for depression in dementia caregivers: Objective and subjective primary stress as predictors. *Psychology and Aging, 14,* 34–43.

Altman, L. K. (1992). Alzheimer's dilemma: Whether to tell people they have the disease. *New York Times,* April 7, p. C3.

American Association of Retired Persons. (1992). *A profile of older Americans.* Washington, DC: AARP.

American Association of Retired Persons. (2001). *Live longer, live healthier—Exercise!* http://www.aarp.org

American Association of Retired Persons (AARP). (2001). Survey on retirement: 1998. Survey summary, Not ready to retire, *Syracuse Post Standard,* April 18, 2001, pp. D1, D10.

American Association of Retired Persons. (2001a). *Funeral and burial costs: What you should know.* www.aarp.org

American Association of Retired Persons. (2001b). Older Americans and preneed burial arrangements: *AARP Research Center Report: Consumer Issues.* www.aarp.org

American Association of Retired Persons. (2001c). Common reactions to loss. *Coping with loss.* www.aarp.org

American Association of Retired Persons. (2001d). *Widows.* www.aarp.org

American Board of Hospice and Palliative Medicine (2001). Certification requirements and standards. http://www.abhpm.org/

American Heart Association (2001a). *Cardiovascular disease statistics.* http://www.americanheart.org

American Heart Association (2001b). *Cholesterol-lowering drugs.* http://www.americanheart.org

American Psychiatric Association. (1994). *Diagnostic and statistical manual of mental disorders (DSM-IV).* (4th ed.). Washington, DC: American Psychiatric Association.

Anders, T. R., Fozard, J. L., & Lillyquist, T. D. (1972). Effects of age upon retrieval from short-term memory. *Developmental Psychology, 6,* 214–217.

Anderson, S. A., Russell, C. S., & Schumm, W. R. (1983). Perceived marital quality and family life-cycle categories: A further analysis. *Journal of Marriage and the Family, 45,* 127–139.

Aneshensel, C. S., Pearlin, L. I., Levy-Storms, L., & Schuler, R. H. (2000). The transition from home to nursing home: Mortality among people with dementia. *Journal of Gerontology, 55B* (3), S152–S162.

Angel, J. L. (2000). Coming of age: Minority elders in the United States. *The Gerontologist, 40* (4), 502–506.

Angel, J. L., Angel, R. J., McClellan, J. L., & Markides, K. S. (1996). Nativity, declining health, and preferences in living arrangements among elderly Mexican Americans: Implications for long-term care. *The Gerontologist, 36,* 464–473.

Angel, R. S., & Angel, J. L. (1995). Mental and physical comorbidity among the elderly: The role of culture and social class. In D. K. Padgett (Ed.), *Handbook on ethnicity, aging, and mental health* (pp. 47–70). Westport, CT: Greenwood Press.

Anthony, J. C., & Aboraya, A. (1992). The epidemiology of selected mental disorders in later life. In J. E. Birren, R. B. Sloane, G. D. Cohen, N. R. Hooyman, B. Leibowitz, M. H. Wykle, & D. E. Deutchman, *Handbook of mental health and aging* (2nd ed.). San Diego: Academic Press.

Antonucci, T. A. (2001). Social relations: An examination of social networks, social support, and sense of control. In J. E. Birren & K. W. Schaie (Eds.), *Handbook of the psychology of aging* (5th ed., pp. 427–453). San Diego: Academic Press.

Antonucci, T. C. (1990). Social supports and social relationships. In R. H. Binstock & K. K. George (Eds.), *Handbook of aging and the social sciences* (3rd ed.). New York: Academic Press.

Antonucci, T. C., & Akiyama, H. (1991a). Social relationships and aging well. *Generations, 15,* 39–44.

Antonucci, T. C., & Akiyama, H. (1991b). Convoys of social support: Generational issues. *Marriage and Family Review, 16,* 103–123.

Aponte, J. F., & Barnes, J. M. (1995). Impact of acculturation and moderator variables on the intervention and treatment of ethnic groups. In J. F. Aponte, R. Y. Rivers, & J. Wohl (Eds.), *Psychological interventions and cultural diversity* (pp. 19–39). Boston: Allyn & Bacon.

Aponte, J. F., Rivers, R. Y., & Wohl, J. (1995). *Psychological interventions and cultural diversity.* Boston: Allyn & Bacon.

Applebaum, P. S., & Grisso, T. (1988). Assessing patients' capacities to consent to treatment. *New England Journal of Medicine, 319,* 1635–1638.

Aranda, M. P., & Knight, B. G. (1997). The influence of ethnicity and culture on the caregiver stress and coping process: A socio-cultural review and analysis. *The Gerontologist, 37,* 342–354.

Argyle, M. (1994). *The psychology of social class.* New York: Routledge.

Arlin, P. K. (1984). Adolescent and adult thought: A structural interpretation. In M. L. Commons, F. A. Richards, & C. Armon (Eds.), *Beyond formal operations: Late adolescent and adult cognitive development.* New York: Praeger.

Arlin, P. K. (1989). Problem solving and problem finding in young artists and young scientists. In M. L. Commons, J. D. Sinnott, F. A. Richards, & C. Armon (Eds.), *Adult development, Vol. 1: Comparisons and applications of developmental models.* New York: Praeger.

Armon, C. (1991). *The development of reasoning about the good life.* Paper presented at the Sixth Adult Development Symposium of the Society for Research in Adult Development, Boston, July.

Asch, D. A., & Christakis, N. A. (1996). Why do physicians prefer to withdraw some forms of life support over others? Intrinsic attribute of life-sustaining treatments are associated with physicians preferences. *Medical Care, 34,* 103–111.

Ascher, B. (1993). *Landscape without gravity.* New York: Delphinivar Books.

Atchley, R. C. (1983). *Aging: Continuity and change.* Belmont, CA: Wadsworth.

Atchley, R. (1999). *Continuity and adaptation in aging: Creating positive experiences.* Baltimore, MD: Johns Hopkins University Press.

Attig, T. (1992). Person-centered death education. *Death Studies, 16,* 357–370.

Ausubel, D. P. (1968). *Educational psychology.* New York: Holt, Rinehart & Winston.

Avorn, J. (1998). Depression in the elderly: Falls and pitfalls. *New England Journal of Medicine, 339* (13), 918–920.

Backman, L., Mantyla, T., & Herlitz, A. (1990). Psychological perspectives on successful aging: The optimization of episodic remembering in old age. In P. B. Baltes & M. M. Baltes (Eds.), *Successful aging* (pp. 118–163). New York: Cambridge University Press.

Backman, L., Small, J. J., & Wahlin, A. (2001). Aging and memory: Cognitive and biological perspectives. In J. E. Birren & K. W. Schaie (Eds.), *Handbook of the psychology of aging* (5th ed.). San Diego: Academic Press.

Baddeley, A. (1994). Working memory: The interface between memory and cognition. In D. L. Schacter & E. Tulving (Eds.), *Memory systems 1994* (pp. 351–368). Cambridge, MA: MIT Press.

Bahrick, H. P., Bahrick, P. O., & Wittlinger, R. P. (1975). Fifty years of memory for names and faces: A cross-sectional approach. *Journal of Experimental Psychology: General, 104,* 54–75.

Bailley, S. E., Kral, M. J., & Dunham, K. (1999). Survivors of suicide do grieve differently: Empirical support for a commonsense proposition. *Suicide and life-threatening behaviors, 29* (3), 256–271.

Baillie, P. H., & Danish, S. J. (1992, March). Understanding the career transition of athletes. *Sport Psychologist, 6,* 77–98.

Balch, D. W. (1997). Long-term healthcare: A family crisis. *Maturity Focus, Eagle Newspapers Supplement,* p. 7.

Baltes, P. B. (1987). Theoretical propositions of life-span developmental psychology: On the dynamics between growth and decline. *Developmental Psychology, 23,* 611–626.

Baltes, P. B. (1993). The aging mind: Potential and limits. *The Gerontologist, 33,* 580–594.

Baltes, P. B. (1997). On the incomplete architecture of human ontogeny: Selection, optimization, and compensation as foundations of developmental theory. *American Psychologist, 52,* 366–380.

Baltes, P. B., & Baltes, M. (1990). Psychological perspectives on successful aging: The model of selective optimization with compensation. In P. B. Baltes & M. Baltes (Eds.), *Longitudinal research and the study of successful (optimal) aging* (pp. 1–49). Cambridge England: Cambridge University Press.

Baltes, P. B., & Graf, P. (1996). Psychological aspects of aging: Facts and frontiers. In D. Magnusson (Ed.), *The life span development of individuals: Behavioral, neurobiological, and psychosocial perspectives* (pp. 427–459). Cambridge: Cambridge University Press.

Baltes, P. B., & Kliegl, R. (1986). On the dynamics between growth and decline in the aging of intelligence and memory. In K. Poeck, H. J. Freund, & H. Ganshirt (Eds.), *Neurology.* Heidelberg, West Germany: Springer-Verlag.

Baltes, P. B., & Kliegl, R. (1992). Further testing of limits of cognitive plasticity: Negative age differences in a mnemonic skill are robust. *Developmental Psychology, 28,* 121–125.

Baltes, P. B., & Lindenberger, U. (1997). Emergence of a powerful connection between sensory and cognitive functions across the adult life span: A new window to the study of cognitive aging? *Psychology and Aging, 12,* 410–432.

Baltes, P. B., & Smith, J. (1997). A systemic-wholistic view of psychological functioning in very old age: Introduction to a collection of articles from the Berlin Aging Study. *Psychology and Aging, 12,* 396–409.

Baltes, P. B., & Staudinger, U. (1993). The search for a psychology of wisdom. *Current Directions in Psychological Science, 2,* 75–80.

Baltes, P. B., & Staudinger, U. M. (2000). Wisdom: A metaheuristic (pragmatic) to orchestrate mind and virtue toward excellence. *American Psychologist, 55,* 122–136.

Baltes, P. B., Lindenberger, U., & Staudinger, U. M. (1998). Life-span theory in developmental psychology. In R. M. Lerner (Ed.), *Handbook of child psychology: Vol. 1. Theoretical models of human development* (5 ed.). New York: Wiley.

Baltes, P. B., Staudinger, U. M., & Lindenberger, U. (1999). Lifespan psychology: Theory and application to intellectual functioning. *Annual Review of Psychology, 50,* 471–507.

Baltes, P. B., Mayer, K. U., Helmchen, H., & Steinhagen-Thiessen, E. (1993). The Berlin Aging Study (BASE): Overview and design. *Aging and Society, 13,* 483–515.

Baltes, P. B., Sowarka, D., & Kliegl, R. (1989). Cognitive training research on fluid intelligence in old age: What can older adults achieve by themselves? *Psychology and Aging, 4,* 217.

Baltes, P. B., Staudinger, U. M., Maeker, A., & Smith, J. (1995). People nominated as wise: A comparative study of wisdom related knowledge. *Psychology and Aging, 10,* 155–166.

Bandura, A. (1982). Self-efficacy in human agency. *American Psychologist, 37,* 122–137.

Barer, B. M. (1994). Men and women aging differently. *International Journal of Aging and Human Development, Special Issue: Social and Cultural Diversity of the Oldest-Old, 38* (1), 29–40.

Barnett, R. C., & Rivers, C. (1996). *She works, he works: How two-income families are happier, healthier, and better off.* San Francisco: Harper & Row.

Barney, D. D. (1995). Use of mental health services by American Indians and Alaska Native elders. In D. K. Padgett (Ed.), *Handbook of ethnicity, aging, and mental health* (pp. 203–214). Westport, CT: Greenwood.

Barron, S. A., Jacobs, L., & Kirkei, W. R. (1976). Changes in size of normal lateral ventricles during aging determined by computerized tomography. *Neurology, 26,* 1011–1013.

Bartoshuk, L. M., Rifkin, B., Marks, L. E., & Bars, P. (1986). Taste and aging. *Journal of Gerontology, 41,* 51–57.

Bartus, R. T. (2000). On neurodegenerative diseases, models, and treatment strategies: Lessons learned and lessons forgotton a generation following the cholinergic hypothesis. *Experimental Neurology, 163,* 495–529.

Bartzokis, G. (2001). Brain still developing in middle age. *Archives of General Psychiatry, 58,* 461–465.

Bashore, T. R. (1993). Differential effects of aging on the neurocognitive functions subserving speeded mental processing. In J. Cerella, J. M. Rybash, W. J. Hoyer, & M. L. Commons (Eds.), *Adult information processing: Limits on loss* (pp. 37–76). San Diego: Academic Press.

Basseches, M. (1984). *Dialectic thinking.* Norwood, NJ: Ablex.

Bassuk, S. S., Glass, T. A., & Berkman, L. F. (1999). Social disengagement and incident cognitive decline in community-dwelling elderly persons. *Annals of Internal Medicine, 131,* 165–173.

Basta, L. L. (1996). *A graceful exit: Life and death on your own terms.* New York: Insight Books-Plenum Press.

Bastida, E. (1987). Sex-typed age norms among older Hispanics. *The Gerontologist, 27,* 59–65.

Baum, C., Edwards, D. F., & Morrow-Howell, N. (1993). Identification and measurement of productive behaviors in servile dementia of the Alzheimer type. *Journal of Gerontology, 33,* 403–408.

Beach, D. L. (1997). Family caregiving: The positive impact on adolescent relationships. *The Gerontologist, 37,* 233–238.

Beckman, A. T. F., Kriegsman, D. M. W., Deeg, D. J. H., & Van Tilburg, W. (1995). The association of physical health and depression in the older population: Age and sex differences. *Social Psychiatry and Psychogeriatric Epidemiology, 30,* 32–38.

Bedford, V. H. (1995). Sibling relationships in middle and old age. In R. Blieszner & V. H. Bedford (Eds.), *Handbook of aging and the family* (pp. 201–222). Westport, CT: Greenwood Press.

Begg, R. K., & Sparrow, W. A. (2000). Characteristics of young and older individuals negotiating a raise surface: Implications for the prevention of fall. *Journal of Gerontology, 55A,* M147–M154.

Beehr, T. A., Glazer, S., Nielson, N. L., & Farmer, S. (2000). Work and nonwork predictors of employees' retirement ages. *Journal of vocational behavior, 57* (2), 206–225.

Beem, E. A. (2001). From earthly to spiritual bliss. *Boston Globe Magazine.* December 23, 2001.

Begley, S. (1993). The puzzle of genius. *Newsweek,* June 28, 46–50.

Bekker, L., DeMoyne, L., & Taylor, C. (1966). Attitudes toward the aged in a multigenerational sample. *Journal of Gerontology, 21,* 115–118.

Beland, F. (1987). Living arrangement preferences among elderly people. *The Gerontologist, 27,* 797–803.

Belasco, J. A. (1991). *Teaching the elephant to dance: The manager's guide to empowering change.* New York: Plume & Penguin Books.

Bell, J. (1992). In search of a discourse on aging. The elderly on television. *The Gerontologist, 32,* 305–311.

Belsky, J. (1981). Early human experience: A family perspective. *Developmental Psychology, 17,* 3–23.

Bem, S. L. (1974). The measurement of psychological androgyny. *Journal of Consulting and Clinical Psychology, 42,* 155–162.

Benbow, C. P., Lubinski, D., Shea, D. L., & Eftekhari-Sanjani, H. (2000). Sex differences in mathematical reasoning ability at age 13: Their status 20 years later. *Psychological Science, 2000,* 11, 474–480.

Benbow, C. P., & Stanley, J. C. (1980). Sex differences in mathematical ability: Fact or artifact? *Science, 210,* 1262–1264.

Bengtson, V. L. (1985). Diversity and symbolism in grandparental roles. In V. L. Bengtson & J. Robertson (Eds.), *Grandparenthood.* Beverly Hills, CA: Sage.

Bengtson, V. L., Mangen, D. G., & Landry, T. J., Jr. (1984). Multigenerational family: Concepts and findings. In V. Garmsholova, E. M. Horning, & D. Schaffer (Eds.), *Intergenerational relationships.* Lewiston, NY: Hogrefe.

Bengtson, V. L., Reedy, M., & Gordon, C. (1985). Aging self conceptions: Personality processes and social context. In J. E. Birren & K. W. Schaie (Eds.), *Handbook of the psychology of aging* (2nd ed.). New York: Van Nostrand Reinhold.

Bennett, P. J., Sekuler, A. B., McIntosh, A. R., & Della-Maggiore, V. (2001). The effects of aging on visual memory: Evidence for functional reorganization of cortical networks. *Acta Psychologica, 107,* 249–273.

Benson, M. (1997). Healthy life often determined by socioeconomic status. *Syracuse Post Standard,* August 18, p. A–4.

Benyamini, Y., Idler, E. L., Leventhal, H., & Leventhal, E. A. (2000). Positive affect and function as influences on self-assessments of health: Expanding our view beyond illness and disability. *Journal of Gerontology, 55B* (2), P107–P116.

Berg, C. A., & Sternberg, R. J. (1992). Adults' conceptions of intelligence across the adult life span. *Psychology and Aging, 7,* 221–231.

Bergstrom, M. J., & Holmes, M. E. (2000). Lay theories of successful aging after the death of a spouse: A network text analysis of bereavement advice. *Health Communication, 12* (4), 377–406.

Berkelman, R. L., & Hughes, J. M. (1993). The conquest of infectious diseases: Who are we kidding? *Annals of Internal Medicine, 119,* 426–427.

Berscheid, E. (1988). Some comments on love's anatomy: Or whatever happened to old-fashioned lust? In R. J. Sternberg & M. L. Barnes (Eds.), *Anatomy of love.* New Haven: Yale University Press.

Berzonsky, M. D. (1978). Formal reasoning in adolescence: An alternative view. *Adolescence, 13,* 279–290.

Biegel, D. E., Bass, D. M., Schulz, R., & Morycz, R. (1993). Predictors of in-home and out-of-home service use by family caregivers of Alzheimer's disease patients. *Journal of Aging and Health, 5,* 419–438.

Billings, J. A., Block, S. D., Finn, J. W. et al. (2002) Initial voluntary program standards for fellowship training in Palliative Medicine. *Journal of Palliative Medicine, 5*(1), 23–33.

Birren, J. E., & Schroots, J. J. F. (2001). History of geropsychology. In J. E. Birren & K. W. Schaie (Eds.), *Handbook of the psychology of aging* (5th ed.). San Diego: Academic Press.

Black, S. A., Goodwin, J. S., & Markides, K. S. (1998). The association between chronic diseases and depressive symptomatology in older Mexican Americans. *Journal of Gerontology: Medical Sciences, 53A,* M188–194.

Black, S. A., & Markides, K. (1994). Americans, Cuban Americans, and Mainland Puerto Ricans. *International Journal of Aging and Human Development, 39,* 97–103.

Blanchard-Fields, F., & Abeles, R. A. (1996). Social cognition and aging. In J. E. Birren & K. W. Schaie (Eds.), *Handbook of the psychology of aging* (4th ed., pp. 150–161). San Diego: Academic Press.

Blazer, D. (1994). Epidemiology of late-life depression. In L. Schneider, C. F. Reynolds, B. Lebowitz, & A. Friedhoff (Eds.), *Diagnosis and treatment of depression in late life* (pp. 9–19). Washington, DC: American Psychiatric Press.

Blazer, D. G. (1993). *Depression in late life* (2nd ed.). St. Louis, MO: C. V. Mosby.

Blieszner, R., & Hatvany, L. E. (1996). Diversity in the experience of late-life widowhood. *Journal of Personal and Interpersonal Loss, 1,* 199–211.

Block, C. E. (2000). Dyadic and gender differences in perceptions of the grandparent-grandchild relationship. *International Journal of Aging and Human Development, 51,* 85–104.

Block, M. R., Davidson, J. L., & Grambs, J. D. (1981). *Women over forty.* New York: Springer.

Bloom, A. (1993). The death of Eros. *New York Times Magazine,* May 23, p. 26.

Blumenthal, J. A., Emery, C. F., Madden, D. J., Schniebolk, S., Walsh-Riddle, M., George, L. K., McKee, D. C., Higgenbotham, M. B., Cobb, F. R., & Coleman, R. E. (1991). Long-term effects of exercise on psychological functioning in older men and women. *Journal of Gerontology: Psychological Science, 46,* P352–361.

Bodnar, J. C., & Kiecolt-Glaser, J. K. (1994). Caregiver depression after bereavement: Chronic stress isn't over when it's over. *Psychology and Aging, 9* (3), 372–380.

Bolger, N., Foster, M., Vinokur, A. D., & Ng, R. (1997). Close relationships and adjustments to a life crisis: The case of breast cancer. *Journal of Personality and Social Psychology, 70,* 283–294.

Bonanno, G. A., Mihalecz, M. C., & LeJeune, J. T. (1999). The core emotion themes of conjugal loss. *Motivation and Emotion, 23* (3), 175–201.

Bookwala, J., & Schulz, R. (1996). Spousal similarity in subjective well-being: The cardiovascular health study. *Psychology and Aging, 11,* 587–590.

Bookwala, J., & Schulz, R. (2000). A comparison of primary stressors, secondary stressors, and depressive symptoms between elderly caregiving husbands and wives: The caregiver caregiver health effects study. *Psychology and Aging, 15* (4), 607–616.

Bookwala, J., Yee, J. L., & Schulz, R. (2000). Caregiving and detrimental mental and physical health outcomes. In G. M. Williamson, P. A. Parmelee, and D. R. Shaffer (Eds.), *Physical illness and depression in older adults: A handbook of theory, research, and practice* (pp. 93–131). New York: Plenum.

Booth-Kewley, S., & Friedman, H. (1987). Psychological predictors of heart disease: A quantitative review. *Psychological Bulletin, 101,* 343–362.

Bortz, W. M., & Bortz, W. M. (1996). How fast do we age? Exercise performance over time as a biomarker. *Journal of Gerontology: Medical Sciences, 51A,* M223–M225.

Bortz, W. M., Wallace, D. H., & Wiley, D. (1999). Sexual function in 1,202 aging males: Differentiating aspects. *Journal of Gerontology: Biological and Medical Sciences, 54A,* M237–M241.

Borup, J. H. (1983). Relocation mortality research: Assessment, reply, and the need to refocus on the issues. *The Gerontologist, 23,* 235–242.

Bosse, R., Aldwin, C. M., Levenson, M. R., Spiro, A., & Mroczek, D. K. (1993). Change in social support after retirement: Longitudinal findings from the normative aging study. *Journal of Gerontology: Psychological Sciences, 48,* P210–P217.

Bosworth, H. B., & Schaie, K. W. (1999). Survival effects in cognitive function, cognitive style, and sociodemographic variables. *Experimental Aging Research, 25,* 121–140.

Botwinick, J. (1977). Intellectual abilities. In J. E. Birren & K. W. Schaie (Eds.), *Handbook of the psychology of aging.* New York: Van Nostrand Reinhold.

Boyd, P. (1969). The valued grandparent: A changing social role. In W. Donahue, J. Kornbluth, & B. Powers (Eds.), *Living in the multigenerational family.* Ann Arbor, MI: Institute of Gerontology.

Bradsher, J. E., Longino, C. F., Jackson, D. J., & Zimmerman, R. S. (1992). Health and geographic mobility among the recently widowed. *Journal of Gerontology: Social Sciences, 47,* S261–S268.

Brainerd, C. J. (1978). The stage question in cognitive developmental theory. *Behavioral and Brain Sciences, 1,* 173–214.

Braithwaite, V. A., Gibson, D. M., and Bosly-Craft, R. (1986). An exploratory study of poor adjustment styles among retirees. *Social Science and Medicine, 23,* 493–499.

Bram, S. (1987). Parenthood or nonparenthood: A comparison of intentional families. *Lifestyles, 8,* 69–84.

Branch, L. G. (1987). Continuing care retirement communities: Self-insuring for long-term care. *The Gerontologist, 27,* 4–8.

Branch, L. G., Friedman, D. J., Cohen, M. A., Smith, N., & Socholitzky, E. (1988). Impoverishing the elderly: A case study of the financial risk of spending down among Massachusetts' elderly. *The Gerontologist, 28,* 648–658.

Brandstaetter, V., Lengfelder, A., & Gollwitzer, P. M. (2001). Implementation intentions and efficient action initiation. *Journal of Personality and Social Psychology, 81,* 946–960.

Brandtstadter, J., Wentura, D., & Greve, W. (1993). Adaptive resources of the aging self: Outlines of an emergent perspective. *International Journal of Behavioral Development, 16,* 323–350.

Breast imaging: Today and tomorrow. (1995). *Harvard Women's Health Watch,* January, p. 2.

Brickel, C. M. (1986). Pet-facilitated therapies: A review of the literature and clinical implementation considerations. *Clinical Gerontologist, 5,* 309–332.

Brill, P. A. (1999). Effective approach toward prevention and rehabilitation in geriatrics. *Activities, Adaptation, and Aging, 23,* 21–32.

Brim, G. (1992). *Ambition: How we manage success and failure throughout our adult lives.* New York: Basic Books.

Brink, S. (1993). Elderly empowerment. *U.S. News and World Report,* April 26, 65–70.

Brock, D. (1989). Death and dying. In R. M. Veatch (Ed.). *Medical ethics* (2nd ed., pp. 363–394).

Brody, H., Campbell, M. L., Faber-Langendoen, K., & Ogle, K. (1997). Withdrawing intensive life sustaining treatment. Recommendations for compassionate clinical management. *New England Journal of Medicine, 336,* 652–657.

Bronfenbrenner, U., McClelland, P., Wethington, E., Moen, P., & Ceci, S. J. (1996). *The state of Americans.* New York: Free Press.

Brown, M., Sinacore, D. R., & Host, H. H. (1995). The relationship of strength to function in the older adult. *Journal of Gerontology, 50A,* 55–59.

Bruner, J. (1986). *Actual minds, possible worlds.* Cambridge, MA: Harvard University Press.

Buchanan, A. (1989). Healthcare delivery and resource allocation. In R. M. Veatch (Ed.), *Medical ethics* (2nd ed., pp. 321–362). Sudbury, MA: Jones and Bartlett.

Buchner, D. M., Cress, M. E., Esselman, P. C., Margherita, A. J., Delateur, B. J., Campbell, A. J., & Wagner, E. H. (1996). Factors associated with changes in gait speed in older adults. *Journal of Gerontology: Medical Sciences, 51A,* 297–302.

Burgio, L. D., Cotter, E. M., & Stevens, A. B. (1996). Treatment in residential settings. In M. Hersen & V. Van Hasselt (Eds.), *Psychological treatment of older adults: An introductory text.* New York: Plenum Press.

Burker, E. J., Wong, H., Sloane, P. D., Mattingly, D., Preisser, J., & Mitchell, C. M. (1995). Predictors of fear of falling in dizzy and nondizzy elderly. *Psychology and Aging, 10,* 104–110.

Burkhauser, R. V., & Salisbury, D. L. (Eds.). (1993). *Pensions in a changing economy.* Washington, DC and Syracuse University: Employee Benefit Research Institute.

Burls, A., Gold, L., & Clark, W. (2001). Systematic review of randomized control trials of sildenafil (Viagra) in the treatment of male erectile dysfunction. *British Journal of General Practice, 473,* 1004–1012.

Burns, P. (1999). Navigation and the mobility of older drivers. *Journal of Gerontology, 54B* (1), S49–S55.

Burrus-Bammel, L. L., & Bammel, G. (1985). Leisure and recreation. In J. E. Birren & K. W. Schaie (Eds.), *Handbook of the psychology of aging* (2nd ed.). New York: Van Nostrand Reinhold.

Burt, J. J., & Meeks, L. B. (1985). *Education for sexuality: Concepts and programs for teaching* (3rd ed.). Philadelphia: Saunders College.

Burton, L. C., German, P. S., Rovner, B. W., Brant, L. J., & Clark, R. D. (1992). Mental illness and the use of restraints in nursing homes. *The Gerontologist, 32,* 164–170.

Burwell, B. (1996). *Medicaid long-term care expenditures in fiscal year 1995.* Cambridge, MA: The Medstat Group.

Butler, R. N. (1963). The life review: An interpretation of reminiscence in the aged. *Psychiatry, 26,* 65–76.

Butler, R. N., Lewis, M., & Sunderland, T. (1991). *Aging and mental health* (4th ed.). New York: Macmillan.

Butters, M. A., Becker, J. T., Nebes, R. D., Zmuda, M. D., Mulsant, B. H., Pollack, B. G., & Reynolds, C. F. (2000). Changes in cognitive functioning following late-life depression. *American Journal of Psychiatry, 157,* 1949–1954.

Cabeza, R. (2001). Cognitive neuroscience of aging: Contributions of functional neuroimaging. *Scandinavian Journal of Neuroscience, 42,* 277–286.

Cabeza, R., Grady, C. L., Nyberg, L., McIntosh, A. R., Tulving, E., Kapur, S., Jennings, J. M., Houle, S., & Craik, F. I. M. (1997). Age-related differences in neural activity during memory encoding and retrieval: A positron emission tomography study. *The Journal of Neuroscience, 17,* 391–400.

Caine, E. D., & Grossman, H. (1992). Neuropsychiatric assessment. In J. E. Birren, R. B. Sloane, & G. D. Cohen (Eds.), *Handbook of mental health and aging* (2nd ed., pp. 603–641). San Diego: Academic Press.

Cairl, R. E., & Kosberg, J. I. (1993). The interface of burden and level of task performance in caregivers of Alzheimer's disease patients: An examination of clinical profiles. *Journal of Gerontological Social Work, 19,* 133–151.

Callahan, C. M. and Wolinsky, F. D. (1995). Hospitalization for major depression among older Americans. *Journal of Gerontology, 50A,* M196–M202.

Callahan, C. M. and Wolinsky, F. D. (1995). Predicting hospital costs among older decedants over time. *Medical Care, 33* (11), 1089–1105.

Callan, M. (1990). *Surviving AIDS.* New York: HarperCollins.

Callan, V. J. (1984). Childlessness and marital adjustment. *Australian Journal of Sex, Marriage, and the Family, 5,* 210–214.

Callan, V. J. (1987). Personal and marital adjustment of voluntary and nonvoluntary childless wives. *Journal of Marriage and the Family, 49,* 847–856.

Camp, C. J., Foss, J. W., O'Hanlon, A. M., & Stevens, A. B. (1996). Memory interventions for persons with dementia. *Applied Cognitive Psychology, 10,* 193–210.

Campbell, D. T., & Stanley, J. C. (1963). *Experimental and quasi-experimental designs for research.* Chicago: Rand McNally.

Campbell, M. K., Bush, T. L., & Hale, W. E. (1993). Medical conditions associated with driving cessation in community-dwelling ambulatory elders. *Journal of Gerontology: Social Sciences, 48,* S230–S234.

Cancer Facts and Figures, 2001. (2001). Clifton, GA: American Cancer Society.

Career Women. (1998). *Career women news: Wage inequity: It's time for working women to earn equal pay! www.careerwomen.com*

Carey, R. G. (1977). The widowed: A year later. *Journal of Counseling Psychology, 24,* 125–131.

Carmelli, D., Swan, G. E., Kelly-Hayes, M., Wolf, P. A., Reed, T., & Miller, B. (2000). Longitudinal changes in the contribution of genetic and environmental influences to symptoms of depression in older male twins. *Psychology and Aging, 15,* 505–510.

Carpenter, B. D., Van Haitsma, R., Ruckdeschel, K., & Lawton, M. P. (2000). Psychosocial preferences of older adults: A pilot examination of content and structure. *The Gerontologist, 40* (3), 335–348.

Carrere, S., & Gottman, J. M. (1999). Predicting divorce among newlyweds from the first three minutes of a marital conflict discussion. *Family Process, 38,* 293–301.

Carrillo, M. C., Stebbins, G. T., Gabrieli, J. D. E., Desmond, J. E., Dirksen, C., Turner, D., & Glover, G. H (1998). *An fMRI study of the effect of aging on frontal activation during semantic encoding.* Paper presented at the 1998 meetings of the Cognitive Neuroscience Society.

Carstensen, L. L. (1998). A life-span approach to social motivation. In J. Heckhausen and C. Dweck (Eds.), *Motivation and self-regulation across the life span* (pp. 341–364). New York: Cambridge University Press.

Carstensen, L. L., Gottman, J. M., & Levenson, R. W. (1995). Emotional behavior in long-term marriage. *Psychology and Aging, 10,* 140–149.

Carstensen, L. L., Isaacowitz, D. M., & Charles, S. T. (1999). Taking time seriously: A theory of socioemotional selectivity. *American Psychologist, 54,* 154–181.

Carstensen, L. L., Pasupathi, M., & Mayr, U. (2000). Emotional experience in everyday life across the adult life span. *Journal of Personality and Social Psychology, 79,* 644–655.

Carstensen, L. L., Pasupathi, M., Mayr, U., & Nesselroade, J. R. (2000). Emotional experience in everyday life across the adult life span. *Journal of Personality and Social Psychology, 79,* 644–655.

Carter, C., Ozee, C., & Bollinger, B. (1998). *Keys to career success.* Englewood Cliffs, N.J.: Prentice-Hall.

Carver, C. S. and Scheier, M. F. (1998). *On the Self-Regulation of Behavior.* N.Y., N.Y.: Cambridge University Press.

Castle, N. G. (2000). Deficiency citations for physical restraint use in nursing homes. *Journal of Gerontology, 55B* (1), S33–S40.

Catania, J. A., Turner, H., Kegeles, S. M., Stall, R., Pollack, L., & Coates, T. J. (1989). Older Americans and AIDS transmission risks and primary prevention research needs. *The Gerontologist, 29,* 373–381.

Ceci, S. J. (1991). How much does schooling influence general intelligence? A reassessment of the evidence. *Developmental Psychology, 27,* 703–722.

Ceci, S. J., & Liker, J. K. (1986). A day at the races: A study of IQ, expertise, and cognitive complexity. *Journal of Experimental Psychology: General, 115,* 255–266.

Center for Work and Family. (2000). *Measuring the impact of workplace flexibility.* Chestnut Hill, MA: Center on Work and Family, Boston College.

Centers for Disease Control. (1997). *Report on AIDS mortality statistics.*

Cerella, J. (1985). Age-related decline in extrafoveal letter perception. *Journal of Gerontology, 40,* 727–736.

Cerella, J. (1990). Aging and information-processing rate. In J. E. Birren & K. W. Schaie (Eds.), *Handbook of the psychology of aging* (3rd ed., pp. 201–221). New York: Academic Press.

Chalke, H. D., Dewhurst, J. R., & Ward, C. W. (1958). Loss of sense of smell in old people. *Public Health, 72,* 223–230.

Chappell, N. L., & Novak, M. (1992). The role of support in alleviating stress among nursing assistants. *The Gerontologist, 32,* 351–359.

Chappell, N. L. and Reid, R. C. (2000). Dimensions of care for dementia sufferers in long-term care institutions: Are They Related to Outcomes? *Journal of Gerontology, 558,* 5234–5244.

Charness, N. (1981). Search in chess: Age and skill differences. *Journal of Experimental Psychology: Human Perception and Performance, 7,* 467–476.

Charness, N. (1985). *Age and expertise: Responding to Talland's challenge.* Paper presented at the George A. Talland Memorial Conference on Aging and Memory, Cape Cod, MA.

Charness, N. (1988). Expertise in chess, music, and physics: A cognitive perspective. In L. K. Obler & D. A. Fein (Eds.), *The neuropsychology of talent and special abilities.* New York: Guilford Press.

Charness, N., & Bosman, E. A. (1992). Human factor and age. In Fergus I. M. Craik & Timothy A. Salthouse (Eds.), *Handbook of aging and cognition* (pp. 495–551). Hillside, NJ: Lawrence Erlbaum.

Charness, N., Kelley, C., Bosman, E. A., & Mottram, M. (2001). Word processing training and retraining: Effects of adult age, experience, and interface. *Psychology and Aging, 16,* 110–127.

Chen, L., Eaton, W. W., Gallo, J. J., Nestadt, G., and Crum, R. M. (2000). Empirical examination of current depression categories in a population-based study symptoms, course, and risk factors: *American Journal of Psychiatry, 157,* 573–580.

Chen, Y. P. (1987). Making assets out of tomorrow's elderly. *The Gerontologist, 27,* 410–416.

Cherlin, A. (1996). *Public and private families: An introduction.* New York: McGraw-Hill.

Cherlin, A., & Furstenberg, F. (1985). Styles and strategies of grandparenting. In V. L. Bengtson & J. Robertson (Eds.), *Granparenthood.* Beverly Hills, CA: Sage.

Cherlin, A., & Furstenberg, F. (1986). Grandparents and family crisis. *Generations, 10,* 26–28.

Chiriboga, D. A. (1982a). Adaptations to marital separation in later and earlier life. *Journal of Gerontology, 37,* 109–114.

Choice in Dying (1996). A living will. *Choice in Dying* (formerly Society for the Right to Die), NY.

Christensen, H., Mackinnon, A. J., Korten, A., & Jorm, T. F. (2001). The common cause hypothesis or cognitive aging: Evidence for not only a common factor but also specific associations of age with vision and grip strength in a cross-sectional analysis. *Psychology and Aging, 16,* 588–599.

Church, D. K., Siegel, M. A., & Foster, C. D. (1988). *Growing old in America.* Wylie, TX: Information Aids.

Claes, R. (2000). Meaning of atypical working: The case of potential telecommuters. *European Review of Applied Psychology, 50* (1), 27–37.

Clancy, S. M., & Hoyer, W. J. (1994). Age and skill in visual search. *Developmental Psychology, 30,* 545–552.

Clancy-Dollinger, S. M., & Hoyer, W. J. (1995). Skill differences in medical laboratory diagnostics. *Applied Cognitive Psychology, 9,* 235–248.

Clark, N. M., Janz, N. K., Dodge, J. A., Schork, M. A., Fingerlin, T. E., Wheeler, J. R. C., Liang, J., Keteyian, S. J., & Santinga, J. T. (2000). Changes in functional health status of older women with heart disease: Evaluation of a program based on self-regulation. *Journal of Gerontology, 55B* (2), S117–S126.

Clebone, B. L., & Taylor, C. M. (1992, February). Family and social attitudes across four generations of women or maternal lineage. *Psychological Reports, 70,* 268–270.

Cloud, J. (2000). A kindler, gentler death. *Time, 156* (no. 12). pp. 60–65.

Cochran, D. L., Brown, D. R., & McGregor, K. C. (1999). Racial differences in the multiple social roles of older women: Implications for depressive symptoms. *The Gerontologist, 39* (4), 465–472.

Cohen, D., & Eisdorfer, C. (1986). *The loss of self.* New York: Norton.

Cohen, D., & Eisdorfer, C. (1989). Depression in family members caring for a relative with Alzheimer's disease. *Journal of the American Geriatrics Society, 36,* 385–389.

Cohen, G. (2000). *The creative age: Awakening human potential in the second half of life.* NY: Avon.

Cohen, G. D. (1988). *The brain in human aging.* New York: Springer.

Cohen, G., & Faulkner, D. (1989). Age differences in source forgetting: Effects of reality monitoring on eyewitness testimony. *Psychology & Aging, 4,* 10–17.

Cohen, G., Conway, M. A., & Maylor, E. A. (1994). Flashbulb memories in older adults. *Psychology and Aging, 9,* 454–463.

Cohen, M. A., Tell, E. J., Batten, H. L., & Larson, M. J. (1988). Attitudes toward joining continuing care retirement communities. *The Gerontologist, 28,* 637–643.

Cohen, S., & Herbert, T. B. (1996). Health psychology: Psychological factors and physical disease from the perspective of human psychneuro-immunology. *Annual Review of Psychology, 47,* 113–142. Palo Alto, CA: Annual Reviews.

Cohen-Mansfield, J., Droge, J. A., and Billig, N. (1992). Factors influencing hospital patients' preferences in the utilization of life-sustaining treatments. *The Gerontologist, 32,* 89–95.

Cohen-Mansfield, J., Werner, P., Marx, M. S., & Freedman, L. (1991). Two studies of pacing in the nursing home. *Journal of Gerontology, 46,* 77–83.

Cohler, B. J. (1992). The myth of successful aging. *Readings: A Journal of Reviews and Commentary in Mental Health,* p. 18–22.

Cohler, B. J., & Grunebaum, H. V. (1981). *Mothers, grandmothers, and daughters: Personality and childcare in three-generation families.* New York: John Wiley.

Colby, A., & Kohlberg, L. (Eds.). (1987). *The measurement of moral judgment, Vol. 1: Theoretical foundations and research validation.* New York: Cambridge University Press.

Colby, A., Kohlberg, L., Gibbs, J. C., & Lieberman, M. (1983). A longitudinal study of moral development. *Monographs of the Society for Research in Child Development, 48* (4), 1–124.

Cole, E. R., & Stewart, A. J. (2001). Invidious comparisons: Imagining a psychology of race and gender beyond differences. *Political Psychology, 22,* 293–308.

Coleman, J. (1988). *Intimate relationships, marriage, and families.* New York: Macmillan.

Coleman, L., & Antonucci, T. (1983). Impact of working on women at midlife. *Developmental Psychology, 19,* 290–294.

Comfort, A. (1980). Sexuality in later life. In J. E. Birren & R. B. Sloane (Eds.), *Handbook of mental health and aging.* New York: Van Nostrand Reinhold.

Commons, M. L., Sinnott, J. D., Richards, F. A., & Armon, C. (1989). *Adult development, Vol. 1: Comparisons and applications of developmental models.* New York: Praeger.

Conger, R. D., Lorenz, F. O., Elder, G. H., Simmons, R. L., & Xiaojia, G. (1993). Husband and wife differences in response to undesirable life events. *Journal of Health and Social Behavior, 34,* 71–88.

Conley, J. J. (1985). Longitudinal stability of personality traits. *Journal of Personality and Social Psychology, 54,* 1266–1282.

Connell, C. M. and Gibson, G. D. (1997). Racial, ethnic, and cultural differences in dementia caregiving. Review and analysis. *The Gerontologist, 37*(3), 355–364.

Connidis, I. A. (1990a). Confidants and companions in later life: The place of friends and family. *Journal of Gerontology: Social Sciences, 45,* S141–S149.

Connidis, I. A., & Davies, L. (1990a). *Family ties and aging.* Toronto: Butterworths.

Connidis, I. G., & Davies, L. (1990b). Confidants and companions in later life: The place of friends and family. *Journal of Gerontology: Social Sciences, 45,* S141–S149.

Connole, C. C. (1999). Adult day care. In J. R. Pratt (Ed.), *Long-term care: Managing across the continuum.* Gaithersburg, MD: Aspen.

Conrad, P. (1990). Qualitative research on chronic illness: A commentary on method and conceptual development. *Social Science Medicine, 30,* 1257–1263.

Conwell, Y. (1994). Suicide and aging: Lessons from the nursing home. *Crisis, 15* (4), 153–154.

Coon, D. W., Rider, K., Gallagher-Thompson, D., and Thompson, L. (1999). Cognitive-behavioral therapy for the treatment of late-life distress. In M. Duffy (ed.), *Handbook of Counseling and Psychotherapy with Older Adults.* N.Y.: John Wiley P. 487–510.

Cooney, T. M., Schaie, K. W., & Willis, S. L. (1988). The relationship between prior functioning on cognitive and personality dimensions and subject attrition in longitudinal research. *Journal of Gerontology: Psychological Science, 43,* P12–P17.

Corder, E. H., & Manton, K. G. (2001, August). *Change in the prevalence of severe dementia among older Americans: 1982 to 1999.* Paper presented at the 24th IUSSP General Population Conference, Salvador, Brazil.

Corder, E. H., Saunders, A. M., Strittmatter, W. J., Schmechel, D. E., Gaskell, P. C., Small, G. W., Roses, A. D., Haines, J. L., & Pericak-Vance, M. A. (1993). Gene dose of apolipoprotein E type 4 allele and the risk of Alzheimer's disease in late onset families. *Science, 261,* 921–926.

Cornelius, S. W., & Capsi, A. (1987). Everyday problem solving in adulthood and old age. *Psychology and Aging, 2,* 144–153.

Coronel, S., & Fulton, D. (1995). *Long-term care insurance in 1993.* Washington, DC: Health Insurance Association of America.

Corporation for National and Community Service (2001). http://www.cns.gov

Corr, C. A. (1992). A task-based approach to coping with dying. *Omega, 24,* 81–94.

Corr, C. A. (2000). What do we know about grieving children and adolescents? In Doka, K. J. (Ed.), *Living with grief: Children, adolescents, and loss.* Washington, DC: Hospice Foundation of America, Brunner Mazel, pp. 21–32.

Corso, J. F. (1977). Auditory perception and communication. In J. E. Birren & K. W. Schaie (Eds.), *Handbook of the psychology of aging* (2nd ed.). New York: Van Nostrand Reinhold.

Costa, P. and McCrae, R. R. (2001). A theoretical context for adult temperament. In T. Wachs and G. A. Kohnstamm (Eds.), *Temperament in context,* (p. 1–21). Mahwah, N.J.: Lawrence Erlbaum.

Costa, P. T., Jr. (1986). *The scope of individuality.* Paper presented at the meeting of the American Psychological Association, Washington, DC.

Costa, P. T., Herbst, J. H., McCrae, R. R., & Siegler, I. C. (2000). Personality at midlife: Stability, intrinsic maturation, and response to life events. *Assessment, Special Issue, (7),* 365–378.

Costa, P. T., Jr., & McCrae, R. R. (1977). Age differences in personality structure revisited: Studies in validity, stability, and change. *Aging and Human Development, 8,* 261–275.

Costa, P. T., Jr., & McCrae, R. R. (1978). Objective personality assessment. In M. Storandt, I. C. Siegler, & M. P. Elias (Eds.), *The clinical psychology of aging.* New York: Plenum.

Costa, P. T., Jr., & McCrae, R. R. (1980). Still stable after all these years: Personality as a key to some issues of adulthood and old age. In P. B. Baltes & O. G. Brim, Jr. (Eds.), *Life-span development and behavior* (Vol. 3). New York: Academic Press.

Costa, P. T., Jr., & McCrae, R. R. (1982). An approach to the attribution of aging: Period and cohort effects. *Psychological Bulletin, 92*, 238–250.

Costa, P. T., Jr., & McCrae, R. R. (1985). Personality as a lifelong determinant of well-being. In C. Malatesta & C. Izard (Eds.), *Affective processes in adult development and aging.* New York: Sage.

Costa, P. T., Jr., & McCrae, R. R. (1986). Cross-sectional studies of personality in a national sample: I. Development and validation of survey measures. *Psychology and Aging, 1*, 140–143.

Costa, P. T., Jr., & McCrae, R. R. (1988). Personality in adulthood: A six-year longitudinal study of self reports and spouse rating in the NEO personality inventory. *Journal of Personality and Social Psychology, 54*, 853–863.

Costa, P. T., Terracciano, A., & McCrae, R. R. (2001). Gender differences in personality traits across cultures: Robust and surprising findings. *Journal of Personality and Social Psychology, 81*, 322–331.

Cotman, C. W. (2000). Homeostatic processes in brain aging: The role of apoptosis, inflammation, and oxidative stress in regulating healthy neural circuitry in the aging brain. In P. C. Stern & L. L. Carstensen (Eds.), *The aging mind: Opportunities in cognitive research* (pp. 114–143). Washington, DC: National Academy Press.

Cotrell, M., & Schulz, R. (1993). The perspective of the patient with Alzheimer's disease: A neglected dimension of dementia research. *The Gerontologist, 33*, 205–211.

Couldrick, A. (1992). Optimizing bereavement outcome: Reading the road ahead. *Social Science and Medicine, 35*, 1521–1523.

Council on Scientific Affairs (American Medical Association). (1996). Alcoholism in the elderly. *Journal of the American Medical Association, 275* (10), 1222–1225.

Covey, H. C. (1988). Historical terminology used to represent older people. *The Gerontologist, 28*, 291–297.

Covinsky, K. E., Kahana, E., Kahana, B., Kercher, K., Schumacher, J. G., & Justice, A. C. (2001). History and mobility exam index to identify community-dwelling elderly persons at risk of falling. *Journal of Gerontology: Medical Sciences, 56A* (4), M253–M259.

Cowgill, D., & Holmes, L. D. (1972). *Aging and modernization.* New York: Appleton-Century-Crofts.

Cox, H. (Ed.). (1997). *Aging* (11th ed.). Guilford, CT: Dushkin Press. *On Aging,* Reprinted from *Administrative Aging,* (1991), #362, pp. 37–40. Washington, DC.

Coyne, J. C., & Fiske, V. (1992). Couples coping with chronic health and catastrophic illness. In T. J. Akamatsu, S. C. Crowther, S. E. Hobfil, & M. A. P. Stevens (Eds.), *Family health psychology* (pp. 129–149). Washington, DC: Hemisphere.

Coyne, J. C., & Racioppo, M. S. (2000). Never the twain shall meet? Closing the gap between coping research and clinical intervention research. *American Psychologist, 55*, 655–664.

Craik, F. I. M., Byrd, M., & Swanson, J. M. (1987). Patterns of memory loss in three elderly samples. *Psychology and Aging, 2*, 79–86.

Craik, F. I. M., Morris, L. W., Morris, R. G., & Loewen, E. R. (1990). Relations between source amnesia and frontal lobe functioning in older adults. *Psychology and Aging, 5*, 148–151.

Cramer, P. (2000). Defense mechanisms in psychology today: Further Processes for Adaptation. *American Psychologist, 55*, 637–646.

Cremation Association of North America. (2001). *Cremation explained: Answers to most frequently asked questions.* http://www.cremationassociation.org

Crohan, S. E., & Antonucci, T. C. (1989). Friends as a source of social support in old age. In R. Adams & R. Blieszner (Eds.), *Older adult friendship: Structure and process.* Beverly Hills, CA: Sage.

Crowley–Robinson, P., Fenwick, C., & Blackshaw, J. K. (1996). A long-term study of elderly people in nursing homes with visiting and resident dogs. *Applied Animal Behaviour Science, Special Issue: Human-animal interactions, 47* (1–2), 137–148.

Csikszentmihalyi, M. (1990). *Flow: The psychology of optimal experience.* New York: Harper & Row.

Csikszentmihalyi, M. (1997). *Finding flow: The psychology of engagement with everyday life.* New York: Basic Books.

Csikszentmihalyi, M. (1999). If we are so rich, why aren't we happy? *American Psychologist, 54*, 821–827.

Cude, R. L., & Jablin, F. M. (1992). Retiring from work: The paradoxical impact of organizational commitment. *Journal of Managerial Issues, 4* (1), 31–45.

Cummings, J. L. (1999). Understanding Parkinson's disease. *Journal of the American Medical Association. 281*, 376–378.

Cunningham, W. R., & Owens, W. A., Jr. (1983). The Iowa study of the adult development of intellectual abilities. In K. W. Schaie (Ed.), *Longitudinal studies of adult psychological development.* New York: Guilford Press.

Curran, J., Jaffe, H., Hardy, A., Morgan, W., Selik, R., & Dondero, T. (1988). Epidemiology of HIV infection and AIDS in the United States. *Science, 239*, 610–616.

Czaja, S. (2001). Technological change and the older worker. In J. E. Birren & K. W. Schaie (Eds.), *Handbook of the psychology of aging* (5th ed.). San Diego: Academic Press.

Danner, D. D., Snowdon, D. A., & Friesen, W. V. (2001). Positive emotions in early life and longevity findings from the nun study. *Journal of Personality and Social Psychology, 80*, 804–813.

Davidson, J. D., & Doka, K. J. (Ed.). (1999). *Living with grief: At work, at school, at worship.* Washington, DC: Hospice Foundation of America, Brunner Mazel.

Davies, B. (1999). *Shadow in the sun: The experience of sibling bereavement in childhood.* Philadelphia: Brunner Mazel.

Davies, B. (2000a). Sibling bereavement: We are grieving too. In J. D. Davidson and K. J. Doka, (eds.), *Living with grief: Children, adolescents, and loss.* Hospice Foundation of America, Washington, DC: Brunner Mazel.

Davies, B. (2000b). Anticipatory mourning and the transition of fading away. In T. Rando (Ed.), *Clinical dimensions of anticipatory mourning: Theory and practice in working with* the dying, their loved ones, and their caregivers (pp. 135–153). Champaign, IL: Research Press.

Davies, R. M., Sieber, K. O., & Hunt, S. L. (1994). Age-cohort differences in treating symptoms of mental illness: A process approach. *Psychology and Aging, 9,* 446–453.

Davis, C. G., Wortman, C. B., Lehman, D. R., & Silver, R. C. (2000). Searching for meaning in loss: Are clinical assumptions correct? *Death studies, 24* (6), 497–540.

Davis, K. E. (1985). Near and dear: Friendship and love compared. *Psychology Today, 19,* 22–30.

DeAngelis, T. (1989). Mania, depression, and genius: Concert, talks inform public about manic-depressive illness. *APA Monitor, 20* (1), 1, 24.

Deeg, J. H. D., Kardaun, P. F., & Fozard, J. L. (1996). In J. E. Birren & K. W. Schaie (Eds.), *Handbook of the psychology of aging* (4th ed., pp. 129–149). San Diego: Academic Press.

D'Eredita, M. A., & Hoyer, W. J. (1999). An examination of the effects of adult age on explicit and implicit learning of figural sequences. *Memory & Cognition, 27,* 890–895.

DeGenova, M. K. (1992). If you had your life to live over again: What would you do differently? *International Journal of Aging and Human Development, 34,* 135–143.

de Groot, A. (1965). *Thought and choice in chess: The Hague:* Mouton.

de la Rochefordiere, A., Asselain, B., & Campena, F. (1993). Age as a prognostic factor in premenopausal breast carcinoma. *Lancet, 341* (8852), 1039–1043.

DeLongis, A., Coyne, J. C., Dakof, S., Folkman, S., & Lazarus, R. S. (1982). Relationship of daily hassles, uplifts, and major life events to health status. *Health Psychology, 1,* 119–136.

De Luca, M., Rose, G., Bonafe, M., Garasto, S., Greco, V., Weir, B. S., Franceschi, C., & Benedictis, G. (2001). Sex-specific longevity associations defined by Tyrosine Hydroxylase-Insulin-Insulin Growth Factor 2 haplotypes on the 11p15.5 chromosomal region. *Experimental Gerontology, 36,* 1663–1671.

Demaris, A. (1984). A comparison of remarriages with first marriages on satisfaction in marriage and its relationship to prior cohabitation. Special Issue: Remarriage and stepparenting. *Family Relations Journal of Applied Family and Child Studies, 33,* 443–449.

Demetriou, A. (1990). Structural and developmental relations between formal and postformal capacities: Towards a comprehensive theory of adolescent and adolescent cognitive development. In M. L. Commons, C. Armon, L. Kohlberg, F. A. Richards, T. A. Groetzer, & J. D. Sinnott (Eds.), *Adult development, vol. 2: Models and methods in the study of adolescent and adult thought.* New York: Praeger.

Denney, N. W. (1984). A model of cognitive development across the life span. *Developmental Review, 4,* 171–191.

Dennis, W. (1966). Creative productivity between the ages of twenty and eighty years. *Journal of Gerontology, 21,* 1–18.

Dennis, W. (1968). Creative productivity between the ages of twenty and eighty years. In B. L. Neugarten (Ed.), *Middle age and aging.* Chicago: University of Chicago Press.

Department of Health and Human Services. (2000). *Healthy people 2010* (Conference Edition). Washington, DC: DHHS.

Department of Labor, Bureau of Women. (2000). *Nontraditional occupations for women in 1999.* Washington, DC: U.S. Department of Labor. http://www.dol.gov/dol/wb/public/wb_pubs/nontra99.htm

Desai, M., Pratt, L. A., Lentzner, H., & Robinson, K. N. (2001). Trends in vision and hearing among older Americans. *Aging Trends:* No. 2. Hyattsville, MD: National Center for Health Statistics.

Deutsch, F. M. (2001). Equally shared parenting. *Current Directions in Psychological Science, 10* (1), 25–28.

deVries, B., Bluck, S., & Birren, J. E. (1993). The understanding of death and dying in a life-span perspective. *The Gerontologist, 33,* 366–372.

Dewji, N. N., & Singer, J. S. (1996). Genetic clues to Alzheimer's disease. *Science, 271,* 159–160.

Dey, E. L., Astin, A. W., & Korn, W. S. (1991). *The American freshman: Twenty-five-year trends.* Los Angeles: Higher Education Research Institute, University of California, Los Angeles.

Dick, L. P., & Gallagher-Thompson, D. (1996). Late-life depression. In M. Hersen & V. B. Van Hasselt (Eds.), *Psychological treatment of older adults: An introductory text* (pp. 181–208). New York: Plenum Press.

Dickens, W. T., & Flynn, J. R. (2001). Heritability estimates versus large environmental effects: The IQ paradox resolved. *Psychological Review, 108,* 346–369.

Dickinson, G. E. (1992). First childhood death experiences. *Omega Journal of Death and Dying, 25,* 169–182.

Diehl, M., Willis, S. L., & Schaie, K. W. (1995). Everyday problem solving in older adults: Observational assessment and cognitive correlates. *Psychology and Aging, 10,* 478–491.

Diener, E. (2000). Subjective well-being: The science of happiness and a proposal for a national index. *American Psychologist, 55,* 34–43.

Diener, E., & Suh, E. (1998). Subjective well-being and age: An international analysis. In K. W. Schaie and M. P. Lawton (Eds.), *Annual review of gerontology and geriatrics (17), Focus on emotional and adult development* (pp. 304–324). New York: Springer.

Diener, E., & Suh, E. (1999). Societies we live in: International comparisons. In D. Kahneman, E. Diener, & N. Schwarz (Eds.), *Well-being: The foundations of hedonic psychology.* New York: Russell Sage Foundation.

Dittmann-Kohli, F., Lachman, M. E., Kliegl, R., & Baltes, P. B. (1991). Effects of cognitive training and testing on intellectual efficacy beliefs in elderly adults. *Journal of Gerontology: Psychological Sciences, 46,* P162–P164.

Dixon, R. A., Kurzman, D., & Friesen, I. C. (1993). Handwriting performance in younger and older adults: Age, familiarity, and practice effects. *Psychology and Aging, 8,* 360–370.

Doka, K. J. (1999). A primer on loss and grief. In J. D. Davidson & K. J. Doka (Eds.), *Living with grief: At work, at school, at worship.* Washington, DC: Hospice Foundation of America, Brunner Mazel.

Doka, K. J. (Ed.) (2000). Living with grief: Children, adolescents, and loss. Hospice Foundation of America, Washington, DC: Brunner Mazel.

Doka, K. J., & Mertz, M. E. (1988). The meaning and significance of great-grandparenthood. *The Gerontologist, 28,* 192–197.

Donaldson, G. (1981). Letter to the editor. *Journal of Gerontology, 36,* 634–636.

Dorfman, L. T. (1992, June). Academics and the transition to retirement. *Educational Gerontology, 18,* 343–363.

Dowdney, L. (2000). Childhood bereavement foloowing parental death. *Journal of Child Psychology and Psychiatry and Allied Disciplines, 41,* 819–830.

Draganich, L. F., Zacny, J., Klafta, J., & Karrison, T. (2001). The effects of antidepressants on obstructed and unobstructed gait in healthy elderly people. *Journal of Gerontology: Medical Sciences, 56A* (1), M36–M41.

Dupree, L. W., & Schonfeld, L. (1996). Substance abuse. In M. Hersen & V. B. Van Hasselt (Eds.), *Psychological treatment of older adults: An introductory text* (pp. 281–297), New York: Plenum Press.

Dupree, L. W., & Schonfeld, L. (1999). Management of alcohol abuse in older adults. In M. Duffy (Ed.), *Handbook of counseling and psychotherapy with older adults* (pp. 632–649). New York: John Wiley.

Durlak, J. A., & Riesenberg, L. A. (1991). The impact of death education. *Death Studies, 15,* 39–58.

Dywan, J., & Jacoby, L. (1990). Effects of aging on source monitoring: Differences in susceptibility to false fame. *Psychology and Aging, 5,* 379–387.

Eaker, E. D., Pinsky, J., & Castelli, W. P. (1992). Myocardial infarction and coronary death among women: Psychosocial predictors from a 20-year follow-up of women in the Framingham Study. *American Journal of Epidemiology, 135,* 854–864.

Eberling, J. L., & Jagust, W. J. (1995). Imaging studies of aging, neurodegenerative disease, and alcoholism. *Alcohol World Health and Research, 19,* 279–286.

Edmonds, S., & Hooker, K. (1992). Perceived changes in life meaning following bereavement. *Omega Journal of Death and Dying, 25,* 307–318.

Eichorn, D., Clausen, J., Haan, N., Honzik, M., & Mussen, P. (Eds.) (1981). *Past and present in middle life.* New York: Academic Press.

Ekerdt, D. J. (1998). Workplace norms for the timing of retirement. In K. W. Schaie & C. Schooler (Eds.), *Impact of work on older adults.* New York: Springer.

Ekerdt, D. J., & DeViney, S. (1990). On defining persons as retired. *Journal of Aging Studies, 4,* 211–229.

Ekerdt, D. J., & DeViney, S. (1993). Evidence for a pre-retirement process among older male workers. *Journal of Gerontology: Social Sciences, 48,* S535–S543.

Ekerdt, D. J., Bosse, R., & Levkoff, S. (1985). An empirical test for phases of retirement: Findings from the normative aging study. *Journal of Gerontology, 40,* 95–101.

Ekerdt, D. J., DeViney, S., & Kosloski, K. (1996). Profiling plans for retirement. *Journal of Gerontology: Social Sciences, 51B,* S140–S149.

Ekerdt, D. J., Kosloski, K., & DeViney, S. (2000). The normative anticipation of retirement by older workers. *Research on Aging, 22* (1), 3–22.

Ekstrom, R. B., French, J. W., & Harman, M. H. (1979). Cognitive factors: Their identification and replication. *Multivariate Behavior Research Monographs* (No. 79.2).

Elder, G. H. (1997). Life-course theory. In R. M. Lerner (Ed.), *Handbook of child psychology: Vol. 1. Theoretical models of human development* (5th ed.). New York: Wiley.

Elder, G. H. (1998). The life course as developmental theory. *Child Development, 69,* 1–12.

Elder, G. H., & Pavalko, E. K. (1993). Work careers in men's later years: Transitions, trajectories, and historical change. *Journal of Gerontology: Social Sciences, 48,* S180–S191.

Elder, G. H., Shanahan, M. J., & Clipp, E. C. (1994). When war comes to men's lives: Life-course patterns in family, work, and health. *Psychology and Aging, 9,* 5–16.

Elias, M. F., Elias, J. W., & Elias, P. K. (1990). Biological and health influences on behavior. In J. E. Birren & K. W. Schaie (Eds.), *Handbook of the psychology of aging* (3rd ed., pp. 80–102). San Diego: Academic Press.

Elias, M. F., Robbins, M., A., Elias, P. K., & Streeten, D. H. (1998). A longitudinal study of blood pressure in relation to performance on the Wechsler Adult Intelligence Scale. *Health Psychology, 17,* 486–493.

Enders-Slegers, M. J. (2000). The meaning of companion animals: Qualitative analysis of the life histories of elderly cat and dog owners. In A. L. Podberscek, E. S. Paul, and J. A. Serpell (Eds.), *Companion animals and us: Exploring relationships between people and pets,* New York: Cambridge University.

Engen, T. (1977). Taste and smell. In J. E. Birren & K. W. Schaie (Eds.), *Handbook of the psychology of aging* (2nd ed.). New York: Van Nostrand Reinhold.

Ericsson, K. A., & Charness, N. (1994). Expert performance: Its structure and acquisition. *American Psychologist, 49,* 725–747.

Ericsson, K. A., & Charness, N. (1995). Abilities: Evidence for talent or characteristics acquired through engagement in relevant activities? *American Psychologist, 50,* 803–804.

Ericsson, K. A., & Crutcher, R. J. (1990). The nature of exceptional performance. In P. B. Baltes, D. L. Featherman, & R. Lerner (Eds.), *Life-span development and behavior* (Vol. 10, pp. 187–217). New York: Academic Press.

Ericsson, K. A., & Simon, H. A. (1984). *Protocol analysis.* Cambridge, MA: Harvard University Press.

Ericsson, K. A., Krampe, R. T., & Tesch-Römer, C. (1993). The role of deliberate practice in the acquisition of expert performance. *Psychological Review, 100,* 363–406.

Erikson, E. H. (1963). *Childhood and society* (2nd ed.). New York: Norton.

Erikson, E. H. (1968). *Identity, youth and crisis.* New York: Norton.

Erikson, E. H. (1982). *The life cycle completed: A review.* New York: Norton.

Erikson, E. H., Erikson, J. M., & Kivnick, H. Q. (1986). *Vital involvement in old age.* New York: Norton.

Erikson, J. M. (1997). *The life cycle completed.* New York: Norton.

Essex, M. J., & Nam, S. (1987). Marital status and loneliness among older women: The differential importance of close family and friends. *Journal of Marriage and the Family, 49,* 93–106.

Esterling, B. A., Kiecolt-Glaser, J. K. Bodnar, J. C., & Glaser, R. (1994). Chronic stress, social support, and persistent alterations in the natural killer response to cytokinesin older adults. *Health Psychology, 13,* 291–298.

Evans, S. I. (2000). Make disappointing treatment outcomes in late-life depression. *British Journal of Psychiatry, 177,* 281–282.

Evans, W. (1992). Body building for the nineties. *Nutrition Action Health Letter, 19,* 5–8. Washington, DC: Center for Science in the Public Interest.

Evans, W. J. (1995a). What is sarcopenia? *Journal of Gerontology, 50A* (Special Issue), 5–10.

Evans, W. J. (1995b). Effects of exercise on body composition and functional capacity of the elderly. *Journal of Gerontology, 50A* (Special Issue), 147–150.

Evans, W., & Rosenberg, I. H., with Thomson, J. (1991). *Biomarkers—The 10 determinants of aging you can control.* New York: Simon & Schuster.

Everard, K. M., Lach, H. W., Fisher, E. B., & Baum, M. C. (2000). Relationship of activity and social support to the functional health of older adults. *Journal of Gerontology, 55,* S208–S212.

Fahey, T. D., Insel, P. M., & Roth, W. T. (2001). *Fit and well* (4th ed.). Mountain View, CA: Mayfield.

Falcon, L. M., & Tucker, K. L. (2000). Prevalence and correlates of depressive symptoms among Hispanic elders in Massachusetts. *Journal of Gerontology, 55B* (2), S108–S116.

Family and Medical Leave Survey. (2000). Washington, DC: Office of the Assistant Secretary of Policy, U. S. Department of Labor. http://www.dol.gov/dol/asp/public/fmla/factsheet.htm

Families and Work Institute. (1997). *National study of the changing workforce, 1997.* New York: Families and Work Institute. http://www.familiesandwork.org//

Families and Work Institute. (1998). *Business work-life study.* New York: Families and Work Institute. http://www.familiesandwork.org//

Farberow, N. L., Gallagher-Thompson, D., Gilewski, M., & Thompson, L. (1992). Changes in grief and mental health. *Journal of Gerontology: Psychological Sciences, 47,* P357–P366.

Farran, C. J. (1997). Theoretical perspectives concerning positive aspects of caring for elderly persons with dementia: Stress, adaptation, and existentialism. *The Gerontologist, 37,* 250–257.

Farrell, M. P., & Rosenberg, S. D. (1981). *Men at midlife.* Boston: Auburn House.

Femia, E. E., Zarit, S. H., & Johansson, B. (2001). The disablement process in very late life: A study of the oldest-old in Sweden. *Journal of Gerontology, 56B* (1), P12–P23.

Ferraro, S. (2001). Early detection is the best cure. *New York Daily News,* June 17, p. 31.

Field, D., & Millsap, R. E. (1991). Personality in advanced old age: Continuity or change. *Journal of Gerontology: Psychological Sciences, 46,* P299–P308.

Field, D., Minkler, M., Falk, R. F., & Leino, E. V. (1993).The influences of health and family contacts and family feelings in advanced old age: A longitudinal study. *Journal of Gerontology: Psychological Sciences, 48,* P18–P28.

Fields, J., & Casper, L. M. (2001). America's families and living arrangements: March, 2000. *Current Population Reports,* pp. 20–537. Washington, DC: United States Census Bureau.

Finch, C. E. (1996). Biological bases for plasticity during aging of individual life histories. In D. Magnusson (Ed.), *The life-span development of individuals: Behavioral, neurobiological, and psychosocial perspectives* (pp. 488–511). New York: Cambridge University Press.

Finch, C. E., & Sapolsky, R. M. (1999). The evolution of Alzheimer's disease, the reproductive schedule, and APOE isoforms. *Neurobiology of aging, 20,* 407–428.

Finkenauer, C., Luminet, O., Gisle, L., El-Ahmadi, A., van der Linden, M., & Philippot, P. (1998). Flashbulb memories and the underlying mechanisms of their formation: Toward an emotional-integrative model. *Memory & Cognition, 26,* 516–531.

Fischer, K. W. (1980). A theory of cognitive development: The control and construction of hierarchies of skills. *Psychological Review, 87,* 477–531.

Fiske, M. L. (1980). Changing hierarchies of commitment in adulthood. In N. J. Smelser & E. Erikson (Eds.), *Theories of love and work in adulthood.* Cambridge, MA: Harvard University.

Fitzgerald, J. M. (1988). Vivid memories and the reminiscence phenomenon: The role of a self-narrative. *Human Development, 31,* 260–270.

Fitzgerald, J. M. (1996).The distribution of self-narrative memories in younger and older adults: Elaborating the self-narrative hypothesis. *Aging, Neuropsychology, and Cognition, 3,* 229–236.

Fitzgerald, J. M., & Lawrence, R. (1984). Autobiographical memory across the life-span. *Journal of Gerontology, 39,* 692–699.

Flavell, J. H. (1977). *Cognitive development.* Englewood Cliffs, NJ: Prentice-Hall.

Flavell, J. H. (1985). *Cognitive development* (2nd ed.). Englewood Cliffs, NJ: Prentice-Hall.

Fletcher, W. L., Hansson, R. O., & Bailey, L. (1992, December). Assessing occupational self-efficacy among middle-aged and older adults. *Journal of Applied Gerontology, 11,* 489–501.

Floyd, M., & Scogin, F. (1997). Effects of memory training on the subjective memory functioning and mental health of older adults: A meta-analysis. *Psychology and Aging, 12,* 150–161.

Flynn, J. R. (1984). The mean IQ of Americans: Massive gains 1932 to 1978. *Psychological Bulletin, 95,* 29–51.

Flynn, J. R. (1987). Massive IQ gains in 14 nations: What IQ tests really measure. *Psychological Bulletin, 101,* 171–191.

Flynn, J. R. (1996). What environmental factors affect intelligence? The relevance of IQ gains over time. In D. K. Detterman (Ed.), *Current topics in human intelligence,* vol. 5 (pp. 17–29), Norwood, NJ: Ablex.

Flynn, J. R. (1999). Searching for justice: The discovery of IQ gains over time. *American Psychologist, 54,* 5–20.

Foldvari, M., Clark, M., Laviolette, L. C., Bernstein, M. A., Kaliton, D., Castaneda, C., Pu, C. T., Hausdorff, J. M., Fielding, R. A., & Singh, M. A. F. (2000). Association of muscle power with functional status in community-dwelling elderly women. *Journal of Gerontology, 55A,* M192–M199.

Folkman, S. (1997). Positive psychological states and coping with severe stress. *Social Science and Medicine, 45,* 1207–1221.

Folkman, S., & Moskowitz, J. T. (2000). Positive affect and the other side of coping. *American Psychologist, 55* (6), 647–654.

Fowler, J. W. (1981). *Stages of faith.* San Francisco: Harper & Row.

Fozard, J. L., & Gordon-Salant, S. (2001). Changes in vision and hearing with aging. In J. E. Birren & K. W. Schaie (Eds.), *Handbook of the psychology of aging* (5th ed.). San Diego: Academic Press.

Franceschi, C., & Fabris, N. (1993). Human longevity: The gender difference. *Aging: Clinical and Experimental Research, 5,* 333–335.

Francis, D. (1990). The significance of work friends in late life. Special Issue: Process, change, and social support. *Journal of Aging Studies, 4,* 405–424.

Frankland, P. W., O'Brien, C., Ohno, M., Kirkwood, A., & Silva, A. J. (2001). A-CAMKII-dependent plasticity in the cortex is required for permanent memory. *Nature, 411,* 309–313.

Frassetto, L. A., Todd, K. M., Morris, C., & Sebastian. (2000). Worldwide incidence of hip fracture in elderly women: Relation to consumption of animal and vegetable foods. *Journal of Gerontology, 55A,* M585–M592.

Frazier, L. D. (2000). Coping with disease-related stressors in Parkinson's disease. *The Geronotologist, 40* (1), 53–63.

Fredrickson, B. L. (1998). What good are positive emotions? *Review of General Psychology, 2,* 300–319.

Fredrickson, B. L. (2001). The role of positive emotions in positive psychology: The broaden and build theory of positive emotions. *American Psychologist, 56,* 218–226.

Freedman, M. (2000). *Prime time: How baby boomers will revolutionize retirement and transform America.* New York: Public Affairs.

Freund, A. M., & Baltes, P. B. (2002). Life-management strategies of selection, optimization, and compensation: Measurement by self-report and construct validity. *Journal of Personality and Social Psychology,*

Fried, L. P., Tangen, C. M., Walston, J., Newman, A. B., Hirsch, C., Gottdiener, J., Seeman, T., Tracy, R., Kop, W. J., Burke, G., & McBurnie, M. A. (2001). Frailty in older adults: Evidence for a phenotype. *Journal of Gerontology, 56A.* M146–M156.

Friedman, M., & Rosenman, R. M. (1974). *Type A behavior and your heart.* New York: Knopf.

Friedmann, E., & Havighurst, R. J. (1954). *The meaning of work and retirement.* Chicago: University of Chicago Press.

Friedmann, E., Katcher, A. H., Lynch, J. J., & Thomas, S. A. (1980). Animal companions and one-year survival of patients after discharge from a coronary care unit. *Public Health Reports, 95,* 307–312.

Fries, J. F. (1997). Can preventive gerontology be on the way? [Editorial.] *American Journal of Public Health, 87,* 1591–1593.

Fries, J. F., & Crapo, L. M. (1981). *Vitality and aging.* San Francisco: Freeman.

Fries, B. E., Morris, J. N., Skarupski, K. A., Blaum, C. S., Galecki, A. Bookstein, F., & Ribbe, M. (2000). Accelerated dysfunction among the very oldest-old in nursing home. *Journal of Gerontology 55A,* M336–M341.

Frieswick, K. (1997). In health: The battle against breast cancer. *Boston Magazine, 84,* 79–91.

Frisoni, G. B., Franzoni, S., Rozzini, R., Ferrucci, L., Boffelli, S., & Trabucchi, M. (1995). Food intake and mortality in the frail elderly. *Journal of Gerontology, 50A,* M203–M210.

Fromm, E. (1955). *The sane society.* New York: Fawcett Books.

Fry, P. S. (1990). A factor analytic investigation of homebound elderly individuals' concerns about death and dying and their coping responses. *Journal of Clinical Psychology, 46,* 737–748.

Fuller-Jonap, F., & Haley, W. E. (1995). Mental and physical health of male caregivers of a spouse with Alzheimer's disease. *Journal of Aging and Health, 7,* 99–118.

Fuller-Thomson, E. (1999–2000). Loss of the kin-keeper? Sibling conflict following parental death. *Omega: Journal of death and dying, 40* (4), 547–559.

Funeral Consumers Alliance. (2000). *Preneed education and information: Statistical report and analysis.* http://www.funerals.org

Futterman, A., Thompson, L. W., Gallagher-Thompson, D., & Ferris, R. (1995). Depression in later life: Epidemiology, assessment, etiology and treatment. In E. E. Beckham & W. R. Leber (Eds.), *Handbook of depression* (2nd ed., pp. 495–525). New York: Guilford Press.

Gabrieli, J. D. E., Brewer, J. E., Desmond, J. E., & Glover, G. H. (1997). Separate neural bases of two fundamental memory processes in the human medial temporal lobe. *Science, 276,* 264–266.

Galinsky, E. (1993). *National study of the changing work force.* New York: Families and Work Institute.

Galinsky, E., & Bond, J. T. (1996). Work and family: The experiences of mothers and fathers in the U.S. labor force. In C. Costello and B. K. Krimgold (Eds.), *The American Woman: 1996–97: Women and work* (pp. 79–103). New York: Norton Press.

Gall, T. L., Evans, D. R., and Howard, J. (1997). The retirement adjustment process: Changes in the well-being of male retirees across time. *Journal of Gerontology, 52B,* P110–P117.

Gallo, J. J., Anthony, J. C., & Muthen, B. O. (1994). Age differences in the symptoms of depression: A latent trait analysis. *Journal of Gerontology, Psychological Sciences, 49,* 251–254.

Gallo, W. T., Bradley, E. H., Siegel, M., and Kasl, S. V. (2001). The impact of involuntary job loss on subsequent alcohol consumption by older workers: Findings from the health and retirement survey. *Journal of Gerontology, 56B* S3–S9.

Gallo, W. T., Bradley, E. H., Siegel, M., & Stanislav, K. V. (2001). The impact of involuntary job loss on subsequent alcohol consumption by older workers: Findings from the health and retirement survey. *Journal of Gerontology, 56B* (1) S3–S9.

Galton, F. (1979). *Heredity and genius: An inquiry into its laws and consequences.* London: Julian Freeman (original work published 1869).

Gambert, S. R. (Ed.). (1987). *Handbook of geriatrics.* New York: Plenum Medical Book Company.

Gardiner, J. M., & Java, R. I. (1990). Recollective experience in word and nonword recognition. *Memory and Cognition, 16,* 309–313.

Gardiner, J. M., & Parkin, A. J. (1990). Attention and recollective experience in recognition memory. *Memory and Cognition, 18,* 23–30.

Gardner, H. (1983). *Frames of mind: The theory of multiple intelligences.* New York: Basic Books.

Gardner, H. (1985). *The mind's new science.* New York: Basic Books.

Gardner, H. (1993a). *Creating minds.* New York: Basic Books.

Gardner, H. (1993b). *Multiple intelligences: The theory in practice.* New York: Basic Books.

Gardner, H. (1995). Why would anyone become an expert? *American Psychologist, 50,* 802–803.

Garret, H. E. (1957). *Great experiments in psychology* (3rd ed.). New York: Appleton-Century-Crofts.

Gatz, M. (2000a). Variations on depression in later life. In S. H. Qualls & N. Abeles (Eds.), *Psychology and the aging revolution: How we adapt to longer life* (pp. 239–258). Washington, DC: American Psychological Association.

Gatz, M. (2000b). Contemporary clinical geropsychology. *The Gerontologist, 40* (5), 627–629.

Gatz, M., Bengtson, V. L., & Blum, M. J. (1990). Caregiving families. In J. E. Birren & K. W. Schaie (Eds.), *Handbook of the psychology of aging* (3rd ed., pp. 404–426). New York: Academic Press.

Gatz, M., Kasl-Godley, J. E., & Karel, M. I. (1996). Aging and mental disorders. In J. E. Birren & K. W. Schaie (Eds.), *Handbook of the psychology of aging* (4th ed., pp. 365–382). San Diego: Academic Press.

Gaugler, J. E., Davey, A., Pearlin, L. J., & Zarit, S. H. (2000). Modeling caregiver adaptation over time: The longitudinal impact of behavior problems. *Psychology and Aging, 15* (3), 437–450.

Gaugler, J. E., Edwards, A. B., Femia, E. E., Zarit, S. H., Stephens, M. P., Townsend, A., & Green, R. (2000). Predictors of institutionalization of cognitively impaired elders: Family help and the timing of placement. *Journal of Gerontology, 55B* (4). P247–P255.

Gavin, R. (1997). Medicare changes would put CNY hospitals under the knife. *Post-Standard,* July 25, pp. 1–2.

Gee, S., & Baillie, J. (1999). Happily ever after? An exploration of retirement expectations. *Educational Gerontology, 25* (2), 109–128.

George, L. K. (1990b). Caregiver stress studies: There really is more to learn. *The Gerontologist, 30,* 580–581.

George, L. K. (1992). Community and home care for mentally ill older adults. In J. E. Birren, R. B. Sloane, & G. D. Cohen (Eds.), *Handbook of mental health and aging* (2nd ed., pp. 793–813). San Diego: Academic Press.

George, L. K., & Gwyther, L. P. (1986). Caregiver well-being: A multidimensional examination of family caregivers of demented adults. *The Gerontologist, 26,* 253–259.

Gergan, K., & Gergan, M. (2001). Happiness and longevity: The nun study. *The Positive Aging Newsletter* (June), p. 2.

Gerhardt, V. (1990). Qualitative research on chronic illness: The issue and the story. *Social Science Medicine, 30,* 1149–1159.

Gescheider, G. A. (1997). *Psychophysics: The fundamentals.* Mahwah, NJ: Erlbaum.

Gescheider, G. A., Bolanowski, S. J., Verillo, R. T., Hall, K. L., & Hoffman, K. E. (1994). The effects of aging on information-processing channels in the sense of touch: I period absolute sensitivity. *Somatosensory and Motor Research, 11,* 345–357.

Gibbs, J. C. (1997). Surprise—and discovery?—in the near-death experience. *Journal of near death studies, 15* (4), Summer, 259–278.

Gibbs, J. C. (1999). Book Review: Light and death: One doctor's fascinating account of near-death experiences. *Journal of near death studies, 18* (2) Winter, 117–127.

Gibson, J. M. and Nathanson, P. S. (1990). Medical treatment guardians: When someone else must decide. *Generations, 14,* 43–46.

Gignac, M. A. M., & Gottlieb, B. H. (1996). Caregivers appraisals of efficacy in coping with dementia. *Psychology and Aging, 11,* 214–225.

Gilley, D. W., Wilson, R. S., Bennett, D. A., Stebbins, G. T., Bernard, B. A., Whalen, M. E., & Fox, J. H. (1991). Cessation of driving and unsafe motor vehicle operation by dementia patients. *Archives of Internal Medicine, 15,* 941–946.

Gillick, M. (2001). Pinning down frailty. *Journal of Gerontology, 56A* (3), M134–M135.

Gilligan, C. (1982). *In a different voice: Psychological theory and women's development.* Cambridge, MA: Harvard University Press.

Gilligan, C., & Belenky, M. F. (1980). A naturalistic study of abortion decisions. *New directions for child development* (No. 7, pp. 69–90). San Francisco: Jossey-Bass.

Ginzberg, E. (1971). *Career guidance.* New York: McGraw-Hill.

Ginzberg, E. (1972). Toward a theory of occupational choice: A restatement. *Vocational Guidance Quarterly, 20,* 169–176.

Ginzberg, E. (1995). *Executive talent: Developing and keeping the best people.* New Brunswick, NJ: Transaction Publishers.

Given, C. W., Given, B. A., Stommel, M., & Azzouz, F. (1999). The impact of new demands for assistance on caregiver depression: Tests using an inception cohort. *The Gerontologist, 39,* (76–85).

Glass, T. A., Prigerson, H., Kasl, S. V., & Mendes de Leon, C. F. (1995). The effects of negative life events on alcohol consumption among older men and women. *Journal of Gerontology, 50B,* S205–S216.

Glover, R. J. (2001) Discriminators of moral orientation: Gender role or personality? *Journal of Adult Development, (8),* 1–7.

Golan, N. (1986). *The perilous bridge: Helping clients through midlife transitions.* New York: Free Press.

Goldberg, A. P., Busby-Whitehead, M. J., Katzel, L. I., Krauss, R. M., Lumpkin, M., & Hagberg, J. M. (2000). Cardiovascular fitness, body composition, and lipoprotein lipid metabolism in older men. *Journal of Gerontology 55A,* M342–M349.

Goleman, D. (1987). Personality: Major traits found stable through life. *New York Times,* March 24, pp. C1, C14.

Goleman, D. (1995). *Emotional intelligence.* New York: Bantam Books.

Gollwitzer, P. M. & Bargh, J. A. (1996). *The psychology of action.* New York: Guilford Press.

Goodman, M., Rubinstein, R. L., Alexander, B. B., & Luborsky, M. (1991). Cultural differences among elderly women in coping with the death of an adult child. *Journal of Gerontology: Social Sciences, 46,* S321–S329.

Gorman, D. G., Benson, F., Vogel, D. G., & Vinters, H. V. (1992, February). Creutzfeldt-Jakob disease in a pathologist. *Neurology, 42,* 463.

Gottleib, G. L. (1992). Economic issues and geriatric mental health. In J. E. Birren, R. B. Sloane, & G. D. Cohen (Eds.), *Handbook of mental health and aging* (2nd ed, pp. 873–890). San Diego: Academic Press.

Gottman, J. M. (1998). Psychology and the study of marital processes. *Annual Review of Psychology, 49,* 169–197.

Gottman, J. M., & Levenson, R. W. (1999). How stable is marital interaction over time? *Family Process, 38,* 159–165.

Gould, R. L. (1972). *Transformations: Growth and change in adult life.* New York: Simon & Schuster.

Gould, R. L. (1980). Transformation tasks in adulthood. *In the course of life, Vol. 3: Adulthood and aging process.* Bethesda, MD: National Institute of Mental Health.

Grady, C. L., McIntosh, A. R., Horwitz, B., Maisog, J. M., Ungerleider, L. G., Mentis, M. J., Pietrini, P., Schapiro, M. B., & Haxby, J. V. (1995). Age-related reductions in human recognition memory due to impaired encoding. *Science, 269,* 218–221.

Grant, R. W. (1995). Interventions with ethnic minority elderly. In J. F. Aponte, R. Y. Rivers, & J. Wohl. (Eds.), *Psychological interventions and cultural diversity* (pp. 199–214). Boston: Allyn & Bacon.

Gratton, G., & Fabiani, M. (2001). The event-related optical signal: A new tool for studying brain function. *International Journal of Psychophysiology, 42,* 109–121.

Greer, S. (1991). Psychological response to cancer and survival. *Psychological Medicine, 21,* 43–49.

Gregoire, J., & Van der Linden, M. (1997). Effect of age on forward and backward digit spans. *Aging, Neuropsychology, and Cognition, 4,* 140–149.

Grober, E., & Buschke, H. (1987). Genuine memory deficits in dementia. *Developmental Neuropsychology, 3,* 13–36.

Group for the Advancement of Psychiatry, Committee on Cultural Psychiatry. (1989). *Suicide and ethnicity in the United States.* Washington, DC: Group for the Advancement of Psychiatry.

Grundman, M. (2000). Vitamin E and Alzheimer's disease: The basis for additional clinical trials. *American Journal of Clinical Nutrition, 71* (suppl.), 630S–636S.

Gubrium, J. F. (1993). *Speaking of life.* New York: deGruyter.

Guilford, J. P. (1959). Three faces of intellect. *American Psychologist, 14,* 469–479.

Guilford, J. P. (1967). *The nature of human intelligence.* New York: McGraw-Hill.

Guinn, B. (1999). Leisure behavior motivation and the life satisfaction of retired persons. *Activities, Adaptation, and Aging, 23* (4), 13–20.

Gump, B. B., & Matthews, K. A. (2000). Are vacations good for your health? The 9-year mortality experience after the multiple risk factor intervention trial. *Psychosomatic Medicine, 62,* 608–612.

Gump, B. B., Polk, D. E., Kamarck, T. W., & Shiffman, S. M. (2001). Partner interactions are associated with reduced blood pressure in the natural environment: Ambulatory monitoring evidence from a healthy, multiethnic adult sample. *Psychosomatic Medicine, 63,* 423–433.

Gutmann, D. L. (1977). The cross-cultural perspective: Notes toward a comparative psychology of aging. In J. E. Birren & K. W. Schaie (Eds.), *Handbook of the psychology of aging* (1st ed.) New York: Van Nostrand Reinhold.

Gutmann, D. L. (1987). *Reclaimed powers: Toward a new psychology of men and women in later life.* New York: Basic Books.

Gutmann, D. L. (1992). Culture and mental health in later life. In J. E. Birren, R. B. Sloane, and G. D. Cohen (Eds.), *Handbook of mental health and aging* (2nd ed., pp. 75–97). San Diego: Academic Press.

Gwyther, L. P. (1992). Proliferation with pizzazz. *The Gerontologist, 33,* 865–867.

Haan, M. N. (1999). Can social engagement prevent cognitive decline in old age? *Annals of Internal Medicine, 131,* 220–221.

Haan, M. N., Shemanski, L., Jagust, W. J., Manolio, T. A., & Kuller, L. (1999). The role of APOE epsilon 4 in modulating effects of other risk factors for cognitive decline in elderly persons. *Journal of the American Medical Association, 282,* 40–46.

Hadley, E. C., Dutta, C., Finkelstein, J., Harris, T. B., Lane, A. A., Roth, G. S., Sherman, S. S., & Starke-Reede, P. E. (2001). Human implications of caloric restriction's effects on aging in laboratory animals: An overview of opportunities for research. *Journal of Gerontology: Biological Sciences and Medical Sciences, 56A,* 5–6.

Hafen, B. Q., & Hoeger, W. W. K. (1994). *Wellness: Guidelines for a healthy lifestyle.* Englewood, CO: Morton Publishing.

Hagberg, B., Samuelsson, G., Lindberg, B., & Dehlin, O. (1991). Stability and change of personality in old age and its relation to survival. *Journal of Gerontology: Psychological Sciences, 46,* P285–P291.

Hagestad, G. O. (1985). Continuity and connectedness. In V. L. Bengtson & J. Robertson (Eds.), *Grandparenthood.* Beverly Hills, CA: Sage.

Haldipur, C. V., & Ward, M. S. (1996). Competence and other legal issues. In M. Hersen & V. B. Van Hasselt (Eds.), *Psychological treatment of older adults: An introductory text.* New York: Plenum Press.

Halevy, A., & Brody, B. (1993). Brain death: Reconciling definitions, criteria, and tests. *Annals of Internal Medicine, 119,* 519–525.

Haley, W. E., Roth, D. L., Coleton, M. I., Ford, G. R., West, C. A., Collins, R. P., & Isobe, T. L. (1996). Appraisal, coping, and social support as mediators of well-being in Black and White family caregivers of patients with Alzheimer's disease. *Journal of Consulting and Clinical Psychology, 64,* 540–552.

Hall, G. S. (1922). *Senescence: The last half of life.* New York: Appleton.

Handelsman, D J. (2002). Male reproductive aging: Human fertility, androgens, and hormone dependent disease. *Novartis Foundation Symposium, 242,* 66–77.

Haney, D. Q. (2001). Mammogram even better than believed. *Syracuse Post Standard,* April, 24, P. 6.

Hanisch, K. A. (1995). Behavioral families and multiple causes: Matching the complexity of responses to the complexity of antecedents. *Current Directions in Psychological Science, 4,* 156–162.

Hanrahan, P., & Luchins, D. J. (1995). Access to hospice programs in end-stage dementia: A national survey of hospice programs. *Journal of the American Geriatric Society, 43,* 56–59.

Hanser, S. B. (1999). Using music therapy in treating psychological problems of older adults. In M. Duffy (Ed.), *Handbook of Counseling and Psychotherapy with Older Adults,* pp. 197–213. John Wiley: NY.

Hansot, E. (1996). A letter from a patient's daughter: *Analysis of Internal Medicine, 125,* 149–151.

Hao, L., & Johnson, R. W. (2000). Economic, cultural, and social origins of emotional well-being: Comparisons of immigrants and natives. *Research on Aging, 22* (6), 599–629.

Harada, N. D., & Kim, L. S. (1995). Use of mental health services by older Asian and Pacific Islander Americans. In D. K. Padgett (Ed.), *Handbook of ethnicity, aging, and mental health* (pp. 184–202). Westport, CT: Greenwood.

Harel, Z., & Biegel, D. E. (1995). Aging, ethnicity, and mental health services: Social work perspectives on need and use. In D. K. Padgett (Ed.), *Handbook of ethnicity, aging, and mental health* (pp. 217–241). Westport, CT: Greenwood.

Harkins, S. W., Price, D. D., & Martinelli, M. (1986). Effects of age on pain perception. *Journal of Gerontology, 41,* 58–63.

Harma, M. I., Hakola, T., & Laitinen, J. (1992). Relation of age of circadian adjustment to night work. Fifth US-Finnish Joint Symposium on Occupational Safety and Health: Occupational epidemics of the 1990s. *Scandinavian Journal of Work, Environment and Health, 18,* Suppl. 2, 116–118.

Harris Interactive. (2000). *Poll, Radcliffe Public Policy Center* (#14119). *Washington Post* Online, 5-3-2000.

Harris, P. B. (1995). Differences among husbands caring for their wives with Alzheimer's disease: Qualitative findings and counseling implications. *Journal of Clinical Geropsychology, 1,* 9–106.

Harris-Wehling, J., Feasley, J. C., & Estes, C. L. (1995). *An evaluation of the long-term care ombudsman programs of the Older Americans Act.* Washington, DC: Institute of Medicine: Division of Health Care Services.

Hart, H. M., McAdams, D. P., Hirsch, B. J., & Bauer, J. J. (2001). Generativity and social involvement among African Americans and white adults. *Journal of Research in Personality, 35,* 208–230.

Harvard Health Letter. (1995). The final chapter, *12.*

Harvard Mental Health Letter. (1995a). Update on Alzheimer's disease, 2.

Harvard Mental Health Letter. (1995b). Update on Alzheimer's disease, Part II, 11 (#9).

Hashimoto, A. (1996). *The gift of generations: Japanese and American perspectives on aging and the social contract.* New York: Cambridge University Press.

Hatch, L. R. (1992). Gender differences in orientation toward retirement from paid labor. *Gender and Society, 6,* 66–85.

Haughie, E., Milne, D., & Elliot, V. (1992). An evaluation of companion pets with elderly psychiatric patients. *Behavioral Psychotherapy, 20,* 367–372.

Havighurst, R. J. (1972). *Developmental tasks and education* (3rd ed.). New York: David McKay.

Hayflick, L. M. (1996). *How and why we age.* New York: Ballantine Books.

Haynie, D. A., Berg, S., Johanson, B., Gatz, M., and Zarit, S. H. (2001). Symptoms of depression in the oldest old: A longitudinal study. *Journal of Gerontology, 56B,* P111–P118.

Hays, J. C., Gold, D. T., & Peiper, C. F. (1997). Sibling bereavement in late life. *Omega: Journal of Death and Dying, 35* (1), 25–42.

Health Care Financing Administration. (1996). *Your medicare handbook, 1996.* Washington, DC: Department of Health and Human Services, U.S. Government Printing Office.

Heidrich, S. M., & Ryff, C. D. (1993). The role of social comparisons. Processes in the psychological adaptation of elderly adults. *Journal of Gerontology: Psychological Sciences, 48,* P127–P136.

Held, B. S. (2001). *Stop smiling, start kvetching: Five steps to creative complaining.* New York: St. Martin's Press.

Helgeson, V. S. (1994). Relation of agency and communion to well-being: Evidence and potential explanations. *Psychological Bulletin, 116,* 412–428.

Hendricks, J., & Cutler, S. J. (2001). The effects of membership in church-related associations and labor unions on age differences in voluntary association affiliations. *The Gerontologist, 41* (2), 250–256.

Henkens, K. (2000). Retirement intentions and spousal support: A multi-actor approach. *Journals of Gerontology: Series A: Biological Sciences and Medical Sciences, 54* (6), S63–S73.

Henretta, J. C., Chan, C. G., & O'Rand, A. M. (1992). Retirement reason versus retirement process: Examining the reasons for retirement typology. *Journals of Gerontology: Social Sciences, 47,* S1–S7.

Herbst, J. H., McCrae, R. R., Costa, P. T., Jr., Feaganes, J. R., & Siegler, I. C. (2000). Self-perceptions of stability and change in personality at midlife: The UNC alumni heart study. *Assessment, Special Issue (7),* 379–388.

Herrnstein, R. J., & Murray, C. (1994). *The bell curve: Intelligence and class structure in American life.* New York: The Free Press.

Hershey, D. A., & Mowen, J. C. (2000). Psychological determinants of financial preparedness for retirement. *The Gerontologist, 40,* 687–697.

Hertzog, C., & Hultsch, D. F. (2000). Metacognition in adulthood and old age. In F. I. M. Craik & T. A. Salthouse (Eds.), *The handbook of aging and cognition* (pp. 417–466). Mahwah, NJ: Erlbaum.

Hertzog, C., & Schaie, K. W. (1988). Stability and change in adult intelligence: 2. Simultaneous analysis of longitudinal means and covariance structures. *Psychology and Aging, 3,* 122–130.

Herzog, A. R., Franks, M. M., Markus, H. R., & Holmberg, D. (1998). Activities and well-being in old age: Effects of self-concept and educational attainment. *Psychology and Aging, 13,* 179–185.

Hess, B. (1971). *Amicability.* Unpublished doctoral dissertation. New Brunswick, NJ: Rutgers University.

Hess, L. A. (1988). *The depiction of grandparents and their relationships with grandchildren in recent children's literature: Content analysis.* Unpublished master's thesis. State College, PA: Penn State University.

Hess, T. M., & Pullen, S. M. (1996). Memory in context. In F. Blanchard-Fields, & T. H., & Hess, (Eds.), *Perspectives on cognitive change in adulthood and aging.* NY: McGraw-Hill.

Heston, L. L., & White, J. A. (1983). *Dementia: A practical guide to Alzheimer's disease and related illnesses.* New York: W.H. Freeman.

Hetherington, E. M., Stanley-Hagan, M., & Anderson, E. R. (1989). Marital transitions: A child's perspective. *American Psychologist, 44,* 303–312.

High, D. M. (1991). A new myth about families of older people. *The Gerontologist, 31,* 611–618.

High, D. M. (1993). Advance directives and the elderly: A study of intervention strategies to increase use. *The Gerontologist, 33,* 342–349.

Hill, E. J., Miller, B. C., Weiner, S. P., & Colihan, J. (1998). Influences of the virtual office on aspects of work and work/life balance. *Personnel Psychology, 51* (3), 667–683.

Hill, R. D., Storandt, M., & Malley, M. (1993). The impact of long-term exercise training on psychological function in older adults. *Journal of Gerontology: Psychological Sciences, 48,* P12–P17.

Hill, T. J. (2000). Legally extending the family: An event history analysis of grandparent visitation rights. *Journal of Family Issues, 21,* 246–261.

Hinrichsen, G. A., & Ramirez, M. (1992). Black and white dementia caregivers: A comparison of their adaptation, adjustment and service utilization. *The Gerontologist, 32,* 375–381.

Hirsch, C. H., Davies, H. D., Boatwright, F., & Ochango, G. (1993). Effects of a nursing-home respite admission on veterans with advanced dementia. *The Gerontologist, 33*(4), 523–528.

Hobfall, S. E. (1998). *Stress, culture, and community.* New York: Plenum.

Hobson, P., & Meara, J. (1999). The detection of dementia and cognitive impairment in a community population of elderly people with Parkinson's disease by use of CAMCOG neuropsychological tests. *Age and Ageing, 28,* 39.

Hoch, C. C., Buysse, D. J., Monk, T. H., & Reynolds, C. F., III. (1992). Sleep disorders and aging. In J. E. Birren, R. B. Sloane, & G. D. Cohen (Eds.), *Handbook of mental health and aging* (2nd ed., pp. 557–581). San Diego: Academic Press.

Hochschild, A. (1997). *The time bind: When work becomes home and home becomes work.* New York: Metropolitan.

Hoeger, L. W., & Hoeger, W. W. K. (1995). *Lifetime: Physical fitness and wellness.* Englewood, CO: Norton.

Hofer, S. M., & Sliwinski, M. J. (2001). Understanding aging: an evaluation of research designs for assessing the interdependence of age-related changes. *Gerontology, 47,* 341–352.

Hoffman, L. W. (1982). Social change and its effects on parents and children: Limitations to knowledge. In P. W. Berman & E. R. Ramey (Eds.), *Women: A developmental perspective.* Washington, DC: U.S. Department of Health and Human Services, Public Health Services, National Institute of Health Publication No. 82-2298.

Holland, J. L. (1996). Exploring careers with a typology: What we have learned and some new directions. *American Psychologist, 51* (4), 397–406.

Holland, J. L. (1997). *Making vocational choices: A theory of vocational personalities and work environments* (3rd edition). Odessa, Fla.: Psychological Assessment Resources.

Holmes, E. R., & Holmes, L. D. (1995). *Other cultures, elder years: An introduction to cultural gerontology* (2nd ed.). Thousand Oaks, CA: Sage.

Holmes, T. H., & Rahe, R. H. (1967). The social readjustment rating scale. *Journal of Psychosomatic Research, 11,* 213–218.

Hong, J. and Seltzer, M. M. (1995). The psychological consequences of multiple role: The nonnormative case. *Journal of Health and Social Behavior, 36,* 386–398.

Hooker, K., Manoogian-O'Dell, M., Monahan, D. J., Frazier, L. D., & Shifren, K. (2000). Does type of disease matter? Gender differences among Alzheimer's and Parkinson's disease spouse caregivers. *The Gerontologist, 40* (5), 568–573.

Hooker, K., & Ventis, G. (1984). Work ethic, daily activities and retirement satisfaction. *Journal of Gerontology, 39,* 478–484.

Horgas, A. L., Wilms, H. U., & Baltes, M. M. (1998). Daily life in very older age: Everyday activities as expression of successful living. *The Gerontologist, 38,* 556–568.

Horn, J. L. (1982). The theory of fluid and crystallized intelligence in relation to concepts of cognitive psychology and aging in adulthood. In F. I. M. Craik & S. Trehub (Eds.), *Aging and cognitive processes* (Vol. 8). New York: Plenum.

Horn, J. L. (1998). A basis for research on age differences in cognitive capabilities. In J. J. McArdle & R. Woodstock (Eds.), *Human cognitive abilities in theory and practice* (pp. 57–91). Mahwah, NJ: Erlbaum.

Horn, J. L., & Donaldson, G. (1976). On the myth of intellectual decline in adulthood. *American Psychologist, 31,* 701–709.

Horn, J. L., & Noll, J. (1994). A system for understanding cognitive capabilities: A theory and the evidence upon which it is based. In D. K. Detterman (Ed.), *Current topics in human intelligence* (Vol. 4.), Norwood, NJ: Ablex.

Horn, J. L., & Noll, J. (1997). Human cognitive abilities: Gf-Gc theory. In D. P. Flanagan & J. L. Genshaft (Eds.), *Contemporary intellectual assessment* (pp. 53–91). New York: Guilford Press.

Hornstein, G. A., & Wapner, S. (1985). Modes of experiencing and adapting to retirement. *International Journal of Aging and Human Development, 21,* 291–315.

Horvath, T. B., & Davis, K. L. (1990). Central nervous system disorders in aging. In E. L. Schneider & J. W. Rowe, (Eds.). *Handbook of the biology of aging* (3rd ed., pp. 306–329). San Diego: Academic Press.

Howard, D. V. (1996). The aging of implicit and explicit memory. In F. Blanchard-Fields & T. M. Hess (Eds.), *Perspective on cognitive change in adulthood and aging* (pp. 221–254). New York: McGraw-Hill.

Howe, M. L., & Courage, M. L. (1993). On resolving the enigma of infantile amnesia. *Psychological Bulletin, 113,* 305–326.

Howland, J., Lachman, M. E., Peterson, E. W., Cote, J., Kasten, L., & Jette, A. (1998). Covariates of fear of falling and associated activity curtailment *The Gerontologist, 38,* 549–555.

Hoyer, W. J. (1998). The older individual in a rapidly changing work context: developmental and cognitive issues. In K. W. Schaie & C. Schooler (Eds.), *Impact of work on older adults.* New York: Springer.

Hoyer, W. J. (2002). Life-span development. In D. J. Eckert (Ed.), *The Macmillan encyclopedia of aging.* New York: Macmillan.

Hoyer, W. J. (2001). Normal brain aging: Behavioral, cognitive, and personality consequences. In N. J. Smelser & P. B. Baltes (Eds.), *International encyclopedia of the social and behavioral sciences.* Oxford: Elsevier.

Hoyer, W. J., & Lincourt, A. E. (1998). Aging and the development of learning. In M. A. Stadler & P. A. Frensch (Eds.), *Handbook of implicit learning* (pp. 445–470). Thousand Oaks, CA: Sage.

Hoyer, W. J., & Rybash, J. M. (1992a). Knowledge factors in everyday visual perception. In R. L. West & J. D. Sinnott (Eds.), *Everyday memory and aging: Current research and methodology* (pp. 215–222). New York: Springer-Verlag.

Hoyer, W. J., & Rybash, J. M. (1992b). Age and visual field differences in computing visual-spatial relations. *Psychology and Aging, 7,* 339–342.

Hoyer, W. J., & Rybash, J. M. (1994). Characterizing adult cognitive development. *Adult Development, 1,* 7–12.

Hoyer, W. J., & Rybash, J. M. (1996). Life-span theory. In J. E. Birren (Ed), *Encyclopedia of gerontology* (pp. 65–71). San Diego: Academic Press.

Hoyer, W. J., & Touron, D. R. (2001). Learning in adulthood. In J. Demick & C. Andreoletti (Eds.), *Handbook of adult development.* New York: Plenum.

Hoyer, W. J., & Touron, D. R. (2002). Learning in adulthood. In J. Demick & C. Andreoletti (Eds.), *Handbook of adult development.* New York: Plenum.

Hsiao, E. T., & Robinovitch, S. N. (2001). Elderly subjects' ability to recover balance with a single backward step associates with body configuration at step contact. *Journal of Gerontology: Medical Science, 56A,* (1), M42–M47.

http://www.hospicefoundation.org (2001). Loss in later life.

http://www.hospicenet.org (2001). Caregivers and bereavement.

Huber, R., Borders, K. Netting, F. E., and Nelson, H. W. (2000). Data from long-term care ombudsman programs in six states: The implications of collecting resident demographics. *The Gerontologist, 41,* 61–68.

Hughes, S. L., Giobbie-Hurder, A., Weaver, F. M., Kubal, J. D., & Henderson, W. (1999). Relationship between caregiver burden and health-related quality of life. *The Gerontologist, 39* (5), 534–545.

Hultsch, D. F. (1971). Adult age differences in free classification and free recall. *Developmental Psychology, 4,* 338–342.

Hultsch, D. F., Hertzog, C., Small, B. J., & Dixon, R. A. (1999). Use it or lose it: Engaged lifestyle as a buffer of cognitive decline in aging? *Psychology & Aging, 14,* 245–263.

Hultsch, D. F., & Plemons, J. K. (1979). Life events and life-span development. In P. B. Baltes & O. G. Brim, Jr. (Eds.), *Life-span development and behavior* (Vol. 2). New York: Academic Press.

Hultsch, D. F., Hammer, M., & Small, B. J. (1993). Age differences in cognitive performance in later life: Relationship to self-reported health and activity life style. *Journal of Gerontology: Psychological Sciences, 48,* P1–P11.

Human Capital Initiative. (1993). *Vitality for life: Psychological research for productive aging.* Washington, DC: American Psychological Society.

Humber, J. M., & Almeder, R. F. (Eds.). *Is there a duty to die?* Totowa, NJ: Biomedical Ethics Review, Humana Press.

Humphrey, D. (1997). *Final exit: Practicalities of self-deliverance and assisted suicide.* N.Y.: Dell.

Hunt, E. (1993). What we need to know about aging. In J. Cerella, J. Rybash, W. Hoyer, & M. L. Commons (Eds.), *Adult information processing: Limits on loss* (pp. 587–589). San Diego: Academic Press.

Hunt, E. (1995). The role of intelligence in modern society. *American Scientist, 83,* 356–368.

Hutchison, T. D., & Scherman, A. (1992). Didactic and experiential death and dying training: Impact upon death anxiety. *Death Studies, 16* (4), 317–330.

Huyck, M. H. (1990). Gender differences in aging. In J. E. Birren & K. W. Schaie (Eds.), *Handbook of the psychology of aging* (3rd ed., pp. 124–132). San Diego: Academic Press.

Huyck, M. H. (1999). Gender roles and gender identity in midlife. In S. L. Willis & J. D. Reid (Eds.), *Life in the middle* (pp. 209–233). San Diego: Academic Press.

Independent Sector. (1998). *America's senior volunteers.* Washington, DC: Independent Sector. Cited in J. Hendricks and S. J. Cutler (2001), The effects of membership in church-related associations and labor unions on age differences in voluntary association affiliations. *The Gerontologist, 41* (2), 250–256.

Ingersoll-Dayton, B., & Antonucci, T. C. (1988). Reciprocal and nonreciprocal social support: Contrasting sides of intimate relationships. *Journal of Gerontology: Social Sciences, 43,* 565–573.

Inhelder, B., & Piaget, J. (1958). *The growth of logical thinking from childhood to adolescence.* New York: Basic Books.

Insel, P. M., Roth, W. T., Rollins, L. M., & Peterson, R. A. (1996). *Core concepts in health* (7th ed.) Mountain View, CA: Mayfield.

Institute of Alcohol Studies. (1997). Alcohol and the elderly. http://www.ias.org.uk/factsheets/elderly.htm

Insurance Institute for Highway Safety. (1992). *Status Report 12,* 1–7. Arlington, VA.

Jacoby, L. L. (1991). A process dissociation framework: Separating automatic from intentional uses of memory. *Journal of Memory and Language, 30,* 513–541.

Jacoby, L. L., Jennings, J. M., & Hay, J. F. (1996). Dissociating automatic from consciously controlled processes: Implications for the diagnosis and treatment of memory disorders. In D. J. Herrmann, C. L. McEvoy, C. Hertzog, P. Hertrel, & M. K. Johnson (Eds.), *Basic and applied memory research: Theory in context* (Vol. 1, pp. 161–193). Hillsdale, NJ: Erlbaum.

Jacoby, L. L., Kelley, C., Brown, J., & Jasechko, J. (1989). Becoming famous overnight: Limits on the ability to avoid unconscious influences of the past. *Journal of Personality and Social Psychology, 56,* 326–338.

Jacoby, L. L., Yonelinas, A. P., & Jennings, J. M. (1996). The relation between conscious and unconscious (automatic) influences: A declaration of independence. In J. D. Cohen & J. W. Schooler (Eds.), *Scientific approaches to consciousness.* (pp. 13–48), Mahwah, NJ: Erlbaum.

James, W. (1890). *Principles of psychology.* New York: Henry Holt.

Janowski, M. J. (1989). When a nurse asks a nurse. *American Journal of Nursing, 89,* p. 1412.

Jansari, A. J., & Parkin, A. J. (1996). Things that go bump in your life: Explaining the reminiscence bump in autobiographical memory. *Psychology and Aging, 11,* 85–91.

Jarvik, L. (1987). *The aging of the brain: How to prevent it.* Paper presented at the annual meeting of the Gerontological Society of America, Washington, DC.

Jecker, N. S. (1990). The role of intimate others in medical decision-making. *The Gerontologist, 30,* 65–71.

Jenkins, L., & Hoyer, W. J. (2000). Memory-based automaticity and aging: Acquisition, reacquisition, and retention. *Psychology and Aging, 15,* 551–565.

Jennings, J. M., & Jacoby, L. L. (1993). Automatic versus intentional uses of memory: Aging, attention, and control. *Psychology and Aging, 8,* 283–293.

Jennings, J. M., & Jacoby, L. L. (1997). An opposition procedure for detecting age-related deficits in recollection: Telling effects of repetition. *Psychology and Aging, 12,* 352–361.

Job Outlook, 2001. (2001). *Planning job choices, 2001.* National Association of Colleges and Employers (44th ed.). Bethlehem, PA: NACE.

Johnson, C. (1999). Fictive kin among oldest-old African Americans in the San Francisco Bay area. *Journal of Gerontology, 54,* S368–S375.

Johnson, C., & Barer, B. (1996). *Life beyond 85 years: The aura of survivorship.* New York: Springer.

Johnson, C. L. (1988). Grandparenting options in divorcing families: An anthropological perspective. In V. L. Bengtson & J. Robertson (Eds.), *Grandparenthood.* Beverly Hills, CA: Sage.

Johnson, C. L., & Barer, B. M. (1993). Coping and a sense of control among the oldest-old: An explanatory analysis. *Journal of Aging Studies, 7,* 67–80.

Johnson, C. L., & Troll, L. (1994). Constraints and facilitators to friendships in late late life. *The Gerontologist, 23,* 612–625.

Joiner, T. E. (2000). Depression: Current developments and controversies. In S. H. Qualls and N. Abeles (Eds.), *Psychology and the aging revolution: How we adapt to longer life* (pp. 223–238). Washington, DC: American Psychological Association.

Jones, C. J., & Meredith, W. (2000). Developmental paths of psychological health from early adolescence to later adulthood. *Psychology and Aging, 15,* 351–360.

Jones, H. E., & Conrad, H. S. (1933). The growth and decline of intelligence: A study of a homogeneous group between the ages of ten and sixty. *Genetic Psychology Monographs, 13,* 223–294.

Jonsen, A. R. (1989). Ethical issues in organ transplantation. In R. M. Veatch (Eds.), Medical ethics (2nd ed., pp. 239–274). Sudbury, MA: Jones & Bartlett.

Judge, J. O., Davis, R. B., & Ounpuu, S. (1996). Step length reductions in advanced aging: The role of ankle and hip kinetics. *Journal of Gerontology: Medical Sciences, 51A,* 303–312.

Jung, C. G. (1933). *Modern man in search of a soul.* New York: Harcourt, Brace, & World.

Kahana, B. (1992). Theoretical and methodological issues in the study of extreme stress in later life. In M. Wykle (Ed.), *Stress and health among the aged* (pp.151–171). New York: Springer.

Kahana, B., & Kahana, E. (1970). Grandparenting from the perspective of the developing grandchild. *Developmental Psychology, 3,* 98–105.

Kalish, R. (1985). The social context of death and dying. In R. H. Binstock & E. Shanas (Eds.), *Handbook of aging and the social sciences* (2nd ed.). New York: Van Nostrand Reinhold.

Kalish, R. A., & Reynolds, D. K. (1981). *Death and ethnicity: A psychosocial study.* Farmingdale, New York: Baywood. (Original work published 1976).

Kaplan, H. S. (1974). *The new sex therapy.* New York: Brunner/Mazel.

Kaplan, M. S., Adamek, M. E., & Calderon, A. (1999). Managing depressed and suicidal geriatric patients: Differences among primary care physicians. *The Gerontologist, 39* (4), 417–425.

Kaplan, M. S., Adamek, M. E., & Geling, O. (1996). Sociodemographic predictions of firearm suicide among older white males. *The Gerontologist, 36,* 530–533.

Kapp, M. B. (1991). Health care decision-making by the elderly: I get by with a little help from my family. *The Gerontologist, 31,* 619–623.

Karpel, M. E., Hoyer, W. J., & Toglia, M. P. (2001). Accuracy and qualities of real and suggested memories: Nonspecific age differences. *Journal of Gerontology: Psychological Sciences.*

Kart, C. S., Metress, E. K., & Metress, S. P. (1992). *Human aging and chronic disease.* London: Jones & Bartlett.

Kasch, F. W., Boyer, J. L., VanCamp, S. P., Verity, L. S., & Wallace, S. P. (1990). The effect of physical activity and inactivity on aerobic power in older men. (a longitudinal study). *Journal of Sports Medicine, 18,* 73–83.

Kaslow, F. W., & Schwartz, L. I. (1987). *The dynamics of divorce: A life cycle perspective.* New York: Brunner/Mazel.

Kastenbaum, R. (1981). *Death, society, and human experience* (2nd ed.). Palo Alto, CA: Mayfield.

Kastenbaum, R. (1985). Death and dying: A life-span approach. In J. E. Birren & K. W. Schaie (Eds.), *Handbook of the psychology of aging* (2nd ed.). New York: Van Nostrand Reinhold.

Kastenbaum, R. (1992). *The psychology of death* (2nd ed.). New York: Springer.

Kastenbaum, R., & Norman, C. (1990). Deathbed scenes imagined by the young and experienced by the old. *Death Studies, 14,* 201–217.

Katchadourian, H. (1987). *Fifty: Midlife in perspective.* New York: W.H. Freeman.

Katon, W., & Sullivan, M. D. (1990). Depression and chronic mental illness. *Journal of Clinical Psychiatry, 51,* 3–11.

Katz, I. R. (1997). Late life suicide and the Euthanasia debate: What should we do about suffering in terminal illness and chronic disease? *The Gerontologist, 37,* 269–271.

Kazanjian, M. A. (1997). The spiritual and psychological explanations for loss experience. *The Hospice Journal, 12,* 17–27.

Keenan, P. A., Ezzat, W. H., Ginsburg, K., & Moore, G. J. (2001). Prefrontal cortex as the site of estrogen's effect on cognition. *Psychoneuroendocrinology, 26,* 577–590.

Keil, C. P. (1998). Loneliness, stress, and human-animal attachment among older adults. In C. C. Wilson, & D. C. Turner (Eds.), *Companion animals in human health* (pp. 123–134). Thousand Oaks, CA: Sage.

Keith, P. M. (2000). Training and educational activities, efficacy, and worry among volunteer ombudsmen in nursing facilities. *Educational Gerontology, 26* (3), 249–260.

Kemp, B. J., & Mitchell, J. M. (1992). Functional assessment in geriatric mental health. In J. E. Birren, R. B. Sloane, & G. D. Cohen (Eds.), *Handbook of mental health and aging* (2nd ed., pp. 671–719). San Diego: Academic Press.

Kemper, S., Greiner, L. H., Marquis, J. G., Prenovost, K., & Mitzner, T. L. (2001). Language decline across the life span: Findings from the nun study. *Psychology and Aging, 16,* 227–239.

Kemper, T. L. (1994). Neuroanatomical and neuropathological changes during aging and in dementia. In M. L. Albert & E. J. E. Knoepfel (Eds.), *Clinical neurology of aging,* (2nd ed.), (pp. 3–67). NY: Oxford University Press.

Kennedy, G. I. (1996). *Suicide and depression in late life: Critical issues in treatment, research, and public policy.* New York: John Wiley & Sons.

Kenshalo, D. R. (1977). Age changes in touch, vibration, temperature, kinesthesis, and pain sensitivity. In J. E. Birren & K. W. Schaie (Eds.), *Handbook of the psychology of aging* (2nd ed.). New York: Van Nostrand Reinhold.

Kessler, R. C., Foster, C., Webster, P. S., & House, J. S. (1992). The relationship between age and depressive symptoms in two national surveys. *Psychology and Aging, 7,* 119–126.

Kiecolt-Glaser, J. K., & Glaser, R. (2001). Stress and immunity: Age enhances the risks. *Current Directions in Psychological Science, 10,* 18–21.

Kiecolt-Glaser, J. K., Malarkey, W. B., Chee, M., Newton, T., Cacioppo, J. T., Mao, H., & Glaser, R. (1993). Negative behavior during marital conflict is associated with immunological down-regulation. *Psychosomatic Medicine, 55,* 395–409.

Kimmel, D. (1995). Lesbians and gay men grow old. In L. A. Bond, S. J. Cutler, & A. Grams (Eds.), *Promoting successful and productive aging.* Thousand Oaks, CA: Sage.

Kimmel, D., & Sang, B. E. (1997). Lesbians and gay men at midlife. In C. J. Patterson & A. R. D'Augelli (Eds.), *Lesbian and gay identities across the life span: Psychological perspectives.* New York: Oxford University Press.

Kimura, R. (1995). Medical ethics; History of subsection: Contemporary Japan. In W. T. Reich (Ed.), *Encyclopedia of Bio-Ethics* (revised ed., pp. 1496–1505). New York: Simon & Schuster/Macmillan.

Kindleberger, R. (1996). Priced out: Assisted living tackles how to make services available to poor and middle-class elderly. *Boston Globe,* November 10, pp. F1–F6.

Kingson, E. R., & O'Grady-LeShane, R. (1993). The effects of caregiving on women's social security benefits. *The Gerontologist, 33,* 230–239.

Kinicki, A. J. (1989). Predicting occupational role choices after involuntary job loss. *Journal of Vocational Behavior, 35,* 204–218.

Kinney, H. C., Korein, J., Panigrahy, A., Dikkes, P., & Goode, R. (1994). Neuropathological findings in the brain of Karen Ann Quinlan. *New England Journal of Medicine, 330* (21), 1469–1475.

Kinoshita, Y., & Kiefer, C. W. (1993). *Refuge of the honored: Social organization in a Japanese retirement community.* Berkeley, CA: University of California Press.

Kissell, J. L. (2000). Grandma, the GNP, and the duty to die. In J. M. Humber and R. F. Almeder (Eds.), *Is there a duty to die?* (pp. 191–204). Totowa, NJ: Biomedical Ethics Review, Humana Press.

Kivnick, H. Q. (1983). Dimensions of grandparental meaning: Deductive conceptualization and empirical derivation. *Journal of Personality and Social Psychology, 44,* 1056–1068.

Klapper, J., Moss, S., Moss, M. S., & Rubinstein, R. (1994). The social context of grief among adult daughters who have lost a parent. *Journal of Aging Studies, 8,* 29–43.

Kliegl, R., Smith, J., & Baltes, P. B. (1990). On the locus and process of magnification of age differences during mnemonic training. *Developmental Psychology, 26,* 894–904.

Kline, D. W., & Scialfa, C. T. (1996). Visual and auditory aging. In J. E. Birren, K. W. Schaie, R. P. Abeles, M. Gatz, & T. A. Salthouse (Eds.), *Handbook of the psychology of aging* (4th ed.). San Diego: Academic Press.

Kline D. W., Kline, T., Fozard, J. L., Kosnik, W., Scheiber, F., & Sekular, R. (1992). Vision, aging and driving: The problems of older drivers. *Journal of Gerontology: Psychological Sciences, 47,* P27–P34.

Klinger, E. (1998). The search for meaning in evolutionary perspective and its clinical implications. In P. T. P. Wong and Fry, P. S. (eds.), *The human quest for meaning: A handbook of psychological research and clinical applications* (p. 27–50). Mahwah, N. J.: Lawrence Erlbaum.

Koenig, H. G. (1995). Religion as a cognitive schema. *International Journal for the Psychology of Religion, 5,* 31–37.

Kogan, N. (1990). Personality and aging. In J. E. Birren, & K. W. Schaie (Eds.), *Handbook of the psychology of aging* (3rd ed., pp. 330–346). San Diego: Academic Press.

Kohlberg, L. (1958). *The development of mode of moral thinking and choice in the years ten to sixteen.* Unpublished doctoral dissertation, University of Chicago.

Kohlberg, L. (1969). Stage and sequence: The cognitive-developmental approach to socialization. In D. Goslin (Ed.), *Handbook of socialization theory and research.* Chicago: Rand McNally.

Kohlberg, L. (1976). Moral stages and moralization: The cognitive-developmental approach. In T. Lickona (Ed.), *Moral development and behavior: Theory, research, and social issues.* New York: Holt, Rinehart & Winston.

Kohlberg, L. (1987). The development of moral judgment and moral action. In L. Kohlberg (Ed.), *Child development and childhood education: A cognitive-developmental view.* New York: Longman Press.

Kohlberg, L. (1990). Which postformal levels are stages? In M. L. Commons, C. Armon, L. Kohlberg, F. A. Richards, T. A. Groetzer, & J. D. Sinnott (Eds.), *Adult development, vol. 2: Models and methods in the study of adolescent and adult thought.* New York: Praeger.

Kohlberg, L., & Candee, D. (1984). The relationship of moral judgment to moral action. In W. M. Kurtines & J. L. Gewirtz (Eds.), *Morality, moral behavior, and moral development.* New York: Wiley.

Kohlberg, L., & Kramer, R. B. (1969). Continuities and discontinuities in childhood and adult moral development. *Human Development, 12,* 93–120.

Kolata, G. (1997). When death begins. *New York Times,* April 20, pp. 1–3.

Kolb, B., & Whishaw, I. Q. (1995). *Fundamentals of human neuropsychology* (3rd ed.). New York: W. H. Freeman.

Konnert, C., Gatz, M., & Hertzsprung, E. A. M. (1999). Preventive interventions for older adults. In M. Duffy (Ed.), *Handbook of counseling and psychotherapy with older adults,* pp. 314–334. New York: John Wiley.

Konradt, U., Schmook, R., Wilm, A., and Hertl, G. (2000). Health circles for teleworkers: Selective results on stress, strain, and coping styles. *Health Education Research, 15,* 327–338.

Koplowitz, H. (1984). A projection beyond Piaget's formal operations stage: A general system stage and a unitary stage. In M. L. Commons, F. A. Richards, & C. Armon (Eds.), *Beyond formal operations: Late adolescent and adult cognitive development.* New York: Praeger.

Kosik, K. S. (1992). Alzheimer's disease: A cell biological perspective. *Science, 256,* 780–783.

Kosnik, W. D., Sekuler, R., & Kline, D. W. (1990). Self-reported visual problems of older drivers. *Human Factors, 32,* 597–608.

Kosnik, W., Winslow, L., Kline, D., Rasinski, K., & Sekuler, R. (1988). Visual changes in daily life throughout adulthood. *Journal of Gerontology: Psychological Sciences, 43,* P63–P70.

Koss-Chioino, J. D. (1995). Traditional and folk approaches among ethnic minorities. In J. F. Aponte, R. Y. Rivers, & J. Wohl (Eds.), Psychological interventions and cultural diversity, (pp. 145–163). Boston: Allyn & Bacon.

Kramer, A. F., Hahn, S., & Gopher, D. (1999). Task coordination and aging: Explorations of executive control processes in the task switching paradigm. *Acta Psychologica, 101,* 339–378.

Kramer, B. (1997a). Gain in the caregiving experience: Where are we? What next? *The Gerontologist, 37,* 218–232.

Kramer, B. (1997b). Differential predictors of strain and gain among husbands caring for wives with dementia. *The Gerontologist, 37,* 239–249.

Kramer, B. J. (1993a). Expanding the conceptualization of caregiver coping: The importance of relationship-focused coping strategies. *Family Relations, 42,* 383–391.

Kramer, B. J. (1993b). Marital history and the prior relationship as predictors of positive and negative outcomes among wife caregivers. *Family Relations, 42,* 367–375.

Kramer, B. J., & Lambert, J. D. (1999). Caregiving as a life course transition among older husbands: A prospective study. *The Gerontologist, 39* (6), 658–667.

Kraus, R. (1978). *Recreation and leisure in modern society* (2nd ed.). Santa Monica, CA: Goodyear.

Krause, N. (1995a). Religiosity and self-esteem among older adults. *Journal of Gerontology: Psychological Sciences, 50B,* 236–246.

Krause, N. (1995b). Stress, alcohol use, and depressive symptoms in late life. *The Gerontologist, 35,* 296–307.

Krause, N. (1998). Stressors in highly valued roles, religious coping, and mortality. *Psychology and Aging, 13* (2), 242–255.

Krause, N., Ingersoll-Dayton, B., Ellison, C. G., & Wulff, K. M. (1999). Aging, religious doubt, and psychological well-being. *The Gerontologist, 39* (5), 525–533.

Krause, N., & Shaw, B. A. (2000). Giving social support to others, socioeconomic status, and changes in self-esteem in later life. *Journal of Gerontology, 55B* (6), S323–S333.

Krueger, J., & Heckhausen, J. (1993). Personality development across the adult life span.: Subjective conceptions vs cross-sectional constraints. *Journal of Gerontology: Psychological Sciences, 48,* P100–P108.

Kübler-Ross, E. (1969). *On death and dying.* New York: Macmillan.

Kübler-Ross, E. (1981). *Living with dying.* New York: Macmillan.

Kuhn, T. S. (1962). *The structure of scientific revolutions.* Chicago: University of Chicago Press.

Kulenovic, A., & Super, D. E. (1995). The five major life roles reviewed cross-nationally. In D. E. Super & B. Sverko (Eds.), *Life roles, values, and careers: International findings of the Work Importance Study* (pp. 252–277). San Francisco: Jossey-Bass.

Kumagai, F. (1996). *Unmasking Japan today: The impact of traditional values on modern Japanese society.* Westport, CT: Greenwood Press.

Kunzmann, U., Little, T. D., & Smith, J. (2000). Is age-related stability of subjective well-being a paradox? Cross-sectional and longitudinal evidence from the Berlin aging study. *Psychology and Aging, 15,* 511–526.

Kurdek, L. A., & Schmitt, J. P. (1986). Relationship quality of gay men in closed or open relationships. *Journal of Homosexuality, 12,* 85–99.

Labouvie-Vief, G. (1982). Dynamic development and mature autonomy. *Human Development, 25,* 161–191.

Labouvie-Vief, G. (1984). Logic and self-regulation from youth to maturity. In M. L. Commons, F. A. Richards, & C. Armon (Eds.), *Beyond formal operations: Late adolescent and adult cognitive development.* New York: Praeger.

Labouvie-Vief, G. (1985). Intelligence and cognition. In J. E. Birren & K. W. Schaie (Eds.), *Handbook of the psychology of aging* (2nd ed.), New York: Van Nostrand Reinhold.

Labouvie-Vief, G., & Schell, D. A. (1982). Learning and memory in later life. In B. B. Wolman (Ed.), *Handbook of developmental psychology.* Englewood Cliffs, NJ: Prentice-Hall.

Lachman, M. E. (Ed.). (2001). Handbook on midlife development. New York: Wiley.

Lachman, M. E., & Burak, O. R. (1993). Planning and control processes across the lifespan: An overview. *International Journal of Behavioral Development, 16,* 131–143.

Lamberson, S. D., & Fischer, K. W. (1988). Optimal and functional levels in cognitive development: The individual's developmental range. *Newsletter of the International Society for the Study of Behavioral Development, 2,* 1–4.

Langer, E. J., & Rodin, J. (1976). The effects of choice and enhanced personal responsibility for the aged: A field experiment in an institutionalized setting. *Journal of Personality and Social Psychology, 34,* 191–198.

Langer, E. J. et al. (1979). Environmental determinants of memory improvement in late adulthood. *Journal of Personality and Social Psychology, 37,* 2003–2013.

Langley, L. K., & Madden, D. J. (2000). Functional neuroimaging of memory: Implications for cognitive aging. *Microscopy Research and Technique, 51,* 75–84.

Langlois, J. A., Keyl, P. M., Guralnick, J. M., Foley, D. J., Marottoli, R., & Wallace, R. B. (1997). Characteristics of older pedestrians who have difficulty crossing the street. *American Journal of Public Health, 87,* 393–397.

Larsen, M. E. (1973). Humbling cases for career counselors. *Phi Delta Kappan, 54,* 374.

Larson, E. B. (1993). Illnesses causing dementia in the very elderly. *New England Journal of Medicine, 328,* 203–205.

Larson, R., Zuzanek, J., & Mannel, R. (1985). Being alone versus being with people: Disengagement in the daily experience of older adults. *Journal of Gerontology, 40,* 375–381.

LaRue, A., Dessonville, C., & Jarvik, L. F. (1985). Aging and mental disorders. In J. E. Birren & K. W. Schaie (Eds.), *Handbook of the psychology of aging* (2nd ed.). New York: Van Nostrand Reinhold.

Lavigne-Pley, C., & Levesque, L. (1992). Reactions of the institutionalized elderly upon learning of the death of a peer. *Death Studies, 16,* 451–461.

La Voie, D. L., & Light, L. L. (1994). Adult age differences in repetition priming: A meta-analysis. *Psychology and Aging, 9,* 539–553.

Lawton, M. P., Moss, M., Kleban, M. H., Glicksman, A., & Rovine, M. (1991). A two-factor model of caregiving appraisal and well-being. *Journal of Gerontology: Psychological Sciences, 46,* P181–P189.

Lawton, M. P., Rajagopal, D., Brody, E., & Kleban, M. (1992). The dynamics of caregiving for a demented elder among black and white families. *Journal of Gerontology: Social Sciences, 47,* S156–S164.

Lazarus, R. S. (1998). Coping with aging: Individuality as a key to understanding. In J. H. Nordhus (Ed.), *Clinical geropsychology* (pp. 109–127). Washington, DC: American Psychological Association.

Lazarus, R. S. (2000). Toward better research on stress and coping. *American Psychologist, 55,* 665–673.

Lazarus, R. S., & Folkman, S. (1984). *Stress, appraisal, and coping.* New York: Springer.

Lee, I., Blair, S. N., Allison, D. B., Folsom, A. R., Harris, T. B., Manson, J. E., & Wing, R. R. (2001). Epidemiologic data on the relationships of caloric intake, energy balance, and weight gain over the life span with longevity and morbidity. *Journal of Gerontology, Special Issue, 56A,* 7–19.

Lee, G. R., Dwyer, J. W., & Coward, R. T. (1993). Gender factors in parent care: Demographic factors and same-gender preferences. *Journal of Gerontology: Social Sciences, 48,* S9–S16.

Lee, I-Min, Blair, S. N., Allison, D. B., Folsom, A. R., Harris, T. B., Manson, J. E., & Wing, R. R. (2001). Epidemiologic data on the relationships of caloric intake, energy balance, and weight gain over the life span with longevity and morbidity. *Journal of Gerontology: Biological Sciences and Medical Sciences, 56A,* 7–19.

Lehman, H. C. (1953). *Age and achievement.* Princeton, NJ: Princeton University Press.

Lehman, H. C. (1960). The age decrement in outstanding scientific creativity. *American Psychologist, 15,* 128–134.

Lemieux, R., & Hale, J. L. (2000). Intimacy, passion, and commitment among married individuals: Further testing of the Triangular Theory of Love. *Psychological Reports, 87,* 941–948.

Lerner, M. J., Somers, D. G., Reid, D., Chiriboga, D., & Tierney, M. (1991). Adult children as caregivers: Egocentric biases in judgments of sibling contributions. *The Gerontologist, 31,* 746–755.

Lerner, R. M. (1984). *On the nature of human plasticity.* New York: Cambridge University Press.

Lerner, R. M. (2001). Concepts and theories of human development. Mahwah, NJ: Erlbaum.

Letzelter, M., Jungeman, R., & Freitag, K. (1986). Swimming performance in old age. *Zeitschrift fur Gerontologie, 19,* 389–395.

Levenson, R. W., Carstensen, L. L., & Gottman, J. M. (1993). Long-term marriage: Age, gender, and satisfaction. *Psychology and Aging, 8,* 301–313.

Leventhal, E. A., Leventhal, H., Schaefer, P., & Easterling, D. (1993). Conservation of energy, uncertainty reduction and swift utilization of medical care among the elderly. *Journal of Gerontology: Psychological Sciences, 48,* P78–P86.

Leventhal, H., Rabin, C., Leventhal, E. A., & Burns, E. (2001). Health, behavior, and aging. In J. E. Birren & K. W. Schaie (Eds.), *Handbook of the psychology of aging* (5th ed.). San Diego: Academic Press.

Levin, J. S., Chatters, L. M., & Taylor, R. J. (1995). Religious effects on health status and life satisfaction among Black Americans. *Journal of Gerontology: Social Sciences, 50B,* S154–S163.

Levin, J. S., Markides, K. S., & Ray, L. A. (1996). Religious attendance and psychological well-being in Mexican Americans: A panel analysis of three generations data. *The Gerontologist, 36,* 454–463.

Levine, D. (1995). Choosing a nursing home: *American Health,* June, 82–84.

Levinson, D. J. (1978). *The seasons of a man's life.* New York: Knopf.

Levinson, D. J. (1986). A conception of adult development. *American Psychologist, 41,* 3–13.

Levinson, D. J. (1996). *Seasons of a woman's life.* New York: Alfred Knopf.

Lichstein, K. L., Durrence, H. H., Bayen, U. J., & Riedel, B. W. (2001). Primary versus secondary insomnia in older adults: Subjective sleep and daytime functioning. *Psychology and Aging, 16,* 264–271.

Lichtenberg, P. A., & Strzepek, D. M. (1990). Assessments of institutionalized dementia patients' competencies to

participate in intimate relationships. *The Gerontologist, 30,* 117–120.

Lieberman, M. A., & Peskin, H. (1992). Adult life crises. In J. E. Birren, R. B. Sloane, & G. D. Cohen (Eds.), *Handbook of mental health and aging* (2nd ed., pp.119–143). San Diego: Academic Press.

Liebman, B. (1995). Exercise: Use it or lose it. *Nutrition Health Letter, 22,* 9–17. Center for Science in the Public Interest: Washington, DC.

Lifson, A. (1988). Do alternative models for transmission of HIV exist? *Journal of the American Medical Association, 259,* 1353–1356.

Light, E., Niederehe, G., & Lebowitz, B. (Eds.). (1994). *Stress effects on family caregivers of Alzheimer's patients: Research and interventions.* New York: Springer.

Lillard, L., Rogowski, J., & Kington, R. (1997). Long-term determinants of patterns of health insurance coverage in the Medicare population. *The Gerontologist, 37,* 314–323.

Lincourt, A. E., Hoyer, W. J., & Cerella, J. (1997, November). *Aging and the development of instance-based automaticity.* Psychonomic Society meetings, Philadelphia, PA.

Lindenberger, U., & Baltes, P. B. (1994). Sensory functioning and intelligence in old age: A strong connection. *Psychology and Aging, 9,* 339–355.

Lindenberger, U., Kliegl, R., & Baltes, P. B. (1992). Professional expertise does not eliminate age differences in imagery-based memory performance during adulthood. *Psychology and Aging, 7,* 585–593.

Lindenberger, U., Mayr, U., & Kliegl, R. (1993). Speed and intelligence in old age. *Psychology and Aging, 8,* 207–220.

Liska, D., Obermaier, K., Lyons, B., & Long, P. (1995). *Medicaid expenditures and beneficiaries: National and state profiles and trends, 1984–1993.* Washington, DC: Kaiser Commission on the Future of Medicaid.

Loevinger, J. (1976). *Ego development.* San Francisco: Jossey-Bass.

Loftus, E. F., & Ketcham, K. (1994). *The myth of repressed memories.* New York: St. Martin's Press.

Lonky, E., Kaus, C., & Roodin, P. A. (1984). Life experience and mode of coping: Relation to moral judgment in adulthood. *Developmental Psychology, 20,* 1159–1167.

Lopata, H. Z. (1979). *Widowhood in an American city.* Cambridge, MA: Schenkman.

Lopata, H. Z. (1987b). *Widows: The Middle East, Asia, and the Pacific.* Durham, NC: Duke University Press.

Lopata, H. Z. (1994). *Circles and settings.* Albany: State University of New York Press.

Lopez-Bushnell, F. K., Tyra, P. A., & Futrell, M. (1992). Alcoholism and the Hispanic older adult. Special Issue: Hispanic aged mental health. *Clinical Gerontologist, 11* (3-4), 123–130.

Loscocco, K. (2000). Age integration as a solution to work-family conflict. *The Gerontologist, 40* (3), 292–300.

Loveridge-Sanonmatsu, J. (1994, April). *Personal communication.* Oswego, NY: SUNY College at Oswego, Department of Communication.

Lowenthal, M., Thurnher, M., & Chiriboga, D. (1975). *Four stages of life: A comparative study of women and men facing transitions.* San Francisco: Jossey-Bass.

Ludwig, A. M. (1996). Mental disturbance and creative achievement. *Harvard Mental Health Letter,* March 4–5.

Lund, D. A. (2001). *Men coping with grief.* Amityville, NY: Baywood.

Lustig, C., May, C. P., & Hasher, L. (2001). Working memory span and the role of proactive interference. *Journal of Experimental Psychology: General, 130,* 199–207.

Lynn, R. and Martin, T. (1997). Gender differences in extraversion, neuroticism, and psychoticism in 37 nations. *Journal of Social Psychology, 137,* 369–373.

Lyons, N. (1983). Two perspectives: On self, relationships, and morality. *Harvard Educational Review, 53,* 125–145.

Lyubomirsky, S. (2001). Why are some people happier than others? The role of cognitive and motivational processes in well-being. *American Psychologist, 56,* 239–249.

Mace, N., & Rabins, P. (1991). *The 36 hour day.* Baltimore, MD: Johns Hopkins University Press.

Mackey, R. A., & O'Brien, B. A. (1999). Adaptation in lasting marriages. *Families in Society, 80,* 587–596.

Madden, D. J. (2000). Speed and timing of behavioral processes. In J. E. Birren & K. W. Schaie (Eds.), *Handbook of the psychology of aging* (5th ed., pp. 288–312). San Diego: Academic Press.

Maddi, S. (1986). *The great stress-illness controversy.* Paper presented at the meeting of the American Psychological Association, Washington, DC.

Majerovitz, S. D. (1995). Role of family adaptability in the psychological adjustment of spouse caregivers to patients with dementia. *Psychology and Aging, 10,* 447–557.

Manton, K. G., Corder, L. S., & Stallard, E. (1993). Estimates of change in chronic disability and institutional incidence and prevalence rates in the U.S. elderly population from the 1982, 1984, and 1989 National Long-Term Care Survey. *Journal of Gerontology: Social Sciences, 48,* S153–S166.

Manton, K. G., & Gu, X. (2001). Changes in the prevalence of chronic disability in the United States black and non-black population above age 65 from 1982 to 1999. *Proceedings of the National Academy of Sciences USA, 98,* 6354–6359.

Marcoen, A. (1994). Spirituality and personal well-being in old age. *Aging and Society, 14,* 521–536.

Marottoli, R. A., Ostfeld, A. M., Merrill, S. S., Perlman, G. D., Foley, D. J., & Cooney, L. M. (1993). Driving cessation and changes in mileage drivers among elderly individuals. *Journal of Gerontology: Social Sciences, 48,* S255–S260.

Marsiglio, W., & Donnelly, D. (1991). Sexual relations in later life: A national survey of married persons. *Journal of Gerontology: Social Sciences, 46,* S338–S344.

Marsiske, M., Klumb, P., & Baltes, M. M. (1997). Everyday activity patterns and sensory functioning in old age. *Psychology and Aging, 12,* 444–457.

Martin, R., Leach, D. J., Norman, P., and Silvester, J. (2000). The role of attributions in psychological reactions to job relocation. *Work and Stress, Special Issue, 14* (4), 347–361.

Martin, T. L. and Doka, K. J. (2000). *Men don't cry . . . women do: Transcending gender stereotypes of grief.* Philadelphia: Brunner/Mazel.

Martino-Saltzman, D., Blasch, B. B., Morris, R. D., & McNeal, L. W. (1992). Travel behavior of nursing home residents perceived as wanderers and nonwanderers. *The Gerontologist, 31,* 666–672.

Marx, J. (1996). Searching for drugs that combat Alzheimer's disease. *Science, 273,* 50–53.

Mason, S. E., & Smith, A. D. (1977). Imagery and the aged. *Experimental Aging Research, 3,* 17–32.

Masoro, E. J. (1984). Food restriction in the aging process. *Journal of the American Geriatrics Society, 32,* 296–300.

Massimini, F., & Delle Fave, A. (2000). Individual development in a biocultural perspective. *American Psychologist, 55,* 24–33.

Masters, H. H., & Johnson, V. E. (1970). *Human sexual inadequacy.* Boston: Little, Brown.

Masters, H. H., Johnson, V. E., & Kolodny, R. C. (1991). *Human sexuality.* Boston: Little, Brown.

Masunaga, H., & Horn, J. L. (2001). Expertise and age-related changes in the components of intelligence. *Psychology and Aging, 16,* 293–311.

Matire, L. M., Stephens, M. A. P., and Atienza, A. A. (1997). The interplay of work and caregiving: Relationships between role satisfaction, role involvement, and well-being. *Journals of Gerontology: Social Sciences, 52B,* S279–S289.

Matthews, K. A., Wing, R. R., Kuller, L. H., Meilahn, E. N., & Owens, J. E. (2000). Menopause as a turning point in midlife. In S. B. Manuck, R. Jennings, B. Rabin, & A. Baum (Eds.), *Behavior, health, and aging.* Mahwah, NJ: Erlbaum.

Matthews, M. (1999). Assisted living/residential care. In J. R. Pratt (Ed.), *Long-term care: Managing across the continuum* (pp. 109–143). Gaithersburg, MD: Aspen.

Matthias, R. E., Lubben, J. E., Atchison, K. A., & Schweitzer, S. O. (1997). Sexual activity and satisfaction among very old adults: Results from a community-dwelling Medicare population survey. *The Gerontologist, 37,* 6–14.

Maurer, T., & Tarulli, B. (1994). Perceived environment, perceived outcome, and person variables in relationship to voluntary development activity by employees. *Journal of Applied Psychology, 79,* 3–14.

Mayr, U. (2001). Age differences in the selection of mental sets: The role of inhibition, stimulus ambiguity, and response-set overlap. *Psychology and Aging, 16,* 96–109.

McAdams, D. P. (1995). What do we know when we know a person? *Journal of Personality, 63,* 365–396.

McAdams, D. P., & Bowman, P. J. (2001). Narrating life's turning points: Redemption and contamination. In D. P. McAdams & R. Josselson (Eds.), *Turns in the road: Narrative studies of lives in transition,* pp. 3–34. Washington, DC: American Psychological Association.

McAdams, D. P., Hart, H. M., & Maruna, S. (1998). The anatomy of generativity. In D. P. McAdams & E. de St. Aubin (Eds.), *Generativity and adult development: How and why we care about the next generation* (pp. 7–44). Washington, DC: American Psychological Association.

McAuley, E., Lox, L., & Duncan, T. E. (1993). Long-term maintenance of exercise, self-efficacy, and physiological change in older adults. *Journal of Gerontology: Psychological Sciences, 48,* P218–P224.

McCain, N. L., & Gramling, L. F. (1992). Living with dying: Coping with HIV disease. *Issues in Mental Health Nursing, 13,* 271–284.

McCartney, J., Izemen, H., Rogers, D., & Cohen, N. (1987). Sexuality in the institutionalized elderly. *Journal of the American Geriatrics Society, 35,* 331–333.

McCay, C. M., & Crowell, M. F. (1934). Prolonging the life span. *Scientific Monthly, 39,* 405–414.

McCrae, R. R., Arenberg, D., & Costa, P. T., Jr. (1987). Declines in divergent thinking with age: Cross-sectional, longitudinal, and cross-sequential analyses. *Psychology and Aging, 2,* 130–137.

McCrae, R. R., Costa, P. T., Jr., de Lima, M. P., Simoes, A., Ostendorf, F., Angleitner, A., Marusic, I., Bratko, D., Caprara, G. V., Barbaranelli, C., Chae, J., & Piedmont, R. I. (1999). Age differences in personality across the adult life span: Parallels in five cultures. *Developmental Psychology, 35,* 466–477.

McDowd, J. M., & Birren, J. E. (1990). Attention and aging. In J. E. Birren & K. W. Schaie (Eds.), *Handbook of the psychology of aging* (3rd ed., pp. 222–233). San Diego: Academic Press.

McDowd, J. M., & Craik, F. I. M. (1988). Effects of aging and task difficulty on divided attention performance. *Journal of Experimental Psychology: Human Perception and Performance, 14,* 267–280.

McDowd, J., & Shaw, R. J. (2000). Attention and aging: A functional perspective. In F. I. M. Craik & T. A. Salthouse (Eds.), *The handbook of aging and cognition* (pp. 221–292). Mahwah, NJ: Erlbaum.

McFadden, S. H. (1996). Religion, spirituality, and aging. In J. E. Birren & K. W. Schaie (Eds.), *Handbook of the psychology of aging* (4th ed., pp. 162–177). San Diego: Academic Press.

McGowin, D. F. (1993). *Living in the labyrinth: A personal journey through Alzheimer's disease.* New York: Delacorte Press.

McIlroy, W. E., & Maki, B. E. (1996). Age-related charges in compensatory stepping in response to unpredictable perturbations. *Journal of Gerontology: Medical Sciences, 51A,* 289–296.

McIntosh, J. L. (1995). Suicide prevention in the elderly (65–99). *Suicide and Life-Threatening Behavior, 25,* 180–192.

McIntosh, J. L. (2001). *U.S.A. suicide, 1998 official final statistics.* American Association of Suicidology. http://www.iusb.edu/~jmcintos/SuicideStats.html

McIntosh, J. L., Santos, J. F., Hubbard, R. W., & Overholser, J. C. (1994). *Elder suicide: Research, theory, and treatment.* Washington, DC: American Psychological Association.

McIntyre, J. S., & Craik, F. I. M. (1987). Age differences in memory for item and source information. *Canadian Journal of Psychology, 41,* 175–192.

McKee, R. D., & Squire, L. R. (1993). On the development of declarative memory. *Journal of Experimental Psychology: Learning, Memory, and Cognition, 19,* 397–404.

McKibben, B. (1998). *Maybe one: A personal and environmental argument for single-child families.* New York: Simon & Schuster.

McLay, P. (1989). The Parkinsonian and driving. *International Disability Studies, 11,* 50–51.

McNeal, M. G., Zareparsi, S, Camicioli, R., Dame, A., Howieson, D., Quinn, J., Ball, M., Kaye, J., & Payami, H. (2001). Predictors of healthy brain aging. *Journal of Gerontology: Biological Sciences and Medical Sciences, 56,* B294–B301.

McNeil, J. K., LeBlanc, E. M., & Joyner, M. (1991). The effects of exercise on depressive symptoms in the moderately depressed elderly. *Psychology and Aging, 6,* 487–488.

Meeks, S., Murrell, S. A., & Mehl, R. C. (2000). Longitudinal relationships between depressive symptoms and health in normal older and middle-aged adults. *Psychology and Aging, 15,* 100–109.

Meinz, E. J. (2000). Experience-based attenuation of age-related differences in music cognition tasks. *Psychology and Aging, 15,* 297–312.

Melvin, D., & Lukeman, D. (2000). Bereavement: A framework for those working with children. *Clinical Child Psychology and Psychiatry, 54* (4), 521–539.

Menon, A. S., Gruber-Baldini, A. L., Hebel, J. R., Kaup, B., Loreck, D., Itkin-Zimmerman, S., Burton, L., German, P., & Magaziner, J. (2001). Relationship between aggressive behaviors and depression among nursing home residents with dementia. *International Journal of Geriatric Psychiatry, 16,* 139–146.

Meyer, B. J. F., Russo, C., & Talbot, A. (1995). Discourse comprehension and problem-solving decisions about the treatment of breast cancer by women across the life-span. *Psychology and Aging, 10,* 84–103.

Miech, R. A., Breitner, J. C., Zandi, P. P., Khachaturian, A. S., Anthony, J. C., Mayer, L. (2002). Incidence of AD may decline in the early 90s for men, later for women: The Cache County study. *Neurology, 58,* 209–218.

Miles, S. H., & Irvine, P. (1992). Deaths caused by physical restraints. *The Gerontologist, 32* (6), 762–766.

Miller, B., Campbell, R. T., Farran, C. J., Kaufman, J. E., & Davis, L. (1995). Race, control, mastery, and caregiver distress. *Journal of Gerontology, 50B,* S374–S382.

Miller, B. (1989). Adult children's perception of caregiver stress and satisfaction. *Journal of Applied Gerontology, 8,* 275–293.

Miller, B., & Lawton, M. P. (1997). Introduction: Finding balance in caregiver research. *The Gerontologist, 37,* 216–217.

Miller, T. Q., Markides, K. S., and Black, S. A. (1997). The factor structure of the CES-D in two surveys of elderly Mexican Americans. *Journals of Gerontology: Psychological Sciences and Social Sciences, 52,* S259–S269.

Mischel, W., Cantor, N., & Feldman, S. (1996). Principles of self-regulation: The nature of willpower and self-control. In E. T. Higgins & A. W. Kruglanski (Eds.), *Social psychology: Handbook of basic principles* (pp. 329–360). New York: Guilford Press.

Mischel, W., & Shoda, Y. (1995). A cognitive-affective system theory of personality: Reconceptualizing situations, dispositions, dynamics, and invariance in personality structure. *Psychological Review, 102,* 246–268.

Mishra, S. (1992). Leisure activities and life satisfaction in old age: A case study of retired government employees living in urban areas. *Activities, Adaptation and Aging, 16*, 7–26.

Mitchell, J. M., & Kemp, B. J. (2000). Quality of life in assisted living homes: A multidimensional analysis. *Journal of Gerontology, 55B* (2), P117–P127.

Mittleman, M. S., Ferris, S. H., Shulman, E., Steinberg, G., Ambinder, A., Mackell, J. A., & Cohen, J. (1995). A comprehensive support program: Effect on depression in spouse-care givers of AD patients. *The Gerontologist, 35*, 729–802.

Molinari, V. (Ed.), (2000). *Professional psychology in long-term care: A comprehensive guide.* N.Y., N.Y. Hatherleigh Press.

Monmaney, T., & MacIver (1995). Marty's gift. *American Health, 14*, 64–69.

Moody, R. A. (1975). *Life after life.* Covington, GA: Mockingbird Books.

Morales, A., Heaton, J. P., & Carson, CC. (2000). *Andropause: A misnomer for a true clinical entity. Journal of Urology, 163*, 705–712.

Morales, P. (1999). The impact of cultural differences in psychotherapy with older clients: Sensitive issues and strategies. In M. Duffy (Ed.), *Handbook of counseling and psychotherapy with older adults,* pp. 132–153. John Wiley, New York.

Mor-Barak, M. E., Scharlach, A. E., Birba, L., & Sokolov, J. (1992). Employment, social networks, and health in the retirement years. *International Journal of Aging and Human Development, 35*, 145–159.

Morgan, D. G. (1992). Neurochemical changes with aging: Predisposition toward age-related mental disorders. In J. E. Birren, R. B. Sloane, & G. D. Cohen (Eds.), *Handbook of mental health and aging* (2nd ed., pp. 175–199). San Diego: Academic Press.

Morgan, D. L., Schuster, T. L., & Butler, E. W. (1991). Role reversals in the exchange of social support. *Journal of Gerontology: Social Sciences, 46*, S278–S287.

Morley, J. E. (2000). The aging athlete. *Journal of Gerontology, 55A*, M627–M629.

Morrison, J. H., & Hof, P. R. (1997). Life and death of neurons in the aging brain. *Science, 278*, 412–419.

Morros, M., Pushkar, D., & Reis, M. (1998). A study of current, former, and new elderly volunteers: A comparison of developmental and trait models of personality. *Journal of Adult Development, 5* (October 4), 219–230.

Morrow, D. G., Menard, W. F., Stine-Morrow, E. A., Teller, T., & Bryant, D. (2001). The influence of expertise and task factors on age differences in pilot communication. *Psychology and Aging, 16*, 31–46.

Moscovitch, M. M. (1994). Memory and working with memory: Evaluation of a component process model and comparison with other models. In D. L. Schacter & E. Tulving (Eds.), *Memory systems 1994.* Cambridge, MA: MIT Press.

Moscovitch, M., & Winocur, G. (1992). The neuropsychology of memory and aging. In F. I. M. Craik & T. A. Salthouse (Eds.), *The handbook of aging and cognition* (pp. 315–372). Hillsdale, NJ: Erlbaum.

Moskowitz, J. T., Acree, M., & Folkman, S. (1998). *The association of positive emotion, negative emotion, and clinical depression in a longitudinal study of caregiving partners of men with AIDS.* Unpublished data. Cited in S. Folkman and J. J. Moskowitz (2000). Positive affect and the other side of coping. *American Psychologist, 55* (6), 647–654.

Moss, M. S., & Moss, S. Z. (1995). Death and bereavement. In R. Blieszner & V. H. Bedford (Eds.), *Handbook of aging and the family* (pp. 422–439). Westport, CT: Greenwood Press.

Moss, M. S., Lawton, M. P., Kleban, M. H., & Duhamel, L. (1993). Time use of caregivers of impaired elders before and after institutionalization. *Journal of Gerontology: Social Sciences, 48*, S102–S111.

Mrazek, P. J. and Haggerty, R. J. (eds.). (1994). *Reducing risks for mental disorders: Frontiers for preventive intervention research.* Washington, D. C.: National Academy Press.

Mui, A. C. (1992). Caregiver strain among Black and White daughter caregivers: A role theory perspective. *The Gerontologist, 32*, 203–212.

Mui, A. C. (1998). Living alone and depression among older Chinese immigrants. *Journal of Gerontological Social Work, 30* (3–4), 147–166.

Mulsant, B. H., Ganguli, M., & Seaberg, E. C. (1997). The relationship between self-rated health and depressive symptoms in an epidemiologic sample of community-dwelling older adults. *Journal of the American Geriatrics Society, 45*, 954–958.

Multi-Society Task Force on PVS. (1994a). Medical aspects of the persistent vegetative state. *New England Journal of Medicine, 330*, 1499–1508.

Multi-Society Task Force on PVS (1994b). Medical aspects of the persistent vegetative state. *New England Journal of Medicine, 330*, 1572–1579.

Mumford, M. D., & Gustafson, S. B. (1988). Creativity syndrome: Integration, application, and innovation. *Psychological Bulletin, 103*, 27–43.

Musick, M. A., Herzog, A. R., & House, J. S. (1999). Volunteering and mortality among older adults: Findings from a national sample. *Journal of Gerontology, 54*, S173–S180.

Mutchler, J. E., & Brallier, S. (1999). English-language proficiency among older Hispanics in the United States. *The Gerontologist, 39*, 310–319.

Mutchler, J. E., Burr, J. A., Pienta, & Massagli, M. P. (1997). Pathways to labor exit: Work transitions and work instability. *Journal of Gerontology: Social Sciences, 52B*, S4–S12.

Myers, J. E. (1999). Adjusting to role loss and leisure in later life. In M. Duffy (Ed.), *Handbook of counseling and psychotherapy with older adults,* p. 41–56. New York: John Wiley.

Myers, D. G. (2000). The funds, friends, and faith of happy people. *American Psychologist, 55*, 56–67.

Myers, J. E., & Shelton, B. (1987). Abuse and older persons: Issues and implications for counselors. *Journal of Counseling and Development, 65*, 376–380.

Namazi, K. H. (1994). Research brief: Management of wandering behavior. *Respite Report: Partners in Caregiving: The Dementia Services Program, 6,* 6.

National Academy on Aging. (1995). Facts on Medicare: Hospital insurance and supplementary medical insurance. *Gerontology News,* October, 9–10.

National Academy on Aging. (1996). Facts on social security: The old age and survivors trust fund. *Gerontology News,* July, 5–6.

National Academy on an Aging Society. (2000a). Who are young retirees and older workers? *Data Profiles: Young retirees and older workers, 2000.* June (#1), Washington, DC: NAAS.

National Academy on an Aging Society. (2000b). How financially secure are young and retirees and older workers? *Data Profiles: Young retirees and older workers, 2000,* August (#2), Washington, DC: NAAS.

National Academy on an Aging Society. (2000c). How healthy are young retirees and older workers? *Data Profiles: Young retirees and older workers, 2000,* October (#3), Washington, DC: NAAS.

National Academy on an Aging Society. (2000d). Do young retirees and older workers differ by race? *Data Profiles: Young retirees and older workers, 2000,* December (#4), Washington, DC: NAAS.

National Center for Health Statistics. (1987a). *Characteristics of the populations below the poverty level.* (Current Population Reports, Series P–60, No. 152). Washington, DC: U.S. Government Printing Office.

National Center for Health Statistics. (2001). Trends in causes of death among the elderly. *Aging Trends, 1.* *http://www.cdc/gov/nchs/releses/01facts/olderame.htm*

National Center for Injury Prevention and Control. (2001). *Center for disease control: Suicide in the United States.* http://www.cdc.gov/ncipc/factsheets/suifacts.htm

National Center for Injury Prevention and Control. (2001a). *Falls and hip fractures among older adults.* http://www.cdc.gov/ncipc/factsheets/falls.htm

National Center for Injury Prevention and Control (2001b). Falls in nursing homes. http://www.cdc.gov/ncipc/factsheets/falls.htm

National Funeral Directors Association. (1997). *Funeral services and expenses.* Office of Public Affairs. Northbrook, Illinois.

National Funeral Directors Association. (2001a). *Consumer resources: U.S. cremation statistics.* http://www.nfda.org/resources/caregiving/cremation.html

National Funeral Directors Association. (2001b). *Consumer resources: NFDA caregiving information, suicide.* http://www.ndfda.org/resources/caregiving/suicide.html

National Hospice and Palliative Care Organization. (2001). *Facts and figures on hospice care in America,* January, pp. 1–2.

National Institute of Alcohol Abuse and Alcoholism. (1998). *Alcohol Alert, 40* (April).

National Institute on Aging. (2001). *AgePage: Aging and alcohol abuse.* www.aoa.dhhs.gov/aoa/PAGES/AGEPAGES/alcohol.html

National Institute of Health. (1988). *Health benefits of pets.* September. A symposium.

National Institute of Mental Health. (2001a). *Suicide facts: Completed suicides.* http://www.nimh.nih.gov/research/suifact.htm

National Institute of Mental Health. (2001b). *Frequently asked questions about suicide.* http://www.nimh.nih.gov/research/suicidefaq.cfm

National Mental Health Association. (2001). *Suicide: General information.* http://www.nmha.org.infoctr/factsheets/81.cfm

National Service—see Corporation for National and Community Service above.

National Service Corps. (2001). *Fact Sheet on Service-Learning and National Service.* www.nationalservice.org

National Vital Statistics. (1999). Suicide. *National Vital Statistics Report, 47* (19), June 30.

Neisser, U. Boodoo, G., Bouchard, T. J., Boykin, A. W., Brody, N., Ceci, S. J., Halpern, D. F., Loehlin, J. C., Perloff, R., Sternberg, R. J., & Urbina, S. (1996). Intelligence: Knowns and unknowns. *American Psychologist, 51,* 77–101.

Nelson, H. W. (1995). Long-term care volunteer roles on trial: Ombudsman effectiveness revisited. *Journal of Gerontological Social Work, 23* (34), 25–46.

Nelson, K. (1993). The psychological and social origins of autobiographical memory. *Psychological Science, 4,* 7–13.

Nesselroade, J. R. (1991). The warp and the woof of the developmental fabric. In R. Downs, L. Liben, & D. Palermo (Eds.), *Visions of aesthetics, the environment, and development: The legacy of Joachim F. Wohlwill* (pp. 213–240). Hillsdale, NJ: Erlbaum.

Neugarten, B. L. (1968). *Personality in middle and late life* (2nd ed.). New York: Atherton Press.

Neugarten, B. L. (1973). Personality change in late life: A developmental perspective. In C. Eisdorfer & M. P. Lawton (Eds.), *The psychology of adult development and aging.* Washington, DC: American Psychological Association.

Neugarten, B. L. (1980a). Act your age: Must everything be a midlife crisis? In *Annual editions: Human development, 1980/1981* (pp. 289–290). Guilford, CT: Dushkin Publishers.

Neugarten, B. L. (1980b, February). Must everything be a midlife crisis? *Prime Time.*

Neugarten, B. L. (1989). Policy issues for an aging society. *The psychology of aging.* Washington, DC: American Psychological Association.

Neugarten, B. L., & Datan, N. (1973). Sociological perspectives on the life cycle. In P. B. Baltes & K. W. Schaie (Eds.), *Life-span developmental psychology.* New York: Academic Press.

Neugarten, B. L., & Neugarten, D. A. (1987). The changing meanings of age. *Psychology Today, 21,* 29–33.

Neugarten, B. L., & Weinstein, K. K. (1984). The changing American grandparent. *Journal of Marriage and the Family, 26,* 199–204.

Neugebauer, R., Rabkin, J. G., & Williams, J. B. (1992). Bereavement reactions among homosexual men experiencing multiple losses in the AIDS epidemic. *American Journal of Psychiatry, 149* (10), 1374–1379.

Neulinger, J. (1981). *The psychology of leisure.* Springfield, IL: Charles C Thomas.

Neumark, Y. D., Van Etten, M. L., & Anthony, J. C. (2000). Alcohol dependence and death: Survival analysis of the Baltimore ECA sample from 1981 to 1995. *Substance Use and Abuse, 35,* 533–549.

New York State Department of Health. (2001). *Do-not-resuscitate orders: A guide for patients and families.* Albany, NY: New York State Department of Health.

Newman, S. (2001). A description and explanation of developmental theories explaining the characteristics of children, youth, and older adults: Tools for intergenerational practitioners. Paper presented at symposium: The evolution of intergenerational studies: An emerging academic field of theory and practice. San Jose, Calif., February, 22–25.

Newmann, J. P., Engel, R., & Jensen, J. E. (1991). Age differences in depressive symptom experiences. *Journal of Gerontology, 46* (5), P224–P235.

Newsom, J. T., & Shulz, R. (1996). Social support as a mediator in the relation between functional status and quality of life in older adults. *Psychology and Aging, 11,* 34–44.

Nilles, J. M. (1998). *Managing telework: Strategies for managing the virtual workforce.* New York, John Wiley.

Nilsson, L. G. (2000). Can genes teach us anything about memory? In E. Tulving (Ed.), *Memory, consciousness, and the brain.* (pp. 28–39). Philadelphia: Psychology Press.

Norem, J. K. (2001a). A very full glass: Adding complexity to our thinking about the implications and applications of optimism and pessimism research. In E. C. Chang (Ed.), *Optimism and pessimism: Implications for theory, research, and practice* (pp. 347–367). Washington, DC: American Psychological Association.

Norem, J. K. (2001b). Defensive pessimism, optimism, and pessimism. In E. C. Chang (Ed.), *Optimism and pessimism: Implications for theory, research, and practice* (pp. 77–100). Washington, DC: American Psychological Association.

Northrup, C. (2001). *The wisdom of menopause: Creating physical and emotional health and healing during the change.* New York: Bantam Books.

Nyberg, L., Cabeza, R., & Tulving, E. (1996). PET studies of encoding and retrieval: The HERA Model. *Psychonomic Bulletin & Review, 3,* 135–148.

O'Bryant, S. L., & Hansson, R. O. (1995). Widowhood. In R. Blieszner & V. H. Bedford (Eds.), *Handbook of aging and the family* (pp. 440–458). Westport, CT: Greenwood Press.

O'Connor, B. P., & Vallerand, R. J. (1998). Psychological adjustment variables as predictors of mortality among nursing home residents. *Psychology and Aging, 13,* 368–374.

O'Connor, P. (1993). Same gender and cross-gender friendships among the frail elderly. *The Gerontologist, 33,* 24–30.

Okun, M. A., Barr, A., & Herzog. A R. (1998). Motivation to volunteer by older adults: A test of competing measurement models. *Psychology and Aging, 13,* 608–621.

Okun, B. F., & Rappaport, L. J. (1980). *Working with other families: An introduction to family therapy.* North Scituate, MA: Duxbury.

Olshansky, S. J., Carnes, B. A., & Butler, R. N. (2001). If humans were built to last. *Scientific American, 284,* 50–55.

Olshansky, S. J., Carnes, B. A., & Cassel, C. K. (1993). The aging of the human species. *Scientific American, 268,* 46–52.

Olshansky, S. J., Carnes, B. A., & Desesquelles, A. (2001). Demography: Prospects for human longevity. *Science, 291,* 1491–1492.

Oman, D., Thoresen, C. E., & McMahon, K. (1999). Volunteerism and mortality among community-dwelling elderly. *Journal of Health Psychology, 4* (3), 301–316.

Orgel, L. E. (1973). Aging of clones of mammalian cells. *Nature, 243,* 441–445.

Ormel, J., Kempen, G. I. J. M., Deeg, D. J. H., Brilman, E. I., Van Sonderen, E., & Relyveld, J. (1998). Functioning, well-being, and health perception in late middle-aged and older people: Comparing the effects of depressive symptoms and chronic medical conditions. *Journal of the American Geriatrics Society, 46,* 39–48.

Ornstein, R., & Thompson, R. F. (1984). *The amazing brain.* Boston: Houghton Mifflin.

Ornstein, S., & Isabella, L. (1990). Age vs. stage models of career attitudes of women: A partial replication and extension. *Journal of Vocational Behavior, 36,* 1–19.

Ory, M. G., Hoffman, R. R., Yee, J. L., Tennstedt, S., & Schulz, R. (1999). Prevalence and impact of caregiving: A detailed comparison between dementia and nondementia caregivers. *The Gerontologist, 39,* 177–185.

Oser, F. K. (1991). The development of religious judgment. *The Gerontologist, 29,* 457–464.

Ostwald, S. K., Hepburn, K. W., Caron, W., Burns, T., and Mantell, R. (1999). Reducing caregiving burden: A randomized psychosocial intervention for caregivers of persons with dementia. *The Gerontologist, 39,* 299–309.

Over, R. (1989). Age and scholar impact. *Psychology and Aging, 4,* 222–225.

Owens, W. A., Jr. (1966). Age and mental abilities: A second adult follow-up. *Journal of Educational Psychology, 51,* 311–325.

Oxman, T. W., & Hull, J. G. (2001). Social support and treatment response in older depressed primary care patients. *Journal of Gerontology, 56B* (1), P35–P45.

Padgett, D. K. (1995). Concluding remarks and suggestions for research and service delivery. In D. K. Padgett (Ed.), *Handbook of ethnicity, aging, and mental health* (pp. 304–319). Westport, CT: Greenwood Press.

Padgett, D. K., Patrick, C., Burns, B. J., & Schlesinger, H. J. (1995). Use of mental health services by black and white elderly. In D. K. Padgett (Eds.), *Handbook of ethnicity, aging, and mental health* (pp. 145–164). Westport, CT: Greenwood Press.

Palmore, E. B. (1990). *Ageism: Negative and positive.* NY: Springer.

Palmore, E. B., & Maeda, D. (1985). *The honorable elders revisited: A revised cross-cultural analysis of aging in Japan.* Durham, NC: Duke University Press.

Palmore, E. B., Burchett, B. M., Fillenbaum, G. C., George, L. K., & Wallman, L. M. (1985). *Retirement: Causes and consequences.* New York: Springer.

Paniagua, F. A. (1994). *Assessing and treating culturally diverse clients: A practical guide.* London: Sage.

Pargament, K. I. (1997). *Psychology of religion and coping: Theory, research, and practice.* New York: Guilford Press.

Parkes, C. M. (1993). Bereavement as a psychosocial transition: Processes of adaptation to change. In M. S. Stroebe, W. Stroebe, and R. O. Hansson (Eds.), *Handbook of bereavement: Theory, research, and intervention* (pp. 91–101). New York: Cambridge University Press.

Parkin, A. J., & Walter, B. M. (1992). Recollective experience, normal aging, and frontal dysfunction. *Psychology and Aging, 7,* 290–298.

Parmelee, P. A., Katz, I. R., & Lawton, M. P. (1991). The relation of pain to depression among institutionalized aged. *Journal of Gerontology: Psychological Sciences, 46,* P15–P21.

Pasupathi, M., Carstensen, L. L., Levenson, R. W., & Gottman, J. M. (1999). Responsive listening in long-married couples. *Journal of Nonverbal Behavior, 23,* 173–193.

Pattison, E. M. (1977). *The experience of dying.* Englewood Cliffs, NJ: Prentice-Hall.

Pearlin, L. I., Mullan, J. T., Semple, S. J., & Skaff, M. M. (1990). Caregiving and the stress process: An overview of concepts and their measures. *The Gerontologist, 30,* 583–594.

Pearson, J. L., Cowan, P. A., Cowan, C. P. and Cohn, D. A. (1993). Adult attachment and adult child–older parent relationships. *American Journal of Orthopsychiatry, 63,* 606–613.

Pennebaker, J. W. (1999). The effects of traumatic disclosure on physical and mental health: The values of writing and talking about upsetting events. *International Journal of Emergency Mental Health (1),* 9–18.

Pepper, L. G. (1976). Patterns of leisure and adjustment to retirement. *The Gerontologist, 16,* 441–446.

Perkins, K. (1992). Psychosocial implications of women and retirement. *Social Work, 37,* 526–532.

Perlmutter, M. (1986). A life-span view of memory. In P. B. Baltes, D. Featherman, & R. Lerner (Eds.), *Advances in life-span development and behavior* (Vol. 7). Hillsdale, NJ: Erlbaum.

Perrone, K. M., & Worthington, E. L. (2001). Factors influencing ratings of marital quality by individuals within dual-career marriages: A conceptual model. *Journal of Counseling Psychology, 48,* 3–9.

Perry, W. B. (1968). *Forms of intellectual and ethical development in the college years: A scheme.* New York: Holt, Rinehart & Winston.

Persson, D. (1993). The elderly driver deciding when to stop. *The Gerontologist, 33,* 88–91.

Peters, K. (1996). Carrier hopes fancy new fitness center pumps up financial wellness. *Syracuse Post-Standard,* September 29, p. D5.

Peters-Davis, N. D., Moss, M. S., & Pruchno, R. A. (1999). Children-in-law in caregiving families. *The Gerontologist, 39* (1), 66–75.

Peterson, C. (2000). The future of optimism. *American Psychologist, 55,* 45–55.

Phillips, C. D., Chu, C. W., Morris, J. N, and Hawes, C. (1993). Effects of cognitive impairment on the reliability of geriatric assessments in nursing homes. *Journal of American Geriatrics Society, 41,* 136–142.

Piaget, J. (1954). *The construction of reality in the child.* New York: Basic Books.

Piaget, J. (1970). Piaget's theory. In P. H. Mussen (Ed.), *Carmichael's manual of child psychology* (3rd ed., vol. 1). New York: Wiley.

Piaget, J. (1972). Intellectual evolution from adolescence to adulthood. *Human Development, 15,* 1–12.

Piaget, J., & Inhelder, B. (1969). *The psychology of the child.* (H. Weaver, trans.). New York: Basic Books (original work published 1932).

Picot, S. J. (1995). Rewards, costs, and coping of African American caregivers. *Nursing Research, 44,* 147–152.

Pierpaoli, W., & Regelson, W. (1995). *The melatonin miracle.* New York: Pocket Books.

Pillemer, K. A. (1986). The dangers of dependency: New findings on domestic violence against the elderly. *Social Problems, 33,* 147–156.

Pillemer, K. A., & Finkelhor, D. (1988). The prevalence of elder abuse: A random sample survey. *The Gerontologist, 28,* 51–57.

Pillemer, K. A., & Wolf, R. S. (1986). *Elder abuse.* Dover, MA: Auburn House.

Pinquart, M., & Sorensen, S. (2000). Influences of socioeconomic status, social network, and competence on subjective well-being in later life: A meta-analysis. *Psychology and Aging, 15,* 187–224.

Plude, D. J., & Hoyer, W. J. (1985). Attention and performance: Identifying and localizing deficits. In N. Charness (Ed.), *Aging and human performance* (pp. 47–99). London: Wiley.

Population 2000. (2000). *Older Americans 2000: Key indicators of well-being.* www.agingstats.gov/chartbook2000/population.html

Posner, M. C., & Wolmark, N. (1994). Indication for breast-preserving surgery and therapy in early breast cancer. *International Surgery (GUP), 79,* 43–47.

Post, G. (1992). Aging and meaning: The Christian tradition. In T. R. Cole, D. D. Van Tassel, & R. Kastenbaum (Eds.), *Handbook of the humanities and aging* (pp. 127–146). New York: Springer.

Prenda, K. M. and Lachman, M. E. (2001). Planning for the future: a life management strategy for increasing control and life satisfaction in adulthood. *Psychology and Aging, Special Issue, 16,* 206–216.

Price, C. A. (2000). Women and retirement: Relinquishing professional identity. *Journal of aging studies, 14* (1), 81–101.

Price, R. W., Sidtis, J., & Rosenblum, M. (1988). The AIDS dementia complex: Some current questions. *Annals of Neurology 23* (Suppl), S27–S33.

Pruchno, R. A., Smyer, M. A., Rose, M. S., Hartman-Stein, P. E., & Henderson-Laribee, D. L. (1995). Competence of long-term care residents to participate in decisions about their medical care: A brief objective assessment. *The Gerontologist, 35* (5), 622–629.

Prull, M. W., Gabrieli, J. D. E., & Bunge, S. A. (2000). Age-related changes in memory: A cognitive-neuroscience perspective. In F. I. M. Craik & T. A. Salthouse (Eds.), *The handbook of aging and cognition* (pp. 91–154). Mahwah, NJ: Erlbaum.

PSA debate continues. (1995). *Johns Hopkins Medical Letter (February)*, 2–3.

Pushkar, D., Arbuckle, T., Conway, M., Chaikelson, J., & Maag, U. (1997). Everyday activity parameters and competence in older adults. *Psychology and Aging, 12,* 600–609.

Quam, J. K., & Whitford, G. S. (1992). Adaptation and age-related expectations of older gay and lesbian adults. *The Gerontologist, 32,* 367–374.

Quinn, J. (2000). Retirement trends in the new century: The end of an era? *TIAA-CREF Participant* (November), 14–15.

Quinn, J. F., & Smeeding, T. M. (1993). The present and future economic well-being of the aged. In D. Salisbury & R. Burkenhauser (Eds.), *Pensions in a changing economy.* Washington, DC: Employee Benefit Research Institute.

Quinn, M., & Tomita, S. (1986). *Elder abuse and neglect: Causes, diagnosis, and intervention strategies.* New York: Springer.

Rabbitt, P. A., & Abson, V. (1990). "Lost and found." Some logical and methodological limitations of self-report questionnaires as tools to study cognitive aging. *British Journal of Psychology, 81,* 1–16.

Rabbitt, P., & McInnis, L. (1988). Do clever older people have earlier and richer first memories? *Psychology and Aging, 3,* 338–341.

Rakfeldt, J., Rybash, J. M., & Roodin, P. A. (1996). Affirmative coping as a marker of success in adult therapeutic intervention. In M. L. Commons, C. Goldberg, & J. Demick (Eds.), *Clinical approaches to adult development* (pp. 295–310). Norwood NJ: Ablex Publishers.

Ramsey, J. L., & Bleiszner, R. (1999). *Spiritual resiliency in older women: Models of strength for challenges through the life span.* Sage Publications: Thousand Oaks, CA.

Rankin, J. K., Wollacott, M. H., Shumway-Cook, A. & Brown, L. A. (2000). Cognitive influence on postural stability: A neuromuscular analysis in young and older adults. *Journal of Gerontology, 55A,* M112–M119.

Rapoport, M., van Reekum, R., & Mayberg, H. (2000). The role of the cerebellum in cognition and behavior. *Journal of Neuropsychiatry and Clinical Neurosciences, 12,* 193–198.

Rapoport, S. I. (1999). How did the human brain evolve? A proposal based on new evidence in vivo brain imaging during attention and ideation. *Brain Research Bulletin, 50,* 149–165.

Raskind, M. A., & Peskind, E. R. (1992). Alzheimer's disease and other dementing disorders. In J. E. Birren, R. B. Sloane, & G. D. Cohen (Eds.), *Handbook of mental health and aging* (2nd ed., pp. 477–513). San Diego: Academic Press.

Rasmusson, D., Rebok, G. W., Bylsma, F. W., & Brandt, J. (1999). Effects of three types of memory training in normal elderly. *Aging, Neuropsychology, and Cognition, 6,* 56–66.

Raz, N. (2000). Aging of the brain and its impact on cognitive performance: Integration of structural and functional findings. In F. I. M. Craik & T. A. Salthouse (Eds.), *The handbook of aging and cognition* (2nd ed., pp. 1–90). Mahwah, NJ: Erlbaum.

Rebok, G. W. (1987). *Life-span cognitive development.* New York: Holt, Rinehart & Winston.

Reed, M. L. (2000). *Grandparents cry twice: Help for bereaved grandparents.* Amityville, NJ: Baywood.

Reese, D. J., & Brown, D. R. (1997). Psychosocial and spiritual care in hospice: Differences between nursing, social work, and clergy. *Hospice Journal, 12,* 29–41.

Regnier, V., & Pynoos, J. (1992). Environmental intervention for cognitively impaired older persons. In J. E. Birren, R. B. Sloane, & G. D. Cohen (Eds.), *Handbook of mental health and aging* (2nd ed., pp. 763–792). San Diego: Academic Press.

Reifler, B. V. (1994). Depression: Diagnosis and Co-morbidity. In L. S. Schneider, C. F. Reynolds, III, B. D. Lebowitz, & A. J. Friedhoff (Eds.), *Diagnosis and treatment of depression in late life* (Vol. 2, pp. 55–59). Washington, DC: American Psychiatric Press.

Reisberg, B., & Bornstein, J. (1986). Clinical diagnosis and assessment. *Drug Therapy, 16,* 43–59.

Reisberg, B., Ferris, S. H., & Franssen, E. (1985). An ordinal functional assessment toll for Alzheimer's-type dementia. *Hospital and Community Psychiatry, 36,* 593–595.

Remafedi, G. (1987). Adolescent homosexuality: Psychosocial and medical implications. *Pediatrics, 79,* 331–337.

Reskin, B. F., & Padavic, I. (1994). Women and men at work. Thousand Oaks, CA: Pine Forge Press.

Reynolds, S. L., Crimmins, E. M., & Saito, Y. (1998). Cohort differences in disability and disease presence. *The Gerontologist, 38* (5), 578–590.

Rhodes, S. L. (1977). A developmental approach to the life cycle of the family. *Social Casework, 58,* 301–311.

Richardson, V., & Kilty, K. M. (1992). Retirement intentions among black professionals: Implications for practice with older black adults. *The Gerontologist, 32,* 7–16.

Richburg, K. B. (2000). Dutch legislators o.k. bill to legalize mercy killings. *Washington Post,* February 12, B7.

Richman, J. (1999). Psychotherapy with the suicidal elderly: A family-oriented approach. In M. Duffy (Ed.), *Handbook of counseling and psychotherapy with older adults,* pp. 650–661. New York: John Wiley.

Riedel, B. W., & Lichstein, K. L. (1998). Objective sleep measures and subjective sleep satisfaction: How do older adults with insomnia define a good night's sleep? *Psychology and Aging, 13,* 159–163.

Riedel, B. W., & Lichstein, K. L. (2000). Insomnia and daytime functioning. *Sleep Medicine Reviews, 4,* 277–298.

Riegel, K. F. (1976). The dialectics of human development. *American Psychologist, 31,* 689–700.

Riegel, K. F., & Riegel, R. M. (1972). Development, drop, and death. *Developmental Psychology, 6,* 306–319.

Rikli, R., & Busch, S. (1986). Motor performance of women as a function of age and physical activity level. *Journal of Gerontology, 41,* 645–649.

Riley, M. W. (1985). Age strata and social systems. In R. H. Binstock & E. Shanas (Eds.), *Handbook of aging and the social sciences* (Vol. 3, pp. 369–411). New York: Van Nostrand Reinhold.

Riley, M. W. (1997). *The hidden age revolution: Emergent integration of all ages.* Policy brief: Center for Policy Research, Syracuse University.

Riley, M. W., & Riley, J. W. (1994). Age integration and the lives of older people. *The Gerontologist, 34,* 110–115.

Riley, M. W., & Riley, J. W. (2000). Age integration: Conceptual and historical background. *The Gerontologist, 40* (3), 266–270.

Ring, K., & Valarino, E. E. (1998). *Lessons from the light: What we can learn from the near-death experience.* New York: Plenum.

Ring, K. (1984). *Heading toward omega: In search of the meaning of the near-death experience.* New York: William Morrow.

Rivers, R. Y. (1995). Clinical issues and intervention with ethnic minority women. In J. F. Aponte, R. Y. Rivers, & J. Wohl (Eds.), Psychological interventions and cultural diversity (pp. 181–198). Boston: Allyn & Bacon.

Roberts, S. B., Pi-Sunyer, X., Kuller, L., Lane, M. A., Ellison, P., Prior, J. C., & Shapses, S. (2001). Physiologic effects of lowering caloric intake in nonhuman primates and nonobese humans. *Journal of Gerontology: Biological Sciences and Medical Sciences, 56A,* 66–75.

Roberts, P., & Newton, P. M. (1987). Levinsonian studies of women's adult development. *Psychology and Aging, 2,* 154–163.

Robertson, J. (1976). Significance of grandparents: Perceptions of young adult grandchildren. *The Gerontologist, 16,* 137–140.

Robertson, K. (1999). *Going beyond telework.* http://klr.com/newslett.htm

Rodin, J. (1986). Aging and health: Effects of the sense of control. *Science, 233,* 1271–1276.

Rodin, J. (1990). Control by any other name: Definitions, concepts, and processes. In J. Rodin, C. Schooler, & K. W. Schaie (Eds.), *Self-directedness cause and effects throughout the life course* (pp. 1–17). Hillsdale, NJ: Lawrence Erlbaum.

Rodin, J., & McAvay, G. (1992). Determinants of change in perceived health in a longitudinal study of older adults. *Journal of Gerontology, 47,* P373–P384.

Rodriguez, O., & O'Donnell, R. M. (1995). Help-seeking and use of mental health services by the Hispanic elderly. In D. K. Padgett (Ed.), *Handbook of ethnicity, aging, and mental health* (pp. 165–184). Westport, CT: Greenwood.

Roediger, H. L., & McDermott, K. B. (1995). Creating false memories: Remembering words not presented in lists. *Journal of Experimental Psychology: Learning, Memory, and Cognition, 21,* 803–814.

Rogaev, E. I., Sherrington, R., Rogaev, E. A., Levesque, G., Ikeda, M., Laing, Y., Chi, H., Lin, C., Holman, K., Tsuda, T., Mar, L., Sorbl, S., Macmias, B., Placentil, S., Amaducci, L., Chumakor, I., Cohen, D., Lannfelt, L., Fraser, P. E., Rommens, J. M., & St. George: Hyslop, P. H. (1995). Familial Alzheimer's disease in kindreds with missense mutations in a gene on chromosome 1 related to the Alzheimer's disease type 3 gene. *Nature, 375,* 775–778.

Rogers, W. A., & Fisk, A. D. (2001). Understanding the role of attention in cognitive aging research. In J. E. Birren & K. W.

Schaie (Eds.), *Handbook of the psychology of aging* (5th ed.). San Diego: Academic Press.

Rogler, L. H., Malgady, R. G., & Rodriguez, O. (1989). Hispanics and mental health: A framework research. Malabar, FL: R. E. Krieger.

Rollins, B. C., & Feldman, H. (1970). Marital satisfaction over the life cycle. *Journal of Marriage and the Family, 32,* 20–28.

Rollins, B. C., & Gallagher, R. (1978). The developing child and marital satisfaction. In R. Lerner & G. Spanier (Eds.), *Child influences on marital interaction: A life-span perspective.* New York: Academic Press.

Romaniuk, J. G., & Romaniuk, M. (1981). Creativity across the life span: A measurement perspective. *Human Development, 24,* 366–381.

Roodin, P. A., Rybash, J. M., & Hoyer, W. J. (1984). Affect in adult cognition: A constructivist view of moral thought and action. In C. Malatesta & C. Izard (Eds.), *The role of affect in adult development and aging.* Beverly Hills, CA: Sage.

Rook, K. S. (2000). The evolution of social relationships in later adulthood. In S. H. Qualls & N. Abeles (Eds.), *Psychology and the aging revolution: How we adapt to longer life,* pp. 173–196. American Psychological Association, Washington, DC.

Rook, K. S. (1987). Reciprocity of social exchange and social satisfaction among older women. *Journal of Personality and Social Psychology, 52,* 145–154.

Rosenblatt, R. A. (2001). First joint federal chartbook shows good news for U.S. Elders. http://www.asaging.org/at/at-215/FedChart.html

Rosenbloom, C. A., & Whittington, F. J. (1993). The effects of bereavement on eating behaviors and nutrient intakes in elderly widowed persons. *Journal of Gerontology, 48,* S223–S229.

Rosengren, K. S., McAuley, E., & Mihalko, S. L. (1998). Gait adjustments in older adults: Activity and efficacy influences. *Psychology and Aging, 13,* 375–386.

Rosenthal, C. J., Martin-Matthews, A., & Matthews, S. A. (1996). Caught in the middle? Occupancy in multiple roles and help to parents in a national probability sample of Canadian adults. *Journal of Gerontology: Social Sciences, 51B,* 274–283.

Rose-Rego, S. K., Strauss, M. E., & Smyth, K. A. (1998). Differences in the perceived well-being of wives and husbands caring for persons with Alzheimer's Disease. *The Gerontologist, 38,* 224–230.

Roubenoff, R., & Hughes, V. (2000). Sarcopenia: Current concepts. *Journal of Gerontology, 55A,* M716–M724.

Rowe, J. W., & Kahn, R. L. (1987). Human aging: Usual and successful. *Science, 237,* 143–149.

Rowe, J. W., & Kahn, R. L. (1997). Successful aging. *The Gerontologist, 37,* 433–440.

Rowe, J. W., & Kahn, R. L. (1999). In K. Dytchwald (Ed.), *Health aging: Challenges and solutions.* Gaithersburg, MD: Aspen.

Rubenstein, C., & Shaver, P. (1981). The experience of loneliness. In L. A. Peplau & D. Perlman (Eds.), *Loneliness: A source book of current theory, research, and therapy.* New York: Wiley Interscience.

Rubenstein, R. L., Alexander, B. B., Goodman, M., & Luborsky, M. (1991). Key relationships of never-married, childless older women: A cultural analysis. *Journal of Gerontology: Social Sciences, 46,* S270–S277.

Rubin, R. M., & Koelln, K. (1993). Out-of-pocket health expenditure differentials between elderly and nonelderly households. *The Gerontologist, 33,* 596–602.

Rubin, Z. (1979, October). Seeking a cure for loneliness. *Psychology Today, 13,* 82–91.

Ruchlin, H. S., & Morris, J. N. (1992, February). Deteriorating health and the cessation of employment among older workers. *Journal of Aging and Health, 4,* 43–57.

Rudberg, M. A., Parzen, M. I., Leonard, L. A., & Cassel, L. K. (1996). Functional limitation pathways and transitions in community-dwelling older persons. *The Gerontologist, 36,* 430–440.

Russell, D. W., Cutrona, C. E., Wallace, R. B., & de la Mora, A. (1997). Loneliness and nursing home admission among rural older adults. *Psychology and Aging, 12,* 574–589.

Rusting, R. L. (1992). Why do we age? *Scientific American, 267,* 130–141.

Ruth, J. E., & Birren, J. E. (1985). Creativity in adulthood and old age: Relations to intelligence, sex, and mode of testing. *International Journal of Behavioral Development, 8,* 99–109.

Ruth, J. E., & Coleman, P. (1996). Personality and aging: Coping and management of the self in later life. In J. E. Birren & K. W. Schaie (Eds.), *Handbook of the psychology of aging* (4th ed., pp. 308–322). San Diego: Academic Press.

Rybarczyk, B., Gallagher–Thompson, D., Rodman, J., and Zeiss, A. (1992). Applying cognitive-behavioral psychotherapy to the chronically ill elderly: Treatment issues and case illustration. *International Psychogeriatrics, 4,* 127–140.

Rybash, J. M. (1996). Aging and implicit memory: A cognitive neuropsychological perspective. *Developmental Neuropsychology, 12,* 127–178.

Rybash, J. M., & Hoyer, W. J. (1996a). Brain reserve capacity and aging: Some unanswered questions. *Brain and Cognition, 30,* 320–323.

Rybash, J. M., & Hoyer, W. J. (1996b). Process dissociation procedure reveals age differences in conscious and unconscious influences on memory for possible and impossible objects. *Aging, Neuropsychology, and Cognition, 3,* 1–13.

Rybash, J. M., & Hrubi, K. L. (1997). Psychometric and psychodynamic correlates of first memories in younger and older adults. *The Gerontologist, 37,* 581–587.

Rybash, J. M., & Hrubi-Bopp, K. L. (2000). Source monitoring and false recognition. *Experimental Aging Research, 26,* 75–87.

Rybash, J. M., & Roodin, P. A. (1989). A comparison of formal and postformal modes of health care decision-making competence. In M. L. Commons, J. D. Sinnott, F. A. Richards, & C. Armon (Eds.), *Adult development: vol. 1. Comparisons and applications of developmental models* (pp. 217–235). New York: Praeger.

Rybash, J. M., Hoyer, W. J., & Roodin, P. A. (1986). *Adult cognition and aging: Developmental changes in processing, knowing, and thinking.* New York: Pergamon.

Rybash, J. M., Roodin, P. A., & Hoyer, W. J. (1983). Expressions of moral thought in later adulthood. *The Gerontologist, 23,* 254–260.

Rybash, J. M., Santoro, K. E., & Hoyer, W. J. (1998). Adult age differences in conscious and unconscious influences on memory for novel associations. *Aging, Neuropsychology, and Cognition, 5,* 14–26.

Ryff, C. D. (1991). Possible selves in adulthood and old age: A tale of shifting horizons. *Psychology and Aging, 6,* 286–295.

Ryff, C. D., & Keyes, C. L. M. (1995). The structure of psychological well-being revisited. *Journal of Personality and Social Psychology, 69,* 719–727.

Ryff, C., & Singer, B. (2000). Interpersonal flourishing: A positive health agenda for the new millennium. *Personality and Social Psychology Review, 4,* 30–44.

Sabom, M. B. (1982). *Recollections of death: A medical investigation.* New York: Harper Row.

Sabom, M. B. (1998). *Light and death: One doctor's fascinating account of near-death experiences.* Grand Rapids, MI: Zondervan.

Sachedina, A. (1995). Islam. In W. T. Reich (Ed.), *Encyclopedia of bio-ethics* (revised ed., Vol. 1. pp. 1289–1297). New York: Simon & Schuster/Macmillan.

Sahyoun, N. R., Lentzner, H., Hoyert, D., & Robinson, K. N. (2001). *Trends in causes of death among the elderly. Aging trends; No. 1.* Hyattsville, MD: National Center for Health Statistics.

Sahyoun, N. R., Pratt, L. A., Lentzner, H., Dey, A., & Robinson, K. N. (2001). The changing profile of nursing home residents: 1985–1997. *Aging Trends, 4,* Hyattsville, MD: Center for Disease Control.

Salthouse, T. A. (1984). Effects of age and skill in typing. *Journal of Experimental Psychology: General, 113,* 345–371.

Salthouse, T. A. (1985). Spread of behavior and its implications for cognition. In J. E. Birren & K. W. Schaie (Eds.), *Handbook of the psychology for aging* (2nd ed.). New York: Van Nostrand Reinhold.

Salthouse, T. A. (1990). Speed of behavior and its implications for cognition. In J. E. Birren & K. W. Schaie (Eds.), *The handbook of the psychology of aging* (2nd ed., 400–426). New York: Van Nostrand Reinhold.

Salthouse, T. A. (1996). Constraints on theories of cognitive aging. *Psychonomic Bulletin & Review, 3,* 287–299.

Salthouse, T. A. (2000). Methodological assumptions in cognitive aging research. In F. I. M. Craik & T. A. Salthouse (Eds.), *The handbook of aging and cognition* (pp. 467–498). Mahwah, NJ: Erlbaum.

Salthouse, T. A., & Maurer, T. J. (1996). Aging, job performance, and career development. In J. E. Birren & K. W. Schaie (Eds.), *Handbook of the psychology of aging* (4th ed., pp. 353–364). San Diego: Academic Press.

Salthouse, T. A., & Somberg, B. L. (1982). Skilled performance: The effects of age and experience on elementary processes. *Journal of Experimental Psychology: General, 111,* 176–207.

Salthouse, T. A., Babcock, R. L., Skovronek, E., Mitchell, D., & Palmon, R. (1990). Age and experience effects in spatial visualization. *Developmental Psychology, 26,* 128–136.

Sarason, I. G., Sarason, B. R., & Pierce, G. R. (1989). *Social support: An interactional view.* NY: Wiley.

Satz, P. (1993). Brain reserve capacity on symptom onset after brain injury: A formulation and review of evidence for threshold theory. *Neuropsychology, 7,* 273–295.

Sauber, M., & Corrigan, E. M. (1970). *The six-year experience of unwed mothers as parents.* New York: Community Council of Greater New York.

Saunders, C. (1977). Dying to live: St. Christopher's Hospice. In H. Feifel (Ed.), *New meanings of death.* New York: McGraw-Hill.

Sax, L. J., Astin, A. W., Korn, W. S., & Mahoney, K. M. (1998). *The American freshman: National norms for fall 1998.* Los Angeles: Higher Education Research Institute, University of California, Los Angeles.

Schacter, D. L. (1994). Priming and multiple memory systems: Perceptual mechanisms of implicit memory. In D. L. Schacter, & E. Tulving, (Eds.), *Memory systems 1994.* Cambridge, MA: MIT Press.

Schacter, D. L. (1996). *Searching for memory.* NY: Basic Books.

Schacter, D. L. (2000). The seven sins of memory: Perspectives from functional neuroimaging. In E. Tulving (Ed.), *Memory, consciousness, and the brain* (pp. 119–137). Philadelphia: Psychology Press.

Schacter, D. L., & Buckner, R. L. (1998). Priming and the brain. *Neuron, 20,* 185–195.

Schacter, D. L., & Tulving, E. (Eds.), (1994). *Memory systems 1994.* Cambridge, MA: MIT Press.

Schacter, D. L., Savage, C. R., Alpert, N. M., Rauch, S. L., & Albert, M. S. (1996). The role of hippocampus and frontal cortex in age-related memory changes: A PET study. *NeuroReport, 7,* 1165–1169.

Schacter, D. L., Wagner, A. D., & Buckner, R. L. (2000). Memory systems of 1999. In E. Tulving & F. I. M. Craik (Eds.), *Handbook of memory* (pp. 627–643). New York: Oxford University Press.

Schaie, K. W. (1985). *Manual for the Schaie-Thurstone Adult Mental Abilities Test* (*STAMAT*). Palo Alto, CA: Consulting Psychologists Press.

Schaie, K. W. (1990). The optimization of cognitive functioning in old age: Prediction based on cohort-sequential and longitudinal data. In P. B. Baltes & M. Baltes (Eds.), *Longitudinal research and the study of successful* (*optimal*) *aging* (pp. 94–117). Cambridge, England: Cambridge University Press.

Schaie, K. W., & Hofer, S. M. (2000). Longitudinal studies in aging research. In J. E. Birren & K. W. Schaie (Eds.), *Handbook of the psychology of aging* (5th ed., pp. 53–77). San Diego: Academic Press.

Schaie, K. W. and Willis, S. L. (1991). Adult personality and psychomotor performance: Cross-sectional and longitudinal analyses. *Journal of Gerontology, 46,* P275–P284.

Schaie, K. W. (1993). The Seattle longitudinal studies of adult intelligence. *Current Directions in Psychological Science, 2,* 171–174.

Schaie, K. W. (1994). The course of adult intellectual development. *American Psychologist, 49,* 304–313.

Schaie, K. W. (1996). *Intellectual development in adulthood: The Seattle longitudinal study.* New York: Cambridge University Press.

Schaie, K. W., & Hertzog, C. (1983). Fourteen-year cohort-sequential studies of adult intelligence. *Developmental Psychology, 19,* 531–543.

Schaie, K. W., Maitland, S. B., Willis, S. L., & Intrieri, R. C. (1998). Longitudinal invariance of adult psychometric ability factor structures across 7 years. *Psychology & Aging, 13,* 8–20.

Schaie, K. W., & Willis, S. L. (1993). Age difference patterns of psychometric intelligence in adulthood: Generalizability within and across ability domains. *Psychology and Aging, 8,* 44–55.

Schaie, K. W., & Willis, S. L. (1996). Psychometric intelligence and aging. In F. Blanchard-Fields, & T. H., & Hess, (Eds.), *Perspectives on cognitive change in adulthood and aging.* NY: McGraw-Hill.

Scheibel, A. B. (1996). Structural and functional changes in the aging brain. In J. E. Birren, K. W. Schaie, R. P. Abeles, M. Gatz, & T. A. Salthouse (Eds.), *Handbook of the psychology of aging* (4th ed.). San Diego: Academic Press.

Schieber, F. (1992). Aging and the senses. In J. E. Birren, R. B. Sloane, & G. D. Cohen (Eds.), *Handbook of mental health and aging* (2nd ed., pp. 252–306). San Diego: Academic Press.

Scheier, M. F., & Carver, S. (1992). Effects of optimism on psychological and physical well-being: Theoretical overview and empirical update. *Cognitive Therapy and Research, 16,* 201–228.

Schiffman, S. (1977). Food recognition by the elderly. *Journal of Gerontology, 32,* 586–592.

Schneider, S. L. (2001). In search of realistic optimism: Meaning, knowledge, and warm fuzziness. *American Psychologist, 56,* 250–263.

Schnelle, J. F., Simmons, S. F., and Ory, M. G. (1992). Risk factors that predict staff failure to release nursing home residents from restraints. *The Gerontologist, 32,* 767–770.

Schnelle, J. F., McNees, P., Crooks, V., & Ouslander, J. G. (1995). The use of a computer-based model to implement an incontinence management program. *The Gerontologist, 35,* 656–665.

Schone, B. S., & Weinick, R. M. (1998). Health-related behaviors and the benefits of marriage for elderly persons. *The Gerontologist, 38* (5), 618–627.

Schonfeld, L. and DuPree, L. W. (1999). Alcohol and misuse in older adults. *Reviews in Clinical Gerontology, 9,* 151–162.

Schonfield, A. E. D., & Robertson, B. A. (1966). Memory storage and aging. *Canadian Journal of Psychology, 20,* 228–236.

Schooler, C., Caplan, L., & Oates, G. (1998). Aging and work: An overview. In K. W. Schaie & C. Schooler (Eds.), *Impact of work on older adults.* New York: Springer.

Schreiner, A. S., Yamamoto, E., & Shiotani, H. (2000). Agitated behavior in elderly nursing home residents with dementia in Japan. *Journal of Gerontology, 55B* (3), P180–P186.

Schroots, J. J. F., & Birren, J. E. (1990). Concepts of time and aging in science. In J. E. Birren & K. W. Schaie (Eds.), *Handbook of the psychology of aging* (3rd ed., pp. 45–64). New York: Academic Press.

Schuckit, M. A., Morrissey, E. R., & O'Leary, M. R. (1979). Alcohol problems in elderly men and women. In D. M. Peterson (Ed.), *Drug use among the aged.* New York: Spectrum.

Schulz, R., & Curnow, C. (1988). Peak performance and age among superathletes: Track and field, swimming, baseball, tennis, and golf. *Journal of Gerontology: Psychological Sciences, 43,* 1113–1120.

Schulz, R., & Williamson, G. M. (1994). Health effects of caregiving: Prevalence of mental and physical illness in Alzheimer's disease caregivers. In E. Light & G. Niederehe (Eds.), *Stress effects on family caregivers of Alzheimer's patients: Research and intervention* (pp. 38–63). New York: Springer.

Schulz, R., Musa, D., Staszewski, J., & Siegler, R. S. (1994). The relation between age and major league baseball performance: Implications for development. *Psychology and Aging, 9. P174–286*

Schulz, R., Bookwala, J., Knapp, J. E., Scheier, M., & Williamson, G. M. (1996). Pessimism, age and cancer mortality. *Psychology and Aging, 11,* 304–309.

Schwartzman, A. E., Gold, D., Andres, D., Arbuckle, T. Y., & Chiakelson, J. (1987). Stability of intelligence: A forty-year follow-up. *Canadian Journal of Psychology, 41,* 244–256.

Seeman, T. W., Bruce, M. L., & McAvay, G. J. (1996). Social network characteristics and onset of ADL disability: MacArthur studies of successful aging. *Journal of Gerontology: Series B: Psychological Sciences and Social Sciences, 51B,* S191–S200.

Sehl, M. E., & Yates, F. E. (2001). Kinetics of human aging: I. Rates of senescence between ages 30 and 70 years in healthy people. *Journal of Gerontology: Biological Sciences, 56A* (5), B199–B208.

Seligman, M. E. P., & Csikszentmihalyi, M. (2000). Positive psychology: An introduction. *American Psychologist, 55,* 5–14.

Selkoe, D. J. (1992). Aging, brain, and mind. *Scientific American, 267,* 134–143.

Selkoe, D. J. (1995). Missense on the membrane. *Nature, 375,* 734–735.

Selkoe, D. J., Bell, D. S., Podlisny, M. B., Price, D. L., & Cork, I. C. (1987). Conservation of brain amyloid proteins in aged mammals and humans. *Science, 235,* 873–877.

Seltzer, B. J., Vasterling, J. J., Yoder, J., & Thompson, K. A. (1997). Awareness of deficit in Alzheimer's disease: Relation to caregiver burden. *Educational Research, 37,* 120–124.

Seltzer, M. M., Greenberg, J. S., & Krauss, M. W. (1995). A comparison of coping strategies of aging mothers of adults with mental illness or mental retardation. *Psychology and Aging, 10,* 64–75.

Selye, H. (1956). *The stress of life.* New York: McGraw-Hill.

Selye, H. (1980). *Selye's guide to stress research.* New York: Van Nostrand.

Seperson, S. B. (2001). Demographics about aging. In S. B. Seperson & C. Hegeman (Eds.), *Service learning and elder care.* Westport, CT: Greenwood.

Shahnasarian, M. (1992). Career development after professional football. *Journal of Career Development, 18,* 299–304.

Shapiro, A. F., Gottman, J. M., & Carrere, S. (2000). The baby and the marriage: Identifying factors that buffer against decline in marital satisfaction after the first baby arrives. *Journal of Family Psychology, 14,* 59–70.

Shaughnessy, J. J., & Zechmeister, E. B. (1996). *Research methods in psychology* (3rd ed.). New York: McGraw-Hill.

Sheehy, G. (1995). *New passages.* New York: Ballantine Books.

Sheehy, G. (1998). *Men's passages.* New York: Ballantine Books.

Sheldon, K. M., & King, L. (2001). Why positive psychology is necessary. *American Psychologist, 56,* 216–217.

Sheridan, C. (1993). *Failure-free activities for the Alzheimer's patient.* San Francisco: Elder Books.

Sherrington, R., Rogaev, E. I., Laing, Y., Rogaeva, E. A., Levesque, G., Ikeda, M., Chi, H., Lin, C., Li, G., Holman, K., Tsuda, T., Mar, L., Foncin, J. F., Bruni, A. C., Montesi, M. P., Sorbl, S., Rainero, I., Pinessi, L., Nee, L., Chumakov, I., Pollen, D., Brookes, A., Sanseau, P., Polinsky, R. J., Wasco, W., DaSilva, H. A. R., Haines, J. L., Pericak-Vancer, M. A., Tansi, R. E., Roses, A. D., Fraser, P. E., Rommens, J. M., & St. George-Hyslop, P. H. (1995). Cloning of a gene bearing missense mutations in early-onset familial Alzheimer's disease. *Nature, 375,* 754–760.

Shi, L. (1993). Family financial and household support exchange between generations: A survey of Chinese rural elderly. *The Gerontologist, 33,* 468–480.

Shneidman, E. (1992). *Death: Current perspectives* (3rd ed.). Mountain View, CA: Mayfield.

Siegel, R. K. (1980). The psychology of life after death. *American Psychologist, 35,* 911–931.

Siegler, I. C. (1983). Psychological aspects of the Duke longitudinal studies. In K. W. Schaie (Ed.), *Longitudinal studies of adult psychological development.* New York: Guilford Press.

Siegler, I. C. and Brummett, B. H. (2000). Associations among NEO personality assessments and well-being at mid-life: facet-level analysis. *Psychology and Aging, 15,* 710–714.

Silverman, N. (2001). *A snapshot in the lives of community-residing elders 85 and older: Their lifestyles, contributions, and concerns.* http://www.asaging.org/at/at-201/old.html

Silverman, P. R. (2000a). When parents die. In Doka, K. J. (Ed.), *Living with grief: Children, adolescents, and loss.* Washington, DC: Hospice Foundation of America. Brunner Mazel, pp. 215–228.

Silverman, P. R. (2000b). *Never too young to know: Death in children's lives.* New York: Oxford University Press.

Silverstein, M., & Marenco, A. (2001). How Americans enact the grandparent role across the family life course. *Journal of Family Issues, 22,* 493–522.

Silverstein, M., & Waite, L. J. (1993). Are blacks more likely than whites to receive and provide social support in middle and old age? Yes, no, and maybe so. *Journal of Gerontology: Social Sciences, 48,* S212–S222.

Simms, L. M., Jones, S. J., & Yoder, K. K. (1982). Adjustment of older persons in nursing homes. *Journal of Gerontological Nursing, 8,* 383–386.

Simoneau, G. G., & Leibowitz, H. W. (1996). Posture, gait, and falls. In J. E. Birren & K. W. Schaie (Eds.), *Handbook of the psychology of aging* (4th ed., pp. 204–235). San Diego: Academic Press.

Simons-Morton, B. G., Greene, W. H., & Gottlieb, N. H. (1995). *Introduction to health education and health promotion* (2nd ed.). Prospect Heights, IL: Wavelength Press.

Simonton, D. K. (1988). Age and outstanding achievement: What do we know after a century of research? *Psychological Bulletin, 104*, 251–267.

Simonton, D. K. (1990). Creativity and wisdom in aging. In J. E. Birren & K. W. Schaie (Eds.), *Handbook of the psychology of aging* (3rd ed., pp. 320–329). San Diego: Academic Press.

Simonton, D. K. (1997). Creative productivity: A predictive and explanatory model of career trajectories and landmarks. *Psychological Review, 104*, 66–89.

Sinnott, J. D. (1981). The theory of relativity: A metatheory for development? *Human Development, 24*, 293–311.

Sinnott, J. D. (1984). Postformal reasoning: The relativistic stage. In M. L. Commons, F. A. Richards, & C. Armon (Eds.), *Beyond formal operations: Late adolescent and adult cognitive development.* New York: Praeger.

Sinnott, J. D. (1989). A model for solution of ill-structured problems: Implications for everyday and abstract problem-solving. In J. D. Sinnott (Ed.), *Everyday problem-solving: Theory and application* (pp. 72–99). New York: Praeger.

Sinnott, J. D. (1994). Development and yearning: Cognitive aspects of spiritual development. *Journal of Adult Development, 1*, 91–99.

Sinnott, J. D., & Shifren, K. (2001). Gender and aging. In J. E. Birren & K. W. Schaie (Eds.), *Handbook of the psychology of aging* (5th ed., pp. 454–476). San Diego: Academic Press.

Siris, E. S., Miller, P. D., Barrett-Connor, E., et al. (2001). Identification and fracture outcomes of undiagnosed low bone mineral density in postmenopausal women: Results from the National Osteoporosis Risk Assessment. *Journal of the American Medical Association, 286*, 2815–2822.

Skaff, M. M., Pearlin, L. I., & Mullan, J. T. (1996). Transitions in the caregiving career. Effects on sense of mastery. *Psychology and Aging, 11*, 247–257.

Skinner, B. F. (1990). Can psychology be a science of mind? *American Psychologist, 45*, 1206–1210.

Sliwinski, M., Lipton, R. B., Buschke, H., & Stewart, W. (1996). The effects of preclinical dementia on estimates of normal cognitive functioning in aging. *Journal of Gerontology: Psychological Sciences, 51B*, P217–P225.

Slomka, J. (1992). The negotiation of death: Clinical decision making at the end of life. *Social Science and Medicine, 35*, 251–259.

Small, B. J., & Backman, L. (1999). Time to death and cognitive performance. *Current Directions in Psychological Science, 8*, 168–172.

Smith, A. D. (1977). Adult age differences in cued recall. *Developmental Psychology, 13*, 326–331.

Smith, A. D., & Earles, J. K. L. (1996). Memory changes in normal aging. In F. Blanchard-Fields & T. M. Hess (Eds.), *Perspective on cognitive change in adulthood and aging* (pp. 192–220). New York: McGraw-Hill.

Smith, J., & Goodnow, J. J. (1999). Unasked for support and unsolicited advice: Age and the quality of social experience. *Psychology and Aging, 14*, 108–121.

Smyer, M. A. (1995). Formal support in later life: Lessons for prevention. In L. A. Bond, S. J. Cutler, & A. Grams (Eds.), *Promoting successful and productive aging* (pp. 186–202). Thousand Oaks, CA: Sage.

Smyer, M. A., & Wilson, M. (1999). Critical issues and strategies in mental health consultation in nursing homes. In M. Duffy (Ed.), *Handbook of counseling and psychotherapy with older adults,* pp. 364–377. New York: John Wiley.

Smyth, J. M., & Pennebaker, J. W. (2001). Preventive management of work stress: Current themes and future challenges. In A. Baum & T. A. Revenson (Eds.), *The handbook of health psychology* (pp. 321–357). Mahweh, NJ: Lawrence Erlbaum.

Snowdon, D. A. (1997). Aging and Alzheimer's disease: Lessons from the Nun Study. *The Gerontologist, 37*, 150–156.

Snowdon, D. D. (2001). *Aging with grace: What the nun study teaches us about longer, healthier, and more meaningful lives.* Random House: New York.

Snowdon, D. D., Greiner, L. H., Kemper, S. J., Nanayakkara, & Mortimer, J. A. (1999). Linguistic ability in early life and longevity: Findings from the nun study. *Paradoxes of Longevity,* pp. 103–113.

Snyder, C. R. (1994). *The psychology of hope: You can get there from here.* New York: Free Press.

Snyder, D. C. (1993). The economic well-being of retired workers by race and Hispanic origin. In D. Salisbury & R. B. Burkenhauser (Eds.), *Pensions in a changing economy* (pp. 67–78). Washington DC: Employee Benefit Research Institute.

Social Security Administration (2001). *A summary of benefits, 2001.*

Sohal, R. S., & Weindruch, R. (1996). Oxidative stress, caloric restriction, and aging, *Science, 273*, 59–63.

Sokolovsky, J. (1986). *Growing old in different societies: Cross-cultural perspectives.* Belmont, CA: Wadsworth.

Soldo, B. J. (1996). Cross-pressures on middle-aged adults: A broader view. *Journal of Gerontology: Psychological Sciences and Social Sciences, 51B*, S271–S273.

Souza, P. E., & Hoyer, W. J. (1996). Age-related hearing loss: Implications for counseling. *Journal of Counseling and Development, 74*, 652–655.

Speare, A., & Avery, R. (1993). Who helps whom in older parent-child families. *Journal of Gerontology, 48*, 564–573.

Spearman, C. (1927). *The abilities of man.* New York: Macmillan.

Spector, A., Davies, S., Woods, B., & Orrell, M. (2000). Reality orientation for dementia: A systematic review of the evidence of effectiveness from randomized controlled trials. *The Gerontologist, 40* (2), 206–212.

Spina, R. J., Miller, T. R., Bogenhagen, W. H., Schechtman, K. B., & Ehsani, A. A. (1996). Gender-related differences in left ventricular filling dynamics in older subjects after endurance exercise training. *Journal of Gerontology: Biological Sciences, 51A* (3), B232–B237.

Squire, L. R. (1994). Declarative and nondeclarative memory: Multiple brain systems supporting learning and memory. In

D. L. Schacter, & E. Tulving, (Eds.). *Memory systems 1994* (pp. 203–232). Cambridge, MA: MIT Press.

Squire, L. R., & Knowlton, B. J. (1995). The organization of memory. In H. Horowitz & J. Singer (Eds.), *The mind, the brain and the CAS: SFI studies in the Sciences of complexity,* Vol XXII, (pp. 63–77) New York: Addison Wesley.

Stall, R., Catania, J., & Pollack, L. (1988). *AIDS as an age-defined epidemic: The social epidemiology of HIV infection among older Americans. Report to the National Institute of Aging.* Unpublished document.

Standon, P., Daniels, K., & Lamond, D. (1999). The home as a workplace: Work-family interaction and psychological well-being in telework. *Journal of Occupational Health Psychology, 4* (4), 368–381.

Staudinger, U. M., & Baltes, P. B. (1996). Interactive minds: A facilitative setting for wisdom related performance. *Journal of Personality and Social Psychology, 71,* 746–762.

Staudinger, U., Lopez, D. F., and Baltes, P. B. (1997). The psychometric location of wisdom-related performance: Intelligence, personality, and more? *Personality and Social Psychology Bulletin, 23* (11), 1200–1214.

Steffens, D. C., Norton, M. C., Plassman, B. L., Tschanz, J. T., Wyse, B. W., Welsh-Bohmer, K. A., Anthony, J. C., & Breitner, J. C. (1999). Enhanced cognitive performance with estrogen use in nondemented community-dwelling women. *Journal of the American Geriatric Society, 47,* 1171–1175.

Stein, S., Linn, M. W., & Stein, E. M. (1985). Patient's anticipation of stress in nursing home care. *The Gerontologist, 25,* 88–94.

Stein, S., Linn, M. W., & Stein, E. M. (1986). *Patient's perceptions of nursing home stress related to quality of care.* Unpublished report, VA Health Services Research Grant (#547). Miami: University of Miami Medical School.

Steinmetz, S. (1978). Battered parents. *Society, 15,* 54–55.

Steinmetz, S. (1981). *Elder abuse.* Aging, January/February, 6–10.

Stephens, M. A. P., Franks, M. M., & Atienza, A. A. (1997). Where two roles intersect: Spillover between parent care and employment. *Psychology and Aging, 12* (10), 30–37.

Stephens, M. A. P., Townsend, A. L., Matire, L. M., and D ruley, J. A. (2001). Balancing parent care with other roles: Interrole conflict of adult daughter caregivers. *Journal of Gerontology, 56B,* P24–P34.

Stephenson, J. S. (1985). *Death, grief, and mourning: Individual and social realities.* New York: Free Press.

Sternbach, H. (1998). Age-associated testosterone decline in men: Clinical issues for psychiatry. *American Journal of Psychiatry, 155,* 1310–1318.

Sternberg, R. J. (1985). *Beyond IQ: A triarchic theory of human intelligence.* New York: Cambridge University Press.

Sternberg, R. J. (1986). A triangular theory of love. *Psychological Review, 93,* 119–135.

Sternberg, R. J. (1988). *Intelligence applied: Understanding and increasing your intellectual skills.* New York: Harcourt Brace Jovanovich.

Sternberg, R. J. (1999a). Intelligence as developing expertise. *Contemporary Educational Psychology, 24,* 359–375.

Sternberg, R. J. (1999b). The theory of successful intelligence. *Review of General Psychology, 3,* 292–316.

Sternberg, R. J. (2001). What is the common thread of creativity? Its dialectical relation to intelligence and wisdom. *American Psychologist, 56,* 360–362.

Sternberg, R. J., Castejon, J. L., Prieto, M. D., Hautamaeki, J., & Grigorenko, E. L. (2001). Confirmatory factor analysis of the Sternberg Triarchic Abilities Test in three international samples: An empirical test of the triarchic theory of intelligence. *European Journal of Psychological Assessment, 17,* 1–16.

Sternberg, R. J., & Lubart, T. I. Wisdom and creativity. In J. E. Birren & K. W. Schaie (Eds.), *Handbook of the psychology of aging* (5th ed.). San Diego: Academic Press.

Sternberg, R. J., Wagner, R. K., Williams, W. M., & Horvath, J. A. (1995). Testing common sense. *American Psychologist, 50,* 912–927.

Sterns, H. L., Barrett, G. V., and Alexander, R. A. (1985). Accidents and the aging individual. In J. E. Birren and K. W. Schaie (Eds.), *Handbook of the psychology of aging* (2nd ed.). New York: Van Nostrand Reinhold.

St. George-Hyslop, P. H., Tanzi, R. E., Polinsky, R. J., Haines, J. L., Nee, L., Watkins, P. C., Myers, R. H., Feldman, R. G., Pollen, D., Drachman, D., Growdon, J., Bruni, A., Foncin, J. F., Salmon, D., Frommelt, P., Amaducci, L., Sorbi, S., Piacentini, S., Steward, G. D., Hobbs, W. J., Conneally, P. M., & Gusella, J. F. (1987). The genetic defect causing familial Alzheimer's disease maps on chromosome 21. *Science, 235,* 885–889.

Stevenson, R. G. (2000). The role of death education in helping students to cope with loss. In Doka, K. J. (Ed.), *Living with grief: Children, adolescents, and loss.* Washington, DC: Hospice Foundation of America, Brunner Mazel, pp. 195–206.

Stewart, A., Harris, H. L., & Mercer, D. L. (2000). A survey of professionals' experiences in delivering death notifications. *Death studies, 24* (7), 611–631.

Stewart, A. J., & Vandewater, E. A. (1999). "If I had to do it all over again . . ." Midlife review, midcourse corrections, and women's well-being at midlife. *Journal of Personality and Social Psychology, 76,* 270–283.

Stokes, J., Pennington, J., Monroe, B., Papadatou, D., & Relf, M. (1999). Developing services for bereaved children. *Mortality, 4* (3), 291–307.

Stone, A. A., et al. (1999). *The science of self-report: Implications for research and practice.* Washington, DC: American Psychological Association.

Stones, J. J., & Kozma, A. (1996). Activity, exercise, & behavior. In J. E. Birren & K. W. Schaie (Eds.), *Handbook of the psychology of aging* (4th ed., pp. 338–364). San Diego: Academic Press.

Stones, M. J., & Dawe, D. (1993). Acute exercise facilitates semantically cued memory in nursing home residents. *Journal of American Geriatrics Society, 41,* 531–534.

Stopping cancer in its tracks (1995). *American Cancer Society,* Washington, D. C.

Stuck, A. E., Van Gorp, W. G., Josephson, K. R., & Morgenstern, H. (1992). Multidimensional risk assessment versus age as criterion for retirement of airline pilots. *Journal of the American Geriatrics Society, 40,* 526–532.

Stull, D. E., & Hatch, L. R. (1984). Unraveling the effects of multiple life changes. *Research on Aging, 6,* 560–571.

Sue, S. (1981). Programmatic issues in the training of Asian-American psychologists. *Journal of Community Psychology, 9* (4), 293–297.

Sue, S. (1998). In search of cultural competence in psychotherapy and counseling. *American Psychologist, 53* (4), 440–448.

Sue, S., Zane, N., & Young, K. (1994). Research on psychotherapy with culturally diverse populations. In A. E. Bergin & S. L. Garfield (Eds.), *Handbook of psychotherapy and behavior change* (4th ed., pp. 783–820). New York: John Wiley.

Sue, S., Fujino, D., Hu, L., Takeuchi, D. T., & Zane, N. W. S. (1992). Community mental health services for ethnic minority groups: A test of the cultural sensitivity hypothesis. *Journal of Consulting and Clinical Psychology, 59,* 533–540.

Suitor, J., & Pillemer, K. (1993). Support and interpersonal stress in the social networks of married daughters caring for parents with dementia. *Journal of Gerontology, 48*(1), S1–S8.

Sullivan, M. (1995). Depression and disability from chronic medical illness. *European Journal of Public Health, 5,* 40–45.

Super, D. E. (1980). A life-span, life-space approach to career development. *Journal of Vocational Behavior, 16,* 282–298.

Super, D. E. (1994). A lifespan, life space, perspective on convergence. In M. L. Savikas and R. W. Lent (eds.), Convergence in career development theories: Implications for science and practice (p. 63–74). Palo Alto, Ca.: U. S. CCP Books.

SUPPORT Principal Investigators. (1995). A controlled study to improve care for seriously ill hospitalized patients: The study to understand prognosis and preferences for outcomes and risks of treatments. *Journal of American Medical Association, 274,* 1591–1598.

Sweet, L. (1994). In memorium: A user's guide on how to behave at funerals of different faiths. *Edmonton Journal,* Aug. 27, p. A10.

Szinovacz, M. E., & Davey, A. (2001). Retirement effects on parent-adult child contacts. *The Gerontologist, 41* (2), 191–200.

Szinovacz, M., & Washo, C. (1992). Gender differences in exposure to life events and adaptation to retirement. *Journals of Gerontology, 47,* S191–S196.

Taylor, S. E. (1983). Adjustment to threatening events: A theory of cognitive adaptation. *American Psychologist, 38,* 1161–1173.

Taylor, S. E., Kemeny, M. E., Aspinwall, L. G., Schneider, S. G., Rodriguez, R., & Heubert, M. (1992). Optimism, coping, psychological distress, and high-risk sexual behavior among men at risk for Acquired Immunodeficiency Syndrome (AIDS). *Journal of Personality and Social Psychology, 63,* 460–473.

Taylor, S. E., Repetti, R. L., & Seeman, T. (1997). Health psychology: What is an unhealthy environment and how does it get under the skin? *Annual Review of Psychology, 58,* 411–447.

Telework America. (2000). *International Telework Association and Council, Executive Summary* http://www.telecommute.org/twa2000/research_results_summary.shtml. U.S. Bureau of Labor Statistics. (2001). *Current population survey: Employed persons by detailed occupation, sex, race, and Hispanic origin.* Washington, DC: U.S. Bureau of Labor. http://stats.bls.gov/cpsaatab.htm#charemp

Teltsch, K. (1991). New study of older workers finds they can become good investments. *New York Times,* May 21, p. A16.

Tennen, H., Affleck, G., Armeli, S., & Carney, M. A. (2000). A daily process approach to coping. *American Psychologist, 55,* 626–636.

Tentori, K., Osherson, D., Hasher, L., & May, C. (2001). Wisdom and aging: Irrational preferences in college students but not older adults. *Cognition, 81,* B87–B96.

Teri, L. (1996). Depression in Alzheimer's disease. In M. Hersen & V. B. Van Hasselt (Eds.), *Psychological treatment of older adults: An introductory text* (pp. 209–222). New York: Plenum Press.

Thomas, J. (1986a). Gender differences in satisfaction with grandparenting. *Psychology and Aging, 1,* 215–219.

Thomas, J. (1986b). Age and sex differences in perceptions of grandparenting. *Journal of Gerontology, 41,* 417–423.

Thomas, L. E., & Eisenhandler, S. A. (1994). Introduction: A human science perspective on aging and the religious dimension. In L. E. Thomas & S. A. Eisenhandler (Eds.), *Aging and the religious dimension* (pp. xvii–xxi). Westport, CT: Auburn House.

Thompson, E. H., Futterman, A. M., Gallagher-Thompson, D., Rose, J. M., & Lovett, S. B. (1993). Social support and caregiving burden in family caregivers of frail elders. *Journal of Gerontology: Social Sciences, 48,* S245–S254.

Thompson, F., & Payne, S. (2000). Bereaved children's questions to a doctor. *Mortality, 5,* 74–96.

Thompson, M. G., Heller, K., & Rody, C. A. (1994). Recruitment challenges in studying late life depression: Do community samples adequately represent depressed older adults? *Psychology and Aging, 9,* 121–125.

Thompson, R. A., Tinsley, B. R., Scalora, M. J., & Parke, R. D. (1989). Grandparents' visitation rights. *American Psychologist, 44,* 1217–1222.

Thorndike, E. L., Bregman, E. O., Tilton, J. W., & Woodyard, E. (1928). *Adult learning.* New York: Macmillan.

Thurstone, L. L. (1938). *Primary mental abilities.* Chicago: University of Chicago Press.

TIAA (1992). *Long-term care.* New York: Teachers Insurance and Annuity Association.

Tideiksaar, R. (1989). *Falling in old age: Its preventions and treatment.* New York: Springer-Verlag.

Tiffany, D. W., & Tiffany, P. G. (1996). Control across the life span: A model for understanding self-direction. *Journal of Adult Development, 3,* 93–108.

Tinsley, B. J., & Parke, R. D. (1987). Grandparents as interactive and socialization agents. In M. Lewis (Ed.), *Beyond the dyad.* New York: Plenum.

Tobin, J. J. (1987). The American idealization of old age in Japan. *The Gerontologist, 27,* 53–58.

Tobin, S. S., & Lieberman, M. (1976). *Last home for the aged.* San Francisco: Jossey-Bass.

Tomiak, M., Berthelot, J. M., Guimond, E., & Mustard, C. A. (2000). Factors associated with nursing-home entry for elders in Manitoba, Canada. *Journal of Gerontology: 55A,* M279–M287.

Tornstan, L. (1994). Gero-transcendence: A theoretical and empirical exploration. In L. E. Thomas & S. A. Eisenhandler (Eds.), *Aging and the religious dimension.* Westport, CT: Greenwood.

Touron, D. R., Hoyer, W. J., & Cerella, J. (2001). Cognitive skill acquisition and transfer in younger and older adults. *Psychology and Aging, 16,* 555–563.

Tower, R. B. and Kasl, S. V. (1996). Depressive symptoms across older spouses: Longitudinal influences. *Psychology and Aging, 11,* 683–697.

Trimble, J. E. (1989). *The enculturation of contemporary psychology.* Paper presented at the annual meetings of the American Psychological Association, New Orleans, August.

Troll, L. E. (1983). Grandparents: The family watchdogs. In T. Brubaker (Ed.), *Family relationships in later life.* Beverly Hills, CA: Sage.

Troll, L. E., & Skaff, M. M. (1997). Perceived continuity of self in very old age. *Psychology and Aging, 12,* 162–169.

Trudel, G., Turgeon, L., & Piche, L. (2000). Marital and sexual aspects of old age. *Sexual and Relationship Therapy, 15,* 381–406.

Tryban, G. M. (1985). Effects of work and retirement within long-term marital relationships. *Lifestyles, 7,* 207–223.

Tsutsumi, T., Don, B. M., Azichowsky, L. D., Takenaka, K., Oka, K., & Ohno, T. (1998). Comparison of high- and moderate-intensity of strength training on mood and anxiety in older adults. *Perceptual and Motor Skills, 87,* 1003–1011.

Tucker, J. S., Friedman, H. S., Tsai, C. M., & Martin, L. R. (1995). Playing with pets and longevity among older persons. *Psychology and Aging, 10,* 3–7.

Tucker, J. S., Schwartz, J. E., Clark, K. M., & Friedman, H. W. (1999). Age-related changes in the associations of social network ties with mortality risk. *Psychology and Aging, 14,* 564–571.

Tulving, E. (1989). Remembering and knowing the past. *American Scientist, 77,* 361–367.

Tulving, E. (1993). Varieties of consciousness and levels of awareness in memory. In A. Baddeley & L. Weiskrantz (Eds.), *Attention: Selection, awareness, and control. A tribute to Donald Broadbent* (pp. 283–299). London: Oxford University Press.

Tulving, E., Hayman, C. A. G., & MacDonald, C. A. (1991). Long-lasting priming in amnesia: A case experiment. *Journal of Experimental Psychology: Learning, Memory, and Cognition, 17,* 595–617.

Turnbull, J. E., & Mui, A. C. (1995). Mental health status and needs of black and white elderly: Differences in depression. In D. K. Padge (Ed.), *Handbook on ethnicity, aging, and mental health.* Westport, CT: Greenwood Press.

Turvey, C. L., Schultz, S., Arndt, S., Wallace, R. B., & Herzog, A. R. (2000). Memory complaint in a community sample aged 70 and older. *Journal of the American Geriatrics Society, 48,* 1435–1441.

Uba, L. (1994). *Asian Americans: Personality patterns, identity, and mental health.* New York: Guilford Press.

Uchino, B. N., Cacioppo, J. T., & Kiecolt-Glaser, J. K. (1996). The relationship between social support and physiological processes: A review with emphasis on underlying mechanisms and implications for health. *Psychological Bulletin, 119,* 488–531.

Uhlenberg, P., Cooney, T., & Boyd, R. (1990). Divorce for women after midlife. *Journal of Gerontology, 45.*

United States Bureau of the Census. (2000). *Statistical abstracts of the United States.* Washington, DC: U.S. Government Printing Office (see the U.S. Census Bureau pages on the internet).

United States Bureau of the Census. (2001). *Statistical abstracts of the United States.* Washington, DC: U.S. Government Printing Office (see the U.S. Census Bureau pages on the internet).

U.S. Department of Agriculture, Human Nutrition Information Service. (1996). *Food guide pyramid.* Bulletin 249.

U.S. Department of Health and Human Services. (2000). *Healthy people 2010.* (Conference edition in two volumes, Washington, DC: U.S. Government Printing Office.

Unverzagt, F. W., Gao, S., Baiyewu, O., et al. (2001). Prevalence of cognitive impairment: Data from the Indianapolis study of health and aging. *Neurology, 57,* 1655–1662.

Usher, J. A., & Neisser, U. (1993). Childhood amnesia and the beginnings of memory for four early life events. *Journal of Experimental Psychology: General, 122,* 155–165.

Valliant, G. (1977). *Adaptation to life.* Boston: Little, Brown.

Vaillant, G. E., & Mukamal, K. (2001). Successful aging. *American Journal of Psychiatry, 158,* 839–847.

Van-Tilburg, T. (1992). Support networks before and after retirement. Special issue: Social networks. *Journal of Social and Personal Relationships, 9,* 433–445.

Van Willigen, M. (2000). Differential benefits of volunteering across the life course. *Journal of Gerontology, 55B* (5) S308–S318.

Vasquez, M. J., & Han, A. L. (1995). Group interventions and treatment with ethnic minorities. In J. F. Aponte, R. Y. Rivers, & J. Wohl (Eds.), *Psychological interventions and cultural diversity* (pp. 109–127). Boston: Allyn & Bacon.

Veevers, J. E. (1980). *Children by choice.* Toronto, Canada: Butterworth.

Verhaeghen, P., & Kliegl, R. (2000). The effects of learning a new algorithm on asymptotic accuracy and execution speed in old age: A reanalysis. *Psychology and Aging, 15,* 648–656.

Verhaeghen, P., Kliegl, R., & Mayr, U. (1997). Sequential and coordinative complexity in time-accuracy functions for mental arithmetic. *Psychology and Aging, 12,* 555–564.

Verhaeghen, P., & Marcoen, A. (1996). On the mechanisms of plasticity in young and older adults after instruction in the method of loci: Evidence for an amplification model. *Psychology and Aging, 11,* 164–178.

Verhaeghen, P., Marcoen, A., & Goossens, L. (1992). Improving memory performance in the aged through mnemonic training: A meta-analytic study. *Psychology and Aging, 7,* 242–251.

Verhaeghen, P., Marcoen, A., & Goossens, L. (1993). Fact and fiction about memory aging: A quantitative integration of research findings. *Journal of Gerontology: Psychological Sciences, 48,* P157–P171.

Verhaeghen, P., Palfai, T., Cerella, J., Buchler, N., Johnson, M. D'Eredita, M. A., Green, D. R., Hoyer, W. J., & Makekau, M. (2000). Age-related dissociations in time accuracy functions for recognition memory: Utilizing semantic support versus building new representations. *Aging, Neuropsychology, and Cognition, 7,* 262–272.

Verhaeghen, P., & Salthouse, T. A. (1997). Meta-analyses of age-cognition relations in adulthood: Estimates of linear and nonlinear age effects and structural models. *Psychological Bulletin, 122,* 231–249.

Vitaliano, P. P., Young, H. M., & Russo, J. (1991). Burden: A review of measures used among caregivers of individuals with dementia. *The Gerontologist, 31,* 67–75.

Wailing, Li, L., Seltzer, M. M., & Greenberg, J. S. (1999). Change in depressive symptoms among daughter caregivers: An 18 month longitudinal study. *Psychology and Aging, 14,* 206–219.

Waldemar, G. (1995). Functional brain imaging with SPECT in normal aging and dementia: Methodological, pathophysiological, and diagnostic aspects. *Cerebrovascular Brain Metaboloic Review, 7,* 89–130.

Waldrop, M. M. (1984). The necessity of knowledge. *Science, 223,* 1279–1283.

Walker, A. J., Martin, S. S. K., & Jones, L. L. (1992). The benefits and costs of caregiving and carereceiving for daughters and mothers. *Journal of Gerontology: Social Sciences, 47,* S130–S139.

Wallace, G. (2001). Grandparent caregivers: Emergent issues in elder law and social work practice. *Journal of Gerontological Social Work, 34,* 127–136.

Wallace, S. P. (2000). American health promotion: Where individualism rules. *The Gerontologist, 40,* (3), 373–376.

Wallerstein, J. S., & Blakeslee, S. (1988). *Second chances: Men, women, and children a decade after divorce.* Boston: Ticknor & Fields.

Warburton, J., LeBrocque, R., & Rosenman, L. (1998). Older people—The reserve army of volunteers? An analysis of volunteerism among older Australians. *International Journal of Aging and Human Development, 46,* 229–245.

Ward, R., Logan, J., & Spitze, G. (1992). The influence of parent and child needs on co-residence in middle and later life. *Journal of Marriage and the Family, 54,* 209–221.

Ward-Wimmer, D., & Napoli, C. (2000). Counseling approaches with children and adolescents. In Doka, K. J. (Ed.), *Living with grief: Children, adolescents, and loss.* Washington, DC: Hospice Foundation of America, Brunner Mazel, pp. 109–122.

Warr, P. (1992). Age and occupational well-being. *Psychology and Aging, 7,* no. 1, 37–45.

Weale, R. A. (1986). Aging and vision. *Vision Research, 26,* 1507–1512.

Webb, W. M., Nasco, S. A., Riley, S., & Headrick, B. (1998). Athlete identity and reactions to retirement from sports. *Journal of Sport Behavior, 21* (3), 338–362.

Webster, J. D., & Cappeliez, P. (1993). Reminiscence and autobiographical memory: Complementary contexts for cognitive aging research. *Developmental Review, 13,* 54–91.

Wechsler, D. (1939). *Measurement of adult intelligence.* Baltimore: Williams & Wilkins.

Weindruch, R., Keenen, K., Carney, J. M., Fernades, G., Feuers, R. J., Floyd, R. A., Halter, J. B., Ramsey, J. J., Richardson, A., Roth, G. S., & Spindler, S. R. (2001). Caloric restriction mimetics: Metabolic interventions. *Journal of Gerontology, Special Issue,* 56A, 20–33.

Weiner, J. (1996). Can medicaid long-term care expenditures for the elderly be reduced? *The Gerontologist, 36,* 800–811.

Weisberg, R. W. (1986). *Creativity.* New York: W. H. Freeman.

Weisman, A. T. (1972). *On dying and denying: A psychiatric study of terminality.* New York: Behavioral Publications.

Weiss, J. C. (1999). The role of art therapy in aiding older adults with life transitions. In M. Duffy (Ed.), *Handbook of counseling and psychotherapy with older adults* (pp. 182–196). New York: John Wiley.

Weiss, L., & Lowenthal, M. (1975). Life course perspectives on friendship. In M. Lowenthal, M. Turnher, & D. Chiriboga (Eds.), *Four stages of life.* San Francisco: Jossey-Bass.

Weiss, R. S. (1973). *Marital separation.* New York: Basic Books.

Welte, J. W., & Mirand, A. L. (1995). Drinking, problem drinking, and life stressors in the elderly general population. *Journal of Studies on Alcoholism, 51,* 67–73.

West, R. L. (1996). An application of prefrontal cortex function theory to cognitive aging. *Psychological Bulletin, 120,* 272–292.

Westermeyer, J. J. (1993). Cross-cultural psychiatric assessment. In A. C. Gaw (Ed.), *Culture, ethnicity and mental illness* (pp. 125–144). Washington, DC: American Psychiatric Press.

Wetherell, J. L., Gatz, M., & Pederson, N. L. (2001). A longitudinal analysis of anxiety and depressive symptoms. *Psychology and Aging, 16,* 187–195.

Wheeler, I. (2001). Parental bereavement: The crisis of meaning. *Death studies, 25* (1), 51–66.

Wheeler, M., Stuss, D. T., & Tulving, E. (1997). Toward a theory of episodic memory: The frontal lobes and autonoetic consciousness. *Psychological Bulletin, 121,* 331–354.

White, N., & Cunningham, W. R. (1988). Is terminal drop pervasive or specific? *Journal of Gerontology: Psychological Sciences, 44,* P141–P144.

White, T. M., Townsend, A. L., & Stephens, M. A. P. (2000). Comparisons of African-American and white women in the parent care role. *The Gerontologist, 40,* (6), 718–728.

Whitehouse, P. J. (1993). Autopsy. *The Gerontologist, 33,* 436–437.

Whitehouse, P. J., Price, D. L., Clark, A. W., Coyle, J. T., & DeLong, M. R. (1981). Alzheimer's disease: Evidence for the selective loss of cholinergic neurons in nucleus basalis. *Annals of Neurology, 10,* 122–126.

Whitten, P. (1992). Just how much do we decline with age? *APA Monitor* (July–August), 17–20.

Wilber, K. H. (1997). Choice, courts, and competency: The coming of age of protective services research. *The Gerontologist, 37,* 272–274.

Wilber, K. H., & McNeilly, D. P. (2001). Elder abuse and victimization. In J. E. Birren & K. W. Schaie (Eds.), *Handbook of the psychology of aging* (5th ed., pp. 569–591). San Diego: Academic Press.

Wilber, K. H., & Reynolds, S. L. (1995). Rethinking alternatives to guardianship. *The Gerontologist, 35* (2), 248–257.

Wilk, C. A., & Kirk, M. A. (1995). Menopause: A developmental stage, not a deficiency disease. *Psychotherapy, 32,* 233–241.

Wilkelgren, I. (1996). For the cortex, neuron loss may be less than thought. *Science, 273,* 48–50.

Williams, K. D., Cheung, C. K. T., & Cho, W. (2000). Cyberostracism: Effects of being ignored over the internet. *Journal of Personality and Social Psychology, 79,* 748–762.

Williamson, G. M., & Schulz, R. (1993). Coping with specific stressors in Alzheimer's disease. *The Gerontologist, 33,* 747–755.

Willis, S. L. (1996). Everyday cognitive competence in elderly persons: Conceptual issues and empirical findings. *The Gerontologist, 36,* 595–601.

Willis, S. L. (2001). Methodological issues in behavioral intervention research with the elderly. In J. E. Birren & K. W. Schaie (Eds.), *Handbook of the psychology of aging* (5th ed., pp. 78–108). San Diego: Academic Press.

Wise, P. M. (1993, June). Hormone regulation during aging. *Paper presented at the NIA Conference on Experimental Psychology of Aging.* University of Michigan.

Wohl, J. (1995). Traditional individual psychotherapy and ethnic minorities. In J. F. Aponte, R. Y. Rivers, & J. Wohl (Eds.), *Psychological interventions and cultural diversity.* Boston: Allyn & Bacon.

Wohlwill, J. F. (1973). *The study of behavioral development.* New York: Academic Press.

Wojik, L. A., Thelen, D. G., Schultz, A. B., Ashton-Miller, J. A., & Alexander, N. B. (1999). Age and gender differences in single-step recovery from a forward fall. *Journal of Gerontology: Medical Science, 54A,* M44–M50.

Wolf, O. T., Kudielka, B. M., Hellhammer, D. H., Hellhammer, J., & Kirschbaum, C. (1998). Opposing effects of DHEA replacement in elderly subjects on declarative memory and attention after exposure to a laboratory stressor. *Psychoneuroendocrinology, 23,* 617–629.

Wolfson, L., Judge, J., Whipple, R., & King, M. (1995). Strength is a major factor in balance, gait, and the occurrence of falls. *Journal of Gerontology, 50A,* 64–67.

Wood, J. V., Taylor, S. E., & Lichtman, R. R. (1985). Social comparison in adjustment to breast cancer. *Journal of Personality and Social Psychology, 49,* 1169–1183.

Woodruff-Pak, D. (1988). *Psychology and aging.* Englewood Cliffs, NJ: Prentice-Hall.

Woodruff-Pak, D. (1993). Neural plasticity as a substrate for cognitive adaptation in adulthood and old age. In J. Cerella, J. M. Rybash, W. J. Hoyer, & M. C. Commons (Eds.), *Adult information processing: Limits on loss* (pp. 13–35). San Diego: Academic Press.

Woodruff-Pak, D. (1997). *The neuropsychology of aging.* Oxford, UK: Blackwell.

Worden, J. W., Davies, B., & McCown, D. (1999). Comparing parent loss with sibling loss. *Death studies, 23* (1), 1–15.

Wurtman, R. J. (1985). Alzheimer's disease. *Scientific American, 252,* 62–74.

Wykle, M. L., & Ford, A. B. (Eds.). (1999). *Serving minority elders in the 21st century.* New York: Springer.

Yankelovich & Gemini Consulting. (1998). *World-wide study of workers.* Agence France Presse (#12201). Published 10-9-2000.

Yates, S. M., & Dunnagan, T. A. (2001). Evaluating the effectiveness of a home-based fall risk reduction program for rural community-dwelling older adults. *Journal of Gerontology: Medical Sciences, 56A* (4), M226–M230.

Yates, M. E., Tennstedt, S., & Chang, B. H. (1999). Contributors to and mediators of psychological well-being for informal caregivers. *Journal of Gerontology, 54B,* (1), P12–P22.

Yee, J. L., & Schulz, R. (2000). Gender differences in psychiatric morbidity among family caregivers: A review and analysis. *The Gerontologist, 40* (2), 147–164.

Youn, G., Knight, B. G., Jeong, H., & Benton, D. (1999). Differences in familism values and caregiving outcomes among Korean, Korean American, and White American dementia caregivers. *Psychology and Aging, 14* (3), 355–364.

Zacks, R. T., Hasher, L., & Li, K. Z. H. (2000). Human memory. In F. I. M. Craik & T. A. Salthouse (Eds.), *The handbook of aging and cognition* (pp. 293–258). Mahwah, NJ: Erlbaum.

Zarit, S. H., Eiler, J., & Hassinger, M. (1985). Clinical assessments. In J. E. Birren & K. W. Schaie (Eds.), *Handbook of the psychology of aging* (2nd ed.). New York: Van Nostrand Reinhold.

Zarit, S. H., & Zarit, J. M. (1983). Cognitive impairment. In P. M. Lewinsohn & L. Teri (Eds.), *Clinical geropsychology: New directions in assessment and treatment.* New York: Pergamon Press.

Zarit, S. H., Orr, N. K., & Zarit, J. M. (1985). *The hidden victims of Alzheimer's disease: Families under stress.* New York: New York University Press.

Zeiss, A. M., Lewinsohn, P. M., Rohde, P., & Seeley, J. R. (1996). Relationship of physical disease and functional impairment to depression in older people. *Psychology and Aging, 11,* 572–581.

Zemke, R. (2000). *Generations at work: Managing the clash of veterans, boomers, X'rs, and next'rs in your workplace.* Saranac Lake, N.Y.: Amacom.

Zweibel, N. R., & Cassel, C. K. (1989). Treatment choices at the end of life: A comparison of decisions by older patients and their physician-selected proxies. *The Gerontologist, 29,* 615–621.

CREDITS

Line Art

Chapter 2

Table 2.1: Common misperceptions about the elderly based on stereotypes
Credit: Republished with permission of Gerontological Society of America, from S. Lubomudrov, "Congressional Perceptions of the Elderly: The Use of Stereotypes in the Legislative Process" in *Journal of Gerontology,* 27:77–81; permission conveyed through Copyright Clearance Center, Inc.
Table 2.2: Examples of masculine and feminine items from Bern's Sex-Role Inventory
Credit: Reproduced by special permission of the publisher, Consulting Psychologists Press, Inc., from the *Bern Sex Role Inventory* of Sandra Bern, Ph.D., copyright 1978. Reprinted with permission.
Figure 2.5: The rectangularization of the human life span
Credit: Reprinted by permission from L. Hayflick (1980), "Cell biology of human aging" in *Scientific American*, 242-58-65.

Chapter 3

Figure 3.1: Osteoporosis: Reducing the risk
Credit: From J. Stevens-Long and M. Commons in *Adult Life.* Copyright ©1992 Mayfield Publishing Company. Reproduced with permission of McGraw-Hill Companies.
Figure 3.3: Average declines in biological function
Credit: From J. Fries and L.M. Crapo (1981). *Vitality and aging.* Reprinted by permission of the W.H. Freeman Company, New York.
Box Figure 3: Changes in the best race times/Changes in average race times
Credit: From M. Letselter, R. Jungeman, and K. Freitag (1986), "Swimming performance in old age" in *Zeitschrift fur Gerontologie,* 19: 389–395.
Figure 3.6: Age-related changes in brain structures
Credit: Adapted from Rybash, Roodin & Hoyer (1995) and D.J. Selkoe (1992)
Figure 3.8: Relationship between age, brain weight, and brain cell counts
Credit: Adapted from Rybash, Roodin & Hoyer (1995) and D.J. Selkoe (1992)
Table 3.4: Global Deterioration Scale for Age-Associated Cognitive. . . .
Credit: From Reisberg, B., Ferris, S.H., de Leon, M.J., and Crook, T., "The global deterioration scale for assessment of primary degenerative dementia" in *American Journal of Psychiatry,* 139:1136–1139, 1982. Adapted with permission.
Box Figure 3.E: Age and Mini-Mental State Exam Score and best fit regression line in.
Credit: From Snowden, D.A. (1977)
Table 3.B: Cognitive Function Test Scores for Sister Mary and the other sisters who died
Credit: From Snowden, D.A. (1977)

Table 3.C: Alzheimer's Disease Lesion Counts and Brain Weight in Sister Mary and the . . .
Credit: From Snowden, D.A. (1977)
Table 3.5: Some Possible Drugs for Preventing or Treating Alzheimer's
Credit: From Marx, J. (1996)

Chapter 4

Table 4.1: The Social Readjustment Rating Scale
Credit: Reprinted from *Journal of Psychosomatic Research,* 11:213–218, T.H. Holmes and R.H. Rahe, "The Social Readjustment Rating Scale," with permission from Elsevier Science.
Box Figure 4.A: Buffering effect of duration of illness and satisfaction . . .
Credit: Republished with permission of Gerontological Society of America, from B.J. Kramer (1997). Differential predictors of strain and gain among husbands caring for wives with dementia. *The Gerontologist,* 37:239–249; permission conveyed through Copyright Clearance Center, Inc.
Table 4.3: Implementation of an AD support group
Credit: From J.N. Henderson, M. Gutierrez-Mayka, J. Garcia, and S. Boyd, "A Mode for Alzheimer's Disease Support Group Development in African-American and Hispanic Populations" in *The Gerontologist,* 33:409–414. Copyright 1993 ©The Gerontological Society of America. Reprinted with permission.
Table 4.4: Types of Appraisals of Coping Efficacy
Credit: From Gignac, M., & Gottlieb, B. (1996)
Research Focus 4.4: Well-Being and Happiness
Credit: From Myers, D.G. (1993)
Figure 4.5: A conceptual model of caregiver adaptation
Credit: Republished with permission of Gerontological Society of America, from Kramer, B.J. (1997a). "Gain in the Caregiving Experience: Where Are We? What Next?" in *The Gerontologist,* 37(2):218–232, p. 239; permission conveyed through Copyright Clearance Center, Inc.
Figure 4.7: Mean reported difficulty on visual driving tasks . . .
Credit: From Kline, D.W., Kline, T.J.B., and Fozard, J.L., (1992). "Vision Aging and Driving: The Problems of older drivers" in *Journal of Gerontology: Psychological Sciences,* 47(1):27–34. figure 1.5 graphs on visual driving tasks. Copyright 1992 ©The Gerontological Society of America. Reprinted with permission.

Chapter 5

Figure 5.1: One-month prevalence rates of any mood disorder . . .
Credit: From Gatz, M.,"Variations on depression in later life" in S.H. Qualls and N. Abeles (Eds.), *Psychology and the Aging Revolution: How we adapt to longer life,* pp. 239–254. Copyright ©2000 by the American Psychological Association. Reprinted with permission.

Figure 5.2: Diatheses-stress model showing the relationship between vulnerability . . .
Credit: From Zubin and Spring in *Journal of Abnormal Psychology,* 1977, Vol. 86, 103–126, figure 2, p. 110. Copyright ©1977 by the American Psychological Association. Reprinted with permission.

Table 5.2: Symptoms of Depression: Diagnostic Criteria for Major Depressive Episodes
Credit: Reprinted with permission from the *Diagnostic and Statistical Manual of Mental Disorders,* Fourth Edition, Text Revision. Copyright 2000 American Psychiatric Association.

Figure 5.3: Suicide Rates by Age, Sex, Race
Credit: From American Association of Suicidology. Reprinted with permission.

Table 5.3: Most important cultural values for therapists to know about
Credit: From L. Uba in *Asian Americans,* p. 246, table 10.1. Copyright ©1994 Guilford Publications, Inc. Reprinted by permission.

Table 5.4: Important ethic-specific problems therapists need to know about
Credit: From L. Uba in *Asian Americans,* p. 246, table 10.2. Copyright ©1994 Guilford Publications, Inc. Reprinted by permission.

Figure 5.4: Drinking Behavior Chain
Credit: From Dupree, L.W. and Schonfeld, L. (1999), "Management of alcohol abuse in older adults," pp. 632–649, in M. Duffy (Ed.) *Handbook of Counseling and Psychotherapy with Older Adults.* Copyright (c)1999 John Wiley & Sons, Inc. Reprinted by permission of John Wiley & Sons, Inc.

Chapter 6
Figure 6.1: Self-rated health of whites, blacks, and hispanic older adults
Credit: ©2002 Wayne Vincent. Reprinted with permission.

Table 6.1: Sources of passive income for retirees by marital status, gender, race, . . .
Credit: data from Richard V. Burkhauser and Dallas L. Salisbury (eds.) *Pensions in a Changing Economy,* Copyright ©National Academy on Aging, Department of Health and Human Services, Washington DC; and data from new Beneficiary Survey, 1982.

Figure 6.2: Median net worth of black and white older adults
Credit: ©2002 Wayne Vincent. Reprinted with permission.

Table 6.2: Assessment of the Home Environment
Credit: From John R. Pratt, *Long-term Care: Managing Across the Continuum,* 1999, p. 209.
Exhibit 7.1. Copyright ©1999 Aspen Publishers. Reprinted with permission.

Figure 6.3: A hierarchical model of functional abilities
Credit: From "Functional Assessment in Geriatric Mental Health" by B.J. Kemp & J.M. Mitchell in *Handbook of Mental Health and Aging,* 2nd ed, edited by J.E. Birren, R.B. Sloane, and G.D. Cohen, pp. 671–719, figure 8, copyright 1992, Elsevier Science (USA). Reprinted with permission.

Table 6.3: Types of Care
Credit: From Long-Term Care–A Guide for the Educational Community. ©1992 Teachers Insurance and Annuity Association (TIAA). Reprinted with permission.

Research Focus 6.3: The use of restraints in nursing homes
Credit: Republished with permission of Gerontological Society of America, from S.H. Miles and P. Irvine (1992), "Deaths caused by physical restraints" in *The Gerontologist* 32(6):762–766; permission conveyed through Copyright Clearance Center, Inc.

Figure 6.4: Disabled versus healthy adults over age 65
Credit: K.G. Manton, L.S. Corder, & E. Stallard, "Estimates of Change in Chronic Disability and Institutional Incidence and Prevalence Rates in the U.S. Elderly Population from the 1982, 1984, and 1989 National Long-Term Care Survey" in *Journal of Gerontology: Social Sciences,* 48:S153–S166; bar graph of disabled/healthy older people; 1993.

Table 6.4: Percentage of persons over 65 years of age reporting difficulty. . .
Source: National Health Interview Survey, National Center for Health Statistics, 1984

Figure 6.6: Patterns of disability and death are shifting
Credit: From S.J. Olshansky, B.A. Carnes, and C.K. Cassel, "The Aging of the Human Species" in *Scientific American* 268:46–52, April 1993, p. 51. Reprinted with permission.

Research Focus 6.6: Preparing for a Longer, Healthier Life
Credit: Reprinted with permission of Simon & Schuster from *BioMarkers* by William Evans, Ph.D and Irwin H. Rosenberg, M.D. Copyright ©1991 by Irwin Rosenberg, Dr. William J. Evans, and Jacqueline Thomson.

Figure 6.7: Cycle of frailty
Credit: Republished with permission of Gerontological Society of America, from Fried, Tangen, Watson in *Journal of Gerontology,* Medical Sciences, 2991 Vol 56A, No. 3, p. M147; permission conveyed through Copyright Clearance Center, Inc.

Table 6.7: Twelve environment-behavior principles for cognitively impaired older persons
Credit: From "Functional Assessment in Geriatric Mental Health" by V. Regnier and J. Pynoos in *Handbook of Mental Health and Aging,* 2nd ed, edited by J.E. Birren, R.B. Sloane, and G.D. Cohen, pp. 763–792, copyright 1992, Elsevier Science (USA). Reprinted with permission.

Figure 6.8: The Increasing Cost of Long-Term Care
Credit: TIAA 2001–PENDING UPDATE APPROVAL

Figure 6.9: Who Pays for Long-Term Care?
Credit: TIAA 2001–PENDING UPDATE APPROVAL

Table 6.8: Characteristic wandering patterns among nursing home residents . . .
Credit: From Martino-Saltzman, Blasch, B.B., Morris, R.D., and McNeal, L.W. (1992). Travel behavior of nursing home residents perceived as wanderers and nonwanderers. *The Gerontologist,* 31(5), 666–672. Adapted with permission.

Table 6.9: Percentage of nondirective independent travel events as selective time
Credit: From Martino-Saltzman, Blasch, B.B., Morris, R.D., and McNeal, L.W. (1992). Travel behavior of nursing home residents perceived as wanderers and nonwanderers. *The Gerontologist,* 31(5), 666–672. Reprinted with permission.

Table 6.10: Some workers cost more
Credit: Adapted from *Syracuse Herald American,* September 29, 1996, p. 5 data: University of Michigan Fitness Research Center

Figure 6.11: Nursing home survivorship curves for three levels of psychological . . .
Credit: From O'Connor, B.P. and Vallerand, R.J., "Psychological adjustment variables as predictors of mortality among nursing home residents" in *Psychology and Aging,* 13, figure 1, p. 372. Copyright ©1998 by the American Psychological Association. Reprinted with permission.

Table 6.11: Cardiorespiratory Fitness Classification
Source: From Preventive Medicine Center, Palo Alto, Calif., and a survey of published sources. As published in Fahey, Insel, & Roth, 1997. Source: G.A. Brooks and T.D. Fahey, *Fundamentals of Human Performance* (New York: Macmillan, 1987)

Figure 6.12: Age and risk of nursing home admission
Credit: From Russell, D.W., Cutrona, C.E., Wallace, R.B., and de la Mora, A., "Loneliness and nursing home admission among rural older adults" in *Psychology and Aging,* 12, figure 4, p. 585. Copyright ©1997 by the American Psychological Association. Reprinted with permission.

Figure 6.13: Two basic room configurations . . .
Credit: From "Environmental Intervention for Cognitively Impaired Older Persons" by V. Regnier and J. Pynoos in *Handbook of Mental Health and*

Aging, 2nd ed, edited by J.E. Birren, R.B. Sloane, and G.D. Cohen, pp. 763–792, copyright 1992, Elsevier Science (USA). Reprinted with permission.

Figure 6.15: Pathways through which psychological factors might influence onset . . .
Credit: With permission, from Cohen, S. & Herbert, T.B. (1996). "Health Psychology: Psychological factors and physical disease from the perspective of human psychoneuroimmunology" in *Annual Review of Psychology,* 47, 113–142, fig. 1, p. 118. ©1996 by Annual Reviews, www.AnnualReviews.org.

Figure 6.16a: Age-Adjusted Cancer Death Rates for Males by Site, US 1930–1997
Credit: Reprinted with the permission of the American Cancer Society, Inc., Surveillance Research, 2001.

Figure 6.16b: Age-Adjusted Cancer Death Rates for Females by Site, US 1930–1997
Credit: Reprinted with the permission of the American Cancer Society, Inc., Surveillance Research, 2001.

Figure 6.17: Adults on a Diet
Credit: Copyright ©2001 Calorie Control Council. Reprinted with permission.

Figure 6.18: Why Do We Fail? – Reasons why Americans not successful at maintaining . . .
Credit: Copyright ©2001 Calorie Control Council. Reprinted with permission.

Figure 6.19: Body-Mass Index Chart, Adults 20 and Older
Credit: Reprinted with the permission of the American Cancer Society, Inc., Surveillance Research, 2001.

Figure 6.21: Tracings of photographs
Credit: Republished with permission of Gerontological Society of America from M. Brown, D.R. Sinacore, and H.H. Host, "The Relationship of Strength to Function in the Older Adult," Program in Physical Therapy, Washington University School of Medicine, St. Louis, in the *Journals of Gerontology* Series A (50A), Special Issue, November 1995, pp. 55–59, figure 6, p. 58; permission conveyed through Copyright Clearance Center, Inc.

Chapter 7

Figure 7.2: Digit span forward and backward. Scores for 1000 research participants . . .
Credit: Adapted from Gregoire, J., & Van der Linden, M. (1997), "Effect of age on forward and backward digit spans" in *Aging, Neuropsychology, and Cognition,* 4, 140–149. Copyright ©1997 Swets Zeitlinger. Reprinted with permission.

Table 7.6: Recognition and recall of names and faces of high school colleagues
Credit: From H.P. Bahrick, P.O. Bahrick, and R.P. Wittlinger, "Fifty years of memory for names and faces: A cross-sectional approach" in *Journal of Experimental Psychology,* 104:54–75, 1975. Copyright ©2000 by the American Psychological Association. Adapted with permission.

Figure 7.7: Older adults' reports of vivid memories
Credit: Republished with permission of Gerontological Society of America from J. Fitzgerald and Lawrence. (1984). Autobiographical memory across the life span in *Journal of Gerontology,* 39, 692–699; permission conveyed through Copyright Clearance Center, Inc.

Chapter 8

Table 8.1: The Primary Mental Abilities
Credit: From *Psychological Testing,* 6th ed. by Anne Anastasi. Copyright (c)1988 by Anne Anastasi. Reprinted by permission of Pearson Education, Inc., Upper Saddle River, NJ.

Figure 8.3: Cross-sectional age differences in several primary mental abilities
Credit: Republished with permission of Gerontological Society of America from K.W. Schaie & S.L. Willis (1993), "Age differences in patterns of psychometric intelligence in adulthood" in *Psychology and Aging,* 8, 44–55; permission conveyed through Copyright Clearance Center, Inc.

Figure 8.6: A comparison of cross-sectional and longitudinal findings concerning . . .
Credit: Data from K.W. Schaie and G. Labouvie-Vief, "Generational versus ontogenetic components of change in adult cognitive behavior: A fourteen-year cross-sequential study" in *Developmental Psychology,* 10:305–320, 1974.

Figure 8.10: An illustration of age-related changes on the everyday problem-solving . . .
Credit: Data from S.W. Cornelius and A. Capsi, "Everyday problem solving in adulthood and old age" in *Psychology and Aging,* 2:144–153.

Chapter 9

Box Figure 9.A: Wisdom-related scores for nominees, clinicians, and controls
Credit: From P.B. Baltes, U. Staudinger, A. Macker and J. Smith, "People nominated as wise: A comparative study of wisdom-related knowledge" in *Psychology and Aging,* 10, figure 1, p. 161. Copyright ©1995 by the American Psychological Association. Reprinted with permission.

Box Figure 9.B: Wisdom-related scores for nominees, clinicians, and controls
Credit: From P.B. Baltes, U. Staudinger, A. Macker and J. Smith, "People nominated as wise: A comparative study of wisdom-related knowledge" in *Psychology and Aging,* 10, figure 3, p. 162. Copyright ©1995 by the American Psychological Association. Reprinted with permission.

Figure 9.1: An illustration of Berzonsky's branching model of formal operations
Credit: From Berzonsky, M.D. (1978) "Formal reasoning in adolescence: An alternative view" in *Journal of Adolescence,* 13, 279–290. Reprinted with permission of Academic Press Ltd.

Figure 9.4: The Berlin model of wisdom . . .
Credit: From P.B. Baltes and U. Staudinger in *Psychological Science,* 2, 75–80. Copyright ©1993 Blackwell Publishers UK. Reprinted by permission.

Table 9.5: Two life review problems
Credit: From U.M. Staudinger, J. Smith, and P.B. Baltes, "Wisdom-related knowledge in a life review task: Age differences and the role of professional specialization" in *Psychology and Aging,* 7, table 2, p. 275. Copyright (c)1992 by the American Psychological Association. Reprinted with permission.

Table 9.6: Illustration of the characteristics of a wise response to life review tasks
Credit: From U.M. Staudinger, J. Smith, and P.B. Baltes, "Wisdom-related knowledge in a life review task: Age differences and the role of professional specialization" in *Psychology and Aging,* 7, table 1, p. 273. Copyright ©1992 by the American Psychological Association. Adapted with permission.

Table 9.7: Illustration of the Principles of Selection, Optimization, and Compensation
Credit: From *Successful Aging: Perspectives from the Behavioral Sciences,* table 9.7, P.B. Baltes (ed.). Reprinted with permission of Cambridge University Press.

Chapter 10

Table 10.1: An overview of Erikson's theory of psychosocial development
Credit: from *Childhood and Society,* 2nd ed. by Erik H. Erikson. Copyright 1950, ©1963 by W.W. Norton & Company, Inc., renewed

©1978, 1991 by Erik H. Erikson. Used by permission of W.W. Norton & Company, Inc.

Table 10.2: Some of the strivings reported by younger, midlife, and older adults
Credit: From D.P. McAdams, E. de St. Aubin, and R. L. Logan, "Generativity among young, midlife, and older adults" in *Psychology and Aging,* 8, p. 228. Copyright ©1993 by the American Psychological Association. Reprinted with permission.

Figure 10.3: An illustration of Costa and McCrae's five-factor model of personality
Credit: Reproduced by special permission of the publisher, Psychological Assessment Resources, Inc., 16204 N. Florida Avenue, Lutz, FL 33549, from the NEO Personality Inventory-Revised, by Paul Costa and Robert McCrae, Copyright 1978, 1985, 1989, 1992 by PAR, Inc. Further reproduction is prohibited without permission of PAR, Inc.

Table 10.3: Loevinger's Six Stages of Ego Devleopment During Adulthood
Credit: Adapted from Loevinger (1976). *Ego development.* San Francsico: Jossey-Bass.

Figure 10.4: Significant change over time
Credit: Republished with permission of Gerontological Society of America from D. Field and R.E. Millsap, " Personality in advanced old age: Continuity or change" in *Journal of Gerontology: Psychological Sciences,* 46:299–308, 1991; permission conveyed through Copyright Clearance Center, Inc.

Table 10.4: An overview of the levels and stages that comprise Kohlberg's theory or moral
Credit: From Lawrence Kohlberg, "Moral Stages and Moralization" in *Moral Development and Behavior*, Thomas Lickona (ed.). Copyright ©1976 by Holt, Rinehart and Winston. Reprinted by permission of Thomas Lickona.

Figure 10.5: A life-events framework
Credit: From D.F. Hultsch and J.K. Plemons, "Life Events and Life Span Development" in *Life Span Development and Behavior* by P.B. Baltes and O.G. Brim, Jr. (Eds.). Copyright ©1979 Academic Press. Reprinted with permission.

Chapter 11

Table 11.A: Rankings of sources of conflict and pleasure for middle-aged and older couples
Credit: From R.W. Levenson, L.L. Carstensen, and J.M. Gottman, "Long-term marriage: Age, gender, and satisfaction" in *Psychology and Aging,* 8, table 2, p. 307. Copyright ©1993 by the American Psychological Association. Reprinted with permission.

Table 11.3: Percent of aging gay men and lesbians indicating different levels . . .
Credit: Republished with permission of Gerontological Society of America from J.K. Quam, and G.S. Whitford, "Adaptation and Age-Related Expectations of Older Gay and Lesbian Adults" in *The Gerontologist,* 32:367–374, 1992; permission conveyed through Copyright Clearance Center, Inc.

Table 11.5: Descriptive data on sexual frequency patterns for married persons 60 years . . .
Credit: Republished with permission of Gerontological Society of America from W. Marsiglio and D. Donnelly, "Sexual Relations in Later Life: A National Study of Married Persons" in *Journal of Gerontology: Social Sciences,* 46:338–344, 1991; permission conveyed through Copyright Clearance Center, Inc.

Figure 11.3: The relationship between marital satisfaction and stage of marriage
Credit: Adapted from S. Anderson, C.S. Russell, W.R. Schumm (1983), "Perceived marital quality and family life-cycle categories: A further analysis" in *Journal of Marriage and the Family,* 45, 127–139. Copyright

©1983 by the National Council on Family Relations. Reprinted by permission.

Chapter 12

Cartoon in ch. 12: Work: The Great Escape
Credit: From *The New York Times,* April 20, 1997. ©Arlie Russell Hochschild. Reprinted with permission.

Table 12.2: The relationship between the functions and meanings of work
Credit: From E. Friedmann and R.J. Havighurst, *The Meaning of Work and Retirement.* Copyright ©1954. The University of Chicago Press. Reprinted with permission.

Table 12.6: Cross-Classification of "Most Important" and "Important" Reasons . . .
Credit: Republished with permission of Gerontological Society of America from J.C. Henrietta, C.G. Chan, and A.M. O'Rand, "Retirement Reason Versus Retirement Process: Examining the Reasons for Retirement Typology" in *Journal of Gerontology: Social Sciences,* 47:1–7, 1992; permission conveyed through Copyright Clearance Center, Inc.

Table 12.7: Dimensions of the four modes of adaption to retirement
Credit: From G.A. Hornstein and S. Wapner,"Modes of Experiencing and Adapting to Retirement" in *International Journal of Aging and Human Development,* 21(4):302–303. Copyright ©1985. Baywood Publishing Company. Reprinted by permission.

Chapter 13

Figure 13.1a: Florida Living Will
Figure 13.1b: Florida Designation of Health Care Surrogate
Credit: Reprinted by permission of Partnership for Caring: America's Voices for the Dying, 1620 Eye Street, NW, Suite 202, Washington, DC 20006, 800–989–9455 *www.partnershipforcaring.org*

Table 13.1: Characteristics of the Persistent Vegetative State, Coma . . .
Credit (on page): From the Multi-Society Task Force on Persistent Vegetative State, "Medical Aspects of the Persistent Vegetative State" in *New England Journal of Medicine,* 330(21):1499–1508. Copyright ©1994 Massachusetts Medical Society. All rights reserved. Reprinted with permission.

Research Focus 13.1: Brain Death Criteria
Credit: From the *Journal of the American Medical Association,* 246: 2184–2186. Copyright ©1981 American Medical Association. Reprinted with permission.

Figure 13.2: The Medical Directive
Credit: Copyright 1995 by Linda L. Emanuel and Ezekiel J. Emanuel. Additional information, copies, and services related to the medical directive may be obtained at the Web site: *www.medicaldirective.org.* Reprinted with permission.

Table 13.2: Reasons for not executing an advance directive
Credit: From D.M. High, "Advance Directives and the Elderly: A Study of Intervention Strategies to Increase Use" in *The Gerontologist,* 33:342–349. Reprinted with permission.

Figure 13.4: Acute, chronic, and terminal phases of the dying process
Credit: Reprinted with the permission of Simon & Schuster, Inc., from *The Experience of Dying* by E. Mansell Pattison, fig. 2, p. 44. Copyright ©1977 by Prentice-Hall, Inc.

Research Focus 13.3: Eight Myths: Children, Adolescents, and Loss
Credit: Copyright ©2000 from K.J. Doka (Ed.), *Living with Grief: Children, adolescents and loss,* pp. 33–34. Reproduced by permission of Taylor & Francis, Inc., http//www.routledge-ny.com

Table 13.4: Funerals of different religions
Credit: Excerpts from "Funeral Etiquette" by Lois Sweet. Reprinted with permission – The Toronto Star Syndicate. Excerpted from The Toronto Star, August 14, 1994.

Photos

Chapter 1
1: © Michael Newman/PhotoEdit; 8: © David Young-Wolff/PhotoEdit;
13 both: © Gail Meese/Meese Photo Research; 14: © AP/Wide World Photos

Chapter 2
21: © Quiel Begonia/Meese Photo Research; 29: © Toni Michaels/Image
Works; 32: © Frank Siteman/Stock Boston; 45l: © Joe Carini/Image Works;
45r: © Myrleen Ferguson Cate/PhotoEdit; 46: Courtesy Patricia M. Peterson

Chapter 3
50: © Earl Dotter/Meese Photo Research; 57l: © KOBAL COLLECTION;
57r: © AP/Wide World Photos; 56: PhotoDisc/Vol. 70; 66 both:
© AP/Wide World Photos; 67: © Michelle D. Bridwell/PhotoEdit;
76: © CNRA/SPL/Photo Researchers; 79: Courtesy Matthew W. Prull

Chapter 4
98: © Owen Franken/Stock Boston; 121: © AP/Wide World Photos;
128: © Susie Leavines/Photo Researchers

Chapter 5
146: © David Young-Wolff/PhotoEdit; 181: © David Harry Stewart/Stone;
194: © Elizabeth Crews/Image Works

Chapter 6
204: © Myrleen Ferguson Cate/PhotoEdit; 222: © David Strickler/Meese
Photo Research; 234: © David Young-Wolff/PhotoEdit

Chapter 7
273: © Roger Allyn Lee/SuperStock; 275: McGraw-Hill, photo by C. P.
Hammond; 278: David Kelly Crow/PhotoEdit; 299: © Gail Meese/Meese
Photo Research

Chapter 8
310: © Martha Tabor/Meese Photo Research; 328: PhotoDisc/Vol. 40;
328: © James Shaffer; 333: © Allen Zak/Meese Photo Research;
336: © AP/Wide World Photos

Chapter 9
343: © Bedrich Grumzweig/Photo Researchers; 349: © Gail Meese/Meese
Photo Research; 357: © Adamsmith/SuperStock; 358: © AP/Wide World
Photos; 364: © Jose Galvez/PhotoEdit

Chapter 10
377: © David Young-Wolff/PhotoEdit; 394l: © David Grossman/Photo
Researchers; 394r: © Dion Ogust/The Image Works; 395: © Charles
Gupton/Stock Boston; 408: © Billy Barnes/PhotoEdit

Chapter 11
428: © Allan Zak/Meese Photo Research; 436: © Merritt
Vincent/PhotoEdit; 437: © J. Nourok/PhotoEdit; 445: © Lawrence
Midgale/Photo Researchers; 446: Courtesy William Hoyer;
451: PhotoDisc/Vol. 100

Chapter 12
461: © Catherine Green/Meese Photo Research; 468: © Bob
Daemmrich/The Image Works; 500: © Gary Walts/The Image Works;
504: © Rick Yamda-Lapides/Meese Photo Research

Chapter 13
514: © A. Ramey/The Image Works; 544: © Jack Kurtz/Image Works;
547: © Etter/Anthro-Photo; 553: © Gail Meese/Meese Photo Research

NAME INDEX

Note: Page numbers in *italics*
   indicate figures; page numbers
   followed by *t* indicate tables.

AARP (American Association
   of Retired Persons), 228,
   254, 486, 550, 551, 552, 556,
   561
ABHP (American Board of
   Hospice and Palliative
   Medicine), 545
Aboraya, A., 160
Abson, V., 275
Achieving and Maintaining Cognitive
   Vitality with Aging, 54
Acree, M., 106
Adamek, M. E., 172, 173
Adams, W. L., 173
Affleck, G., 110
Agronin, M. E., 148
Ai, A. L., 139
Ajrouch, K. J., 164
Akiyama, H., 131, 508
Albert, M., 74, 75
Albert, M. S., 77, 80, 300
Aldwin, C., 100, 101, 103, 104,
   105, 110, 508
Alexander, B. B., 450, 557
Alexander, N. B., 265
Alexander, R. A., 476
Allison, D. B., 34, 248
Almeida, D. M., 44
Alpaugh, P., 338
Alpert, N. M., 300
Alspaugh, M. E. L., 115, 167
Altman, L. K., 119
Alvarez, H., 32
AMA (American Medical
   Association), 173, 514
Amaducci, L., 86
Ambinder, A., 164
American Association of Retired
   Persons (AARP), 228, 254,
   486, 550, 551, 552, 556, 561

American Board of Hospice
   and Palliative Medicine
   (ABHP), 545
American Cancer Society, *249, 252*
American Heart Association, 247,
   249, 250, *250,* 253
American Medical Association
   (AMA), 173, 514
American Psychiatric Association,
   148, 161, 162*t*
Anders, T. R., 279
Anderson, S. A., 438
Andres, D., 318
Aneshensel, C. S., 230
Angel, J. L., 131, 153, 154, 155
Angel, R. S., 131, 154, 155
Angleitner, A., 396
Anthony, J. C., 34, 55, 160
Antonucci, T., 486
Antonucci, T. A., 16, 432, 438
Antonucci, T. C., 131, 164, 431,
   432–433, 508
Aponte, J. F., 157, 174, 178,
   180, 182
Applebaum, P. S., 198
Aranda, M. P., 129
Arbuckle, T., 103, 318
Arenberg, D., 339
Arlin, P. K., 351, 353
Armeli, S., 110
Armon, C., 412
Arndt, S., 274
Asch, D. A., 525
Ascher, B., 103, 554
Ashton-Miller, J. A., 265
Aspinwall, L. G., 100, 542
Asselain, B., 243
Astin, A. W., 8, *9*
Atchison, K. A., 456
Atchley, R. C., 501, 502, *502,* 508
Atienza, A. A., 112
Attig, T., 534
Ausubel, D. P., 334
Avery, R., 111, 130

Avorn, J., 266
Azichowsky, L. D., 254
Azzouz, F., 167

Backman, L., 273, 325
Baddeley, A., 278
Bahrick, H. P., 288
Bahrick, P. O., 288
Bailey, L., 474
Bailley, S. E., 562
Baillie, J., 492, 507
Baillie, P. H., 466
Balch, D. W., 227
Ball, M., 54, *54*
Baltes, M. M., 66, 372, 372*t,*
   492, 493*t*
Baltes, P. B., 6, 9, 16, 324, 326,
   327, 329, 361, 362, 365, 366,
   367, 367*t, 368,* 368*t,* 369,
   370, *371,* 372, 372*t,* 373,
   373, 374, 399
Bammel, G., 488
Bandura, A., 10
Barbaranelli, C., 396
Barer, B. M., 100, 132, 164, 386
Barnes, J. M., 157, 178, 180, 182
Barnett, R. C., 494
Barney, D. D., 157
Barr, A., 196
Barrett, G. V., 476
Bars, P., 66
Bartoshuk, L. M., 66
Bashore, T. R., 78
Bass, D. M., 116
Basseches, M., 351
Bassuk, S. S., 431
Basta, L. L., 528, 529
Bastida, E., 40
Bauer, J. J., 443
Baum, C., 114, 114*t*
Baum, M. C., 209
Bayen, U. J., 252
Beach, D. L., 125
Becker, J. T., 168

Beckman, A. T. F., 165
Bedford, V. H., 558
Beehr, T. A., 500
Beem, E. A., 449
Begg, R. K., 266
Begley, S., 340
Bekker, L., 447
Belasco, J. A., 480
Belenky, M. F., 415
Bell, J., 490
Bem, S. L., 42, 43*t*
Benbow, C. P., 341
Bengtson, V. L., 45, 116, 446, 447
Bennett, D. A., 137
Benson, F., 92
Benson, M., 252
Benton, D., 130
Benyamini, Y., 215, 419
Berg, S., 164
Bergstrom, M. J., 561
Berkelman, R. L., 34
Berkman, L. F., 431
Bernard, B. A., 137
Bernstein, M. A., 262, 263
Berscheid, E., 430
Berthelot, J. M., 229
Berzonsky, M. D., 348, 349, *350*
Biegel, D. E., 116, 151, 155
Billig, N., 518
Binet, A., 311
Birba, L., 508
Birren, J. E., 298, 338, 339, 532
Black, S. A., 153, 177
Blackshaw, H. J., 194
Blair, S. N., 34, 248
Blakeslee, S., 454
Blasch, B. B., 233, 235, *236*
Blaum, C. S., 258
Blazer, D. G., 162, 163
Blieszner, R., 140, 560–561, 562
Bloom, A., 429
Bluck, S., 532
Blum, M. J., 116
Blumenthal, J. A., 491

SUBJECT INDEX

Reliability, A–3, A–4 to A–6, A–28
Religion
 aging and, 141
 attitudes toward death and, 531
 diversity and, 140–141
 health and coping, 139–140, 143
 spirituality and, 138
Remarriage, 454, 560
Reminiscence, 383
Reminiscence bump, 288,
  289, 290
Reminiscence therapy, 192
Reminiscing, death and, 287–288
Remote phase of retirement,
  502, *502*
Reorganization and recovery, 553
Reorientation phase of retirement,
  502, 503
Representative sample, A–27
Reproduction, changes in, 61–62
Research
 cross-cultural studies, 419
 cross-sectional studies of
   intelligence, 316–317, *317,*
   318, 341
 efficacy research, 185–186
 on formal operations, 348
 methodological weaknesses in,
   126, 128–129
 on postformal operations,
   352–354
 stereotyping in, 39, 40*t*
 See also Longitudinal studies
Research methods, A–2 to A–29
 behavioral research, A–8
 between-subject manipulations,
   A–15
 correlational *vs.* experimental
   studies, A–13 to A–15
 measurement issues, A–4 to A–7
 meta-analysis, A–26
 physiological, A–10
 problems of sampling in, A–26 to
   A–28
 quasi-experiments, A–15 to
   A–25, A–18*t*
 research design, A–13 to A–17,
   A–29
 research design strategies, A–13
   to A–17
 settings for, A–8 to A–9
 standardized tests, A–9
Reserve capacity, 6
 of brain, 78, 80, 87, 329
 cognitive, 329, *365,* 365–366
Resistance exercises, 262–263
Respeto, 154
Respiratory system, 60
Respite care, 121–122, 123*t*
Responsive listening, 440
Restraints, use of, 233, 237–238,
  239, *239*

Re-testing, internal validity and,
  A–17, A–19 to A–21
Retired Senior Volunteer Program
  (RSVP), 195, 508
Retirement, 185, *494–497,*
  494–511, 498*t*
 career development and, 467
 as challenge to coping, 132
 demographics of, *495,* 495–496
 early retirement, 494–495, *495*
 economic issues in, 491, 497, 500
 factors related to, 478, 499–501,
   501*t,* 508–509
 leisure in, 492–494, 493*t*
 lifestyle and, 439
 mandatory, BFOQs and, 498, 499
 pensions and, 497
 phases of, 501–503, *502*
 satisfaction with, 507–508
 styles of adjustment to, 503–509
 theories of, 509
 work following, 486, 500–501, 508
 See also Leisure; Social Security;
   Work
Retirement communities, 38
Retirement stage in career planning,
  469, *469*
Retrieval deficit, 301
Reversibility of fitness, 254
RFT (rod-and-frame task), *400,*
  400–401, *401*
Rheumatoid arthritis, 240
RIASEC theory of career choice,
  468–469
Rod-and-frame task (RFT), *400,*
  400–401, *401*
Role satisfaction, 444
Roman Catholic funerals, 547*t*–548*t*
Route planning, 135–136
Routine events, 106
R response, 283
RSVP (Retired Senior Volunteer
  Program), 195, 508
Running, 71, *71*

Sampling problems, A–26 to A–28,
  A–29
Sandwich generation, 112–113
Santeria, 155
Sarcomas, 241
Sarcopenia, 262, 263, *264*
Sati, 546, 547*t*
Satisfaction
 leisure activities and, 493
 life satisfaction, 191
 marital, parenting and, 436–437
 occupational, 471–474, *473*
 with retirement, 507–508
 role satisfaction, 444
 as stable trait, 398
Schaie-Thurstone Adult Mental
  Abilities Test, 312

School Sisters of Notre Dame, 87,
  417–418
Scrapie, 92
Search for meaning, 107–109, *109,*
  139, 554
"Seasons of life," 387–390, *388*
Seattle Longitudinal Study (SLS),
  8, 319, *320,* 323, 397
Secondary aging, 51–52
Secondary appraisal, 104, *104,*
  119–120
Secondary insomnia, 252
Secondary memory, 276
Secondary stressors, 167
Second career pattern, 487
Selection, 372, 372*t,* A–16
Selection and entry stage in career
  planning, 469, *469*
Selective attention, 278, 298
Selective dropout, 324, A–20, A–21
Selective optimization with
  compensation, 372–374,
  372*t,* *373*
Selective prevention, 150
Self, development of, 392
Self-assessment
 of driving skills, 137
 of physical health, 214–216
 of work behavior, 479
Self-concept, 465–467
Self-determination, 519
Self-esteem, 196
Self-image, 108–109, *109,* 117–118
Selfish grief, 559–560
Self-knowledge, 469
Self-report inventories, 394
Self-worth, 456
Semantic elaboration, 284
Semantic memory, 281–282,
  283, *283*
Senescence. *See* Normal aging
Senile plaques, 76, 81, 87
Senior Companions program, 195
Sensation, 62
Sensorimotor development, 94–95
Sensorimotor stage of cognitive
  development, 346
Sensory acuity, 326–327, *327*
Sensory deprivation hypothesis, 326
Sensory processes, 62–68, 94–95
 hearing, 64–66, 65*t*
 taste, smell, and touch, 66–67
 temperature, pain, and
   kinesthesis, 67–68
 vestibular system, 263, *264*
 vision, *62,* 62–64, 63*t*
Sentence completion method, 390
Service delivery, 189
Service economy
 employment in, 496, *497*
 hourly wages, 486, *487*
 skills for, 463, *463,* 464*t*

Settings of death, 542–545, 544*t*
Sex roles
 androgyny and, 42–44, 43*t*
 changes in, 42–46, 48
 dominant orientations view of, 45
 ego mastery styles, 44–45
 in later life, 45–46
 See also Gender; Men; Women
Sexuality, 454–457, 459
 attitudes and behavior, 454
 institutionalized elderly and, 458
 in late adulthood, 456–457, 457*t*
 male climacteric, 456
 menopause, 454–455, 455*t*
Shock, 514, 515, 551
Short Portable Mental Status
  Questionnaire (SPMSQ), 431
Short-term memory
 capacity of, 277
 long-term memory and, 275–280,
   276, 277
 memory search, *279,* 279–280
Sibling, death of, 555, 558
Significance tests, A–12 to A–13
Single lifestyle, 449–450, *450*
Single parents, 482
Skin, 57
Sleep, 54
Sleep disturbances, 252
SLS (Seattle Longitudinal Study),
  8, 319, *320,* 323, 397
Smell, sense of, 66, 67
Social activities, 54
Social age, 12, 14
Social class, 35–36, 488
Social clock, 103, 403
Social cognition, 354
Social convoys, 431–432, 508
Social development, 46–47
Social domain, 18
Social engagement, 431
Social environment, 403
Social interaction
 postformal thinking and, 354
 well-being and, 131–132
 widowhood and, 561–562
 wisdom in context of, 367
Social isolation, 431, 432
Social multipliers, 321
Social networks, 131
Social personality, 468
Social perspectives, 409*t*–410*t,*
  413–414
Social readjustment rating scale,
  102, 102*t*
Social Security
 health-care costs and, 208
 long-term health care and, 217,
   218, 219*t*
 retirement and, 496, 497, 498*t*
Social Security system, 34, 37, 497
Social status, 41

Social stigma, of AD, 118, 119
Social support
caregiver burden and, 120–121
as community-based intervention, 190–191
convoy model of, 431–432, 508
culture and, 154–155
divorce and, 453
health and, 209
importance of, 113
lack of, suicide and, 172, 173
mortality rates and, 209–210
provided by religion, 140
stress-buffering effects of, 163–164
subjective well-being and, 419–420, *420*
for widows, 561–562
Societal events, 7–9, *9*
Socioeconomic factors, 174, 420
Socioemotional selectivity theory, 131–132
Sociohistorical contexts, 408
Sociohistorical/sociocultural views of death, 530–535
SOC strategies, 373
Soma, 73
Source memory, 285–286, 291
Spatial frequency, 64
Spatial reasoning, 312*t*
Specific Affect Coding System, 435
Speeded subtest, 316
Spending down, 225
Spirituality, 138, 139, 143, 552
Split dreams, 390
SPMSQ (Short Portable Mental Status Questionnaire), 431
Sports
careers of professional athletes, 466
as leisure pursuit, 490
master athletes, 258, 260
performance in, *70,* 70–71, *71,* 361, 363
See also Exercise; *specific sports*
Spousal abuse, 448–449
Spouse, death of, 439–440, *442,* 560–562, 560*t*
Stability of personality
Berkeley study of, 397–399, *398*
conclusions about, 399–402
as personal illusion, 396
survival rates and, *400,* 400–401, *401*
Stability phase of retirement, *502,* 503
Stages of dying, 536–538, 563
Stage theories, 5–6
of cognitive development, 345, 346, 374–375
Piaget's, 344, 346–351
Stage theories of personality development, 379–392, 423

conclusions about, 390–392, *391*
Erikson's stages, 379–380, 381*t,* 382–384, 383*t,* 386
Freud's stages and, 380
gero-transcendence and, 384–386, 385*t*
Levinson's "seasons of life," 387–390, *388,* 423
Loevinger's ego development theory, 386, 387*t,* 423
Standard deviation, A–10
Standardization, A–9
Standardized tests, A–9
Standard phase of moral development, 415
Statistical methods, A–6
Statistical significance, A–13
Stereotyping, 39, 40*t*
Strategic retrieval, 300
Strength, 59, 261, 267
Strength training, 259–261, 266–267, 270
Stress
abusive relationships and, 448–449
of AD, *127,* 127–128
career transition and, 466
of caregiving, 101, 130–132, *133,* 142–143
coping with, 99, 111, 163–164
diathesis-stress model, 148–149, *149,* 199
immune system and, 240, *240*
of job, vacations and, 476
in life-events framework, *404,* 404–405
life expectancy and, 29
management of, 101, *101*
measurement of, 101–102, 102*t*
oxidative, 55
physiological response to, 100
proximal and distal aspects of, 105
reduction of, 54
religion as buffer, 140
responses to, 102–103
of unemployment, 481
well-being and, 130–131
Stress buffering, 163–164
Stressors, 167, 400
Stroke, 91, *91,* 251
Structural equation modeling, 326
Structural magnetic resonance imaging (MRI), 77
Structured wholeness, 345, 349
Subjective caregiver burden, 113
Subjective well-being, 418–421, *420,* 424–425
Substitution hypothesis, 233
Successful aging, 9
active lifestyle in, 206
components of, 13

defined, 208–209
in Hindu tradition, 41–42
"intellectual aging," 372
lifestyle choices and, 206
normal aging distinguished, 51
pathways to, 47
personal control and, 10
work and, 481
Suicide
demographics of, 170
ethnicity and, 170–172, *171*
impact of, 562–563
physician-assisted, 528–529
risks and treatment of, 172–173, 200
Sundowning, 236
Super's theory of occupational choice, 465–467
Supplementary Medical Insurance—Medicare Part B, 217, 222, 226
Supplementation hypothesis, 233
Surgery, 246
Survey method, 390–391
Survival, personality and, *400,* 400–401, *401*
Survivorship, 33–34, 171, 386
Survivorship curve, 33, *33*
"Swan songs," 536
Swimming, 70, *70,* 260
Syncope, 137–138

Tacrine, 90
Tactile sensitivity, 66, 67
Talent-based approach to expertise, 362–363
Task switching, 298–299
Taste, declines in, 66–67
Telework, 464–465, 489
Temperature sensitivity, 67
Temporal lobe, 73
Tension-reduction hypothesis, 176, 177, 201
Tentative stage of occupational choice, 467
Terminal drop, 325
Terminal phase of dying, 539, *539*
Termination phase of retirement, *502,* 503
Testamentary capacity, 198–199
Testing limits of cognitive reserve, 364–366, *365*
Testosterone, 455
Test-retest reliability, A–5
Theoretical issues, 4–7, 5*t*
Theory of Multiple Intelligences, 334
Therapeutic interventions, 183–190, 201
community-based, 190–191, 192, 195–197, *196*
with elderly, illustrated, 190–199

ethnicity and. *See* Ethnic elderly populations
goals of, 186–187, 186*t*
institutional, 191–193
intergenerational, 192
kinds of functioning, 187
in late adulthood, 184–185
legal intervention, 197–199
in middle adulthood, 183–184
options in, 185–186, 186*t*
pet therapy, 193–195
physical health and, *210,* 210–211
settings and agents for, 186*t,* 190
symptoms, 188
techniques of, 188–189
volunteering, 195–197, *196*
Thinking, 355
Threshold model, 79
Thyroid disorders, 94
TIAs (transient ischemic attacks), 91, *91*
Time-sequential research design, A–18*t,* *A–22,* A–22 to A–23, A–24, *A–25*
Timing of events, 103
Tinnitus, 65
Tobacco use, 34
Total cholesterol/HDL ratio, 261
Total recall, *306,* 307, *307*
Trait(s), 393–394
Trait approach to personality, 392–402, 423
Baltimore Longitudinal Study of Aging, 394, *395,* 396–397
Berkeley Older Generation Study, 397–399, *398*
Berlin Aging Study, 399
characteristics of traits, 393–394
Seattle Longitudinal Study, 397
stability of personality, 399–402
Trait theorists, 392
Trajectory of life, 538–539, *539*
Transcendental NDEs, 535
Transient ischemic attacks (TIAs), 91, *91*
Transitions
in life cycle, 388, 466, 503, 505*t*–506*t*
to postformal operations, 356–357
Transurethral resection (TUR), 245
Treatment programs for alcoholism, 174–175, *175*
Triarchic Theory of Intelligence, 335
Trust *vs.* mistrust, 380, 381*t*
TUR (transurethral resection), 245
Type A personality, 251
Type B personality, 251
Typing, 359

Uncontrollable factors, 9
Unemployment, 176, 481–482
Unfinished business, 192
Unidirectional change, 7
United Network for Organ
　　Sharing, 526
Universal prevention, 150
Universal progression, 345
Untimely deaths. *See* Difficult
　　deaths
Upgrading kinship relationships, 153
Uplifts, 106–107, 405
Upswing hypothesis, 438, *438*
Upward social comparisons, 108

Vacations, 476
Validity of measurement, A–3, A–6
　　to A–7, A–28
Variability, measures of, A–10
Variables
　cognitive variables, 104–105
　correlations between, A–11 to
　　A–12
　fuzzy variables, 351
Ventricular fibrillation, 249
Verbal comprehension, 312*t*
Verguenza, 154
Vestibular sensory system,
　263, *264*
Viagra, 456
Vision
　ability to drive and, 135–137, *136*
　changes in, *62,* 62–64, 63*t,* 94–95
Visitation rights of grandparents, 447
Visual acuity, 63, 64, 136
Visual field, 63–64, *400,* 400–401
Visual identification tasks, 360
Visual scratch pad, 278
Visual search tasks, 298, 360–361
Vitamins, 55
Volunteering
　busy ethic and, 507–508
　as preventive intervention, 150
　as therapeutic intervention,
　　195–197, *196*

VO₂max (maximal oxygen uptake),
　257–258, 257*t,* 259

WAIS-R (Wechsler Adult
　　Intelligence Scale), 314,
　　314*t,* 341
Wandering, 233, 235–237, *236,*
　236t, 237*t*
Wayfinding, 135–136
Wear-and-tear theory, 52
Wechsler Adult Intelligence Scale
　　(WAIS-R), 314, 314*t,* 341
Weight management, 246–249,
　248, 249
Well-being, 143
　caregiving and, 120, 419
　coping with stress and,
　　130–131, 134
　dimensions of, 132, *133*
　happiness and, 134
　occupational, 474
　sense of control and, 132–133
　sex differences in, 384
　subjective, 418–421, *420*
　subjective, age and, *373,* 373–374
　volunteerism and, 196, *196*
Wellness. *See* Health promotion
White matter, 75
Widowhood, 439–440, *442,*
　560–562, 560*t*
Will, execution of, 198–199
Wisdom, 344, 361–367, *363*
　aging and, 366–367, 367*t,*
　　368, 368*t*
　biology, society and, 374
　mechanics and pragmatics,
　　362, 364
　professional expertise and,
　　369–370, 369*t,* 370*t, 371*
Women
　adjustment to retirement,
　　508–509
　affirmative coping by, 415
　breast cancer in, 241, 243–244
　career tracks for, *485,* 486–488

in caregiving roles, 111–112,
　115–116
clinical depression in, 160
fear of falling, 264–265
female friendships, 432
grief in, 553
HIV and, 246
Kohlberg's theory and, 414–415
life dreams of, 184
menopause and. *See* Menopause
minority, wages of, 483
nontraditional employment of,
　483–484, *484*
occupational concerns of,
　470–471
in part-time work, 482
personality development in, 405
shift to careers, 474
social convoys of, 431–432
split dreams of, 390
workplace concerns of, 472
See also Gender; Men; Sex roles
Women's Health Initiative
　Study, 89
Word fluency, 312*t*
Word naming task, 294
Word-stem completion, 293, 294
Work, 462–488, 509–510
　adjustment to, *463,* 470–471
　age discrimination and, 478
　age integration in, 473
　bridge employment, 508
　career of professional athlete, 466
　career planning, 469, *469*
　career tracks for women, *485,*
　　486–488
　choice of profession, wisdom
　　and, 366
　culture of work environment, 480
　daily hassles and, 105–106
　death and grieving and, 556
　decisions about, 477–479,
　　479*t, 480*
　experience of flow in, 490
　families and, 472, 480, 482–488

following retirement, 486,
　500–501, 508
gender and, 483–484, *484, 485,*
　485*t,* 486
generations and, 471
historical context of, 462–465
intelligence and, 329, 332, *332*
job counseling programs, 481–482
job withdrawal and, 478
in late adulthood, 475–476,
　486, *487*
midlife career change, 474–475
modern workplace, 463,
　463, 464*t*
nontraditional, by women,
　483–484, *484*
occupation, entering, 470
occupational choice, 465–469
over life cycle, 465–479
part-time employment, 479, *480,*
　482, 486
performance, aging and, 477
physical fitness and,
　256–257, 256*t*
satisfaction, productivity and,
　471–474, *473*
in service economy, 496, *497*
successful aging and, 481
telework, 464–465, 489
unemployment and, 481–482
vacations and, 476
See also Careers; Occupational
　choice
Working memory, 277–279
Workplace support, 472
Work withdrawal, 478
World population, *26,* 26–27

Young adulthood, 389
　career development in, 466
　friendships in, 431
　impact of suicide in, 562
　intimacy *vs.* isolation in, 380, 382
　leisure in, 491–492
　postformal thinking in, 353–354